Structured Programming in Assembly Language for the IBM PC® and PS/2®

RECENT COMPUTER SCIENCE TITLES FROM PWS PUBLISHING COMPANY

SECOND EDITION

Structured Programming in Assembly Language for the IBM PC® and PS/2®

WILLIAM C. RUNNION

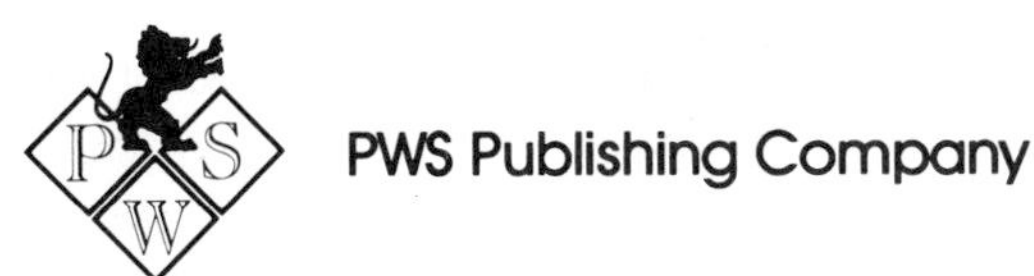

I(T)P An International Thomson Publishing Company

New York • London • Bonn • Boston • Detroit • Madrid • Melbourne • Mexico City • Paris
Singapore • Tokyo • Toronto • Washington • Albany NY • Belmont CA • Cincinnati OH

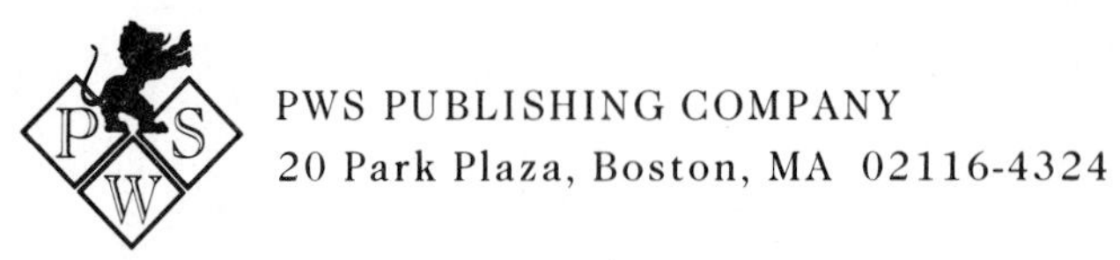

International Thomson Publishing
The trademark ITP is used under license.

Library of Congress Cataloging-in-Publication Data

Runnion, William C.
Structured programming in assembly language for the IBM PC and PS/2 William C. Runnion.—2nd ed.
p. cm.
Includes index.
ISBN 0-534-93268-1
1. IBM Personal Computer—Programming. 2. Assembler language (Computer program language) 3. Structured programming. I. Title.
QA76.8.I2594R86 1994 94-286
005.265--dc20 CIP

Sponsoring Editor: *Michael Sugarman*
Developmental Editor: *Susan McCulley Gay*
Assistant Editor: *Ken Morton*
Production Editor: *Monique Calello*
Marketing Manager: *Nathan Wilbur*
Manufacturing Manager: *Ellen Glisker*
Interior/Cover Designer: *Monique Calello*
Compositor: *Santype International Limited*
Cover Photo/Art: *Rob Atkins, The Image Bank®*
Cover Printer: *Henry Sawyer Co.*
Text Printer and Binder: *Courier Westford, Inc.*

Printed and bound in the United States of America.
00 01 02 03 - 10 9 8 7 6 5 4

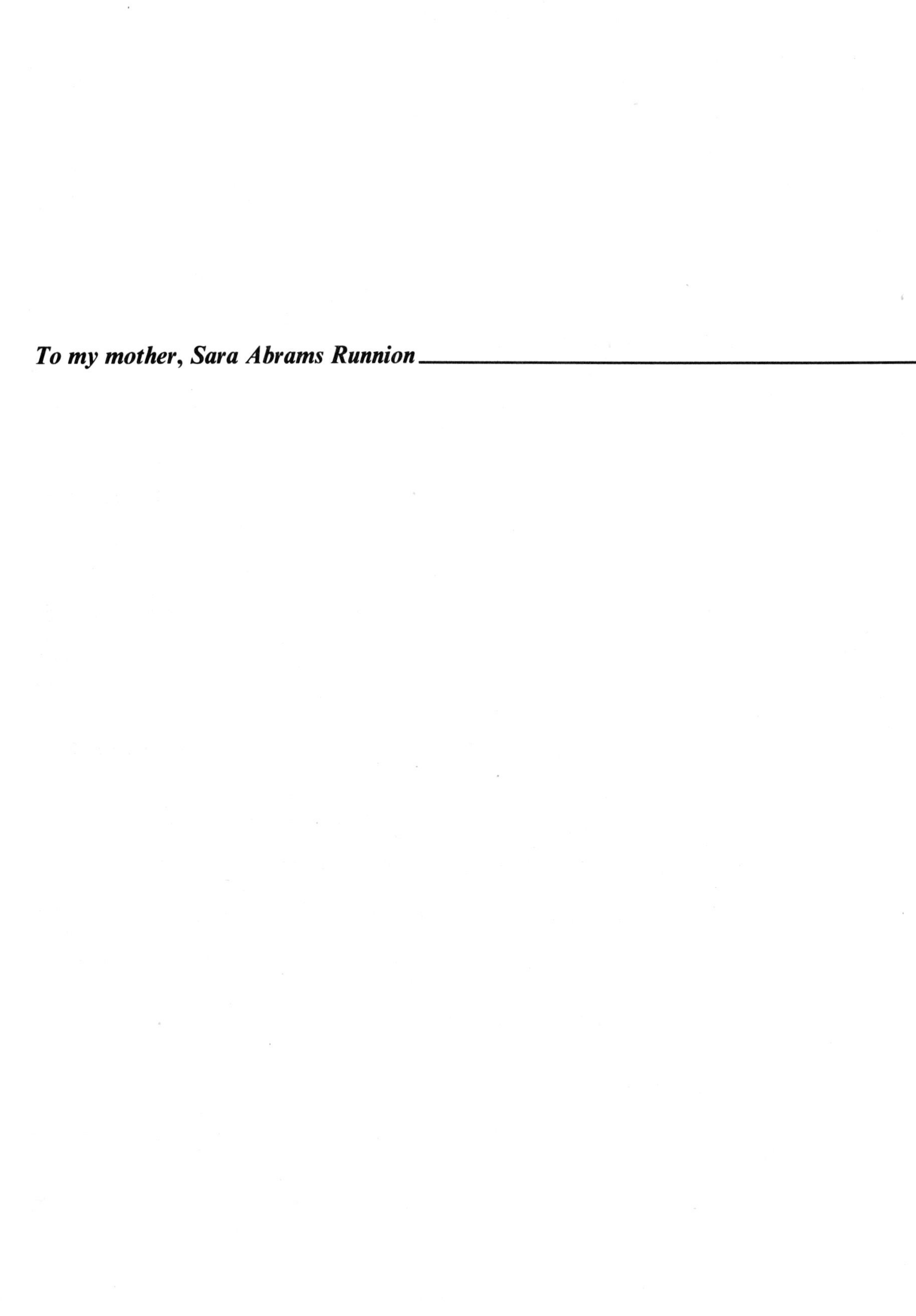

To my mother, Sara Abrams Runnion

Preface

The purpose of *Structured Programming in Assembly Language for the IBM PC and PS/2, Second Edition* is to teach structured assembly language programming to computer science students while introducing them to computer organization. The intended audience is students at the sophomore or junior level who are taking a concentration in computer science. Students are expected to have successfully completed one high-level language programming course. They will be at an advantage if that high-level language course emphasized structured programming.

A course in assembly language is still an essential part of the computer science curriculum. The demand for assembly language programmers has increased in recent years due largely to the need for high-performance software for microcomputers. However, the justification for an assembly language course should never be based on the need for assembly language programmers. The development of good assembly language programmers is obviously not accomplished through one course in assembly language, but rather through years of experience. Instead, the justification for an assembly language course stems from its value in bridging the gap between computer programming and computer science. The computer programmer needs to know how things work in the virtual machine provided by the operating system and the high-level programming language being used. The computer scientist needs to know how things work at the real-machine level. A course in assembly language provides an introduction to how things work at the machine level.

This text is based on the CS 3 course in *ACM Curriculum '78*. The main emphasis is on structured programming in assembly language, which keeps students on familiar ground—that of solving problems with computer programs—and enables them to relate constructs appearing in high-level languages to implementations of those constructs at the machine level. Computer organization is woven throughout the text to give students a clearer understanding of how things work at the machine level.

The stand-alone environment of a microcomputer enhances the CS 3 course and allows the student to experiment with capabilities, such as direct input/output, that are hidden by the operating system in a time-shared environment. Where possible, the advantages of the stand-alone environment have been exploited in this book.

The basic approach of this book is to teach by example in an incremental fashion. Most chapters concentrate on a particular subset of the 8088/8086 assembly language instructions. The capabilities provided by a particular subset of instructions are presented in detail. Short instruction sequences are used to illustrate the instructions of the subset, and example programs or procedures are used to illustrate the use of the instructions in the solution of a problem. The example programs are designed to emphasize the use of the subset of instructions just presented while reinforcing the use of instructions from subsets covered in previous chapters.

Second Edition Revisions

Two major revisions have been incorporated throughout the second edition:

1. The text has been updated to conform to Version 6.0 of the Microsoft Macro Assembler (MASM).
   a. In addition to DEBUG, the CodeView debugger is covered in Chapters 1, 2, and 3.
   b. Simplified segment directives, introduced in MASM 5.1 and enhanced in MASM 6.0, are used in example programs throughout the book. Full segment definitions are introduced in Chapter 1 and presented in detail in Chapter 12.
   c. The decision- and loop-generating macro directives of MASM 6.0 are introduced in Chapter 4 and are used in selected example programs throughout the remainder of the book. Other example programs in those chapters demonstrate primitive implementations of decision and loop structures. This technique further emphasizes the relationship between high-level control structures and machine-level implementations of those control structures, an important emphasis of the first edition.
   d. Subprocedure interface features, introduced in MASM 5.1 and enhanced in MASM 6.0, are presented from a user standpoint in Chapter 5 and discussed in detail in Chapters 8 and 10.
   e. Local stack variables, a MASM 6.0 feature, are presented from a user standpoint in Chapter 5 and discussed in detail in Chapters 8 and 10.

   Although the text has been written for Version 6.0 of MASM, information has been included to render the book effective for MASM 5.1 users as well. (*All information pertaining to MASM 5.1 is encased within a vertical rule that appears in the text margin.*)

2. The text has been updated for compatibility with any computer in the IBM PC or the IBM PS/2 family of microcomputers or with a computer that is compatible with an IBM PC or PS/2.
   a. Chapter 1 has been updated to describe the organization of the Intel 8086 microprocessor as well as the Intel 8088 microprocessor. The primary emphasis of the book is 8088/8086 assembly language programming. In addition, there are sections, where appropriate, that present additional capabilities in the 80286 assembly language.
   b. Chapter 7 has been updated to include a section on the organization of the

Intel 80386 microprocessor and assembly language programming on 80386-based microcomputers. In subsequent chapters, there are sections, where appropriate, that present additional capabilities in the 80386 assembly language.

c. Chapter 13 has been updated to include information on the EGA, VGA, and MCGA video subsystems as well as the MDA and CGA video adapters.

In addition to these comprehensive revisions, four other revisions appear in the second edition:

1. Chapter 7 includes a brief section that addresses 80486 assembly language programming.
2. Chapter 9 has been revised to include a section on DOS user services (interrupt Type 21H).
3. Chapter 9 has been revised to include a section on disk file input/output.
4. Chapter 12 has been revised to include a section on high-level language interface.

Text Features

Several unique features set this book apart from other books on the subject of 8088/8086 assembly language:

Input/Output Subprocedure Package The object code for a comprehensive set of input/output subprocedures is included on the diskette that accompanies this book. These subprocedures enable the student to write meaningful assembly language programs without first having to encounter the difficult-to-master concept of input/output at the machine level. These subprocedures are used in the example programs of the book for all input/output operations. The source code for one of these procedures is gradually revealed in the book, and the source code for two others is revealed in Chapter 9 (the chapter on interrupts and input/output). These I/O subprocedures have been class-tested since the fall of 1984. There are two versions of the I/O subprocedure package, an 8088/8086 version and an 80386 version. The I/O subprocedures and their interface specifications are described in Appendix D.

Example Programs Each chapter contains one or more programs or subprocedures to illustrate the major topics of that chapter. The example programs illustrate topics from the current chapter and reinforce the topics covered in previous chapters. These are not just program fragments but complete programs or subprocedures that provide a solution to an interesting problem. The source code for each of these example programs is included on the enclosed diskette.

Pseudocode Comments All the programs used in this text are documented using a high-level pseudocode, which appears as in-line comments in the assembly language code. Each pseudocode statement appears as the comment on the first of the sequence of assembly language instructions that implement the statement. A control structure, such as REPEAT-UNTIL, brackets the sequence of instructions that implement the structure. Indentation is used in the pseudocode comments to emphasize the nesting of control structures. The pseudocode comments provide the following advantages:

1. They facilitate the reading and understanding of the example programs. Students

can first read the pseudocode to gain an understanding of the algorithm being implemented by the program; they can then concentrate on the assembly language code corresponding to each control structure in the pseudocode to see how that control structure is actually implemented.

2. They enable students to relate high-level constructs to machine-level implementations of those constructs.
3. They provide a general description of the algorithm being implemented by the program. This description is an algorithm design that can be implemented in any programming language. The student could readily implement the algorithm in another language for comparison.
4. They encourage good programming style and demonstrate the value of structured programming, even at the machine level.

The pseudocode used in the example programs is described in detail in Appendix C.

Reference Appendixes

The six appendixes at the end of this book eliminate the need for a separate reference manual to support programming in the 8088/8086, 80286, and 80386 assembly languages.

Appendix A summarizes the instruction set of the 8088/8086 microprocessor, and the real-mode instructions of the 80286, 80386, and 80486 microprocessors. For each instruction, Appendix A provides a description of the operation performed, the general form for the instruction, the allowable operands, and its effect on the bits of the flags register.

Appendix B summarizes the pseudo-operations (assembler directives) recognized by version 6.0 of the Microsoft Macro Assembler. For each pseudo-operation, Appendix B provides a description of the operation performed by the assembler, the general form for the pseudo-operation, and information about the operands.

Appendix C describes the high-level pseudocode used for the statement of algorithms and as in-line comments in all example programs.

Appendix D describes the input/output subprocedures referenced in the example programs and available on the diskette that accompanies the book. For each subprocedure, Appendix D provides a description of the function performed by the procedure and its interface requirements. Both versions of the I/O subprocedures are described in this appendix.

Appendix E summarizes the extended ASCII character set with respect to both video monitors and dot matrix printers.

Appendix F provides information on the following support software programs:

CodeView	Library Manager (LIB)
Cross Reference (CREF)	Line Editor (EDLIN)
DEBUG,	Linkage Editor (LINK)
Disk Operating System (DOS)	Microsoft Macro Assembler (Version 5.1 and 6.0)

Pedagogical Paths

This book contains more than enough material for a one-semester course in assembly language. Several paths could be taken through the material, depending on the inclination of the instructor. The following chart shows the dependencies of the chapter.

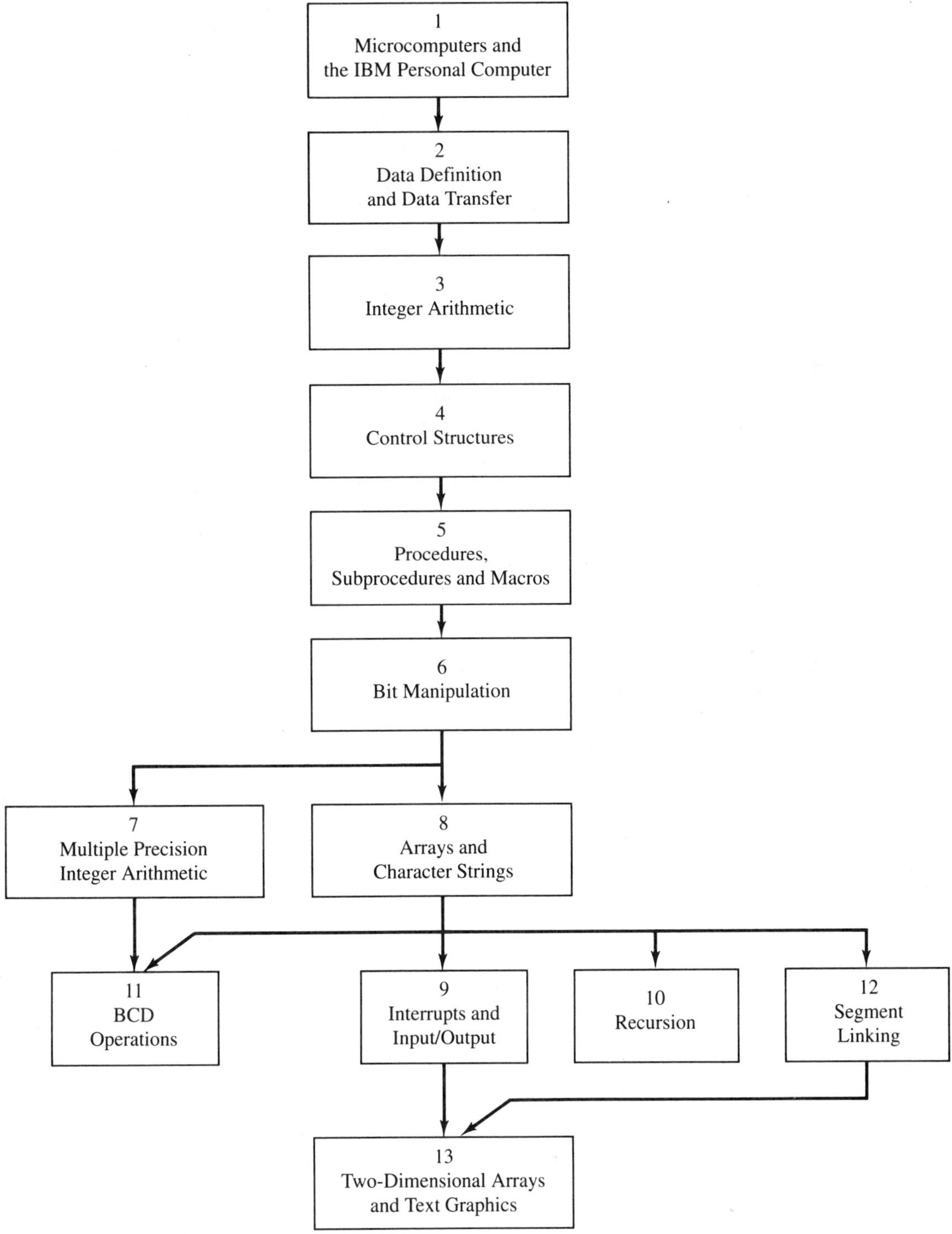

Ancillary Material

An *Instructor's Solutions Manual* with software and transparency masters is available to accompany the text. The manual contains complete solutions to all exercises in the book and also contains all the listings for test programs and selected exercises. The software, available on a $3\frac{1}{2}''$ data disk format, includes the source code for test programs, I/O subprocedures, and BCD subprocedures. The ISM also contains transparency masters of selected figures, tables, and listings from the main text.

Acknowledgments

I would like to express my appreciation to the staff of PWS Publishing Company who were directly involved with the second edition of this project. Thanks to Mike Sugarman, Mary Thomas, Susan McCulley Gay, and Ken Morton for their patience during the review process. Thanks to Monique Calello for her help during the production phase. Working with Monique was a real pleasure. She did much to provide a happy ending to a laborious process.

The following people were involved in reviewing all or part of the second edition manuscript: James R. Aman, Wilmington College; John J. Currano, Roosevelt University; Ronald L. Danilowicz, Utica College of Syracuse University; Robert Forward, Texarkana College; and E. B. Trent, Southern College of Technology. I appreciate your comments and your enthusiasm for this project.

I would like to express my gratitude to my family, Ann, Paul, and K.C. for their patience and understanding during a long and tedious process.

My dear friend, Bob Williams-Neal deserves a special word of appreciation. Bob brought humor into my life at a time when it was greatly needed. In addition to being a true friend, Bob served as my pastor for a year. I will always be grateful that our paths met and joined together.

William C. Runnion

Contents

CHAPTER 

Procedures, Subprocedures, and Macros 221

CHAPTER 

Bit Manipulation 283

CHAPTER 7 Multiple Precision Integer Arithmetic Using the Carry Flag 309

CHAPTER 8 Arrays and Character Strings 371

CHAPTER 

Interrupts and Input/Output 429

CHAPTER 10

Recursion 488

CHAPTER 11

BCD Operations 516

CHAPTER 1

Microcomputers and the IBM Personal Computer

This book combines structured assembly language programming with an introduction to computer organization. Microcomputers provide a single-user environment that makes them an excellent vehicle for the study of assembly language and computer organization. They allow access to instructions that are hidden by the operating system in a time-shared environment (e.g., direct input/output instructions). This book presents the architecture and assembly language for the IBM PC and the IBM PS/2 Model 30 and other microcomputers that are based on the Intel 8088 and Intel 8086 microprocessors. For the purpose of elementary assembly language programming, the Intel 8088 and Intel 8086 microprocessors can be treated as one and the same. The designation Intel 8088/8086 (or simply, 8088/8086) is used in this book when the discussion applies to both of these microprocessors. The architectural differences between the two microprocessors are discussed in Section 1.4. Specific sections of this book discuss some additional capabilities available in the assembly language of the Intel 80286 microprocessor and in the assembly language of the Intel 80386 microprocessor.

This chapter provides background material and establishes a foundation for the study of the IBM PC and the IBM PS/2 Model 30 and their architectures. It begins with a brief discussion of the IBM PC and IBM PS/2 families of microcomputers and the microprocessors on which they are based. The notion of a microprocessor's machine language and its symbolic form (i.e., assembly language) are introduced. The architecture of microcomputers in general and the architectures of the IBM PC and the Intel 8088 microprocessor and of the IBM PS/2 Model 30 and the Intel 8086 microprocessor are discussed. The chapter includes a section on number systems in general and the binary and hexadecimal number systems in particular. The binary number system is used by most digital computers. The hexadecimal number system is used as an abbreviation for the binary number system. The basic components of an 8088/8086 assembly language program for translation by the Microsoft Macro Assembler (MASM) Version 6.0 are presented. The chapter concludes with a brief discussion of some system software packages that are available to support 8088/8086 assembly language programmers.

1.1 IBM Personal Computer and Personal System/2

The IBM Corporation has developed two families of microcomputers: the *Personal Computer (PC) family* and the *Personal System/2 (PS/2) family*. The PC family includes the IBM PC, the IBM PC Convertible, the IBM PCjr, the IBM Portable PC, the IBM PC/XT, and the IBM PC/AT. The microcomputers in these two families are designed around the Intel family of microprocessors, which includes the Intel 8088, the Intel 8086, the Intel 80286, the Intel 80386, and the Intel 80486. The IBM PC family of microcomputers is designed around the Intel 8088 microprocessor on the low end and the Intel 80286 microprocessor on the high end. The IBM PS/2 family is designed around the Intel 8086 on the low end, the Intel 80286 in the middle range, and the Intel 80386 on the high end.

A **microprocessor** interprets and executes **machine language**, which is a set of general-purpose instructions. Machine language is a numeric language, which means that all machine language instructions and the data on which those instructions operate are in numeric form. Each microprocessor has its own machine language. A family of microprocessors may have a common machine language or compatible machine languages. For example, the machine language of the Intel 8088 microprocessor is exactly the same as the machine language of the 8086 microprocessor and is a subset of the machine language of the 80286 microprocessor. The machine language of the 80286 microprocessor is a subset of the machine language of the 80386 microprocessor. This compatibility allows any program that executes on the 8088/8086 to execute on the 80286 and 80386, and it allows any program that executes on the 80286 to execute on the 80386. Such **upward compatibility** exists when, as we move upward in the family of microprocessors (i.e., from older designs to newer designs), software still executes correctly. However, some programs that execute on the 80386 cannot execute on the 80286, and some programs that execute on the 80286 cannot execute on the 8088/8086. The reason is that the 80386 machine language contains instructions that are not available in the 80286 machine language and the 80286 machine language contains instructions that are not available in the 8088/8086 machine language. Even though the machine language for the Intel 8088/8086 is a subset of the machine language for the Intel 80286, the two microprocessors interpret a few of the common instructions in a slightly different manner. Most example programs in this book execute the same on the 8088/8086 and the 80286. When instructions interpret differently between the two microprocessors, this difference is explained.

A machine language program is a sequence of numbers that represents instructions and data. Since both instructions and data are represented by numbers, the microprocessor cannot tell the difference between instructions and data simply by appearance. By the way a program is written and by specifying where in the program execution is to begin, the programmer tells the processor how to interpret the contents of each memory location (i.e., as an instruction or as a data item). Since the microprocessor gets its instructions and data from the memory component of the computer, a machine language program must be loaded into memory before it can be executed. Therefore, to program in machine language, a programmer must specify the contents of memory locations both for instructions and data.

Assembly language is just a symbolic form of machine language. Numeric operation codes are replaced by mnemonics; numeric memory addresses are replaced by symbolic names; data values may be specified in a number system other than the computer's number system; and numeric codes are replaced by symbolic codes. To program in assembly language, the programmer must specify the contents of memory locations, both for instructions and data, in a symbolic form. There is a one-to-one correspondence between assembly language entities and machine language entities: Each assembly language instruction translates to one machine language instruction, and each assembly language data value translates to one machine language data value. The **assembler** program performs the translation from assembly language to machine language.

Microcomputer Architecture

A microcomputer consists of three components: the *central processing unit* (*CPU*), the *memory*, and the *I/O subsystem.* They are connected by a bus system. A **bus** is a set of parallel wires over which digital data in transmitted. Figure 1.1 shows a simple block diagram of the microcomputer components. The bus system in the figure includes an address bus, a data bus, and a control bus.

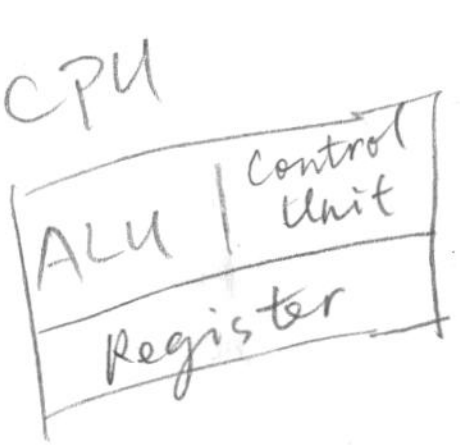

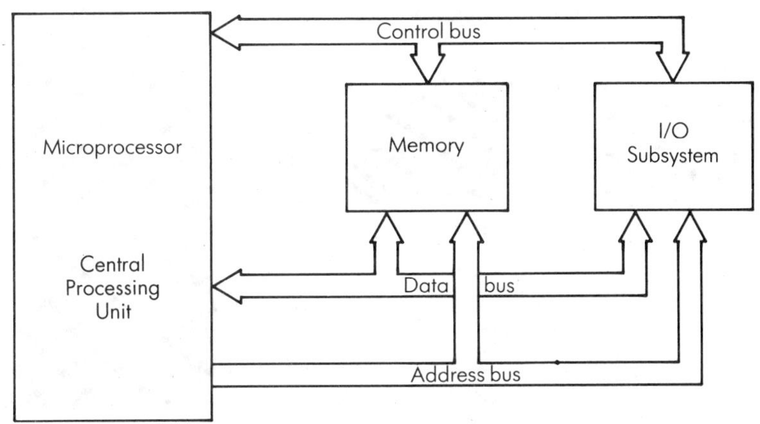

FIGURE 1.1
Microcomputer block diagram

Microprocessors

The **CPU** of a microcomputer is a microprocessor. A microprocessor includes three major components: the *control unit* (*CU*), the *arithmetic logic unit* (*ALU*), and a set of *registers.* Figure 1.2 shows a simple block diagram of the CPU components. The **control unit** of a microprocessor interprets machine language instructions and transmits signals that control the various components of the computer system as they perform the operations necessary to execute the instructions. The **ALU** performs arithmetic computations (e.g., addition and subtraction) and logical operations (e.g., logical conjunction and disjunction). These operations are performed under the control of the CU. The **register set** provides the capability for temporary storage of numeric data within the CPU itself. The registers act like a "scratch pad" for the microprocessor; they keep track of the instructions, data, memory addresses, and status indicators the microprocessor is working with. The following types of registers

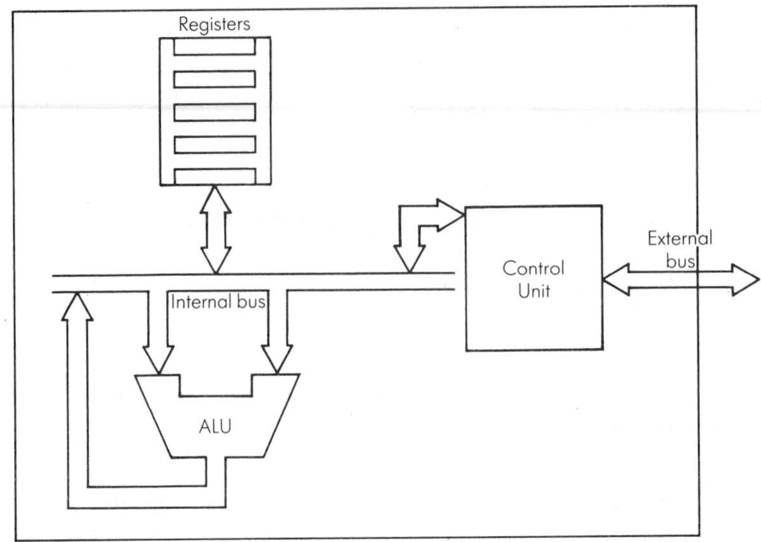

FIGURE 1.2
Microprocessor block diagram

are typically found in microprocessors:

Instruction register This register holds the instruction that the microprocessor is currently decoding and executing.

Program counter This register holds the memory address of the next instruction to be executed.

Accumulator registers These registers are used to hold operands for ALU operations and to hold the result of ALU operations.

Index registers These registers are used as counters (to perform operations such as loop control) and as subscripts (to access elements of data structures like arrays and strings).

Processor status word This register contains information regarding the current state of the CPU. Among other things, the processor status word contains information that describes the result of the ALU's latest arithmetic or logic operation (e.g., whether the result was negative, zero, or positive or whether the result was too large to be stored in an accumulator register).

A microprocessor performs a cyclic process, as shown in Figure 1.3. It fetches an

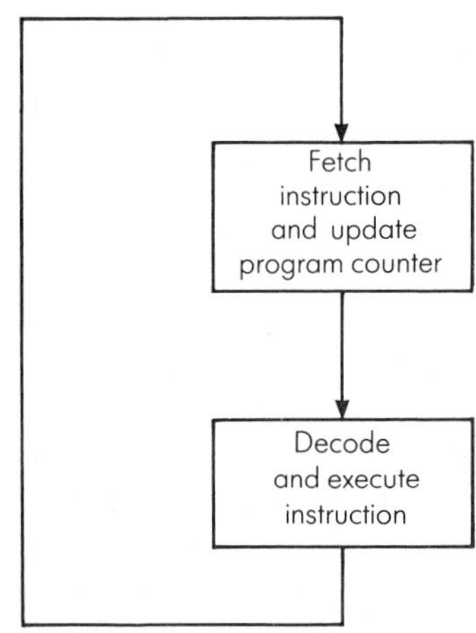

FIGURE 1.3
Cyclic process performed by a microprocessor

instruction from memory, updates the program counter, decodes the instruction, and sends the appropriate control signals to the affected components of the computer system to direct execution of the instruction. The microprocessor then repeats the process over and over until it receives a special halt instruction or a specific external event occurs (i.e., the operator presses a halt button or the power is removed). Execution of an instruction may involve operations that can be performed entirely within the microprocessor (e.g., adding two operands that are already in processor registers). However, instruction execution may involve operations that require the services of other components of the computer system (e.g., fetching an operand from memory or storing the result of a computation in memory).

The kinds of instructions that can be interpreted and executed by a typical microprocessor include:

- Arithmetic operations, for example:
  - Add two numbers.
  - Subtract two numbers.
- Logical operations, for example:
  - AND two truth values.
  - Invert a truth value.
- Data transfer operations, for example:
  - Move a value from memory to a CPU register.
  - Exchange the values of two CPU registers.
- Transfer of control operations, for example:
  - Fetch the next instruction from a specified memory location.
  - Fetch the next instruction from a specified memory location only if a certain condition holds True. Otherwise, continue with sequential instruction execution.

Memory

The instructions that the microprocessor interprets and executes and the data required for execution of those instructions are obtained from memory. The **memory** of a microcomputer can be viewed as a linear array of storage cells in which each cell is capable of holding a fixed size number (i.e., a fixed number of digits), the size being the same for all storage cells in a given computer's memory. Each storge cell is identified by a unique number, called its **address**. For a memory with n storage cells, the addresses generally range from 0 to $n - 1$, as shown in Figure 1.4.

A microcomputer's memory is somewhat analogous to a set of post office boxes in a post office. Each box has a unique number (the box number) by which it is identified (addressed). The analogy fails, however, when the notion of contents is considered. A post office box may be empty, it may contain a single letter, or it may contain many letters, and the letters in a post office box may be of different sizes. The contents of a memory cell, on the other hand, are always exactly one m-digit number, in which m digits is the fixed size of each storage cell. A memory cell can never be empty; it always contains a value. However, the value of a given storage cell may not have meaning to the program that is executing. Whenever a new m-digit number is stored in a given storage cell, it replaces the m-digit number previously stored in that cell. When the contents are fetched from a storage cell, the contents are not removed. Only a copy of the contents of that cell is obtained. The value in the storage cell remains unchanged. The m-digit number in a storage cell may be interpreted in many

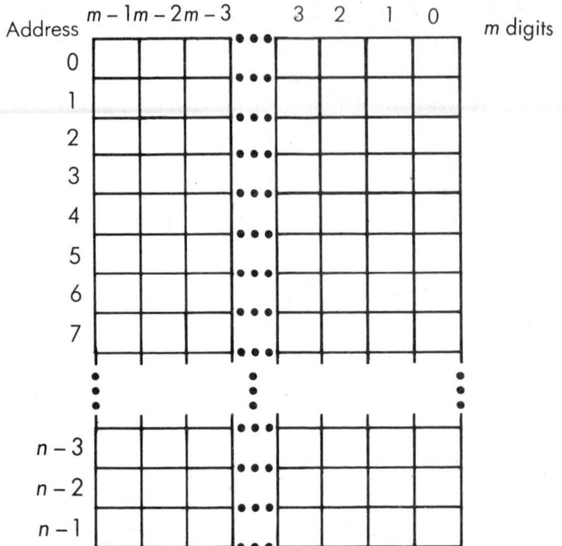

FIGURE 1.4 *n*-cell by *m*-digit memory

ways: It may be interpreted as an instruction or as part of an instruction; it may be interpreted as an integer, as part of an integer, or as several integers; and it may be interpreted as one or more characters in a character string.

The CPU can perform two operations with respect to memory: The CPU may fetch the contents of a memory cell, or it may replace the contents of (store a new value in) a memory cell. To fetch a copy of a memory cell's contents, the CPU places the address of the memory cell on the address bus (see Figure 1.1) and sends a control signal on the control bus to memory, instructing the memory to perform a fetch operation. The memory reads the address from the address bus, extracts a copy of the contents of the specified memory cell, and places that value on the data bus. The CPU then reads the copy of the memory cell's contents from the data bus.

To store a new value in a memory cell, the CPU places the address of the memory cell on the address bus, places the data to be stored at that address on the data bus, and sends a control signal to memory, instructing it to perform a store operation. The memory reads the address from the address bus and replaces the value of the specified memory cell with a copy of the value read from the data bus.

I/O Subsystem

The **I/O subsystem** provides the communications link between the microprocessor/memory and the input/output devices (e.g., keyboard, display monitor, and printer). The I/O subsystem in its simplest form consists of a set of **I/O ports**, which is similar to a set of memory locations. The main difference between a memory location and an I/O port is that a port has an electrical connection to some external device. As in the case of memory, the set of I/O ports is connected to the bus system. To select a specified I/O port, its address is placed on the address bus. Data can be transmitted to or received from the selected port via the data bus. A signal on the control bus is used to indicate whether the bus system is being used to communicate with memory or to communicate with an I/O port. An I/O port temporarily holds numeric data that is being transmitted between the microprocessor and an external device. A port may be used for transmitting data to or receiving data from a device, transmitting control information to a device, or receiving status information from a device.

Hypothetical Computer

Consider the hypothetical machine whose architecture is shown in Figure 1.5. (For discussion purposes, the hypothetical computer in this book uses the decimal number system.) The characteristics of this hypothetical machine are described as follows:

Main Memory The main memory of the machine contains 1000 storage locations addressed by the consecutive integers 000 to 999. Each memory location holds a five-digit decimal integer (i.e., the word size of the machine is five decimal digits). The value stored in a memory location can represent either a single machine language instruction or a nonnegative integer.

Central Processing Unit The CPU of the machine contains a control unit (not shown in Figure 1.5), an arithmetic logic unit, and the following registers:

Arithmetic registers These two registers supply operands to the ALU for arithmetic operations and receive results from the ALU. Each of the arithmetic registers is capable of holding a five-digit decimal integer. The A-register is the main arithmetic register. The B-register is used as an extension of the A-register for multiply and divide operations. That is, the combined A- and B-register can hold a 10-digit decimal integer.

FIGURE 1.5
Hypothetical machine

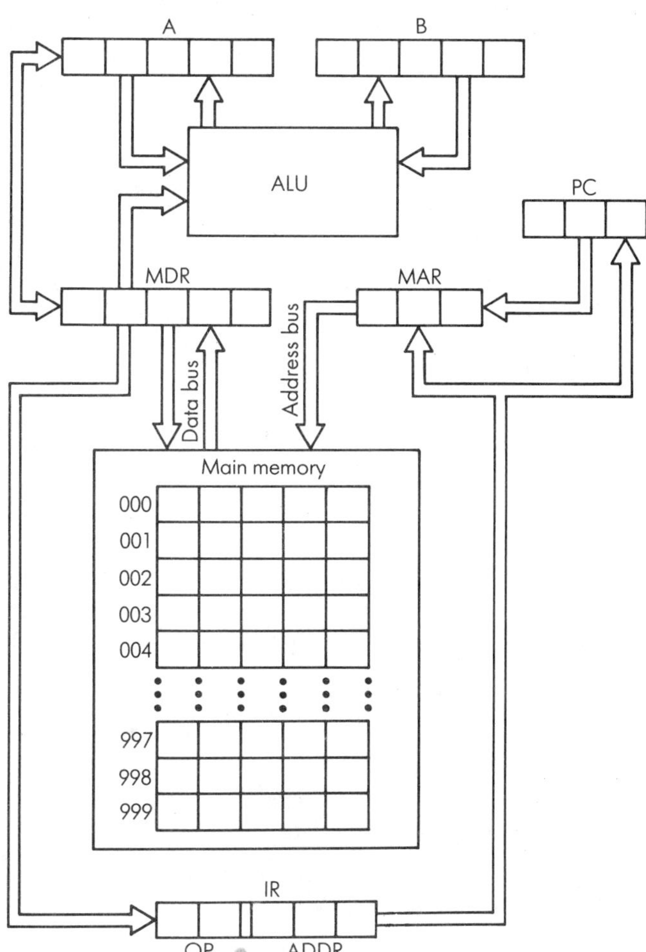

Program counter (*PC*) The PC-register is the register that holds the main memory address of the next instruction to be executed. The size of the PC-register is dependent on the size of the main memory. It must be capable of holding a value at least as large as the highest memory address (999). The PC-register in Figure 1.5 can hold a three-digit decimal integer.

Instruction register (*IR*) The instruction register holds the machine instruction currently being executed. Its size is dependent on the machine language. The instruction register in Figure 1.5 can hold a five-digit decimal integer.

Memory address register (*MAR*) The memory address register holds the address of the memory location where an instruction or data value is to be fetched or stored. Its size is dependent on the size of the main memory. It must be capable of holding a value at least as large as the highest memory address. The memory address register in Figure 1.5 can hold a three-digit decimal integer.

Memory data register (*MDR*) The memory data register holds the instruction or data value just fetched from memory or about to be stored in memory. Its size is dependent on the word size of the machine. The memory data register in Figure 1.5 can hold a five-digit decimal integer.

Everything outside the main memory in Figure 1.5 is part of the CPU. The connection between the MAR and the main memory represents the address bus, and the connections between the MDR and the main memory represent the bidirectional data bus. All other connections are part of the CPU's internal bus.

A machine language instruction for the hypothetical machine is represented by a five-digit decimal integer. Figure 1.6 shows the format for this machine language instruction. The **operation code** (**op code**) field is made up of the first two digits and identifies the operation to be performed. The address field is made up of the last three digits and identifies the memory location that contains the operand. Not all machine language instructions require an operand from memory; which means the address field may have another meaning in some instructions. Table 1.1 describes the operations performed for a selected subset of machine language op codes for this hypothetical machine.

FIGURE 1.6 Instruction format for the hypothetical machine

The instruction execution cycle for the hypothetical machine includes the operations shown in Figure 1.3. The process labeled "Fetch instruction and update program counter" consists of the following steps in the hypothetical machine:

1. Move PC value to the MAR.
2. Activate memory to perform a fetch operation. To perform the fetch operation, memory receives the address from the MAR via the address bus, extracts a copy of the contents of the specified memory location, and transmits the extracted value to the MDR via the data bus.
3. Update the value of the PC-register. The PC-register value is incremented by 1 so that it addresses the next instruction in sequence.
4. Move the fetched instruction from the MDR to the IR.

TABLE 1.1
Machine language operations for the hypothetical machine

Op Code	Operation Performed
01	Load the A-register with a copy of the contents of the memory location specified by the address in the instruction's address field.
02	Store a copy of the value of the A-register in the memory location specified by the address in the instruction's address field.
03	Exchange the contents of the A-register with the contents of the B-register. The address field of the instruction is ignored.
04	Load the A-register with the value zero. The address field of the instruction is ignored.
20	Add the contents of the memory location specified by the address in the address field to the contents of the A-register, leaving the result in the A-register.
21	Subtract the contents of the memory location specified by the address in the address field from the contents of the A-register, leaving the result in the A-register.
22	Multiply the contents of the memory location specified by the address in the address field by the contents of the A-register, leaving the result in the combined A- and B-register.
23	Divide the contents of the combined A- and B-register by the contents of the memory location specified by the address in the address field, leaving the quotient in the A-register and the remainder in the B-register.
30	Set the program counter (PC-register) to the value in the address field of the instruction; that is, jump to the instruction in the memory location specified by the address in the address field.
99	Halt instruction execution.

The steps of the process labeled "Decode and execute instruction" in Figure 1.3 depend on the operation code of the instruction itself. The steps of this process are shown by tracing an example program fragment. Suppose the state of the machine at the beginning of the instruction cycle is as shown in Figure 1.7. The PC-register indicates that memory location 000 contains the next instruction to be executed. Figures 1.8–1.14 trace the execution of three instructions in this machine.

The first iteration of the instruction execution cycle begins with an instruction fetch. The PC-register identifies the location in memory of the next instruction to be fetched. The PC-register value (000) is copied into the memory address register, and a memory fetch operation is initiated. While the memory fetch operation is being performed, the processor increments the value in the PC-register (from 000 to 001). The memory fetch operation includes the following steps:

1. The contents of the MAR (000) are placed on the address bus.
2. The contents (01999) of the memory location specified by the address on the address bus (000) are copied onto the data bus.
3. The value on the data bus (01999) is copied into the MDR.

The value fetched from memory (01999) is copied from the MDR into the instruction register, completing the instruction fetch portion of the execution cycle. After completing the instruction fetch, the state of the machine is as shown in Figure 1.8.

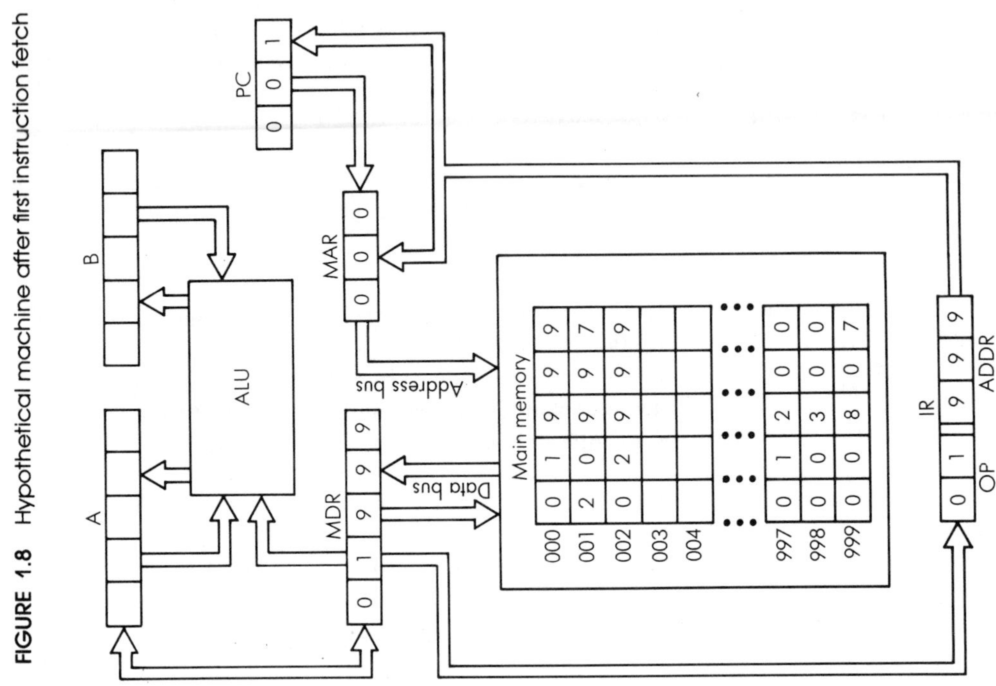

FIGURE 1.8 Hypothetical machine after first instruction fetch

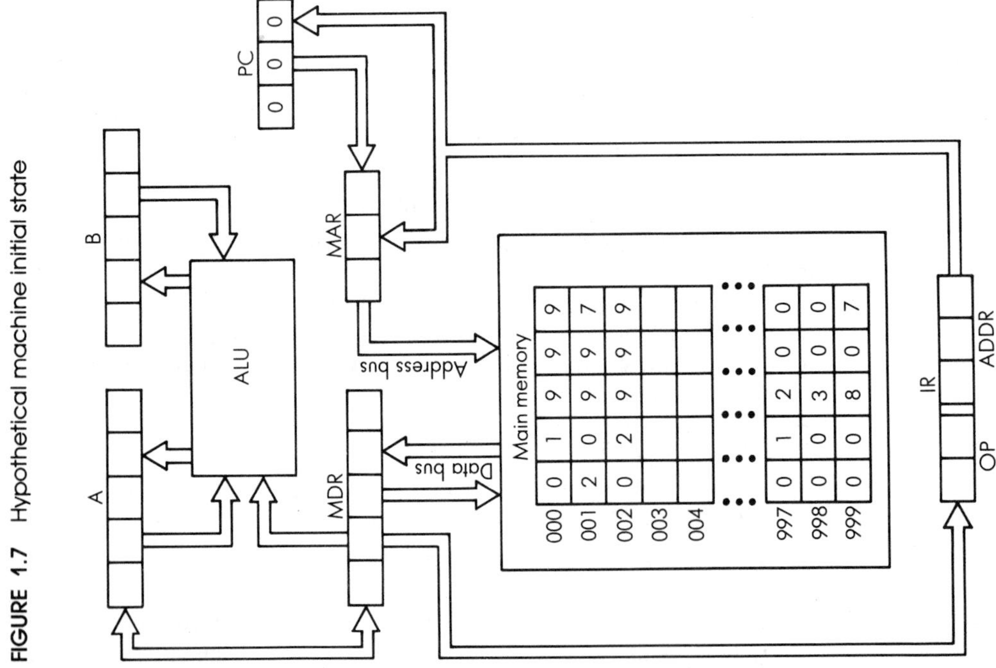

FIGURE 1.7 Hypothetical machine initial state

The first iteration of the instruction execution cycle continues with the instruction decode phase. During this phase, the control unit determines the operations to be performed in executing the instruction in the instruction register. The operation code in the first two digits of the instruction register value (01) indicates that a "load A-register from memory" operation is to be performed.

The execution phase for this instruction begins with a data fetch. The last three digits of the value in the instruction register identify the memory location of the data to be fetched. The address field of the instruction register (999) is copied from the instruction register into the memory address register, and a memory fetch operation is initiated. The steps for this data fetch operation are similar to those for the instruction fetch operation discussed previously. The value fetched from memory (00807) is copied from the MDR into the A-register, completing the execution phase for the instruction. After completing the first iteration of the execution cycle—that is, after completing the execution of the first instruction—the state of the machine is as shown in Figure 1.9.

The second iteration of the instruction execution cycle also begins with an instruction fetch. The PC-register again identifies the location in memory (001) of the next instruction to be fetched. The steps of the instruction fetch are similar to those for the first instruction fetch. After completing the second instruction fetch, the state of the machine is as shown in Figure 1.10.

The second iteration of the instruction execution cycle continues with the instruction decode phase. During this phase, the control unit determines the operations to be performed in executing the instruction in the instruction register. The op code in the first two digits of the instruction register value (20) indicates that an "add to A-register from memory" operation is to be performed.

The execution phase for this instruction begins with a data fetch. The last three digits of the value in the instruction register (997) identify the memory location of the data to be fetched. After completing the data fetch operation, the state of the machine is as shown in Figure 1.11. The next step in the execution phase is the addition operation. This operation is performed by the ALU. The ALU receives its operands from the A-register (00807) and the memory data register (01200). The result of the addition operation (02007) is returned to the A-register. After completing the second iteration of the instruction execution cycle—that is, after completing the execution of the addition instruction—the state of the machine is as shown in Figure 1.12.

The third iteration of the instruction execution cycle also begins with an instruction fetch. The PC-register again identifies the memory location (002) of the next instruction to be fetched. After completing the third instruction fetch, the state of the machine is as shown in Figure 1.13.

The third iteration of the cycle continues with the instruction decode phase. During this phase, the control unit determines the operations to be performed in executing the instruction in the instruction register. The operation code in the first two digits of the instruction register value (02) indicates that a "store from A-register into memory" operation is to be performed.

The execution phase for this instruction involves a data store operation. The last three digits of the value in the instruction register (999) identify the memory location where the data is to be stored. The value of the A-register (02007) is the value that is to be stored in that memory location. The contents of the address field of the instruction register (999) are copied into the memory address register, the A-register value (02007) is copied into the memory data register, and a memory store operation

FIGURE 1.9 Hypothetical machine after first instruction execution

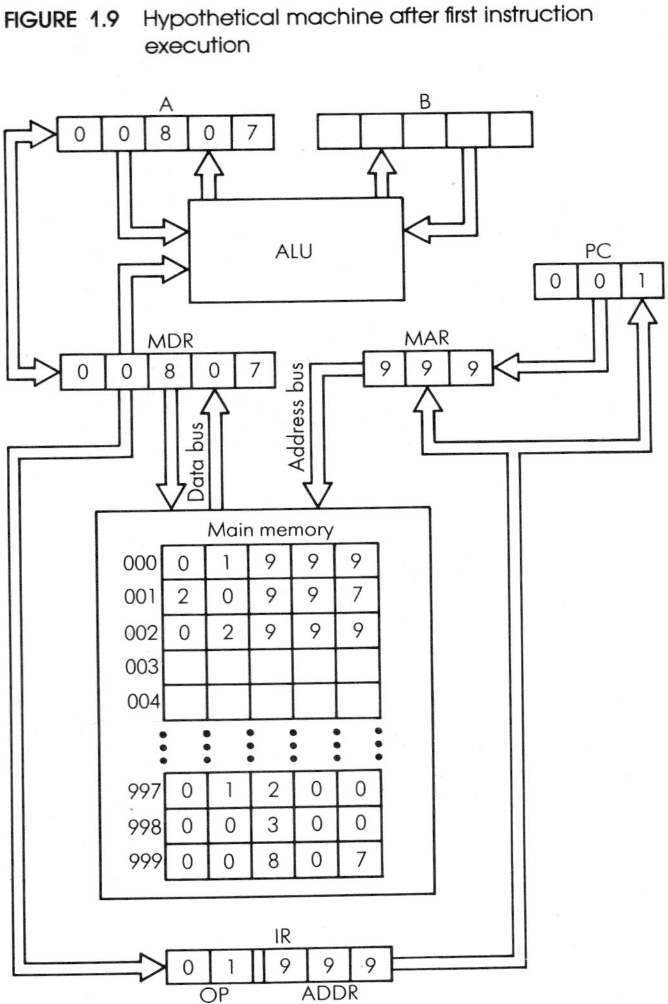

FIGURE 1.10 Hypothetical machine after second instruction fetch

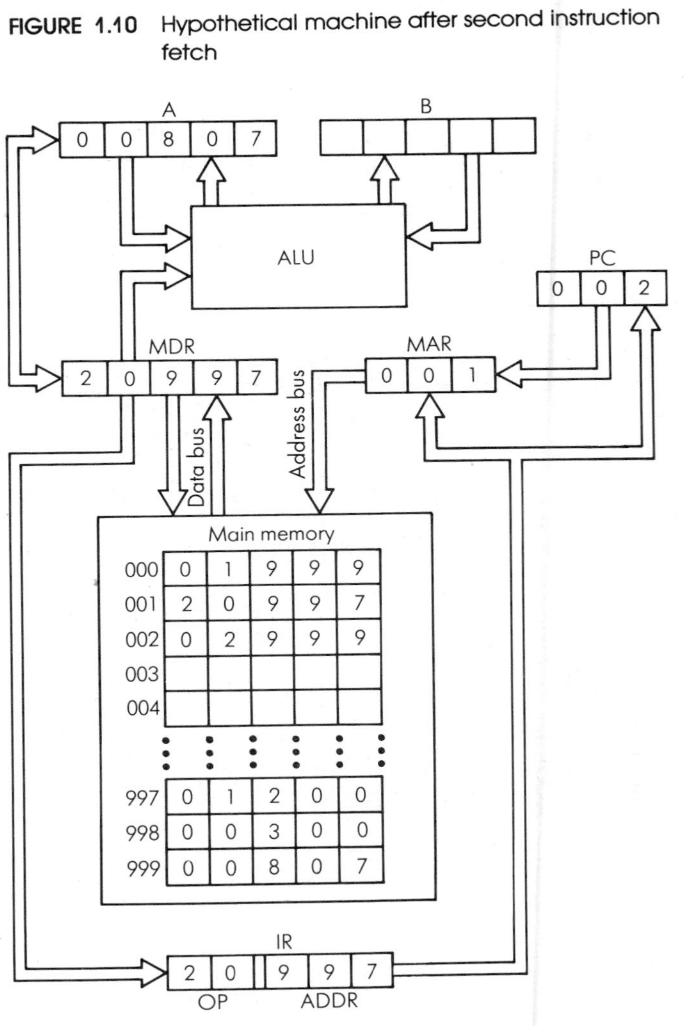

FIGURE 1.11 Hypothetical machine after data fetch for second instruction

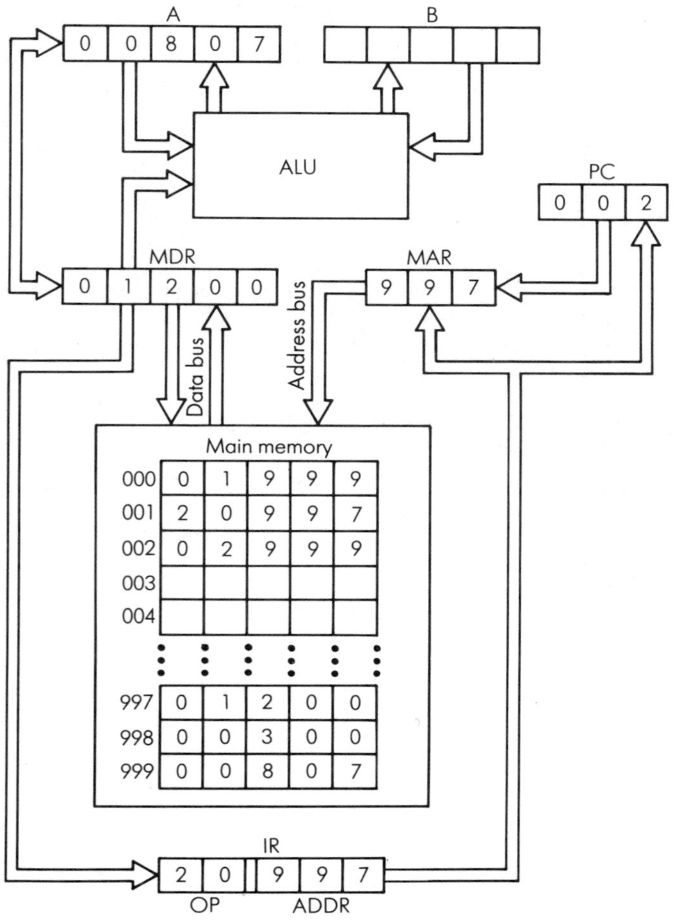

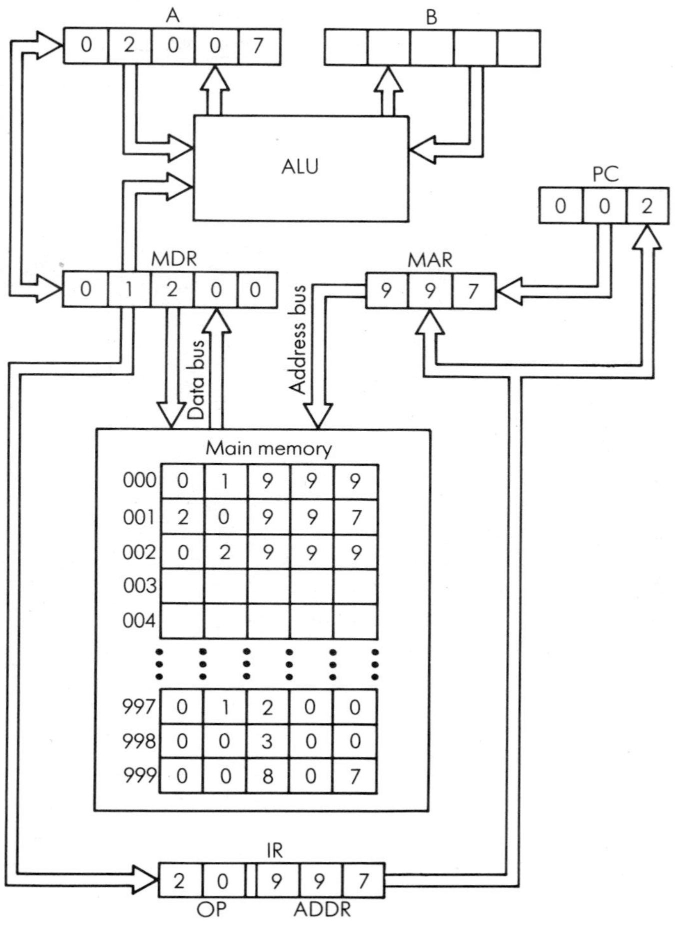

FIGURE 1.12 Hypothetical machine after second instruction execution

is initiated. The memory store operation includes the following steps:

1. The contents of the MAR (999) are placed on the address bus.
2. The contents of the MDR (02007) are placed on the data bus.
3. The contents of the memory location specified by the address on the address bus (999) are replaced by the value on the data bus (02007).

After completing the third iteration of the instruction execution cycle—that is, after completing the execution of the store operation—the state of the machine is as shown in Figure 1.14. The instruction execution cycle continues in this manner, as the microprocessor steps its way through the instructions of a machine language program.

The machine language program fragment shown in the memory of the hypothetical machine is in a numeric form, the form understood by the machine, but machine language is not a convenient form for humans to use for writing programs. Assembly language provides a more convenient form for writing programs because it is a symbolic representation of the machine language. Table 1.2 shows the assembly

TABLE 1.2
Symbolic form of machine language operations

Machine Code	Assembler Format	Operation Performed
01	LDA *addr*	Load the A-register with a copy of the contents of the memory location specified by the symbolic name in the *addr* field of the instruction.
02	STA *addr*	Store a copy of the value of the A-register in the memory location specified by the symbolic name in the *addr* field of the instruction.
03	XAB	Exchange the contents of the A-register with the contents of the B-register.
04	CLA	Load the A-register with the value zero.
20	ADD *addr*	Add the contents of the memory location specified by the symbolic name in the *addr* field to the contents of the A-register, leaving the result in the A-register.
21	SUB *addr*	Subtract the contents of the memory location specified by the symbolic name in the *addr* field from the contents of the A-register, leaving the result in the A-register.
22	MUL *addr*	Multiply the contents of the memory location specified by the symbolic name in the *addr* field by the contents of the A-register, leaving the result in the combined A- and B-register.
23	DIV *addr*	Divide the contents of the combined A- and B-register by the contents of the memory location specified by the symbolic name in the *addr* field, leaving the quotient in the A-register and the remainder in the B-register.
30	JMP *addr*	Set the program counter (PC-register) to the value specified by the symbolic name in the *addr* field of the instruction; that is, jump to the instruction in the memory location specified by the symbolic name in the *addr* field.
99	HLT	Halt instruction execution.

FIGURE 1.13 Hypothetical machine after third instruction fetch

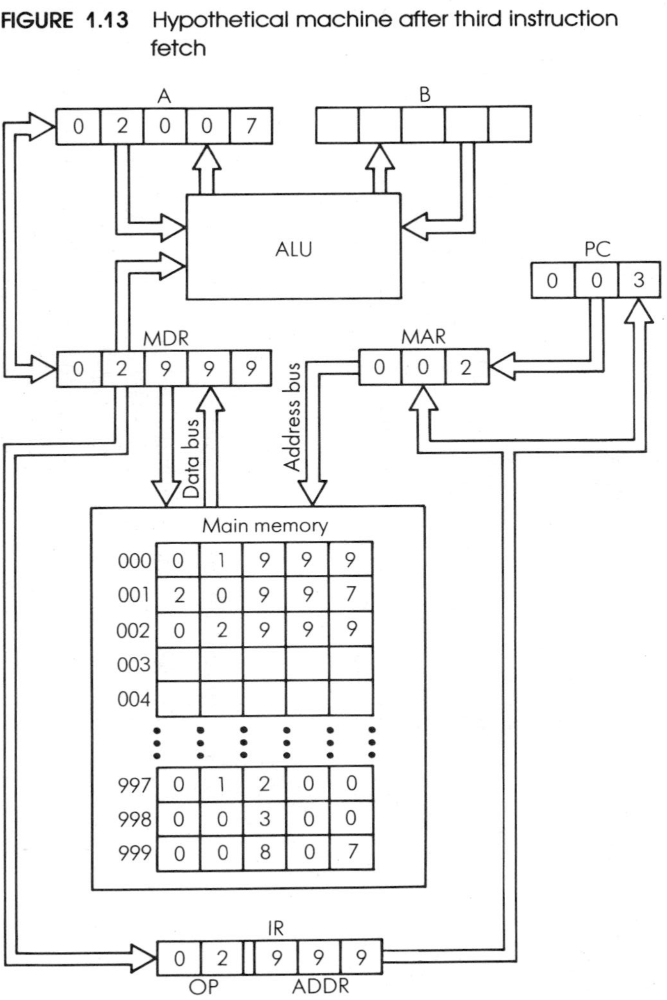

FIGURE 1.14 Hypothetical machine after third instruction execution

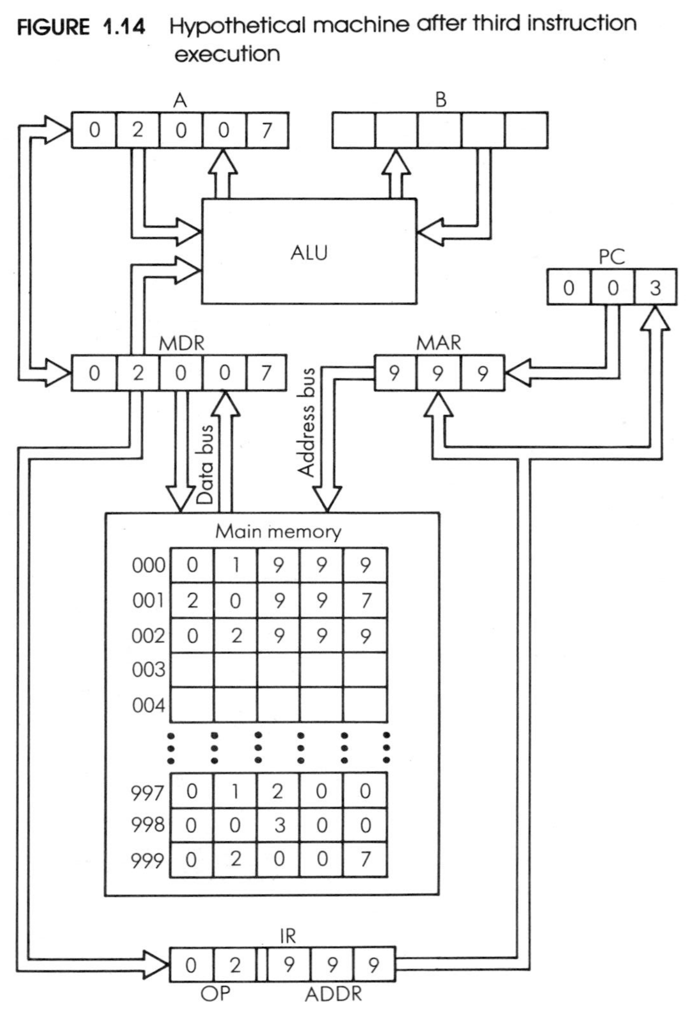

language version of the machine language given in Table 1.1. The decimal operation codes are replaced by three-character mnemonics, and the decimal memory addresses are replaced by symbolic names that are used to represent memory addresses. The machine language program fragment shown in the memory of the hypothetical machine could be translated into the following assembly language code:

```
   LDA  Z
   ADD  X
   STA  Z
     .
     .
     .
X  DEC  01200
Y  DEC  00300
Z  DEC  00807
```

The operation code DEC is referred to as a *pseudo-operation.* It does not represent a machine language operation code but is a directive to the assembler. The directive

```
X  DEC  01200
```

tells the assembler to allocate a storage cell in memory to be associated with the symbolic name X and to give that storage cell an initial value of 1200. Thus, whenever X is used in the program, it is a reference to this storage cell. In assembly language, the programmer does not need to determine or even to know the storage cell associated with a symbolic name. The assembler, in conjunction with other support software, determines the storage cell to be associated with any specific symbolic name. Any time the symbolic name is referenced, it refers to the same storage cell.

1.3 Positional Number Systems

Most people are familiar with the decimal number system, which is a **positional number system**. Each positional number system has a base, or **radix**, that defines the number of symbols used to represent numbers in that system. With a positional number system, the value given to each digit is determined by its position relative to a reference point, called the **radix point**. The position values of digits to the left of the radix point are based on the right-to-left progression of the nonnegative powers of the base. The position values of digits to the right of the radix point are based on the left-to-right progression of the negative powers of the base.

Decimal Number System

The **decimal number system** is a positional number system in which the base is 10, and the radix point is referred to as the **decimal point**. The decimal number system uses 10 symbols, the digits 0, 1, 2, 3, 4, 5, 6, 7, 8, and 9. The position values of digits to the left of the decimal point are based on the right-to-left progression of the nonnegative powers of 10. The position values of digits to the right of the decimal point are based on the left-to-right progression of the negative powers of 10.

EXAMPLE

The number 1427.73 in the base 10 number system represents

$$1 \times 10^3 + 4 \times 10^2 + 2 \times 10^1 + 7 \times 10^0 + 7 \times 10^{-1} + 3 \times 10^{-2}$$

$$1000 + \quad 400 + \quad 20 + \quad 7 + \quad .7 + \quad .03$$ ■

Consider the notion of counting in the decimal number system. We begin with 0, the lowest-valued digit, and count through the digits, in order, by value (0, 1, 2, 3, 4, 5, 6, 7, 8, and 9). When we reach the highest-valued digit, we place a 0 in that position and increment the next higher position by 1, producing 10 in this case. We then count through the digits again (10, 11, 12, 13, 14, 15, 16, 17, 18, and 19). Having reached the highest-valued digit, we place a 0 in that position and increment the next higher position by 1, producing 20 in this case. We then count through the digits again (20, 21, 22, 23, 24, 25, 26, 27, 28, and 29). The process continues until we reach 90, 91, 92, 93, 94, 95, 96, 97, 98, and 99. Having reached the highest-valued digit, we place a 0 in that position and increment the next higher position by 1. However, we also have reached the highest-valued digit in that position. Therefore, we place a 0 in that position too and increment the next higher position by 1, producing 100.

This procedure for counting can be stated in algorithm form. When counting from the *n*-digit decimal integer

$$d_{n-1}d_{n-2} \ldots d_2 d_1 d_0$$

to its successor, we perform the following steps:

```
I = 0
WHILE dI = 9
       dI = 0
        I = I + 1
ENDWHILE
dI = successor of dI
```

The preceding algorithm instructs you to start with the rightmost digit of the number and work left. When the highest-valued digit (9 in the case of decimal) is encountered, set that digit to 0 and carry a 1 into the next digit position. When a digit that is less than the highest-valued digit is reached, set it to its successor (i.e., add 1 to it) and stop the process.

EXAMPLE

The successor of 13499 is

13499 (the digits 499 struck through)

13500 ■

Binary Number System

The binary number system is the number system that is native to the digital computer. An assembly language programmer must be competent with the binary number system. The components of a computer system are two-state devices. That is, they can be in only one of two possible states at any given time.

EXAMPLES

Magnetic materials such as the tiny magnetic cores used in the main memory of some computers are magnetized either in one direction or in the opposite direction.

电晶体
Transistors are either conducting or nonconducting.
Switches are either open or closed.
Electrical pulses are either present or absent. ■

This two-state property gives rise to the base 2 number system, called the **binary number system**. The binary number system is a positional number system with a base of 2 and uses two symbols to represent numbers: 0 and 1. The radix point is referred to as the **binary point**, and a single **binary** dig**it** is called a **bit**.

Counting in Binary

Counting in binary can be described using a slight modification to the decimal counting algorithm already given. When counting from the *n*-bit binary integer

$$b_{n-1}b_{n-2} \dots b_2 b_1 b_0$$

to its successor, we perform the following steps:

```
I = 0
WHILE bI = 1
      bI = 0
       I = I + 1
ENDWHILE
bI = successor of bI
```

The preceding algorithm instructs you to start with the rightmost digit of the number and work left. When the highest-valued digit (1 in the case of binary) is encountered, set that digit to 0 and carry a 1 into the next digit position. When a digit that is less than the highest-valued digit is reached, set it to its successor (i.e., add 1 to it) and stop the process. Table 1.3 compares counting in binary to counting in decimal.

TABLE 1.3
Counting in binary and decimal

Binary	Decimal	Binary	Decimal	Binary	Decimal
0	0	1000	8	10000	16
1	1	1001	9	10001	17
10	2	1010	10	10010	18
11	3	1011	11	10011	19
100	4	1100	12	10100	20
101	5	1101	13	10101	21
110	6	1110	14	10110	22
111	7	1111	15	10111	23

Binary-to-Decimal Conversion

Since the binary number system is a positional number system, the value given to each digit in a binary number is determined by its position relative to the binary point. The position values of digits to the left of the binary point are based on the right-to-left progression of the nonnegative powers of 2 (10 in binary). The position values of digits to the right of the binary point are based on the left-to-right progression of the negative powers of 2. The number 10110.101 in the binary number system represents

$$1 \times 10^{100} + 0 \times 10^{11} + 1 \times 10^{10} + 1 \times 10^{1} + 0 \times 10^{0} + 1 \times 10^{-1}$$
$$+ 0 \times 10^{-10} + 1 \times 10^{-11}$$

Note that this expression is written entirely in binary.

To convert a number from binary to decimal, first express that number in terms of powers of the base. Then convert that expression to decimal and carry out the arithmetic in the decimal number system. The binary number 10110.101, previously expressed in terms of powers of the base, converts to the following decimal expression:

$$1 \times 2^{4} + 0 \times 2^{3} + 1 \times 2^{2} + 1 \times 2^{1} + 0 \times 2^{0} + 1 \times 2^{-1} + 0 \times 2^{-2}$$
$$+ 1 \times 2^{-3}$$

Carrying out the arithmetic in the decimal number system yields

$$16 + 0 + 4 + 2 + 0 + 0.5 + 0.0 + 0.125 = 22.625$$

Therefore, 22.625 is the decimal equivalent of the binary number 10110.101.

Consider another example. The binary number 110101011.011 is expressed as

$$1 \times 10^{1000} + 1 \times 10^{111} + 0 \times 10^{110} + 1 \times 10^{101} + 0 \times 10^{100} + 1 \times 10^{11}$$
$$+ 0 \times 10^{10} + 1 \times 10^{1} + 1 \times 10^{0} + 0 \times 10^{-1} + 1 \times 10^{-10}$$
$$+ 1 \times 10^{-11}$$

Converting this expression to decimal yields

$$1 \times 2^{8} + 1 \times 2^{7} + 0 \times 2^{6} + 1 \times 2^{5} + 0 \times 2^{4} + 1 \times 2^{3} + 0 \times 2^{2} + 1 \times 2^{1}$$
$$+ 1 \times 2^{0} + 0 \times 2^{-1} + 1 \times 2^{-2} + 1 \times 2^{-3}$$

Carrying out the arithmetic in decimal yields

$$256 + 128 + 0 + 32 + 0 + 8 + 0 + 2 + 1 + 0.0 + 0.25 + 0.125$$
$$= 427.375$$

Note that as you move left in a binary number, the value associated with each digit position is twice the value of the previous digit position, and as you move right in a binary number, the value associated with each digit position is one-half the value of the previous digit position.

EXAMPLE

101101011.1011

1	0	1	1	0	1	0	1	1	1	0	1	1
×	×	×	×	×	×	×	×	×	×	×	×	×
256	128	64	32	16	8	4	2	1	.5	.25	.125	.0625
256	+0	+64	+32	+0	+8	+0	+2	+1	+.5	+0	+.125	+.0625

= 363.6875

The decimal equivalent of the binary integer 101101011.1011 is 363.6875. ■

Decimal-to-Binary Conversion

To convert decimal numbers to binary, first separate the integer and fractional portions of the decimal number, convert the two portions separately, and then rejoin the two converted parts to get the equivalent binary number.

To convert the integer portion of the decimal number to binary, perform the following algorithm, in which NUMBER represents the decimal integer to be converted and is an input to the algorithm:

```
I = 0
REPEAT
     I = I + 1
     DIGIT(I)  = NUMBER mod 2
     NUMBER    = NUMBER / 2 (truncated to an integer)
UNTIL NUMBER = 0
WHILE I ≠ 0
     OUTPUT DIGIT(I)
     I = I - 1
ENDWHILE
```

Note that the mod operator provides the remainder from an unsigned division operation.

The algorithm just given can be summarized as follows: Repeatedly divide NUMBER by 2 and replace NUMBER with the quotient of the division each time. Continue this division process until NUMBER becomes zero. Writing down the remainders of these divisions in the reverse order from which they were produced provides the equivalent binary integer. Table 1.4 traces this process for the decimal integer 327. Writing down the remainders in the reverse order from which they were produced provides 101000111, which is the binary number equivalent to the decimal integer 327.

TABLE 1.4
Conversion of 327 from decimal to binary

Number / 2	= Quotient	Remainder
327 / 2	163	1
163 / 2	81	1
81 / 2	40	1
40 / 2	20	0
20 / 2	10	0
10 / 2	5	0
5 / 2	2	1
2 / 2	1	0
1 / 2	0	1
0		

To convert the fractional portion of the decimal number to binary, perform the following algorithm, in which FRACTION represents the decimal fraction to be converted and COUNT represents the number of fractional digits to be produced. FRACTION and COUNT are the inputs to the algorithm:

```
OUTPUT binary point
REPEAT
     NUMBER = FRACTION * 2
     OUTPUT integer portion of NUMBER
     FRACTION = fractional portion of NUMBER
     COUNT = COUNT - 1
UNTIL COUNT = 0 or FRACTION = 0
```

The algorithm can be summarized as follows: Repeatedly multiply FRACTION by 2 and replace FRACTION with the fractional portion of the product each time. The integer portion of the product becomes the next digit to the right of the binary point. Repeat the process until FRACTION becomes zero or until the desired number of fractional digits has been produced. Table 1.5 traces this process for the decimal fraction .3125. The binary fraction that is equivalent to the decimal fraction .3125 is .0101. Joining the integer and fractional portions from the previous two examples gives

327.3125 decimal = 101000111.0101 binary

TABLE 1.5
Conversion of .3125 from decimal to binary

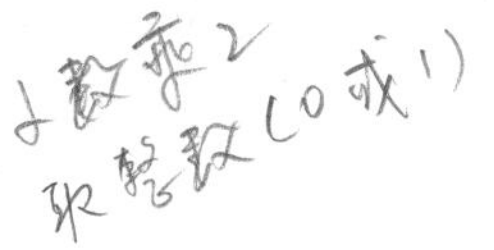

Fraction * 2	= Number	Binary Digit	Next Fraction
.3125 * 2	0.625	0	.625
.625 * 2	1.250	1	.25
.25 * 2	0.500	0	.5
.5 * 2	1.0	1	.0

Table 1.6 traces the fractional conversion process for the decimal FRACTION .1, using a digit COUNT of 10. The binary fraction that is equivalent to the decimal fraction .1 is .00011001100110011 ... Note that the binary fraction is a repeating fraction. That is, the decimal fraction .1 cannot be represented in binary with a finite number of digits. When representing decimal fractions in a computer, you can only store a finite number of digits. Thus, the fraction stored in the machine may only be an approximation to the decimal fraction that it represents. This representational error can be significant in certain computations.

TABLE 1.6
Conversion of .1 from decimal to binary

Fraction * 2	= Number	Binary Digit	Next Fraction
.1 * 2	0.2	0	.2
.2 * 2	0.4	0	.4
.4 * 2	0.8	0	.8
.8 * 2	1.6	1	.6
.6 * 2	1.2	1	.2
.2 * 2	0.4	0	.4
.4 * 2	0.8	0	.8
.8 * 2	1.6	1	.6
.6 * 2	1.2	1	.2
.2 * 2	0.4	0	.4

Octal Number System

Two number systems are widely used for abbreviations of binary numbers: the octal and hexadecimal number systems. The **octal number system** is a positional number system with base 8. The octal number system uses eight symbols (0, 1, 2, 3, 4, 5, 6, and 7) to represent numbers. The radix point is referred to as the **octal point**. Counting works the same in the octal number system as it does in any other positional number system. Table 1.7 compares counting in octal to counting in decimal.

TABLE 1.7
Counting in octal and decimal

Octal	Decimal	Octal	Decimal	Octal	Decimal
0	0	10	8	20	16
1	1	11	9	21	17
2	2	12	10	22	18
3	3	13	11	23	19
4	4	14	12	24	20
5	5	15	13	25	21
6	6	16	14	26	22
7	7	17	15	27	23

Since the octal number system is a positional number system, the value given to each digit in an octal number is determined by its position relative to the octal point. The position values of digits to the left of the octal point are based on the right-to-left progression of the nonnegative powers of 8 (10 in octal). The position values of digits to the right of the octal point are based on the left-to-right progression of the negative powers of 8. The octal number 217.43 may be expressed as

$$2 \times 10^2 + 1 \times 10^1 + 7 \times 10^0 + 4 \times 10^{-1} + 3 \times 10^{-2}$$

Note that this expression is written entirely in octal.

Octal-to-Decimal Conversion

To convert a number from octal to decimal, express the number in terms of powers of the base, convert that expression to decimal, and carry out the arithmetic in the decimal number system. The octal number 217.43, previously expressed in terms of powers of the base, converts to the following decimal expression:

$$2 \times 8^2 + 1 \times 8^1 + 7 \times 8^0 + 4 \times 8^{-1} + 3 \times 8^{-2}$$

Carrying out the arithmetic in the decimal number system produces

$$(2 \times 64) + (1 \times 8) + (7 \times 1) + (4 \times .125) + (3 \times .015625)$$

$$128 \quad + \quad 8 \quad + \quad 7 \quad + \quad .5 \quad + \quad .046875 = 143.546875$$

Therefore, 143.546875 is the decimal equivalent of the octal number 217.43.

Decimal-to-Octal Conversion

Decimal-to-octal conversion can be performed using an algorithm similar to the one that was used for decimal-to-binary conversion. The difference is that the division in the integer conversion and the multiplication in the fractional conversion are by 8 rather than by 2. Tables 1.8 and 1.9 show the steps in converting 143.546875 from

TABLE 1.8
Conversion of 143 from decimal to octal

Number / 8	= Quotient	Remainder
143 / 8	17	7
17 / 8	2	1
2 / 8	0	2
0		

TABLE 1.9
Conversion of .546875 from decimal to octal

Fraction * 8	= Number	Octal Digit	Next Fraction
.546875 * 8	4.375	4	.375
.375 * 8	3.0	3	.0

decimal to octal. Copying the remainders from Table 1.8 in the reverse order from which they were produced provides 217, the octal equivalent of the decimal integer 143. Copying the integer portion of each of the products from Table 1.9 provides .43, the octal equivalent of the decimal fraction .546875. That is,

$$143.546875 \text{ decimal} = 217.43 \text{ octal}$$

Binary-to-Octal Conversion

The octal number system is useful in dealing with binary numbers because there is a direct translation between the two systems. Table 1.10 shows each octal digit along with its three-digit binary equivalent. Note that all possible combinations of three binary digits are consumed in representing the eight octal digits. This situation occurs because the base of the octal number system (8) is a power of the base of the binary number system (2): $2^3 = 8$.

To convert a binary number to octal, start at the binary point and work in both directions, collecting the bits into groups of threes. Leading zeros can be added to the integer to complete a group of three, and trailing zeros must be added to the fraction to complete a group of three. Then use Table 1.10 to convert each three-bit group to the corresponding octal digit.

TABLE 1.10
Binary equivalents of octal digits

Octal	Binary
0	000
1	001
2	010
3	011
4	100
5	101
6	110
7	111

EXAMPLE

10101110.10001
Grouping the bits by threes about the binary point and converting each group to its octal equivalent produces

```
010 101 110.100 010
 \/  \/  \/  \/  \/
 2   5   6 . 4   2
```

Therefore, the octal equivalent of the binary number 10101110.10001 is 256.42. ■

Octal-to-Binary Conversion

To convert an octal number to binary, simply translate each octal digit to its three-bit binary equivalent. Then eliminate any leading zeros in the integer and any trailing zeros in the fraction.

713.34

Converting each octal digit to its binary equivalent produces 111 001 011.011 100. Therefore, the binary equivalent is 111001011.0111. ■

Hexadecimal Number System

The **hexadecimal number system** is a positional number system with base 16. The hexadecimal number system uses 10 digits (0, 1, 2, 3, 4, 5, 6, 7, 8, and 9) and 6 letters (A, B, C, D, E, and F). Table 1.11 shows the decimal equivalents of the hexadecimal digits. The radix point is referred to as the **hex point.** Counting works the same in the hexadecimal number system as it does in any other positional number system. Table 1.12 compares counting in hexadecimal to counting in decimal.

TABLE 1.11
Decimal equivalents of hexadecimal digits

Hexadecimal	Decimal	Hexadecimal	Decimal
0	0	8	8
1	1	9	9
2	2	A	10
3	3	B	11
4	4	C	12
5	5	D	13
6	6	E	14
7	7	F	15

TABLE 1.12
Counting in hexadecimal and decimal

Hex	Decimal	Hex	Decimal	Hex	Decimal
0	0	C	12	18	24
1	1	D	13	19	25
2	2	E	14	1A	26
3	3	F	15	1B	27
4	4	10	16	1C	28
5	5	11	17	1D	29
6	6	12	18	1E	30
7	7	13	19	1F	31
8	8	14	20	20	32
9	9	15	21	21	33
A	10	16	22	22	34
B	11	17	23	23	35

Since the hexadecimal number system is a positional number system, the value given to each digit in a hexadecimal number is determined by its position relative to the hex point. The position values of digits to the left of the hex point are based on the right-to-left progression of the nonnegative powers of 16 (10 in hexadecimal). The position values of digits to the right of the hex point are based on the left-to-right progression of the negative powers of 16. The hexadecimal number 4AF.9 may be expressed as

$$4 \times 10^2 + A \times 10^1 + F \times 10^0 + 9 \times 10^{-1}$$

Note that this expression is written entirely in hexadecimal.

Hexadecimal-to-Decimal Conversion

To convert a number from hexadecimal to decimal, express the number in terms of powers of the base, convert that expression to decimal, and carry out the arithmetic in the decimal number system. The hexadecimal number 4AF.9, previously expressed in terms of powers of the base, converts to the following decimal expression:

$$4 \times 16^2 + 10 \times 16^1 + 15 \times 16^0 + 9 \times 16^{-1}$$

Carrying out the arithmetic in the decimal number system produces

$$(4 \times 256) + (10 \times 16) + (15 \times 1) + (9 \times .0625)$$

$$1024 \quad + \quad 160 \quad + \quad 15 \quad + \quad .5625 = 1199.5625$$

Therefore, 1199.5625 is the decimal equivalent of the hexadecimal number 4AF.9.

Decimal-to-Hexadecimal Conversion

Decimal-to-hexadecimal conversion can be performed using an algorithm similar to the one that was used for decimal-to-binary conversion. The difference is that the division in the integer conversion and the multiplication in the fractional conversion are by 16 rather than by 2. The remainders produced by division and the integer portions of the products produced by multiplication will be integers in the range 0–15. These integers must be converted to the corresponding hexadecimal digits (see Table 1.11). Tables 1.13 and 1.14 show the steps in converting 1004.546875 from decimal to hexadecimal. Copying the hexadecimal digits that correspond to the remainders from Table 1.13 in the reverse order from which they were produced provides 3EC, the hexadecimal equivalent of the decimal integer 1004. Copying the hexadecimal equivalents of the integer portion of each of the products from Table 1.14 produces .8C, the hexadecimal equivalent of the decimal fraction .546875. That is,

1004.546875 decimal = 3EC.8C hexadecimal

TABLE 1.13
Conversion of 1004 from decimal to hex

Number / 16	=	Quotient	Remainder	Hex Digit
1004 / 16		62	12	C
62 / 16		3	14	E
3 / 16		0	3	3
0				

TABLE 1.14
Conversion of .546875 from decimal to hex

Fraction * 16	=	Number	Hex Digit	Next Fraction
.546875 * 16		8.75	8	.75
.75 * 16		12.0	C	.0

Binary-to-Hexadecimal Conversion

The hexadecimal number system also is useful in dealing with binary numbers because there is a direct translation between the two systems. Table 1.15 shows each hexadecimal digit along with its four-bit binary equivalent. Note that all possible combinations of four binary digits are consumed in representing the 16 hexadecimal digits. This situation occurs because the base of the hexadecimal number system (16) is a power of the base of the binary number system (2): $2^4 = 16$.

To convert a binary number to hexadecimal, start at the binary point and work in both directions, collecting the bits into groups of fours. Leading zeros can be added to the integer to complete a group of four, and trailing zeros must be added to the fraction to complete a group of four. Then use Table 1.15 to convert each four-bit group to the corresponding hexadecimal digit.

TABLE 1.15
Binary equivalents of hexadecimal digits

Hexadecimal	Binary	Hexadecimal	Binary
0	0000	8	1000
1	0001	9	1001
2	0010	A	1010
3	0011	B	1011
4	0100	C	1100
5	0101	D	1101
6	0110	E	1110
7	0111	F	1111

EXAMPLE

1101011100.10111
Grouping the bits by fours about the binary point and converting each group to its hexadecimal equivalent produces

```
0011 0101 1100.1011 1000
 \/   \/   \/   \/   \/
 3    5    C  . B    8
```

Therefore, the hexadecimal equivalent of the binary number 1101011100.10111 is 35C.B8. ■

Hexadecimal-to-Binary Conversion

To convert a hexadecimal number to binary, simply translate each hexadecimal digit to its four-bit binary equivalent. Then eliminate any leading zeros in the integer and any trailing zeros in the fraction.

EXAMPLE

2A7.C4
Converting each hexadecimal digit to its four-bit binary equivalent produces 0010 1010 0111.1100 0100. Therefore, the binary equivalent is 1010100111.110001.
■

In converting numbers between the octal and decimal number systems or between the decimal and hexadecimal number systems, you will find it somewhat easier to convert to binary first. Such a conversion avoids having to deal with the powers of 8 or 16 and avoids multiplication and division by 8 or 16.

EXAMPLE

Convert the hexadecimal number 5F.C8 to decimal, as follows:

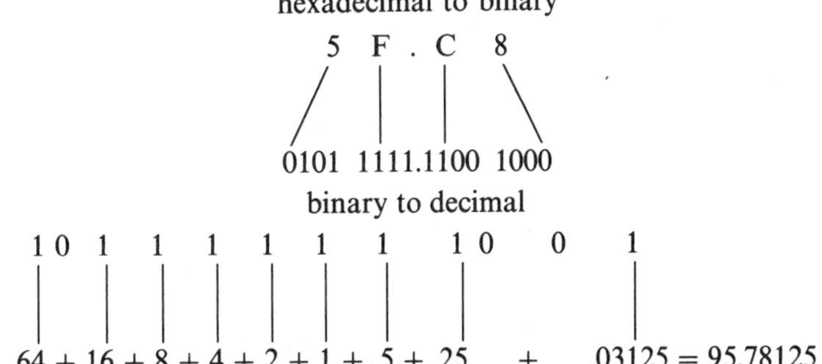

■

An assembly language program describes the contents of memory locations including both instructions and data. The assembler program translates a program from assembly language into machine language. The output of the assembler can include a binary object program (machine language) and a listing of each line of the assembly language program with its machine language equivalent. To save space in the listing, most assemblers display the machine language in either octal or hexadecimal, rather than binary. The Microsoft Macro Assembler displays the machine language in hexadecimal.

The Microsoft Disk Operating System (MS-DOS) includes a utility program called *DEBUG*, and the Microsoft Macro Assembler (MASM) includes a utility program called *CodeView*. These utility programs provide for the execution of a program one instruction at a time with user intervention allowed between instruction executions. Between instruction executions, the user can inspect and/or change the contents of registers and memory locations. This capability allows the user to trace program execution instruction by instruction. If an error is detected during the trace, the user can repair instructions and damaged data before continuing with the execution. With utility programs such as these, the memory addresses and the contents of registers and memory locations are generally displayed in hexadecimal. The values entered by the user might also have to be entered in hexadecimal. Therefore, an 8088/8086 assembly language programmer needs to be proficient in using the hexadecimal number system and in performing conversions among the binary, decimal, and hexadecimal number systems.

1.4 IBM PC and IBM PS/2 Model 30 Architecture

The IBM PC is designed around the Intel 8088 microprocessor, and the IBM PS/2 Model 30 is designed around the Intel 8086 microprocessor. The Intel 8088 is a 16-bit microprocessor internally and an 8-bit microprocessor externally. It can perform 16-bit arithmetic; its registers are 16-bit registers; and its internal bus system is a 16-bit bus system. The external data bus is an 8-bit bus; that is, data is transmitted between the microprocessor and memory or between the microprocessor and the I/O ports 8 bits at a time. The Intel 8086 is a 16-bit microprocessor both internally and externally. Data can be transmitted between the microprocessor and the I/O ports either 8 bits at a time or 16 bits at a time. This difference in data transmission rate is the primary reason why the Intel 8086 can execute instructions faster than can the Intel 8088.

IBM PC and IBM PS/2 Model 30 Memory Organization

The IBM PC and the IBM PS/2 Model 30 can address up to 1,048,576 storage cells (1024K, where 1K = 1024). From the software point of view (the logical view), these storage cells are addressed by the integers in the range 0–1,048,575 decimal (00000–FFFFF hexadecimal). Each storage cell in this memory holds an 8-bit binary number called a **byte**. Two consecutive bytes can be treated as a single 16-bit binary number called a **word**. When a word is stored in memory, it must be stored as two consecutive byte values. The low-order byte is stored first, followed by the high-order byte, as shown in Figure 1.15.

From the hardware point of view (the physical view), the memory in the IBM PC is quite different from the memory in the IBM PS/2 Model 30. The IBM PC has a single bank of memory that contains 1024K storage cells addressed by the integers in the range 00000–FFFFF hexadecimal. Each storage cell in memory holds a byte value. In the IBM PC, the byte is the unit of data transmission between the microprocessor, the memory, and the I/O ports; that is, each memory fetch operation fetches a single byte, and each memory store operation stores a single byte. When a word is stored in the memory of the IBM PC, it is stored as two consecutive byte values. The low-order byte is stored first, followed by the high-order byte. See Figure 1.15(a).

FIGURE 1.15
Sixteen-bit word stored in memory as two 8-bit bytes (low-order byte followed by high-order byte)

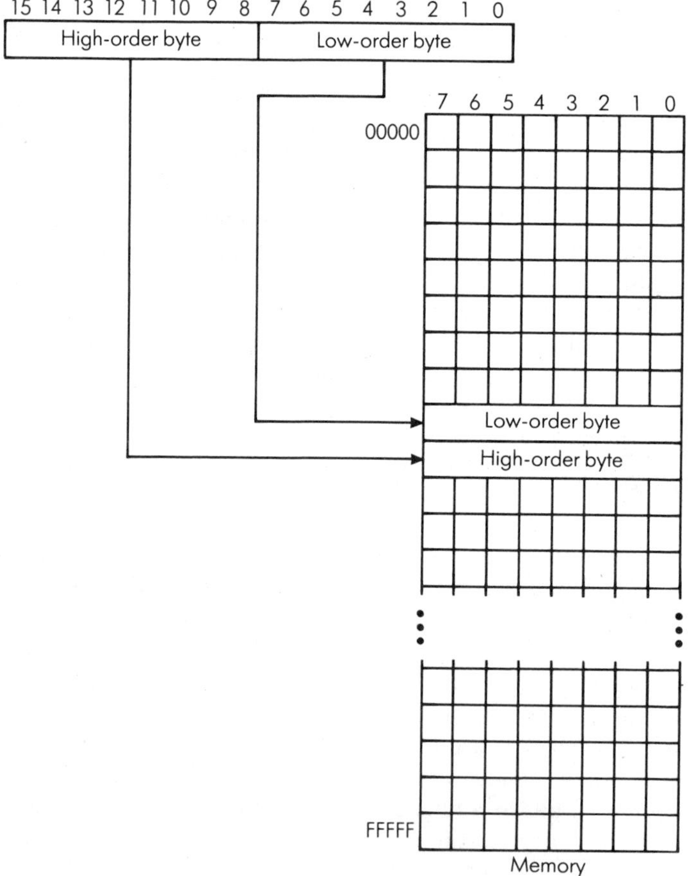

(a) Single-bank memory of an 8088-based microcomputer

The IBM PS/2 Model 30 has two banks of memory. Each bank contains 512K storage cells addressed by the integers in the range 00000–7FFFF hexadecimal. These hardware addresses are called **physical addresses**. Each storage cell in these memory banks holds a byte value. Logically (i.e., as the programmer sees it), these two memory banks make up a single memory of 1024K storage cells addressed by the integers in the range 00000–FFFFF hexadecimal. These addresses are called **logical addresses**. The two banks are organized in such a way that all the logical storage cells with even addresses are in memory bank 0 and those with odd addresses are in memory bank 1. See Figure 1.15(b). That is, the storage cells with logical addresses 00000, 00002, 00004, ..., FFFFE are the storage cells in memory bank 0 with physical addresses 00000, 00001, 00002, ..., 7FFFF, respectively, and the storage cells with logical addresses 00001, 00003, 00005, ..., FFFFF are the storage cells in memory bank 1 with physical addresses 00000, 00001, 00002, ..., 7FFFF, respectively. This type of memory organization, with adjacent logical storage cells being in different banks of physical memory, is called **memory interleaving**. Note that the low-order bit of the logical address is the bank indicator and that the high-order 19 bits of the logical address make up the physical address within the bank.

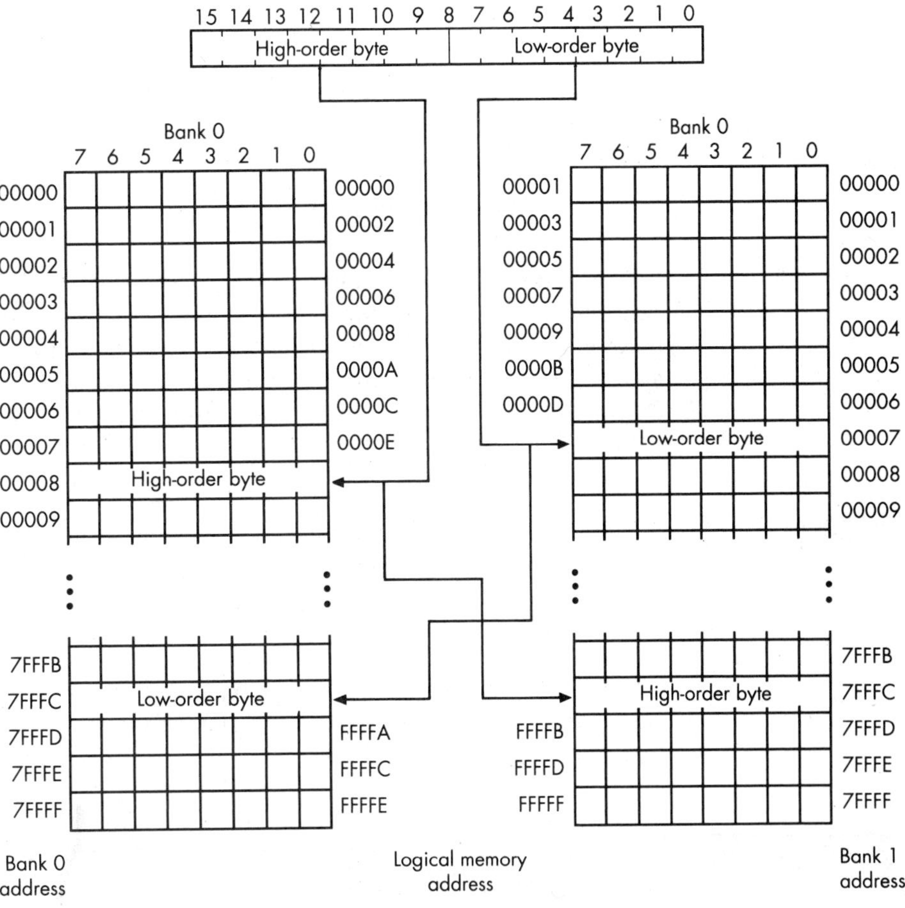

(b) Two-bank memory of an 8086-based microcomputer

EXAMPLE

(a) If the logical address is

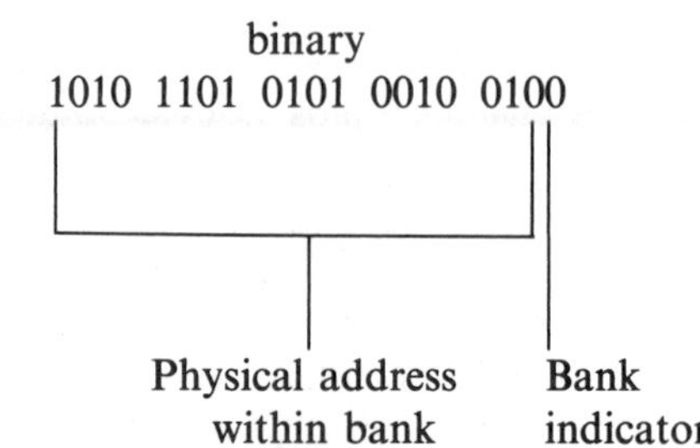

then the corresponding physical address in memory bank 0 is

binary	hexadecimal
101 0110 1010 1001 0010	56A92

(b) If the logical address is

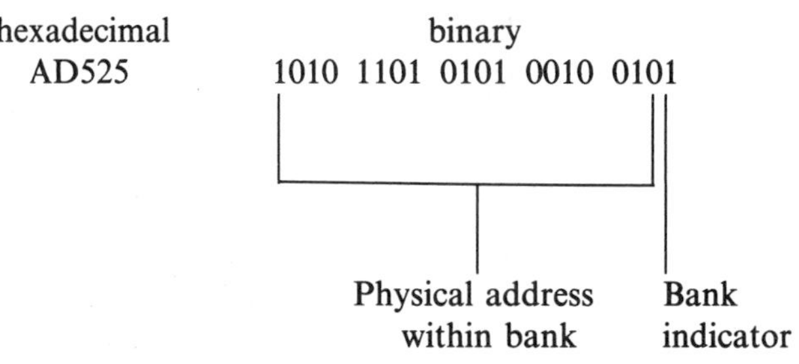

then the corresponding physical address in memory bank 1 is

binary	hexadecimal
101 0110 1010 1001 0010	56A92

■

When a word is stored in the memory of the IBM PS/2 Model 30, it is stored as two consecutive byte values. The low-order byte is stored first in logical memory, followed immediately by the high-order byte. Thus, the two bytes of a word are stored in separate memory banks. Refer to Figure 1.15(b) again. If the low-order byte is stored in a storage cell with an even logical address (i.e., in a storage cell in bank 0), then the higher-order byte is stored in bank 1 at the same physical address.

EXAMPLE

In the lower portion of Figure 1.15(b), a word is stored with the low-order byte at logical address FFFF8 (physical address 7FFFC in bank 0) and the high-order byte at logical address FFFF9 (physical address 7FFFC in bank 1). The physical address is the same in both banks. ■

However, if the low-order byte is stored in a storage cell with an odd logical address (i.e., in a storage cell in bank 1), then the high-order byte is stored in bank 0 at the next highest physical address.

EXAMPLE

In the upper portion of Figure 1.15(b), a word is stored with the low-order byte at logical address 0000F (physical address 00007 in bank 1) and the high-order byte at logical address 00010 (physical address 00008 in bank 0). The physical addresses are different in the two banks. ■

In the IBM PS/2 Model 30, the two memory banks share a common address bus but have separate data buses. Thus, a word can be transmitted between the microprocessor and memory with simultaneous bank operations if the physical address is the same in both banks (see the first of the two preceding examples). However, two sequential bank operations are required if the physical addresses are different in the two banks (see the second of the two preceding examples). Therefore, word operations in the IBM PS/2 Model 30 are more efficient if the words are aligned in memory so that the low-order byte is stored in a storage cell with an even logical address. Such word operations are discussed in more detail later in this section and in Chapter 2.

Figure 1.16 shows the basic memory map for the 1-megabyte (1024K bytes) address space of the IBM PC and the IBM PS/2 Model 30. There is from 256K to 640K of *random-access memory* (*RAM*) with addresses in the range 00000–9FFFF for the operating system and user programs; up to 128K of RAM with addresses in the range A0000–BFFFF for video display buffers (the location and size of the video display buffer depend on the video adapter present in the microcomputer system); up to 128K of *read-only memory* (*ROM*) with addresses in the range C0000–DFFFF for installable ROM modules (e.g., the IBM PC/XT has an 8K fixed disk controller installed in ROM beginning at location C8000); and up to 128K of permanent ROM with addresses in the range E0000–FFFFF for the start-up program, the Basic Input/Output System (BIOS), and the ROM BASIC interpreter. The first 1K of RAM (addresses 00000–003FF) is an interrupt vector table and is not available for general use. Interrupt vectors are discussed in Chapter 9. The next 512 locations of RAM (addresses 00400–005FF) also are not available for general use. This memory space is used for system software data areas (256 locations for BIOS and 256 locations for

FIGURE 1.16
IBM PC and IBM PS/2 Model 30 memory map

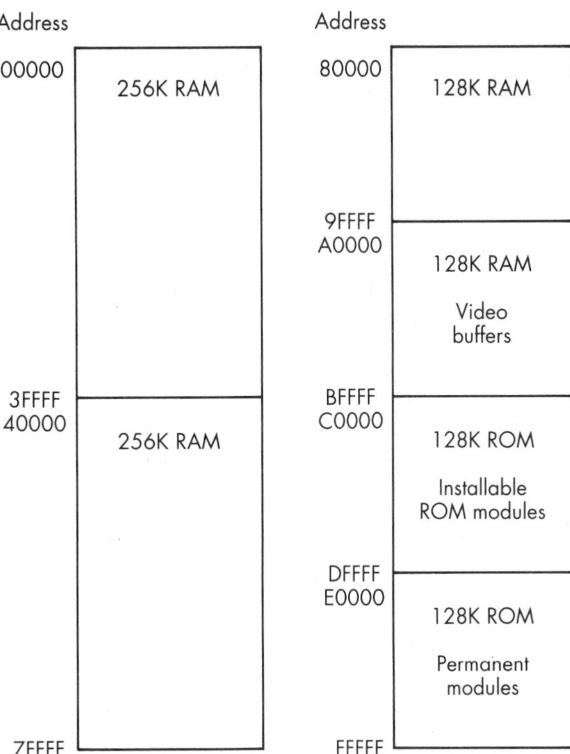

DOS and BASIC). Portions of the memory map shown in Figure 1.16 are discussed in more detail in later chapters; video adapters and video buffers, for example, are discussed further in Chapters 9 and 13.

It is important to realize that a particular microcomputer system may have less than a full megabyte of memory and that the memory may not be contiguous. For example, an IBM PC with a monochrome video monitor, in its minimum configuration, has 256K of RAM with addresses 00000–3FFFF, 4K of RAM with addresses B0000–B0FFF for the video buffer, and 40K of ROM with addresses F6000–FFFFF for BIOS and the BASIC interpreter.

Intel 8088 and Intel 8086 Microprocessors

The **Intel 8088 microprocessor** is the CPU in the IBM PC. Figure 1.17 shows a block diagram of this microprocessor. The **Intel 8086 microprocessor** is the CPU in the IBM PS/2 Model 30. The block diagram of the Intel 8086 differs only slightly from that of the Intel 8088. The differences are pointed out at the appropriate places in the following subsections. The 8088/8086 microprocessor consists of two separate processing units: the *execution unit* (*EU*) and the *bus interface unit* (*BIU*). The EU interprets and executes instructions, and the BIU performs bus operations (e.g., instruction fetch, operand fetch, data store, and communication with I/O devices).

FIGURE 1.17 Intel 8088 microprocessor

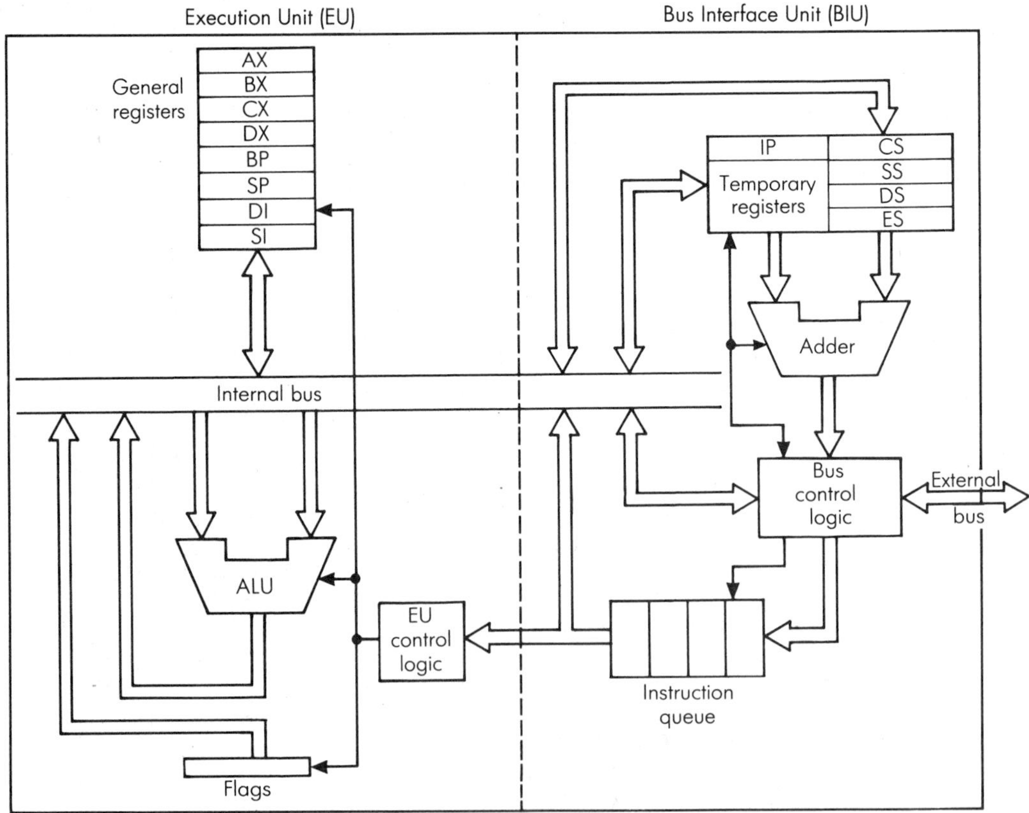

Execution Unit

The **EU** contains control logic for decoding and executing instructions, an ALU for performing arithmetic and logical operations, a set of general-purpose registers, and a control register called the *flags register*. The control logic within the EU interprets machine language instructions and controls the operations necessary for carrying out those instructions. The EU receives instruction bytes from the instruction queue in the order in which they were inserted into the instruction queue by the BIU. When the EU needs an operand from memory or needs to store a result in memory, it directs the BIU to perform the required operation. The EU provides the components needed by the BIU to compute the physical memory address for the fetch or store operation. The ALU receives its operands via the internal bus from the general registers, from instruction bytes, or from the BIU (i.e., operands fetched from memory). The ALU is capable of performing both 8-bit computations (byte computations) and 16-bit computations (word computations).

Bus Interface Unit

The **BIU** contains bus control logic that controls all external bus operations; an instruction queue for holding instruction bytes for the EU; an adder for generating physical memory addresses; and a set of registers that includes four segment registers, an instruction pointer, and some internal communications registers. The BIU is responsible for controlling all external bus operations, including communications with both memory and I/O ports. The external address bus is used to select a specific memory location or I/O port.

The BIU fetches instruction bytes and places them into the instruction queue for the EU (see Figure 1.17). The BIU can prefetch up to four bytes of instruction code in the 8088 and up to six bytes in the 8086. That is, the size of the instruction queue is four bytes in the 8088 and six bytes in the 8086. While the EU is processing one instruction byte, the BIU can be prefetching another instruction byte. As long as the EU is not requesting that the BIU perform a data fetch or data store, the BIU is free to prefetch instruction bytes. Data fetch and data store operations take priority over the instruction prefetch operation. Instruction prefetch allows the BIU and the EU to work in parallel, thus increasing the performance of the microprocessor. This form of computer architecture is known as a **pipeline architecture**, in which instruction bytes are said to be queued up in a pipeline fashion.

Bus System and Bus Operations

The Intel 8088 and the Intel 8086 are both housed in a 40-pin integrated circuit chip. A **pin** is a point of connection between the chip and its external environment. At a specific point in time, one bit may be input to the circuitry in the chip or one bit may be output from the circuitry in the chip via a given pin.

Of the 40 pins on the Intel 8088 microprocessor chip, 20 are allocated to the external address and data buses used to communicate with memory and the I/O ports. Figure 1.18(a) shows the pin numbers and standard labels used for these 20 pins. These 20 pins are connected to the 20-bit address bus. The *most significant bit* (*MSB*) of the address bus is connected at pin A_{19}; the *least significant bit* (*LSB*), at pin AD_0. Pins AD_7–AD_0 are also connected to the 8-bit data bus. The MSB of the 8-bit data bus is connected at pin AD_7; the LSB, at pin AD_0. Pins AD_7–AD_0 are **multiplexed**, which means that they have different functions at different points in time.

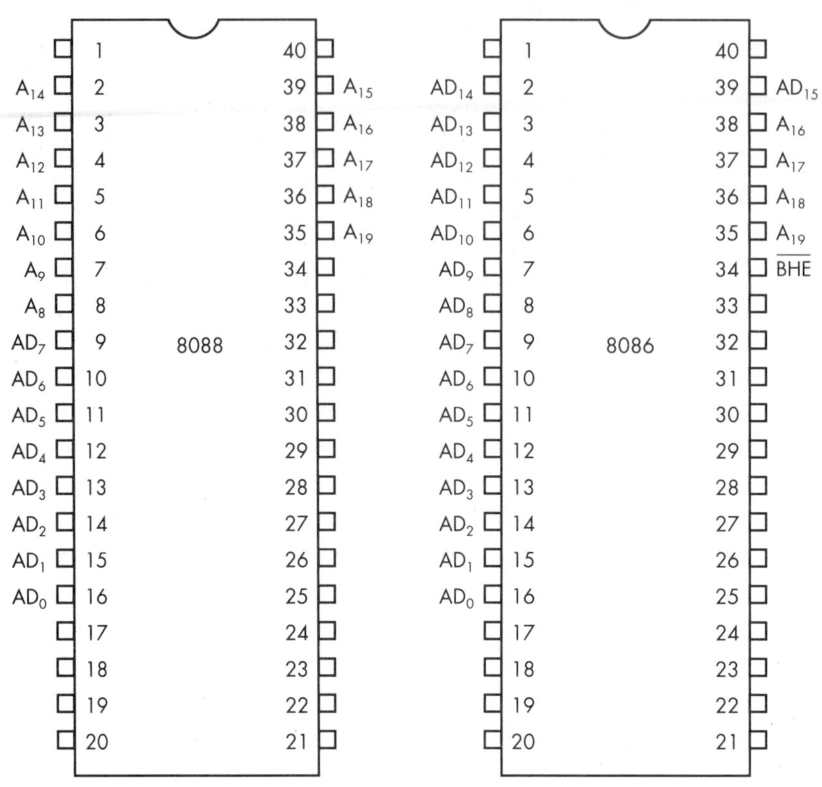

FIGURE 1.18
Pin assignments for address and data buses

(a) Intel 8088 microprocessor chip (b) Intel 8086 microprocessor chip

Of the 40 pins on the Intel 8086 microprocessor chip, 20 are allocated to the external address and data buses. Figure 1.18(b) shows the pin numbers and standard labels used for these 20 pins. These 20 pins are connected to the 20-bit address bus. The MSB of the address bus is connected at pin A_{19}; the LSB, at pin AD_0. Pins AD_{15}–AD_0 are also connected to the 16-bit data bus. The MSB of the 16-bit data bus is connected at pin AD_{15}; the LSB, at pin AD_0. Pins AD_{15}–AD_0 are multiplexed. Note that pin 34 is labeled $\overline{BHE}$ (bus high enable). The overbar indicates that it is active when in the low or zero state. This pin is connected to one of the lines of the control bus. For the most part, control signals have been eliminated from this discussion in order to focus attention on address and data involvement in memory operations. However, the $\overline{BHE}$ control signal is extremely critical for understanding operations on the two-bank memory organization of the IBM PS/2 Model 30. It is, nonetheless, important to realize that control signals are necessary to indicate whether a bus operation is a memory or an I/O operation and whether it is a fetch or a store operation.

In the IBM PC and the IBM PS/2 Model 30, a memory operation is a four-phase process, called a **bus cycle**. The four phases of the bus cycle are typically referred to as T_1, T_2, T_3, and T_4. The operations within the bus cycle are somewhat different in the two machines because of the differences in their memory organization (i.e., the single-bank organization of the IBM PC versus the two-bank organization of the IBM PS/2 Model 30).

With the IBM PC, the 20-bit address bus and the 8-bit data bus are both connected to the single memory bank. During phase T_1 of the bus cycle, the address is transmitted from the microprocessor to the address bus via pins A_{19}–AD_0. For a fetch operation, the contents of the memory location specified by the address on the address bus are placed on the data bus during phase T_2, and the microprocessor reads the data from the data bus, via pins AD_7–AD_0, during phase T_3. For a store operation, the data to be stored is transmitted from the microprocessor to the data bus, via pins AD_7–AD_0, during phase T_2, and during phase T_3, memory stores the byte that is on the data bus in the memory location specified by the address on the address bus.

EXAMPLE

To store the byte value 6A hexadecimal at memory location C3A24 hexadecimal, the following bus operations are performed in the IBM PC:

During phase T_1, the microprocessor outputs the address via pins A_{19}–AD_0. The bit values at these pins would be

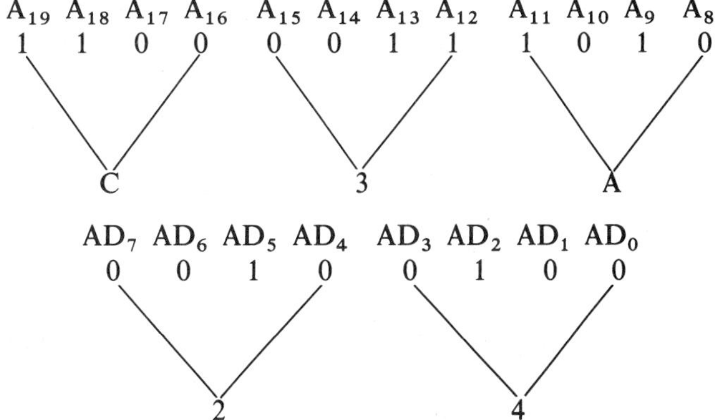

During phase T_2, the microprocessor outputs the data via pins AD_7–AD_0. The bit values at these pins would be

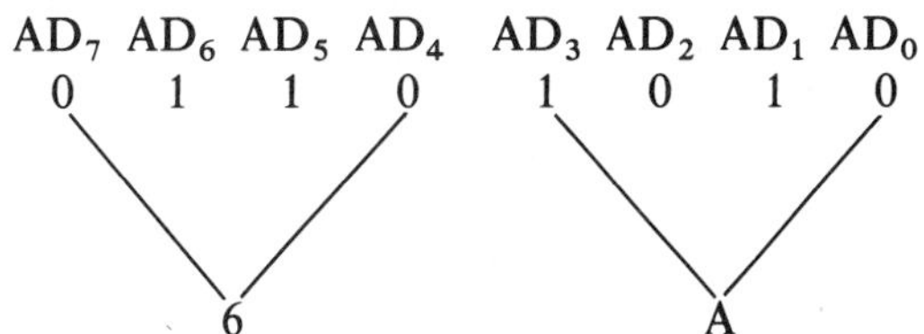

During phase T_3, memory stores the byte value 6A hexadecimal at location C3A24. ■

In the IBM PC, two bus cycles (i.e., two memory operations) are required to fetch or store a word. The first cycle transfers the low-order byte, and the second cycle transfers the high-order byte.

EXAMPLE

To fetch the word value whose low-order byte of 7B hexadecimal is stored at location 36F4D hexadecimal and whose high-order byte of A5 hexadecimal is stored at location 36F4E hexadecimal, the following bus operations are performed in the IBM PC:

During phase T_1 of the first bus cycle, the microprocessor outputs the address of the low-order byte via pins A_{19}–AD_0. The bit values at these pins would be

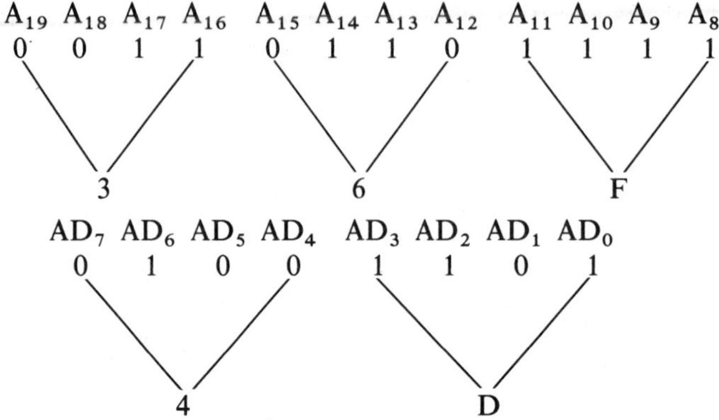

During phase T_2 of the first bus cycle, the memory places the contents of location 36F4D on the data bus, and during phase T_3, the microprocessor reads the data from the data bus via pins AD_7–AD_0. The bit values at these pins would be

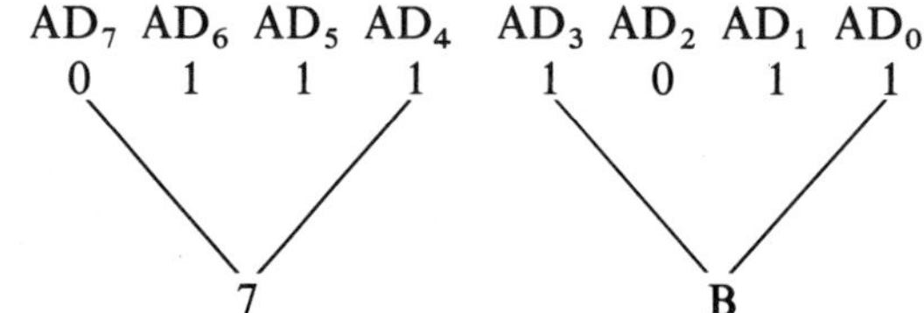

During phase T_1 of the second bus cycle, the microprocessor outputs the address of the high-order byte via pins A_{19}–AD_0. The bit values at these pins would be

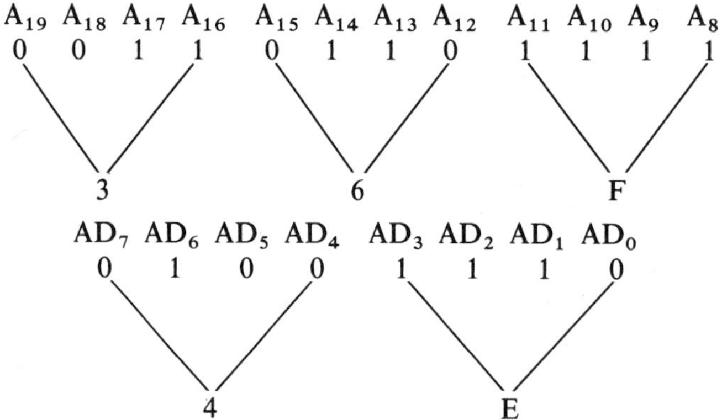

During phase T_2 of the second bus cycle, the memory places the contents of location 36F4E on the data bus, and during phase T_3, the microprocessor reads the data from the data bus via pins AD_7–AD_0. The bit values at these pins would be

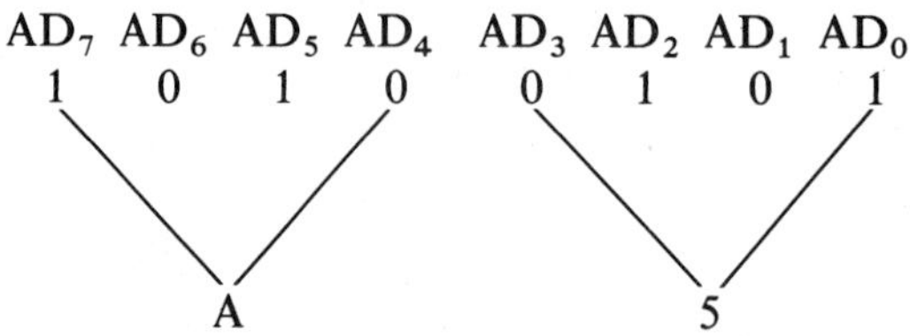

■

With the IBM PS/2 Model 30, the 20-bit address bus is connected to both memory banks. The low-order 8 bits of the 16-bit data bus are connected to memory bank 0, and the high-order 8 bits of the 16-bit data bus are connected to memory bank 1. That is, the low-order 8 bits of the data bus constitute the data bus for memory bank 0, and the high-order 8 bits constitute the data bus for memory bank 1.

Consider a byte operation involving a logical memory address that is even (i.e., the physical address is in bank 0). During phase T_1 of the bus cycle, the logical address is transmitted from the microprocessor to the address bus via pins A_{19}–AD_0, and $\overline{BHE}$ is set to 1. Since the logical address is even, the bit value at AD_0 is 0. The combination of $AD_0 = 0$ and $\overline{BHE} = 1$ tells memory that this operation is a byte operation involving bank 0. For a fetch operation, the contents of the bank 0 memory location specified by the 19-bit address on the high-order 19 bits of the address bus are placed on the low-order 8 bits of the data bus during phase T_2, and the microprocessor reads the data from the low-order half of the data bus, via pins AD_7–AD_0, during phase T_3. For a store operation, the data to be stored is transmitted from the microprocessor to the low-order 8 bits of the data bus, via pins AD_7–AD_0, during phase T_2, and during phase T_3, memory stores the byte on the low-order half of the data bus in the bank 0 memory location specified by the 19-bit address on the high-order 19 bits of the address bus.

EXAMPLE

To store the byte value 6A hexadecimal at the logical memory location C3A24 hexadecimal, the following bus operations are performed in the IBM PS/2 Model 30:

During phase T_1, the microprocessor outputs the logical address via pins A_{19}–AD_0 and sets $\overline{BHE}$ to 1. The bit values at these pins would be

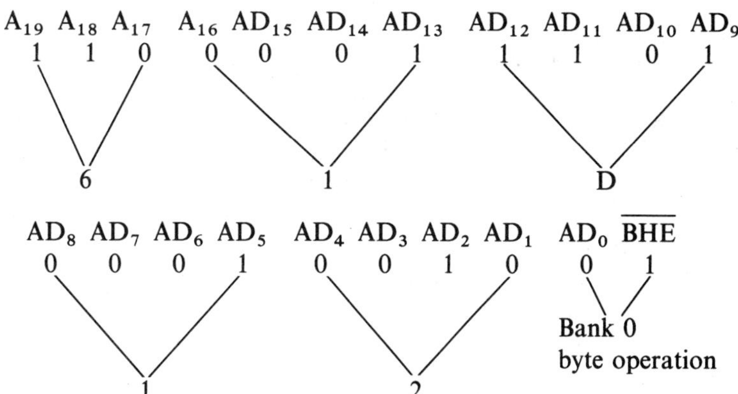

During phase T_2, the microprocessor outputs the data via pins AD_7–AD_0. The bit values at these pins would be

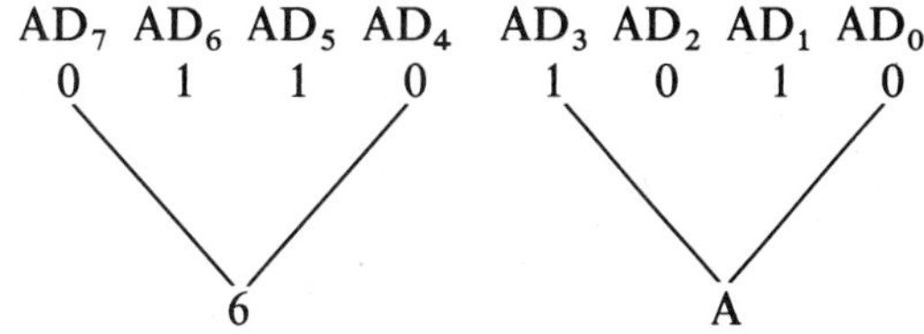

During phase T_3, memory bank 0 stores the byte value 6A hexadecimal at its physical location 61D12. ■

Consider a byte operation involving a logical memory address that is odd (i.e., the physical address is in bank 1). During phase T_1 of the bus cycle, the logical address is transmitted from the microprocessor to the address bus via pins A_{19}–AD_0, and $\overline{BHE}$ is set to 0. Since the logical address is odd, the bit value at AD_0 is 1. The combination of $AD_0 = 1$ and $\overline{BHE} = 0$ tells memory that this operation is a byte operation involving bank 1. For a fetch operation, the contents of the bank 1 memory location specified by the 19-bit address on the high-order 19 bits of the address bus are placed on the high-order 8 bits of the data bus during phase T_2, and the microprocessor reads the data from the high-order half of the data bus, via pins AD_{15}–AD_8, during phase T_3. For a store operation, the data to be stored is transmitted from the microprocessor to the high-order 8 bits of the data bus, via pins AD_{15}–AD_8, during phase T_2, and during phase T_3, memory stores the byte on the high-order half of the data bus in the bank 1 memory location specified by the 19-bit address on the high-order 19 bits of the address bus.

EXAMPLE

To store the byte value 7B hexadecimal at the logical memory location C3A25 hexadecimal, the following bus operations are performed in the IBM PS/2 Model 30:

During phase T_1, the microprocessor outputs the logical address via pins A_{19}–AD_0 and sets $\overline{BHE}$ to 0. The bit values at these pins would be

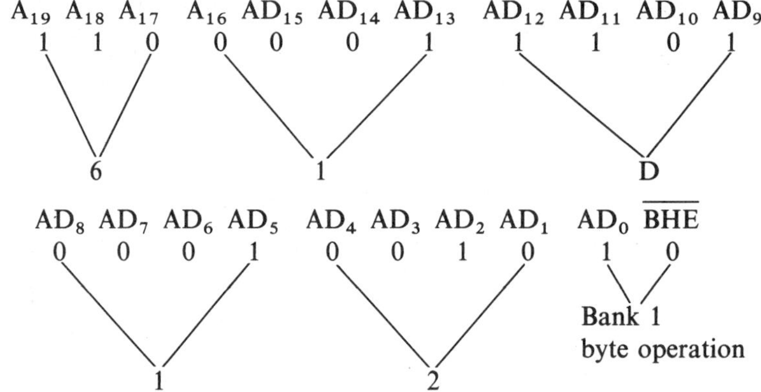

During phase T_2, the microprocessor outputs the data via pins AD_{15}–AD_8. The bit values at these pins would be

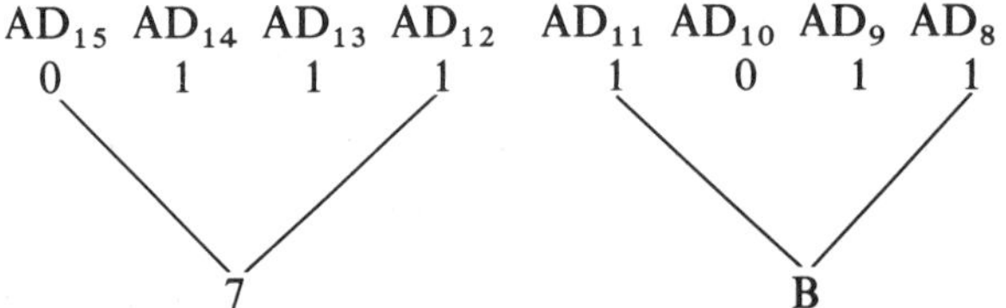

During phase T_3, memory bank 1 stores the byte value 7B hexadecimal at its physical location 61D12. ■

In the IBM PS/2 Model 30, a word is fetched or stored in one bus cycle if the logical address is even. However, two bus cycles are required if the logical address is odd.

Consider a word operation involving a logical memory address that is even. In this case, the low-order byte is fetched from or stored into bank 0, the high-order byte is fetched from or stored into bank 1, and the physical address for each bank operation is the same. Refer back to Figure 1.15(b) for verification. During phase T_1 of the bus cycle, the logical address is transmitted from the microprocessor to the address bus via pins A_{19}–AD_0, and $\overline{BHE}$ is set to 0. Since the logical address is even, the bit value at AD_0 is 0. The combination of $AD_0 = 0$ and $\overline{BHE} = 0$ tells memory that this operation is a word operation involving both bank 0 and bank 1. For a fetch operation, the contents of the bank 0 and bank 1 memory locations specified by the 19-bit address on the high-order 19 bits of the address bus are placed on the 16-bit data bus during phase T_2, and the microprocessor reads the word from the 16-bit data bus, via pins AD_{15}–AD_0, during phase T_3. The byte from bank 0 is placed on the low-order 8 bits of the data bus, which is connected to pins AD_7–AD_0, and the byte from bank 1 is placed on the high-order 8 bits of the data bus, which is connected to pins AD_{15}–AD_8. The two banks fetch their respective bytes concurrently. For a store operation, the word to be stored is transmitted from the microprocessor to the data bus, via pins AD_{15}–AD_0, during phase T_2, and during phase T_3, memory stores the word on the data bus in the bank 0 and bank 1 memory locations specified by the 19-bit address on the high-order 19 bits of the address bus. The low-order 8 bits from the data bus are stored in bank 0, and the high-order 8 bits are stored in bank 1. The two banks store their respective bytes concurrently.

EXAMPLE

To fetch the word whose value of 369C hexadecimal is stored at logical address 2468A hexadecimal (i.e., whose low-order byte of 9C is stored at logical address 2468A and whose high-order byte of 36 is stored at logical address 2468B), the following bus operations are performed in the IBM PS/2 Model 30:

During phase T_1, the microprocessor outputs the logical address via pins A_{19}–AD_0 and sets $\overline{BHE}$ to 0. The bit values at these pins would be

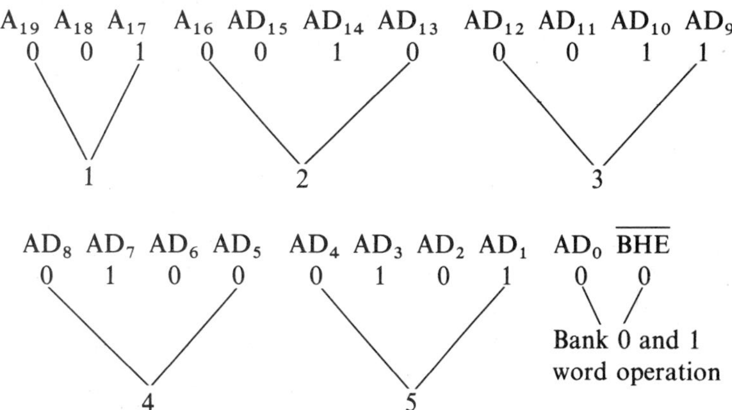

During phase T_2, memory bank 0 places the contents of its location 12345 hexadecimal on the low-order half of the data bus, and memory bank 1 places the contents of its location 12345 hexadecimal on the high-order half of the data bus. Since the address within the two banks is the same, these transfers can be done concurrently.

During phase T_3, the microprocessor reads the word from the data bus via pins AD_{15}–AD_0. The bit values at these pins would be

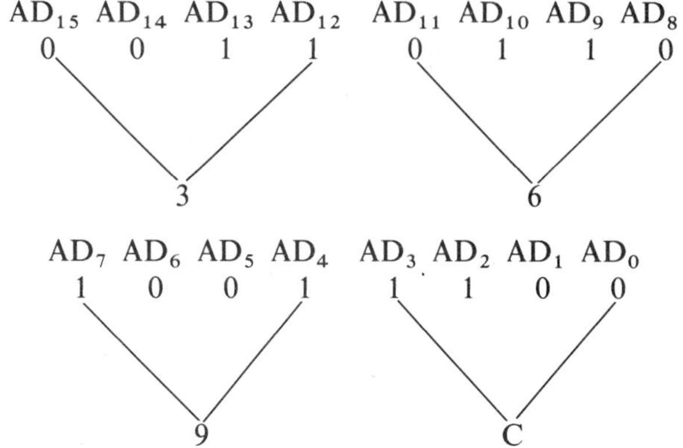

■

Consider a word operation involving a logical memory address that is odd. In this case, the low-order byte is fetched from or stored into bank 1, the high-order byte is fetched from or stored into bank 0, and the physical address for the bank 0 operation is one higher than the physical address for the bank 1 operation. Refer back to Figure 1.15(b) for verification. The operation is performed in two bus cycles. During the first bus cycle, a byte operation is performed on bank 1, and during the second bus cycle, a byte operation is performed on bank 0.

EXAMPLE

To store the word whose value is AD73 hexadecimal at logical address 2C1A5 hexadecimal, the following bus operations are performed in the IBM PS/2 Model 30:

During phase T_1 of the first bus cycle, the microprocessor outputs the logical address for the low-order byte via pins A_{19}–AD_0 and sets $\overline{BHE}$ to 0. The bit values at these pins would be

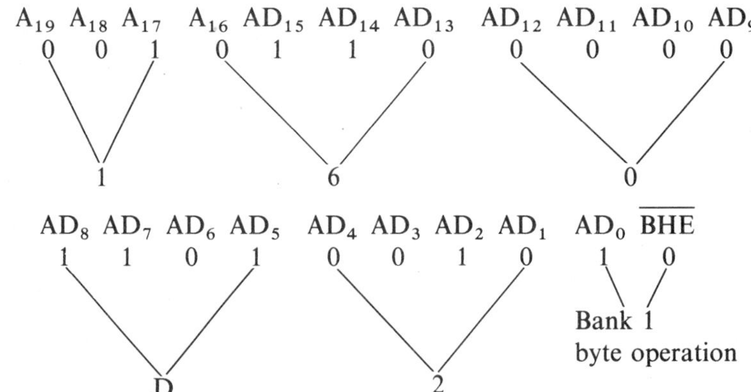

During phase T_2 of the first bus cycle, the microprocessor outputs the low-order byte of the data via pins AD_{15}–AD_8. The bit values at these pins would be

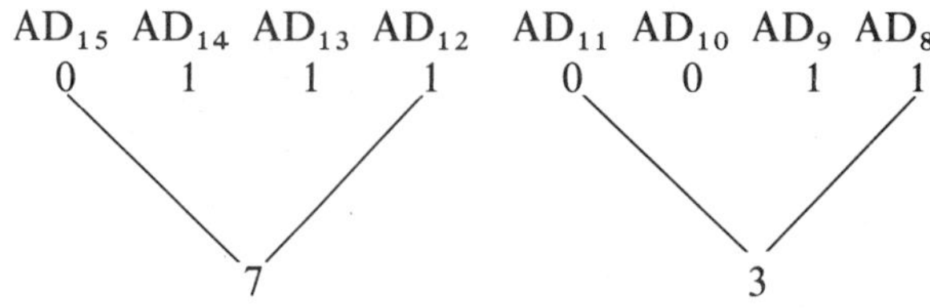

During phase T_3 of the first bus cycle, memory bank 1 stores the byte value 73 hexadecimal at its physical location 160D2.

During phase T_1 of the second bus cycle, the microprocessor outputs the logical address for the high-order byte via pins A_{19}–AD_0 and sets $\overline{BHE}$ to 1. The bit values at these pins would be

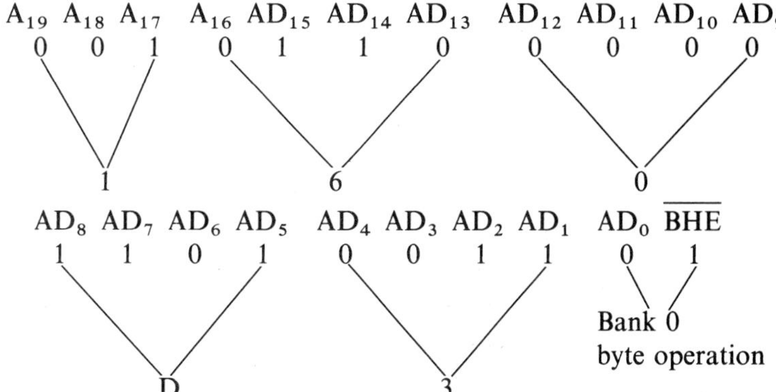

During phase T_2 of the second bus cycle, the microprocessor outputs the high-order byte of the data via pins AD_7–AD_0. The bit values at these pins would be

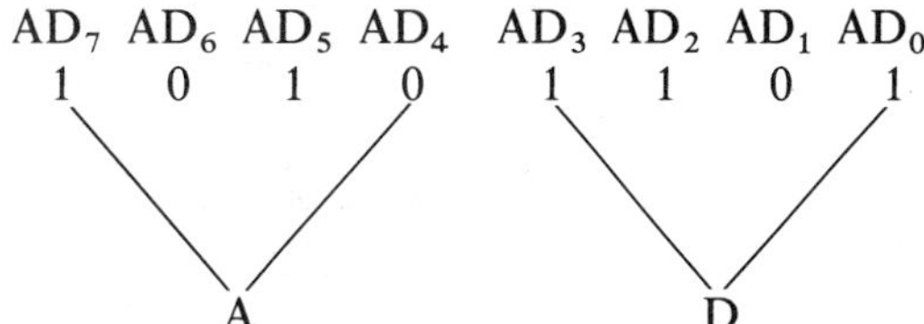

During phase T_3 of the second bus cycle, memory bank 0 stores the byte value AD hexadecimal at its physical location 160D3. ■

Intel 8088/8086 Register Set

An assembly language programmer's primary interface with the hardware components of the computer is through the microprocessor's register set. The Intel 8088/8086 microprocessor contains fourteen 16-bit registers that can be directly or indirectly manipulated by assembly language programs. The BIU contains four segment registers and an instruction pointer register. The EU contains eight general-purpose registers and the flags register. These registers are illustrated in Figure 1.19 and are discussed in the following sections.

Segment Registers

An assembly language program is divided into segments. Each segment can be as large as 64K bytes. A program can have many segments, but only four segments can be active at any one time during program execution. The **start address** (origin address) of each active segment is specified by the contents of one of the four segment registers.

In an 8088/8086 machine language program, all memory addresses are specified by a **segment origin** (the contents of a segment register) and an offset relative to the segment origin. The BIU **adder** is used to add the offset to the segment origin to generate the physical memory address, which is 20 bits wide. Each of the four

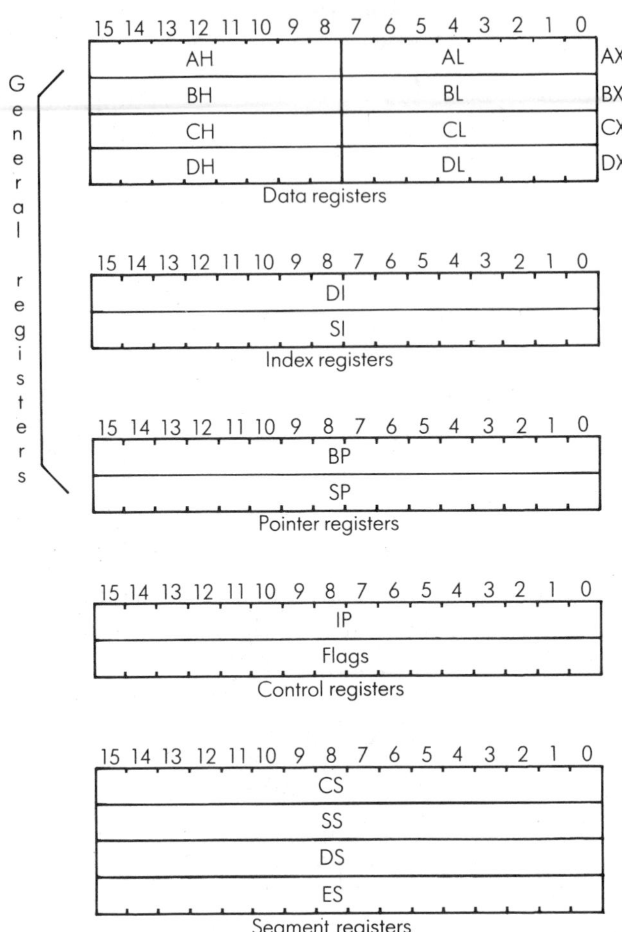

FIGURE 1.19
Intel 8088/8086 registers

segment registers is 16 bits wide. How can a 20-bit segment origin address be specified by the contents of a 16-bit segment register? This specification is accomplished by the requirement that all segments begin on a **paragraph boundary**, a memory address that is divisible by 16. Being divisible by 16 means that the low-order 4 bits of the base address are 0000, which means that only the high-order 16 bits of the segment origin address must be stored in the segment register. In other words, the segment register contains the high-order, 16-bit address of the segment origin and the low-order 4 bits are assumed to be 0000.

The four segment registers of the BIU are as follows:

CS-Register The CS-register specifies the address of the origin of the currently active code segment. A *code segment* contains executable instructions.

SS-Register The SS-register specifies the address of the origin of the currently active stack segment. A *stack segment* contains dynamic data whose storage is allocated and deallocated on demand during execution.

DS-Register The DS-register specifies the address of the origin of the currently active data segment. A *data segment* usually contains static data whose storage is allocated prior to execution and is deallocated at program termination. Static data storage remains fixed throughout program execution.

ES-Register The ES-register specifies the address of the origin of the currently active extra segment. An *extra segment*, like a data segment, usually contains static data.

Each of these types of segments is discussed in more detail in Section 1.5.

Instruction Pointer Register

The **IP-register** is the instruction pointer register and always contains the 16-bit offset, within the currently active code segment, of the next instruction byte to be fetched from memory. The CS:IP register pair always specifies the 20-bit memory address of the next instruction byte to be fetched from memory. The CS-register contents specify the segment origin address of the code segment, and the IP-register contains the offset from this origin address to (i.e., the difference between this origin address and) the address of the instruction byte to be fetched. The CS:IP register pair is said to point to the next instruction byte to be fetched from memory and is like the program counter in the hypothetical machine.

General Registers

There are eight 16-bit general registers in the EU. These registers are divided into three groups in Figure 1.19. There are four **data registers** (AX, BX, CX, and DX), two **index registers** (DI and SI), and two **pointer registers** (BP and SP). Each of these registers can be used to supply a 16-bit operand to and receive the 16-bit result from an arithmetic or logical operation performed by the ALU. The four data registers can each be divided into two 8-bit registers: The high-order half of the AX-register is referred to as the AH-register, and the low-order half is referred to as the AL-register. Similarly, BH and BL are the designators for the two halves of the BX-register, CH and CL for the CX-register, and DH and DL for the DX-register. Each of these eight 8-bit data registers can be used to supply an 8-bit operand to and receive an 8-bit result from an arithmetic or logical operation performed by the ALU. In addition to supplying operands to and receiving results from the ALU, each register has a specific purpose, as follows:

AX-Register The AX-register is the **accumulator register** and can be used as a single 16-bit word register or as two 8-bit byte registers. Where possible, the AX-register should be used to accumulate the result of 16-bit arithmetic and logical operations. The AL-register should be used to accumulate the result of 8-bit arithmetic and logical operations. Even though any of the other general registers can be used as the accumulator in most arithmetic and logical operations, use of the AX and AL registers produces more efficient machine code. They also are used implicitly in multiply and divide operations. (Arithmetic operations are discussed in Chapter 3.) In addition, the AX and AL registers are used in input/output operations.

BX-Register The BX-register is the **base register** and is used to access an item in a data structure (e.g., an element of an array).

CX-Register The CX-register is the **count register** and is used as a counter in loop operations. It also is used as a shift counter in multibit shift operations. (Loop operations are discussed in Chapter 4, and a special type of loop operation is presented in Chapter 8. Shift operations and use of the CL-register as a shift counter are discussed in Chapter 6.)

DX-Register The DX-register is the **data register**. It is used as an extension to the AX-register for multiplication and division operations and for 32-bit arithmetic.

DI-Register The DI-register is the **destination index register**. It is used with a special set of instructions, called *string instructions*, that are used for manipulating the elements of character strings and arrays.

SI-Register The SI-register is the **source index register**. It, like the DI-register, is used with the string instructions. (The string instructions and their use of the SI-register and DI-register are discussed in Chapter 8.)

SP-Register The SP-register is the **stack pointer**. It always contains the offset within the stack segment of the current top-of-stack item. The SS:SP register pair always specifies the 20-bit memory address of the 16-bit word that is the current top-of-stack item. The SS-register contents specify the segment origin address of the stack segment, and the SP-register contains the offset from this origin to the address of the current top-of-stack item. That is, the SS:SP register pair points to the item at the top of the stack. (The concept of a stack and its push and pop operations are discussed further in Section 1.5 and in Chapter 2.)

BP-Register The BP-register is the **base pointer register**. It is useful as an auxiliary stack segment pointer when arguments are passed to subprocedures via the stack. (Passing arguments via the stack and the use of the BP-register are discussed in Chapter 5, in the addressing modes section of Chapter 8, and in Chapter 10.)

Flags Register

The **flags register** is a 16-bit register contained in the EU. Only 9 of the 16 bits are implemented, as shown in Figure 1.20. Each of these 9 bits has a distinct purpose and indicates something about the current state of the microprocessor. Three of the bits are control flags: the *direction flag* (*DF*), the *interrupt flag* (*IF*), and the *trap flag* (*TF*). The other 6 bits are status flags. The 9 flag bits indicate the following:

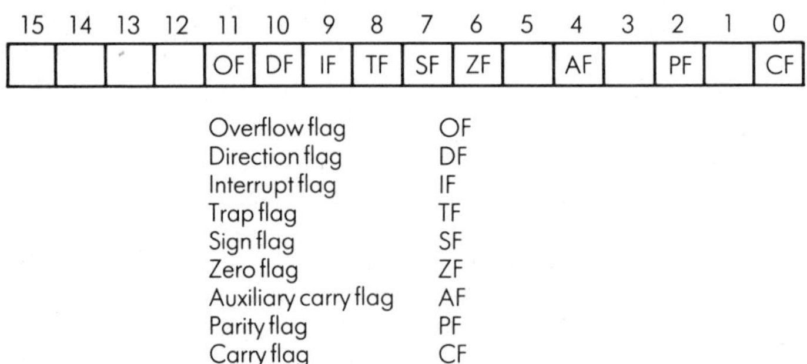

FIGURE 1.20
Flags register

Overflow Flag (OF) When the operands of an addition or subtraction operation are interpreted as signed integer values, the OF bit in the flags register indicates whether or not the result of the operation is too large to be stored in the register or memory location that is designated to receive the result. Producing a result that is too large to be stored is a condition known as an *arithmetic overflow*. The OF bit also is used to indicate whether or not the most significant bit changes on a shift operation. (The interpretation of binary numbers is discussed in Chapter 2. The concept of arithmetic overflow is discussed in Chapters 3, 6, and 7.)

Direction Flag (DF) String instructions automatically update the SI- and/or DI-register to point to the next (or previous) character in a string or element in an array. The DF bit in the flags register is used to control whether this automatic update is an increment (DF = 0) to the next character or array element or a decrement (DF = 1) to the previous character or array element. (Manipulation of the DF bit is discussed in Chapters 6 and 8.)

Interrupt Flag (IF) An external interrupt is a request for service from some external device (e.g., a keyboard, printer, or display screen). The IF bit in the flags register controls whether the microprocessor processes external interrupts (IF = 1) or ignores external interrupts (IF = 0). (Interrupts and input/output operations are discussed in Chapter 9.)

Trap Flag (TF) The microprocessor has a *single-step mode* that allows for program intervention after each instruction execution of another program. That is, the single-step mode allows one program to trace the execution of another program. The DEBUG and CodeView utility programs help programmers trace the execution of their programs. They use the single-step mode to provide this service. The TF bit in the flags register controls whether the microprocessor is in the single-step mode (TF = 1) or is not in the single-step mode (TF = 0). (The DEBUG and CodeView programs are discussed at various points in this book. The single-step mode is discussed in Chapter 9.)

Sign Flag (SF) The SF bit is used to hold a copy of the most significant bit of the result of arithmetic and logical operations. If the result is being interpreted as a signed integer, then the SF bit reflects the sign of that result (SF = 0 implies nonnegative; SF = 1 implies negative). The sign flag is used when binary numbers are compared. In conjunction with the zero flag, the sign flag is used to determine which of two unequal binary numbers is the larger.

Zero Flag (ZF) The ZF bit is used to indicate whether or not the result of an arithmetic or logical operation is zero (ZF = 1 implies the result is zero; ZF = 0 implies the result is nonzero). The zero flag is used when binary numbers are compared. It reflects whether or not two binary numbers are equal. (The comparison of binary numbers, for the purpose of making decisions in assembly language programs, is discussed in Chapter 4.)

Auxiliary Carry Flag (AF) The AF bit of the flags register is used to reflect the carry out of or borrow into bit position 3 on an addition or subtraction operation. It is used in computations involving *binary coded decimal* (*BCD*) numbers. (Carry and borrow are discussed in Chapters 3 and 7. The use of the AF bit is discussed in Chapter 11.)

Parity Flag (PF) A technique that detects single-bit errors in the transmission of binary data is to add a parity bit to each bit pattern transmitted. The parity bit is chosen in such a way that the number of 1 bits in the bit pattern being transmitted is always odd (odd parity code) or always even (even parity code). If the receiving device receives a bit pattern that has the wrong parity, then it knows that an error has occurred in transmission. The PF bit of the flags register reflects the parity of the low-order 8 bits of the result of an arithmetic or logical operation (PF = 0 implies odd parity; PF = 1 implies even parity).

Carry Flag (CF) The CF bit is used to reflect the carry out of or borrow into the most significant bit in an addition or subtraction operation. The CF bit also is used to record the last bit shifted out of a register or memory operand in a binary shift operation. The CF bit of the flags register reflects overflow of an addition or subtraction operation when the operands and the result are interpreted as unsigned integers. (Carry and borrow are discussed in Chapters 3 and 7. Shift operations are discussed in Chapter 6.)

A bit is said to be **set** if it is a 1. It is said to be **reset** or **cleared** if it is a 0. The bits in the flags register are set and cleared by the execution of machine language instructions. The flag bits indicate conditions that involve some of the operations being performed by the microprocessor. A set of assembly language instructions called *jump instructions* allows the program to make decisions based on these conditions. Jump instructions and their use in implementing decision structures are discussed in Chapter 4.

To describe the execution of an assembly language instruction completely, its effect on the flags register must be described. As each assembly language instruction is discussed in this text, its effect on the bits of the flags register is presented.

1.5 Anatomy of an 8088/8086 Assembly Language Program

An 8088/8086 assembly language program is divided into units called **segments**. The various segments that make up a program can be defined in one or more assembly modules. An **assembly module** contains the definition of one or more segments and the links required for names that are used in the assembly module but are defined in other assembly modules. A **segment definition** consists of assembly language instructions, data, and directives to the assembler program that direct the assembler in performing the translation to machine language. Assembler directives are also called *pseudo-operations.*

An assembly module is one complete input to the assembler program. The assembler translates an assembly module into an object module. An **object module** contains machine language instructions, data, and a list of external references (names used in the assembly module that produced the object module that are defined in other assembly modules).

The *Linkage Editor program* (*LINK*) combines object modules produced by the assembler into a complete executable program. The assembler and LINK programs are discussed in more detail later in this chapter.

There are three distinct types of segments in 8088/8086 assembly language programs: the *stack segment*, the *data segment*, and the *code segment*. An 8088/8086 assembly language program must contain exactly one stack segment, one or more code segments, and zero or more data segments.

Stack Segment

The **stack segment** contains dynamic data. Storage for dynamic data is allocated and deallocated on demand as the program executes. In the abstract, a stack is a data structure of unlimited capacity. It is a list of data items in which all insertions and deletions are made at one end, called the **top of the stack**. Inserting a new data item in a stack is called **pushing** the data item on top of the stack. Removing a data item from the stack is called **popping** the data item from the top of the stack. When a data item is pushed on the stack, it becomes the new top-of-stack data item. All data items previously in the stack are pushed down one position relative to the top of the stack. When the top-of-stack data item is popped from the stack, the data items remaining in the stack pop up one position relative to the top of the stack. The new top-of-stack data item is the one that was at the top of the stack just before the popped item was pushed. At any point in time, the only item that can be popped from the stack is the item at the top of the stack, the last item that was pushed on the stack. A stack is also called a **LIFO**, or **last-in-first-out**, data structure.

Theoretically, there is no limit to the number of items that can be pushed onto a stack. However, when implemented on a computer, there must be some upper limit to the number of items that the stack can contain. The stack segment definition in an 8088/8086 assembly language program defines the size of the program's stack (i.e., the maximum number of data items that the stack can hold at any point in time). The address of the origin of the stack segment is contained in the SS-register. The offset from this origin to the current top-of-stack data item is contained in the SP-register. The SS-register and SP-register are automatically maintained by the microprocessor as it executes push and pop operations. Normally, these registers are not directly manipulated by the program. The stack segment of a program is used primarily for the temporary storage of data. It is discussed in more detail in Chapter 2.

Data Segment

A **data segment** contains static data. Storage for static data is allocated prior to execution of the program and is deallocated at program termination. In other words, storage for static data exists throughout the entire execution of the program. Data in the data segment are referenced by name. The name is translated, by the assembler, to an offset from the beginning of the data segment. The address of the origin of the data segment is contained in either the DS-register, the ES-register, or both. The DS- and/or ES-register must be initialized and maintained by the program. Data segment definitions are discussed in detail in Chapter 2.

Code Segment

A **code segment** contains machine language instructions and consists of one or more procedure definitions. A procedure is a block of machine language instructions that has a name by which it can be called into execution. It is either the main procedure or a subprocedure. The main procedure is the one that receives control when the executable program is placed into execution by the operating system. A subprocedure receives execution control when it is called into execution by another procedure in the program. When a subprocedure terminates, it returns execution control to the procedure that called it into execution. When the main procedure terminates, it returns control to the operating system, thus terminating the executable program.

The address of the origin of the code segment that contains the currently executing procedure is maintained in the CS-register. The offset from this origin to the next instruction byte to be fetched from memory is contained in the IP-register. That is, the CS:IP register pair always specifies the address of the next instruction byte to be fetched from memory. The CS-register and IP-register are automatically maintained by the microprocessor as it executes instructions. Normally, these registers are not directly manipulated by the program.

Assembly Language Coding Formats

The assembly language syntax and coding formats presented in this book are recognized by the Microsoft Macro Assembler Version 6.0 (MASM 6.0). In some cases, where MASM 6.0 differs significantly from previous versions of the Microsoft Macro Assembler, MASM 5.1 syntax and coding formats are also presented.

A line of code in an assembly module is categorized as a comment line, a mnemonic representation of a machine language instruction, or a pseudo-operation (a directive to the assembler program):

Comment Line Any line in an 8088/8086 assembly language program whose first nonblank character is a semicolon (;) is a **comment line**. A comment line is essentially ignored by the assembler. It enables the programmer to embed documentation in the program, but it has no effect on the translation to machine language.

Mnemonic Representation of a Machine Language Instruction A machine language instruction that is written in symbolic form is a **mnemonic representation** of that instruction. It specifies an operation to be performed during program execution.

Pseudo-Operation A **pseudo-operation** looks like a mnemonic representation of a machine language instruction, but it is a directive to the assembler program. It specifies an operation to be performed during the translation from assembly language to machine language.

When discussing the various machine operations and pseudo-operations of the 8088/8086 assembly language, this text provides the general form for each operation. The following conventions are used for such general forms:

1. Items shown in capital letters must be coded exactly as shown.
2. Items enclosed in pointed brackets (⟨ ⟩) must be supplied by the programmer.
3. Items enclosed in square brackets ([ ]) are optional.

A line that specifies a machine operation or a pseudo-operation is divided into four fields:

⟨*name*⟩ ⟨*operation code*⟩ ⟨*operand list*⟩ [⟨*comment*⟩]

The fields must be coded in the order shown and must be separated by one or more spaces and/or TAB characters.

The ⟨*name*⟩ field specifies a symbolic name that is to be associated with a memory location. It can contain up to 247 significant characters (31 in previous versions of MASM). A symbolic name may include any of the following characters:

Alphabetic	A–Z (Note that lowercase letters are converted to uppercase letters on input.)
Numeric	0–9
Special	?, @, _, and $

The first character of a symbolic name must be alphabetic or a special character. (In previous versions of MASM, a period was allowed as the first character of a symbolic name.) The ⟨*name*⟩ field does not have to begin in the first character position of a line, but in the example programs in this book, that particular convention is followed. The use of labels, or symbolic names, is discussed in more detail in Chapters 2 and 4.

The ⟨*operation code*⟩ field contains a mnemonic operation code that represents a machine instruction or a pseudo-operation. The ⟨*operand list*⟩ field contains expressions that specify the operands required by the operation specified by the entry in the ⟨*operation code*⟩ field.

The ⟨*comment*⟩ field is used for documentation purposes. It is essentially ignored by the assembler. It also is echoed in the listing generated by the assembler. A semicolon (;) denotes that the remainder of the line is the ⟨*comment*⟩ field.

The only required field in a noncomment line is the ⟨*operation code*⟩ field. For some operation codes, the ⟨*name*⟩ field is required; for others, it is optional; and for still others, it must be omitted. Some operation codes require operands; others do not. If the ⟨*operand list*⟩ field contains more than one operand, then the operands are separated by the delimiter comma (,). Any line may end with a ⟨*comment*⟩ field.

Example Assembly Module

Program Listing 1.1 is an example of an 8088/8086 assembly module. It contains the definitions of three segments of a thirteen-segment program and the links for the names that are used in these three segments but are defined in one of the other segments. The ten segments not defined in this assembly module listing are a data segment and nine code segments that are included in the input/output subprocedure library available on diskette to accompany this book. Each of the nine code segments contains a single input/output subprocedure that is referenced directly or indirectly by the program in Program Listing 1.1. The I/O subprocedures available on this library are described in Appendix D. The method of linking a program (such as the one in Program Listing 1.1) with library procedures is discussed later in this chapter.

Line 1 in Program Listing 1.1 is a pseudo-operation that sets the page size for the assembler-generated listing. The listing generated by the assembler expands the lines from the source code file to include the machine code or data allocation, if any, that is generated for that line during the translation from source code to machine code. The listing requires more than 80 characters per line. However, the default line length used by the assembler is 80 characters. To direct the assembler to expand the line length, the PAGE pseudo-operation is used. The **PAGE pseudo-operation** has the following general form:

```
PAGE  ⟨lines/page⟩,⟨char/line⟩
```

in which ⟨*lines/page*⟩ is an integer constant in the range 10–255 that specifies the maximum number of lines per page of the listing and ⟨*char/line*⟩ is an integer constant in the range 60–255 (60–132 in previous versions of MASM) that specifies the maximum number of characters per line of the listing.

Most dot matrix printers can print 6 lines per inch (66 lines per page) or 8 lines per inch (88 lines per page). They can print 80 characters per line (normal mode) or 132 characters per line (compressed mode). The pseudo-operation PAGE 80,132 (line 1 of Program Listing 1.1) directs the assembler to generate the listing with 80 lines per page and 132 characters per line. Note that the PAGE pseudo-operation does not cause the printer to be placed in compressed mode. The printer mode is changed via the DOS MODE command, which is presented in Chapter 3. The PAGE pseudo-

```
            PAGE    80,132
;========================================================================
;                 PROGRAM LISTING 1.1
;
; PROGRAM TO PRINT NUMBER SYSTEM TRANSLATION TABLES
;========================================================================
                                              ;PROCEDURES TO
            EXTRN   CLEAR:FAR                 ;CLEAR SCREEN
            EXTRN   NEWLINE:FAR               ;DISPLAY NEWLINE CHARACTER
            EXTRN   PAUSE:FAR                 ;PAUSE UNTIL KEY STROKE
            EXTRN   PUTBIN:FAR                ;DISPLAY BINARY (BYTE OR WORD)
            EXTRN   PUTDEC:FAR                ;DISPLAY 16-BIT DECIMAL INT.
            EXTRN   PUTHEX:FAR                ;DISPLAY HEX   (BYTE OR WORD)
            EXTRN   PUTOCT:FAR                ;DISPLAY OCTAL (BYTE OR WORD)
            EXTRN   PUTSTRNG:FAR              ;DISPLAY CHARACTER STRING
;========================================================================
;S T A C K   S E G M E N T   D E F I N I T I O N
;
STACK       SEGMENT STACK
            DB      256 DUP(?)
STACK       ENDS
;========================================================================
;D A T A   S E G M E N T   D E F I N I T I O N
;
DATA        SEGMENT
HEADERS     DB      'DECIMAL         '
            DB      'BINARY                 '
            DB      'OCTAL        '
            DB      'HEXADECIMAL '
SPACES      DB      '      '
PAUSE_MSG   DB      '    ANY KEY CONTINUES'
DATA        ENDS
;========================================================================
;C O D E   S E G M E N T   D E F I N I T I O N
;
CODE        SEGMENT 'CODE'
            ASSUME  CS:CODE,DS:NOTHING,ES:DATA,SS:STACK
EX_1_1:
            MOV     AX,SEG DATA               ;SET ES-REGISTER TO POINT TO
            MOV     ES,AX                     ;DATA SEGMENT
;
            MOV     AX,-128                   ;NUMBER = -128
NUM_LOOP:                                     ;REPEAT
            CALL    CLEAR                     ;   CLEAR SCREEN
            LEA     DI,HEADERS                ;   DISPLAY HEADERS
            MOV     CX,61
            CALL    PUTSTRNG
            MOV     CX,24                     ;   LOOP_COUNT = 24
PAGE_LOOP:                                    ;   REPEAT
            CALL    NEWLINE                   ;      DISPLAY NEWLINE CHAR.
            PUSH    CX                        ;      PUSH LOOP_COUNT
            MOV     BH,+1                     ;      DISPLAY NUMBER IN
            CALL    PUTDEC                    ;      DECIMAL RIGHT JUSTIFIED
            LEA     DI,SPACES                 ;      DISPLAY 3 SPACES
            MOV     CX,3
            CALL    PUTSTRNG
            MOV     BL,0                      ;      DISPLAY LOWER 8 BITS
            CALL    PUTBIN                    ;      OF NUMBER IN BINARY
            MOV     CX,1                      ;      DISPLAY 1 SPACE
            CALL    PUTSTRNG
            MOV     BL,1                      ;      DISPLAY NUMBER IN
            CALL    PUTBIN                    ;      BINARY
            MOV     CX,3                      ;      DISPLAY 3 SPACES
            CALL    PUTSTRNG
            MOV     BL,0                      ;      DISPLAY LOWER 8 BITS
            CALL    PUTOCT                    ;      OF NUMBER IN OCTAL
            MOV     CX,1                      ;      DISPLAY 1 SPACE
```

```
68:            CALL    PUTSTRNG
69:            MOV     BL,1                ;       DISPLAY NUMBER IN
70:            CALL    PUTOCT              ;       OCTAL
71:            MOV     CX,5                ;       DISPLAY 5 SPACES
72:            CALL    PUTSTRNG
73:            MOV     BL,0                ;       DISPLAY LOWER 8 BITS
74:            CALL    PUTHEX              ;       OF NUMBER IN HEX
75:            MOV     CX,1                ;       DISPLAY 1 SPACE
76:            CALL    PUTSTRNG
77:            MOV     BL,1                ;       DISPLAY NUMBER IN HEX
78:            CALL    PUTHEX
79:            POP     CX                  ;       POP LOOP_COUNT
80:            INC     AX                  ;       NUMBER = NUMBER + 1
81:            LOOP    PAGE_LOOP           ;       DECREMENT LOOP_COUNT
82:                                        ;    UNTIL LOOP_COUNT = 0
83:            PUSH    AX                  ;    PUSH NUMBER
84:            LEA     DI,PAUSE_MSG        ;    PAUSE AND WAIT FOR
85:            MOV     CX,20               ;    KEY STROKE
86:            CALL    PAUSE
87:            POP     AX                  ;    POP NUMBER
88:            CMP     AX,256
89:            JGE     RETURN              ;UNTIL NUMBER = 256
90:            JMP     NUM_LOOP
91: RETURN:
92:            MOV     AX,4C00H            ;RETURN TO OS
93:            INT     21H
94: CODE       ENDS
95:            END     EX_1_1
```

operation affects only the format of the assembler-generated listing. The 80-line page is specified rather than the 88-line page to allow for one inch of margin. The use of the assembler-generated listing is discussed further in Chapter 3.

Lines 2–6 in Program Listing 1.1 are comment lines that act as a prologue to explain the function performed by the program. All example programs in this book contain a prologue for each main procedure and subprocedure. The prologues explain the purpose of each procedure or subprocedure (not how it does it, but what it does). In addition, the prologue for a subprocedure contains a description of its input/output interface.

Lines 7–15 identify symbolic names that are used in this assembly module but are defined in other assembly modules. External names are declared to the assembler by using the **EXTRN pseudo-operation**, which has the following general form:

EXTRN 〈*ext-name-list*〉 [〈*comment*〉]

in which 〈*ext-name-list*〉 is a list of external name specifications of the form 〈*name*〉:〈*type*〉, where 〈*name*〉 is a symbolic name and 〈*type*〉 is one of the following type attributes: BYTE, SBYTE, WORD, SWORD, DWORD, SDWORD, FWORD, NEAR, or FAR.

The EXTRN pseudo-operation identifies to the assembler the symbolic names that are referenced in this assembly module but are defined in other assembly modules. The EXTRN pseudo-operation also identifies the type attribute for each of these external names so that the assembler can determine whether or not the names are being used properly. Line 15, for example, defines PUTSTRNG as the external (EXTRN) name of a subprocedure that is defined in another code segment (FAR). The comment at the end of line 15 explains that this procedure will display a character string. The function of this subprocedure and its interface requirements are described in Appendix D.

Lines 16–18 are comment lines that indicate that a stack segment definition follows. The stack segment definition itself appears in lines 19–21. Every segment definition begins with a SEGMENT pseudo-operation and terminates with an ENDS pseudo-operation. The **SEGMENT pseudo-operation** has the following general form:

⟨*seg-name*⟩ SEGMENT [⟨*align*⟩] [⟨*combine*⟩] [⟨*class*⟩] [⟨*comment*⟩]

in which ⟨*seg-name*⟩ is the symbolic name to be associated with the memory location where the segment is to begin, ⟨*align*⟩ identifies the type of boundary for the beginning of the segment, ⟨*combine*⟩ indicates the way in which the segment is to be combined with other segments at program link time, and ⟨*class*⟩ is a symbolic name used to group segments at link time. (All segments with the same class name are to be contiguous in memory.) The ⟨*seg-name*⟩ field is required. Every segment defined in an assembly module must be given a name.

Most of the optional operands can be omitted at this point. The ⟨*align*⟩ type is required to be PARA (paragraph) for all segments that are not to be combined with other segments, which simply means that at program load time, the segment is to be aligned so as to begin on a paragraph boundary (an address that is divisible by 16). Since the default for ⟨*align*⟩ type is PARA, the operand can be omitted.

A ⟨*combine*⟩ type of STACK indicates that the segment is to be part of the run-time stack segment for the program. All segments with a ⟨*combine*⟩ type of STACK are combined into a single stack segment at link time. If the ⟨*combine*⟩ type operand is omitted, then the segment is to be logically separate from other segments in the program, regardless of its placement relative to other segments. Chapter 12 discusses the SEGMENT pseudo-operation operands in more detail.

The **ENDS pseudo-operation** has the following general form:

⟨*seg-name*⟩ ENDS [⟨*comment*⟩]

in which ⟨*seg-name*⟩ is the symbolic name to be associated with the segment and must match the ⟨*seg-name*⟩ used on the SEGMENT pseudo-operation that marked the beginning of the segment definition. The ENDS pseudo-operation marks the physical end of a segment definition.

The SEGMENT and ENDS pseudo-operations in lines 19 and 21, respectively, delimit the stack segment definition for the example program. The DB pseudo-operation in line 20 defines the size of the stack segment as 256 decimal (100 hex) bytes. The DB pseudo-operation is discussed further in Chapter 2.

Lines 22–24 are comment lines that indicate that a static data segment definition follows. The data segment definition itself appears in lines 25–32. The segment definition begins with the SEGMENT pseudo-operation and ends with the ENDS pseudo-operation. Both of these pseudo-operations specify the name of the segment being defined. The data-defining pseudo-operations appearing in lines 26–31 are discussed in Chapter 2.

Lines 33–35 are comment lines that indicate that a code segment definition follows. The code segment definition itself begins with the SEGMENT pseudo-operation in line 36 and ends with the ENDS pseudo-operation in line 94. The SEGMENT pseudo-operation in line 36 specifies a class name of 'CODE'. This class name is used to satisfy a requirement of the assembler. For the assembler to generate CodeView source information, code segments must have a class name that ends with 'CODE'. For the example programs in this book, class names that end with 'CODE' are specified in all code segment definitions.

Line 37 in the code segment definition is an ASSUME pseudo-operation. The **ASSUME pseudo-operation** has the following general form:

ASSUME ⟨*seg-reg-assign-list*⟩ [⟨*comment*⟩]

in which ⟨*seg-reg-assign-list*⟩ is a list of segment register assignments of the form ⟨*seg-reg*⟩:⟨*seg-name*⟩ or ⟨*seg-reg*⟩:NOTHING or ⟨*seg-reg*⟩:ERROR, where ⟨*seg-reg*⟩ is one of the segment register designators CS, SS, DS, or ES and ⟨*seg-name*⟩ is the symbolic name of a segment defined by a SEGMENT pseudo-operation in the same assembly module.

The ASSUME pseudo-operation tells the assembler how the segment registers will be associated with the program segments at execution time. The assignment of the DS-register to NOTHING in the code segment of Program Listing 1.1 signifies to the assembler that the DS-register will not be used in this code segment. The operand DS:NOTHING could be omitted, and the effect would be the same. An assignment of a segment register to ERROR signifies to the assembler that an assembly error is to be generated if that segment register is inadvertently used in the code that follows.

The CS-register and SS-register are initialized by the operating system as part of program invocation. The CS-register is automatically updated by the microprocessor when control is transferred to or from a subprocedure. The DS-register and ES-register must be initialized and maintained by the program itself. The ASSUME pseudo-operation does not perform this initialization; it simply tells the assembler what initialization is to be performed at execution time. Segment register initialization is discussed in detail in Chapters 2 and 3.

Lines 38–93 are machine language instructions written in symbolic form. These instructions constitute the main procedure of this program. Each of the following chapters in this book is devoted to a specific class of assembly language instructions.

The assembly module in Program Listing 1.1 terminates with an END pseudo-operation in line 95. The **END pseudo-operation** has the following general form:

END [⟨*label*⟩] [⟨*comment*⟩]

in which ⟨*label*⟩ is the symbolic name that specifies the entry point for the executable program (i.e., the label of the instruction where execution is to begin). The END pseudo-operation defines the physical end of an 8088/8086 assembly module. It must be the last line of every assembly language source module. The optional ⟨*label*⟩ is required on the END pseudo-operation in the assembly module that contains the main procedure definition and must be the label of an instruction in the main procedure. The optional ⟨*label*⟩ must be omitted from the END pseudo-operation in any assembly module that contains only subprocedure definitions.

The algorithm implemented by the program in Program Listing 1.1 is not discussed here. It requires information from several future chapters. The purpose of this example is to show the form of an 8088/8086 assembly language program. It demonstrates the use of a number of subprocedures in the I/O library. You may wish to refer back to this program for examples of the use of these subprocedures.

Example Assembly Module—An Alternative

MASM 6.0 and MASM 5.1 both provide a set of simplified segment directives for defining the segments in an assembly module. Program Listing 1.2 is an example of an 8088/8086 assembly module whose segments are defined with simplified segment directives. This assembly module is identical to that of Program Listing 1.1, except for the segment-defining pseudo-operations used. The segments of the assembly module are defined with full segment definitions in Program Listing 1.1 and with simplified segment definitions in Program Listing 1.2. This discussion concentrates on the differences between the two listings.

When the various object modules that make up an executable program are

```
            PAGE    80,132
;====================================================================
;                PROGRAM LISTING 1.2
;
; PROGRAM TO PRINT NUMBER SYSTEM TRANSLATION TABLES
;====================================================================
            DOSSEG
            .MODEL  SMALL,BASIC
;====================================================================
                                        ;PROCEDURES TO
            EXTRN   CLEAR:FAR           ;CLEAR SCREEN
            EXTRN   NEWLINE:FAR         ;DISPLAY NEWLINE CHARACTER
            EXTRN   PAUSE:FAR           ;PAUSE UNTIL KEY STROKE
            EXTRN   PUTBIN:FAR          ;DISPLAY BINARY (BYTE OR WORD)
            EXTRN   PUTDEC:FAR          ;DISPLAY 16-BIT DECIMAL INT.
            EXTRN   PUTHEX:FAR          ;DISPLAY HEX    (BYTE OR WORD)
            EXTRN   PUTOCT:FAR          ;DISPLAY OCTAL (BYTE OR WORD)
            EXTRN   PUTSTRNG:FAR        ;DISPLAY CHARACTER STRING
;====================================================================
;S T A C K   S E G M E N T   D E F I N I T I O N
;
            .STACK  256
;====================================================================
;C O N S T A N T   S E G M E N T   D E F I N I T I O N
;
            .CONST
HEADERS     DB      'DECIMAL         '
            DB      'BINARY                   '
            DB      'OCTAL       '
            DB      'HEXADECIMAL '
SPACES      DB      '        '
PAUSE_MSG   DB      '   ANY KEY CONTINUES'
;====================================================================
;C O D E   S E G M E N T   D E F I N I T I O N
;
            .CODE
            ASSUME  DS:NOTHING,ES:DGROUP
EX_1_2:
            MOV     AX,DGROUP           ;SET ES-REGISTER TO POINT TO
            MOV     ES,AX               ;CONSTANT DATA SEGMENT
;
            MOV     AX,-128             ;NUMBER = -128
NUM_LOOP:                               ;REPEAT
            CALL    CLEAR               ;   CLEAR SCREEN
            LEA     DI,HEADERS          ;   DISPLAY HEADERS
            MOV     CX,61
            CALL    PUTSTRNG
            MOV     CX,24               ;   LOOP_COUNT = 24
PAGE_LOOP:                              ;   REPEAT
            CALL    NEWLINE             ;      DISPLAY NEWLINE CHAR.
            PUSH    CX                  ;      PUSH LOOP_COUNT
            MOV     BH,+1               ;      DISPLAY NUMBER IN
            CALL    PUTDEC              ;      DECIMAL RIGHT JUSTIFIED
            LEA     DI,SPACES           ;      DISPLAY 3 SPACES
            MOV     CX,3
            CALL    PUTSTRNG
            MOV     BL,0                ;      DISPLAY LOWER 8 BITS
            CALL    PUTBIN              ;      OF NUMBER IN BINARY
            MOV     CX,1                ;      DISPLAY 1 SPACE
            CALL    PUTSTRNG
            MOV     BL,1                ;      DISPLAY NUMBER IN
            CALL    PUTBIN              ;      BINARY
            MOV     CX,3                ;      DISPLAY 3 SPACES
            CALL    PUTSTRNG
            MOV     BL,0                ;      DISPLAY LOWER 8 BITS
            CALL    PUTOCT              ;      OF NUMBER IN OCTAL
            MOV     CX,1                ;      DISPLAY 1 SPACE
```

```
68:              CALL    PUTSTRNG
69:              MOV     BL,1             ;      DISPLAY NUMBER IN
70:              CALL    PUTOCT           ;      OCTAL
71:              MOV     CX,5             ;      DISPLAY 5 SPACES
72:              CALL    PUTSTRNG
73:              MOV     BL,0             ;      DISPLAY LOWER 8 BITS
74:              CALL    PUTHEX           ;      OF NUMBER IN HEX
75:              MOV     CX,1             ;      DISPLAY 1 SPACE
76:              CALL    PUTSTRNG
77:              MOV     BL,1             ;      DISPLAY NUMBER IN HEX
78:              CALL    PUTHEX
79:              POP     CX               ;      POP LOOP_COUNT
80:              INC     AX               ;      NUMBER = NUMBER + 1
81:              LOOP    PAGE_LOOP        ;      DECREMENT LOOP_COUNT
82:                                       ;   UNTIL LOOP_COUNT = 0
83:              PUSH    AX               ;   PUSH NUMBER
84:              LEA     DI,PAUSE_MSG     ;   PAUSE AND WAIT FOR
85:              MOV     CX,20            ;   KEY STROKE
86:              CALL    PAUSE
87:              POP     AX               ;   POP NUMBER
88:              CMP     AX,256
89:              JGE     RETURN           ;UNTIL NUMBER = 256
90:              JMP     NUM_LOOP
91: RETURN:
92:              MOV     AX,4C00H         ;RETURN TO OS
93:              INT     21H
94:              END     EX_1_2
```

linked together using the Linkage Editor (LINK), the segments of the program are organized in a particular sequence. With the full segment definitions used in Program Listing 1.1, the segments without class names are organized in the sequence in which they are encountered by LINK, followed by the segments with class names being grouped by class name. Within a given class, the segments are again organized in the sequence in which they are encountered by LINK. The assembly module of Program Listing 1.2 alters this sequence of segments by using the DOSSEG pseudo-operation in line 7. The **DOSSEG pseudo-operation** has the following general form:

DOSSEG [〈*comment*〉]

MASM 6.0 allows either DOSSEG or .DOSSEG to be used in the operation code field of this pseudo-operation. The dot form is provided for consistency with other simplified segment directives. The DOSSEG pseudo-operation causes the segments of the executable program to be organized in memory according to segment type. All code segments appear first in memory, followed by all data segments, followed by the stack segment. Within a given type, the segments are grouped according to class name. When defined using simplified segment directives, segments are given a default class name.

The sequence of segments is not an important issue at this point. However, it becomes an important issue when assembly modules are linked with modules written in high-level languages. The DOSSEG ordering is the same as the standard order required by Microsoft high-level languages.

Line 8 of Program Listing 1.2 is a pseudo-operation that enables the use of simplified segment directives. The .MODEL directive must appear in the assembly module prior to any simplified segment directive. The **.MODEL pseudo-operation** has the following general form:

.MODEL 〈*mem-model*〉 [,〈*lang-type*〉] [,〈*os*〉] [,〈*stack-type*〉]

in which 〈*mem-model*〉 specifies the memory model (TINY, SMALL, MEDIUM,

COMPACT, LARGE, HUGE, or FLAT), ⟨*lang-type*⟩ specifies compatibility with a high-level language (PASCAL, BASIC, FORTRAN, C, SYSCALL, or STDCALL) in terms of naming conventions and procedure-calling conventions, ⟨*os*⟩ specifies the operating system being used (OS_DOS or OS_OS2), and ⟨*stack-type*⟩ specifies whether the stack segment is to be placed into a group with the data segments (NEARSTACK) or is to be in a segment by itself (FARSTACK). The .MODEL directive in MASM 5.1 has only the ⟨*mem-model*⟩ and ⟨*lang-type*⟩ options in its general form.

When assembly language modules are linked with high-level language modules, the memory model of the assembly module should be the same as that for the high-level language module. For stand-alone assembly language programs, the memory model is not a critical item. In general, the smallest model that will accommodate the code and data will be the most efficient. The TINY memory model is not sufficient for assembly modules that have external procedure references (e.g., those that reference procedures from the input/output subprocedure library).

The language type BASIC is chosen here because it specifies the calling conventions that are presented in Chapter 5 for passing parameters via the stack. The default for the operating system option is OS_DOS, and since DOS is the operating system assumed in this book, the ⟨*os*⟩ option is omitted from the .MODEL directive in all example programs. The default for the stack type option is NEARSTACK. Using the default values for the operating system option and the stack type option makes the program compatible with MASM 5.1.

Lines 22, 26, and 36 of Program Listing 1.2 are the simplified segment directives of this assembly module. A simplified segment directive ends the definition of one segment and begins the definition of another segment. The .STACK pseudo-operation in line 22 marks the beginning of the stack segment definition for this assembly module. The **.STACK pseudo-operation** has the following general form:

.STACK ⟨*stack-size*⟩ [⟨*comment*⟩]

in which ⟨*stack-size*⟩ specifies the size of the stack segment in bytes. The .STACK pseudo-operation in line 22 defines a 256-byte stack segment.

The .CONST pseudo-operation in line 26 marks the end of the stack segment definition and the beginning of the definition of a data segment that is to contain only constants—in this case, string constants. The **.CONST pseudo-operation** has the following general form:

.CONST [⟨*comment*⟩]

The string constants to be contained in this segment are defined by the pseudo-operations in lines 27–32.

The .CODE pseudo-operation in line 36 marks the end of the constant data segment definition and the beginning of the code segment definition. The **.CODE pseudo-operation** has the following general form:

.CODE [⟨*seg-name*⟩] [⟨*comment*⟩]

in which ⟨*seg-name*⟩ is the symbolic name to be associated with the memory location where the segment is to begin. Since the optional segment name is omitted from the .CODE pseudo-operation in line 36, a default segment name of _TEXT is assigned by the assembler. The assembler also assigns a default class name of 'CODE', which is required if the assembler is to generate CodeView source information.

The END pseudo-operation in line 94 marks the end of the code segment definition, marks the end of the assembly module, and tells the assembler that execution of the program is to begin with the instruction labeled EX_1_2. .

Compare the ASSUME pseudo-operation in line 37 of Program Listing 1.2 to the one in line 37 of Program Listing 1.1. With simplified segment directives, the assembler generates the ASSUME statements automatically. The ASSUME pseudo-operation in line 37 of Program Listing 1.2 alters the assumptions made by the assembler. The assembler assumes that the DS-register will be used to contain the origin of the data group that is made up of the stack segment (defined in line 22) and the constant data segment (defined in lines 26–32). The ASSUME pseudo-operation in line 37 tells the assembler that the ES-register will be used instead.

1.6 Support Software

Several software packages are available for support of 8088/8086 assembly language programming. Among the more popular are those developed by the Microsoft Corporation, which include the *Disk Operating System*, the *Macro Assembler*, and their utility programs. These software packages were used in developing the example programs in this book and are discussed briefly in this section. A more detailed discussion can be found in Appendix F.

This section also contains a brief discussion of the I/O subprocedure library referenced in the example programs. A description of each of the subprocedures in this library appears in Appendix D.

Disk Operating System

The **Disk Operating System (DOS)** is a set of programs that aids in operation of the microcomputer. The memory-resident portion of DOS is usually loaded when the machine is turned on and remains in memory while the machine is in use. DOS provides the interface between the user and the resources of the microcomputer. These resources include both hardware and software. DOS provides the interface via a command language. The user enters a command from the keyboard in response to a DOS prompt. A command is, in effect, a request for DOS to execute some program, either a utility program or a user program. DOS interprets the command and invokes the program that provides the service requested.

If the program that provides a requested service is not part of the memory-resident portion of DOS, then DOS loads the program from diskette into memory and begins program execution. While a requested program is executing, it is in control and may prompt the user for input. In most cases, when the requested program terminates, it returns control to DOS, which then prompts the user for another command.

If DOS cannot interpret the command as entered or the requested program is not available to be loaded, then DOS displays an appropriate diagnostic message and prompts the user for another command. Consult your DOS manual for a list of the diagnostic messages displayed.

The commands recognized by DOS can be divided into the following categories:

Commands that provide the capability to batch DOS commands (i.e., to collect DOS commands into a group that can be invoked by name)

Commands that facilitate the creation, maintenance, and deletion of files on the fixed disk and on diskettes

Commands that set and display the system date and time

- Commands that request and control output to the display screen
- Commands that request and control output to the printer
- Commands that customize the system configuration and that install device drivers

Appendix F describes some of the more commonly used DOS commands, although the discussion is by no means exhaustive. Your DOS manual can provide further information. Also, tutorials on DOS are available at many colleges and universities. You should learn to do at least the following with DOS before proceeding to the next chapter:

- Bootstrap load the DOS program
- Enter the date and time
- Format a diskette
- Display a directory of the files on a diskette
- Copy a file from one diskette to the same or another diskette
- Erase a file from a diskette
- Display the contents of a text file on the display screen
- Print the contents of a text file on the printer
- Print a copy of the display screen on the printer
- Set the default disk drive

The finer points of DOS can be picked up as needed.

Editor

You should be familiar with one editor or word processor for use in creating source code files. When using a word processor, you must be careful to produce an ASCII text file. (*ASCII* stands for *A*merican *S*tandard *C*ode for *I*nformation *I*nterchange.) Word processing files contain numerous control characters that are not recognized by the assembler.

Macro Assembler

The **Macro Assembler (MASM)** program translates a program (or part of a program) from assembly language to machine language. The input to MASM is a disk file that contains a complete assembly module. This input file is called the **source code file**. The output produced by MASM is a disk file that contains the machine language translation of the source code file. This output file is called the **object code file**.

Under DOS, the name of a disk file can be from one to eight characters in length, optionally followed by a filename extension, which is a period (.) followed by from one to three characters. The following characters are allowed in filenames and extensions: A–Z, 0–9, and $, &, #, @, !, %, ‘, ’, (,), –, {,}, and _. The following reserved device names should not be used as filenames: CLOCK$, CON, AUX, COM1, COM2, COM3, COM4, PRN, LPT1, LPT2, LPT3, and NUL.

EXAMPLES

DATE_CNV.ASM
EX01.OBJ
A.B
XYZ.$$$ ■

An **explicit file specification** is a filename that is preceded by a **disk drive identifier**, which is the letter designator for the disk drive (e.g., A or B) followed by a colon (:). If the disk drive identifier is omitted, then the default drive identifier specified in the DOS prompt is assumed.

By convention, the suffix .ASM is used as the file extension for a source code file, and the suffix .OBJ is used as the file extension for an object code file. As long as these conventions are used, the file extension may be omitted from filenames appearing in commands that invoke the assembler. It is a good idea to use the suffix .ASM for the file extension on all source code files.

MASM 6.0

In its simplest form, the command used to invoke Version 6.0 of the Microsoft Macro Assembler has the following general form:

`ml` [⟨*options*⟩] ⟨*source*⟩

in which ⟨*options*⟩ is a list of commands that control the way the assembler performs its task and ⟨*source*⟩ identifies the input source code file. The ⟨*source*⟩ entry must be present and is an explicit file specification that identifies the disk drive, the filename, and the filename extension. The filename extension cannot be omitted.

The options in the options list begin with a forward slash (/) or a dash (–). The forward slash is used throughout this book. Three command-line options will be introduced at this point. The /c option tells the assembler to assemble only (i.e., not to also invoke the Linkage Editor). The /Zi option tells the assembler to generate CodeView information in the object file. This option is important if the CodeView debugger is going to be used in debugging the program. The /Fo⟨*filename*⟩ option tells the assembler where to save the object code file. The ⟨*filename*⟩ may be specified in any of the following ways:

The ⟨*filename*⟩ can be an explicit file specification that identifies the disk drive and the filename. If the filename extension is omitted, then the suffix .OBJ is assumed.

The ⟨*filename*⟩ can be a disk drive identifier (e.g., A:), which specifies that the object file is to be placed on the diskette in the indicated drive using the same name as the source file but with the suffix .OBJ as the filename extension.

The entry can be the mnemonic NUL, which specifies that the object file is not to be generated.

The /Fo⟨*filename*⟩ option can be omitted from the command line, which specifies that the object file is to be placed on the diskette in the default drive using the same name as the source file but with the suffix .OBJ as the filename extension.

It is important to note that the case of letters is significant for the command-line options. The letter c in the option /c must be a lowercase c. The letters Z and i in the option /Zi must be an uppercase Z and a lowercase i. The letters F and o in the option /Fo⟨*filename*⟩ must be an uppercase F and a lowercase o.

Consider the assembly module in Program Listing 1.1. Suppose this assembly module has already been entered using an editor and has been saved on a diskette with EX_1_1.ASM as the filename. Suppose further that we have a fixed disk system, the Macro Assembler is on the fixed disk, the source code file is on the diskette in drive A, and the fixed disk drive is the default drive. To assemble this assembly module, the following command can be entered in response to the C⟩ prompt from DOS:

```
ml  /c  /Zi  /FoA:  A:ex_1_1.asm
```

This command instructs MASM 6.0 to translate the assembly module in file EX_1_1.ASM to machine language. MASM 6.0 places the object code file on the diskette in drive A with EX_1_1.OBJ as the filename. When the command line does not specify a filename for the object code file, MASM 6.0 uses the same filename as that of the source code file, with the filename extension changed from .ASM to .OBJ.

When MASM 6.0 encounters an error in the assembly module it is translating, it displays the line number of the line of code that contains the error, an error number, and a diagnostic message. The *Microsoft Macro Assembler Programmer's Guide—Version 6.0* contains a list of these error numbers with a brief description of the probable cause.

The complete form of the MASM 6.0 command line is described in Appendix F and in the MASM 6.0 programmer's guide. The abbreviated form given here will suffice for now.

MASM 5.1

In its simplest form, the command used to invoke Version 5.1 of the Microsoft Macro Assembler has the following general form:

MASM [⟨*options*⟩] ⟨*source*⟩ [,⟨*object*⟩];

in which ⟨*options*⟩ is a list of commands that control the way the assembler performs its task, ⟨*source*⟩ identifies the input source code file, and ⟨*object*⟩ identifies the output object code file. The ⟨*source*⟩ entry must be present and is an explicit file specification that identifies the disk drive and the filename. If the filename extension is omitted, then the suffix .ASM is assumed. The ⟨*object*⟩ entry may be specified in any of the following ways:

The entry can be an explicit file specification that identifies the disk drive and the filename. If the filename extension is omitted, then the suffix .OBJ is assumed.

The entry can be omitted or left blank, which specifies that the object file is to be placed on the diskette in the default drive using the same name as the source file but with the suffix .OBJ as the filename extension.

The entry can be the mnemonic NUL, which specifies that the object file is not to be generated.

The entry can be a disk drive identifier (e.g., B:), which specifies that the object file is to be placed on the diskette in the indicated drive using the same name as the source file but with the suffix .OBJ as the filename extension.

The options in the options list begin with a forward slash (/) or a dash (–). The forward slash is used throughout this book. One command-line option will be introduced at this point. The /ZI option tells the assembler to generate CodeView information in the object file. This option is important if the CodeView debugger is going to be used in debugging the program. It is important to note that the case of letters is *not* significant for the command-line options in MASM 5.1. /ZI and /zi will produce the same result.

In its complete form, the MASM command contains two additional entries: one to specify an output listing file and one to specify an output cross-reference file. The semicolon (;), shown in the general form, indicates that these two entries are being omitted and that the assembler is not to generate the corresponding output files.

Consider the assembly module in Program Listing 1.1. Suppose this assembly module has already been entered using an editor and has been saved on a diskette with EX_1_1.ASM as the filename. Suppose further that we have a fixed disk system, the Macro Assembler is on the fixed disk, the source code file is on the diskette in drive A, and the fixed disk drive is the default drive. To assemble this assembly module, the following command can be entered in response to the C> prompt from DOS:

```
masm  /zi  A:ex_1_1,  A:;
```

This command instructs MASM 5.1 to translate the assembly module in file EX_1_1.ASM to machine language. MASM 5.1 places the object code file on the diskette in drive A with EX_1_1.OBJ as the filename. When the command line does not specify a filename for the object code file, MASM 5.1 uses the same filename as that of the source code file, with the filename extension changed from .ASM to .OBJ.

When MASM 5.1 encounters an error in the assembly module it is translating, it displays the line number of the line of code that contains the error, an error number, and a diagnostic message. The *Microsoft Macro Assembler 5.1 Programmer's Guide* contains a list of these error numbers with a brief description of the probable cause.

The complete form of the MASM 5.1 command line is described in Appendix F and in the MASM 5.1 programmer's guide. The abbreviated form given here will suffice for now.

Linkage Editor

Assembly language programs are often divided into several assembly modules. The individual assembly modules that make up a program are each assembled separately by the assembler, producing separate object code files. In such a form, the object code files cannot be loaded and executed. They first must be combined into one executable machine language program.

For example, the assembly module in Program Listing 1.1 is only part of a program. The procedure defined in that assembly module references eight external procedures, each of which appears in a separate assembly module. In fact, one of the eight external procedures references a ninth external procedure that appears in yet another assembly module. Therefore, the program, of which Program Listing 1.1 is a part, consists of ten assembly modules, each of which is assembled separately, producing ten object code files. Nine of these object code files already exist in the I/O subprocedure library. The object code file produced from the assembly module in Program Listing 1.1 must be combined with the other nine modules to produce a complete and executable program.

The program that combines object code files into a complete executable machine language program is the **Linkage Editor (LINK)** program. The input to LINK is a sequence of object code files. The output is a relocatable object code module called a **run file**, or **executable file**, which contains a complete program that can be loaded and executed.

By convention, the suffix .OBJ is used as the filename extension for object code files, the suffix .EXE is used as the filename extension for the executable code file, and the suffix .LIB is used for libraries of object files. As long as these conventions are used, the filename extension may be omitted from filenames appearing in commands that invoke LINK.

The command used to invoke LINK has the following general form:

`link` [⟨*options*⟩] ⟨*obj-list*⟩,⟨*runfile*⟩,⟨*loadmap*⟩,⟨*lib-list*⟩

in which ⟨*options*⟩ is a list of commands that control the way the Linkage Editor performs its task, ⟨*obj-list*⟩ is a list of object file specifications separated by spaces or plus (+) signs, ⟨*runfile*⟩ identifies the file that is to receive the relocatable object module (i.e., the executable file), ⟨*loadmap*⟩ identifies the file that is to receive the load map listing, and ⟨*lib-list*⟩ is a list of library specifications separated by spaces or plus (+) signs.

The options in the options list begin with a forward slash (/). One command-line option will be introduced at this point. The /CO option tells LINK to generate CodeView information in the executable file. This option is important if the CodeView debuffer is going to be used in debugging the program. The LINK options are not case sensitive.

The ⟨*obj-list*⟩ entry identifies object files that are to be linked to create an executable program. There must be at least one item in this list, and each item in the list must be an explicit file specification that identifies the disk drive and the filename. If the file extension is omitted from a filename, then the suffix .OBJ is assumed. The need for more than one entry in the ⟨*obj-list*⟩ will not exist until Chapter 5.

The ⟨*runfile*⟩ entry may be specified in any of the following ways:

> The entry can be an explicit file specification that identifies the disk drive and the filename. If the filename extension is omitted from the filename, then the suffix .EXE is assumed.
>
> The entry can be omitted or left blank, which specifies that the executable file is to be placed on the diskette in the default drive using the same name as the first file in the ⟨*obj-list*⟩ but with the suffix .EXE as the filename extension.
>
> The entry can be a disk drive identifier (e.g., B:), which specifies that the executable file is to be placed on the diskette in the indicated drive using the same name as the first file in the ⟨*obj-list*⟩ but with the suffix .EXE as the filename extension.

Another option for the ⟨*runfile*⟩ entry is given in Appendix F. The ones given here more than suffice for now.

The LINK program can be directed to generate and output a load map. The **load map** shows where each segment will be loaded in memory relative to the other segments in the executable file. The map also shows the size in bytes for each segment in the executable program. The ⟨*loadmap*⟩ entry in the command line that invokes the LINK program specifies whether this load map is to be generated and where it is to be output. The ⟨*loadmap*⟩ entry may be specified in one of the following ways:

> The entry can be the mnemonic NUL, which specifies that the load map is not to be generated.
>
> The entry can be the mnemonic CON, which specifies that the load map is to be generated and displayed on the video screen.

Other options for the ⟨*loadmap*⟩ entry are given in Appendix F. The NUL entry is probably the most often used by beginning 8088/8086 assembly language programmers.

The ⟨*lib-list*⟩ entry identifies library files that are to be searched for other object files needed to complete the executable program. Each item in the list must be an explicit file specification that identifies the disk drive and the filename. If the filename extension is omitted, then the suffix .LIB is assumed.

Consider again the assembly module in Program Listing 1.1. Suppose this assembly module has already been assembled and the object file has been saved on a diskette with EX_1_1.OBJ as the filename. Suppose further that we have a fixed disk system, the Linkage Editor and the I/O subprocedure library IO.LIB are on the fixed disk, the object code file is on the diskette in drive A, and the fixed disk drive is the default drive. To link file EX_1_1.OBJ with the appropriate object code files from IO.LIB, the following command can be entered in response to the C⟩ prompt from DOS:

```
link  /co  a:ex_1_1,a:,nul,io
```

This command instructs the LINK program to combine file EX_1_1.OBJ from the diskette in drive A with the appropriate object files from the library IO.LIB on the fixed disk and to place the executable code file on the diskette in drive A using EX_1_1.EXE as the filename. The load map listing is not generated.

The complete form of the LINK command is described in Appendix F and in the LINK chapter of the MASM programmer's guide. The abbreviated form given here suffices for most of this book.

DEBUG and CodeView

The **DEBUG** and **CodeView** programs provide the capability for tracing the execution of a machine language program by executing one instruction or a selected group of instructions at a time. Between instruction group executions, these programs provide the user with the opportunity to inspect and/or change the contents of registers and memory locations.

DEBUG is a primitive debugger in that it is rather simple to learn. Following each instruction execution, DEBUG displays the contents of all of the processor registers and also displays the next instruction to be executed. The next instruction to be executed is displayed in machine code form and in a symbolic form that is obtained by unassembling the machine code. Source code is not available to DEBUG. If the user needs to see additional information, such as the contents of memory locations, then it must be requested through commands to DEBUG.

CodeView is a more sophisticated debugger. Through windows set up by the user, a variety of information can be viewed while tracing the instructions of a program. For example, the user may wish to view four windows—one showing a portion of the source code, one showing the registers, one showing the stack segment, and one showing the data segment. Source code is available to CodeView via the /Zi option on the Macro Assembler command line and the /CO option on the LINK command line.

Descriptions of a DEBUG session and a CodeView session are included at the end of Chapter 2. Appendix F has a section devoted to DEBUG. The Microsoft Macro Assembler package provides documentation on CodeView.

Input/Output Subprocedure Library

A set of input/output subprocedures has been developed by the author so that beginning 8088/8086 assembly language programmers can start writing programs without first having to master the difficult concepts of input and output at the machine level. These I/O subprocedures and their interface requirements are described in Appendix D. An object file library containing the object code files for these subprocedures is available. The name of the library is IO.LIB.

NUMERIC EXERCISES

1.1 Fill in the blanks in the following table:

Decimal	Binary	Octal	Hexadecimal
237.4375			
	11010111.10101		
		237.35	
			C4.B4

1.2 Fill in the blanks in the following table:

Decimal	Binary	Hexadecimal
482		
	1101011101	
		6E
234.5		
	1010101.01	
		234.5

1.3 Assume the two-bank memory organization of an 8086-based microcomputer. In the following table, for each logical address given in hexadecimal, fill in the corresponding bank address (i.e., bank number and physical address within the bank).

Logical Address	Bank	Address within Bank
002A4		
003C5		
0A3E7		
3B014		
3B015		

1.4 Assume the two-bank memory organization of an 8086-based microcomputer. In the following table, for each physical address given in hexadecimal, fill in the corresponding logical address in hexadecimal.

Bank	Address within Bank	Logical Address
0	002A4	
1	002A4	
0	0A3E7	
1	0A3E7	
1	7FFFF	

1.5 For each of the following memory operations, state the bus operations that would be performed in the IBM PC.

a. Store the byte value 5A hexadecimal at memory location A1B2C hexadecimal.
b. Fetch the byte value 3C hexadecimal stored at memory location 3D4E5 hexadecimal.
c. Store the word value 3C5A hexadecimal at memory location 12ABC hexadecimal.

1.6 For each of the following memory operations, state the bus operations that would be performed in the IBM PS/2 Model 30.

a. Store the byte value 5A hexadecimal at memory location A1B2C hexadecimal.
b. Fetch the byte value 3C hexadecimal stored at memory location 3D4E5 hexadecimal.
c. Store the word value 3C5A hexadecimal at memory location 12ABC hexadecimal.

PROGRAMMING EXERCISES

1.1 Enter the program in Program Listing 1.1 and save it on diskette using PR_1_1.ASM as the filename. Assemble the program and link it with the I/O subprocedures from IO.LIB. Execute the program. The program will display a table on the video screen and then pause, waiting for you to press a key at the keyboard. When you press any key, the program will display another page and pause again. Continue this process until 16 pages of output have been displayed. Can you print each screenful at the printer? Try it.

1.2 Enter the program in Program Listing 1.3 and save it on diskette using PR_1_2.ASM as the filename. Assemble the program and link it with the I/O subprocedures from IO.LIB. Execute the program.

1.3 Modify the assembly module of Program Listing 1.3 using simplified segment directives for all segment definitions. Save the modified version on diskette using PR_1_3.ASM as the filename. Assemble the program and link it with the I/O subprocedures from IO.LIB. Execute the program.

```
           PAGE     80,132
;===================================================================
;                    PROGRAM LISTING 1.3
;
; PROGRAM TO ACCEPT AN INTEGER IN SIGNED DECIMAL FORM AND TO
; DISPLAY THE RESULTING BIT PATTERN ALONG WITH  ITS  UNSIGNED
; DECIMAL INTERPRETATION
;===================================================================
;                                          ;PROCEDURES TO
           EXTRN    GETDEC:FAR             ;INPUT SIGNED DECIMAL INTEGER
           EXTRN    NEWLINE:FAR            ;DISPLAY NEWLINE CHARACTER
           EXTRN    PUTBIN:FAR             ;DISPLAY BINARY INTEGER
           EXTRN    PUTDEC:FAR             ;DISPLAY SIGNED DECIMAL INT.
           EXTRN    PUTDEC$:FAR            ;DISPLAY UNSIGNED DECIMAL INT
           EXTRN    PUTSTRNG:FAR           ;DISPLAY CHARACTER STRING
;===================================================================
; S T A C K   S E G M E N T   D E F I N I T I O N
;
STACK      SEGMENT STACK
           DB       256 DUP(?)
STACK      ENDS
;===================================================================
; D A T A   S E G M E N T   D E F I N I T I O N
;
DATA       SEGMENT
;
PROMPT     DB       'ENTER AN INTEGER IN THE RANGE -32768 TO +32767'
BIN_MSG    DB       'THE INTERNAL BIT PATTERN FOR THE INPUT NUMBER IS:
DEC_MSG    DB       'THE UNSIGNED INTEGER INTERPRETATION OF THIS '
           DB       'BIT PATTERN IS:'
;
DATA       ENDS
;===================================================================
; C O D E   S E G M E N T   D E F I N I T I O N
;
CODE       SEGMENT 'CODE'
           ASSUME   CS:CODE,SS:STACK,ES:DATA,DS:NOTHING
PR_1_2:
           MOV      AX,SEG DATA            ;SET ES-REGISTER TO ADDRESS
           MOV      ES,AX                  ;DATA SEGMENT
           LEA      DI,PROMPT              ;PROMPT FOR INTEGER
           MOV      CX,46
           CALL     PUTSTRNG
           CALL     NEWLINE
           CALL     GETDEC                 ;GET INTEGER (SIGNED DECIMAL)
           CALL     NEWLINE
           LEA      DI,BIN_MSG             ;DISPLAY INTEGER IN BINARY
```

```
                MOV     CX,50
                CALL    PUTSTRNG
                MOV     BL,1
                CALL    PUTBIN
                CALL    NEWLINE
                LEA     DI,DEC_MSG          ;DISPLAY INTEGER AS AN
                MOV     CX,59               ;   UNSIGNED DECIMAL INTEGER
                CALL    PUTSTRNG
                MOV     BH,1
                CALL    PUTDEC$
                CALL    NEWLINE
                MOV     AX,4C00H            ;RETURN TO DOS
                INT     21H
CODE            ENDS
                END     PR_1_2
```

CHAPTER 2

Data Definition and Data Transfer

The previous chapter identified the basic components of an 8088/8086 assembly language program. As discussed, the major component is the segment definition, which consists of symbolic representations of machine language instructions and directives to the assembler. This chapter is concerned with the definition of data and the movement of data within the computer. It first presents some traditional methods for representing data in a computer, and it then discusses the pseudo-operations used in the definition of stack and data segments in an 8088/8086 assembly language program. With these pseudo-operations, the user can define 8-bit or 16-bit variables in memory, assign initial values to those variables, and assign names to constants used in the program. The assembly language instructions for the movement of data between the memory and the microprocessor registers of the 8088/8086 microprocessor also are discussed.

2.1 Computer Representations of Data

Data are represented in the computer by groups of two-state components. A lamp is an example of a two-state device: Assuming that a lamp has a two-way switch and no dimming device, then the lamp is either on or off. Figure 2.1(a) shows the two possible states of a single lamp, and Figure 2.1(b) shows the possible states of a group of two lamps. By adding a second lamp, the number of possible states has been doubled from two to four. Figure 2.1(c) shows the possible states of a group of three lamps. By adding a third lamp, the number of possible states has been doubled again from four to eight. Note that the first four states in Figure 2.1(c) contain all possible states of lamps 2 and 3 with lamp 1 off and that the last four states contain all possible states of lamps 2 and 3 with lamp 1 on. In this manner, the number of possible states is doubled each time a new lamp is added to the group. Each of the possible states can

FIGURE 2.1
The possible states of groups of lamps

(a) Single lamp

Off	Off	
Off	On	
On	Off	
On	On	2 lamps => 4 states => 2^2

(b) Two lamps

Off	Off	Off	
Off	Off	On	
Off	On	Off	
Off	On	On	
On	Off	Off	
On	Off	On	
On	On	Off	
On	On	On	3 lamps => 8 states => 2^3

(c) Three lamps

be used to represent some information: With a single lamp, two pieces of information can be represented; with a group of two lamps, four pieces of information can be represented; with a group of three lamps, eight pieces of information can be represented; and so on. In general, with a group of n lamps, 2^n pieces of information can be represented.

A single, two-state component can store one binary digit (i.e., one of the two states represents a binary 0, and the other state represents a binary 1). The bits in the computer's main memory are organized into fixed size units called **memory cells**. That is, each memory cell is a fixed size group of two-state components. Each memory cell has associated with it a unique number, called its **address**, by which it is referenced. If a memory has n cells, then the addresses generally range from 0 to $n-1$. This addressable memory cell is the unit of data transmission in the computer. That is, whenever data is stored in memory or retrieved from memory, it is done one memory cell at a time by address. In the 8088/8086, this addressable unit of storage is called a **byte**, and its size is 8 bits. The 8088/8086 also provides the capability to combine two contiguous 8-bit bytes into a 16-bit **word**. If the size of a memory cell is n bits, then the binary bit pattern contained in that cell will be one of 2^n possible bit patterns. These bit patterns can be used to represent integers, either nonnegative integers only or both negative and nonnegative integers. These bit patterns also can be used to represent textual data. The following subsections discuss one number system for representing nonnegative integers, four number systems for representing both negative and nonnegative integers, and a code for representing text characters.

Modulo 2^n (Unsigned)

Suppose the size of a memory cell is 8 bits and that the bit pattern contained in a memory cell represents the corresponding nonnegative binary integer. Table 2.1 shows the range of nonnegative decimal integers that can be represented by the 256

TABLE 2.1
Range of integer values for the 8-bit modulo 2^8 number system

Bit Pattern	Modulo 2^8 Integer
00000000	0
00000001	1
00000010	2
00000011	3
00000100	4
00000101	5
00000110	6
00000111	7
.	.
.	.
.	.
01111100	124
01111101	125
01111110	126
01111111	127
10000000	128
10000001	129
10000010	130
10000011	131
.	.
.	.
.	.
11111000	248
11111001	249
11111010	250
11111011	251
11111100	252
11111101	253
11111110	254
11111111	255

possible values of an 8-bit binary number. This number system is referred to as the **modulo 2^8 (modulo 256) number system.**

With 8-bit binary numbers, the integers in the modulo 2^8 number system (i.e., integers in the range 0 to $2^8 - 1$ or 0 to 255) can be represented. In general, with *n*-bit binary numbers, the integers in the modulo 2^n number system (i.e., integers in the range 0 to $2^n - 1$) can be represented. The 8088/8086 microprocessor uses the modulo 2^n number system to represent unsigned integers.

Sign Magnitude

The **sign magnitude number system** provides for both negative and nonnegative integers. With the sign magnitude number system, the leftmost bit in a bit pattern is used to represent the sign of the integer (0 for positive and 1 for negative), and the remaining bits in the bit pattern represent the magnitude of the integer.

EXAMPLES

The 8-bit binary number 00010101 represents the decimal integer +21. The leftmost bit represents the sign (0 implies +), and the remaining bits are the binary representation for the decimal integer 21.

The 8-bit binary number 10010101 represents the decimal integer −21. The leftmost bit represents the sign (1 implies −), and the remaining bits are the binary representation for the decimal integer 21. ■

Table 2.2 shows the range of integers that can be represented in the sign magnitude number system using 8-bit binary bit patterns. This range is from $-(2^7 - 1)$ to $+(2^7 - 1)$, which is −127 to +127. In general, the range of integers that can be represented by n-bit binary integers in sign magnitude form is from $-(2^{n-1} - 1)$ to $+(2^{n-1} - 1)$. To negate a number in the sign magnitude number system, simply invert the leftmost bit, the **sign bit**. The magnitude bits remain the same.

The sign magnitude number system takes the available bit patterns and chooses half of them to represent positive integers and the other half to represent negative integers. Note that in sign magnitude form there are two representations for zero: positive zero and negative zero. This method runs contrary to standard mathematics where zero is neither positive nor negative.

TABLE 2.2
Range of integer values for the 8-bit sign magnitude number system

Bit Pattern	Sign Magnitude Integer
00000000	0
00000001	1
00000010	2
00000011	3
00000100	4
00000101	5
00000110	6
00000111	7
.	.
.	.
.	.
01111100	124
01111101	125
01111110	126
01111111	127
10000000	−0
10000001	−1
10000010	−2
10000011	−3
.	.
.	.
.	.
11111000	−120
11111001	−121
11111010	−122
11111011	−123
11111100	−124
11111101	−125
11111110	−126
11111111	−127

One's Complement

The **one's complement number system** provides for both negative and nonnegative integers. Table 2.3 shows the range of integers that can be represented by the 8-bit

TABLE 2.3
Range of integer values for the 8-bit one's complement number system

Bit Pattern	One's Complement Integer
00000000	0
00000001	1
00000010	2
00000011	3
00000100	4
00000101	5
00000110	6
00000111	7
.	.
.	.
.	.
01111100	124
01111101	125
01111110	126
01111111	127
10000000	−127
10000001	−126
10000010	−125
10000011	−124
.	.
.	.
.	.
11111000	−7
11111001	−6
11111010	−5
11111011	−4
11111100	−3
11111101	−2
11111110	−1
11111111	−0

one's complement number system. This range is from $-(2^7 - 1)$ to $+(2^7 - 1)$, which is -127 to $+127$. In general, the range of integers that can be represented by n-bit binary integers in one's complement form is from $-(2^{n-1} - 1)$ to $+(2^{n-1} - 1)$.

In the one's complement number system, all negative integers have a 1 in the leftmost bit position, and all positive integers have a 0 in the leftmost bit position. The leftmost bit is, therefore, the sign bit. To negate an integer in the one's complement number system, simply invert every bit of the integer (i.e., change each 0 to a 1, and change each 1 to a 0).

EXAMPLES

The bit pattern 00010101 represents the integer +21 in the 8-bit one's complement number system. Inverting each bit of this bit pattern gives the bit pattern 11101010, which represents the integer −21 in the 8-bit one's complement number system.

The bit pattern 00000000 represents the integer 0 in the 8-bit one's complement number system. Inverting each bit of this bit pattern gives the bit pattern 11111111, which represents the integer −0 in the 8-bit one's complement number system. ■

The one's complement number system takes the available bit patterns and chooses half of them to represent positive integers and the other half to represent negative integers. Note that in one's complement form there are two representations for zero: positive zero and negative zero. This method runs contrary to standard mathematics where zero is neither positive nor negative.

Two's Complement

The **two's complement number system** provides for both negative and nonnegative integers. The 8088/8086 microprocessor uses the two's complement number system to represent signed integers. Table 2.4 shows the range of integers that can be represented by the 8-bit two's complement number system. This range is from -2^7 to $+2^7 - 1$, which is -128 to $+127$. In general, with n-bit binary numbers in the two's complement number system, the integers in the range -2^{n-1} to $+2^{n-1} - 1$ can be represented.

TABLE 2.4
Range of integer values for the 8-bit two's complement number system

Bit Pattern	Two's Complement Integer
00000000	0
00000001	1
00000010	2
00000011	3
00000100	4
00000101	5
00000110	6
00000111	7
.	.
.	.
.	.
01111100	124
01111101	125
01111110	126
01111111	127
10000000	−128
10000001	−127
10000010	−126
10000011	−125
.	.
.	.
.	.
11111000	−8
11111001	−7
11111010	−6
11111011	−5
11111100	−4
11111101	−3
11111110	−2
11111111	−1

In the two's complement number system, all negative integers have a 1 in the leftmost bit position, and all nonnegative integers have a 0 in the leftmost bit position. The leftmost bit is, therefore, the sign bit.

In the two's complement number system, negating an integer is a two-step process:

1. Invert each bit in the binary number (i.e., change each 1 to a 0, and change each 0 to a 1). The result of this step is called the **one's complement** of the original binary number.
2. Then add 1 to the result of step 1 using modulo 2^n addition, in which n is the number of bits in the binary number being negated.

An alternate method for negating an integer in the two's complement number system is as follows:

1. Copy all bits up to and including the first bit that is a 1 (start with the rightmost bit of the binary number and work left).
2. Invert all of the remaining bits to the left.

EXAMPLES

Method 1	*Method 2*	
00001100	0 0 0 0 1 1 0 0	
11110011	I I I I I C C C	I → Invert; C → Copy
+ 1		
11110100	1 1 1 1 0 1 0 0	

Method 1	*Method 2*	
11101000	1 1 1 0 1 0 0 0	
00010111	I I I I C C C C	I → Invert; C → Copy
+ 1		
00011000	0 0 0 1 1 0 0 0	

■

Negating a number in the two's complement number system is called "taking the two's complement" of the number. The negative of a number is called the **two's complement** of that number.

The two's complement number system takes the available bit patterns and chooses half of them to represent negative integers and the other half to represent nonnegative integers. Note that in two's complement form there is only one representation for zero. As well, there is one negative integer that has no corresponding positive integer: -128 (i.e., -2^7). In the n-bit two's complement number system, this extra negative integer is -2^{n-1}, which is represented by the n-bit pattern having a 1 in the leftmost bit and a 0 in all other bit positions.

Excess 2^{n-1}

The **excess 2^{n-1} number system** provides for both negative and nonnegative integers. Table 2.5 shows the range of integers that can be represented by the 8-bit excess 2^7 (excess 128) number system. This range is from -2^7 to $+2^7 - 1$, which is -128 to $+127$. In general, with n-bit binary numbers in the excess 2^{n-1} number system, integers in the range -2^{n-1} to $+2^{n-1} - 1$ can be represented.

TABLE 2.5
Range of integer values for the 8-bit excess 2^7 number system

Bit Pattern	Excess 2^7 Integer
00000000	−128
00000001	−127
00000010	−126
00000011	−125
00000100	−124
00000101	−123
00000110	−122
00000111	−121
.	.
.	.
.	.
01111100	−4
01111101	−3
01111110	−2
01111111	−1
10000000	0
10000001	1
10000010	2
10000011	3
.	.
.	.
.	.
11111000	120
11111001	121
11111010	122
11111011	123
11111100	124
11111101	125
11111110	126
11111111	127

In the excess 2^{n-1} number system, the n-bit binary number used to represent an integer is 2^{n-1} larger than the integer that it represents; that is, the binary bit pattern is in excess by 2^{n-1} of the integer that it represents. In this number system, all negative integers have a 0 in the leftmost bit position, and all nonnegative integers have a 1 in the leftmost bit position. The leftmost bit is, again, an indication of the sign.

It is interesting to note that in the excess 2^{n-1} number system the bit pattern used to represent a given integer is the same as the bit pattern used to represent that integer in the two's complement number system with the sign bit inverted. To negate an integer in the excess 2^{n-1} number system, simply take the two's complement of that integer.

The excess 2^{n-1} number system takes the available bit patterns and chooses half of them to represent negative integers and the other half to represent nonnegative integers. Note that in excess 2^{n-1} form there is only one representation for zero. As well, there is one negative integer that has no corresponding positive integer: -128 (i.e., -2^7). In the n-bit excess 2^{n-1} number system, this extra negative integer is -2^{n-1}, which is represented by the bit pattern that contains all zeros. An excess 2^{n-1} number system often is used to represent the exponent of a floating-point number.

ASCII Code

The **American Standard Code for Information Interchange (ASCII)** is a 7-bit code adopted by the American National Standards Institute (ANSI). ASCII code is used to represent characters such as A, $, b, 7, ?, and] using binary bit patterns. With a 7-bit code, a total of 128 characters can be represented. The first 32 binary codes in the ASCII character set (0000000 to 0011111, which is 00 HEX to 1F HEX) are used to represent control characters, such as form feed and line feed for the printer. The remaining binary codes (0100000 to 1111111, which is 20 HEX to 7F HEX) are used to represent the printable characters, including the uppercase and lowercase letters, the decimal digits, and special characters such as $, ?, SPACEBAR,], and /.

For the IBM PC and PS/2 families of microcomputers, the ASCII character code has been extended to an 8-bit code, in which the first 128 codes in the extended ASCII character set (00000000 to 01111111, which is 00 HEX to 7F HEX) are used to represent the standard ASCII character set. The remaining 128 binary codes in the extended ASCII character set (10000000 to 11111111, which is 80 HEX to FF HEX) are used to represent a variety of symbols that include graphics symbols, math symbols, and Greek letters. The IBM extended ASCII character set also provides for an additional 32 graphics symbols (00000000 to 00011111, which is 00 HEX to 1F HEX) that can be interpreted as special graphics symbols rather than control characters when the codes are output to the display. The tables in Appendix E show both the standard ASCII character set and the IBM extended ASCII character set.

2.2 Data-Defining Pseudo-Operations

A data segment definition includes a series of pseudo-operations that describes to the assembler how the static data is to be organized. These pseudo-operations provide the following information:

- Size of (i.e., number of bytes in) the static data segment
- Symbolic names that are to be associated with specific locations in the static data segment
- Initial values to be placed in specific locations in the static data segment
- Symbolic names that are to be associated with a constant value

Variable Definitions

Variables are defined in a static data segment using the DB, BYTE, SBYTE, DW, WORD, and SWORD pseudo-operations.

MASM 5.1

Only the DB and DW pseudo-operations are available in MASM 5.1.

With full segment definitions, these data-defining pseudo-operations are bracketed by the SEGMENT and ENDS pseudo-operations (see Program Listing 1.1). With simplified segment definitions, these data-defining pseudo-operations are preceded by the .CONST pseudo-operation for data segments containing only constant definitions (see Program Listing 1.2) or by the .DATA, .DATA?, .FARDATA, and .FARDATA? pseudo-operations for data segments containing variable definitions.

The **.DATA**, **.DATA?**, **.FARDATA**, and **.FARDATA? pseudo-operations** have the following general forms:

```
.DATA                          [⟨comment⟩]
.DATA?                         [⟨comment⟩]
.FARDATA     [⟨seg-name⟩]      [⟨comment⟩]
.FARDATA?    [⟨seg-name⟩]      [⟨comment⟩]
```

in which ⟨*seg-name*⟩ is the symbolic name to be associated with the memory location where the segment is to begin. These pseudo-operations mark the end of the previous segment definition and the beginning of a data segment definition. The .DATA pseudo-operation is used to define a near data segment for initialized data, and the .DATA? pseudo-operation is used to define a near data segment for uninitialized data. The .FARDATA pseudo-operation is used to define a far data segment for initialized data, and the .FARDATA? pseudo-operation is used to define a far data segment for uninitialized data. A **near data segment** will be combined with other near data and stack segments to form a data group. The data segments in the group can all be accessed through a common segment register. A **far data segment** is physically separate from other data segments and must be addressed through its own segment register. If the total amount of data for a program is less than 64K bytes and is placed in a single data segment to be addressed by the DS-register, then it makes no difference whether a near or a far data segment is used. However, if the total amount of data exceeds 64K bytes, then segment register switching can decrease the efficiency of the program. In this case, frequently used data should appear in a near data segment addressed by the DS-register, and infrequently used data should be placed in far data segments.

The data-defining pseudo-operations for defining byte data, **DB**, **BYTE**, and **SBYTE**, have the following general forms:

```
[⟨name⟩]  DB        ⟨byte-constant-list⟩  [⟨comment⟩]
[⟨name⟩]  BYTE      ⟨byte-constant-list⟩  [⟨comment⟩]
[⟨name⟩]  SBYTE     ⟨byte-constant-list⟩  [⟨comment⟩]
```

in which ⟨*name*⟩ is the symbolic name to be associated with the memory location in which the sequence of data bytes is to begin and ⟨*byte-constant-list*⟩ is a list of byte constants separated by commas.

A ⟨*byte-constant*⟩ is one of the following:

1. A **binary byte constant** is a signed or an unsigned string of up to eight significant binary digits followed by the letter B (upper case or lower case).
2. An **octal byte constant** is a signed or an unsigned string of octal digits followed by either the letter O or the letter Q (upper case or lower case). The octal value must lie in the range 0–377.
3. A **hexadecimal byte constant** is a signed or an unsigned string of up to two significant hexadecimal digits followed by the letter H (upper case or lower case). The first character in the string must be a digit 0–9; for example, the hexadecimal constant F8 would have to be written as 0F8H. This rule allows the assembler to distinguish between the hexadecimal constant F8H and the symbolic name F8H.
4. A **decimal byte constant** is a signed or an unsigned string of decimal digits optionally followed by the letter D (upper case or lower case). The decimal string must be in the range 0–255.
5. A string of characters enclosed in apostrophes (') or double quotation marks ("), in which each character in the string defines one byte constant.

6. A question mark (?), which indicates that a byte of storage is to be allocated but that an initial value is not being specified. The initial value for the allocated byte is unknown.

Each ⟨*byte-constant*⟩ with the exception of a string constant specifies the allocation of one byte of storage. The value of the constant specifies the initial value of that byte. The order of the constants in the list specifies the order in which the storage bytes are to appear in the static data segment. The symbolic ⟨*name*⟩ is associated with the first byte in the list.

Note that a binary, octal, hexadecimal, or decimal byte constant may be signed or unsigned. A minus sign (−) in front of a byte constant simply instructs the assembler to perform the two's complement of the binary representation of the constant.

EXAMPLES

The octal constant 377Q is translated by the assembler to the binary bit pattern 11111111. The octal constant −377Q is translated to the two's complement of this bit pattern, producing the bit pattern 00000001.

The decimal constant 144 is translated by the assembler to the binary bit pattern 10010000. The decimal constant −144 is translated to the two's complement of this bit pattern, producing the bit pattern 01110000. Note that the decimal integer 144 is within the range for 8-bit unsigned integers. However, the decimal integer −144 is *not* within the range for 8-bit signed two's complement integers. Unfortunately, the assembler does not flag this occurrence as an error. It translates −144 to the binary representation for 112 decimal. ■

With versions of MASM prior to Version 6.0, the DB pseudo-operation was used to define both unsigned and signed byte variables. The decimal range of unsigned integer byte values is from 0 to 255. The decimal range of signed integer byte values is from −128 to +127. So that one pseudo-operation could be used to cover both of these ranges, these earlier versions of MASM treated a constant in the ⟨*byte-constant-list*⟩ as a sign magnitude value. The magnitude, which could be in the range 0–255, was converted to an unsigned binary integer. Then, if the sign was minus (−), that value was negated (i.e., a two's complement operation was performed on the value). The resulting value was the initial value of the variable.

EXAMPLES

The decimal byte constant 228, appearing as an initial value in a DB pseudo-operation, produced the binary byte value 11100100.

The decimal byte constant 28, appearing as an initial value in a DB pseudo-operation, produced the binary byte value 00011100.

The bogus decimal byte constant −228, appearing as an initial value in a DB pseudo-operation, was converted to a binary byte value in a two-step process: First the magnitude (228) was converted to binary, producing the byte value 11100100. Then, because of the minus sign, this binary byte value was negated, producing the byte value 00011100. Note that the resulting value is actually the 8-bit binary representation of 28. ■

With MASM 6.0, three pseudo-operations can be used to define byte variables: DB, BYTE, and SBYTE. We would reasonably expect the DB pseudo-operation to be consistent with previous versions of MASM, the BYTE pseudo-operation to accept integers only in the range 0–255, and the SBYTE pseudo-operation to accept integers only in the range from −128 to +127. Unfortunately, all three pseudo-operations accept integers in the range from −255 to 255. The reader should therefore verify these ranges on future versions of MASM, which, hopefully, will correct this apparent oversight.

The use of the BYTE and SBYTE pseudo-operations, rather than the DB pseudo-operation, becomes important when variables are used in decision- and loop-generating macro directives. These directives are discussed in detail in Chapter 4.

EXAMPLE

The following data segment definition instructs the assembler to generate a 12-byte static data segment with the symbolic names and initial values as shown in Table 2.6:

```
            .FARDATA    DATA
NUMBER      DB          8CH
COUNT       DB          ?
TWELVE      DB          12
NEG_ONE     DB          -1
ALL_ONES    DB          11111111B
ONE         DB          -377Q
STRING      DB          'A1 (2)'
```

■

TABLE 2.6
Twelve-byte data segment

Symbolic Name	Byte Offset	Hex Contents
NUMBER	0000	8C
COUNT	0001	?
TWELVE	0002	0C
NEG_ONE	0003	FF
ALL_ONES	0004	FF
ONE	0005	01
STRING	0006	41
	0007	31
	0008	20
	0009	28
	000A	32
	000B	29

(? means initial value unknown)

The data-defining pseudo-operations for defining word data, **DW**, **WORD**, and **SWORD**, have the following general forms:

[⟨*name*⟩] DW ⟨*word-constant-list*⟩ [⟨*comment*⟩]
[⟨*name*⟩] WORD ⟨*word-constant-list*⟩ [⟨*comment*⟩]
[⟨*name*⟩] SWORD ⟨*word-constant-list*⟩ [⟨*comment*⟩]

in which ⟨*name*⟩ is the symbolic name to be associated with the memory location in which the sequence of data words is to begin and ⟨*word-constant-list*⟩ is a list of word constants separated by commas.

A ⟨*word-constant*⟩ is one of the following:

1. A **binary word constant** is a signed or an unsigned string of up to 16 significant binary digits followed by the letter B (upper case or lower case).

2. An **octal word constant** is a signed or an unsigned string of octal digits followed by either the letter O or the letter Q (upper case or lower case). The octal value must lie in the range 0–177777.
3. A **hexadecimal word constant** is a signed or an unsigned string of up to four significant hexadecimal digits followed by the letter H (upper case or lower case). The first character in the string must be a digit 0–9.
4. A **decimal word constant** is a signed or an unsigned string of decimal digits optionally followed by the letter D (upper case or lower case). The decimal string must be in the range 0–65535.
5. A label, which represents a 16-bit offset within a segment.
6. A question mark (?), which indicates that two bytes (one word) of storage are to be allocated but that an initial value is not being specified. The initial value for the allocated word is unknown.

Each ⟨*word-constant*⟩ specifies the allocation of two consecutive bytes (one word) of storage, with the value of the constant being the initial value of that word. The low-order byte of the 16-bit initial value is stored in the first byte, and the value's high-order byte is stored in the second byte. The order of the constants in the list specifies the order in which the words are to appear in the static data segment. The symbolic ⟨*name*⟩ is associated with the first word in the list.

Note that a binary, octal, hexadecimal, and decimal word constant may be signed or unsigned. A minus sign (−) in front of a word constant simply instructs the assembler to perform the two's complement of the binary representation of the constant.

With versions of MASM prior to Version 6.0, the DW pseudo-operation was used to define both unsigned and signed word variables. The decimal range of unsigned integer word values is from 0 to 65535. The decimal range of signed integer word values is from −32768 to +32767. So that one pseudo-operation could be used to cover both of these ranges, these earlier versions of MASM treated a constant in the ⟨*word-constant-list*⟩ as a sign magnitude value. The magnitude, which could be in the range 0–65535, was converted to an unsigned binary integer. Then, if the sign was minus (−), that value was negated (i.e., a two's complement operation was performed on the value). The resulting value was the initial value of the variable.

With MASM 6.0, three pseudo-operations can be used to define word variables: DW, WORD, and SWORD. We would reasonably expect the DW pseudo-operation to be consistent with previous versions of MASM, the WORD pseudo-operation to accept integers only in the range 0–65535, and the SWORD pseudo-operation to accept integers only in the range from −32768 to +32767. Unfortunately, all three pseudo-operations accept integers in the range from −65535 to 65535. The reader should therefore verify these ranges on future versions of MASM, which, hopefully, will correct this apparent oversight.

The use of the WORD and SWORD pseudo-operations, rather than the DW pseudo-operation, becomes important when variables are used in decision- and loop-generating macro directives. These directives are discussed in detail in Chapter 4.

EXAMPLE

The following data segment definition instructs the assembler to generate a 6-word (12-byte) static data segment with the symbolic names and initial values as shown in Table 2.7:

```
            .FARDATA    DATA
X           DW          ?
Y           DW          -377Q
ORDER       DW          12ABH
ADDRESS     DW          ORDER
HUNDRED     DW          100
MINUS_ONE   DW          -1
```

TABLE 2.7
Six-word data segment

Symbolic Name	Byte Offset	Hex Contents
X	0000	?
	0001	?
Y	0002	01
	0003	FF
ORDER	0004	AB
	0005	12
ADDRESS	0006	04
	0007	00
HUNDRED	0008	64
	0009	00
MINUS_ONE	000A	FF
	000B	FF

(? means initial value unknown)

The entry

```
ADDRESS    DW                ORDER
```

allocates a word of storage and assigns as the initial value the offset associated with the symbolic name ORDER (0004). ADDRESS is said to be a **pointer** to the variable ORDER. ■

A constant list that contains repetition can be abbreviated somewhat by the use of a duplicate clause. A **duplicate clause** has the following general form:

⟨*repeat-count*⟩ DUP (⟨*constant-list*⟩)

This clause specifies that the ⟨*constant-list*⟩ is to be duplicated ⟨*repeat-count*⟩ times in succession. The ⟨*constant-list*⟩ itself may contain a duplicate clause. That is, duplicate clauses may be nested.

EXAMPLES

The duplicate clause

```
12 DUP(0)
```

is an abbreviation for the constant list

```
0, 0, 0, 0, 0, 0, 0, 0, 0, 0, 0, 0
```

The duplicate clause

```
3 DUP (3 DUP(0), 1)
```

is an abbreviation for the constant list

```
0, 0, 0, 1, 0, 0, 0, 1, 0, 0, 0, 1
```

■

Byte and word data-defining pseudo-operations can be used in the same data segment definition.

EXAMPLE

The following data segment definition instructs the assembler to generate a 24-byte static data segment with the symbolic names and initial values as shown in Table 2.8:

```
          .FARDATA    DATA
PROMPT    DB          'ENTER  N', ODH, OAH
N         DW          ?
HUNDRED   DW          100
ARRAY     DW          5  DUP(?)
FLAG      DB          0
```

TABLE 2.8
Twenty-four-byte data segment

Symbolic Name	Byte Offset	Hex Contents
PROMPT	0000	45
	0001	4E
	0002	54
	0003	45
	0004	52
	0005	20
	0006	4E
	0007	0D
	0008	0A
N	0009	?
	000A	?
HUNDRED	000B	64
	000C	00
ARRAY	000D	?
	000E	?
	000F	?
	0010	?
	0011	?
	0012	?
	0013	?
	0014	?
	0015	?
	0016	?
FLAG	0017	00

(? means initial value unknown)

The entry

```
ARRAY    DW              5  DUP(?)
```

allocates five consecutive words (10 bytes) of storage. The name ARRAY is the symbolic name to be associated with the first of these five words. The question mark (?) means that an initial value is not being specified for any of the five words. The entry, in effect, defines a 5-word array named ARRAY. (The definition and use of arrays is discussed in detail in Chapter 8.) Note that the word variables N and HUNDRED and the words of ARRAY all begin at an odd address (i.e., an odd byte offset). This alignment means that any access to these words requires two bus cycles on an 8086-

based machine. To force these words to begin at an even address, the EVEN pseudo-operation is inserted between the definition of variable PROMPT and the definition of variable N. This insertion causes the variable N to begin at offset 000A, the variable HUNDRED to begin at offset 000C, and ARRAY to begin at offset 000E. The byte at offset 0009 is unused. The form of the EVEN pseudo-operation is described in Appendix B. ■

Constant Definitions

Two kinds of constant definitions can appear in an 8088/8086 assembly module. One is a symbolic constant that is known only during the assembly process, and the other allocates and initializes storage cells to which the assembler will allow fetch operations but not store operations.

A constant can be given a symbolic name in an 8088/8086 assembly module. This symbolic name can then be used anywhere in the assembly module that a constant can be used; it is simply another name for that constant. A symbolic name is assigned to a constant by means of the EQU (equate) pseudo-operation. The **EQU pseudo-operation** has the following general form:

⟨*name*⟩ EQU ⟨*constant-expression*⟩

in which ⟨*name*⟩ is the symbolic name to be associated with the value of the ⟨*constant-expression*⟩ and ⟨*constant-expression*⟩ can be, among other things, a word constant or a byte constant.

EXAMPLE

```
FALSE  EQU  0
TRUE   EQU  1
```

The symbolic name FALSE can be used anywhere in the assembly module that the constant 0 can be used. The values of FALSE and TRUE cannot be changed during execution. ■

A symbolic constant defined by the EQU pseudo-operation is known only during the assembly process. The assembler changes all occurrences of the symbolic name to the equated constant prior to translation of the assembly module. The purpose of the symbolic constant is simply to render the assembly module more readable.

A static data segment can be defined in such a way that the values of the data items in the segment are intended to remain constant. That is, the items are intended to be used but not modified during execution. With simplified segment definitions, the definition of a constant data segment begins with the .CONST pseudo-operation. The .CONST pseudo-operation was introduced in Chapter 1 in the discussion of Program Listing 1.2. The constant data segment definition in Program Listing 1.2 contains the definitions of string constants that are used for annotation in the program's output. With full segment definitions, the definition of a constant data segment begins with a SEGMENT pseudo-operation that has the operand READONLY. If the SEGMENT pseudo-operation in line 25 of Program Listing 1.1 were changed to

```
DATA  SEGMENT  READONLY
```

then the static data segment would be a constant data segment.

The assembler checks all references in the assembly module to data items in constant data segments. If there is an instruction in the assembly module that would potentially modify (i.e., that would store into) a data item in a constant data segment, then that instruction is flagged by the assembler with a warning message. Note that warnings do not keep the assembler from producing the object module. Thus, if warning messages are ignored, it is possible to produce an executable program that modifies data items in a constant data segment.

2.3 Memory Addressing

The Intel 8088/8086 microprocessor can address 1,048,576 bytes (1 megabyte) of memory. To address this amount of memory, a 20-bit address is required. All memory addresses in an 8088/8086 machine language program are in the form of a segment origin and an offset within the segment. This setup is used whether the address is for an instruction fetch, a data fetch, or a data store. The segment origin is specified by the contents of one of the four segment registers in the BIU of the microprocessor. The offset within the segment can be specified in the machine language instruction itself by the contents of a pointer register (SP, BP, or IP), by the contents of an index register (DI or SI), or by some combination of these three.

EXAMPLES The memory address of the next instruction byte to be fetched is specified by the contents of the CS:IP register pair. That is, the contents of the CS-register specifies the start address of the current code segment, and the contents of the IP-register is the offset within that code segment of the instruction byte to be fetched.

The memory address of the top-of-stack item for a push or pop operation is specified by the contents of the SS:SP register pair. That is, the contents of the SS-register specifies the start address of the stack segment, and the contents of the SP-register is the offset within the stack segment of the top-of-stack item. ■

Address Computation

The generation of a 20-bit physical memory address from a segment origin and an offset within the segment is performed by the BIU, which contains an adder (see Figure 1.17) that converts a memory address from a 16-bit segment origin and a 16-bit offset to a 20-bit physical memory address. Figure 2.2 describes the operation performed by this adder. First the contents of the specified segment register are expanded from 16 bits to 20 bits by concatenating 0000 (binary) onto the lower end of the segment register value. Recall that all segments must begin on a paragraph boundary (i.e., a memory cell whose address is divisible by 16), which means that the 20-bit start address of a segment always ends with 0000, and the 0000 is not stored in the segment register. Only the high-order 16 bits of the start address are stored in the segment register. The 0000 is concatenated to the contents of the segment register before adding an offset. Next the 16-bit offset is added to the expanded 20-bit segment origin address to produce the 20-bit physical memory address.

EXAMPLE Suppose the BIU is about to fetch the next instruction byte and the contents of the CS and IP registers are as follows:

$$CS = 0928 \text{ hex}$$

$$IP = 0022 \text{ hex}$$

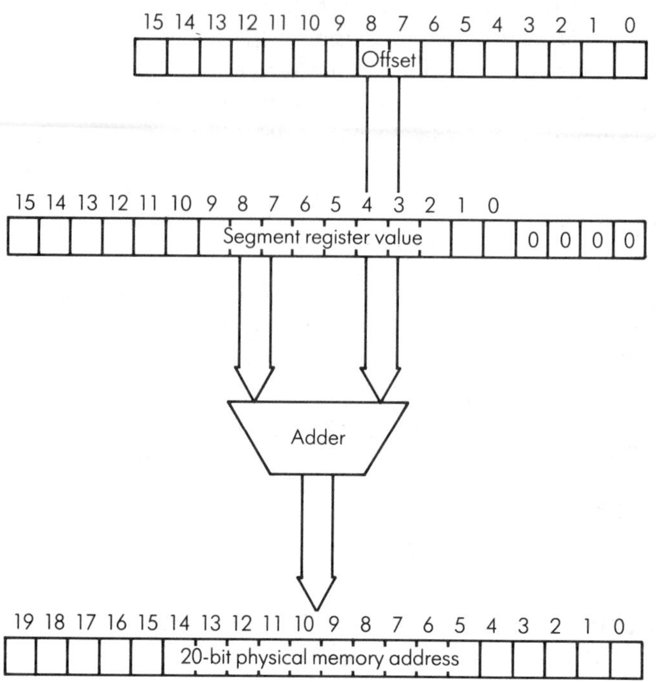

FIGURE 2.2 8088/8086 memory address generation

The 16-bit contents of the CS-register specifies the 20-bit base address as 09280 hex. Therefore, the adder performs the following operation:

```
 09280
  0022
 -----
 092A2
```

The physical memory address of the next instruction byte to be fetched is thus 092A2 hex. ■

Addressing Modes

Some of the instructions in the machine language of the Intel 8088/8086 microprocessor specify the location of one or more operands to be used in execution of the instruction. For example, an addition instruction specifies the locations of two 8-bit operands or two 16-bit operands to be added together. An operand of such an instruction may be the contents of a general register, a value contained in the instruction itself (an immediate value), or the contents of a memory location. The example programs presented in the early chapters of this book deal primarily with scalar (single-valued) data items and use three assembly language addressing modes to specify operands.

Register Addressing

With **register addressing**, the operand is the contents of one of the 8-bit or 16-bit registers. A specific register is addressed by coding its two-character symbolic name in the operand field of the instruction. The two-character register designators recognized by the Macro Assembler are given in Table 2.9.

TABLE 2.9
Register designators used in register addressing

General Registers		
8-Bit	16-Bit	Segment Registers
AL	AX	CS
BL	BX	SS
CL	CX	DS
DL	DX	ES
AH	BP	
BH	SP	
CH	DI	
DH	SI	

Immediate Addressing

With **immediate addressing**, the operand is an 8-bit or 16-bit constant contained in the machine language representation of the instruction. A specific immediate value is referenced by coding a constant representation for the value in the operand field of the instruction. The various constant forms allowed in the MASM assembly language were discussed in Section 2.2.

Direct Addressing

With **direct addressing**, the operand is the 8-bit contents of a memory location or the 16-bit contents of two consecutive memory locations. A specific memory location is addressed directly by coding its symbolic name into the operand field of the instruction.

With a direct address, the symbolic name identifies both a segment and an offset within the segment; thus, it identifies a unique memory location. In most cases, the symbolic name used in a direct address is completely defined in the same assembly module. The assembler knows the segment in which the symbolic name is defined, and through the ASSUME pseudo-operation, it knows which segment register is to contain the address of that segment's origin during program execution. The segment register is specified (implicitly or explicitly) in the machine language representation of the instruction. The offset associated with the symbolic name is dependent on the order in which items are defined in the segment that contains the symbolic name. Therefore, the assembler has the information to determine the offset within the segment. The offset is also part of the machine language representation of the instruction. Several additional methods for specifying operands from memory are discussed in Chapter 8.

2.4 Data Transfer Instructions

There are three types of data transfer instructions in the 8088/8086 assembly language:

1. Instructions for moving data among CPU registers and between memory and CPU registers (MOV and XCHG instructions)
2. Instructions for moving data on and off the stack (PUSH, POP, PUSHF, and POPF instructions)

3. Instructions for moving the address of a memory location to a CPU register (LEA instruction)

Figure 2.3 shows the data transfer capabilities provided by the MOV, XCHG, PUSH, POP, PUSHF, and POPF instructions. The LEA instruction does not appear in Figure 2.3 because it transfers the address of the memory cell and the ones shown transfer the contents of a register or memory cell. Each of these instructions is discussed in the following subsections.

FIGURE 2.3
Data transfer instructions

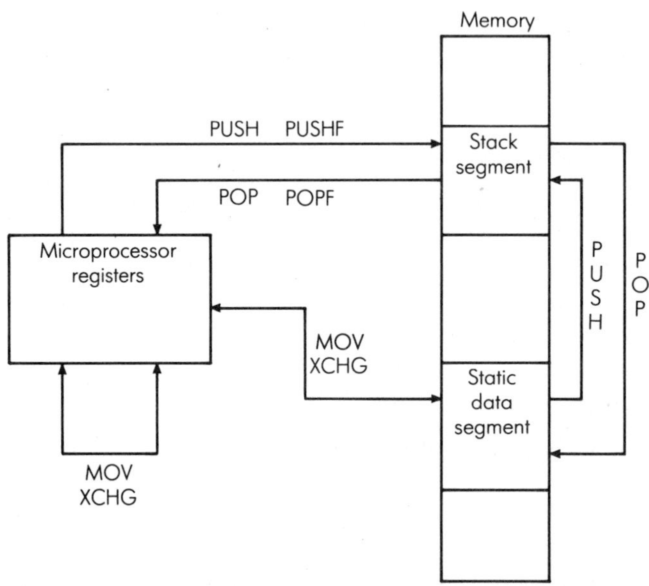

MOV and XCHG Instructions

The two instructions for moving data among CPU registers and between CPU registers and memory are MOV and XCHG.

The **MOV instruction** has the following general form:

[⟨*label*⟩] `MOV` ⟨*destination*⟩, ⟨*source*⟩ [⟨*comment*⟩]

in which ⟨*label*⟩ is the symbolic name to be associated with the memory location in which the instruction is to begin, ⟨*source*⟩ identifies the location of the data that is to be copied, and ⟨*destination*⟩ identifies where the data is to be moved. The MOV instruction causes a copy of the value of the source operand to replace the value of the destination operand. The value of the source operand is not modified by execution of the MOV instruction. The type attribute of the source and destination operands must match (i.e., both must be byte or both must be word). For technical reasons, not all combinations of destination and source operands are allowed. Figure 2.4 shows the permissible combinations of destination and source operands. Each arrow in the figure indicates a permissible combination of operands for the MOV instruction. That is, an arrow originates at the source operand and points to a destination operand. For example, a MOV instruction can copy the contents of a general register into a segment register (i.e., an arrow leads from general register to segment register). However, the figure also illustrates that a MOV instruction cannot copy the contents of one memory location into another memory location (i.e, no

FIGURE 2.4
Allowable operands for the MOV instruction

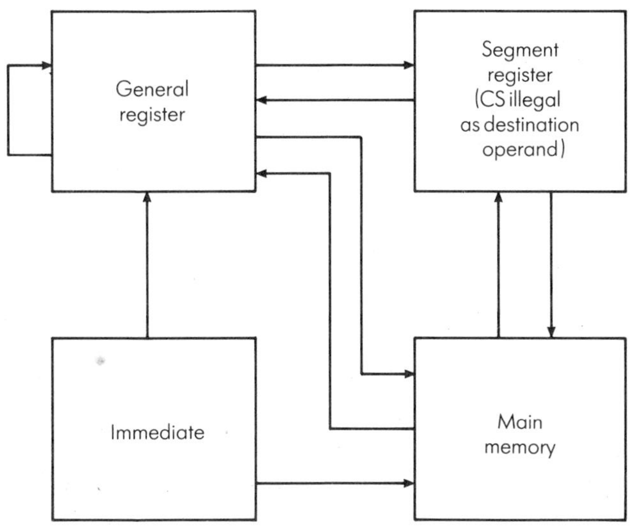

arrow leads from main memory to main memory). None of the bits in the flags register are affected by the execution of a MOV instruction.

EXAMPLES

```
MOV  BH, AL
```

copies the 8-bit value of the AL-register into the BH-register.

```
MOV  AX, COUNT
```

copies the 16-bit value that begins at the memory location specified by COUNT into the AX-register.

```
MOV  CX, 40
```

copies the 16-bit constant 40 from the instruction into the CX-register. ■

The **XCHG instruction** has the following general form:

[⟨*label*⟩] XCHG ⟨*destination*⟩,⟨*source*⟩ [⟨*comment*⟩]

in which ⟨*source*⟩ and ⟨*destination*⟩ identify the locations of the values to be exchanged. This instruction causes the value of the source operand to replace the value of the destination operand and, at the same time, causes the value of the destination operand to replace the value of the source operand; that is, the values of the two operands are interchanged. Figure 2.5 shows the possible combinations of oper-

FIGURE 2.5
Allowable operands for the XCHG instruction

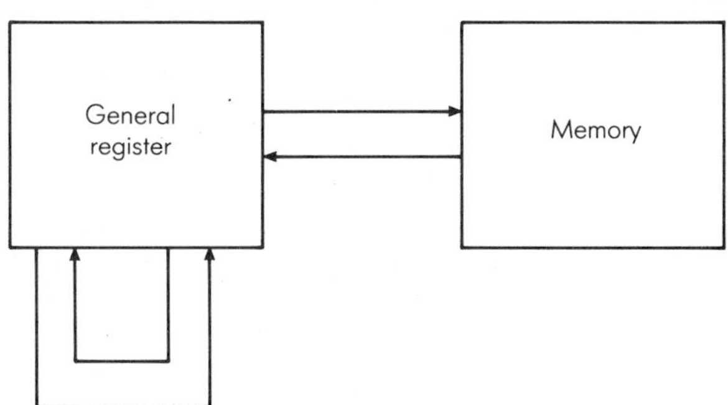

ands. Both source and destination operands can be general registers, or one operand can be a general register and the other a memory location. None of the bits in the flags register are affected by the execution of an XCHG instruction.

EXAMPLE

```
XCHG  AX, DX
```

interchanges the values of the AX and DX registers. ■

Stack Operations

The stack segment is a list of data words (*not bytes*) in which all insertions and deletions are made at one end of the stack, which is called the **top of the stack**. Inserting a new word in the stack segment is referred to as **pushing** the word onto the top of the stack. Removing a word from the stack is referred to as **popping** the word off the top of the stack. When a word is pushed onto the stack, it becomes the new top-of-stack data item. All data items previously in the stack are pushed down one position relative to the top of the stack. When the word at the top of the stack is popped from the stack, the data items remaining in the stack pop up one position relative to the top of the stack. The new top-of-stack data item is the word that was at the top of the stack when the popped item was pushed. The only item that can be popped from the stack is the word at the top of the stack, which is also the last word that was pushed onto the stack.

During execution of an 8088/8086 assembly language program, the SS:SP register pair always addresses the top-of-stack data item. The SS-register contains the address of the origin of the stack segment, and the SP-register contains the offset within the stack segment of the current top-of-stack data item. The bottom of the stack is fixed at the highest offset, and the top of the stack changes dynamically as push and pop operations are performed. The SS and SP registers are automatically maintained by the microprocessor and are not directly manipulated by the program.

The instructions for moving data on and off the stack are PUSH, POP, PUSHF, and POPF.

The **PUSH instruction** has the following general form:

[⟨*label*⟩] `PUSH` ⟨*source*⟩ [⟨*comment*⟩]

in which ⟨*source*⟩ identifies the location of a 16-bit value to be pushed onto the stack. This instruction causes the value of the SP-register to be decremented by 2 and then the 16-bit value of the source operand to be stored in the stack segment at the location pointed to by the SS:SP register pair (i.e., the new top of the stack). The source operand can be either a general register, a segment register, or a memory location. The type attribute of the source operand must be word. None of the bits in the flags register are affected by the execution of a PUSH instruction.

The **POP instruction** has the following general form:

[⟨*label*⟩] `POP` ⟨*destination*⟩ [⟨*comment*⟩]

in which ⟨*destination*⟩ identifies the location in which the data popped from the top of the stack is to be placed. This instruction causes a copy of the 16-bit stack segment value pointed to by the SS:SP register pair (i.e., the top-of-stack value) to replace the 16-bit value of the destination operand and then the SP-register to be incremented by 2. The increment of the SP-register logically pops up all subsequent stack segment values one position relative to the top of the stack. The new top-of-stack value is the one that was at the top of the stack when the value just copied was pushed onto the stack. The destination operand can be either a general register, a segment register other than the CS-register, or a memory location. The type attribute of the destination operand must be word. None of the bits in the flags register are affected by the execution of a POP instruction.

The **PUSHF instruction** has the following general form:

[⟨*label*⟩] PUSHF [⟨*comment*⟩]

This instruction causes the value of the SP-register to be decremented by 2 and the 16-bit value of the flags register to be stored in the stack segment at the location pointed to by the SS:SP register pair (i.e., the new top of the stack). None of the bits in the flags register are modified by the execution of a PUSHF instruction.

The **POPF instruction** has the following general form:

[⟨*label*⟩] POPF [⟨*comment*⟩]

This instruction causes a copy of the 16-bit stack segment value pointed to by the SS:SP register pair (i.e., the top-of-stack value) to replace the 16-bit value of the flags register and the SP-register to be incremented by 2. All of the bits in the flags register are potentially modified by the execution of a POPF instruction. Note that the POPF instruction provides the only way for a program to modify explicitly certain bits of the flags register. Explicit modification of flags register bits is discussed in Chapter 6.

EXAMPLES

```
PUSH  AX
```

pushes the 16-bit value of the AX-register onto the stack.

```
POP  BX
```

pops the 16-bit value from the top of the stack and places it in the BX-register.

```
PUSHF
```

pushes the 16-bit value of the flags register onto the stack.

```
POPF
```

pops the 16-bit value from the top of the stack and places it in the flags register. ■

Figures 2.6–2.10 show the mechanics of stack operations in an 8088/8086 assembly language program. The stack segment shown is an 8-word (16-byte) stack segment.

Figure 2.6 shows how the stack is initialized to empty. In the figure, the SS-register contains the address of the origin of the stack segment, and the SP-register contains the offset of the memory location immediately following the stack segment.

Data is pushed onto the stack and popped from the stack in units of 16 bits (1 word). A push operation first decrements the offset in the SP-register by 2 (i.e., 2 bytes or 1 word) and then stores a 16-bit word at memory locations SS:SP (low-order byte) and SS:SP + 1 (high-order byte). A pop operation copies the word at memory locations SS:SP (low-order byte) and SS:SP + 1 (high-order byte) and then increments the contents of the SP-register by 2. The SS:SP register pair always specifies the memory address of the top-of-stack data item.

Figure 2.7 shows the result of pushing the hexadecimal value 4A9F onto the empty stack. The SP-register has been decremented to 000E, the offset of the top-of-stack item 4A9F. Note that the two bytes of the 16-bit value 4A9F are stored in

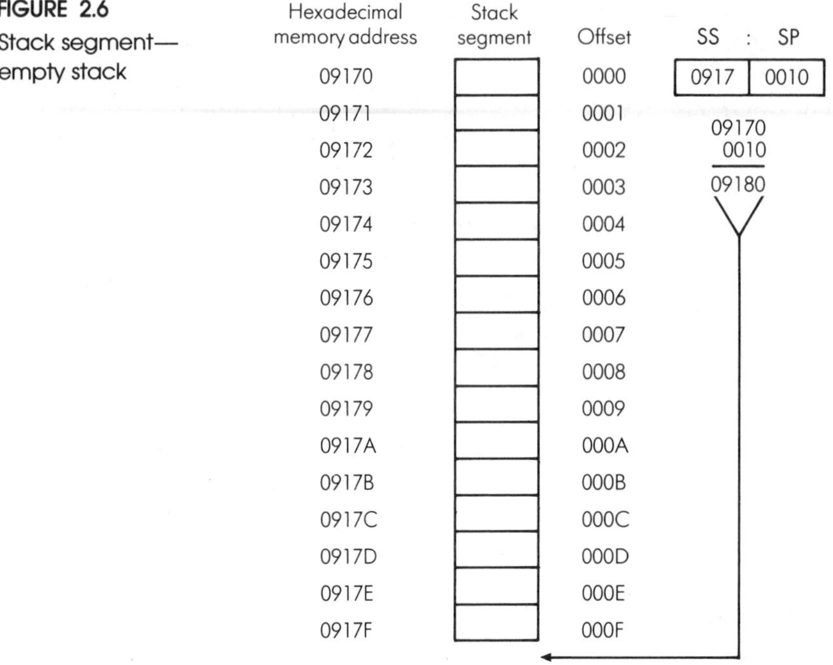

FIGURE 2.6
Stack segment—empty stack

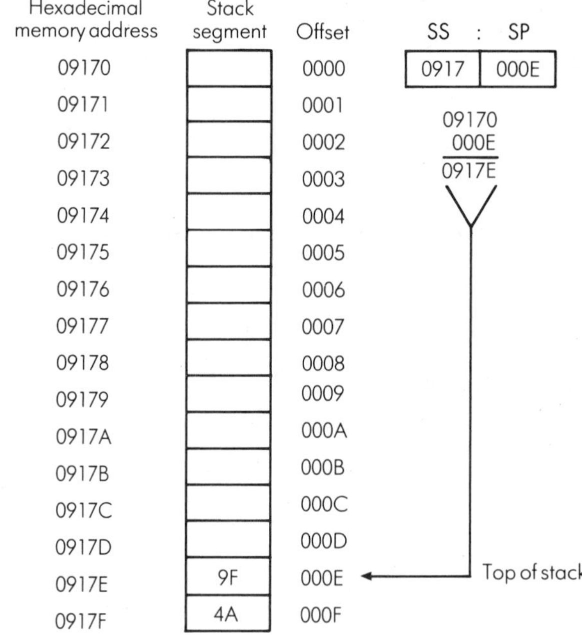

FIGURE 2.7
Stack segment—after push of 4A9F

reverse order beginning at offset 000E; that is, the low-order byte (9F) is stored at offset 000E, and the high-order byte (4A) is stored at offset 000F.

Figure 2.8 shows the result of pushing the hexadecimal value 373F onto the stack. The SP-register has been decremented to 000C, the offset of the new top-of-stack item 373F. Again, the two bytes of the value are stored in reverse order.

A pop operation would copy the hexadecimal value 373F to the destination operand and leave the stack segment as shown in Figure 2.9. The SP-register has been incremented to 000E, the offset of the new top-of-stack item 4A9F. This item is the item that was at the top of the stack at the time that 373F, the value just popped, was pushed onto the stack. Note that the value 373F is still in the stack segment, but it is not included in the logical stack. The logical stack begins with the word pointed to by the top-of-stack pointer (i.e., the SS:SP register pair) and goes through the end

FIGURE 2.8
Stack segment—after push of 4A9F and 373F

Hexadecimal memory address	Stack segment	Offset
09170		0000
09171		0001
09172		0002
09173		0003
09174		0004
09175		0005
09176		0006
09177		0007
09178		0008
09179		0009
0917A		000A
0917B		000B
0917C	3F	000C
0917D	37	000D
0917E	9F	000E
0917F	4A	000F

SS : SP
0917 000C
09170
000C
0917C
Top of stack

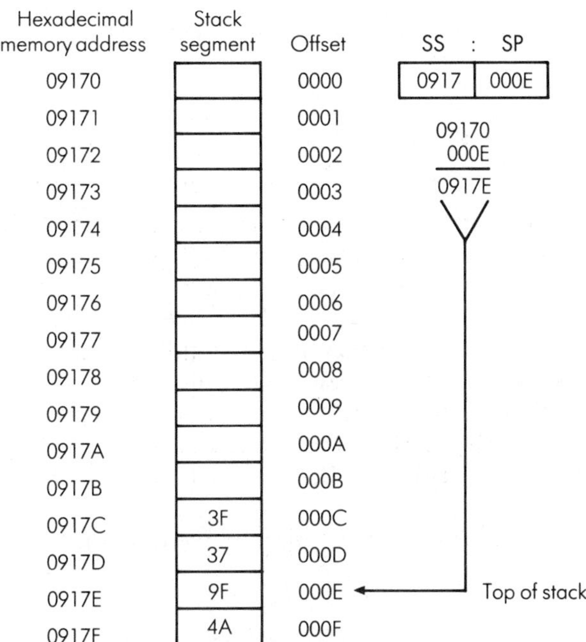

FIGURE 2.9
Stack segment—after push of 4A9F and 373F and pop of 373F

of the stack segment, which is the bottom of the logical stack. The storage cells from the origin of the stack segment up to but not including the word pointed to by the SS:SP register pair currently are not part of the logical stack.

Figure 2.10 shows the result of pushing the hexadecimal value 60C2 onto the stack. The SP-register has been decremented to 000C, the offset of the new top-of-stack item 60C2. Note that the value 60C2 replaces the value 373F that had previously been stored in these locations.

FIGURE 2.10
Stack segment—after push of 4A9F and 373F, pop of 373F, and push of 60C2

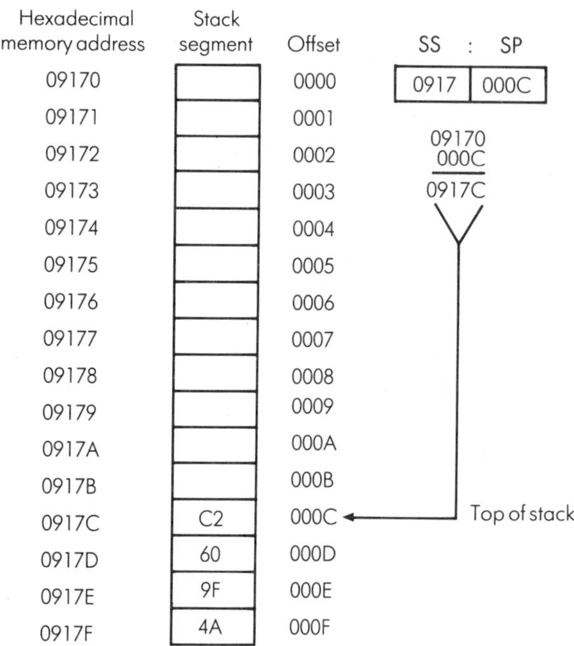

The SS and SP registers are automatically maintained by the microprocessor as it executes push and pop operations. These registers are not normally manipulated directly by the program.

Address-Accessing Operators and Instructions

It is often necessary in an assembly language program to obtain the memory address of a data value rather than the value itself. Several of the I/O subprocedures referenced in this book require as an input the beginning address of a memory area in the caller's environment. This address identifies either memory locations that contain the data to be output or memory locations in which the input data are to be stored. Recall that all memory addresses in the 8088/8086 machine language are in the form of a segment origin (value of a segment register) and an offset within the segment. The two operators SEG and OFFSET and the LEA (load effective address) instruction are used to obtain either the segment or offset portion of the address of a memory location.

The **SEG operator** is a value-returning operator that appears as follows:

`SEG` ⟨*symbolic-name*⟩

in which ⟨*symbolic-name*⟩ is either a variable name or the label of an instruction. This operator, when used with a ⟨*symbolic-name*⟩, is an immediate operand whose 16-bit value is the high-order 16 bits of the segment portion of the memory address associated with the ⟨*symbolic-name*⟩. This operator can be used in any instruction that allows an immediate operand.

The **OFFSET operator** is a value-returning operator that appears as follows:

OFFSET ⟨*symbolic-name*⟩

in which ⟨*symbolic-name*⟩ is either a variable name or the label of an instruction. This operator, when used with a ⟨*symbolic-name*⟩, is an immediate operand whose 16-bit value is the offset portion of memory address associated with the ⟨*symbolic-name*⟩. It can be used in any instruction that allows an immediate operand.

EXAMPLES

```
MOV  AX, SEG  DATA
```

moves to the AX-register the high-order 16 bits of the segment portion of the address of the variable DATA.

```
MOV  DI, OFFSET  MSG
```

moves to the DI-register the offset portion of the address of the variable MSG. ■

The **LEA (load effective address) instruction** generates the offset portion of a memory address as an operand. The LEA instruction has the following general form:

[⟨*label*⟩] LEA ⟨*destination*⟩, ⟨*source*⟩ [⟨*comment*⟩]

in which ⟨*destination*⟩ is the designation of the 16-bit general register whose value is to be replaced by the offset and ⟨*source*⟩ is the address expression from which the offset is to be computed. This instruction causes the value of the 16-bit general register specified as the destination operand to be replaced by the computed offset of the memory location specified by the source operand. None of the bits of the flags register are affected by the execution of an LEA instruction.

EXAMPLE

```
LEA  DI, PROMPT
```

computes the offset portion of the address of the memory location associated with the name PROMPT and places that value in the DI-register. ■

The two instructions

```
LEA  DI, PROMPT
```

and

```
MOV  DI, OFFSET  PROMPT
```

have the same effect: Both load the DI-register with the offset portion of the address of the variable PROMPT. The OFFSET operator actually directs the assembler to compute the offset of variable PROMPT and to embed that value in the machine language instruction as an immediate operand, which means that the operand of the OFFSET operator must be a symbolic name whose offset is known at assembly time. The LEA instruction, on the other hand, causes the offset of PROMPT to be computed when the LEA instruction is executed, which means that the source operand of an LEA instruction can be any address expression. The various forms of memory addresses that can appear in memory-referencing instructions are discussed in Section 8.4.

2.5 Example Program—Demonstrate Data Definition and Data Transfer

Explanation of Program

Program Listing 2.1 illustrates a program that demonstrates the data definition pseudo-operations and data transfer instructions presented in earlier sections of this chapter. It shows a complete 8088/8086 assembly language program that consists of three segments: a stack segment, a data segment, and a code segment.

```
           PAGE    80,132
;==========================================================================
;                         PROGRAM LISTING 2.1
;
; PROGRAM TO DEMONSTRATE
;          1. DATA DEFINITION PSEUDO-OPERATIONS
;          2. DATA TRANSFER INSTRUCTIONS
;==========================================================================
           .MODEL  SMALL,BASIC,FARSTACK
;==========================================================================
; S T A C K   S E G M E N T   D E F I N I T I O N
;
           .STACK  16
;==========================================================================
; C O N S T A N T   D E F I N I T I O N
;
ZERO_ONE   EQU     55H                     ;55 HEX
;==========================================================================
; D A T A   S E G M E N T   D E F I N I T I O N
;
           .FARDATA DATA
                                           ;BYTE           WORD
BYTE1      DB      0                       ;00 HEX
BYTE2      DB      ZERO_ONE                ;55 HEX
BYTE3      DB      0AAH                    ;AA HEX
BYTE4      DB      377Q                    ;FF HEX
WORD3      DW      1010101011111111B       ;FF HEX         AAFF HEX
                                           ;AA HEX
WORD4      DW      000125Q                 ;55 HEX         0055 HEX
                                           ;00 HEX
WORD1      EQU     WORD PTR BYTE1          ;BYTE2:BYTE1  = 5500 HEX
WORD2      EQU     WORD PTR BYTE3          ;BYTE4:BYTE3  = FFAA HEX
;==========================================================================
; C O D E   S E G M E N T   D E F I N I T I O N
           .CODE
           ASSUME  DS:DATA
EX_2_1:    MOV     AX,SEG DATA             ;SET DS-REGISTER TO ORIGIN
           MOV     DS,AX                   ;OF DATA SEGMENT
           NOP
                                           ;AH AL BH BL CH CL DH DL
           MOV     AL,BYTE1                ;   00
           MOV     AH,AL                   ;00 00
           MOV     AL,ZERO_ONE             ;00 55
           MOV     BX,WORD3                ;00 55 AA FF
           MOV     CX,WORD2                ;00 55 AA FF FF AA
           MOV     DX,WORD4                ;00 55 AA FF FF AA 00 55
           XCHG    DH,DL                   ;00 55 AA FF FF AA 55 00
           PUSH    AX                      ;00 55 AA FF FF AA 55 00
           PUSH    CX                      ;00 55 AA FF FF AA 55 00
           POP     AX                      ;FF AA AA FF FF AA 55 00
           POP     CX                      ;FF AA AA FF 00 55 55 00
           XCHG    CX,DX                   ;FF AA AA FF 55 00 00 55
```

```
53: ;
54:         MOV     WORD1,BX            ;WORD1 BYTE1    FF HEX
55:                                     ;      BYTE2    AA HEX
56:         MOV     BYTE3,DL            ;WORD2 BYTE3    55 HEX
57:         MOV     BYTE4,CL            ;      BYTE4    00 HEX
58:         MOV     WORD3,CX            ;WORD3          00 HEX
59:                                     ;               55 HEX
60:         MOV     WORD4,AX            ;WORD4          AA HEX
61:                                     ;               FF HEX
62:         .EXIT                       ;RETURN TO DOS
63: ;
64:         END     EX_2_1
```

The program begins with the PAGE pseudo-operation (line 1), which sets the page size for the assembler-generated listing. The PAGE pseudo-operation is followed by a prologue (lines 2–8) that explains the function of the program. This program does not implement an algorithm for solving a specific problem; it simply demonstrates the pseudo-operations and instructions covered in this chapter.

The .MODEL pseudo-operation in line 9 enables the use of simplified segment directives. It also tells the assembler to create a data group called DGROUP and to assume that, at execution time, the DS-register will specify the origin of this group. This group will contain the stack segment if it is a near stack segment, and it will contain any data segment whose definition begins with a .CONST, .DATA, or .DATA? pseudo-operation. Since the .MODEL pseudo-operation in line 9 specifies FARSTACK, the stack segment will not be a part of this data group but will be a separate and distinct segment.

The definition of the program's stack segment appears in lines 10–13. Lines 10–12 are comment lines that indicate that a stack segment definition follows; the actual definition of the stack segment appears in line 13. The .STACK pseudo-operation defines the size of the stack segment as 16 bytes (8 words).

The comments in lines 14–16 indicate that a constant definition follows, and the EQU pseudo-operation in line 17 equates the symbolic name ZERO_ONE with the 8-bit constant 55 hex (01010101 binary). Anywhere that the symbolic name ZERO_ONE appears, the assembler substitutes the constant 55 hex. The symbolic name ZERO_ONE is simply another way of saying 55H in this assembly module. ZERO_ONE is not a variable name, and the value associated with the symbolic name ZERO_ONE cannot be changed during program execution.

The comments in lines 18–20 indicate that a static data segment definition follows. The data segment definition begins with the .FARDATA pseudo-operation in line 21 and terminates with the next simplified segment directive, the .CODE pseudo-operation in line 35. Since the data segment definition begins with the .FARDATA pseudo-operation, the data segment will not be a part of the data group DGROUP, which the assembler created in response to the .MODEL pseudo-operation in line 9. Instead, it will be a separate and distinct segment.

By choosing the stack and data segments to be separate and distinct segments, the offsets within the segments begin at 0000, which will simplify the tracing of these segments in the DEBUG and CodeView traces presented later in this section. If the two segments are combined into a group, then all offsets are relative to the origin of the group rather than to the origins of segments. Therefore, the programmer has to know how the group is organized in order to be able to trace data items in a DEBUG or CodeView trace.

The .FARDATA pseudo-operation in line 21 also specifies that DATA is to be the name of the data segment. The organization of the data segment generated by this definition is described in Table 2.10.

TABLE 2.10
Organization of the static data segment defined in Program Listing 2.1

Symbolic Name(s)	Offset from Beginning of Segment	Initial Value (Hexadecimal)
BYTE1/WORD1	0000	00
BYTE2	0001	55
BYTE3/WORD2	0002	AA
BYTE4	0003	FF
WORD3	0004	FF
	0005	AA
WORD4	0006	55
	0007	00

The size of the data segment is 8 bytes as defined by the DB and DW pseudo-operations in lines 23–29. The first byte in the data segment, the byte at offset 0000 from the beginning of the data segment, is defined by the DB pseudo-operation in line 23. This byte can be referenced by the symbolic name BYTE1 and is assigned an initial value of zero. The second byte in the data segment (offset 0001) is defined by the DB pseudo-operation in line 24. It can be referenced by the symbolic name BYTE2 and has the initial value 55 hex (01010101 binary). The constant that appears in the operand field of line 24 is the named constant ZERO_ONE, whose definition appears in line 17. The third byte in the data segment (offset 0002) is defined by the DB pseudo-operation in line 25. It can be referenced by the symbolic name BYTE3 and has the initial value AA hex (10101010 binary). The fourth byte in the data segment (offset 0003) is defined by the DB pseudo-operation in line 26. It can be referenced by the symbolic name BYTE4 and has the initial value 377 octal (FF hex or 11111111 binary).

The fifth and sixth bytes in the data segment (offsets 0004 and 0005) are defined by the DW pseudo-operation in line 27. These two bytes can be referenced collectively as a 16-bit word by the symbolic name WORD3. The initial value of this 16-bit word is 1010101011111111 binary (AAFF hex). In an IBM PC's or IBM PS/2's memory, a 16-bit word is stored as two consecutive 8-bit bytes. The low-order byte is stored first, followed by the high-order byte. This sequencing means that the fifth byte of the data segment has the initial value 11111111 binary (FF hex), and the sixth byte has the initial value 10101010 binary (AA hex).

The seventh and eighth bytes in the data segment (offsets 0006 and 0007) are defined by the DW pseudo-operation in line 29. These two bytes can be referenced collectively as a 16-bit word by the symbolic name WORD4. The initial value of this 16-bit word is 000125 octal (0055 hex or 0000000001010101 binary). Since the low-order byte is stored first, followed by the high-order byte, the initial value of the seventh byte is 01010101 binary (55 hex), and the initial value of the eighth byte is zero.

The initial value of a variable is the value of that variable at the time program execution begins. A variable's value can be changed during program execution. The initial value of a variable remains until replaced by a new value during program execution.

Each of the symbolic names BYTE1, BYTE2, BYTE3, and BYTE4 has a type attribute of BYTE and is a reference to an 8-bit operand in the data segment. Each of the symbolic names WORD3 and WORD4 has a type attribute of WORD and is a reference to a 16-bit operand in the data segment.

Lines 31 and 32 demonstrate an additional capability provided by the EQU pseudo-operation. In line 31, this pseudo-operation equates the symbolic name WORD1 to the same offset that is referenced by the symbolic name BYTE1, offset 0000. The operator PTR with the WORD type prefix overrides the type attribute of the symbolic name BYTE1 with the type attribute WORD; that is, the symbolic name WORD1 has a type attribute of WORD. A reference to the symbolic name WORD1 is a reference to the 16-bit value beginning at offset 0000 within the data segment. Since the low byte is stored first, followed by the high byte, the 16-bit initial value of WORD1 is 5500 hex. The EQU pseudo-operation in line 32 equates the symbolic name WORD2 to the same offset that is referenced by the symbolic name BYTE3, offset 0002. The symbolic name WORD2 has type attribute WORD, whereas the symbolic name BYTE3 has type attribute BYTE. A reference to the symbolic name WORD2 is a reference to the 16-bit value beginning at offset 0002 within the data segment. The initial value of WORD2 is FFAA hex.

The comments in lines 33–34 indicate that a code segment definition follows. The code segment definition begins with the .CODE pseudo-operation in line 35 and terminates with the END pseudo-operation in line 64.

The ASSUME pseudo-operation in line 36 tells the assembler to assume that, at execution time, the DS-register will specify the origin of the data segment. With simplified segment definitions, the assembler automatically makes segment register assumptions in response to the simplified segment directives. The explicit ASSUME pseudo-operation in line 36 is needed to override one of the automatic assumptions. In the case of the assembly module of Program Listing 2.1, the .MODEL pseudo-operation (line 9) directs the assembler to assume that the DS-register will specify the origin of the data group DGROUP. However, none of the segments in this assembly module will be a part of DGROUP. The .FARDATA pseudo-operation in line 21 specifies that the data segment is to be a separate and distinct segment, but it does not direct the assembler to change its assumption about the DS-register. The ASSUME pseudo-operation in line 36 is therefore needed to tell the assembler to change this assumption. Note that the SS and CS registers are not included in the ASSUME pseudo-operation in line 36. The .STACK pseudo-operation in line 13 directs the assembler to assume that, at execution time, the SS-register will specify the origin of the stack segment being defined, and the .CODE pseudo-operation in line 35 directs the assembler to assume that, at execution time, the CS-register will specify the origin of the code segment being defined.

All machine language addresses generated by the assembler specify a segment register and an offset from the segment origin specified by that segment register. Each symbolic name referenced in the assembly module has associated with it an offset within the segment in which it is defined. For example, the symbolic name BYTE4 in the assembly module of Program Listing 2.1 references the byte at offset 0003 from the beginning of the data segment. The ASSUME pseudo-operation in line 36 tells the assembler to assume that the origin of the data segment will be in the DS-register at execution time. The address generated by the assembler for BYTE4 is thus offset 0003 relative to the origin specified by the contents of the DS-register (DS:0003).

The main procedure of the program consists of the symbolic instructions specified in lines 37–61 and the macro instruction in line 62 of Program Listing 2.1. The main procedure of a program is the one where execution of the program begins. Since no subprocedures are referenced by this program, the main procedure contains all of the executable instructions of the program.

The segment register assumptions, both the ones implied by the simplified segment directives and the ones explicitly stated by the ASSUME pseudo-operation, tell the assembler what the segment registers are to contain at execution time. The code segment and stack segment origins in the CS and SS registers are initialized automatically by DOS when the program is placed into execution. However, it is the program's responsibility to initialize the DS- and/or ES-register to contain the segment origins that the assembler was told to assume they would contain. In the case of Program Listing 2.1, it is the program's responsibility to initialize the DS-register with the origin of the data segment, and this initialization must be done prior to the first reference to an item in the data segment.

Before DOS loads an executable program and places the main procedure of that program into execution, it sets up a 256-byte memory block called the **program segment prefix (PSP)**. The PSP is set up at the lowest available paragraph boundary in memory, and the program is loaded immediately following the PSP. The PSP is the communications link between DOS and the executable program. When DOS passes control to the main procedure of an executable program, both the DS- and ES-registers specify the segment origin of the PSP.

The two instructions in lines 37 and 38 initialize the DS-register to contain the origin of the data segment defined in lines 21–32. The MOV instruction in line 37 moves to the AX-register the high-order 16 bits of the segment portion of the memory address associated with the symbolic name DATA. This instruction loads the AX-register with the origin of the data segment. The MOV instruction in line 38 moves this segment origin from the AX-register to the DS-register. Two instructions are required here because the instruction

```
MOV  DS, SEG  DATA
```

is syntactically illegal. The operand SEG DATA is an immediate operand, and a MOV instruction whose destination operand is a segment register cannot have an immediate value as its source operand (see Figure 2.4).

The instruction in line 39 has an op code NOP, which stands for *N*o *OP*eration and performs no operation. That is, this instruction has no effect on the program. Its purpose is discussed later in this section.

The instructions in lines 41–61 demonstrate various forms of the MOV, XCHG, PUSH, and POP instructions using the data defined in the data segment. The comments on the instructions in lines 41–52 show the resulting value in the AX (AH and AL), BX (BH and BL), CX (CH and CL), and DX (DH and DL) registers. A blank indicates that the value of that register is unknown.

The MOV instruction in line 41 moves the value of the variable BYTE1, which in this case is zero, to the AL-register. This instruction performs a copy operation, so the value of variable BYTE1 is not modified. In this MOV instruction, the destination operand is an 8-bit general register (AL-register), and the source operand is the 8-bit contents of the memory location specified by BYTE1.

The MOV instruction in line 42 moves to the AH-register a copy of the value of the AL-register (zero). The AL-register is not modified by execution of this instruction. In this MOV instruction, the destination operand is an 8-bit general register (AH-register), and the source operand is another 8-bit general register (AL-register).

The MOV instruction in line 43 moves to the AL-register a constant byte value of 55 hex, which is contained in memory immediately following the first byte of the MOV instruction. In this MOV instruction, the destination operand is an 8-bit general register (AL-register), and the source operand is an immediate value (a constant value that is part of the machine language representation of the MOV instruction). Recall that the symbolic name ZERO_ONE is a name for the constant 55 hex. It was defined by the EQU pseudo-operation in line 17.

The MOV instruction in line 44 moves to the BX-register a copy of the 16-bit value of the variable WORD3 (AAFF hex). The MOV instruction in line 45 moves to the CX-register a copy of the 16-bit value of the variable WORD2 (FFAA hex). The MOV instruction in line 46 moves to the DX-register a copy of the 16-bit value of the variable WORD4 (0055 hex). In each of these MOV instructions, the destination operand is a 16-bit general register, and the source operand is the 16-bit contents of two consecutive memory locations. In each case, the source operand (the memory operand) is not modified by execution of the instruction.

The XCHG instruction in line 47 interchanges the values of two 8-bit general registers (DH and DL registers). Prior to execution of this XCHG instruction, the DH-register had the value 00 hex, and the DL-register had the value 55 hex. After execution of this XCHG instruction, the DH-register has the value 55 hex, and the DL-register has the value 00 hex.

The PUSH and POP instructions in lines 48–51 interchange the values of the 16-bit AX and CX registers. The PUSH instruction in line 48 pushes the 16-bit value of the AX-register onto the top of the stack. The PUSH instruction in line 49 pushes the 16-bit value of the CX-register onto the top of the stack, which pushes the AX-register value down one position relative to the top of the stack. The POP instruction in line 50 pops the top-of-stack value (a copy of the CX-register value) into the AX-register, which returns the previous AX-register value to the top of the stack. The POP instruction in line 51 pops the top-of-stack value (the previous AX-register value) into the CX-register. Prior to execution of these PUSH and POP instructions, the AX-register had the value 0055 hex, and the CX-register had the value FFAA hex. After execution, the AX-register has the value FFAA hex, and the CX-register has the value 0055 hex.

The XCHG instruction in line 52 interchanges the values of two 16-bit general registers (CX- and DX-registers). Prior to this execution, the CX-register had the value 0055 hex, and the DX-register had the value 5500 hex. After execution, the CX-register has the value 5500 hex, and the DX-register has the value 0055 hex.

At this point, the variables defined in the data segment still have their initial values as shown in Table 2.10, and the general registers have the values shown in Table 2.11.

TABLE 2.11
General register values at line 53 of Program Listing 2.1

Register	AX		BX		CX		DX	
	AH	AL	BH	BL	CH	CL	DH	DL
Hex Value	FF	AA	AA	FF	55	00	00	55

The MOV instruction in line 54 replaces the 16-bit value of the two memory locations specified by the symbolic name WORD1 with a copy of the value of the BX-register (AAFF hex). Since a 16-bit value is stored in memory with low byte followed by high byte, BYTE1 receives the value FF hex, and BYTE2 receives the value AA hex. The value of the BX-register is not modified by execution of this MOV instruction. In this instruction, the destination operand is a 16-bit memory location (the one specified by the symbolic name WORD1), and the source operand is a 16-bit general register (BX-register).

The MOV instruction in line 56 replaces the 8-bit value of the memory location specified by the symbolic name BYTE3 with a copy of the value in the DL-register (55 hex). The MOV instruction in line 57 replaces the 8-bit value of the memory location specified by the symbolic name BYTE4 with a copy of the value in the CL-register (00 hex). In each of these MOV instructions, the destination operand is an 8-bit byte in memory, and the source operand is an 8-bit general register. In each case, the source operand (the 8-bit general register) is not modified by execution of the instruction.

The MOV instruction in line 58 replaces the 16-bit value of the two memory locations specified by the symbolic name WORD3 with a copy of the value in the CX-register (5500 hex). The MOV instruction in line 60 replaces the 16-bit value of the two memory locations specified by the symbolic name WORD4 with a copy of the value in the AX-register (FFAA hex). In each of these MOV instructions, the destination operand is a 16-bit word in memory, and the source operand is a 16-bit general register. In each case, the source operand (the 16-bit general register) is not modified by execution of the instruction.

At this point, the general registers still have the values shown in Table 2.11, and the variables defined in the data segment have the values shown in Table 2.12.

TABLE 2.12
Data segment values at line 61 of Program Listing 2.1

Symbolic Name(s)	Offset from Beginning of Segment	Value (Hexadecimal)
BYTE1/WORD1	0000	FF
BYTE2	0001	AA
BYTE3/WORD2	0002	55
BYTE4	0003	00
WORD3	0004	00
	0005	55
WORD4	0006	AA
	0007	FF

The .EXIT pseudo-operation in line 62 directs the assembler to generate the assembly language instructions that, when executed, will return control to DOS. Prior to translating the program to machine language, the assembler substitutes the two instructions

```
MOV  AH, 04CH
INT  021H
```

for the .EXIT pseudo-operation. The INT instruction is an interrupt instruction, which, in this case, is a call to a DOS service procedure. The AH-register provides the input to this DOS procedure. An input of 4C hexadecimal tells DOS that the program is terminating and that DOS should take over control of the processor. (Interrupts, the INT instruction, and DOS service calls are discussed in Chapter 9.) The .EXIT pseudo-operation behaves like a macro instruction. (Macro instructions are discussed in Chapter 5.)

MASM 5.1

The .EXIT pseudo-operation is not available in MASM 5.1. MASM 5.1 users should substitute the instructions

```
MOV  AH,04CH
INT  021H
```

for the .EXIT pseudo-operation in their programs.

The END pseudo-operation in line 64 marks the end of the code segment definition and the end of the assembly module. This operation tells the assembler that program execution is to begin with the instruction whose symbolic name is EX_2_1. This instruction is the first instruction in the code segment of Program Listing 2.1. It should be noted that execution does not have to begin with the first instruction in the code segment. However, in a structured program, execution begins with the first instruction of the main procedure.

DEBUG Trace of Program

DEBUG Listing 2.2 shows a trace of the program of Program Listing 2.1 using the DEBUG utility program. This listing is a hard copy of the inputs and outputs that appeared on the display during the DEBUG session. To get a printout of a DEBUG session, press Ctrl-Print Screen at the keyboard before invoking DEBUG. (Press Ctrl-Print Screen upon completion of the DEBUG session to turn off the print screen function.) The command

```
debug ex_2_1.exe
```

loads the DEBUG program, begins execution of the DEBUG program, and has the DEBUG program load the executable module ex_2_1.exe for tracing (see DEBUG Listing 2.2). The hyphen (-) prompt in DEBUG Listing 2.2 is the prompt output by DEBUG to indicate that it is ready to accept commands.

The first command in DEBUG Listing 2.2, the **r (register) command**, asks for the display of the current value of each of the processor registers. DEBUG responds by displaying three lines (see DEBUG Listing 2.2). Note that all values in this display are in hexadecimal.

The first line of the DEBUG response shows the values of the eight general registers just prior to execution of the first instruction of the program. The AX, BX, DX, BP, SI, and DI registers have been initialized to zero by the DEBUG program. DOS will *not* perform such initializations. Therefore, a program *must never* depend on registers being initialized to zero automatically. The CX-register is initialized by the DEBUG program to contain the length, in bytes, of the executable program. DOS does *not* perform this initialization either. The SP-register is initialized to the offset from the origin of the stack segment of the memory location immediately following the end of the stack segment. This initialization denotes an empty stack.

The second line of the DEBUG response shows the values of the four segment registers, the IP-register, and the flags register prior to execution of the first instruction of the program. Recall that the value in a segment register is the high-order 16 bits of a 20-bit address and that the low-order 4 bits are always zero. The initial value of the DS-register and the ES-register is the origin of the program segment prefix (hexadecimal location 1DFC0 in this case). The initial value of the SS-register is the origin of the stack segment (hexadecimal location 1E100 in this case). The SS:SP register pair always points to the memory location within the stack segment that contains the current top-of-stack data word. The stack segment for this program was defined to have a size of 16 bytes (see line 13 of Program Listing 2.1). Since the stack's origin is location 1E100, the stack segment ends at location 1E10F. The SS:SP register pair currently points to location 1E110 (1E100 + 0010). This location is one location beyond the end of the stack segment, thus denoting an empty stack.

The initial value of the CS-register is the origin of the code segment (hexadecimal location 1E0C0 in this case). The initial value of the IP-register is zero, the offset of the first location in the code segment. The CS:IP register pair always

DEBUG LISTING 2.2

```
debug ex_2_1.exe
-r
AX=0000  BX=0000  CX=0178  DX=0000  SP=0010  BP=0000  SI=0000  DI=0000
DS=1DFC  ES=1DFC  SS=1E10  CS=1E0C  IP=0000   NV UP EI PL NZ NA PO NC
1E0C:0000 B8111E        MOV     AX,1E11
-t

AX=1E11  BX=0000  CX=0178  DX=0000  SP=0010  BP=0000  SI=0000  DI=0000
DS=1DFC  ES=1DFC  SS=1E10  CS=1E0C  IP=0003   NV UP EI PL NZ NA PO NC
1E0C:0003 8ED8          MOV     DS,AX
-t

AX=1E11  BX=0000  CX=0178  DX=0000  SP=0010  BP=0000  SI=0000  DI=0000
DS=1E11  ES=1DFC  SS=1E10  CS=1E0C  IP=0005   NV UP EI PL NZ NA PO NC
1E0C:0005 90            NOP
-t

AX=1E11  BX=0000  CX=0178  DX=0000  SP=0010  BP=0000  SI=0000  DI=0000
DS=1E11  ES=1DFC  SS=1E10  CS=1E0C  IP=0006   NV UP EI PL NZ NA PO NC
1E0C:0006 A00000        MOV     AL,[0000]                         DS:0000=00
-d ds:0,7
1E11:0000  00 55 AA FF FF AA 55 00                          .U....U.
-t

AX=1E00  BX=0000  CX=0178  DX=0000  SP=0010  BP=0000  SI=0000  DI=0000
DS=1E11  ES=1DFC  SS=1E10  CS=1E0C  IP=0009   NV UP EI PL NZ NA PO NC
1E0C:0009 8AE0          MOV     AH,AL
-t

AX=0000  BX=0000  CX=0178  DX=0000  SP=0010  BP=0000  SI=0000  DI=0000
DS=1E11  ES=1DFC  SS=1E10  CS=1E0C  IP=000B   NV UP EI PL NZ NA PO NC
1E0C:000B B055          MOV     AL,55
-t

AX=0055  BX=0000  CX=0178  DX=0000  SP=0010  BP=0000  SI=0000  DI=0000
DS=1E11  ES=1DFC  SS=1E10  CS=1E0C  IP=000D   NV UP EI PL NZ NA PO NC
1E0C:000D 8B1E0400      MOV     BX,[0004]                         DS:0004=AAFF
-t

AX=0055  BX=AAFF  CX=0178  DX=0000  SP=0010  BP=0000  SI=0000  DI=0000
DS=1E11  ES=1DFC  SS=1E10  CS=1E0C  IP=0011   NV UP EI PL NZ NA PO NC
1E0C:0011 8B0E0200      MOV     CX,[0002]                         DS:0002=FFAA
-t

AX=0055  BX=AAFF  CX=FFAA  DX=0000  SP=0010  BP=0000  SI=0000  DI=0000
DS=1E11  ES=1DFC  SS=1E10  CS=1E0C  IP=0015   NV UP EI PL NZ NA PO NC
1E0C:0015 8B160600      MOV     DX,[0006]                         DS:0006=0055
-t

AX=0055  BX=AAFF  CX=FFAA  DX=0055  SP=0010  BP=0000  SI=0000  DI=0000
DS=1E11  ES=1DFC  SS=1E10  CS=1E0C  IP=0019   NV UP EI PL NZ NA PO NC
1E0C:0019 86F2          XCHG    DH,DL
-t

AX=0055  BX=AAFF  CX=FFAA  DX=5500  SP=0010  BP=0000  SI=0000  DI=0000
DS=1E11  ES=1DFC  SS=1E10  CS=1E0C  IP=001B   NV UP EI PL NZ NA PO NC
1E0C:001B 50            PUSH    AX
-t

AX=0055  BX=AAFF  CX=FFAA  DX=5500  SP=000E  BP=0000  SI=0000  DI=0000
DS=1E11  ES=1DFC  SS=1E10  CS=1E0C  IP=001C   NV UP EI PL NZ NA PO NC
1E0C:001C 51            PUSH    CX
-t

AX=0055  BX=AAFF  CX=FFAA  DX=5500  SP=000C  BP=0000  SI=0000  DI=0000
```

```
DS=1E11  ES=1DFC  SS=1E10  CS=1E0C  IP=001D   NV UP EI PL NZ NA PO NC
1E0C:001D 58            POP     AX
-d ss:0,f
1E10:0000  00 00 55 00 00 00 1D 00-0C 1E BF 18 AA FF 55 00   ..U..........U.
-t

AX=FFAA  BX=AAFF  CX=FFAA  DX=5500  SP=000E  BP=0000  SI=0000  DI=0000
DS=1E11  ES=1DFC  SS=1E10  CS=1E0C  IP=001E   NV UP EI PL NZ NA PO NC
1E0C:001E 59            POP     CX
-d ss:0,f
1E10:0000  00 00 55 00 AA FF 00 00-1E 00 0C 1E BF 18 55 00   ..U..........U.
-t

AX=FFAA  BX=AAFF  CX=0055  DX=5500  SP=0010  BP=0000  SI=0000  DI=0000
DS=1E11  ES=1DFC  SS=1E10  CS=1E0C  IP=001F   NV UP EI PL NZ NA PO NC
1E0C:001F 87CA          XCHG    CX,DX
-t

AX=FFAA  BX=AAFF  CX=5500  DX=0055  SP=0010  BP=0000  SI=0000  DI=0000
DS=1E11  ES=1DFC  SS=1E10  CS=1E0C  IP=0021   NV UP EI PL NZ NA PO NC
1E0C:0021 891E0000      MOV     [0000],BX                          DS:0000=5500
-t

AX=FFAA  BX=AAFF  CX=5500  DX=0055  SP=0010  BP=0000  SI=0000  DI=0000
DS=1E11  ES=1DFC  SS=1E10  CS=1E0C  IP=0025   NV UP EI PL NZ NA PO NC
1E0C:0025 88160200      MOV     [0002],DL                          DS:0002=AA
-t

AX=FFAA  BX=AAFF  CX=5500  DX=0055  SP=0010  BP=0000  SI=0000  DI=0000
DS=1E11  ES=1DFC  SS=1E10  CS=1E0C  IP=0029   NV UP EI PL NZ NA PO NC
1E0C:0029 880E0300      MOV     [0003],CL                          DS:0003=FF
-t

AX=FFAA  BX=AAFF  CX=5500  DX=0055  SP=0010  BP=0000  SI=0000  DI=0000
DS=1E11  ES=1DFC  SS=1E10  CS=1E0C  IP=002D   NV UP EI PL NZ NA PO NC
1E0C:002D 890E0400      MOV     [0004],CX                          DS:0004=AAFF
-t

AX=FFAA  BX=AAFF  CX=5500  DX=0055  SP=0010  BP=0000  SI=0000  DI=0000
DS=1E11  ES=1DFC  SS=1E10  CS=1E0C  IP=0031   NV UP EI PL NZ NA PO NC
1E0C:0031 A30600        MOV     [0006],AX                          DS:0006=0055
-t

AX=FFAA  BX=AAFF  CX=5500  DX=0055  SP=0010  BP=0000  SI=0000  DI=0000
DS=1E11  ES=1DFC  SS=1E10  CS=1E0C  IP=0034   NV UP EI PL NZ NA PO NC
1E0C:0034 B44C          MOV     AH,4C
-d ds:0,7
1E11:0000  FF AA 55 00 00 55 AA FF                           ..U..U..
-t

AX=4CAA  BX=AAFF  CX=5500  DX=0055  SP=0010  BP=0000  SI=0000  DI=0000
DS=1E11  ES=1DFC  SS=1E10  CS=1E0C  IP=0036   NV UP EI PL NZ NA PO NC
1E0C:0036 CD21          INT     21
-q
```

points to the memory location that contains the next instruction byte to be fetched. Initially, the CS:IP register pair points to the location of the first byte of the first instruction in the program.

The flag bits in the flags register are all cleared (i.e., set to 0) initially. Table 2.13 shows the abbreviations used for the flags register display.

The third line of the response in DEBUG Listing 2.2 shows the next instruction to be executed, which, in this case, is the first instruction in the program. The hexadecimal pair 1E0C:0000 is the segment origin and offset of the memory location that

TABLE 2.13
Abbreviations used by DEBUG in the flags register display

Flag Bit	Abbreviation for 0 (Clear)	Abbreviation for 1 (Set)
OF	NV	OV
DF	UP	DN
IF	DI	EI
SF	PL	NG
ZF	NZ	ZR
AF	NA	AC
PF	PO	PE
CF	NC	CY

contains the first byte of the instruction. The segment value 1E0C is the contents of the CS-register, and the offset value 0000 is the contents of the IP-register. The three-byte hexadecimal value B8111E is the machine language representation of the instruction. The string

```
MOV    AX,1E11
```

is an assembly language interpretation of the machine language instruction B8111E. This interpretation corresponds to the instruction

```
MOV    AX,SEG DATA
```

that appears in line 37 of Program Listing 2.1. The operand SEG DATA represents an immediate operand that is inserted into the executable module by the DOS loader program. The decision of where in memory to place various segments of the executable program is made by DOS at load time. The DEBUG program traces the execution of machine language instructions that it obtains from the executable module file (ex_2_1.exe). It knows that the machine language instruction B8111E is an instruction to move the immediate value 1E11 to the AX-register. However, DEBUG does not know that the immediate value 1E11 is the high-order 16-bits of the origin of the data segment. Therefore, an assembly language instruction displayed by DEBUG is its interpretation of a machine language instruction.

Following the three-line DEBUG response, the hyphen (-) prompt is displayed to indicate that DEBUG is ready to accept the next command. There are two DEBUG commands that are used for the execution of instructions in single-step mode: the **t (trace) command** and the **p (proceed) command**. For the instructions of the program in Program Listing 2.1, the two are virtually equivalent. The two commands differ in the way in which they handle a CALL instruction. The CALL instruction is the instruction that, when executed, invokes a subprocedure. The t command causes DEBUG to execute the CALL instruction in single-step mode, thus allowing the user to trace into the subprocedure. The user can then trace the instructions of the subprocedure in single-step mode. The p command causes DEBUG to execute the entire subprocedure as if it were a single step; that is, DEBUG allows instructions to be executed continuously, stopping just prior to the execution of the instruction that immediately follows the CALL instruction. The t and p commands differ in a similar manner for loop instructions (Chapter 4), string instructions with repeat prefixes (Chapter 8), and INT instructions (Chapter 9). Since there are no CALL, loop, string, or INT instructions in this program, the t and p commands behave in the same way for the instructions of this program.

The trace command (t), entered in response to the second hyphen prompt in

DEBUG Listing 2.2, is a request for DEBUG to trace execution of one instruction. The instruction that is to be executed is the one that appeared at the end of the three-line DEBUG response, the MOV AX,1E11 instruction. DEBUG executes the instruction and displays the three-line register display again. A comparison of the two register displays shows part of the effect of executing the MOV AX,1E11 instruction. Only two registers have changed. The AX-register, the destination operand of the MOV instruction, now has the value 1E11 hexadecimal, the value of the immediate source operand. Since the source operand is an immediate operand, it is embedded in the machine language representation of the instruction, which is B8111E. Note that the last two bytes of this three-byte machine language instruction are 111E, which is the hexadecimal value 1E11 stored low-byte followed by high-byte. The IP-register has been incremented by 3, the size in bytes of the machine language instruction just executed. The CS:IP register pair (1E0C:0003) now points to the location of the first byte of the next instruction to be executed. The last line of the three-line register display shows the next instruction to be executed. This instruction begins at the memory location whose address is the hexadecimal number 1E0C3. The machine language representation of the instruction is the two-byte hexadecimal number 8ED8. The assembly language interpretation of the machine language instruction is

```
MOV    DS,AX
```

Again, the hyphen prompt is displayed in DEBUG Listing 2.2 to indicate that DEBUG is ready to accept another command. The next trace command t causes the MOV DS,AX instruction to be executed and the three-line register display to be displayed once again. The MOV instruction replaced the value of the DS-register with a copy of the value of the AX-register. The DS-register now has the value 1E11 hexadecimal, and the AX-register is unchanged. The IP-register has been incremented by 2, the size in bytes of the machine language instruction just executed. The CS:IP register pair (1E0C:0005) now points to the location of the first byte of the next instruction to be executed. The last line of the three-line register display shows the next instruction to be executed. The address of the first byte of the instruction is 1E0C5. The machine language representation of the instruction is 90 hexadecimal. The assembly language interpretation of the instruction is

```
NOP
```

Again, the hyphen prompt is displayed to indicate that DEBUG is ready to accept another command. The next trace command causes the NOP instruction to be executed. The only thing that has changed is the value of the IP-register. The NOP instruction caused no operation to be performed. The reason for having the NOP instruction in the program is to facilitate the tracing of the program on 8088/8086-based machines. The DEBUG program uses the single-step mode of the microprocessor to implement the trace command. When in the single-step mode, the microprocessor generates a single-step interrupt following most instruction executions. The DEBUG program is the interrupt service procedure that is invoked to service the single-step interrupt. The 8088/8086 microprocessor will not generate a single-step interrupt following a MOV or POP instruction whose destination operand is a segment register. Therefore, no single-step interrupt is generated following the execution of the MOV DS,AX instruction. The 8088/8086 microprocessor will execute the NOP instruction before generating the single-step interrupt and returning control to DEBUG. The NOP instruction was used so that only one significant instruction would be executed in response to the trace command with 8088/8086-based machines. The 80286 and 80386 microprocessors will not generate a single-step interrupt following a MOV or POP instruction whose destination operand is the SS-register. Since this is a MOV with the DS-register as the destination operand, the single-step interrupt is generated between the MOV and the NOP on the 80286 and 80386 microprocessors. The DEBUG trace shown in DEBUG Listing 2.2 was generated on an 80386-based machine. The single-step interrupt is discussed in detail in Chapter 9.

The IP-register has been incremented by 1, the size in bytes of the machine language instruction (i.e., the NOP instruction) just executed. The CS:IP register pair (1E0C:0006) now points to the location of the first byte of the next instruction to be executed.

The next command issued to DEBUG after the hyphen (-) prompt (see DEBUG Listing 2.2) is the **d (dump) command**

```
d ds:0,7
```

which is a request to DEBUG to display the contents of the memory locations specified by the remainder of the command line. This command line specifies that data segment locations 0000–0007 are to be displayed. The first value displayed in response to this command (see DEBUG Listing 2.2) is 1E11:0000, which is the segment and offset (DS:0000) of the first memory location to be dumped. The remainder of the display shows the contents of consecutive memory locations beginning with the specified location. The eight values

```
00 55 AA FF FF AA 55 00
```

are the initial values of the eight bytes defined in the data segment. Compare this dump to Table 2.10.

The remainder of the display (.U....U.) is the ASCII interpretation of the values of the eight bytes that appeared previously on the line. A period (.) indicates that the corresponding ASCII code is a nonprintable control character or an extended ASCII character. In this dump, 55 is the ASCII code for U, AA is an extended ASCII character, and 00 and FF are ASCII codes for nonprintable control characters. This part of the display is quite useful when the locations being dumped contain ASCII codes for characters in character strings because it precludes the need for human translation from hexadecimal to character.

If this dump command had been issued earlier in the DEBUG session, then the first eight bytes of the program segment prefix (PSP) would have been displayed instead of the data segment. At the beginning of the DEBUG session, the DS-register contained the origin of the PSP. It was not until the trace of the MOV DS,AX instruction that the DS-register was set to contain the origin of the data segment.

The following six trace commands execute the six MOV instructions in lines 41–46 of Program Listing 2.1. An inspection of the register displays shows the effects of execution of the corresponding instructions. Note that the flag bits in the flags register do not change during execution of the six MOV instructions because none of the bits in the flags register are affected by execution of a MOV instruction. Note also the display form of the last of these six MOV instructions, which looks like the following:

```
1E0C:0015 8B160600 MOV DX, [0006] DS:0006=0055
```

The machine language instruction begins at location 1E0D5 hexadecimal and is four bytes in length. The machine language instruction is 8B160600 and has the following assembly language interpretation:

```
MOV DX, [0006]
```

The square brackets indicate that the value 0006 is the offset within the data segment of the memory location that contains the operand. The rightmost part of the display (DS:0006 = 0055) indicates that the word that begins at offset 0006 within the data segment currently has the hexadecimal value 0055. That is, the value 0055 is the value that is moved into the DX-register when the instruction is executed. The register display that follows indicates that this is the case.

The next trace command causes the instruction

```
XCHG  DH, DL
```

to be executed. The register display that contains this instruction shows a DX-register value of 0055 hexadecimal; that is, the DH-register contains 00, and the DL-register contains 55 hex just prior to execution of the instruction. The following register display shows a DX-register value of 5500 hexadecimal; that is, the DH-register contains 55 hex, and the DL-register contains 00 just after execution of the instruction.

The next two trace commands cause the PUSH instructions in lines 48 and 49 of Program Listing 2.1 to be executed. The first of these two instructions pushes a copy of the value in the AX-register (0055 hex) onto the stack. The second one pushes a copy of the value in the CX-register (FFAA hex) onto the stack. With each of these instructions, the SP-register is decremented by 2 so that the SS:SP register pair points to the new top-of-stack item. The current status of the stack segment is shown in Figure 2.11.

The next command issued to DEBUG (see DEBUG Listing 2.2) is the d command

```
d ss:0,f
```

which is a request to display the contents of the stack segment. This command line

FIGURE 2.11 Status of stack segment after execution of instruction in line 49 of Program Listing 2.1

Hexadecimal memory address	Contents
1E100	?
1E101	?
1E102	?
1E103	?
1E104	?
1E105	?
1E106	?
1E107	?
1E108	?
1E109	?
1E10A	?
1E10B	?
1E10C	AA
1E10D	FF
1E10E	55
1E10F	00

SS	SP
1E10	000C

Top of stack (→ 1E10C)

(? means value unknown)

specifies that stack segment locations 0000–000F are to be displayed. The SS:SP register pair indicates that the top-of-stack item begins at 1E10:000C, which is memory address 1E10C. Therefore, the current stack begins at location 1E10C and goes through location 1E10F. The remaining stack segment locations (1E100–1E10B) are not part of the current stack. Compare this display of the stack segment in DEBUG Listing 2.2 to the predicted values shown in Figure 2.11.

The next trace command causes the POP instruction in line 50 of Program Listing 2.1 to be executed. Execution of this POP instruction causes the value at the top of the stack, FFAA hex (the previous CX-register value), to be copied into the AX-register and the SP-register to be incremented by 2. After execution, the SS:SP register pair points to the new top-of-stack value, 0055 hex (the previous AX-register value). The current status of the stack segment is shown in Figure 2.12. Note that the value FFAA still exists in the physical stack segment. However, the SP-register has been updated so that this value is not part of the logical stack.

FIGURE 2.12 Status of stack segment after execution of instruction in line 50 of Program Listing 2.1

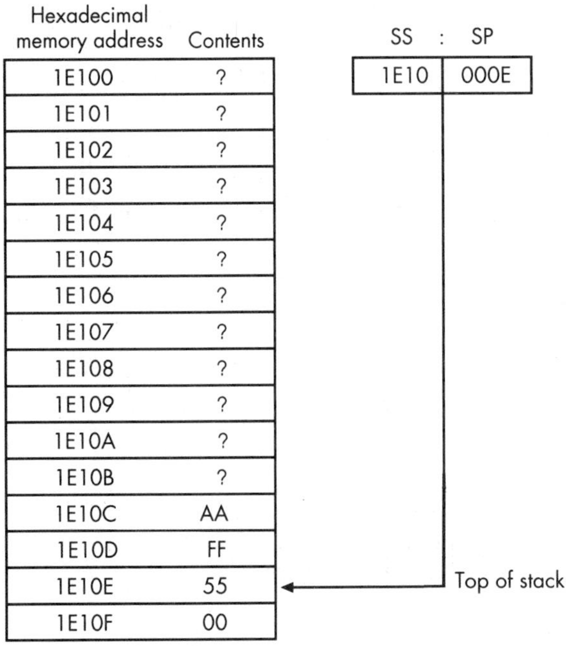

Hexadecimal memory address	Contents
1E100	?
1E101	?
1E102	?
1E103	?
1E104	?
1E105	?
1E106	?
1E107	?
1E108	?
1E109	?
1E10A	?
1E10B	?
1E10C	AA
1E10D	FF
1E10E	55
1E10F	00

(? means value unknown)

SS	SP
1E10	000E

The next command issued to DEBUG (see DEBUG Listing 2.2) is another request to display the contents of the stack segment. Compare this display to the predicted values shown in Figure 2.12. Note that the value FFAA is no longer in the stack segment; it has been replaced by the value 18BF. How did this value get into the stack segment? It appears that no other PUSH operations have been performed. The reason this value has changed is that during the transition between the user program and the single-step interrupt service procedure (part of DEBUG), the flags register and the address of the next instruction to be executed in the user program are saved on the user program's stack. The three items above the user program's top of stack are 18BF, 1E0C, and 001E, the first of which is the flags register value and the last two of which are the CS and IP register values for the next instruction to be executed in the user program. (The mechanism by which these values are pushed onto the stack is discussed in Chapter 9.) These values are popped from the stack as part of returning control from the interrupt service procedure to the user program.

The next trace command causes the POP instruction in line 51 of Program Listing 2.1 to be executed. Execution of this POP instruction causes the top-of-stack value, 0055 hex, to be copied into the CX-register and the SP-register to be incremented by 2. After execution, the SS:SP register pair points one location beyond the end of the stack segment, indicating that the stack is empty once again.

The next trace command causes the instruction

```
XCHG  CX, DX
```

to be executed. The register display that contains this instruction shows a DX-register value of 5500 hexadecimal and a CX-register value of 0055 hexadecimal. The following register display shows a DX-register value of 0055 hexadecimal and a CX-register value of 5500 hexadecimal.

The next five trace commands in DEBUG Listing 2.2 cause the five MOV instructions in lines 54–60 of Program Listing 2.1 to be executed. The destination operand in each of these MOV instructions is the location of a byte or word in the data segment. These five instructions modify the data segment values. The next command to the DEBUG program is a request to dump the contents of the data segment. Compare the current values of the data segment shown in this display to the initial values of the data segment shown in Table 2.10 and the predicted final values of the data segment shown in Table 2.12.

The next trace command in DEBUG Listing 2.2 causes the instruction

```
MOV      AH,4CH
```

to be executed. This instruction is the first of the two instructions generated by the .EXIT pseudo-operation in line 62 of Program Listing 2.1. The following register display shows that the value of the AH-register has changed to 4C hex. Note also that the value of the AL-register is not modified by the execution of this MOV instruction. The register display also shows that the next instruction to be executed is an

```
INT      21
```

instruction, which is the second of the two instructions generated by the .EXIT pseudo-operation in line 62 of Program Listing 2.1.

The last command issued to DEBUG in DEBUG Listing 2.2 is the **q (quit) command**. This command terminates DEBUG and causes control to be returned to DOS.

CodeView Trace of Program

CodeView is a debugging tool that divides the video screen into windows. Each window keeps track of a different part of the run-time environment of the program (i.e., processor registers, code segment, stack segment, data segment) as the instructions of the program are being traced. The command

```
cv  /tsf  ex_2_1
```

loads the CodeView program, begins execution of the CodeView program, and has the CodeView program load the executable module ex_2_1.exe for tracing. The /tsf command-line option directs CodeView to begin execution with its default configuration of windows. The CodeView program records the current configuration of windows being displayed. When CodeView is invoked, it begins execution with the same configuration of windows that it was displaying the last time it terminated execution unless the /tsf option directs it to begin with the default configuration. The /tsf option is used here so that the reader is able to reproduce this trace.

When CodeView is invoked with the command just given, the video screen looks like the one in Screen Image 2.1. The top line of the screen shows the names of the menus available with CodeView. The menu names are File, Edit, View, Search, Run, Watch, Options, Calls, and Help. These menus provide much of the interface between the user and CodeView. CodeView also uses the function keys for part of its interface with the user. The bottom line of the screen shows the commands that are entered to CodeView via five of these function keys. The bottom line is also used for messages from CodeView to the user. Between the top line and the bottom line, the screen is divided into windows.

SCREEN IMAGE 2.1

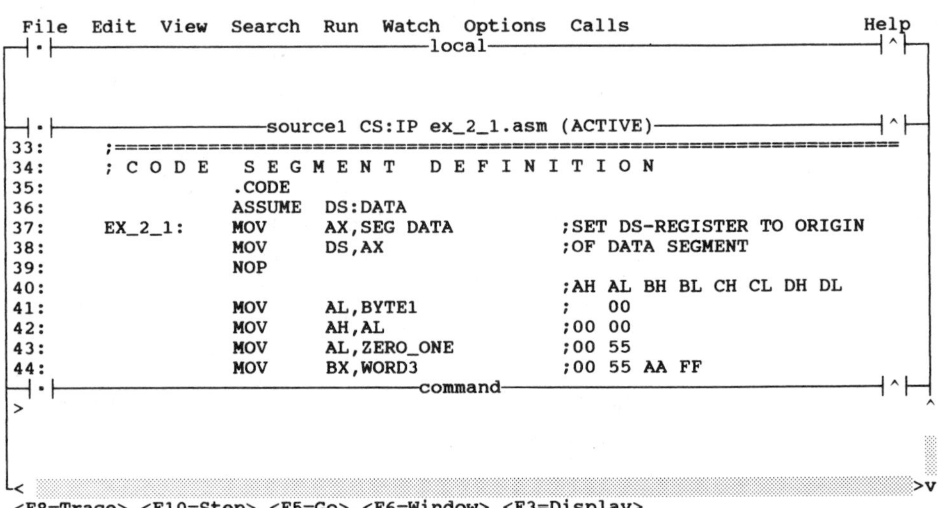

```
File  Edit  View  Search  Run  Watch  Options  Calls                    Help
---------------------------------local---------------------------------

---------------------sourcel CS:IP ex_2_1.asm (ACTIVE)------------------
        ;=====================================================================
        ; C O D E     S E G M E N T    D E F I N I T I O N
                      .CODE
                      ASSUME  DS:DATA
        EX_2_1:       MOV     AX,SEG DATA           ;SET DS-REGISTER TO ORIGIN
                      MOV     DS,AX                 ;OF DATA SEGMENT
                      NOP
                                                    ;AH AL BH BL CH CL DH DL
                      MOV     AL,BYTE1              ;   00
                      MOV     AH,AL                 ;00 00
                      MOV     AL,ZERO_ONE           ;00 55
                      MOV     BX,WORD3              ;00 55 AA FF
--------------------------------command---------------------------------
>

<                                                                      >v
<F8=Trace> <F10=Step> <F5=Go> <F6=Window> <F3=Display>
```

The default screen shown in Screen Image 2.1 is divided into three windows. The top window is labeled “local” and is used to monitor the local variables of a subprocedure. The middle window is labeled “sourcel CS:IP ex_2_1.asm (ACTIVE)” and is used to trace the instructions of the assembly language program. The bottom window is labeled “command” and is used to enter commands to CodeView.

The first step in this trace is that of reconfiguring the windows in order to look at the information that is most helpful in the tracing of this program. Since there are no local variables in this program, the local window can be eliminated. The commands needed in this trace can be entered via menu selections and function keys. Therefore, the command window can also be eliminated.

The commands for closing windows (i.e., for eliminating windows from the display) are found in the View menu. To gain access to the menu list on the top line of the screen, press the Alt key. Pressing this key causes the first letter of each menu name to be highlighted. To select a menu, press the letter key corresponding to the first letter of the menu name. To select the View menu, press the V key. Pressing this key causes the pull-down View menu to be displayed over the windows, as shown in Screen Image 2.2. The top five items in the second section of the View menu (i.e., Register, 8087, Local, Watch, and Command) behave like toggle switches. Selecting the item opens the corresponding window (i.e., adds the window to the screen) if that

SCREEN IMAGE 2.2

```
 File  Edit  View  Search  Run  Watch  Options  Calls                      Help
-|•|-----------┌──────────────────────┐──local────────────────────────|^|-
               │ Source               │
               │ Memory               │
-|•|-----------├──────────────────────┤IP ex_2_1.asm (ACTIVE)─────────|^|-
33:        ;== │ Register          F2 │==========================================
34:        ; C │•Local                │   D E F I N I T I O N
35:            │ Watch                │
36:            │•Command              │A
37:        EX_ │ Help                 │ DATA          ;SET DS-REGISTER TO ORIGIN
38:            ├──────────────────────┤               ;OF DATA SEGMENT
39:            │ Output            F4 │
40:            ├──────────────────────┤               ;AH AL BH BL CH CL DH DL
41:            │ Maximize  Ctrl+F10   │E1             ;   00
42:            │ Size       Ctrl+F8   │               ;00 00
43:            │ Close      Ctrl+F4   │O_ONE          ;00 55
44:            └──────────────────────┘D3             ;00 55 AA FF
-|•|--------------------------------------command------------------------|^|-
>                                                                          ^



<                                                                          >v
<F8=Trace> <F10=Step> <F5=Go> <F6=Window> <F3=Display> <ESC=Cancel>
```

window is currently closed. Selecting the item closes the corresponding window (i.e., removes the window from the screen) if that window is currently open. Note that, in this menu, the items Local and Command have a dot displayed in front of them, which indicates that these windows are currently open. To close one of these windows, simply press the key corresponding to the highlighted letter in the menu item. Pressing the L key causes the local window to be removed from the screen.

Pressing the Alt key followed by the V key causes the View menu to be displayed again. Pressing the C key causes the command window to be removed from the screen. The source1 window now takes up the entire window space.

To facilitate the tracing of this program, there are several windows that need to be opened. Three windows will be opened: the register window for monitoring the processor registers, a memory window for monitoring the data segment, and a second memory window for monitoring the stack segment. Again, the View menu is accessed by pressing the Alt key followed by the V key. Pressing the R key causes the register window to be added to the screen. The register window is a vertical window appearing on the right-hand side of the screen, as shown in Screen Image 2.3.

SCREEN IMAGE 2.3

```
 File  Edit  View  Search  Run  Watch  Options  Calls                      Help
-|•|----------source1 CS:IP ex_2_1.asm (ACTIVE)------------|^|--|•|reg|^|-
33:      ;=================================================^   AX = 0000
34:      ; C O D E   S E G M E N T   D E F I N I T I O N       BX = 0000
35:                 .CODE                                      CX = 0000
36:                 ASSUME   DS:DATA                           DX = 0000
37:      EX_2_1:    MOV      AX,SEG DATA       ;SET DS-REGISTER T  SP = 0010
38:                 MOV      DS,AX             ;OF DATA SEGMENT    BP = 0000
39:                 NOP                                        SI = 0000
40:                                            ;AH AL BH BL CH CL  DI = 0000
41:                 MOV      AL,BYTE1          ;   00          DS = 1CC4
42:                 MOV      AH,AL             ;00 00          ES = 1CC4
43:                 MOV      AL,ZERO_ONE       ;00 55          SS = 1CD8
44:                 MOV      BX,WORD3          ;00 55 AA FF    CS = 1CD4
45:                 MOV      CX,WORD2          ;00 55 AA FF FF AA  IP = 0000
46:                 MOV      DX,WORD4          ;00 55 AA FF FF AA  FL = 0200
47:                 XCHG     DH,DL             ;00 55 AA FF FF AA
48:                 PUSH     AX                ;00 55 AA FF FF AA  NV UP EI PL
49:                 PUSH     CX                ;00 55 AA FF FF AA  NZ NA PO NC
50:                 POP      AX                ;FF AA AA FF FF AA
51:                 POP      CX                ;FF AA AA FF 00 55
52:                 XCHG     CX,DX             ;FF AA AA FF 55 00
53:      ;
<                                                         >v
<F8=Trace> <F10=Step> <F5=Go> <F6=Window> <F3=Display>
```

To open a memory window and to specify what is to be monitored in the window, both the View menu and the Options menu are utilized. First, the View menu is accessed by pressing the Alt key followed by the V key. The Source and Memory items in the View menu do not behave like toggle switches. Selecting one of these items always opens a window of the specified type. This mechanism allows for more than one source window and/or more than one memory window. Pressing the M key causes a memory window to be opened. Next, the Options menu is accessed by pressing the Alt key followed by the O key. The Memory Window item is selected by pressing the M key. Selecting this item causes an input window to be opened, as shown in Screen Image 2.4. This window allows the user to specify what the memory window will monitor and in what form the data in the memory window is to be displayed. The first section of this input window allows the user to specify the form in which the data is to be displayed (e.g., bytes in hexadecimal, ASCII characters, decimal integers). The current selection is shown by a dot in the parentheses to the left of the item. The up-arrow and down-arrow cursor keys are used to change the selection. For the trace here, Byte (8-bit hex) was selected.

SCREEN IMAGE 2.4

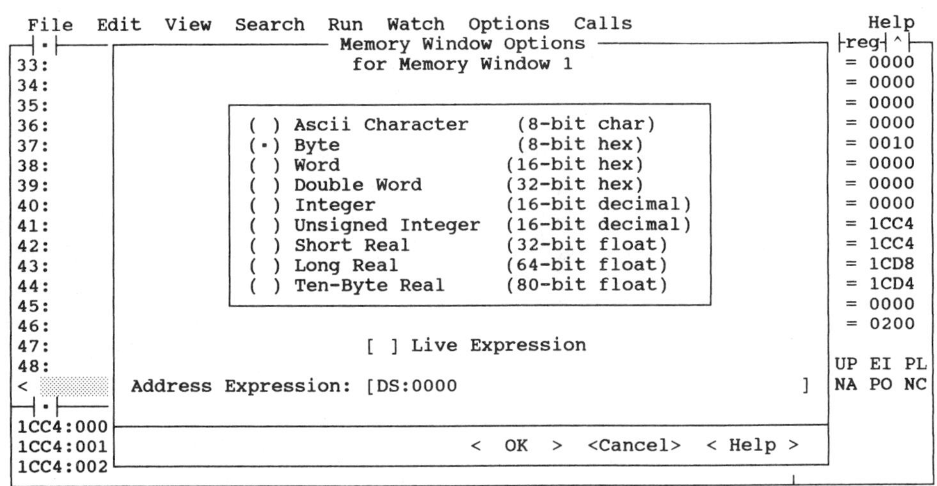

To move the cursor to the next section of this input window, press the TAB key. This section is labeled "[ ] Live Expression", which refers to the Address Expression appearing in the next section of this input window. The address expression has the form ⟨*segment*⟩:⟨*offset*⟩, and it specifies the start address for the storage cells that are to be displayed in the window. The number of storage cells to be displayed depends on the size of the window. The default address expression for a memory window is DS:0000. It is possible that, during program execution, the value of the address expression might change. For example, in the case of the default address expression, the value of the DS-register might change during program execution. If the address expression is a live expression, then a change in the value of the address expression causes a different set of storage cells to be displayed in the window. If the address expression is not a live expression, then a change in the value of the address expression has no effect on the storage cells being displayed in the window. For the trace of the program of Program Listing 2.1, the default address expression will be selected for the first of the two memory windows, and it needs to be a live expression. Upon entry to the program, the DS-register contains the origin of the program segment prefix

(PSP). The program initializes the DS-register to address its data segment. By making this a live expression, execution of the instructions that initialize the DS-register will cause CodeView to update the memory window to display the program's data segment. With the cursor in the brackets to the left of Live Expression, pressing the up-arrow key causes the letter X to be displayed in the brackets, which shows that the address expression is to be a live expression. (Pressing the down-arrow key would remove the X.)

Pressing the TAB key causes the cursor to move to the next section of the input window. This section allows the user to specify the address expression. No entry is required here if the default expression is the desired address expression. Pressing the TAB key again causes the cursor to move to the last section of the input window.

The last section of the input window allows the user either to enter the information shown in the input window by selecting ⟨OK⟩ or to reject the information by selecting ⟨Cancel⟩. To select ⟨OK⟩, press the Enter key. (To select ⟨Cancel⟩, first press the TAB key to move the cursor to ⟨Cancel⟩, and then press the Enter key.) The current state of the trace is shown in Screen Image 2.5.

SCREEN IMAGE 2.5

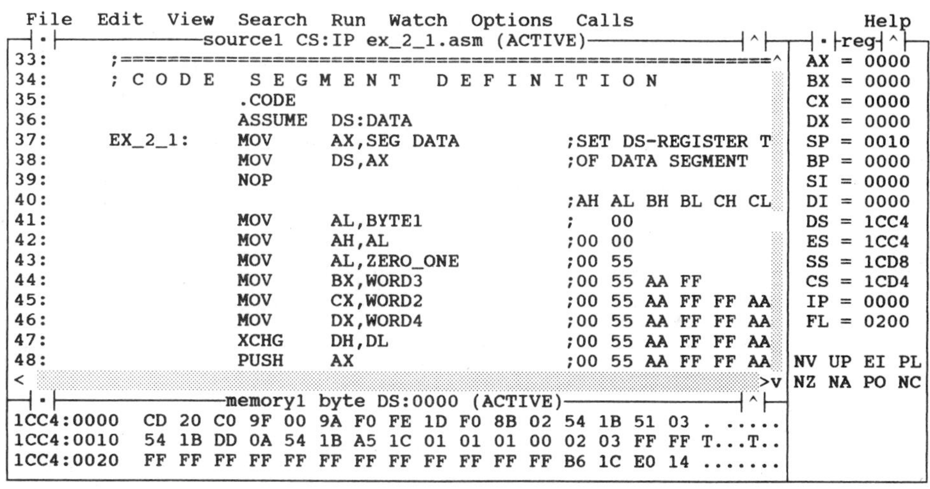

```
 File  Edit  View  Search  Run  Watch  Options  Calls                    Help
 -sourcel CS:IP ex_2_1.asm (ACTIVE)-                                      reg
33:     ;=============================================          AX = 0000
34:     ; C O D E    S E G M E N T    D E F I N I T I O N       BX = 0000
35:                  .CODE                                      CX = 0000
36:                  ASSUME  DS:DATA                            DX = 0000
37:     EX_2_1:      MOV     AX,SEG DATA        ;SET DS-REGISTER T   SP = 0010
38:                  MOV     DS,AX              ;OF DATA SEGMENT     BP = 0000
39:                  NOP                                        SI = 0000
40:                                             ;AH AL BH BL CH CL   DI = 0000
41:                  MOV     AL,BYTE1           ;   00          DS = 1CC4
42:                  MOV     AH,AL              ;00 00          ES = 1CC4
43:                  MOV     AL,ZERO_ONE        ;00 55          SS = 1CD8
44:                  MOV     BX,WORD3           ;00 55 AA FF    CS = 1CD4
45:                  MOV     CX,WORD2           ;00 55 AA FF FF AA   IP = 0000
46:                  MOV     DX,WORD4           ;00 55 AA FF FF AA   FL = 0200
47:                  XCHG    DH,DL              ;00 55 AA FF FF AA
48:                  PUSH    AX                 ;00 55 AA FF FF AA   NV UP EI PL
<                                                          >v   NZ NA PO NC
 -memoryl byte DS:0000 (ACTIVE)-
1CC4:0000  CD 20 C0 9F 00 9A F0 FE 1D F0 8B 02 54 1B 51 03 . .....
1CC4:0010  54 1B DD 0A 54 1B A5 1C 01 01 01 00 02 03 FF FF T...T..
1CC4:0020  FF FF FF FF FF FF FF FF FF FF FF FF B6 1C E0 14 .......

<F8=Trace> <F10=Step> <F5=Go> <F6=Window> <F3=Display>
```

To open a memory window for monitoring the stack segment, the View and Options menus are utilized once again. First, the View menu is accessed by pressing the Alt key followed by the V key, and the Memory item is selected by pressing the M key. Thus, a second memory window is opened. Next, the Options menu is accessed by pressing the Alt key followed by the O key, and the Memory Window item is selected by pressing the M key. Thus, the Memory Window Options input window is again displayed, as shown in Screen Image 2.6. Note that this input window is for Memory Window 2 (see header at top of input window). Since the second memory window is for monitoring the program's stack segment and since the stack is a word-oriented structure, the stack segment will be displayed in word form rather than byte form. Pressing the down-arrow key one time causes the selection dot to move from Byte (8-bit hex) to Word (16-bit hex). Pressing the TAB key causes the cursor to move to the Live Expression section of the input window. The SS-register is initialized to the origin of the program's stack segment prior to execution and remains fixed throughout execution of the program. Therefore, there is no need here for the address expression to be a live expression. Pressing the TAB key causes the cursor to move to

SCREEN IMAGE 2.6

```
File  Edit  View  Search  Run  Watch  Options  Calls                    Help
                          Memory Window Options                         reg
33:                        for Memory Window 2                           = 0000
34:                                                                      = 0000
35:                                                                      = 0000
36:        ( ) Ascii Character      (8-bit char)                         = 0000
37:        (•) Byte                 (8-bit hex)                          = 0010
38:        ( ) Word                (16-bit hex)                          = 0000
39:        ( ) Double Word         (32-bit hex)                          = 0000
40:        ( ) Integer             (16-bit decimal)                      = 0000
41:        ( ) Unsigned Integer    (16-bit decimal)                      = 1CC4
42:        ( ) Short Real          (32-bit float)                        = 1CC4
43:        ( ) Long Real           (64-bit float)                        = 1CD8
44:        ( ) Ten-Byte Real       (80-bit float)                        = 1CD4
<                                                                        = 0000
                                                                         = 0200
1CC4:000                  [ ] Live Expression
1CC4:001                                                                 UP EI PL
1CC4:002  Address Expression: [DS:0000                              ]    NA PO NC

1CC4:000
1CC4:001                         <  OK  >  <Cancel>  < Help >
1CC4:002

<F1=Help> <Enter> <ESC=Cancel> <TAB=Next Field>
```

the Address Expression section of the input window. To change the address expression shown in the input window, simply type the new expression, which is ss:0 in this case. The resulting state of the input window is shown in Screen Image 2.7. There is no need to move the cursor to the last section of the input window. Pressing the Enter key enters the input window in its present state. The resulting window configuration is shown in Screen Image 2.8.

SCREEN IMAGE 2.7

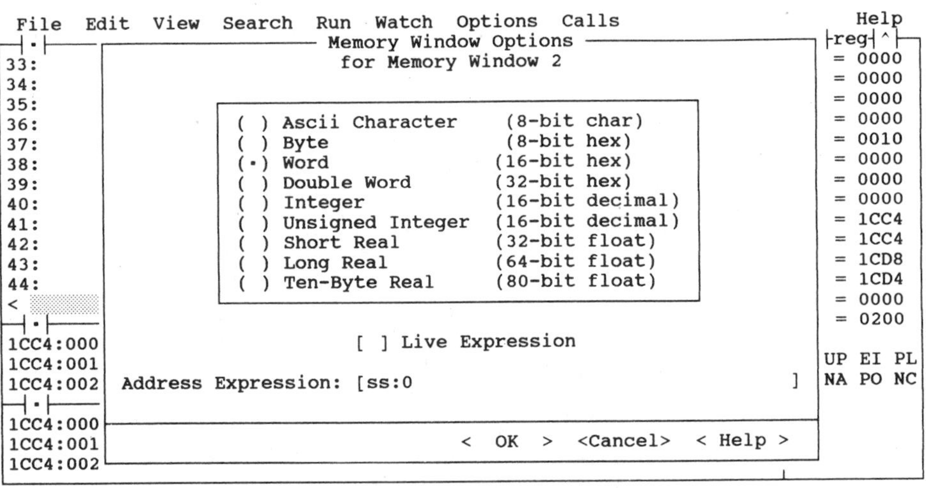

The size of the data segment for the program being traced is only 8 bytes, but CodeView is displaying 48 bytes in the memory1 window. Also, the size of the stack segment for the program is 8 words, but CodeView is displaying 24 words in the memory2 window. The sizes of the two memory windows can be reduced, thus leaving more space for the source1 window, by moving the two horizontal boundaries of the memory1 window. To change the size of a window, the cursor must be in that window. The cursor is currently in the source1 window. Note that the window that contains the cursor has its last line shaded (see last line of source1 window in Screen

SCREEN IMAGE 2.8

```
 File  Edit  View  Search  Run  Watch  Options  Calls                 Help
┤•├────────────sourcel CS:IP ex_2_1.asm (ACTIVE)──────────────┤^├─┤•├reg┤^├
33:      ;===============================================^  AX = 0000
34:      ; C O D E   S E G M E N T   D E F I N I T I O N    BX = 0000
35:                  .CODE                                  CX = 0000
36:                  ASSUME  DS:DATA                        DX = 0000
37:      EX_2_1:     MOV     AX,SEG DATA       ;SET DS-REGISTER T  SP = 0010
38:                  MOV     DS,AX             ;OF DATA SEGMENT    BP = 0000
39:                  NOP                                    SI = 0000
40:                                            ;AH AL BH BL CH CL  DI = 0000
41:                  MOV     AL,BYTE1          ;   00       DS = 1CC4
42:                  MOV     AH,AL             ;00 00       ES = 1CC4
43:                  MOV     AL,ZERO_ONE       ;00 55       SS = 1CD8
44:                  MOV     BX,WORD3          ;00 55 AA FF CS = 1CD4
<                                                       >v  IP = 0000
┤•├──────────────memory1 byte DS:0000─────────────────┤^├   FL = 0200
1CC4:0000  CD 20 C0 9F 00 9A F0 FE 1D F0 8B 02 54 1B 51 03 . .....
1CC4:0010  54 1B DD 0A 54 1B A5 1C 01 01 01 00 02 03 FF FF T...T..  NV UP EI PL
1CC4:0020  FF FF FF FF FF FF FF FF FF FF FF FF B6 1C E0 14 .......  NZ NA PO NC
┤•├────────────memory2 word ss:0 (ACTIVE)─────────────┤^├
1CD8:0000  0000 0000 0000 0000 0000 0000 0000 0000
1CD8:0010  5500 FFAA AAFF 0055 424E 3230 00EE 0000
1CD8:0020  0000 0000 0038 0000 0000 0001 650A 5F78

<F8=Trace> <F10=Step> <F5=Go> <F6=Window> <F3=Display>
```

Image 2.8). Pressing the F6 function key causes the cursor to move from the source1 window to the memory1 window.

In order to change the size of the window containing the cursor, the View menu can be utilized. The View menu is accessed by pressing the Alt key followed by the V key. Note that the Size item in the View menu has Ctrl+F8 displayed next to it, indicating that the window size function can be accessed directly (i.e., without first accessing the View menu) by holding down the Ctrl key and pressing the F8 function key. From the View menu, the Size item is selected by pressing the Z key. Pressing the Z key causes the message

```
Use arrow key to select window edge - ESC to cancel
```

to appear at the bottom of the screen. Pressing the down-arrow cursor key causes the bottom edge of the window to be selected and the message

```
Use arrow keys to resize windows - CR to finish - Esc to cancel
```

to appear at the bottom of the screen. Pressing the down-arrow key two more times causes the border between the two memory windows to move down two lines. Pressing the Enter key completes the resizing operation. This resizing operation reduced the memory2 window to one line and expanded the memory1 window to five lines, as shown in Screen Image 2.9.

The memory1 window can now be reduced by moving its top edge down. The size function can be accessed by holding down the Ctrl key and pressing the F8 function key. Pressing the up-arrow cursor key causes the top edge of the memory1 window to be selected. Pressing the down-arrow key four times causes the border between the source1 window and the memory1 window to move down four lines. Pressing the Enter key completes the resizing operation. This resizing operation reduced the memory1 window to one line and expanded the source1 window, as shown in Screen Image 2.10.

With the desired window configuration established, the next step is that of tracing the execution of the program's instructions. The processor state shown in Screen Image 2.10 is the state that exists just prior to the execution of the first instruction of the program. The register window shows the values of the processor registers just prior to execution of the first instruction. The AX, BX, CX, DX, BP, SI,

SCREEN IMAGE 2.9

```
 File  Edit  View  Search  Run  Watch  Options  Calls                    Help
-|.|-----------source1 CS:IP ex_2_1.asm (ACTIVE)-----------|^|- -|.|reg|^|-
33:      ;=====================================================  AX = 0000
34:      ; C O D E   S E G M E N T   D E F I N I T I O N          BX = 0000
35:                .CODE                                           CX = 0000
36:                ASSUME  DS:DATA                                 DX = 0000
37:      EX_2_1:   MOV     AX,SEG DATA        ;SET DS-REGISTER TO  SP = 0010
38:                MOV     DS,AX              ;OF DATA SEGMENT     BP = 0000
39:                NOP                                             SI = 0000
40:                                           ;AH AL BH BL CH CL   DI = 0000
41:                MOV     AL,BYTE1           ;   00               DS = 1CC4
42:                MOV     AH,AL              ;00 00               ES = 1CC4
43:                MOV     AL,ZERO_ONE        ;00 55               SS = 1CD8
44:                MOV     BX,WORD3           ;00 55 AA FF         CS = 1CD4
45:                MOV     CX,WORD2           ;00 55 AA FF FF AA   IP = 0000
-|.|-----------memory1 byte DS:0000 (ACTIVE)---------------|^|-   FL = 0200
1CC4:0000  CD 20 C0 9F 00 9A F0 FE 1D F0 8B 02 54 1B 51 03 . ....^
1CC4:0010  54 1B DD 0A 54 1B A5 1C 01 01 01 00 02 03 FF FF T...T.  NV UP EI PL
1CC4:0020  FF FF FF FF FF FF FF FF FF FF FF FF B6 1C E0 14 ......  NZ NA PO NC
1CC4:0030  E6 18 14 00 18 00 C4 1C FF FF FF FF 00 00 00 00 ......
<                                                               >v
-|.|-----------------memory2 word ss:0---------------------|^|-
1CD8:0000  0000 0000 0000 0000 0000 0000 0000 0000

<F8=Trace> <F10=Step> <F5=Go> <F6=Window> <F3=Display> <Sh+F3=Memory Format>
```

SCREEN IMAGE 2.10

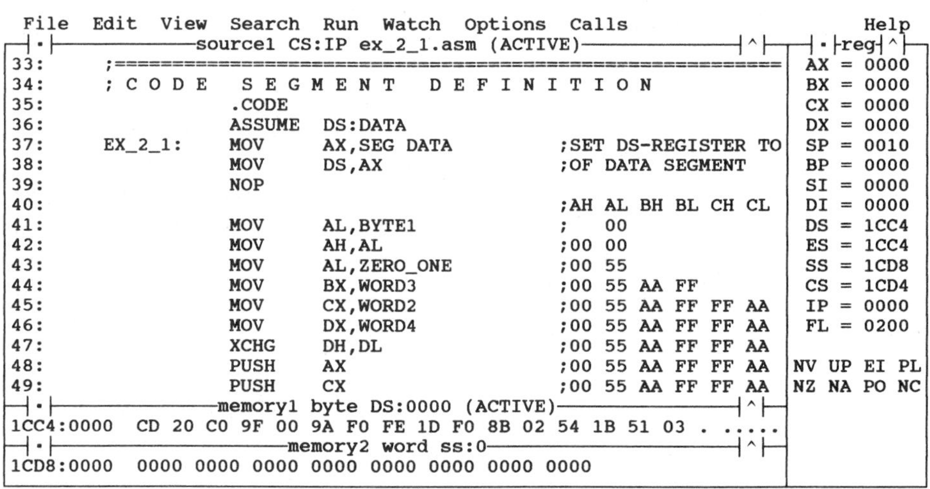

```
 File  Edit  View  Search  Run  Watch  Options  Calls                    Help
-|.|-----------source1 CS:IP ex_2_1.asm (ACTIVE)-----------|^|- -|.|reg|^|-
33:      ;=====================================================  AX = 0000
34:      ; C O D E   S E G M E N T   D E F I N I T I O N          BX = 0000
35:                .CODE                                           CX = 0000
36:                ASSUME  DS:DATA                                 DX = 0000
37:      EX_2_1:   MOV     AX,SEG DATA        ;SET DS-REGISTER TO  SP = 0010
38:                MOV     DS,AX              ;OF DATA SEGMENT     BP = 0000
39:                NOP                                             SI = 0000
40:                                           ;AH AL BH BL CH CL   DI = 0000
41:                MOV     AL,BYTE1           ;   00               DS = 1CC4
42:                MOV     AH,AL              ;00 00               ES = 1CC4
43:                MOV     AL,ZERO_ONE        ;00 55               SS = 1CD8
44:                MOV     BX,WORD3           ;00 55 AA FF         CS = 1CD4
45:                MOV     CX,WORD2           ;00 55 AA FF FF AA   IP = 0000
46:                MOV     DX,WORD4           ;00 55 AA FF FF AA   FL = 0200
47:                XCHG    DH,DL              ;00 55 AA FF FF AA
48:                PUSH    AX                 ;00 55 AA FF FF AA  NV UP EI PL
49:                PUSH    CX                 ;00 55 AA FF FF AA  NZ NA PO NC
-|.|-----------memory1 byte DS:0000 (ACTIVE)---------------|^|-
1CC4:0000  CD 20 C0 9F 00 9A F0 FE 1D F0 8B 02 54 1B 51 03 . .....
-|.|-----------------memory2 word ss:0---------------------|^|-
1CD8:0000  0000 0000 0000 0000 0000 0000 0000 0000

<F8=Trace> <F10=Step> <F5=Go> <F6=Window> <F3=Display> <Sh+F3=Memory Format>
```

and DI registers have been initialized to zero by the CodeView program. DOS will *not* perform such initializations. Therefore, a program *must never* depend on registers being initialized to zero automatically.

The SP-register is initialized to the offset from the origin of the stack segment of the memory location immediately following the end of the stack segment. This initialization denotes an empty stack. The initial value of the SS-register specifies the origin of the stack segment (hexadecimal location 1CD80 in this case). The SS:SP register pair points to the memory location within the stack segment that contains the current top-of-stack data word. The stack segment for this program was defined to have a size of 16 bytes (see line 13 of Program Listing 2.1). Since the stack's origin is location 1CD80, the stack segment ends at location 1CD8F. The SS:SP register pair currently points to location 1CD90 (1CD80 + 0010). This location is one location beyond the end of the stack segment, thus denoting an empty stack.

The initial value of the DS-register and the ES-register specifies the origin of the program segment prefix (hexadecimal location 1CC40 in this case). Recall that the value in a segment register is the high-order 16 bits of a 20-bit address and that the low-order 4 bits are always zero.

The initial value of the CS-register specifies the origin of the code segment (hexadecimal location 1CD40 in this case). The initial value of the IP-register is zero, the offset of the first location in the code segment. The CS:IP register pair always points to the memory location that contains the next instruction byte to be fetched. Initially, the CS:IP register pair points to the location of the first byte of the first instruction in the program.

The flags register value is displayed in two ways: Its value is displayed in hexadecimal, and selected bits are interpreted using abbreviations. The flags register display in Screen Image 2.10 appears as follows:

```
FL = 0200

NV  UP  EI  PL
NZ  NA  PO  NC
```

Table 2.13 shows the abbreviations used for the interpretation part of the flags register display. The flag bits in the flags register, with the exception of the interrupt flag, are cleared (i.e., set to 0) initially.

The source1 window shows the first few instructions of the assembly language program. CodeView highlights the instruction that is addressed by the CS:IP register pair (i.e., the next instruction to be executed). At this point, the highlighted instruction is the first instruction in the program, the MOV AX,SEG DATA instruction.

The memory1 window currently shows the first 16 bytes of the program segment prefix. Upon entry to the program, the DS-register addresses the program segment prefix. The memory2 window shows the 8 words (16 bytes) of the stack segment.

There are two function keys that are used for the execution of instructions in single-step mode: the **F8 (trace into)** and the **F10 (step over) function keys**. For the instructions of the program in Program Listing 2.1, the two are virtually equivalent. The two functions differ in the way in which they handle a CALL instruction. The CALL instruction is the instruction that, when executed, invokes a subprocedure. The F8 function key causes CodeView to execute the CALL instruction in single-step mode, thus allowing the user to "trace into" the subprocedure. The user can then trace the instructions of the subprocedure in single-step mode. The F10 function key causes CodeView to "step over" the entire subprocedure as if it were a single step; that is, CodeView allows instructions to be executed continuously, stopping just prior to the execution of the instruction that immediately follows the CALL instruction. The F8 and F10 functions differ in a similar manner for loop instructions (Chapter 4), string instructions with repeat prefixes (Chapter 8), and INT instructions (Chapter 9). Since there are no CALL, loop, string, or INT instructions in this program, F8 and F10 behave in the same way for the instructions of this program.

Pressing F10 causes the instruction

```
MOV     AX,SEG DATA
```

to be executed and control to be returned to CodeView. CodeView highlights the items on the video screen that changed because of the execution of this instruction. The AX-register changed from 0000 to 1CD9, which is the value of the immediate operand SEG DATA. The value 1CD9 is the high-order 16 bits of the 20-bit address (1CD90) of the origin of the program's data segment. The IP-register changed from 0000 to 0003, which indicates that the instruction just executed is a three-byte instruction in machine language. The CS:IP register pair now addresses the first byte of the next instruction in sequence, the MOV DS,AX instruction, which is now highlighted in the source1 window.

It should also be noted that five words in the stack segment have changed. How did these values get into the stack segment? The instruction just executed is not a PUSH instruction. The reason these values appear in the stack is that during the transition between the user program and the single-step interrupt service procedure (part of CodeView), the flags register and the address of the next instruction to be executed in the user program are saved on the user program's stack. (The mechanism by which these values are pushed onto the stack is discussed in Chapter 9.) In addition, CodeView pushes two more words onto the user program's stack. These two words are the values of the DS-register and the AX-register. CodeView uses these two registers and therefore must save them for the user program. CodeView pops these two words from the stack and restores the DS- and AX-registers prior to returning control to the user program. The other three words are popped from the stack as part of returning control from the interrupt service procedure to the user program. Note that the value of the SP-register shown in the register window of CodeView's display is the value that existed in the SP-register prior to these extra items being pushed onto the stack.

Pressing F10 again causes the instruction

```
MOV     DS,AX
```

to be executed and control to be returned to CodeView. The processor state at this point in the trace is shown in Screen Image 2.11. The DS-register changed from 1CC4 (the segment address of the origin of the program segment prefix) to 1CD9 (the segment address of the origin of the program's data segment). Since the address expression for the memory1 window (DS:0000) is a live expression, the memory1 window now displays the program's data segment. The first eight bytes of the data shown in this window,

```
00 55 AA FF FF AA 55 00
```

are the initial values of the eight bytes defined in the data segment definition of Program Listing 2.1. Compare this display to Table 2.10.

The IP-register changed from 0003 to 0005, which indicates that the instruction

SCREEN IMAGE 2.11

```
File  Edit  View  Search  Run  Watch  Options  Calls                       Help
-source1 CS:IP ex_2_1.asm (ACTIVE)-                                        reg
     ;===========================================================  AX = 1CD9
     ; C O D E   S E G M E N T   D E F I N I T I O N               BX = 0000
                .CODE                                              CX = 0000
                ASSUME  DS:DATA                                    DX = 0000
     EX_2_1:    MOV     AX,SEG DATA         ;SET DS-REGISTER TO    SP = 0010
                MOV     DS,AX               ;OF DATA SEGMENT       BP = 0000
                NOP                                                SI = 0000
                                            ;AH AL BH BL CH CL     DI = 0000
                MOV     AL,BYTE1            ;   00                 DS = 1CD9
                MOV     AH,AL               ;00 00                 ES = 1CC4
                MOV     AL,ZERO_ONE         ;00 55                 SS = 1CD8
                MOV     BX,WORD3            ;00 55 AA FF           CS = 1CD4
                MOV     CX,WORD2            ;00 55 AA FF FF AA     IP = 0005
                MOV     DX,WORD4            ;00 55 AA FF FF AA     FL = 0202
                XCHG    DH,DL               ;00 55 AA FF FF AA
                PUSH    AX                  ;00 55 AA FF FF AA   NV UP EI PL
                PUSH    CX                  ;00 55 AA FF FF AA   NZ NA PO NC
-memory1 byte DS:0000 (ACTIVE)-
1CD9:0000   00 55 AA FF FF AA 55 00 4E 42 30 32 EE 00 00 00 .U....U
-memory2 word ss:0-
1CD8:0000   0000 0000 0000 1CD9 1CD9 0005 1CD4 0102

<F8=Trace> <F10=Step> <F5=Go> <F6=Window> <F3=Display> <Sh+F3=Memory Format>
```

just executed is a two-byte instruction in machine language. The CS:IP register pair now addresses the NOP instruction, which is now highlighted in the source1 window.

Pressing F10 again causes the NOP instruction to be executed. The IP-register changed from 0005 to 0006 (NOP is a one-byte instruction in machine language), and the next instruction is highlighted in the source1 window. Nothing else changed because of the execution of this instruction. That is, execution of a NOP instruction causes no operation to be performed. The reason for having the NOP instruction in the program is to facilitate the tracing of the program on 8088/8086-based machines. The CodeView program uses the single-step mode of the microprocessor to implement the trace command. When in the single-step mode, the microprocessor generates a single-step interrupt following most, but not all, instruction executions. The CodeView program is the interrupt service procedure that is invoked to service the single-step interrupt. The 8088/8086 microprocessor will not generate a single-step interrupt following a MOV or POP instruction whose destination operand is a segment register. Therefore, no single-step interrupt is generated following the execution of the MOV DS,AX instruction. The 8088/8086 microprocessor will execute the NOP instruction before generating the single-step interrupt and returning control to CodeView. The NOP instruction was used so that only one significant instruction would be executed in response to the trace command with 8088/8086-based machines. The 80286 and 80386 microprocessors will not generate a single-step interrupt following a MOV or POP instruction whose destination operand is the SS-register. Since this is a MOV with the DS-register as the destination operand, the single-step interrupt is generated between the MOV and the NOP on the 80286 and 80386 microprocessors. The CodeView trace described here was generated on an 80386-based machine. The single-step interrupt is discussed in detail in Chapter 9.

Pressing F10 six more times causes the six MOV instructions in lines 41–46 of Program Listing 2.1 to be executed in single-step mode. The reader should perform these steps slowly, making sure that he or she can account for the changes that occur with each step. The processor state that exists after the execution of these six MOV instructions is shown in Screen Image 2.12.

Pressing F10 again causes the instruction

```
XCHG  DH,DL
```

to be executed. The DX-register value changed from 0055 hexadecimal (DH = 00 and

SCREEN IMAGE 2.12

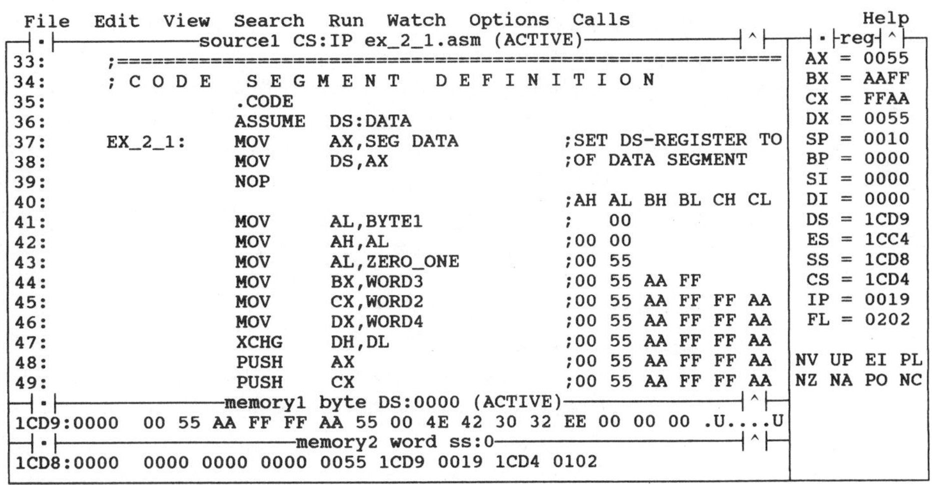
File Edit View Search Run Watch Options Calls Help
source1 CS:IP ex_2_1.asm (ACTIVE)
reg
33: ;==
34: ; C O D E S E G M E N T D E F I N I T I O N
35: .CODE
36: ASSUME DS:DATA
37: EX_2_1: MOV AX,SEG DATA ;SET DS-REGISTER TO
38: MOV DS,AX ;OF DATA SEGMENT
39: NOP
40: ;AH AL BH BL CH CL
41: MOV AL,BYTE1 ; 00
42: MOV AH,AL ;00 00
43: MOV AL,ZERO_ONE ;00 55
44: MOV BX,WORD3 ;00 55 AA FF
45: MOV CX,WORD2 ;00 55 AA FF FF AA
46: MOV DX,WORD4 ;00 55 AA FF FF AA
47: XCHG DH,DL ;00 55 AA FF FF AA
48: PUSH AX ;00 55 AA FF FF AA
49: PUSH CX ;00 55 AA FF FF AA
AX = 0055
BX = AAFF
CX = FFAA
DX = 0055
SP = 0010
BP = 0000
SI = 0000
DI = 0000
DS = 1CD9
ES = 1CC4
SS = 1CD8
CS = 1CD4
IP = 0019
FL = 0202
NV UP EI PL
NZ NA PO NC
memory1 byte DS:0000 (ACTIVE)
1CD9:0000 00 55 AA FF FF AA 55 00 4E 42 30 32 EE 00 00 00 .U....U
memory2 word ss:0
1CD8:0000 0000 0000 0000 0055 1CD9 0019 1CD4 0102
<F8=Trace> <F10=Step> <F5=Go> <F6=Window> <F3=Display> <Sh+F3=Memory Format>

DL = 55) to 5500 hexadecimal (DH = 55 and DL = 00). That is, the values of the DH and DL registers were interchanged by the execution of this instruction.

Pressing F10 two more times causes the PUSH instructions in lines 48 and 49 of Program Listing 2.1 to be executed. The processor state at this point in the trace is shown in Screen Image 2.13. The first of these two instructions pushes a copy of the value in the AX-register (0055 hex) onto the stack. The second one pushes a copy of the value in the CX-register (FFAA hex) onto the stack. With each of these instructions, the SP-register is decremented by 2 so that the SS:SP register pair points to the new top-of-stack item. The current status of the stack segment is shown in Figure 2.13. Compare the stack segment in the memory2 window of Screen Image 2.13 to the predicted values in Figure 2.13.

SCREEN IMAGE 2.13

```
File  Edit  View  Search  Run  Watch  Options  Calls                        Help
-|.|-----------source1 CS:IP ex_2_1.asm (ACTIVE)----------------|^|-|-|.|-reg-|^|-
45:              MOV     CX,WORD2           ;00 55 AA FF FF AA   AX = 0055
46:              MOV     DX,WORD4           ;00 55 AA FF FF AA   BX = AAFF
47:              XCHG    DH,DL              ;00 55 AA FF FF AA   CX = FFAA
48:              PUSH    AX                 ;00 55 AA FF FF AA   DX = 5500
49:              PUSH    CX                 ;00 55 AA FF FF AA   SP = 000C
50:              POP     AX                 ;FF AA AA FF FF AA   BP = 0000
51:              POP     CX                 ;FF AA AA FF 00 55   SI = 0000
52:              XCHG    CX,DX              ;FF AA AA FF 55 00   DI = 0000
53:      ;                                                       DS = 1CD9
54:              MOV     WORD1,BX           ;WORD1 BYTE1    FF H  ES = 1CC4
55:                                         ;      BYTE2    AA H  SS = 1CD8
56:              MOV     BYTE3,DL           ;WORD2 BYTE3    55 H  CS = 1CD4
57:              MOV     BYTE4,CL           ;      BYTE4    00 H  IP = 001D
58:              MOV     WORD3,CX           ;WORD3          00 H  FL = 0202
59:                                         ;               55 H
60:              MOV     WORD4,AX           ;WORD4          AA H NV UP EI PL
61:                                         ;               FF H NZ NA PO NC
-|.|-----------memory1 byte DS:0000 (ACTIVE)--------------------|^|-
1CD9:0000  00 55 AA FF FF AA 55 00 4E 42 30 32 EE 00 00 00 .U....U
-|.|-----------------memory2 word ss:0--------------------------|^|-
1CD8:0000  0000 0055 1CD9 001D 1CD4 0102 FFAA 0055
<F8=Trace> <F10=Step> <F5=Go> <F6=Window> <F3=Display> <Sh+F3=Memory Format>
```

Pressing F10 again causes the POP instruction in line 50 of Program Listing 2.1 to be executed. The processor state at this point in the trace is shown in Screen Image 2.14. Execution of this POP instruction causes the value at the top of the stack, FFAA hex (the previous CX-register value), to be copied into the AX-register and the SP-register to be incremented by 2. After execution, the SS:SP register pair points to the new top-of-stack value, 0055 hex (the previous AX-register value). The current status of the stack segment is shown in Figure 2.14. Note that the value FFAA still exists in the physical stack segment. However, the SP-register has been updated so that this value is not part of the logical stack. Compare the stack segment in the memory2 window of Screen Image 2.14 to the predicted values shown in Figure 2.14. The value FFAA does not still appear in the stack segment shown in Screen Image 2.14 because, again, CodeView uses the user program's stack.

Pressing F10 again causes the POP instruction in line 51 of Program Listing 2.1 to be executed. Execution of this POP instruction causes the top-of-stack value, 0055 hex, to be copied into the CX-register and the SP-register to be incremented by 2. After execution, the SS:SP register pair points one location beyond the end of the stack segment, indicating that the stack is empty once again.

Pressing F10 again causes the instruction

```
XCHG  CX,DX
```

to be executed. The DX-register value changed from 5500 hexadecimal to 0055 hexa-

FIGURE 2.13 Status of stack segment after execution of instruction in line 49 of Program Listing 2.1

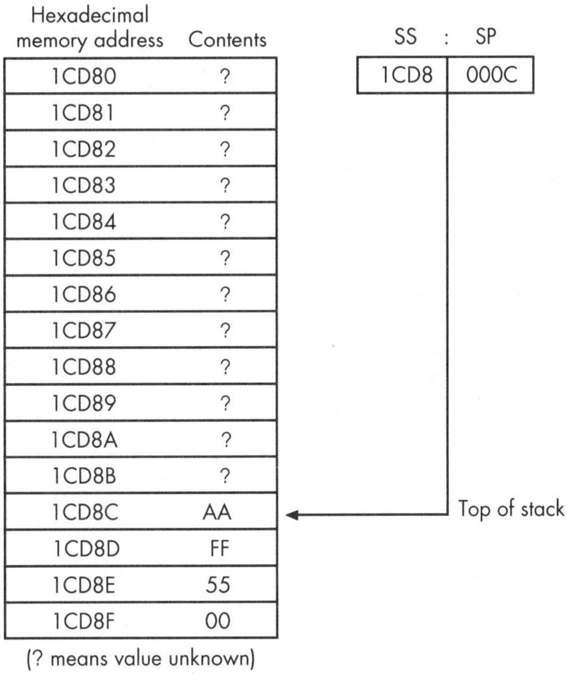

Hexadecimal memory address	Contents
1CD80	?
1CD81	?
1CD82	?
1CD83	?
1CD84	?
1CD85	?
1CD86	?
1CD87	?
1CD88	?
1CD89	?
1CD8A	?
1CD8B	?
1CD8C	AA
1CD8D	FF
1CD8E	55
1CD8F	00

(? means value unknown)

SS	:	SP
1CD8		000C

Top of stack (1CD8C)

SCREEN IMAGE 2.14

```
 File  Edit  View  Search  Run  Watch  Options  Calls                                Help
─┤•├──────────sourcel CS:IP ex_2_1.asm (ACTIVE)──────────────┤^├──┤•├reg┤^├─
45:              MOV     CX,WORD2               ;00 55 AA FF FF AA    AX = FFAA
46:              MOV     DX,WORD4               ;00 55 AA FF FF AA    BX = AAFF
47:              XCHG    DH,DL                  ;00 55 AA FF FF AA    CX = FFAA
48:              PUSH    AX                     ;00 55 AA FF FF AA    DX = 5500
49:              PUSH    CX                     ;00 55 AA FF FF AA    SP = 000E
50:              POP     AX                     ;FF AA AA FF FF AA    BP = 0000
51:              POP     CX                     ;FF AA AA FF 00 55    SI = 0000
52:              XCHG    CX,DX                  ;FF AA AA FF 55 00    DI = 0000
53:      ;                                                            DS = 1CD9
54:              MOV     WORD1,BX               ;WORD1 BYTE1    FF H  ES = 1CC4
55:                                             ;      BYTE2    AA H  SS = 1CD8
56:              MOV     BYTE3,DL               ;WORD2 BYTE3    55 H  CS = 1CD4
57:              MOV     BYTE4,CL               ;      BYTE4    00 H  IP = 001E
58:              MOV     WORD3,CX               ;WORD3          00 H  FL = 0202
59:                                             ;               55 H
60:              MOV     WORD4,AX               ;WORD4          AA H NV UP EI PL
61:                                             ;               FF H NZ NA PO NC
─┤•├──────────memory1 byte DS:0000 (ACTIVE)──────────────┤^├─
1CD9:0000   00 55 AA FF FF AA 55 00 4E 42 30 32 EE 00 00 00 .U....U
─┤•├──────────────memory2 word ss:0──────────────────────┤^├─
1CD8:0000   0000 0055 FFAA 1CD9 001E 1CD4 0102 0055

<F8=Trace> <F10=Step> <F5=Go> <F6=Window> <F3=Display> <Sh+F3=Memory Format>
```

decimal, and the CX-register value changed from 0055 hexadecimal to 5500 hexadecimal. That is, the values of the DX and CX registers were interchanged by the execution of this instruction.

Pressing F10 five more times causes the five MOV instructions in lines 54–60 of Program Listing 2.1 to be executed. The destination operand in each of these MOV instructions is the location of a byte or word in the data segment. These five instructions modify the data segment values. The reader should perform these steps slowly, making sure that he or she can account for the changes that occur with each step,

FIGURE 2.14 Status of stack segment after execution of instruction in line 50 of Program Listing 2.1

Hexadecimal memory address	Contents
1CD80	?
1CD81	?
1CD82	?
1CD83	?
1CD84	?
1CD85	?
1CD86	?
1CD87	?
1CD88	?
1CD89	?
1CD8A	?
1CD8B	?
1CD8C	AA
1CD8D	FF
1CD8E	55
1CD8F	00

SS	SP
1CD8	000E

SS : SP 1CD8:000E → 1CD8E (Top of stack)

(? means value unknown)

especially changes to the data segment shown in the memory1 window. The processor state that exists after the execution of these five MOV instructions is shown in Screen Image 2.15.

To terminate execution of the CodeView program, the File menu is utilized. The File menu is accessed by pressing the Alt key followed by the F key. Pressing the X key selects the Exit item, which causes CodeView to return control to DOS.

SCREEN IMAGE 2.15

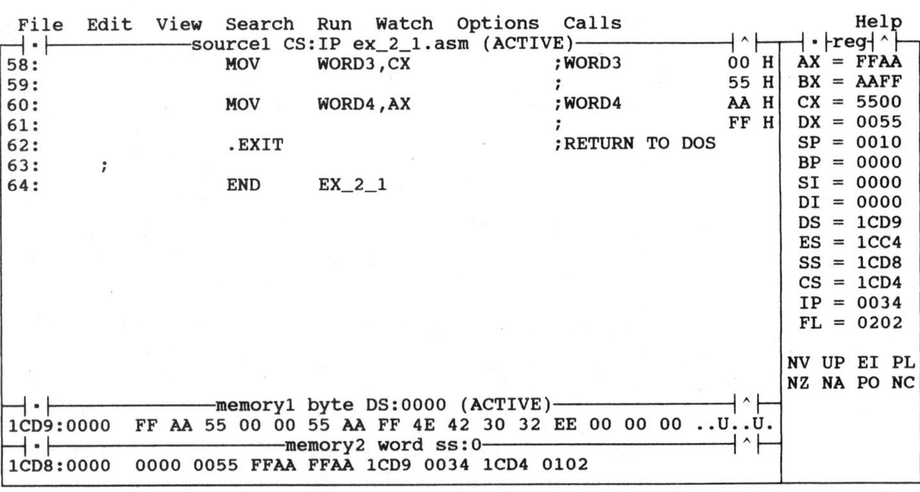

```
 File  Edit  View  Search  Run  Watch  Options  Calls                     Help
-source1 CS:IP ex_2_1.asm (ACTIVE)-                                      -reg-
58:            MOV     WORD3,CX                ;WORD3          00 H  AX = FFAA
59:                                            ;               55 H  BX = AAFF
60:            MOV     WORD4,AX                ;WORD4          AA H  CX = 5500
61:                                            ;               FF H  DX = 0055
62:            .EXIT                           ;RETURN TO DOS        SP = 0010
63:     ;                                                            BP = 0000
64:            END     EX_2_1                                        SI = 0000
                                                                     DI = 0000
                                                                     DS = 1CD9
                                                                     ES = 1CC4
                                                                     SS = 1CD8
                                                                     CS = 1CD4
                                                                     IP = 0034
                                                                     FL = 0202

                                                                    NV UP EI PL
                                                                    NZ NA PO NC
-memory1 byte DS:0000 (ACTIVE)-
1CD9:0000  FF AA 55 00 00 55 AA FF 4E 42 30 32 EE 00 00 00 ..U..U.
-memory2 word ss:0-
1CD8:0000  0000 0055 FFAA FFAA 1CD9 0034 1CD4 0102
<F8=Trace> <F10=Step> <F5=Go> <F6=Window> <F3=Display> <Sh+F3=Memory Format>
```

2.6 Additional Capabilities in the 80286 Assembly Language

The 80286 assembly language provides several additional capabilities for stack operations in data transfer instructions. The PUSH instruction can have an immediate operand.

EXAMPLE

The instruction

```
PUSH    324
```

is legal in the 80286 assembly language. In the 8088/8086 assembly language, this instruction would have to be replaced with two instructions like the following:

```
MOV   AX, 324
PUSH  AX
```

■

As well, two stack manipulation instructions are provided: PUSHA (push all) and POPA (pop all). The **PUSHA instruction** has the following general form:

[⟨*label*⟩] PUSHA [⟨*comment*⟩]

The PUSHA instruction causes the values of all eight 16-bit general registers to be pushed onto the stack. The order in which the general registers are pushed onto the stack is AX, CX, DX, BX, SP, BP, SI, and DI. The value that is pushed onto the stack for the SP-register is the value that the SP-register had before the first register (AX) was pushed onto the stack.

The **POPA instruction** has the following general form:

[⟨*label*⟩] POPA [⟨*comment*⟩]

The POPA instruction causes the top eight words on the stack to be popped into the eight general registers. The order in which the registers are popped from the stack is DI, SI, BP, SP, BX, DX, CX, and AX. The fourth value popped is actually discarded rather than being popped into the SP-register. The SP-register is automatically incremented by 2 as each word is popped from the stack.

The PUSHA and POPA instructions are convenient for saving and restoring the general registers in a subprocedure, and they are discussed further in Chapter 5.

There is one difference in execution of PUSH between the Intel 8088/8086 microprocessor and the Intel 80286 and higher microprocessors. This difference occurs in the case where the PUSH operand is the SP-register. The instruction

```
PUSH  SP
```

in the Intel 80286 pushes the value that existed in the SP-register just prior to execution of the instruction. In the Intel 8088/8086, the SP-register is first decremented by 2 and the resulting value then is pushed onto the stack.

The instruction

```
POP  SP
```

executes the same in both microprocessors. The value in the SP-register after execution is the value that was at the top of the stack just prior to the execution, and there is no additional increment of the SP-register by 2.

EXAMPLE Suppose the SP-register contains the value 0100 hexadecimal when the instructions

```
PUSH  SP
POP   SP
```

are executed. With the Intel 8088/8086 microprocessor, the resulting SP-register value is 00FE hex. With the Intel 80286 microprocessor, the resulting SP-register value is 0100 hex. ■

NUMERIC EXERCISES

2.1 Fill in the blanks in the following table:

Eight-Bit Binary Bit Pattern	Modulo 2^8 Interpretation	Two's Complement Interpretation
10110111		
	145	
		−115

2.2 Fill in the blanks in the following table:

Eight-Bit Binary Bit Pattern	Sign Magnitude Interpretation	One's Complement Interpretation	Excess 128 Interpretation
10110111			
	125		
		−115	

2.3 State the range of integers that can be represented with 12-bit binary numbers using (a) the modulo 2^{12} number system, (b) the two's complement number system, (c) the one's complement number system, (d) the sign magnitude number system, and (e) the excess 2^{11} number system.

2.4 Translate the character string

```
IBM PC
```

to six 8-bit binary codes (one per character) using the extended ASCII character code table in Appendix E. State the codes in both binary and hexadecimal.

2.5 Represent each of the following decimal integers as a 16-bit signed binary integer in two's complement form.

a. 324 **b.** −324 **c.** 5284
d. −3333 **e.** −16

2.6 Represent each of the following decimal integers as a 16-bit unsigned binary integer in modulo 65536 form.

a. 397 **b.** 500 **c.** 1000
d. 24000 **e.** 61440

PROGRAMMING EXERCISES

2.1 The program in Program Listing 2.3 contains four checkpoints indicated by comments in lines 36, 44, 50, and 55. Fill in the blanks in the following table to show the hexadecimal values of the AX, BX, CX, DX, SP, and flags registers at each of these points during program execution. Fill in the blanks in the second table to show the hexadecimal values in the stack segment at each of these points during program execution. Use the question mark character (?) for values that are unknown. Verify your answers by tracing the program with DEBUG or CodeView.

Register Values at Each Checkpoint						
Checkpoint	AX	BX	CX	DX	SP	Flags
A						
B						
C						
D						

Stack Segment Values at Each Checkpoint

Stack Segment Offset	Stack Segment Value at Checkpoint A	B	C	D
0000				
0001				
0002				
0003				
0004				
0005				
0006				
0007				
0008				
0009				
000A				
000B				
000C				
000D				
000E				
000F				

2.2 The program in Program Listing 2.4 contains three checkpoints indicated by comments in lines 37, 45, and 50. Place the symbolic names ALPHA, BETA, GAMMA, LAMDA, and OMEGA in the appropriate positions in the first column of the following table. Fill in the blanks in the third, fourth, and fifth columns with the hexadecimal values that would appear in the data segment at the indicated points during program execution. Verify your answers by tracing the program with DEBUG or CodeView.

Data Segment Values at Each Checkpoint

Symbolic Name	Data Segment Offset	Value at Checkpoint A	B	C
	0000			
	0001			
	0002			
	0003			
	0004			
	0005			
	0006			
	0007			

```
            PAGE    80,132
;==========================================================
;
;                        PROGRAM LISTING 2.3
;
;                      PROGRAM FOR EXERCISE 2.1
;
;==========================================================
            .MODEL  SMALL,BASIC,FARSTACK
;==========================================================
;
; S T A C K   S E G M E N T   D E F I N I T I O N
;
            .STACK  16
;==========================================================
;
; D A T A   S E G M E N T   D E F I N I T I O N
;
            .FARDATA DATA
;
FLAGS       DW      0000110011010101B
;==========================================================
;
; C O D E   S E G M E N T   D E F I N I T I O N
;
            .CODE
            ASSUME  DS:DATA
PR_2_1:     MOV     AX,SEG DATA
            MOV     DS,AX
            NOP
;
```

```
            MOV     AX,0123H
            MOV     BX,4567H
            MOV     CX,89ABH
            MOV     DX,0CDEFH
;*** CHECKPOINT A ***
            PUSH    FLAGS
            POPF
            PUSH    AX
            PUSH    BX
            PUSHF
            PUSH    CX
            PUSH    DX
;*** CHECKPOINT B ***
            POP     AX
            POP     BX
            POPF
            PUSH    AX
            PUSH    BX
;*** CHECKPOINT C ***
            POP     DX
            POP     CX
            POP     BX
            POP     AX
;*** CHECKPOINT D ***
            .EXIT                           ;RETURN TO DOS
            END     PR_2_1
```

```
            PAGE    80,132
;====================================================================
;
;                     PROGRAM LISTING 2.4
;
;                   PROGRAM FOR EXERCISE 2.2
;
;====================================================================
            .MODEL  SMALL,BASIC,FARSTACK
;====================================================================
;
; S T A C K   S E G M E N T   D E F I N I T I O N
;
            .STACK  16
;====================================================================
;
; D A T A   S E G M E N T   D E F I N I T I O N
;
           .FARDATA DATA
ALPHA       DB      35
BETA        DW      01ABH
GAMMA       DW      45EFH
LAMDA       DB      CONSTANT
OMEGA       DW      67CDH
CONSTANT    EQU     10001001B
;
;====================================================================
;
; C O D E   S E G M E N T   D E F I N I T I O N
;
            .CODE
            ASSUME  DS:DATA
PR_2_2:
            MOV     AX,SEG DATA             ;SET DS-REGISTER TO POINT
            MOV     DS,AX                   ;TO DATA SEGMENT
            NOP
;*** CHECKPOINT A ***
```

```
            MOV     AH,CONSTANT
            MOV     AL,ALPHA
            MOV     BX,GAMMA
            XCHG    AH,BH
            XCHG    AX,BETA
            MOV     ALPHA,AH
            MOV     LAMDA,AL
;*** CHECKPOINT B ***
            MOV     CX,OMEGA
            XCHG    BL,CH
            MOV     GAMMA,BX
            MOV     OMEGA,CX
;*** CHECKPOINT C ***
            .EXIT                               ;RETURN TO DOS
            END     PR_2_2
```

CHAPTER 3

Integer Arithmetic

The previous chapter presented various ways of representing data inside a computer. The pseudo-operations for defining and initializing data in an 8088/8086 assembly language program and the instructions for data transfer were discussed. To solve some simple, meaningful problems with assembly language programs, instructions for performing arithmetic computations are needed. Integer arithmetic operations are the subject of this chapter. Integer addition and subtraction in the binary number system are discussed first. Then the instructions for performing integer arithmetic operations in an 8088/8086 assembly language program are presented. As well, the notion of arithmetic overflow is discussed in detail.

3.1 Binary Arithmetic

This section is devoted to arithmetic in binary number systems with finite bounds, the type of number systems used in computers. In mathematics, we are accustomed to working with unbounded number systems, number systems that range from negative infinity to positive infinity. Within the finite bounds of a digital computer, we are restricted to working with bounded number systems. The discussion is limited to addition and subtraction in the modulo 2^n and two's complement number systems (the number systems of the 8088/8086). Table 3.1 shows the range of integer values that can be represented by 8-bit binary numbers in both the unsigned and the signed two's complement number systems.

Addition

To add the n-bit binary integer

$$A_{n-1}A_{n-2} \cdots A_2 A_1 A_0$$

TABLE 3.1
Range of integer values for 8-bit unsigned and signed two's complement number systems

Bit Pattern	Unsigned	Signed Two's Complement
00000000	0	0
00000001	1	1
00000010	2	2
00000011	3	3
00000100	4	4
00000101	5	5
00000110	6	6
00000111	7	7
.	.	.
.	.	.
.	.	.
01111100	124	124
01111101	125	125
01111110	126	126
01111111	127	127
10000000	128	−128
10000001	129	−127
10000010	130	−126
10000011	131	−125
.	.	.
.	.	.
.	.	.
11111000	248	−8
11111001	249	−7
11111010	250	−6
11111011	251	−5
11111100	252	−4
11111101	253	−3
11111110	254	−2
11111111	255	−1

to the n-bit binary integer

$$B_{n-1}B_{n-2} \cdots B_2 B_1 B_0$$

the following algorithm can be used:

```
CARRY = 0
I = 0
WHILE I < n
      SUM = A_I + B_I + CARRY
      S_I = rightmost bit of SUM
      CARRY = SUM with rightmost bit removed
      I = I + 1
ENDWHILE
```

The output of this algorithm is the n-bit binary sum

$$S_{n-1}S_{n-2} \cdots S_2 S_1 S_0$$

and the carry out of the most significant bit position, CARRY. There are only eight possibilities for the addition

$A_I + B_I +$ CARRY

which produces a sum bit, S_I, and a carry into the next-highest bit position. These possibilities are summarized in Table 3.2. Due to similarities, only four possibilities are significant:

1. All three bits are zero:

   $0 + 0 + 0 = 00 \qquad S_I = 0 \qquad \text{Carry} = 0$

2. Exactly one of the three bits is a 1:

   $0 + 0 + 1 = 01 \qquad S_I = 1 \qquad \text{Carry} = 0$

3. Exactly two of the three bits are 1:

   $0 + 1 + 1 = 10 \qquad S_I = 0 \qquad \text{Carry} = 1$

4. All three bits are 1:

   $1 + 1 + 1 = 11 \qquad S_I = 1 \qquad \text{Carry} = 1$

TABLE 3.2 Addition of two corresponding bits and a carry (in) producing a sum bit and a carry (out)

A_I	B_I	Carry (In)	Carry (Out)	S_I
0	0	0	0	0
0	0	1	0	1
0	1	0	0	1
0	1	1	1	0
1	0	0	0	1
1	0	1	1	0
1	1	0	1	0
1	1	1	1	1

EXAMPLES

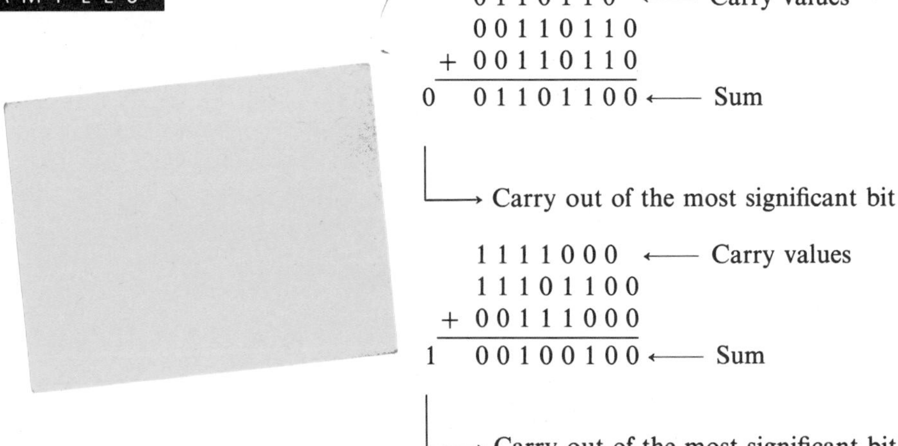

```
       0 1 1 0 1 1 0   <---- Carry values
       0 0 1 1 0 1 1 0
     + 0 0 1 1 0 1 1 0
     -----------------
  0    0 1 1 0 1 1 0 0 <---- Sum
  |
  |___> Carry out of the most significant bit

       1 1 1 1 0 0 0   <---- Carry values
       1 1 1 0 1 1 0 0
     + 0 0 1 1 1 0 0 0
     -----------------
  1    0 0 1 0 0 1 0 0 <---- Sum
  |
  |___> Carry out of the most significant bit
```

■

As far as the computer is concerned, binary addition can be handled in the same manner for both the modulo 2^n and the two's complement number systems. The difference is the way in which the operands and the sum are interpreted. Note that, in this regard, a two's complement machine has the advantage over a one's complement machine. With a two's complement machine, one circuit can perform two kinds of additions. With a one's complement machine, separate circuits are needed for unsigned and signed addition. Table 3.3 shows some examples of 8-bit binary addition in both the modulo 2^8 and the two's complement number systems.

TABLE 3.3
Binary addition with both modulo 2^8 and two's complement number systems

Addition Operation	Modulo 2^8 Interpretation (Unsigned)	Two's Complement Interpretation (Signed)
11111000	248	−8
00000101	5	5
0 11111101	253	−3
00110110	54	54
00110110	54	54
0 01101100	108	108
11011100	220	−36
00001100	12	12
0 11101000	232	−24
↑ Carry		

Subtraction

Most computers perform subtraction by adding the two's complement of the subtrahend to the minuend. That is, the subtraction operation is replaced by a two's complement operation followed by an addition operation. As far as the computer is concerned, binary subtraction can be handled in this manner for both the modulo 2^n and the two's complement number systems. The difference is, again, the way in which the operands and the result are interpreted. Table 3.4 shows some examples of 8-bit

TABLE 3.4
Binary subtraction with both modulo 2^n and two's complement interpretations

Subtraction Operation	Modulo 2^n Interpretation (Unsigned)	Two's Complement Interpretation (Signed)
01101011 Minuend	107	107
−00110100 Subtrahend	−52	−52
01101011 Minuend		107
+11001100 Two's complement		+(−52)
1 00110111	55	55
11100111 Minuend	231	−25
−10111100 Subtrahend	−188	−(−68)
11100111 Minuend		−25
+01000100 Two's complement		+68
1 00101011	43	43
11011011 Minuend	219	−37
−00011001 Subtrahend	−25	−25
11011011 Minuend		−37
+11100111 Two's complement		+(−25)
1 11000010	194	−62
↑ Carry		

binary subtractions and their interpretations in both the modulo 2^n and the two's complement number systems.

Arithmetic Overflow

The range of integers that can be represented with n-bit binary numbers is 0 to $2^n - 1$ in the modulo 2^n number system and -2^{n-1} to $+2^{n-1} - 1$ in the two's complement number system. For $n = 8$, the ranges are 0 to 255 and -128 to $+127$, respectively. If an arithmetic operation produces a result that is outside the range of integers for the number system being used, then a condition called **arithmetic overflow** occurs, which is discussed in Section 3.4. Table 3.5 shows some examples of 8-bit binary additions that result in an arithmetic overflow in at least one of the two number systems. Note that in each of the examples in Table 3.5, if the sum is extended by one bit, the carry bit, then the sum is correct. Thus, on overflow, the sum produced is actually the lower n bits (8 bits in Table 3.5) of the correct sum.

TABLE 3.5 Binary addition with both modulo 2^n and two's complement interpretations

Addition Operation	Modulo 2^n Interpretation (Unsigned)	Two's Complement Interpretation (Signed)
01111110	126	126
01111100	124	124
0 11111010	250	−6
		(Overflow)
11111100	252	−4
00001100	12	12
1 00001000	8	8
	(Overflow)	
10000001	129	−127
10011001	153	−103
1 00011010	26	26
↑ Carry	(Overflow)	(Overflow)

3.2 Integer Arithmetic Instructions

The Intel 8088/8086 provides a set of instructions for performing integer arithmetic operations. These instructions can operate on either 8-bit or 16-bit operands, which can be interpreted as either unsigned integer values (modulo 2^8 and modulo 2^{16} number systems) or signed integer values (two's complement number system). Table 3.1 shows the range of integer values that can be represented by 8-bit binary numbers in both unsigned form and signed two's complement form. For 16-bit operands, the ranges are 0 to 65,535 for the unsigned integer form, and −32,768 to +32,767 for the signed two's complement form.

For addition and subtraction operations, the microprocessor is unaware of the interpretation being applied to the operands, and the same instructions are used for both types of operands. For multiplication and division operations, the microprocessor must know the interpretation being applied to the operands, and it provides two sets of instructions, one set for unsigned operands and the other for signed two's complement operands. Programs must be written in such a way that consistent interpretations are applied.

The interpretation of a binary integer is applied when a value is input for the integer or when the value of the integer is being output. The I/O subprocedures used in the example programs of this book include two procedures for 16-bit decimal input (GETDEC and GETDEC$) and two procedures for 16-bit decimal output (PUTDEC and PUTDEC$).

GETDEC This procedure accepts a 16-bit integer from the keyboard in signed decimal form and returns it to the caller. The range of integers allowed is −32,768 to +32,767. The procedure does not prompt for the input—that responsibility belongs to the caller. Error messages are output to the video display in response to input errors, and then another input is accepted. The procedure expects no inputs from the caller. The input value is returned to the caller in the AX-register.

GETDEC$ This procedure accepts a 16-bit integer from the keyboard in unsigned decimal form and returns it to the caller. The range of integers allowed is 0 to 65,535. The procedure does not prompt for the input—that responsibility belongs to the caller. Error messages are output to the video display in response to input errors, and then another input is accepted. The procedure expects no inputs from the caller. The input value is returned to the caller in the AX-register.

PUTDEC This procedure displays a 16-bit integer in signed decimal form, beginning at the current cursor position on the video screen. The procedure expects the value to be displayed in the AX-register and a display code in the BH-register. The display code is interpreted as follows:

$BH < 0 \rightarrow$ Left-justify output in a six-character field

$BH = 0 \rightarrow$ Display with no leading or trailing blanks

$BH > 0 \rightarrow$ Right-justify output in a six-character field

PUTDEC$ This procedure displays a 16-bit integer in unsigned decimal form, beginning at the current cursor position on the video screen. The procedure expects the value to be displayed in the AX-register and a display code in the BH-register. The display code is interpreted as follows:

$BH < 0 \rightarrow$ Left-justify output in a six-character field

$BH = 0 \rightarrow$ Display with no leading or trailing blanks

$BH > 0 \rightarrow$ Right-justify output in a six-character field

Addition and Subtraction

The general-purpose binary addition instruction is the ADD instruction, and the general-purpose subtraction instruction is the SUB instruction. The **ADD instruction** has the following general form:

[⟨*label*⟩] ADD ⟨*destination*⟩,⟨*source*⟩ [⟨*comment*⟩]

in which ⟨*source*⟩ identifies the location of the addend and ⟨*destination*⟩ identifies the location of the augend that is to be replaced by the sum. This instruction causes the source operand to be added to the destination operand, and the destination operand to be replaced by the sum.

The **SUB instruction** has the following general form:

[<*label*>] SUB <*destination*>,<*source*> [<*comment*>]

in which <*source*> identifies the location of the subtrahend and <*destination*> identifies the location of the minuend that is to be replaced by the difference. This instruction causes the source operand to be subtracted from the destination operand, and the destination operand to be replaced by the difference. The subtraction is actually performed by adding the minuend (destination operand), the one's complement of the subtrahend (source operand), and 1. This operation, in effect, adds the two's complement of the subtrahend to the minuend.

The type attribute of the two operands must match for both the ADD and SUB instructions (i.e., both byte or both word). Figure 3.1 shows the possible combinations of destination and source operands. If the destination operand is a general register, then the source operand can be either a general register, a memory location, or an immediate value. If the destination operand is a memory location, then the source operand can be either a general register or an immediate value.

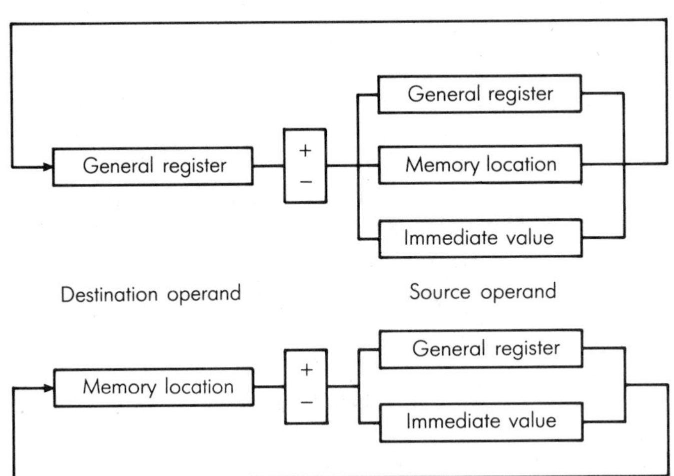

FIGURE 3.1 Allowable operands for ADD and SUB instructions

EXAMPLES

The instruction

```
ADD  BH, DL
```

adds the 8-bit value in the DL-register to the 8-bit value in the BH-register, leaving the sum in the BH-register.

The instruction

```
ADD  DX, 17
```

adds the constant 17 to the 16-bit value in the DX-register, leaving the sum in the DX-register.

Suppose the data segment definition for a program contains the following definitions

```
X  DW  ?
Y  DW  ?
Z  DW  ?
```

and that the GETDEC procedure has been used to input signed integer values for X and Y. The following instructions implement the assignment:

```
Z = 2X - 2Y

MOV  AX,X
ADD  AX,X
SUB  AX,Y
SUB  AX,Y
MOV  Z,AX
```

The first instruction places a copy of the value of variable X into the AX-register. The second instruction adds the value of variable X to the value of the AX-register, leaving the result in the AX-register. The AX-register now contains the value $X + X = 2X$. The third instruction subtracts the value of variable Y from the value of the AX-register, leaving the result in the AX-register. The AX-register now contains the value $2X - Y$. The fourth instruction again subtracts the value of variable Y from the value of the AX-register, leaving the result in the AX-register. The AX-register now contains the value $2X - 2Y$. The last instruction replaces the value of variable Z with a copy of the result (the value in the AX-register). ■

The ADD and SUB instructions perform straight binary addition and subtraction. The same instructions are used for both unsigned and signed integer operations. It is the programmer's responsibility to make sure that interpretation of the operands is consistent (i.e., both operands are interpreted as unsigned integers, or both operands are interpreted as signed two's complement integers). Table 3.3 and Table 3.5 show some examples of 8-bit binary additions and their interpretations for both unsigned and signed integer forms. Table 3.4 shows some examples of 8-bit binary subtractions and their interpretations for both unsigned and signed integer forms.

The OF, SF, ZF, PF, CF, and AF bits of the flags register are all affected by execution of ADD and SUB instructions.

OF In an addition operation, if the carry into the most significant bit differs from the carry out of the most significant bit, then the OF bit is set. Otherwise, the OF bit is cleared. (Recall that subtraction is performed by complement and addition.) If the two operands represent signed two's complement integers, then the OF bit reflects whether or not execution of the ADD or SUB instruction resulted in an overflow.

SF The SF bit is a copy of the most significant bit of the result of the addition or subtraction operation. If the two operands represent signed two's complement numbers, then the SF bit reflects the sign of the result.

ZF If the result of the addition or subtraction operation is zero, then the ZF bit is set. Otherwise, the ZF bit is cleared.

PF The PF bit is set to reflect the parity of the low-order 8 bits of the result. (See the discussion of the flags register in Chapter 1.)

CF If an addition operation produces a carry of 1 out of the most significant bit (bit 7 for byte addition, bit 15 for word addition), or if a subtraction operation requires a borrow into the most significant bit, then the CF bit is set. Otherwise, the CF bit is cleared. If the two operands represent unsigned integer values, then the CF bit reflects whether or not execution of the ADD or SUB instruction resulted in an overflow. (Arithmetic overflow is discussed in detail in Section 3.4.) The CF bit also is useful in performing addition and subtraction operations on operands that are longer than 16 bits. (See Chapter 7 for more details on this subject.)

AF The AF bit is handled in a manner similar to the CF bit. However, the AF bit reflects the carry out of or the borrow into bit 3. The AF bit is used in addition and subtraction operations involving binary coded decimal (BCD) numbers. (The AF bit is discussed further in Chapter 11.)

Incrementing and Decrementing

The 8088/8086 assembly language includes two instructions expressly for the frequently used operations of adding 1 to a value and subtracting 1 from a value: the INC and DEC instructions. The **INC instruction** has the following general form:

[⟨*label*⟩] `INC` ⟨*destination*⟩ [⟨*comment*⟩]

in which ⟨*destination*⟩ identifies the location of the value to be incremented. This instruction causes the value in the register or memory location specified by the ⟨*destination*⟩ operand to be incremented by 1.

The **DEC instruction** has the following general form:

[⟨*label*⟩] `DEC` ⟨*destination*⟩ [⟨*comment*⟩]

in which ⟨*destination*⟩ identifies the location of the value to be decremented. This instruction causes the value in the register or memory location specified by the ⟨*destination*⟩ operand to be decremented by 1.

For both the INC and DEC instructions, the ⟨*destination*⟩ operand can be a general register (byte or word) or a memory location (byte or word).

Both the INC and DEC instructions affect the OF, SF, ZF, AF, and PF bits in the flags register.

OF In an addition operation, if the carry into the most significant bit differs from the carry out of the most significant bit, then the OF bit is set. Otherwise, the OF bit is cleared. If the operand represents a signed two's complement integer, then the OF bit reflects whether or not the increment or decrement resulted in an overflow.

SF The SF bit is a copy of the most significant bit of the result of the increment or decrement operation. If the operand represents a signed two's complement number, then the SF bit reflects the sign of the result.

ZF If the result of the increment or decrement operation is zero, then the ZF bit is set. Otherwise, the ZF bit is cleared.

AF If an increment operation produces a carry of 1 from bit 3 or a decrement operation produces a borrow into bit 3, then the AF bit is set. Otherwise, the AF bit is cleared.

PF The PF bit is set to reflect the parity of the low-order 8 bits of the result.

Note that the CF bit is not affected by execution of an INC or DEC instruction, which is important to remember when using the INC instruction or the DEC instruction with unsigned integer values. This pitfall is illustrated in Program Listing 4.1.

Negation

The 8088/8086 assembly language provides an instruction to perform the unary minus operation (negation): the NEG instruction. The **NEG instruction** has the following general form:

[⟨*label*⟩] NEG ⟨*destination*⟩ [⟨*comment*⟩]

in which ⟨*destination*⟩ identifies the location of the value to be negated. This instruction performs the two's complement of the value in the general register or memory location specified by the ⟨*destination*⟩ operand. The two's complement operation is actually performed by subtracting the destination operand from zero. Recall that subtraction is performed by adding the minuend (zero in this case), the one's complement of the subtrahend (the value to be negated in this case), and 1. The ⟨*destination*⟩ operand can be a general register (byte or word) or a memory location (byte or word). The destination operand must be interpreted as a signed two's complement integer value for the NEG operation to have meaning.

Execution of a NEG instruction affects the OF, SF, ZF, AF, PF, and CF bits in the flags register.

OF In an addition operation, if the carry into the most significant bit differs from the carry out of the most significant bit, then the OF bit is set. Otherwise, the OF bit is cleared. The 8088/8086 represents signed integers in two's complement form, and, as mentioned, the NEG operation has meaning only for signed integers. With the two's complement representation, the range of integers that can be represented is −128 to +127 for byte operands and −32,768 to +32,767 for word operands. In each case, one value cannot be successfully negated: For byte operands, this value is −128 (i.e., there is no representation for +128 in 8-bit two's complement); for word operands, this value is −32,768 (i.e., there is no representation for +32,768 in 16-bit two's complement). Taking the two's complement of the byte value −128 or the word value −32,768 results in an arithmetic overflow and in the setting of the OF bit. In all other cases, the OF bit is cleared.

SF The SF bit is a copy of the most significant bit (sign bit) of the result of the negation operation. That is, the SF bit reflects the sign of the result.

ZF If the result of the negation operation is zero, then the ZF bit is set. Otherwise, the ZF bit is cleared.

AF If the NEG operation requires a borrow into bit 3, then the AF bit is set. Otherwise, the AF bit is cleared.

PF The PF bit is set to reflect the parity of the low-order 8 bits of the result.

CF If the result of the negation operation is nonzero, then the CF bit is set. Otherwise, the CF bit is cleared. This situation occurs because of the way in which the 8088/8086 microprocessor performs the two's complement operation. The destination operand value is subtracted from zero. A subtraction is performed by adding the minuend, the one's complement of the subtrahend, and 1. Since this is a subtraction, the carry out of the sign bit is automatically inverted to reflect a borrow. That is, any nonzero value that is subtracted from zero requires a borrow into the most significant bit. However, zero can be subtracted from zero without borrowing. Table 3.6 lists some examples of the negation operation on byte values and the resulting value of the CF bit.

TABLE 3.6
Setting of the carry flag by execution of a NEG instruction

Destination Operand	Operation Performed
00000000	00000000 11111111 1 1 00000000 0 → CF
00000001	00000000 11111110 1 0 11111111 1 → CF
01111111	00000000 10000000 1 0 10000001 1 → CF
11111111	00000000 00000000 1 0 00000001 1 → CF

Multiplication

The 8088/8086 assembly language provides two integer multiply instructions: one for unsigned integer values (MUL) and one for signed two's complement integer values (IMUL). The **MUL instruction** has the following general form:

[⟨*label*⟩] MUL ⟨*source*⟩ [⟨*comment*⟩]

in which ⟨*source*⟩ identifies the location of the multiplier. The ⟨*source*⟩ operand can be either a general register (byte or word) or a memory location (byte or word). If the source operand has a type attribute of byte, then the MUL instruction causes the

8-bit unsigned integer value in the AL-register to be multiplied by the 8-bit unsigned integer value of the source operand. This multiplication produces a 16-bit unsigned integer product that replaces the value in the AX-register. If the source operand has a type attribute of word, then the MUL instruction causes the 16-bit unsigned integer value in the AX-register to be multiplied by the 16-bit unsigned integer value of the source operand. This multiplication produces a 32-bit unsigned integer product that replaces the value in the DX:AX register pair.

Execution of a MUL instruction affects the SF, ZF, AF, PF, OF, and CF bits in the flags register:

1. The SF, ZF, AF, and PF bits are undefined following execution of a MUL instruction.
2. If the upper half of the product (AH-register for byte multiplication, DX-register for word multiplication) is nonzero, then the OF and CF bits are set. Otherwise, the OF and CF bits are cleared. These bits indicate whether or not the product overflows 8 bits for byte multiplication or 16 bits for word multiplication.

EXAMPLES

The instruction

```
MUL BL
```

multiplies the 8-bit unsigned integer value in the AL-register by the 8-bit unsigned integer value in the BL-register, leaving the 16-bit unsigned integer product in the AX-register. If the AH-register is nonzero (i.e., the product does not fit in the 8-bit AL-register), then the OF and CF bits of the flags register are set.

Suppose the data segment definition for a program contains the variable definition

```
TWO DW  2
```

The instruction

```
MUL TWO
```

multiplies the 16-bit unsigned integer value in the AX-register by the 16-bit unsigned integer value of variable TWO, leaving the 32-bit unsigned integer product in the DX:AX register pair. If the DX-register is nonzero (i.e., the product does not fit in the 16-bit AX-register), then the OF and CF bits of the flags register are set. Note that the instruction

```
MUL TWO
```

could not be replaced by

```
MUL 2   ; SYNTACTICALLY ILLEGAL
```

because the MUL instruction cannot have an immediate operand. ■

The **IMUL instruction** has the following general form:

[⟨*label*⟩] IMUL ⟨*source*⟩ [⟨*comment*⟩]

in which ⟨*source*⟩ identifies the location of the multiplier. The source operand can be either a general register (byte or word) or a memory location (byte or word). If the source operand has a type attribute of byte, then the IMUL instruction causes the 8-bit signed integer value in the AL-register to be multiplied by the 8-bit signed integer value of the source operand. This multiplication produces a 16-bit signed integer product that replaces the value in the AX-register. If the source operand has a type attribute of word, then the IMUL instruction causes the 16-bit signed integer value in the AX-register to be multiplied by the 16-bit signed integer value of the source operand. This multiplication produces a 32-bit signed integer product that replaces the value in the DX:AX register pair.

Execution of an IMUL instruction affects the SF, ZF, AF, PF, OF, and CF bits of the flags register:

1. The SF, ZF, AF, and PF bits are undefined following execution of an IMUL instruction.
2. If the upper half of the product (AH-register for byte multiplication, DX-register for word multiplication) is the sign extension of the lower half, then the OF and CF bits are cleared. Otherwise, the OF and CF bits are set. These bits indicate whether or not the product overflows 8 bits for byte multiplication or 16 bits for word multiplication.

EXAMPLES

The instruction

```
IMUL BL
```

multiplies the 8-bit signed integer value in the AL-register by the 8-bit signed integer value in the BL-register, leaving the 16-bit product in the AX-register. If the AH-register is not the sign extension of the AL-register (i.e., if the product does not fit in the 8-bit AL-register), then the OF and CF bits of the flags register are set.

Suppose the data segment definition for a program contains the variable definition

```
MINUSTWO DW  -2
```

The instruction

```
IMUL MINUSTWO
```

multiplies the 16-bit signed integer value in the AX-register by the 16-bit signed integer value of variable MINUSTWO, leaving the 32-bit signed integer product in the DX:AX register pair. If the DX-register is not the sign extension of the AX-register (i.e., the product does not fit in the 16-bit AX-register), then the OF and CF bits of the flags register are set. Note that the instruction

```
IMUL MINUSTWO
```

could not be replaced by

```
IMUL -2  ; SYNTACTICALLY ILLEGAL
```

because the IMUL instruction cannot have an immediate operand. ■

Note that for both the MUL and IMUL instructions, the ⟨*source*⟩ operand cannot be an immediate value. Also, the destination operand is implicit. The multiplicand must always be in the AL-register for byte multiplication and in the AX-register for word multiplication. The double-length product is always left in the AX-register for byte multiplication and in the DX:AX register pair for word multiplication.

Table 3.7 lists some examples of byte multiplications for both signed and unsigned interpretations. The effect of the multiplication on the carry and overflow flags is also shown. Note that in the third example in the table, the AL and BL register values are specified as 11101000 and 00000101:

1. For the unsigned integer interpretation, these bit patterns represent 232 and 5. When multiplied using the MUL instruction, the product is 0000010010001000 (1160 decimal). The upper half of the product is nonzero, which means the product is greater than 255. Therefore, the OF and CF flag bits are set.
2. For the signed integer interpretation, these bit patterns represent −24 and 5. When multiplied using the IMUL instruction, the product is 1111111110001000 (−120 decimal). The upper half of the product is the sign extension of the lower half, which means the product is in the range −128 to +127. Therefore, the OF and CF flag bits are cleared.

TABLE 3.7
Signed and unsigned integer multiplication showing the influence of carry and overflow flags

AL and BL Registers	MUL BL				IMUL BL			
00011000	AH	AL	OF	CF	AH	AL	OF	CF
00000101	00000000	01111000	0	0	00000000	01111000	0	0
00111100	AH	AL	OF	CF	AH	AL	OF	CF
00000011	00000000	10110100	0	0	00000000	10110100	1	1
11101000	AH	AL	OF	CF	AH	AL	OF	CF
00000101	00000100	10001000	1	1	11111111	10001000	0	0
11111111	AH	AL	OF	CF	AH	AL	OF	CF
00000001	00000000	11111111	0	0	11111111	11111111	0	0
10000000	AH	AL	OF	CF	AH	AL	OF	CF
11111110	01111111	00000000	1	1	00000001	00000000	1	1

Division

The 8088/8086 assembly language provides two integer division instructions: one for unsigned integer values (DIV) and one for signed two's complement integer values (IDIV). The **DIV instruction** has the following general form:

[⟨*label*⟩] `DIV` ⟨*source*⟩ [⟨*comment*⟩]

in which ⟨*source*⟩ identifies the location of the divisor. The ⟨*source*⟩ operand can be either a general register (byte or word) or a memory location (byte or word). If the source operand has a type attribute of byte, then the DIV instruction causes the 16-bit unsigned integer value in the AX-register to be divided by the 8-bit unsigned integer value of the source operand. This division produces an 8-bit unsigned integer quotient and an 8-bit unsigned integer remainder. The quotient replaces the value in the AL-register, and the remainder replaces the value in the AH-register. If the source operand has a type attribute of word, then the DIV instruction causes the 32-bit unsigned integer value in the DX:AX register pair to be divided by the 16-bit unsigned integer value of the source operand. This division then produces a 16-bit unsigned integer quotient and a 16-bit unsigned integer remainder. The quotient replaces the value in the AX-register, and the remainder replaces the value in the DX-register.

The OF, SF, ZF, AF, PF, and CF bits of the flags register are undefined following execution of a DIV instruction. If the division results in a quotient that is too large for the destination (AL-register for byte division, AX-register for word division), then the quotient and remainder are undefined, and the processor generates a Type 0 interrupt. This condition occurs if the divisor is not greater than the high-order half of the dividend. Note that a divisor of zero is one such case. DOS services the Type 0 interrupt by displaying the message

```
Divide overflow
```

on the screen and then aborting program execution. Interrupts are discussed in Chapter 9.

EXAMPLES

The instruction

```
DIV BL
```

divides the 16-bit unsigned integer value in the AX-register by the 8-bit unsigned integer value in the BL-register, leaving the 8-bit unsigned integer quotient in the AL-register and the 8-bit unsigned integer remainder in the AH-register.

Supose the data segment definition for a program contains the variable definition

```
THREE DW  3
```

The instruction

```
DIV THREE
```

divides the 32-bit unsigned integer value in the DX:AX register pair by the 16-bit unsigned integer value of variable THREE, leaving the 16-bit unsigned integer quotient in the AX-register and the 16-bit unsigned integer remainder in the DX-register. Note that the instruction

```
DIV THREE
```

could not be replaced by

```
DIV 3  ; SYNTACTICALLY ILLEGAL
```

because the DIV instruction cannot have an immediate operand. ■

The **IDIV instruction** has the following general form:

[⟨*label*⟩] IDIV ⟨*source*⟩ [⟨*comment*⟩]

in which ⟨*source*⟩ identifies the location of the divisor. The ⟨*source*⟩ operand can be either a general register (byte or word) or a memory location (byte or word). If the source operand has a type attribute of byte, then the IDIV instruction causes the 16-bit signed integer value in the AX-register to be divided by the 8-bit signed integer value of the source operand. This division produces an 8-bit signed integer quotient and an 8-bit signed integer remainder. The quotient replaces the value in the AL-register, and the remainder replaces the value in the AH-register. If the source operand has a type attribute of word, then the IDIV instruction causes the 32-bit signed integer value in the DX:AX register pair to be divided by the 16-bit signed integer value of the source operand. This division produces a 16-bit signed integer quotient and a 16-bit signed integer remainder. The quotient replaces the value in the AX-register, and the remainder replaces the value in the DX-register.

The OF, SF, ZF, AF, PF, and CF bits in the flags register are undefined following execution of an IDIV instruction. If the division results in a quotient that is too large for the destination (AL-register for byte division, AX-register for word division), then the quotient and remainder are undefined, and the processor generates a Type 0 interrupt. This condition occurs if the divisor is not greater in magnitude than the high-order 9 bits of the dividend for byte division or the high-order 17 bits of the dividend for word division.

EXAMPLES

The instruction

```
IDIV BL
```

divides the 16-bit signed integer value in the AX-register by the 8-bit signed integer value in the BL-register, leaving the 8-bit signed integer quotient in the AL-register and the 8-bit signed integer remainder in the AH-register.

Suppose the data segment definition for a program contains the variable definition

```
MINUS3 DW  -3
```

The instruction

```
IDIV MINUS3
```

divides the 32-bit signed integer value in the DX:AX register pair by the 16-bit signed integer value of variable MINUS3, leaving the 16-bit signed integer quotient in the AX-register and the 16-bit signed integer remainder in the DX-register. Note that the instruction

```
IDIV MINUS3
```

could not be replaced by

```
IDIV -3   ; SYNTACTICALLY ILLEGAL
```

because the IDIV instruction cannot have an immediate operand. ■

Note that for both the DIV and IDIV instructions, the ⟨*source*⟩ operand cannot be an immediate value. Also, the destination operand is implicit. The dividend must always be in the AX-register for byte division and the DX:AX register pair for word division. The quotient is always left in the AL-register for byte division and in the AX-register for word division. The remainder is always left in the AH-register for byte division and in the DX-register for word division.

When performing a byte division, it is often necessary to expand the dividend from 8 bits to 16 bits prior to the division operation. As well, when performing a word division, it is often necessary to expand the dividend from 16 bits to 32 bits prior to the division operation. For unsigned integer division, this expansion is simply a matter of moving zero into the upper half of the double-length dividend. That is, to expand the 8-bit unsigned integer value in the AL-register to a 16-bit integer value in the AX-register, use the instruction

```
MOV AH, 0
```

As well, to expand the 16-bit unsigned integer value in the AX-register to a 32-bit value in the DX:AX register pair, use the instruction

```
MOV DX, 0
```

For signed two's complement integer values, this expansion requires extending the sign of the lower half throughout the upper half. The 8088/8086 assembly language provides two instructions for expanding an 8-bit or a 16-bit signed integer value to double length: change byte to word (CBW) and change word to double word (CWD).

The **CBW instruction** has the following general form:

[⟨*label*⟩] CBW [⟨*comment*⟩]

Execution of a CBW instruction causes the signed integer value in the AL-register to be expanded into a word that replaces the value in the AX-register. This expansion is accomplished by extending the sign bit (bit 7 of the AL-register) through the entire AH-register.

The **CWD instruction** has the following general form:

[⟨*label*⟩] CWD [⟨*comment*⟩]

Execution of a CWD instruction causes the signed integer value in the AX-register to be expanded to 32 bits, replacing the value in the DX:AX register pair. This expansion is accomplished by extending the sign bit (bit 15 of the AX-register) through the entire DX-register.

None of the bits in the flags register are affected by the execution of a CBW or a CWD instruction.

EXAMPLES

Suppose the data segment definition for a program contains the following variable definitions

```
N  DB  ?
X  DW  ?
```

Suppose further that the variable N has been given an unsigned integer value and that the variable X has been given a signed integer value.

The following instructions load the CL-register with the value of CEILING(N/2), the smallest integer that is greater than or equal to N/2:

```
MOV  AL,N
MOV  AH,0
MOV  DL,2
DIV  DL
ADD  AL,AH
MOV  CL,AL
```

The first instruction loads the AL-register with the unsigned integer value of the variable N. The second instruction expands this value to a 16-bit unsigned integer value in the AX-register. The third instruction loads the DL-register with the 8-bit divisor. The fourth instruction divides the 16-bit expansion of the value of the variable N by 2, leaving the quotient in the AL-register and the remainder in the AH-register. The remainder of the division is either 0 or 1. If the remainder is 0, then the quotient is the ceiling of N/2. If the remainder is 1, then 1 must be added to the quotient to produce the ceiling of N/2. That is, adding the remainder to the quotient produces the ceiling of N/2, which is the job of the fifth instruction. The last instruction moves the ceiling of N/2 to the CL-register.

The following instructions divide the signed integer value of variable X by 3, replacing the value of variable X with the quotient:

```
MOV   AX,X
CWD
MOV   BX,3
IDIV  BX
MOV   X,AX
```

Since the value of X is being interpreted as a signed integer value, the CWD instruction must be used to expand the dividend from 16 bits (in the AX-register) to 32 bits (in the DX:AX register pair). The CWD instruction copies the sign of the AX-register throughout the DX-register.

3.3 Programming Examples

This section presents two example programs. The first involves signed two's complement integers; the second involves unsigned integers.

Fahrenheit-to-Centigrade Conversion

Consider the problem of converting a temperature from degrees Fahrenheit to degrees centigrade. The formula to be used is as follows:

$$C = 5 * (F - 32)/9$$

in which F is temperature in degrees Fahrenheit and C is temperature in degrees centigrade. The resulting centigrade temperature is to be rounded to the nearest integer.

Program Listing 3.1. shows an 8088/8086 assembly language program that performs this conversion. Lines 2–10 are the prologue that explains the program's function. Lines 15–18 identify the external procedures that are called by this program. The GETDEC procedure is used to input the temperature in degrees Fahrenheit. The PUTDEC procedure is used to output the temperature in degrees centigrade. The PUTSTRNG procedure is used to display a prompt message to the user and to annotate the output. Lines 19–23 define the stack segment in the standard way.

Lines 24–30 define the constant data segment for the program. Two entries appear in the constant data segment definition. Line 29 defines a 42-character prompt message to ask the user to 'ENTER TEMPERATURE IN DEGREES FAHRENHEIT'. Line 30 defines a 42-character annotation message that describes the output as 'TEMPERATURE IN DEGREES CENTIGRADE'.

Lines 31–61 define the code segment for the program. The code segment contains the instructions for the main procedure of the program. The main procedure begins by initializing the segment register (lines 37 and 38). The ES-register is being used to point to the data group DGROUP because the constant data segment (see lines 28–30) is the only segment in DGROUP and both of its entries are going to be inputs to the PUTSTRNG procedure. The PUTSTRNG procedure expects the string address to be input in the ES:DI register pair.

Note that no ASSUME pseudo-operation is needed here to tell the assembler that the ES-register rather than the DS-register will be used to address DGROUP. The ASSUME pseudo-operation is not needed because the assembler does not have to generate the segment portion of the address for any of the references to the items in

```
           PAGE    80,132
;====================================================================
;
;                  PROGRAM LISTING 3.1
;
; PROGRAM  TO  CONVERT  A  TEMPERATURE  FROM
; FAHRENHEIT TO CENTIGRADE USING THE FORMULA
;
; C = 5*(F-32)/9  ROUNDED TO NEAREST INTEGER
;====================================================================
           DOSSEG
           .MODEL  SMALL,BASIC,FARSTACK
;====================================================================
                                       ;PROCEDURES TO
           EXTRN   GETDEC:FAR          ;GET 16-BIT DECIMAL INTEGER
           EXTRN   NEWLINE:FAR         ;DISPLAY NEWLINE CHARACTER
           EXTRN   PUTDEC:FAR          ;DISPLAY 16-BIT DECIMAL INTEGER
           EXTRN   PUTSTRNG:FAR        ;DISPLAY CHARACTER STRING
;====================================================================
;
; S T A C K   S E G M E N T   D E F I N I T I O N
;
           .STACK  256
;====================================================================
;
; C O N S T A N T   S E G M E N T   D E F I N I T I O N
;
           .CONST
PROMPT     DB      'ENTER TEMPERATURE IN DEGREES FAHRENHEIT   '
ANNOTATION DB      '      TEMPERATURE IN DEGREES CENTIGRADE   '
;====================================================================
;
; C O D E   S E G M E N T   D E F I N I T I O N
;
           .CODE
EX_3_1:
           MOV     AX,SEG DGROUP       ;SET ES-REGISTER TO ADDRESS
           MOV     ES,AX               ;    DGROUP
;
           LEA     DI,PROMPT           ;PROMPT FOR F_TEMP
           MOV     CX,42
           CALL    PUTSTRNG
           CALL    GETDEC              ;GET F_TEMP
           SUB     AX,32               ;C_TEMP = (F_TEMP -32) * 5 / 9
           MOV     BX,5
           IMUL    BX
           MOV     BX,9
           IDIV    BX
           XCHG    AX,DX               ;REMAIN = (F_TEMP-32)*5 rem 9
           MOV     BL,5                ;ROUND  = REMAIN / 5
           IDIV    BL
           CBW
           ADD     AX,DX               ;C_TEMP = C_TEMP + ROUND
;
           LEA     DI,ANNOTATION       ;DISPLAY C_TEMP
;          MOV     CX,42
           CALL    PUTSTRNG
           MOV     BH,0
           CALL    PUTDEC
           CALL    NEWLINE
           .EXIT                       ;RETURN TO DOS
;
           END     EX_3_1
;====================================================================
```

the constant data segment. The constants PROMPT and ANNOTATION are referenced only in LEA instructions. For an LEA instruction, the assembler has to generate only the offset portion of the address of the source operand.

Lines 40–42 display the prompt message on the screen using the PUTSTRNG subroutine. The call to GETDEC in line 43 is used to accept a signed integer value from the keyboard. GETDEC returns the input value in the AX-register. This discussion assumes that the input value is 11 (i.e., the value in the AX-register is now 11).

The SUB instruction in line 44 subtracts 32 from the AX-register, leaving a value of −21 in the AX-register. Lines 45 and 46 are used to multiply the value in the AX-register by 5. Note that it is *not* possible to replace these two instructions with the single instruction

```
IMUL 5
```

because the IMUL instruction cannot have an immediate value as its operand. The constant 5 is moved into the BX-register, and then the value in the AX-register is multiplied by the value in the BX-register. The IMUL instruction is used because temperature values can be positive or negative. The product (−105 in this example) is in the combined DX:AX register pair.

The next step is to divide this product by 9. If 16-bit division is used, then the 32-bit dividend must be in the combined DX:AX register pair. The product is already in the DX:AX register pair. Therefore, there is no need to worry about expanding the dividend before the divide. This situation is often the case when a division operation follows a multiplication operation. The division by 9 is performed by the two instructions in lines 47 and 48. Again, these two instructions could *not* be replaced by the single instruction

```
IDIV 5
```

because the IDIV instruction cannot have an immediate value as its operand. The IDIV instruction is used because the computation involves signed two's complement integer values. The quotient of the division (−11 in this example) is in the AX-register, and the remainder (−6 in this example) is in the DX-register.

The next step is to round the quotient to the nearest integer. The remainder of a division by 9 is in the range 0 to 8 if the dividend is positive and is in the range 0 to −8 if the dividend is negative. A remainder of *n* represents a fraction of *n*/9. If *n* is greater than or equal to 5, then 1 must be added to the quotient. If *n* is less than or equal to −5, then −1 must be added to the quotient. Otherwise, the quotient is left as is. This rounding can be accomplished by dividing the remainder by 5 and then adding the quotient of that division (either 0, 1, or −1) to the quotient of the division by 9, which is accomplished in lines 49–53 of Program Listing 3.1. In line 49, the remainder (−6) is moved into the AX-register, and the quotient (−11) is moved into the DX-register. Since the AX-register already contains the dividend in 16-bit form, and since the value in the DX-register must be protected, a byte division is performed. The constant 5 is moved into the BL-register (line 50), and the byte division is performed by the IDIV instruction in line 51. The quotient (−1) is in the AL-register, and the remainder (−1) is in the AH-register. The next step is to add the quotient of this division (−1 in the AL-register) to the quotient of the division by 9 (−11 in the DX-register). However, one of these quotients is a byte operand, and the other is a word operand. The two operands must be of the same type before the addition operation can be performed. The CBW instruction in line 52 expands the byte operand in the AL-register into a word operand in the AX-register by extending the sign of the AL-register through the entire AH-register. With the ADD instruction in line 53, the operand in the DX-register (−11) is added to the operand in the AX-register (−1), leaving the sum (−12) in the AX-register. This quantity in the AX-register is the centigrade temperature.

The instructions in lines 55–57 display the annotation message on the screen. Note that line 56 is a comment line—it is not an instruction to move 42 to the CX-register. Such an instruction would be redundant. The value 42 was moved to the CX-register by the MOV instruction in line 41, and none of the instructions between line 41 and line 56 modify the value of the CX-register. Therefore, the value 42 remains in the CX-register. The comment line in line 56 serves documentation purposes. It indicates that the string being displayed is 42 characters in length. The MOV instruction in line 58 sets the alignment code for the PUTDEC procedure in the BH-register (0 implies that the value is to be displayed with no leading or trailing blanks). The call to PUTDEC in line 59 displays the centigrade temperature in the AX-register according to the alignment code in the BH-register. There is no need to worry that the call to PUTSTRNG in line 57 would destroy the centrigrade temperature in the AX-register because all I/O procedures save and restore the registers that they use.

The .EXIT pseudo-operation in line 61 directs the assembler to generate the instructions that, when executed, will return control to DOS.

The following are the results from some executions of this program:

```
ENTER TEMPERATURE IN DEGREES FAHRENHEIT -20
      TEMPERATURE IN DEGREES CENTIGRADE -29

ENTER TEMPERATURE IN DEGREES FAHRENHEIT 32
      TEMPERATURE IN DEGREES CENTIGRADE 0

ENTER TEMPERATURE IN DEGREES FAHRENHEIT 100
      TEMPERATURE IN DEGREES CENTIGRADE 38

ENTER TEMPERATURE IN DEGREES FAHRENHEIT 212
      TEMPERATURE IN DEGREES CENTIGRADE 100
```

Sum of Cubes of First *n* Positive Integers

Consider the problem of computing the sum of the cubes of the first n positive integers using the following formula:

$$1^3 + 2^3 + 3^3 + \cdots + n^3 = [n(n + 1)/2]^2$$

The value of n will be supplied as an input. Since n is a positive integer, and the computation deals with only positive integers, unsigned integer arithmetic is used in performing this computation.

Program Listing 3.2 shows an 8088/8086 assembly language program that performs this computation. Lines 2–9 contain the prologue, which explains the program's function. Lines 14–17 identify the external procedures that are called by the program. The GETDEC$ procedure inputs the unsigned integer value of n. The PUTDEC$ procedure outputs the value of n and the sum of the cubes of the first n positive integers. The PUTSTRNG procedure displays a prompt message to the user and annotates the output. Lines 18–20 define the stack segment in the standard way.

```
             PAGE    80,132
;===============================================================
;                    PROGRAM LISTING 3.2
;
; GIVEN AN INTEGER VALUE FOR n, THIS PROGRAM COMPUTES THE SUM OF
; THE CUBES  OF THE FIRST n POSITIVE INTEGERS USING THE FORMULA:
;  3    3    3          3                       2
; 1  + 2  + 3  + ... + n  = [n(n + 1)/2]
;===============================================================
             DOSSEG
             .MODEL  SMALL,BASIC,FARSTACK
;===============================================================
                                        ;PROCEDURES TO
             EXTRN   GETDEC$:FAR        ;GET 16-BIT UNSIGNED DEC INT
             EXTRN   NEWLINE:FAR        ;DISPLAY NEWLINE CHARACTER
             EXTRN   PUTDEC$:FAR        ;DISPLAY 16-BIT UNSIGNED INT
             EXTRN   PUTSTRNG:FAR       ;DISPLAY CHARACTER STRING
;===============================================================
; S T A C K   D E F I N I T I O N
             .STACK  256
;===============================================================
; C O N S T A N T   D E F I N I T I O N S
             .CONST
PROMPT       DB      'ENTER A POSITIVE INTEGER VALUE   '
MESSAGE_1    DB      'THE SUM OF THE FIRST '
MESSAGE_2    DB      ' CUBE(S) IS '
TWO          DW      2                  ;CONSTANT 2
;===============================================================
; V A R I A B L E   D E F I N I T I O N S
             .DATA
N            DW      ?                  ;NUMBER OF CUBES TO SUM
SUM          DW      ?                  ;SUM OF FIRST N CUBES
;===============================================================
; C O D E   S E G M E N T   D E F I N I T I O N
             .CODE   EX_3_2
             .STARTUP                   ;GENERATE STARTUP CODE
             PUSH    DS                 ;SET ES-REGISTER TO ADDRESS
             POP     ES                 ;    DGROUP
             LEA     DI,PROMPT          ;PROMPT FOR N
             MOV     CX,33
             CALL    PUTSTRNG
             CALL    GETDEC$            ;GET N
             MOV     N,AX
             INC     AX                 ;SUM = [N(N + 1)/2] ** 2
             MUL     N
             DIV     TWO
             MUL     AX
             MOV     SUM,AX
             CALL    NEWLINE            ;DISPLAY NEWLINE CHARACTER
             LEA     DI,MESSAGE_1       ;DISPLAY 'THE SUM OF THE FIRST
             MOV     CX,21
             CALL    PUTSTRNG
             MOV     AX,N               ;DISPLAY N
             MOV     BH,0
             CALL    PUTDEC$
             LEA     DI,MESSAGE_2       ;DISPLAY ' CUBE(S) IS '
             MOV     CX,12
             CALL    PUTSTRNG
             MOV     AX,SUM             ;DISPLAY SUM
             CALL    PUTDEC$
             .EXIT                      ;RETURN TO DOS
;
             END
;===============================================================
```

Lines 21–27 define the constant data segment for the program. Four entries appear in the constant data segment definition. Line 24 defines a 33-character prompt message that asks the user to 'ENTER A POSITIVE INTEGER VALUE'. Lines 25 and 26 define two messages used for annotation of the output. By displaying the value of *n* after the first message and the value of the sum after the second message, the output line will look like the following:

```
THE SUM OF THE FIRST 5 CUBE(S) IS 225
```

Line 27 defines a word constant with symbolic name TWO, and it initializes its value to 2. This constant is used as the operand in a DIV instruction. The immediate operand 2 is not legal as the operand in a DIV instruction.

Lines 28–32 define the variable data segment for the program. Line 31 defines a word variable N, which holds the input value. The N variable is not given an initial value. Line 32 defines a word variable SUM, which holds the sum of the cubes of the first *n* positive integers. The SUM variable is not given an initial value.

Lines 33–61 define the code segment for the program. The code segment contains the instructions for the main procedure of the program. The main procedure begins by initializing the segment registers (lines 36–38). The .STARTUP pseudo-operation in line 36 directs the assembler to generate the assembly language instructions that, when executed, will initialize the DS-register to the origin of DGROUP. With simplified segment directives, the assembler automatically assumes that the DS-register will be used to contain the origin of DGROUP. The .STARTUP pseudo-operation directs the assembler to generate the instructions that will perform the initialization to comply with this assumption. In the program generated from the assembly module of Program Listing 3.2, DGROUP will contain the constant data segment, which is defined in lines 21–27, and the variable data segment, which is defined in lines 28–32. Since the stack segment is defined as a far stack segment (see line 11), it will not be included in DGROUP. Prior to translating the program to machine language, the assembler substitutes the two instructions

```
MOV  DX,DGROUP
MOV  DS,DX
```

for the .STARTUP pseudo-operation. If the stack segment had been defined as a near stack segment, then the assembler would include some additional instructions in the substitution for the purpose of adjusting the SP-register. These additional instructions include shift instructions, which are covered in Chapter 6. Therefore, to avoid the use of these instructions until they have been covered, far stack segments are used in the example programs in Chapters 2–5. The .STARTUP pseudo-operation, like the .EXIT pseudo-operation, behaves like a macro instruction. Macro instructions are discussed in Chapter 5.

MASM 5.1

The .STARTUP pseudo-operation is not available in MASM 5.1. MASM 5.1 users should substitute the instructions

```
MOV  DX,DGROUP
MOV  DS,DX
```

for the .STARTUP pseudo-operation in their programs.

The two instructions in lines 37 and 38 set the ES-register to address the origin of DGROUP. The DS-register already contains the origin of DGROUP as a result of the code generated in response to the .STARTUP directive. The ES-register can be initialized by copying the value of the DS-register into the ES-register. This copy operation cannot be performed with a single MOV instruction because the MOV instruction cannot have segment registers for both of its operands (see Figure 2.4). The operation can be performed by pushing a copy of the DS-register value onto the stack (line 37) and then popping that value from the stack into the ES-register (line 38).

The reader may wonder why the instruction

```
MOV  ES,DX
```

was not used to initialize the value of the ES-register. The DX-register also contains the origin of DGROUP as a result of the code generated in response to the .STARTUP directive. To use the MOV ES,DX instruction would be to assume that future versions of the Macro Assembler will continue to use DX as the intermediate register in the code generated for .STARTUP. This assumption is not necessarily a safe one. With the PUSH and POP instructions, it is more likely that the program will be compatible with future versions of the Macro Assembler.

Both the DS-register and the ES-register are used to point to DGROUP. The ES-register addresses DGROUP because several of the entries in the constant data segment (lines 24–26) are strings to be displayed by the PUTSTRNG procedure, which expects the string's address to be in the ES:DI register pair. The DS-register addresses DGROUP because its use leads to more efficient machine language representations of memory-referencing instructions. Several of the entries in the two data segment definitions (lines 27, 31, and 32) are used in memory-referencing instructions (e.g., lines 43, 45, 46, and 48). The default segment register for a memory-referencing instruction is the DS-register. If a register other than the DS-register is required in a memory-referencing instruction, then a 1-byte segment prefix, which identifies that segment register, must be appended to the beginning of that instruction's machine language representation. If the ES-register alone is used to address DGROUP, then the additional instruction byte is required. However, if the DS-register also addresses DGROUP, then the assembler can use the more efficient machine language representation.

Lines 39–41 display the prompt message to the user. The call to GETDEC$ in line 42 is used to accept a 16-bit unsigned integer value from the keyboard. GETDEC$ returns the input value in the AX-register. This discussion assumes that the input value is 5; thus, the AX-register now contains 5. The MOV instruction in line 43 copies the value in the AX-register into the memory location identified by the symbolic name N. The input value of 5 is now the value of variable N as well as the value in the AX-register.

The INC instruction in line 44 increments the value in the AX-register, which now contains 6, the value (N + 1). Line 45 causes the value in the AX-register to be multiplied by the value of variable N, N(N + 1) (30 in this example). The product is in the DX:AX register pair. The MUL instruction is used rather than the IMUL instruction because unsigned integer arithmetic is being used.

The next step is to divide the product by 2. As in Program Listing 3.1, a multiply precedes a divide. Therefore, the dividend is already expanded to 32 bits. The DIV instruction in line 46 divides the 32-bit value in the DX:AX register pair (30) by the 16-bit value of constant TWO (2), leaving the quotient (15) in the AX-register and the remainder (0) in the DX-register.

The value in the AX-register represents [N(N + 1)/2]. The MUL instruction in line 47 multiplies the value in the AX-register (15) by the value in the AX-register (15), leaving the result (225) in the DX:AX register pair. This 32-bit unsigned integer value is the sum of the cubes of the first N = 5 positive integers. This program assumes that the value can fit into 16 bits. The MOV instruction in line 48 moves the lower 16 bits of the 32-bit result into the variable SUM.

The instructions in lines 50–52 display the first part of the output annotation:

```
THE SUM OF THE FIRST
```

The instructions in lines 53–55 display the value of N. The MOV instruction in line 53 places the value of variable N in the AX-register. The MOV instruction in line 54 sets the alignment code in the BH-register (0 implies that the number is to be displayed with no leading or trailing blanks). In line 55, the PUTDEC$ procedure is called to display the value in the AX-register, according to the code in the BH-register. The instructions in lines 56–58 display the last part of the output annotation:

```
CUBE(S) IS
```

The instructions in lines 59 and 60 display the value of the variable SUM. The alignment code now does not have to be set in the BH-register because the value of the BH-register has not changed since the last call to PUTDEC$.

The .EXIT pseudo-operation in line 61 directs the assembler to generate the instructions that, when executed, will return control to DOS. Note that the END pseudo-operation (line 63) does not specify where program execution is to begin. This specification is not required when the .STARTUP macro directive is used (line 36). The assembler assumes that program execution is to begin with the instructions generated by the assembler in response to the .STARTUP macro directive.

The following are the results from some executions of this program:

```
ENTER A POSITIVE INTEGER VALUE 3
THE SUM OF THE FIRST 3 CUBE(S) IS 36

ENTER A POSITIVE INTEGER VALUE 8
THE SUM OF THE FIRST 8 CUBE(S) IS 1296

ENTER A POSITIVE INTEGER VALUE 22
THE SUM OF THE FIRST 22 CUBE(S) IS 64009

ENTER A POSITIVE INTEGER VALUE 23
THE SUM OF THE FIRST 23 CUBE(S) IS 10640
```

Note that the sum of the cubes of the first 23 positive integers is less than the sum of the cubes of the first 22 positive integers, which obviously is *not* correct. The sum has to increase as n increases. By hand calculation, it is easy to see that 64009 is the correct output for an input of 22 but that 10640 is not the correct output for an input of 23. To locate the problem, a DEBUG or CodeView trace is used.

To facilitate the DEBUG trace, an assembler-generated listing of the program can be obtained. In the MASM 6.0 command line, the /Fl⟨*filename*⟩ option identifies the listing file and the /S options specify what is to be included in the listing file. The rules for expressing these options are summarized in Appendix F. Suppose we have a fixed disk system, the Macro Assembler is on the fixed disk, the source code file is on the diskette in drive A, and the fixed disk drive is the default drive. The command

```
ml /c /Zi /FoA: /Sa /FlA: A:ex_3_2.asm
```

instructs MASM 6.0 to translate the assembly module in file EX_3_2.ASM to machine language and to generate a listing file, which includes all available information (/Sa option). MASM 6.0 places the object code file on the diskette in drive A with

EX_3_2.OBJ as the filename (/Fo option), and it places the listing file on the diskette in drive A with EX_3_2.LST as the filename (/Fl option). When the command line does not specify a filename for the listing file, MASM 6.0 uses the same filename as that of the source code file, with the filename extension changed from .ASM to .LST.

MASM 5.1

In the MASM 5.1 command line, the third argument identifies the listing file. Suppose we have a fixed disk system, the Macro Assembler is on the fixed disk, the source code file is on the diskette in drive A, and the fixed disk drive is the default drive. The command

```
masm /zi  A:ex_3_2,A:,A:;
```

instructs MASM 5.1 to translate the assembly module in file EX_3_2.ASM to machine language and to generate a listing file. MASM 5.1 places the object code file on the diskette in drive A with EX_3_2.OBJ as the filename, and it places the listing file on the diskette in drive A with EX_3_2.LST as the filename. When the command line does not specify a filename for the listing file, MASM 5.1 uses the same filename as that of the source code file, with the filename extension changed from .ASM to .LST.

Assembler Listing 3.3 is a copy of the listing file for the assembly module in Program Listing 3.2. (Note that the comment in line 3 was changed before assembly for identification purposes.) The PAGE pseudo-operation in line 1 directs the assembler to generate the listing with 80 lines per page and 132 characters per line. To print the listing file in this form, the printer must be in the compressed mode. To place the printer in the compressed mode, use the DOS command

```
mode lpt1:132,8
```

To print the listing file, use the DOS command

```
print a:ex_3_2.lst
```

To return the printer to its normal mode, use the DOS command

```
mode lpt1:80,6
```

The right-hand portion of the assembler-generated program listing is the assembly language source code as entered via the editor. The left-hand portion of the listing is the machine language translation of the source code, which is given in hexadecimal. The first column of the machine code listing gives offset relative to the beginning of the segment, and the subsequent columns give the contents of consecutive memory locations beginning with that offset. For example, the lines

```
0036 20 43 55 42 45 28      MESSAGE_2  DB      'CUBE(S) IS'
      53 29 20 49 53 20
```

indicate that the character string MESSAGE_2 begins at offset 0036 hexadecimal within the constant data segment and that the initial values to be stored in the constant data segment from offset 0036 through 0041 are the hexadecimal values 20, 43, 55, 42, 45, 28, 53, 29, 20, 49, 53, and 20, which are the ASCII representations of the characters of the string 'CUBE(S) IS'. As another example, the line

```
0023  F7 E0                                           MUL AX
```

indicates that the instruction MUL AX begins at offset 0023 within the code segment and is a two-byte instruction whose machine language representation is F7E0 hexadecimal.

The execution problem encountered in Program Listing 3.2 appears to be in the computation. Tracing the execution of the initialization instructions at the beginning of the program is of no value, as is tracing the execution of the PUTSTRNG and GETDEC$ procedures. It would be nice to begin the trace after return from the GETDEC$ procedure (i.e., just prior to execution of the MOV N,AX instruction). Assembler Listing 3.3 indicates that the MOV N,AX instruction begins at offset 0017 within the code segment.

```
Microsoft (R) Macro Assembler Version 6.00B              05/04/93 11:05:20
ex_3_3.asm                                               Page 1 - 1
                                     PAGE    80,132
                               ;============================================================
                               ;                  ASSEMBLER LISTING 3.3
                               ;
                               ; GIVEN AN INTEGER VALUE FOR n, THIS PROGRAM COMPUTES THE SUM OF
                               ; THE CUBES  OF THE FIRST n POSITIVE INTEGERS USING THE FORMULA:
                               ;  3    3    3           3              2
                               ; 1  + 2  + 3  + ... + n  = [n(n + 1)/2]
                               ;============================================================
                                     DOSSEG
                                     .MODEL  SMALL,BASIC,FARSTACK
                               ;============================================================
                                                               ;PROCEDURES TO
                                     EXTRN   GETDEC$:FAR       ;GET 16-BIT UNSIGNED DEC INT
                                     EXTRN   NEWLINE:FAR       ;DISPLAY NEWLINE CHARACTER
                                     EXTRN   PUTDEC$:FAR       ;DISPLAY 16-BIT UNSIGNED INT
                                     EXTRN   PUTSTRNG:FAR      ;DISPLAY CHARACTER STRING
                               ;============================================================
                               ; S T A C K   D E F I N I T I O N
                                     .STACK  256
                               ;============================================================
                               ; C O N S T A N T   D E F I N I T I O N S
0000                                 .CONST
0000 45 4E 54 45 52 20         PROMPT      DB    'ENTER A POSITIVE INTEGER VALUE   '
     41 20 50 4F 53 49
     54 49 56 45 20 49
     4E 54 45 47 45 52
     20 56 41 4C 55 45
     20 20 20
0021 54 48 45 20 53 55         MESSAGE_1   DB    'THE SUM OF THE FIRST '
     4D 20 4F 46 20 54
     48 45 20 46 49 52
     53 54 20
0036 20 43 55 42 45 28         MESSAGE_2   DB    ' CUBE(S) IS '
     53 29 20 49 53 20
0042 0002                      TWO         DW    2                 ;CONSTANT 2
                               ;============================================================
                               ; V A R I A B L E   D E F I N I T I O N S
0000                                 .DATA
0000 0000                      N           DW    ?                 ;NUMBER OF CUBES TO SUM
0002 0000                      SUM         DW    ?                 ;SUM OF FIRST N CUBES
                               ;============================================================
                               ; C O D E   S E G M E N T   D E F I N I T I O N
0000                                 .CODE   EX_3_2
                                     .STARTUP                      ;GENERATE STARTUP CODE
0000                        *@Startup:
0000  BA ---- R             *       mov     dx, DGROUP
```

```
0003  8E DA             *       mov     ds, dx
0005  1E                        PUSH    DS              ;SET ES-REGISTER TO ADDRESS
0006  07                        POP     ES              ;    DGROUP
0007  BF 0000 R                 LEA     DI,PROMPT       ;PROMPT FOR N
000A  B9 0021                   MOV     CX,33
000D  9A ---- 0000 E            CALL    PUTSTRNG
0012  9A ---- 0000 E            CALL    GETDEC$         ;GET N
0017  A3 0000 R                 MOV     N,AX
001A  40                        INC     AX              ;SUM = [N(N + 1)/2] ** 2
001B  F7 26 0000 R              MUL     N
001F  F7 36 0042 R              DIV     TWO
0023  F7 E0                     MUL     AX
0025  A3 0002 R                 MOV     SUM,AX
0028  9A ---- 0000 E            CALL    NEWLINE         ;DISPLAY NEWLINE CHARACTER
002D  BF 0021 R                 LEA     DI,MESSAGE_1    ;DISPLAY 'THE SUM OF THE FIRST '
0030  B9 0015                   MOV     CX,21
0033  9A ---- 0000 E            CALL    PUTSTRNG
0038  A1 0000 R                 MOV     AX,N            ;DISPLAY N
003B  B7 00                     MOV     BH,0
003D  9A ---- 0000 E            CALL    PUTDEC$
0042  BF 0036 R                 LEA     DI,MESSAGE_2    ;DISPLAY ' CUBE(S) IS '
0045  B9 000C                   MOV     CX,12
0048  9A ---- 0000 E            CALL    PUTSTRNG
004D  A1 0002 R                 MOV     AX,SUM          ;DISPLAY SUM
0050  9A ---- 0000 E            CALL    PUTDEC$
                                .EXIT                   ;RETURN TO DOS
0055  B4 4C             *       mov     ah, 04Ch
0057  CD 21             *       int     021h
                        ;
                                END
                        ;==============================================================

Microsoft (R) Macro Assembler Version 6.00B              05/04/93 11:05:20
ex_3_3.asm                                                 Symbols 2 - 1

Segments and Groups:

                N a m e             Size    Length  Align   Combine Class

DGROUP . . . . . . . . . . . . .   GROUP
_DATA  . . . . . . . . . . . . .   16 Bit  0004    Word    Public  'DATA'
STACK  . . . . . . . . . . . . .   16 Bit  0100    Para    Stack   'STACK'
CONST  . . . . . . . . . . . . .   16 Bit  0044    Word    Public  'CONST'     ReadOnly
EX_3_2 . . . . . . . . . . . . .   16 Bit  0059    Word    Public  'CODE'
_TEXT  . . . . . . . . . . . . .   16 Bit  0000    Word    Public  'CODE'

Microsoft (R) Macro Assembler Version 6.00B              05/04/93 11:05:20
ex_3_3.asm                                                 Symbols 3 - 1

Symbols:

                N a m e             Type    Value   Attr

@CodeSize  . . . . . . . . . . .   Number  0000h
@DataSize  . . . . . . . . . . .   Number  0000h
@Interface . . . . . . . . . . .   Number  0006h
@Model . . . . . . . . . . . . .   Number  0002h
@Startup . . . . . . . . . . . .   L Near  0000    EX_3_2
@code  . . . . . . . . . . . . .   Text    EX_3_2
@data  . . . . . . . . . . . . .   Text    DGROUP
@fardata?  . . . . . . . . . . .   Text    FAR_BSS
@fardata . . . . . . . . . . . .   Text    FAR_DATA
```

```
@stack . . . . . . . . . . . . . .    Text    STACK
GETDEC$ . . . . . . . . . . . . .    L Far   0000    External BASIC
MESSAGE_1 . . . . . . . . . . . .    Byte    0021    CONST
MESSAGE_2 . . . . . . . . . . . .    Byte    0036    CONST
NEWLINE . . . . . . . . . . . . .    L Far   0000    External BASIC
N . . . . . . . . . . . . . . . .    Word    0000    _DATA
PROMPT . . . . . . . . . . . . . .   Byte    0000    CONST
PUTDEC$ . . . . . . . . . . . . .    L Far   0000    External BASIC
PUTSTRNG . . . . . . . . . . . . .   L Far   0000    External BASIC
SUM . . . . . . . . . . . . . . .    Word    0002    _DATA
TWO . . . . . . . . . . . . . . .    Word    0042    CONST

            0 Warnings
            0 Errors
```

DEBUG Trace of Program

DEBUG Listing 3.4 shows a DEBUG session that begins the trace at the MOV N,AX instruction. The second command issued to DEBUG is the **G (go) command**.

DEBUG LISTING 3.4

```
DEBUG EX_3_2.EXE
-R
AX=0000  BX=0000  CX=0300  DX=0000  SP=0100  BP=0000  SI=0000  DI=0000
DS=1FAB  ES=1FAB  SS=1FEB  CS=1FBC  IP=0000   NV UP EI PL NZ NA PO NC
1FBC:0000 BAE61F        MOV     DX,1FE6
-G 17
ENTER A POSITIVE INTEGER VALUE   23

AX=0017  BX=0000  CX=0021  DX=1FE6  SP=0100  BP=0000  SI=0000  DI=000C
DS=1FE6  ES=1FE6  SS=1FEB  CS=1FBC  IP=0017   NV UP EI PL NZ NA PO NC
1FBC:0017 A30800        MOV     [0008],AX                      DS:0008=0000
-T

AX=0017  BX=0000  CX=0021  DX=1FE6  SP=0100  BP=0000  SI=0000  DI=000C
DS=1FE6  ES=1FE6  SS=1FEB  CS=1FBC  IP=001A   NV UP EI PL NZ NA PO NC
1FBC:001A 40            INC     AX
-T

AX=0018  BX=0000  CX=0021  DX=1FE6  SP=0100  BP=0000  SI=0000  DI=000C
DS=1FE6  ES=1FE6  SS=1FEB  CS=1FBC  IP=001B   NV UP EI PL NZ NA PE NC
1FBC:001B F7260800      MUL     WORD PTR [0008]                DS:0008=0017
-T

AX=0228  BX=0000  CX=0021  DX=0000  SP=0100  BP=0000  SI=0000  DI=000C
DS=1FE6  ES=1FE6  SS=1FEB  CS=1FBC  IP=001F   NV UP EI PL NZ AC PE NC
1FBC:001F F7364E00      DIV     WORD PTR [004E]                DS:004E=0002
-T

AX=0114  BX=0000  CX=0021  DX=0000  SP=0100  BP=0000  SI=0000  DI=000C
DS=1FE6  ES=1FE6  SS=1FEB  CS=1FBC  IP=0023   NV UP EI NG NZ AC PO CY
1FBC:0023 F7E0          MUL     AX
-T

AX=2990  BX=0000  CX=0021  DX=0001  SP=0100  BP=0000  SI=0000  DI=000C
DS=1FE6  ES=1FE6  SS=1FEB  CS=1FBC  IP=0025   OV UP EI PL NZ NA PO CY
1FBC:0025 A30A00        MOV     [000A],AX                      DS:000A=0000
-Q
```

The command

```
G 17
```

directs the DEBUG program to begin execution with the instruction addressed by the

CS:IP register pair (the instruction at location IFBC:0000 in the example) and to continue executing instructions until the instruction at offset 0017 within the code segment is reached. The instructions executed in response to this command include the PUTSTRNG and GETDEC$ procedures. The DEBUG display shows that immediately following the G 17 command, the prompt message is displayed by the PUTSTRNG procedure, the value 23 is entered by the user, and DEBUG regains control with the CS:IP register pair addressing the MOV N,AX instruction at offset 0017. The value in the AX-register at this point (0017 hex) is the input value (23 decimal) returned by the GETDEC$ procedure.

The remainder of the DEBUG session is the single-step trace of the computation. The first trace command causes the instruction

```
MOV N,AX
```

to be executed. The second trace command causes the instruction

```
INC AX
```

to be executed. The value in the AX-register is incremented from 17 hex to 18 hex (23 decimal to 24 decimal, which is the value N + 1. The third trace command causes the instruction

```
MUL N
```

to be executed, which performs the computation

```
(N+1)*N = 24(23)
```

which produces the product 552 decimal (228 hex) in the DX:AX register pair. The fourth trace command causes the instruction

```
DIV TWO
```

to be executed, which performs the computation

```
(N+1)*N/2 = 552/2
```

which produces the quotient 276 decimal (114 hex) in the AX-register. The fifth trace command causes the instruction

```
MUL AX
```

to be executed, which performs the computation

$$((N+1)*N/2)^2 = (276)^2$$

which produces the product 76,176 decimal (12990 hex) in the DX:AX register pair. Note that the OF and CF bits of the flags register are set by execution of this MUL instruction; thus, the product cannot be reduced to 16 bits. However, the program assumes that the product can be reduced to 16 bits, and the next instruction to be executed,

```
MOV SUM,AX
```

stores the lower 16 bits of the product. In the example traced in DEBUG Listing 3.4, the value 2990 hex (10,640 decimal) will be stored for the SUM, which is the value that is displayed when the program is executed with an input of 23.

Arithmetic overflow occurred in the computation but is not detected by the program. Chapter 4 discusses the making of a decision in a program based on a condition such as arithmetic overflow.

CodeView Trace of Program

The command

```
cv /tsf ex_3_2
```

loads the CodeView program, begins execution of the CodeView program, and has the CodeView program load the executable module ex_3_2.exe for tracing. The /tsf option directs CodeView to begin with its default configuration of windows.

The first step in the trace is that of reconfiguring the windows. The local and command windows will be closed, and the register window will be opened. Pressing the Alt key followed by the V key causes the View menu to be displayed. Pressing the L key causes the local window to be closed. Pressing the Alt key followed by the V key causes the View menu to be displayed again. Pressing the C key causes the command window to be closed. Pressing the Alt key followed by the V key causes the View menu to be displayed again. Pressing the R key causes the register window to be opened. The current state of the trace is shown in Screen Image 3.1.

SCREEN IMAGE 3.1

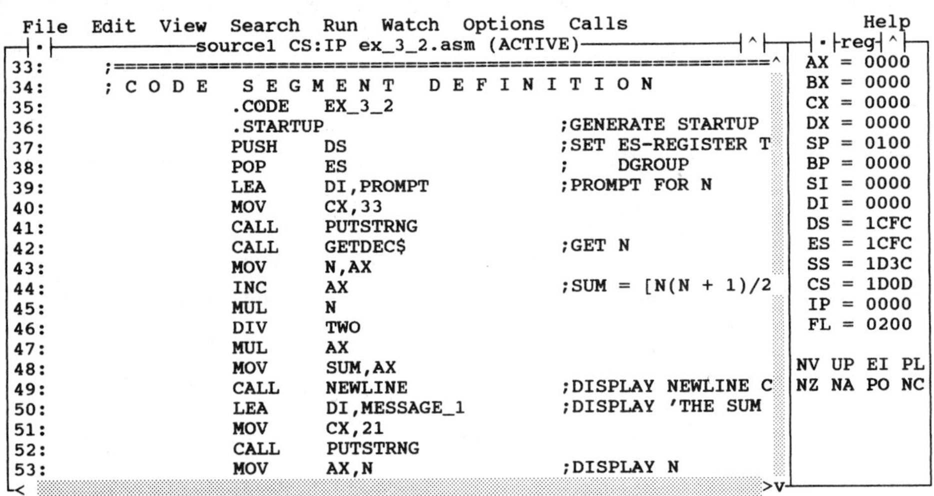
File Edit View Search Run Watch Options Calls Help
source1 CS:IP ex_3_2.asm (ACTIVE)
reg
33: ;===
34: ; C O D E S E G M E N T D E F I N I T I O N
35: .CODE EX_3_2
36: .STARTUP ;GENERATE STARTUP
37: PUSH DS ;SET ES-REGISTER T
38: POP ES ; DGROUP
39: LEA DI,PROMPT ;PROMPT FOR N
40: MOV CX,33
41: CALL PUTSTRNG
42: CALL GETDEC$;GET N
43: MOV N,AX
44: INC AX ;SUM = [N(N + 1)/2
45: MUL N
46: DIV TWO
47: MUL AX
48: MOV SUM,AX
49: CALL NEWLINE ;DISPLAY NEWLINE C
50: LEA DI,MESSAGE_1 ;DISPLAY 'THE SUM
51: MOV CX,21
52: CALL PUTSTRNG
53: MOV AX,N ;DISPLAY N
AX = 0000
BX = 0000
CX = 0000
DX = 0000
SP = 0100
BP = 0000
SI = 0000
DI = 0000
DS = 1CFC
ES = 1CFC
SS = 1D3C
CS = 1D0D
IP = 0000
FL = 0200
NV UP EI PL
NZ NA PO NC
<F8=Trace> <F10=Step> <F5=Go> <F6=Window> <F3=Display>

Another window is needed to monitor the variables N and SUM. A memory window could be opened to monitor these variables; however, an alternative is to open a watch window. With a watch window, selected variables can be monitored by name. Pressing the Alt key followed by the W key causes the Watch menu to be displayed, as shown in Screen Image 3.2. We need to select the Add Watch item from this menu. Note that holding down the Ctrl key and pressing the W key can be used to select the Add Watch function directly (i.e., without first accessing the Watch menu). To select the Add Watch item from the Watch menu, press the A key. Pressing this key causes CodeView to display the Add Watch input window, as shown in Screen Image 3.3. To select a variable to be monitored in the watch window, simply type the symbolic name of that variable and then press the Enter key. Typing the variable name N followed by pressing the Enter key causes CodeView to open the watch window and to display the variable N along with its current value in that window, as shown in Screen Image 3.4. Holding down the Ctrl key and pressing the W key causes the Add Watch input window to be displayed again. Typing the variable name SUM followed by pressing the Enter key causes CodeView to add the variable SUM to the watch window, as shown in Screen Image 3.5.

SCREEN IMAGE 3.2

```
 File  Edit  View  Search  Run  Watch  Options  Calls                     Help
-sourcel CS:IP                                                            reg
33:      ;=====================  Add Watch...          Ctrl+W  ====^   AX = 0000
34:      ; C O D E   S E G M E   Delete Watch...       Ctrl+U          BX = 0000
35:                 .CODE    EX_ Set Breakpoint...         F9          CX = 0000
36:                 .STARTUP     Edit Breakpoints...           TUP     DX = 0000
37:                 PUSH     DS  Quick Watch...      Shift+F9  ER T    SP = 0100
38:                 POP      ES                                        BP = 0000
39:                 LEA      DI,PROMPT            ;PROMPT FOR N        SI = 0000
40:                 MOV      CX,33                                     DI = 0000
41:                 CALL     PUTSTRNG                                  DS = 1CFC
42:                 CALL     GETDEC$              ;GET N               ES = 1CFC
43:                 MOV      N,AX                                      SS = 1D3C
44:                 INC      AX                   ;SUM = [N(N + 1)/2   CS = 1D0D
45:                 MUL      N                                         IP = 0000
46:                 DIV      TWO                                       FL = 0200
47:                 MUL      AX
48:                 MOV      SUM,AX                                    NV UP EI PL
49:                 CALL     NEWLINE              ;DISPLAY NEWLINE C   NZ NA PO NC
50:                 LEA      DI,MESSAGE_1         ;DISPLAY 'THE SUM
51:                 MOV      CX,21
52:                 CALL     PUTSTRNG
53:                 MOV      AX,N                 ;DISPLAY N
<F8=Trace> <F10=Step> <F5=Go> <F6=Window> <F3=Display> <ESC=Cancel>
```

SCREEN IMAGE 3.3

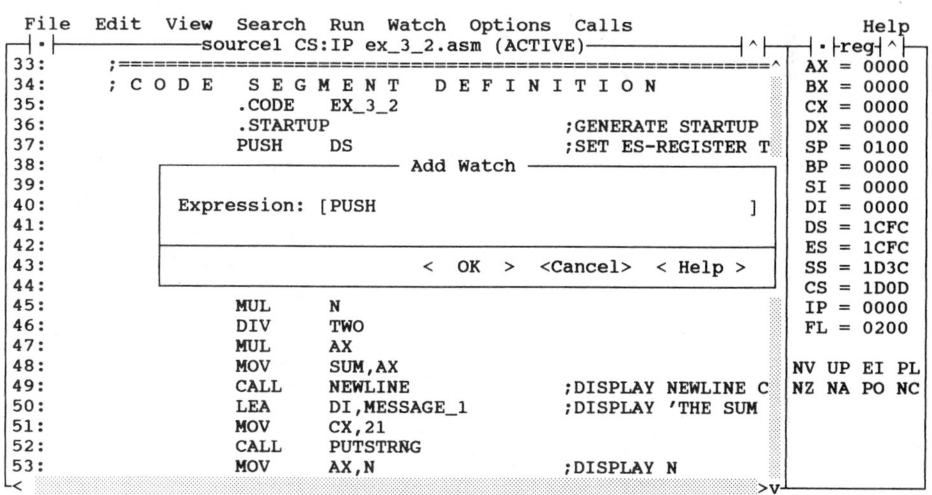

```
 File  Edit  View  Search  Run  Watch  Options  Calls                     Help
-sourcel CS:IP ex_3_2.asm (ACTIVE)                                        reg
33:      ;=================================================^   AX = 0000
34:      ; C O D E   S E G M E N T   D E F I N I T I O N       BX = 0000
35:                 .CODE    EX_3_2                            CX = 0000
36:                 .STARTUP              ;GENERATE STARTUP    DX = 0000
37:                 PUSH     DS           ;SET ES-REGISTER T   SP = 0100
38:          ---------- Add Watch ----------                   BP = 0000
39:                                                            SI = 0000
40:          Expression: [PUSH                          ]      DI = 0000
41:                                                            DS = 1CFC
42:                                                            ES = 1CFC
43:                       <  OK  >  <Cancel>  < Help >         SS = 1D3C
44:                                                            CS = 1D0D
45:                 MUL      N                                 IP = 0000
46:                 DIV      TWO                               FL = 0200
47:                 MUL      AX
48:                 MOV      SUM,AX                            NV UP EI PL
49:                 CALL     NEWLINE      ;DISPLAY NEWLINE C   NZ NA PO NC
50:                 LEA      DI,MESSAGE_1 ;DISPLAY 'THE SUM
51:                 MOV      CX,21
52:                 CALL     PUTSTRNG
53:                 MOV      AX,N         ;DISPLAY N
<F1=Help> <Enter> <ESC=Cancel> <TAB=Next Field>
```

SCREEN IMAGE 3.4

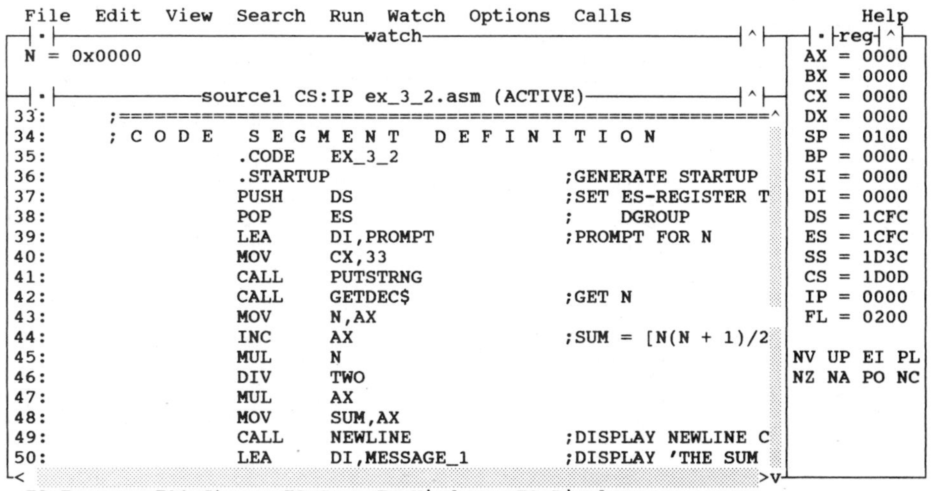

```
 File  Edit  View  Search  Run  Watch  Options  Calls                     Help
-watch                                                                    reg
 N = 0x0000                                                    AX = 0000
                                                               BX = 0000
-sourcel CS:IP ex_3_2.asm (ACTIVE)                             CX = 0000
33:      ;=================================================^   DX = 0000
34:      ; C O D E   S E G M E N T   D E F I N I T I O N       SP = 0100
35:                 .CODE    EX_3_2                            BP = 0000
36:                 .STARTUP              ;GENERATE STARTUP    SI = 0000
37:                 PUSH     DS           ;SET ES-REGISTER T   DI = 0000
38:                 POP      ES           ;    DGROUP          DS = 1CFC
39:                 LEA      DI,PROMPT    ;PROMPT FOR N        ES = 1CFC
40:                 MOV      CX,33                             SS = 1D3C
41:                 CALL     PUTSTRNG                          CS = 1D0D
42:                 CALL     GETDEC$      ;GET N               IP = 0000
43:                 MOV      N,AX                              FL = 0200
44:                 INC      AX           ;SUM = [N(N + 1)/2
45:                 MUL      N                                 NV UP EI PL
46:                 DIV      TWO                               NZ NA PO NC
47:                 MUL      AX
48:                 MOV      SUM,AX
49:                 CALL     NEWLINE      ;DISPLAY NEWLINE C
50:                 LEA      DI,MESSAGE_1 ;DISPLAY 'THE SUM
<F8=Trace> <F10=Step> <F5=Go> <F6=Window> <F3=Display>
```

SCREEN IMAGE 3.5

```
File  Edit  View  Search  Run  Watch  Options  Calls                       Help
-----------------------------watch--------------------------------      -reg-
 N = 0x0000                                                              AX = 0000
 SUM = 0x0000                                                            BX = 0000
--------------source1 CS:IP ex_3_2.asm (ACTIVE)-------------------       CX = 0000
        ;=======================================================         DX = 0000
        ; C O D E    S E G M E N T    D E F I N I T I O N                 SP = 0100
                   .CODE    EX_3_2                                       BP = 0000
                   .STARTUP                     ;GENERATE STARTUP        SI = 0000
                   PUSH     DS                  ;SET ES-REGISTER T       DI = 0000
                   POP      ES                  ;    DGROUP              DS = 1CFC
                   LEA      DI,PROMPT           ;PROMPT FOR N            ES = 1CFC
                   MOV      CX,33                                        SS = 1D3C
                   CALL     PUTSTRNG                                     CS = 1D0D
                   CALL     GETDEC$             ;GET N                   IP = 0000
                   MOV      N,AX                                         FL = 0200
                   INC      AX                  ;SUM = [N(N + 1)/2
                   MUL      N                                           NV UP EI PL
                   DIV      TWO                                         NZ NA PO NC
                   MUL      AX
                   MOV      SUM,AX
                   CALL     NEWLINE             ;DISPLAY NEWLINE C
                   LEA      DI,MESSAGE_1        ;DISPLAY 'THE SUM
<F8=Trace> <F10=Step> <F5=Go> <F6=Window> <F3=Display>
```

In this CodeView trace, the source1 window will be reconfigured so that we will have a view of both the assembly language code and the machine language code. This reconfiguration is accomplished via the Options menu. Pressing the Alt key followed by the O key causes the Options menu to be displayed. Pressing the S key selects the Source Window item from this menu, which causes CodeView to display the Source Window Options input window, as shown in Screen Image 3.6. Pressing the TAB key moves the cursor to the Display Mode section of this input window. Pressing the down-arrow key moves the selection dot to the option labeled "( ) Mixed Source and Assembly." Pressing the Enter key inputs this change to CodeView. CodeView responds by displaying both assembly code and machine code in the source1 window, as shown in Screen Image 3.7. Under each assembly code instruction is the corresponding machine code instruction.

Note that under the first assembly language instruction, which is PUSH DS, there are three machine language instructions. The first two of these instructions were generated in response to the .STARTUP pseudo-operation. The third is the PUSH DS instruction itself. Since the .STARTUP pseudo-operation immediately precedes

SCREEN IMAGE 3.6

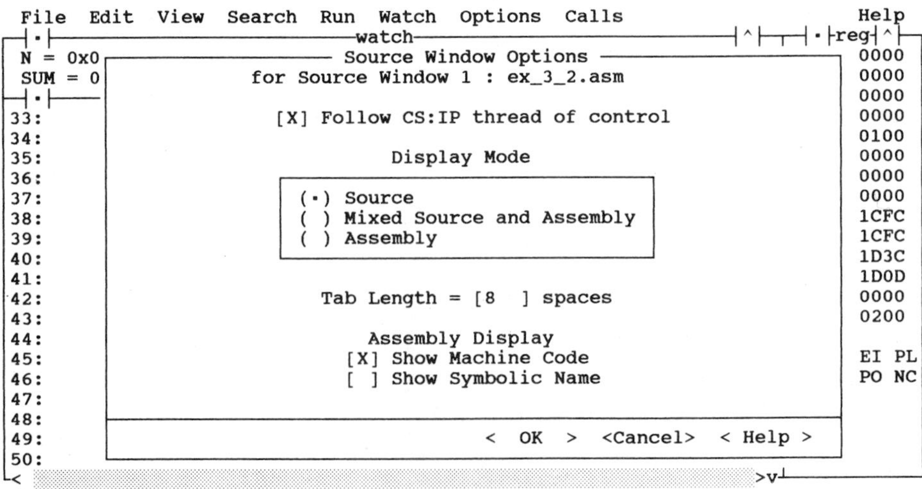

SCREEN IMAGE 3.7

```
File  Edit  View  Search  Run  Watch  Options  Calls                   Help
-|•|---------------------------watch--------------------------|^|--|•|reg|^|-
 N = 0x0000                                                      AX = 0000
 SUM = 0x0000                                                    BX = 0000
-|•|--------------sourcel CS:IP ex_3_2.asm (ACTIVE)-----------|^|- CX = 0000
37:                 PUSH    DS                ;SET ES-REGISTER T^  DX = 0000
1D0D:0000 BA371D          MOV       DX,1D37                      SP = 0100
1D0D:0003 8EDA            MOV       DS,DX                        BP = 0000
1D0D:0005 1E              PUSH      DS                           SI = 0000
38:                 POP     ES                ;    DGROUP        DI = 0000
1D0D:0006 07              POP       ES                           DS = 1CFC
39:                 LEA     DI,PROMPT         ;PROMPT FOR N      ES = 1CFC
1D0D:0007 BF0C00          MOV       DI,000C                      SS = 1D3C
40:                 MOV     CX,33                                CS = 1D0D
1D0D:000A B92100          MOV       CX,0021                      IP = 0000
41:                 CALL    PUTSTRNG                             FL = 0200
1D0D:000D 9A0000171D      CALL      1D17:0000
42:                 CALL    GETDEC$           ;GET N             NV UP EI PL
1D0D:0012 9A0000251D      CALL      1D25:0000                    NZ NA PO NC
43:                 MOV     N,AX
1D0D:0017 A30800          MOV       Word Ptr [0008],AX
44:                 INC     AX                ;SUM = [N(N + 1)/2
1D0D:001A 40              INC       AX
<                                                              >v
<F8=Trace> <F10=Step> <F5=Go> <F6=Window> <F3=Display>
```

the PUSH DS instruction in the program, the code generated for it is displayed with the PUSH DS instruction. Pressing the F10 function key three times causes these three instructions to be executed. Pressing the F10 function key three more times causes the POP, LEA, and MOV instructions (lines 38–40 of Program Listing 3.2) to be executed.

The next instruction to be executed is the CALL PUTSTRNG instruction (line 41 of Program Listing 3.2). Here is where the F8 and F10 function keys differ in their effect. Pressing the F8 key would cause CodeView to execute the CALL instruction and to stop at the first instruction of the subprocedure, which would allow the user to trace the instructions of the subprocedure. Pressing the F10 key would cause CodeView to execute the entire subprocedure and to stop upon return from the subprocedure. The F10 function key is used in the trace described here. The state of the trace after executing the subprocedure is shown in Screen Image 3.8.

At any point in the trace, the user can direct CodeView to switch from its window display to the display of the output screen. The output screen is the one that existed prior to invoking the CodeView program. It is the screen that you would see if you were executing the program from DOS without the aid of a debugging tool.

SCREEN IMAGE 3.8

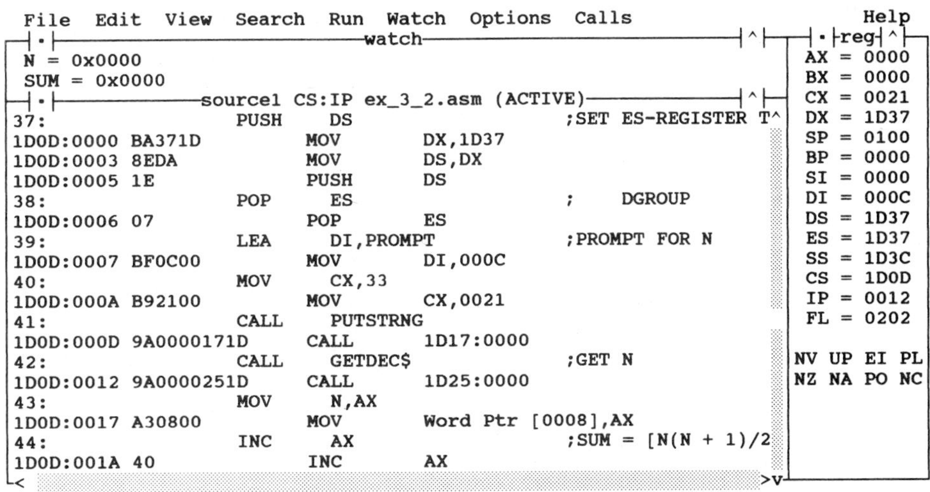

```
File  Edit  View  Search  Run  Watch  Options  Calls                   Help
-|•|---------------------------watch--------------------------|^|--|•|reg|^|-
 N = 0x0000                                                      AX = 0000
 SUM = 0x0000                                                    BX = 0000
-|•|--------------sourcel CS:IP ex_3_2.asm (ACTIVE)-----------|^|- CX = 0021
37:                 PUSH    DS                ;SET ES-REGISTER T^  DX = 1D37
1D0D:0000 BA371D          MOV       DX,1D37                      SP = 0100
1D0D:0003 8EDA            MOV       DS,DX                        BP = 0000
1D0D:0005 1E              PUSH      DS                           SI = 0000
38:                 POP     ES                ;    DGROUP        DI = 000C
1D0D:0006 07              POP       ES                           DS = 1D37
39:                 LEA     DI,PROMPT         ;PROMPT FOR N      ES = 1D37
1D0D:0007 BF0C00          MOV       DI,000C                      SS = 1D3C
40:                 MOV     CX,33                                CS = 1D0D
1D0D:000A B92100          MOV       CX,0021                      IP = 0012
41:                 CALL    PUTSTRNG                             FL = 0202
1D0D:000D 9A0000171D      CALL      1D17:0000
42:                 CALL    GETDEC$           ;GET N             NV UP EI PL
1D0D:0012 9A0000251D      CALL      1D25:0000                    NZ NA PO NC
43:                 MOV     N,AX
1D0D:0017 A30800          MOV       Word Ptr [0008],AX
44:                 INC     AX                ;SUM = [N(N + 1)/2
1D0D:001A 40              INC       AX
<                                                              >v
<F8=Trace> <F10=Step> <F5=Go> <F6=Window> <F3=Display>
```

Pressing the F4 function key causes CodeView to switch to the output screen. On the output screen, you see the history of the commands you performed just prior to invoking CodeView, the command you used to invoke CodeView, and the prompt message just displayed by the execution of subprocedure PUTSTRNG. Pressing the F4 function key again causes CodeView to switch back to its window display.

Pressing F10 again causes CodeView to execute the GETDEC$ subprocedure, stopping again upon return from GETDEC$. Since GETDEC$ is an input subprocedure, it will not return control until an input value has been entered by the user. Note that CodeView switched to the output screen before executing the CALL instruction. Since GETDEC$ has control of the processor, the output screen is being displayed and GETDEC$ is waiting for an input from the user. Enter the value 23, the value that resulted in an erroneous output. Once the value is entered, GETDEC$ continues. When GETDEC$ returns control to the main procedure, CodeView stops the execution once again, as shown in Screen Image 3.9. Note that the input value, 0017 hex (23 decimal), appears in the AX-register. GETDEC$ returned the input value in the AX-register.

SCREEN IMAGE 3.9

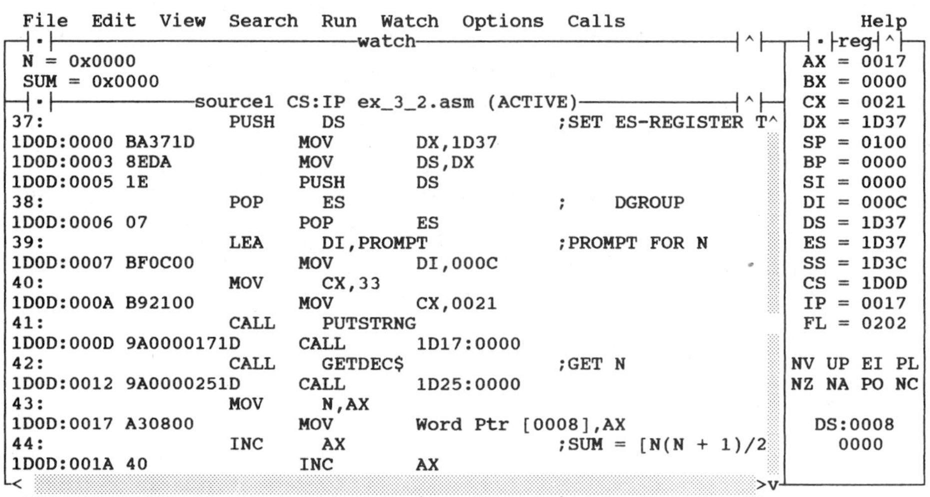

```
File  Edit  View  Search  Run  Watch  Options  Calls                     Help
watch                                                                    reg
 N = 0x0000                                                          AX = 0017
 SUM = 0x0000                                                        BX = 0000
source1 CS:IP ex_3_2.asm (ACTIVE)                                    CX = 0021
37:                   PUSH    DS                  ;SET ES-REGISTER T^ DX = 1D37
1D0D:0000 BA371D            MOV      DX,1D37                         SP = 0100
1D0D:0003 8EDA              MOV      DS,DX                           BP = 0000
1D0D:0005 1E                PUSH     DS                              SI = 0000
38:                   POP     ES                  ;     DGROUP       DI = 000C
1D0D:0006 07                POP      ES                              DS = 1D37
39:                   LEA     DI,PROMPT           ;PROMPT FOR N      ES = 1D37
1D0D:0007 BF0C00            MOV      DI,000C                         SS = 1D3C
40:                   MOV     CX,33                                  CS = 1D0D
1D0D:000A B92100            MOV      CX,0021                         IP = 0017
41:                   CALL    PUTSTRNG                               FL = 0202
1D0D:000D 9A0000171D        CALL     1D17:0000
42:                   CALL    GETDEC$             ;GET N             NV UP EI PL
1D0D:0012 9A0000251D        CALL     1D25:0000                       NZ NA PO NC
43:                   MOV     N,AX
1D0D:0017 A30800            MOV      Word Ptr [0008],AX               DS:0008
44:                   INC     AX                  ;SUM = [N(N + 1)/2    0000
1D0D:001A 40                INC      AX
<F8=Trace> <F10=Step> <F5=Go> <F6=Window> <F3=Display>
```

Pressing F10 again causes the instruction

```
MOV N,AX
```

(line 43 of Program Listing 3.2) to be executed. This instruction causes the input value to be copied from the AX-register to the memory location identified by variable N. CodeView updates variable N in the watch window, as shown in Screen Image 3.10.

Pressing F10 again causes the instruction

```
INC AX
```

to be executed. The value in the AX-register is incremented from 17 hex to 18 hex (23 decimal to 24 decimal), which is the value N + 1. Pressing F10 again causes the instruction

```
MUL N
```

to be executed, which performs the computation

```
(N+1)*N = 24(23)
```

SCREEN IMAGE 3.10

```
 File  Edit  View  Search  Run  Watch  Options  Calls                      Help
┤•├──────────────────────────watch──────────────────────────────┤^├──┤•├reg┤^├
 N = 0x0017                                                         AX = 0017
 SUM = 0x0000                                                       BX = 0000
┤•├───────────sourcel CS:IP ex_3_2.asm (ACTIVE)─────────────────┤^├  CX = 0021
37:                  PUSH    DS                    ;SET ES-REGISTER T^  DX = 1D37
1D0D:0000 BA371D           MOV         DX,1D37                        SP = 0100
1D0D:0003 8EDA             MOV         DS,DX                          BP = 0000
1D0D:0005 1E               PUSH        DS                             SI = 0000
38:                  POP     ES                    ;     DGROUP       DI = 000C
1D0D:0006 07               POP         ES                             DS = 1D37
39:                  LEA     DI,PROMPT             ;PROMPT FOR N      ES = 1D37
1D0D:0007 BF0C00           MOV         DI,000C                        SS = 1D3C
40:                  MOV     CX,33                                    CS = 1D0D
1D0D:000A B92100           MOV         CX,0021                        IP = 001A
41:                  CALL    PUTSTRNG                                 FL = 0202
1D0D:000D 9A0000171D       CALL        1D17:0000
42:                  CALL    GETDEC$               ;GET N            NV UP EI PL
1D0D:0012 9A0000251D       CALL        1D25:0000                     NZ NA PO NC
43:                  MOV     N,AX
1D0D:0017 A30800           MOV         Word Ptr [0008],AX
44:                  INC     AX                    ;SUM = [N(N + 1)/2
1D0D:001A 40               INC         AX
<                                                                  >v
 <F8=Trace> <F10=Step> <F5=Go> <F6=Window> <F3=Display>
```

which produces the product 552 decimal (228 hex) in the DX:AX register pair. Pressing F10 again causes the instruction

```
DIV TWO
```

to be executed, which performs the computation

```
(N+1)*N/2 = 552/2
```

which produces the quotient 276 decimal (114 hex) in the AX-register. Pressing F10 again causes the instruction

```
MUL AX
```

to be executed, which performs the computation

$$((N+1)*N/2)^2 = (276)^2$$

which produces the product 76,176 decimal (12990 hex) in the DX:AX register pair. Note that the OF and CF bits of the flags register are set by execution of this MUL instruction, as shown in Screen Image 3.11; thus, the product cannot be reduced to 16

SCREEN IMAGE 3.11

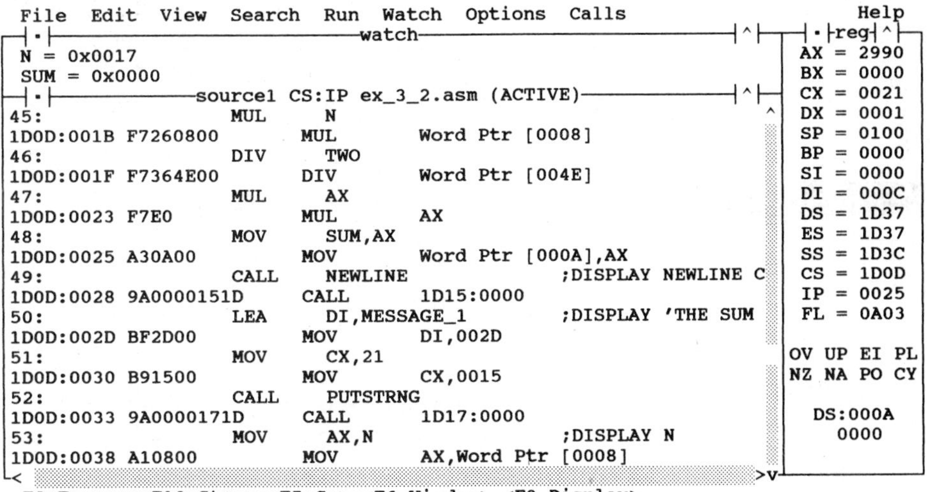

```
 File  Edit  View  Search  Run  Watch  Options  Calls                      Help
┤•├──────────────────────────watch──────────────────────────────┤^├──┤•├reg┤^├
 N = 0x0017                                                         AX = 2990
 SUM = 0x0000                                                       BX = 0000
┤•├───────────sourcel CS:IP ex_3_2.asm (ACTIVE)─────────────────┤^├  CX = 0021
45:                  MUL     N                                  ^  DX = 0001
1D0D:001B F7260800         MUL         Word Ptr [0008]                SP = 0100
46:                  DIV     TWO                                      BP = 0000
1D0D:001F F7364E00         DIV         Word Ptr [004E]                SI = 0000
47:                  MUL     AX                                       DI = 000C
1D0D:0023 F7E0             MUL         AX                             DS = 1D37
48:                  MOV     SUM,AX                                   ES = 1D37
1D0D:0025 A30A00           MOV         Word Ptr [000A],AX             SS = 1D3C
49:                  CALL    NEWLINE               ;DISPLAY NEWLINE C  CS = 1D0D
1D0D:0028 9A0000151D       CALL        1D15:0000                      IP = 0025
50:                  LEA     DI,MESSAGE_1          ;DISPLAY 'THE SUM  FL = 0A03
1D0D:002D BF2D00           MOV         DI,002D
51:                  MOV     CX,21                                   OV UP EI PL
1D0D:0030 B91500           MOV         CX,0015                       NZ NA PO CY
52:                  CALL    PUTSTRNG
1D0D:0033 9A0000171D       CALL        1D17:0000                      DS:000A
53:                  MOV     AX,N                  ;DISPLAY N            0000
1D0D:0038 A10800           MOV         AX,Word Ptr [0008]
<                                                                  >v
 <F8=Trace> <F10=Step> <F5=Go> <F6=Window> <F3=Display>
```

bits. However, the program assumes that the product can be reduced to 16 bits, and the next instruction to be executed,

```
MOV SUM,AX
```

stores the lower 16 bits of the product. In this example, the value 2990 hex (10,640 decimal) will be stored for the SUM, which is the value that is displayed when the program is executed with an input of 23.

Arithmetic overflow occurred in the computation but is not detected by the program. Chapter 4 discusses the making of a decision in a program based on a condition such as arithmetic overflow.

3.4 Overflow Detection

Overflow detection depends on the integer interpretation being used. With the two's complement interpretation, overflow can be detected in addition and subtraction operations by comparing the signs of the operands with the sign of the result. The method for detecting overflow on an addition operation with the two's complement interpretation is as follows:

1. If the operands have different signs, then overflow is impossible.
2. If the operands have the same sign, then the sign of the sum must be the same as the sign of the operands. If the sign of the sum is *not* the same as that of the two operands, then an arithmetic overflow has occurred.

There is also an alternate method for detecting overflow on an addition operation with the two's complement interpretation:

1. If the carry into the sign bit differs from the carry out of the sign bit, then arithmetic overflow has occurred.
2. If the carry into the sign bit is the same as the carry out of the sign bit, then arithmetic overflow has *not* occurred.

The first method is probably the more convenient method for humans. The alternate method is easier to implement in the circuitry of a digital computer.

Subtraction in the 8088/8086 is performed by adding the minuend, the one's complement of the subtrahend, and 1. All of the preceding rules for detection of overflow in addition also apply to detection of overflow in subtraction.

EXAMPLES

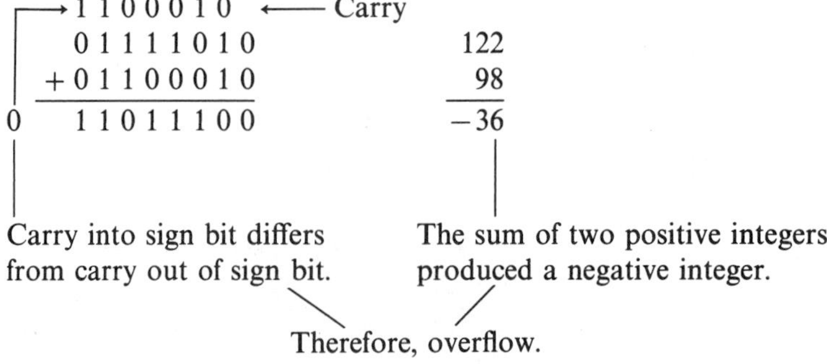

1 1 0 0 0 1 0 ← Carry
0 1 1 1 1 0 1 0
+0 1 1 0 0 0 1 0
0 1 1 0 1 1 1 0 0
122
98
−36
Carry into sign bit differs from carry out of sign bit.
The sum of two positive integers produced a negative integer.
Therefore, overflow.

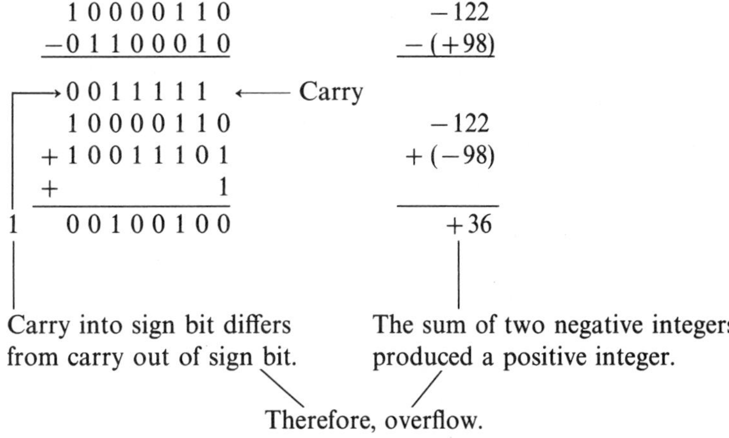

1 0 0 0 0 1 1 0
−0 1 1 0 0 0 1 0
−122
−(+98)
0 0 1 1 1 1 1
Carry
1 0 0 0 0 1 1 0
+1 0 0 1 1 1 0 1
+ 1
1 0 0 1 0 0 1 0 0
−122
+(−98)
+36
Carry into sign bit differs from carry out of sign bit.
The sum of two negative integers produced a positive integer.
Therefore, overflow.

Recall that with the two's complement interpretation, the range of integers that can be represented with n-bit binary numbers is -2^{n-1} to $+2^{n-1}-1$. Note that there is always one negative integer for which there is no corresponding positive integer: -2^{n-1}. For $n = 8$, the negative integer that has no corresponding positive integer is −128, which cannot be negated successfully. An attempt to take the two's complement of this integer automatically results in an arithmetic overflow. In the 8088/8086, the two's complement operation is implemented by a subtraction operation. To take the two's complement of an integer, the 8088/8086 simply subtracts the integer from zero. Therefore, the overflow generated by negating the largest-magnitude negative number is detected in the same way that overflow on subtraction is detected.

EXAMPLE

To negate 10000000:

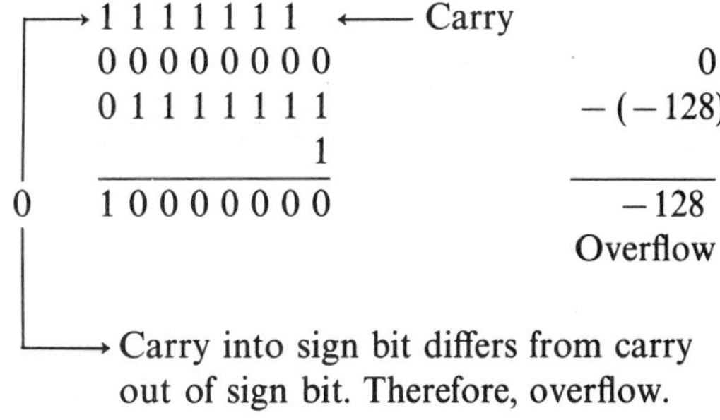

1 1 1 1 1 1 1
Carry
0 0 0 0 0 0 0 0
0 1 1 1 1 1 1 1
1
0 1 0 0 0 0 0 0 0
0
−(−128)
−128
Overflow
Carry into sign bit differs from carry out of sign bit. Therefore, overflow.

With the unsigned integer interpretation, overflow occurs whenever there is a carry out of the most significant bit in addition or a borrow into the most significant bit in subtraction. When subtraction is performed by adding the minuend, the one's complement of the subtrahend, and 1, the carry out of the most significant bit in the addition is the inverse of the borrow into the most significant bit for the subtraction. That is:

1. If the carry out of the most significant bit in the addition portion of the operation is 0, then the borrow into the most significant bit for the subtraction is a 1.
2. If the carry out of the most significant bit in the addition portion of the operation is 1, then the borrow into the most significant bit for the subtraction is a 0.

EXAMPLES

```
     1111100  ←—Carry
     11111100           252
    +00001100          + 12
  1  00001000             8
  |
  └→ Carry of 1 from the most significant bit. Therefore, overflow.
```

```
   00001100          12
  -00001110        - 14

    0000001  ←—Carry
    00001100
   +11110001
           1
0   11111110        254
|
└→ Carry of 0 from the most significant bit means a borrow of 1 into the most
   significant bit. Therefore, overflow.
```

■

The Intel 8088/8086 microprocessor detects overflow in addition, subtraction, and negation operations and sets the OF and/or CF bit in the flags register to indicate the overflow condition. In an addition operation or the addition portion of a subtraction or negation operation, if the carry into the most significant bit differs from the carry out of the most significant bit, then the OF bit is set in the flags register. Otherwise, the OF bit is cleared following these operations. In an addition operation, the carry out of the most significant bit is recorded in the CF bit of the flags register. In a subtraction or negation operation, the inverse of the carry out of the most significant bit (i.e., the borrow into the most significant bit) is recorded in the CF bit of the flags register. Therefore, the CF bit in the flags register is actually a carry/borrow flag.

In a multiplication operation, arithmetic overflow is impossible. When multiplying two n-bit binary numbers, a $2n$-bit product is produced. Regardless of the magnitude of the two operands, the product will fit in $2n$ bits. The Intel 8088/8086 microprocessor does, however, provide an overflow check on multiplication. It is an indication of whether or not the product can be reduced to n bits without loss of significant digits. For an unsigned integer multiplication operation, if the upper half of the product is nonzero, then the CF and OF bits in the flags register are set. Otherwise, both the CF and OF bits in the flags register are cleared following execution of an unsigned integer multiply instruction. For a signed two's complement integer multiplication operation, if the upper half of the product is *not* the sign extension of the lower half, then the CF and OF bits in the flags register are set. Otherwise, the CF and OF bits in the flags register are cleared following execution of a signed integer multiply instruction.

In a division operation, overflow is possible. For an unsigned integer division operation, overflow occurs if the divisor is not greater than the high-order half of the dividend. For an n-bit signed integer division operation, overflow occurs if the divisor is not greater than the high-order $n + 1$ bits of the dividend. The Intel 8088/8086 microprocessor detects overflow on a division operation and responds to the condition by generating a Type 0 interrupt.

Note that for addition, subtraction, negation, and multiplication operations, the microprocessor detects arithmetic overflow but does nothing about it, except for setting the CF and/or OF bit in the flags register. These flag bits can be tested by the assembly language program, and a decision can be made based on their values. Chapter 4 is devoted to decisions and loops (i.e., control structures) in assembly language programs and discusses an example of how a program can react to an arithmetic overflow condition. Program Listing 3.2 is modified to include an overflow check.

3.5 Additional Capabilities in the 80286 Assembly Language

The 80286 assembly language provides two additional forms for the IMUL instruction that allow multiplication of a 16-bit register or memory location by an immediate value. With the 80286 microprocessor, the IMUL instruction may have the following general form:

[⟨*label*⟩] `IMUL` ⟨*destination*⟩, ⟨*immediate*⟩ [⟨*comment*⟩]

in which ⟨*destination*⟩ identifies the location of the multiplicand that is to be replaced by the product and ⟨*immediate*⟩ is an immediate value representing the multiplier. This instruction causes the destination operand to be multiplied by the immediate value and the destination operand to be replaced by the product. It is important to note that the product is a single-length product. The destination operand can be any 16-bit general register.

With the 80286 microprocessor, the IMUL instruction may also have the following general form:

[⟨*label*⟩] `IMUL` ⟨*destination*⟩, ⟨*source*⟩, ⟨*immediate*⟩ [⟨*comment*⟩]

in which ⟨*source*⟩ identifies the location of the multiplicand, ⟨*immediate*⟩ is an immediate value representing the multiplier, and ⟨*destination*⟩ identifies the register whose value is to be replaced by the product. This instruction causes the source operand to be multiplied by the immediate value and the destination operand to be replaced by the product. The destination operand can be any 16-bit general register. The source operand can be any 16-bit general register or the 16-bit contents of two consecutive memory locations.

The flags register is affected in the same way for these forms of the IMUL instruction as it is for the single-operand form presented previously in this chapter. Since the product produced is a single-length product, the OF and CF bits of the flags register indicate whether or not overflow occurred.

These two forms do not exist for the MUL instruction. There is no need for them. When multiplying two 16-bit integers, the lower 16 bits of the product will be the same whether the two 16-bit integers being multiplied are interpreted as signed or unsigned. That is, these two additional forms of the IMUL instruction can be used for both signed and unsigned operands. However, it should be noted that the OF and CF bits of the flags register indicate overflow only for the signed interpretation.

EXAMPLES

The instruction

```
IMUL BX,7
```

multiplies the 16-bit value of the BX-register by 7, leaving the 16-bit product in the

BX-register. If the product (signed interpretation) is too large to fit in the BX-register, then the OF and CF bits of the flags register are set.

The instruction

```
IMUL DX,LNGTH,2
```

multiplies the 16-bit value of the variable LNGTH by 2, leaving the 16-bit product in the DX-register. If the product (signed interpretation) is too large to fit in the DX-register, then the OF and CF bits of the flags register are set. ■

NUMERIC EXERCISES

3.1 Perform the following additions involving 8-bit binary integers in the modulo 2^8 number system. In each case, state whether or not overflow occurs.

a. 00111011 01011001	**b.** 10110101 00110011
c. 10110011 01011011	**d.** 11101011 11110010

3.2 Perform the following additions involving 8-bit binary integers in the two's complement number system. In each case, state whether or not overflow occurs.

a. 00111011 01011001	**b.** 10110101 00110011
c. 10110011 01011011	**d.** 11101011 11110010

3.3 Perform the following subtractions involving 8-bit binary integers in the modulo 2^8 number system by adding the two's complement of the subtrahend to the minuend. In each case, state whether or not overflow occurs.

a. 00111011 01011001	**b.** 10110101 00110011
c. 10110011 01011011	**d.** 11101011 11110010

3.4 Perform the following subtractions involving 8-bit binary integers in the two's complement number system by adding the two's complement of the subtrahend to the minuend. In each case, state whether or not overflow occurs.

a. 00111011 01011001	**b.** 10110101 00110011
c. 10110011 01011011	**d.** 11101011 11110010

PROGRAMMING EXERCISES

3.1 Design an algorithm to convert a temperature from degrees centrigrade to degrees Fahrenheit using the formula

$$F = (9/5)C + 32$$

in which C is temperature in degrees centigrade and F is temperature in degrees Fahrenheit. Round the Fahrenheit temperature to the nearest integer. Implement your algorithm with an 8088/8086 assembly language program. Your input should be the centigrade temperature entered via the keyboard. Your output should be the Fahrenheit temperature with appropriate annotation. Be sure to prompt the user for the input.

3.2 Design an algorithm to convert a time from seconds to hours, minutes, and seconds. Implement your algorithm with an 8088/8086 assembly language program. Your input should be the time in seconds entered via the keyboard. The input value will be in the range 0 to 65,535. Your output should be the equivalent time in the form HH:MM:SS. For example, for an input of 7272 seconds, the program should output 2:1:12. Demonstrate your program with each of the following input values: 0, 59, 60, 3599, 3600, 7272, 32,000, 32,072, and 65,535.

3.3 Design an algorithm to accept as input an integer value for x and to compute and output the corresponding value for y using the function

$$y = x^3 - 11x^2 + 98x - 24$$

Implement your algorithm with an 8088/8086 assembly language program. Your input should be a signed integer value for x entered via the keyboard. Your output should be the corresponding value for y with appropriate annotation. Use 16-bit arithmetic in your program. Demonstrate your program with the following set of input values: -30, -29, -28, -27, -12, 0, 12, 30, 31, and 32.

3.4 DEBUG Listing 3.5 shows a useful feature of DEBUG. This DEBUG session verifies the third example in Table 3.7. The first command issued to DEBUG in this session is the A (assemble) command, which provides the capability for entering assembly language instructions. DEBUG assembles the instructions as they are entered and loads the machine language representation directly into memory. All numeric values appearing in the instructions entered must be specified in hexadecimal. An address may be included with the A command to specify where in memory the instruction sequence is to begin. If no address is specified, DEBUG chooses the start address of an available block of memory. The machine language representations of the instructions entered are stored in successive memory locations.

In DEBUG Listing 3.5, DEBUG responds to the A command by displaying the address 1DEB:0100 on the screen. The instruction

```
MOV AL, E8
```

is entered via the keyboard to be assembled into memory beginning at that location. DEBUG assembles the instruction into memory and then displays the address of the next available memory location, 1DEB:0102, on the screen. The procedure continues until all desired instructions have been entered. Pressing only Enter in response to an address terminates the assemble command. The last instruction (the NOP instruction) acts as a marker for the end of the instruction sequence.

A register display shows that DEBUG is ready to execute the first instruction of the sequence. The remainder of the DEBUG session is a single-step trace of this instruction sequence. Compare the results to those of Table 3.7.

Use the assemble feature to determine the quotient and remainder for each of the following divisions involving signed decimal integers:

a. $\frac{17}{3}$ **b.** $\frac{-17}{3}$ **c.** $\frac{17}{-3}$ **d.** $\frac{-17}{-3}$

DEBUG LISTING 3.5

```
DEBUG
-A
1DEB:0100 MOV AL,E8
1DEB:0102 MOV BL,5
1DEB:0104 MUL BL
1DEB:0106 MOV AL,E8
1DEB:0108 IMUL BL
1DEB:010A NOP
1DEB:010B
-R
AX=0000  BX=0000  CX=0000  DX=0000  SP=FFEE  BP=0000  SI=0000  DI=0000
DS=1DEB  ES=1DEB  SS=1DEB  CS=1DEB  IP=0100   NV UP EI PL NZ NA PO NC
1DEB:0100 B0E8          MOV     AL,E8
-T

AX=00E8  BX=0000  CX=0000  DX=0000  SP=FFEE  BP=0000  SI=0000  DI=0000
DS=1DEB  ES=1DEB  SS=1DEB  CS=1DEB  IP=0102   NV UP EI PL NZ NA PO NC
1DEB:0102 B305          MOV     BL,05
-T

AX=00E8  BX=0005  CX=0000  DX=0000  SP=FFEE  BP=0000  SI=0000  DI=0000
DS=1DEB  ES=1DEB  SS=1DEB  CS=1DEB  IP=0104   NV UP EI PL NZ NA PO NC
1DEB:0104 F6E3          MUL     BL
-T

AX=0488  BX=0005  CX=0000  DX=0000  SP=FFEE  BP=0000  SI=0000  DI=0000
DS=1DEB  ES=1DEB  SS=1DEB  CS=1DEB  IP=0106   OV UP EI PL NZ AC PE CY
1DEB:0106 B0E8          MOV     AL,E8
-T

AX=04E8  BX=0005  CX=0000  DX=0000  SP=FFEE  BP=0000  SI=0000  DI=0000
DS=1DEB  ES=1DEB  SS=1DEB  CS=1DEB  IP=0108   OV UP EI PL NZ AC PE CY
1DEB:0108 F6EB          IMUL    BL
-T

AX=FF88  BX=0005  CX=0000  DX=0000  SP=FFEE  BP=0000  SI=0000  DI=0000
DS=1DEB  ES=1DEB  SS=1DEB  CS=1DEB  IP=010A   NV UP EI NG NZ AC PE NC
1DEB:010A 90            NOP
-Q
```

CHAPTER 4

Control Structures

The program of Program Listing 3.1 converts temperature from degrees Fahrenheit to degrees centigrade. That program would be more useful if it produced a table of Fahrenheit temperatures and the corresponding centigrade temperatures for some specified range. This task could be accomplished by adding a loop structure to the program. The program of Program Listing 3.2 computes the sum of the cubes of the first *n* positive integers. That program could display an incorrect result due to the undetected condition of arithmetic overflow. To produce a more meaningful output, the program needs a decision structure that is based on whether or not overflow occurs during the computation.

This chapter presents two types of control structures: the decision structure and the loop structure. To implement control structures in assembly language programs, a class of instructions called **transfer of control instructions** is needed. In 8088/8086 terminology, this class of instructions is called *JUMP instructions.* The 8088/8086 assembly language also contains some additional transfer of control instructions that are called *LOOP instructions.* These instructions are used for implementing certain types of loop structures. This chapter discusses the use of JUMP and LOOP instructions to implement control structures in 8088/8086 assembly language programs.

4.1 JUMP Instructions

Figure 4.1 presents a loose description of the instruction execution cycle for the Intel 8088/8086 microprocessor. The "Instruction fetch" step is the memory fetch for the first byte of an instruction. That first byte indicates the operation to be performed and the size of the instruction (i.e., the number of additional bytes to be fetched for the instruction). The "Update IP-register" step increments the IP-register by 1 so that the CS:IP register pair points to the memory location that contains the next instruc-

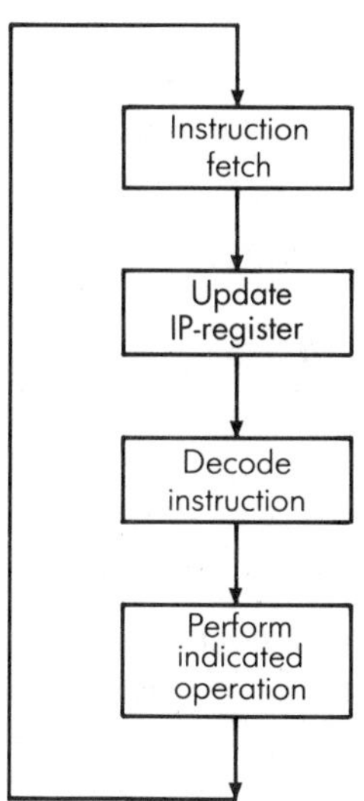

FIGURE 4.1
Instruction execution cycle

the CS:IP register pair points to the memory location that contains the next instruction byte to be fetched (i.e., the next byte of this instruction or the first byte of the next instruction). The "Decode instruction" step decodes the first byte of the instruction to determine the specific steps for the operation to be performed. The "Perform indicated operation" box includes different steps for different instructions. For the instruction

```
MOV  AL,COUNT
```

the detail of the "Perform indicated operation" box would include the following steps:

1. Fetch the next two bytes of the instruction that contains the offset of the operand COUNT.
2. Update the IP-register.
3. Add the offset to the appropriate segment register value to obtain the effective address of the data.
4. Fetch the data from the memory location specified by the effective address.
5. Move the fetched data to the AL-register.

Following execution of an instruction, the CS:IP register pair points to the first byte of the next instruction to be executed. For the instructions that have been considered thus far, this instruction is the one that immediately follows the instruction just executed. JUMP instructions provide a mechanism for altering the sequence of instruction executions, which is accomplished by altering the CS:IP register pair as part of the "Perform indicated operation" step of the instruction execution cycle. There are two types of JUMP instructions: conditional JUMP instructions and unconditional JUMP instructions. A **conditional JUMP instruction** may cause the CS:IP register pair to be altered depending on the current state of the flags register. An **unconditional JUMP instruction** always causes the CS:IP register pair to be altered.

Conditional JUMP Instructions

The "Perform indicated operation" step in the instruction execution cycle for a conditional JUMP instruction includes a decision. Depending on the outcome of this decision, one of two events happens:

1. No operation is performed, meaning that instruction execution continues with the next instruction in sequence.
2. The CS:IP register pair is altered so that instruction execution continues with the instruction at the address specified by the operand of the JUMP instruction.

In the 8088/8086 assembly language, the conditional JUMP instructions are divided into three groups:

Group 1 This group provides the capability to make decisions based on the current values of unsigned integers. The instructions in this group are described in Table 4.1. The first column of this table gives the operation code mnemonic. In each case, a choice of two operation code mnemonics is given for the operation. The second column gives an interpretation for the operation code mnemonics. The third column gives the flag settings that cause the CS:IP register pair to be altered for the given instruction. In the table, the term "above" for unsigned integers is analogous to the term "greater than" for signed integers, and the term "below" for unsigned integers is analogous to the term "less than" for signed integers.

Group 2 This group provides the capability to make decisions based on the current values of signed integers. The instructions in this group are described in Table 4.2. This table has the same form as that of Table 4.1.

Group 3 This group provides the capability to make decisions based on the current state of a specific flag in the flags register. The instructions in this group are described in Table 4.3, which also has the same form as that of Table 4.1.

The **conditional JUMP instructions** have the following general form:

[⟨*label*⟩] ⟨*op-code*⟩ ⟨*short-label*⟩ [⟨*comment*⟩]

in which ⟨*op-code*⟩ is one of the operation code mnemonics listed in Table 4.1, Table 4.2, or Table 4.3 and ⟨*short-label*⟩ is the label of an instruction elsewhere in the

TABLE 4.1
Conditional JUMP instructions for unsigned numbers

Operation Code Mnemonic	Description	Will Jump If
JA/JNBE	Jump if above Jump if not below nor equal	CF = 0 and ZF = 0
JAE/JNB	Jump if above or equal Jump if not below	CF = 0
JB/JNAE	Jump if below Jump if not above nor equal	CF = 1
JBE/JNA	Jump if below or equal Jump if not above	CF = 1 or ZF = 1
JE/JZ	Jump if equal to zero	ZF = 1
JNE/JNZ	Jump if not equal to zero	ZF = 0

procedure. This label must be the label of a memory location that is in the range −128 to +127 from the memory location immediately following the JUMP instruction. The operand value contained in the machine language representation of this instruction is an 8-bit two's complement integer. If the specific condition is met, then this value (extended to 16 bits) is added to the IP-register. None of the bits in the flags register are affected by execution of conditional JUMP instructions.

TABLE 4.2
Conditional JUMP instructions for signed numbers

Operation Code Mnemonic	Description	Will Jump If
JG/JNLE	Jump if greater than Jump if not less nor equal	ZF = 0 and SF = OF
JGE/JNL	Jump if greater than or equal Jump if not less than	(SF xor OF) = 0 (i.e., SF = OF)
JL/JNGE	Jump if less than Jump if not greater nor equal	(SF xor OF) = 1 (i.e., SF ≠ OF)
JLE/JNG	Jump if less than or equal Jump if not greater than	ZF = 1 or SF ≠ OF
JE/JZ	Jump if equal to zero	ZF = 1
JNE/JNZ	Jump if not equal to zero	ZF = 0

TABLE 4.3
Conditional JUMP instructions for the flags register

Operation Code Mnemonic	Description	Will Jump If
JC	Jump if carry	CF = 1
JNC	Jump if no carry	CF = 0
JO	Jump if overflow	OF = 1
JNO	Jump if no overflow	OF = 0
JS	Jump if sign negative	SF = 1
JNS	Jump if nonnegative sign	SF = 0
JZ	Jump if zero	ZF = 1
JNZ	Jump if not zero	ZF = 0
JP/JPE	Jump if parity even	PF = 1
JNP/JPO	Jump if parity odd	PF = 0

Consider the instruction

```
JE ALPHA
```

The assembler computes the difference between the offset of the memory location specified by ALPHA and the offset of the memory location immediately following the JE instruction. If this offset difference is not in the range −128 to +127, then the assembler generates an error message. MASM 6.0 generates the following message:

```
error A2075: jump destination too far : by n byte(s)
```

MASM 5.1

MASM 5.1 generates the following error message:

```
error A2053: Jump out of range by n byte(s)
```

In each case, n is the number of bytes out of range. When within range, the 1-byte offset difference is the operand in the machine language representation of the JE instruction.

EXAMPLES

Suppose that in the current code segment the offset of the JE instruction is 0055 hex, the offset of the instruction that follows the JE instruction is 0057 hex, and the offset of the instruction that contains the label ALPHA is 0033 hex. The offset difference is computed as follows:

0033 hex	0000000000110011 binary
−0057 hex	−0000000001010111 binary
0033 hex	0000000000110011 binary
+ FFA9 hex	+ 1111111110101001 binary
FFDC hex	1111111111011100 binary

Since the offset difference is in the range −128 to +127, it is reduced to 1 byte (DC hex or 11011100 binary) and stored as the operand in the machine language representation of the JE instruction.

Suppose that in the current code segment the offset of the JE instruction is 0018 hex, the offset of the instruction that follows the JE instruction is 001A hex, and the offset of the instruction that contains the label ALPHA is 0024 hex. The offset difference is computed as follows:

0024 hex	0000000000100100 binary
−001A hex	−0000000000011010 binary
0024 hex	0000000000100100 binary
+FFE6 hex	+1111111111100110 binary
000A hex	0000000000001010 binary

Since the offset difference is in the range −128 to +127, it is reduced to 1 byte (0A hex or 00001010 binary) and stored as the operand in the machine language representation of the JE instruction. ■

The "Perform indicated operation" step in the instruction cycle for execution of the JE ALPHA instruction would include the following steps:

1. Fetch the next byte of the instruction that contains the offset difference between the offset of ALPHA and the offset of the next instruction in sequence.
2. Update the IP-register, which forces the CS:IP register pair to point to the next instruction in sequence:

```
IF ZF = 1
THEN
        Expand offset difference to 16 bits
        Add expanded offset difference to IP-register
ENDIF
```

The resulting CS:IP register value identifies the next instruction to be executed. Note that the CS:IP register pair does not change if the condition (ZF = 1) is not True; that is, the CS:IP register pair continues to point to the instruction following the JE instruction.

Unconditional JUMP Instruction

In the 8088/8086 assembly language, the unconditional JUMP instruction is the **JMP instruction**, which has the following general form:

[⟨*label*⟩] JMP ⟨*target*⟩ [⟨*comment*⟩]

in which ⟨*target*⟩ is one of the following: a label with type attribute NEAR, a label with type attribute FAR, a variable with type attribute WORD, a variable with type attribute DOUBLE WORD, a 16-bit general register. Execution of a JMP instruction causes an unconditional transfer of control to the instruction that begins at the memory location specified by ⟨*target*⟩. Sequential execution continues from that point until another transfer of control instruction is encountered. None of the bits in the flags register are affected by execution of an unconditional JUMP instruction.

If the target operand is a label with type attribute NEAR, then the assembler computes the difference between the offset of the memory location specified by the target label and the offset of the memory location immediately following the JMP instruction. This difference is the operand in the machine language representation of the JMP instruction. This machine language operand can be either byte or word. The SHORT operator can be placed prior to the label in a JMP instruction to force the assembler to use a byte-offset difference in the machine language representation of the instruction. For example, consider the instruction

```
JMP SHORT ALPHA
```

In this case, the offset difference must be in the range -128 to $+127$. If it is not, then the assembler generates the "jump out of range" message. If the SHORT operator is omitted, then the target label can be anywhere within the current code segment. The SHORT operator is used to conserve memory space.

The SHORT operator is not needed in MASM 6.0. MASM 6.0 automatically generates the byte-offset form of the machine language instruction if the computed offset is in the range -128 to $+127$. Otherwise, it generates the word-offset form of the instruction.

Other possibilities for a target operand in a JMP instruction are beyond the scope of this book. The JUMP instructions used in the example programs involve labels that are defined in the same procedure as the jump itself.

The JMP instruction does not have a range restriction as do the conditional JUMP instructions. In fact, the JMP instruction can be used to get around the range restriction of a conditional JUMP instruction. Consider the following code fragment:

```
REPEAT:
        MOV  AX,BX
              .
              .
              .
        DEC  BX
        JNE  REPEAT
        LEA  DI,STRING
```

Following execution of the DEC instruction, the flags are set to reflect the value in the BX-register. If the BX-register value is nonzero, then the JNE instruction transfers control to the MOV instruction with label REPEAT. If the BX-register value is zero, then execution continues with the next instruction in sequence, the LEA instruction.

Suppose the JNE instruction causes a "jump out of range" error. The code fragment can be modified as follows to eliminate this error:

```
REPEAT:
          MOV  AX,BX
               .
               .
               .
          DEC  BX
          JE   CONTINUE
          JMP  REPEAT
CONTINUE:
          LEA  DI,STRING
```

Following execution of the DEC instruction, the flags are set to reflect the value in the BX-register. If the BX-register value is nonzero, then the JE instruction passes control to the next instruction in sequence, the JMP instruction, which transfers control to the MOV instruction with label REPEAT. If the BX-register value is zero, then the JE instruction transfers control to the LEA instruction with label CONTINUE.

Both of the preceding code fragments are equivalent logically. The second one corrects an out-of-range error in the first one at the expense of one JMP instruction.

4.2 Decision Structures

Decision structures in programs are based on conditions. Conditions are logical expressions that have a **truth value**. That is, a **logical expression** is one that evaluates to either True or False. The program decision then is based on the truth value of the condition. Most high-level languages provide relational expressions as one form for expressing conditions. The **relational expression** has the following general form:

$\langle arith\ expr\rangle\langle relational\ op\rangle\langle arith\ expr\rangle$

in which $\langle arith\ expr\rangle$ is an arithmetic expression and $\langle relational\ op\rangle$ is one of the following relational operators: $<$ (is less than), $\leq$ (is less than or equal to), $=$ (is equal to), $\neq$ (is not equal to), $>$ (is greater than), or $\geq$ (is greater than or equal to). To evaluate a relational expression, the two arithmetic expressions must be evaluated first. The value of the relational expression is True if the value of the first arithmetic expression has the specified relationship to the value of the second arithmetic expression. Otherwise, the value of the relational expression is False.

EXAMPLE

X**2 + Y**2 < Z**2

The value of the preceding relational expression is True if the value of the expression X**2 + Y**2 is less than the value of the expression Z**2. Otherwise, the value of the preceding relational expression is False. ■

In assembly language, one method of evaluating a relational expression is first to write the instructions to evaluate the two arithmetic expressions and then subtract the value of the second arithmetic expression from the value of the first arithmetic expression. The resulting value will have the same relationship to zero as the value of the first arithmetic expression has to the value of the second arithmetic expression. The bits in the flags register will reflect this relationship.

EXAMPLE

Consider the relational expression

$$SIDE3 < (SIDE1 + SIDE2)$$

This relational expression is equivalent to the relational expression

$$(SIDE3 - (SIDE1 + SIDE2)) < 0$$

which was obtained by subtracting

$$(SIDE1 + SIDE2)$$

from both sides of the inequality. To set the flags register to reflect this relationship, the following instructions can be used:

```
MOV  AX,SIDE3
SUB  AX,SIDE1
SUB  AX,SIDE2
```

■

Once the bits in the flags register have been set to reflect the desired relationship, the appropriate conditional JUMP instruction is used to make the decision.

Single-Alternative Decision

Two types of decision structures are introduced at this point: the single-alternative decision and the double-alternative decision.

A **single-alternative decision** structure either performs a sequence of instructions or skips that sequence of instructions depending on the value of a condition. If the condition evaluates to True, then the sequence of instructions is performed. If the condition evaluates to False, then the sequence of instructions is skipped.

The flowchart in Figure 4.2 represents a single-alternative decision structure. The pseudocode used in this book for a single-alternative decision structure is as follows:

```
IF     ⟨condition⟩
THEN
       ⟨sequence of control structures⟩
ENDIF
```

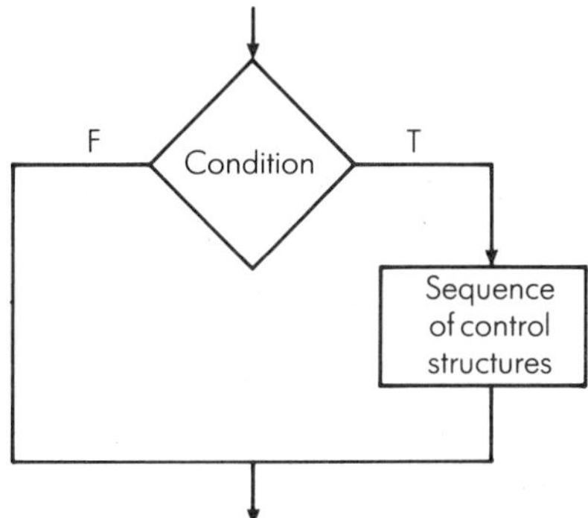

FIGURE 4.2
Flowchart of a single-alternative decision structure

EXAMPLE

Suppose the data segment definition for a program contains the following variable definitions for three unsigned integer variables:

```
X    DW  ?
Y    DW  ?
SUM  DW  ?
```

The following instructions implement the single-alternative decision structure:

```
STRUCTURE:
     IF    X/Y ≠ Y
     THEN
           SUM = SUM + Y
     ENDIF

IMPLEMENTATION:
                MOV  AX,X
                MOV  DX,0
                DIV  Y
                SUB  AX,Y
                JE   END_IF
                MOV  AX,Y
                ADD  SUM,AX
     END_IF:
```

The first two MOV instructions load the AX-register with the unsigned integer value of variable X and expand it to 32 bits in the DX:AX register pair. The DIV instruction computes the value of the left-hand arithmetic expression X/Y. The value of the right-hand arithmetic expression is the value of variable Y. The SUB instruction computes the difference between the two arithmetic expressions, (X/Y) − Y. The difference has the same relationship to zero as the value of the left-hand arithmetic expression has to the value of the right-hand arithmetic expression. The SUB instruction sets the flags to reflect this relationship. The JE instruction makes the decision based on this relationship. If the difference is nonzero, then the MOV and ADD instructions are executed (i.e., the jump to END_IF is not taken). If the difference is zero, then the MOV and ADD instructions are skipped (i.e., the jump to END_IF is taken). The MOV and ADD instructions implement the assignment

$$SUM = SUM + Y$$

The assignment is the single alternative that is either selected or skipped based on the value of the relational expression. ■

Double-Alternative Decision

A **double-alternative decision** structure selects one of two sequences of instructions to perform depending on the value of a condition. If the condition evaluates to True, then the first sequence of instructions is selected. If the condition evaluates to False, then the second sequence of instructions is selected.

The flowchart in Figure 4.3 represents a double-alternative decision structure.

FIGURE 4.3 Flowchart of a double-alternative decision structure

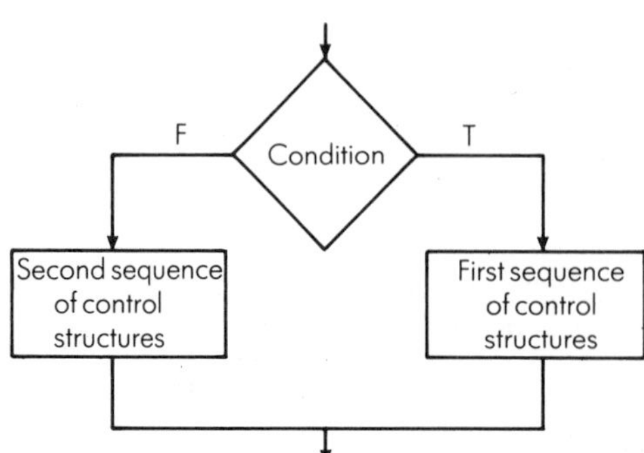

The pseudocode used in this book for a double-alternative decision structure is as follows:

```
IF    ⟨condition⟩
THEN
      ⟨first sequence of control structures⟩
ELSE
      ⟨second sequence of control structures⟩
ENDIF
```

EXAMPLE

Suppose the data segment definition for a program contains the following variable definitions for two signed integers:

```
X  DW  ?
Y  DW  ?
```

The following instructions implement the double-alternative decision structure:

```
STRUCTURE:
     IF    X ≤ 3
     THEN
           Y = 2X - 1
     ELSE
           Y = 5
     ENDIF

IMPLEMENTATION:
                  MOV    AX,X
                  SUB    AX,3
                  JG     ELSE1
                  MOV    AX,X  ;
                  ADD    AX,X  ;       TRUE ALTERNATIVE
                  DEC    AX    ;
                  MOV    Y,AX  ;
                  JMP    ENDIF1
         ELSE1:
                  MOV    Y,5  ;     FALSE ALTERNATIVE
         ENDIF1:
```

The first two instructions compute the value X − 3, which has the same relationship to zero as X has to 3. The SUB instruction sets the flags to reflect this relationship. The JG instruction makes the decision based on this relationship. The decision selects one of the two alternatives to be executed. If X − 3 is less than or equal to zero, then the jump to ELSE1 is not taken, the four instructions of the TRUE ALTERNATIVE are executed, and the JMP instruction causes the FALSE ALTERNATIVE to be skipped. If X − 3 is greater than zero, then the jump to ELSE1 is taken, the TRUE ALTERNATIVE is skipped, and the one instruction of the FALSE ALTERNATIVE is executed. No matter which alternative is selected, after the alternative instructions have been executed, sequential execution continues with the instruction at label ENDIF1. ■

Compare Instruction

Suppose a decision in a program is to be based on the relationship between the value in the AX-register and the immediate value 15. The instruction

```
SUB AX,15
```

sets the bits in the flags register to reflect this relationship. However, the value in the AX-register now is modified, and that value may be needed in one or both of the alternatives of the decision that is based on this relationship.

The 8088/8086 assembly language provides a compare instruction, the CMP instruction, that behaves like the SUB instruction except that the destination operand is not modified (i.e., the difference is not saved). The **CMP instruction** has the following general form:

[⟨*label*⟩] `CMP` ⟨*destination*⟩,⟨*source*⟩ [⟨*comment*⟩]

in which ⟨*destination*⟩ and ⟨*source*⟩ identify the locations of the two values being compared. This instruction causes the destination operand to be compared to the source operand and the flags to be set to reflect the relationship of the destination operand to the source operand. This task is accomplished by subtracting the source operand from the destination operand and setting the flags to reflect this difference. Neither the source operand nor the destination operand is modified.

For the CMP instruction, the type attribute of the two operands must match (i.e., both byte or both word). Figure 4.4 illustrates the possible combinations of the destination and source operands. If the destination operand is a general register, then the source operand can be a general register, a memory location, or an immediate value. If the destination operand is a memory location, then the source operand can be either a general register or an immediate value.

FIGURE 4.4 Allowable operands for CMP instruction

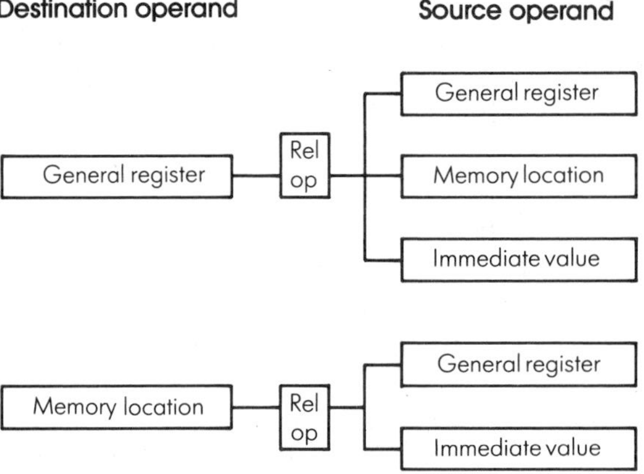

(Rel op stands for relational operator)

Note that the mnemonics of the conditional JUMP instructions were designed to have meaning when used in conjunction with the CMP instruction. For a conditional JUMP instruction that immediately follows a CMP instruction, the jump is taken when the destination operand is related to the source operand in the specified way.

EXAMPLE

With the instructions

```
CMP  AX,BX
JG   ENDIFF
```

the jump to ENDIFF is taken if the signed integer value in the AX-register is greater than the signed integer value in the BX-register. ■

Execution of a CMP instruction affects the flags in exactly the same way as they would be affected by execution of a SUB instruction with the same operands. See Section 3.2 for an explanation of the flag settings for execution of a SUB instruction.

EXAMPLE

In the double-alternative decision example, the instruction

```
MOV AX,X
```

appeared twice because the SUB instruction modified the value in the AX-register and the original value was needed in the TRUE ALTERNATIVE. Use of the CMP instruction rather than the SUB instruction allows for the elimination of one of the two MOV instructions. Either of the following instruction sequences can be substituted for the sequence in that previous example:

Sequence A:

```
        MOV  AX,X
        CMP  AX,3
        JG   ELSE1
        ADD  AX,X
        DEC  AX
        MOV  Y,AX
        JMP  ENDIF1
ELSE1:
        MOV  Y,5
ENDIF1:
```

Sequence B:

```
        CMP  X,3
        JG   ELSE2
        MOV  AX,X
        ADD  AX,X
        DEC  AX
        MOV  Y,AX
        JMP  ENDIF2

ELSE2:
        MOV  Y,5
ENDIF2:
```

■

Decision-Generating Macro Directives

MASM 6.0 provides some macro directives that facilitate the implementation of decision structures. For the single-alternative decision structure, the decision-generating macro directives have the following general form:

.IF ⟨*conditional-expr*⟩
⟨*instruction-list*⟩
.ENDIF

in which ⟨*instruction-list*⟩ is the list of assembly language instructions to be executed if the ⟨*conditional-expr*⟩ evaluates to True, and ⟨*conditional-expr*⟩, in its simplest form, is a relational expression of the form

⟨*destination*⟩ ⟨*rel-op*⟩ ⟨*source*⟩

Here, ⟨*destination*⟩ is the destination operand for the CMP instruction to be generated by the assembler, ⟨*source*⟩ is the source operand for the CMP instruction, and ⟨*rel-op*⟩ is one of the following relational operators: < (is less than), <= (is less than or equal to), == (is equal to), != (is not equal to), > (is greater than), or >= (is greater than or equal to). The .IF directive causes the assembler to generate the instruction

```
CMP  <destination>,<source>
```

followed by a conditional JUMP instruction that jumps over the instructions of the ⟨*instruction-list*⟩ if the ⟨*conditional-expr*⟩ is False (i.e., if the reverse of the ⟨*conditional-expr*⟩ is True). The assembler also generates a unique label, which is the operand of the conditional JUMP instruction and is the label of the instruction that immediately follows the .ENDIF directive. The unique labels generated by the assembler in response to the decision-generating macro directives are selected from the set of reserved labels in the range @C0001–@CFFFF.

EXAMPLE

Suppose the data segment definition for a program contains the following variable definitions for three unsigned integer variables:

```
X    WORD  ?
Y    WORD  ?
SUM  WORD  ?
```

The single-alternative decision structure

```
IF    X/Y ≠ Y
THEN
      SUM = SUM + Y
ENDIF
```

can be implemented by the code

```
MOV     AX,X
MOV     DX,0
DIV     Y
.IF     AX != Y
MOV     AX,Y
ADD     SUM,AX
.ENDIF
```

from which the assembler (MASM 6.0) might generate the following code to be translated into machine language:

```
         MOV    AX,X
         MOV    DX,0
         DIV    Y
         cmp    ax,y
         je     @C0001
         MOV    AX,Y
         ADD    SUM,AX
@C0001:
```

Note the lowercase form for the instructions that are generated by the assembler in response to the macro directives. This form is the form in which these instructions appear in the assembler-generated listing. ■

For the double-alternative decision structure, the decision-generating macro directives have the following general form:

```
.IF ⟨conditional-expr⟩
⟨first-instruction-list⟩
.ELSE
⟨second-instruction-list⟩
.ENDIF
```

in which ⟨*first-instruction-list*⟩ is the list of assembly language instructions to be executed if the ⟨*conditional-expr*⟩ evaluates to True, ⟨*second-instruction-list*⟩ is the list of assembly language instructions to be executed if the ⟨*conditional-expr*⟩ evaluates to False, and ⟨*conditional-expr*⟩, in its simplest form, is a relational expression of the form

```
⟨destination⟩ ⟨rel-op⟩ ⟨source⟩
```

in which ⟨*destination*⟩ and ⟨*source*⟩ are the operands for the CMP instruction to be generated by the assembler and ⟨*rel-op*⟩ is one of the following relational operators: <, <=, ==, !=, >, or >=. The .IF directive causes the assembler to generate the instruction

```
CMP ⟨destination⟩,⟨source⟩
```

followed by a conditional JUMP instruction that jumps over the instructions of the ⟨*first-instruction-list*⟩ if the ⟨*conditional-expr*⟩ is False (i.e., if the reverse of the ⟨*conditional-expr*⟩ is True). The assembler also generates a unique label, which is the operand of the conditional JUMP instruction and is the label of the instruction that immediately follows the .ELSE directive (i.e., the first instruction in the ⟨*second-instruction-list*⟩). The .ELSE directive causes the assembler to generate a JMP instruction that jumps over the instructions of the ⟨*second-instruction-list*⟩. The assembler also generates another unique label, which is the operand of the JMP instruction and is the label of the instruction that immediately follows the .ENDIF directive.

EXAMPLE

Suppose the data segment definition for a program contains the following variable definitions for two signed integers:

```
X SWORD ?
Y SWORD ?
```

The double-alternative decision structure

```
IF   X ≤ 3
THEN
     Y = 2X - 1
ELSE
     Y = 5
ENDIF
```

can be implemented by the code

```
.IF        X <= 3
MOV        AX,X
ADD        AX,AX
DEC        AX
MOV        Y,AX
.ELSE
MOV        Y,5
.ENDIF
```

from which the assembler (MASM 6.0) might generate the following code to be translated into machine language:

```
            cmp     x,003h
            jg      @C0002
            MOV     AX,X
            ADD     AX,AX
            DEC     AX
            MOV     Y,AX
            JMP      @C0004
@C0002:
            MOV     Y,5
@C0004:
```

Note that a label is skipped between the two labels that are generated by the assembler. There is a triple-alternative form for the decision-generating macro directives that makes use of this skipped label. The triple-alternative form is not discussed here.

Note also that it is necessary to define X with the SWORD pseudo-operation. If X had been defined with either the DW pseudo-operation or the WORD pseudo-operation, then the assembler would have assumed that X was an unsigned variable and would have generated the conditional JUMP instruction

```
ja  @C0002
```

Since X was defined with the SWORD pseudo-operation, the assembler knew that X was a signed variable and thus generated the instruction

```
jg  @C0002
```

Note again the lowercase form for the instructions that are generated by the assembler in response to the macro directives. Constants appearing in these assembler-generated instructions are always in hexadecimal form. ■

Programming Examples

In this section, two problems are considered. The first problem, computing the sum of the cubes of the first *n* positive integers, was introduced in Chapter 3. The program to perform that computation here is modified to include an overflow check. The second problem is that of evaluating a particular step function.

Sum of Cubes of First *n* Positive Integers

Program Listing 3.2 shows the implementation of an algorithm to compute the sum of the cubes of the first *n* positive integers. A check for arithmetic overflow in the computation is not performed. Therefore, for any input value of *n* that is greater than 22, the program displays an incorrect result. A better way to handle such inputs would be to display a message to the user that indicates that the input is beyond the program's capability. Program Listing 4.1 shows a modified version of Program Listing 3.2. In the modified version, if an overflow occurs in the computation, then the program displays the message

```
ARITHMETIC OVERFLOW OCCURRED
```

This discussion concentrates on the differences between Program Listing 4.1 and Program Listing 3.2. One line (line 11) has been added to the prologue to explain

```
            PAGE    80,132
;====================================================================
;                      PROGRAM LISTING 4.1
;
; GIVEN AN INTEGER VALUE FOR n, THIS PROGRAM COMPUTES THE SUM OF
; THE CUBES OF THE FIRST n POSITIVE INTEGERS USING THE FORMULA:
;
;  3    3    3          3              2
; 1  + 2  + 3  + ... + n  = [n(n + 1)/2]
;
; AN OVERFLOW CHECK IS PROVIDED
;====================================================================
            DOSSEG
            .MODEL  SMALL,BASIC,FARSTACK
;====================================================================
                                        ;PROCEDURES TO
            EXTRN   GETDEC$:FAR         ;GET 16-BIT UNSIGNED DEC INT
            EXTRN   NEWLINE:FAR         ;DISPLAY NEWLINE CHARACTER
            EXTRN   PUTDEC$:FAR         ;DISPLAY 16-BIT UNSIGNED INT
            EXTRN   PUTSTRNG:FAR        ;DISPLAY CHARACTER STRING
;====================================================================
; S T A C K   D E F I N I T I O N
            .STACK  256
;====================================================================
; C O N S T A N T   D E F I N I T I O N S
            .CONST
;
PROMPT      DB      'ENTER A POSITIVE INTEGER VALUE   '
MESSAGE_1   DB      'THE SUM OF THE FIRST '
MESSAGE_2   DB      ' CUBE(S) IS '
OVRFLO_MSG  DB      'ARITHMETIC OVERFLOW OCCURRED'
TWO         DW      2                   ;CONSTANT 2
;
;====================================================================
; V A R I A B L E   D E F I N I T I O N S
            .DATA
;
N           DW      ?                   ;NUMBER OF CUBES TO SUM
SUM         DW      ?                   ;SUM OF FIRST N CUBES
;
;====================================================================
; C O D E   S E G M E N T   D E F I N I T I O N
            .CODE   EX_4_1
            .STARTUP                    ;GENERATE STARTUP CODE
;
            PUSH    DS                  ;SET ES REGISTER TO POINT TO
            POP     ES                  ;DATA GROUP
            LEA     DI,PROMPT           ;PROMPT FOR N
            MOV     CX,33
            CALL    PUTSTRNG
            CALL    GETDEC$             ;GET N
            MOV     N,AX
            ADD     AX,1                ;SUM = [N(N + 1)/2] ** 2
            JC      OVRFLO              ;IF   NO OVERFLOW
            MUL     N
            JC      OVRFLO
            DIV     TWO
            MUL     AX
            JC      OVRFLO
            MOV     SUM,AX              ;THEN
            CALL    NEWLINE             ;      SKIP TO NEXT LINE ON DISP.
            LEA     DI,MESSAGE_1        ;      DISPLAY
            MOV     CX,21               ;      'THE SUM OF THE FIRST '
            CALL    PUTSTRNG
            MOV     AX,N                ;      DISPLAY N
            MOV     BH,0
            CALL    PUTDEC$
```

```
68:              LEA    DI,MESSAGE_2          ;      DISPLAY ' CUBE(S) IS '
69:              MOV    CX,12
70:              CALL   PUTSTRNG
71:              MOV    AX,SUM                ;      DISPLAY SUM
72:              CALL   PUTDEC$
73:              JMP    RETURN
74: OVRFLO:                                   ;ELSE
75:              LEA    DI,OVRFLO_MSG         ;      DISPLAY OVERFLOW MESSAGE
76:              MOV    CX,28
77:              CALL   PUTSTRNG
78: RETURN:                                   ;ENDIF
79:              .EXIT                        ;RETURN TO DOS
80: ;
81:              END
```

that an overflow check is provided by the program. As well, one line (line 31) has been added in the constant data segment that defines the message to be displayed to the user in the event that the program detects an overflow in the computation.

The computation performed by the program is

$$[n(n + 1)/2]^2$$

where n is the input value. Arithmetic overflow could occur at one of three places in this computation: If the input value for n is 65,535, then overflow occurs when $n + 1$ is performed; if the input value for n is 1000, then overflow occurs when $n(n + 1)$ is performed; if the input value for n is 23, then overflow occurs when $[n(n + 1)]^2$ is performed.

One common misconception of beginning assembly language programmers is that, once the overflow or carry flag is set, it stays set until it is cleared by an explicit instruction that clears the flags. This situation is *not* the case with the 8088/8086. Each integer arithmetic instruction in the computation sets or clears the OF and CF bits in the flags register depending on whether or not execution of that instruction resulted in an overflow condition. Therefore, an overflow check has to be made after each part of the computation that could potentially cause an overflow condition. In Program Listing 4.1, the computation involves unsigned integer values. Recall that with unsigned integer values, the CF bit in the flags register is the overflow indicator.

The instructions in lines 52–60 perform the computation and provide the overflow checks. The ADD instruction in line 53 performs the computation $n + 1$. Note that this is done with an ADD instruction rather than the INC instruction used in Program Listing 3.2. ADD is used here because the INC instruction does not affect the CF bit in the flags register and the ADD instruction does. Execution of the ADD instruction sets the condition. That is, ADD sets or clears the CF bit in the flags register depending on whether or not an overflow occurred in the addition operation. The JC instruction in line 54 makes a decision based on this condition—either to continue with the computation if the CF bit in the flags register is 0 or to skip the remainder of the computation and transfer control to the instruction labeled OVRFLO if the CF bit in the flags register is 1. That is,

```
JC OVRFLO
```

is a conditional JUMP instruction that causes the program to jump to the instruction labeled OVRFLO if the CF bit in the flags register is set. Otherwise, the instruction causes the program to continue to the next instruction in sequence.

The MUL instruction in line 55 performs the computation $n(n + 1)$. Execution of the MUL instruction sets the condition. It sets or clears the CF bit in the flags register depending on whether or not an overflow occurred in the multiplication operation. The JC instruction in line 56 again makes a decision based on this condition—either to continue the computation (CF = 0) or to skip the remainder of the computation (CF = 1). Recall that with integer multiplication instructions, both the CF and OF bits are set or cleared depending on whether or not overflow occurred. Thus, the JC instruction in line 56 could be changed to a JO instruction without affecting the correctness of the program. The JC instruction is used for consistency in dealing with unsigned integer values.

The DIV instruction in line 57 performs the computation $n(n + 1)/2$. For all positive integer values for n, where $n(n + 1)$ does not cause overflow, the value of $n(n + 1)$ is greater than or equal to 2 and is even. Therefore, this division cannot cause an overflow. Division overflow is handled via interrupts and is discussed further in Chapter 9.

The MUL instruction in line 58 performs $[n(n + 1)/2]^2$. Execution of the MUL instruction sets the condition. It sets or clears the CF bit in the flags register depending on whether or not an overflow occurred in the multiplication operation. The JC instruction in line 59 again makes a decision based on this condition—either to save and display the results of the computation (lines 60–72) or to skip the instructions that display the result and to execute the instructions (lines 74–77) to display the message

```
ARITHMETIC OVERFLOW OCCURRED
```

From a high-level pseudocode standpoint, the program includes a computation followed by a double-alternative decision (see the pseudocode in Program Listing 4.1). The double-alternative decision says that, if no overflow occurred during the computation, then display the results of the computation. Otherwise, display the overflow message.

The following are the results from some executions of this program:

```
ENTER A POSITIVE INTEGER VALUE          18
THE SUM OF THE FIRST 18 CUBE(S) IS 29241

ENTER A POSITIVE INTEGER VALUE          23
ARITHMETIC OVERFLOW OCCURRED

ENTER A POSITIVE INTEGER VALUE        1000
ARITHMETIC OVERFLOW OCCURRED

ENTER A POSITIVE INTEGER VALUE       65535
ARITHMETIC OVERFLOW OCCURRED
```

Step Function Evaluation

Consider the problem of computing the value of y for the following step function, given an integer value for x:

$$
\begin{aligned}
y &= -5 && \text{for } x \leq -2 \\
y &= 2x - 1 && \text{for } -2 \leq x \leq 3 \\
y &= 5 && \text{for } x \geq 3
\end{aligned}
$$

Figure 4.5 graphs this step function. The following pseudocode describes an

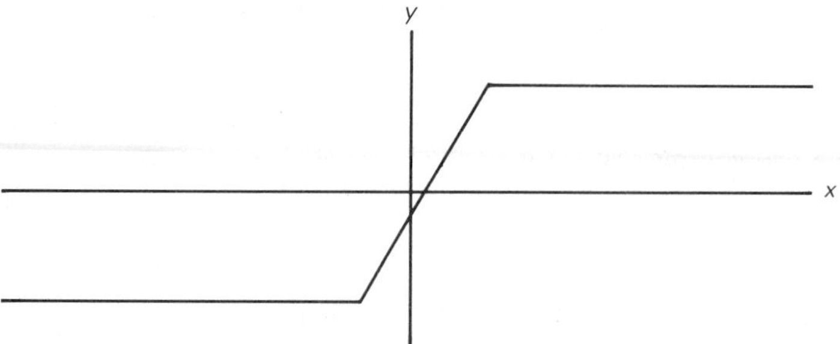

FIGURE 4.5
Graph of a step function

algorithm for solving the preceding step function:

```
GET X
IF   X < -2
THEN
     Y = -5
ELSE
     IF   X ≤ 3
     THEN
          Y = 2X - 1
     ELSE
          Y = 5
     ENDIF
ENDIF
DISPLAY Y
```

This algorithm contains two double-alternative decision structures. The second alternative of one of the double-alternative decision structures is the other double-alternative decision structure. This algorithm illustrates **nested decision structures**. Nested control structures are considered in detail in Section 4.4.

Program Listing 4.2 shows an implementation of the preceding algorithm. The prologue in lines 2–10 explains the program's function, the .MODEL pseudo-operation in line 11 enables the use of simplified segment directives, the external definitions in lines 14–17 identify the input/output procedures that are referenced by the program, and the stack segment definition in lines 18–21 is the standard one used in the example programs of this book.

The constant data segment is defined in lines 22–27. Two string constants are defined in the data segment: a message that prompts the user to enter an integer value for X (line 26) and a message used for annotation of the output (line 27).

The code segment is defined in lines 28–62 and contains the instructions for the main procedure of the program. The main procedure begins in the standard way by initializing the segment register (lines 33 and 34). These two MOV instructions set the ES-register to address DGROUP.

The instructions in lines 35–37 display the prompt message to the user, and the call to GETDEC in line 38 accepts a signed integer value for X from the keyboard into the AX-register. In this implementation of the algorithm, the AX-register is used to hold the values of both X and Y. In two of the three cases, Y is a constant; in the third case, Y is computed as a function of X. In all three cases, once the value of Y has been determined, the value of X is no longer needed. Therefore, the value of Y can replace the value of X in the AX-register. This double use of the AX-register is convenient because procedure GETDEC leaves the input value (X) in the AX-register and procedure PUTDEC expects the output value (Y) in the AX-register.

```
             PAGE     80,132
;=====================================================================
;                     PROGRAM LISTING 4.2
;
; COMPUTE Y GIVEN INTEGER X WHERE
;      Y = -5            FOR X <= -2
;      Y = 2X-1          FOR -2 <= X <= 3
;      Y = 5             FOR X >= 3
;
;=====================================================================
             .MODEL   SMALL,BASIC,FARSTACK
;=====================================================================
                                                ;PROCEDURES TO
             EXTRN    GETDEC:FAR                ;GET DECIMAL INTEGER
             EXTRN    NEWLINE:FAR               ;DISPLAY NEWLINE CHARACTER
             EXTRN    PUTDEC:FAR                ;DISPLAY DECIMAL INTEGER
             EXTRN    PUTSTRNG:FAR              ;DISPLAY CHARACTER STRING
;=====================================================================
; S T A C K   D E F I N I T I O N
;
             .STACK   256
;=====================================================================
; C O N S T A N T   D E F I N I T I O N S
             .CONST
;
PROMPT       DB       'ENTER INTEGER VALUE FOR X',0DH,0AH
ANNOTATION   DB       0DH,0AH,'Y = '
;=====================================================================
; C O D E   S E G M E N T   D E F I N I T I O N
;
             .CODE
EX_4_2:
             MOV      AX,DGROUP                 ;SET ES-REGISTER TO ADDRESS
             MOV      ES,AX                     ;DGROUP
             LEA      DI,PROMPT
             MOV      CX,27                     ;PROMPT FOR X
             CALL     PUTSTRNG
             CALL     GETDEC                    ;GET X
IF_1:                                           ;IF   X < -2
             CMP      AX,-2
             JGE      ELSE_1
             MOV      AX,-5                     ;THEN Y = -5
             JMP      ENDIF_1
ELSE_1:                                         ;ELSE
IF_2:
             CMP      AX,3                      ;      IF   X <= 3
             JG       ELSE_2
             ADD      AX,AX                     ;      THEN Y = 2X-1
             DEC      AX
             JMP      ENDIF_2
ELSE_2:                                         ;      ELSE Y = 5
             MOV      AX,5
ENDIF_2:                                        ;      ENDIF
ENDIF_1:                                        ;ENDIF
             LEA      DI,ANNOTATION
             MOV      CX,6                      ;DISPLAY ANNOTATION
             CALL     PUTSTRNG
             MOV      BH,0
             CALL     PUTDEC                    ;DISPLAY Y
             CALL     NEWLINE
             .EXIT                              ;RETURN TO DOS
;
             END      EX_4_2
```

The outer double-alternative decision structure is implemented in lines 39–54. The labels IF_1, ELSE_1, and ENDIF_1 have been used to emphasize the parts of this structure. The test of the condition is performed by the CMP instruction in line 40. This instruction subtracts −2 from the value of X in the AX-register and sets the flags to reflect the result. The value in the AX-register is not modified by execution of this CMP instruction. The conditional JUMP instruction in line 41 makes the decision based on this condition. If the value of X is less than −2, then the jump is *not* taken and execution continues with the MOV instruction in line 42 (the beginning of the True alternative, or the "then" portion of the double-alternative decision). However, if the value of X is greater than or equal to −2, then the jump is taken to the instruction in lines 44–46 (the beginning of the False alternative, or the "else" portion of the double-alternative decision). Note that ELSE_1 and IF_2 are labels for the instruction in line 46; both are not necessary but are placed there for emphasis.

If the value of X is less than −2, the MOV instruction in line 42 sets the value of Y in the AX-register to −5 and the unconditional JUMP instruction in line 43 transfers control to the end of the double-alternative decision structure (lines 54 and 55, labeled ENDIF_1).

If the value of X is greater than or equal to −2, the inner double-alternative decision structure is entered, which is implemented in lines 45–53. The labels IF_2, ELSE_2, and ENDIF_2 have been used to emphasize the parts of this structure. The test of the condition is performed by the CMP instruction in line 46. This instruction subtracts 3 from the value of X in the AX-register and sets the flags to reflect the result. Again, the value in the AX-register is not modified by execution of this CMP instruction. The conditional JUMP instruction in line 47 makes the decision based on this condition. If the value of X is less than or equal to 3, then the jump is *not* taken and execution continues with the ADD instruction in line 48 (the beginning of the True alternative, or the "then" portion of the double-alternative decision). However, if the value of X is greater than 3, then the jump is taken to the instruction in lines 51 and 52 (the beginning of the False alternative, or the "else" portion of the double-alternative decision).

If the value of X is less than or equal to 3, the instructions in lines 48–50 are executed. The instructions in lines 48 and 49 compute the value (2X − 1) in the AX-register. This value is the value of Y for the case −2 <= X <= 3. The unconditional JUMP instruction in line 50 transfers control to the end of the inner double-alternative decision structure (lines 53–55, labeled ENDIF_2), which is also the end of the outer double-alternative decision structure.

If the value of X is greater than 3, the MOV instruction in line 52 is executed. This instruction sets the value of Y in the AX-register to 5. The next instruction to be executed is the instruction in line 55. That is, the end of the two double-alternative decision structures has been reached.

The instructions in lines 55–60 display the value of Y along with the annotation message. The .EXIT macro directive in line 61 causes the assembler to generate the instructions that will return control to DOS.

The following are the results from some executions of this program:

```
ENTER INTEGER VALUE FOR X
-3
Y = -5

ENTER INTEGER VALUE FOR X
-1
Y = -3
```

```
ENTER INTEGER VALUE FOR X
0

Y = -1


ENTER INTEGER VALUE FOR X
2

Y = 3


ENTER INTEGER VALUE FOR X
4

Y = 5
```

The decision structures implemented in lines 39–54 of Program Listing 4.2 could have been implemented using the decision-generating macro directives available in MASM 6.0. With MASM 6.0, the code in lines 39–54 of Program Listing 4.2 can be replaced with the following code:

```
.IF      SWORD PTR AX < -2    ;IF   X < -2
MOV      AX,-5                ;THEN Y = -5
.ELSE                         ;ELSE
.IF      SWORD PTR AX <= 3    ;     IF   X <= 3
ADD      AX,AX                ;     THEN Y = 2X - 1
DEC      AX
.ELSE                         ;     ELSE
MOV      AX,5                 ;          Y = 5
.ENDIF                        ;     ENDIF
.ENDIF                        ;ENDIF
```

The assembler performs the substitutions for the decision-generating macro directives .IF, .ELSE, and .ENDIF, and the assembly language code that is translated to machine language is the following:

```
          cmp    sword ptr ax, - 002h
          jge    @C0001
          MOV    AX,-5
          jmp    @C0003
@C0001:
          cmp    sword ptr ax, 003h
          jg     @C0004
          ADD    AX,AX
          DEC    AX
          jmp    @C0006
@C0004:
          MOV    AX,5
@C0006:
@C0003:
```

Compare this assembly language code to the code in lines 39–54 of Program Listing 4.2.

Note the use of the SWORD type specifier and the PTR operator in the .IF macro directives. Since the operands of the .IF directive are a register designator and an immediate value, the assembler does not know whether the operands are signed or unsigned values. If the assembler does not know the type attribute of the operands for a .IF directive, then it assumes that they are unsigned and generates an unsigned conditional JUMP instruction following the CMP instruction. The operand SWORD

PTR AX tells the assembler that the AX-register contains a signed integer value; therefore, the assembler knows to generate a signed conditional JUMP instruction. That is, the directive

```
.IF  AX < -2
```

causes the assembler to generate

```
cmp  ax, - 002h
jae  @C0001
```

but the directive

```
.IF  SWORD PTR AX < -2
```

causes the assembler to generate

```
cmp  ax, - 002h
jge  @C0001
```

The latter code is correct for the program of Program Listing 4.2 because the program manipulates signed integer values.

The diskette that accompanies this book includes a source code file named EX_4_2A.ASM. This source file provides an alternative implementation of the algorithm of Program Listing 4.2. This alternative implementation uses decision-generating macro directives.

Labels

At this point, a discussion of labels is in order. The label for an instruction can be on the same line as the instruction or on a separate line between the instruction and the one that immediately precedes it. That is, a label is associated with the first instruction that follows it in the code. In Program Listing 4.2, the labels ELSE_1 and IF_2 are both labels for the CMP instruction in line 46. The advantage of placing the label on a separate line is for ease in program editing. Suppose a program that contains the instruction

```
ALPHA:  ADD  AX,Y
```

needs to be modified to the instructions

```
ALPHA:  MOV  AX,X
        ADD  AX,Y
```

This modification requires that an instruction be added and that the label be moved to the instruction that was added. However, if the original version had been

```
ALPHA:
            ADD  AX,Y
```

then the modification to

```
ALPHA:

            MOV  AX,X
            ADD  AX,Y
```

could be accomplished by addition of a single instruction. The label is moved automatically.

Labels have type attributes associated with them. The value of this type attribute is either NEAR or FAR. A label with type attribute NEAR has as its value a

2-byte offset. This is the offset within the segment of the memory location that is identified by that label. A label with type attribute NEAR can be referenced only from instructions within the same code segment. A label with type attribute FAR has as its value a 2-byte segment address and a 2-byte offset within the segment. The segment address and offset is the address of the actual memory location identified by that label. A label with type attribute FAR can be referenced from instructions in any code segment of the program. The colon (:) appended to a label gives a label the type attribute NEAR. The ⟨*short-label*⟩ operand in a conditional JUMP instruction must be a label with type attribute NEAR. The target operand in an unconditional JUMP instruction may be a label with a type attribute of either NEAR or FAR. Most of the labels appearing in the program listings in this book have colons (:) appended (i.e., they have type attribute NEAR).

4.3 Loop Structures

A **loop structure** provides a mechanism for repeating a set of instructions based on the value of a condition. A loop structure consists of two parts: the loop test and the loop body. The **loop body** is the sequence of instructions to be repeated. The **loop test** is the evaluation of the condition on which the decision to execute the loop body is based. Two condition-controlled loop structures are discussed in this section: the WHILE loop and the REPEAT-UNTIL loop.

WHILE Loop

With a **WHILE loop structure**, the loop test is at the top of the loop. While the value of the condition is True, the loop body is executed. When the value of the condition is False, the loop is terminated. Since the test is at the top of the loop, it is possible that the loop body will not be executed at all.

The flowchart in Figure 4.6 represents a WHILE loop structure. The pseudocode used in this book for a WHILE loop structure is as follows:

```
WHILE  ⟨condition⟩
    ⟨sequence of control structures⟩
ENDWHILE
```

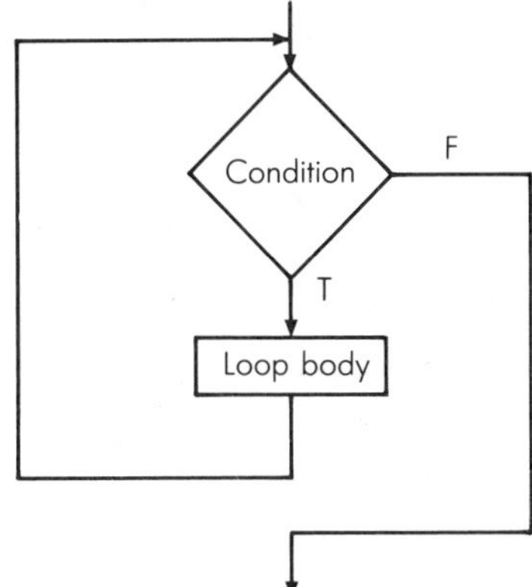

FIGURE 4.6
Flowchart of a WHILE loop structure

EXAMPLE

To find the smallest value of n for which

$$1^2 + 2^2 + 3^2 + \cdots + n^2 > 1000$$

the following WHILE loop could be used:

```
SUM = 1
N = 1
WHILE SUM ≤ 1000
   N = N + 1
   SUM = SUM + N*N
ENDWHILE
```

The following instructions implement the pseudocode in 8088/8086 assembly language. The BX-register is used to maintain the value of SUM, and the CX-register is used to maintain the value of N:

```
            MOV    BX,1
            MOV    CX,1
WHILETOP:
            CMP    BX,1000
            JA     ENDWHILE
            INC    CX
            MOV    AX,CX
            MUL    CX
            ADD    BX,AX
            JMP    WHILE_TOP
ENDWHILE:
```

The first two MOV instructions initialize the values of SUM and N, respectively. The label WHILE_TOP marks the top of the loop. It is the label of the instruction that begins the loop test. The CMP and JA instructions perform the loop test. If the SUM (BX-register value) is greater than 1000, then the jump to ENDWHILE is taken, exiting the loop with the desired value of N in the CX-register. If the SUM is less than or equal to 1000, then the loop body

```
INC    CX
MOV    AX,CX
MUL    CX
ADD    BX,AX
```

is executed. After each execution of the loop body, the JMP instruction transfers control to the loop test at the top of the loop. ■

REPEAT-UNTIL Loop

With a **REPEAT-UNTIL loop structure**, the loop test is at the bottom of the loop. The loop body is executed and, as long as the condition evaluates to False, is repeated. When the condition evaluates to True, the loop is terminated. Since the test is at the bottom of the loop, the loop body always is executed at least once.

The flowchart in Figure 4.7 represents a REPEAT-UNTIL loop structure. The pseudocode used in this book for a REPEAT-UNTIL loop structure is as follows:

```
REPEAT
    ⟨sequence of control structures⟩
UNTIL  ⟨condition⟩
```

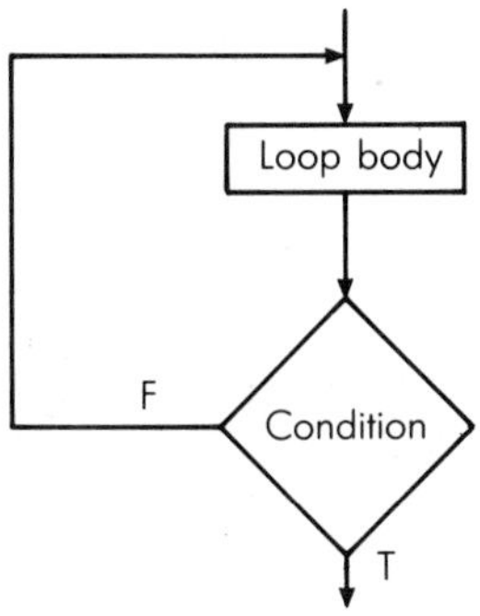

FIGURE 4.7
Flowchart of a REPEAT-UNTIL loop structure

EXAMPLE

To find the smallest value of n for which

$$1^2 + 2^2 + 3^2 + \cdots + n^2 > 1000$$

the following REPEAT-UNTIL loop could be used:

```
SUM = 1
N = 1
REPEAT
   N = N + 1
   SUM = SUM + N*N
UNTIL SUM > 1000
```

The following instructions implement this pseudocode in 8088/8086 assembly language. The BX-register is used to maintain the value of SUM, and the CX-register is used to maintain the value of N:

```
          MOV    BX,1
          MOV    CX,1
REPEAT1:
          INC    CX
          MOV    AX,CX
          MUL    CX
          ADD    BX,AX
          CMP    BX,1000
          JBE    REPEAT1
```

The first two MOV instructions initialize the values of SUM and N, respectively. The label REPEAT1 marks the top of the loop. It is the label of the first instruction of the loop body. The last two instructions (the CMP and JBE instructions) perform the loop test. If the SUM (BX-register value) is less than or equal to 1000, then the jump to REPEAT1 is taken, causing the loop body to execute again. If the SUM is greater than 1000, then the loop is exited (i.e., execution continues with the instruction that follows the JBE instruction). ■

With a condition-controlled loop, there must be something in the loop body that potentially can alter the value of the condition. Otherwise, an endless loop is created.

LOOP Instructions

The condition that controls a loop may be based on a count. That is, the count specifies the exact number of times that the loop body is to be executed. When implementing such count-controlled loops in the 8088/8086 assembly language, the LOOP instruction may be of use. The **LOOP instruction** uses the CX-register as a counter and has the following general form:

[⟨*label*⟩] LOOP ⟨*short-label*⟩ [⟨*comment*⟩]

in which ⟨*short-label*⟩ is the label of an instruction whose memory location is within −128 to +127 bytes from the memory location immediately following the LOOP instruction. This instruction causes the value in the CX-register to be decremented by 1. If the resulting value in the CX-register is nonzero, then control is transferred to the instruction that begins at the memory location specified by the ⟨*short-label*⟩. Otherwise, execution continues with the next instruction in sequence. None of the bits in the flags register are affected by execution of the LOOP instruction.

Consider the loop skeleton described in the flowchart and pseudocode of Figure 4.8. The code that implements this loop structure is as follows:

```
            MOV   CX,N          ;COUNT = N
LOOPTOP:                        ;REPEAT
            ⟨loop body⟩         ;    ⟨loop body⟩
            LOOP  LOOPTOP       ;    COUNT = COUNT - 1
                                ;UNTIL COUNT = 0
```

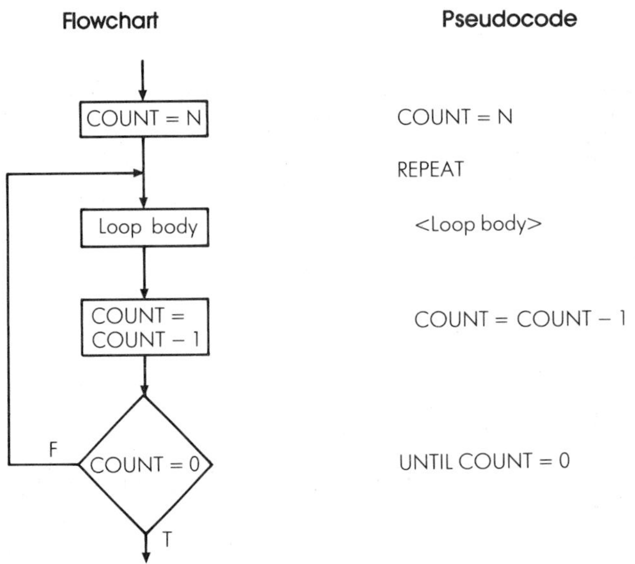

FIGURE 4.8
Loop skeleton

The LOOP instruction performs both the decrement of the COUNT and the test of the COUNT.

A condition-controlled loop can be based on a multiple condition. The loop instructions loop on equal, LOOPE (loop on zero, LOOPZ), and loop on not equal, LOOPNE (loop on nonzero, LOOPNZ), provide a capability of this type.

The **LOOPE (LOOPZ) instruction** has one of the following general forms:

[⟨*label*⟩] LOOPE ⟨*short-label*⟩ [⟨*comment*⟩]
[⟨*label*⟩] LOOPZ ⟨*short-label*⟩ [⟨*comment*⟩]

in which ⟨*short-label*⟩ is the label of an instruction whose memory location is within −128 to +127 bytes from the memory location following the LOOPE (LOOPZ) instruction. This instruction causes the value in the CX-register to be decremented by 1. If the resulting value in the CX-register is nonzero and the ZF bit in the flags register is set to 1, then control is transferred to the instruction that begins at the memory location specified by the operand. Otherwise, execution continues with the next instruction in sequence. None of the bits in the flags register are affected by execution of this instruction.

The **LOOPNE (LOOPNZ) instruction** has one of the following general forms:

```
[⟨label⟩]  LOOPNE  ⟨short-label⟩  [⟨comment⟩]
[⟨label⟩]  LOOPNZ  ⟨short-label⟩  [⟨comment⟩]
```

in which ⟨*short-label*⟩ is the label of an instruction whose memory location is within −128 to +127 bytes from the memory location following the LOOPNE (LOOPNZ) instruction. This instruction causes the value in the CX-register to be decremented by 1. If the resulting value in the CX-register is nonzero and the ZF bit in the flags register is cleared to 0, then control is transferred to the instruction that begins at the memory location specified by the operand. Otherwise, execution continues with the next instruction in sequence. None of the bits in the flags register are affected by execution of this instruction.

The LOOPE (LOOPZ) and LOOPNE (LOOPNZ) instructions are useful in searching arrays and character strings. The count in the CX-register defines a maximum for the number of times to execute the loop body. The loop is terminated when the desired element is found or when the entire array has been searched. Arrays and character strings are discussed in Chapter 8.

Loop-Generating Macro Directives

MASM 6.0 provides some macro directives that facilitate the implementation of loop structures. For the REPEAT-UNTIL loop structure, the loop-generating macro directives have the following general form:

```
.REPEAT
⟨instruction-list⟩
.UNTIL  ⟨conditional-expr⟩
```

in which ⟨*instruction-list*⟩ is the list of assembly language instructions to be executed until the ⟨*conditional-expr*⟩ evaluates to True (i.e., the instructions of the loop body) and ⟨*conditional-expr*⟩, in its simplest form, is a relational expression of the form

```
⟨destination⟩  ⟨rel-op⟩  ⟨source⟩
```

in which ⟨*destination*⟩ and ⟨*source*⟩ are the operands for the CMP instruction to be generated by the assembler and ⟨*rel-op*⟩ is one of the following relational operators: <, <=, ==, !=, >, or >=. The .REPEAT directive causes the assembler to generate a unique label, which is the label of the first instruction in the ⟨*instruction-list*⟩ (i.e., the label of the first instruction in the loop body). The .UNTIL directive causes the assembler to generate the instruction

```
CMP  ⟨destination⟩,⟨source⟩
```

followed by a conditional JUMP instruction that jumps back to the top of the loop if the ⟨*conditional-expr*⟩ is False (i.e., if the reverse of the ⟨*conditional-expr*⟩ is True). The operand of the conditional JUMP instruction is the unique label that was generated in response to the .REPEAT directive. The unique labels generated by the assembler in response to the loop-generating macro directives are selected from the set of reserved labels in the range @C0001–@CFFFF.

The assembler responds to a macro directive by generating assembly language instructions to replace the macro directive in the source code. This instruction generation is done prior to translating the source code to machine language. If the loop body is large, the conditional JUMP instruction, which is generated in response to the .UNTIL directive, may be an out-of-range jump. This out-of-range condition is detected when the assembler translates the assembler-generated instruction to machine language, and it is handled like any other out-of-range jump (i.e., the assembler generates an out-of-range error message).

EXAMPLE

To find the smallest value of n for which

$$1^2 + 2^2 + 3^2 + \cdots + n^2 > 1000$$

the following REPEAT-UNTIL loop could be used:

```
SUM = 1
N = 1
REPEAT
     N = N + 1
     SUM = SUM + N*N
UNTIL SUM > 1000
```

The following instructions implement this pseudocode in 8088/8086 assembly language. The BX-register is used to maintain the value of SUM, and the CX-register is used to maintain the value of N:

```
MOV      BX,1
MOV      CX,1
.REPEAT
INC      CX
MOV      AX,CX
MUL      CX
ADD      BX,AX
.UNTIL BX > 1000
```

From these instructions, the assembler (MASM 6.0) might generate the following code to be translated into machine language:

```
          MOV    BX,1
          MOV    CX,1
@C0001:
          INC    CX
          MOV    AX,CX
          MUL    CX
          ADD    BX,AX
          cmp    bx, 003E8h
          jbe    @C0001
```

Note the lowercase form for the instructions that are generated by the assembler in response to the macro directives. This form is the form in which these instructions appear in the assembler-generated listing. Constants appearing in these assembler-generated instructions are always in hexadecimal form. ■

For the WHILE loop structure, the loop-generating macro directives have the following general form:

```
.WHILE ⟨conditional-expr⟩
⟨instruction-list⟩
.ENDW
```

in which ⟨*instruction-list*⟩ is the list of assembly language instructions to be executed while the ⟨*conditional-expr*⟩ evaluates to True (i.e., the instructions of the loop body) and ⟨*conditional-expr*⟩, in its simplest form, is a relational expression of the form

⟨*destination*⟩ ⟨*rel-op*⟩ ⟨*source*⟩

in which ⟨*destination*⟩ and ⟨*source*⟩ are the operands for the CMP instruction to be generated by the assembler and ⟨*rel-op*⟩ is one of the following relational operators: <, < =, = =, ! =, >, or > =. MASM 6.0 implements the WHILE loop structure as a special case of the bottom-tested loop. The loop test follows the loop body, as is the case with a REPEAT-UNTIL loop, but there is an unconditional JUMP (JMP) instruction prior to the loop body that transfers control to the loop test. This JMP instruction is outside of the loop and thus is executed only once, upon entry into the loop. The .WHILE directive causes the assembler to generate a JMP instruction and a unique label, which is the operand of the JMP instruction and is the label of the first instruction of the loop test. The assembler also generates a second unique label, which is the label of the first instruction in the ⟨*instruction-list*⟩ (i.e., the label of the first instruction in the loop body). The .ENDW directive causes the assembler to generate the instruction

CMP ⟨*destination*⟩,⟨*source*⟩

followed by a conditional JUMP instruction that jumps back to the first instruction of the loop body if the ⟨*conditional-expr*⟩ is True. The operand of the conditional JUMP instruction is the second of the two unique labels generated in response to the .WHILE directive. The first of the two unique labels generated in response to the .WHILE directive is the label of the CMP instruction.

EXAMPLE

To find the smallest value of n for which

$$1^2 + 2^2 + 3^2 + \cdots + n^2 > 1000$$

the following WHILE loop could be used:

```
SUM = 1
N = 1
WHILE SUM ≤ 1000
     N = N + 1
     SUM = SUM + N*N
ENDWHILE
```

The following instructions implement this pseudocode in 8088/8086 assembly language. The BX-register is used to maintain the value of SUM, and the CX-register is used to maintain the value of N:

```
MOV       BX,1
MOV       CX,1
.WHILE    BX <= 1000
INC       CX
MOV       AX,CX
MUL       CX
ADD       BX,AX
.ENDW
```

From these instructions, the assembler (MASM 6.0) might generate the following code to be translated into machine language:

```
         MOV    BX,1
         MOV    CX,1
         jmp    @C0001
@C0002:
         INC    CX
         MOV    AX,CX
         MUL    CX
         ADD    BX,AX
@C0001:
         cmp    bx, 003E8h
         jbe    @C0002
```

■

For the count-controlled loop structure, the loop-generating macro directives have the following general form:

.REPEAT
⟨*instruction-list*⟩
.UNTILCXZ

in which ⟨*instruction-list*⟩ is the list of assembly language instructions to be executed the specified number of times (i.e., the instructions of the loop body). The CX-register is used to maintain the count and therefore must be initialized prior to the .REPEAT directive. The .REPEAT directive causes the assembler to generate a unique label, which is the label of the first instruction in the ⟨*instruction-list*⟩ (i.e., the label of the first instruction in the loop body). The .UNTILCXZ directive causes the assembler to generate a LOOP instruction that decrements the count in the CX-register and jumps back to the top of the loop if the resulting CX-register value is nonzero. The operand of the LOOP instruction is the unique label that was generated in response to the .REPEAT directive.

EXAMPLE

To compute the sum of the first 100 positive integers, the following count-controlled loop could be used:

```
SUM = 0
COUNT = 100
REPEAT
     SUM = SUM + COUNT
     COUNT = COUNT - 1
UNTIL COUNT = 0
```

The following instructions implement this pseudocode in 8088/8086 assembly language. The AX-register is used to maintain the value of SUM, and the CX-register is used to maintain the value of COUNT:

```
MOV     AX,0
MOV     CX,100
.REPEAT
ADD     AX,CX
.UNTILCXZ
```

From these instructions, the assembler (MASM 6.0) might generate the following code to be translated into machine language:

```
         MOV    AX,0
         MOV    CX,100
```

```
@C0001:
            ADD     AX,CX
            loop    @C0001
```

■

Programming Examples

In this section, the implementations of two algorithms designed to solve the same problem are discussed. The problem is defined as follows:

> The square of an integer n is equal to the sum of the first $|n|$ odd, positive integers:
>
> $$3^2 = 1 + 3 + 5$$
>
> $$7^2 = 1 + 3 + 5 + 7 + 9 + 11 + 13$$
>
> Design an algorithm to accept as input an integer n and to compute n^2 by summing the first $|n|$ odd, positive integers. Implement the algorithm with an 8088/8086 assembly language program.

REPEAT-UNTIL Loop Solution

The following pseudocode describes an algorithm using a REPEAT-UNTIL loop structure for solving the problem just defined:

```
SQUARE = 0
ODDINT = 1
GET NUMBER
LOOP_COUNT = |NUMBER|
REPEAT
   SQUARE = SQUARE + ODDINT
   ODDINT = ODDINT + 2
   LOOP_COUNT = LOOP_COUNT - 1
UNTIL LOOP_COUNT = 0
DISPLAY NUMBER
DISPLAY SQUARE
```

The absolute value of the input NUMBER is used for the LOOP_COUNT so that the algorithm can compute the square for both positive and negative integers. Each time through the loop, the next odd, positive integer (ODDINT) is added to the sum (SQUARE), and the value of ODDINT is incremented by 2 to the next odd, positive integer. With loop termination, NUMBER and its SQUARE are displayed.

Program Listing 4.3 shows an implementation of this algorithm. The prologue in lines 2–9 explains the program's function, the .MODEL pseudo-operation in line 10 enables the use of simplified segment directives, the external definitions in lines 13–17 identify the input/output procedures that are referenced by the program, and the stack segment definition in lines 18–20 is the standard one used in the example programs of this book.

The variable data segment is defined in lines 22–28. Three variables are defined in the data segment: one to hold the input value (NUMBER, defined in line 26), one to hold an odd, positive integer (ODDINT, defined in line 27), and one to hold the sum (SQUARE, defined in line 28). NUMBER is left uninitialized. ODDINT is initialized to 1, the first odd, positive integer. SQUARE is initialized to 0, the sum before any odd, positive integers are added. The variable NUMBER is defined as a signed two's complement integer because the input value can be either positive or negative.

```
            PAGE    80,132
;====================================================================
;                       PROGRAM LISTING 4.3
;
;PROGRAM TO COMPUTE THE SQUARE OF AN
;INTEGER, N, BY  SUMMING  THE  FIRST
;|N| ODD POSITIVE INTEGERS.
;
;====================================================================
            .MODEL  SMALL,BASIC,FARSTACK
;====================================================================
                                          ;PROCEDURES TO
            EXTRN   GETDEC:FAR            ;INPUT DECIMAL INTEGER
            EXTRN   NEWLINE:FAR           ;DISPLAY NEWLINE CHARACTER
            EXTRN   PUTDEC:FAR            ;DISPLAY SIGNED DECIMAL INT.
            EXTRN   PUTDEC$:FAR           ;DISPLAY UNSIGNED DECIMAL INT.
            EXTRN   PUTSTRNG:FAR          ;DISPLAY CHARACTER STRING
;====================================================================
; S T A C K   D E F I N I T I O N
            .STACK  256
;
;====================================================================
; V A R I A B L E   D E F I N I T I O N S
            .DATA
;
NUMBER      SWORD   ?                     ;INPUT NUMBER
ODDINT      DW      1                     ;ODD POSITIVE INTEGER
SQUARE      DW      0                     ;SQUARE OF INPUT NUMBER
;====================================================================
; C O N S T A N T   D E F I N I T I O N S
            .CONST
;
PROMPT      DB      'ENTER INTEGER VALUE',0DH,0AH
MSGOUT1     DB      'THE SQUARE OF '
MSGOUT2     DB      ' IS '
OFLMSG      DB      'OVERFLOW OCCURRED',0DH,0AH
;
;====================================================================
; C O D E   S E G M E N T   D E F I N I T I O N
;
            .CODE   EX_4_3
            .STARTUP                      ;GENERATE STARTUP CODE
;
            PUSH    DS                    ;SET ES-REGISTER TO ADDRESS
            POP     ES                    ;DGROUP
;
            LEA     DI,PROMPT             ;PROMPT USER TO ENTER AN INTEGER
            MOV     CX,21
            CALL    PUTSTRNG
            CALL    GETDEC                ;GET NUMBER
            MOV     NUMBER,AX             ;ABSNUM = NUMBER
            CMP     AX,0                  ;IF   ABSNUM < 0
            JGE     ENDABS
            NEG     AX                    ;THEN ABSNUM = -ABSNUM
ENDABS:                                   ;ENDIF
            MOV     CX,AX                 ;LOOP_COUNT = ABSNUM
LOOPTOP:                                  ;REPEAT
            MOV     AX,ODDINT             ;    SQUARE = SQUARE + ODDINT
            ADD     SQUARE,AX
            JC      OVRFLO                ;    EXIT TO OVRFLO ON OVERFLOW
            ADD     ODDINT,2              ;    ODDINT = ODDINT + 2
            LOOP    LOOPTOP               ;    LOOP_COUNT = LOOP_COUNT - 1
                                          ;UNTIL LOOP_COUNT = 0
            CALL    NEWLINE
            LEA     DI,MSGOUT1
            MOV     CX,14
            CALL    PUTSTRNG
```

```
68:             MOV     AX,NUMBER           ;DISPLAY NUMBER
69:             MOV     BH,0
70:             CALL    PUTDEC
71:             LEA     DI,MSGOUT2
72:             MOV     CX,4
73:             CALL    PUTSTRNG
74:             MOV     AX,SQUARE           ;DISPLAY SQUARE OF NUMBER
75:             CALL    PUTDEC$
76:             CALL    NEWLINE
77:             .EXIT                       ;RETURN TO DOS
78: ;
79: ;_______________________________________________________________
80: ; O V E R F L O W   H A N D L I N G
81: OVRFLO:
82:             LEA     DI,OFLMSG           ;DISPLAY OVERFLOW MESSAGE
83:             MOV     CX,19
84:             CALL    PUTSTRNG
85:             CALL    NEWLINE
86:             .EXIT                       ;RETURN TO DOS
87: ;
88: ;_______________________________________________________________
89:             END
```

The values of variables ODDINT and SQUARE are interpreted as unsigned integer values, which gives SQUARE an upper limit of 65,535.

The constant data segment is defined in lines 29–36. Four character strings are defined in the data segment: a message that prompts the user to enter an integer value (line 33), two messages used for annotation of the output (lines 34 and 35), and a message that is displayed if an overflow occurs during the computation (line 36).

The code segment is defined in lines 38–88 and contains the instructions for the main procedure of the program. The main procedure begins in the standard way by initializing the segment registers (lines 42–45).

The instructions in lines 47–49 display the prompt message to the user, and the call to GETDEC in line 50 accepts a signed integer value into the AX-register. The MOV instruction in line 51 stores the input value as the value of the variable NUMBER.

The three instructions in lines 52–55 compute the absolute value of the signed two's complement integer in the AX-register. The CMP instruction in line 52 sets the bits in the flags register to reflect the relationship of the input value to zero. The conditional JUMP instruction in line 53 causes the NEG instruction in line 54 to be skipped if the input value is already greater than or equal to zero. However, if the input value is less than zero, then the jump is *not* taken and the NEG instruction in line 54 is executed. In either event, when control reaches the instruction in lines 55 and 56, the AX-register contains the absolute value of the input integer. The value in variable NUMBER is still the original input number, and the value in the AX-register is the absolute value of that number.

The instructions in lines 52–55 implement a single-alternative decision. The conditional JUMP instruction in line 53 makes the decision either to execute the NEG instruction in line 54 or to skip that instruction depending on the value of the condition tested by the CMP instruction in line 52.

The instruction in line 56 moves the absolute value of the input number into the CX-register, which is being used to hold the loop count. This step is the initialization for the REPEAT-UNTIL loop.

The REPEAT-UNTIL loop is implemented in lines 57–63. The loop body appears in lines 58–61, and the loop test is the LOOP instruction in line 62. The two instructions in lines 58 and 59 add the value of variable ODDINT to the value of variable SQUARE, leaving the sum as the new value of variable SQUARE. The ADD instruction in line 59 sets or clears the CF bit in the flags register depending on whether or not the addition of the two unsigned integer values resulted in an arithmetic overflow condition. The JC instruction in line 60 makes a decision based on this condition—either to continue with execution of the loop body (CF = 0) or to exit the loop abruptly (CF = 1) and display an error message.

Normally, such an abrupt exit from the middle of a REPEAT-UNTIL loop is frowned on in structured programming. However, when a catastrophic event occurs, such as an arithmetic overflow, it is often acceptable to abandon the current sequence of instruction executions and jump to a sequence of instructions provided specifically for handling the current condition. In the pseudocode, such exiting would be shown by the statement

EXIT TO 〈*label*〉 ON 〈*condition*〉

in the loop body. The catastrophic condition handler appears at the end of the code segment and is bracketed by horizontal lines (see Program Listing 4.3).

If the ADD instruction in line 59 does not cause an overflow condition, then execution of the loop body continues with the ADD instruction in line 61. This instruction increments the value of variable ODDINT by 2 to the next odd, positive integer.

Execution of the LOOP instruction in line 62 causes the following sequence of events:

1. The value in the CX-register, the loop count, is decremented by 1.
2. If the value in the CX-register is nonzero, then the loop body is repeated. That is, a jump is made to the instruction with label LOOPTOP. If the value in the CX-register is zero, then execution continues with the next instruction in sequence. That is, the loop is terminated.

With normal loop exit (i.e., the LOOP instruction decrements the CX-register value to zero), the instructions in lines 64–76 are executed. These instructions display NUMBER and its SQUARE. The .EXIT macro directive in line 77 causes the assembler to generate the instructions that will return control to DOS.

The overflow handler (lines 78–87) is executed only if an overflow condition is detected in the accumulation of the sum (SQUARE) in the REPEAT-UNTIL loop body. The overflow handler simply displays an overflow message to the user (lines 82–85) and then returns control to DOS (line 86).

The loop structure implemented in lines 57–63 of Program Listing 4.3 could have been implemented using the loop-generating macro directives available in MASM 6.0. With MASM 6.0, the code in lines 57–63 of Program Listing 4.3 can be replaced with the following code:

```
.REPEAT                  ;REPEAT
MOV      AX,ODDINT       ;    SQUARE = SQUARE + ODDINT
ADD      SQUARE,AX
JC       OVRFLO          ;    EXIT TO OVRFLO ON OVERFLOW
ADD      ODDINT,2        ;    ODDINT = ODDINT + 2
.UNTILCXZ                ;    LOOP_COUNT = LOOP_COUNT - 1
                         ;UNTIL LOOP_COUNT = 0
```

The assembler performs the substitutions for the loop-generating macro directives

.REPEAT and .UNTILCXZ, and the assembly language code that is translated into machine language is the following:

```
@C0003:
          MOV     AX,ODDINT
          ADD     SQUARE,AX
          JC      OVRFLO
          ADD     ODDINT,2
          loop    @C0003
```

Compare this assembly language code to the code in lines 57–63 of Program Listing 4.3.

The diskette that accompanies this book includes a source code file named EX_4_3A.ASM. This source file provides an alternative implementation of the algorithm of Program Listing 4.3. This alternative implementation uses loop-generating and decision-generating macro directives.

The following are the results from some executions of the program of Program Listing 4.3:

```
ENTER INTEGER VALUE
16

THE SQUARE OF 16 IS 256


ENTER INTEGER VALUE
-16

THE SQUARE OF -16 IS 256


ENTER INTEGER VALUE
255

THE SQUARE OF 255 IS 65025


ENTER INTEGER VALUE
-255

THE SQUARE OF -255 IS 65025


ENTER INTEGER VALUE
256
OVERFLOW OCCURRED


ENTER INTEGER VALUE
0
OVERFLOW OCCURRED
```

Note that for an input of 0, the program displays the message

```
OVERFLOW OCCURRED
```

This output obviously is *not* correct. The square of 0 is 0, and the program should be able to handle this trivial case. The sum of the first 0 odd, positive integers is 0. To see why this case fails, trace program execution for an input of 0. The value stored in the CX-register in line 56 is the absolute value of 0, or 0; that is, the loop count is 0. Thus, the loop body should be executed zero times, leaving the value of SQUARE at its initial value, 0. However, the loop body of a REPEAT-UNTIL loop always is executed at least once. When the LOOP instruction in line 62 is executed the first time, it decrements the value in the CX-register from 0 to −1. This value is nonzero, so the jump to LOOPTOP is taken and the loop body is repeated. The CX-register cycles through the following values: −1, −2, −3, ..., −32,767, −32,768, 32,767, 32,766, ..., 3, 2, 1, and 0 before the loop terminates, which means the loop body would be executed 65,536 times. That is, the sum of the first 65,536 odd, positive integers (the square of 65,536) would be computed. Obviously, there would be an overflow along the way—the wrong type of loop was chosen for this solution. This problem can be avoided by using a WHILE loop structure rather than a REPEAT-UNTIL loop structure.

WHILE Loop Solution

The following pseudocode describes an algorithm using a WHILE loop structure for solving the problem defined previously:

```
SQUARE = 0
ODDINT = 1
GET NUMBER
LOOP_COUNT = |NUMBER|
WHILE LOOP_COUNT ≠ 0
   SQUARE = SQUARE + ODDINT
   ODDINT = ODDINT + 2
   LOOP_COUNT = LOOP_COUNT - 1
ENDWHILE
DISPLAY NUMBER
DISPLAY SQUARE
```

The only difference between this algorithm and the previous algorithm is that the REPEAT-UNTIL loop has been changed to a WHILE loop. In this algorithm, if the LOOP_COUNT is zero at the time of loop entry, the loop terminates without the loop body being executed. Since the value of SQUARE is initialized to zero, the program output will be correct for an input of zero.

Implementation of this algorithm uses the jump if CX-register equals zero (JCXZ) instruction. The **JCXZ instruction** has the following general form:

[⟨*label*⟩] JCXZ ⟨*short-label*⟩ [⟨*comment*⟩]

in which ⟨*short-label*⟩ is the label of an instruction whose memory location is within −128 to +127 bytes from the memory location immediately following the JCXZ instruction. If the value in the CX-register is zero, then this instruction causes a transfer of control to the instruction that begins at the memory location specified by the operand. If the value in the CX-register is nonzero, then this instruction causes no operation to be performed (i.e., execution continues with the next instruction in sequence). None of the bits in the flags register are affected by execution of a JCXZ instruction.

Program Listing 4.4 is the same as Program Listing 4.3, except for the loop structure. The WHILE loop structure is implemented in lines 57–65. The loop begins with the loop test in line 58, which is followed by the loop body in lines 59–63. The last instruction in the loop is an unconditional JUMP instruction (line 64) that returns control to the test at the top of the loop.

The JCXZ instruction in line 58 tests the value in the CX-register and then makes a decision based on that value. If the value in the CX-register is zero, then control is transferred to the instruction with label LOOPEND (i.e., the first instruction in the sequence of instructions that displays the result). That is, if the value in the

```
            PAGE    80,132
;====================================================================
;                   PROGRAM LISTING 4.4
;
;PROGRAM TO COMPUTE THE SQUARE OF AN
;INTEGER, N, BY  SUMMING  THE  FIRST
;|N| ODD POSITIVE INTEGERS.
;
;====================================================================
            .MODEL  SMALL,BASIC,FARSTACK
;====================================================================
                                        ;PROCEDURES TO
            EXTRN   GETDEC:FAR          ;INPUT DECIMAL INTEGER
            EXTRN   NEWLINE:FAR         ;DISPLAY NEWLINE CHARACTER
            EXTRN   PUTDEC:FAR          ;DISPLAY SIGNED DECIMAL INT.
            EXTRN   PUTDEC$:FAR         ;DISPLAY UNSIGNED DECIMAL INT.
            EXTRN   PUTSTRNG:FAR        ;DISPLAY CHARACTER STRING
;====================================================================
; S T A C K   S E G M E N T   D E F I N I T I O N
            .STACK  256
;
;====================================================================
; V A R I A B L E   D E F I N I T I O N S
            .DATA
;
NUMBER      SWORD   ?                   ;INPUT NUMBER
ODDINT      DW      1                   ;ODD POSITIVE INTEGER
SQUARE      DW      0                   ;SQUARE OF INPUT NUMBER
;====================================================================
; C O N S T A N T   D E F I N I T I O N S
            .CONST
;
PROMPT      DB      'ENTER INTEGER VALUE',0DH,0AH
MSGOUT1     DB      'THE SQUARE OF '
MSGOUT2     DB      ' IS '
OFLMSG      DB      'OVERFLOW OCCURRED',0DH,0AH
;
;====================================================================
; C O D E   S E G M E N T   D E F I N I T I O N
;
            .CODE   EX_4_4
            .STARTUP                    ;GENERATE STARTUP CODE
;
            PUSH    DS                  ;SET ES-REGISTER TO ADDRESS
            POP     ES                  ;DGROUP
;
            LEA     DI,PROMPT           ;PROMPT USER TO ENTER AN INTEGER
            MOV     CX,21
            CALL    PUTSTRNG
            CALL    GETDEC              ;GET NUMBER
            MOV     NUMBER,AX           ;ABSNUM = NUMBER
            CMP     AX,0                ;IF   ABSNUM < 0
            JGE     ENDABS
            NEG     AX                  ;THEN ABSNUM = -ABSNUM
ENDABS:                                 ;ENDIF
            MOV     CX,AX               ;LOOP_COUNT = ABSNUM
LOOPTOP:                                ;WHILE LOOP_COUNT <> 0
            JCXZ    LOOPEND
            MOV     AX,ODDINT           ;   SQUARE = SQUARE + ODDINT
            ADD     SQUARE,AX
            JC      OVRFLO              ;   EXIT TO OVRFLO ON OVERFLOW
            ADD     ODDINT,2            ;   ODDINT = ODDINT + 2
            DEC     CX                  ;   LOOP_COUNT = LOOP_COUNT - 1
            JMP     LOOPTOP             ;ENDWHILE
LOOPEND:                                ;
            CALL    NEWLINE
            LEA     DI,MSGOUT1
```

```
68:              MOV     CX,14
69:              CALL    PUTSTRNG
70:              MOV     AX,NUMBER               ;DISPLAY NUMBER
71:              MOV     BH,0
72:              CALL    PUTDEC
73:              LEA     DI,MSGOUT2
74:              MOV     CX,4
75:              CALL    PUTSTRNG
76:              MOV     AX,SQUARE               ;DISPLAY SQUARE OF NUMBER
77:              CALL    PUTDEC$
78:              CALL    NEWLINE
79:              .EXIT                           ;RETURN TO DOS
80: ;
81: ;____________________________________________________________________
82: ; O V E R F L O W   H A N D L I N G
83: OVRFLO:
84:              LEA     DI,OFLMSG               ;DISPLAY OVERFLOW MESSAGE
85:              MOV     CX,19
86:              CALL    PUTSTRNG
87:              CALL    NEWLINE
88:              .EXIT                           ;RETURN TO DOS
89: ;
90: ;____________________________________________________________________
91:              END
```

CX-register is zero, then the loop is terminated. If the value in the CX-register is nonzero, then execution continues with the next instruction in sequence. That is, if the value in the CX-register is nonzero, then the loop body is executed again.

The first four instructions of the loop body (lines 59–62) are identical to the loop body in the REPEAT-UNTIL loop in Program Listing 4.3. The DEC instruction in line 63 has been added to the loop body to decrement the loop count each time through the loop. (This decrement was handled by the LOOP instruction in the REPEAT-UNTIL loop version.)

The following are the results from some executions of this program:

```
ENTER INTEGER VALUE
16

THE SQUARE OF 16 IS 256


ENTER INTEGER VALUE
-16

THE SQUARE OF -16 IS 256


ENTER INTEGER VALUE
-255


THE SQUARE OF -255 IS 65025


ENTER INTEGER VALUE
256
OVERFLOW OCCURRED


ENTER INTEGER VALUE
0

THE SQUARE OF 0 IS 0
```

The loop structure implemented in lines 57–65 of Program Listing 4.4 could have been implemented using the loop-generating macro directives available in MASM 6.0. With MASM 6.0, the code in lines 57–65 of Program Listing 4.4 can be replaced with the following code:

```
.WHILE     CX != 0        ;WHILE LOOP_COUNT <> 0
MOV        AX,ODDINT      ;    SQUARE = SQUARE + ODDINT
ADD        SQUARE,AX
JC         OVRFLO         ;    EXIT TO OVRFLO ON OVERFLOW
ADD        ODDINT,2       ;    ODDINT = ODDINT + 2
DEC        CX             ;    LOOP_COUNT = LOOP_COUNT - 1
.ENDW                     ;ENDWHILE
```

The assembler performs the substitutions for the loop-generating macro directives .WHILE and .ENDW, and the assembly language code that is translated into machine language is the following:

```
           jmp    @C0003
@C0004:
           MOV    AX,ODDINT
           ADD    SQUARE,AX
           JC     OVRFLO
           ADD    ODDINT,2
           DEC    CX
@C0003:
           or     cx,cx
           jne    @C0004
```

Compare this assembly language code to the code in lines 57–65 of Program Listing 4.4.

Note that the loop test is not implemented with a CMP instruction and thus illustrates a special case of the conditional expression in decision-generating and in loop-generating macro directives. When the source operand is the immediate value 0, the assembler generates the instruction

OR 〈*destination*〉,〈*destination*〉

rather than the instruction

CMP 〈*destination*〉,〈*source*〉

The logical OR of a value with itself leaves the value unchanged but sets the flags to reflect that value; it is simply a more efficient way of comparing a value to zero. The OR instruction is discussed in detail in Chapter 6.

The diskette that accompanies this book includes a source code file named EX_4_4A.ASM. This source file provides an alternative implementation of the algorithm of Program Listing 4.4. This alternative implementation uses loop-generating and decision-generating macro directives.

4.4 Nested Control Structures

As noted earlier, control structures may be nested. In structured programming, **nesting of control structures** is allowed as long as one control structure is contained completely within another. If a control structure is nested in a decision structure, then it must be contained completely within one of the alternatives of the decision structure. If a control structure is nested in a loop structure, then it must be contained completely within the loop body of the loop structure. Control structures may be nested to any level required by the algorithm.

Programming Example

To illustrate nested control structures, design an algorithm to classify each of the integers in the range 2–100 as perfect, abundant, or deficient. Implement the algorithm with an 8088/8086 assembly language program. Take note of the following definitions:

The **proper divisors** of an integer *n* are those integers less than *n* that divide *n* evenly:

integer	proper divisors
6	1, 2, 3
9	1, 3
12	1, 2, 3, 4, 6
18	1, 2, 3, 6, 9

An integer is said to be a **perfect number** if it is equal to the sum of its proper divisors. The number 6 is the first perfect number:

$$6 = 1 + 2 + 3$$

An integer is said to be an **abundant number** if it is less than the sum of its proper divisors. The number 12 is an abundant number:

$$12 < 1 + 2 + 3 + 4 + 6$$

An integer is said to be a **deficient number** if it is greater than the sum of its proper divisors. The number 9 is a deficient number:

$$9 > 1 + 3$$

The following pseudocode describes an algorithm for classifying each of the positive integers in the range 2–100 as deficient, abundant, or perfect:

```
LOOP_COUNT = 99
NUMBER = 2
REPEAT
   DIVISOR_SUM = 1
   DIVISOR = 2
   UPPER_LIMIT = NUMBER / 2
   WHILE DIVISOR ≤ UPPER_LIMIT
      QUOTIENT = NUMBER / DIVISOR
      REMAINDER = NUMBER mod DIVISOR
      IF   REMAINDER = 0
      THEN
           DIVISOR_SUM = DIVISOR_SUM + DIVISOR
           IF   DIVISOR < > QUOTIENT
           THEN
                DIVISOR_SUM = DIVISOR_SUM + QUOTIENT
           ENDIF
           UPPER_LIMIT = QUOTIENT - 1
      ENDIF
      DIVISOR = DIVISOR + 1
      ENDWHILE
```

```
        IF   DIVISOR_SUM = NUMBER
        THEN
             DISPLAY 'PERFECT'
        ELSE
             IF   DIVISOR_SUM < NUMBER
             THEN
                  DISPLAY 'DEFICIENT'
             ELSE
                  DISPLAY 'ABUNDANT'
             ENDIF
        ENDIF
        DISPLAY NUMBER
        NUMBER = NUMBER + 1
        LOOP_COUNT = LOOP_COUNT - 1
   UNTIL LOOP_COUNT = 0
```

The algorithm contains a REPEAT-UNTIL loop structure. Nested within the REPEAT-UNTIL loop is a WHILE loop structure, which is followed by a double-alternative decision structure. Nested within the WHILE loop is a single-alternative decision structure that itself contains a single-alternative decision structure. Nested within the second alternative of the double-alternative decision structure is another double-alternative decision structure.

Program Listing 4.5 shows an implementation of the preceding algorithm. The program is arranged in the standard way. A prologue (lines 2–8) is followed by the .MODEL pseudo-operation (line 9) and the external procedure definitions (lines 10–14). Next is the standard stack segment definition (lines 15–18), followed by the variable data segment definitions (lines 19–26), the constant data segment definitions (lines 27–34), and the code segment definition (lines 35–97). Concluding the program is an END pseudo-operation (line 98).

Three variables are defined in the variable data segment. All three have type attribute WORD, and all three are uninitialized. The variable NUMBER, defined in line 23, holds the integer currently being classified. The variable SUM, defined in line 24, accumulates the sum of the proper divisors of the integer currently being classified. The variable LIMIT, defined in line 25, keeps track of an upper limit on the proper divisors of the integer currently being classified. Three classification messages are defined in the constant data segment (lines 31–33): DEFICIENT, ABUNDANT, and PERFECT.

The named constant defined in line 34 equates the name MSG_LNGTH with the constant specified by the expression $ – PERFECT. The $ refers to the current value of the location counter, and PERFECT refers to the offset portion of the address of the string constant PERFECT (defined in line 33). The **location counter** is a counter maintained by the assembler, and it identifies the current offset within the segment being translated by the assembler.

Assembler Listing 4.6 is the assembler-generated listing for the assembly module of Program Listing 4.5. The left-hand column in this listing shows the offset portion of the address for each item being defined. The assembler uses its location counter to determine the offset. For example, consider the constant data segment defined in lines 27–34 of Program Listing 4.5. When the .CONST directive is encountered (line 29), the assembler initializes the location counter to zero. Therefore, when the definition of the constant DEFICIENT is encountered (line 31), the location counter has the value 0000, which becomes the offset portion of the address associated with the symbolic name DEFICIENT (see Assembler Listing 4.6). The constant DEFICIENT is a string constant that is represented internally by the ASCII values 44, 45, 46, 49, 43, 49, 45,

```
             PAGE    80,132
;====================================================================
;                       PROGRAM LISTING 4.5
;
;PROGRAM TO CLASSIFY EACH OF THE POSITIVE INTEGERS
;2 - 100  AS DEFICIENT, ABUNDANT, OR PERFECT.
;
;====================================================================
             .MODEL  SMALL,BASIC,FARSTACK
;====================================================================
                                         ;PROCEDURES TO
             EXTRN   NEWLINE:FAR         ;DISPLAY NEWLINE CHARACTER
             EXTRN   PUTDEC:FAR          ;DISPLAY DECIMAL INTEGER
             EXTRN   PUTSTRNG:FAR        ;DISPLAY CHARACTER STRING
;====================================================================
; S T A C K   S E G M E N T   D E F I N I T I O N
             .STACK  256
;
;====================================================================
; V A R I A B L E   D E F I N I T I O N S
             .DATA
;
NUMBER       DW      ?                   ;NUMBER BEING CLASSIFIED
SUM          DW      ?                   ;SUM OF DIVISORS OF NUMBER
LIMIT        DW      ?                   ;UPPER LIMIT FOR DIVISORS
;
;====================================================================
; C O N S T A N T   D E F I N I T I O N S
             .CONST
;
DEFICIENT    DB      'DEFICIENT   '
ABUNDANT     DB      'ABUNDANT    '
PERFECT      DB      'PERFECT     '
MSG_LNGTH    EQU     $ - PERFECT
;====================================================================
; C O D E   S E G M E N T   D E F I N I T I O N
;
             .CODE   EX_4_5
             .STARTUP                    ;GENERATE STARTUP CODE
;
             PUSH    DS                  ;SET ES-REGISTER TO ADDRESS
             POP     ES                  ;DGROUP
;
             MOV     CX,99               ;LOOP_COUNT = 99
             MOV     NUMBER,2            ;NUMBER = 2
             .REPEAT                     ;REPEAT
             MOV     SUM,1               ;   SUM = 1
             MOV     BX,2                ;   DIVISOR = 2
             MOV     AX,NUMBER           ;   UPPER_LIMIT = NUMBER/2
             MOV     DX,0
             DIV     BX
             MOV     LIMIT,AX
;
             .WHILE  BX <= LIMIT         ;   WHILE DIVISOR <= UPPER_LIMIT
;
             MOV     AX,NUMBER           ;      QUO = NUMBER/DIVISOR
             MOV     DX,0                ;      REM = NUMBER mod
             DIV     BX                  ;                 DIVISOR
             .IF     DX == 0             ;      IF   REM = 0
;
             ADD     SUM,BX              ;      THEN SUM = SUM + DIVISOR
             .IF     BX != AX            ;           IF   DIVISOR<>QUO
                                         ;           THEN
             ADD     SUM,AX              ;                SUM = SUM+QUO
             .ENDIF                      ;           ENDIF
             DEC     AX                  ;           UPPER_LIMIT = QUO-1
             MOV     LIMIT,AX
```

```
68:            .ENDIF                    ;        ENDIF
69:            INC      BX               ;        DIVISOR = DIVISOR + 1
70: ;
71:            .ENDW                     ;    ENDWHILE
72:            PUSH     CX               ;    PUSH LOOP_COUNT
73:            MOV      CX,MSG_LNGTH
74:            MOV      AX,NUMBER
75:            .IF      SUM == AX        ;    IF    SUM = NUMBER
76: ;
77:                                      ;    THEN
78:            LEA      DI,PERFECT       ;         DISPLAY 'PERFECT'
79:            .ELSE                     ;    ELSE
80:            .IF      SUM < AX         ;         IF    SUM < NUMBER
81:            LEA      DI,DEFICIENT     ;         THEN DISPLAY 'DEFICIENT'
82: ;
83:            .ELSE                     ;         ELSE
84:            LEA      DI,ABUNDANT      ;              DISPLAY 'ABUNDANT'
85:            .ENDIF                    ;         ENDIF
86:            .ENDIF                    ;    ENDIF
87:            CALL     PUTSTRNG
88:            MOV      AX,NUMBER
89:            MOV      BH,-1
90:            CALL     PUTDEC           ;    DISPLAY NUMBER
91:            CALL     NEWLINE
92:            POP      CX               ;    POP LOOP COUNT
93:            INC      NUMBER           ;    NUMBER = NUMBER + 1
94:            .UNTILCXZ                 ;    LOOP_COUNT = LOOP_COUNT - 1
95:                                      ;UNTIL LOOP_COUNT = 0
96:            .EXIT                     ;RETURN TO DOS
97: ;
98:            END
```

4E, 54, 20, 20, and 20 (see Assembler Listing 4.6). Because there are 12 characters in the string constant, the assembler increments its location counter by 12 to 000C hexadecimal. Therefore, when the definition of the constant ABUNDANT is encountered (line 32), the location counter has the value 000C, which becomes the offset portion of the address associated with symbolic name ABUNDANT (see Assembler Listing 4.6). The constant ABUNDANT is also a string constant with 12 characters. Again, the assembler increments its location counter by 12 to 0018 hexadecimal. Therefore, when the definition of the constant PERFECT is encountered (line 33), the location counter has the value 0018, which becomes the offset portion of the address associated with symbolic name PERFECT (see Assembler Listing 4.6). The constant PERFECT is also a string constant with 12 characters. Again, the assembler increments its location counter by 12 to 0024 hexadecimal.

When the definition of the named constant MSG_LNGTH is encountered (line 34), the location counter has the value 0024 hexadecimal (36 decimal). The constant value assigned to the symbolic name MSG_LNGTH is the value of the expression $ – PERFECT. That is, the value assigned to MSG_LNGTH is the current value of the location counter (0024 hex or 36 decimal) minus the offset associated with symbolic name PERFECT (0018 hex or 24 decimal), which is the value 000C hexadecimal (12 decimal). This value is the length of each of the three string constants. Therefore, the assembler can be used to compute the length of a string constant. In general, a string constant and its length are defined as follows:

⟨string-name⟩ DB *⟨string-constant⟩*
⟨length-name⟩ EQU $–*⟨string-name⟩*

```
Microsoft (R) Macro Assembler Version 6.00B            01/25/94 10:08:19
ex_4_6.asm                                              Page 1 - 1

                                        PAGE    80,132
                                ;================================================================
                                ;               ASSEMBLER LISTING 4.6
                                ;
                                ;PROGRAM TO CLASSIFY EACH OF THE POSITIVE INTEGERS
                                ;2-100  AS DEFICIENT, ABUNDANT, OR PERFECT
                                ;
                                ;================================================================
                                        .MODEL  SMALL,BASIC,FARSTACK
                                ;================================================================
                                                                ;PROCEDURES TO
                                        EXTRN   NEWLINE:FAR     ;DISPLAY NEWLINE CHARACTER
                                        EXTRN   PUTDEC:FAR      ;DISPLAY DECIMAL INTEGER
                                        EXTRN   PUTSTRNG:FAR    ;DISPLAY CHARACTER STRING
                                ;================================================================
                                ; S T A C K   S E G M E N T   D E F I N I T I O N
                                        .STACK  256
                                ;
                                ;================================================================
                                ; V A R I A B L E   D E F I N I T I O N S
 0000                                   .DATA
                                ;
 0000 0000                      NUMBER  DW      ?               ;NUMBER BEING CLASSIFIED
 0002 0000                      SUM     DW      ?               ;SUM OF DIVISORS OF NUMBER
 0004 0000                      LIMIT   DW      ?               ;UPPER LIMIT FOR DIVISORS
                                ;
                                ;================================================================
                                ; C O N S T A N T   D E F I N I T I O N S
 0000                                   .CONST
                                ;
 0000 44 45 46 49 43 49         DEFICIENT DB    'DEFICIENT   '
      45 4E 54 20 20 20
 000C 41 42 55 4E 44 41         ABUNDANT  DB    'ABUNDANT    '
      4E 54 20 20 20 20
 0018 50 45 52 46 45 43         PERFECT   DB    'PERFECT     '
      54 20 20 20 20 20
 0024 = 000C                    MSG_LNGTH EQU   $ - PERFECT
                                ;================================================================
                                ; C O D E   S E G M E N T   D E F I N I T I O N
                                ;
 0000                                   .CODE   EX_4_5
                                        .STARTUP                ;GENERATE STARTUP CODE
 0000                          *@Startup:
 0000  BA ---- R               *        mov     dx, DGROUP
 0003  8E DA                   *        mov     ds, dx
                                ;
 0005  1E                               PUSH    DS              ;SET ES-REGISTER TO ADDRESS
 0006  07                               POP     ES              ;DGROUP
                                ;
 0007  B9 0063                          MOV     CX,99           ;LOOP_COUNT = 99
 000A  C7 06 0000 R 0002                MOV     NUMBER,2        ;NUMBER = 2
                                        .REPEAT                 ;REPEAT
 0010                          *@C0001:
 0010  C7 06 0002 R 0001                MOV     SUM,1           ;  SUM = 1
 0016  BB 0002                          MOV     BX,2            ;  DIVISOR = 2
 0019  A1 0000 R                        MOV     AX,NUMBER       ;  UPPER_LIMIT = NUMBER/2
```

```
001C  BA 0000                      MOV    DX,0
001F  F7 F3                        DIV    BX
0021  A3 0004 R                    MOV    LIMIT,AX
                        ;
                                   .WHILE  BX <= LIMIT        ;  WHILE DIVISOR <= UPPER_LIMIT
0024  EB 1D             *      jmp    @C0002
0026                    *@C0003:
                        ;
0026  A1 0000 R                    MOV    AX,NUMBER           ;     QUO = NUMBER/DIVISOR
0029  BA 0000                      MOV    DX,0                ;     REM = NUMBER mod
002C  F7 F3                        DIV    BX                  ;                  DIVISOR
                                   .IF    DX == 0             ;     IF   REM = 0
002E  0B D2             *      or   dx, dx
0030  75 10             *      jne    @C0004
                        ;
0032  01 1E 0002 R                 ADD    SUM,BX              ;     THEN SUM = SUM + DIVISOR
                                   .IF    BX != AX            ;          IF   DIVISOR<>QUO
0036  3B D8             *      cmp    bx, ax
0038  74 04             *      je     @C0006
                                                              ;          THEN
003A  01 06 0002 R                 ADD    SUM,AX              ;               SUM = SUM+QUO
                                   .ENDIF                     ;          ENDIF
003E                    *@C0006:
003E  48                           DEC    AX                  ;          UPPER_LIMIT = QUO-1
003F  A3 0004 R                    MOV    LIMIT,AX
                                   .ENDIF                     ;     ENDIF
0042                    *@C0004:
0042  43                           INC    BX                  ;     DIVISOR = DIVISOR + 1
                        ;
                                   .ENDW                      ;  ENDWHILE
0043                    *@C0002:
0043  3B 1E 0004 R      *      cmp    bx, LIMIT
0047  76 DD             *      jbe    @C0003
0049  51                           PUSH   CX                  ;  PUSH LOOP_COUNT
004A  B9 000C                      MOV    CX,MSG_LNGTH
004D  A1 0000 R                    MOV    AX,NUMBER
                                   .IF    SUM == AX           ;  IF   SUM = NUMBER
0050  39 06 0002 R      *      cmp    SUM, ax
0054  75 05             *      jne    @C0009
                        ;
                                                              ;  THEN
0056  BF 0018 R                    LEA    DI,PERFECT          ;       DISPLAY 'PERFECT'
                                   .ELSE                      ;  ELSE
0059  EB 0E             *      jmp    @C000B
005B                    *@C0009:
                                   .IF    SUM < AX            ;       IF   SUM < NUMBER
005B  39 06 0002 R      *      cmp    SUM, ax
005F  73 05             *      jae    @C000C
0061  BF 0000 R                    LEA    DI,DEFICIENT        ;       THEN DISPLAY 'DEFICIENT'
                        ;
                                   .ELSE                      ;       ELSE
0064  EB 03             *      jmp    @C000E
0066                    *@C000C:
0066  BF 000C R                    LEA    DI,ABUNDANT         ;            DISPLAY 'ABUNDANT'
                                   .ENDIF                     ;       ENDIF
                                   .ENDIF                     ;  ENDIF
0069                    *@C000E:
0069                    *@C000B:
0069  9A ---- 0000 E               CALL   PUTSTRNG
```

```
006E  A1 0000 R                           MOV    AX,NUMBER
0071  B7 FF                               MOV    BH,-1
0073  9A ---- 0000 E                      CALL   PUTDEC        ;  DISPLAY NUMBER
0078  9A ---- 0000 E                      CALL   NEWLINE
007D  59                                  POP    CX            ;  POP LOOP_COUNT
007E  FF 06 0000 R                        INC    NUMBER        ;  NUMBER = NUMBER + 1
                                          .UNTILCXZ            ;  LOOP_COUNT = LOOP_COUNT - 1
0082  E2 8C                *      loop    @C0001
                                                               ;UNTIL LOOP_COUNT = 0
                                          .EXIT                ;RETURN TO DOS
0084  B4 4C                *      mov     ah, 04Ch
0086  CD 21                *      int     021h
                               ;
                                          END
```

in which ⟨*string-name*⟩ is the symbolic name to be associated with the memory location where the string constant is to begin, ⟨*string-constant*⟩ is the characters of the string enclosed in apostrophes ('), and ⟨*length-name*⟩ is the symbolic name to be associated with the length of the string.

The code segment contains the instructions for the main procedure of the program. The procedure begins in the standard way by initializing the segment registers (lines 39–42).

The decision and loop structures in the algorithm are implemented with decision-generating and loop-generating macro directives. Assembler Listing 4.6 shows the instructions generated by the assembler in response to the decision-generating and loop-generating macro directives used in Program Listing 4.5.

The classification loop, the REPEAT-UNTIL loop implemented in lines 46–95 of Program Listing 4.5, executes 99 times, once for each value of NUMBER from 2–100. The MOV instruction in line 44 initializes the loop count in the CX-register to 99, and the MOV instruction in line 45 initializes the value of variable NUMBER to 2. Each iteration of the REPEAT-UNTIL loop (lines 46–95) computes and displays the classification for a single integer. The loop body of this REPEAT-UNTIL loop (lines 47–93) performs the following sequence of steps:

1. The MOV instruction in line 47 initializes the SUM of the proper divisors to 1. Since 1 is a proper divisor of all positive integers, there is no need to test it. It can be added to the SUM initially.
2. The MOV instruction in line 48 initializes the trial divisor to 2. The trial divisor is maintained in the BX-register.
3. The instructions in lines 49–52 initialize the upper limit for trial divisors of the current NUMBER to one-half the current NUMBER. There can be no proper divisor of n that is greater than $n/2$. Thus, there is no need to test values greater than $n/2$.
4. The WHILE loop, implemented in lines 54–71, computes the SUM of the proper divisors of the current NUMBER. (This nested loop structure is discussed in detail in the following paragraphs.)
5. The PUSH instruction in line 72 saves the value in the CX-register (the REPEAT-UNTIL loop's loop count) because the CX-register is needed to hold a parameter for the PUTSTRNG procedure, which is used to display the classification.
6. The MOV instruction in line 73 stores the length of the classification strings in the CX-register, which is one of the parameters for the PUTSTRNG procedure.

7. The double-alternative decision structure, implemented in lines 74–86, determines the classification to be displayed based on the relationship between the current NUMBER and the SUM of its proper divisors. (This decision structure is discussed in detail in the following paragraphs.)
8. The call to the PUTSTRNG procedure in line 87 displays the classification.
9. The instructions in lines 88–91 display the current NUMBER followed by a NEWLINE character.
10. The POP instruction in line 92 restores the CX-register with the REPEAT-UNTIL loop's loop count, which was saved by the PUSH instruction in line 72.
11. The INC instruction in line 93 increments the value of variable NUMBER to the integer to be classified on the next iteration of the REPEAT-UNTIL loop body.

The .UNTILCXZ directive in line 94 causes the assembler to generate a LOOP instruction, which is the loop count decrement and test for the REPEAT-UNTIL loop. The loop count in the CX-register is decremented by 1. If the resulting value is nonzero, then a jump is made to the instruction in line 47 (the instruction immediately following the .REPEAT directive) and the loop body is executed again. If the resulting value is zero, then the REPEAT-UNTIL loop is terminated and the code generated in response to the .EXIT directive in line 96 is executed, returning control to DOS.

The nested WHILE loop implemented in lines 54–71 computes the SUM of the proper divisors of the current NUMBER. The initialization for this loop is performed by the instructions in lines 47–53, which were discussed previously. The WHILE loop test is generated by the assembler in response to the .WHILE directive in line 54 and the .ENDW directive in line 71 (see Assembler Listing 4.6). The WHILE loop is terminated when the trial divisor becomes greater than the upper LIMIT. However, if the trial divisor is less than or equal to the upper LIMIT, then the loop body is executed.

The WHILE loop body is implemented in lines 56–69 and performs the following sequence of steps:

1. The instructions in lines 56–58 divide the current NUMBER by the current trial divisor.
2. The single-alternative decision structure in lines 59–68 performs the following sequence of steps if the remainder of the preceding division is zero (i.e., if the trial divisor divides the NUMBER evenly):
   a. The ADD instruction in line 61 adds the trial divisor to the SUM.
   b. The single-alternative decision structure in lines 62–65 adds the quotient of the preceding division to the SUM if the quotient is not equal to the trial divisor. That is, if the remainder of the division is zero, then both the divisor and the quotient are proper divisors of the NUMBER and therefore can be added to the SUM. However, if the divisor and the quotient are equal, then only one of them should be added to the SUM; to add both of them would include one of the proper divisors twice.
   c. The instructions in lines 66 and 67 set the upper LIMIT to 1 less than the quotient of the preceding division. As the divisor increases, the quotient of the division decreases. Since the quotient is added to the SUM whenever the divisor is added to the SUM (unless they are equal), the quotient minus 1 becomes the new upper LIMIT on divisors that must be tested.
   d. The instruction in line 69 increments the trial divisor by 1.

The nested double-alternative decision structure in lines 74–86 determines the classification. The MOV instruction in line 74 loads the AX-register with the NUMBER currently being classified. The code generated by the assembler in response to the .IF directive in line 75 (see Assembler Listing 4.6) compares the NUMBER to the SUM of its proper divisors and makes a decision based on the result of the comparison. If the SUM is equal to the NUMBER, then the DI-register is loaded with the offset of the message PERFECT (line 78) and control is transferred to the instruction in line 87 (i.e., the instruction immediately following the .ENDIF directive in line 86). If the SUM is not equal to the NUMBER, then control is transferred to the double-alternative decision structure in lines 80–85. The code generated by the assembler in response to the .IF directive in line 80 (see Assembler Listing 4.6) again compares the NUMBER to the SUM of its proper divisors and makes a decision based on the result of the comparison. If the SUM is less than the NUMBER, then the DI-register is loaded with the offset of the message DEFICIENT (line 81) and control is transferred to the instruction in line 87 (i.e., the instruction immediately following the .ENDIF directive in line 85). If the SUM is not less than the NUMBER, then control is transferred to the instruction in line 84. The DI-register is loaded with the offset of the message ABUNDANT, and control continues with the next instruction in sequence, the instruction in line 87. The DI-register is used as one of the inputs to the PUTSTRNG procedure. In all three cases, after loading the DI-register, control is transferred to the instruction in line 87, and the selected classification message is displayed.

The diskette that accompanies this book includes a source code file named EX_4_5A.ASM. This source file provides an alternative implementation of the algorithm of Program Listing 4.5. This alternative implementation does not use loop-generating and decision-generating macro directives.

When executed, this example program displays 99 lines of output, which is certainly more than one screenful. In Programming Exercise 4.11 at the end of this chapter, a technique is presented for stopping the display, under program control, after each screenful.

PROGRAMMING EXERCISES

4.1 Given a positive integer $n1$, a sequence of positive integers $n1, n2, n3, \ldots, 1$ can be generated using the following rules:

1. If ni is odd, then $n(i+1)$ is computed by

$$n(i + 1) = 3 * ni + 1$$

2. If ni is even, then $n(i+1)$ is computed by

$$n(i + 1) = ni/2$$

3. The sequence is terminated at the first occurrence of the integer 1.

It has been conjectured (but to the author's knowledge never proven) that the length of a sequence is always finite. That is, for any positive integer value of $n1$, the sequence eventually reaches the integer 1 and terminates. The length of a sequence is the number of integers in the sequence.

EXAMPLE

For $n1 = 22$, the sequence is

22	11	34	17	52	26	13	40
20	10	5	16	8	4	2	1

The length of the sequence is 16. ■

Design an algorithm to accept as input a positive integer $n1$ and to compute and output the sequence $n1, n2, n3, \ldots, 1$ and its length. The sequence is to be generated according to the preceding rules. Implement your algorithm with an 8088/8086 assembly language program. Your input should be the first integer in the sequence entered via the keyboard. Your output should be the sequence and length displayed on the screen. The sequence should be displayed 10 integers per line, and the length should be displayed on a separate line following the sequence. Your program should detect any overflow in the sequence generation. If overflow occurs, then terminate the sequence and display an appropriate diagnostic message in place of the length output. Demonstrate your program using the following input values:

1, 22, 38834, 38836, 38838, 93, 97, 9995, 9997

In *Using Basic: An Introduction to Computer Programming*, Third Edition, by Julien Hennefeld (PWS Publishing Company), this phenomenon is referred to as *Ulam's conjecture*. Such a sequence is referred to as an *Ulam sequence*, and the length of the sequence is referred to as the *Ulam length*.

4.2 Modify your program from Programming Exercise 3.3 to include an overflow check. If overflow is detected, then display an appropriate diagnostic message. Demonstrate your program with the set of inputs specified in the problem statement.

4.3 Design an algorithm to find and output the count of the number of ways to make change for a dollar using half-dollars, quarters, dimes, nickels, and pennies. Implement your algorithm with an 8088/8086 assembly language program. There is no input to your program. Your output should be the count of the number of ways to make change for a dollar displayed on the screen.

4.4 Design an algorithm to find and output all three-digit integers that are equal to the sum of the cubes of their digits. The integer 371 is an example of such an integer:

$$371 = 3^3 + 7^3 + 1^3 = 27 + 343 + 1$$

Implement your algorithm with an 8088/8086 assembly language program. There is no input to your program. Your output should be the sequence of three-digit integers that have the given property.

4.5 The four-digit integer 3025 has the property that the square of the sum of the integer formed by its first two digits and the integer formed by its last two digits is equal to the integer itself. That is,

$$3025 = (30 + 25)^2 = (55)^2$$

Design an algorithm to find and output all four-digit integers that have this property. Implement your algorithm with an 8088/8086 assembly language program. There is no input to your program. Your output should be the sequence of four-digit integers that have the given property.

4.6 Euclid's algorithm for finding the greatest common divisor (GCD) of two positive integers is given. Implement this algorithm with an 8088/8086 assembly language program. Your input should be two positive integers entered via the keyboard. Your output should be the GCD of the two input integers. The output is to be displayed on the screen.

```
EUCLID'S ALGORITHM:

      GET X and Y
      WHILE Y ≠ 0
            X = X mod Y
            INTERCHANGE X and Y
      ENDWHILE
      DISPLAY X
```

Recall that X mod Y is the remainder of X divided by Y.

4.7 Design an algorithm to accept as input two 16-bit integers that represent a departure time and an arrival time based on a 24-hour clock (0000–2359) and to compute and output the flight duration in hours and minutes.

EXAMPLES

Departure Time	Arrival Time	Flight Duration
1048	1324	2 hr 36 min
2135	0212	4 hr 37 min

■

You may assume that no flight lasts longer than 24 hours. Implement your algorithm with an 8088/8086 assembly language program. Your input should be two 16-bit integers in the range 0000–2359 entered via the keyboard. Your output should be the hours and minutes of flight duration displayed on the screen. Demonstrate your program using the following inputs:

Departure Time	Arrival Time
1054	1323
2145	0252
0842	0842
1843	1124

4.8 Given a positive integer $n1$, a sequence of positive integers $n1, n2, n3, \ldots$ can be generated using the following rule:

$$n(i + 1) = \text{sum of squares of digits of } ni$$

Either one of two events will happen in the sequence:

1. The integer 1 is produced; therefore, all subsequent integers in the sequence are 1.
2. The integer 4 is produced, and the subsequent integers in the sequence are 16, 37, 58, 89, 145, 42, 20, 4, ... That is, the sequence contains a cycle, and the integer 1 is never produced in the sequence.

Any positive integer whose sequence eventually produces 1 is said to be an *insipid* integer.

EXAMPLES

8 64 52 29 85 89 145 42 20 4 16 37 58 89 ...

The number 8 is not an insipid integer.

23 13 10 1 ...

The number 23 is an insipid integer. ■

Design an algorithm to accept a positive integer as input and to output the sequence generated by the preceding rule until either the integer 1 or the integer 4 is produced. Implement your algorithm with an 8088/8086 assembly language program. Your input should be a positive integer. Your output should be the sequence of integers produced and the word 'INSIPID' if the integer 1 is produced in the sequence.

4.9 A Pythagorean triple is a sequence of three positive integers (x, y, z) that satisfy the equation

$$z^2 = x^2 + y^2$$

For example, the sequence (3, 4, 5) is a Pythagorean triple:

$$5^2 = 3^2 + 4^2$$

$$25 = 9 + 16$$

Design an algorithm to find and output all Pythagorean triples whose integers are in the range 1–50. Be sure that your algorithm does not produce any duplicates, such (3, 4, 5) and (4, 3, 5). Implement your algorithm with an 8088/8086 assembly language program. There is no input to your program. Your output should be a list of the Pythagorean triples displayed on the screen, one triple per line.

4.10 Design an algorithm to compute and print a table of Fahrenheit temperatures and the corresponding centigrade temperatures for Fahrenheit temperatures in the range −60 degrees to 150 degrees in increments of 10 degrees. Implement your algorithm with an 8088/8086 assembly language program. There is no input to your program. Your output should be the table of temperature values displayed on the screen.

4.11 The PAUSE procedure in the I/O subprocedure library displays a message on the screen, clears the keyboard input buffer, and waits for a keystroke from the keyboard. When the keystroke is received, control is returned to the caller. The message to be displayed is supplied by the caller. The PAUSE procedure thus provides the capability for a program to pause during execution and then to continue when the user presses a key on the keyboard. The inputs to the PAUSE procedure are the same as the inputs for the PUTSTRNG procedure. Modify Program Listing 4.5 to pause and wait for a keystroke after each 20 lines of output.

CHAPTER 5

Procedures, Subprocedures, and Macros

The program listings in Chapters 1–4 show a single code segment containing a single procedure, the main procedure for the program. Most of these listings also show external references (i.e., EXTRN pseudo-operations) that identify subprocedures to be combined with the main procedure by the Linkage Editor. The object code for these subprocedures already exists in the I/O subprocedure library.

The subprocedure is an important tool for the assembly language programmer. Programming in assembly language becomes much more efficient once a comprehensive library of subprocedures has been developed. The I/O subprocedure library on the diskette that accompanies this book is only a start in this direction. It enables users to develop meaningful programs without having to encounter machine-level input/output operations. Up to this point, the user has made use of already existing subprocedures. This chapter shows how to develop subprocedures and how to link procedures together to form a complete and executable program. This chapter also introduces the assembler's macro feature, which allows a programmer to define new operations in terms of existing machine-level instructions.

5.1 Terminology

An **executable program** in the 8088/8086 consists of one or more code segments, a stack segment, and zero or more static data segments. The code segments consist of exactly one main procedure and zero or more subprocedures. The **main procedure** receives execution control of the processor when the executable program initially is placed into execution by the operating system. A **subprocedure** receives execution control of the processor by being referenced or called from another procedure (possibly itself). The procedure that invokes a subprocedure is referred to as the **caller** of the subprocedure. The term **procedure** is used to refer to either a main procedure or a subprocedure.

An **assembly module** is one complete input to the assembler program, and it consists of one or more segment definitions. An assembly module does not have to be a complete program. Object modules produced by assembling various assembly modules are combined into a complete executable program by the Linkage Editor program (LINK).

5.2 Subprocedures

A subprocedure is similar in many ways to a main procedure. It can perform the same actions as a main procedure. That is, a subprocedure can accept input data, perform computations, and return results (output). However, many differences exist between a main procedure and a subprocedure. One such difference, the way in which they are invoked, was discussed in Section 5.1. A main procedure receives its inputs from a source external to the computer and sends its outputs to a destination external to the computer. Even though subprocedures can communicate with external devices, they generally receive their inputs from the caller and return results back to the caller. Termination of a main procedure terminates execution of the entire executable program. Termination of a subprocedure returns execution control of the processor to the caller of the subprocedure. A subprocedure may be called from more than one place in a procedure. Each time the subprocedure terminates, control is returned to the instruction in the calling procedure that immediately follows the instruction that called the subprocedure into execution. This sequence is shown in Figure 5.1.

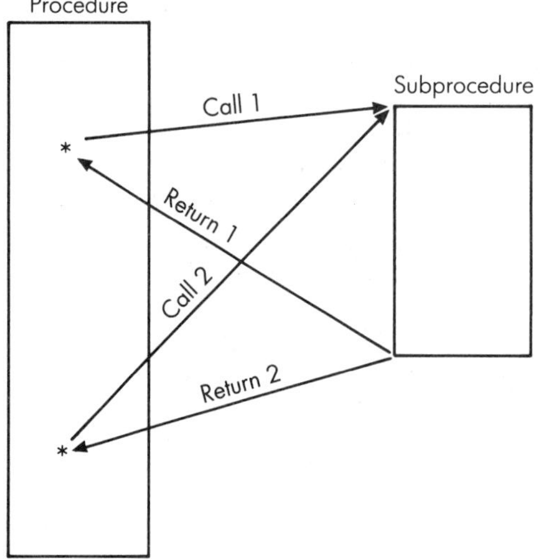

FIGURE 5.1 Multiple subprocedure calls

Uses of Subprocedures

Subprocedures are used in two basic ways:

1. Subprocedures provide a set of instructions that appear only once in an executable program but can be executed more than once to manipulate different sets of input data.

EXAMPLE

Given the coordinates of three vertices of a triangle, ($x1$, $y1$), ($x2$, $y2$), and ($x3$, $y3$), the area of the triangle can be computed as follows:

(a) Compute the lengths of the three sides of the triangle:

$$A = \sqrt{(y2 - y1)^2 + (x2 - x1)^2}$$
$$B = \sqrt{(y3 - y2)^2 + (x3 - x2)^2}$$
$$C = \sqrt{(y1 - y3)^2 + (x1 - x3)^2}$$

(b) Compute the semiperimeter:

$$S = 1/2(A + B + C)$$

(c) Compute the area:

$$\text{AREA} = \sqrt{S(S - A)(S - B)(S - C)}$$

The instructions to compute the square root of a positive real number are needed four times in this computation. Rather than writing the instructions in four places in the program with only slight modifications to accommodate data, the instructions can be written once as a subprocedure that accepts a positive real number as input and returns the square root of that number as its output. ■

2. Subprocedures facilitate the dividing of a problem into smaller independent subproblems, each of which can be solved separately. The solution to each subproblem is implemented as a subprocedure, and the subprocedures eventually are integrated into a unit using a main procedure that calls the subprocedures in the proper sequence. This modularity feature allows the work of a large programming project to be divided among several programmers, with the programmers able to do much of the work independently of one another.

EXAMPLE

Consider the problem of writing a program that detects palindromes. A palindrome is a word, phrase, or sentence that is spelled the same backward as forward. The following are examples of palindromes:

No radar on.
Madam I'm Adam.
Able was I ere I saw Elba.
Rats live on no evil star.

Note that there are several considerations to this problem. Characters other than letters must be ignored. The type case of a letter must be ignored; "A" and "a" must be treated the same, for example. The problem could be divided into subproblems as follows:

(a) Design an algorithm to accept as input a character string and to produce as output the input string with all nonletters removed.
(b) Design an algorithm to accept as input a character string and to produce as output the input string with each lowercase letter changed to the corresponding uppercase letter.
(c) Design an algorithm to accept as input a character string and to produce as output the reverse of the input string.
(d) Design an algorithm to accept as input two equal-length character strings and to return as output an indication of whether or not the two strings are the same.
(e) Design a main program to accept as input a character string, use the subprocedures from (a) and (b) to convert the input string into an uppercase letter string, use the subprocedure from (c) to reverse the uppercase letter string, and use

the subprocedure from (d) to compare the uppercase letter string to its reverse to determine whether the original input string is a palindrome.

The problem of designing an algorithm to detect palindromes seems to be a rather complex task. However, designing an algorithm to solve any of the subproblems listed is a rather simple task. The original problem has been simplified by modularization. ■

Types of Subprocedures

Two classes of subprocedures are available in most high-level programming languages: value-returning procedures (functions) and nonvalue-returning procedures (subroutines). A **function** returns an explicit result and is invoked by a reference to the function that appears as an operand in an expression. During evaluation of the expression, when it is time for that operand to be evaluated, the function is invoked. The function is applied to its arguments (inputs). The value returned by the function is used as the value of the function reference in the evaluation of the expression.

EXAMPLE

The Pascal programming language provides the predefined function sqrt, which accepts a positive real number as input and returns the square root of that real number as output. The sqrt function can be referenced in an assignment statement like the following:

```
R1 := (-B + sqrt(B*B - 4*A*C))/(2*A)
```

The subexpression

```
sqrt(B*B - 4*A*C)
```

is an operand in the arithmetic expression on the right-hand side of the assignment operator. When the value of that operand is needed in the evaluation of the arithmetic expression, the subexpression

```
B*B - 4*A*C
```

is evaluated, and then the sqrt function is invoked with the value of this subexpression as its input argument. The value returned by the sqrt function takes the place of the operand

```
sqrt(B*B - 4*A*C)
```

in the evaluation of the arithmetic expression. ■

A **subroutine** does not return an explicit value. It is invoked at time of execution by a special subprocedure invocation statement that references the subroutine.

EXAMPLE

The Pascal programming language provides the predefined procedure write, which specifies output to the standard output file. The statement

```
write (X)
```

indicates that the write procedure is to be invoked with the value of variable X as its input argument. The procedure outputs the value of variable X to the standard output file. ■

5.3 Subprocedure Interface

The interface between a subprocedure and its caller can be described by the occurrence of the following four events:

1. The transfer of control from the caller to the subprocedure (calling the subprocedure)
2. The return of control from the subprocedure to the caller (returning from the subprocedure)
3. The saving and restoring of the state of the processor for the caller
4. The passing of inputs from the caller to the subprocedure and the returning of outputs from the subprocedure to the caller (parameter passing)

Calling a Subprocedure

Calling a subprocedure requires the following:

1. Altering the program count (the CS:IP register pair in the 8088/8086) from its current sequence to the memory location where execution is to begin in the subprocedure
2. Saving the address of the instruction that is to be executed when the subprocedure returns control to the caller (the caller's return address)

In the 8088/8086 assembly language, a subprocedure is invoked by a **CALL instruction**, which has the following general form:

[⟨*label*⟩] `CALL` ⟨*target*⟩ [⟨*comment*⟩]

in which ⟨*target*⟩ is the name of the procedure that is being invoked (direct CALL) or an address expression that specifies the memory location that contains the address of the procedure being invoked (indirect CALL). The CALL instruction causes the address of the instruction immediately following the CALL instruction (i.e., the return address) to be pushed onto the top of the stack. The CS:IP register pair then is modified to point to the memory location where the first instruction of the called procedure begins.

Returning from a Subprocedure

Returning from a subprocedure requires returning the program count (the CS:IP register pair in the 8088/8086) to the instruction in the calling procedure that immediately follows the instruction that invoked the subprocedure. In the 8088/8086 assembly language, the **RET instruction** is used to return from a subprocedure to its caller, and it has the following general form:

[⟨*label*⟩] `RET` [⟨*pop-value*⟩] [⟨*comment*⟩]

in which ⟨*pop-value*⟩ is an immediate value that specifies the number of argument bytes to be popped from the stack and discarded. The RET instruction causes the return address to be popped from the top of the stack and placed in the CS:IP register pair. The value of the immediate operand is then added to the SP-register to pop arguments from the stack. The use of the stack for passing arguments is introduced from a user perspective later in this section and is discussed in detail in Chapters 8 and 10.

Saving and Restoring Registers

The state of the processor at any point in time is described by the values in the registers, including the flags register. To save the state of the processor, the desired register values are pushed onto the stack using the PUSH and PUSHF instructions. To restore the state of the processor, these values are popped from the stack into the registers from which they came using the POP and POPF instructions. There are two approaches to **saving and restoring the state of the processor**:

1. The burden of saving and restoring the state of the processor can be placed on the caller. Prior to calling the subprocedure, the caller saves the registers it needs and, on return from the subprocedure, restores these registers. With this approach, only the registers that need to be protected are saved and restored, although this method places a sometimes aggravating burden on the subprocedure user.
2. The burden of saving and restoring the state of the processor can be placed on the subprocedure. At the beginning of the subprocedure, all registers used by the subprocedure, including the flags register, are saved. Just prior to return to the caller, these registers are restored. This approach centralizes the saving and restoring of the processor state to one place rather than requiring that it appear around each call. However, the subprocedure must save and restore all of the registers that it uses, whether or not a caller needs them saved.

The author's preference is to use the second approach. The I/O procedure package and the example programs in this book were designed using this philosophy.

Parameter Passing

In high-level languages, subprocedures receive their inputs through parameters defined in the subprocedure definition. The actual inputs for a specific invocation of a subprocedure are specified by arguments that appear in the subprocedure reference and that are bound to the corresponding parameters as part of the subprocedure invocation. In high-level programming languages, **parameter passing** is accomplished through two popular mechanisms: call-by-value and call-by-location. With **call-by-value**, the value of the argument is bound to the parameter. The argument simply provides an initial value for the parameter on invocation of that subprocedure. The subprocedure's assignment of a new value to the parameter has no effect on the caller's environment. With **call-by-location**, the address of the argument is bound to the parameter. The parameter is just another name for the memory location that contains the argument. The subprocedure's assignment of a new value to the parameter is an assignment of a new value to the corresponding argument in the caller's environment, which is one way for a subprocedure to return values to the caller.

An important feature of subprocedures is this ability to parameterize their behaviors. The parameters allow the net effect of the subprocedure to be characterized. That is, a subprocedure takes certain inputs and produces certain outputs. The subprocedure can be viewed as a black box of the form shown in Figure 5.2.

From the user's point of view, the parameters characterize the entire effect of the named subprocedure. The way in which the outputs are produced from the inputs is

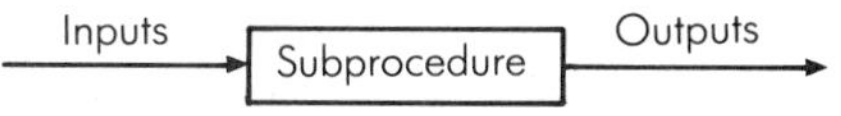

FIGURE 5.2 Subprocedure as a black box

of no concern to the user. The user needs to know only what the procedure does and what the interface is, not how the subprocedure performs its function. The subprocedures in the I/O library of this book have been used in this way; Appendix D describes the function and interface requirements for each of these subprocedures, but it does not describe how the subprocedures perform their functions. The information contained in Appendix D is sufficient for users of these procedures.

In the 8088/8086 assembly language, there are three typical ways to pass inputs to a subprocedure and receive outputs from a subprocedure:

1. The input values can be placed in processor registers by the caller, and the subprocedure can pick them up from there. The subprocedure can leave the output values in processor registers, and the caller can pick them up from there. The I/O procedure PUTDEC receives its inputs in this way. For a function subprocedure that returns a single value to be used in further computation, the following conventions typically are used:
   a. If the value being returned is a byte value, then it is returned in the AL-register.
   b. If the value being returned is a word value, then it is returned in the AX-register.
   c. If the value being returned is a double-word value (32 bits), then it is returned in the DX:AX register pair.

   The I/O procedure GETDEC is a function procedure that returns its output in the AX-register.
2. The addresses of arguments can be placed in processor registers by the caller. The subprocedure then has access to a part of the caller's environment. By changing the values at these addresses, the subprocedure can return outputs to the caller. The I/O procedure PUTSTRNG obtains the address of the string to be displayed in this way. The I/O procedure GETSTRNG places the input string at the address specified by the caller.
3. The input values (or their addresses) can be placed in the stack by the caller, and the subprocedure can pick them up from there. The subprocedure can leave the output values in the stack, and the caller can pick them up from there. This method, used by some high-level language compilers, can be used in implementing recursive algorithms, which are discussed in Chapter 10.

The first of these three approaches is used to implement call-by-value parameter passing, the second is used to implement call-by-location parameter passing, and the third can be used to implement either call-by-value or call-by-location.

5.4 8088/8086 Assembly Language Subprocedures

In the 8088/8086 assembly language, a code segment definition contains the definition of one or more procedures. In each of the example programs in Chapters 1–4, the code segment definition contains only the instructions for the main procedure of the program. A code segment definition may contain: (a) only the instructions for the main procedure, or (b) the instructions of the main procedure plus the definitions of one or more subprocedures, or (c) just the definitions of one or more subprocedures. A subprocedure definition begins with a PROC pseudo-operation and terminates with an ENDP pseudo-operation. The **PROC pseudo-operation** has the following general form:

⟨*proc-name*⟩ `PROC` [⟨*attributes*⟩] [`USES` ⟨*reg-list*⟩] [,⟨*parameter-list*⟩] [⟨*comment*⟩]

in which ⟨*attributes*⟩ is a list of attributes (separated by spaces) for the procedure, ⟨*reg-list*⟩ is the list of register designators for the registers used by the subprocedure that must be saved and restored, and ⟨*parameter-list*⟩ is the list of parameters (separated by commas) whose arguments are to be passed via the stack.

The ⟨*attributes*⟩ specified in the PROC pseudo-operation include the following:

Type attribute This attribute, which specifies the scope of the procedure name, can be either NEAR or FAR. NEAR means that the subprocedure is local to the code segment that contains it and can be invoked only by procedures defined in the same code segment. FAR means that the subprocedure can be made available to be invoked by procedures in any code segment of the executable program. (NEAR and FAR subprocedures are discussed in detail in the following two subsections.) If the type attribute is not explicitly specified in the PROC pseudo-operation, then it is implicitly specified. If full segment definitions are being used, the default type attribute for the PROC pseudo-operation is always NEAR. If simplified segment directives are being used, the type attribute is implicitly specified by the memory model declared with the .MODEL pseudo-operation. For the TINY, SMALL, COMPACT, and FLAT models, the default type attribute is NEAR. For the MEDIUM, LARGE, and HUGE models, the default type attribute is FAR.

Language attribute This attribute, which specifies the subprocedure interface, can be BASIC, FORTRAN, PASCAL, C, STDCALL, or SYSCALL. For a language attribute of BASIC, FORTRAN, or PASCAL, the assembler will (a) convert the subprocedure name to uppercase, (b) expect the arguments to be pushed on the stack in left-to-right order, and (c) convert all of the RET instructions in the subprocedure to RET instructions that pop the arguments from the stack. For a language attribute of C or STDCALL, the assembler will prefix the subprocedure name with an underscore (_) character if the visibility attribute of the subprocedure is PUBLIC or EXPORT. For a language attribute of C, STDCALL, or SYSCALL, the assembler will expect the arguments to be pushed on the stack in right-to-left order.

Visibility attribute This attribute, which specifies whether the subprocedure is available to other assembly modules, can be PRIVATE, PUBLIC, or EXPORT. Subprocedures with visibility attribute PRIVATE are not available to be called from procedures defined in other assembly modules. Those with visibility attribute PUBLIC are available to be called from procedures defined in other assembly modules. The visibility attribute EXPORT is beyond the scope of this book.

MASM 5.1

In MASM 5.1, the attributes field includes only the type attribute, which can be either NEAR or FAR. The default value for the type attribute is chosen according to the same rules as those for MASM 6.0.

The ⟨*parameter-list*⟩, separated from the ⟨*attributes*⟩ or the USES ⟨*reg-list*⟩ clause by a comma, is a list of parameter specifications of the form ⟨*parameter-name*⟩:⟨*type*⟩, where ⟨*parameter-name*⟩ is the symbolic name of the parameter and ⟨*type*⟩ is one of the following type attributes: BYTE, SBYTE, WORD, SWORD, DWORD, SDWORD, FWORD, NEAR, or FAR.

EXAMPLE

The pseudo-operation

```
CLR_BLK  PROC  FAR BASIC PUBLIC USES AX BX CX DX DI ES,
               R1:WORD,C1:WORD,R2:WORD,C2:WORD
```

begins the definition of a FAR, PUBLIC subprocedure named CLR_BLK. The subprocedure uses the AX, BX, CX, DX, DI, and ES registers, and it saves and restores them for the caller. The subprocedure expects four arguments on the stack in left-to-right order. The subprocedure pops the arguments from the stack before returning to the caller. The calling sequence

```
PUSH    ULR
PUSH    ULC
PUSH    BX
PUSH    AX
CALL    CLR_BLK
```

invokes subprocedure CLR_BLK with the value of variable ULR as the initial value of parameter R1, the value of variable ULC as the initial value of parameter C1, the BX-register value as the initial value of parameter R2, and the AX-register value as the initial value of parameter C2. The subprocedure can move new values to the parameters without affecting the arguments because the storage cells for the parameters are stack locations. The parameter passing described here takes the call-by-value approach. ■

The **ENDP pseudo-operation**, which terminates a subprocedure definition, has the following general form:

⟨*proc-name*⟩ `ENDP` [⟨*comment*⟩]

in which ⟨*proc-name*⟩ is the symbolic name to be associated with the subprocedure and must match the ⟨*proc-name*⟩ used on the PROC pseudo-operation that marks the beginning of the subprocedure definition. The ENDP pseudo-operation marks the physical end of a subprocedure definition.

The assembly language CALL instruction is translated to one of two different machine language call instructions, depending on whether the subprocedure being called is type NEAR or type FAR. A RET instruction appearing in a subprocedure definition is translated to one of two different machine language return instructions, depending on whether the subprocedure containing the RET instruction is defined as type NEAR or type FAR.

NEAR Subprocedures

A NEAR subprocedure is one that is defined in the same code segment as the procedure(s) that references it. It is known by and can be invoked only by procedures in the code segment in which it is defined. The names of variables, labels, and procedures defined within a given assembly module are available to all procedures within that assembly module.

A **NEAR subprocedure** is declared by using the type attribute NEAR in the PROC pseudo-operation that identifies the beginning of the procedure definition:

```
⟨proc-name⟩ PROC NEAR [⟨comment⟩]
```

The machine language instruction that calls a NEAR subprocedure causes only the value of the IP-register to be pushed onto the stack. The IP-register then is set to the offset within the code segment of the subprocedure name. That is, the IP-register is set to the offset of the first instruction in the called subprocedure. The value of the CS-register does not have to be saved or modified since the subprocedure is in the same code segment as its caller.

The machine language instruction that returns from a NEAR subprocedure pops a single value from the stack and places that value in the IP-register. A NEAR subprocedure must be written in such a way that the offset pushed onto the stack by the CALL instruction that invoked the subprocedure is again at the top of the stack when any RET instruction in the subprocedure is executed. Then, the value popped into the IP-register becomes the offset of the first byte of the instruction that immediately follows the CALL instruction that invoked the subprocedure.

Programming Example—Display Binary Integer (PUTBIN Version 1, NEAR Subprocedure)

The assembly module in Program Listing 5.1 has a code segment definition (lines 17–111) that contains two procedure definitions. One is a NEAR subprocedure that displays an 8-bit or a 16-bit integer in binary form, and the other is a main procedure that was designed to demonstrate the subprocedure. The subprocedure is called PUTBIN because, from a functional standpoint, it behaves exactly like the PUTBIN procedure in the I/O procedure package that accompanies this book. However, this subprocedure is not the version of PUTBIN that is included in that package.

The subprocedure PUTBIN appears in lines 61–110. This subprocedure begins with a prologue (lines 61–72) that describes the subprocedure's function, the inputs expected by the subprocedure, and the outputs produced by the subprocedure. From a user standpoint, the subprocedure is characterized by the way in which the input arguments are passed to the subprocedure and the way in which outputs are returned to the caller. The PUTBIN subprocedure expects two inputs:

1. A display code is expected in the BL-register. A code of zero implies that an 8-bit value is to be displayed, and a nonzero code implies that a 16-bit value is to be displayed.
2. The value to be displayed is expected in the AL-register for byte output, and it is expected in the AX-register for word output.

PUTBIN returns nothing to the caller. Its output goes to the display screen.

The prologue should contain all of the information required by a user. A user should have no need to look at the code. The prologue should explain what the subprocedure does and how a calling procedure is to interface with the subprocedure. The prologue does not need to give the details of how the subprocedure's function is implemented. This information is provided in the pseudocode comments and in the code itself.

The subprocedure definition begins with the PROC pseudo-operation in line 73 and terminates with the ENDP pseudo-operation in line 110. Both of these pseudo-operations have the name of the subprocedure (PUTBIN) in their label field. The

```
            PAGE    80,132
;====================================================================
;                   PROGRAM LISTING 5.1
;
;PROGRAM TO DEMONSTRATE SUBROUTINE INTERFACE
;
;====================================================================
            .MODEL  SMALL,BASIC,FARSTACK
;====================================================================
                                        ;PROCEDURES TO
            EXTRN   NEWLINE:FAR         ;DISPLAY NEWLINE CHARACTER
            EXTRN   PUTDEC:FAR          ;DISPLAY DECIMAL INTEGER
;====================================================================
; S T A C K   D E F I N I T I O N
;
            .STACK  256
;====================================================================
; C O D E   S E G M E N T   D E F I N I T I O N
;
            .CODE
;
EX_5_1:
            MOV     BL,1                ;SET CODE FOR WORD DISPLAY
            MOV     AX,0001H            ;LOAD AX WITH
                                        ;
                                        ;0000000000000001
                                        ;
            CALL    PUTBIN              ;DISPLAY CONTENTS OF AX
            CALL    NEWLINE             ;SKIP TO NEXT LINE ON DISPLAY
            MOV     AX,5555H            ;LOAD AX WITH
                                        ;
                                        ;0101010101010101
                                        ;
            CALL    PUTBIN              ;DISPLAY CONTENTS OF AX
            CALL    NEWLINE             ;SKIP TO NEXT LINE ON DISPLAY
            MOV     AX,0AAAAH           ;LOAD AX WITH
                                        ;
                                        ;1010101010101010
                                        ;
            CALL    PUTBIN              ;DISPLAY CONTENTS OF AX
            CALL    NEWLINE             ;SKIP TO NEXT LINE ON DISPLAY
            MOV     AX,0FFFFH           ;LOAD AX WITH
                                        ;
                                        ;1111111111111111
                                        ;
            CALL    PUTBIN              ;DISPLAY CONTENTS OF AX
            CALL    NEWLINE             ;SKIP TO NEXT LINE ON DISPLAY
            MOV     BL,0                ;SET CODE FOR BYTE DISPLAY
            MOV     AX,55AAH            ;LOAD AH  AND  AL WITH
                                        ;
                                        ;01010101 AND 10101010
                                        ;
            CALL    PUTBIN              ;DISPLAY CONTENTS OF AL
            CALL    NEWLINE             ;SKIP TO NEXT LINE ON DISPLAY
            XCHG    AL,AH               ;EXCHANGE AL AND AH REGISTERS
            CALL    PUTBIN              ;DISPLAY CONTENTS OF AL
            CALL    NEWLINE             ;SKIP TO NEXT LINE ON DISPLAY
            .EXIT                       ;RETURN TO DOS
;
            PAGE
;====================================================================
; PROCEDURE TO DISPLAY AN 8- OR 16-BIT VALUE IN BINARY FORM
;
; INPUT:  AL-REG  8-BIT  VALUE TO BE DISPLAYED
;         BL=0    CODE FOR  8-BIT DISPLAY
;               OR
;         AX-REG  16-BIT VALUE TO BE DISPLAYED
```

```
 68: ;          BL<>0   CODE FOR 16-BIT DISPLAY
 69: ;
 70: ; OUTPUT: INPUT VALUE DISPLAYED IN BINARY FORM ON THE
 71: ;          SCREEN BEGINNING AT CURRENT CURSOR POSITION
 72: ;=================================================================
 73: PUTBIN      PROC     NEAR               ;PROCEDURE PUTBIN(NUMBER,CODE)
 74:             PUSH     AX                      ;SAVE REGISTERS
 75:             PUSH     DX
 76:             PUSH     DI
 77:             PUSH     BX
 78:             PUSH     CX
 79:             PUSHF                            ;SAVE FLAGS
 80:             CMP      BL,0                    ;IF   CODE = BYTE (BL=0)
 81:             JNZ      _ELSE
 82:             MOV      AH,0                    ;THEN EXPAND NUMBER TO 16 BITS
 83:             MOV      CX,8                    ;      BIT_COUNT = 8
 84:             JMP      _ENDIF
 85: _ELSE:                                      ;ELSE
 86:             MOV      CX,16                   ;      BIT_COUNT = 16
 87: _ENDIF:                                     ;ENDIF
 88:             MOV      BX,2
 89:             MOV      DI,CX                   ;SAVE BIT_COUNT
 90: LOOPTOP:                                    ;REPEAT
 91:             MOV      DX,0                    ;    BIT = NUMBER mod 2
 92:             DIV      BX                      ;    NUMBER = NUMBER / 2
 93:             PUSH     DX                      ;    PUSH BIT
 94:             LOOP     LOOPTOP                 ;    DECREMENT BIT_COUNT
 95:                                              ;UNTIL BIT_COUNT = 0
 96:             MOV      CX,DI                   ;RESTORE BIT_COUNT
 97:             MOV      BH,0                    ;<DISPLAY CODE>
 98: _REPEAT:                                    ;REPEAT
 99:             POP      AX                      ;    POP BIT
100:             CALL     PUTDEC                  ;    DISPLAY BIT
101:             LOOP     _REPEAT                 ;    DECREMENT BIT_COUNT
102:                                              ;UNTIL BIT_COUNT = 0
103:             POPF                             ;RESTORE FLAGS
104:             POP      CX                      ;RESTORE REGISTERS
105:             POP      BX
106:             POP      DI
107:             POP      DX
108:             POP      AX
109:             RET                              ;RETURN
110: PUTBIN      ENDP                        ;END PUTBIN
111:             END      EX_5_1
```

PROC pseudo-operation specifies that the subprocedure is of type NEAR. That is, the subprocedure can be called only from procedures that are defined in the same code segment in which this subprocedure is defined.

The subprocedure begins by saving the values currently in the registers that it will be using. The PUSH instructions in lines 74–78 save the AX, DX, DI, BX, and CX register values on the stack, and the PUSHF instruction in line 79 saves the flags register value on the stack. The subprocedure terminates by restoring the values of the registers that it used and returning to the caller. The POPF instruction in line 103 restores the value of the flags register, and the POP instructions in lines 104–108 restore the values of the CX, BX, DI, DX, and AX registers. Note that the POP operations are in the reverse order from the corresponding PUSH operations in lines 74–79. This situation occurs because the stack is a **last-in-first-out** data structure. These PUSH and POP operations ensure that the state of the processor is the same on return to the caller as it was at the point of call to the subprocedure. The RET instruction in line 109 returns execution control to the caller by popping the return address offset from the stack into the IP-register.

The instructions in lines 80–102 implement the subprocedure's function. The double-alternative decision structure in lines 80–87 tests the input code in the BL-register to determine whether 8-bit or 16-bit output is required and stores the appropriate bit count (8 or 16) in the CX-register. The MOV instruction in line 89 saves a copy of the bit count in the DI-register, which is used to control the number of iterations of the REPEAT-UNTIL loop in lines 90–95 and the REPEAT-UNTIL loop in lines 98–102.

The REPEAT-UNTIL loop in lines 90–95 repeatedly divides the number by 2, pushing the remainder onto the stack and saving the quotient as the number to be divided on the next iteration of the loop. The sequence of remainders is the sequence of bits in the binary representation of the input number. This sequence is produced in right-to-left order and must be displayed in left-to-right order, which is why each bit produced is pushed onto the stack. Since the stack is a last-in-first-out data structure, the bits are popped off in the reverse order from which they were produced (i.e., left-to-right order). Note that the input value is treated as an unsigned integer value and that unsigned integer division is used. As an exercise, try to explain what happens if the division is changed to signed integer division.

The MOV instruction in line 96 restores the CX-register with the bit count so that it can be used to control the second REPEAT-UNTIL loop. The MOV instruction in line 97 sets the display code for the external procedure PUTDEC. The PUTDEC procedure is used to display the individual bits of the binary number. A display code of zero causes each bit to be displayed with no leading or trailing blanks. In Chapter 9, a version of PUTBIN is presented that uses the Basic I/O System (BIOS) interrupt procedures to output the individual bits.

The REPEAT-UNTIL loop in lines 98–102 pops the bits from the stack and displays them using the PUTDEC procedure. On each iteration of the loop, one bit is popped and displayed.

The main procedure, EX_5_1, appears in lines 22–59 of Program Listing 5.1. The instructions in lines 23 and 24 set up the inputs for a call to the NEAR subprocedure PUTBIN. The MOV instruction in line 23 sets the display code (BL = 1) to indicate that the 16-bit value in the AX-register is to be displayed. The MOV instruction in line 24 places the value to be displayed (hexadecimal 1) in the AX-register. The call to the PUTBIN procedure in line 28 causes the value 0000000000000001 to be displayed on the screen beginning at the current cursor position. The call to the NEWLINE procedure in line 29 then moves the cursor to the beginning of the next line of the display.

The MOV instruction in line 30 puts the hexadecimal value 5555 in the AX-register in preparation for another call to the PUTBIN procedure. The display code does not have to be set in the BL-register again; nothing has changed its value since it was last set in line 23. Both the PUTBIN and the NEWLINE procedures preserve registers for their callers. The call to the PUTBIN procedure in line 34 causes the value 0101010101010101 to be displayed on the screen beginning at the current cursor position. The call to the NEWLINE procedure in line 35 then moves the cursor to the beginning of the next line of the display.

Similarly, the instructions in lines 36, 40, and 41 cause the value 1010101010101010 to be displayed, and the instructions in lines 42, 46, and 47 cause the value 1111111111111111 to be displayed. Each value is displayed on a separate line.

The MOV instruction in line 48 sets the display code for PUTBIN (BL = 0) to indicate that the 8-bit value in the AL-register is to be displayed. The MOV instruction in line 49 places the value 01010101 in the AH-register and the value 10101010 in the AL-register. The call to PUTBIN in line 53 causes the AL-register value 10101010 to be displayed. The XCHG instruction in line 55 places the value 10101010 in the AH-register and the value 01010101 in the AL-register. The call to PUTBIN in line 56 causes the AL-register value 01010101 to be displayed. The complete output for this program is as follows:

```
0000000000000001
0101010101010101
1010101010101010
1111111111111111
10101010
01010101
```

Note that both the main procedure and the PUTBIN subprocedure are part of the same code segment, which begins with the .CODE pseudo-operation in line 20 and ends with the END pseudo-operation in line 111. A NEAR procedure *must* be defined in the same code segment as the procedures that reference it.

Note also that the external procedure declarations (lines 11 and 12) include only PUTDEC (called by PUTBIN) and NEWLINE (called by the main procedure). PUTBIN does not appear in the external procedure declarations because it is defined internally to this assembly module. That is, this program references the internal procedure PUTBIN defined in this program, not the external procedure PUTBIN defined in the I/O library.

Finally, note the PAGE pseudo-operation in line 60. A PAGE pseudo-operation with no operand field causes the assembler to insert a page eject into the assembler-generated listing. Thus, the subprocedure definition will appear on a separate page in the assembler-generated listing.

FAR Subprocedures

A FAR subprocedure is one that can be invoked by procedures in other code segments. It can be defined in a code segment that is physically separate from other code segments of the executable program. It can be developed and maintained in a separate assembly module. The assembly module that contains a FAR subprocedure can also contain stack segments and data segments, in addition to the code segment. At link time, the stack segments are concatenated with other stack segments of the executable program to produce a single stack segment. An executable program contains exactly one stack segment. The data segments can be concatenated with, overlayed on, or separate from other data segments in the executable program. These options are specified in the operand field of the SEGMENT pseudo-operation that marks the beginning of the segment definition when full segment definitions are used. Segmentation features are discussed in detail in Chapter 12.

A **FAR subprocedure** is declared by using the type attribute FAR in the PROC pseudo-operation that identifies the beginning of the subprocedure definition:

⟨*proc-name*⟩ PROC FAR [⟨*comment*⟩]

The machine language instruction that calls a FAR subprocedure causes the value in the CS-register and then the value in the IP-register to be pushed onto the stack. The CS:IP register pair then is set to the segment and offset associated with the FAR subprocedure name. That is, the CS:IP register pair is set to the segment and offset of the first instruction in the called subprocedure.

The machine language instruction that returns from a FAR subprocedure pops a value from the stack and places that value in the IP-register, and then it pops a second value from the stack and places that value in the CS-register. A FAR subprocedure must be written in such a way that the segment and offset pushed onto the stack by the CALL instruction that invoked the subprocedure are again at the top of the stack when any RET instruction in the subprocedure is executed. Then, the values popped by the return instruction are the segment and offset of the first byte of the instruction that immediately follows the CALL instruction that invoked the subprocedure.

In addition to the call and return mechanisms, two other mechanisms are needed for a FAR subprocedure that is defined in an assembly module separate from the procedure(s) that references it:

A Mechanism to Resolve External References (LINK) A call to an external subprocedure cannot be translated fully by the assembler because it does not know the relative load address for the subprocedure. The best that the assembler can do is to set aside memory space for the address (segment and offset) of the subprocedure and have that memory space filled in with the address at some later point.

A Mechanism to Declare External Names (EXTRN, PUBLIC) If a procedure in one assembly module is to invoke a subprocedure in another assembly module, then the assembler must be informed that the subprocedure being referenced is external to this assembly module and will be supplied at a later point. Otherwise, the assembler expects the referenced subprocedure to be defined in the assembly module.

If a subprocedure in one assembly module is to be invoked by procedures in other assembly modules, then its name must be made available to the procedures in other assembly modules. However, the names of some subprocedures in the assembly module may need to be hidden from the procedures in other assembly modules. There must be a way to identify the subprocedures that are to be known to procedures in other assembly modules.

The mechanism to resolve external references is the utility program LINK. The **LINK program** combines object modules into a single executable program. It checks to see if all external references in the object modules are resolved and, if not, displays appropriate error messages.

In the 8088/8086 assembly language, the mechanism to declare external names is a pair of pseudo-operations: EXTRN and PUBLIC. The **EXTRN pseudo-operation** is used in an assembly module to identify symbolic names that are referenced in the assembly module but that are defined in another assembly module, and it has the following general form:

`EXTRN` ⟨*ext-spec-list*⟩ [⟨*comment*⟩]

in which ⟨*ext-spec-list*⟩ is a list of external specifications of the form ⟨*name*⟩:⟨*type*⟩ (items in the list are separated by commas), where ⟨*name*⟩ is the symbolic name of a label, variable, or procedure that is defined in another assembly module, and ⟨*type*⟩ is the type attribute of the symbolic name and may be one of the following: BYTE, SBYTE, WORD, SWORD, DWORD, SDWORD, FWORD, NEAR, or FAR.

At this point, only external procedures of the FAR type are of interest. An EXTRN pseudo-operation may be placed anywhere in an assembly module as long as it appears before the first reference to the names that it defines. In the program listings used in this book, EXTRN pseudo-operations are placed at the beginning of the assembly module immediately after the prologue.

The **PUBLIC pseudo-operation** is used in an assembly module to identify symbolic names defined in the assembly module that are to be available to procedures in other assembly modules, and it has the following general form:

PUBLIC ⟨*name-list*⟩ [⟨*comment*⟩]

in which ⟨*name-list*⟩ is a list of symbolic names of the variables, labels, and procedures that are to be known outside of this assembly module. PUBLIC pseudo-operations may be placed anywhere in an assembly module. With MASM 6.0, a subprocedure name can be declared PUBLIC by specifying the PUBLIC visibility attribute on the PROC pseudo-operation that begins the subprocedure definition.

The LINK program matches external names in one object module (defined by EXTRN pseudo-operations in the corresponding assembly module) with the PUBLIC names in other object modules (defined by PUBLIC pseudo-operations in the corresponding assembly modules). The LINK program fills in addresses (segment and offset) in the machine code to resolve external references.

Programming Example—Display Binary Integer (PUTBIN Version 1, FAR Subprocedure)

The assembly module in Program Listing 5.3 contains the definition of a FAR subprocedure that displays an 8-bit or a 16-bit integer in binary form, and the assembly module in Program Listing 5.2 contains the definition of a main procedure that was designed to demonstrate the subprocedure. The object modules produced by assembling these two modules are to be linked to produce a single, executable program. Program Listings 5.2 and 5.3 are basically the same as Program Listing 5.1, but the subprocedure has been converted from an internal NEAR procedure to an external FAR procedure. This discussion concentrates on the differences between the programs.

The assembly module in Program Listing 5.2 contains the definition of the stack segment for the program and the definition for the main procedure. The reference to PUTDEC has been removed from the external procedure declarations. PUTDEC is referenced by PUT_BIN, and procedure PUT_BIN now is defined in a separate assembly module. Since PUT_BIN is defined separately, a declaration for the PUT_BIN procedure has been added to the external procedure declarations (line 12). The name of the subprocedure has been changed from PUTBIN to PUT_BIN so that it is obvious that the subprocedure being used is not the external PUTBIN procedure in the I/O library.

The code segment of this assembly module, defined in lines 17–59, contains only the main procedure, EX_5_2, which is the same as the EX_5_1 procedure in Program Listing 5.1, except that the CALL instructions in lines 28, 34, 40, 46, 53, and 56 have been modified to reflect the new name of the subprocedure.

The assembly module in Program Listing 5.3 contains the definition of the PUT_BIN procedure. A number of items were added or changed when the subprocedure was extracted and placed in a separate assembly module. The PAGE pseudo-operation (line 1) and the .MODEL pseudo-operation (line 13) were copied into this new assembly module. The external declaration for the referenced PUTDEC procedure was extracted and embedded in this assembly module (line 15). Since an assembly module consists of one or more segment definitions, the definition of the PUT_BIN subprocedure (lines 20–57) had to be embedded in a code segment; the code segment definition begins with the .CODE pseudo-operation in line 18 and ends

```
            PAGE    80,132
;====================================================================
;                    PROGRAM LISTING 5.2
;
;PROGRAM TO DEMONSTRATE SUBROUTINE INTERFACE
;
;====================================================================
            .MODEL  SMALL,BASIC,FARSTACK
;====================================================================
                                        ;PROCEDURES TO
            EXTRN   NEWLINE:FAR         ;DISPLAY NEWLINE CHARACTER
            EXTRN   PUT_BIN:FAR         ;DISPLAY BINARY INTEGER
;====================================================================
; S T A C K   D E F I N I T I O N
;
            .STACK  256
;====================================================================
; C O D E   S E G M E N T   D E F I N I T I O N
;
            .CODE
;
EX_5_2:
            MOV     BL,1                ;SET CODE FOR WORD DISPLAY
            MOV     AX,0001H            ;LOAD AX WITH
                                        ;
                                        ;0000000000000001
                                        ;
            CALL    PUT_BIN             ;DISPLAY CONTENTS OF AX
            CALL    NEWLINE             ;SKIP TO NEXT LINE ON DISPLAY
            MOV     AX,5555H            ;LOAD AX WITH
                                        ;
                                        ;0101010101010101
                                        ;
            CALL    PUT_BIN             ;DISPLAY CONTENTS OF AX
            CALL    NEWLINE             ;SKIP TO NEXT LINE ON DISPLAY
            MOV     AX,0AAAAH           ;LOAD AX WITH
                                        ;
                                        ;1010101010101010
                                        ;
            CALL    PUT_BIN             ;DISPLAY CONTENTS OF AX
            CALL    NEWLINE             ;SKIP TO NEXT LINE ON DISPLAY
            MOV     AX,0FFFFH           ;LOAD AX WITH
                                        ;
                                        ;1111111111111111
                                        ;
            CALL    PUT_BIN             ;DISPLAY CONTENTS OF AX
            CALL    NEWLINE             ;SKIP TO NEXT LINE ON DISPLAY
            MOV     BL,0                ;SET CODE FOR BYTE DISPLAY
            MOV     AX,55AAH            ;LOAD AH  AND  AL WITH
                                        ;
                                        ;01010101 AND 10101010
                                        ;
            CALL    PUT_BIN             ;DISPLAY CONTENTS OF AL
            CALL    NEWLINE             ;SKIP TO NEXT LINE ON DISPLAY
            XCHG    AL,AH               ;EXCHANGE AL AND AH REGISTERS
            CALL    PUT_BIN             ;DISPLAY CONTENTS OF AL
            CALL    NEWLINE             ;SKIP TO NEXT LINE ON DISPLAY
            .EXIT                       ;RETURN TO DOS
;
            END     EX_5_2
```

```
 1:             PAGE    80,132
 2: ;===================================================================
 3: ;                     PROGRAM LISTING 5.3
 4: ; PROCEDURE TO DISPLAY AN 8- OR 16-BIT VALUE IN BINARY FORM
 5: ; INPUT:  AL-REG  8-BIT  VALUE TO BE DISPLAYED
 6: ;         BL=0    CODE FOR  8-BIT DISPLAY
 7: ;               OR
 8: ;         AX-REG  16-BIT VALUE TO BE DISPLAYED
 9: ;         BL<>0   CODE FOR 16-BIT DISPLAY
10: ; OUTPUT: INPUT VALUE DISPLAYED IN BINARY FORM ON THE
11: ;         SCREEN BEGINNING AT CURRENT CURSOR POSITION
12: ;===================================================================
13:             .MODEL  SMALL,BASIC
14:                                        ;PROCEDURE TO
15:             EXTRN   PUTDEC:FAR         ;DISPLAY DECIMAL INTEGER
16: ;===================================================================
17: ; C O D E   S E G M E N T   D E F I N I T I O N
18:             .CODE   EX_5_3
19: ;
20: PUT_BIN     PROC    FAR PUBLIC USES AX BX CX DX DI
21:                                     ;PROCEDURE PUT_BIN(NUMBER,CODE)
22:                                        ;SAVE REGISTERS - (ASSEMBLER
23:                                        ;     GENERATES  APPROPRIATE
24:                                        ;     PUSH  INSTRUCTIONS  IN
25:                                        ;     RESPONSE TO USES LIST)
26:             PUSHF                      ;SAVE FLAGS
27:             CMP     BL,0               ;IF   CODE = BYTE (BL=0)
28:             JNZ     _ELSE
29:             MOV     AH,0               ;THEN EXPAND NUMBER TO 16 BITS
30:             MOV     CX,8               ;     BIT_COUNT = 8
31:             JMP     _ENDIF
32: _ELSE:                                 ;ELSE
33:             MOV     CX,16              ;     BIT_COUNT = 16
34: _ENDIF:                                ;ENDIF
35:             MOV     BX,2
36:             MOV     DI,CX              ;SAVE BIT_COUNT
37: LOOPTOP:                               ;REPEAT
38:             MOV     DX,0               ;   BIT = NUMBER mod 2
39:             DIV     BX                 ;   NUMBER = NUMBER / 2
40:             PUSH    DX                 ;   PUSH BIT
41:             LOOP    LOOPTOP            ;   DECREMENT BIT_COUNT
42:                                        ;UNTIL BIT_COUNT = 0
43:             MOV     CX,DI              ;RESTORE BIT_COUNT
44:             MOV     BH,0               ;<DISPLAY CODE>
45: _REPEAT:                               ;REPEAT
46:             POP     AX                 ;   POP BIT
47:             CALL    PUTDEC             ;   DISPLAY BIT
48:             LOOP    _REPEAT            ;   DECREMENT BIT_COUNT
49:                                        ;UNTIL BIT_COUNT = 0
50:             POPF                       ;RESTORE FLAGS
51:                                        ;RESTORE REGISTERS ---
52:                                        ;    (ASSEMBLER GENERATES
53:                                        ;     THE APPROPRIATE POP
54:                                        ;     INSTRUCTIONS IN
55:                                        ;     RESPONSE TO USES LIST)
56:             RET                        ;RETURN
57: PUT_BIN     ENDP                    ;END PUT_BIN
58:             END
```

with the END pseudo-operation in line 58. The code segment contains the definition for a single procedure, the PUT_BIN subprocedure.

The definition of the PUT_BIN subprocedure begins with the PROC pseudo-operation in line 20 and ends with the ENDP pseudo-operation in line 57. The PROC pseudo-operation specifies that the PUT_BIN subprocedure is of type FAR, which means that the PUT_BIN subprocedure can be called from procedures defined in the same or different code segments. The PROC pseudo-operation also specifies that the PUT_BIN subprocedure has visibility PUBLIC, which means that the name PUT_BIN is to be available for reference by procedures in other assembly modules. The LINK program links procedures by replacing external procedure names in one object module with the address associated with the corresponding PUBLIC names in other object modules. The PROC pseudo-operation also specifies that the PUT_BIN subprocedure uses the AX, BX, CX, DX, and DI registers. Note that the PUSH instructions in lines 74–78 and the corresponding POP instructions in lines 104–108 of Program Listing 5.1 do not appear in the subprocedure definition in Program Listing 5.3. These PUSH and POP instructions have been removed because the clause

```
USES AX BX CX DX DI
```

on the PROC pseudo-operation in line 20 of Program Listing 5.3 causes the assembler to generate the instructions

```
push  ax
push  bx
push  cx
push  dx
push  di
```

prior to the first instruction of the subprocedure and to generate the instructions

```
pop  di
pop  dx
pop  cx
pop  bx
pop  ax
```

prior to any RET instruction in the subprocedure.

Because Program Listing 5.3 is the code for a complete assembly module, it must terminate with the END pseudo-operation (line 58).

The object modules that correspond to the two assembly modules in Program Listings 5.2 and 5.3 must be linked along with the library routines that they reference to form an executable program. This task is accomplished via LINK. Suppose the assembly module in Program Listing 5.2 is in a file on the diskette in drive A under the name EX_5_2.ASM, and suppose the assembly module in Program Listing 5.3 is in a file on the same diskette under the name EX_5_3.ASM. Suppose further that we have a fixed disk system, the Macro Assembler and the Linkage Editor are on the fixed disk, and the fixed disk drive is the default drive. The DOS commands

```
ml  /c  /Zi  /Foa:  a:ex_5_2.asm
ml  /c  /Zi  /Foa:  a:ex_5_3.asm
```

assemble these two source code modules, creating the two object modules

```
A:EX_5_2.OBJ
A:EX_5_3.OBJ
```

MASM 5.1

Two features of MASM 6.0 that are used in the assembly module of Program Listing 5.3 are not supported by MASM 5.1. In MASM 5.1, the .CODE segment directive does not include a segment name field as it does in MASM 6.0. Also in

MASM 5.1, the PROC pseudo-operation does not include the visibility attribute as it does in MASM 6.0. A separate PUBLIC pseudo-operation is required in MASM 5.1 to declare the subprocedure name as PUBLIC. If lines 18–21 of Program Listing 5.3 are changed to the following, this assembly module can then be translated by MASM 5.1:

```
          .CODE
;
PUT_BIN   PROC    FAR USES AX BX CX DX DI
          PUBLIC PUT_BIN      ;PROCEDURE PUT_BIN(NUMBER,CODE)
```

Suppose the assembly module in Program Listing 5.2 is in a file on the diskette in drive A under the name EX_5_2.ASM, and suppose the assembly module in Program Listing 5.3, modified as just shown, is in a file on the same diskette under the name EX_5_3.ASM. Suppose further that we have a fixed disk system, the Macro Assembler and the Linkage Editor are on the fixed disk, and the fixed disk drive is the default drive. The DOS commands

```
masm /zi  a:ex_5_2,a:;
masm /zi  a:ex_5_3,a:;
```

assemble these two source code modules, creating the two object modules

```
A:EX_5_2.OBJ
A:EX_5_3.OBJ
```

To link these two object modules into a complete executable program, the following DOS command can be used:

```
link a:ex_5_2 a:ex_5_3,a:,nul,io
```

Note the separator between the file specifications for the two object modules. It is either a space or a plus sign (+), not a comma (,). A comma marks the end of the list of object modules, which may contain any number of object module specifications, and the object module specifications may be in any order. The preceding LINK command links the two object modules and any referenced library procedures from IO.LIB, creating an executable program module named A:EX_5_2.EXE. When no name is specified in the LINK command for the executable program module, the name that is used is the same as the name of the first object module in the object module list, with the suffix replaced by EXE.

The output of this program is exactly the same as that for the program of Program Listing 5.1. The subprocedures in Program Listings 5.1 and 5.3 are examples of subroutines (nonvalue-returning procedures).

5.5 Local Data Segments

It is often the case that an external subprocedure requires its own local data. The assembly module that contains the subprocedure also may contain one or more data segments. The data in these segments is available to any procedure defined in the code segment of the same assembly module. If a subprocedure defined in the code segment of one assembly module is to be invoked by procedures defined in other assembly modules, then the subprocedure should assume that the caller is using both the DS and ES registers. To use one of these segment registers to point to a local data segment, the subprocedure is responsible for performing the following operations:

1. On entry, the subprocedure must save the value of the segment register for the caller and then set the segment register to point to the local data segment.
2. Just prior to return to the caller, the subprocedure must restore the value of the segment register for the caller.

This protocol allows the caller and the callee to use their own private data segments. It is possible for procedures defined in separate assembly modules to share data segments. Data segment sharing is discussed in Chapter 12.

The data contained in a local data segment for a subprocedure is static in nature. That is, the storage for the data exists prior to the first invocation of the subprocedure and persists through the last invocation of the subprocedure, which means that the values of the variables in the local data segment persist from one invocation of the subprocedure to the next invocation.

Programming Example—Random Number Generator

Applications involving simulation often require a sequence of random numbers. A **random number generator** is a procedure that provides the capability of producing a sequence of pseudorandom numbers in some specified range. Program Listing 5.4 is the definition of such a procedure. This random number generator is a function subprocedure that returns an integer in the range LOWER to UPPER, where LOWER and UPPER are the inputs to the subprocedure. The integer is produced by evaluating an expression. One of the variables in the expression changes on each invocation of the subprocedure, which means that the expression evaluation potentially produces different values on successive invocations of the subprocedure. A sequence of n calls to the subprocedure produces n pseudorandom integers in the specified range.

The algorithm used to produce the pseudorandom integers is an application of the technique known as the **mixed linear congruential method**. This particular algorithm was introduced by P. Grogono.[1] The following formula is used by Grogono to produce an integer in the range 0–65,535:

$$\text{SEED} = (\text{SEED} * 25173 + 13849) \bmod 65536$$

The following formulas convert this integer to an integer in the range LOWER to UPPER:

$$\text{RANGE} = \text{UPPER} - \text{LOWER} + 1$$

$$\text{RANDOM} = (\text{SEED} * \text{RANGE})/65536 + \text{LOWER}$$

The value of RANDOM, which is an integer in the range LOWER to UPPER, is the pseudorandom integer returned by the function subprocedure. The value of SEED, an integer in the range 0–65,535, is saved for the next call to the subprocedure. On each call to the subprocedure, the previous SEED value is used to compute a new value for SEED, and the new SEED value is used to compute the pseudorandom integer (RANDOM) to be returned to the caller. The SEED value must persist from one invocation of the subprocedure to the next. A local data segment is used to maintain the value of SEED.

The assembly module in Program Listing 5.4 is an implementation of this

[1] Peter Grogono, *Programming in Pascal*, Second Edition (pp. 136), © 1984 by Addison-Wesley Publishing Company, Inc. Reprinted by permission of the publisher.

```
            PAGE    80,132
;=======================================================================
;                     PROGRAM LISTING 5.4
;       r a n d o m   n u m b e r   g e n e r a t o r
;
; GENERATES PSEUDO-RANDOM INTEGERS IN THE RANGE LOWER TO UPPER
; INPUT:  TWO STACK PARAMETERS - LOWER AND UPPER ENDS OF RANGE
; OUTPUT: AX-REG CONTAINS RANDOM INTEGER
; CALLING SEQUENCE:       PUSH    <LOWER END OF RANGE>
;                         PUSH    <UPPER END OF RANGE>
;                         CALL    RANDOM
;=======================================================================
            .MODEL  SMALL,BASIC
;=======================================================================
FALSE       EQU     0                       ;CONSTANT FALSE
TRUE        EQU     1                       ;CONSTANT TRUE
;=======================================================================
; D A T A   S E G M E N T   D E F I N I T I O N
            .FARDATA RAND_DATA
SEED        DW      ?                       ;SEED FOR RANDOM NUMBER GEN.
MULTIPLIER DW       25173                   ;MULTIPLIER AND
ADDEND      DW      13849                   ;ADDEND FOR MIXED
                                            ;LINEAR CONGRUENTIAL METHOD
FIRST_CALL DB       TRUE                    ;FIRST CALL FLAG
;=======================================================================
; C O D E   S E G M E N T   D E F I N I T I O N
;
            .CODE   EX_5_4
            ASSUME  DS:RAND_DATA
;
RANDOM      PROC    FAR PUBLIC USES CX DX DS,
                    LOWER:WORD, UPPER:WORD
                                          ;FUNCTION RANDOM(LOWER,UPPER)
                                            ;SAVE REGISTERS (USES LIST)
            PUSHF                           ;SAVE FLAGS
            MOV     AX,SEG RAND_DATA        ;SET DS-REGISTER TO POINT
            MOV     DS,AX                   ;TO LOCAL DATA SEGMENT
;
            .IF     FIRST_CALL == TRUE      ;IF   FIRST_CALL
                                            ;THEN
            MOV     FIRST_CALL,FALSE        ;     FIRST_CALL = FALSE
            MOV     AH,0                    ;     SEED = LOWER HALF OF
            INT     1AH                     ;             TIME OF DAY CLOCK
            MOV     SEED,DX
            .ENDIF                          ;ENDIF
            MOV     AX,SEED                 ;X = SEED * MULTIPLIER mod
            MUL     MULTIPLIER              ;                      65536
            ADD     AX,ADDEND               ;SEED = (X + ADDEND) mod 65536
            MOV     SEED,AX
            MOV     CX,UPPER                ;RANGE = UPPER - LOWER + 1
            SUB     CX,LOWER
            INC     CX
            MUL     CX                      ;RANDOM = (SEED*RANGE)/65536
            ADD     DX,LOWER                ;                     + LOWER
            MOV     AX,DX
            POPF                            ;RESTORE FLAGS
                                            ;RESTORE REGISTERS (ASSEMBLER
                                            ;   GENERATES INSTRUCTIONS TO
                                            ;   RESTORE REGISTERS - USES)
            RET                             ;RETURN (RANDOM)
RANDOM      ENDP                          ;END RANDOM
            END
```

random number generator as an 8088/8086 assembly language external FAR subprocedure with its own local data segment. The assembly module begins with a PAGE pseudo-operation followed by a prologue (lines 2–12) that explains the procedure's function, inputs, and outputs. The inputs for the procedure are two stack parameters that specify the LOWER and UPPER limits for the pseudorandom integer to be returned by the function. The SEED for the random number generator is maintained in a local data segment. The only output is the function value (the pseudorandom integer), and it is returned in the AX-register. The prologue also specifies the calling sequence for the subprocedure (lines 9–11). Three steps are required to invoke the subprocedure. The first step is to push the LOWER limit for the range of integers onto the stack, the second step is to push the UPPER limit for the range of integers onto the stack, and the final step is to call subprocedure RANDOM into execution.

Two named constants are defined in the assembly module: the Boolean constants True and False. The label FALSE is equated to the constant 0 (line 15), and the label TRUE is equated to the constant 1 (line 16). The EQU pseudo-operations are directives to the assembler to indicate that the label FALSE is to be treated as the constant 0 and that the label TRUE is to be treated as the constant 1. FALSE and TRUE are *not* symbolic names to be associated with memory locations. Whenever the assembler encounters the name FALSE in this assembly module, it is to substitute the constant 0. Similarly, it is to substitute 1 for the name TRUE. For example, the intruction

```
MOV  FIRST_CALL,FALSE
```

is really the instruction

```
MOV  FIRST_CALL,0
```

in this assembly module.

The local data segment for the procedure is defined in lines 17–24. The actual definition of the segment begins with the .FARDATA pseudo-operation in line 19. The symbolic name for the data segment is RAND_DATA. The SEED of the random number generator is defined in line 20. It has type attribute WORD and is uninitialized. It receives an initial value on first invocation of the random number generator. The MULTIPLIER used in the formula to compute the new SEED value is defined in line 21. It is given an initial value of 25,173 and is treated as a constant by the random number generator. The ADDEND used in the formula to compute the new SEED value is defined in line 22. It is given an initial value of 13,849 and is also treated as a constant by the random number generator. If the SEED variable is going to be given an initial value on the first call to the random number generator, then the random number generator must be able to detect its first call. To accomplish this task, a Boolean variable and the two Boolean constants, True and False, are defined. The Boolean constants are defined in lines 15 and 16. The Boolean variable FIRST_CALL is defined in line 24. It has type attribute BYTE and is initialized to TRUE (1). The local data segment definition terminates with the beginning of the code segment definition (line 28).

The function subprocedure that returns the pseudorandom integer is defined in a code segment that begins with the .CODE pseudo-operation in line 28 and ends with the END pseudo-operation in line 62. In addition to the random number generator definition, the code segment contains an ASSUME pseudo-operation (line 29) that instructs the assembler to assume that, when the subprocedure is executed, the

DS-register will address the local data segment, RAND_DATA. The DS-register has to be set by the subprocedure itself.

The function subprocedure, called RANDOM, is defined in lines 31–61. The PROC pseudo-operation in lines 31 and 32 defines the subprocedure to be a FAR subprocedure since it has to be invoked by procedures defined in other code segments, and it defines the subprocedure to be PUBLIC since it is to be invoked by procedures defined in other assembly modules. The USES clause in the PROC pseudo-operation directs the assembler to generate the code to save and restore the CX, DX, and DS registers for the caller. The PROC pseudo-operation also specifies two stack parameters, LOWER and UPPER, both of which are specified to be of type WORD. Because BASIC was chosen to be the language interface for subprocedure RANDOM (see line 13), the caller must PUSH the arguments onto the stack in the left-to-right order of the parameters in the PROC pseudo-operation. That is, the caller must first push the value for LOWER onto the stack, next push the value for UPPER onto the stack, and then call RANDOM into execution. This calling sequence is specified in the prologue (see lines 9–11).

The procedure begins by saving the registers that it will be using, including the flags register. Because of the USES clause and the presence of parameter specifications in the PROC pseudo-operation, the assembler will generate the following instructions at the very beginning of the procedure:

```
push bp
mov  bp, sp
push cx
push dx
push ds
```

The first two of these instructions are generated in response to the parameter specifications in the PROC pseudo-operation, and the last three are generated in response to the USES clause in the PROC pseudo-operation. The registers are pushed onto the stack in the order in which they appear in the USES clause. Included in the registers being saved is the DS-register, which will be used by the subprocedure to address the local data segment. The assembler uses the BP-register to access the arguments in the stack.

The instruction

```
push bp
```

saves the value of the BP-register for the caller, and the instruction

```
mov  bp, sp
```

sets the SS:BP register pair to address a known position within the stack segment. The state of the top portion of the stack segment following the execution of these two instructions is as shown in Figure 5.3. The subsequent execution of PUSH and POP

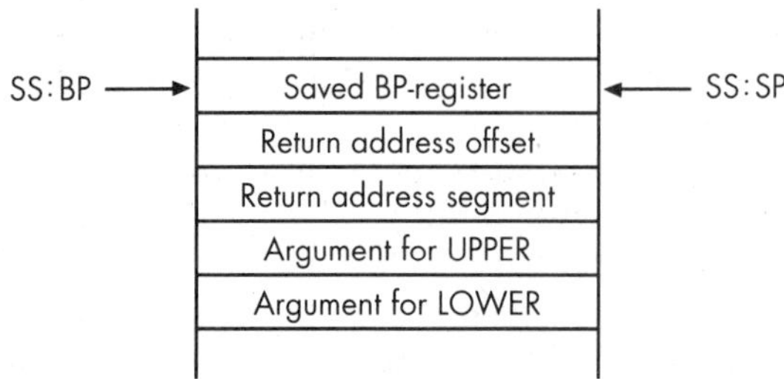

FIGURE 5.3 Stack segment after execution of the push bp and mov bp, sp instructions

instructions alters the address specified by the SS:SP register pair but does not modify the SS:BP register pair. For example, following the execution of the instructions

```
push  cx
push  dx
push  ds
```

the state of the stack segment is as shown in Figure 5.4. With the SS:BP register pair

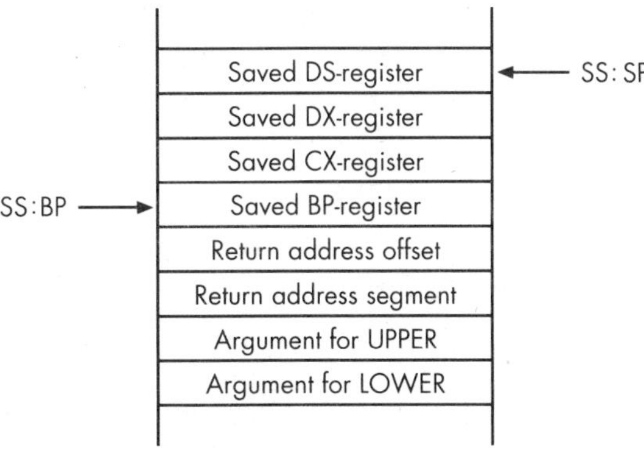

FIGURE 5.4 Stack segment after execution of the push cx, push dx, and push ds instructions

addressing a known point in the stack, the assembler can generate memory addresses (segment and offset) for the references to the parameters LOWER and UPPER (lines 50, 51, and 54). The segment portion of the address, in both cases, is the run-time contents of the SS-register. The offset portion of the address of UPPER is the run-time contents of the BP-register plus 6. Similarly, the offset portion of the address of LOWER is the run-time contents of the BP-register plus 8. The method of specifying such an address in assembly language is discussed in Chapter 8. At this point, stack parameters are dealt with from a user standpoint.

The PUSHF instruction in line 35 saves the flags register value for the caller. Apparently, MASM 6.0 does not provide a way to specify the flags register in a USES clause.

The MOV instructions in lines 36 and 37 set the DS-register to point to the local data segment. This task must be done prior to executing any instruction that references an item defined in the local data segment.

The single-alternative decision structure in lines 39–45 tests the FIRST_CALL flag to see if it is the first call to the RANDOM procedure. If it is the first call (i.e., FIRST_CALL has the value TRUE), then the instructions in lines 41–44 are executed. The MOV instruction in line 41 sets the value of the FIRST_CALL flag to FALSE so that lines 41–44 are not executed on subsequent calls to RANDOM. The two instructions in lines 42 and 43 are the calling sequence for a BIOS function procedure that returns the current value of the microprocessor's time-of-day clock in the CX:DX register pair (which is one reason why the CX-register must be saved and restored for the caller). The instruction in line 43 generates a software interrupt that causes the BIOS procedure that references the time-of-day clock to be executed. It can be viewed as a procedure call. The INT instruction executes similarly to a CALL instruction. The MOV instruction in line 42 sets up the input parameter for this BIOS procedure in the AH-register. An input parameter of 0 means read the current clock value. Interrupts and interrupt service procedures are discussed in detail in Chapter 9. The MOV instruction in line 44 sets the initial SEED value to the lower half of the time-of-day clock value returned by the BIOS procedure, which means that each time a program that uses this random number generator is executed, it starts the SEED at a different initial value.

The instructions in lines 46–49 compute the new value of the SEED using the following formula:

$$\text{SEED} = [(\text{SEED} * \text{MULTIPLIER}) + \text{ADDEND}] \bmod 65536$$

Recall that 16-bit unsigned integers in the 8088/8086 represent a modulo 65536 number system. Multiplying two 16-bit unsigned integers produces a 32-bit product. The low-order 16 bits is the product in the modulo 65536 number system. Adding two 16-bit unsigned integers produces the sum in the modulo 65536 number system. To perform modulo 65536 arithmetic, simply ignore overflow. The preceding formula is actually implemented using the equivalent formula

$$\text{SEED} = [(\text{SEED} * \text{MULTIPLIER}) \bmod 65536 + \text{ADDEND}] \bmod 65536$$

The MUL instruction in line 47 produces a 32-bit product in the DX:AX register pair. Ignoring the overflow in the DX-register, the AX-register contains the value

$$X = (\text{SEED} * \text{MULTIPLIER}) \bmod 65536$$

The ADD instruction in line 48 adds to the lower half of the product, ignoring the upper half. Ignoring overflow, the AX-register contains

$$(X + \text{ADDEND}) \bmod 65536$$

The MOV instruction in line 49 stores this sum as the new SEED value.

The instructions in lines 50–55 compute the pseudorandom integer in the range LOWER to UPPER to be returned to the caller. The integer is computed by the following formula:

$$[\text{SEED} * (\text{UPPER} - \text{LOWER} + 1)]/65536$$

The instructions in lines 50–52 compute the value of UPPER − LOWER + 1 in the CX-register. The MUL instruction in line 53 multiplies this value by the SEED value in the AX-register, leaving the 32-bit product in the DX:AX register pair. The quotient of a 32-bit integer divided by 65,536 is simply the upper half of that 32-bit number. The ADD instruction in line 54 essentially performs the division by adding LOWER to the upper half of the 32-bit number. The sum is then moved to the AX-register for return to the caller (line 55).

The POPF instruction in line 56 restores the flags register for the caller. The RET instruction in line 60 causes the assembler to generate the following sequence of intructions:

```
pop  ds
pop  dx
pop  cx
pop  bp
ret  00004h
```

The first three of these instructions restore the registers specified in the USES clause in the PROC pseudo-operation. The instruction

```
pop  bp
```

restores the register that was used to access the arguments in the stack. The instruction

```
ret  00004h
```

returns control to the caller with the pseudorandom integer in the AX-register and pops the two arguments from the stack. When this ret instruction is executed, the following steps are performed:

1. The top-of-stack value is popped into the IP-register.
2. The next top-of-stack value is popped into the CS-register.
3. The ret instruction operand (00004h) is added to the SP-register. This step essentially pops the two argument words (4 bytes) from the stack and discards them.

The ENDP pseudo-operation in line 61 marks the end of the definition of the RANDOM procedure.

Using the arguments 0 and 99 and beginning with an initial SEED value of 4824, the first 12 computed values of SEED and the corresponding pseudorandom integers are as follows:

SEED	Random Integer
10193	15
28798	43
52207	79
27252	41
63133	96
12858	19
5979	9
52560	80
425	0
30006	45
52487	80
63340	96

Note that the integer 96 is produced twice from different SEED values. This situation is possible because the random integer range (0–99) is much smaller than the SEED range (0–65,535). In fact, with a small range (e.g., 1–6 to simulate the rolling of a die), it is possible to produce the same value several times in succession.

5.6 Additional Capabilities in the 80286 Assembly Language

The 80286 assembly language provides a single instruction to save the contents of all eight general registers onto the stack and a single instruction to restore the contents of all eight general registers by popping the top eight stack items into these registers. These two instructions are the PUSHA and POPA instructions (see Chapter 2), which are 1-byte instructions. In the 8088/8086 assembly language, it takes eight 1-byte instructions to push the values of all eight general registers onto the stack and another eight 1-byte instructions to restore the values of the eight general registers. That is, two 1-byte instructions in the 80286 assembly language can do the job of sixteen 1-byte instructions in the 8088/8086 assembly language. If a subprocedure must save and restore a small number of general registers, say three or less, then the individual PUSH and POP instructions could be used in the 80286 assembly language to avoid using more stack locations than are needed. However, if a subprocedure must save and restore four or more of the general registers, then the PUSHA and POPA instructions could be used since the savings in instruction bytes compensates for the unneeded stack locations that are used. It should be noted that instruction bytes represent permanent storage and that stack locations represent temporary storage. A savings in instruction bytes often is worth the use of extra stack locations.

5.7 Assembler Macros

The assembler's macro feature is a programming tool that provides the capability for programmers to define operation codes in terms of existing machine operations. For example, the MUL and IMUL instructions do not allow an immediate operand. To multiply the unsigned integer value in the AX-register by 7, the following instructions might be used:

```
MOV  BX,7
MUL  BX
```

The macro feature provides the capability to assign an operation code to represent this sequence of instructions. Each time the assembler encounters the user-defined operation code, it substitutes in the corresponding sequence of instructions. User-defined operation codes can have operands, which allows the operands in the corresponding sequence of instructions to be different each time that operation code appears in the assembly module. In the case of the preceding multiply immediate example, the immediate operand can be different each time the multiply immediate operation code appears in the assembly module.

Macro directives, such as .STARTUP, .EXIT, and .WHILE–.ENDW, used in the example programs of previous chapters, are special cases of the assembler macro feature. The macro directive .EXIT is an operation code that represents the instruction sequence

```
MOV  AH,4CH
INT  21H
```

The macro directive

```
.IF  AX < 7
```

is an operation code with operands that represents an instruction sequence like the following:

```
CMP  AX,7
JAE  @C0001
```

These macro directives could be referred to as *system-defined* macros. They have been defined as part of the assembler and are available for assembly language programmers to use. This section concentrates on *user-defined* macros.

Macro Definition and Expansion

Two steps are involved in using macros: macro definition and macro expansion. **Macro definition** gives the macro a name (the user-defined operation code) and identifies the sequence of instructions that are represented by this name. **Macro expansion** occurs whenever the assembler encounters the macro name used as an operation code, at which time the assembler substitutes the sequence of instructions specified in the macro definition for the macro reference.

A **macro definition** has the following general form:

```
⟨mac-name⟩ MACRO  ⟨arg-list⟩   [⟨comment⟩]
                  ⟨macro-body⟩
           ENDM                [⟨comment⟩]
```

in which ⟨*mac-name*⟩ is the symbolic name of the macro (the user-defined operation code), ⟨*arg-list*⟩ is a list of dummy arguments separated by commas, and ⟨*macro-body*⟩ is the sequence of instructions that are represented by the ⟨*mac-name*⟩. The dummy arguments in the ⟨*arg-list*⟩ are symbolic names that can be used as operation codes or operands in the ⟨*macro-body*⟩ instructions. These dummy arguments are replaced by actual arguments whenever macro expansion occurs.

A **macro reference** looks like a mnemonic representation of a machine instruction, and it has the following general form:

```
[⟨label⟩]  ⟨mac-name⟩  ⟨opnd-list⟩  [⟨comment⟩]
```

in which ⟨*label*⟩ is the symbolic name to be associated with the memory location in which the macro body instructions are to begin, ⟨*mac-name*⟩ is the name of the macro to be expanded (the user-defined operation code), and ⟨*opnd-list*⟩ is the list of operands for the user-defined operation code. The number of operands in the ⟨*opnd-list*⟩ must agree with the number of dummy arguments in the ⟨*arg-list*⟩ of the macro definition. An operand in the ⟨*opnd-list*⟩ must be compatible with the corresponding dummy argument in the macro body of the macro definition. Otherwise, assembly errors occur at time of macro expansion.

When the assembler encounters a macro reference, it expands the macro by substituting the instructions of the macro body for the macro reference. Each dummy argument appearing in the macro body is replaced by the corresponding operand from the operand list in the macro reference. Operands are matched to dummy arguments by position.

EXAMPLES

The multiply immediate operation code for unsigned integers, mentioned previously, can be defined by the following macro definition:

```
muli MACRO const
     MOV   BX,const
     MUL   BX
     ENDM
```

The name of the macro is muli. It has one operand represented in the macro body by the dummy argument const. The macro body is the instruction sequence

```
MOV  BX,const
MUL  BX
```

On encountering the macro reference

```
muli  7
```

the assembler substitutes the instructions

```
MOV  BX,7
MUL  BX
```

The dummy argument const is replaced by the operand 7 when the macro is expanded. On encountering the macro reference

```
muli  3
```

the assembler substitutes the instructions

```
MOV  BX,3
MUL  BX
```

The dummy argument const is replaced by the operand 3 for this reference. The preceding macro can be generalized to accommodate either signed or unsigned integers by using a dummy argument for the operation code of the second instruction in the macro body. The modified macro definition might be as follows:

```
muli MACRO op,const
     MOV   BX,const
     op    BX
     ENDM
```

On encountering the macro reference

```
muli  MUL,12
```

the assembler substitutes the instructions

```
MOV  BX,12
MUL  BX
```

On encountering the macro reference

```
muli  IMUL,-12
```

the assembler substitutes the instructions

```
MOV   BX,-12
IMUL  BX
```

■

Programming Example—Compute Date of Easter Sunday

Program Listing 5.5 is an implementation of an algorithm to compute the date of Easter Sunday (month and day) given the year. The following pseudocode describes the algorithm:

```
GET YEAR
CYCLE_YEAR = YEAR mod 19
FULL_MOON = (19*CYCLE_YEAR + 24) mod 30
CALENDAR_ADJUSTMENT = 2(YEAR mod 4) + 4(YEAR mod 7) + 5
DATE_ADJUSTMENT = (6*FULL_MOON + CALENDAR_ADJUSTMENT) mod 7
DATE = 21 + FULL_MOON + 1 + DATE_ADJUSTMENT
IF   DATE > 31
THEN DATE = DATE - 31
     IF   DATE = 26
     THEN DATE = 19
     ENDIF
     DISPLAY 'APRIL ', DATE
ELSE
     DISPLAY 'MARCH ', DATE
ENDIF
```

```
            PAGE    80,132
;====================================================================
;                   PROGRAM LISTING 5.5
;
; PROGRAM  TO COMPUTE THE DATE OF
; EASTER  SUNDAY,  GIVEN THE YEAR
;====================================================================
            .MODEL  SMALL,BASIC,FARSTACK
;====================================================================
                                       ;PROCEDURES TO
            EXTRN   GETDEC$:FAR        ;GET 16-BIT UNSIGNED DEC INT
            EXTRN   NEWLINE:FAR        ;DISPLAY NEWLINE CHARACTER
            EXTRN   PUTDEC$:FAR        ;DISPLAY UNSIGNED DECIMAL INT
            EXTRN   PUTSTRNG:FAR       ;DISPLAY CHARACTER STRING
;====================================================================
; S T A C K   D E F I N I T I O N
            .STACK  256
;====================================================================
; V A R I A B L E   D E F I N I T I O N S
            .DATA
;
CAL_ADJ     DW      ?                  ;CALENDAR ADJUSTMENT (THERE
                                       ;ARE 14 POSSIBLE CALENDARS)
FM          DW      ?                  ;FULL MOON RELATIVE TO MAR 21
YEAR        DW      ?                  ;YEAR OF EASTER SUNDAY
;====================================================================
; C O N S T A N T   D E F I N I T I O N S
            .CONST
;
PROMPT      DB      'ENTER YEAR - '
PROMPT_LNG  EQU     $ - PROMPT
ANNOTATE    DB      'EASTER SUNDAY WAS (WILL BE) ON '
ANNOTATE_L  EQU     $ - ANNOTATE
MARCH       DB      'MARCH '
APRIL       DB      'APRIL '
MONTH_LNG   EQU     APRIL - MARCH
;====================================================================
; M A C R O   D E F I N I T I O N S
;-------------------------------------------------------------
;FUNCTION  x modulo y   COMPUTES REMAINDER OF UNSIGNED x/y
;                       |  x AND y CAN BE WORD REGISTER,  |
;                       |  WORD MEMORY, OR IMMEDIATE.     |
;                       |  USES AX, BX, AND DX REGISTERS  |
;                       LEAVES  x modulo y  IN AX-REGISTER
modulo      MACRO   x,y
            MOV     AX,x
            MOV     BX,y
            MOV     DX,0
            DIV     BX
            MOV     AX,DX
            ENDM
;-------------------------------------------------------------
;MULTIPLY IMMEDIATE (UNSIGNED)
;                   const SHOULD BE IMMEDIATE
;                   USES BX-REGISTER
;                   LEAVES PRODUCT IN DX:AX
muli        MACRO   const
            MOV     BX,const
            MUL     BX
            ENDM
;-------------------------------------------------------------
; E N D   O F   M A C R O   D E F I N I T I O N S
;====================================================================
            PAGE
;====================================================================
;C O D E   S E G M E N T   D E F I N I T I O N
;
```

```
               .CODE    EX_5_5
;
               .STARTUP                     ;GENERATE STARTUP CODE
;
               PUSH     DS                  ;SET ES-REGISTER TO POINT TO
               POP      ES                  ;DATA GROUP
;
               LEA      DI,PROMPT           ;PROMPT FOR YEAR
               MOV      CX,PROMPT_LNG
               CALL     PUTSTRNG
               CALL     GETDEC$             ;GET YEAR
               MOV      YEAR,AX
               LEA      DI,ANNOTATE         ;DISPLAY ANNOTATION
               MOV      CX,ANNOTATE_L
               CALL     PUTSTRNG
               modulo   AX,19               ;CYCL_YR = YEAR mod 19
               muli     19                  ;FM = (19*CYCL_YR + 24) mod 30
               ADD      AX,24
               modulo   AX,30
               MOV      FM,AX
               modulo   YEAR,4              ;CAL_ADJ = 2(YEAR mod 4)
               muli     2
               MOV      CAL_ADJ,AX
               modulo   YEAR,7              ;         + 4(YEAR mod 7)
               muli     4
               ADD      AX,5                ;         + 5
               ADD      CAL_ADJ,AX
               MOV      AX,FM               ;DATE_ADJ = (6*FM + CAL_ADJ)
               muli     6                   ;                        mod 7
               ADD      AX,CAL_ADJ
               modulo   AX,7
               PAGE
               ADD      AX,FM               ;DATE = DATE_ADJ + FM + 22
               ADD      AX,22
               CMP      AX,31               ;IF   DATE > 31
               JLE      ELSE1
               SUB      AX,31               ;THEN DATE = DATE - 31
               CMP      AX,26               ;     IF   DATE = 26
               JNE      ENDIF2
               MOV      AX,19               ;     THEN DATE = 19
ENDIF2:                                     ;     ENDIF
               LEA      DI,APRIL            ;     DISPLAY 'APRIL '
               JMP      ENDIF1
ELSE1:                                      ;ELSE
               LEA      DI,MARCH            ;     DISPLAY 'MARCH '
ENDIF1:                                     ;ENDIF
               MOV      CX,MONTH_LNG
               CALL     PUTSTRNG
               CALL     PUTDEC$             ;DISPLAY DATE
               CALL     NEWLINE
               .EXIT                        ;RETURN TO DOS
;
               END
```

Easter Sunday is the Sunday following the first full moon on or after the vernal equinox (March 21). A full moon occurs every 29 days, 12 hours, and 44.05 minutes, which is every 29.5305902 days. The algorithm assumes that a full moon occurs every $29\frac{1}{2}$ days and thus is not 100% accurate. The program has been tested for all years between 1900 and 2012, inclusive, and was found to fail for only one year in that range, the year 1954. For an input of 1954, the program produces the date April 25, and Easter actually occurred on April 18 in that year. In addition, the algorithm assumes that a leap year occurs every four years. However, a year that is divisible by

100 is not a leap year unless it is also divisible by 400. This assumption limits the range of years for which the algorithm is valid to the range 1900–2099.

The algorithm contains several multiplications by a constant; therefore, the previously defined multiply immediate macro is useful The algorithm also contains several instances of the mod function; therefore, a mod function macro is also useful.

The assembly module in Program Listing 5.5 implements this algorithm. A complete description is not provided here. Only the use of macros in this implementation is discussed.

The multiply immediate macro is defined in lines 57–60 (which is the same macro definition that was presented in a previous example). The prologue in lines 52–56 explains the macro's function, specifies the type of operand expected, identifies the registers used by the macro, and indicates where the macro leaves its result. This information is provided mainly for instructional purposes. However, it is extremely helpful to provide this information for any macro that is to be used in more than one program or by more than one programmer.

The mod function macro is defined in lines 45–51. The symbolic name of the macro is modulo. The symbolic name mod is a reserved word in MASM 6.0 and therefore cannot be used as a macro name. The macro has two operands that are represented in the macro body by the symbolic names x and y. The macro body instruction sequence divides the unsigned integer value of the dummy argument x by the unsigned integer value of the dummy argument y, and then the instruction sequence moves the remainder of that division (the value x modulo y) into the AX-register. The prologue in lines 39–44 provides important information about the macro for users.

The program input is the year, entered via the keyboard. The GETDEC$ procedure (line 78) accepts the input from the keyboard. The MOV instruction in line 79 replaces the value of the variable YEAR with a copy of this input value. At the beginning of the computation, the AX-register and the variable YEAR both contain a copy of the input value.

The computation appears in lines 83–113. The modulo reference in line 83 implements the assignment

$$\text{CYCL\_YR} = \text{YEAR mod } 19$$

leaving the result in the AX-register. This instruction is a macro reference that is expanded by the assembler to the following instruction sequence:

```
MOV  AX,AX
MOV  BX,19
MOV  DX,0
DIV  BX
MOV  AX,DX
```

This sequence divides the value in the AX-register (the year) by 19, leaving the remainder in the AX-register. Note that the first instruction of the macro body is

```
MOV  AX,x
```

and the first operand in the macro reference

```
modulo  AX,19
```

is the register designator AX. Thus, the assembler substitutes the operand AX for the dummy argument x, producing the redundant instruction

```
MOV  AX,AX
```

This instruction is legal, as it does exactly what it says it does; it moves a copy of the contents of the AX-register into the AX-register.

The instructions in lines 84–87 implement the assignment

$$FM = (19 * CYCL\_YR + 24) \bmod 30$$

The muli macro reference in line 84 multiplies the value in the AX-register (the value of the pseudocode variable CYCL_YR) by 19, leaving the result in the DX:AX register pair. This instruction is a macro reference expanded by the assembler to the following instruction sequence:

```
MOV  BX,19
MUL  BX
```

Given any reasonable value for the year, none of the computations in this algorithm can cause overflow. Therefore, it is safe to assume that the product of this multiplication fits in the AX-register. The ADD instruction in line 85 adds 24 to the product in the AX-register. The instructions generated for the macro reference in line 86 cause the value in the AX-register (19 * CYCL_YR + 24) to be divided by 30 and the remainder of the division (19 * CYCL_YR + 24) mod 30) to be moved to the AX-register. The MOV instruction in line 87 stores this remainder as the value of variable FM.

The instructions in lines 88–94 implement the assignment

$$CAL\_ADJ = 2(YEAR \bmod 4) + 4(YEAR \bmod 7) + 5$$

The instructions generated for the macro reference in line 88 divide the value of the variable YEAR by 4 and move the remainder of that division to the AX-register. The instructions generated for the macro reference in line 89 multiply this remainder (YEAR mod 4) by 2, leaving the product in the DX:AX register pair. Again, this product fits in the AX-register. The MOV instruction in line 90 stores this product as the value of variable CAL_ADJ. The instructions generated for the macro reference in line 91 compute the value YEAR mod 7, leaving the result in the AX-register. The instructions generated for the macro reference in line 92 multiply this value by 4, leaving the product in the AX-register. The ADD instruction in line 93 adds 5 to the product in the AX-register, and the ADD instruction in line 94 adds this result to the value of variable CAL_ADJ.

The instructions in lines 95–98 implement the assignment

$$DATE\_ADJ = (6 * FM + CAL\_ADJ) \bmod 7$$

The MOV instruction in line 95 loads the AX-register with the value of variable FM. The instructions generated for the macro reference in line 96 multiply this value by 6, leaving the result in the AX-register. The ADD instruction in line 97 adds the value of variable CAL_ADJ to this result, leaving the value (6 * FM + CAL_ADJ) in the AX-register. The instructions generated for the macro reference in line 98 divide this value by 7 and move the remainder of that division to the AX-register. At this point, the AX-register contains the value of the pseudocode variable DATE_ADJ.

The instructions in lines 100 and 101 implement the assignment

$$DATE = DATE\_ADJ + FM + 22$$

The value of the pseudocode variable DATE is left in the AX-register and is an integer in the range 22–57, inclusive. A value in the range 22–31 represents a date in March. A value greater than 31 represents a date in April and must be decremented by 31. Note that Easter cannot fall after April 25, but the formula can produce April

26 as a date. The year 1981 is an example: If this situation occurs, then the correct date for Easter Sunday is April 19. The nested decision structure in lines 102–113 makes the appropriate adjustments to the pseudocode variable DATE and displays the appropriate month.

The following are the results from some sample executions of this program:

```
C>ex_5_5
ENTER YEAR - 1989
EASTER SUNDAY WAS (WILL BE) ON MARCH 26

C>ex_5_5
ENTER YEAR - 1990
EASTER SUNDAY WAS (WILL BE) ON APRIL 15

C>ex_5_5
ENTER YEAR - 1991
EASTER SUNDAY WAS (WILL BE) ON MARCH 31

C>ex_5_5
ENTER YEAR - 1992
EASTER SUNDAY WAS (WILL BE) ON APRIL 19

C>ex_5_5
ENTER YEAR - 1993
EASTER SUNDAY WAS (WILL BE) ON APRIL 11

C>ex_5_5
ENTER YEAR - 1994
EASTER SUNDAY WAS (WILL BE) ON APRIL 3
```

Assembler Listing 5.6 shows the first three pages of the assembler-generated listing for Program Listing 5.5. Note that no machine code is shown for the macro definition. The macro definition simply identifies, to the assembler, the sequence of instructions that is to be substituted each time the macro name is encountered as an operation code. Note also that each reference to the macro is followed by the assembly language instructions generated for that reference. Each instruction of the expansion is preceded by a 1 in the listing. As well, note that the instructions of the expansion are translated to machine language. No machine code is shown for the macro reference itself. The substitution of the macro body for the macro reference takes place before the translation to machine language.

INCLUDE Pseudo-Operation

A macro may be useful in a number of programs or procedures. For example, many of the example programs in this book output an annotation string followed by an integer value in decimal form. The main procedure in Program Listing 5.5 displays a month string followed by the integer value representing the day of the month. The main procedure in Program Listing 4.4 displays the string THE SQUARE OF followed by the value of variable NUMBER, and then it displays the string IS followed by the value of variable SQUARE.

The macros defined in Program Listing 5.7 provide the capability to display a string followed by the value in the AX-register with a single macro instruction. The macro displ$ (lines 13–19) displays the AX-register value in unsigned form, and the macro displ (lines 31–37) displays the AX-register value in signed form.

The macros displ$ and displ have three arguments: the symbolic name of the string, the length of the string, and the input code for PUTDEC$ or PUTDEC. The three EQU definitions in lines 39–41 are provided so that the user can specify

```
Microsoft (R) Macro Assembler Version 6.00B             05/22/93 03:29:46
EX_5_6.asm                                              Page 1 - 1


                                        PAGE    80,132
                                ;===============================================================
                                ;               ASSEMBLER LISTING 5.6
                                ;
                                ; PROGRAM  TO COMPUTE THE DATE OF
                                ; EASTER  SUNDAY,  GIVEN THE YEAR
                                ;===============================================================
                                        .MODEL  SMALL,BASIC,FARSTACK
                                ;===============================================================
                                                                ;PROCEDURES TO
                                        EXTRN   GETDEC$:FAR     ;GET 16-BIT UNSIGNED DEC INT
                                        EXTRN   NEWLINE:FAR     ;DISPLAY NEWLINE CHARACTER
                                        EXTRN   PUTDEC$:FAR     ;DISPLAY UNSIGNED DECIMAL INT
                                        EXTRN   PUTSTRNG:FAR    ;DISPLAY CHARACTER STRING
                                ;===============================================================
                                ; S T A C K   D E F I N I T I O N
                                        .STACK  256
                                ;===============================================================
                                ; V A R I A B L E   D E F I N I T I O N S
0000                                    .DATA
                                ;
0000 0000                       CAL_ADJ  DW     ?               ;CALENDAR ADJUSTMENT (THERE
                                                                ;ARE 14 POSSIBLE CALENDARS)
0002 0000                       FM       DW     ?               ;FULL MOON RELATIVE TO MAR 21
0004 0000                       YEAR     DW     ?               ;YEAR OF EASTER SUNDAY
                                ;===============================================================
                                ; C O N S T A N T   D E F I N I T I O N S
0000                                    .CONST
                                ;
0000 45 4E 54 45 52 20          PROMPT   DB     'ENTER YEAR - '
     59 45 41 52 20 2D
     20
000D = 000D                     PROMPT_LNG EQU  $ - PROMPT
000D 45 41 53 54 45 52          ANNOTATE DB     'EASTER SUNDAY WAS (WILL BE) ON '
     20 53 55 4E 44 41
     59 20 57 41 53 20
     28 57 49 4C 4C 20
     42 45 29 20 4F 4E
     20
002C = 001F                     ANNOTATE_L EQU  $ - ANNOTATE
002C 4D 41 52 43 48 20          MARCH    DB     'MARCH '
0032 41 50 52 49 4C 20          APRIL    DB     'APRIL '
= 0006                          MONTH_LNG EQU   APRIL - MARCH
                                ;===============================================================
                                ; M A C R O   D E F I N I T I O N S
                                ;-------------------------------------------------------
                                ;FUNCTION  x modulo y   COMPUTES REMAINDER OF UNSIGNED x/y
                                ;                       ¦ x AND y CAN BE WORD REGISTER, ¦
                                ;                       ¦ WORD MEMORY, OR IMMEDIATE.    ¦
                                ;                       ¦ USES AX, BX, AND DX REGISTERS ¦
                                ;                       LEAVES  x modulo y  IN AX-REGISTER
                                modulo  MACRO   x,y
                                        MOV     AX,x
                                        MOV     BX,y
                                        MOV     DX,0
```

```
                                DIV     BX
                                MOV     AX,DX
                                ENDM
                        ;------------------------------------------------------------
                        ;MULTIPLY IMMEDIATE (UNSIGNED)
                        ;               const SHOULD BE IMMEDIATE
                        ;               USES BX-REGISTER
                        ;               LEAVES PRODUCT IN DX:AX
                        muli    MACRO   const
                                MOV     BX,const
                                MUL     BX
                                ENDM
                        ;------------------------------------------------------------
                        ;E N D   O F   M A C R O   D E F I N I T I O N S
                        ;=================================================================

Microsoft (R) Macro Assembler Version 6.00B             05/22/93 03:29:46
EX_5_6.asm                                              Page 2 - 1

                                PAGE
                        ;=================================================================
                        ;C O D E   S E G M E N T   D E F I N I T I O N
                        ;
 0000                           .CODE   EX_5_5
                        ;
                                .STARTUP                ;GENERATE STARTUP CODE
 0000                  *@Startup:
 0000  BA ---- R       *        mov     dx, DGROUP
 0003  8E DA           *        mov     ds, dx
                        ;
 0005  1E                       PUSH    DS              ;SET ES-REGISTER TO POINT TO
 0006  07                       POP     ES              ;DATA GROUP
                        ;
 0007  BF 0000 R                LEA     DI,PROMPT       ;PROMPT FOR YEAR
 000A  B9 000D                  MOV     CX,PROMPT_LNG
 000D  9A ---- 0000 E           CALL    PUTSTRNG
 0012  9A ---- 0000 E           CALL    GETDEC$         ;GET YEAR
 0017  A3 0004 R                MOV     YEAR,AX
 001A  BF 000D R                LEA     DI,ANNOTATE     ;DISPLAY ANNOTATION
 001D  B9 001F                  MOV     CX,ANNOTATE_L
 0020  9A ---- 0000 E           CALL    PUTSTRNG
                                modulo  AX,19           ;CYCL_YR = YEAR mod 19
 0025  8B C0           1        MOV     AX,AX
 0027  BB 0013         1        MOV     BX,19
 002A  BA 0000         1        MOV     DX,0
 002D  F7 F3           1        DIV     BX
 002F  8B C2           1        MOV     AX,DX
                                muli    19              ;FM = (19*CYCL_YR + 24) mod 30
 0031  BB 0013         1        MOV     BX,19
 0034  F7 E3           1        MUL     BX
 0036  83 C0 18                 ADD     AX,24
                                modulo  AX,30
 0039  8B C0           1        MOV     AX,AX
 003B  BB 001E         1        MOV     BX,30
 003E  BA 0000         1        MOV     DX,0
 0041  F7 F3           1        DIV     BX
 0043  8B C2           1        MOV     AX,DX
 0045  A3 0002 R                MOV     FM,AX
                                modulo  YEAR,4          ;CAL_ADJ = 2(YEAR mod 4)
```

```
0048  A1 0004 R          1          MOV     AX,YEAR
004B  BB 0004            1          MOV     BX,4
004E  BA 0000            1          MOV     DX,0
0051  F7 F3              1          DIV     BX
0053  8B C2              1          MOV     AX,DX
                                    muli    2
0055  BB 0002            1          MOV     BX,2
0058  F7 E3              1          MUL     BX
005A  A3 0000 R                     MOV     CAL_ADJ,AX
                                    modulo  YEAR,7           ;        + 4(YEAR mod 7)
005D  A1 0004 R          1          MOV     AX,YEAR
0060  BB 0007            1          MOV     BX,7
0063  BA 0000            1          MOV     DX,0
0066  F7 F3              1          DIV     BX
0068  8B C2              1          MOV     AX,DX
                                    muli    4
006A  BB 0004            1          MOV     BX,4
006D  F7 E3              1          MUL     BX
006F  83 C0 05                      ADD     AX,5             ;        + 5
0072  01 06 0000 R                  ADD     CAL_ADJ,AX
0076  A1 0002 R                     MOV     AX,FM            ;DATE_ADJ = (6*FM + CAL_ADJ)
                                    muli    6                ;                         mod 7
0079  BB 0006            1          MOV     BX,6
007C  F7 E3              1          MUL     BX
007E  03 06 0000 R                  ADD     AX,CAL_ADJ
                                    modulo  AX,7
0082  8B C0              1          MOV     AX,AX
0084  BB 0007            1          MOV     BX,7
0087  BA 0000            1          MOV     DX,0
008A  F7 F3              1          DIV     BX
008C  8B C2              1          MOV     AX,DX


Microsoft (R) Macro Assembler Version 6.00B            05/22/93 03:29:46
EX_5_6.asm                                              Page 3 - 1


                                    PAGE
008E  03 06 0002 R                  ADD     AX,FM            ;DATE = DATE_ADJ + FM + 22
0092  83 C0 16                      ADD     AX,22
0095  83 F8 1F                      CMP     AX,31            ;IF   DATE > 31
0098  7E 10                         JLE     ELSE1
009A  83 E8 1F                      SUB     AX,31            ;THEN DATE = DATE - 31
009D  83 F8 1A                      CMP     AX,26            ;     IF   DATE = 26
00A0  75 03                         JNE     ENDIF2
00A2  B8 0013                       MOV     AX,19            ;     THEN DATE = 19
00A5                     ENDIF2:                             ;     ENDIF
00A5  BF 0032 R                     LEA     DI,APRIL         ;     DISPLAY 'APRIL '
00A8  EB 03                         JMP     ENDIF1
00AA                     ELSE1:                              ;ELSE
00AA  BF 002C R                     LEA     DI,MARCH         ;     DISPLAY 'MARCH '
00AD                     ENDIF1:                             ;ENDIF
00AD  B9 0006                       MOV     CX,MONTH_LNG
00B0  9A ---- 0000 E                CALL    PUTSTRNG
00B5  9A ---- 0000 E                CALL    PUTDEC$          ;DISPLAY DATE
00BA  9A ---- 0000 E                CALL    NEWLINE
                                    .EXIT                    ;RETURN TO DOS
00BF  B4 4C              *      mov ah, 04Ch
00C1  CD 21              *      int 021h
                         ;
                                    END
```

```
;=====================================================================
;           PROGRAM LISTING 5.7
;---------------------------------------------------------------------
; MACRO TO:
;           DISPLAY A CHARACTER STRING
;           DISPLAY THE UNSIGNED DECIMAL INTEGER IN THE AX-REGISTER
;
; ARGUMENTS:
;           string --- STRING TO BE DISPLAYED
;           lngth ---- LENGTH OF STRING TO BE DISPLAYED
;           code ----- DISPLAY CODE FOR PUTDEC$
;---------------------------------------------------------------------
displ$      MACRO   string,lngth,code
            LEA     DI,string
            MOV     CX,lngth
            CALL    PUTSTRNG
            MOV     BH,code
            CALL    PUTDEC$
            ENDM
;---------------------------------------------------------------------
;---------------------------------------------------------------------
; MACRO TO:
;           DISPLAY A CHARACTER STRING
;           DISPLAY THE SIGNED DECIMAL INTEGER IN THE AX-REGISTER
;
; ARGUMENTS:
;           string --- STRING TO BE DISPLAYED
;           lngth ---- LENGTH OF STRING TO BE DISPLAYED
;           code ----- DISPLAY CODE FOR PUTDEC
;---------------------------------------------------------------------
displ       MACRO   string,lngth,code
            LEA     DI,string
            MOV     CX,lngth
            CALL    PUTSTRNG
            MOV     BH,code
            CALL    PUTDEC
            ENDM
;=====================================================================
LJ          EQU     -1                      ;code FOR LEFT  JUSTIFY
NJ          EQU      0                      ;code FOR NO JUSTIFICATION
RJ          EQU     +1                      ;code FOR RIGHT JUSTIFY
;=====================================================================
```

the code for PUTDEC$ or PUTDEC in mnemonic form. On encountering the macro reference

```
displ$  MSG,MSG_LNG,LJ
```

the assembler substitutes the instructions

```
LEA   DI,MSG
MOV   CX,MSG_LNG
CALL  PUTSTRNG
MOV   BH,-1
CALL  PUTDEC$
```

On encountering the macro reference

```
displ  ANNOTATE,LNG,RJ
```

the assembler substitutes the instructions

```
LEA   DI,ANNOTATE
MOV   CX,LNG
CALL  PUTSTRNG
```

```
MOV   BH,+1
CALL  PUTDEC
```

In many programs, a macro like displ$ or displ would be referenced one time only. Defining a macro and then referencing it only once leads to more work than coding the individual instructions. The INCLUDE pseudo-operation makes it feasible to use macros that are referenced only once in an assembly module by providing the capability to embed text from one source code file into the text of another source code file during the assembly process. The **INCLUDE pseudo-operation** has the following general form:

INCLUDE ⟨*file-spec*⟩ [⟨*comment*⟩]

in which ⟨*file-spec*⟩ is an explicit file specification that identifies the disk drive and the filename. When the assembler encounters an INCLUDE pseudo-operation, it replaces that pseudo-operation with the text from the file specified by the ⟨*file-spec*⟩ operand.

EXAMPLE

Suppose the macro definitions shown in Program Listing 5.7 are on the diskette in drive A under the filename EX_5_7.MAC. On encountering the pseudo-operation

```
INCLUDE  A:EX_5_7.MAC
```

in an assembly module, the assembler substitutes the definitions of the displ$ and displ macros that appear in the file EX_5_7.MAC. ■

Labels in Macros

The need to use labels in macros leads to the need for a special kind of label. Consider the following macro definition that is designed to compute the absolute value of the contents of a general register or memory location and to leave the result as the new value of that register or memory location:

```
abs      MACRO num
         CMP   num,0
         JGE   ENDABS
         NEG   num
ENDABS:
         ENDM
```

If this macro is referenced more than once in the assembly module, then the assembler generates the label ENDABS more than once. MASM 6.0 generates the following error message at each definition of the ENDABS after the first:

```
error A2005: symbol redefinition : ENDABS
```

MASM 5.1

MASM 5.1 generates the following error messages at each definition of the ENDABS after the first:

```
error A2004: Redefinition of symbol
error A2005: Symbol is multidefined: ENDABS
```

In addition, MASM 5.1 generates the following error message at each reference to the multidefined symbol:

```
error A2026: Reference to multidefined symbol
```

If labels are to be allowed in macros, then there must be a way to direct the assembler to generate unique labels during macro expansion. The **LOCAL pseudo-operation for generating unique labels** has the following general form:

LOCAL ⟨*dummy-label-list*⟩ [⟨*comment*⟩]

in which ⟨*dummy-label-list*⟩ is a list of dummy labels separated by commas. At the time of macro expansion, the LOCAL pseudo-operation directs the assembler to generate a unique label for each dummy label in the ⟨*dummy-label-list*⟩ and substitute that unique label for each occurrence of the corresponding dummy label in the macro body. The labels generated by the assembler are the labels in the range ??0000–??FFFF. The LOCAL pseudo-operation must appear between the MACRO pseudo-operation that marks the beginning of the macro definition and the first instruction of the macro body.

MASM 5.1

In MASM 5.1, there can be no intervening comment lines between the MACRO and LOCAL pseudo-operations.

EXAMPLE

The following macro definition corrects the absolute value macro defined earlier:

```
abs       MACRO num
          LOCAL ENDABS
          CMP   num,0
          JGE   ENDABS
          NEG   num
ENDABS:
          ENDM
```

If the first reference to the macro is

```
abs  X
```

then the instruction sequence substituted by the assembler might be as follows:

```
          CMP  X,0
          JGE  ??0000
          NEG  X
??0000:
```

If the second reference to the macro is

```
abs  BX
```

then the instruction sequence substituted by the assembler might be as follows:

```
          CMP  BX,0
          JGE  ??0001
          NEG  BX
??0001:
```

The actual code generated would depend on the existence of other macros with local labels. On encountering a reference to the abs macro, the assembler selects the next available label from the list ??0000–??FFFF and substitutes it for the dummy label ENDABS in the expansion. ■

Local Stack Variables

MASM 6.0 provides a second form for the LOCAL pseudo-operation. (In versions prior to 6.0, the LOCAL pseudo-operation could be used only in a macro definition to define labels that had to be unique in each expansion of the macro.) With MASM 6.0, the LOCAL pseudo-operation can also be used in a subprocedure definition to create stack-based variables that exist for a single invocation of the subprocedure. The **LOCAL pseudo-operation for defining local stack variables** has the following general form:

```
        LOCAL  ⟨local-stack-variable-list⟩
```

in which ⟨*local-stack-variable-list*⟩ is a list of variable definitions separated by commas. The variable definitions in the list have the form

```
⟨name⟩  [[⟨count⟩]][:⟨type⟩]
```

in which ⟨*name*⟩ is the symbolic name to be associated with the stack location in which storage for the variable is to begin, ⟨*count*⟩ is the number of elements for an array variable, and ⟨*type*⟩ is the type attribute for the variable. Note that the optional ⟨*count*⟩, if it is included, must be enclosed in square brackets. If ⟨*count*⟩ is omitted, then the variable being defined is a scalar variable. Storage space for local stack variables is allocated in the stack upon entry to the subprocedure and is deleted from the stack just prior to returning control to the caller. LOCAL pseudo-operations for defining local stack variables must appear between the PROC pseudo-operation and the first instruction of the procedure body.

EXAMPLE

The pseudo-operations

```
EASTER  PROC   FAR PUBLIC USES AX BX DX ES, YEAR:WORD
        LOCAL  CAL_ADJ:WORD, FM:WORD
```

mark the beginning of the definition of a subprocedure named EASTER. The subprocedure has one parameter, YEAR, which is passed via the stack. The subprocedure also has two local variables, CAL_ADJ and FM, which are maintained in the stack. Within the procedure body, these variables may be referenced by name. The assembler will translate the name to the address of the stack location that the name represents as it translates the assembly module from assembly language to machine language. The programmer uses symbolic names, and the assembler keeps track of the storage cells associated with the names. ■

The use of the stack for storing local variables is introduced from a user perspective in this chapter and is discussed in detail in Chapters 8 and 10.

Conditional Assembly

It is possible in an assembly module to identify a sequence of instructions and pseudo-operations that is to be included in or omitted from the assembly depending on the value of a constant expression. This mechanism is known as **conditional assembly**, and its specification has the following general form:

```
IFxxxx  ⟨argument⟩
        ⟨block⟩
[ELSE
        ⟨block⟩]
ENDIF
```

in which IFxxxx is one of the conditional pseudo-operations from Table 5.1, ⟨*argument*⟩ is a constant expression or symbolic name depending on the conditional pseudo-operation, and ⟨*block*⟩ is a sequence of instructions and pseudo-operations to be included in or omitted from the assembly.

TABLE 5.1
Conditional pseudo-operations

Pseudo-Operation		Explanation
IF	⟨*expr*⟩	True if the constant expression (⟨*expr*⟩) evaluates to a nonzero value.
IFE	⟨*expr*⟩	True if the constant expression (⟨*expr*⟩) evaluates to zero.
IFDEF	⟨*symbol*⟩	True if the symbolic name (⟨*symbol*⟩) is defined or has been declared as external by the EXTRN pseudo-operation.
IFNDEF	⟨*symbol*⟩	True if the symbolic name (⟨*symbol*⟩) is not defined and has not been declared as external by the EXTRN pseudo-operation.
IFB	⟨⟨*arg*⟩⟩	The pointed brackets around ⟨*arg*⟩ are required. Usually used inside a macro definition. True in a specific macro expansion if the operand corresponding to the dummy argument (⟨*arg*⟩) is blank.
IFNB	⟨⟨*arg*⟩⟩	The pointed brackets around ⟨*arg*⟩ are required. Usually used inside a macro definition. True in a specific macro expansion if the operand corresponding to the dummy argument (⟨*arg*⟩) is not blank.

Note that the clause

```
[ELSE
        ⟨block⟩]
```

is optional. The ⟨*block*⟩ in this clause is included in the assembly if the conditional pseudo-operation selects to omit the required ⟨*block*⟩. The required ⟨*block*⟩ is included in the assembly if the specified condition is True; it is omitted from the assembly if the condition is False. Table 5.1 explains some of the conditional pseudo-operations.

Conditional assembly is especially useful in macros. For a specific expansion, the decision to include or omit some of the instructions in the macro body can be based on the operand associated with a specific dummy argument.

Consider again the macros displ$ and displ defined earlier in this chapter. Program Listing 5.8 shows an alternative for these macro definitions. The listing contains the definition of a single macro named displ (lines 16–29), which uses conditional assembly to select either a call to PUTDEC$ or a call to PUTDEC and to select whether or not to make a call to NEWLINE at the end of the display.

The displ macro defined in Program Listing 5.8 has five arguments:

string, the symbolic name of the character string to be displayed

lngth, the length of the string to be displayed

```
 1: ;==================================================================
 2: ;            PROGRAM LISTING 5.8
 3: ;
 4: ; MACRO TO:
 5: ;            DISPLAY A CHARACTER STRING
 6: ;            DISPLAY THE DECIMAL INTEGER IN THE AX-REGISTER
 7: ;            DISPLAY A NEWLINE CHARACTER (IF REQUESTED)
 8: ;
 9: ; ARGUMENTS:
10: ;            string --- STRING TO BE DISPLAYED
11: ;            lngth  --- LENGTH OF STRING TO BE DISPLAYED
12: ;            code ----- DISPLAY CODE FOR PUTDEC AND PUTDEC$
13: ;            type ----- TYPE OF OUTPUT (SIGNED OR UNSIGNED)
14: ;            flag ----- FLAG FOR REQUESTING CALL TO NEWLINE
15: ;==================================================================
16: displ      MACRO   string,lngth,code,type,flag:=<0>
17:            LEA     DI,string
18:            MOV     CX,lngth
19:            CALL    PUTSTRNG
20:            MOV     BH,code
21:            IF      type
22:            CALL    PUTDEC$
23:            ELSE
24:            CALL    PUTDEC
25:            ENDIF
26:            IF      flag
27:            CALL    NEWLINE
28:            ENDIF
29:            ENDM
30: ;==================================================================
31: LJ         EQU     -1                  ;code FOR LEFT  JUSTIFY
32: NJ         EQU      0                  ;code FOR NO JUSTIFICATION
33: RJ         EQU     +1                  ;code FOR RIGHT JUSTIFY
34: PD         EQU     0                   ;type FOR SELECTING PUTDEC
35: PD$        EQU     1                   ;type FOR SELECTING PUTDEC$
36: NL         EQU     1                   ;flag FOR REQUESTING NEWLINE
37: ;==================================================================
```

code, the display code for PUTDEC$ or PUTDEC

type, which specifies whether the output is to be unsigned (type = 1) or signed (type = 0)—in effect, whether to call PUTDEC$ or PUTDEC

flag, which specifies whether to call NEWLINE (flag = 1 specifies a call to NEWLINE)

Note that the argument flag is followed by the specification :=⟨0⟩. This entry specifies a default value of 0 for the argument. That is, if the fifth argument is omitted from a reference to the macro displ, then the default value 0 is assumed for that argument.

MASM 5.1

MASM 5.1 does not support default values for macro arguments.

The conditional assembly specification in lines 21–25 of Program Listing 5.8 directs the assembler to include the instruction

```
CALL  PUTDEC$
```

in the macro expansion if the type argument has a nonzero value and to include the instruction

```
CALL  PUTDEC
```

if type has a value of zero. The conditional assembly specification in lines 26–28 directs the assembler to include the intruction

```
CALL  NEWLINE
```

in the macro expansion if the flag argument has a nonzero value.

The six EQU definitions in lines 31–36 are provided so that the user can specify the arguments code, type, and flag in mnemonic form. The macro reference

```
displ  MSG,MSG_LNG,RJ,PD$
```

would be expanded to the instruction sequence

```
LEA   DI,MSG
MOV   CX,MSG_LNG
CALL  PUTSTRNG
MOV   BH,+1
CALL  PUTDEC$
```

The macro reference

```
displ  MSG,MSG_LNG,NJ,PD,NL
```

would be expanded to the instruction sequence

```
LEA   DI,MSG
MOV   CX,MSG_LNG
CALL  PUTSTRNG
MOV   BH,0
CALL  PUTDEC
CALL  NEWLINE
```

Programming Example—Compute Dates of 21 Easter Sundays

Program Listing 5.9 is an implementation of an algorithm to compute the dates of 21 consecutive Easter Sundays given the starting year. The assembly module contains the definition of the stack segment for the program (lines 21–23), the definition of a constant data segment (lines 24–32), and the definition of the main procedure (lines 39–62). The main procedure prompts for and accepts from the keyboard a value for the beginning year (lines 43–46), displays a header for the output (lines 47–50), and then enters a REPEAT-UNTIL loop (lines 51–60). The loop executes 21 times, once for each of 21 consecutive years beginning with the year that was input via the keyboard. The body of the loop displays the year (line 54), invokes the external subprocedure EASTER (lines 55 and 56) to compute and display the date of Easter Sunday for that year, and then increments to the next year (line 57). The year is maintained in the AX-register.

The assembly module of Program Listing 5.10 contains the definition of a constant data segment for the subprocedure EASTER (lines 19–25) and the definition of the subprocedure EASTER (lines 64–103). The EASTER subprocedure computes and displays the date of an Easter Sunday given the year. The year is passed to the EASTER subprocedure via the stack. The date of Easter Sunday for that year (month and day) is displayed on the screen beginning at the current cursor position. The EASTER subprocedure in Program Listing 5.10 implements the same algorithm as the main procedure in Program Listing 5.5. The main difference between the two implementations is the interface. The EASTER subprocedure in Program Listing 5.10

```
            PAGE    80,132
;====================================================================
;                   PROGRAM LISTING 5.9
;
; PROGRAM  TO  COMPUTE  THE  DATE  OF 21
; EASTER SUNDAYS GIVEN THE STARTING YEAR
;
;====================================================================
            .MODEL  SMALL,BASIC,FARSTACK
;====================================================================
                                        ;PROCEDURES TO
            EXTRN   EASTER:FAR          ;COMPUTE AND DISPLAY  DATE OF
                                        ;EASTER SUNDAY GIVEN THE YEAR
            EXTRN   GETDEC$:FAR         ;GET  16-BIT UNSIGNED DEC INT
            EXTRN   NEWLINE:FAR         ;DISPLAY NEWLINE CHARACTER
            EXTRN   PUTDEC$:FAR         ;DISPLAY UNSIGNED DECIMAL INT
            EXTRN   PUTSTRNG:FAR        ;DISPLAY CHARACTER STRING
;====================================================================
; M A C R O   D E F I N I T I O N
            INCLUDE A:EX_5_8.MAC        ;displ MACRO
;====================================================================
; S T A C K   D E F I N I T I O N
            .STACK  256
;====================================================================
; C O N S T A N T   D E F I N I T I O N S
            .CONST
PROMPT      DB      'ENTER YEAR - '
PROMPT_LNG EQU      $ - PROMPT
HEADER      DB      'EASTER SUNDAYS:'
HEADER_LNG EQU      $ - HEADER
SPACES      DB      '            '
SP_LNG      EQU     $ - SPACES
;====================================================================
            PAGE
;====================================================================
; C O D E   S E G M E N T   D E F I N I T I O N
            .CODE   EX_5_9
;
            .STARTUP                    ;GENERATE STARTUP CODE
            PUSH    DS                  ;SET ES-REGISTER TO ADDRESS
            POP     ES                  ;DGROUP
;
            LEA     DI,PROMPT           ;PROMPT FOR YEAR
            MOV     CX,PROMPT_LNG
            CALL    PUTSTRNG
            CALL    GETDEC$             ;GET YEAR
            LEA     DI,HEADER           ;DISPLAY HEADER
            MOV     CX,HEADER_LNG
            CALL    PUTSTRNG
            CALL    NEWLINE             ;DISPLAY NEWLINE CHARACTER
            MOV     CX,21               ;LOOP_COUNT = 21
            .REPEAT                     ;REPEAT
            PUSH    CX
            displ   SPACES,SP_LNG,NJ,PD$;   DISPLAY YEAR
            PUSH    AX                  ;   CALL EASTER(YEAR)
            CALL    EASTER
            INC     AX                  ;   YEAR = YEAR + 1
            POP     CX
            .UNTILCXZ                   ;   LOOP_COUNT = LOOP_COUNT-1
                                        ;UNTIL LOOP_COUNT = 0
            .EXIT                       ;RETURN TO DOS
;
            END
```

```
            PAGE    80,132
;====================================================================
;                   PROGRAM LISTING 5.10
;
; PROCEDURE TO COMPUTE AND DISPLAY THE
; DATE OF EASTER SUNDAY GIVEN THE YEAR
;
; CALLING SEQUENCE:
;                   PUSH    <YEAR>
;                   CALL    EASTER
;
;====================================================================
            .MODEL  SMALL,BASIC
;====================================================================
                                        ;PROCEDURES TO
            EXTRN   NEWLINE:FAR         ;DISPLAY NEWLINE CHARACTER
            EXTRN   PUTDEC$:FAR         ;DISPLAY UNSIGNED DECIMAL INT
            EXTRN   PUTSTRNG:FAR        ;DISPLAY CHARACTER STRING
;====================================================================
; C O N S T A N T   D E F I N I T I O N S
            .CONST
MARCH       DB      ' - MARCH '
MAR_L       EQU     $ - MARCH
APRIL       DB      ' ---------- APRIL '
APR_L       EQU     $ - APRIL
;====================================================================
;
;
;
;
;====================================================================
; M A C R O   D E F I N I T I O N S
;----------------------------------------------------------
;FUNCTION  x modulo y   COMPUTES REMAINDER OF UNSIGNED x/y
;                       |  x AND y CAN BE WORD REGISTER, |
;                       |  WORD MEMORY, OR IMMEDIATE.    |
;                       |  USES AX, BX, AND DX REGISTERS |
;                       LEAVES  x modulo y  IN AX-REGISTER
modulo      MACRO   x,y
            MOV     AX,x
            MOV     BX,y
            MOV     DX,0
            DIV     BX
            MOV     AX,DX
            ENDM
;----------------------------------------------------------
;MULTIPLY IMMEDIATE (UNSIGNED)
;                   const SHOULD BE IMMEDIATE
;                   USES BX-REGISTER
;                   LEAVES PRODUCT IN DX:AX
muli        MACRO   const
            MOV     BX,const
            MUL     BX
            ENDM
;----------------------------------------------------------
            INCLUDE A:EX_5_8.MAC        ;displ MACRO
;----------------------------------------------------------
; E N D   O F   M A C R O   D E F I N I T I O N S
;====================================================================
;====================================================================
;C O D E   S E G M E N T   D E F I N I T I O N
;
            .CODE   EX_5_10
EASTER      PROC    FAR PUBLIC USES AX BX DX ES, YEAR:WORD
                                    ;PROCEDURE EASTER(YEAR)
```

```
 66:            LOCAL   CAL_ADJ:WORD
 67:            LOCAL   FM:WORD
 68: ;
 69:            MOV     AX,DGROUP           ;SET ES-REGISTER TO
 70:            MOV     ES,AX               ;ADDRESS DGROUP
 71:            modulo  YEAR,19             ;CYCL_YR = YEAR mod 19
 72:            muli    19                  ;FM = (19*CYCL_YR + 24) mod 30
 73:            ADD     AX,24
 74:            modulo  AX,30
 75:            MOV     FM,AX
 76:            modulo  YEAR,4              ;CAL_ADJ = 2(YEAR mod 4)
 77:            muli    2
 78:            MOV     CAL_ADJ,AX
 79:            modulo  YEAR,7              ;         + 4(YEAR mod 7)
 80:            muli    4
 81:            PAGE
 82:            ADD     AX,5                ;         + 5
 83:            ADD     CAL_ADJ,AX
 84:            MOV     AX,FM               ;DATE_ADJ = (6*FM + CAL_ADJ)
 85:            muli    6                   ;                       mod 7
 86:            ADD     AX,CAL_ADJ
 87:            modulo  AX,7
 88:            ADD     AX,FM               ;DATE = DATE_ADJ + FM + 22
 89:            ADD     AX,22
 90:            .IF     AX > 31             ;IF   DATE > 31
 91:                                        ;THEN
 92:            SUB     AX,31               ;     DATE = DATE - 31
 93:            .IF     AX == 26            ;     IF   DATE = 26
 94:                                        ;     THEN
 95:            MOV     AX,19               ;          DATE = 19
 96:            .ENDIF                      ;     ENDIF
 97:            displ   APRIL,APR_L,NJ,PD$,NL;     DISPLAY 'APRIL ',DATE
 98: ;
 99:            .ELSE                       ;ELSE
100:            displ   MARCH,MAR_L,NJ,PD$,NL;     DISPLAY 'MARCH ',DATE
101:            .ENDIF                      ;ENDIF
102:            RET                         ;RETURN TO CALLER
103: EASTER     ENDP                     ;END EASTER
104:            END
```

receives its input via the stack, and the main procedure in Program Listing 5.5 receives its input via the keyboard.

Program Listings 5.9 and 5.10 are two parts of a single program that uses three macros. The macros modulo and muli are defined in Program Listing 5.10 (lines 31–59) and were discussed and illustrated in Program Listing 5.5. The macro displ is defined in a separate source code file. The file A:EX_5_8.MAC contains the definition of the displ macro in Program Listing 5.8 (which was discussed in the previous section).

The INCLUDE pseudo-operation incorporates the definition of the displ macro into the assembly modules in Program Listings 5.9 and 5.10. The INCLUDE pseudo-operation in line 20 of Program Listing 5.9 and the one in line 56 of Program Listing 5.10 cause the assembler to replace each of those lines with a copy of the text contained in file EX_5_8.MAC on the diskette in drive A.

Assembler Listing 5.11 shows the first two pages of the assembler-generated listing for the assembly module in Program Listing 5.9. Note that the INCLUDE pseudo-operation is immediately followed by the lines of text from the EX_5_8.MAC

```
Microsoft (R) Macro Assembler Version 6.00B              05/24/93 11:59:18
EX_5_11.asm                                               Page 1 - 1


                                         PAGE    80,132
                                  ;==============================================================
                                  ;              ASSEMBLER LISTING 5.11
                                  ;
                                  ; PROGRAM  TO  COMPUTE  THE  DATE  OF 21
                                  ; EASTER SUNDAYS GIVEN THE STARTING YEAR
                                  ;
                                  ;==============================================================
                                         .MODEL  SMALL,BASIC,FARSTACK
                                  ;==============================================================
                                                                   ;PROCEDURES TO
                                         EXTRN   EASTER:FAR        ;COMPUTE AND DISPLAY  DATE OF
                                                                   ;EASTER SUNDAY GIVEN THE YEAR
                                         EXTRN   GETDEC$:FAR       ;GET  16-BIT UNSIGNED DEC INT
                                         EXTRN   NEWLINE:FAR       ;DISPLAY NEWLINE CHARACTER
                                         EXTRN   PUTDEC$:FAR       ;DISPLAY UNSIGNED DECIMAL INT
                                         EXTRN   PUTSTRNG:FAR      ;DISPLAY CHARACTER STRING
                                  ;==============================================================
                                  ; M A C R O   D E F I N I T I O N
                                         INCLUDE A:EX_5_8.MAC      ;displ MACRO
                                C ;==============================================================
                                C ;          PROGRAM LISTING 5.8
                                C ;
                                C ; MACRO TO:
                                C ;          DISPLAY A CHARACTER STRING
                                C ;          DISPLAY THE DECIMAL INTEGER IN THE AX-REGISTER
                                C ;          DISPLAY A NEWLINE CHARACTER (IF REQUESTED)
                                C ;
                                C ; ARGUMENTS:
                                C ;          string --- STRING TO BE DISPLAYED
                                C ;          lngth  --- LENGTH OF STRING TO BE DISPLAYED
                                C ;          code ----- DISPLAY CODE FOR PUTDEC AND PUTDEC$
                                C ;          type ----- TYPE OF OUTPUT (SIGNED OR UNSIGNED)
                                C ;          flag ----- FLAG FOR REQUESTING CALL TO NEWLINE
                                C ;==============================================================
                                C displ    MACRO    string,lngth,code,type,flag:=<0>
                                C          LEA      DI,string
                                C          MOV      CX,lngth
                                C          CALL     PUTSTRNG
                                C          MOV      BH,code
                                C          IF       type
                                C          CALL     PUTDEC$
                                C          ELSE
                                C          CALL     PUTDEC
                                C          ENDIF
                                C          IF       flag
                                C          CALL     NEWLINE
                                C          ENDIF
                                C          ENDM
                                C ;==============================================================
 =-0001                         C LJ       EQU     -1              ;code FOR LEFT  JUSTIFY
 = 0000                         C NJ       EQU      0              ;code FOR NO JUSTIFICATION
 = 0001                         C RJ       EQU     +1              ;code FOR RIGHT JUSTIFY
 = 0000                         C PD       EQU     0               ;type FOR SELECTING PUTDEC
 = 0001                         C PD$      EQU     1               ;type FOR SELECTING PUTDEC$
```

```
= 0001                  C NL         EQU     1                  ;flag FOR REQUESTING NEWLINE
                        C ;=============================================================
                        C
                        C
                          ;=============================================================
                          ; S T A C K   D E F I N I T I O N
                                  .STACK  256
                          ;=============================================================
                          ; C O N S T A N T   D E F I N I T I O N S
0000                              .CONST
0000 45 4E 54 45 52 20    PROMPT      DB      'ENTER YEAR - '
     59 45 41 52 20 2D
     20
000D = 000D               PROMPT_LNG EQU     $ - PROMPT
000D 45 41 53 54 45 52    HEADER      DB      'EASTER SUNDAYS:'
     20 53 55 4E 44 41
     59 53 3A
001C = 000F               HEADER_LNG EQU     $ - HEADER
001C 20 20 20 20 20 20    SPACES      DB      '               '
     20 20 20 20 20 20
     20 20 20
002B = 000F               SP_LNG      EQU     $ - SPACES
                          ;=============================================================
```

```
Microsoft (R) Macro Assembler Version 6.00B               05/24/93 11:59:18
EX_5_11.asm                                                Page 2 - 1


                                  PAGE
                          ;=============================================================
                          ; C O D E   S E G M E N T   D E F I N I T I O N
0000                              .CODE   EX_5_9
                          ;
                                  .STARTUP                        ;GENERATE STARTUP CODE
0000                     *@Startup:
0000  BA ---- R          *        mov     dx, DGROUP
0003  8E DA              *        mov     ds, dx
0005  1E                          PUSH    DS                      ;SET ES-REGISTER TO ADDRESS
0006  07                          POP     ES                      ;DGROUP
                          ;
0007  BF 0000 R                   LEA     DI,PROMPT               ;PROMPT FOR YEAR
000A  B9 000D                     MOV     CX,PROMPT_LNG
000D  9A ---- 0000 E              CALL    PUTSTRNG
0012  9A ---- 0000 E              CALL    GETDEC$                 ;GET YEAR
0017  BF 000D R                   LEA     DI,HEADER               ;DISPLAY HEADER
001A  B9 000F                     MOV     CX,HEADER_LNG
001D  9A ---- 0000 E              CALL    PUTSTRNG
0022  9A ---- 0000 E              CALL    NEWLINE                 ;DISPLAY NEWLINE CHARACTER
0027  B9 0015                     MOV     CX,21                   ;LOOP_COUNT = 21
                                  .REPEAT                         ;REPEAT
002A                     *@C0001:
002A  51                          PUSH    CX
                                  displ   SPACES,SP_LNG,NJ,PD$;   DISPLAY YEAR
002B  BF 001C R            1      LEA     DI,SPACES
002E  B9 000F              1      MOV     CX,SP_LNG
0031  9A ---- 0000 E       1      CALL    PUTSTRNG
0036  B7 00                1      MOV     BH,NJ
0038  9A ---- 0000 E       1      CALL    PUTDEC$
```

```
003D 50                        PUSH   AX            ;  CALL EASTER(YEAR)
003E 9A ---- 0000 E            CALL   EASTER
0043 40                        INC    AX            ;  YEAR = YEAR + 1
0044 59                        POP    CX
                               .UNTILCXZ            ;  LOOP_COUNT = LOOP_COUNT-1
0045 E2 E3         1     loop  @C0001
                                                    ;UNTIL LOOP_COUNT = 0
                               .EXIT                ;RETURN TO DOS
0047 B4 4C         1     mov   ah, 04Ch
0049 CD 21         1     int   021h
                      ;
                               END
```

file and that each of these lines is preceded by the letter C in the listing. Note also that no machine code is generated for these lines. Each line from the INCLUDE file is either a comment line or part of a macro definition. Assembler Listing 5.11 also shows the expansion for the reference to the displ macro. The reference

```
displ  SPACES,SP_LNG,NJ,PD$
```

was expanded to the instruction sequence

```
LEA   DI,SPACES
MOV   CX,SP_LNG
CALL  PUTSTRNG
MOV   BH,NJ
CALL  PUTDEC$
```

Note that a call to NEWLINE was *not* generated because the fifth argument was omitted from the macro reference and the default value for the fifth argument is 0.

Assembler Listing 5.12 shows the first three pages of the assembler-generated listing for the assembly module in Program Listing 5.10. Note again the lines inserted as a result of the INCLUDE pseudo-operation (i.e., the lines preceded by the letter C). Assembler Listing 5.12 also shows the expansion for each reference to the displ macro. The reference

```
displ  APRIL,APR_L,NJ,PD$,NL
```

was expanded to the instruction sequence

```
LEA   DI,APRIL
MOV   CX,APR_L
CALL  PUTSTRNG
MOV   BH,NJ
CALL  PUTDEC$
CALL  NEWLINE
```

and the reference

```
displ  MARCH,MAR_L,NJ,PD$,NL
```

was expanded to the instruction sequence

```
LEA   DI,MARCH
MOV   CX,MAR_L
CALL  PUTSTRNG
MOV   BH,NJ
CALL  PUTDEC$
CALL  NEWLINE
```

```
Microsoft (R) Macro Assembler Version 6.00B              05/24/93 11:59:27
EX_5_12.asm                                              Page 1 - 1


                                   PAGE    80,132
                             ;====================================================================
                             ;                  ASSEMBLER LISTING 5.12
                             ;
                             ; PROCEDURE TO COMPUTE AND DISPLAY THE
                             ; DATE OF EASTER SUNDAY GIVEN THE YEAR
                             ;
                             ; CALLING SEQUENCE:
                             ;                  PUSH    <YEAR>
                             ;                  CALL    EASTER
                             ;
                             ;====================================================================
                                   .MODEL  SMALL,BASIC
                             ;====================================================================
                                                               ;PROCEDURES TO
                                   EXTRN   NEWLINE:FAR         ;DISPLAY NEWLINE CHARACTER
                                   EXTRN   PUTDEC$:FAR         ;DISPLAY UNSIGNED DECIMAL INT
                                   EXTRN   PUTSTRNG:FAR        ;DISPLAY CHARACTER STRING
                             ;====================================================================
                             ;C O N S T A N T   D E F I N I T I O N S
0000                               .CONST
0000 20 2D 20 4D 41 52       MARCH      DB      ' - MARCH '
     43 48 20
0009 = 0009                  MAR_L      EQU     $ - MARCH
0009 20 2D 2D 2D 2D 2D       APRIL      DB      ' ---------- APRIL '
     2D 2D 2D 2D 2D 20
     41 50 52 49 4C 20
001B = 0012                  APR_L      EQU     $ - APRIL
                             ;====================================================================
                             ;
                             ;
                             ;
                             ;
                             ;====================================================================
                             ;M A C R O   D E F I N I T I O N S
                             ;-----------------------------------------------------------
                             ;FUNCTION  x modulo y   COMPUTES REMAINDER OF UNSIGNED x/y
                             ;                       | x AND y CAN BE WORD REGISTER, |
                             ;                       | WORD MEMORY, OR IMMEDIATE.    |
                             ;                       | USES AX, BX, AND DX REGISTERS |
                             ;                       LEAVES  x modulo y  IN AX-REGISTER
                             modulo     MACRO   x,y
                                        MOV     AX,x
                                        MOV     BX,y
                                        MOV     DX,0
                                        DIV     BX
                                        MOV     AX,DX
                                        ENDM
                             ;-----------------------------------------------------------
                             ;MULTIPLY IMMEDIATE (UNSIGNED)
                             ;                  const SHOULD BE IMMEDIATE
                             ;                  USES BX-REGISTER
                             ;                  LEAVES PRODUCT IN DX:AX
                             muli       MACRO   const
                                        MOV     BX,const
```

```
                          MUL     BX
                          ENDM
                   ;--------------------------------------------------------
                          INCLUDE A:EX_5_8.MAC        ;displ MACRO
                 C ;================================================================
                 C ;          PROGRAM LISTING 5.8
                 C ;
                 C ; MACRO TO:
                 C ;          DISPLAY A CHARACTER STRING
                 C ;          DISPLAY THE DECIMAL INTEGER IN THE AX-REGISTER
                 C ;          DISPLAY A NEWLINE CHARACTER (IF REQUESTED)
                 C ;
                 C ; ARGUMENTS:
                 C ;          string --- STRING TO BE DISPLAYED
                 C ;          lngth  --- LENGTH OF STRING TO BE DISPLAYED
                 C ;          code ----- DISPLAY CODE FOR PUTDEC AND PUTDEC$
                 C ;          type ----- TYPE OF OUTPUT (SIGNED OR UNSIGNED)
                 C ;          flag ----- FLAG FOR REQUESTING CALL TO NEWLINE
                 C ;================================================================
                 C displ      MACRO   string,lngth,code,type,flag:=<0>
                 C            LEA     DI,string
                 C            MOV     CX,lngth
                 C            CALL    PUTSTRNG
                 C            MOV     BH,code
                 C            IF      type
```

Microsoft (R) Macro Assembler Version 6.00B 05/24/93 11:59:27
EX_5_12.asm Page 2 - 1

```
                 C            CALL    PUTDEC$
                 C            ELSE
                 C            CALL    PUTDEC
                 C            ENDIF
                 C            IF      flag
                 C            CALL    NEWLINE
                 C            ENDIF
                 C            ENDM
                 C ;================================================================
 =-0001          C LJ         EQU     -1             ;code FOR LEFT  JUSTIFY
 = 0000          C NJ         EQU      0             ;code FOR NO JUSTIFICATION
 = 0001          C RJ         EQU     +1             ;code FOR RIGHT JUSTIFY
 = 0000          C PD         EQU     0              ;type FOR SELECTING PUTDEC
 = 0001          C PD$        EQU     1              ;type FOR SELECTING PUTDEC$
 = 0001          C NL         EQU     1              ;flag FOR REQUESTING NEWLINE
                 C ;================================================================
                 C
                 C
                   ;--------------------------------------------------------
                   ;E N D   O F   M A C R O   D E F I N I T I O N S
                   ;================================================================
                   ;================================================================
                   ;C O D E   S E G M E N T   D E F I N I T I O N
                   ;
 0000                     .CODE   EX_5_10
 0000              EASTER PROC    FAR PUBLIC USES AX BX DX ES, YEAR:WORD
                                                        ;PROCEDURE EASTER(YEAR)
                          LOCAL   CAL_ADJ:WORD
                          LOCAL   FM:WORD
```

```
                                   ;
0000  55                 *        push   bp
0001  8B EC              *        mov    bp, sp
0003  83 C4 FC           *        add    sp, 0FFFCh
0006  50                 *        push   ax
0007  53                 *        push   bx
0008  52                 *        push   dx
0009  06                 *        push   es
000A  B8 ---- R                   MOV     AX,DGROUP      ;SET ES-REGISTER TO
000D  8E C0                       MOV     ES,AX          ;ADDRESS DGROUP
                                  modulo  YEAR,19        ;CYCL_YR = YEAR mod 19
000F  8B 46 06           1        MOV     AX,YEAR
0012  BB 0013            1        MOV     BX,19
0015  BA 0000            1        MOV     DX,0
0018  F7 F3              1        DIV     BX
001A  8B C2              1        MOV     AX,DX
                                  muli    19             ;FM = (19*CYCL_YR + 24) mod 30
001C  BB 0013            1        MOV     BX,19
001F  F7 E3              1        MUL     BX
0021  83 C0 18                    ADD     AX,24
                                  modulo  AX,30
0024  8B C0              1        MOV     AX,AX
0026  BB 001E            1        MOV     BX,30
0029  BA 0000            1        MOV     DX,0
002C  F7 F3              1        DIV     BX
002E  8B C2              1        MOV     AX,DX
0030  89 46 FC                    MOV     FM,AX
                                  modulo  YEAR,4         ;CAL_ADJ = 2(YEAR mod 4)
0033  8B 46 06           1        MOV     AX,YEAR
0036  BB 0004            1        MOV     BX,4
0039  BA 0000            1        MOV     DX,0
003C  F7 F3              1        DIV     BX
003E  8B C2              1        MOV     AX,DX
                                  muli    2
0040  BB 0002            1        MOV     BX,2
0043  F7 E3              1        MUL     BX
0045  89 46 FE                    MOV     CAL_ADJ,AX
                                  modulo  YEAR,7         ;         + 4(YEAR mod 7)
0048  8B 46 06           1        MOV     AX,YEAR
004B  BB 0007            1        MOV     BX,7
004E  BA 0000            1        MOV     DX,0
0051  F7 F3              1        DIV     BX
0053  8B C2              1        MOV     AX,DX
                                  muli    4
0055  BB 0004            1        MOV     BX,4
0058  F7 E3              1        MUL     BX

Microsoft (R) Macro Assembler Version 6.00B              05/24/93 11:59:27
EX_5_12.asm                                               Page 3 - 1

                                  PAGE
005A  83 C0 05                    ADD     AX,5           ;         + 5
005D  01 46 FE                    ADD     CAL_ADJ,AX
0060  8B 46 FC                    MOV     AX,FM          ;DATE_ADJ = (6*FM + CAL_ADJ)
                                  muli    6              ;                        mod 7
0063  BB 0006            1        MOV     BX,6
0066  F7 E3              1        MUL     BX
```

```
0068  03 46 FE                            ADD     AX,CAL_ADJ
                                          modulo  AX,7
006B  8B C0              1                MOV     AX,AX
006D  BB 0007            1                MOV     BX,7
0070  BA 0000            1                MOV     DX,0
0073  F7 F3              1                DIV     BX
0075  8B C2              1                MOV     AX,DX
0077  03 46 FC                            ADD     AX,FM            ;DATE = DATE_ADJ + FM + 22
007A  83 C0 16                            ADD     AX,22
                                          .IF     AX > 31          ;IF  DATE > 31
007D  83 F8 1F           *         cmp    ax, 01Fh
0080  76 24              *         jbe    @C0001
                                                                   ;THEN
0082  83 E8 1F                            SUB     AX,31            ;    DATE = DATE - 31
                                          .IF     AX == 26         ;    IF  DATE = 26
0085  83 F8 1A           *         cmp    ax, 01Ah
0088  75 03              *         jne    @C0003
                                                                   ;    THEN
008A  B8 0013                             MOV     AX,19            ;        DATE = 19
                                          .ENDIF                   ;    ENDIF
                                          displ   APRIL,APR_L,NJ,PD$,NL;    DISPLAY 'APRIL ',DATE
008D                     *@C0003:
008D  BF 0009 R          1                LEA     DI,APRIL
0090  B9 0012            1                MOV     CX,APR_L
0093  9A ---- 0000 E     1                CALL    PUTSTRNG
0098  B7 00              1                MOV     BH,NJ
009A  9A ---- 0000 E     1                CALL    PUTDEC$
009F  9A ---- 0000 E     1                CALL    NEWLINE
                            ;
                                          .ELSE                    ;ELSE
00A4  EB 17              *         jmp    @C0005
00A6                     *@C0001:
                                          displ   MARCH,MAR_L,NJ,PD$,NL;    DISPLAY 'MARCH ',DATE
00A6  BF 0000 R          1                LEA     DI,MARCH
00A9  B9 0009            1                MOV     CX,MAR_L
00AC  9A ---- 0000 E     1                CALL    PUTSTRNG
00B1  B7 00              1                MOV     BH,NJ
00B3  9A ---- 0000 E     1                CALL    PUTDEC$
00B8  9A ---- 0000 E     1                CALL    NEWLINE
                                          .ENDIF                   ;ENDIF
00BD                     *@C0005:
                                          RET                      ;RETURN TO CALLER
00BD  07                 *         pop    es
00BE  5A                 *         pop    dx
00BF  5B                 *         pop    bx
00C0  58                 *         pop    ax
00C1  8B E5              *         mov    sp, bp
00C3  5D                 *         pop    bp
00C4  CA 0002            *         ret    00002h
00C7                            EASTER    ENDP                   ;END EASTER
                                          END
```

Note that a call to NEWLINE *was* generated because the fifth argument was NL, which stands for the constant 1.

Note also the code that was generated by the assembler at the beginning and at the end of the subprocedure EASTER. The following code was generated at the beginning of the subprocedure:

```
push  bp
mov   bp, sp
add   sp, 0FFFCh
push  ax
push  bx
push  dx
push  es
```

The first two of these instructions were generated in response to the parameter specifications in the PROC pseudo-operation, the third was generated in response to the two LOCAL pseudo-operations, and the last four were generated in response to the USES clause in the PROC pseudo-operation. The assembler uses the BP-register to access the argument in the stack (YEAR) and to access the two local stack variables (CAL_ADJ and FM).

The instruction

```
push  bp
```

saves the value of the BP-register for the caller, and the instruction

```
mov  bp, sp
```

sets the SS:BP register pair to address a known position within the stack segment. The state of the top portion of the stack segment following the execution of these two instructions is as shown in Figure 5.5. Again, the subsequent execution of PUSH and POP instructions alters the address specified by the SS:SP register pair but not the address specified by the SS:BP register pair.

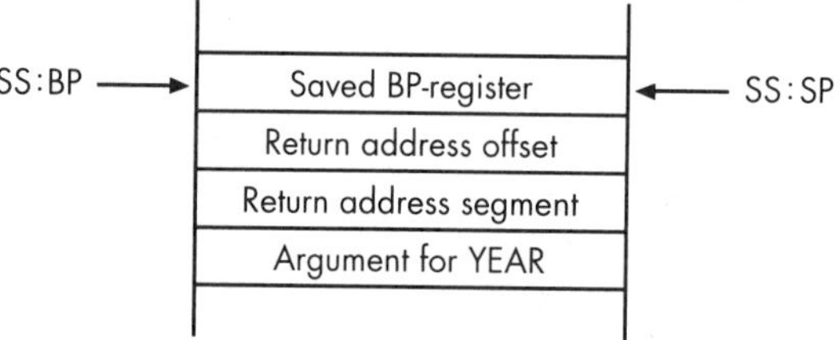

FIGURE 5.5 Stack segment after execution of the push bp and mov bp,sp instructions

The instruction

```
add  sp, 0FFFCh
```

has the effect of adding −4 to (i.e., subtracting 4 from) the value in the SP-register. This operation allocates space in the stack for the two local variables CAL_ADJ and FM. The state of the top portion of the stack segment following the execution of this instruction is as shown in Figure 5.6.

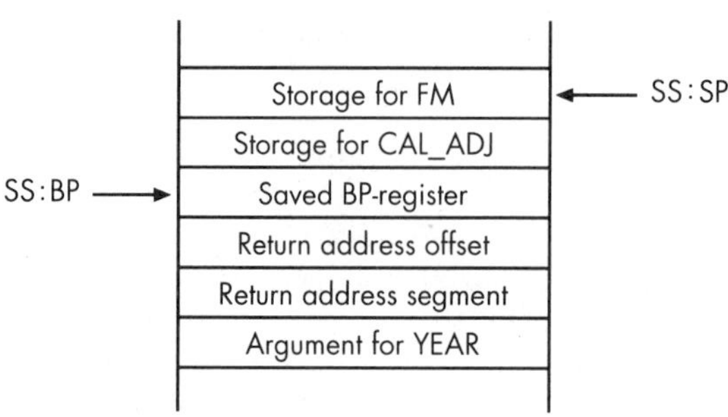

FIGURE 5.6 Stack segment after execution of the add sp,0FFFCh instruction

The four instructions

```
push  ax
push  bx
push  dx
push  es
```

save the registers specified in the USES clause of the PROC pseudo-operation. Following the execution of these four instructions, the state of the top portion of the stack segment is as shown in Figure 5.7. With the SS:BP register pair addressing a known point in the stack, the assembler can generate memory addresses (segment and offset) for the references to the parameter YEAR and for the references to the local variables CAL_ADJ and FM. The segment portion of the address, in each case, is the run-time contents of the SS-register. The offset portion of the address of YEAR is the run-time contents of the BP-register plus 6. Similarly, the offset portion of the address of CAL_ADJ is the run-time contents of the BP-register minus 2, and the offset for FM is the run-time contents of the BP-register minus 4. The method of specifying such an address in assembly language is discussed in Chapter 8. At this point, stack parameters and local stack variables are dealt with from a user standpoint.

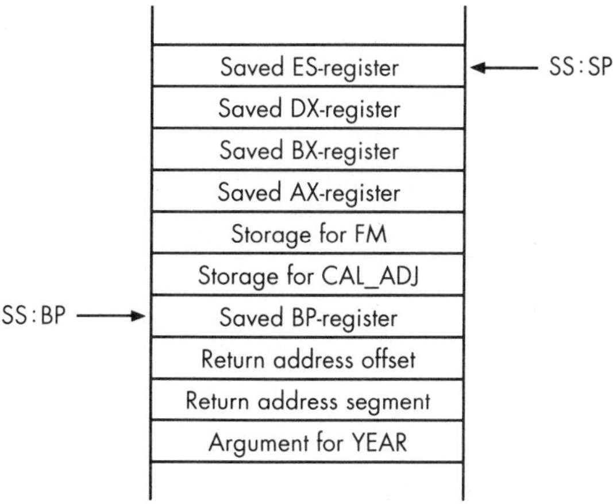

FIGURE 5.7
Stack segment after execution of the push ax, push bx, push dx, and push es instructions

The following code was generated at the end of subprocedure EASTER in place of the RET instruction:

```
pop  es
pop  dx
pop  bx
pop  ax
mov  sp, bp
pop  bp
ret  00002h
```

The state of the top portion of the stack segment just prior to the execution of these instructions should, once again, be as shown in Figure 5.7. The first four of these instructions restore the registers specified in the USES clause in the PROC pseudo-operation. Following the execution of these four POP instructions, the state of the top portion of the stack segment should, once again, be as shown in Figure 5.6.

The instruction

```
mov  sp, bp
```

has the effect of deallocating the storage space for the two local variables, thus returning the top portion of the stack to the state shown in Figure 5.5. The instruction

```
pop  bp
```

restores the register that was used to access the parameters and the local variables in the stack. The instruction

```
ret  00002h
```

returns control to the caller and pops the 2-byte argument from the stack.

The following is the result from a sample execution of the program of Program Listings 5.9 and 5.10:

```
ENTER YEAR - 1990
EASTER SUNDAYS:
                  1990 ---------- APRIL 15
                  1991 - MARCH 31
                  1992 ---------- APRIL 19
                  1993 ---------- APRIL 11
                  1994 ---------- APRIL 3
                  1995 ---------- APRIL 16
                  1996 ---------- APRIL 7
                  1997 - MARCH 30
                  1998 ---------- APRIL 12
                  1999 ---------- APRIL 4
                  2000 ---------- APRIL 23
                  2001 ---------- APRIL 15
                  2002 - MARCH 31
                  2003 ---------- APRIL 20
                  2004 ---------- APRIL 11
                  2005 - MARCH 27
                  2006 ---------- APRIL 16
                  2007 ---------- APRIL 8
                  2008 - MARCH 23
                  2009 ---------- APRIL 12
                  2010 ---------- APRIL 4
```

5.8 Macro versus Subprocedure

The subprocedure and the macro are both important tools in assembly language programming and important concepts for the beginning assembly language programmer to master. One key to proficiency in assembly language programming is having a good library of subprocedures and macros available. From the viewpoint of a beginning assembly language programmer, a subprocedure and a macro may appear to be quite similar. In both cases, a block of instructions is written once by the programmer but can be used in many places in the program. However, the two are quite different with respect to memory space and execution time.

The difference between macros and subprocedures can be viewed from the standpoint of when certain events occur during program translation and execution. The subprocedure instructions appear only once in a machine language program. When the assembler encounters a subprocedure definition, it translates the subprocedure instructions to machine language. Each time the assembler encounters a reference to that subprocedure, for example, a CALL instruction that names the subprocedure, it translates that instruction to a machine language call instruction. During program execution, execution of the machine language call instruction causes control to be transferred to the single copy of the machine language instructions of the subprocedure. Subsequent execution of a return instruction should return control to the instruction that immediately follows the call instruction. The memory space required for subprocedure instructions is not dependent on the number of times the subprocedure is referenced (called).

A macro's instructions may appear more than once in a machine language program. When the assembler encounters a macro definition, no translation to machine language takes place. However, each time the assembler encounters a reference to the macro (i.e., the macro name used as an operation code), the macro body instructions are translated to machine language. The memory space required for the macro instructions is dependent on the number of times the macro is referenced.

Some extra processing is required to execute a subprocedure that is not required to execute macro instructions. There are usually instructions in the calling procedure to set up the inputs for the subprocedure. There is a call instruction to transfer control to the subprocedure. There are usually instructions in the subprocedure to save and restore the state of the processor for the caller. There is a return instruction to transfer control back to the caller. All these instructions require extra memory space and increase execution time, which is referred to as the **overhead** of using a subprocedure.

The decision of whether to use a macro or a subprocedure is often based on the tradeoff of memory space per copy of the macro versus the subprocedure overhead. The macro was chosen for the multiply immediate and mod operations of the Easter Sunday algorithm because the overhead of a subprocedure was considered to equal or exceed the memory space required for the macro instructions. For the display of signed decimal integer capability, provided by the PUTDEC procedure, a subprocedure was chosen because the memory requirements for a macro were felt to be too restrictive for large programs in which signed decimal output is frequently needed. Effective use of macros and subprocedures makes assembly language programming more feasible.

PROGRAMMING EXERCISES

5.1 In Programming Exercise 4.1, the notion of an Ulam sequence and its length was introduced. Design a subalgorithm to accept a positive integer as input and to return the length of the Ulam sequence for that integer as output. As well, design a main algorithm that uses the subalgorithm to find an integer in the range 1–100 whose Ulam sequence has the largest length. The algorithm is to output that integer and the length of its Ulam sequence. The main algorithm is to reference the subalgorithm 100 times, once for each integer in the range 1–100.

Implement your subalgorithm with an 8088/8086 assembly language NEAR function subprocedure. The input to your subprocedure should be a positive integer passed in the AX-register. The length of the Ulam sequence for the input integer should be returned to the caller in the AX-register. Implement your main algorithm with an 8088/8086 assembly language program that uses your NEAR subprocedure to compute the length of the Ulam sequence for each of the integers in the given range. There is no input to your program. Your output should be the integer whose Ulam sequence has the largest length and that largest-length value. The two integers are to be displayed on the screen.

5.2 Design an algorithm to perform integer exponentiation. Your input to the algorithm should be a signed integer value that represents the BASE and an unsigned integer value that represents the positive exponent. Your output should be the value of BASE raised to the EXPONENT. For example, if the inputs are BASE = 2 and EXPONENT = 5, then the output should be $2^5 = 32$. Your algorithm must detect overflow.

Implement your algorithm with an 8088/8086 assembly language FAR subprocedure. The input to your subprocedure should be an 8-bit signed integer value in the AL-register that represents the BASE and an 8-bit unsigned integer value in the AH-register that represents the EXPONENT. Your subprocedure is to return the result, a 16-bit signed integer value, in the AX-register and to return an overflow indicator in the BL-register (BL-register = 0 implies no overflow). Your subprocedure must save and restore all registers used for purposes other than subprocedure output. The registers being saved and restored must include the flags register and the BH-register if it is being used.

5.3 Program Listing 5.4 shows an external subprocedure called RANDOM that returns pseudorandom integers in a specified range. The subprocedure uses a local data segment to maintain a SEED for the random number generator function used and contains some logic to initialize the SEED value at the time of first invocation of the subprocedure. Remove the first call logic from the RANDOM subprocedure. Instead, provide a second FAR subprocedure called RESEED that is defined in the same code segment. The RESEED subprocedure simply sets the SEED value as specified by the caller. Your input to the RESEED procedure should be a code in the BL-register and possibly a 16-bit unsigned integer value in the AX-register. The interpretation for the code in the BL-register is as follows:

BL = 0 → Use the lower half of the time-of-day clock as the new SEED value

BL ≠ 0 → Use the value in the AX-register as the new SEED value

Design an algorithm that uses RANDOM and RESEED to perform the following tasks:

a. Call RANDOM 200 times to produce a sequence of 200 pseudorandom integers in the range 0–9999.

b. Call RESEED prior to the first call to RANDOM to initialize the SEED value to 5555 hexadecimal.

c. Call RESEED after the one-hundredth call to RANDOM to reinitialize the SEED value to the value in the lower half of the time-of-day clock.

d. Display the sequence of random integers on the screen, 10 per line.

e. Count the number of integers in the sequence that are (a) odd, (b) even, (c) high (i.e., in the range 5000–9999), and (d) low (i.e., in the range 0000–4999).

f. Display the results of the four preceding counts on the screen.

Implement your algorithm with an 8088/8086 assembly language program. There is no input to your program. Link your program with RANDOM, RESEED, and the local data segment to produce a complete, executable program. Your output should look something like the following:

```
 832 6809 8658 1206 5968 8066 3916 5338 8185 6129
2739 7450 3575 8968 2470 1758  732 7051 2952 4983
 751 3347 6531 6342 7225 3324 8049 7555 6248 4952
4850 2840 6413 8699 6778 8916 8815 7534 6177 5001
7047 6925 7890 2816 7203 4842 9262 6577 7876 1753
 135 3005  160  627 2854 1317 7650 6932 2263 3233
6438 8638 5704 2971 5119 6213 3023 7251 4787 2626
6563 5290 9034 3346 1166 8807 3955 6341 4179 2022
8144 2080 5443 1652 2695 3532 7302 6918 1200 6166
4602 9537 9754 7950 4684 3728 6950 9353 7393 6211
5836 1678 2634 2458 1358 3222 9880 3012 6851 7277
5455 6622 7158 5560 5455 1258 9623 2290 8471 7388
4090 4187 5600 7980 2903  468  433 8505  905 2852
9065 6929 5441 5559   90 3723 6353 5307 4601 1855
5986 1315 6192 6793 9184 5301  957 6507 3290 1485
7490 1465 8148 6584 6884 4636 6101 9818 2733 1488
1994 2906 1131 9991 3170   66  671  613 9473 8017
2448 6323 3247 5978   55 2589 9335 5667 9585 7381
5082 1304 9634 1167  330 9607 1293 6916 7424 9794
8158   96 1208 3585 6321 8677 9025 5198 4377 3127
ODD = 98    EVEN = 102    HIGH = 109    LOW = 91
C>
```

5.4 In Programming Exercise 4.6, Euclid's algorithm for finding the greatest common divisor (GCD) of two positive integers was introduced. Implement Euclid's algorithm with an 8088/8086 assembly language FAR function subprocedure called GCD. Your input should be two 16-bit unsigned integers in the AX and BX registers. Your subprocedure should return the GCD of these two integers in the AX-register. Your subprocedure must protect all registers used. The programs in Programming Exercise 5.5 or 5.6 can be used to demonstrate your subprocedure.

5.5 In Programming Exercise 4.9, the notion of Pythagorean triples was introduced. Your solution probably produced some Pythagorean triples that were integer multiples of other triples produced. For example, the triple (6, 8, 10) is an integer multiple of the triple (3, 4, 5). If each pair of integers in the triple is relatively prime, then the triple is not an integer multiple of some other triple. Two positive integers are relatively prime if their GCD is 1.

EXAMPLES

$GCD(3, 4) = GCD(3, 5) = GCD(4, 5) = 1$

Therefore, (3, 4, 5) is not a multiple.

$$GCD(6, 8) = GCD(6, 10) = GCD(8, 10) = 2$$

Therefore, (6, 8, 10) is a multiple. ■

Modify your solution to Programming Exercise 4.9 to eliminate the display of triples that are integer multiples of other triples. Use your GCD subprocedure from Programming Exercise 5.4 to determine whether a given triple is a multiple. Increase the range of integers considered from 1–50 to 1–100.

5.6 Programming Exercises 4.9 and 5.5 involve algorithms for producing Pythagorean triples. Your solution to these problems probably included three nested loops. You probably noticed some hesitation in the display of the triples, especially in the second version that considered a wider range of integers. The following algorithm contains only two nested loops and is a much more efficient algorithm for computing Pythagorean triples:

```
ALGORITHM:
     U = 2
     REPEAT
          IF    U is even
          THEN
               V = 1
          ELSE
               V = 2
          ENDIF
          REPEAT
               IF    GCD(U,V) = 1
               THEN
                    CALL TRIPLE(U,V)
               ENDIF
               V = V + 2
          UNTIL V > U
          U = U + 1
     UNTIL U = 10

SUBALGORITHM:
     TRIPLE(U,V)
          Z = U*U + V*V
          Y = U*U - V*V
          X = 2*U*V
          IF    X > Y
          THEN
               INTERCHANGE X & Y
          ENDIF
          DISPLAY X, Y, Z
          RETURN
     END TRIPLE
```

It is based on the following result: Given positive integers U and V, such that either U or V is odd and the other is even and that U and V are relatively prime, the triple ($2UV$, $U^2 - V^2$, $U^2 + V^2$) is a unique Pythagorean triple and is not an integer multiple of some other Pythagorean triple.

Implement this algorithm with an 8088/8086 assembly language program. There is no input to your program. Your output should be a list of the Pythagorean triples displayed on the screen, one triple per line. Implement the subalgorithm with an 8088/8086 assembly language NEAR subprocedure. Your input should be the two positive integers U and V in the BX- and CX-registers, respectively. Your output should be the Pythagorean triple displayed on the screen on a line by itself. Your program should also include your GCD subprocedure from Programming Exercise 5.4.

5.7 In Programming Exercise 4.8, the notion of an insipid integer was introduced. Design a Boolean subalgorithm to accept a positive integer as input and to return True if that integer is insipid; otherwise, it should return False. Design a main algorithm to find and output all positive integers in the range 1–1500 that are insipid. Your algorithm is to use your Boolean subalgorithm to determine whether a given integer is insipid.

Implement your subalgorithm with an 8088/8086 assembly language NEAR Boolean function subprocedure. Your input should be a positive integer passed in the AX-register. The Boolean result should be returned to the BL-register (0 for False, 1 for True).

Implement your main algorithm with an 8088/8086 assembly language program that uses your NEAR subprocedure to test each of the integers in the range 1–1500 to determine whether it is insipid. There is no input to your program. Your output should be the list of insipid integers in the range 1–1500. The integers are to be displayed on the screen, 10 per line.

5.8 The modulo function macro used in Program Listing 5.5 will fail if the operand associated with the dummy argument y is the AX-register. Why? Rewrite the modulo function macro to eliminate this problem. Your solution should not create the same problem with a different register. (*Hint*: Consider use of the stack and/or data storage embedded in the macro.)

5.9 In Programming Exercise 4.6, Euclid's algorithm for finding the GCD of two positive integers was introduced. Implement Euclid's algorithm with an 8088/8086 assembly language macro named GCD. The macro is to compute the GCD of the two 16-bit unsigned integers in the AX- and BX-registers, leaving the result in the AX-register. Complete Programming Exercise 5.5 or 5.6 with the GCD macro replacing the GCD subprocedure.

5.10 Rewrite the multiply immediate macro used in Program Listing 5.5 to perform either byte or word multiplication depending on the operand associated with a second dummy argument called byte:

byte = 0 → Perform word multiplication

byte = 1 → Perform byte multiplication

For example, the macro reference

```
muli  7,0
```

should generate the instructions

```
MOV  BX,7
MUL  BX
```

and the macro reference

```
muli  12,1
```

should generate the instructions

```
MOV  BL,12
MUL  BL
```

5.11 Modify the assembly module of Program Listing 4.4 (in file EX_4_4.ASM on the accompanying diskette) to use the displ macro defined in Program Listing 5.8 (in file EX_5_8.MAC on the diskette). Replace lines 67–78 of Program Listing 4.4 with two references to the displ macro. Use the INCLUDE pseudo-operation to incorporate the macro definition into the assembly module of Program Listing 4.4.

5.12 Design an algorithm that uses the random number generator of Program Listing 5.4 to simulate the tossing of a coin. Your algorithm should display the result (H for heads and T for tails) of successive tosses of the coin, terminating the display when four consecutive heads are tossed. Implement your algorithm with an 8088/8086 assembly language program. The output of your program should be different each time it is executed. The output for a given execution might look something like the following:

```
H H T H T T T H T H H T T H
                              H T T T T H H T H H H H
```

CHAPTER 6

Bit Manipulation

In assembly language programming, you often need to perform operations on individual bits. For example, the solution to Programming Exercise 4.1 requires that you determine whether an integer is odd or even. To do so, you can test that integer's least significant bit (the remainder of division by 2 yields the least significant bit of an integer) and determine whether that bit value is 1 or 0. As a second example, the PUTBIN procedure in Program Listing 5.1 isolates each bit of an 8-bit or a 16-bit integer by repeatedly dividing by 2. Each remainder represents one bit of the binary number. This technique produces the bits of a binary number in right-to-left order. To display the bits in left-to-right order, PUTBIN had to reverse them.

Bit manipulation instructions provide access to an individual bit or a group of bits in a binary number. With these instructions, a programmer can inspect, change, or make a decision based on the value of an individual bit or group of bits. This chapter discusses the two types of bit manipulation instructions available in the 8088/8086 assembly language: *shift instructions* and *logical instructions.* The chapter shows how to use these instructions to implement alternative solutions to the problems previously identified.

6.1 Shift Operations

A **shift operation** is the bit-to-bit movement of the contents of a register or memory location. Figure 6.1 depicts both a byte and a word with the individual bits numbered from right to left, according to the convention used in the IBM PC and IBM PS/2 documentation. The most significant bit (MSB) is bit 7 for a byte and bit 15 for a word. The least significant bit (LSB) is bit 0.

A 1-bit left-shift operation moves bit i to bit $i + 1$ ($14 \leq i \leq 0$ for word shifts; $6 \leq i \leq 0$ for byte shifts). The MSB is shifted into the CF bit of the flags register. The

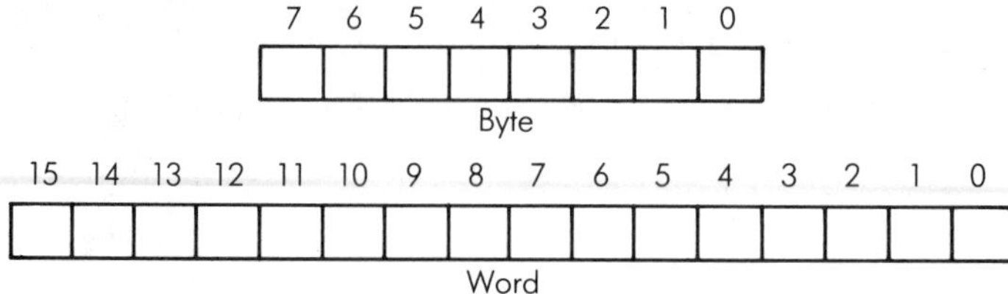

FIGURE 6.1
Byte and word with individual bits numbered

bit value that is shifted into the LSB depends on the type of shift operation. A multi-bit, left-shift operation behaves like a sequence of single-bit, left-shift operations.

A 1-bit right-shift operation moves bit i to bit $i - 1$ ($15 \leq i \leq 1$ for word shifts; $7 \leq i \leq 1$ for byte shifts). The LSB is shifted into the CF bit of the flags register. The bit value that is shifted into the MSB depends on the type of shift operation. A multibit, right-shift operation behaves like a sequence of single-bit, right-shift operations.

All shift operations affect the OF bit in the flags register in the same way. If the MSB changes with the 1-bit shift, then the OF bit in the flags register is set; otherwise, the OF bit is cleared. Since a multibit shift operation behaves like a sequence of single-bit shift operations, the OF bit in the flags register reflects a change in the MSB on the last bit shifted.

The **shift instructions** in the 8088/8086 assembly language have the following general form:

[⟨*label*⟩] ⟨*op-code*⟩ ⟨*destination*⟩,⟨*shift-count*⟩ [⟨*comment*⟩]

in which ⟨*op-code*⟩ is one of the following operation codes: SAR, SHR, ROR, RCR, SAL, SHL, ROL, or RCL; ⟨*destination*⟩ specifies the register or memory location containing the value to be shifted; and ⟨*shift-count*⟩ is either the constant 1 or the register designator CL. The constant 1 specifies a single-bit shift; the register designator CL specifies a multibit shift, with the shift count being the value in the CL-register.

Execution of a shift instruction that uses the CL-register as a shift count does *not* alter the value in the CL-register. The value is used but *not* changed.

Arithmetic Shift

There are three types of shift operations: the *arithmetic shift*, the *logical shift*, and the *rotate*. An **arithmetic shift** operation treats the operand as a signed binary number in two's complement form. The operation code for an **arithmetic right-shift** is **SAR**. With the SAR instruction, the bit value that is shifted into the MSB is a copy of the sign bit (Figure 6.2). Note in the figure that the sign bit does not change during the shift,

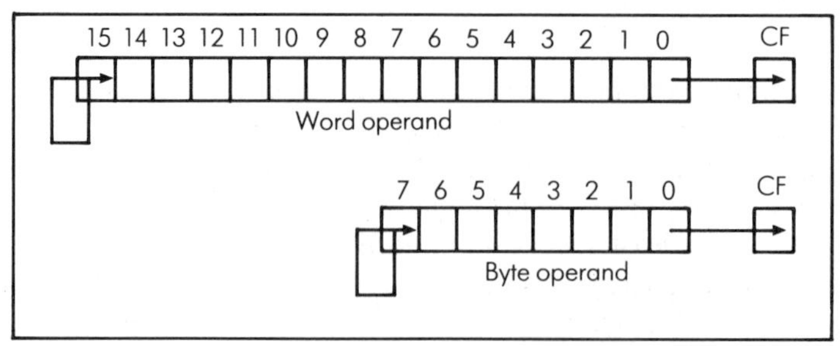

FIGURE 6.2
SAR instruction

which means that the overflow flag is always cleared by execution of the SAR instruction. The SAR instruction extends the sign bit as it shifts right. Given a signed integer value x, an arithmetic right-shift of n bits produces the signed integer value $\lfloor x/2^n \rfloor$ in which $\lfloor y \rfloor$ (read floor of y) is the greatest integer that is less than or equal to y. If y is an integer, then $\lfloor y \rfloor = y$.

EXAMPLES

			CF
Value before shift	00101000	= 40	?
After right-shift of 1	00010100	= 20 = 40/2	0
After right-shift of 2	00001010	= 10 = 40/4	0
After right-shift of 3	00000101	= 5 = 40/8	0
After right-shift of 4	00000010	= 2 = $\lfloor 40/16 \rfloor$	1

			CF
Value before shift	11011000	= −40	?
After right-shift of 1	11101100	= −20 = −40/2	0
After right-shift of 2	11110110	= −10 = −40/4	0
After right-shift of 3	11111011	= −5 = −40/8	0
After right-shift of 4	11111101	= −3 = $\lfloor -40/16 \rfloor$	1

■

The operation code for an **arithmetic left-shift** operation is **SAL**. With the SAL instruction, the bit value that is shifted into the LSB is always 0 (Figure 6.3). Given a signed integer value x, an arithmetic left-shift of n bits produces the signed integer value $x \times 2^n$.

FIGURE 6.3
SAL and SHL instructions

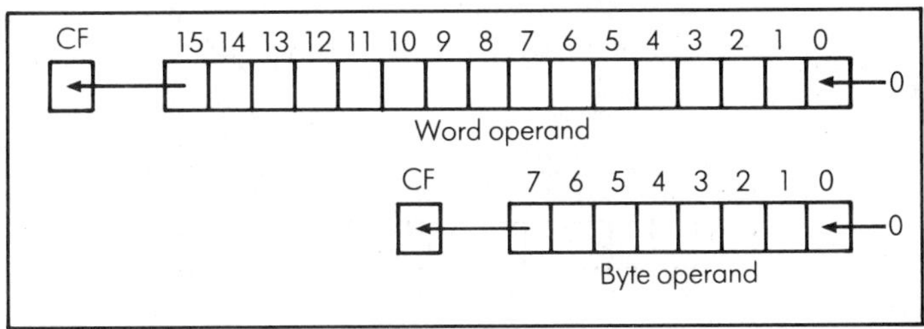

If the sign bit changes on the last bit shifted, then the OF bit in the flags register is set; otherwise, the OF bit is cleared. For an arithmetic left-shift of 1, the OF bit in the flags register is a true indication of overflow when dealing with signed two's complement integer values. For a multibit left-shift of a signed integer value, if the sign bit ever changes during the shift, then overflow has occurred. Therefore, the OF bit in the flags register is *not* a true indication of overflow when dealing with a multi-bit left-shift of a signed integer value.

EXAMPLES

	OF	CF	bit pattern	signed interpretation
Value before shift	?	?	00001010	= 10
After left-shift of 1	0	0	00010100	= 20 = 10∗2
After left-shift of 2	0	0	00101000	= 40 = 10∗4
After left-shift of 3	0	0	01010000	= 80 = 10∗8
After left-shift of 4	1	0	10100000	= overflow
After left-shift of 5	1	1	01000000	= overflow

■

The arithmetic shift operation provides an extremely efficient method for multiplying and dividing signed integer values by powers of 2. To double a signed integer value, simply perform an arithmetic left-shift of 1 bit. For signed integer values, the OF bit in the flags register will correctly reflect whether or not an overflow occurred because of the shift operation. To divide a signed integer value in half, simply perform an arithmetic right-shift of 1 bit. The CF bit in the flags register is the remainder of this division by 2.

In addition to the CF and OF bits, the arithmetic shift instructions affect the SF, ZF, AF, and PF bits in the flags register:

If the result of the shift operation has the MSB (sign bit) set, then the SF bit in the flags register is set following execution of an arithmetic shift instruction; otherwise, the SF bit is cleared.

If the result of the arithmetic shift operation is zero, then the ZF bit in the flags register is set; otherwise, the ZF bit is cleared.

The AF bit in the flags register is undefined following execution of an arithmetic shift instruction.

The PF bit in the flags register reflects the parity of the low-order 8 bits of the result of the arithmetic shift operation.

Logical Shift

A **logical shift** operation treats the operand as an unsigned integer value. The operation code for a **logical right-shift** is **SHR**. With the SHR instruction, the bit that is shifted into the MSB is always 0 (Figure 6.4). Given an unsigned integer value x, a logical right-shift of n bits produces the unsigned integer value $\lfloor x/2^n \rfloor$.

FIGURE 6.4
SHR instruction

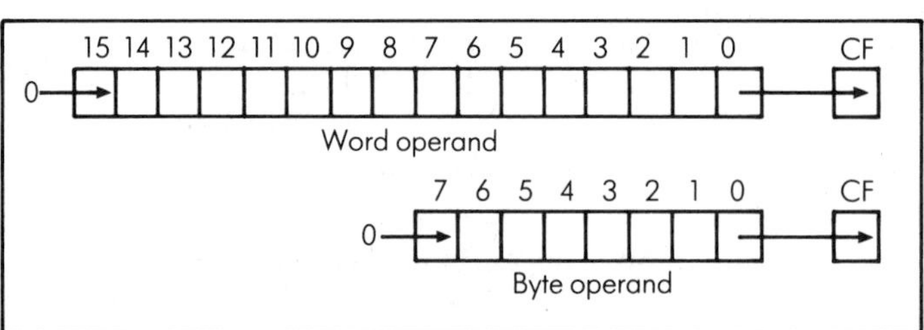

EXAMPLES

			CF
Value before shift	00101000	= 40	?
After right-shift of 1	00010100	= 20 = 40/2	0
After right-shift of 2	00001010	= 10 = 40/4	0
After right-shift of 3	00000101	= 5 = 40/8	0
After right-shift of 4	00000010	= 2 = $\lfloor 40/16 \rfloor$	1

			CF
Value before shift	11011000	= 216	?
After right-shift of 1	01101100	= 108 = 216/2	0
After right-shift of 2	00110110	= 54 = 216/4	0
After right-shift of 3	00011011	= 27 = 216/8	0
After right-shift of 4	00001101	= 13 = $\lfloor 216/16 \rfloor$	1

■

The operation code for a **logical left-shift** operation is **SHL**, which behaves exactly like the SAL instruction (Figure 6.3). In fact, SAL and SHL are two operation codes that produce exactly the same machine language instruction.

The logical shift operation provides an extremely efficient method for multiplying and dividing unsigned integer values by powers of 2. To double an unsigned integer value, simply perform a logical left-shift of 1 bit. The CF bit in the flags register will correctly reflect overflow. For a multibit left-shift of an unsigned integer value, if the CF bit in the flags register ever receives a 1 during the shift operation, even though its final value may not be a 1, then overflow has occurred. Therefore, the CF bit in the flags register is *not* a true indication of overflow in the case of the multibit left-shift of an unsigned integer.

The following example shows a sequence of single-bit, left-shift operations on an 8-bit value. Both signed and unsigned integer interpretations are given, and the effect on the OF and CF bits of the flags register is shown.

EXAMPLE

OF	CF	bit pattern	signed interpretation	unsigned interpretation
0	0	00001010	= 10	= 10
0	0	00010100	= 20 = 10*2	= 20 = 10*2
0	0	00101000	= 40 = 10*4	= 40 = 10*4
0	0	01010000	= 80 = 10*8	= 80 = 10*8
1	0	10100000	= overflow	= 160 = 10*16
1	1	01000000	= overflow	= overflow

■

To divide an unsigned integer value in half, simply perform a logical right-shift of 1 bit. The CF bit in the flags register is the remainder of this division by 2.

In addition to the CF and OF bits, the logical shift instructions affect the SF, ZF, AF, and PF bits in the flags register:

> If the result of the shift operation has the MSB set, then the SF bit in the flags register is set following execution of a logical shift instruction; otherwise, the SF bit is cleared.
>
> If the result of the logical shift operation is zero, then the ZF bit in the flags register is set; otherwise, the ZF bit is cleared.
>
> The AF bit in the flags register is undefined following execution of a logical shift instruction.
>
> The PF bit in the flags register reflects the parity of the low-order 8 bits of the result of the logical shift operation.

Rotate

A **rotate** operation treats the operand as if it were a circular collection of bits. That is, it treats the MSB as if it were physically adjacent to the LSB. Bit values shifted from one end of the operand are shifted back into the other end. The 8088/8086 assembly language has two types of rotate operations: the *straight rotate* and the *rotate-through-carry flag*.

Straight Rotate

A **straight rotate** operation treats the carry flag as if it were separate from the operand itself. The carry flag is used to record the last bit rotated from one end of the operand

and into the other end. The operation code for a **right rotate** instruction is **ROR**. With the ROR instruction, the bit value that is shifted into the MSB is the bit value that was shifted from the LSB (Figure 6.5).

FIGURE 6.5
ROR instruction

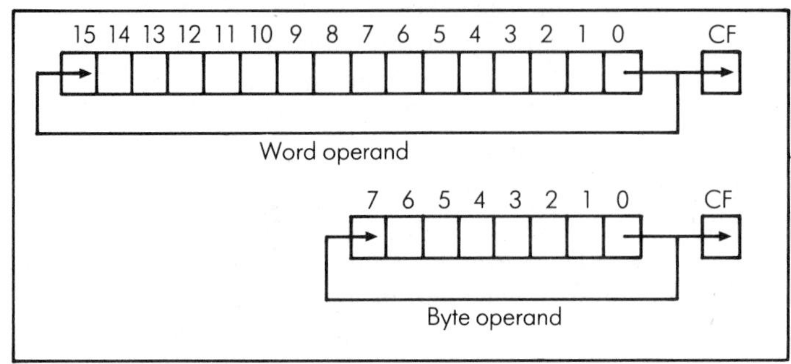

The operation code for a **left rotate** instruction is **ROL**. With the ROL instruction, the bit value that is shifted into the LSB is the bit value that was shifted from the MSB (Figure 6.6).

FIGURE 6.6
ROL instruction

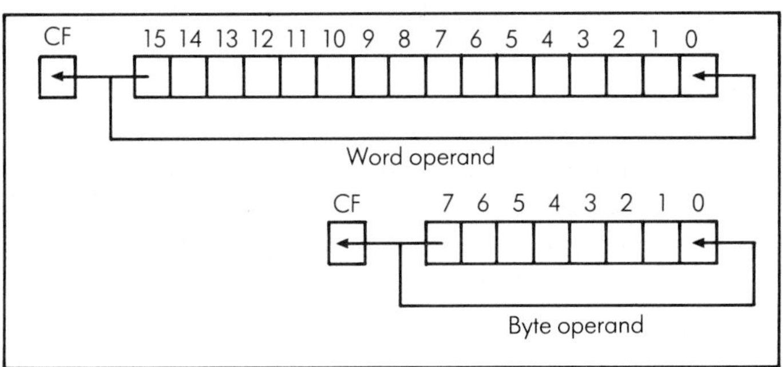

Rotate-through-Carry Flag

A **rotate-through-carry flag** operation treats the carry flag as a 1-bit extension of the operand. The carry flag is treated as a bit that lies between the MSB and the LSB of the operand. The operation code for the **right rotate-through-carry** operation is **RCR**. With the RCR instruction, the bit value that is shifted out of the LSB is shifted into the carry flag, and the bit value that is shifted from the carry flag is shifted into the MSB (Figure 6.7).

FIGURE 6.7
RCR instruction

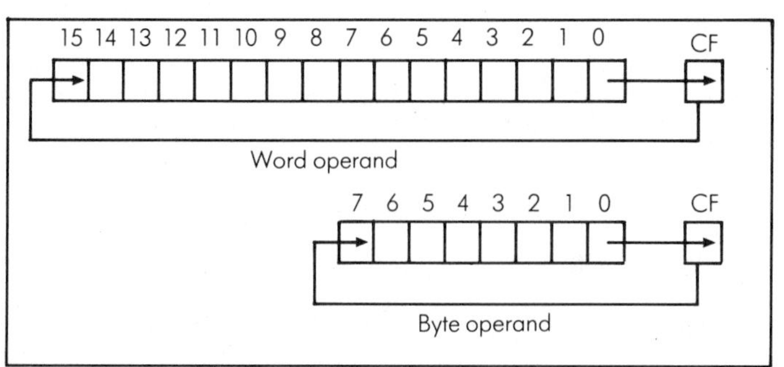

The operation code for the **left rotate-through-carry** operation is **RCL**. With the RCL instruction, the bit value that is shifted from the MSB is shifted into the carry flag, and the bit that is shifted from the carry flag is shifted into the LSB (Figure 6.8).

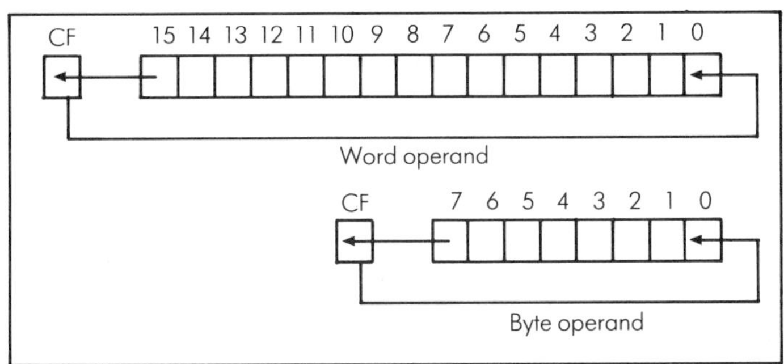

FIGURE 6.8
RCL instruction

Programming Example—Shift Instructions

Program Listing 6.1 demonstrates the various shift operations in the 8088/8086 assembly language. The program places a value in the AX-register and then moves through a sequence of shift operations. After each shift operation, a call to the PUTBIN procedure is made to display the resulting register value in binary form.

The MOV instruction in line 23 sets the display code for the PUTBIN procedure to request word output. Since the BL-register is not used for any other purpose in the program and since the BL-register value is protected by all external procedures referenced, this MOV operation has to be performed only once. That is, the BL-register value remains constant as far as this program is concerned and therefore does not have to be set up for subsequent calls to PUTBIN.

The MOV instruction in line 24 initializes the AX-register value to AAAB hexadecimal. The two CALL instructions in lines 28 and 29 then cause the value 1010101010101011 to be displayed in binary on a line by itself.

The ROL instruction in line 30, a rotate operation, shifts this value left 1 bit position; thus, the bit shifted out on the left (1) is shifted back into the vacated bit position on the right. The bit rotated out on the left and back in on the right (1) is also recorded in the CF bit of the flags register. The two CALL instructions in lines 34 and 35 display the resulting value, 0101010101010111, by itself on the next line of the display screen.

The MOV instruction in line 36 sets the CL-register to 3 in preparation for a 3-bit shift operation. The ROR instruction in line 37, a rotate operation, shifts the value in the AX-register right 3 bit positions; thus, the three bits shifted out on the right (111) are shifted back into the vacated bit positions on the left. The last bit rotated out on the right and back in on the left (1) is also recorded in the CF bit of the flags register. The resulting value in the AX-register, 1110101010101010, is displayed by itself on the next line of the display screen (lines 41 and 42).

The SAR instruction in line 43, an arithmetic right-shift operation, shifts this value right 1 bit position; thus, the bit shifted out on the right (0) is recorded in the CF bit of the flags register, and a copy of the sign bit (1) is shifted into the vacated bit position on the left. The resulting value in the AX-register, 1111010101010101, is displayed by itself on the next line of the display screen (lines 47 and 48).

Since the value in the CL-register is still 3, the SAL instruction in line 49, an arithmetic left-shift operation, shifts the value in the AX-register left 3 bit positions;

```
        PAGE    80,132
;====================================================================
;                   PROGRAM LISTING 6.1
;
;PROGRAM TO DEMONSTRATE SHIFT AND ROTATE INSTRUCTIONS
;
;====================================================================
        .MODEL  SMALL,BASIC
;====================================================================
                                        ;PROCEDURES TO
        EXTRN   NEWLINE:FAR             ;DISPLAY NEWLINE CHARACTER
        EXTRN   PUTBIN:FAR              ;DISPLAY BINARY INTEGER
;====================================================================
; S T A C K   D E F I N I T I O N
;
        .STACK  256
;
;====================================================================
; C O D E   S E G M E N T   D E F I N I T I O N
;
        .CODE   EX_6_1
        .STARTUP                        ;GENERATE STARTUP CODE
        MOV     BL,1                    ;DISPLAY CODE - WORD OUTPUT
        MOV     AX,0AAABH               ;LOAD AX WITH
                                        ;
                                        ;1010101010101011
                                        ;
        CALL    PUTBIN                  ;DISPLAY CONTENTS OF AX
        CALL    NEWLINE                 ;DISPLAY NEWLINE CHARACTER
        ROL     AX,1                    ;LEFT ROTATE AX 1 GIVING
                                        ;
                                        ;0101010101010111
                                        ;
        CALL    PUTBIN                  ;DISPLAY CONTENTS OF AX
        CALL    NEWLINE                 ;DISPLAY NEWLINE CHARACTER
        MOV     CL,3                    ;MOVE SHIFT COUNT TO CL
        ROR     AX,CL                   ;RIGHT ROTATE AX 3 GIVING
                                        ;
                                        ;1110101010101010
                                        ;
        CALL    PUTBIN                  ;DISPLAY CONTENTS OF AX
        CALL    NEWLINE                 ;DISPLAY NEWLINE CHARACTER
        SAR     AX,1                    ;ARITH SHIFT RIGHT 1 GIVING
                                        ;
                                        ;1111010101010101
                                        ;
        CALL    PUTBIN                  ;DISPLAY CONTENTS OF AX
        CALL    NEWLINE                 ;DISPLAY NEWLINE CHARACTER
        SAL     AX,CL                   ;ARITH SHIFT LEFT 3 GIVING
                                        ;
                                        ;1010101010101000
                                        ;
        CALL    PUTBIN                  ;DISPLAY CONTENTS OF AX
        CALL    NEWLINE                 ;DISPLAY NEWLINE CHARACTER
;
;
        MOV     CL,2                    ;MOVE SHIFT COUNT TO CL
        SHR     AX,CL                   ;LOG. SHIFT RIGHT 2 GIVING
                                        ;
                                        ;0010101010101010
                                        ;
        CALL    PUTBIN                  ;DISPLAY CONTENTS OF AX
        CALL    NEWLINE                 ;DISPLAY NEWLINE
        MOV     CL,3                    ;MOVE SHIFT COUNT TO CL
        SHL     AX,CL                   ;LOG.SHIFT LEFT 3 GIVING
                                        ;
                                        ;0101010101010000
```

```
 68:                                                ;
 69:                                                ;AND CARRY FLAG = 1
 70:            CALL    PUTBIN                      ;DISPLAY CONTENTS OF AX
 71:            CALL    NEWLINE                     ;DISPLAY NEWLINE CHARACTER
 72:            RCL     AX,1                        ;LEFT ROTATE AX 1 THROUGH
 73:                                                ;CARRY GIVING
 74:                                                ;
 75:                                                ;1010101010100001
 76:                                                ;
 77:                                                ;AND CARRY FLAG = 0
 78:            CALL    PUTBIN                      ;DISPLAY CONTENTS OF AX
 79:            CALL    NEWLINE                     ;DISPLAY NEWLINE CHARACTER
 80:            MOV     CL,2
 81:            RCR     AX,CL                       ;RIGHT ROTATE AX 2 THROUGH
 82:                                                ;CARRY GIVING
 83:                                                ;
 84:                                                ;1010101010101000
 85:                                                ;
 86:            CALL    PUTBIN                      ;DISPLAY CONTENTS OF AX
 87:            CALL    NEWLINE                     ;DISPLAY NEWLINE CHARACTER
 88:            MOV     CL,4                        ;MOVE SHIFT COUNT TO CL
 89:            SAR     AL,CL                       ;ARITH RIGHT SHIFT AL 4 GIVING
 90:                                                ;
 91:                                                ;1010101011111010
 92:                                                ;
 93:            CALL    PUTBIN                      ;DISPLAY CONTENTS OF AX
 94:            CALL    NEWLINE                     ;DISPLAY NEWLINE CHARACTER
 95:            ROL     AL,CL                       ;LEFT ROTATE AL 4 GIVING
 96:                                                ;
 97:                                                ;1010101010101111
 98:                                                ;
 99:            CALL    PUTBIN                      ;DISPLAY CONTENTS OF AX
100:            CALL    NEWLINE                     ;DISPLAY NEWLINE CHARACTER
101:            .EXIT                               ;RETURN TO DOS
102: ;
103:            END
```

thus, the three bits (111) shifted out on the left are lost—except for the last bit (1), which is recorded in the CF bit of the flags register—and zeros are shifted into the vacated bit positions on the right. The resulting value in the AX-register, 1010101010101000, is displayed by itself on the next line of the display screen (lines 53 and 54).

The MOV instruction in line 57 sets the CL-register to 2 in preparation for a 2-bit shift operation. The SHR instruction in line 58, a logical right-shift operation, shifts the value in the AX-register right 2 bit positions; thus, the first zero shifted out on the right is lost, the second zero shifted out on the right is recorded in the CF bit of the flags register, and zeros are shifted into the vacated bit positions on the left. The resulting value in the AX-register, 0010101010101010, is displayed by itself on the next line of the display screen (lines 62 and 63).

The MOV instruction in line 64 sets the CL-register to 3 in preparation for a 3-bit shift operation. The SHL instruction in line 65, a logical left-shift operation, shifts the value in the AX-register left 3 bit positions; thus, the three bits (001) shifted out on the left are lost—except for the last bit (1), which is recorded in the CF bit of the flags register—and zeros are shifted into the vacated bit positions on the right. The resulting value in the AX-register, 0101010101010000, is displayed by itself on the next line of the display screen (lines 70 and 71).

Since the last bit shifted out on the previous shift operation (line 65) was a 1 and since PUTBIN and NEWLINE save and restore the flags register for the caller, the value in the CF bit of the flags register is a 1 just prior to execution of the RCL instruction in line 72. This instruction, a rotate-through-carry operation, shifts the value in the AX-register left 1 bit position; thus, the value in the CF bit of the flags register (1) is shifted into the vacated bit position on the right, and the bit shifted out on the left (0) is recorded in the CF bit of the flags register. The resulting value in the AX-register, 1010101010100001, is displayed by itself on the next line of the display screen (lines 78 and 79).

The MOV instruction in line 80 sets the CL-register to 2 in preparation for a 2-bit shift operation. The CF bit in the flags register is zero, the result of the previous shift operation. The RCR instruction in line 81 shifts the value in the AX-register (extended to include the CF bit of the flags register) right 2 bit positions. The 17-bit value being shifted is 0 1010101010100001. Since this is a rotate operation, the two bits rotated out on the right (01) are rotated into the vacated bit positions on the left. (The 1 goes into bit 15 of the AX-register, and the 0 goes into the CF bit of the flags register.) The resulting value in the AX-register, 1010101010101000, is displayed by itself on the next line of the display screen (lines 86 and 87).

The MOV instruction in line 88 sets the CL-register to 4 in preparation for a 4-bit shift operation. The SAR instruction in line 89, an arithmetic right-shift operation, shifts the value in the AL-register right 4 bit positions; thus, the last bit (1) of the 1000 shifted out on the right is recorded in the CF bit of the flags register, and a copy of the sign bit (1) is copied into the 4 vacated bit positions on the left. Since this is an AL-register shift, the value in the AH-register is unchanged by execution of this instruction. The resulting value in the AX-register, 1010101011111010, is displayed by itself on the next line of the display screen (lines 93 and 94).

The ROL instruction in line 95, a rotate operation, shifts the value in the AL-register left 4 bit positions; thus, the four bits rotated out on the left (1111) are rotated back into the vacated bit positions on the right. The last bit rotated out on the left and back in on the right (1) is also recorded in the CF bit of the flags register. Since this is a shift of the AL-register, the AH-register is not changed by execution of this instruction. The resulting value in the AX-register, 1010101010101111, is displayed by itself on the next line of the display screen (lines 99 and 100).

The complete output for this program is as follows:

```
1010101010101011
0101010101010111
1110101010101010
1111010101010101
1010101010101000
0010101010101010
0101010101010000
1010101010100001
1010101010101000
1010101011111010
1010101010101111
```

To see this program's operation more vividly, especially with regard to the setting of the CF bit of the flags register, trace its execution using the DEBUG or the CodeView utility program.

6.2 Logical Operations

The **logical operations** treat each bit of an operand as a **Boolean value**. A bit value of 0 represents the Boolean value False, and a bit value of 1 represents the Boolean value

True. In the 8088/8086 assembly language, the logical instructions provide the Boolean operations AND, inclusive OR, exclusive OR, and NOT.

The AND operation is provided by the **AND instruction**, which has the following general form:

[<*label*>] AND <*destination*>,<*source*> [<*comment*>]

Execution of an AND instruction ANDs each bit of the destination operand with the corresponding bit of the source operand, replacing that bit in the destination operand with the result. Table 6.1 is a truth table that defines the AND operation.

Figure 6.9 shows the possible combinations of destination and source operands for the AND instruction. If the destination operand is a general register, then the source operand can be either a general register, a memory location, or an immediate value. If the destination operand is a memory location, then the source operand can be either a general register or an immediate value. The types of the two operands must match (i.e., both must be byte, or both must be word).

TABLE 6.1
Definition of the AND operation

Source Bit	Destination Bit	AND
0	0	0
0	1	0
1	0	0
1	1	1

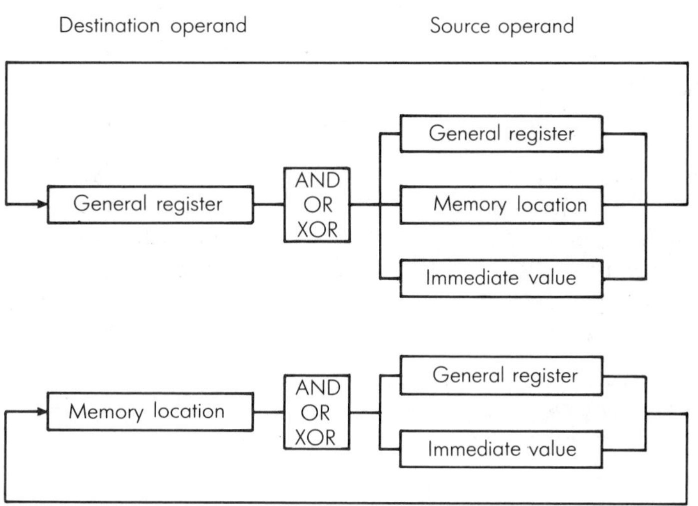

FIGURE 6.9
Allowable operands for AND, OR, and XOR instructions

EXAMPLE

AND AL,BL
AND each bit in the AL-register with the corresponding bit in the BL-register, leaving the result in that bit of the AL-register:

00110011	AL-register before execution of AND
01010101	BL-register
00010001	AL-register after execution of AND

■

The inclusive OR operation is provided by the **OR instruction**, which has the following general form:

[⟨*label*⟩] `OR` ⟨*destination*⟩,⟨*source*⟩ [⟨*comment*⟩]

Execution of an OR instruction performs the inclusive OR of each bit of the destination operand with the corresponding bit of the source operand, replacing that bit in the destination operand with the result. Table 6.2 is a truth table that defines the inclusive OR operation. Figure 6.9 also shows the possible combinations of destination and source operands for the OR operation. The types of the two operands must match (i.e., both must be byte, or both must be word).

TABLE 6.2
Definition of the OR operation

Source Bit	Destination Bit	OR
0	0	0
0	1	1
1	0	1
1	1	1

EXAMPLE

OR AL,55H
OR each bit in the AL-register with the corresponding bit in the immediate value 01010101, leaving the result in that bit of the AL-register:

00110011 AL-register before execution of OR
01010101 Immediate operand
01110111 AL-register after execution of OR ■

The exclusive OR operation is provided by the **XOR instruction**, which has the following general form:

[⟨*label*⟩] `XOR` ⟨*destination*⟩,⟨*source*⟩ [⟨*comment*⟩]

Execution of an XOR instruction performs the exclusive OR of each bit of the destination operand with the corresponding bit of the source operand, replacing that bit in the destination operand with the result. Table 6.3 is a truth table that defines the exclusive OR operation. Figure 6.9 also shows the possible combinations of destination and source operands for the XOR operation. The types of the two operands must match (i.e., both must be byte, or both must be word).

TABLE 6.3
Definition of the XOR operation

Source Bit	Destination Bit	XOR
0	0	0
0	1	1
1	0	1
1	1	0

EXAMPLE

XOR AL,33H
Exclusive OR each bit in the AL-register with the corresponding bit in the immediate value 00110011, leaving the result in that bit of the AL-register:

01010101 AL-register before execution of XOR
00110011 Immediate operand
01100110 AL-register after execution of XOR ■

The AND, OR, and XOR instructions affect the OF, SF, ZF, AF, PF, and CF bits of the flags register:

> The OF bit in the flags register is cleared by the execution of an AND, OR, or XOR instruction.
>
> If the result of the logical operation has the MSB set, then the SF bit in the flags register is set; otherwise, the SF bit is cleared.
>
> If the result of the logical operation is zero, then the ZF bit in the flags register is set; otherwise, the ZF bit is cleared.
>
> The AF bit in the flags register is undefined following execution of an AND, OR, or XOR instruction.
>
> If the low-order 8 bits of the result of the logical operation have an even number of 1 bits, then the PF bit in the flags register is set; otherwise, the PF bit is cleared.
>
> The CF bit in the flags register is cleared by execution of an AND, OR, or XOR instruction.

The AND operation is frequently used to isolate a bit or group of bits (i.e., to clear out the bits that are not needed). The OR operation is frequently used to set certain bits or to merge bits together.

EXAMPLE

Suppose the byte value in the variable COUNTS represents two 4-bit mod 16 counters. A mod 16 counter is one that counts from 0 to 15 and back to 0 again, producing the following sequence of binary counts:

```
0000
0001
0010
0011
  .
  .
  .
1101
1110
1111
0000
0001
0010
0011
  .
  .
  .
```

The following sequence of instructions will increment the counter in the low-order 4 bits (right nibble), leaving the counter in the high-order 4 bits (left nibble) unchanged:

```
MOV  AL,COUNTS
INC  AL
AND  AL,0FH
AND  COUNTS,0F0H
OR   COUNTS,AL
```

The first instruction moves a copy of the two counters into the AL-register. The second instruction increments the counter in the right nibble of the AL-register, which may cause an overflow into the counter in the left nibble of the AL-register, but the counter in the right nibble has been correctly incremented in a mod 16 fashion. The third instruction clears the left nibble of the AL-register, which now has its left nibble clear, and its right nibble contains the incremented low-order counter. The fourth instruction clears the counter in the right nibble of the variable COUNTS, which now has its right nibble clear, and its left nibble has the high-order counter unchanged. The last instruction merges the two counters into the two nibbles of the variable COUNTS.

Traces of this instruction sequence for two initial values of COUNTS are given:

```
                  COUNTS      AL-register
                  0110 0101
MOV AL,COUNTS     0110 0101   0110 0101
INC AL            0110 0101   0110 0110
AND AL,0FH        0110 0101   0000 0110
AND COUNTS,0F0H   0110 0000   0000 0110
OR  COUNTS,AL     0110 0110   0000 0110

                  COUNTS      AL-register
                  0011 1111
MOV AL,COUNTS     0011 1111   0011 1111
INC AL            0011 1111   0100 0000
AND AL,0FH        0011 1111   0000 0000
AND COUNTS,0F0H   0011 0000   0000 0000
OR  COUNTS,AL     0011 0000   0000 0000
```

■

The NOT operation is provided by the **NOT instruction**, which has the following general form:

[⟨*label*⟩] NOT ⟨*destination*⟩ [⟨*comment*⟩]

Execution of the NOT instruction inverts each bit of the destination operand, thus performing the one's complement operation. Table 6.4 is a truth table that defines the NOT operation. The destination operand can be either a general register or a memory location, and it can be either byte or word. None of the flags are affected by execution of this instruction.

TABLE 6.4 Definition of the NOT operation

Destination Bit	NOT
0	1
1	0

EXAMPLE

NOT AL

Invert each bit in the AL-register:

00110101	AL-register before execution of NOT
11001010	AL-register after execution of NOT

■

The NOT operation inverts every bit of a bit pattern. The XOR instruction can be used to invert certain bits of a bit pattern.

EXAMPLE

Suppose the PF bit in the flags register is to be inverted. The following instructions invert the PF bit, leaving the other flag bits unchanged:

```
PUSHF
POP    AX
XOR    AX,0004H
PUSH   AX
POPF
```

The first two instructions copy the flags register into the AX-register. The third instruction inverts bit 2 of the AX-register. Bit 2 of the flags register is the PF bit. The last two instructions copy the modified flags from the AX-register to the flags register. ■

The AND operation can be used to test a single bit to see if it is set. For example, to determine whether an integer is odd or even, a test of the least significant bit (LSB) can be made: If the LSB is 1, then the integer is odd; if the LSB is 0, then the integer is even. To determine whether the value in the AX-register is odd or even, the following instructions can be used:

```
AND  AX,0001
JZ   EVEN
```

If the jump is taken, then the number that was in the AX-register just before execution of the AND instruction was even; if the jump is *not* taken, then that number was odd. The value in the AX-register is modified by execution of the AND instruction. However, that value may be needed in one or both decision alternatives.

The 8088/8086 assembly language provides a bit test instruction, the **TEST instruction**, that behaves like the AND instruction except that the destination operand is not modified (i.e., the result is not saved). This instruction has the following general form:

[〈*label*〉] TEST 〈*destination*〉,〈*source*〉 [〈*comment*〉]

Execution of a TEST instruction ANDs each bit of the destination operand with the corresponding bit of the source operand and sets the flags to reflect the result. Neither the source operand nor the destination operand is modified. Note that the TEST instruction relates to the AND instruction in the same way that the CMP instruction relates to the SUB instruction.

Figure 6.10 shows the possible combinations of destination and source oper-

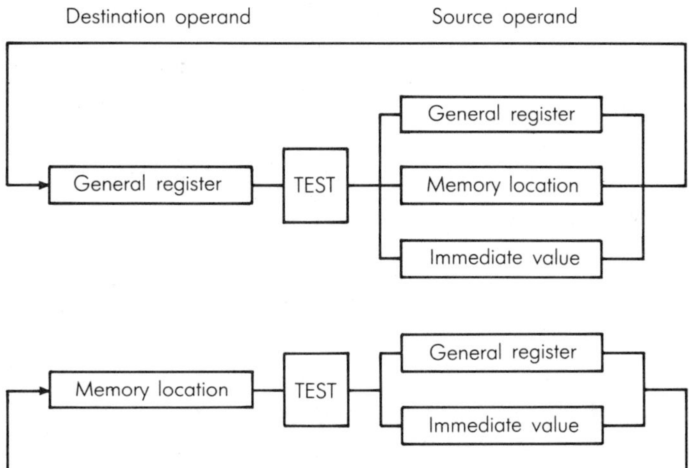

FIGURE 6.10
Allowable operands for the TEST instruction

ands for the TEST instruction. If the destination operand is a general register, then the source operand can be either a general register, a memory location, or an immediate value. If the destination operand is a memory location, then the source operand can be either a general register or an immediate value. The types of the two operands must match (i.e., both must be byte, or both must be word). The bits of the flags register are affected in exactly the same way as they are for the AND instruction.

EXAMPLE

To test the value in the AX-register to determine whether it is odd or even, without changing this value, the following instructions can be used:

```
TEST  AX,0001
JZ    EVEN
```

If the jump is taken, then the value in the AX-register is even; if the jump is *not* taken, then the value in the AX-register is odd. In either case, the value in the AX-register is not modified by this decision. ■

Programming Example—Logical Instructions

Program Listing 6.2 demonstrates the various logical operations in the 8088/8086 assembly language. The program places a value in the AX-register and then goes through a sequence of logical operations, each involving the AX-register. After each logical operation, a call to the PUTBIN procedure is made to display the resulting value in binary form.

The MOV instruction in line 23 sets the display code for the PUTBIN procedure to request word output. This value remains in the BL-register throughout program execution and does not have to be re-established prior to each call to PUTBIN.

The MOV instruction in line 25 initializes the AX-register value to 5555 hexadecimal. The two CALL instructions in lines 27 and 28 then cause the value 0101010101010101 to be displayed on a line by itself.

The MOV instruction in line 30 loads the CX-register with the value 3F3F hexadecimal, which is 0011111100111111 in binary. The AND instruction in line 31 ANDs the AX-register value with the CX-register value, leaving the result in the AX-register. The operation performed is shown as follows:

AX-register	0101010101010101
AND CX-register	0011111100111111
AX-register	0001010100010101

The two CALL instructions in lines 34 and 35 then cause the resulting value, 0001010100010101, to be displayed on a line by itself.

The OR instruction in line 37 ORs the AX-register value with the immediate value 4343 hexadecimal, which is 0100001101000011 in binary, leaving the result in the AX-register. The operation performed is shown as follows:

AX-register	0001010100010101
OR immediate	0100001101000011
AX-register	0101011101010111

The two CALL instructions in lines 40 and 41 then cause the resulting value, 0101011101010111, to be displayed on a line by itself.

The XOR instruction in line 43 performs the bit-by-bit exclusive OR of the

```
          PAGE    80,132
;====================================================================
;                 PROGRAM LISTING 6.2
;
; PROGRAM TO DEMONSTRATE LOGICAL INSTRUCTIONS
;
;====================================================================
          .MODEL  SMALL,BASIC
;====================================================================
                                        ;PROCEDURES TO
          EXTRN   NEWLINE:FAR           ;DISPLAY NEWLINE CHARACTER
          EXTRN   PUTBIN:FAR            ;DISPLAY BINARY NUMBERS
;====================================================================
; S T A C K   D E F I N I T I O N
;
          .STACK  256
;
;====================================================================
; C O D E   S E G M E N T   D E F I N I T I O N
;
          .CODE   EX_6_2
          .STARTUP                      ;GENERATE STARTUP CODE
          MOV     BL,1                  ;MOVE CODE FOR WORD OUTPUT TO BL
                                        ;
          MOV     AX,5555H              ;LOAD AX WITH 0101010101010101
                                        ;
          CALL    PUTBIN                ;DISPLAY CONTENTS OF AX
          CALL    NEWLINE               ;SKIP TO NEXT LINE
                                        ;
          MOV     CX,3F3FH              ;LOAD CX WITH 0011111100111111
          AND     AX,CX                 ;AND AX WITH CX
                                        ;GIVING       0001010100010101
                                        ;
          CALL    PUTBIN                ;DISPLAY CONTENTS OF AX
          CALL    NEWLINE               ;SKIP TO NEXT LINE
                                        ;
          OR      AX,4343H              ;OR AX WITH   0100001101000011
                                        ;GIVING       0101011101010111
                                        ;
          CALL    PUTBIN                ;DISPLAY CONTENTS OF AX
          CALL    NEWLINE               ;SKIP TO NEXT LINE
                                        ;
          XOR     AX,33CCH              ;EXCLUSIVE OR AX WITH
                                        ;
                                        ;             0011001111001100
                                        ;GIVING       0110010010011011
                                        ;
          CALL    PUTBIN                ;DISPLAY CONTENTS OF AX
          CALL    NEWLINE               ;SKIP TO NEXT LINE
                                        ;
          NOT     AX                    ;TAKE 1'S COMPLEMENT OF AX
                                        ;GIVING       1001101101100100
                                        ;
          CALL    PUTBIN                ;DISPLAY CONTENTS OF AX
          CALL    NEWLINE               ;SKIP TO NEXT LINE
                                        ;
          OR      AH,AL                 ;OR AH WITH AL
                                        ;GIVING       1111111101100100
                                        ;
          CALL    PUTBIN                ;DISPLAY CONTENTS OF AX
          CALL    NEWLINE               ;SKIP TO NEXT LINE
          .EXIT                         ;RETURN TO DOS
;
          END
```

AX-register value with the immediate value 33CC hexadecimal, which reads 0011001111001100 in binary, leaving the result in the AX-register. The operation performed is shown as follows:

AX-register	0101011101010111
XOR immediate	0011001111001100
AX-register	0110010010011011

The two CALL instructions in lines 48 and 49 then cause the resulting value, 0110010010011011, to be displayed on a line by itself.

The NOT instruction in line 51 inverts every bit of the value in the AX-register, leaving the result, 1001101101100100, in the AX-register. The two CALL instructions in lines 54 and 55 cause the resulting value, 1001101101100100, to be displayed on a line by itself.

The OR instruction in line 57 ORs the AH-register value with the AL-register value, leaving the result in the AH-register. The AL-register value is not modified by execution of this instruction. The operation performed is shown as follows:

AH-register	10011011
OR AL-register	01100100
AH-register	11111111

The two CALL instructions in lines 60 and 61 cause the entire AX-register value, 1111111101100100, to be displayed on a line by itself.

The complete output for this program is as follows:

```
0101010101010101
0001010100010101
0101011101010111
0110010010011011
1001101101100100
1111111101100100
```

To see this program's operation more vividly, trace its execution using the DEBUG or the CodeView utility program.

6.3 Flag Bit Operations

Some applications require direct manipulation of certain bits in the flags register. As will be seen in Chapter 8, a group of 8088/8086 assembly language instructions (string instructions) automatically update an index register to address the next (or previous) character in a string or element in an array. The DF bit in the flags register is used to determine whether this automatic update is an increment or a decrement to the next character or array element. Therefore, the program must be able to set or clear the DF bit in the flags register directly.

As will be seen in Chapter 9, the IF bit in the flags register indicates whether or not external interrupts are enabled. Interrupt service procedures and input/output procedures must be able to set or clear the IF bit in the flags register directly.

Seven instructions provide for direct manipulation of bits in the flags register, and they have the following general form:

[⟨*label*⟩] ⟨*op-code*⟩ [⟨*comment*⟩]

in which ⟨*op-code*⟩ is one of the following seven operation codes: CMC, CLC, CLD, CLI, STC, STD, or STI.

The **CMC instruction** complements the CF bit of the flags register.
The **CLC instruction** clears the CF bit in the flags register.
The **STC instruction** sets the CF bit in the flags register.
The **CLD instruction** clears the DF bit in the flags register.
The **STD instruction** sets the DF bit in the flags register.
The **CLI instruction** clears the IF bit in the flags register.
The **STI instruction** sets the IF bit in the flags register.

Only the indicated flag bit is affected by execution of one of these instructions. All other bits in the flags register remain unchanged.

To manipulate any of the other bits in the flags register, the flags register value must first be loaded into one of the general registers. The flags register value can be copied into the AX-register with the following sequence of instructions:

```
PUSHF
POP    AX
```

Once the flags register value has been copied into one of the general registers, the individual bits of this copy can be manipulated using shift and logical instructions. For example, the AND instruction is used to clear some bits while protecting the others; the OR instruction is used to set some bits while protecting the others; the XOR instruction is used to toggle some bits while protecting the others. See Table 6.5 for a summary of these operations. The modified copy of the flags register can then be copied back to the flags register, replacing the previous value of the flags register. The AX-register value can be copied into the flags register with the following sequence of instructions:

```
PUSH  AX
POPF
```

TABLE 6.5
Bit manipulations

Operation	Result	Explanation
x AND 0	0	AND with 0 to clear a bit
x AND 1	*x*	AND with 1 to copy a bit
x OR 0	*x*	OR with 0 to copy a bit
x OR 1	1	OR with 1 to set a bit
x XOR 0	*x*	XOR with 0 to copy a bit
x XOR 1	NOT *x*	XOR with 1 to toggle a bit

The 8088/8086 assembly language provides two additional instructions for moving values between the flags register and the accumulator register (AX-register), the **LAHF** and **SAHF instructions**, which have the following general forms:

[⟨*label*⟩] LAHF [⟨*comment*⟩]
[⟨*label*⟩] SAHF [⟨*comment*⟩]

The LAHF instruction loads the AH-register with a copy of the value in the low-order half of the flags register, which is diagrammed in Figure 6.11. The SAHF instruction copies the AH-register value into the low-order half of the flags register.

These two instructions are provided in the Intel 8088/8086 machine language for compatibility with the Intel 8085/8080 microprocessors. They are not very useful for beginning 8088/8086 assembly language programmers.

FIGURE 6.11
Low-order half of flags register

7	6	5	4	3	2	1	0
SF	ZF		AF		PF		CF

In most of the example programs of the previous chapters, the stack segment was defined to be a FAR segment, and this stack type was specified via the FARSTACK option in the .MODEL pseudo-operation. In the assembly modules of Program Listings 6.1 and 6.2, the FARSTACK option is omitted from the .MODEL pseudo-operation (see line 8 of each listing). Without the FARSTACK option, the stack segment is implicitly defined to be a NEAR segment. A NEAR stack segment is combined with the other segments of the group DGROUP. The code generated by the assembler in response to the .STARTUP pseudo-operation includes the code that adjusts the SS:SP register pair so that the SS-register contains the origin of DGROUP and the SP-register is relative to this origin. The following code is generated in response to the .STARTUP pseudo-operation:

```
mov  dx, DGROUP
mov  ds, dx
mov  bx, ss
sub  bx, dx
shl  bx, 001h
shl  bx, 001h
shl  bx, 001h
shl  bx, 001h
cli
mov  ss, dx
add  sp, bx
sti
```

This generated code illustrates the flag bit operations CLI and STI as well as the use of a shift instruction.

The two instructions

```
mov  dx, DGROUP
mov  ds, dx
```

set the DS-register to address the origin of DGROUP. The SS:SP register pair has already been initialized as if it were going to be a FAR segment immediately following DGROUP. (This initialization was performed by DOS prior to placing the program into execution.) For the sake of this discussion, suppose that DGROUP begins at location 1A28:0000 (1A280) hexadecimal and that the stack segment begins at location 1A4B:0000 (1A4B0) hexadecimal. Therefore, the DS-register (and also the DX-register) now contains 1A28, and the SS-register contains 1A4B. For a 256-byte stack, the SP-register would contain 0100 hexadecimal; therefore, the SS:SP register pair would address location 1A4B:0100 (1A5B0). The instructions

```
mov  bx, ss
sub  bx, dx
```

set the BX-register to the difference between the origin of the stack segment and the origin of DGROUP. Using the register values given previously, the BX-register would contain 0023 hexadecimal (1A4B − 1A28). Because this value was computed from two segment register values, it is the high-order 16 bits of the 20-bit address difference between the origin of the stack segment and the origin of DGROUP. To expand this high-order 16 bits of the address difference to the correct 20-bit address difference, the value can be shifted left 4 bit positions, replacing the vacated bits with zeros. This task is accomplished by the four shl instructions:

```
shl  bx, 001h
shl  bx, 001h
shl  bx, 001h
shl  bx, 001h
```

Note the hexadecimal form used for the shift count in these instructions. This form is used by the assembler in the instructions that it generates. With the values being assumed, this 4-bit shift would leave the value 0230 hexadecimal in the BX-register. The instruction

```
mov  ss, dx
```

moves the origin of DGROUP (1A28 in this example) into the SS-register, and the instruction

```
add  sp, bx
```

adds the 20-bit address difference (0230 hexadecimal) to the SP-register value (0100 hexadecimal), which adjusts the SP-register value to be relative to the origin of DGROUP. With the values being assumed, this addition would leave the value 0330 hexadecimal in the SP-register. The SS:SP register pair still specifies the address 1A5B0 (1A280 + 0330), but the SP-register value, which is now 0330, is relative to a different segment origin, 1A28. Note that the instructions

```
mov  ss, dx
add  sp, bx
```

are surrounded by the instructions CLI and STI. These two instructions ensure that the MOV and ADD instructions will be executed without external interrupt. The need for these two instructions is discussed in Chapter 9.

6.4 Programming Example—Display Binary Integer (PUTBIN, Version 2)

Program Listing 6.3 shows an external procedure called PUT_BIN that displays an 8-bit or a 16-bit integer in binary form. From a functional standpoint, this procedure behaves exactly like the external subprocedure in Program Listing 5.3. It accepts a code in the BL-register that specifies whether 8-bit (BL = 0) or 16-bit (BL ≠ 0) output is desired. It also accepts the value to be displayed in either the AL-register (8-bit display) or the AX-register (16-bit display). It displays the input value in binary form on the screen beginning at the current cursor position.

This version of the PUT_BIN procedure implements an algorithm different from the version in Program Listing 5.3. The previous version repeatedly divides by 2, saving the remainder each time until either 8 or 16 remainders have been produced. The remainders (0s and 1s) are displayed in the reverse order from which they are produced. The version in Program Listing 6.3 tests each individual bit of the input value, displaying a 1 if the bit is set and a 0 if the bit is not set.

Except for the algorithm itself, Program Listing 6.3 looks like Program Listing 5.3, and this discussion thus concentrates on the algorithm being implemented. The double-alternative decision structure in lines 25–33 tests the input code in the BL-register (line 25). If the BL-register value is 0 (byte output), then the value to be

```
 1:               PAGE     80,132
 2: ;=====================================================================
 3: ;                      PROGRAM LISTING 6.3
 4: ;
 5: ; PROCEDURE TO DISPLAY AN 8- OR 16-BIT VALUE IN BINARY FORM
 6: ;
 7: ; INPUT:   AL-REG   8-BIT  VALUE TO BE DIAPLAYED
 8: ;          BL=0     CODE FOR  8-BIT DISPLAY
 9: ;                OR
10: ;          AX-REG   16-BIT VALUE TO BE DISPLAYED
11: ;          BL<>0    CODE FOR 16-BIT DISPLAY
12: ;
13: ; OUTPUT:  INPUT VALUE DISPLAYED IN BINARY FORM ON THE
14: ;          SCREEN BEGINNING AT CURRENT CURSOR POSITION
15: ;=====================================================================
16:               .MODEL   SMALL,BASIC
17: ;=====================================================================
18:                                          ;PROCEDURE TO
19:               EXTRN    PUTDEC:FAR        ;DISPLAY DECIMAL INTEGER
20: ;=====================================================================
21:               .CODE    EX_6_3
22: PUT_BIN       PROC     FAR PUBLIC USES AX BX CX DX
23:                                       ;PROCEDURE PUT_BIN(NUMBER,CODE)
24:               PUSHF                      ;SAVE FLAGS
25:               .IF      BL == 0           ;IF    CODE = BYTE (BL=0)
26: ;
27:               MOV      CL,8              ;THEN LEFT JUSTIFY 8-BIT NUMBER
28:               SHL      AX,CL             ;      IN 16-BIT AX-REGISTER
29:               MOV      CX,8              ;      BIT_COUNT = 8
30: ;
31:               .ELSE                      ;ELSE
32:               MOV      CX,16             ;      BIT_COUNT = 16
33:               .ENDIF                     ;ENDIF
34:               MOV      DX,AX             ;SAVE NUMBER IN DX
35:               MOV      BH,0              ;<PUTDEC DISPLAY CODE>
36:               .REPEAT                    ;REPEAT
37:               TEST     DX,8000H          ;   IF    BIT 15 OF NUMBER = 0
38:               JNZ      ONE
39:               MOV      AX,0              ;   THEN DISPLAY 0
40:               JMP      DISPLAY
41: ONE:                                     ;   ELSE
42:               MOV      AX,1              ;        DISPLAY 1
43: DISPLAY:
44:               CALL     PUTDEC            ;   ENDIF
45:               ROL      DX,1              ;   ROTATE NUMBER LEFT 1 BIT
46:                                          ;   TO GET NEXT BIT IN POS. 15
47:               .UNTILCXZ                  ;   DECREMENT BIT_COUNT
48:                                          ;UNTIL BIT_COUNT = 0
49:               POPF                       ;RESTORE FLAGS
50:               RET                        ;RETURN
51: PUT_BIN       ENDP                    ;END PUT_BIN
52:               END
```

displayed is shifted to the upper half of the AX-register (lines 27 and 28) and the bit count in the CX-register is set to 8 (line 29). If the BL-register value is nonzero, then the bit count in the CX-register is set to 16 (line 32). The rest of the algorithm tests and displays the first 8 or 16 bits of the AX-register depending on the value of the bit count in the CX-register.

The input number is moved to the DX-register (line 34). The DX-register is used as the working register since the AX-register is needed for displaying individual bits. The external PUTDEC procedure is used to display the individual bits. The display code, an input to the PUTDEC procedure, is placed in the BH-register (line 35), which causes each bit to be displayed as a single digit with no leading or trailing blanks.

The REPEAT-UNTIL loop in lines 36–48 tests and displays the first 8 or 16 bits of the DX-register. The double-alternative decision structure in lines 37–44 tests the next bit in the DX-register and displays a 1 or a 0 depending on whether or not the bit is set. The TEST instruction in line 37 checks to see if bit 15 of the DX-register (the next bit of the input number) is set. If it is set, then the jump in line 38 is taken and the instruction in line 42 moves the value 1 into the AX-register; if it is reset, then the jump in line 38 is *not* taken and the instruction in line 39 moves the value 0 into the AX-register. In both cases, a CALL is made to PUTDEC (line 44) to display the value just moved into the AX-register (0 or 1) with no leading or trailing blanks. The rotate instruction in line 45 shifts the next bit of the input number into bit position 15 of the DX-register in preparation for the next iteration of the REPEAT-UNTIL loop. The TEST instruction in line 37 always tests bit 15 of the DX-register. The ROL instruction in line 45 ensures that a different bit (the next bit) of the input number is in bit position 15 on each iteration of the loop. The LOOP instruction generated for the macro directive in line 47 decrements the bit count and transfers control to the top of the loop if the bit count has not reached zero.

In the preceding algorithm, the bit pattern used for the test remains constant (1000000000000000). The value being displayed is rotated on each iteration to get its next bit into bit position 15 for testing. An alternative approach would be to keep the input number constant and to vary the bit pattern being used for the test. To accomplish such a task, add the DI-register to the USES clause in the PROC pseudo-operation and change lines 36–46 to the following code:

```
          MOV      DI,8000H  ;I = 15
          .REPEAT            ;REPEAT
          TEST     DX,DI     ;    IF   BIT I OF NUMBER = 0
          JNZ      ONE
          MOV      AX,0      ;    THEN DISPLAY 0
          JMP      DISPLAY
ONE:                         ;    ELSE
          MOV      AX,1      ;         DISPLAY 1
DISPLAY:
          CALL     PUTDEC    ;    ENDIF
          SHR      DI,1      ;    I = I - 1
```

The bit manipulation instructions are quite useful in certain character string operations and in operations involving BCD numbers. Character strings and BCD numbers are covered in detail in Chapters 8 and 11, respectively.

6.5 Conditional Expressions Revisited

The conditional expression appearing in a .IF, .WHILE, or .UNTIL pseudo-operation may be a compound expression formed by combining simple relational expressions using the logical operators && (AND), || (OR), and ! (NOT).

EXAMPLE The instructions

```
.IF      BX >= 80 && BX < 90
INC      BCOUNT
.ENDIF
```

cause the assembler to generate code like the following:

```
         cmp  bx, 050h
         jb   @C0001
         cmp  bx, 05Ah
         jae  @C0001
         INC  BCOUNT
@C0001:
```

■

6.6 Additional Capabilities in the 80286 Assembly Language

In the 80286 assembly language, the ⟨*shift-count*⟩ operand in a shift or rotate instruction can be either the constant 1, the register designator CL, or an 8-bit immediate value.

EXAMPLE When a NEAR stack segment is defined in an assembly module, the code generated for a .STARTUP pseudo-operation includes the four instructions

```
shl  bx, 001h
shl  bx, 001h
shl  bx, 001h
shl  bx, 001h
```

which combine to shift the BX-register left 4 bit positions. The two instructions

```
mov  cl, 004h
shl  bx, cl
```

could have been generated instead, but this alternative requires the use of an additional register. When generating code for an 80286 or higher microprocessor, the assembler generates the instruction

```
shl  bx, 004h
```

in place of the four 1-bit shift instructions. ■

PROGRAMMING EXERCISES

6.1 Design a subalgorithm to compute the parity of a 16-bit integer value. Implement your algorithm with an 8088/8086 assembly language external FAR subprocedure called PARITY. Your input should be a 16-bit value in the AX-register. Your output should be reflected in the PF bit of the flags register, in which

PF = 1 → Parity of the input value is even

PF = 0 → Parity of the input value is odd

Your subprocedure should save and restore all registers used including the flags register, except for the PF bit of the flags register that is used for the procedure output.

6.2 Write an 8088/8086 external FAR subprocedure called PUTFLAGS to display the flags register value. Your input should be the flags register. Your output should have the following form:

```
OF DF IF TF SF ZF AF PF CF
x1 x2 x3 x4 x5 x6 x7 x8 x9
```

in which *xi* is 0 or 1 depending on whether the corresponding flag bit is cleared or set.

6.3 Write an 8088/8086 assembly language program to demonstrate your subprocedures from Programming Exercises 6.1 and 6.2. Your program should perform the following steps in sequence:

a. Accept a 16-bit integer input via the keyboard.
b. Display the input in binary.
c. Call PUTFLAGS to display the flags register value.
d. Call PARITY to compute the parity of the input value.
e. Call PUTFLAGS to display the flags register. The PF bit in the flags register should correctly reflect the parity of the input value. All other flag bits should remain unchanged from the previous call to PUTFLAGS.

Demonstrate your program and subprocedures with the following inputs:

0, 32767, 33023, 33024, 21845, 54613

6.4 Modify Program Listing 6.1 to use your PUTFLAGS subprocedure from Programming Exercise 6.2 to display the flags register prior to the display of each binary value. To obtain the entire output on one screen, display the binary value at the end of the second line of the flags display.

6.5 Design an algorithm to convert an n-bit binary number

$$b_1 b_2 b_3 \ldots b_n$$

to an n-bit gray code number

$$g_1 g_2 g_3 \ldots g_n$$

The following formulas describe this conversion process:

$$g_1 = b_1$$
$$g_i = b_i \oplus b_{i-1} \qquad \text{for } 2 \le i \le n$$

in which $\oplus$ is the exclusive OR operation. Implement your algorithm with an 8088/8086 assembly language external FAR subprocedure called BIN_GRAY. Your input should be a 16-bit binary integer in the AX-register. Your output should be the corresponding gray code integer in the AX-register.

6.6 Design an algorithm to convert an n-bit gray code number

$$g_1 g_2 g_3 \ldots g_n$$

to an n-bit binary number

$$b_1 b_2 b_3 \ldots b_n$$

The following formulas describe this conversion process:

$$b_1 = g_1$$
$$b_i = g_i \oplus b_{i-1} \qquad \text{for } 2 \le i \le n$$

in which $\oplus$ is the exclusive OR operation. Implement your algorithm with an 8088/8086 assembly language external FAR subprocedure called GRAY_BIN. Your input should be a 16-bit gray code integer in the AX-register. Your output should be the corresponding binary integer in the AX-register.

6.7 Write an 8088/8086 assembly language program to demonstrate your subprocedures from Programming Exercises 6.5 and 6.6. Your program should perform the following steps in sequence:

a. Accept a 16-bit integer input via the keyboard in decimal.
b. Call the PUTBIN subprocedure to display the input integer in binary.
c. Call your BIN_GRAY subprocedure to convert the input integer to gray code.
d. Call the PUTBIN subprocedure to display the gray code number.
e. Call your GRAY_BIN subprocedure to convert the integer back to binary.
f. Call the PUTBIN subprocedure to display the binary number.

Demonstrate your program and subprocedures with the following inputs:

5A0F, 00FF, 694B, 33CC

6.8 If the 8088/8086 were a one's complement machine rather than a two's complement machine, then the SAL instruction might execute as follows for a 1-bit shift of a 16-bit operand:

Bit i is shifted into bit $i + 1$ for $14 \le i \le 0$.

Bit 15 is shifted into the CF bit of the flags register and replaces the vacated bit, bit 0.

If the sign bit (bit 15) changes, then the OF bit in the flags register is set; otherwise, the OF bit is cleared.

All other flags are handled the same as for the two's complement SAL instruction.

A multibit shift would behave like a sequence of 1-bit shift operations. The SAL instruction for an 8-bit operand would execute in a similar manner.

Write an 8088/8086 external FAR subprocedure called SAL_1C to perform the left-shift of a signed integer in one's complement form according to the preceding specifications. Your inputs should be as follows:

1. AX-register contains the 16-bit value to be shifted.

2. BL-register contains a nonzero value to specify a word shift.
3. CL-register contains the shift count.

or

1. AL-register contains the 8-bit value to be shifted.
2. BL-register contains zero to specify a byte shift.
3. CL-register contains the shift count.

Your outputs should be the shifted value in the AX-register (AL-register), and the flags register should be modified according to the preceding specifications. All registers used by your subprocedure, except the ones used for subprocedure output, must be saved and restored.

6.9 The Boolean operator implication, denoted by the operator symbol ⇒, is defined by the following truth table:

A	B	A⇒B
0	0	1
0	1	1
1	0	0
1	1	1

Note that the implication operation is not commutative.

Write an 8088/8086 external FAR subprocedure to perform the implication operation on two 8-bit or two 16-bit operands. Your inputs should be as follows:

1. AX-register contains the 16-bit left operand.
2. DX-register contains the 16-bit right operand.
3. BL-register contains a nonzero value to specify a word operation.

or

1. AL-register contains the 8-bit left operand.
2. AH-register contains the 8-bit right operand.
3. BL-register contains zero to specify a byte operation.

Your output should be the result of the implication operation in the AX-register (AL-register), with the flags register affected the same way as for the AND, OR, and XOR instructions. All registers used by your subprocedure, except the ones used for subprocedure output, must be saved and restored.

6.10 Write a macro named STF that sets bit *i* of the flags register, in which *i* is the operand for the macro. Your macro can assume that *i* is an immediate value in the range 0–15, inclusive. That is, the macro reference

```
STF 11
```

should generate the code to set the OF bit of the flags register.

Write a macro named CLF that clears bit *i* of the flags register, in which *i* is the operand for the macro. Your macro can assume that *i* is an immediate value in the range 0–15, inclusive. That is, the macro reference

```
CLF 11
```

should generate the code to clear the OF bit of the flags register.

CHAPTER 7

Multiple Precision Integer Arithmetic Using the Carry Flag

Chapter 3 introduced 8-bit and 16-bit integer arithmetic in the 8088/8086. The ranges of integers that can be manipulated by these instructions are summarized in Table 7.1. The solution to a specific problem might require a larger range of integer values. For example, Program Listings 3.2 and 4.1 show programs that compute the sum of the first *n* cubes. The largest value of *n* that can be accommodated by the 16-bit integer arithmetic of these programs is 22. But, suppose the sum of the first 300 cubes is required. If the program could be modified to perform 32-bit integer arithmetic, then the largest value of *n* that could be accommodated would be over 300. Table 7.1 shows the signed and unsigned integer ranges for 32-bit binary numbers.

This chapter presents techniques for storing and performing arithmetic on integers that are larger than 16 bits. It introduces addition and subtraction instructions designed to aid in performing multiple precision integer arithmetic operations. The shift operations presented in Chapter 6 are expanded to accommodate integers whose size is a multiple of 8 or 16 bits.

This chapter also presents the expanded register and instruction sets of the 80386 microprocessor. The 80386 microprocessor has the same set of 8-bit and 16-bit registers that are available in the 8088/8086. However, in the 80386, each 16-bit general register is actually the low-order half of an expanded 32-bit register. The expanded instruction set of the 80386 includes integer arithmetic and bit manipulation instructions that operate on the expanded 32-bit operands. The 80386 provides the capability to perform 8-bit, 16-bit, or 32-bit operations. The techniques for performing 32-bit arithmetic on the 8088/8086, which are presented in this chapter, can be applied on the 80386 to perform 64-bit arithmetic.

TABLE 7.1
Integer ranges: 8-, 16-, and 32-bit

Integer Ranges	Unsigned Integers	Signed Two's Complement
8-bit	0–255	−128–+127
16-bit	0–65535	−32768–+32767
32-bit	0–4294967295	−2147483648–+2147483647

7.1 Addition and Subtraction Using Carry/Borrow Flag

The CF bit of the flags register is used to record the carry out of the most significant bit on an addition operation and to record the borrow into the most significant bit on a subtraction operation, and it is required for multiple precision addition and subtraction operations. To add two 32-bit binary integers using 16-bit integer arithmetic, the following procedure can be used:

1. Add the low-order 16 bits of one operand to the low-order 16 bits of the second operand, producing the low-order 16 bits of the sum and the carry out of bit 15 into bit 16.
2. Add the high-order 16 bits of one operand, the high-order 16 bits of the other operand, and the carry from the addition of the low-order halves of the two operands. This addition produces the high-order 16 bits of the sum and the carry out of its most significant bit (MSB).

Figure 7.1 illustrates this procedure giving hexadecimal and decimal equivalences. Note that the carry out of the MSB is zero, which means that overflow does not occur for the unsigned integer interpretation. The result (2148309336 decimal) is within the 32-bit unsigned integer range specified in Table 7.1. Note also that the carry into the MSB (1) differs from the carry out of the MSB (0), which means that overflow does occur for the signed integer interpretation. The result (2148309336 decimal) is not within the 32-bit signed integer range specified in Table 7.1.

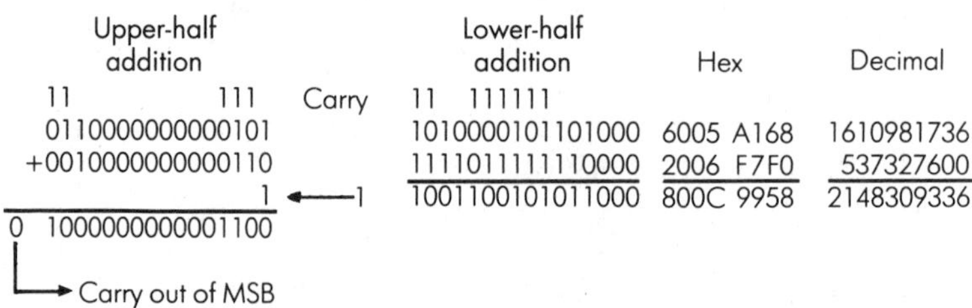

FIGURE 7.1
32-bit addition

To subtract two 32-bit binary integers using 16-bit integer arithmetic, the following procedure can be used:

1. Subtract the low-order 16 bits of the subtrahend from the low-order 16 bits of the minuend, producing the low-order 16 bits of the difference and the borrow from bit 16 into bit 15.
2. Subtract from the high-order 16 bits of the minuend, the high-order 16 bits of the

subtrahend, and the borrow into the low-order half of the subtraction. This subtraction produces the high-order 16 bits of the difference and the borrow into the MSB.

Figure 7.2 illustrates this procedure giving hexadecimal and decimal equivalences. The subtraction operations are shown as complement and add operations. Note that the borrow into the MSB is zero for the high-order half of the subtraction, which means that overflow does not occur for the unsigned integer interpretation. The result (1073654136) is within the 32-bit unsigned integer range specified in Table 7.1. Note also that on both upper-half additions, the carry into the MSB is the same as the carry out of the MSB, which means that overflow does not occur for the signed integer interpretation. The result (1073654136) is within the 32-bit signed integer range specified in Table 7.1.

FIGURE 7.2
32-bit subtraction

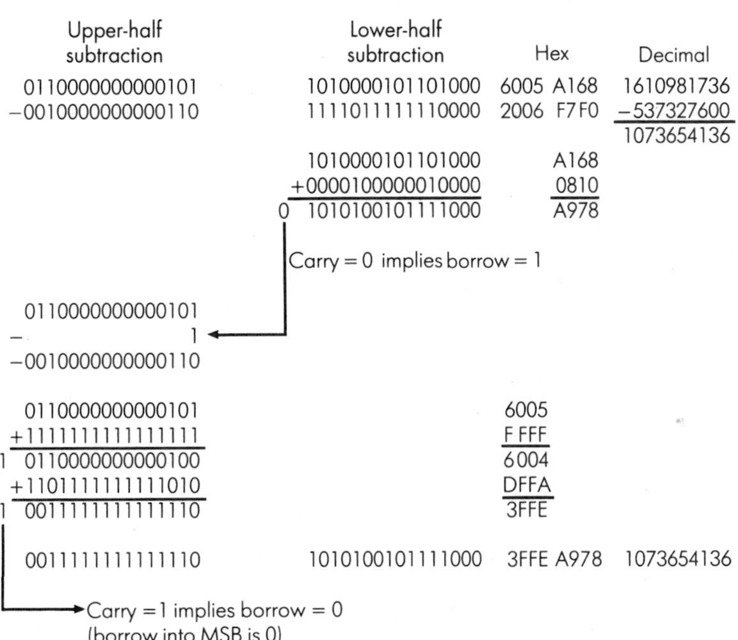

The 8088/8086 assembly language includes an addition instruction and a subtraction instruction that are useful in multiple precision integer arithmetic operations: the add with carry (ADC) instruction and the subtract with borrow (SBB) instruction. The **ADC instruction** has the following general form:

[⟨*label*⟩] `ADC` ⟨*destination*⟩, ⟨*source*⟩ [⟨*comment*⟩]

This instruction causes the source operand, the destination operand, and the CF bit of the flags register to be added together, producing a sum that replaces the value of the destination operand.

The **SBB instruction** has the following general form:

[⟨*label*⟩] `SBB` ⟨*destination*⟩, ⟨*source*⟩ [⟨*comment*⟩]

This instruction causes the source operand and the CF bit of the flags register to be subtracted from the destination operand, producing a difference that replaces the value of the destination operand.

Figure 7.3 shows the possible combinations of destination and source operands for the ADC and SBB instructions. If the destination operand is a general register, then the source operand can be either a general register, a memory location, or an immediate value. If the destination operand is a memory location, then the source operand can be either a general register or an immediate value. The types of the two operands must match (i.e., both must be word, or both must be byte).

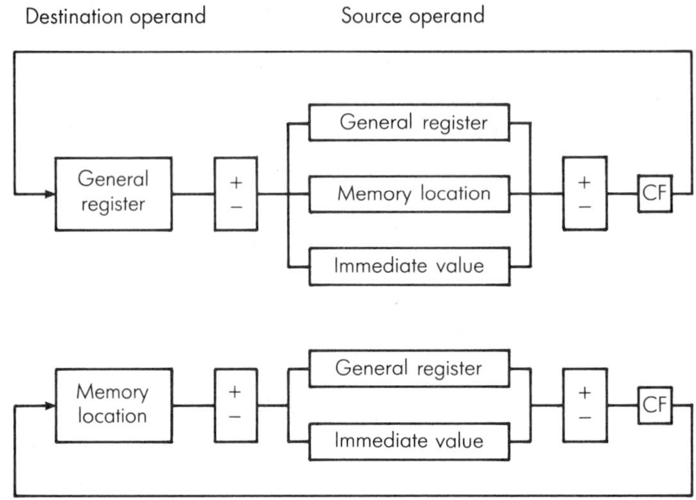

FIGURE 7.3 Allowable operands for ADC and SBB instructions

The OF, SF, ZF, AF, PF, and CF bits of the flags register are all affected by execution of ADC and SBB instructions:

> If the carry into the MSB differs from the carry out of the MSB on the addition operation, then the OF bit is set; otherwise, the OF bit is cleared. (Recall that subtraction is performed by complement and addition.) If the two operands represent signed two's complement integers, then the OF bit reflects whether or not execution of the ADC or SBB instruction resulted in an overflow.
>
> The SF bit is a copy of the MSB of the result of the addition or subtraction operation. If the two operands represent signed two's complement numbers, then the SF bit reflects the sign of the result.
>
> If the result of the addition or subtraction operation is zero, then the ZF bit is set; otherwise, the ZF bit is cleared.
>
> The PF bit is set to reflect the parity of the low-order 8 bits of the result.
>
> If an addition operation produces a carry of 1 from the MSB (bit 7 for byte addition; bit 15 for word addition) or if a subtraction operation requires a borrow into the MSB, then the CF bit is set; otherwise, the CF bit is cleared. If the two operands represent unsigned integer values, then the CF bit reflects whether or not execution of the ADC or SBB instruction resulted in an overflow.
>
> The AF bit is handled in a manner similar to the CF bit. However, the AF bit reflects the carry out of or borrow into bit 3.

The ADC and SBB instructions are used primarily for multiple precision integer arithmetic. Suppose a 32-bit variable is defined in the data segment as follows:

```
TIME DW ?,?
```

The value for this variable is stored in memory beginning at the location identified by the symbolic name TIME. This 32-bit value could be interpreted as shown in Figure 7.4. To give this variable an initial value of 1, the data definition could be

```
TIME DW 1,0
```

FIGURE 7.4 Storage for a 32-bit integer

TIME	Low-order byte of least significant word
TIME+1	High-order byte of least significant word
TIME+2	Low-order byte of most significant word
TIME+3	High-order byte of most significant word

To add the 32-bit value of TIME to the 32-bit value in the DX:AX register pair leaving the result in that register pair, the following sequence of instructions could be used:

```
ADD  AX,TIME
ADC  DX,TIME+2
```

The ADD instruction adds the low-order halves of the two operands, leaving the result in the AX-register. The ADC instruction adds the high-order halves of the two operands along with the carry from the addition of the low-order halves, leaving the result in the DX-register. The organization of the bits for this 32-bit addition is shown in Figure 7.5.

FIGURE 7.5 Organization of bits for a 32-bit addition of variable TIME to DX:AX register pair

	31 24	23 16	15 8	7 0
	DH	DL	AH	AL
	DX-register		AX-register	
+	TIME+3	TIME+2	TIME+1	TIME
	Word at TIME+2		Word at TIME	
	DH	DL	AH	AL
	DX-register		AX-register	

To subtract the 32-bit value beginning at the memory location specified by the symbolic name TIME from the 32-bit value in the DX:AX register pair leaving the result in that register pair, the following sequence of instructions could be used:

```
SUB  AX,TIME
SBB  DX,TIME+2
```

The SUB instruction subtracts the low-order half of the 32-bit value beginning at the memory location identified by the label TIME from the low-order half of the DX:AX register pair, leaving the result in the AX-register. The SBB instruction subtracts from the high-order half of the DX:AX register pair the high-order half of the 32-bit value of TIME and the borrow into the subtraction of the low-order halves, leaving the result in the DX-register.

These techniques can be extrapolated to techniques for performing addition and subtraction operations involving integers whose lengths are any multiple of 8 or 16 bits.

EXAMPLE

Consider the following definition for a 40-bit variable named DATA:

```
DATA  DW  6050H,8000H
      DB  1H
```

The initial value of variable data is 0180006050 hex or 6442475600 decimal. To add the 40-bit value of DATA to the 40-bit value in the BL:DX:AX register group, the following sequence of instructions could be used:

```
ADD  AX,DATA
ADC  DX,DATA+2
ADC  BL,BYTE PTR DATA+4
```

The result of the addition is in the BL:DX:AX register group. The BYTE PTR operators are required in the second ADC instruction because the symbolic name DATA is defined with a type attribute of word, but the reference DATA+4 is used to access a byte. Figure 7.6 shows the bit organization for this addition using the hexadecimal values shown:

	BL:DX:AX	009000C6D0
+	DATA	0180006050
	BL:DX:AX	0210012720

■

FIGURE 7.6

Organization of bits for a 40-bit addition of variable DATA to BL:DX:AX register group

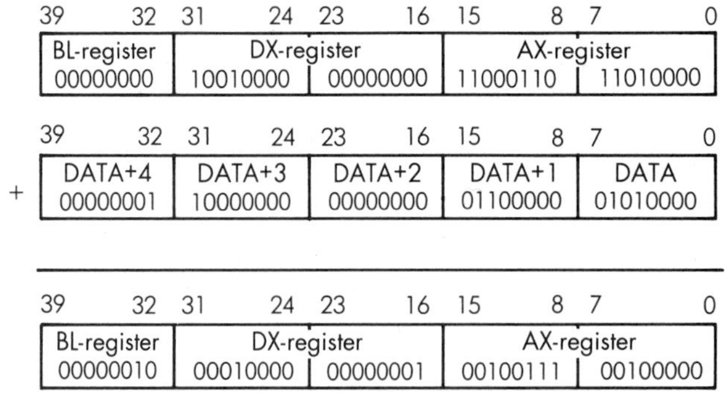

	39–32	31–24	23–16	15–8	7–0
	BL-register	DX-register		AX-register	
	00000000	10010000	00000000	11000110	11010000
	DATA+4	DATA+3	DATA+2	DATA+1	DATA
+	00000001	10000000	00000000	01100000	01010000
	BL-register	DX-register		AX-register	
	00000010	00010000	00000001	00100111	00100000

7.2 Multiple Register Shifts

In multiple precision integer arithmetic operations, it is often necessary to perform shift operations on multiple precision values. Recall from Chapter 6 that a left-shift operation is like multiplication by a power of 2 and a right-shift operation is like division by a power of 2. Multiplication and division by a power of 2 can be performed much more efficiently by a shift operation than by the multiplication and division instructions. In multiple precision integer arithmetic, multiplication and division must be performed by some algorithm. If the multiplication or division operation is by a power of 2, then the multiple precision shift operation is by far the most efficient approach.

It is important to remember two things in the implementation of multiple precision shift operations:

1. With any shift or rotate instruction, the last bit shifted out is recorded in the CF bit of the flags register.
2. There are two rotate instructions that include the CF bit of the flags register as part of the value being rotated: the rotate-through-carry instructions presented in Section 6.1.

Suppose the 32-bit signed integer value in the DX:AX register pair must be shifted right 1 bit position. The value in the DX-register is first shifted right 1 bit position using an arithmetic shift operation. The bit shifted from the low-order end of the DX-register is recorded in the CF bit of the flags register. The value in the AX-register is then shifted right 1 bit position using a rotate-through-carry operation. The value of the CF bit in the flags register (i.e., the bit shifted from the low-order end of the DX-register) is rotated into the MSB of the AX-register as the bits of the AX-register are shifted right 1 bit position. The bit shifted from the low-order end of the AX-register is recorded in the CF bit of the flags register. This arithmetic right-shift of the 32-bit value in the DX:AX register pair is performed by the following two instructions:

```
SAR  DX,1
RCR  AX,1
```

These instructions divide the signed integer value in the DX:AX register pair by 2, leaving the quotient in the DX:AX register pair and the remainder (0 or 1) in the CF bit of the flags register. Figure 7.7 shows the operation of these two instructions for the 32-bit value 1111111100001001 0110100111110000.

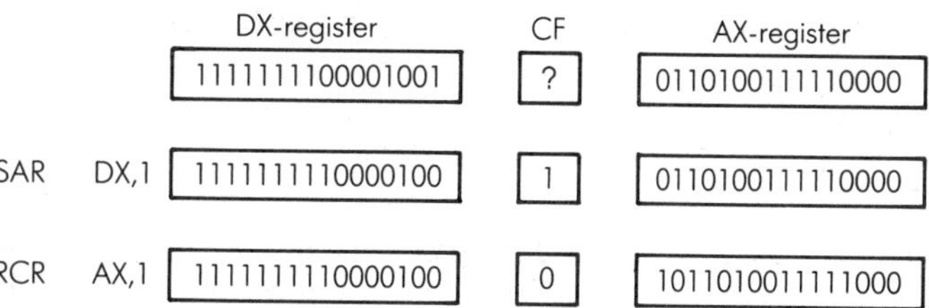

FIGURE 7.7 32-bit arithmetic right-shift operation

Suppose the 32-bit signed integer value in the DX:AX register pair must be shifted right 3 bit positions. In multiple precision shift operations, the CL-register cannot be used as a shift count for the individual shift instructions because a shift of 1 bit position requires multiple shift operations. It is these multiple shift operations (e.g., the two shift instructions shown previously) that must be repeated to implement the multibit, multiple precision shift operation. A loop can be used to repeat the multiple shift operations the desired number of times. The following loop shifts the

32-bit signed integer value in the DX:AX register pair right 3 bit positions:

```
            MOV   CX,3
SHFT_LOOP:
            SAR   DX,1
            RCR   AX,1
            LOOP  SHFT_LOOP
```

Figure 7.8 shows the operation of this loop for the 32-bit value 1111111111110101 0000110000000110.

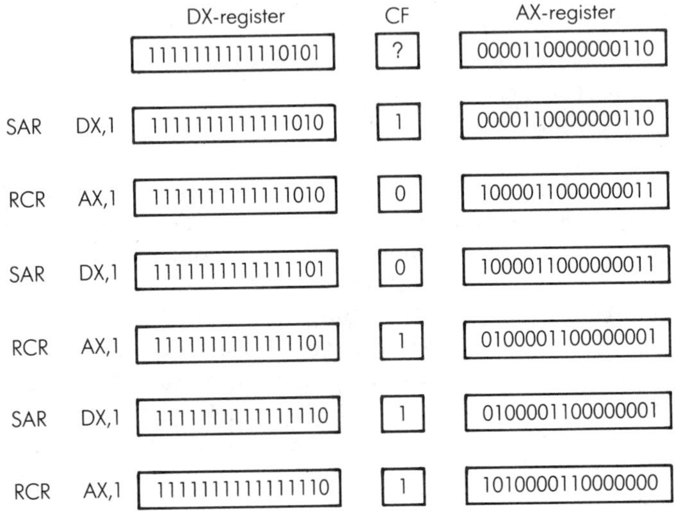

FIGURE 7.8 32-bit arithmetic right-shift by 3 bit positions

Note that, when a multibit, right-shift operation is used for division by a power of 2, the remainder of the division is not available. The most significant bit of the remainder appears in the CF bit of the flags register, but the other bits of the remainder are lost during the shift. The preceding loop can be modified so that the remainder is shifted into another register and therefore not lost (see Programming Exercise 7.12 at the end of this chapter).

Multiple precision left-shift operations are implemented in a similar manner. To shift the 32-bit signed integer value in the DX:AX register pair left 1 bit position, the following sequence of instructions can be used:

```
SAL  AX,1
RCL  DX,1
```

To shift the 32-bit signed integer value in the DX:AX register pair left 3 bit positions, these instructions can be placed in the body of a loop as follows:

```
            MOV   CX,3
SHFT_LOOP:
            SAL   AX,1
            RCL   DX,1
            LOOP  SHFT_LOOP
```

A left-shift of a signed integer value is like a multiplication by a power of 2 and can therefore produce an overflow. The RCL instruction affects the OF bit in the flags register as follows:

If the sign bit changes on the last bit shifted, then the OF bit in the flags register is set.

If the sign bit does *not* change on the last bit shifted, then the OF bit in the flags register is cleared.

For a single-bit, multiple precision shift (i.e., a multiply by 2), the OF bit in the flags register correctly reflects signed integer overflow. However, for a multibit, multiple precision shift, the OF bit does *not* correctly reflect signed integer overflow. For a multibit shift, if the sign bit ever changes during the shift, then overflow has occurred. However, if the sign bit *never* changes during the shift, then overflow has *not* occurred.

EXAMPLE

Consider the 32-bit value

`0100000000000010 0110100111000011    (4002 69C3 hex)`

interpreted as a signed integer value. Figure 7.9 shows the steps of a 3-bit left-shift of this value. At the end of this 3-bit shift operation, the OF bit of the flags register is cleared. The sign bit of the DX-register did not change on the last bit shifted, and the OF bit was cleared. However, the sign bit (MSB of DX-register) changed from 0 to 1 on the first bit shifted. The OF bit was set at that point, correctly reflecting the signed integer overflow. ■

FIGURE 7.9
32-bit left-shift by 3-bit positions

OF	CF	DX-register	AX-register	
?	?	0100000000000010	0110100111000011	
1	0	0100000000000010	1101001110000110	SAL AX,1
1	0	1000000000000100	1101001110000110	RCL DX,1
0	1	1000000000000100	1010011100001100	SAL AX,1
1	1	0000000000001001	1010011100001100	RCL DX,1
1	1	0000000000001001	0100111000011000	SAL AX,1
0	0	0000000000010011	0100111000011000	RCL DX,1

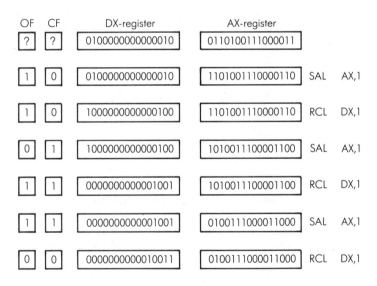

To detect overflow during the 3-bit left-shift of the 32-bit signed integer value in the DX:AX register pair, the following loop can be used:

```
            MOV   OVERFLO,0
            MOV   CX,3
SHFT_LOOP:
            SAL   AX,1
            RCL   DX,1
            JNO   SLOOP_END
            MOV   OVERFLO,1
SLOOP_END:
            LOOP  SHFT_LOOP
```

If the sign bit ever changed during the shift, then the variable OVERFLO has the value 1 at loop exit; otherwise, OVERFLO has the value 0 at loop exit.

For multiple precision shifts of unsigned integer values, simply replace SAR and SAL instructions with SHR and SHL instructions, respectively, in each of the preceding examples except the overflow detection example. Recall that the SAL and SHL instructions are equivalent. For the single-bit, left-shift of a multiple precision unsigned integer value, the CF bit in the flags register correctly reflects overflow. However, for a multibit, multiple precision shift, the CF bit does *not* correctly reflect an unsigned integer overflow. For a multibit, left-shift of a multiple precision unsigned integer value, if the CF bit in the flags register is ever set to 1 during the shift, then overflow has occurred.

EXAMPLE

Consider again the 32-bit value

```
0100000000000010 0110100111000011    (4002 69C3 hex)
```

interpreted as an unsigned integer value. Figure 7.9 shows the steps of a 3-bit left-shift of this value. At the end of this 3-bit left-shift operation, the CF bit of the flags register is cleared. The last bit shifted from the DX-register (0) was recorded in the CF bit. However, a significant bit was shifted from the MSB of the DX-register on the second bit shifted. The CF bit was set at that point, correctly reflecting the unsigned integer overflow. ■

To detect overflow during the 3-bit left-shift of the 32-bit unsigned integer value in the DX:AX register pair, the following loop can be used:

```
            MOV   OVERFLO,0
            MOV   CX,3
SHFT_LOOP:
            SHL   AX,1
            RCL   DX,1
            JNC   SLOOP_END
            MOV   OVERFLO,1
SLOOP_END:
            LOOP  SHFT_LOOP
```

If the CF bit in the flags register was ever set during the shift (i.e., a significant bit was shifted out), then the variable OVERFLO has the value 1 at loop exit; otherwise, OVERFLO has the value 0 at loop exit.

These procedures can be extrapolated to procedures for performing shift operations involving integers whose lengths are any multiple of 8 or 16 bits. For example, to shift the 40-bit signed integer value in the BL:DX:AX register group right 3-bit positions, the following loop can be used:

```
            MOV   CX,3
SHFT_LOOP:
            SAR   BL,1
            RCR   DX,1
            RCR   AX,1
            LOOP  SHFT_LOOP
```

7.3 Programming Examples

The programming examples in this chapter present two implementations of an algorithm for performing integer multiplication using addition and shift operations. The goal is to produce a procedure to perform 32-bit integer multiplication. The algorithm used in these example programs is known as the *Russian Peasant's Method.* The first implementation of this algorithm is an internal procedure for performing 16-bit unsigned integer multiplication. The second implementation is an external procedure for performing 32-bit signed integer multiplication.

The programming exercises at the end of this chapter introduce other algorithms for multiplication and an algorithm for division. Algorithms for multiplication and division are presented for two reasons:

1. Such algorithms are needed to perform multiple precision multiplication and division operations.
2. Some microprocessors do not have multiplication and division instructions in their machine language. Therefore, a software algorithm is needed to perform these operations.

The Russian Peasant's Method can be explained through examination of the standard multiplication method taught in elementary schools. The following is an example of the multiplication of two 6-bit unsigned binary integers using the long multiplication method that is normally used when two decimal numbers are multiplied using pencil and paper:

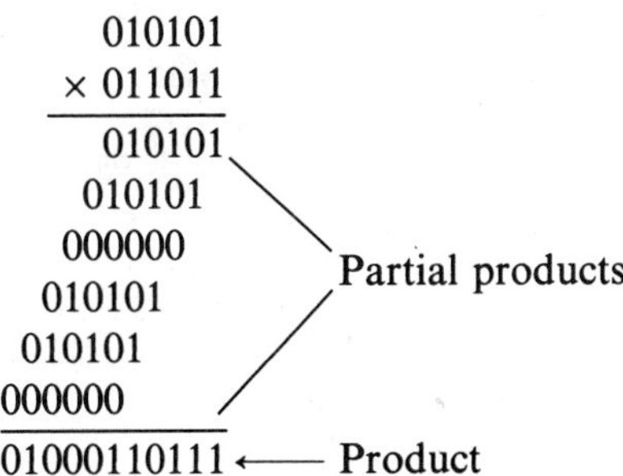

Note that a given partial product is either 000000 or a copy of the multiplicand (010101) shifted left the appropriate number of bit positions necessary to place its least significant bit (LSB) under the multiplier bit that produced it. Recall from Chapter 6 that shifting an unsigned binary integer value left n bit positions is the equivalent to multiplying that value by 2^n. The partial products can be rewritten as shown:

```
        010101
      × 011011
      --------
        010101 (2^0 × multiplicand) × 1
       0101010 (2^1 × multiplicand) × 1
      00000000 (2^2 × multiplicand) × 0
     010101000 (2^3 × multiplicand) × 1
    0101010000 (2^4 × multiplicand) × 1
   00000000000 (2^5 × multiplicand) × 0
   -----------
   01000110111 ←— Product
```

The interpretation states each successive partial product as the next higher power of 2 (starting with 2^0) multiplied by the multiplicand, which is multiplied by the next higher multiplier bit (starting with the LSB).

In general, the product of a 6-bit unsigned binary integer multiplicand and a 6-bit unsigned binary integer multiplier, M5 M4 M3 M2 M1 M0, can be computed by summing the following six partial products:

$$2^0 \times \text{multiplicand} \times \text{M0}$$

$$2^1 \times \text{multiplicand} \times \text{M1}$$

$$2^2 \times \text{multiplicand} \times \text{M2}$$

$$2^3 \times \text{multiplicand} \times \text{M3}$$

$$2^4 \times \text{multiplicand} \times \text{M4}$$

$$2^5 \times \text{multiplicand} \times \text{M5}$$

Note that the only partial products that need to be summed are those that are produced by a multiplier bit (M*i*) of 1. The *i*th bit of the multiplier from the right will be a 1 only if the multiplier / 2^i is odd.

This process leads to the following algorithm, the Russian Peasant's Method, for computing the product of two unsigned binary integers:

```
FUNCTION MULTIPLY (MULTIPLICAND, MULTIPLIER)
    PRODUCT = 0
    WHILE   MULTIPLIER > 0
       IF   MULTIPLIER IS ODD
       THEN PRODUCT = PRODUCT + MULTIPLICAND
       ENDIF
       MULTIPLICAND = MULTIPLICAND * 2
       MULTIPLIER = MULTIPLIER / 2
                             truncated to an integer
    ENDWHILE
    RETURN (PRODUCT)
  END MULTIPLY
```

Table 7.2 shows a trace, in both binary and decimal, of this algorithm for the two values (21 and 27) used in the preceding binary examples.

Russian Peasant's Multiply—16-Bit Implementation

Program Listing 7.1 shows a program that contains an internal subprocedure that is an implementation of the Russian Peasant's Method algorithm for 16-bit unsigned integers and a main procedure that demonstrates the subprocedure. This discussion concentrates on the subprocedure defined in lines 63–106 of Program Listing 7.1.

The subprocedure begins with a prologue (lines 63–71) that explains the function of and the interface for the procedure. The 16-bit unsigned integer multiplicand is expected in the BX-register, and the 16-bit unsigned integer multiplier is expected in the AX-register. The 32-bit unsigned integer product is returned in the DX:AX register pair. The OF and CF bits of the flags register are set to reflect whether or not the product overflows 16 bits. If the high-order 16 bits of the product are zero, then the OF and CF bits are cleared. However, if there is a 1 anywhere in the high-order 16 bits of the product, then the OF and CF bits are set. Note that both the OF and CF bits are affected, which was done to make the MULTIPLY procedure consistent with the MUL instruction. However, there is a slight inconsistency between the MUL instruction and the MULTIPLY procedure. The MUL instruction leaves the AF, PF,

TABLE 7.2
Trace of Russian Peasant's Method algorithm

Step	Multiplier Conditions >0	Multiplier Conditions Odd	Multiplicand	Multiplier	Product
Enter function			000000010101 (21)	011011 (27)	
Product = 0					000000000000 (000)
Loop test	T				
Decision test		T			
Product = Product + Multiplicand					000000010101 (21)
Multiplicand = Multiplicand * 2			000000101010 (42)		
Multiplier = Multiplier / 2				001101 (13)	
Loop test	T				
Decision test		T			
Product = Product + Multiplicand					000000111111 (63)
Multiplicand = Multiplicand * 2			000001010100 (84)		
Multiplier = Multiplier / 2				000110 (6)	
Loop test	T				
Decision test		F			
Multiplicand = Multiplicand * 2			000010101000 (168)		
Multiplier = Multiplier / 2				000011 (3)	
Loop test	T				
Decision test		T			
Product = Product + Multiplicand					000011100111 (231)
Multiplicand = Multiplicand * 2			000101010000 (336)		
Multiplier = Multiplier / 2				000001 (1)	
Loop test	T				
Decision test		T			
Product = Product + Multiplicand					001000110111 (567)
Multiplicand = Multiplicand * 2			001010100000 (672)		
Multiplier = Multiplier / 2				000000 (0)	
Loop test	F				
Return					001000110111 (567)

```
            PAGE    80,132
;======================================================================
;                    PROGRAM LISTING 7.1
;
;PROGRAM TO DEMONSTRATE RUSSIAN PEASANT MULTIPLY PROCEDURE
;
;======================================================================
            .MODEL  SMALL,BASIC
;======================================================================
                                        ;PROCEDURES TO
            EXTRN   GETDEC$:FAR         ;GET UNSIGNED DECIMAL INTEGER
            EXTRN   NEWLINE:FAR         ;DISPLAY NEWLINE CHARACTER
            EXTRN   PUTDC32$:FAR        ;DISPLAY 32-BIT UNSIGNED INT
            EXTRN   PUTSTRNG:FAR        ;DISPLAY CHARACTER STRING
;======================================================================
; S T A C K   D E F I N I T I O N
;
            .STACK  256
;======================================================================
; C O N S T A N T   D E F I N I T I O N S
;
            .CONST
;
PROMPT1     DB      'ENTER MULTIPLICAND (NON-NEGATIVE) '
PROMPT2     DB      'ENTER MULTIPLIER   (NON-NEGATIVE) '
PROMPT_LNG EQU      PROMPT2-PROMPT1     ;LENGTH OF PROMPT MESSAGES
ANNOTATE    DB      'PRODUCT = '
ANNOTATE_L EQU      $-ANNOTATE          ;LENGTH OF ANNOTATION MESSAGE
;
;======================================================================
; C O D E   S E G M E N T   D E F I N I T I O N
;
            .CODE   EX_7_1
            .STARTUP                    ;GENERATE STARTUP CODE
            PUSH    DS                  ;SET ES-REGISTER TO ADDRESS
            POP     ES                  ;DGROUP
;
            CALL    NEWLINE
            LEA     DI,PROMPT1          ;PROMPT FOR MULTIPLICAND
            MOV     CX,PROMPT_LNG
            CALL    PUTSTRNG
            CALL    GETDEC$             ;GET MCAND
            MOV     BX,AX               ;<MCAND TO BX>
;
            LEA     DI,PROMPT2          ;PROMPT FOR MULTIPLIER
;
            CALL    PUTSTRNG
            CALL    GETDEC$             ;GET MPLIER
;
            CALL    MULTIPLY            ;PRODUCT = MULTIPLY(MCAND,MPLIER)
            LEA     DI,ANNOTATE         ;DISPLAY 'PRODUCT = '
            MOV     CX,ANNOTATE_L
            CALL    PUTSTRNG
            MOV     BH,-1               ;DSPL_CODE = LEFT JUSTIFY
            JNC     LEFT                ;IF  PRODUCT OVERFLOWED 16 BITS
            MOV     BH,1                ;THEN DSPL_CODE = RIGHT JUST.
LEFT:                                   ;ENDIF
            CALL    PUTDC32$            ;DISPLAY PRODUCT ACCORDING TO
            CALL    NEWLINE             ;                 DSPL_CODE
            .EXIT                       ;RETURN TO DOS
;
;
;======================================================================
; PROCEDURE TO PERFORM 16-BIT UNSIGNED INTEGER MULTIPLICATION
; USING THE RUSSIAN PEASANT'S METHOD.
;
; INPUTS:  AX-REGISTER CONTAINS MULTIPLIER
```

```
 68: ;           BX-REGISTER CONTAINS MULTIPLICAND
 69: ; OUTPUTS: DX:AX REGISTER PAIR CONTAINS PRODUCT
 70: ;           OF AND CF BITS OF FLAGS REGISTER SET TO REFLECT OVERFLOW
 71: ;==================================================================
 72: MULTIPLY   PROC    NEAR USES BX CX DI
 73:                                    ;FUNCTION MULTIPLY(MULTIPLICAND,
 74:                                    ;                  MULTIPLIER)
 75:                                      ;SAVE REGISTERS (USES CLAUSE)
 76:            PUSHF                     ;SAVE FLAGS
 77:            MOV     DI,AX
 78:            MOV     CX,0              ;EXPAND MULTIPLICAND TO
 79:                                      ;           32 BITS IN CX:BX
 80:            MOV     DX,CX             ;PRODUCT = 0
 81:            MOV     AX,DX             ;           <PRODUCT IN DX:AX>
 82: LOOPTOP:                             ;WHILE MULTIPLIER > 0
 83:            CMP     DI,0
 84:            JE      LOOPEND
 85:            SHR     DI,1              ;   IF   MULTIPLIER IS ODD
 86:            JNC     UPDATE
 87:            ADD     AX,BX             ;   THEN PRODUCT=PRODUCT +
 88:            ADC     DX,CX             ;                 MULTIPLICAND
 89: UPDATE:                              ;   ENDIF
 90:            SAL     BX,1              ;   MULTIPLICAND=MULTIPLICAND*2
 91:            RCL     CX,1
 92:                                      ;   MULTIPLIER=MULTIPLIER / 2
 93:                                      ;   (DONE IN IF TEST ABOVE)
 94:            JMP     LOOPTOP
 95: LOOPEND:                             ;ENDWHILE
 96:            POP     BX                ;FLAGS = SAVED FLAGS
 97:            AND     BX,0F7FEH         ;CLEAR OF AND CF IN FLAGS
 98:            CMP     DX,0              ;IF   UPPER HALF OF
 99:            JE      RESTORE           ;     PRODUCT <> 0
100:            OR      BX,0801H          ;THEN SET OF AND CF IN FLAGS
101: RESTORE:                             ;ENDIF
102:            PUSH    BX                ;SAVED FLAGS = FLAGS
103:            POPF                      ;RESTORE FLAGS
104:                                      ;RESTORE REGISTERS (USES CLS)
105:            RET                       ;RETURN (PRODUCT)
106: MULTIPLY   ENDP                    ;END MULTIPLY
107:            END
```

SF, and ZF bits of the flags register undefined, and the MULTIPLY procedure leaves them unchanged.

The subprocedure definition begins with the PROC pseudo-operation in line 72 and terminates with the ENDP pseudo-operation in line 106. The subprocedure itself begins by saving the registers specified in the USES clause (line 72) and by saving the contents of the flags register (line 76).

The MOV instruction in line 77 stores the input multiplier as the value of the DI-register. The MOV instruction in line 78 expands the input multiplicand to 32 bits in the CX:BX register pair by setting the upper 16 bits (CX-register) to zero. The MOV instructions in lines 80 and 81 initialize the 32-bit product in the DX:AX register pair to zero. Since the product of two 16-bit integers is a 32-bit integer, the product is maintained by the procedure as a 32-bit value. Since the product is accumulated by adding powers of 2 multiplied by the multiplicand, the multiplicand is maintained by the procedure as a 32-bit value. The 32-bit multiplicand is doubled on each iteration of the WHILE loop.

The WHILE loop in lines 82–95 computes the product of the multiplicand and the multiplier. The instructions in lines 83 and 84 provide the loop test. While the multiplier is greater than zero, there are still nonzero partial products to be added to the product sum, so the loop body is executed. When the multiplier becomes zero, there are no further nonzero partial products to be added to the product sum, so the loop is terminated (i.e., the jump in line 84 is taken). The loop body consists of the instructions in lines 85–91.

The single-alternative decision structure in lines 85–89 tests the current value of the multiplier to see if it is odd. If it is odd, then the current value of the multiplicand is added to the product sum; if it is even, then nothing is added to the product sum (i.e., the partial product for the current multiplier bit is zero). The SHR instruction in line 85 performs two functions. It tests the current value of the multiplier to see if it is odd, and it divides the multiplier by 2, discarding the remainder, in preparation for the next loop test and the next iteration of the loop body. A logical right-shift of 1 divides an unsigned integer by 2. The bit shifted from the right is recorded in the CF bit of the flags register. The bit shifted out is actually the remainder of the division by 2. If this remainder is 1 (i.e., CF = 1), then the value of the multiplier was odd prior to the division operation. If this remainder is 0 (i.e., CF = 0), then the value of the multiplier was even prior to the division operation. The JNC instruction in line 86 makes the decision based on this condition. If the CF bit in the flags register is 1, then the jump is not taken and the instructions in lines 87 and 88 are executed. If the CF bit in the flags register is 0, then the instructions in lines 87 and 88 are skipped.

The two instructions in lines 87 and 88 add the 32-bit value in the CX:BX register pair (the current value of the multiplicand) to the 32-bit value in the DX:AX register pair (the current value of the product sum), leaving the result in the DX:AX register pair (the new value of the product sum). The ADD instruction in line 87 adds the low-order halves of the two 32-bit operands, leaving the result in the AX-register. The ADC instruction in line 88 adds the high-order halves of the two operands plus the carry from the addition of the low-order halves, leaving the result in the DX-register.

Following the single-alternative decision structure, the 32-bit value of the multiplicand in the CX:BX register pair is multiplied by 2. This task is accomplished by the double-register, left-shift operation in lines 90 and 91. The SAL instruction in line 90 shifts the BX-register left 1 bit position. The value shifted from the MSB of the BX-register is recorded in the CF bit of the flags register. The RCL instruction in line 91 shifts the CX-register value left 1 bit position, shifting the CF bit of the flags register into the LSB of the CX-register. The bit shifted from the MSB of the CX-register is recorded in the CF bit of the flags register and will always be zero; that is, the 32-bit multiplicand does not overflow during the computation. This situation occurs because the high-order 16 bits are initially zero (line 78), and the double-register, left-shift occurs, at most, 16 times before the multiplier reduces to zero. The comments in lines 92 and 93 indicate that the division of the multiplier by 2 was performed by the SHR instruction in line 85.

The JMP instruction in line 94 returns control to the WHILE loop test beginning in line 83. At the time of loop exit, the instructions in lines 96–105 are executed, and the completed product is in the DX:AX register pair.

The instructions in lines 96–102 set the OF and CF bits in the flags register to reflect whether or not the product overflows 16 bits. If the high-order half of the product is nonzero, then the OF and CF bits in the flags register are set; if the high-order half of the product is zero, then the OF and CF bits in the flags register are cleared. Again, both bits are affected for consistency with the MUL instruction that is being simulated. The POP instruction in line 96 pops the flags register value, which is saved on entry to the subprocedure, from the stack into the BX-register. The AND instruction in line 97 clears the OF and CF bits in this flags register value.

The single-alternative decision structure in lines 98–101 sets the OF and CF bits in this flags register value if the upper half of the product is nonzero. The CMP instruction in line 98 tests the DX-register (the high-order half of the product) to see if it is nonzero. The JE instruction in line 99 makes the decision based on this condition. If the DX-register does not contain zero, then the jump is not taken and the OR instruction in line 100 is executed. The OR instruction sets the OF and CF bits in the flags register value in the BX-register. Following the single-alternative decision structure, the PUSH instruction in line 102 is executed, which pushes the modified flags register value back onto the stack.

The subprocedure ends by restoring the flags (line 103), restoring the registers specified in the USES clause, and returning control to the caller (line 105). The unsigned integer product is returned in the DX:AX register pair. Note that the OF and CF bits in the saved and restored flags register value have been modified by this subprocedure. All other bits in the flags register have been preserved. This subprocedure simulates the 8088/8086 assembly language MUL instruction for 16-bit operands. However, it does not leave the SF, ZF, AF, and PF bits in the flags register undefined, as does the MUL instruction.

The main procedure defined in lines 34–61 in Program Listing 7.1 performs the following steps:

1. Prompts for the multiplicand (lines 38–41).
2. Accepts the input value for the multiplicand in the AX-register (line 42).
3. Moves the multiplicand to the BX-register (line 43).
4. Prompts for the multiplier (lines 44–47).
5. Accepts the input value for the multiplier in the AX-register (line 48).
6. Calls the MULTIPLY subprocedure to compute the product of the multiplicand and the multiplier (line 50).
7. Displays the product left-justified in an 11-character field if the product did not overflow 16 bits, right-justified in an 11-character field if the product overflowed 16 bits (lines 51–59).

The following are the results from some sample executions of this program:

```
C>ex_7_1

ENTER MULTIPLICAND (NON-NEGATIVE) 2400
ENTER MULTIPLIER   (NON-NEGATIVE) 12
PRODUCT = 28800

C>ex_7_1

ENTER MULTIPLICAND (NON-NEGATIVE) 21845
ENTER MULTIPLIER   (NON-NEGATIVE) 3
PRODUCT = 65535

C>ex_7_1

ENTER MULTIPLICAND (NON-NEGATIVE) 4
ENTER MULTIPLIER   (NON-NEGATIVE) 16384
PRODUCT =       65536

C>ex_7_1

ENTER MULTIPLICAND (NON-NEGATIVE) 32100
ENTER MULTIPLIER   (NON-NEGATIVE) 64200
PRODUCT   2060820000
```

Note that in the first two executions the product is displayed immediately after the annotation message (ie., left-justified in the 11-character field) and that in the last two executions it is separated from the annotation message by some spaces (i.e., right-justified in the 11-character field). These differences demonstrate the setting of the CF bit by the MULTIPLY procedure.

Russian Peasant's Multiply—32-Bit Implementation

A slight change to the Russian Peasant's Method algorithm produces an algorithm that handles signed integer values as follows:

```
FUNCTION MULTIPLY (MULTIPLICAND,MULTIPLIER)
    SIGN = +1
    IF    MULTIPLICAND < 0
    THEN
          SIGN = - SIGN
          MULTIPLICAND = - MULTIPLICAND
    ENDIF
    IF    MULTIPLIER < 0
    THEN
          SIGN = - SIGN
          MULTIPLIER = - MULTIPLIER
    ENDIF
    PRODUCT = 0
    WHILE   MULTIPLIER > 0
       IF   MULTIPLIER IS ODD
       THEN
            PRODUCT = PRODUCT+MULTIPLICAND
       ENDIF
       MULTIPLICAND = MULTIPLICAND*2
       MULTIPLIER = MULTIPLIER/2
    ENDWHILE
    IF    SIGN = -1
    THEN  PRODUCT = - PRODUCT
    ENDIF
    RETURN (PRODUCT)
END MULTIPLY
```

The two single-alternative decision structures that appear before the WHILE loop set both the multiplicand and multiplier to nonnegative and set a sign flag to indicate the required sign of the product. The WHILE loop is the same as in the previous algorithm: It produces a nonnegative product from a nonnegative multiplicand and a nonnegative multiplier. The single-alternative decision structure that appears after the WHILE loop negates the product if the sign flag indicates that the product should be negative.

The assembly module in Program Listing 7.3 contains an external subprocedure that is an implementation of the modified Russian Peasant's Method algorithm for 32-bit signed binary integers in two's complement form. The assembly module in Program Listing 7.2 contains a main procedure that demonstrates the external subprocedure. This section concentrates on the subprocedure and concludes with a brief discussion of the main procedure.

The assembly module in Program Listing 7.3 begins with a prologue (lines 2–11) that describes the function of the external subprocedure defined in the assembly

```
            PAGE    80,132
;===================================================================
;                   PROGRAM LISTING 7.2
;
;PROGRAM TO DEMONSTRATE RUSSIAN PEASANT MULTIPLY PROCEDURE
;
;===================================================================
            .MODEL  SMALL,BASIC
;===================================================================
                                        ;PROCEDURES TO
            EXTRN   GETDEC32:FAR        ;GET 32-BIT SIGNED DEC. INT.
            EXTRN   MULTIPLY:FAR        ;PERFORM 32-BIT MULTIPLY USING
                                        ;THE RUSSIAN PEASANT'S METHOD
            EXTRN   NEWLINE:FAR         ;DISPLAY NEWLINE CHARACTER
            EXTRN   PUTBIN:FAR          ;DISPLAY BINARY INTEGER
            EXTRN   PUTDEC32:FAR        ;DISPLAY 32-BIT SIGNED INT
            EXTRN   PUTSTRNG:FAR        ;DISPLAY CHARACTER STRING
;
;===================================================================
; S T A C K   D E F I N I T I O N
;
            .STACK  256
;===================================================================
; C O N S T A N T   D E F I N I T I O N S
;
            .CONST
PROMPT1     DB      'ENTER MULTIPLICAND '
PROMPT2     DB      'ENTER MULTIPLIER   '
ANNOTATE    DB      'PRODUCT = '
PROMPT_LNG  EQU     PROMPT2-PROMPT1     ;LENGTH OF PROMPT MESSAGES
ANNOTATE_L  EQU     $-ANNOTATE          ;LENGTH OF ANNOTATION MESSAGE
;
;===================================================================
; C O D E   S E G M E N T   D E F I N I T I O N
;
            .CODE   EX_7_2
            .STARTUP                    ;GENERATE STARTUP CODE
;
            PUSH    DS                  ;SET ES-REGISTER TO ADDRESS
            POP     ES                  ;DGROUP
;
            CALL    NEWLINE
;
            LEA     DI,PROMPT2          ;PROMPT FOR MPLIER
            MOV     CX,PROMPT_LNG
            CALL    PUTSTRNG
            CALL    GETDEC32            ;GET MPLIER
            MOV     BL,1                ;PUTBIN CODE = WORD
            XCHG    DX,AX               ;DISPLAY MPLIER IN BINARY
            CALL    PUTBIN
            XCHG    DX,AX
            CALL    PUTBIN
            CALL    NEWLINE
            CALL    NEWLINE
            MOV     DI,DX               ;<MPLIER IN DI:SI>
            MOV     SI,AX
            PUSH    DI
            LEA     DI,PROMPT1          ;PROMPT FOR MCAND
;
            CALL    PUTSTRNG
            POP     DI
            CALL    GETDEC32            ;GET MCAND
            XCHG    DX,AX               ;DISPLAY MCAND IN BINARY
            CALL    PUTBIN
            XCHG    DX,AX
            CALL    PUTBIN
            CALL    NEWLINE
```

```
68:                CALL     NEWLINE
69:                CALL     MULTIPLY                ;PRODUCT = MULTIPLY(MCAND,
70:                PUSH     DI                      ;                    MPLIER)
71:                LEA      DI,ANNOTATE             ;DISPLAY 'PRODUCT = '
72:                MOV      CX,ANNOTATE_L
73:                CALL     PUTSTRNG
74:                POP      DI
75:                MOV      BL,1                    ;PUTBIN CODE = WORD
76:                JNO      _ELSE                   ;IF   OVERFLOW
77:                PUSH     AX                      ;THEN
78:                CALL     NEWLINE
79:                MOV      AX,DI                   ;       DISPLAY BITS 63 - 48
80:                CALL     PUTBIN                  ;               OF PRODUCT
81:                MOV      AX,SI                   ;       DISPLAY BITS 47 - 32
82:                CALL     PUTBIN                  ;               OF PRODUCT
83:                MOV      AX,DX                   ;       DISPLAY BITS 31 - 16
84:                CALL     PUTBIN                  ;               OF PRODUCT
85:                POP      AX                      ;       DISPLAY BITS 15 - 00
86:                CALL     PUTBIN                  ;               OF PRODUCT
87:                JMP      _ENDIF
88: _ELSE:                                          ;ELSE
89:                MOV      BH,0                    ;       DISPLAY PRODUCT IN DEC.
90:                CALL     PUTDEC32
91: _ENDIF:                                         ;ENDIF
92:                CALL     NEWLINE
93:                .EXIT                            ;RETURN TO DOS
94: ;
95:                END
```

module and describes the interface requirements for that subprocedure. The subprocedure multiplies two 32-bit signed integers, producing a 64-bit signed integer product. The subprocedure expects the 32-bit multiplicand in the DX:AX register pair, and it expects the 32-bit multiplier in the DI:SI register pair. The product is returned to the caller in the DI:SI:DX:AX register group. Both the product and the multiplicand are maintained by the subprocedure as 64-bit values. Each time the multiplicand is added to the product, a 64-bit addition operation is performed.

The assembly module contains the definition of a local data segment (lines 13–23). The data in this local data segment are referenced by the MULTIPLY procedure defined in the same assembly module. Two variables are defined in the local data segment: MPCAND and MPLIER. MPCAND is defined in lines 16–19 as four consecutive 16-bit words (i.e., 64 bits). MPLIER is defined in lines 20 and 21 as two consecutive 16-bit words (i.e., 32 bits). The physical order of the storage of the 8 bytes of MPCAND and the 4 bytes of MPLIER is shown in Figure 7.10. The bytes are stored in reverse order. The local data segment also contains a SIGN flag that is initialized to +1 (line 22). The flag indicates whether the final product should be positive or negative.

The macro definition in lines 27–32 is that of a user-defined operation code to negate a 32-bit value. The high-order half of the value to be negated is identified by the first macro operand (msreg), and the low-order half is identified by the second macro operand (lsreg). For example, the macro reference

```
NEG32  DX,AX
```

generates the instructions to negate the 32-bit value in the DX:AX register pair. The macro body appears in lines 28–31. Recall that the two's complement of a binary integer is equivalent to the one's complement of the binary integer plus 1. The two NOT instructions in lines 28 and 29 perform the one's complement of the 32-bit value

```
            PAGE    80,132
;====================================================================
;                   PROGRAM LISTING 7.3
;
; PROCEDURE TO PERFORM 32-BIT SIGNED INTEGER MULTIPLICATION
; USING THE RUSSIAN PEASANT'S METHOD.
; INPUTS:  DX:AX REGISTER PAIR CONTAINS MULTIPLICAND
;          DI:SI REGISTER PAIR CONTAINS MULTIPLIER
; OUTPUTS: DI:SI:DX:AX REGISTER GROUP CONTAINS PRODUCT
;          OF AND CF BITS OF FLAGS REGISTER SET TO REFLECT OVERFLOW
;====================================================================
            .MODEL  SMALL,BASIC
;====================================================================
; L O C A L   D A T A   D E F I N I T I O N S
            .FARDATA MULT_DATA
MPCAND      DW      ?                ;64-BIT EXPANDED MULTIPLICAND
            DW      ?
            DW      ?
            DW      ?
MPLIER      DW      ?                ;32-BIT MULTIPLIER
            DW      ?
SIGN        DB      1                ;SIGN OF PRODUCT (INIT +1)
;
;====================================================================
; M A C R O   D E F I N I T I O N
;
NEG32       MACRO   msreg,lsreg      ;NEGATE 32-BIT INTEGER
            NOT     msreg
            NOT     lsreg
            ADD     lsreg,1
            ADC     msreg,0
            ENDM
;====================================================================
; C O D E   S E G M E N T   D E F I N I T I O N
;
            .CODE   EX_7_3
            ASSUME  DS:MULT_DATA
MULTIPLY    PROC    FAR PUBLIC USES BX CX DS
                                     ;FUNCTION MULTIPLY(MPCAND,MPLIER)
                                         ;SAVE REGISTERS SPECIFIED
                                         ;     IN USES CLAUSE
            PUSHF                        ;SAVE FLAGS
            MOV     BX,SEG MULT_DATA     ;SET DS-REGISTER TO ADDRESS
            MOV     DS,BX                ;LOCAL DATA SEGMENT
            .IF     SWORD PTR DX < 0     ;IF   MPCAND < 0
;
            NEG     SIGN                 ;THEN SIGN = - SIGN
            NEG32   DX,AX                ;     MPCAND = - MPCAND
            .ENDIF                       ;ENDIF
            MOV     MPCAND,AX            ;EXPAND MPCAND TO 64-BITS
            MOV     MPCAND+2,DX
            MOV     MPCAND+4,0
            MOV     MPCAND+6,0
            .IF     SWORD PTR DI < 0     ;IF   MPLIER < 0
;
            NEG     SIGN                 ;THEN SIGN = - SIGN
            NEG32   DI,SI                ;     MPLIER = - MPLIER
            .ENDIF                       ;ENDIF
            MOV     MPLIER,SI
            MOV     MPLIER+2,DI
;
            MOV     AX,0                 ;PRODUCT = 0
            MOV     DX,AX
            MOV     SI,AX
            MOV     DI,AX
LOOPTOP:                                 ;WHILE MPLIER > 0
            CMP     MPLIER,0
```

```
 68:            JNE      CONTINUE
 69:            CMP      MPLIER+2,0
 70:            JE       LOOPEND
 71: CONTINUE:
 72:            SHR      MPLIER+2,1           ;     IF   MPLIER IS ODD
 73:            RCR      MPLIER,1
 74:            JNC      UPDATE
 75:            ADD      AX,MPCAND            ;     THEN PRODUCT = PRODUCT +
 76:            ADC      DX,MPCAND+2          ;                    MPCAND
 77:            ADC      SI,MPCAND+4
 78:            ADC      DI,MPCAND+6
 79: UPDATE:                                  ;     ENDIF
 80:            SAL      MPCAND,1             ;     MPCAND = MPCAND * 2
 81:            RCL      MPCAND+2,1
 82:            RCL      MPCAND+4,1
 83:            RCL      MPCAND+6,1
 84:                                          ;     MPLIER = MPLIER / 2
 85:                                          ;     (DONE IN IF TEST ABOVE)
 86:            JMP      LOOPTOP
 87: LOOPEND:                                 ;ENDWHILE
 88:            .IF      SBYTE PTR SIGN < 0   ;IF    SIGN < 0
 89: ;
 90:            NOT      DI                   ;THEN PRODUCT = - PRODUCT
 91:            NOT      SI
 92:            NOT      DX
 93:            NOT      AX
 94:            ADD      AX,1
 95:            ADC      DX,0
 96:            ADC      SI,0
 97:            ADC      DI,0
 98:            .ENDIF                        ;ENDIF
 99:            POP      BX                   ;FLAGS = SAVED FLAGS
100:            AND      BX,0F7FEH            ;CLEAR OF AND CF IN FLAGS
101:            PUSH     DX                   ;IF    UPPER HALF OF PRODUCT
102:            MOV      CL,15                ;      IS NOT SIGN EXTENSION
103:            SAR      DX,CL                ;      OF THE LOWER HALF
104:            .IF      DI != DX || SI != DX
105:            OR       BX,0801H             ;THEN SET OF AND CF IN FLAGS
106:            .ENDIF                        ;ENDIF
107:            POP      DX
108:            PUSH     BX                   ;SAVED FLAGS = FLAGS
109:            POPF                          ;RESTORE FLAGS
110:                                          ;RESTORE REGISTERS SPECIFIED
111:                                          ;          IN USES CLAUSE
112:            RET                           ;RETURN (PRODUCT)
113: MULTIPLY   ENDP                      ;END MULTIPLY
114:            END
```

in msreg:lsreg, leaving the result in msreg:lsreg. The ADD and ADC instructions add 1 to this value, completing the two's complement operation.

The external subprocedure MULTIPLY is defined in lines 38–113. It begins by saving the registers specified in the USES clause and flags (line 42) for its caller. The MOV instructions in lines 43 and 44 set the DS-register to the origin of the local data segment.

The single-alternative decision structure in lines 45–49 tests the multiplicand in the DX:AX register pair to see if it is negative. If it is negative, then the instructions in lines 47 and 48 are executed; if it is nonnegative, then these instructions are skipped. The NEG instruction in line 47 negates the value of the SIGN flag. The instructions generated by the macro reference in line 48 negate the value of the multiplicand in the DX:AX register pair.

Note that the 32-bit negation operation is designed to convert the multiplicand from signed two's complement form to unsigned integer form, with the sign main-

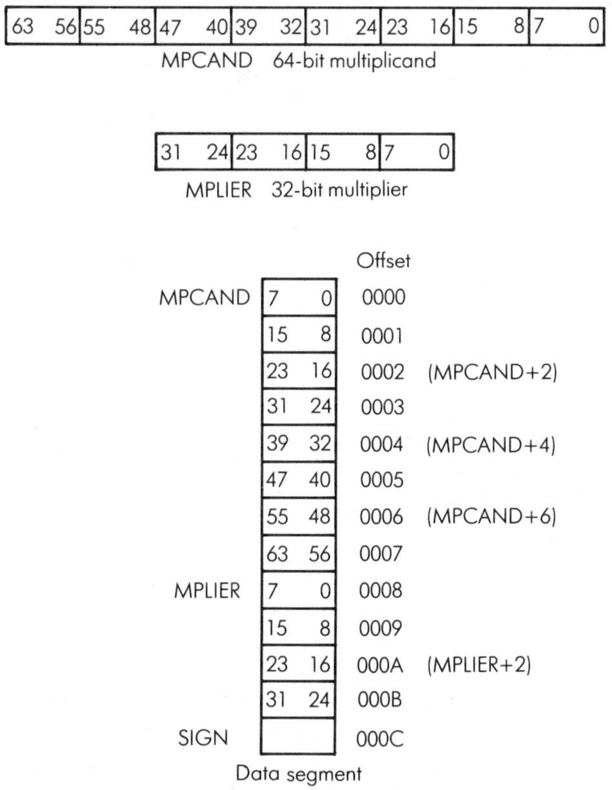

FIGURE 7.10 Organization of local data segment

63 56	55 48	47 40	39 32	31 24	23 16	15 8	7 0

MPCAND 64-bit multiplicand

31 24	23 16	15 8	7 0

MPLIER 32-bit multiplier

	Bits	Offset	
MPCAND	7 0	0000	
	15 8	0001	
	23 16	0002	(MPCAND+2)
	31 24	0003	
	39 32	0004	(MPCAND+4)
	47 40	0005	
	55 48	0006	(MPCAND+6)
	63 56	0007	
MPLIER	7 0	0008	
	15 8	0009	
	23 16	000A	(MPLIER+2)
	31 24	000B	
SIGN		000C	

Data segment

tained separately. Recall that the range of integers that can be represented with 32-bit binary numbers in two's complement form is −2,147,483,648 to +2,147,483,647. Thus, the 32-bit signed integer value −2,147,483,648 cannot successfully be negated since the integer +2,147,483,648 cannot be represented in the 32-bit two's complement number system. However, this integer can be represented in 32-bit unsigned integer form, and the 32-bit negation operation is performed to convert it from signed form to unsigned form. The value −2,147,483,648 is represented in 32-bit two's complement form by the hexadecimal value 80000000. Taking the two's complement of this value produces the same hexadecimal value 80000000, which is the 32-bit unsigned integer representation of +2,147,483,648. This situation means that any negative integer in two's complement form can be converted to the corresponding positive integer in unsigned form by performing the negation (two's complement) operation on that negative integer.

The four MOV instructions in lines 50–53 expand the 32-bit unsigned integer multiplicand now in the DX:AX register pair to a 64-bit value beginning at the memory location specified by the symbolic name MPCAND. The first two MOV instructions move the 32-bit contents of the DX:AX register pair to the lower 32 bits of MPCAND. The last two MOV instructions set the upper 32 bits of MPCAND to zero.

The single-alternative decision structure in lines 54–58 tests the multiplier in the DI:SI register pair to see if it is negative. If it is negative, then the instructions in lines 56 and 57 are executed; if it is nonnegative, then these instructions are skipped. The NEG instruction in line 56 negates the value of the SIGN flag. The instructions generated by the macro reference in line 57 negate the value of the multiplier in the

DI:SI register pair. Again, this negation operation is performed by taking the one's complement of the value in the DI:SI register pair and then adding 1 to that result.

The two MOV instructions in lines 59 and 60 move a copy of the 32-bit value of the multiplier to the four consecutive bytes of memory that begin at the memory location specified by the symbolic name MPLIER. The first MOV instruction moves a copy of the contents of the SI register to the lower 16 bits of MPLIER. The second MOV instruction moves a copy of the contents of the DI-register to the upper 16 bits of MPLIER.

At this point, the variable MPCAND contains a 64-bit unsigned integer multiplicand, and the variable MPLIER contains a 32-bit unsigned integer multiplier. The SIGN flag indicates whether or not the unsigned integer product, to be produced by the Russian Peasant's Method algorithm, will need to be negated to produce the correct signed integer product. The SIGN flag is initialized to +1 (line 22). If the original multiplicand and multiplier are both nonnegative, then the NEG instructions (lines 47 and 56) are not executed and the value of SIGN remains at 1. If the multiplicand and multiplier are both negative, then both NEG instructions are executed. The first instruction changes the value of SIGN to −1, and the second returns the value of SIGN to +1. If the multiplicand and the multiplier do not have the same sign (i.e., one is negative, and one is nonnegative), then exactly one of the two NEG instructions is executed, setting SIGN to −1, which indicates that the product must be negated.

The four MOV instructions in lines 62–65 initialize the product in the DI:SI:DX:AX register group to zero. The MOV instruction in line 62 moves the immediate value zero to the AX-register. The three MOV instructions in lines 63–65 copy zero from the AX-register to the DX, SI, and DI registers, respectively. The register-to-register moves are 2-byte instructions, and the immediate-to-register move is a 3-byte instruction. That is, the sequence

```
MOV  AX,0
MOV  DX,AX
MOV  SI,AX
MOV  DI,AX
```

requires three fewer instruction bytes than does the sequence

```
MOV  AX,0
MOV  DX,0
MOV  SI,0
MOV  DI,0
```

In addition to the memory savings, a register-to-register move executes faster than an immediate-to-register move.

The WHILE loop in lines 66–87 computes the product of the multiplicand and the multiplier. The instructions in lines 67–70 provide the loop test. The two 16-bit halves of the multiplier have to be compared to zero separately. As long as the multiplier is nonzero, there are still nonzero partial products to be added to the product sum—thus the loop body is executed. When both halves of the multiplier become zero, no further nonzero partial products are to be added to the product sum, so the loop is terminated (i.e., the jump in line 70 is taken). The loop body consists of the instructions in lines 72–83.

The single-alternative decision structure in lines 72–79 tests the current value of the multiplier to see if it is odd. If it is odd, then the current value of the multiplicand is added to the product sum; if it is even, then nothing is added to the product sum (i.e., the partial product for the current multiplier bit is zero). The SHR and RCR instructions in lines 72 and 73 perform two functions. They test the current value of the 32-bit multiplier to see if it is odd, and they divide the 32-bit multiplier by 2 in preparation for the next loop test and the next iteration of the loop body The bit shifted from the right of the 32-bit operand, MPLIER, is recorded in the CF bit of the flags register. The bit shifted out is the remainder of the division by 2, and it indicates whether the value of the 32-bit multiplier was odd or even prior to the division operation. The JNC instruction in line 74 makes the decision based on this condition. If the CF bit in the flags register is 1, then the jump is not taken and the instructions in lines 75–78 are executed; if the CF bit in the flags register is 0, then the instructions in lines 75–78 are skipped.

The four instructions in lines 75–78 perform a 64-bit addition operation. They add the 64-bit value of the MPCAND variable (the current value of the multiplicand) to the 64-bit value in the DI:SI:DX:AX register group (the current value of the product sum), leaving the result in the DI:SI:DX:AX register group (the new value of the product sum). The ADD instruction in line 75 adds bits 15 to 0 of the two 64-bit operands, leaving the result in the AX-register. The ADC instruction in line 76 adds bits 31 to 16 of the two 64-bit operands and the carry from bit 15, leaving the result in the DX-register. The ADC instruction in line 77 adds bits 47 to 32 of the two 64-bit operands and the carry from bit 31, leaving the result in the SI-register. The ADC instruction in line 78 adds bits 63 to 48 of the two 64-bit operands and the carry from bit 47, leaving the result in the DI-register. The carry out of bit 63 (the MSB) is recorded in the CF bit of the flags register.

Following the single-alternative decision structure, the 64-bit value of MPCAND, the current value of the multiplicand, is multiplied by 2. This task is accomplished by the multiple-word, left-shift operation in lines 80–83. The comments in lines 84 and 85 indicate that the division of the multiplier by 2 was performed by the SHR and RCR instructions in lines 72 and 73.

The JMP instruction in line 86 returns control to the WHILE loop test beginning in line 66. At loop exit, the complete unsigned integer product is in the DI:SI:DX:AX register group, and the instructions in lines 88–112 are executed.

The single-alternative decision structure in lines 88–98 negates the 64-bit product in the DI:SI:DX:AX register group if the SIGN flag indicates that the product should be negative. The instructions generated for the macro directive in line 88 test the SIGN flag and make the decision based on the condition of the SIGN flag. If the SIGN flag has the value −1, then the instructions in lines 90–97 are executed; otherwise, these instructions are skipped. The instructions in lines 90–97 perform the two's complement of the 64-bit value in the DI:SI:DX:AX register group. The four NOT instructions perform the one's complement of this 64-bit value, and the four addition instructions add 1 to the one's complement, producing the two's complement. The resulting 64-bit signed integer product is left in the DI:SI:DX:AX register group.

The instructions in lines 99–108 set the OF and CF bits in the flags register to reflect whether or not the 64-bit signed integer product overflows 32 bits. If the high-order half of the product is not the sign extension of the low-order 32 bits, then the signed integer product does not fit in 32 bits and the OF and CF bits in the flags register are set. If the high-order half of the product is the sign extension of the low-order 32 bits, then the OF and CF bits in the flags register are cleared. The POP instruction in line 99 pops the flags register value, which is saved on entry to the subprocedure (line 42), into the BX-register. The AND instruction in line 100 clears the OF and CF bits in this flags register value.

The single-alternative decision structure in lines 101–107 sets the OF and CF bits in the flags register value in the BX-register if the high-order half of the 64-bit product is not the sign extension of the low-order half. The sign bit of the DX-register is the sign of the low-order half of the product. If the sign bit of the DX-register is extended throughout the SI and DI registers, then the product fits in the 32 bits of the DX:AX register pair. The PUSH instruction in line 101 saves the value of the DX-register so that the DX-register can be used to create a sign extension of the DX-register. The MOV and SAR instructions in lines 102 and 103 perform a 15-bit arithmetic right-shift of the DX-register value. Since the shift is an arithmetic shift, the sign bit is extended throughout the DX-register. If both the DI- and SI-registers are equal to this DX-register value, then the DI:SI register pair is a sign extension of the DX:AX register pair. Otherwise, the DI:SI is not a sign extension of the DX:AX. The code generated in response to the .IF pseudo-operation in line 104 causes the OR instruction in line 105 to be executed if either the DI-register value or the SI-register value is not equal to the DX-register value. These instructions cause the OR instruction to be skipped if both the DI-register value and the SI-register value are equal to the DX-register value. The OR instruction in line 105 sets the OF and CF bits in the flags register value in the BX-register. The POP instruction in line 107 restores the DX-register value, which was saved by the PUSH instruction in line 101. Following this single-alternative decision structure, the PUSH instruction in line 108 is executed, which pushes the modified flags register value back onto the stack.

The subprocedure ends by restoring the flags (line 109), restoring the registers specified in the USES clause, and returning control to the caller (line 112). The signed integer product is returned in the DI:SI:DX:AX register group. The OF and CF bits in the saved and restored flags register value have been modified. All other bits in the flags register have been preserved.

Compound conditional expressions were introduced in Chapter 6 (see Section 6.5). The subprocedure MULTIPLY, defined in Program Listing 7.3, provides two examples of compound conditional expressions. One example is implemented with the primitive instructions of the 8088/8086 assembly language, and the other is implemented with the decision-generating macro directives of MASM 6.0.

In line 66 of Program Listing 7.3, the pseudocode statement

```
WHILE MPLIER > 0
```

must be implemented with the equivalent compound conditional

```
WHILE  low-order half of  MPLIER  ≠  0
    or high-order half of  MPLIER  ≠  0
```

in the 8088/8086 assembly language. Since MPLIER is a 32-bit operand and since the 8088/8086 assembly language instructions can manipulate only 8-bit or 16-bit operands, the two 16-bit halves of the 32-bit operand must be tested separately. The CMP instruction in line 67 compares the low-order half of MPLIER to zero, and the JNE instruction in line 68 transfers control to the beginning of the loop body if the low-order half is nonzero. If the low-order half is zero, then the CMP instruction in line 69 compares the high-order half of MPLIER to zero, and the JE instruction in line 70 causes the loop to be terminated if the high-order half is zero. If the high-order half is nonzero, then control flows to the beginning of the loop body. The net effect of the instructions in lines 67–70 is to exit the loop if both halves of MPLIER are zero and to execute the loop body if either the low-order half or the high-order half of MPLIER is nonzero. The loop in lines 66–87 of Program Listing 7.3 can also be implemented with loop-generating macro directives as follows:

```
          .WHILE  MPLIER != 0 || MPLIER+2 != 0
                                ;WHILE MPLIER > 0
          SHR  MPLIER+2,1       ;    IF   MPLIER IS ODD
          RCR  MPLIER,1
          JNC  UPDATE
          ADD  AX,MPCAND        ;    THEN PRODUCT = PRODUCT +
          ADC  DX,MPCAND+2      ;                   MPCAND
          ADC  SI,MPCAND+4
          ADC  DI,MPCAND+6
UPDATE:                         ;    ENDIF
          SAL  MPCAND,1         ;    MPCAND = MPCAND * 2
          RCL  MPCAND+2,1
          RCL  MPCAND+4,1
          RCL  MPCAND+6,1
                                ;    MPLIER = MPLIER / 2
                                ;    (DONE IN IF TEST ABOVE)
          .ENDW                 ;ENDWHILE
```

The single-alternative decision structure in lines 101–107 of Program Listing 7.3 is partially implemented with decision-generating macro directives (see lines 104–106). The assembler translates lines 104–106 into the following primitive instructions:

```
          cmp  di,dx
          jne  @C0008
          cmp  si,dx
          je   @C0007
@C0008:
          OR   BX,0801H
@C0007:
```

The OR instruction is executed if either the DI-register value is not equal to the DX-register value or the SI-register value is not equal to the DX-register value. The OR instruction is skipped if both the DI-register value and the SI-register value are equal to the DX-register value. The single-alternative decision structure in lines 101–107 of Program Listing 7.3 can also be implemented with the primitive instructions of the assembly language as follows:

```
          PUSH  DX          ;IF   UPPER HALF OF PRODUCT
          MOV   CL,15       ;     IS NOT SIGN EXTENSION
          SAR   DX,CL       ;     OF THE LOWER HALF
          CMP   DI,DX
          JNE   THEN1
          CMP   SI,DX
          JE    ENDIF1
THEN1:                      ;THEN
          OR    BX,0801H    ;     SET OF AND CF IN FLAGS
ENDIF1:                     ;ENDIF
          POP   DX
```

The main procedure defined in lines 37–94 in Program Listing 7.2 performs the following steps:

1. Prompts for the multiplier (lines 44–46).
2. Accepts the input value for the multiplier in the DX:AX register pair (line 47).
3. Displays the multiplier in binary form (lines 48–54).
4. Moves the multiplier to the DI:SI register pair (lines 55–56).

5. Prompts for the multiplicand (lines 57–61).
6. Accepts the input value for the multiplicand in the DX:AX register pair (line 62).
7. Displays the multiplicand in binary form (lines 63–68).
8. Calls the MULTIPLY subprocedure to compute the product of the multiplicand and the multiplier (line 69).
9. Displays the product in binary form if the product overflowed 32 bits, in decimal if the product did not overflow 32 bits (lines 70–91).

The following are the results from some sample executions of this program:

```
C>EX_7_2
ENTER MULTIPLIER   32767
00000000000000000111111111111111

ENTER MULTIPLICAND -32767
11111111111111111000000000000001

PRODUCT = -1073676289

C>EX_7_2
ENTER MULTIPLIER   62100
00000000000000001111001010010100

ENTER MULTIPLICAND -12
11111111111111111111111111110100

PRODUCT = -745200

C>EX_7_2
ENTER MULTIPLIER   65535
00000000000000001111111111111111

ENTER MULTIPLICAND -65535
11111111111111110000000000000001

PRODUCT =
1111111111111111111111111111111100000000000000011111111111111111

C>EX_7_2
ENTER MULTIPLIER   -131072
11111111111111100000000000000000

ENTER MULTIPLICAND -524287
11111111111110000000000000000001

PRODUCT =
0000000000000000000000000000111111111111111111100000000000000000
```

7.4 Intel 80386 Assembly Language Programming

The Intel 8088/8086 microprocessor was designed for a single-process environment. A **single-process environment** is an environment in which only one program executes at a time. The Intel 80286 microprocessor was designed with some multiprocessing features, and the Intel 80386 microprocessor was designed for a multiprocess environment. A **multiprocess environment** is an environment in which two or more programs can execute simultaneously.

The Intel 80286 microprocessor has two modes of operation: real mode and protected mode. A **real-mode 80286** emulates an enhanced 8088/8086; it is faster and has an expanded instruction set. Some of the instructions in this expanded instruction set have already been presented (see sections entitled "Additional Capabilities in the 80286 Assembly Language"). The protected mode of the 80286 provides some memory protection features that facilitate multiprocessing. Only the real mode of the 80286 is considered in this book. Protected-mode programming is beyond the scope of this book.

The Intel 80386 microprocessor has three modes of operation: real mode, protected mode, and virtual mode. A **real-mode 80386** emulates an enhanced real-mode 80286; it is faster, has an extended register set, and has an expanded instruction set. Only the real mode of the 80386 is considered in detail in this book. For the most part, protected-mode and virtual-mode programming are beyond the scope of this book. However, from a computer organization standpoint, a contrast of real mode and protected mode is often helpful in studying real-mode operations. Therefore, some aspects of protected mode are considered in this chapter.

The 8088/8086 and 80286 microprocessors provide registers and instructions for performing integer arithmetic and bit manipulation operations on either 8-bit or 16-bit operands, which can be interpreted as either unsigned or signed integer values. The 80386 microprocessor provides registers and instructions for performing integer arithmetic and bit manipulation operations on either 8-bit, 16-bit, or 32-bit operands, which can be interpreted as either unsigned or signed integer values. Table 7.1, near the beginning of this chapter, shows the range of integer values that can be represented by 8-bit, 16-bit, and 32-bit binary numbers in both unsigned form and signed two's complement form.

The instructions and registers used in 8088/8086 and 80286 assembly language programs can also be used in 80386 assembly language programs for 8-bit and 16-bit operations. The expanded instruction set of the 80386 includes some additional instructions that can also be used for 8-bit and 16-bit operations. For 32-bit operations, the 80386 provides an extended register set and an expanded instruction set. The extended registers can be used with the basic integer arithmetic and bit manipulation instructions, which the 80386 inherited from the older microprocessors in the Intel family. In addition, the expanded instruction set of the 80386 includes instructions specifically designed for 32-bit operations.

Intel 80386 Register Set

The Intel 80386 microprocessor contains ten 32-bit registers and six 16-bit registers that can be directly or indirectly manipulated by real-mode assembly language programs. These registers are shown in Figure 7.11 and are discussed in the following subsections.

Segment Registers

The Intel 80386 has six 16-bit segment registers: CS, SS, DS, ES, FS, and GS. The CS, SS, DS, and ES registers have exactly the same function as the corresponding registers in the older microprocessors in the family. The FS and GS registers, like the ES-register, contain the origin of currently active static data segments. Thus, there

FIGURE 7.11
Intel 80386 registers

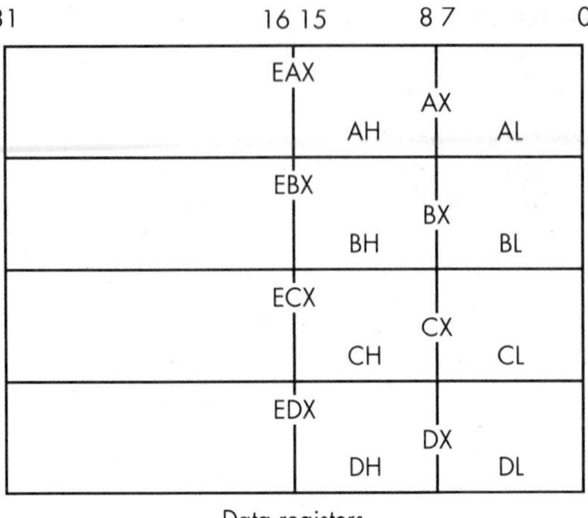

Data registers

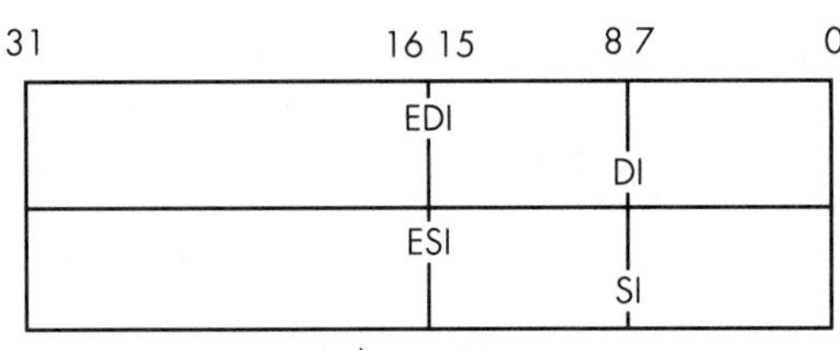

Index registers

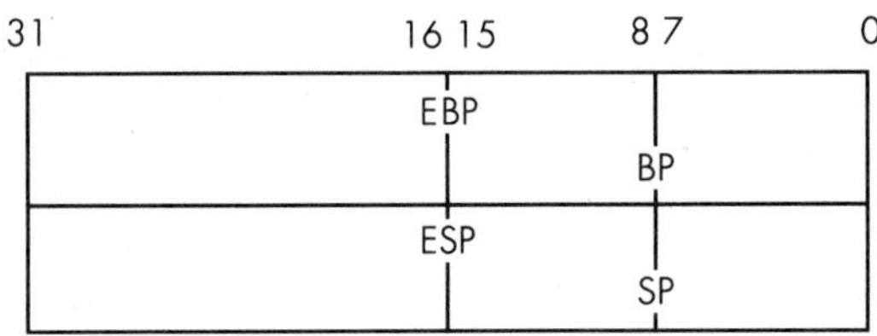

Pointer registers

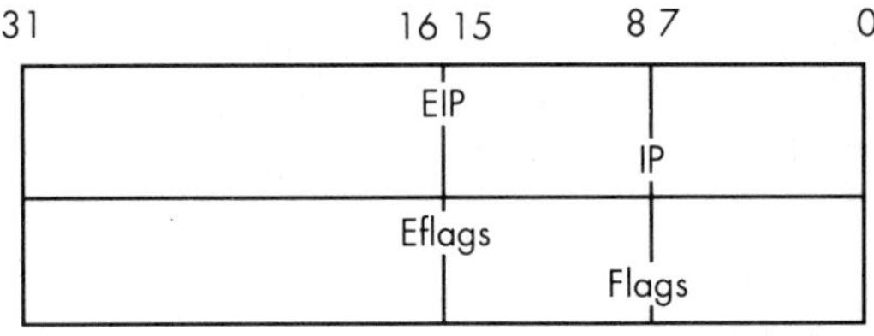

Control registers

15   0
CS
SS
DS
ES
FS
GS

Segment registers

can be up to four active static data segments for an 80386 program, which are addressed by the DS, ES, FS, and GS registers.

Instruction Pointer Register

The instruction pointer register has the same function in the 80386 microprocessor as it does in the older microprocessors in the family. The combination of the code segment register and the instruction pointer register provides the information necessary for the processor to compute the address of the next instruction byte to be fetched from memory. The instruction pointer register contains the offset within the currently active code segment of the next instruction byte to be fetched. If the 80386 is operating in real mode, then the instruction pointer is the 16-bit contents of the IP-register, and the maximum code segment size is 64K bytes. If the 80386 is operating in protected mode, then the instruction pointer is the 32-bit contents of the EIP-register, and the maximum segment size is 4 gigabytes (4,194,304K bytes).

General Registers

There are eight 32-bit general registers in the 80386 microprocessor. These registers are divided into three groups in Figure 7.11. There are four data registers (EAX, EBX, ECX, and EDX), two index registers (EDI and ESI), and two pointer registers (EBP and ESP). Each of these registers can be used to supply a 32-bit operand to and receive the 32-bit result from an arithmetic or bit manipulation operation performed by the ALU. The low-order 16 bits of these registers can be used to supply a 16-bit operand to and receive a 16-bit result from an arithmetic or bit manipulation operation performed by the ALU. The register designator for the low-order half of a 32-bit register is the register designator for that 32-bit register with the E omitted. That is, the AX-register is the low-order 16 bits of the EAX-register, the BX-register is the low-order 16 bits of the EBX-register, and so on (see Figure 7.11). The low-order half of each of the four data registers can be divided into two 8-bit registers. The high-order half of the AX-register (bits 8–15 of the EAX-register) is referred to as the AH-register, and the low-order half (bits 0–7 of the EAX) is referred to as the AL-register. Similarly, BH and BL are the designators for the two halves of the BX-register, CH and CL for the CX-register, and DH and DL for the DX-register (see Figure 7.11). Each of these eight 8-bit data registers can be used to supply an 8-bit operand to and receive an 8-bit result from an arithmetic or bit manipulation operation performed by the ALU.

In addition to supplying operands to and receiving results from the ALU, each general register has a specific purpose as follows:

EAX-Register The EAX-register is the accumulator register for 32-bit operations.

ECX-Register The ECX-register is the **32-bit count register** and can be used as a counter in loop operations. The CX-register is the default count register used with the LOOP instruction in real mode, and the ECX-register is the default count register used with the LOOP instruction in protected mode. However, in either mode, it is possible to override the default count register and use the other count register in a loop operation.

EDX-Register The EDX-register is used as an extension to the EAX-register for multiplication and division operations and for 64-bit arithmetic.

ESP-Register The **stack pointer** has the same function in the 80386 microprocessor as it does in the older microprocessors in the family. The combination of the stack segment register and the stack pointer provides the information necessary for the processor to compute the address of the top-of-stack data word. The stack pointer contains the offset within the stack segment of the top-of-stack data word. If the 80386 is operating in real mode, then the stack pointer is the 16-bit contents of the SP-register. If the 80386 is operating in protected mode, then the stack pointer is the 32-bit contents of the ESP-register.

EDI, ESI, EBX, and EBP Registers These registers are the index and pointer registers for specifying 32-bit offsets in protected mode. The DI, SI, BX, and BP registers are the index and pointer registers for specifying 16-bit offsets in real mode.

Eflags Register

The Eflags register is a 32-bit register, as shown in Figure 7.12. The low-order half of the Eflags register is identical to the flags register of the 80286 microprocessor, and the low-order 12 bits of the Eflags register are identical to the low-order 12 bits of the 8088/8086 flags register. (The high-order 4 bits of the 8088/8086 flags register are unused.)

FIGURE 7.12
Eflags register

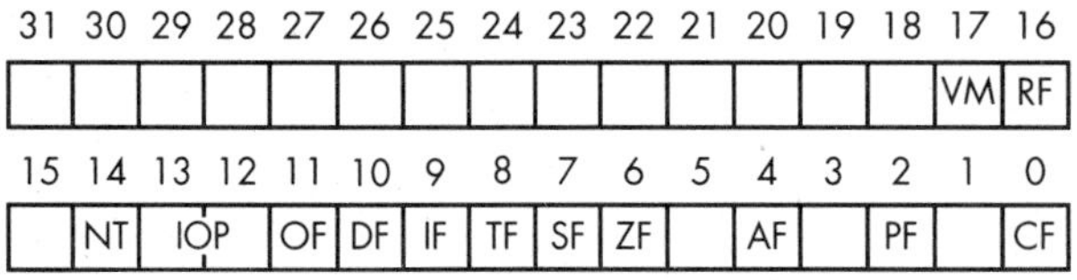

31	30	29	28	27	26	25	24	23	22	21	20	19	18	17	16
														VM	RF

15	14	13	12	11	10	9	8	7	6	5	4	3	2	1	0
	NT	IOP		OF	DF	IF	TF	SF	ZF		AF		PF		CF

80386	
Virtual 8086 mode	VM
Resume flag	RF
80286/80386	
Nested task	NT
I/O protection level	IOP
8088/8086/80286/80386	
Overflow flag	OF
Direction flag	DF
Interrupt flag	IF
Trap flag	TF
Sign flag	SF
Zero flag	ZF
Auxiliary carry flag	AF
Parity flag	PF
Carry flag	CF

Data-Defining Pseudo-Operations

The data-defining pseudo-operations for defining double-word (32-bit) data, **DD**, **DWORD**, and **SDWORD**, have the following general forms:

[⟨*name*⟩] `DD` ⟨*double-word-constant-list*⟩ [⟨*comment*⟩]
[⟨*name*⟩] `DWORD` ⟨*double-word-constant-list*⟩ [⟨*comment*⟩]
[⟨*name*⟩] `SDWORD` ⟨*double-word-constant-list*⟩ [⟨*comment*⟩]

in which <*name*> is the symbolic name to be associated with the memory location in which the sequence of double words is to begin and <*double-word-constant-list*> is a list of double-word constants separated by commas. A double-word constant can be specified in binary, octal, hexadecimal, or decimal. The rules for specifying double-word constants in these four forms are the same as those for specifying byte and word constants, with the ranges expanded to the appropriate 32-bit ranges.

Each double-word constant specifies the allocation of 4 consecutive bytes (one double word) of storage, with the value of the constant being the initial value of that double word. The 4 bytes of that 32-bit initial value are stored in order from low-order byte to high-order byte. The order of the constants in the list specifies the order in which the double words are to appear in the static data segment. The symbolic <*name*> is associated with the first double word in the list.

A question mark (?) can be used in place of a double-word constant. A question mark indicates that 4 bytes (one double word) of storage are to be allocated but that an initial value is not being specified. The initial value for the allocated double word is unknown.

EXAMPLE

The following data segment definition instructs the assembler to generate a 19-byte static data segment with the symbolic names and initial values as shown in Table 7.3:

```
            .FARDATA  DATA
HUNDRED     DB        100
THOUSAND    DW        1000
MILLION     DD        1000000
BILLION     DD        1000000000
HEX_DIGITS  DD        01234567H,89ABCDEFH
```

■

TABLE 7.3
A 19-byte data segment

Symbolic Name	Byte Offset	Hex Contents
HUNDRED	0000	64
THOUSAND	0001	E8
	0002	03
MILLION	0003	40
	0004	42
	0005	0F
	0006	00
BILLION	0007	00
	0008	CA
	0009	9A
	000A	3B
HEX_DIGITS	000B	67
	000C	45
	000D	23
	000E	01
	000F	EF
	0010	CD
	0011	AB
	0012	89

8088/8086 Instructions with 80386 Registers

The 80386 assembly language is a superset of the 8088/8086 assembly language. This upward compatibility means that the instructions of the 8088/8086 assembly language are all available in the 80386 assembly language. In the 80386 assembly language, the instructions inherited from the 8088/8086 assembly language can operate on either 8-bit, 16-bit, or 32-bit operands. This expansion of the basic 8088/8086 instructions to allow 32-bit operands is accomplished in the 80386 machine language by a 1-byte instruction prefix.

The 8088/8086 machine language becomes two different machine languages on the 80386 microprocessor, depending on whether the 80386 is operating in real mode or in protected mode. With the 80386 operating in real mode, the machine language instructions are interpreted the same as they are on an 8088/8086. This equivalent interpretation means that an executable program that was developed on an 8088/8086-based computer can be executed on an 80386-based computer without having to be modified or reassembled and relinked. However, with the 80386 operating in protected mode, some of the machine language instructions are interpreted in a different way than they are on the 8088/8086. As a general rule, 8088/8086 machine language instructions with byte operands have the same interpretation on the 80386 in both real mode and protected mode, and those instructions with word operands have the same interpretation on the 80386 in real mode but have a different interpretation on the 80386 in protected mode. The word operands become double-word operands in protected mode. These similarities and differences are best illustrated with a few examples. Table 7.4 shows four 8088/8086 machine language instructions along with the corresponding instructions in 8088/8086 assembly language, 80386 real-mode assembly language, and 80386 protected-mode assembly language. The first row of Table 7.4 shows the following:

> On the 8088/8086, on the 80386 in real mode, and on the 80386 in protected mode, execution of the 2-byte machine language instruction B7 01 causes the value of the BH-register to be replaced with the immediate value 1.

The second row of Table 7.4 shows the following:

> On the 8088/8086 and on the 80386 in real mode, execution of the 2-byte machine language instruction 8B C2 causes the value of the AX-register to be replaced with a copy of the value of the DX-register. However, on the 80386 in protected mode, execution of this instruction causes the value of the EAX-register to be replaced with a copy of the value of the EDX-register.

TABLE 7.4
Machine language with corresponding assembly code

Machine Language	8088/8086 Assembly Language	80386 Real-Mode Assembly Language	80386 Protected-Mode Assembly Language
B7 01	MOV BH,1	MOV BH,1	MOV BH,1
8B C2	MOV AX,DX	MOV AX,DX	MOV EAX,EDX
50	PUSH AX	PUSH AX	PUSH EAX
F7 E3	MUL BX	MUL BX	MUL EBX

Limited to the instructions of the 8088/8086 machine language, the 80386 microprocessor can manipulate only 8-bit and 16-bit operands when operating in real mode and only 8-bit and 32-bit operands when operating in protected mode. How, then, can all three operand sizes be made available in both real mode and protected mode? This is where the 1-byte instruction prefix comes into play. None of the instructions in the 8088/8086 machine language begin with the byte value 66 hexadecimal. The 80386 machine language uses this byte value as an instruction prefix. When operating in real mode, this instruction prefix instructs the processor to interpret the prefixed instruction as it would if it were operating in protected mode. When operating in protected mode, this instruction prefix instructs the processor to interpret the prefixed instruction as it would if it were operating in real mode. The effect of the instruction prefix is best illustrated with a few examples. Table 7.5 shows three 80386 machine language instructions with and without the operand-size instruction prefix (66 hexadecimal). The first row of Table 7.5 shows the following:

> With the 80386 operating in real mode, execution of the unprefixed machine language instruction 8B C2 causes the value of the AX-register to be replaced with a copy of the value of the DX-register. However, with the 80386 operating in protected mode, execution of this instruction causes the value of the EAX-register to be replaced with a copy of the value of the EDX-register.

The second row of Table 7.5 shows the following:

> With the 80386 operating in real mode, execution of the prefixed machine language instruction 66 8B C2 causes the value of the EAX-register to be replaced with a copy of the value of the EDX-register. However, with the 80386 operating in protected mode, execution of this instruction causes the value of the AX-register to be replaced with a copy of the value of the DX-register.

TABLE 7.5
80386 machine language with and without 1-byte prefix

Machine Language	80386 Real-Mode Assembly Language	80386 Protected-Mode Assembly Language
8B C2	MOV AX,DX	MOV EAX,EDX
66 8B C2	MOV EAX,EDX	MOV AX,DX
50	PUSH AX	PUSH EAX
66 50	PUSH EAX	PUSH AX
F7 E3	MUL BX	MUL EBX
66 F7 E3	MUL EBX	MUL BX

Fortunately, 80386 assembly language programmers do not have to keep track of this operand-size instruction prefix. Through the use of pseudo-operations, which will be presented later in this chapter, the programmer instructs the assembler to generate code either for real-mode execution or for protected-mode execution. In addition, the 80386 assembly language recognizes the 32-bit register designators and provides additional instruction mnemonics that indicate the desired operand size. Therefore, in the 80386 assembly language, the instructions inherited from the 8088/8086 assembly language can operate on either 8-bit, 16-bit, or 32-bit operands.

EXAMPLES

The instruction

```
ADD  EAX,EDI
```

causes the 32-bit value of the EDI-register to be added to the 32-bit value of the EAX-register, leaving the 32-bit sum in the EAX-register and setting the flags to reflect the sum.

The instruction

```
MUL  EBX
```

causes the 32-bit unsigned integer value of the EAX-register to be multiplied by the 32-bit unsigned integer value of the EBX-register, leaving the 64-bit product in the EDX:EAX register pair. The OF and CF bits of the flags register reflect whether or not the product overflows 32 bits.

The instruction

```
IDIV  EBX
```

causes the 64-bit signed integer dividend in the EDX:EAX register pair to be divided by the 32-bit signed integer divisor in the EBX-register, leaving the 32-bit quotient in the EAX-register and the 32-bit remainder in the EDX-register. ■

Stack operations on the 80386 microprocessor can involve either word or double-word operands. When word operands are involved, the stack pointer is adjusted by 2 with each push or pop operation. When double-word operands are involved, the stack pointer is adjusted by 4 with each push or pop operation.

EXAMPLES

The instruction

```
PUSH  ECX
```

causes the value of the SP-register (ESP-register in protected mode) to be decremented by 4 and the 4-byte (32-bit) value of the ECX-register to be stored in the stack segment beginning at the location addressed by the SS:SP register pair (SS:ESP in protected mode). The bytes are stored in order from low-order byte to high-order byte.

The instruction

```
POP  ESI
```

causes a copy of the 4-byte (32-bit) stack segment value addressed by the SS:SP register pair (SS:ESP in protected mode) to replace the value of the ESI-register and the SP-register to be incremented by 4 (ESP-register in protected mode). The incrementing of the SP-register (ESP) has the effect of removing 4 bytes (2 words) from the logical stack. ■

When the operand of a PUSH instruction is either a register designator or a variable name, the assembler knows the appropriate operand size. However, when the operand is an immediate value, it is not clear to the assembler whether the operand size should be 16 bits or 32 bits. Beginning with the 80286 microprocessor, the microprocessors of the Intel family have allowed the operand of a PUSH instruction to be an immediate value (see Section 2.6). For 80386 assembly, MASM 6.0 makes the assumption that a PUSH instruction with an immediate operand is intended to be a 16-bit push operation in real mode and a 32-bit push operation in protected mode. Even when the value of the immediate operand lies outside of the 16-bit range,

MASM 6.0 assumes that the operand was intended to be a 16-bit operand if it is translating for real-mode operations. In this case, MASM 6.0 truncates the binary representation of the immediate operand and uses only the low-order 16 bits. For example, when translating for real-mode operations, MASM 6.0 translates the instruction

```
PUSH  65536
```

to the machine language instruction 6A00, which is equivalent to the instruction

```
PUSH  0
```

MASM 6.0 does provide two alternative operation codes for the PUSH operation code: PUSHW (push word) and PUSHD (push double word). These alternative operation codes are used with immediate operands to inform the assembler of the desired operand size. They can also be used with register and memory operands, apparently with the intent of providing type checking on the source operand.[1] These alternative operation codes are not available in MASM 5.1.

EXAMPLE

The instruction

```
PUSH  327
```

causes the 16-bit value 0147 hex to be pushed onto the stack in real mode and the 32-bit value 00000147 hex to be pushed onto the stack in protected mode.

The instruction

```
PUSHD  327
```

can be used in real mode to cause the 32-bit value 00000147 hex to be pushed onto the stack, and the instruction

```
PUSHW  327
```

can be used in protected mode to cause the 16-bit value 0147 hex to be pushed onto the stack. ■

Loop operations on the 80386 microprocessor can involve either a word or a double-word count register. The default count register for the LOOP, LOOPE (LOOPZ), and LOOPNE (LOOPNZ) instructions is the CX-register in real mode and the ECX-register in protected mode. The 80386 machine language uses the operand-size instruction prefix (66 hexadecimal) to override these defaults (i.e., to use the ECX-register as the count register in real mode or to use the CX-register as the count register in protected mode). MASM 6.0 provides alternative operation codes for explicitly specifying the count register in its 80386 assembly language. The alternative mnemonics are LOOPW, LOOPEW (LOOPZW), and LOOPNEW (LOOPNZW) for specifying that the CX-register is to be used as the count register, and LOOPD, LOOPED (LOOPZD), and LOOPNED (LOOPNZD) for specifying that the ECX-register is to be used as the count register. These alternative operation codes are not available in MASM 5.1.

---

[1] Unfortunately, MASM 6.0 seems to be inconsistent with its handling of PUSHW and PUSHD. MASM 6.0 does not allow a 32-bit register designator or a double-word variable to be used as the source operand for a PUSHW instruction. However, it does allow a 16-bit register designator and a word variable to be used as the source operand for a PUSHD instruction. For example, PUSHD AX is translated as if it were PUSHD EAX.

EXAMPLES

Following the execution of the instructions

```
          MOV   EAX,0
          MOV   ECX,66666
LOOPTOP:
          INC   EAX
          LOOP  LOOPTOP
```

the EAX-register contains the value 1130 because the count register is the CX-register (the low-order half of the ECX-register). That is, 66666 decimal = 1046A hex, which, when truncated to 16 bits, is 046A hex (1130 decimal).

Following the execution of the instructions

```
          MOV    EAX,0
          MOV    ECX,66666
LOOPTOP:
          INC    EAX
          LOOPD  LOOPTOP
```

the EAX-register contains the value 66666 because the count register is the ECX-register. ■

The 80386 assembly language provides two operation code mnemonics for the jump if count register is zero instruction: JCXZ (jump if CX-register is zero) and JECXZ (jump if ECX-register is zero). JCXZ is translated to the same unprefixed machine language instruction in real mode as JECXZ is translated to in protected mode. When JECXZ is used in real mode or JCXZ is used in protected mode, the same machine language instruction is prefixed with the operand-size prefix (66 hexadecimal). The JECXZ mnemonic is available in both MASM 6.0 and MASM 5.1.

New Instructions in the 80386 Expanded Instruction Set

The expanded instruction set of the 80386 assembly language includes two additional data transfer instructions: the MOVZX and MOVSX instructions. These instructions replace the destination operand with a copy of the smaller source operand, zero-extended or sign-extended to fit the larger operand size. The **MOVZX** and **MOVSX instructions** have the following general forms:

[⟨*label*⟩] MOVZX ⟨*destination*⟩,⟨*source*⟩ [⟨*comment*⟩]
[⟨*label*⟩] MOVSX ⟨*destination*⟩,⟨*source*⟩ [⟨*comment*⟩]

in which ⟨*source*⟩ identifies the location of the data that is to be copied and extended and ⟨*destination*⟩ identifies where the data is to be moved.

The MOVZX instruction causes a copy of the value of the source operand, with zero extension, to replace the value of the destination operand. The MOVSX instruction causes a copy of the value of the source operand, with sign extension, to replace the value of the destination operand. The value of the source operand is not modified by execution of the MOVZX or the MOVSX instruction. The type attribute of the destination operand must be larger than the type attribute of the source operand. The type attribute of the source operand can be either byte or word. If the source operand has a type attribute of byte, then the type attribute of the destination operand must be either word or double word. If the source operand has a type attribute of word, then the type attribute of the destination operand must be double word. The source operand can be either a general register or a memory location. The destination operand must be a general register.

EXAMPLES

The instruction

```
MOVZX  ESI,CX
```

causes the 16-bit value of the CX-register to be copied into the low-order 16 bits of the ESI-register and the high-order 16 bits of the ESI-register to be set to zero.

The instruction

```
MOVSX  EAX,DL
```

causes the 8-bit value of the DL-register to be copied into the low-order 8 bits of the EAX-register and the sign bit of the DL-register to be copied throughout the high-order 24 bits of the EAX-register. ■

EXAMPLE

To find the smallest value of n for which

$$1^2 + 2^2 + 3^2 + \cdots + n^2 > 1{,}000{,}000{,}000$$

the following REPEAT-UNTIL loop could be used:

```
          MOV    EBX,1              ;SUM = 1
          MOV    CX,1               ;N = 1
REPEAT1:                            ;REPEAT
          INC    CX                 ;     N = N + 1
          MOVZX  EAX,CX             ;     SUM = SUM + N*N
          MUL    EAX
          ADD    EBX,EAX
          CMP    EBX,1000000000     ;UNTIL SUM > 1000000000
          JBE    REPEAT1
```

The value of SUM is maintained in the 32-bit EBX-register. A 32-bit register is required because the value of variable SUM can exceed 1 billion. The value of N is maintained in the 16-bit CX-register. SUM and N are both initialized to 1. In the loop body, the value of N is incremented by 1, and the square of the new value of N is added to SUM. The MOVZX instruction copies the value of the CX-register (the value of pseudocode variable N) to the EAX-register, zero-extending the value to 32 bits. The MUL instruction squares the value in the EAX-register (i.e., computes N∗N), leaving the 64-bit product in the EDX:EAX register pair. Because the value of N fits in 16 bits, the value of N∗N will fit in 32 bits. Therefore, the high-order 32 bits of the product can be ignored. The ADD instruction adds the 32-bit value of N∗N in the EAX-register to the 32-bit value of SUM in the EBX-register. The CMP and JBE instructions implement the loop test. The value of SUM in the EBX-register is compared to the immediate value 1 billion. The loop body is repeated if the value in the EBX-register is below or equal to 1 billion. The loop terminates when the value in the EBX-register exceeds 1 billion. ■

The expanded instruction set of the 80386 assembly language includes four additional stack operation instructions: the PUSHAD, PUSHFD, POPAD, and POPFD instructions. The **PUSHAD instruction** has the following general form:

[⟨*label*⟩]   PUSHAD [⟨*comment*⟩]

The PUSHAD instruction causes values of all eight 32-bit general registers to be pushed onto the stack. The order in which the general registers are pushed onto the stack is EAX, ECX, EDX, EBX, ESP, EBP, ESI, and EDI. The value that is pushed onto the stack for the ESP-register is the value that the ESP-register had before the first register (EAX) was pushed onto the stack.

The **POPAD instruction** has the following general form:

[⟨*label*⟩] `POPAD` [⟨*comment*⟩]

The POPAD instruction causes the top eight double words on the stack to be popped into the eight 32-bit general registers. The order in which the registers are popped from the stack is EDI, ESI, EBP, ESP, EBX, EDX, ECX, and EAX. The fourth double word popped is actually discarded rather than being popped into the ESP-register. The SP-register (ESP-register in protected mode) is automatically incremented by 4 as each double word is popped from the stack.

The **PUSHFD instruction** has the following general form:

[⟨*label*⟩] `PUSHFD` [⟨*comment*⟩]

The PUSHFD instruction causes the value of the SP-register (ESP-register in protected mode) to be decremented by 4 and the 32-bit value of the Eflags register to be stored in the stack segment at the location addressed by the SS:SP register pair (SS:ESP in protected mode).

The **POPFD instruction** has the following general form:

[⟨*label*⟩] `POPFD` [⟨*comment*⟩]

The POPFD instruction causes a copy of the 32-bit stack segment value addressed by the SS:SP register pair (SS:ESP register pair in protected mode) to replace the 32-bit value of the Eflags register and the SP-register (ESP-register in protected mode) to be incremented by 4.

None of the bits in the flags register are affected by the execution of a PUSHAD, a POPAD, or a PUSHFD instruction. All of the bits in the flags register are potentially modified by execution of a POPFD instruction.

The expanded instruction set of the 80386 assembly language includes two additional integer arithmetic instructions: CDQ (change double word to quad word) and CWDE (change word to double word extended). It also provides additional operand combinations for the IMUL instruction.

The **CDQ instruction** has the following general form:

[⟨*label*⟩] `CDQ` [⟨*comment*⟩]

Execution of a CDQ instruction causes the signed integer value in the EAX-register to be expanded into a quad word (64-bit value) that replaces the value in the EDX:EAX register pair. This expansion is accomplished by extending the sign bit (bit 31 of the EAX-register) through the entire EDX-register.

The **CWDE instruction** has the following general form:

[⟨*label*⟩] `CWDE` [⟨*comment*⟩]

Execution of a CWDE instruction causes the signed integer value in the AX-register to be expanded into a double word (32-bit value) that replaces the value in the EAX-register. This expansion is accomplished by extending the sign bit (bit 15 of the AX-register) through the entire upper-half of the EAX-register.

None of the bits in the flags register are affected by the execution of a CDQ or a CWDE instruction.

The 80386 assembly language provides an additional form for the IMUL instruction, which allows multiplication of a 16-bit or 32-bit register by a 16-bit or 32-bit register or memory location. With the 80386 microprocessor, the **IMUL instruction** may have the following general form:

[⟨*label*⟩] IMUL ⟨*destination*⟩, ⟨*source*⟩ [⟨*comment*⟩]

in which ⟨*destination*⟩ identifies the location of the multiplicand that is to be replaced by the product and ⟨*source*⟩ identifies the location of the multiplier. This instruction causes the destination operand to be multiplied by the source operand and the destination operand to be replaced by the product.

The type attributes of the two operands must match (i.e., both must be word, or both must be double word). The destination operand must be a general register, and the source operand can be a general register or a memory location. It is important to note that the product is a single-length product.

The flags register is affected in the same way for this form of the IMUL instruction as it is for the forms presented in Chapter 3. Because the product is a single-length product, the OF and CF bits of the flags register indicate whether or not overflow occurred.

This form does not exist for the MUL instruction. There is no need for it. When multiplying two *n*-bit integers, the lower *n* bits of the product will be the same whether the two *n*-bit integers being multiplied are interpreted as signed or unsigned. That is, the additional form for the IMUL instruction can be used for both signed and unsigned operands. However, note that the OF and CF bits of the flags register indicate overflow only for the signed interpretation.

EXAMPLES

The instruction

```
IMUL  BX,DI
```

multiplies the 16-bit value of the BX-register by the 16-bit value of the DI-register, leaving the 16-bit product in the BX-register. If the product (signed interpretation) is too large to fit in the BX-register, then the OF and CF bits of the flags register are set.

The instruction

```
IMUL  ESI,LNGTH
```

multiplies the 32-bit value of the ESI-register by the 32-bit value of variable LNGTH, leaving the 32-bit product in the ESI-register. The variable LNGTH must have a type attribute of double word. That is, LNGTH must have been defined with either the DD, the DWORD, or the SDWORD pseudo-operation. If the product (signed interpretation) is too large to fit in the ESI-register, then the OF and CF bits of the flags register are set. ■

The expanded instruction set of the 80386 assembly language includes eight additional bit manipulation instructions, which include two bit scan instructions (BSF and BSR), four bit test instructions (BT, BTC, BTR, and BTS), and two shift instructions (SHLD and SHRD).

The **bit scan instructions** have the following general forms:

[⟨*label*⟩] BSF ⟨*destination*⟩,⟨*source*⟩ [⟨*comment*⟩]
[⟨*label*⟩] BSR ⟨*destination*⟩,⟨*source*⟩ [⟨*comment*⟩]

in which ⟨*source*⟩ identifies the location of the binary value that is to be scanned and ⟨*destination*⟩ identifies the general register that is to receive the bit index of the first set bit (i.e., bit with value 1) found in the scan. The BSF (bit scan forward) instruction scans the source operand from bit 0 toward the most significant bit (MSB). The BSR (bit scan reverse) instruction scans the source operand from the MSB toward bit 0. For both instructions, if a set bit is found, then the value of the destination operand is replaced by the bit index of the first set bit found, and the ZF bit of the flags register is cleared. If no set bit is found (i.e., if the value of the source operand is zero), then the ZF bit of the flags register is set, and the destination operand is not modified.

The type attributes of the two operands must match (i.e., both must be word, or both must be double word). The destination operand must be a general register, and the source operand can be either a general register or a memory location. The ZF bit is the only bit in the flags register that is affected by the execution of a BSF or a BSR instruction.

EXAMPLES

Suppose the EBX-register contains the following 32-bit value

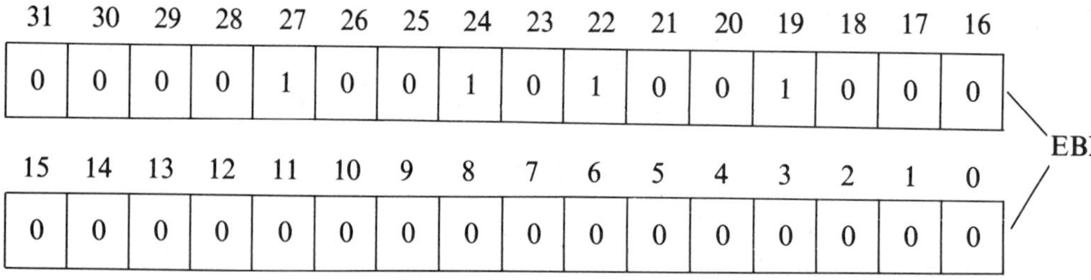

31	30	29	28	27	26	25	24	23	22	21	20	19	18	17	16
0	0	0	0	1	0	0	1	0	1	0	0	1	0	0	0

15	14	13	12	11	10	9	8	7	6	5	4	3	2	1	0
0	0	0	0	0	0	0	0	0	0	0	0	0	0	0	0

EBX

The instruction

```
BSF  EDX,EBX
```

causes the value of the EDX-register to be replaced with the value 19 decimal (13 hexadecimal) and the ZF bit of the flags register to be cleared.

The instruction

```
BSR  EDX,EBX
```

causes the value of the EDX-register to be replaced with the value 27 decimal (1B hexadecimal) and the ZF bit of the flags register to be cleared.

Both the instruction

```
BSF  DX,BX
```

and the instruction

```
BSR  DX,BX
```

cause the ZF bit of the flags register to be set and leave the DX-register value unchanged. ■

The **bit test instructions** have the following general forms:

[⟨*label*⟩] BT ⟨*destination*⟩,⟨*source*⟩ [⟨*comment*⟩]
[⟨*label*⟩] BTC ⟨*destination*⟩,⟨*source*⟩ [⟨*comment*⟩]

[⟨*label*⟩] BTR ⟨*destination*⟩,⟨*source*⟩ [⟨*comment*⟩]
[⟨*label*⟩] BTS ⟨*destination*⟩,⟨*source*⟩ [⟨*comment*⟩]

in which ⟨*source*⟩ specifies a bit position and ⟨*destination*⟩ identifies the location of the binary number that is to have a bit tested and, in the case of BTC, BTR, and BTS, modified.

These instructions cause the bit of the destination operand, whose bit position is specified by the source operand, to be copied into the CF bit of the flags register. Following this copy operation, the **BT** (bit test) instruction leaves the destination operand unchanged, the **BTC** (bit test and complement) instruction complements (toggles) the specified bit of the destination operand, the **BTR** (bit test and reset) instruction resets (clears) the specified bit of the destination operand, and the **BTS** (bit test and set) instruction sets the specified bit of the destination operand.

Except in the case of an immediate source operand, the type attributes of the two operands must match (i.e., both must be word, or both must be double word). An immediate source operand is always a byte value. The destination operand can be either a general register or a memory location, and the source operand can be either a general register or an immediate value. The CF bit is the only bit in the flags register that is affected by the execution of a BT, a BTC, a BTR, or a BTS instruction.

EXAMPLE

Figure 7.13 shows the instruction-by-instruction effect of the execution of a sequence of bit test instructions. ■

FIGURE 7.13 Instruction-by-instruction effect of a sequence of bit test instructions

BX-register

	15	14	13	12	11	10	9	8	7	6	5	4	3	2	1	0	CF
MOV BX,3333H	0	0	1	1	0	0	1	1	0	0	1	1	0	0	1	1	?
BT BX,14	0	0	1	1	0	0	1	1	0	0	1	1	0	0	1	1	0
BT BX,13	0	0	1	1	0	0	1	1	0	0	1	1	0	0	1	1	1
BTC BX,8	0	0	1	1	0	0	1	0	0	0	1	1	0	0	1	1	1
BTC BX,7	0	0	1	1	0	0	1	0	1	0	1	1	0	0	1	1	0
BTR BX,6	0	0	1	1	0	0	1	0	1	0	1	1	0	0	1	1	0
BTR BX,5	0	0	1	1	0	0	1	0	1	0	0	1	0	0	1	1	1
BTS BX,4	0	0	1	1	0	0	1	0	1	0	0	1	0	0	1	1	1
BTS BX,3	0	0	1	1	0	0	1	0	1	0	0	1	1	0	1	1	0

EXAMPLE

The following program fragment counts the bits that are set (1 bits) in the EAX-register value:

```
          MOV    DX,0       ;COUNT = 0
          MOV    ECX,32     ;BIT_POS = 32
LOOPTOP:                    ;WHILE BIT_POS <> 0
          JECXZ  LOOPEND
          DEC    ECX        ;    BIT_POS = BIT_POS - 1
          BT     EAX,ECX    ;    IF   BIT_POS OF EAX
          JNC    ENDIF1     ;         CONTAINS A 1
```

```
            INC    DX          ;   THEN COUNT = COUNT + 1
ENDIF1:                        ;   ENDIF
            JMP    LOOPTOP     ;ENDWHILE
LOOPEND:
```
■

The **SHLD** and **SHRD instructions** have the following general forms:

[⟨*label*⟩] SHLD ⟨*destination*⟩,⟨*source*⟩,⟨*shift-count*⟩ [⟨*comment*⟩]
[⟨*label*⟩] SHRD ⟨*destination*⟩,⟨*source*⟩,⟨*shift-count*⟩ [⟨*comment*⟩]

in which ⟨*destination*⟩ specifies the register or memory location containing the value to be shifted, ⟨*source*⟩ specifies the register containing the bits that are to replace the vacated bits, and ⟨*shift-count*⟩ is either an 8-bit immediate value or the register designator CL. The SHLD instruction causes the value of the destination operand to be shifted left n bit positions, replacing the vacated bits with the n most significant bits of the source operand, where n is the value of the shift count operand. The SHRD instruction causes the value of the destination operand to be shifted right n bit positions, replacing the vacated bits with the n least significant bits of the source operand, where n is the value of the shift count operand. The source operand and the shift count operand are not modified.

The type attributes of the source and destination operands must match (i.e., both must be word, or both must be double word). The destination operand can be either a general register or a memory location, and the source operand must be a general register. The flags register is affected in the same way for these instructions as it is for the SHL and SHR instructions.

EXAMPLES

Suppose the AX-register contains C3C3 hexadecimal and the BX-register contains A5A5 hexadecimal. The instruction

```
SHLD  AX,BX,6
```

leaves the value F0E9 hexadecimal in the AX-register. This operation is depicted as follows:

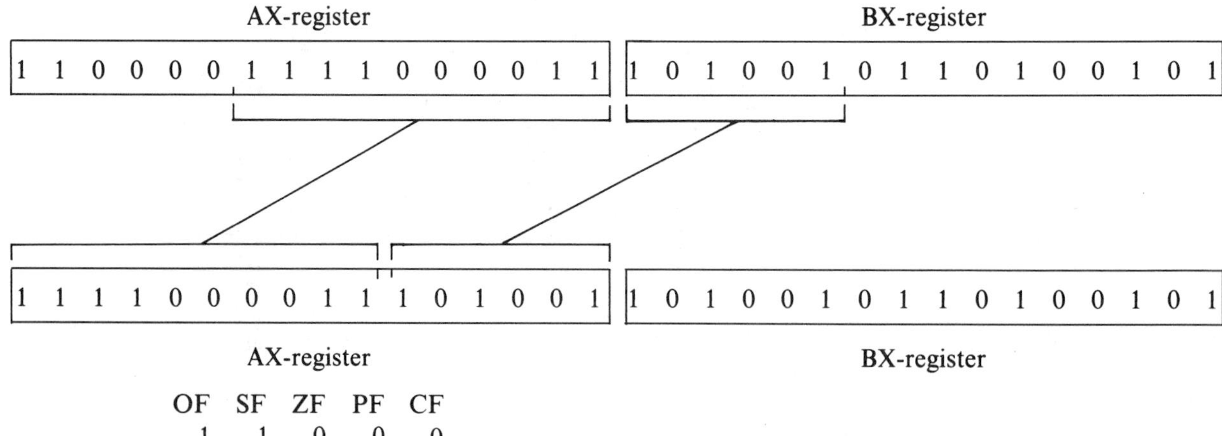

Suppose the AX-register contains C3C3 hexadecimal and the BX-register contains A5A5 hexadecimal. The instruction

```
SHRD  AX,BX,6
```

leaves the value 970F hexadecimal in the AX-register. This operation is depicted as follows:

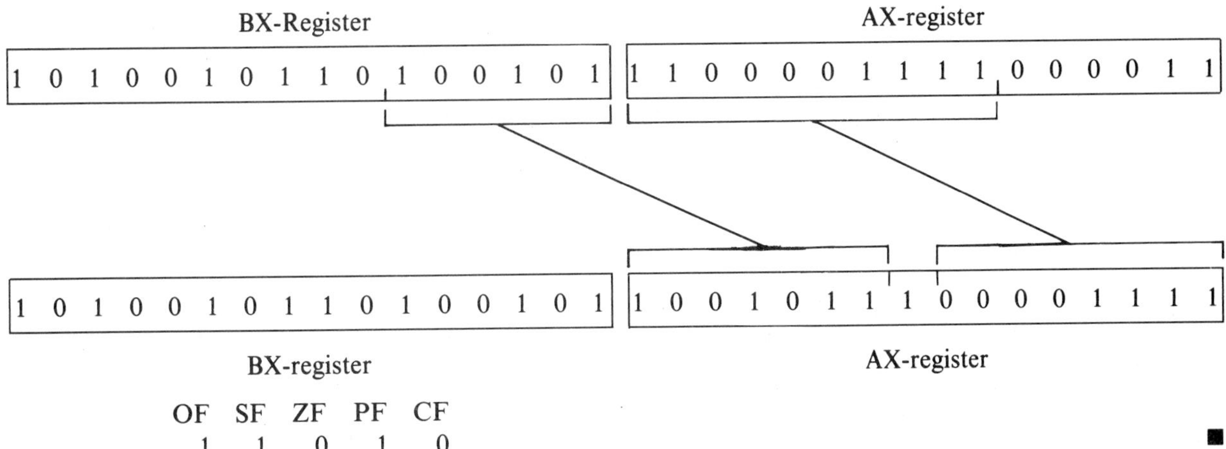

OF	SF	ZF	PF	CF
1	1	0	1	0

■

EXAMPLE The flags register has the following form:

15	14	13	12	11	10	9	8	7	6	5	4	3	2	1	0
				OF	DF	IF	TF	SF	ZF		AF		PF		CF

Suppose a program needs a copy of the flags register value converted to the following form:

15	14	13	12	11	10	9	8	7	6	5	4	3	2	1	0
							OF	DF	IF	TF	SF	ZF	AF	PF	CF

The following program fragment will produce the desired value in the BX-register:

```
          PUSHF
          POP    AX
          MOV    CX,3
LOOPTOP:
          SHRD   BX,AX,1
          ROR    AX,2
          LOOP   LOOPTOP
          SHRD   BX,AX,6
          SHR    BX,7
```

A trace of the AX- and BX-registers through the execution of this program fragment follows. In the trace, a bit value of × indicates that the actual bit value is unimportant in the problem at hand:

Just prior to the first execution of the loop body:

AX-register

15	14	13	12	11	10	9	8	7	6	5	4	3	2	1	0
×	×	×	×	OF	DF	IF	TF	SF	ZF	×	AF	×	PF	×	CF

BX-register

15	14	13	12	11	10	9	8	7	6	5	4	3	2	1	0
×	×	×	×	×	×	×	×	×	×	×	×	×	×	×	×

Just after the first execution of the loop body:

AX-register

15	14	13	12	11	10	9	8	7	6	5	4	3	2	1	0
×	CF	×	×	×	×	OF	DF	IF	TF	SF	ZF	×	AF	×	PF

BX-register

15	14	13	12	11	10	9	8	7	6	5	4	3	2	1	0
CF	×	×	×	×	×	×	×	×	×	×	×	×	×	×	×

Just after the second execution of the loop body:

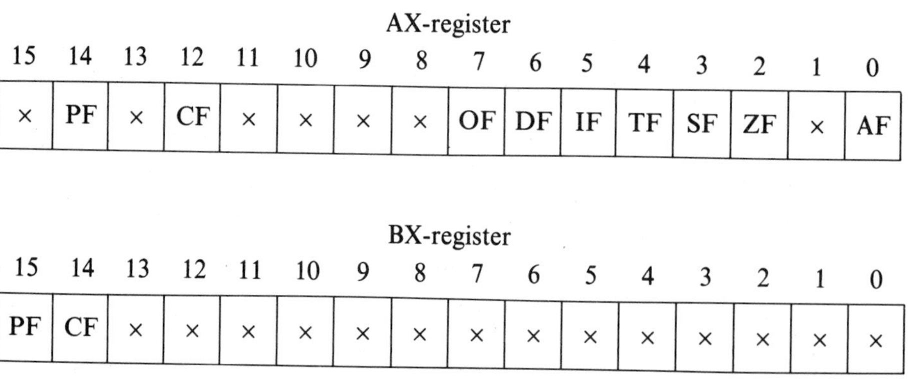

AX-register

15	14	13	12	11	10	9	8	7	6	5	4	3	2	1	0
×	PF	×	CF	×	×	×	×	OF	DF	IF	TF	SF	ZF	×	AF

BX-register

15	14	13	12	11	10	9	8	7	6	5	4	3	2	1	0
PF	CF	×	×	×	×	×	×	×	×	×	×	×	×	×	×

Just after the third and final execution of the loop body:

AX-register

15	14	13	12	11	10	9	8	7	6	5	4	3	2	1	0
×	AF	×	PF	×	CF	×	×	×	×	OF	DF	IF	TF	SF	ZF

BX-register

15	14	13	12	11	10	9	8	7	6	5	4	3	2	1	0
AF	PF	CF	×	×	×	×	×	×	×	×	×	×	×	×	×

Just after the execution of the instruction SHRD BX, AX 6:

AX-register

15	14	13	12	11	10	9	8	7	6	5	4	3	2	1	0
×	AF	×	PF	×	CF	×	×	×	×	OF	DF	IF	TF	SF	ZF

BX-register

15	14	13	12	11	10	9	8	7	6	5	4	3	2	1	0
OF	DF	IF	TF	SF	ZF	AF	PF	CF	×	×	×	×	×	×	×

Just after the execution of the SHR instruction:

BX-register

15	14	13	12	11	10	9	8	7	6	5	4	3	2	1	0
×	×	×	×	×	×	×	OF	DF	IF	TF	SF	ZF	AF	PF	CF

■

The expanded instruction set of the 80386 assembly language includes 18 conditional SET instructions, which set a byte to either 0 or 1 depending on the value of a condition. The **conditional SET instructions** have the following general form:

[⟨*label*⟩] ⟨*op-code*⟩ ⟨*destination*⟩ [⟨*comment*⟩]

in which ⟨*op-code*⟩ is one of the operation code mnemonics listed in Table 7.6 and ⟨*destination*⟩ identifies the location of the byte value that is to be replaced by 0 or 1 depending on the value of the condition specified by the operation code. A conditional SET instruction causes the destination operand to be replaced with 1 if the specified condition is True; with 0, if the specified condition is False. None of the bits in the flags register are affected by execution of conditional SET instructions.

The type attribute of the destination operand must be byte. The destination operand can be either a general register or a memory location.

EXAMPLES

The instructions

```
CMP   AX,7
SETE  BL
```

set the BL-register to 1 if the value of the AX-register is equal to 7. They set the BL-register to 0 if the value of the AX-register is not equal to 7.

The instructions

```
PUSHF
POP    AX
BT     AX,11
SETC   BL
```

set the BL-register to 1 if the OF bit of the flags register is set. They set the BL-register to 0 if the OF bit of the flags register is zero. ■

The expanded instruction set of the 80386 assembly language includes two sets

TABLE 7.6
Conditional SET instructions

Operation Code Mnemonic	Description	Will Set to 1 If
SETA/SETNBE	Set if above Set if not below nor equal	CF = 0 and ZF = 0
SETAE/SETNB	Set if above or equal Set if not below	CF = 0
SETB/SETNAE	Set if below Set if not above nor equal	CF = 1
SETBE/SETNA	Set if below or equal Set if not above	CF = 1 or ZF = 1
SETG/SETNLE	Set if greater than Set if not less nor equal	ZF = 0 and SF = OF
SETGE/SETNL	Set if greater than or equal Set if not less than	(SF xor OF) = 0 (i.e., SF = OF)
SETL/SETNGE	Set if less than Set if not greater nor equal	(SF xor OF) = 1 (i.e., SF ≠ OF)
SETLE/SETNG	Set if less than or equal Set if not greater than	ZF = 1 or SF ≠ OF
SETC SETNC	Set if carry Set if no carry	CF = 1 CF = 0
SETO SETNO	Set if overflow Set if no overflow	OF = 1 OF = 0
SETS SETNS	Set if sign negative Set if nonnegative sign	SF = 1 SF = 0
SETE/SETZ SETNE/SETNZ	Set if equal to zero Set if not equal to zero	ZF = 1 ZF = 0
SETP/SETPE SETNP/SETPO	Set if parity even Set if parity odd	PF = 1 PF = 0

of conditional JUMP instructions. The two sets use the same operation code mnemonics and differ only in the operand. The conditional JUMP instructions that were inherited from the 8088/8086 assembly language have a short label for the operand. A short label is the label of a memory location, in the machine language translation, that is in the range −128 to +127 bytes from the memory location immediately following the JUMP instruction (see Section 4.1). The conditional JUMP instructions that were added in the expanded instruction set of the 80386 assembly language have an extended short label for the operand. An extended short label is the label of a memory location, in the machine language translation, that is in the range −32,768 to +32,767 bytes from the memory location immediately following the JUMP instruction.

The distinction between the two sets of conditional JUMP instructions is more evident in machine language than in assembly language. In machine language, a short jump is a 2-byte instruction, and an extended short jump is a 4-byte instruction. The assembler makes the distinction transparent to the assembly language programmer. When translating a conditional JUMP instruction, the assembler generates the 2-byte machine language form of the instruction if the operand is the label of an instruction that lies within the short range (−128 to +127 bytes from the instruction following the JUMP); it generates the 4-byte machine language form of the instruction if the operand is the label of an instruction that lies outside of the short range but within the extended short range (−32,768 to +32,767 bytes from the instruction following the JUMP); and it generates a "jump out of range" error message if the operand is the label of an instruction that lies outside of the extended short range. The extra set of conditional JUMP instructions simply means that the 80386 assembly language programmer will encounter out-of-range conditional jumps far less frequently than will the 8088/8086 assembly language programmer.

It should be noted that in the 80386 assembly language, the operand for LOOP instructions and for the JCXZ and JECXZ instructions must be a short label. The expansion to allow extended short labels does not include these instructions.

Programming Example

Program Listings 3.2 and 4.1 show two implementations of an algorithm to compute the sum of the cubes of the first *n* positive integers using the formula

$$1^3 + 2^3 + 3^3 + \cdots + n^3 = [n(n + 1)/2]^2$$

These two implementations use 16-bit arithmetic and therefore are limited to values of *n* that are less than or equal to 22. Values of *n* greater than 22 lead to overflow in the computation. Program Listing 7.4 shows an 80386 assembly language implementation of a similar algorithm that uses 32-bit arithmetic and produces tables of values of *n* along with the corresponding values of the sum of the first *n* cubes. Each table consists of one header line and 24 lines of data (i.e., one screenful). The program pauses and waits for a keystroke from the user after each table is displayed. The tables include all positive values of *n* for which the sum of the first *n* cubes can be represented by a 32-bit unsigned integer. The tables also indicate the point at which the sum of the first *n* cubes becomes too large to be represented as a 16-bit unsigned integer. (See the prologue in lines 2–19 of Program Listing 7.4.)

The sequence of the two pseudo-operations in lines 20 and 21 is critical for the proper translation of an 80386 assembly module. The .386 directive directs the assembler to translate the assembly module for execution on an 80386 microprocessor. The .386 directive tells the assembler to expect (and to allow) the use of the extended register set and the expanded instruction set in this assembly module. However, the assembler also needs to know whether it is to translate the assembly module for 80386 real-mode or protected-mode operation. Recall from Table 7.5 that certain instructions (e.g., MOV EAX,EDX) differ in their real-mode and protected-mode machine language representations by the presence or absence of a 1-byte instruction prefix (66 hexadecimal). The assembler needs to know whether or not to generate this operand-size instruction prefix for a given instruction. It is the order of the .MODEL and .386 directives that tells the assembler whether to translate for real-mode or protected-mode operation. If the .MODEL directive precedes the .386 directive, as is the case in Program Listing 7.4, then the assembler is being directed to translate for real-mode operation. However, if the .386 directive precedes the .MODEL directive, then the assembler is being directed to translate for protected-mode operation.

The external definitions for the assembly module appear in lines 23–29 of Program Listing 7.4. These subprocedures should be quite familiar to you by now. However, for some of these subprocedures, the interface is slightly different for the 80386 version than it is for the 8088/8086 version. Appendix D describes the interface for both versions of the I/O subprocedures. An object file library containing the

```
            PAGE    80,132
;===================================================================
;                       PROGRAM LISTING 7.4
;
; GIVEN AN INTEGER VALUE FOR n, THIS PROGRAM COMPUTES THE SUM OF
; THE CUBES OF THE FIRST n POSITIVE INTEGERS USING THE FORMULA:
;
;  3     3     3           3               2
; 1  + 2  + 3  + ... + n  = [n(n + 1)/2]
;
; THE PROGRAM BEGINS WITH n=1  AND CONTINUES THROUGH THE LARGEST
; VALUE OF n  FOR WHICH THE SUM OF THE FIRST n CUBES WILL FIT IN
; 32 BITS.
; THE PROGRAM USES THE PUTDC32$ DISPLAY CODE  TO SHOW  THE POINT
; AT WHICH THE SUM  OF THE FIRST n CUBES OVERFLOWS 16 BITS.  THE
; SUM IS DISPLAYED WITHOUT LEADING OR TRAILING BLANKS (CODE = 0)
; WHILE THE SUM FITS IN 16 BITS AND IS DISPLAYED RIGHT JUSTIFIED
; (CODE = 1) AFTER THE SUM OVERFLOWS 16 BITS.
;===================================================================
            .MODEL  SMALL,BASIC
            .386
;===================================================================
                                        ;PROCEDURES TO
            EXTRN   CLEAR:FAR           ;CLEAR SCREEN
            EXTRN   NEWLINE:FAR         ;DISPLAY NEWLINE CHARACTER
            EXTRN   PAUSE:FAR           ;PAUSE AND WAIT FOR KEYSTROKE
            EXTRN   PUTDEC$:FAR         ;DISPLAY 16-BIT UNSIGNED INT.
            EXTRN   PUTDC32$:FAR        ;DISPLAY 32-BIT UNSIGNED INT.
            EXTRN   PUTSTRNG:FAR        ;DISPLAY CHARACTER STRING
;===================================================================
; S T A C K   S E G M E N T   D E F I N I T I O N
;
            .STACK  256
;===================================================================
; C O N S T A N T   D A T A   S E G M E N T   D E F I N I T I O N
;
            .CONST
HEADER      DB      '     n   SUM OF THE FIRST n CUBES'
HEADER_LNG  EQU     $-HEADER            ;LENGTH OF HEADER
PAUSE_MSG   DB      '       PRESS ANY KEY TO CONTINUE'
PAUSE_LNG   EQU     $-PAUSE_MSG         ;LENGTH OF PAUSE MESSAHE
TWENTY_4    DW      24                  ;CONSTANT 24
;===================================================================
; V A R I A B L E   D A T A   S E G M E N T   D E F I N I T I O N
;
            .DATA
N           DW      1                   ;NUMBER OF CUBES TO SUM
SUM         DD      1                   ;SUM OF FIRST N CUBES
;===================================================================
; C O D E   S E G M E N T   D E F I N I T I O N
            .CODE   EX_7_4
            .STARTUP                    ;GENERATE STARTUP CODE
            PUSH    DS                  ;SET ES-REGISTER TO ADDRESS
            POP     ES                  ;DGROUP
;
            LEA     DI,HEADER           ;DISPLAY HEADER
            MOV     CX,HEADER_LNG
            CALL    PUTSTRNG
            CALL    NEWLINE             ;DISPLAY NEWLINE CHARACTER
REPEAT1:                                ;REPEAT
            MOV     AX,N                ;   DISPLAY N
            MOV     BH,1
            CALL    PUTDEC$
            LEA     DI,HEADER           ;   DISPLAY 5 SPACES
            MOV     CX,5
            CALL    PUTSTRNG
            MOV     EAX,SUM             ;   DISPLAY SUM
```

```
68:              CMP     EAX,65535
69:              SETA    BH
70:              CALL    PUTDC32$
71:              MOV     AX,N                 ;   IF    N mod 24 = 0
72:              MOV     DX,0
73:              DIV     TWENTY_4
74:              CMP     DX,0
75:              JNE     ENDIF1
76:              LEA     DI,PAUSE_MSG         ;   THEN
77:              MOV     CX,PAUSE_LNG         ;         DISPLAY PAUSE MESSAGE
78:              CALL    PAUSE                ;         WAIT FOR KEYSTROKE
79:              CALL    CLEAR                ;         CLEAR SCREEN
80:              LEA     DI,HEADER            ;         DISPLAY HEADER
81:              MOV     CX,HEADER_LNG
82:              CALL    PUTSTRNG
83: ENDIF1:                                   ;   ENDIF
84:              CALL    NEWLINE              ;   DISPLAY NEWLINE CHARACTER
85:              INC     N                    ;   N = N + 1
86:              MOVZX   EAX,N                ;   SUM = [N(N + 1)/2] ** 2
87:              MOV     EBX,EAX
88:              INC     EBX
89:              MUL     EBX
90:              SHR     EDX,1
91:              RCR     EAX,1
92:              MUL     EAX
93:              MOV     SUM,EAX
94:              JNC     REPEAT1              ;UNTIL OVERFLOW
95:              .EXIT                        ;RETURN TO DOS
96: ;
97:              END
```

object code files for the 80386 version of the I/O subprocedures is included on the diskette that accompanies this book. The name of the library is I0386.LIB.

The size of the stack segment is defined in line 33 as 256 bytes, which is the same stack size that has been used in previous example programs. Note that for many of the I/O subprocedures, the stack requirements for the 80386 version are greater than those for the 8088/8086 version because the 80386 version is saving and restoring 32-bit registers rather than 16-bit registers. The increased stack needs of the 80386 I/O subprocedures must be considered in writing 80386 assembly language programs. The 256-byte stack size is adequate for the program of Program Listing 7.4.

Lines 34–42 define the constant data for the program. Line 38 defines the header line for the tables, and line 39 equates the symbolic name HEADER_LNG with the constant expression whose value is the length of the header line. Line 40 defines the message to be displayed when the program pauses after the display of each table, and line 41 equates the symbolic name PAUSE_LNG with the constant expression whose value is the length of the pause message. Line 42 defines a word constant with symbolic name TWENTY_4 and with value 24 decimal. The constant TWENTY_4 is used in the computation to determine when all 24 lines of a table have been displayed, after which the program pauses and waits for a keystroke from the user.

Lines 43–48 define the variable data for the program. Line 47 defines a word variable with symbolic name N, which represents the number of cubes to sum. Variable N is initialized to 1. Line 48 defines a double-word variable with symbolic name SUM, which represents the sum of the first N cubes. Variable SUM is initialized to 1 (the sum of the first 1 cubes).

Lines 49–96 define the code segment for the program. The code segment contains the instructions for the main procedure of the program. The main procedure begins by initializing the DS and ES registers (lines 52–54) to address the origin of the data group DGROUP. Lines 56–59 display the header for the first table. The header is displayed on a line by itself.

The body of the REPEAT-UNTIL loop in lines 60–94 executes once for each value of N from its initial value (1) to the largest value of N for which the sum of the first N cubes can be represented as a 32-bit unsigned integer. The loop body begins by displaying the current value of variable N (lines 61–63), followed by five spaces (lines 64–66), followed by the current value of variable SUM (lines 67–70). The 80386 version of PUTDC32$ expects two inputs: The 32-bit value to be displayed is input via the EAX-register, and a display code is input via the BH-register. The MOV instruction in line 67 loads the EAX-register with the current value of variable SUM. The display of the value of variable SUM also indicates the point at which the value of SUM becomes too large to be represented as a 16-bit unsigned integer. The SUM is displayed with no leading or trailing blanks (display code 0) if its value is less than or equal to 65,535. The SUM is displayed right-justified in an 11-character field (display code 1) if its value is greater than 65,535. This conditional setting of the BH-register (so that it will contain the appropriate display code) is accomplished by the instructions in lines 68 and 69. The CMP instruction in line 68 tests the condition, and the SETA (set above) instruction in line 69 sets the BH-register based on the condition. The BH-register is set to 1 if the value in the EAX-register is above 65,535; it is set to 0 if the value in the EAX-register is below or equal to 65,535.

The single-alternative decision structure in lines 71–83 determines whether or not the display of a table has been completed. If the current value of N is divisible by 24, then the display of a table has been completed, and the program must pause and wait for a keystroke from the user. Lines 71–73 perform the 16-bit division of N by 24. The CMP instruction in line 74 compares the remainder of this division to zero. The JNE instruction in line 75 causes the single alternative (lines 76–82) to be skipped if the remainder is nonzero (i.e., if the current value of N is not divisible by 24). If the remainder of the division is zero (i.e., if N is divisible by 24), then the instructions in lines 76–82 are executed. The instructions in lines 76–78 invoke procedure PAUSE to display the pause message and wait for a keystroke. The return from PAUSE will not occur until a key is depressed at the keyboard, which gives the user a chance to inspect the displayed table before proceeding to the display of the next table. The table can be printed by pressing the Print Screen key (Shift-PrtSc on older keyboards). When control is returned from PAUSE, the program clears the screen (line 79) and the header is displayed for the next table (lines 80–82).

Following the single-alternative decision structure, a call to NEWLINE is made (line 84) in preparation for displaying the next line of the table. Calling NEWLINE must be done whether the program just displayed a data line or the header for the next table.

The remainder of the loop body computes the next values of N and SUM. The INC instruction in line 85 increments the value of variable N to the next highest integer. The instructions in lines 86–93 compute the next value of SUM from the updated value of N. The value of N is a 16-bit value, and the value of SUM is a 32-bit value. Therefore, the value of N must be expanded to 32 bits so that the computation of SUM can be performed with 32-bit arithmetic. The MOVZX instruction in line 86 takes a copy of the value of variable N, zero-extends it to 32-bits, and moves it into the EAX-register. The MOV instruction in line 87 moves a copy of this value into the EBX-register. Both the EAX- and EBX-registers now contain a copy of the expanded value of variable N. The INC instruction in line 88 leaves the value N+1 in the EBX-register. The MUL instruction in line 89 multiplies the value of the EAX-register (N) by the value of the EBX-register (N+1), leaving the 64-bit product, N(N+1), in the EDX:EAX register pair. The instructions in lines 90 and 91 perform a 64-bit right-shift of this product, thus dividing it by 2 and producing the value N(N+1)/2 in the EDX:EAX register pair. The upper half of this 64-bit value can be ignored because we know that it must be zero. N started as a 16-bit value. Therefore, N(N+1)/2 cannot overflow 32 bits. We also know that the remainder of this division by 2 is zero because N(N+1) is even for all positive integer values of N. The MUL instruction in line 92 multiplies the value of the EAX-register by itself, leaving the 64-bit product $[N(N+1)/2]^2$ in the EDX:EAX register pair. The MOV instruction in line 93 stores the lower 32 bits of this product as the new value of variable SUM. If the 64-bit product can be represented in 32 bits, then the loop body should be executed again to display the new values of N and SUM and to compute their next values. However, if the 64-bit product cannot be represented in 32 bits, then the loop should be terminated. The MUL instruction in line 92 set the CF bit of the flags register to reflect whether or not the 64-bit product could be reduced to 32 bits. The JNC instruction in line 94 performs the loop test based on the value of the CF bit of the flags register. If the CF bit of the flags register is not set, then control is transferred to the instruction labeled REPEAT1, and the loop body is repeated. If the CF bit is set, then the jump is not taken, and control continues with the instructions generated in response to the macro directive in line 95.

Output Listing 7.5 shows the first two tables produced by the execution of this program. Note that the sum of the first 22 cubes is displayed with no leading blanks (display code 0) and that the sum of the first 23 cubes is displayed right-justified (display code 1). N = 23 is the point at which the sum overflows 16 bits. (You can execute the program to see all of the tables and to see the point at which the sum overflows 32 bits.)

In linking this program to the I/O subprocedures, the library I0386.LIB must be used. Suppose this assembly module has already been assembled, and suppose the object file has been saved on a diskette with EX_7_4.OBJ as the filename. Suppose further that we have a fixed disk system, the Linkage Editor and the I/O subprocedure library I0386.LIB are on the fixed disk, the object code file is on the diskette in drive A, and the fixed disk drive is the default drive. To link file EX_7_4.OBJ with the appropriate object code files from I0386.LIB, one of the following commands can be entered in response to the DOS C> prompt:

```
link  a:ex_7_4,a:,nul,io386
link  /co a:ex_7_4,a:,nul,io386
```

These commands instruct the LINK program to combine file EX_7_4.OBJ from the diskette in drive A with the appropriate object files from the library I0386.LIB on the fixed disk and to place the executable code file on the diskette in drive A using EX_7_4.EXE as the filename. The second of these two commands further instructs the LINK program to prepare the executable code file for execution with CodeView.

7.5 Intel 80486 Assembly Language Programming

From an assembly language programming standpoint, the 80386 and the 80486 are virtually the same microprocessor. There are two real-mode instructions in the 80486 assembly language which do not exist in the 80386 assembly language: the compare

```
OUTPUT LISTING 7.5

 n    SUM OF THE FIRST n CUBES
 1      1
 2      9
 3      36
 4      100
 5      225
 6      441
 7      784
 8      1296
 9      2025
10      3025
11      4356
12      6084
13      8281
14      11025
15      14400
16      18496
17      23409
18      29241
19      36100
20      44100
21      53361
22      64009
23            76176
24            90000       PRESS ANY KEY TO CONTINUE


 n    SUM OF THE FIRST n CUBES
25             105625
26             123201
27             142884
28             164836
29             189225
30             216225
31             246016
32             278784
33             314721
34             354025
35             396900
36             443556
37             494209
38             549081
39             608400
40             672400
41             741321
42             815409
43             894916
44             980100
45            1071225
46            1168561
47            1272384
48            1382976       PRESS ANY KEY TO CONTINUE
```

and exchange instruction (CMPXCHG) and the exchange and add instruction (XADD). These two instructions are covered in Appendix A.

The numeric coprocessor is the major difference between the two microprocessors. The numeric coprocessor extends the assembly language instruction set to include a set of floating point instructions. It is a built-in feature of the 80486 microprocessor and is an add-on feature to the 80386 microprocessor, as it was to the 8088, 8086, and 80286 microprocessors.

NUMERIC EXERCISES

7.1 Fill in the blanks in the following table:

Before Execution		Instruction Executed	After Execution
EAX-Register	BX-Register		EAX-Register
F731137F	E620	MOVZX AX,BL	
F731137F	E620	MOVZX EAX,BL	
F731137F	E620	MOVZX AX,BH	
F731137F	E620	MOVZX EAX,BH	
F731137F	E620	MOVZX EAX,BX	
F731137F	E620	MOVSX AX,BL	
F731137F	E620	MOVSX EAX,BL	
F731137F	E620	MOVSX AX,BH	
F731137F	E620	MOVSX EAX,BH	
F731137F	E620	MOVSX EAX,BX	

7.2 Fill in the blanks in the following table:

DX:AX register pair before execution	3579:8C63	3579:8C63	3579:8C63
DI:SI register pair before execution	1614:C3A4	1614:C3A4	2468:36C8
Instructions executed	ADD AX,SI ADC DX,DI	SUB AX,SI SBB DX,DI	ADD AX,SI ADC DX,DI
DX:AX register pair after execution			
DI:SI register pair after execution			
OF, SF, ZF, CF after execution			

7.3 Fill in the blanks in the following table:

Before Execution	Instruction Executed	After Execution		
EAX-Register		EAX-Register	EBX-Register	ZF
00300C00	BSF EBX,EAX			
00300C00	BSR EBX,EAX			
E0000000	BSF EBX,EAX			
E0000000	BSR EBX,EAX			
00000000	BSF EBX,EAX			
00000000	BSR EBX,EAX			

7.4 Fill in the blanks in the following table:

Before Execution	Instruction Executed	After Execution	
EAX-Register		EAX-Register	CF
EC800137	BT EAX,29		
EC800137	BT EAX,28		
EC800137	BTC EAX,26		
EC800137	BTC EAX,25		
EC800137	BTR EAX,23		
EC800137	BTR EAX,22		
EC800137	BTS EAX,6		
EC800137	BTS EAX,5		

7.5 Fill in the blanks in the following table:

Before Execution		Instruction Executed	After Execution	
DX-Register	AX-Register		DX-Register	AX-Register
C5A3	73E6	SHRD DX,AX,5		
C5A3	73E6	SHRD AX,DX,5		
C5A3	73E6	SHLD DX,AX,5		
C5A3	73E6	SHLD AX,DX,5		
C5A3	73E6	SHLD AX,DX,8		

7.6 What is the value in the BH-register after the execution of the instruction sequence

```
MOV   BH,0A3H
CMP   AX,0
SETL  BH
NEG   BH
SETG  BH
```

a. if the value in the AX-register is zero?
b. if the value in the AX-register is 84B6 hexadecimal?
c. if the value in the AX-register is 6B48 hexadecimal?

PROGRAMMING EXERCISES

7.1 In Programming Exercise 4.1, the notion of an Ulam sequence and its length was introduced. Programming Exercise 5.1 also involved Ulam sequences. This exercise expands Programming Exercise 5.1. Design a subalgorithm to accept a positive integer as input and to return the length of the Ulam sequence for that integer as output. Design a main algorithm that uses the subalgorithm to find the integer in the range 1–65,535 whose Ulam sequence has the largest length. The algorithm is to output that integer and the length of its Ulam sequence. The main algorithm will reference the subalgorithm 65,535 times, once for each integer in the range 1–65,535.

Implement your subalgorithm with an 8088/8086 assembly language external FAR function subprocedure. Your input should be a 16-bit unsigned integer in the AX-register. The length of the Ulam sequence for the input integer will be returned to the caller in the AX-register. Use 32-bit arithmetic in your subprocedure to accommodate large integers in the Ulam sequence. (*Hint*: You can avoid the need for a 32-bit multiply by using $3x + 1 = 2x + x + 1$.) In the event that 32-bit arithmetic is not sufficient for all integers in the given range, your subprocedure should return an Ulam length of zero if overflow is detected during computation of the Ulam sequence.

Implement your main algorithm with an 8088/8086 assembly language program that uses your external subprocedure to compute the length of the Ulam sequence for each of the integers in the given range. There is no input to your program. Your output should be a list of integers whose Ulam sequence produced an integer that overflowed 32 bits and the integer whose Ulam sequence had the largest length along with that largest length. The output is to be displayed on the screen. (*Warning*: Allow approximately five minutes for this program to execute.)

7.2 Design an algorithm to perform integer exponentiation. Your inputs should be a signed integer value that represents the BASE and an unsigned integer value that represents the positive EXPONENT. Your output should be the value of BASE raised to EXPONENT. For example, if the inputs are BASE = -2 and EXPONENT = 5, then the output should be $(-2)^5 = -32$. Your algorithm must detect overflow.

Implement your algorithm with an 8088/8086 assembly language external FAR subprocedure. Your input should be an 8-bit signed integer value in the AL-register that represents BASE and an 8-bit unsigned integer value in the AH-register that represents EXPONENT. Your subprocedure is to return the result, a 32-bit signed integer, in the DX:AX register pair and an overflow indicator in the OF bit of the flags register (OF = 1 implies overflow). Your subprocedure must save and restore all registers used for purposes other than procedure output. The OF bit must be the only bit of the flags register that is modified by your subprocedure.

Alternate implementation Implement your algorithm with an 80386 assembly language external FAR subprocedure. Your input shoud be a 16-bit signed integer value in the AX-register that represents BASE and an 8-bit unsigned integer value in the DL-register that represents EXPONENT. Your subprocedure is to return the result, a 32-bit signed integer, in the EAX-register and an overflow indicator in the OF bit of the flags register (OF = 1 implies overflow). Your subprocedure must save and restore all registers used for purposes other than procedure output. The OF bit must be the only bit of the flags register that is modified by your subprocedure.

7.3 The MULTIPLY procedure presented in Program Listing 7.3 contains one known bug: The procedure may not execute correctly if called more than once from another procedure. For example, if MULTIPLY is called with inputs of -12 and $+16$ and then called a second time with inputs of -12 and $+16$, the product from the second call will be $+192$. Use the main procedure in Program Listing 7.6 and see what happens.

Repair the bug in Program Listing 7.3. Demonstrate the modified procedure by using the main procedure in Program Listing 7.6 with the inputs in Table 7.7.

TABLE 7.7 Inputs for Programming Exercises 7.3–7.6

Multiplicand	Multiplier
0	5281
150	150
−160	−160
32767	−1
−32768	32767
65536	−32768
−16384	−131072
20	−102261127

7.4 The following algorithm is an alternative to the algorithm for signed integer multiplication presented in the section "Russian Peasant's Multiply—32-Bit Implementation":

```
            PAGE    80,132
;===================================================================
;                   PROGRAM LISTING 7.6
;
;PROGRAM TO DEMONSTRATE MULTIPLY PROCEDURES
;===================================================================
            .MODEL  SMALL,BASIC
;===================================================================
                                       ;PROCEDURES TO
            EXTRN   GETDEC32:FAR       ;GET 32-BIT SIGNED DEC. INT.
            EXTRN   MULTIPLY:FAR       ;PERFORM 32-BIT MULTIPLY
            EXTRN   NEWLINE:FAR        ;DISPLAY NEWLINE CHARACTER
            EXTRN   PUTBIN:FAR         ;DISPLAY BINARY INTEGER
            EXTRN   PUTDEC32:FAR       ;DISPLAY 32-BIT SIGNED INT.
            EXTRN   PUTSTRNG:FAR       ;DISPLAY CHARACTER STRING
;===================================================================
; S T A C K   D E F I N I T I O N
;
            .STACK  256
;===================================================================
; C O N S T A N T   D E F I N I T I O N S
;
            .CONST
PROMPT1     DB      'ENTER MULTIPLICAND '
PROMPT2     DB      'ENTER MULTIPLIER   '
ANNOTATE    DB      'PRODUCT = '
PROMPT_LNG EQU      PROMPT2-PROMPT1    ;LENGTH OF PROMPT MESSAGES
ANNOTATE_L EQU      $-ANNOTATE         ;LENGTH OF ANNOTATION MESSAGE
;===================================================================
; C O D E   S E G M E N T   D E F I N I T I O N
;
            .CODE   EX_7_6
;
            .STARTUP                   ;GENERATE STARTUP CODE
            PUSH    DS                 ;SET ES-REGISTER TO ADDRESS
            POP     ES                 ;DGROUP
            CALL    NEWLINE
            LEA     DI,PROMPT2         ;PROMPT FOR MPLIER
            MOV     CX,PROMPT_LNG
            CALL    PUTSTRNG
            CALL    GETDEC32           ;GET MPLIER
            MOV     BL,1               ;PUTBIN CODE = WORD
            XCHG    DX,AX              ;DISPLAY MPLIER IN BINARY
            CALL    PUTBIN
            XCHG    DX,AX
            CALL    PUTBIN
            CALL    NEWLINE
            CALL    NEWLINE
            MOV     DI,DX              ;<MPLIER IN DI:SI>
            MOV     SI,AX
            PUSH    DI
            LEA     DI,PROMPT1         ;PROMPT FOR MCAND
;
            CALL    PUTSTRNG
            POP     DI
            CALL    GETDEC32           ;GET MCAND
            XCHG    DX,AX              ;DISPLAY MCAND IN BINARY
            CALL    PUTBIN
            XCHG    DX,AX
            CALL    PUTBIN
            CALL    NEWLINE
            CALL    NEWLINE
            PUSH    DX                 ;PUSH MCAND
            PUSH    AX
            PUSH    DI                 ;PUSH MPLIER
            PUSH    SI
            CALL    MULTIPLY           ;PRODUCT = MULTIPLY(MCAND,
                                       ;                   MPLIER)
```

```
                CALL    PUTPROD             ;DISPLAY PRODUCT
                POP     SI                  ;POP MPLIER
                POP     DI
                POP     AX                  ;POP MCAND
                POP     DX
                CALL    MULTIPLY            ;PRODUCT = MULTIPLY(MCAND,
                                            ;                   MPLIER)
                CALL    PUTPROD             ;DISPLAY PRODUCT
                .EXIT                       ;RETURN TO DOS
;
;=====================================================================
; PROCEDURE TO DISPLAY PRODUCT IN DI:SI:DX:AX REGISTER GROUP
;=====================================================================
PUTPROD         PROC    NEAR                ;PROCEDURE PUTPROD(PRODUCT)
                PUSH    DI
                LEA     DI,ANNOTATE         ;DISPLAY 'PRODUCT = '
                MOV     CX,10
                CALL    PUTSTRNG
                POP     DI
                MOV     BL,1                ;PUTBIN CODE = WORD
                JNO     ELSE1               ;IF   OVERFLOW
                PUSH    AX                  ;THEN
                MOV     AX,DI               ;     DISPLAY BITS 63 - 48
                CALL    PUTBIN              ;             OF PRODUCT
                MOV     AX,SI               ;     DISPLAY BITS 47 - 32
                CALL    PUTBIN              ;             OF PRODUCT
                MOV     AX,DX               ;     DISPLAY BITS 31 - 16
                CALL    PUTBIN              ;             OF PRODUCT
                POP     AX                  ;     DISPLAY BITS 15 - 00
                CALL    PUTBIN              ;             OF PRODUCT
                JMP     ENDIF1
ELSE1:                                      ;ELSE
                MOV     BH,0                ;     DISPLAY PRODUCT IN
                CALL    PUTDEC32            ;                  DECIMAL
ENDIF1:                                     ;ENDIF
                CALL    NEWLINE
                RET                         ;RETURN TO CALLER
PUTPROD         ENDP                        ;END PUTPROD
                END
```

```
FUNCTION MULTIPLY(MULTIPLICAND,MULTIPLIER)
     IF      MULTIPLIER <0
     THEN
            MULTIPLICAND = - MULTIPLICAND
            MULTIPLIER   = - MULTIPLIER
     ENDIF
     PRODUCT = 0
     WHILE    MULTIPLIER > 0
       IF     MULTIPLIER IS ODD
       THEN
              PRODUCT = PRODUCT + MULTIPLICAND
       ENDIF
       MULTIPLICAND = MULTIPLICAND*2
       MULTIPLIER =   MULTIPLIER/2
     ENDWHILE
     RETURN (PRODUCT)
END MULTIPLY
```

Implement this algorithm with an 8088/8086 assembly language external FAR subprocedure. Your input should be a 32-bit signed integer multiplicand in the DX:AX register pair and a 32-bit signed integer multiplier in the DI:SI register pair. Your output should be the 64-bit signed integer product in the DI:SI:DX:AX register group, with the OF and CF bits of the flags register set to reflect whether or not the product overflows 32 bits. Your subprocedure must save and restore all registers used for purposes other than procedure output. All flags register bits other than the OF and CF bits must be saved and restored.

Use the main procedure in Program Listing 7.6 to demonstrate your subprocedure, and use the inputs in Table 7.7 in your demonstration.

7.5 The following algorithm, the Shift and Add Method, is an alternative to the Russian Peasant's Method for performing signed integer multiplication:

```
FUNCTION MULTIPLY(MULTIPLICAND,MULTIPLIER)
   EXP_MPCAND = MULTIPLICAND EXPANDED TO 2N BITS
   PARTIAL_PRODUCT = 0
   IF   MSB OF MULTIPLIER = 1
   THEN
        PARTIAL_PRODUCT = 2'S COMPLEMENT OF EXP_MPCAND
```

```
    ENDIF
    BIT_COUNT = N-1
    REPEAT
      SHIFT PARTIAL_PRODUCT LEFT 1 BIT POSITION
      SHIFT MULTIPLIER LEFT 1 BIT POSITION
      IF   MSB OF MULTIPLIER = 1
      THEN
           PARTIAL_PRODUCT = PARTIAL_PRODUCT + EXP_MPCAND
      ENDIF
      BIT_COUNT = BIT_COUNT - 1
    UNTIL BIT_COUNT = 0
    RETURN (PARTIAL_PRODUCT)
END MULTIPLY
```

It accepts an n-bit multiplicand and an n-bit multiplier and produces a $2n$-bit product. Implement this algorithm with an 8088/8086 assembly language external FAR subprocedure. Your input should be a 32-bit signed integer multiplicand in the DX:AX register pair and a 32-bit signed integer multiplier in the DI:SI register pair. Your output should be the 64-bit signed integer product in the DI:SI:DX:AX register group, with the OF and CF bits of the flags register set to reflect whether or not the product overflows 32 bits. Your subprocedure must save and restore all registers used for purposes other than procedure output. All flags register bits other than the OF and CF bits must be saved and restored.

Use the main procedure in Program Listing 7.6 to demonstrate your subprocedure, and use the inputs in Table 7.7 in your demonstration.

7.6 The following algorithm, the Add and Shift Method, is another alternative for performing signed integer multiplication:

```
FUNCTION MULTIPLY(MULTIPLICAND,MULTIPLIER)
   PARTIAL_PRODUCT = 0
   BIT_COUNT = N-1
   REPEAT
      IF      LSB OF MULTIPLIER = 1
      THEN    ADD MULTIPLICAND TO UPPER HALF OF PARTIAL_PRODUCT
              IF     OVERFLOW
              THEN SHIFT PARTIAL_PRODUCT RIGHT 1 BIT SHIFTING
                     IN CARRY
              ELSE
                     SHIFT PARTIAL PRODUCT
                     RIGHT 1 BIT SHIFTING
                     IN COPY OF SIGN
              ENDIF
      ELSE
              SHIFT PARTIAL_PRODUCT RIGHT 1 BIT SHIFTING IN COPY
              OF SIGN
      ENDIF
      SHIFT MULTIPLIER RIGHT 1 BIT POSITION
      BIT_COUNT = BIT_COUNT - 1
   UNTIL    BIT_COUNT = 0
   IF    LSB OF MULTIPLIER = 1
   THEN
       ADD 2'S COMPLEMENT OF MULTIPLICAND TO UPPER HALF OF
       PARTIAL_PRODUCT
   ENDIF
   SHIFT PARTIAL_PRODUCT RIGHT 1 BIT SHIFTING IN COPY OF SIGN
   IF    PARTIAL_PRODUCT = -2^(2N-2)
   THEN
         PARTIAL_PRODUCT = +2^(2N-2)
   ENDIF
   RETURN (PARTIAL_PRODUCT)
END MULTIPLY
```

It accepts an n-bit multiplicand and an n-bit multiplier and produces a $2n$-bit product. Implement this algorithm with an 8088/8086 assembly language external FAR subprocedure. Your input should be a 32-bit signed integer multiplicand in the DX:AX register pair and a 32-bit signed integer multiplier in the DI:SI register pair. Your output should be the 64-bit signed integer product in the DI:SI:DX:AX register group, with the OF and CF bits of the flags register set to reflect whether or not the product overflows 32 bits. Your subprocedure must save and restore all registers used for purposes other than procedure output. All flags register bits other than the OF and CF bits must be saved and restored.

Use the main procedure in Program Listing 7.6 to demonstrate your subprocedure, and use the inputs in Table 7.7 in your demonstration.

7.7 The following algorithm, the Restoring Method, provides a method for performing signed integer division:

```
PROCEDURE DIVIDE (DIVIDEND,DIVISOR,QUOTIENT,REMAINDER)
    QUOTIENT = 0
    IF  SIGN OF DIVIDEND ≠ SIGN OF DIVISOR
    THEN
        TRIAL_DIV = DIVISOR
        RESTORE = - DIVISOR
    ELSE
        TRIAL_DIV = - DIVISOR
        RESTORE = DIVISOR
    ENDIF
    SIGN = SIGN OF DIVIDEND
    EXP_DIV = DIVIDEND EXPANDED TO 2N BITS
    BIT_COUNT = N
    REPEAT
       SHIFT EXP_DIV LEFT 1 BIT POSITION
       ADD TRIAL_DIV TO UPPER HALF OF EXP_DIV
       SHIFT QUOTIENT LEFT 1 BIT POSITION
       IF     EXP_DIV = 0OR
              SIGN = SIGN OF EXP_DIV
       THEN
              QUOTIENT = QUOTIENT + 1
       ENDIF
       BIT_COUNT = BIT_COUNT - 1
    UNTIL BIT_COUNT = 0
    REMAINDER = UPPER HALF OF EXP_DIV
    IF   SIGN OF DIVIDEND ≠ SIGN OF DIVISOR
    THEN
         QUOTIENT = - QUOTIENT
    ENDIF
    RETURN
END DIVIDE
```

The algorithm accepts an n-bit dividend and an n-bit divisor and produces an n-bit quotient and an n-bit remainder. Implement this algorithm with an 8088/8086 assembly language external FAR subprocedure. Your input should be a 32-bit signed integer dividend in the DX:AX register pair and a 32-bit signed integer divisor in the CX:BX register pair. Your output should be the 32-bit signed integer quotient in the DX:AX register pair and the 32-bit signed integer remainder in the CX:BX register pair. Your subprocedure must save and restore all registers used for purposes other than procedure output, including the flags register.

Use the main procedure in Program Listing 7.7 to demonstrate your subprocedure, and use the following inputs in your demonstration:

Dividend	Divisor
2147483635	117
2147483635	−117
−2147483635	117
−2147483635	−117
0	−123456789
123456789	1
−20	2
−23	4
2147483647	−2147483648
−2147483648	2147483647

7.8 The following sequence of positive integers, 1, 1, 2, 3, 5, 8, 13, 21, 34, 55, 89 ..., is called the *Fibonacci sequence.* The first number in the sequence, F_1, is 1. The second number in the sequence, F_2, is 1. Each subsequent number in the sequence, F_i, is the sum of the two numbers previous to it in the sequence. That is,

$$F_i = F_{i-1} + F_{i-2} \qquad \text{for } i > 2$$

Design an algorithm to find and display the largest value of i for which F_i can be represented as a 64-bit unsigned binary integer. Implement your algorithm with an 8088/8086 assembly language program. There is no input to your program. Your output should be the appropriate value of i displayed in decimal and the corresponding value of F_i displayed in binary.

Alternate implementation: Implement your algorithm with an 80386 assembly language program. There is no input to your program. Your output should be the appropriate value of i displayed in decimal and the corresponding value of F_i displayed in decimal.

7.9 The factorial of a nonnegative integer n can be defined as follows:

$$n! = 1 \qquad \text{if } n = 0$$

$$n! = (n)(n-1)(n-2)\cdots(2)(1) \qquad \text{if } n > 0$$

```
                PAGE     80,132
;===================================================================
;                        PROGRAM LISTING 7.7
;
;PROGRAM TO DEMONSTRATE INTEGER DIVISION SUBPROCEDURE
;===================================================================
                .MODEL   SMALL,BASIC
;===================================================================
                                             ;PROCEDURES TO
                EXTRN    DIVIDE:FAR          ;PERFORM 32-BIT SIGNED DIVIDE
                EXTRN    GETDEC32:FAR        ;GET 32-BIT SIGNED DEC. INT.
                EXTRN    NEWLINE:FAR         ;DISPLAY NEWLINE CHARACTER
                EXTRN    PUTDEC32:FAR        ;DISPLAY 32-BIT SIGNED INT.
                EXTRN    PUTSTRNG:FAR        ;DISPLAY CHARACTER STRING
;===================================================================
; S T A C K   D E F I N I T I O N
;
                .STACK   256
;===================================================================
; C O N S T A N T   D E F I N I T I O N S
;
                .CONST
PROMPT1         DB       'ENTER DIVIDEND  '
PROMPT2         DB       'ENTER DIVISOR   '
OUTPUT1         DB       'DIVIDEND   =  '
OUTPUT2         DB       'DIVISOR    =  '
OUTPUT3         DB       'QUOTIENT   =  '
OUTPUT4         DB       'REMAINDER  =  '
PROMPT_LNG EQU           PROMPT2-PROMPT1     ;LENGTH OF PROMPT MESSAGES
OUTPUT_LNG EQU           OUTPUT2-OUTPUT1     ;LENGTH OF OUTPUT MESSAGES
;===================================================================
; V A R I A B L E   D E F I N I T I O N S
;
                .DATA
DVDEND          DW       ?                   ;DIVIDEND
```

```
            DW      ?
DVISOR      DW      ?                         ;DIVISOR
            DW      ?
;===================================================================
; C O D E   S E G M E N T   D E F I N I T I O N
;
            .CODE   EX_7_7
;
            .STARTUP                          ;GENERATE STARTUP CODE
            PUSH    DS                        ;SET ES-REGISTER TO ADDRESS
            POP     ES                        ;DGROUP
            LEA     DI,PROMPT1                ;PROMPT FOR DIVIDEND
            MOV     CX,PROMPT_LNG
            CALL    PUTSTRNG
            CALL    GETDEC32                  ;GET DIVIDEND
            MOV     DVDEND,AX
            MOV     DVDEND+2,DX
            CALL    NEWLINE
            LEA     DI,PROMPT2                ;PROMPT FOR DIVISOR
;
            CALL    PUTSTRNG
            CALL    GETDEC32                  ;GET DIVISOR
            MOV     DVISOR,AX
            MOV     DVISOR+2,DX
            CALL    NEWLINE
            MOV     AX,DVDEND                 ;CALL DIVIDE(DIVIDEND,DIVISOR,
            MOV     DX,DVDEND+2               ;        QUOTIENT,REMAINDER)
            MOV     BX,DVISOR
            MOV     CX,DVISOR+2
            CALL    DIVIDE
            PUSH    BX
            PUSH    CX
            PUSH    AX
            PUSH    DX
            LEA     DI,OUTPUT1                ;OUTPUT DIVIDEND
            MOV     CX,OUTPUT_LNG
            CALL    PUTSTRNG
            MOV     AX,DVDEND
            MOV     DX,DVDEND+2
            MOV     BH,0
            CALL    PUTDEC32
            CALL    NEWLINE
            LEA     DI,OUTPUT2                ;OUTPUT DIVISOR
;
            CALL    PUTSTRNG
            MOV     AX,DVISOR
            MOV     DX,DVISOR+2
            CALL    PUTDEC32
            CALL    NEWLINE
            LEA     DI,OUTPUT3                ;OUTPUT QUOTIENT
;
            CALL    PUTSTRNG
            POP     DX
            POP     AX
            CALL    PUTDEC32
            CALL    NEWLINE
            LEA     DI,OUTPUT4                ;OUTPUT REMAINDER
;
            CALL    PUTSTRNG
            POP     DX
            POP     AX
            CALL    PUTDEC32
            CALL    NEWLINE
            .EXIT                             ;RETURN TO DOS
;
            END
```

That is, $n!$ is the product of the first n positive integers for $n > 0$.

Design an algorithm to find the largest value of n for which $n!$ can be represented as a 32-bit unsigned binary integer. Implement your algorithm with an 8088/8086 assembly language program. There is no input to your program. Your output should be the appropriate value of n and the corresponding value of $n!$ displayed in decimal. You will need a 32-bit unsigned integer multiply procedure in your program. The assembly module in Program Listing 7.3 with slight modifications can satisfy this need.

7.10 Write an 8088/8086 assembly language macro named ROL32 to perform a left-rotate operation on a 32-bit value in the DX:AX register pair. Your macro should have one operand, an immediate value that specifies the shift count. It should affect the flags register in exactly the same way that the ROL instruction affects the flags register. It also should protect registers for the user.

Write an 8088/8086 assembly language macro named ROR32 to perform a right-rotate operation on a 32-bit value in the DX:AX register pair. Your macro should have one operand, an immediate value that specifies the shift count. It should affect the flags register in exactly the same way that the ROR instruction affects the flags register. It also should protect registers for the user.

7.11 Write a 32-bit version of the PUT_BIN subprocedure in Program Listing 6.3. Use the same basic algorithm as in Program Listing 6.3, eliminating the logic that tests the code in the BL-register. You *may not* call the PUTBIN subprocedure in your solution. Your subprocedure should be named PUTBIN32. Your input should be a 32-bit value in the DX:AX register pair. Your subprocedure should display the value in binary form on the screen beginning at the current cursor position.

7.12 Write an 8088/8086 assembly language macro named SHR32 to perform a logical right-shift of the 32-bit value in the DX:AX register pair. This macro is to be used for division by a power of 2, so your macro should leave the remainder of the division (the bits shifted from the DX:AX register pair) in the BX:CX register pair (right-justified). It should have one operand, an immediate value that specifies the shift count. You may assume that the shift count will be in the range 1–32.

7.13 Implement the Russian Peasant's Method algorithm for the multiplication of signed integers (see the section entitled "Russian Peasant's Multiply—32-Bit Implementation") with an 80386 assembly language external FAR subprocedure named MULTIPLY. Your input should be a 64-bit signed integer multiplicand in the EDX:EAX register pair and a 64-bit signed integer multiplier in the EDI:ESI register pair. Your output should be the 128-bit signed integer product in the EDI:ESI:EDX:EAX register group, with the OF and CF bits of the flags register set to reflect whether or not the product overflows 64 bits. Your subprocedure must save and restore all registers used for purposes other than procedure output. All flags register bits other than the OF and CF bits must be saved and restored. Use the main procedure in file EX_7_8.ASM on the accompanying diskette to demonstrate your program.

7.14 Write an 80386 assembly language macro named SHR64 to perform a logical right-shift of the 64-bit value in the EDX:EAX register pair. This macro is to be used for division by a power of 2, so your macro should leave the remainder of the division (the bits shifted from the EDX:EAX register pair) in the EBX:ECX register pair (right-justified). It should have one operand, an immediate value that specifies the shift count. You may assume that the shift count will be in the range 1–64.

7.15 Suppose you are given 1 penny on the first day, 2 pennies on the second day, 4 pennies on the third day, 8 pennies on the fourth day, and so on. The number of pennies you are given doubles each day. After 10 days, you would have $10.23. Write an 80386 assembly language program to determine and display the number of days it would take for you to become a billionaire and the total amount of money you would have on that day. Display the total amount in dollars and cents.

7.16 Write an 80386 assembly language macro named DXAXEAX to copy the 32-bit value from the DX:AX register pair to the EAX-register. The EAX-register should be the only register modified by your macro. Then, write an 80386 assembly language macro named EAXDXAX to copy the 32-bit value from the EAX-register to the DX:AX register pair. The DX-register should be the only register modified by your macro. Explain why these macros might be useful in an 80386 assembly language program.

CHAPTER 8

Arrays and Character Strings

The example programs in previous chapters primarily involved single-valued data items called *scalars*. They included character strings, but these were used exclusively to display messages to the program's user. This chapter introduces one type of multivalued data item, the *array*. The *character string*, which is a special kind of array, is also discussed in more detail. Assuming you are already familiar with one- and two-dimensional arrays in some high-level language, this book explores how arrays are stored in a computer's memory and the machine-level techniques that are used to manipulate an array's elements. This chapter is restricted to one-dimensional arrays. Two-dimensional arrays are covered in Chapter 13.

8.1 One-Dimensional Array

An **array** is an ordered list of homogeneous data items called **array elements**. The term *ordered* refers to the fact that the list has a first element, a second element, a third element, and so on. The term *homogeneous* means that all elements in the list are of the same data type; that is, an array is a list of integers, a list of real numbers, a list of characters, a list of arrays (i.e., a multidimensional array). A **character string** is a special kind of array; it is an array of characters.

Figure 8.1 shows the logical arrangement of the elements of an *n*-element array. Representing an array in computer memory is quite natural. Its elements are stored in contiguous memory locations, with the first element stored first, immediately followed by the second element, immediately followed by the third element, and so on. Figure 8.1 can be viewed as a block of contiguous memory. The address of the first element of the array, called the **base address** of the array, and the size of an array element are the only items needed to compute an element's address. The address of a given element is computed from an offset relative to the base address. Figure 8.1 shows the offset for each element relative to the base address. Memory itself can be

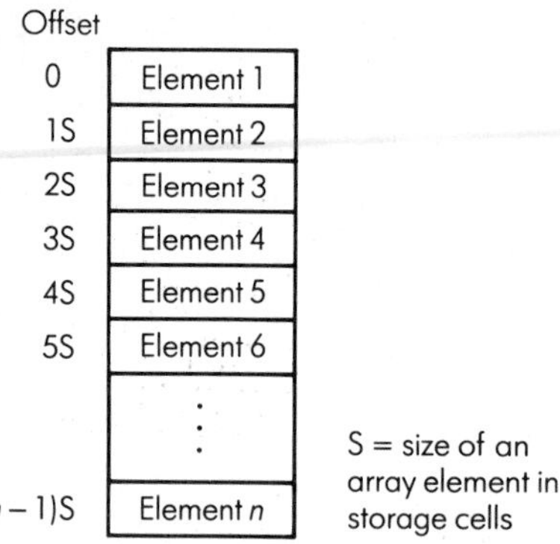

FIGURE 8.1
Organization of array elements

viewed as an array of storage cells. In fact, the segment–offset approach to memory addressing is based on this viewpoint: The segment portion of the address is a base address, and the offset portion is an offset relative to that base address.

The example programs in this chapter illustrate arrays of integers (word arrays) and character strings (byte arrays). One program introduces BCD numbers (nibble arrays). BCD numbers and BCD arithmetic are discussed in detail in Chapter 11.

8.2 Defining and Initializing Arrays

In the 8088/8086 assembly language, arrays are defined and initialized with data-defining pseudo-operations, such as DB and DW. Recall that the DB and DW pseudo-operations have the following general forms:

[⟨*label*⟩] DB ⟨*byte constant-list*⟩ [⟨*comment*⟩]
[⟨*label*⟩] DW ⟨*word constant-list*⟩ [⟨*comment*⟩]

in which ⟨*constant-list*⟩ is a list of constants (named constants, literal constants, or the null constant) separated by commas. Also, recall that a list of constants that contains a constant or group of constants that is repeated in a sequence can be abbreviated with a duplicate clause (see Section 2.2).

In array definitions, the DB and DW pseudo-operations specify the name of the array. The ⟨*constant-list*⟩ defines the size of the array and the initial values of the array's elements. The following data segment definition provides some examples of array definitions along with the translation listing generated by MASM 5.1 (note that the array elements are stored in a contiguous sequence of memory locations):

```
                                           .DATA
0000  0064[                       TABLE    DW      100 DUP(?)
          ????
                         ]

00C8  0032[                       COUNTS   DW      50 DUP(0)
          0000
                         ]

012C  0000 0001 0002 0003 ARRAY    DW      0,1,2,3,4,5,6,7,8,9
      0004 0005 0006 0007
      0008 0009
0140  54 48 49 53 20 49   STRING   DB      'THIS IS A STRING'
      53 20 41 20 53 54
      52 49 4E 47
```

```
0150  0028[                  INSTRNG  DB      40 DUP(' ')
          20
                         ]
                                  END
```

TABLE is defined as a word array with 100 elements (64 hex) whose elements are not initialized. COUNTS is defined as a word array with 50 elements (32 hex) whose elements are all initialized to 0. ARRAY is defined as a word array with 10 elements whose first element is initialized to 0 and whose second element is initialized to 1. In general, the *n*th element is initialized to $n - 1$. STRING is defined as a byte array with 16 elements whose first element is initialized to "T" (ASCII code 54 hex) and whose second element is initialized to "H." The sixteenth element of STRING is initialized to "G." INSTRNG is defined as a byte array with 40 elements (28 hex) whose elements are all initialized to the character SPACE (ASCII code 20 hex). Note that 40 DUP(20H) or 40 DUP(32) could also have been used to define INSTRNG.

The following listing shows the same data segment definition along with the machine language translation generated by MASM 6.0:

```
0000                                   .DATA
0000   0064 [                  TABLE    DW      100 DUP(?)
        0000
       ]
00C8   0032 [                  COUNTS   DW      50 DUP(0)
        0000
       ]
012C  0000 0001 0002 0003  ARRAY    DW      0,1,2,3,4,5,6,7,8,9
       0004 0005 0006
       0007 0008 0009
0140  54 48 49 53 20 49    STRING   DB      'THIS IS A STRING'
       53 20 41 20 53 54
       52 49 4E 47
0150   0028 [                  INSTRNG  DB      40 DUP(' ')
        20
       ]
                                   END
```

Note that MASM 6.0 treated the question mark (?) as a zero in the translation of TABLE. Unfortunately, MASM 6.0 seems inconsistent in its treatment of the ? as an initializer.[1] This discrepancy is not a problem for the programmer as long as the programmer consistently treats the ? initializer as meaning that the initial value is unknown.

8.3 Accessing Array Elements

Array elements can be accessed by specifying an index (offset) relative to the base address (start address) of the array or by using a special set of 8088/8086 assembly language instructions called *string instructions*.

---

[1] *Microsoft Macro Assembler Programmer's Guide—Version 6.0* (Redmond, Wash.: Microsoft Corporation, 1991), p. 115.

Indexing into Arrays

To select and use an array element, an operation known as **subscripting**, or **indexing**, is used. A **subscript** is an offset that is added to the base address of the array, thus providing the address of a specific element. The base address of an array is the address of the first element. In array definition examples given previously, the name in the label field of the DB or DW pseudo-operation is the name of the array. It is actually the symbolic name of the memory location where contiguous storage for the array elements begins; that is, it is the symbolic name for the array's first element. Therefore, this name is used symbolically to specify the base address of the array. **Index registers** are used to hold offsets from this base address. In the 8088/8086 assembly language, the BX-, DI-, SI-, and BP- registers are used for indexing (subscripting) into arrays. Note that the BP-register is designed for use as an auxiliary pointer in the stack segment. However, it can also be used as an index register for a static array. Its use is discussed further in Section 8.4. If an operand is to be subscripted, then the index register name appears in square brackets following the operand. Such notation indicates that the value in the index register is to be added to the address specified by the operand, which then provides the address of the desired array element.

EXAMPLES

Suppose a byte array is defined as follows:

```
TABLE  DB  10 DUP(0)
```

This byte array is described in Figure 8.2(a). TABLE is the symbolic name associated with the first element of the array, the element with index 0. The *i*th element is indexed by the integer $i - 1$; that is, to reach the *i*th element, $i - 1$ must be added to the array's base address, which is associated with the symbolic name TABLE.

Suppose the AL-register contains 17 hex and the BX-register contains 3 hex. Then the instruction

```
MOV  TABLE[BX],AL
```

will move 17 hex into the fourth element of TABLE; see Figure 8.2(b). The offset portion of the effective address specified by the operand TABLE[BX] is the offset of TABLE plus the contents of the BX-register. The segment portion of the effective address is the address of the segment that contains the TABLE definition.

FIGURE 8.2
Byte array table

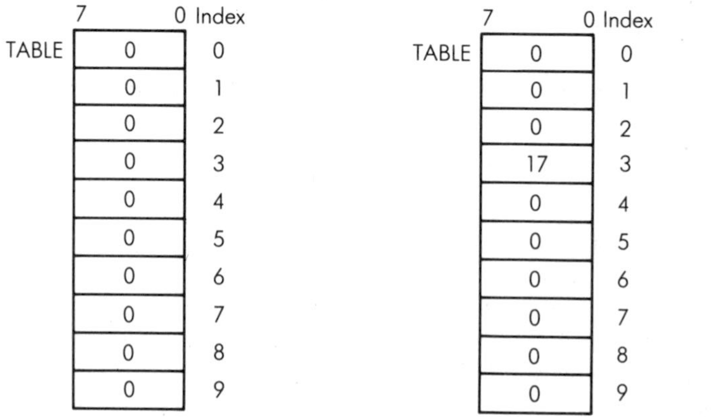

(a) Before MOV TABLE[BX],AL

	7 0	Index
TABLE	0	0
	0	1
	0	2
	0	3
	0	4
	0	5
	0	6
	0	7
	0	8
	0	9

(b) After MOV TABLE[BX],AL

	7 0	Index
TABLE	0	0
	0	1
	0	2
	17	3
	0	4
	0	5
	0	6
	0	7
	0	8
	0	9

Suppose TABLE had been defined as a word array:

```
TABLE  DW  10 DUP(0)
```

This word array is described in Figure 8.3(a). TABLE is the symbolic name associated with the first element (word) of the array (bytes 0 and 1). The ith element is the word in bytes $2(i-1)$ and $2(i-1)+1$ of the array. Therefore, the ith element is the word indexed by the integer $2(i-1)$; that is, to reach the ith element of a word array, $2(i-1)$ must be added to the array's base address, which is associated with the symbolic name TABLE.

FIGURE 8.3
Word array table

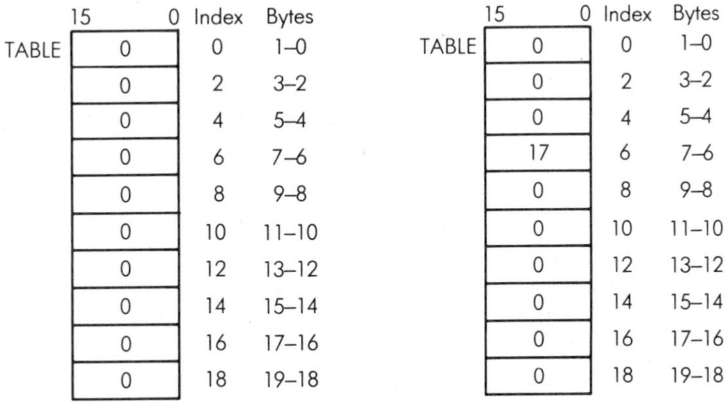

(a) Before MOV TABLE[BX],AX

	15 … 0	Index	Bytes
TABLE	0	0	1–0
	0	2	3–2
	0	4	5–4
	0	6	7–6
	0	8	9–8
	0	10	11–10
	0	12	13–12
	0	14	15–14
	0	16	17–16
	0	18	19–18

(b) After MOV TABLE[BX],AX

	15 … 0	Index	Bytes
TABLE	0	0	1–0
	0	2	3–2
	0	4	5–4
	17	6	7–6
	0	8	9–8
	0	10	11–10
	0	12	13–12
	0	14	15–14
	0	16	17–16
	0	18	19–18

Suppose the AX-register contains 17 hex and the BX-register contains 6 hex. Then the instruction

```
MOV  TABLE[BX],AX
```

will move 17 hex into the fourth element of TABLE; see Figure 8.3(b). ■

To perform some function on every element of an array, a loop can be used. The loop body can execute once for each element in the array. Each time through the loop body, the array index is incremented (or decremented) to move to the next element.

EXAMPLE

Consider the following array definitions:

```
BTABLE  DB  100 DUP(?)
WTABLE  DW  100 DUP(?)
```

BTABLE is defined as a byte array of 100 elements, and WTABLE is defined as a word array of 100 elements. To initialize both arrays to the values 1, 2, 3, 4, ..., 99, 100, the following loop could be used:

```
          MOV   CX,100           ;LOOP_CNT = 100
LOOPTOP:                         ;REPEAT
          MOV   BX,CX            ;    I = LOOP_CNT - 1
          DEC   BX
          MOV   BTABLE[BX],CL    ;    BTABLE[I] = LOOP_CNT
          SAL   BX,1             ;    I = I*2
```

```
        MOV   WTABLE[BX],CX  ;    WTABLE[I] = LOOP_CNT
        LOOP  LOOPTOP        ;    DECREMENT LOOP_CNT
                             ;UNTIL LOOP_CNT = 0
```

The first instruction sets the loop count to 100. Each iteration of the loop initializes one element in each array. The label LOOPTOP marks the top of the loop. The loop body consists of the five instructions that follow the label LOOPTOP. LOOPTOP is actually the label of the first instruction of the loop body. The first two instructions in the loop body set the index to the loop count minus 1. As the loop count moves from 100 to 1, the index moves from 99 to 0. The third instruction in the loop body stores the low-order 8 bits of the loop count in the BTABLE element specified by the index in the BX-register. The fourth instruction in the loop body converts the BX-register value from a byte index to a word index, which is done by shifting the BX-register left 1 bit position (i.e., multiplying it by 2). The last instruction in the loop body stores the loop count in the WTABLE element specified by the index in the BX-register. The LOOP instruction that follows the loop body performs the loop test. It decrements the loop count by 1 and returns to LOOPTOP if the resulting value of the loop count is nonzero. Table 8.1 traces the first and last three iterations of the loop. ■

TABLE 8.1
Iterations of BTABLE/WTABLE initialization loop

Loop Count	Byte Index	BTABLE Store	Word Index	WTABLE Store
100	99	BTABLE(99) = 100	198	WTABLE(99) = 100
99	98	BTABLE(98) = 99	196	WTABLE(98) = 99
98	97	BTABLE(97) = 98	194	WTABLE(97) = 98
.	.	.	.	.
.	.	.	.	.
.	.	.	.	.
3	2	BTABLE(2) = 3	4	WTABLE(2) = 3
2	1	BTABLE(1) = 2	2	WTABLE(1) = 2
1	0	BTABLE(0) = 1	0	WTABLE(0) = 1

8088/8086 String Instructions

The **string instructions** in the 8088/8086 assembly language are really a set of array instructions that operate on either byte arrays (e.g., character strings) or word arrays. With these instructions, the following conventions are used:

1. Source array elements are addressed by the DS:SI register pair.
2. Destination array elements are addressed by the ES:DI register pair.
3. The SI- and/or DI-register is automatically updated at the end of execution of a string instruction, which allows for addressing of the next array element in sequence. This update is an increment (decrement) by 2 for word arrays or an increment (decrement) by 1 for byte arrays.
4. The direction flag (DF bit in the flags register) is used to determine whether the SI/DI register update is an increment or a decrement. If the DF bit in the flags register is 0, then the update is an increment; if the DF bit is 1, then the update is a decrement.

Two instructions in the 8088/8086 assembly language manipulate the DF bit in the flags register: the CLD and STD instructions. The **CLD instruction** *clears* the DF bit in the flags register to denote incrementing. The **STD instruction** *sets* the DF bit in the flags register to denote decrementing. These instructions have the following general forms:

```
[<label>]  CLD                 [<comment>]
[<label>]  STD                 [<comment>]
```

Only the DF bit in the flags register is affected by execution of a CLD or an STD instruction.

Move, Load, and Store String Instructions

There are two move string instructions: MOVSB and MOVSW. The **MOVSB instruction** has the following general form:

```
[<label>]  MOVSB               [<comment>]
```

It causes the processor to replace the byte addressed by the ES:DI register pair with a copy of the byte addressed by the DS:SI register pair and then to update the DI and SI registers to point to the next byte in their respective strings. If the DF bit in the flags register is 0, then DI and SI are both incremented by 1; if the DF bit in the flags register is 1, then DI and SI are both decremented by 1.

The **MOVSW instruction** has the following general form:

```
[<label>]  MOVSW               [<comment>]
```

It causes the processor to replace the word addressed by the ES:DI register pair with a copy of the word addressed by the DS:SI register pair and then to update the DI and SI registers to point to the next word in their respective arrays. If the DF bit in the flags register is 0, then DI and SI are both incremented by 2; if the DF bit in the flags register is 1, then DI and SI are both decremented by 2.

EXAMPLES

Consider the segments DATA and EXTRA defined and illustrated in Figure 8.4. The .FARDATA pseudo-operation is being used to define static data segments, which are physically separate and addressed by separate segment registers (see Section 2.2). The ASSUME pseudo-operation instructs the assembler as to how the segment registers are to be used during execution (see Section 1.5). At the beginning of the main procedure, the instructions

```
MOV  AX,SEG DATA   ;SET DS-REGISTER TO ADDRESS
MOV  DS,AX         ;SEGMENT DATA
MOV  AX,SEG EXTRA  ;SET ES-REGISTER TO ADDRESS
MOV  ES,AX         ;SEGMENT EXTRA
```

should appear to initialize the segment registers consistent with the assumptions given the assembler in the ASSUME pseudo-operation. Suppose that after the execution of these instructions, the DS-register contains 0926 hex (the base address of segment DATA) and the ES-register contains 0927 hex (the base address of segment EXTRA).

Suppose the SI-register contains 000A (the offset of string COUNTRY within segment DATA) and the DI-register contains 0000 (the offset of string CITY within segment EXTRA). That is, the DS:SI register pair specifies the base address of byte array COUNTRY (0926:000A), and the ES:DI register pair specifies the base address

FIGURE 8.4
DATA and EXTRA segment definitions for string instruction examples

```
        .FARDATA   DATA
TABLE   DW         100, 200, 300, 400, 500
COUNTRY DB         'POLAND'

        .FARDATA   EXTRA
CITY    DB         'KRAKOW'
LIST    DW         200, 400, 600, 800, 1000
        ASSUME     DS:DATA,ES:EXTRA
```

Address	DATA segment	
0926:0000	64	TABLE
0926:0001	00	
0926:0002	C8	
0926:0003	00	
0926:0004	2C	
0926:0005	01	
0926:0006	90	
0926:0007	01	
0926:0008	F4	
0926:0009	01	
0926:000A	50	COUNTRY
0926:000B	4F	
0926:000C	4C	
0926:000D	41	
0926:000E	4E	
0926:000F	44	

Address	EXTRA segment	
0927:0000	4B	CITY
0927:0001	52	
0927:0002	41	
0927:0003	4B	
0927:0004	4F	
0927:0005	57	
0927:0006	C8	LIST
0927:0007	00	
0927:0008	90	
0927:0009	01	
0927:000A	58	
0927:000B	02	
0927:000C	20	
0927:000D	03	
0927:000E	E8	
0927:000F	03	

of byte array CITY (0927:0000). Suppose further that the DF bit of the flags register is 0 (for automatic incrementing). The instruction MOVSB moves a copy of the byte addressed by the DS:SI register pair (50 hex, the ASCII code for P) to the byte addressed by the ES:DI register pair and then increments the DI- and SI-registers by 1. The result is shown in Figure 8.5. The DS:SI register pair now addresses the second element of array COUNTRY (0926:000B), and the ES:DI register pair now addresses the second element of array CITY (0927:0001).

Suppose the SI-register contains 0004, the DI-register contains 000C, and the DF bit of the flags register is set to 1. That is, the DS:SI register pair specifies the address of the third element of word array TABLE (0926:0004), the ES:DI register pair specifies the address of the fourth element of word array LIST (0927:000C), and the direction flag is set for automatic decrementing. The instruction MOVSW replaces the word addressed by the ES:DI register pair with the word addressed by the DS:SI register pair and then decrements the DI- and SI-registers by 2 (1 word). The result is shown in Figure 8.6. The DS:SI register pair now addresses the second element of array TABLE (0926:0002), and the ES:DI register pair now addresses the third element of array LIST (0927:000A).

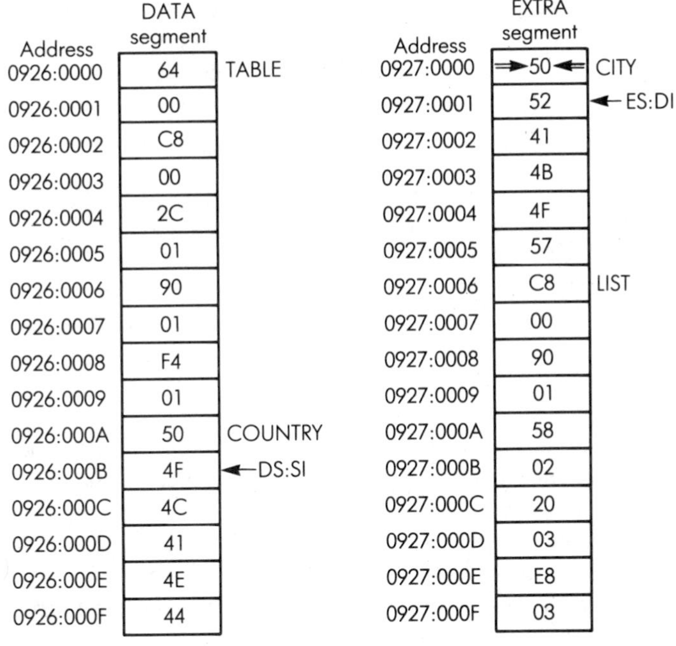

FIGURE 8.5
DATA and EXTRA segments after MOVSB

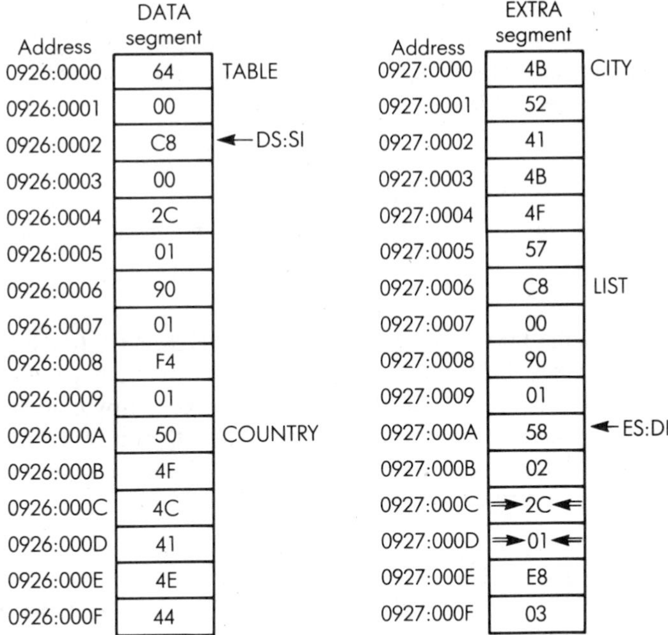

FIGURE 8.6
DATA and EXTRA segments after MOVSW

There are two load string instructions: LODSB and LODSW. The **LODSB instruction** has the following general form:

[⟨*label*⟩] `LODSB` [⟨*comment*⟩]

It causes the processor to load the AL-register with a copy of the byte addressed by the DS:SI register pair and then to update the SI-register to point to the next byte in the string. If the DF bit in the flags register is 0, then the SI-register is incremented by 1; if the DF bit in the flags register is 1, then the SI-register is decremented by 1.

The **LODSW instruction** has the following general form:

[⟨*label*⟩] `LODSW` [⟨*comment*⟩]

It causes the processor to load the AX-register with a copy of the word addressed by the DS:SI register pair and then to update the SI-register to point to the next word in the array. If the DF bit in the flags register is 0, then the SI-register is incremented by 2; if the DF bit in the flags register is 1, then the SI-register is decremented by 2.

There are two store string instructions: STOSB and STOSW. The **STOSB instruction** has the following general form:

[⟨*label*⟩] `STOSB` [⟨*comment*⟩]

It causes the processor to replace the byte addressed by the ES:DI register pair with a copy of the byte in the AL-register and then to update the DI-register to point to the next byte in the string. If the DF bit in the flags register is 0, then the DI-register is incremented by 1; if the DF bit in the flags register is 1, then the DI-register is decremented by 1.

The **STOSW instruction** has the following general form:

[⟨*label*⟩] `STOSW` [⟨*comment*⟩]

It causes the processor to replace the word addressed by the ES:DI register pair with a copy of the word in the AX-reigster and then to update the DI-register to point to the next word in the array. If the DF bit in the flags register is 0, then the DI-register is incremented by 2; if the DF bit in the flags register is 1, then the DI-register is decremented by 2.

EXAMPLES

Consider again the segments DATA and EXTRA defined and illustrated in Figure 8.4.

Suppose the DS:SI register pair contains 0926:000C (the address of the third element of byte array COUNTRY) and the DF bit of the flags register is 0. The instruction LODSB loads the AL-register with a copy of the byte addressed by the DS:SI register pair (4C hex, the ASCII code for L) and then increments the SI-register by 1. The result is shown in Figure 8.7. The DS:SI register pair now addresses the fourth element of array COUNTRY (0926:000D).

Suppose the ES:DI register pair contains 0927:000A (the address of the third element of word array LIST), the DF bit of the flags register is set to 1, and the AX-register contains the hexadecimal value 12AC. The instruction STOSW replaces the word addressed by the ES:DI register pair (0258) with a copy of the AX-register value (12AC) and then decrements the DI-register by 2. The result is shown in Figure 8.8. The ES:DI register pair now addresses the second element of array LIST (0927:0008). ■

None of the flag bits in the flags register are affected by execution of a move, load, or store string instruction.

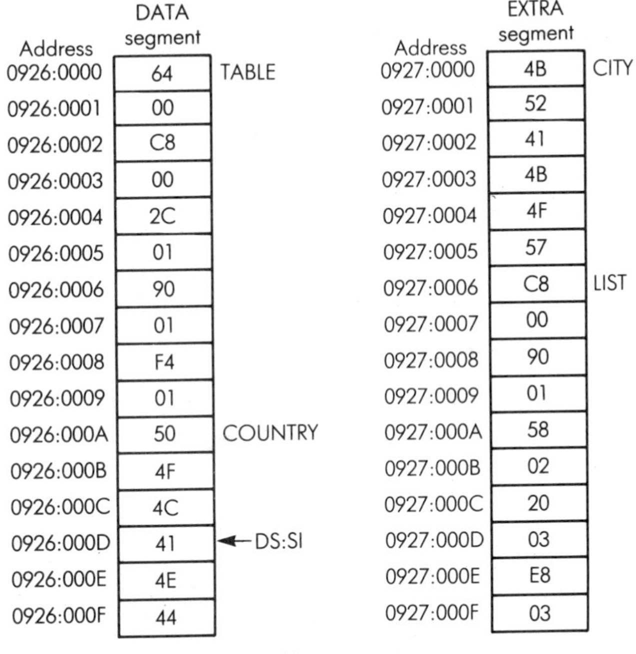

FIGURE 8.7
DATA and EXTRA segments after LODSB

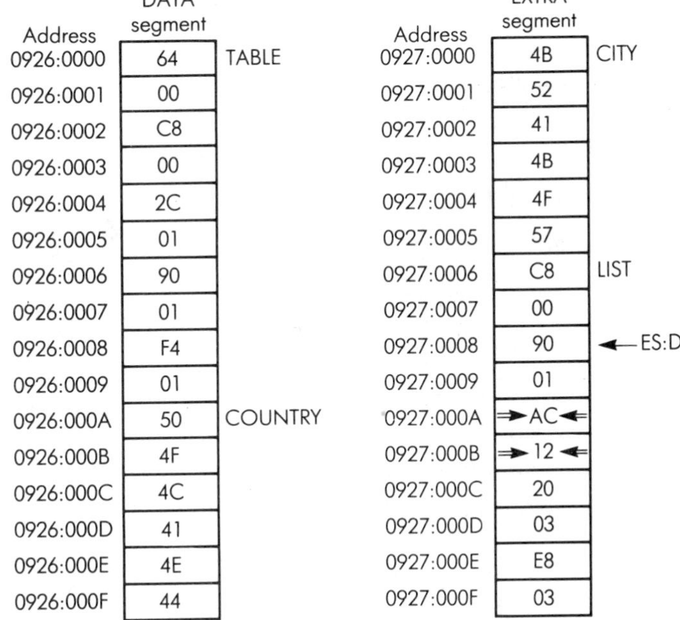

FIGURE 8.8
DATA and EXTRA segments after STOSW

Compare and Scan String Instructions

There are two compare string instructions: CMPSB and CMPSW. The **CMPSB instruction** has the following general form:

[⟨*label*⟩] `CMPSB` [⟨*comment*⟩]

It causes the processor to compare the byte addressed by the DS:SI register pair to the byte addressed by the ES:DI register pair, to set the flags to reflect this relationship, and then to update the DI- and SI-registers to point to the next byte in their respective strings. If the DF bit in the flags register is 0, then the DI- and SI-registers are both incremented by 1; if the DF bit in the flags register is 1, then the DI- and SI-registers are both decremented by 1. To perform the comparison, the processor subtracts the byte addressed by the ES:DI register pair from the byte addressed by the DS:SI register pair and sets the bits in the flags register to reflect the result. Neither byte is modified by execution of this instruction.

The **CMPSW instruction** has the following general form:

[⟨*label*⟩] CMPSW [⟨*comment*⟩]

It causes the processor to compare the word addressed by the DS:SI register pair to the word addressed by the ES:DI register pair, to set the flags to reflect this relationship, and then to update the DI- and SI-registers to point to the next word in their respective arrays. If the DF bit in the flags register is 0, then the DI- and SI-registers are both incremented by 2; if the DF bit in the flags register is 1, then the DI- and SI-registers are both decremented by 2. To perform the comparison, the processor subtracts the word addressed by the ES:DI register pair from the word addressed by the DS:SI register pair and sets the bits in the flags register to reflect the result. Neither word is modified by execution of this instruction.

It is important to note that the CMPSB and CMPSW string instructions follow a different philosophy than does the CMP compare instruction. CMP compares the destination to the source operand; that is, it sets the flags to reflect the value of destination operand minus source operand. CMPSB and CMPSW compare the item addressed by the DS:SI register pair (source operand) to the item addressed by the ES:DI register pair (destination operand); that is, they set the flags to reflect the value of source operand minus destination operand.

There are two scan string instructions: SCASB and SCASW. The **SCASB instruction** has the following general form:

[⟨*label*⟩] SCASB [⟨*comment*⟩]

It causes the processor to compare the byte in the AL-register to the byte addressed by the ES:DI register pair, to set the flags to reflect this relationship, and then to update the DI-register to point to the next byte in the string. If the direction flag is 0, then the DI-register is incremented by 1; if the direction flag is 1, then the DI-register is decremented by 1. To perform the comparison, the processor subtracts the byte addressed by the ES:DI register pair from the byte in the AL-register and sets the flags to reflect the result. Neither byte is modified by execution of this instruction.

The **SCASW instruction** has the following general form:

[⟨*label*⟩] SCASW [⟨*comment*⟩]

It causes the processor to compare the word in the AX-register to the word addressed by the ES:DI register pair, to set the flags to reflect this relationship, and then to update the DI-register to point to the next word in the array. If the direction flag is 0, then the DI-register is incremented by 2; if the direction flag is 1, then the DI-register is decremented by 2. To perform the comparison, the processor subtracts the word addressed by the ES:DI register pair from the word in the AX-register and sets the flags to reflect the result. Neither word is modified by execution of this instruction.

The OF, SF, ZF, AF, PF, and CF bits in the flags register are affected by execution of a compare or scan string instruction:

> If the subtraction operation results in a signed integer, arithmetic overflow, then the OF bit in the flags register is set; otherwise, the OF bit in the flags register is cleared.
>
> The SF bit in the flags register will contain a copy of the sign bit of the result of the subtraction operation. That is, if the result of the subtraction is negative, then the SF bit in the flags register is set; otherwise, the SF bit is cleared.
>
> If the result of the subtraction operation is zero, then the ZF bit in the flags register is set; otherwise, the ZF bit is cleared.
>
> If the result of the subtraction operation has an even number of 1 bits in the low-order byte, then the PF bit in the flags register is set; if the result has an odd number of 1 bits in the low-order byte, then the PF bit in the flags register is cleared.
>
> If the subtraction operation requires a borrow into the most significant bit, then the CF bit in the flags register is set; otherwise, the CF bit is cleared.
>
> The AF bit in the flags register is set if there is a borrow into bit 3 during the subtraction operation; otherwise, the AF bit is cleared.

EXAMPLES

Consider again the segments DATA and EXTRA defined and illustrated in Figure 8.4.

Suppose the DS:SI register pair contains 0926:0000 (the address of the first element of word array TABLE), the ES:DI register pair contains 0927:0006 (the address of the first element of word array LIST), and the DF bit of the flags register is 0. The instruction CMPSW subtracts the word addressed by the ES:DI register pair (00C8) from the word addressed by the DS:SI register pair (0064), sets the flags to reflect the result, and then increments the DI- and SI-registers by 2. The subtraction performed is

$$\begin{array}{r} 0064 \\ -\ \underline{00C8} \\ \end{array} \qquad \begin{array}{r} 0064 \\ +\ \underline{FF38} \\ FF9C \end{array}$$

The six flags affected are set as follows:

OF	SF	ZF	AF	PF	CF
0	1	0	1	1	1

The DS:SI register pair now addresses the second element of array TABLE (0926:0002), and the ES:DI register pair now addresses the second element of array LIST (0927:0008). Neither array is modified.

Suppose the ES:DI register pair contains 0927:0005 (the address of the last element of byte array CITY), the DF bit of the flags register is 1, and the AL-register contains 59 hex. The instruction SCASB subtracts the byte addressed by the ES:DI register pair (57 hex) from the byte in the AL-register (59 hex), sets the flags to reflect the result, and decrements the DI-register by 1. The subtraction performed is

$$\begin{array}{r} 59\text{ hex} \\ -\ \underline{57\text{ hex}} \\ 02\text{ hex} \end{array}$$

The six flags affected are set as follows:

OF	SF	ZF	AF	PF	CF
0	0	0	0	0	0

The ES:DI register pair now addresses the fifth element of array CITY (0927:0004). Neither the array nor the AL-register is modified. ■

Generic Forms for String Instructions

Note that there is also a generic form for each of the five string instructions previously discussed:

```
[⟨label⟩]  MOVS  ⟨destination⟩,⟨source⟩        [⟨comment⟩]
[⟨label⟩]  LODS  ⟨source⟩                      [⟨comment⟩]
[⟨label⟩]  STOS  ⟨destination⟩                 [⟨comment⟩]
[⟨label⟩]  CMPS  ⟨source⟩,⟨destination⟩        [⟨comment⟩]
[⟨label⟩]  SCAS  ⟨destination⟩                 [⟨comment⟩]
```

An operand in the generic form of a string instruction is the symbolic name of an array. When two operands are required (i.e., with MOVS or CMPS), the type attributes of the two operands must match (i.e., both must be byte, or both must be word). When the generic form of a string instruction is used, the assembler generates the code for one of the two corresponding standard string instructions depending on the type attribute of the operand(s). For example, when the generic form MOVS is used, the assembler generates the machine code for either MOVSB or MOVSW depending on the type attribute of the two operands. The explicit statement of the operands provides several advantages:

1. By explicitly identifying the arrays involved, the program is better documented.
2. It allows the assembler to check the types of the operands.
3. It allows the assembler to check the accessibility of the operands. That is, the assembler can check to see that the arrays identified by the explicit operands are in the proper segments for the specified string instruction.

It is important to realize, however, that the string instructions use the ES:DI register pair and/or the DS:SI register pair (not the explicit operands) to locate the array elements. The operands in the generic string instructions are there only to provide type- and accessibility-checking information for the assembler; that is, the operands could be incorrect, and yet the instruction generated by the assembler might be the instruction desired.

EXAMPLE

Consider the following data segment definition shown with its assembler-generated output:

```
0000                         .DATA
0000 50 4F 4C 41 4E 44       COUNTRY  DB  'POLAND'
0006 4B 52 41 4B 4F 57       CITY     DB  'KRAKOW'
000C 0014 0028 003C 0050     LIST     DW  20,40,60,80,100
     0064
```

Suppose the assembler has already encountered the statement

```
ASSUME  ES:DGROUP
```

and the instructions

```
.STARTUP
PUSH    DS
POP     ES
```

which, at execution time, initialize the DS and ES registers to address the data group DGROUP. The ASSUME pseudo-operation instructs the assembler as to how the ES-register is to be used during execution, and the PUSH and POP instructions actually initialize the ES-register during execution.

The following sequence of instructions is designed to move a SPACE character to each element of array CITY:

```
          CLD
          LEA    DI,CITY
          MOV    CX,6
          MOV    AL,' '
LOOPTOP:
          STOSB
          LOOP   LOOPTOP
```

The STOSB instruction could be replaced by the generic form

```
STOS  CITY
```

and the assembler would generate exactly the same code. The assembler would use the symbolic name CITY to verify that the named array (CITY) is defined in the segment ASSUMEd to be addressed by the ES-register (the register used by a store string instruction). The assembler would then generate the machine code for an STOSB instruction since CITY is defined with a type attribute of byte.

The STOSB instruction could also be replaced by the generic form

```
STOS  COUNTRY
```

and again the assembler would generate exactly the same code. The assembler would use the symbolic name COUNTRY to verify that the named array (COUNTRY) is defined in the segment ASSUMEd to be addressed by the ES-register (the register used by a store string instruction). The assembler would then generate the machine code for an STOSB instruction since COUNTRY is defined with a type attribute of byte.

At execution time, the store string operation uses the ES:DI register pair to identify the array element. With both generic forms given previously, the translated program is exactly the same. However, in one case, the documentation is consistent with the array used:

```
LEA   DI,CITY
   .
   .
   .
STOS  CITY
```

In the other case, it is not consistent with the array used:

```
LEA   DI,CITY
   .
   .
   .
STOS  COUNTRY
```

■

The generic forms of the string instructions are generally not used in the example programs of this book.

Repeat Prefixes

The string instructions operate on a single character of a string or on a single element of an array, although there are times you may wish to perform some operation on every character in a string or on every element of an array. To accomplish this task, a repeat prefix can be placed on a string instruction to specify that the instruction is to be repeated some number of times. With a repeat prefix, the CX-register is used as a counter to control the number of times the string instruction is to be executed.

There are three repeat prefixes that can be used with the string instructions: REP, REPE/REPZ, and REPNE/REPNZ.

REP

The **REP prefix** has the following general form:

[⟨*label*⟩] REP ⟨*string-op*⟩ ⟨*operands*⟩ [⟨*comment*⟩]

in which ⟨*string-op*⟩ is the operation code of one of the string instructions and ⟨*operands*⟩ is the operand list (if any) for the string instruction. The REP prefix on a string instruction causes the processor to execute the string instruction the number of times specified by the value in the CX-register, which is decremented after each execution of the string instruction. The REP prefix on a string instruction causes the following loop to be executed:

REPEAT
    Execute string instruction (updating SI and/or DI)
    Decrement CX-register by 1
UNTIL *CX-register is 0*

This loop is given in flowchart form in Figure 8.9. Note that each time the string

FIGURE 8.9
REP prefix

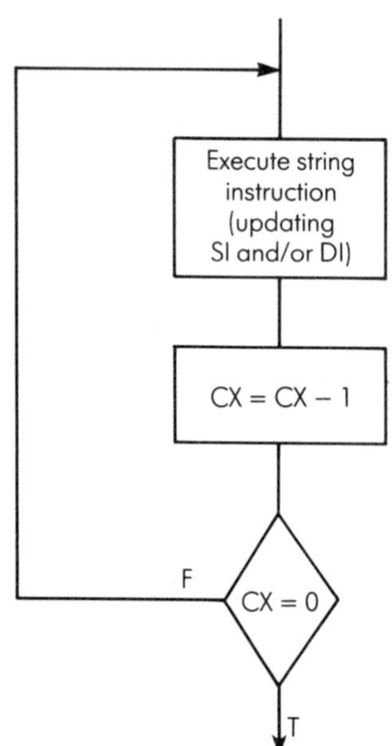

instruction is executed, the SI- and/or DI-register is automatically updated so that a different array element is (different array elements are) processed on each execution of the string instruction.

The REP prefix should be used only with the move, load, and store string instructions. It makes no sense to repeatedly execute a compare or scan string instruction. A compare or scan string instruction should be followed by a decision based on the result of the comparison made by that instruction. The REPE/REPZ and REPNE/REPNZ prefixes, which are discussed in the next two subsections, provide the capability for the repeated execution of the string instruction to be based on a condition as well as a count.

EXAMPLE

Suppose a character string is defined in a static data segment as follows:

```
STRING  DB  40 DUP(?)
```

Also, suppose the ES-register currently specifies the address of the origin of this data segment. The following code sets every character in STRING to an asterisk (*):

```
      CLD
      LEA    DI,STRING
      MOV    CX,40
      MOV    AL,'*'
REP   STOSB
```

The CLD instruction clears the DF bit in the flags register so that the store string instruction automatically increments the DI-register. The LEA instruction sets the DI-register to the offset of STRING, which means that the ES:DI register pair now specifies the address of the first element of array STRING. The first MOV instruction sets the CX-register to 40, the number of elements in array STRING. The store string instruction containing the REP prefix is to be executed 40 times, once for each element in array STRING. The second MOV instruction places the ASCII representation of the character * in the AL-register, which is the value that is to be stored in each element of array STRING.

The store string instruction is executed 40 times. The REP prefix causes the store string instruction to be executed repeatedly as the CX-register counts from 40 to 0. Each time the store string instruction is executed, the DI-register is automatically incremented by 1 so that the ES:DI register pair specifies the address of the next character (byte) of the string (array). On each execution of the store string instruction, an * character is stored in the byte addressed by the ES:DI register pair.

On the first execution of the store string instruction, the first character of STRING is replaced by *. On the second execution of the store string instruction, the second character of STRING is replaced by *. In general, on the *n*th execution of the store string instruction, the *n*th character of STRING is replaced by *. On the last execution of the store string instruction, the fortieth character of STRING is replaced by *. ■

REPE/REPZ

The **REPE/REPZ prefix** has the following general form (either form is acceptable):

[⟨*label*⟩] REPE ⟨*string-op*⟩ ⟨*operands*⟩ [⟨*comment*⟩]
[⟨*label*⟩] REPZ ⟨*string-op*⟩ ⟨*operands*⟩ [⟨*comment*⟩]

in which ⟨*string-op*⟩ is the operation code of one of the string instructions and

⟨*operands*⟩ is the operand list (if any) for the string instruction. The REPE or REPZ prefix on a string instruction causes the processor to execute the string instruction repeatedly as long as the ZF bit in the flags register is set. The value in the CX-register specifies the maximum number of times that the string instruction is to be executed, and it is decremented after each execution of the string instruction. The REPE/REPZ prefix on a string instruction causes the following loop to be executed:

REPEAT
    Execute string instruction (updating SI and/or DI)
    Decrement CX-register by 1
UNTIL *CX-register is 0 or ZF = 0*

This loop is given in flowchart form in Figure 8.10.

FIGURE 8.10
REPE/REPZ prefix

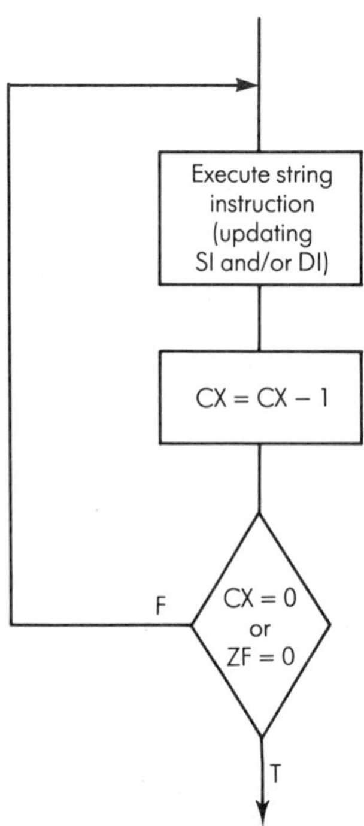

The REPE/REPZ prefix should be used only with the compare and scan string instructions. It makes no sense to base the repeated execution of a move, load, or store string instruction on a condition because these string instructions cannot potentially change the value of the condition.

EXAMPLE

Suppose a character string is defined in a static data segment as follows:

```
STRING  DB  40 DUP(?)
```

Also, suppose the ES-register currently specifies the address of the origin of this data segment and STRING has been given a value. The following code sets the ES:DI register pair to address the first nonblank character in STRING:

```
        CLD
        LEA    DI,STRING
        MOV    CX,40
        MOV    AL,' '
```

```
REPE  SCASB
      JE      ALL_BLANKS
      DEC     DI
```

The CLD instruction clears the DF bit in the flags register so that the scan string instruction automatically increments the DI-register. The LEA instruction sets the DI-register to the offset of STRING, which means that the ES:DI register pair now specifies the address of the first element of array STRING. The first MOV instruction sets the CX-register to 40, the number of elements in array STRING. The scan string instruction containing the REPE prefix is to be executed a maximum of 40 times. The second MOV instruction places the ASCII code for SPACE in the AL-register.

The scan string instruction repeatedly executes as long as the character being scanned is a space (blank), up to a maximum of 40 times. It terminates if either a nonblank character is found or all 40 characters of STRING have been scanned.

Following repeated execution of the scan string instruction, it must be determined which of the two conditions caused the instruction to terminate execution. The JE instruction makes this determination. If the ZF bit in the flags register is still set, then the CX-register must have reached zero, causing the scan string instruction to terminate; that is, the jump is taken when all 40 characters are scanned without finding a character that is not equal to blank. However, if the ZF bit in the flags register is not set, then the last character scanned was a nonblank character, and the ES:DI register pair has already been updated to specify the address of the byte immediately following that nonblank character. Therefore, if the jump fails, the DI-register must be decremented so that the ES:DI register pair specifies the address of the byte containing the first nonblank character in STRING. This task is accomplished by the DEC instruction. ■

REPNE/REPNZ

The **REPNE/REPNZ prefix** has the following general form (either form is acceptable):

[⟨*label*⟩] REPNE ⟨*string-op*⟩ ⟨*operands*⟩ [⟨*comment*⟩]
[⟨*label*⟩] REPNZ ⟨*string-op*⟩ ⟨*operands*⟩ [⟨*comment*⟩]

in which ⟨*string-op*⟩ is the operation code of one of the string instructions and ⟨*operands*⟩ is the operand list (if any) for the string instruction. The REPNE or REPNZ prefix on a string instruction causes the processor to execute the string instruction repeatedly as long as the ZF bit in the flags register is *not* set. The value in the CX-register specifies the maximum number of times that the string instruction is to be executed, and it is decremented after each execution of the string instruction. The REPNE/REPNZ prefix on a string instruction causes the following loop to be executed:

REPEAT
    Execute string instruction (updating SI and/or DI)
    Decrement CX-register by 1
UNTIL *CX-register is 0 or ZF = 1*

This loop is given in flowchart form in Figure 8.11.

The REPNE/REPNZ prefix should be used only with the compare and scan string instructions. It makes no sense to base the repeated execution of a move, load, or store string instruction on a condition because these string instructions cannot potentially change the value of the condition.

FIGURE 8.11
REPNE/REPNZ prefix

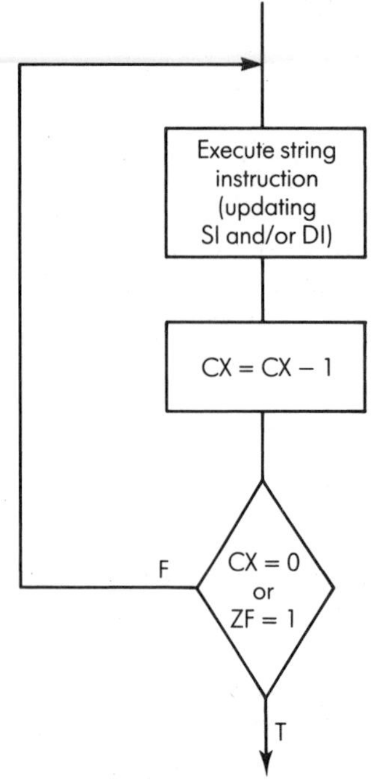

EXAMPLE

Suppose a word array is defined in a static data segment as follows:

```
ARRAY     DW  99 DUP(?)
ARRAYEND  DW  ?
```

Note that ARRAY is defined as a word array of size 100 and that each element is left uninitialized. ARRAY is the symbolic name associated with the first array element, and ARRAYEND is the symbolic name associated with the last (one-hundredth) array element. This setup allows for sequential processing to begin at either end of the array.

Also, suppose the DS- and ES-registers currently specify the address of the origin of this data segment and the elements of ARRAY have been given values. The following code sets the ES:DI register pair to address the last element of ARRAY that has a value of zero:

```
      STD
      LEA   DI,ARRAYEND
      MOV   CX,100
      MOV   AX,0
REPNE SCASW
      JNE   NOT_FOUND
      INC   DI
      INC   DI
```

The STD instruction sets the DF bit in the flags register so that the scan string instruction automatically decrements the DI-register. The LEA instruction sets the DI-register to the offset of ARRAYEND, the last word in the array, which means that the ES:DI register pair now specifies the address of the last element of the array. The first MOV instruction sets the CX-register to 100, the number of elements in ARRAY. The scan string instruction containing the REPNE prefix is to be executed a maximum of 100 times (i.e., at most once for each element of ARRAY). The second MOV instruction places the value 0 in the AX-register.

The scan string instruction repeatedly executes as long as the value being scanned is *not* zero, up to a maximum of 100 times. It terminates if either a value of zero is found or all 100 elements of ARRAY have been scanned. Since the scan is from the last element to the first element in the array, the first element found whose value is zero is the last element in the array whose value is zero.

Following repeated execution of the scan string instruction, it must be determined which of the two conditions caused the instruction to terminate execution. The JNE instruction makes this determination. If the ZF bit in the flags register is still cleared, then the CX-register must have reached zero, causing the scan string instruction to terminate; that is, the jump is taken when all 100 elements are scanned without finding a zero value. However, if the ZF bit in the flags register is set, then the last element scanned was a zero value, and the ES:DI register pair has already been updated to specify the address of the word immediately preceding that zero value. Therefore, if the jump fails, the DI-register must be incremented by 2 (2 bytes or 1 word) so that the ES:DI register pair specifies the address of the word found to be zero. This task is accomplished by the two INC instructions. The instruction

```
ADD  DI,2
```

could replace the two INC instructions. The two INC instructions require less memory space than the single ADD instruction. However, the ADD instruction executes faster than the two INC instructions. ■

The repeat prefixes translate to 1111001Z in machine code, in which $Z = 1$ for REP and REPE/REPZ and $Z = 0$ for REPNE/REPNZ. For the move, load, and store string instructions, the repeat prefix causes the string instruction to be repeated until the CX-register counts down to zero, regardless of the value of Z. For the scan and compare string instructions, the repeat prefix causes the string instruction to be repeated until the ZF bit in the flags register is not equal to Z or the CX-register counts down to zero. MASM 6.0 allows the REP prefix to be used only with move, load, and store string instructions and the REPE/REPZ and REPNE/REPNZ prefixes to be used only with compare and scan string instructions. MASM 6.0 generates the message

```
error A2068: instruction prefix not allowed
```

when the REP prefix is used with a compare or scan string instruction or the REPE/REPZ or REPNE/REPNZ prefix is used with a move, load, or store string instruction.

MASM 5.1

MASM 5.1 allows the repeat prefixes to be used with any string instruction. If the REP prefix is used with a compare or scan string instruction, it behaves exactly like REPE/REPZ. If the REPE/REPZ or REPNE/REPNZ prefix is used with a move, load, or store string instruction, it behaves exactly like REP. That is, the ZF bit of the flags register has no effect when REPE/REPZ or REPNE/REPNZ is used with a move, load, or store string instruction.

None of the flags are affected by a repeat prefix. However, the string instruction being repeated affects the flags in the normal manner.

Programming Example— BCD-to-ASCII Conversion

It is possible to store numbers in the computer in decimal rather than in binary form and to perform computations on those decimal numbers. To do so, a binary code is used to represent the individual digits of a decimal number. One such code is called **binary coded decimal (BCD)**. The BCD code for each of the 10 decimal digits is given in Table 8.2, in which each decimal digit is represented by a 4-bit binary code. Note that the six 4-bit codes 1010, 1011, 1100, 1101, 1110, 1111 are not used and in fact are illegal in the BCD number system. To represent a 5-digit decimal number, a total of 20 bits (4 per digit) are needed. Table 8.3 shows some 4-digit BCD numbers, the corresponding 4-digit decimal numbers, and the corresponding binary numbers.

TABLE 8.2
BCD codes

Decimal Digit	BCD Code
0	0000
1	0001
2	0010
3	0011
4	0100
5	0101
6	0110
7	0111
8	1000
9	1001

TABLE 8.3
Examples of corresponding numbers in the BCD, decimal, and binary number systems

BCD	Decimal	Binary
0000 0000 0000 0000	0000	0
1001 1001 1001 1001	9999	10011100001111
1000 0001 1001 0001	8191	1111111111111
0010 0111 0011 0101	2735	101010101111
0100 0110.0010 0101	46.25	101110.01

Program Listing 8.1 shows an implementation of an algorithm to convert a BCD number to an ASCII character string for output. The input is a packed array of BCD digits and a count of the number of BCD digits in the array. A **packed array** is one in which the BCD digits are packed 2 per byte. This kind of array is also called a **nibble array** because each element of the array is a 4-bit nibble (one-half a byte). The output of the algorithm is a character string (i.e., an ASCII array). Figure 8.12 shows the hexadecimal contents of a BCD array and the corresponding ASCII array. Each of the two arrays in the figure contains the 7-digit decimal number 2147483.

Program Listing 8.1 shows an external subprocedure that performs this BCD-to-ASCII conversion. The prologue (lines 2–14) explains the function of the procedure and its interface requirements. On entry to the subprocedure, the DS:SI register pair must specify the base address of the BCD array, the ES:DI register pair must specify the base address of the array in which the ASCII character string is to be stored, and the CX-register must contain a count of the number of digits in the BCD

```
 1:            PAGE    80,132
 2: ;====================================================================
 3: ;                    PROGRAM LISTING 8.1
 4: ;
 5: ; PROCEDURE TO CONVERT A BCD NUMBER TO ASCII
 6: ;
 7: ; INPUT:   DS:SI POINTS TO ARRAY CONTAINING BCD   NUMBER
 8: ;          ES:DI POINTS TO ARRAY TO CONTAIN ASCII NUMBER
 9: ;          CX    CONTAINS SIZE OF BCD NUMBER (DIGIT_COUNT)
10: ;
11: ; OUTPUT: UPON RETURN, THE ARRAY POINTED TO BY ES:DI WILL
12: ;          CONTAIN AN ASCII NUMBER EQUIVALENT  TO  THE BCD
13: ;          NUMBER IN THE ARRAY POINTED TO BY DS:SI.
14: ;====================================================================
15:            .MODEL  SMALL,BASIC
16: ;====================================================================
17: ; C O D E   S E G M E N T   D E F I N I T I O N
18:            .CODE   EX_8_1
19: ;
20: BCDASCII   PROC    FAR PUBLIC USES AX CX DX DI SI
21:                                     ;PROCEDURE BCDASCII(DIGIT_COUNT,
22:                                     ;                    DS:SI,ES:DI)
23:                                        ;SAVE REGISTERS SPECIFIED
24:                                        ;       IN USES CLAUSE
25:            PUSHF                       ;SAVE FLAGS
26:            CLD                         ;SET DF FOR INCREMENTING
27:            MOV     DX,-1               ;LR_FLAG = LEFT
28: LOOP_TOP:                              ;REPEAT
29:            PUSH    CX                  ;   SAVE DIGIT_COUNT
30:            CMP     DX,0                ;   IF   LR_FLAG = LEFT
31:            JG      ELSE1
32:            LODSB                       ;   THEN PAIR = DS:SI -> BYTE
33:                                        ;        SI = SI + 1
34:            MOV     AH,AL
35:            MOV     CL,4                ;        DIGIT = LEFT NIBBLE
36:            SHR     AL,CL               ;                OF PAIR
37:            JMP     ENDIF1
38: ELSE1:                                 ;   ELSE
39:            MOV     AL,AH
40:            AND     AL,0FH              ;        DIGIT = RIGHT NIBBLE
41:                                        ;                OF PAIR
42: ENDIF1:                                ;   ENDIF
43:            ADD     AL,'0'              ;   CHAR = DIGIT + ASCII(0)
44:            STOSB                       ;   ES:DI -> BYTE = CHAR
45:                                        ;   DI = DI + 1
46:            NEG     DX                  ;   REVERSE LR_FLAG
47:            POP     CX                  ;   RESTORE DIGIT_COUNT
48:            LOOP    LOOP_TOP            ;   DECREMENT DIGIT_COUNT
49:                                        ;UNTIL DIGIT_COUNT = 0
50: LOOP_END:
51:            POPF                        ;RESTORE FLAGS
52:            RET                         ;RESTORE REGISTERS SPECIFIED
53:                                        ;        IN USES CLAUSE AND
54:                                        ;        RETURN TO CALLER
55: BCDASCII   ENDP                     ;END BCDASCII
56:            END
```

array. On return to the caller, the array addressed by the ES:DI register pair will contain an ASCII number equivalent to the BCD number in the array addressed by the DS:SI register pair.

The subprocedure begins by saving the registers specified in the USES clause (line 20) and saving the flags register (line 25). Note that the DI and SI are among the registers that are saved. They are updated as the procedure works its way through the two arrays. The DS:SI register pair always specifies the address of the next pair of

FIGURE 8.12
BCD and ASCII arrays for 7-digit number 2147483

BCD array	Offset	ASCII array
21	0000	32
47	0001	31
48	0002	34
3?	0003	37
	0004	34
	0005	38
	0006	33

(? means value unknown)

BCD digits to be fetched from the BCD array. The ES:DI register pair always specifies the address of the ASCII array element where the next ASCII character is to be stored. On return to the caller, the DS:SI register pair and the ES:DI register pair must once again specify the base addresses of the respective arrays.

The CLD instruction in line 26 clears the DF bit in the flags register so that string instructions automatically increment the DI- and/or SI-register. The MOV instruction in line 27 initializes a LEFT/RIGHT flag to LEFT, and this flag is maintained in the DX-register. The LEFT/RIGHT flag indicates whether the BCD digit currently being processed is from the left or right nibble of a byte; that is, each byte extracted from the BCD array contains two BCD digits, one in the left nibble and one in the right nibble. The flag indicates which of the two is currently being converted to ASCII.

The body (lines 29–47) of the REPEAT_UNTIL loop (lines 28–49) executes once for each digit in the BCD array. The digit count, input to the subprocedure in the CX-register, controls execution of this loop. Each iteration of the loop translates one BCD digit to ASCII and stores the result in the ASCII array. A byte is extracted from the BCD array on every odd iteration of the loop (i.e., every time a left nibble is to be translated).

The PUSH instruction in line 29 saves the digit count so that the CL-register can be used as a shift count within the loop body. The double-alternative decision structure in lines 30–42 selects the next BCD digit to be translated. The selection is based on the LEFT/RIGHT flag. The CMP instruction in line 30 tests the flag. If the flag indicates LEFT, then the instructions in lines 32–37 are executed. The LODSB instruction in line 32 extracts the next two BCD digits from the BCD array (the byte pointed to by the DS:SI register pair) and increments the SI-register by 1 so that the DS:SI register pair addresses the next byte in the BCD array. The pseudocode reference DS:SI → BYTE means the byte addressed (or pointed to) by the DS:SI register pair. The DS:SI register pair behaves like a pointer variable in a high-level language. (Pascal is a language that provides pointer variables.) The byte just extracted is in the AL-register. The MOV instruction in line 34 saves a copy of this byte in the AH-register for use in the next iteration of the loop. This iteration of the loop translates the left nibble of the byte just extracted, and the next iteration, if needed, translates the right nibble of the byte just extracted. The instructions in lines 35 and 36 shift the byte in the AL-register right 4 bit positions, pushing out the right nibble and right-justifying the left nibble; that is, the leftmost BCD digit of the byte is now in the rightmost 4 bits of the AL-register. If the flag indicates RIGHT, then the instructions in lines 39 and 40 are executed. The MOV instruction in line 39 moves the copy (saved in line 34) of the byte extracted from the BCD array on the last iteration of the loop from the AH-register to the AL-register. The AND instruction in line 40 clears the left nibble of the byte, leaving the right nibble in the rightmost 4 bits of the AL-register. When the ENDIF is reached (line 42), the AL-register contains a single BCD digit.

The ADD instruction in line 43 converts the BCD digit in the AL-register to ASCII by adding the ASCII code for zero to the BCD code. The STOSB instruction in line 44 stores the ASCII code in the ASCII array at the address specified by the ES:DI register pair, and then it increments the DI-register by 1 so that the ES:DI register pair addresses the next byte in the ASCII array.

The NEG instruction in line 46 reverses the direction of the LEFT/RIGHT flag for the next iteration of the loop. The POP instruction in line 47 restores the digit count to the CX-register. The LOOP instruction in line 48 decrements the digit count in the CX-register by 1, and, if the resulting digit count is nonzero, it transfers control to the top of the loop (line 28). Otherwise, the loop is terminated. At loop exit, the flags register is restored for the caller (line 51), the registers specified in the USES clause are restored, and control is returned to the caller (line 52).

8.4 Addressing Modes

The one-dimensional array is a good vehicle for studying the various addressing modes available in the 8088/8086 assembly language. An instruction such as MOV or ADD specifies the addresses of operands to be used in execution of the instruction. Such an operand may be the contents of a general register, an immediate value (i.e., a value contained in the instruction itself), or the contents of a memory location. The example programs in previous chapters dealt exclusively with **scalar** (single-valued) data items. Three addressing modes were used in those example programs.

Register Addressing With register addressing, the operand is the contents of one of the 8-bit or 16-bit registers. A specific register is addressed by coding its two-character symbolic name into the operand field of the instruction, as in the following examples:

```
INC  AL
MOV  BX,DX
```

Register addressing can be used for either the source operand, the destination operand, or both.

Direct Addressing With direct addressing, the operand is the 8-bit contents of a memory location or the 16-bit contents of two consecutive memory locations. A specific memory location is addressed directly by coding its symbolic name into the operand field of the instruction, as in the following examples:

```
INC  COUNT
MOV  SUM,0
```

Direct addressing can be used for either the source operand or the destination operand, but not both.

With a direct address, the symbolic name identifies both a segment and an offset within the segment, thus identifying a unique memory location. In most cases, the symbolic name used in a direct address is completely defined in the same assembly module. The assembler knows the segment in which the symbolic name is defined and, through the ASSUME pseudo-operation, knows which segment register is to contain the base address of that segment during program execution. Recall that an ASSUME pseudo-operation is implicit in the .MODEL directive. That is, when simplified segment directives are being used, the assembler automatically assumes that the DS-register will contain the origin of DGROUP. The segment register is specified (implicitly or explicitly) in the machine language representation of the instruction. The offset associated with the symbolic name is dependent on the order in which items are defined in the segment that contains the symbolic name. Therefore, the assembler has the information to determine the offset within the segment. The offset is also part of the machine language representation of the instruction.

Immediate Addressing With immediate addressing, the operand is an 8- or a 16-bit constant that is contained in the machine language representation of the instruction. A specific immediate value is referenced by coding its literal in the operand field of the instruction, as in the following examples:

```
MOV  COUNT,16
CMP  CHAR,'*'
ADD  AX,-4
```

An immediate value can only be a source operand; it cannot be a destination operand.

Memory Addressing Modes

With register and immediate addressing modes, the operands are directly accessible by the execution unit of the Intel 8088/8086 microprocessor (see Figure 1.17). The general registers are part of the EU, and the immediate operands are contained in the instruction queue. Memory operands, on the other hand, are accessible only through the bus interface unit of the microprocessor. The EU directs the BIU to perform a data fetch or data store operation, and it provides the offset portion of the address. The offset portion is also called the **effective address**. The BIU adds the shifted contents of the appropriate segment register to the effective address, producing a 20-bit physical memory address. The BIU then performs the appropriate bus operations to fetch or replace the contents of the memory location identified by the physical address.

The effective address, a 16-bit unsigned integer, is computed by the EU according to information contained in the second byte of the machine language instruction. The second byte of a memory-referencing instruction has the form shown in Figure 8.13. The effective address is computed from one or more of the following components:

An 8-bit or a 16-bit displacement contained in the third or the third and fourth bytes of the machine language instruction

The 16-bit contents of an index register, either the DI-register or the SI-register

The 16-bit contents of a base register, either the BX-register or the BP-register

FIGURE 8.13
Second byte of memory-referencing instruction

7 6	5 3	2 0
MOD	REG	R/M

Table 8.4 shows the various ways that the effective address can be computed by the EU of the Intel 8088/8086 microprocessor. It also states the addressing mode and gives the MOD and R/M field encodings for each of the possible address computations.

TABLE 8.4
Effective address computations for memory addressing modes

MOD	R/M	Effective Address Computation	Addressing Mode
00	110	EA = DISP_16	Direct
00	100	EA = (SI)	Register indirect
00	101	EA = (DI)	Register indirect
00	111	EA = (BX)	Register indirect
01	100	EA = (SI) + DISP_8	Indexed
01	101	EA = (DI) + DISP_8	Indexed
10	100	EA = (SI) + DISP_16	Indexed
10	101	EA = (DI) + DISP_16	Indexed
01	110	EA = (BP) + DISP_8	Base
01	111	EA = (BX) + DISP_8	Base
10	110	EA = (BP) + DISP_16	Base
10	111	EA = (BX) + DISP_16	Base
00	000	EA = (BX) + (SI)	Base indexed
00	001	EA = (BX) + (DI)	Base indexed
00	010	EA = (BP) + (SI)	Base indexed
00	011	EA = (BP) + (DI)	Base indexed
01	000	EA = (BX) + (SI) + DISP_8	Base indexed
01	001	EA = (BX) + (DI) + DISP_8	Base indexed
01	010	EA = (BP) + (SI) + DISP_8	Base indexed
01	011	EA = (BP) + (DI) + DISP_8	Base indexed
10	000	EA = (BX) + (SI) + DISP_16	Base indexed
10	001	EA = (BX) + (DI) + DISP_16	Base indexed
10	010	EA = (BP) + (SI) + DISP_16	Base indexed
10	011	EA = (BP) + (DI) + DISP_16	Base indexed

Direct Addressing

Direct addressing is one of several memory addressing modes. With direct addressing, the effective address of the memory operand is the 16-bit displacement contained in the third and fourth bytes of the machine language representation of the instruction. In the assembly language representation of an instruction, a direct address is specified by encoding the symbolic name of memory location in the appropriate operand field of the instruction.

EXAMPLE

```
MOV  CX,COUNT
```

The offset portion of the address of the memory location associated with symbolic name COUNT is the displacement stored in the third and fourth bytes of the machine language representation of the instruction. ■

Register Indirect Addressing

With **register indirect addressing**, the effective address of the memory operand is the 16-bit contents of the BX-, DI-, or SI-register. In the assembly language representation of an instruction, a register indirect address is specified by enclosing the two-character symbolic name of the register (BX, DI, or SI) in square brackets in the appropriate operand field of the instruction.

When the BX-, DI-, or SI-register is used as an indirect address, the DS-register contents are assumed to specify the segment portion of the address unless a segment override prefix explicitly specifies the use of another segment register. A **segment override prefix** is a segment register designator followed by a colon (e.g., ES:), and it precedes the operand.

EXAMPLES

Suppose an array is defined in the data segment as follows:

```
TABLE  DW  100 DUP(?)
```

Also, suppose the DS-register contains the origin of the segment or group containing TABLE. The following sequence of instructions sets each element of TABLE to zero:

```
           LEA   DI,TABLE  ;PTR = ADDRESS OF TABLE
           MOV   CX,100    ;COUNT = 100
           MOV   AX,0
LOOP_TOP:                  ;REPEAT
           MOV   [DI],AX   ;    PTR->WORD = 0
           ADD   DI,2      ;    PTR = PTR + 2
           LOOP  LOOP_TOP  ;    COUNT = COUNT - 1
                           ;UNTIL COUNT = 0
```

The DS:DI register pair addresses an element of the array. The pseudocode pointer variable PTR represents the DS:DI register pair. This loop does the same thing as an STOSB instruction with the REP prefix, except the STOSB instruction uses the ES:DI register pair to address an array element.

Now, suppose the ES-register contains the origin of the segment or group containing TABLE. The following sequence of instructions also sets each element of TABLE to zero:

```
     CLD                 ;SET DF FOR INCREMENTING
     LEA    DI,TABLE     ;PTR = ADDRESS OF TABLE
     MOV    CX,100       ;COUNT = 100
     MOV    AX,0
REP  STOSW               ;REPEAT
                         ;    PTR->WORD = 0
                         ;    PTR = PTR + 2
                         ;    COUNT = COUNT - 1
                         ;UNTIL COUNT = 0
```

■

Programming Example

Program Listing 8.2 shows an implementation of the algorithm to convert a BCD number to an ASCII character string that differs from the one shown in Program Listing 8.1 in two major ways:

1. The implementation of Program Listing 8.1 uses string instructions and that of Program Listing 8.2 does not.
2. The implementation of Program Listing 8.1 accesses the BCD array once for each pair of BCD digits and then uses that pair on two successive iterations of the loop. The implementation of Program Listing 8.2 accesses the BCD array twice for each pair of BCD digits, updating the pointer only on the second access.

The CLD instruction in line 26 in Program Listing 8.1 has been eliminated in Program Listing 8.2. Because the string instructions are not being used in this implementation, there is no need for the direction flag.

```
 1:             PAGE    80,132
 2: ;==================================================================
 3: ;                   PROGRAM LISTING 8.2
 4: ;
 5: ; PROCEDURE TO CONVERT A BCD NUMBER TO ASCII
 6: ;
 7: ; INPUT:   DS:SI POINTS TO ARRAY CONTAINING BCD   NUMBER
 8: ;          ES:DI POINTS TO ARRAY TO CONTAIN ASCII NUMBER
 9: ;          CX    CONTAINS SIZE OF BCD NUMBER (DIGIT_COUNT)
10: ;
11: ; OUTPUT: UPON RETURN, THE ARRAY POINTED TO BY ES:DI WILL
12: ;          CONTAIN AN ASCII NUMBER EQUIVALENT  TO  THE BCD
13: ;          NUMBER IN THE ARRAY POINTED TO BY DS:SI.
14: ;==================================================================
15:             .MODEL  SMALL,BASIC
16: ;==================================================================
17: ; C O D E   S E G M E N T   D E F I N I T I O N
18:             .CODE   EX_8_2
19: ;
20: BCDASCII    PROC    FAR PUBLIC USES AX CX DX DI SI
21:                                     ;PROCEDURE BCDASCII(DIGIT_COUNT,
22:                                     ;                   SPTR, DPTR)
23:                                        ;SAVE REGISTERS SPECIFIED
24:                                        ;     IN USES CLAUSE
25:             PUSHF                      ;SAVE FLAGS
26:             MOV     DX,-1              ;LR_FLAG = LEFT
27:             .REPEAT                    ;REPEAT
28:             PUSH    CX                 ;  SAVE DIGIT_COUNT
29:             .IF     SWORD PTR DX < 0   ;  IF   LR_FLAG = LEFT
30:                                        ;  THEN
31:             MOV     AL,[SI]            ;       PAIR = SPTR -> BYTE
32:             MOV     CL,4               ;       DIGIT = LEFT NIBBLE
33:             SHR     AL,CL              ;               OF PAIR
34: ;
35:             .ELSE                      ;  ELSE
36:             MOV     AL,DS:[SI]         ;       PAIR = SPTR -> BYTE
37:             INC     SI                 ;       SPTR = SPTR + 1
38:             AND     AL,0FH             ;       DIGIT = RIGHT NIBBLE
39:                                        ;               OF PAIR
40:             .ENDIF                     ;  ENDIF
41:             ADD     AL,'0'             ;  CHAR = DIGIT + ASCII(0)
42:             MOV     ES:[DI],AL         ;  DPTR -> BYTE = CHAR
43:             INC     DI                 ;  DPTR = DPTR + 1
44:             NEG     DX                 ;  REVERSE LR_FLAG
45:             POP     CX                 ;  RESTORE DIGIT_COUNT
46:             .UNTILCXZ                  ;  DECREMENT DIGIT_COUNT
47:                                        ;UNTIL DIGIT_COUNT = 0
48:             POPF                       ;RESTORE FLAGS
49:                                        ;RESTORE REGISTERS SPECIFIED
50:                                        ;       IN USES CLAUSE AND
51:             RET                        ;       RETURN TO CALLER
52: BCDASCII    ENDP                    ;END BCDASCII
53:             END
```

The STOSB instruction in line 44 in Program Listing 8.1 has been replaced by the two instructions in lines 42 and 43 in Program Listing 8.2. The MOV instruction (line 42) moves a copy of the byte in the AL-register to the byte in the ASCII array addressed by the ES:DI register pair (an example of register indirect addressing with a segment override prefix). The prefix, ES:, is required because the default segment register for the DI-register is the DS-register. The INC instruction (line 43) increments the DI-register by 1 so that the ES:DI register pair addresses the next byte in the ASCII array. These two instructions perform the same function as does the STOSB instruction, except INC affects the flags and STOSB does not.

The double-alternative decision structure in lines 29–40 of Program Listing 8.2 differs from the corresponding structure in lines 30–42 of Program Listing 8.1. The decision structure of Program Listing 8.2 is implemented using the decision-generating macro directives of MASM 6.0. The decision is based on the LEFT/RIGHT flag in the DX-register. If the flag indicates LEFT, then the instructions in lines 31–33 are executed. The MOV instruction in line 31 extracts the next two BCD digits from the BCD array (the byte pointed to by the DS:SI register pair). The operand [SI] is an example of register indirect addressing. The SI-register contains the effective address of the operand rather than the operand itself. This MOV instruction moves to the AL-register a copy of the byte in the BCD array addressed by the DS:SI register pair. The DS-register is the default segment register when the SI-register is used as an indirect address. The SI-register is not updated here. Therefore, the DS:SI register pair continues to address the same byte in the BCD array, which allows this byte to be extracted on the next iteration of the REPEAT_UNTIL loop (i.e., the iteration that will process the right nibble of the byte). The instructions in lines 32 and 33 shift the byte in the AL-register right 4 bit positions, pushing out the right nibble and right-justifying the left nibble; that is, the leftmost BCD digit of the byte is now in the rightmost 4 bits of the AL-register. If the flag indicates RIGHT, then the instructions in lines 36–38 are executed. The MOV instruction in line 36 moves to the AL-register a copy of the byte in the BCD array addressed by the DS:SI register pair (an example of register indirect addressing). The prefix, DS:, is not required because the default segment register for the SI-register is the DS-register. The two MOV instructions in lines 31 and 36 are equivalent. The INC instruction in line 37 increments the SI-register by 1 so that the DS:SI register pair addresses the next byte in the BCD array. The instructions in lines 36 and 37 perform the same function as does the LODSB instruction, except INC affects the flags and LODSB does not. The AND instruction in line 38 clears the left nibble of the byte, leaving the right nibble in the rightmost 4 bits of the AL-register. As is the case with the corresponding decision structure in Program Listing 8.1, when the ENDIF is reached (line 40), the AL-register contains a single BCD digit.

There is one other difference between Program Listing 8.1 and Program Listing 8.2. The pseudocode of Program Listing 8.2 uses symbolic pointers, while the pseudocode of Program Listing 8.1 shows the actual registers used for the pointers. The explicit pointers ES:DI and DS:SI have been replaced by the symbolic pointers DPTR and SPTR, respectively. The register form is used in Program Listing 8.1 to more explicitly show how pointers are handled in the 8088/8086 family of microprocessors. The symbolic form for pointers used in Program Listing 8.2 is more in keeping with the high-level nature of the pseudocode and will be used in all subsequent example programs.

Indexed Addressing

With **indexed addressing**, the effective address of the memory operand is the sum of the displacement contained in the machine language representation of the instruction and the 16-bit contents of an index register (DI or SI). In the assembly language representation of an instruction, an indexed address can be specified by encoding the symbolic name of a memory location followed by the two-character designator for an index register enclosed in square brackets.

EXAMPLE

Suppose an array is defined in the data segment as follows:

```
TABLE DW 100 DUP(?)
```

The following sequence of instructions sets each element of TABLE to zero:

```
            MOV   CX,100          ;COUNT = 100
            MOV   DI,0            ;I = 0
            MOV   AX,0
LOOP_TOP:                         ;REPEAT
            MOV   TABLE[DI],AX    ;    TABLE[I] = 0
            ADD   DI,2            ;    I = I + 2
            LOOP  LOOP_TOP        ;    COUNT = COUNT - 1
                                  ;UNTIL COUNT = 0
```

The index, DI, selects an element of the array. The offset of TABLE within the data segment (i.e., the offset of the base address of array TABLE) is the displacement in the machine language representation of the instruction. The effective address is the sum of the displacement and the contents of the DI-register, an offset relative to the base address of array TABLE. ■

Base Addressing

With **base addressing**, the effective address of the memory operand is the sum of the displacement contained in the machine language representation of the instruction and the 16-bit contents of a base register (BX or BP). In the assembly language representation of an instruction, a base address can be specified by encoding a constant followed by the two-character designator for a base register enclosed in square brackets.

When the BP-register is used as a base address, the SS-register is assumed to be the segment register unless a segment override prefix is used. Base addressing with the BP-register facilitates the accessing of data embedded in the stack.

Programming Example

Arguments to a subprocedure can be passed via the stack, as was demonstrated earlier by the random number generator of Program Listing 5.4. In Chapter 5, stack arguments were considered from a user perspective. In this chapter, the use of base addressing to access stack arguments is considered in detail.

Recall that subprocedure RANDOM of Program Listing 5.4 uses a feature of the assembler (introduced in MASM 5.1) that allows the programmer to assign symbolic names to arguments received via the stack. The programmer can then use those symbolic names in instructions that access the arguments. The assembler converts these symbolic references to base address references that use the BP-register. The PROC pseudo-operation of Program Listing 5.4 (lines 31 and 32) defines LOWER as the symbolic name for the first argument pushed onto the stack and UPPER as the symbolic name for the second argument pushed onto the stack. The arguments are then referenced by name in the subprocedure body (see lines 50, 51, and 54).

Program Listing 8.3 shows an implementation of the same random number generator. This implementation does not assign symbolic names to the arguments. Assembly of the two versions produces exactly the same object code. (The reader is encouraged to assemble the two versions producing the assembler-generated listing in each case, and to compare the machine code in the two listings.)

The calling sequence for subprocedure RANDOM is

```
PUSH  〈lower end of range〉
PUSH  〈upper end of range〉
CALL  RANDOM
```

```
             PAGE     80,132
;======================================================================
;                     PROGRAM LISTING 8.3
;      r a n d o m   n u m b e r   g e n e r a t o r
;
; GENERATES PSEUDO-RANDOM INTEGERS IN THE RANGE LOWER TO UPPER
; INPUT:  TWO STACK PARAMETERS - LOWER AND UPPER ENDS OF RANGE
; OUTPUT: AX-REG CONTAINS RANDOM INTEGER
; CALLING SEQUENCE:     PUSH    <LOWER END OF RANGE>
;                       PUSH    <UPPER END OF RANGE>
;                       CALL    RANDOM
;======================================================================
             .MODEL  SMALL,BASIC
;======================================================================
FALSE        EQU     0                        ;CONSTANT FALSE
TRUE         EQU     1                        ;CONSTANT TRUE
;======================================================================
; D A T A   S E G M E N T   D E F I N I T I O N
             .FARDATA RAND_DATA
SEED         DW      ?                        ;SEED FOR RANDOM NUMBER GEN.
MULTIPLIER   DW      25173                    ;MULTIPLIER AND
ADDEND       DW      13849                    ;ADDEND FOR MIXED
                                              ;LINEAR CONGRUENTIAL METHOD
FIRST_CALL   DB      TRUE                     ;FIRST CALL FLAG
;======================================================================
; C O D E   S E G M E N T   D E F I N I T I O N
             .CODE   EX_8_3
             ASSUME  DS:RAND_DATA
;
RANDOM       PROC    FAR PUBLIC           ;FUNCTION RANDOM(LOWER.UPPER)
             PUSH    BP                       ;SAVE BP-REGISTER
             MOV     BP,SP
             PUSH    CX                       ;SAVE REGISTERS
             PUSH    DX
             PUSH    DS
             PUSHF                            ;SAVE FLAGS
             MOV     AX,SEG RAND_DATA         ;SET DS-REGISTER TO POINT
             MOV     DS,AX                    ;TO LOCAL DATA SEGMENT
             .IF     FIRST_CALL == TRUE       ;IF   FIRST_CALL
                                              ;THEN
             MOV     FIRST_CALL,FALSE         ;     FIRST_CALL = FALSE
             MOV     AH,0                     ;     SEED = LOWER HALF OF
             INT     1AH                      ;            TIME OF DAY CLOCK
             MOV     SEED,DX
             .ENDIF                           ;ENDIF
             MOV     AX,SEED                  ;X = SEED * MULTIPLIER mod
             MUL     MULTIPLIER               ;                      65536
             ADD     AX,ADDEND                ;SEED = (X + ADDEND) mod 65536
             MOV     SEED,AX
             MOV     CX,6[BP]                 ;RANGE = UPPER - LOWER + 1
             SUB     CX,8[BP]
             INC     CX
             MUL     CX                       ;RANDOM = SEED/65536 * RANGE
             ADD     DX,8[BP]                 ;                    + LOWER
             MOV     AX,DX
             POPF                             ;RESTORE FLAGS
             POP     DS                       ;RESTORE REGISTERS
             POP     DX
             POP     CX
             POP     BP
             RET     4                        ;RETURN (RANDOM)
RANDOM       ENDP                         ;END RANDOM
             END
```

Figure 8.14 shows the state of the stack at time of entry to the RANDOM sub-procedure. The instructions (lines 31 and 32)

```
PUSH  BP
MOV   BP,SP
```

save the BP-register for the caller and set the BP-register so that the SS:BP register

FIGURE 8.14 Stack at entry to RANDOM

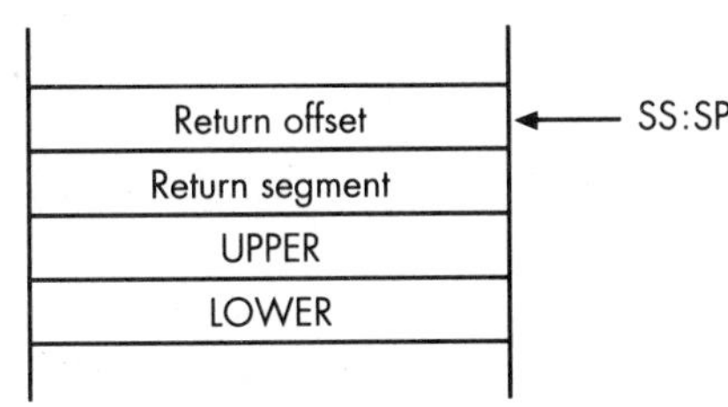

pair addresses the current top-of-stack element. Figure 8.15 shows the state of the stack just after execution of these two instructions. The SS:BP register pair is not modified by further PUSH and POP operations (see Figure 8.16); it provides a reference point in the stack. An offset relative to this reference point is the technique for referencing the two arguments.

FIGURE 8.15 Stack just after initialization of BP-register

FIGURE 8.16 Stack after saving of registers and flags

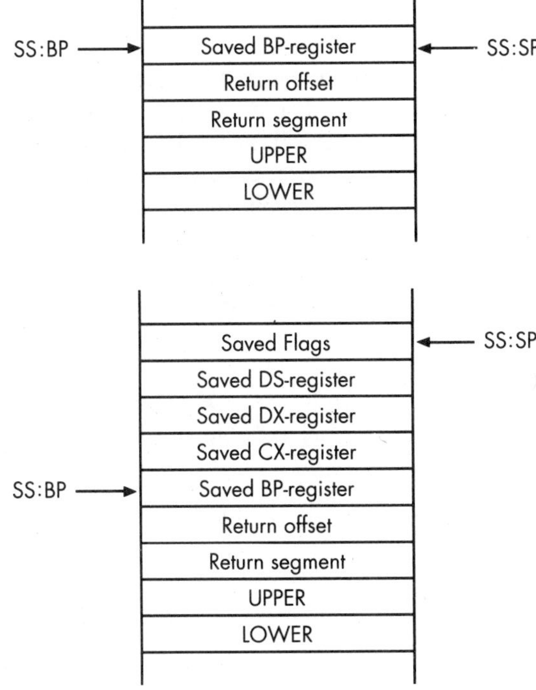

The instruction (line 50)

```
MOV  CX,6[BP]
```

moves to the CX-register a copy of the stack segment value located 6 bytes (3 words) from the stack segment location addressed by the SS:BP register pair. The value at stack location SS:(BP + 6) is the value of argument UPPER. The instruction (line 51)

```
SUB  CX,8[BP]
```

subtracts from the CX-register the stack segment value located 8 bytes (4 words) from the stack segment location addressed by the SS:BP register pair. The value at stack location SS:(BP+8) is the value of argument LOWER. The operands 6[BP] and 8[BP] are examples of base addressing.

Base Indexed Addressing

With **base indexed addressing**, the effective address of the memory operand is one of the following sums:

> Sum of the 16-bit contents of a base register (BX or BP) and the 16-bit contents of an index register (DI or SI)
>
> Sum of the displacement contained in the machine language representation of the instruction, the 16-bit contents of a base register (BX or BP), and the 16-bit contents of an index register (DI or SI)

In the assembly language representation of an instruction, a base indexed address can be specified in any of the following five forms:

⟨*name*⟩[⟨*base*⟩][⟨*index*⟩]
[⟨*base*⟩ + ⟨*constant*⟩][⟨*index*⟩]
[⟨*base*⟩][⟨*index*⟩ + ⟨*constant*⟩]
[⟨*base*⟩ + ⟨*index*⟩ + ⟨*constant*⟩]
[⟨*base*⟩ + ⟨*constant*⟩ + ⟨*index*⟩]

in which ⟨*name*⟩ is the symbolic name associated with a memory location, ⟨*base*⟩ is the two-character designator of a base register (BX or BP), ⟨*index*⟩ is the two-character designator of an index register (DI or SI), and ⟨*constant*⟩ is any legal 8-bit or 16-bit constant. Base indexed addressing can be used to access the elements of two-dimensional arrays, and this application is discussed further in Chapter 13.

Base indexed addressing can also be used to access the elements of an array that is defined as a local stack-based variable in a subprocedure definition. The concept of local stack-based variables was introduced in Section 5.7.

EXAMPLE

The following code fragment is the beginning of a subprocedure definition that includes a local stack-based array variable and a loop to initialize each element of the array to zero:

```
BASEINDEX PROC   NEAR USES AX CX SI
                                    ;PROCEDURE BASEINDEX
          LOCAL  TABLE[100]:WORD
          MOV    CX,100                ;COUNT = 100
          MOV    SI,0                  ;I = 0
          MOV    AX,0
LOOP_TOP:                              ;REPEAT
          MOV    TABLE[SI],AX          ;    TABLE[I] = 0
          ADD    SI,2                  ;    I = I + 2
          LOOP   LOOP_TOP              ;    COUNT = COUNT = 1
                                       ;UNTIL COUNT = 0
          .
          .
          .
BASEINDEX ENDP                      ;END BASEINDEX
```

The assembler generates the following instructions and places them at the very beginning of the subprocedure (just prior to the MOV CX,100 instruction):

```
push  bp
mov   bp, sp
add   sp, 0FF38h
push  ax
push  cx
push  si
```

The instructions

```
push  bp
mov   bp, sp
```

save the BP-register for the caller and set the BP-register so that the SS:BP register pair addresses the current top-of-stack element. The SS:BP register pair is not modified by further PUSH and POP operations; it provides a reference point in the stack. The instruction

```
add  sp, 0FF38h
```

allocates space in the stack for the local array TABLE. The hexadecimal value FF38 is equivalent to the signed decimal value −200. Therefore, this instruction is equivalent to the instruction

```
SUB  SP,200
```

which allocates 200 bytes (100 words) on the stack. The instructions

```
push  ax
push  cx
push  si
```

save the registers specified in the USES clause of the PROC pseudo-operation.

Figure 8.17 shows the state of the stack following execution of these assembler-

FIGURE 8.17
Stack after execution of assembler-generated instructions

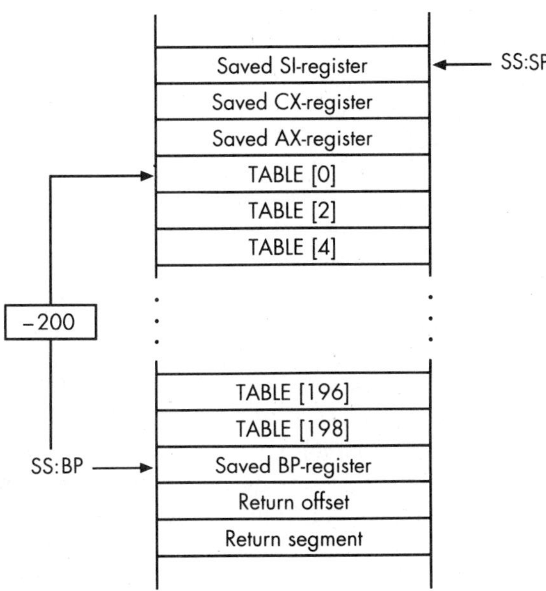

generated instructions. The instruction

```
MOV  TABLE[SI],AX
```

is equivalent to the instruction

```
MOV  OFF38H[BP][SI],AX
```

and is an example of base indexed addressing. The assembler translates the symbolic name TABLE to the base address 0FF38H[BP], which is equivalent to the base address −200[BP]. This base address is the address, within the stack segment, of the first element of the array TABLE. This base address is then indexed by the SI-register to select the desired element of array TABLE. The complete address is the base indexed address 0FF38H[BP][SI].

The RET instruction at the end of this subprocedure causes the assembler to generate the following instructions:

```
pop  si
pop  cx
pop  ax
mov  sp, bp
pop  bp
ret
```

The first three POP instructions restore the registers specified in the USES clause of the PROC pseudo-operation. The MOV instruction, in effect, pops the 100 words of array TABLE from the stack. The next POP instruction restores the BP-register for the caller, and the RET instruction returns control to the caller. ■

8.5 Programming Examples

This section contains three example programs that demonstrate most of the topics discussed in this chapter: character strings, integer word arrays, and integer byte arrays. As well, many of the addressing modes described are illustrated in these examples.

Secret Message Translation

Program Listing 8.4 shows an implementation of an algorithm to translate a secret message. The input is an encoded message, and the output is the decoded message. The translation scheme is as follows:

Encoded alphabet: `JEKPQBWALR.MSCUTDVNFZGYHIOX$`

Decoded alphabet: `ABCDEFG.HIJKLMNO PQRSTUVWXYZ`

The algorithm accepts an encoded message such as KTCVYGQFDZKRQUKQ and decodes and displays the decoded message: COMPUTER SCIENCE. The decoding is accomplished by translating the K to a C, the T to an O, the C to an M, and so on. The translation algorithm places an asterisk (*) in the decoded message for any character in the encoded message that is not in the encoded alphabet.

The program that performs this translation includes both constant data definitions (lines 21–27) and variable data definitions (lines 33–36). The array SECRTMSG

```
            PAGE    80,132
;===================================================================
;                   PROGRAM LISTING 8.4
;
;PROGRAM TO TRANSLATE A SECRET MESSAGE
;===================================================================
            .MODEL  SMALL,BASIC
;===================================================================
                                        ;PROCEDURES TO
            EXTRN   GETSTRNG:FAR        ;INPUT A CHARACTER STRING
            EXTRN   PUTSTRNG:FAR        ;DISPLAY CHARACTER STRING
            EXTRN   NEWLINE:FAR         ;DISPLAY NEWLINE CHARACTER
;===================================================================
; S T A C K   S E G M E N T   D E F I N I T I O N
;
            .STACK  256
;===================================================================
; C O N S T A N T   D E F I N I T I O N S
;
            .CONST
DECODED     DB      'ABCDEFG.HIJKLMNO PQRSTUVWXYZ'
ENCODED     DB      'JEKPQBWALR.MSCUTDVNFZGYHIOX$'
PROMPT      DB      'ENTER SECRET MESSAGE',0DH,0AH
TMSG        DB      'TRANSLATED MESSAGE',0DH,0AH
CODE_LNGTH EQU      ENCODED-DECODED     ;LENGTH OF CODE STRINGS
PROMPT_LNG EQU      TMSG - PROMPT       ;LENGTH OF PROMPT MESSAGE
TMSG_LNG    EQU     $ - TMSG            ;LENGTH OF TMSG
;
;===================================================================
; V A R I A B L E   D E F I N I T I O N S
;
            .DATA
SECRTMSG    DB      40 DUP(?)           ;SECRET MESSAGE
TRANSMSG    DB      40 DUP(?)           ;TRANSLATED MESSAGE
COUNT       DW      ?                   ;CHARACTER COUNT OF MESSAGE
MSG_LNG     EQU     TRANSMSG - SECRTMSG ;LENGTH OF SECRET MESSAGE
;
;===================================================================
; C O D E   S E G M E N T   D E F I N I T I O N
;
            .CODE   EX_8_4
            .STARTUP                    ;GENERATE STARTUP CODE
            PUSH    DS                  ;SET ES-REGISTER TO ADDRESS
            POP     ES                  ;DGROUP
            CALL    NEWLINE
;
            LEA     DI,PROMPT           ;PROMPT FOR SECRET_MSG
            MOV     CX,PROMPT_LNG
            CALL    PUTSTRNG
            LEA     DI,SECRTMSG         ;GET SECRET_MSG AND MSG_LENGTH
            MOV     CX,MSG_LNG
            CALL    GETSTRNG
            CALL    NEWLINE
            CLD                         ;SET DF FOR INCREMENTING
            MOV     COUNT,CX            ;COUNT = MSG_LENGTH
            MOV     BX,0                ;INDEX = 0
NEXT_CHAR:                              ;REPEAT
            MOV     AL,SECRTMSG[BX]     ;   CHAR = SECRET_MSG (INDEX)
            PUSH    CX
            MOV     CX,CODE_LNGTH       ;   SRCH_CNT = CODE_LNGTH
            LEA     DI,ENCODED          ;   SET EPTR TO BASE ADDRESS
                                        ;       OF ENCODED STRING
      REPNE SCASB                       ;   FOUND = FALSE
                                        ;   REPEAT
                                        ;      IF   EPTR->BYTE = CHAR
                                        ;      THEN FOUND = TRUE
                                        ;      ENDIF
```

```
68:                                               ;       EPTR = EPTR + 1
69:                                               ;       DECREMENT SRCH_CNT
70:                                               ;    UNTIL FOUND OR SRCH_CNT=0
71:             JE      FOUND                     ;    IF   NOT FOUND
72:             MOV     TRANSMSG[BX],'*'          ;    THEN TRANS_MSG(INDEX) = *
73:             JMP     LOOPEND
74: FOUND:                                        ;    ELSE
75:             DEC     DI                        ;       EPTR = EPTR - 1
76:             MOV     SI,DI                     ;       DPTR = EPTR
77:             SUB     SI,OFFSET ENCODED         ;         - BASE ADDR OF ENCODED
78:             ADD     SI,OFFSET DECODED         ;         + BASE ADDR OF DECODED
79:             LODSB                             ;       TRANS_MSG(INDEX) =
80:             MOV     TRANSMSG[BX],AL           ;         DPTR->BYTE
81: LOOPEND:                                      ;    ENDIF
82:             INC     BX                        ;    INDEX = INDEX + 1
83:             POP     CX
84:             LOOP    NEXT_CHAR                 ;    DECREMENT MSG_LENGTH
85:                                               ;UNTIL MSG_LENGTH = 0
86:             LEA     DI,TMSG                   ;DISPLAY TRANS_MSG
87:             MOV     CX,TMSG_LNG
88:             CALL    PUTSTRNG
89:             LEA     DI,TRANSMSG
90:             MOV     CX,COUNT
91:             CALL    PUTSTRNG
92:             CALL    NEWLINE
93:             .EXIT                             ;RETURN TO DOS
94: ;
95:             END
```

(defined in line 33) is a 40-character string whose characters are uninitialized, and it is used to hold the input encoded string. The array TRANSMSG (defined in line 34) is also a 40-character string whose characters are uninitialized, and it is used to build the decoded string. The scalar variable COUNT (defined in line 35) holds the actual length of the secret message. The symbolic name MSG_LNG is equated to the constant that represents the maximum length of the secret message (line 36), the size of the arrays SECRTMSG and TRANSMSG.

The array DECODED (defined in line 21) is a 28-character string that is initialized to contain the characters of the decoded alphabet. The array ENCODED (defined in line 22) is also a 28-character string that is initialized to contain the characters of the encoded alphabet. The two strings ENCODED and DECODED have been initialized in such a way that the *i*th character of the ENCODED string translates to the *i*th character of the DECODED string. For each character of SCRTMSG, the algorithm searches the ENCODED string for the same character. If the character is found in the ENCODED string, then the corresponding character in the DECODED string is copied into the next position of TRANSMSG. If the character is not found in the ENCODED string, then an asterisk is copied into the next position of TRANSMSG. The symbolic name CODE_LNGTH is equated to the fixed length of the encoded and decoded alphabets (line 25).

The array PROMPT and the array TMSG (defined in lines 23 and 24) are prompt and annotation messages, respectively. Character strings have been used for these purposes in example programs throughout this book. The ASCII characters 0D hex and 0A hex are RETURN and LINE FEED, respectively. These two characters are displayed by the NEWLINE subprocedure. The symbolic name PROMPT_LNG is equated to the length of the array PROMPT (line 26), and the symbolic name TMSG_LNG is equated to the length of the array TMSG (line 27).

The program begins in the standard manner by setting the DS- and ES-registers to address DGROUP (lines 42–44). The instructions in lines 47–49 display the prompt message that asks the user to enter a secret message. The instructions in lines 50–52 are the calling sequence for the GETSTRNG procedure, the procedure that accepts a character string from the keyboard and then returns it to the caller. GETSTRNG expects two inputs: the ES:DI register pair that points to the array that is to receive the input string and the CX-register that contains the size of that array. The LEA instruction in line 50 sets up the first of these two inputs, and the MOV instruction in line 51 sets up the second. The GETSTRNG procedure returns the input character string to the caller in the caller's array, with the actual length of the string in the CX-register.

The instructions in lines 54–56 perform initialization for the loop that translates the characters of the secret message, one character per loop iteration. The CLD instruction in line 54 clears the DF bit in the flags register so that string instructions automatically increment the index registers. The MOV instruction in line 55 saves the input string length as the value of variable COUNT. The string length in the CX-register controls the loop that translates the secret message. The value of variable COUNT restores the string length when the translated message is displayed. The MOV instruction in line 56 initializes to zero the index for arrays SECRTMSG and TRANSMSG.

The REPEAT-UNTIL loop in lines 57–85 translates the secret message. Each iteration of the loop translates one character of the message. The MOV instruction in line 58 copies the next character of the secret message into the AL-register (an example of base addressing). The effective address is the sum of the offset of symbolic name SECRTMSG and the contents of the BX-register, which is an index from the base address of array SECRTMSG.

The instructions in lines 59–61 perform initialization for the loop that searches the encoded alphabet for the character just extracted from the secret message. The PUSH instruction in line 59 saves the outer loop counter, the remaining message length, so that the CX-register can be used to control the inner loop. The MOV instruction in line 60 initializes the CX-register to the length of the encoded alphabet. This CX-register value defines the maximum number of times that the inner loop body is to be executed. The LEA instruction in line 61 sets the ES:DI register pair to address the first character of the string ENCODED.

The entire inner loop is implemented by the SCASB instruction that contains the REPNE prefix (line 63). The comments in lines 63–70 describe the loop that is implemented by this repeated instruction. The SCASB instruction repeatedly executes until a character is found in the encoded string that matches the character in the AL-register or until all characters of the encoded string have been scanned. That is, the SCASB instruction terminates for either one of the following two reasons:

1. A match is found between the character just scanned in ENCODED and the character in the AL-register. In this case, the ZF bit in the flags register is set.
2. The CX-register reaches zero, meaning that the entire ENCODED string has been scanned. In this case, the ZF bit in the flags register is cleared unless the character is found to match the last character of ENCODED.

On termination of the inner loop, the program must determine which of the two reasons caused the loop exit.

The double-alternative decision structure in lines 71–81 determines the condition that caused the loop exit and performs the appropriate translation based on this condition. The JE instruction in line 71 makes the decision based on this condition. If the character from SECRTMSG was not found in the ENCODED string, then the jump is not taken and the instructions in lines 72 and 73 are executed. The MOV instruction in line 72 stores an asterisk in the string TRANSMSG. The BX-register is used as an index into the string TRANSMSG. This index is the same as that for the string SECRTMSG (line 58), which means that the translated character is inserted at the same position in TRANSMSG as the character being translated appeared in SECRTMSG. The JMP instruction in line 73 causes the second alternative of the double-alternative decision structure to be skipped.

If the character from SECRTMSG is found in the ENCODED string, then the jump in line 71 is taken and the instructions in lines 75–80 are executed. Since the SCASB instruction updates the DI-register after the comparison is made, the ES:DI register pair addresses the character in ENCODED that immediately follows the one that matches the character from SECRTMSG. The DEC instruction in line 75 sets the ES:DI register pair to address the character in ENCODED that matches the character from SECRTMSG. The instructions in lines 76–78 set the DS:SI register pair to address the character in DECODED that corresponds to the character in ENCODED that is addressed by the ES:DI register pair. Figure 8.18 shows an example of this address conversion. The MOV instruction in line 76 copies the offset from the DI-register to the SI-register. At this point in the program, the ES:DI register pair and the DS:SI register pair address the same character in ENCODED. The SI-register contains the offset of this character relative to the origin of the data segment; see Figure 8.18(a). The SUB instruction in line 77 subtracts the offset of the origin of the string ENCODED from the offset in the SI-register. The SI-register now contains the offset of the matching character in ENCODED relative to its origin, which is also the offset of the corresponding character in DECODED relative to its origin; see Figure 8.18(b). The ADD instruction in line 78 adds the offset of the origin of the string DECODED to the offset in the SI-register. The SI-register now contains

FIGURE 8.18 Computation to convert address of character in the ENCODED string to address of corresponding character in the DECODED string

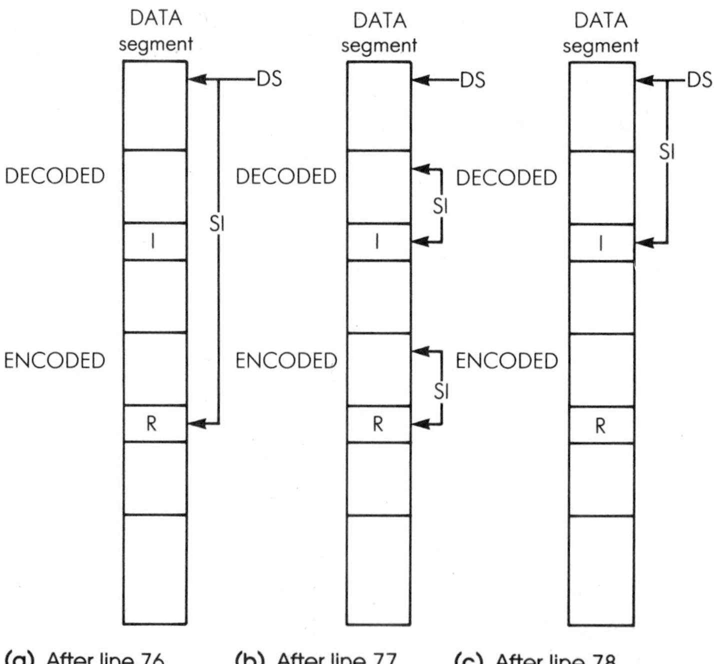

the offset of the corresponding character in DECODED relative to the origin of the data segment; see Figure 8.18(c). That is, the DS:SI register pair now addresses the character in DECODED that is the translation of the character from SECRTMSG. The LODSB instruction in line 79 loads the character addressed by the DS:SI register pair into the AL-register, and the MOV instruction in line 80 stores this character in the string TRANSMSG. Again, the BX-register is used as the index into the string TRANSMSG.

When line 81 (the end of the double-alternative decision structure) is reached, a new character has been inserted into the string TRANSMSG in the same position as that of the character extracted from SECRTMSG in line 58. Following the double-alternative decision structure, some loop maintenance operations are performed. The INC instruction in line 82 increments the index into SECRTMSG and TRANSMSG for the next iteration of the outer loop. The POP instruction in line 83 restores the value of the outer loop counter, the remaining message length, to the CX-register. The LOOP instruction in line 84 decrements the loop counter in the CX-register and transfers control to the top of the loop (line 57) if the resulting value is nonzero.

On termination of the outer loop, the translated message is displayed on the video screen. The instructions in lines 86–88 display the annotation message, and the instructions in lines 89–91 display the translated message itself. The LEA instruction in line 89 sets the ES:DI register pair to address the origin of TRANSMSG. The MOV instruction in line 90 loads the saved length of the secret message (i.e., the length of the translated message) into the CX-register. The call to the PUTSTRNG procedure in line 91 then causes the translated message to be displayed on the screen.

The following are the results from some sample executions of this program:

```
C>ex_8_4

ENTER SECRET MESSAGE
MKDJFFRHQPDRUDPQKQCEQFDJZDVSJUUQP

TRANSLATED MESSAGE
KC ARRIVED IN DECEMBER AS PLANNED

C>ex_8_4

ENTER SECRET MESSAGE
VJYSDIJZDJSFQJPXDLQFQ

TRANSLATED MESSAGE
PAUL WAS ALREADY HERE
```

Sieve of Eratosthenes

Program Listing 8.5 shows an implementation of an algorithm to compute prime numbers. The algorithm is called the *Sieve of Eratosthenes.* The algorithm can be stated as follows:

> Fill the sieve with the consecutive integers from 2 through *n*.
> Repeat
>   Find the smallest integer in the sieve. It is a prime number, so display it.
>   Remove this prime number and remove all multiples of this prime number from the sieve.
> Until sieve is empty.

The implementation of this algorithm uses two internal subprocedures for the purpose of modularity. One of the subprocedures finds the next prime number (the

```
            PAGE    80,132
;====================================================================
;                   PROGRAM LISTING 8.5
;
; PROGRAM TO DISPLAY THE PRIME NUMBERS THAT ARE LESS THAN 16000.
; THE PROGRAM USES THE SIEVE OF ERATOSTHENES.
;====================================================================
            .MODEL  SMALL,BASIC
            .DOSSEG
;====================================================================
                                        ;PROCEDURES TO
            EXTRN   NEWLINE:FAR         ;DISPLAY NEWLINE CHARACTER
            EXTRN   PAUSE:FAR           ;PAUSE UNTIL KEYSTROKE
            EXTRN   PUTDEC$:FAR         ;DISPLAY UNSIGNED DECIMAL INT.
;====================================================================
; S T A C K   S E G M E N T   D E F I N I T I O N
            .STACK  256
;====================================================================
; C O N S T A N T   D E F I N I T I O N S
;
            .CONST
PAUSE_MSG   DB      'PRESS ANY KEY TO CONTINUE'
;-------------------------------------------------
PAUSE_LNG   EQU     $ - PAUSE_MSG
SIZE$       EQU     15999
MAX_INDEX   EQU     2*SIZE$
;-------------------------------------------------
;====================================================================
; V A R I A B L E   D E F I N I T I O N S
;
            .DATA?
SIEVE       DW      SIZE$ DUP(?)
;====================================================================
; C O D E   S E G M E N T   D E F I N I T I O N
;
            .CODE   EX_8_5
;
            .STARTUP                    ;GENERATE STARTUP CODE
            PUSH    DS                  ;SET ES-REGISTER TO ADDRESS
            POP     ES                  ;DGROUP
;
                                        ;<INITIALIZE SIEVE>
            CLD                         ;SET DF FOR INCREMENTING
            MOV     CX,SIZE$            ;LOOP_COUNT = SIZE OF SIEVE
            LEA     DI,SIEVE            ;SET DPTR TO BASE ADDRESS
                                        ;          OF SIEVE
            MOV     AX,2                ;VALUE = 2
LOADLOOP:                               ;REPEAT
            STOSW                       ;   DPTR -> WORD = VALUE
                                        ;   DPTR = DPTR + 2
            INC     AX                  ;   VALUE = VALUE + 1
            LOOP    LOADLOOP            ;   LOOP_COUNT = LOOP_COUNT - 1
                                        ;UNTIL LOOP_COUNT = 0
            MOV     BX,0                ;INDEX = 0
            MOV     CX,0                ;PRIME_COUNT = 0
            CALL    FINDPRIM            ;CALL FINDPRIME(INDEX,PRIME)
;
PRIMELOOP:                              ;REPEAT
            CALL    SIFTSIEVE           ;   CALL SIFTSIEVE(PRIME,INDEX)
                                        ;   <SIFT OUT MULTIPLES OF PRIME>
            PUSH    BX
            MOV     BH,1                ;   DISPLAY PRIME
            CALL    PUTDEC$
            INC     CX                  ;   PRIME_COUNT = PRIME_COUNT + 1
            MOV     AX,CX               ;   IF   PRIME_COUNT mod 10 = 0
            MOV     DX,0
            MOV     BX,10
```

```
 68:             DIV     BX
 69:             CMP     DX,0
 70:             JNE     NEXTPRIME
 71:             CALL    NEWLINE           ;   THEN DISPLAY NEWLINE CHAR
 72:             MOV     DX,0              ;        IF   PRIME_COUNT mod 240
 73:             MOV     BX,24             ;             = 0
 74:             DIV     BX
 75:             CMP     DX,0
 76:             JNE     NEXTPRIME
 77:             PUSH    CX                ;        THEN
 78:             LEA     DI,PAUSE_MSG      ;             PAUSE FOR PRINT
 79:             MOV     CX,PAUSE_LNG      ;             OF DISPL SCREEN
 80:             CALL    PAUSE
 81:             POP     CX
 82:                                       ;        ENDIF
 83: NEXTPRIME:                            ;   ENDIF
 84:             POP     BX
 85:             CALL    FINDPRIM          ;   CALL FINDPRIME(INDEX,PRIME)
 86:             CMP     AX,0
 87:             JNE     PRIMELOOP         ;UNTIL SIEVE IS EMPTY
 88:             CALL    NEWLINE
 89:             .EXIT                     ;RETURN TO DOS
 90: ;
 91: ;=================================================================
 92: ; SIFT MULTIPLES OF PRIME OUT OF SIEVE
 93: ;
 94: ; INPUT:  AX-REG CONTAINS PRIME NUMBER
 95: ;         BX-REG CONTAINS SIEVE INDEX OF PRIME NUMBER
 96: ;
 97: ; OUTPUT: SIEVE WITH MULTIPLES OF PRIME REMOVED
 98: ;=================================================================
 99: SIFTSIEVE   PROC    NEAR           ;PROCEDURE SIFTSIEVE(PRIME,INDEX)
100:             PUSH    AX                ;SAVE REGISTERS
101:             PUSH    BX
102:             MOV     SIEVE[BX],0       ;SIEVE(INDEX) = 0
103:             SAL     AX,1              ;OFFSET = PRIME * 2
104:                                       ;<OFFSET BETWEEN MULTIPLES
105:                                       ;                 OF PRIME>
106: SIFTLOOP:                             ;WHILE (INDEX+OFFSET) < MAX_INDEX
107:             ADD     BX,AX             ;   INDEX = INDEX + OFFSET
108:             CMP     BX,MAX_INDEX
109:             JAE     RETURN1
110:             MOV     SIEVE[BX],0       ;   SIEVE(INDEX) = 0
111:             JMP     SIFTLOOP
112: RETURN1:                              ;ENDWHILE
113:             POP     BX                ;RESTORE REGISTERS
114:             POP     AX
115:             RET                       ;RETURN
116: SIFTSIEVE   ENDP                   ;END SIFTSIEVE
117: ;*****************************************************************
118: ;
119: ; I N S E R T   P R O C E D U R E   F I N D P R I M
120: ;
121: ;*****************************************************************
122:             END
```

smallest integer left) in the sieve, and the other removes a given prime number and all of its multiples from the sieve. An integer array is used for the sieve.

The program includes both a constant data segment definition (lines 18–27) and a variable data segment definition (lines 28–32). The named constant SIZE$ (defined in line 25) defines the size of the sieve in words; its value here is 15,999. To modify the program to process a different size sieve, you only need to modify the value of SIZE$. The named constant MAX_INDEX (defined in line 26) is the index of the word that immediately follows the end of the sieve; its value here is twice the value of SIZE$. The sieve itself is defined in line 32 as a word array of length SIZE$ (15,999 in the implementation shown). It is initialized by the main procedure to contain the integers 2–16,000. As stated in the prologue (lines 5 and 6), the program displays the prime numbers that are less than 16,000. The character string defined in line 22 is displayed at the end of each page of display. The program pauses at the end of each page of display to allow the user to print a hard copy of the display. The symbolic name PAUSE_LNG is equated to the length of this pause message (line 24).

The variable data segment, which contains only the array SIEVE, is defined with the .DATA? directive. This directive used in conjunction with the .DOSSEG directive (line 9) conserves space in the executable file (.EXE file) stored on the disk. The .DOSSEG directive specifies a particular ordering of the segments in the executable program. This ordering places the stack segment at the very end of the list of segments, and it places segments that contain only uninitialized data (defined by the DUP operator under the .DATA? directive) just prior to the stack segment. The Linkage Editor LINK does not store such segments as part of the executable file. Storage space is allocated in memory for these segments when the executable program file is loaded into memory for execution. Without the .DOSSEG directive, the .EXE file, for the completed program, would be over 32,000 bytes larger. This extra storage space is wasted disk space because both the stack and the array SIEVE are uninitialized data structures.

The code segment definition begins in line 33 and contains a main procedure and two internal NEAR subprocedures. The two subprocedures are used to divide the problem into simpler subproblems. The 15,999-element array that represents the sieve is initialized to contain the consecutive integers 2–16,000. To remove a prime and its multiples from the sieve, the SIFTSIEVE subprocedure replaces those values with zeros. The subprocedure performs this removal process given the index in the sieve of a prime number. To find the next prime number in the sieve, a search, using the FINDPRIM subprocedure (not shown here), is performed for the next nonzero element. The search can begin at the position (index) of the last prime number found and removed from the sieve.

The SIFTSIEVE subprocedure is defined in lines 91–116. The prologue in lines 91–98 states the interface requirements for the procedure, which expects a prime number in the AX-register and the sieve index of that prime number in the BX-register. The procedure sets the indexed sieve element to zero and also sets to zero any sieve element that is a multiple of that prime number.

The subprocedure begins by saving the registers that it uses (lines 100–101). The MOV instruction in line 102 removes the prime number from the sieve by setting to zero the element of SIEVE that is indexed by the value in the BX-register. The SAL instruction in line 103 computes the offset (i.e., difference in index) between consecutive multiples of the prime number just removed. Since this is a word array, the prime number is multiplied by 2 to compute this offset.

The WHILE loop in lines 106–112 removes the multiples of the specified prime number from the sieve. On each iteration of the loop, the index of the next multiple is computed from the index of the multiple removed on the previous iteration, and the multiple at this new index is replaced with zero (i.e., removed). The ADD instruction in line 107 computes the index of the next multiple by adding the offset between multiples (computed in line 103) to the index in the BX-register. Figure 8.19 shows several iterations of this index computation for the prime number 3. The CMP instruction in line 108 performs the loop test, and the JAE instruction in line 109 makes the decision based on this test. If the new index is less than or equal to the

FIGURE 8.19 Computation of sieve index of next multiple of a prime from index of current multiple of the prime

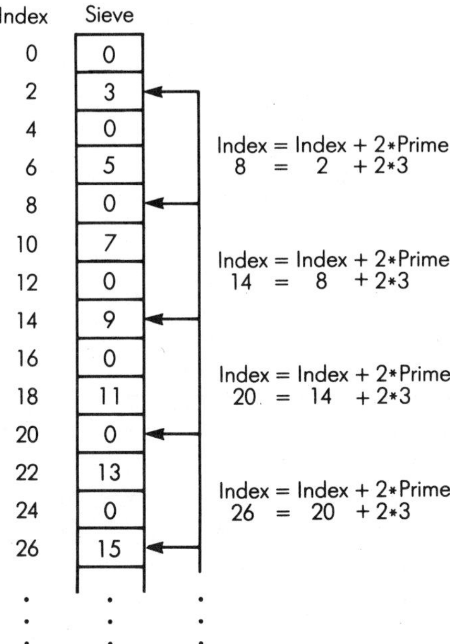

index of the last element in the sieve (less than MAX_INDEX), then the jump is not taken and the loop continues; if the new index is greater than the maximum index, the jump is taken and the loop is terminated. The MOV instruction in line 110 sets to zero the element of array SIEVE that is indexed by the value of the BX-register. This step removes the current multiple of the specified prime number. The JMP instruction in line 111 returns control to the top of the loop (line 106).

At loop exit, the registers are restored for the caller (lines 113 and 114), and control is returned to the caller (line 115). The clause USES AX BX could be added to the PROC pseudo-operation to eliminate the need for the PUSH instructions in lines 100 and 101 and the POP instructions in lines 113 and 114. The USES clause directs the assembler to generate the PUSH and POP instructions.

The subprocedure FINDPRIM is not shown in Program Listing 8.5 (the task is left to Programming Exercise 8.10), although the interface requirements of FINDPRIM are discussed here. The FINDPRIM procedure expects a sieve index in the BX-register. This index specifies the position in array SIEVE at which the search for the prime number is to begin. The procedure starts at the specified position and searches for the first nonzero element. If a nonzero element is found, then the sieve index of that element is returned in the BX-register and the element itself (i.e., the next prime number) is returned in the AX-register. If the end of array SIEVE is reached without finding a nonzero element, then zero is returned in the AX-register, which indicates to the caller that the sieve is empty.

The main procedure for this program is defined in lines 38–89 of Program Listing 8.5. The program begins in the standard manner by initializing the segment registers (lines 38–40). Both the ES- and DS-registers specify the address of the origin of the data group DGROUP.

The instructions in lines 43–47 perform initialization for the loop that initializes SIEVE. The CLD instruction in line 43 clears the DF bit of the flags register so that string instructions increment their way through the sieve. The MOV instruction in line 44 sets the loop counter, the CX-register, to the size of the sieve. The LEA instruction in line 45 sets the ES:DI register pair to specify the base address of array SIEVE. The MOV instruction in line 47 sets the AX-register to 2, the first value in the range of integers to be placed in the sieve.

The REPEAT-UNTIL loop in lines 48–52 places the consecutive integers 2–16,000 into consecutive locations of array SIEVE. The STOSW instruction in line 49 copies the value of the AX-register into the word of array SIEVE addressed by the ES:DI register pair, and then it increments the DI-register by 2 so that the ES:DI register pair addresses the next element in array SIEVE. The INC instruction in line 51 increments the value in the AX-register by 1, producing the value to be stored in that next element of array SIEVE. The LOOP instruction in line 52 performs the loop test. It decrements the loop count in the CX-register by 1 and, if the resulting value is nonzero, transfers control to the top of the loop (line 48).

At loop exit, the instructions in lines 54–56 are executed. These instructions perform initialization for the loop that finds and displays the prime numbers. The MOV instruction in line 54 initializes the BX-register, the index into array SIEVE, to zero. At this point, the address expression SIEVE[BX] addresses the first element of array SIEVE. The MOV instruction in line 55 initializes the count of prime numbers displayed to zero. This count is maintained in the CX-register. The CALL instruction in line 56 invokes the FINDPRIM procedure to locate the first prime number in the sieve. FINDPRIM returns with the first prime number, 2, in the AX-register and with the BX-register set to the index within SIEVE of that prime number. Since the first prime number in the sieve is the first element in array SIEVE, FINDPRIM finds that element immediately. In fact, the CALL instruction could be replaced by the instruction

```
MOV  AX,SIEVE[BX]
```

obviously rendering the program more efficient.

The REPEAT-UNTIL loop in lines 58–87 finds and displays the prime numbers, one prime number per iteration. At the beginning of each iteration of the loop body, the AX-register contains the next prime number in the sieve, and the BX-register contains the index within array SIEVE of that prime number. The CALL instruction in line 59 invokes the SIFTSIEVE procedure to remove that prime number and its multiples from the sieve. On return from the SIFTSIEVE procedure, the AX-register still contains the prime number, and the BX-register still contains the index within array SIEVE. That index is used as the starting point for the search of array SIEVE for the next prime number. The PUSH instruction in line 61 saves the sieve index so that the BX-register can be used for other purposes. The two instructions in lines 62 and 63 display the prime number, and the INC instruction in line 64 increments the count of prime numbers displayed. The nested, single-alternative decision structure in lines 65–83 handles line and page control for the display of the prime numbers. This nested structure is discussed in detail shortly.

On completion of the nested decision structure, the sieve index is restored (line 84). The CALL to FINDPRIM in line 85 locates the next prime number in the sieve if the sieve is not empty. On return from the FINDPRIM procedure, either the AX-register contains the next prime number in the sieve or it contains zero (indicating that the sieve is empty). If the AX-register contains a prime number, then the BX-register contains the index within array SIEVE of that prime number. The CMP instruction in line 86 performs the loop test, and the JNE instruction in line 87 makes the decision based on this test. If a prime number is in the AX-register, then the jump is taken to the top of the REPEAT-UNTIL loop (line 58); if the AX-register contains zero, then the sieve is empty and the loop is terminated. At loop exit, control is returned to DOS (line 89).

The prime numbers are displayed on the screen 10 per line. Each number is displayed right-justified in a six-character field (lines 62 and 63). After each 24 lines of display, a pause is made to allow the user to print the display screen. The continuation of the display is under user control. The display control is performed by the nested, single-alternative decision structure in lines 65–83. The instructions in lines 65–69 test to see if the count of primes displayed (CX-register value) is divisible by 10, and the JNE instruction in line 70 makes the decision based on this test. If the count is not divisible by 10 (i.e., remainder of division by 10 is nonzero), then the jump is taken to the end of the nested decision structure (line 83); if the count is divisible by 10, then a display line has just been completed and the instructions in lines 71–82 are executed. The call to the NEWLINE procedure in line 71 moves the cursor to the beginning of the next line on the display. Lines 72–82 implement the inner decision structure.

The inner decision structure determines whether a page of display has been completed. The quotient of the division of the count by 10 (line 68) represents a line count. The instructions in lines 72–75 test to see if the line count is divisible by 24, and the JNE instruction in line 76 makes the decision based on this test. If the line count is not divisible by 24 (i.e., the remainder of the division by 24 is nonzero), then the jump is taken to the end of the nested decision structure (line 83); if the line count is divisible by 24, then a display page has just been completed and the instructions in lines 77–81 are executed. The PUSH instruction in line 77 saves the CX-register value, the count of primes displayed, so that the CX-register can be used for input to the PAUSE procedure. The instructions in lines 78–80 are the calling sequence for the PAUSE procedure. The input requirements for PAUSE are the same as those for PUTSTRNG. In fact, PAUSE calls PUTSTRNG to display the specified message beginning at the current cursor position. The PAUSE procedure then clears the input buffer and waits for a keystroke. When the keystroke is received, the PAUSE procedure calls the NEWLINE procedure to move the cursor to the beginning of the next display line and then returns to the caller. On return from PAUSE, the count of primes displayed is restored in the CX-register (line 81), and the end of the decision structure is reached (line 83). Output Listing 8.6 is a printout of the first two pages of the display generated by this program.

Large Integer Values

Program Listing 8.7 demonstrates a technique for processing decimal integers that are too large to be represented directly in binary with 8, 16, or even 32 bits. The technique is demonstrated using a program that computes large factorial values.

Given an integer n, the factorial of n (denoted by $n!$) is the product of the first n positive integers:

$$n! = n(n-1)(n-2) \cdots (3)(2)(1)$$

One interesting property of the factorial function is the rate at which $n!$ grows as n gets larger. The limit for 8-bit unsigned integers is $5! = 120$; the limit for 16-bit unsigned integers is $8! = 40{,}320$; and the limit for 32-bit unsigned integers is $12! = 479{,}001{,}600$. The value of $20!$ requires 19 decimal digits and 63 binary digits.

To compute arbitrarily large factorial values, a byte array is used to represent a single decimal integer. Each element of the array represents one decimal digit of the integer value. The number of decimal digits in the integer value being represented is

OUTPUT LISTING 8.6

```
     2     3     5     7    11    13    17    19    23    29
    31    37    41    43    47    53    59    61    67    71
    73    79    83    89    97   101   103   107   109   113
   127   131   137   139   149   151   157   163   167   173
   179   181   191   193   197   199   211   223   227   229
   233   239   241   251   257   263   269   271   277   281
   283   293   307   311   313   317   331   337   347   349
   353   359   367   373   379   383   389   397   401   409
   419   421   431   433   439   443   449   457   461   463
   467   479   487   491   499   503   509   521   523   541
   547   557   563   569   571   577   587   593   599   601
   607   613   617   619   631   641   643   647   653   659
   661   673   677   683   691   701   709   719   727   733
   739   743   751   757   761   769   773   787   797   809
   811   821   823   827   829   839   853   857   859   863
   877   881   883   887   907   911   919   929   937   941
   947   953   967   971   977   983   991   997  1009  1013
  1019  1021  1031  1033  1039  1049  1051  1061  1063  1069
  1087  1091  1093  1097  1103  1109  1117  1123  1129  1151
  1153  1163  1171  1181  1187  1193  1201  1213  1217  1223
  1229  1231  1237  1249  1259  1277  1279  1283  1289  1291
  1297  1301  1303  1307  1319  1321  1327  1361  1367  1373
  1381  1399  1409  1423  1427  1429  1433  1439  1447  1451
  1453  1459  1471  1481  1483  1487  1489  1493  1499  1511
PRESS ANY KEY TO CONTINUE

  1523  1531  1543  1549  1553  1559  1567  1571  1579  1583
  1597  1601  1607  1609  1613  1619  1621  1627  1637  1657
  1663  1667  1669  1693  1697  1699  1709  1721  1723  1733
  1741  1747  1753  1759  1777  1783  1787  1789  1801  1811
  1823  1831  1847  1861  1867  1871  1873  1877  1879  1889
  1901  1907  1913  1931  1933  1949  1951  1973  1979  1987
  1993  1997  1999  2003  2011  2017  2027  2029  2039  2053
  2063  2069  2081  2083  2087  2089  2099  2111  2113  2129
  2131  2137  2141  2143  2153  2161  2179  2203  2207  2213
  2221  2237  2239  2243  2251  2267  2269  2273  2281  2287
  2293  2297  2309  2311  2333  2339  2341  2347  2351  2357
  2371  2377  2381  2383  2389  2393  2399  2411  2417  2423
  2437  2441  2447  2459  2467  2473  2477  2503  2521  2531
  2539  2543  2549  2551  2557  2579  2591  2593  2609  2617
  2621  2633  2647  2657  2659  2663  2671  2677  2683  2687
  2689  2693  2699  2707  2711  2713  2719  2729  2731  2741
  2749  2753  2767  2777  2789  2791  2797  2801  2803  2819
  2833  2837  2843  2851  2857  2861  2879  2887  2897  2903
  2909  2917  2927  2939  2953  2957  2963  2969  2971  2999
  3001  3011  3019  3023  3037  3041  3049  3061  3067  3079
  3083  3089  3109  3119  3121  3137  3163  3167  3169  3181
  3187  3191  3203  3209  3217  3221  3229  3251  3253  3257
  3259  3271  3299  3301  3307  3313  3319  3323  3329  3331
  3343  3347  3359  3361  3371  3373  3389  3391  3407  3413
PRESS ANY KEY TO CONTINUE
```

limited only by the array size. Program Listing 8.7 uses a 60-byte array called FAC to represent a factorial value. The factorial value is represented in the following way:

`FAC(0)` *contains the most significant digit*
`FAC(1)` *contains the next most significant digit*

.

.

.

`FAC(57)` *contains the hundreds digit*
`FAC(58)` *contains the tens digit*
`FAC(59)` *contains the units digit*

```
             PAGE    80,132
;=====================================================================
;                    PROGRAM LISTING 8.7
;
;PROGRAM TO COMPUTE LARGE FACTORIAL VALUES.   A LARGE INTEGER IS
;REPRESENTED BY A BYTE ARRAY. EACH ELEMENT OF THE ARRAY CONTAINS
;ONE DIGIT OF THE LARGE INTEGER. A TABLE OF FACTORIAL VALUES  IS
;DISPLAYED.  THE USER ENTERS THE LARGEST VALUE OF N FOR WHICH N!
;IS TO BE DISPLAYED. OVERFLOW WILL TERMINATE THE PROGRAM EARLY.
;=====================================================================
                                          ;PROCEDURES TO
             EXTRN   GETDEC$:FAR          ;GET UNSIGNED DECIMAL INTEGER
             EXTRN   PUTDEC$:FAR          ;DISPLAY UNSIGNED DECIMAL INT.
             EXTRN   NEWLINE:FAR          ;DISPLAY NEWLINE CHARACTER
             EXTRN   PUTSTRNG:FAR         ;DISPLAY CHARACTER STRING
             EXTRN   PUTLGINT:FAR         ;DISPLAY LARGE INTEGERS
;=====================================================================
             .MODEL  SMALL,BASIC
;=====================================================================
; S T A C K   S E G M E N T   D E F I N I T I O N
;
             .STACK  256
;
;=====================================================================
; V A R I A B L E   D E F I N I T I O N S
;
             .DATA
SIZE$        EQU     60
FAC          DB      (SIZE$-1) DUP(0)
FAC_END      DB      1
CARRY        DW      ?
;=====================================================================
; C O N S T A N T   D E F I N I T I O N S
             .CONST
PROMPT       DB      'ENTER LARGEST VALUE',0DH,0AH
             DB      'FOR WHICH TO COMPUTE',0DH,0AH
             DB      'FACTORIAL',0DH,0AH
PROMPT_LNG EQU       $ - PROMPT           ;LENGTH OF PROMPT MESSAGE
;=====================================================================
; C O D E   S E G M E N T   D E F I N I T I O N
;
             .CODE   EX_8_7
             .STARTUP                     ;GENERATE STARTUP CODE
             PUSH    DS                   ;SET ES-REGISTER TO ADDRESS
             POP     ES                   ;DGROUP
;
             LEA     DI,PROMPT            ;PROMPT FOR MAXN
             MOV     CX,PROMPT_LNG
             CALL    PUTSTRNG
             CALL    GETDEC$              ;GET MAXN
             MOV     CX,AX                ;OUTER_LOOP_COUNT = MAXN
             MOV     BL,1                 ;N = 1
OUTERLOOP:   JCXZ    LOOP_END             ;WHILE OUTER_LOOP_COUNT <> 0
             MOV     CARRY,0              ;   CARRY = 0
             LEA     DI,FAC_END           ;   PTR = END ADDRESS OF FAC
             STD                          ;   SET DF FOR DECREMENTING
             MOV     BH,SIZE$             ;   INNER_LOOP_COUNT = SIZE$
INNERLOOP:                                ;   REPEAT
             MOV     AL,BYTE PTR ES:[DI]  ;      TEMP = (PTR->BYTE * N
             MUL     BL                   ;                    + CARRY)
             ADD     AX,CARRY
             MOV     DX,0
             MOV     SI,10
             DIV     SI
             MOV     CARRY,AX             ;      CARRY = TEMP / 10
             XCHG    AX,DX                ;      PTR->BYTE = TEMP mod 10
             STOSB                        ;      PTR = PTR - 1
```

```
68:              DEC     BH                 ;        DECR INNER_LOOP_COUNT
69:              JNZ     INNERLOOP          ;    UNTIL INNER_LOOP_COUNT = 0
70:              CMP     CARRY,0            ;    IF   CARRY = 0
71:              JNE     ELSE1
72:              PUSH    CX                 ;    THEN
73:              LEA     DI,FAC             ;         DISPLAY FAC
74:              MOV     CX,SIZE$
75:              CALL    PUTLGINT
76:              MOV     BH,1
77:              MOV     AL,BL              ;         DISPLAY N
78:              MOV     AH,0
79:              CALL    PUTDEC$
80:              CALL    NEWLINE            ;         DISPLAY NEWLINE CHAR
81:              POP     CX
82:              JMP     ENDIF1
83: ELSE1:                                  ;    ELSE
84:              MOV     CX,1               ;         OUTER_LOOP_COUNT = 1
85:                                         ;         <FORCE LOOP EXIT>
86: ENDIF1:                                 ;    ENDIF
87:              INC     BL                 ;    N = N + 1
88:              DEC     CX                 ;    DECR OUTER_LOOP_COUNT
89:              JMP     OUTERLOOP          ;ENDWHILE
90: LOOP_END:
91:              .EXIT                      ;RETURN TO DOS
92: ;
93:              END
```

The program computes a table of factorial values of the consecutive integers 1–n. For simplification, the program makes use of the relationship $n! = n(n-1)!$. That is, each factorial value can be computed from the previous factorial value, as in the following example:

$$10! = 3{,}628{,}800$$

$$11! = 11(10!) = 11(3{,}628{,}800) = 39{,}916{,}800$$

The series of diagrams in Figure 8.20 demonstrates the technique that is used in Program Listing 8.7 for computing one factorial value from the previous factorial value. The figure shows the computing of 11! from 10!. Starting with the last digit of array FAC (i.e., starting with the least significant digit of the 10! value) and working toward the beginning of the array (i.e., toward the most significant digit of the 10! value), the following operations are performed on each digit in turn:

1. The digit is multiplied by 11, and the carry from the previous digit is added.
2. The result of step 1 is divided by 10.
3. The remainder of the division in step 2 (i.e., the rightmost digit of the result of step 1) is the new digit for this position of the number.
4. The quotient of the division in step 2 (i.e., the result of step 1 with its rightmost digit removed) is the carry into the next digit position.

Figure 8.20 shows these steps being performed on the rightmost nine digits of 10!, producing the rightmost nine digits of 11!. The other 51 iterations of these steps simply produce 51 leading zeros.

Program Listing 8.7 shows an implementation of the technique just described. It references a subprocedure called PUTLGINT (see the EXTRN pseudo-operation in line 16) that displays a large integer that is stored in a byte array, one digit per byte, beginning with the most significant digit. The PUTLGINT procedure expects the

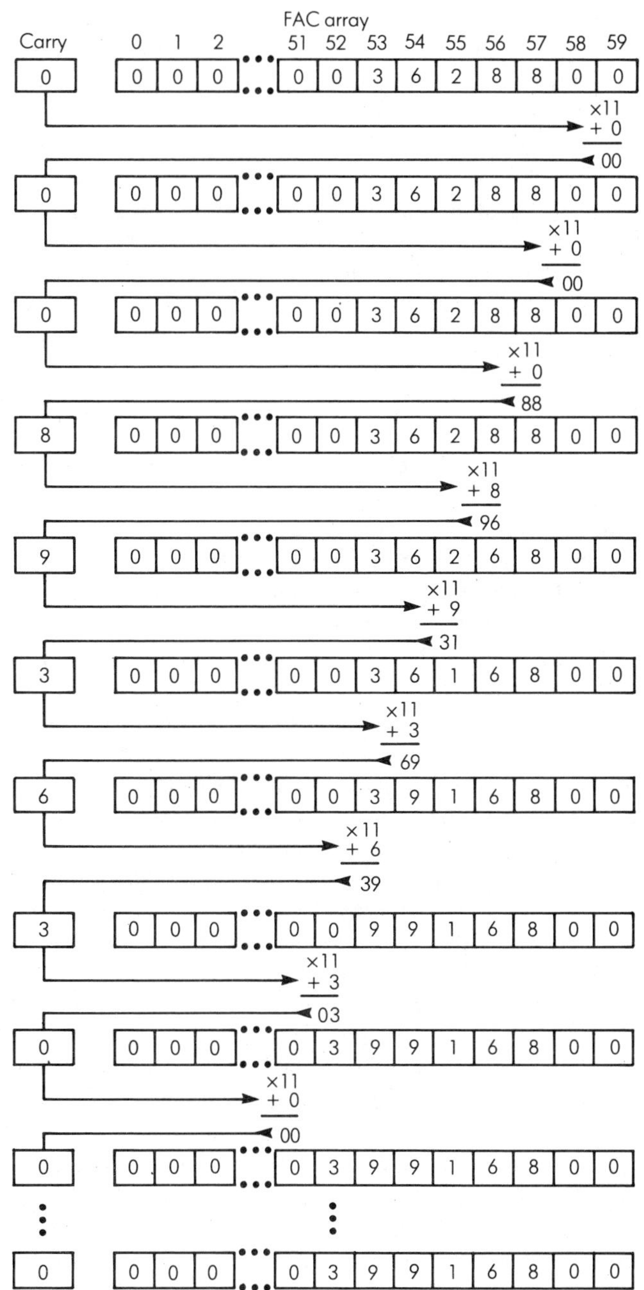

FIGURE 8.20
Computation of 11! from 10!

ES:DI register pair to specify the base address of the array that contains the integer to be displayed and the CX-register to contain the size in bytes of that array. The procedure displays blanks for leading zeros so that the integer contained in an n-element array is displayed right-justified in an n-character field. (The PUTLGINT procedure is left to Programming Exercise 8.12.)

The program includes both a variable data segment definition (lines 24–31) and a constant data segment definition (lines 32–38). The named constant defined in line 28 is the size of the FAC array (i.e., the number of decimal digits in the large integer).

To modify the program to handle a different size factorial value, simply change the value of this named constant. The FAC array is defined in lines 29 and 30 as a 60-byte array with symbolic names for both the first and last elements. FAC is the symbolic name for the first element, and FAC_END is the symbolic name for the last element. Such labeling makes it easy to begin sequential processing from either end of the array. The elements of array FAC are initialized to zero, except for the last element (the least significant digit), which is initialized to 1—initializing the factorial value to 0! = 1.

The word variable CARRY (line 31) holds the carry from one digit position to the next in the computation of a factorial value from the previous factorial value. The character string defined in lines 35–37 is a prompt message that is displayed on the screen to prompt the user to enter the maximum value for N. The string is 54 characters in length and is displayed on three lines. The length of the string is equated to the symbolic name PROMPT_LNG (line 38).

The program begins in the standard manner by setting the DS- and ES-registers to address DGROUP (lines 43–45). The instructions in lines 47–49 prompt the user for the maximum value for which to compute the factorial. The GETDEC$ subprocedure is called (line 50) to perform the input. The value received from the keyboard by GETDEC$ is returned in the AX-register.

The program contains nested loops. The outer loop is a WHILE loop that executes once for each factorial value computed. It is controlled by a counter that counts from MAXN (the input value) to zero. On each iteration of the outer loop, a factorial value is computed and displayed. The MOV instruction in line 51 initializes the outer loop counter to the input value (MAXN). The CX-register maintains the outer loop counter so that the JCXZ instruction (line 53) can be used for the loop test. The MOV instruction in line 52 initializes the value of N to 1. N is the value whose factorial will be computed on the next iteration of the outer loop. The value of N is maintained in the BL-register. The body of the outer loop appears in lines 54–88.

The inner loop performs the computation illustrated in Figure 8.20. It computes a new factorial value from the previous factorial value and executes once for each element of array FAC. It is controlled by a counter that counts from SIZE$ (the size of the FAC array) to zero. The instructions at the beginning of the outer loop body (lines 54–57) perform the initialization for the inner loop. The MOV instruction in line 54 initializes the carry from the previous digit to zero (i.e., the carry into the least significant digit position is always zero). The LEA instruction in line 55 sets the DI-register to the offset of FAC_END so that the ES:DI register pair addresses the last element of array FAC (i.e., the least significant digit of the previous factorial value). The STD instruction in line 56 sets the DF bit in the flags register so that string instructions automatically decrement the DI-register. This step allows processing to proceed from the end of array FAC toward the beginning. The MOV instruction in line 57 initializes the inner loop counter to the size of array FAC. This count is maintained in the BH-register.

The inner loop body appears in lines 59–68. The MOV instruction in line 59 copies to the AL-register the digit of the FAC array that is addressed by the ES:DI register pair. The MUL instruction in line 60 multiplies the digit by the value of N (BL-register value), and the ADD instruction in line 61 adds the carry from the previous digit position. The instructions in lines 62–64 divide the result by 10 to separate the new digit for this position from the carry into the next digit position. The quotient of this division is the carry into the next digit position and is stored as the value of variable CARRY (line 65). The remainder of this division is the new digit for this position. The STOSB instruction in line 67 stores this new digit in the byte of array

FAC addressed by the ES:DI register pair, and it decrements the DI-register so that the ES:DI register pair addresses the previous element of array FAC (the next higher digit of the previous factorial value). The DEC instruction in line 68 decrements the inner loop counter, and the JNZ instruction in line 69 transfers control to the top of the inner loop (line 58) if the inner loop count is nonzero. If the decrement operation leaves the inner loop counter at zero, then the inner loop is terminated.

On termination of the inner loop, the double-alternative decision structure in lines 70–86 is executed. The decision is based on the value of CARRY, the carry out of the most significant digit of the factorial value just computed. The CMP instruction in line 70 tests the condition, and the JNE instruction in line 71 makes the decision based on the condition. If the carry is zero, then the instructions in lines 72–82 are executed. The PUSH instruction in line 72 saves the outer loop counter so that the CX-register can be used for input to the PUTLGINT subprocedure. The instructions in lines 73–75 cause the factorial value to be displayed, and the instructions in lines 76–79 cause the value of N to be displayed. The POP instruction in line 81 restores the outer loop counter. The JMP instruction in line 82 skips the False alternative of the decision structure. If the carry from the most significant digit is nonzero (i.e., if overflow has occurred in the factorial computation), then the instruction in line 84 is executed. This MOV instruction sets the outer loop counter to 1, which forces loop exit on the next decrement and test of the outer loop counter.

Following the double-alternative decision structure, the instructions in lines 87–89 are executed. The INC instruction in line 87 increments the value of N (BL-register) in preparation for the next iteration of the outer loop. The DEC instruction in line 88 decrements the outer loop counter, and the JMP instruction in line 89 transfers control to the loop test (line 53). On termination of the outer loop, control is returned to DOS (line 91).

The following are the results from a sample execution of this program:

```
ENTER LARGEST VALUE
FOR WHICH TO COMPUTE
FACTORIAL
19
                                                   1   1
                                                   2   2
                                                   6   3
                                                  24   4
                                                 120   5
                                                 720   6
                                                5040   7
                                               40320   8
                                              362880   9
                                             3628800  10
                                            39916800  11
                                           479001600  12
                                          6227020800  13
                                         87178291200  14
                                       1307674368000  15
                                      20922789888000  16
                                     355687428096000  17
                                    6402373705728000  18
                                  121645100408832000  19
```

8.6 Additional Capabilities in the 80386 Assembly Language

The expanded instruction set of the 80386 assembly language includes five string instructions for manipulating arrays of double words. These string instructions have the following general forms:

```
[<label>]  LODSD                                   [<comment>]
[<label>]  STOSD                                   [<comment>]
[<label>]  MOVSD                                   [<comment>]
[<label>]  CMPSD                                   [<comment>]
[<label>]  SCASD                                   [<comment>]
```

These instructions behave in a manner similar to the corresponding byte and word string instructions. For example, execution of an STOSD instruction causes the processor to replace the double word addressed by the ES:DI register pair with a copy of the double word in the EAX-register and then to update the DI-register to point to the next double word in the array. If the DF bit in the flags register is 0, then the DI-register is incremented by 4; if the DF bit in the flags register is 1, then the DI-register is decremented by 4.

PRACTICAL EXERCISES

8.1 Suppose the CX-register contains the value 12, and suppose the DS:SI register pair and the ES:DI register pair are currently pointing to two character strings as indicated here:

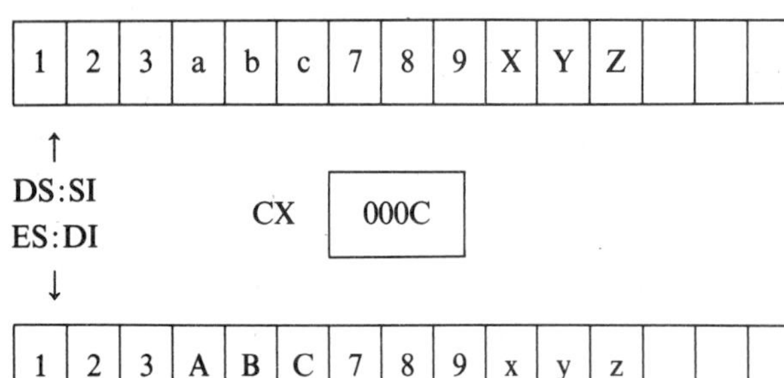

Fill in the following diagram and show the value of the CX-register, the values of the two strings, and the position within the strings pointed to by the DS:SI register pair and the ES:DI register pair after execution of the following sequence of instructions:

```
      CLD
REPE  CMPSB
REP   MOVSB
```

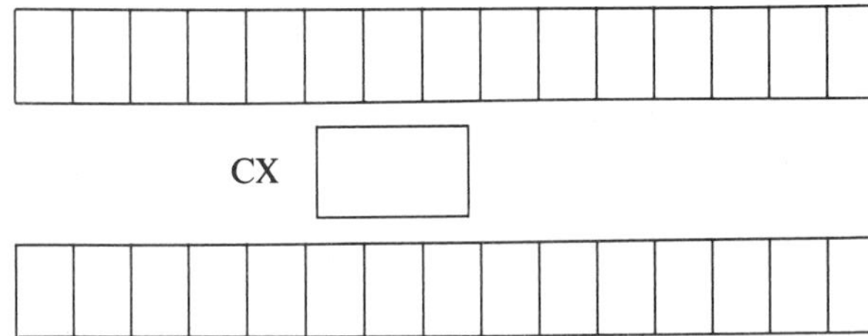

8.2 Suppose the CX-register contains the value 12, and suppose the DS:SI register pair and the ES:DI register pair are currently pointing to two character strings as indicated here:

1	2	3	a	B	c	7	8	9	X	Y	Z			

↑
DS:SI   CX 000C
ES:DI
↓

0	1	2	A	B	C	7	8	9	x	y	z			

Fill in the following diagram and show the value of the CX-register, the values of the two strings, and the position within the strings pointed to by the DS:SI register pair and the ES:DI register pair after execution of the following sequence of instructions:

```
      CLD
REPNE CMPSB
REP   MOVSB
```

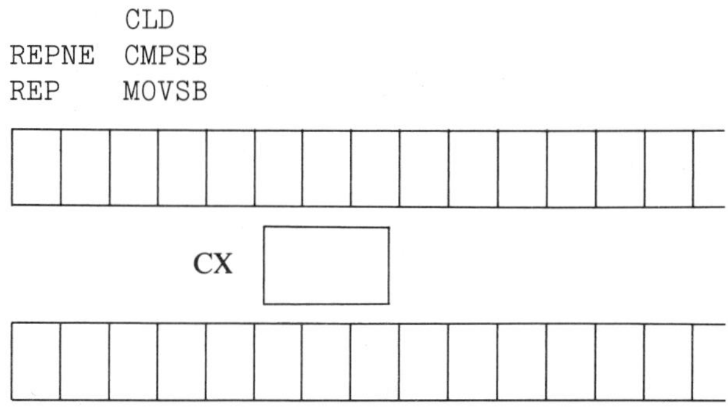

8.3 Suppose the CX-register contains the value 12, and suppose the DS:SI register pair and the ES:DI register pair are currently pointing to two character strings as indicated here:

0	1	2	a	b	c	7	6	5	X	Y	Z			

↑
DS:SI

CX 000C

ES:DI
↓

1	2	3	A	B	C	7	8	9	x	y	z			

Fill in the following diagram and show the value of the CX-register, the values of the two strings, and the position within the strings pointed to by the DS:SI register pair and the ES:DI register pair after execution of the following sequence of instructions:

```
      CLD
REPNE CMPSB
      LODSB
REP   STOSB
```

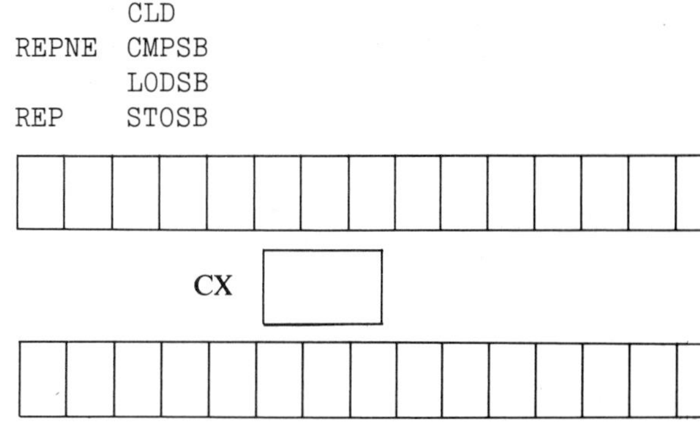

8.4 The example of base indexed addressing in Section 8.4 shows the beginning of a subprocedure definition and shows the assembler-generated instructions that would be placed at the beginning of the subprocedure. Figure 8.17 shows the state of the stack segment following execution of these assembler-generated instructions. The example also shows that the following instructions would be generated by the assembler in response to the RET instruction:

```
pop  si
pop  cx
pop  ax
mov  sp, bp
pop  bp
ret
```

Assume that the state of the stack segment just prior to execution of these assembler-generated instructions is the same as shown in Figure 8.17.

a. Draw a diagram to show the state of the stack segment after execution of the following instructions:

```
pop  si
pop  cx
pop  ax
```

b. Draw a diagram to show the state of the stack segment after execution of the following instruction:

```
mov  sp, bp
```

PROGRAMMING EXERCISES

8.1 Design an algorithm to accept as input a byte array that contains an ASCII number and to produce as output a byte array that contains the same number in packed BCD form (2 BCD digits per byte). The size of the array is also an input to the algorithm.

Implement your algorithm with an 8088/8086 assembly language external FAR subprocedure. The name of your procedure should be ASCIIBCD. Your inputs should be as follows:

DS:SI register pair addresses the beginning of the array that contains the ASCII number.

ES:DI register pair addresses the beginning of the array that is to contain the result (i.e., the corresponding BCD number).

CX-register contains the number of digits in the ASCII number.

On return from your subprocedure, the array addressed by the ES:DI register pair should contain the BCD number equivalent of the ASCII number in the array addressed by the DS:SI register pair. Your subprocedure should save and restore all registers used.

8.2 Design an algorithm to accept a character string as input and to return as output the input string with all nonletters removed.

Implement your algorithm with an 8088/8086 assembly language external FAR subprocedure called REMOVE. Your inputs should be as follows:

DS:SI register pair addresses the first character of the input string.
CX-register contains the length of the input string.
ES:DI register pair addresses the first character of the output string.

(Note that DS:SI and ES:DI may address the same string.)

On return to the calling procedure, the output string is to contain the input string with all nonalphabetic characters removed, and the CX-register is to contain the length of the output string. Your subprocedure should save and restore all registers used, except for the CX-register, which is used for subprocedure output.

8.3 Design an algorithm to accept a character string as input and to return as output the input string with each lowercase letter converted to the corresponding uppercase letter.

Implement your algorithm with an 8088/8086 assembly language FAR subprocedure called UP_SHIFT. Your inputs should be as follows:

DS:SI register pair addresses the first character of the input string.
CX-register contains the length of the input string.
ES:DI register pair addresses the first character of the output string.

(Note that DS:SI and ES:DI may address the same string.)

On return to the calling procedure, the output string is to contain the input string with all lowercase letters converted to uppercase letters. Your subprocedure should save and restore all registers used.

8.4 Design an algorithm to accept a character string as input and to return as output the reverse of the input string.

Implement your algorithm with an 8088/8086 assembly language external FAR subprocedure called REVERSE. Your inputs should be as follows:

DS:SI register pair addresses the first character of the input string.
CX-register contains the length of the input string.
ES:DI register pair addresses the first character of the output string.

(Note that DS:SI and ES:DI may address the same string.)

On return to the calling procedure, the output string is to contain the reverse of the input string. Your subprocedure should save and restore all registers used.

8.5 Design an algorithm to accept two character strings as input, compare the two strings, and return the result of the comparison to the caller. The algorithm should allow for the fact that the two strings may be of different lengths. In the case of different string lengths, the smaller string is to be viewed as being padded on the right-hand side with blanks.

Implement your algorithm with an 8088/8086 assembly language external FAR subprocedure called CMP_STR. Your inputs should be as follows:

ES:DI register pair addresses the first character of the destination string.
DS:SI register pair addresses the first character of the source string.
CH-register contains the length of the destination string.
CL-register contains the length of the source string.

Your subprocedure should return to the caller with the SF and ZF bits of the flags register set to reflect the relationship of the source string to the destination string. As well, your subprocedure should save and restore all registers used.

8.6 A palindrome is a word, sentence, or phrase that is spelled the same backward as forward. The following are several palindromes: Madam I'm Adam; Able was I ere I saw Elba; A man, a plan, a canal, Panama!

Design and implement in 8088/8086 assembly language an algorithm that uses the subalgorithms of Programming Exercises 8.2–8.5 to detect palindromes. Your algorithm should perform the following steps:

a. Use GETSTRNG to input a character string from the keyboard.
b. Call REMOVE to remove all nonalphabetic characters from the input string.
c. Call UP_SHIFT to convert the letter string produced in (b) to an uppercase letter string.
d. Call REVERSE to obtain the reverse of the uppercase letter string.
e. Call CMP_STR to compare the uppercase letter string in (c) to the reverse string in (d).
f. Display the string

```
THE STRING IS A PALINDROME
```

or the string

```
THE STRING IS NOT A PALINDROME
```

depending on the outcome of (e).

8.7 Design an algorithm to find the first occurrence of a source string within a destination string. Your inputs should be the two byte arrays that contain the two character strings. The first byte in each array contains the length of the string contained in the subsequent bytes of the array. Your output should be the index within the destination string's array of the first character of the first occurrence of the source string. The algorithm should return an index of zero if the source string does not appear in the destination string.

Implement your algorithm with an 8088/8086 assembly language external FAR subprocedure called INDEX. Your inputs should be as follows:

> ES:DI register pair addresses the first byte of the destination string's array.
> DS:SI register pair addresses the first byte of the source string's array.

On return to the caller, the BX-register should contain the index within the destination string's array of the first occurrence of the source string. The BX-register should contain zero if the source string does not appear within the destination string. Your subprocedure should save and restore all registers used, except the BX-register, which is used for procedure output.

8.8 The sequence of positive integers that begins 1, 1, 2, 3, 5, 8, 13, 21, 34, 55, 89 ... is called the *Fibonacci sequence*. The first number in the sequence, F_1, is 1. The second number in the sequence, F_2, is 1. Each subsequent number in the sequence, F_i, is the sum of the two numbers previous to it in the sequence. That is,

$$F_i = F_{i-1} + F_{i-2} \qquad \text{for } i > 2$$

This sequence grows at a fairly rapid pace. The fourteenth number in the sequence, 377, is too large for 8-bit unsigned integers. The twenty-fifth number in the sequence, 75,025, is too large for 16-bit unsigned integers. The fiftieth number in the sequence, 12,586,296,025, is too large for 32-bit unsigned integers.

Design an algorithm to compute arbitrarily large Fibonacci numbers. Use the technique presented in Section 8.5 for maintaining large integers. Your input should be an integer value of n, and your output should be the nth integer in the Fibonacci sequence.

Implement your algorithm with an 8088/8086 assembly language program. Your input value for n should be entered via the keyboard. The nth Fibonacci number is to be displayed on the screen. Your program should be able to produce Fibonacci numbers up to 72 digits in length.

8.9 Design an algorithm to simulate the following procedure:

a. Place 500 cups in a row, and number the cups consecutively from 1 to 500.
b. Place a marble in each cup.
c. Remove the marble from every other cup beginning with cup 2.
d. Check every third cup beginning with cup 3. If the cup contains a marble, then remove it; otherwise, place a marble in the cup.
e. Check every fourth cup beginning with cup 4. If the cup contains a marble, then remove it; otherwise, place a marble in the cup.
f. Continue this process until every five-hundredth cup is checked beginning with cup 500.
g. Display the number of each cup that contains a marble.

Implement your algorithm with an 8088/8086 assembly language program. There is no input to your program. Your output should be the list of cup numbers displayed on the screen.

8.10 Complete Program Listing 8.5 by implementing the internal subprocedure FINDPRIM with interface specifications as described in Section 8.5. If your implementation requires the size of the sieve or the maximum index within array SIEVE, be sure to use the named constants defined in lines 25 and 26 of Program Listing 8.5.

Assemble, link, and execute the completed program in Program Listing 8.5. Change the value of SIZE$ in line 25 to 1199, and then assemble, link, and execute the program once again. Then change the value of SIZE$ in line 25 to 3099, and assemble, link, and execute the program one more time.

8.11 Design an algorithm to compute and display a table of the first 64 powers of 2. Use the technique presented in Section 8.5 to maintain large integers.

Implement your algorithm with an 8088/8086 assembly language program. There is no input to your program. Your output should be the table of powers of 2 displayed one entry per line, 16 lines per page. Each line should contain a value of n followed by the value of 2^n, which should be right-justified.

8.12 Design an algorithm to display a large integer that is stored in a byte array using the technique described in Section 8.5. Your input should be the base address and size of the array. Your output should be the large integer displayed on the screen right-justified in an n-character field, in which n is the size of the input array. Leading zeros are to be replaced by spaces in the output.

Implement your algorithm with an 8088/8086 assembly language external FAR subprocedure called PUTLGINT. Your input should be the address of the array in the ES:DI register pair and the size of the array in the CX-register. Your output should be displayed on the screen as described previously. The PUTDEC or PUTDEC$ procedure can be used to display the integer's individual digits.

8.13 Character strings can be defined with a special character that marks the end of the string. Two characters are typically used for marking the end of a character string: the null character (ASCII 0) and the dollar sign ($). The following string definition gives an example of a null-terminated string:

```
PROMPT  DB  'Enter an unsigned integer.',0
```

The following string definition gives an example of a $-terminated string:

```
PROMPT  DB  'Enter an unsigned integer.$'
```

Write a subprocedure called PUTTEXT to display a null-terminated character string. The input to your subprocedure will be the address of the string in the ES:DI register pair. Your subprocedure should compute the length of the string and then call PUTSTRNG to display the string. The null character should *not* be included in the length of the string.

The Microsoft Macro Assembler package includes the utility program LIB, which allows programmers to build and maintain libraries of object code files. With LIB on the fixed disk and the library IO.LIB and the object file PUTTEXT.OBJ on the diskette in drive A, the following sequence of steps will add the object file PUTTEXT.OBJ to IO.LIB. (*Warning:* These steps should only be performed to a copy of IO.LIB. The original copy of IO.LIB should be preserved as is for backup purposes.)

1. Type the following command in response to the DOS prompt:

   ```
   lib a:io
   ```

   This command causes DOS to load the LIB program and causes LIB to access the file A:IO.LIB as its input file. The LIB program then outputs the following prompt message:

   ```
   Operations:
   ```

2. Enter the operation

   ```
   +a:puttext
   ```

   and press the Enter key. This command causes LIB to add a copy of the object file A:PUTTEXT.OBJ to the library A:IO.LIB. The LIB program then outputs the following prompt message:

   ```
   List file:
   ```

3. Enter the filename

   ```
   a:io.lst
   ```

   and press the Enter key. This command tells LIB to create a listing file for the updated library and to place it on the diskette in drive A with the filename IO.LST. The LIB program then outputs the following prompt message:

   ```
   Output library:
   ```

4. Enter the library name

   ```
   a:io.lib
   ```

   and press the Enter key. This command tells LIB to place the updated library on the diskette in drive A with the library name IO.LIB. The old library is renamed IO.BAK and remains on the diskette as backup. When the LIB program completes its task, it returns control to DOS.

Display or print a copy of the file A:IO.LST to see a list of the files contained on the updated library.

A programming exercise at the end of the next chapter specifies a version of PUTTEXT that performs its own output and therefore does not need to call PUTSTRNG. This programming exercise includes instructions on the use of the LIB program to replace an object file on the library. Appendix F contains a section that summarizes the LIB commands.

CHAPTER 9

Interrupts and Input/Output

In the example programs of previous chapters, input/output operations were performed by a set of input/output subprocedures. To use these subprocedures, you only had to know the interface requirements for each. From the standpoint of a user, how a given subprocedure performs its function is of no concern. This chapter introduces I/O operations at the machine level. To understand machine-level I/O operations, an understanding of interrupts is required. This chapter discusses interrupts in general and the interrupt structure of the 8088/8086 microprocessor in particular.

I/O operations have already been viewed from the user level. In this chapter, I/O operations are studied from three lower levels. The read-only memory (ROM) in the IBM PC and IBM PS/2 contains a set of primitive I/O procedures known as the *Basic Input/Output System* (*BIOS*), which can be invoked from assembly language programs via software interrupts. The I/O subprocedures used in preceding chapters were implemented using I/O procedures of the BIOS level. The interface requirements for a number of BIOS procedures are discussed in this chapter, and several additional I/O subprocedures are presented.

The 8088/8086 assembly language has two instructions that provide for *direct machine-level communication* between a program and I/O devices. BIOS procedures are implemented using these machine-level I/O instructions. This chapter introduces these machine-level I/O instructions and provides some examples that demonstrate their use.

The *Disk Operating System* (*DOS*) also contains a set of I/O procedures that can be invoked from assembly language programs via software interrupts. The interface requirements for a number of DOS I/O procedures are discussed in this chapter, and file I/O using features provided by these DOS I/O procedures is introduced.

9.1 Interrupts

An **interrupt** is an external request for service—a request for the processor to stop executing a procedure and to begin executing a procedure that has been previously designated to service interrupts of the designated type. On completion of the interrupt service procedure, the processor normally is instructed to resume execution of the interrupted procedure. An interrupt can be viewed as an unscheduled procedure invocation.

An interrupt often signals some event (e.g., the completion of an I/O operation, the end of a time interval, or an attempt to divide by zero). It is said to be **maskable** if it can be ignored by the hardware or **nonmaskable** if it must be acknowledged by the hardware. All interrupts can be ignored by software—by writing an interrupt service procedure that simply returns control to the interrupted procedure.

Three hardware mechanisms are required for the handling of interrupts:

1. A mechanism for recognizing interrupt requests
2. A mechanism for stopping the currently executing procedure and initiating a designated procedure to service the external request
3. A mechanism for restoring the state of the processor so that the interrupted procedure can continue execution once the interrupt service procedure has performed its function

In the Intel 8088/8086 microprocessor, each interrupt has associated with it an integer in the range 0–255 that is called the **interrupt type** and is used to identify the procedure that is to be executed to service an interrupt. The first 1024 bytes of memory (addresses 00000–003FF) are reversed for **interrupt vectors**, which are the addresses (segment and offset) of interrupt service procedures. The interrupt vector for the Type 0 interrupt is stored in the 4 bytes at memory locations 00000–00003. The interrupt vector for the Type 1 interrupt is stored in the 4 bytes at memory locations 00004–00007. In general, the interrupt vector for the Type t interrupt is stored in the 4 bytes at memory locations $4t$ through $4t + 3$. Each interrupt vector requires 4 bytes (2 words): The first 2 bytes hold the offset portion of the address of the interrupt service procedure, and the last 2 bytes hold the segment portion.

The Intel 8088/8086 checks for pending interrupts at the end of most instruction executions. When an interrupt is detected, the following steps are performed by the processor:

1. The flags register is pushed onto the stack.
2. The trap flag and the interrupt flag are cleared.
3. The CS-register is pushed onto the stack.
4. The location of the interrupt vector is computed from the interrupt type.
5. The second word of the interrupt vector is loaded into the CS-register.
6. The IP-register is pushed onto the stack.
7. The first word of the interrupt vector is loaded into the IP-register.

Steps 1, 3, and 6 save the return address and the flags register for the interrupted procedure. Any general registers and/or segment registers used by the interrupt service procedure must be saved and restored by the interrupt service procedure itself.

Step 2 ensures that the interrupt service procedure will not execute in the single-step mode and that the interrupt service procedure will not be interrupted. Steps 4, 5, and 7 set the CS:IP register pair to address the beginning of the interrupt service procedure, which transfers control to that procedure. The next instruction to be executed is the first instruction of the interrupt service procedure.

The interrupt service procedure returns control to the interrupted procedure by executing the **IRET instruction**, which has the following general form:

[⟨*label*⟩] `IRET` [⟨*comment*⟩]

Its execution causes the processor to pop the top-of-stack item into the IP-register, pop the new top-of-stack item into the CS-register, and then pop the new top-of-stack item into the flags register. This sequence returns control to the interrupted procedure. Thus, the next instruction to be executed is the instruction that logically follows the instruction that was executed just prior to detection of the interrupt.

Interrupts can be classified as external or internal. An *external interrupt* is generated by some event that occurs outside the microprocessor. An *internal interrupt* is generated by some event that occurs within the microprocessor itself. The Intel 8088/8086 microprocessor provides for both external and internal interrputs.

External Interrupts

An **external interrupt** is generated by a device that is external to the microprocessor in order to request some service by the microprocessor. For example, when a key is pressed on the keyboard, an interrupt is generated to tell the microprocessor that a key has been pressed and that the **key identifier code**, called a **scan code**, is available at the input port. The BIOS keyboard interrupt service procedure in the IBM PC and IBM PS/2 accepts the scan code, converts it to an extended ASCII code, and stores both codes in the next available location in its keyboard input buffer. It can queue up to 15 scan code:character code pairs in its input buffer.

Except for the Type 2 interrupt (discussed shortly), all external interrupts are maskable. To disable external interrupts, clear the IF bit in the flags register by using the CLI instruction. To enable external interrupts, set the IF bit in the flags register by using the STI instruction.

The 8088/8086 microprocessor has two lines that can be used for signaling external interrupts: the **nonmaskable interrupt (NMI) line** and the **interrupt request (INTR) line**. Interrupts arriving on the NMI line cannot be disabled by clearing the interrupt flag (IF bit of the flags register). The 8088- and 8086-based models of the IBM PC and IBM PS/2 use the NMI line to report memory and I/O parity errors. Interrupts arriving on the INTR line are enabled and disabled by the IF bit of the flags register. In the 8088- and 8086-based models of the IBM PC and IBM PS/2, the INTR line is driven by an interrupt controller, the Intel 8259A interrupt controller, which is programmed to provide the interrupt type when the interrupt is acknowledged by the microprocessor. The interrupt controller can report interrupts from eight different devices. In the IBM PC and IBM PS/2, these interrupts are identified with interrupt Types 8 through F hex.

Internal Interrupts

An **internal interrupt** is generated within the microprocessor itself, and it can be generated in any of the following ways:

1. An internal interrupt is generated when execution of a DIV or an IDIV instruction produces a quotient that is too large to fit in the AL-register (byte division) or AX-register (word division). For unsigned integer division, overflow occurs if the divisor is not greater than the high-order half of the double-length dividend. For signed integer division, overflow occurs if the n-bit divisor is not greater in magnitude than the high-order $n + 1$ bits of the dividend, in which $n = 8$ for byte division and $n = 16$ for word division. Division by zero is one case that causes a divide overflow.

2. An internal interrupt is generated following execution of most instructions when the microprocessor is in the single-step mode. The microprocessor is in the single-step mode when the trap flag (i.e., the TF bit in the flags register) is set. The single-step interrupt is discussed in detail in Section 9.2.

3. An internal interrupt is generated by execution of the **INT instruction**, which has the following general form:

   [⟨*label*⟩] `INT` ⟨*int-type*⟩ [⟨*comment*⟩]

   in which ⟨*int-type*⟩ is an integer in the range 0–255 that specifies the specific interrupt being generated. Execution of an INT instruction causes an interrupt of Type ⟨*int-type*⟩ to be generated. The microprocessor immediately acknowledges the interrupt by performing the seven steps described previously.

Internal interrupts have many uses in assembly language programming. The single-step interrupt can be used to trace program execution, one instruction at a time. The DEBUG program uses this single-step feature to implement its trace (T) command. The CodeView program uses this single-step feature to implement its trace into (F8) command. Internal interrupts can also be used to provide a set of system software procedures, such as the **Basic Input/Output System (BIOS)**, for general use in assembly language programs. BIOS is a set of primitive I/O procedures that appear in the read-only memory (ROM) of the IBM PC and IBM PS/2. Each BIOS procedure can be invoked by execution of an INT instruction. Interrupt Types 10 hex through 1C hex are assigned to specific BIOS procedures. Another use of internal interrupts is the simulation of external interrupts. Any external interrupt can be simulated by execution of an INT instruction with the appropriate interrupt type.

Internal interrupts are nonmaskable. That is, the IF bit in the flags register has no effect on internal interrupts.

IBM PC and IBM PS/2 Interrupt Assignments

Interrupts in the Intel 8088 and 8086 microprocessors can be classified as predefined interrupts or 8088/8086 user-defined interrupts. Predefined interrupts are those that were defined by Intel at the time the 8088 or 8086 microprocessor was designed; 8088/8086 user-defined interrupts are those that are available for definition by the user of the 8088 or 8086 microprocessor. In the case of the IBM PC and IBM PS/2, the user is the IBM Corporation. That is, IBM uses the 8088 or 8086 as the microprocessor in certain models of its PC and PS/2, and the 8088/8086 user-defined interrupts are available for definition by IBM in the development of these microcomputers. The 8088/8086 user-defined interrupts can be further classified as system-defined interrupts or IBM PC (IBM PS/2) user-defined interrupts. System-defined interrupts are those assigned to the various system software packages, such as BIOS and DOS. IBM PC (IBM PS/2) user-defined interrupts are those available to assembly language programmers, the users of the IBM PC (IBM PS/2). Table 9.1 summarizes the interrupt assignments in the IBM PC and IBM PS/2.

TABLE 9.1
IBM PC and IBM PS/2 interrupt assignments

Type	Vector Offset	Class	IBM PC	IBM PS/2
0	0000–0003	Predefined	Divide overflow	
1	0004–0007		Single step	
2	0008–000B		Nonmaskable	
3	000C–000F		Breakpoint	
4	0010–0013		Overflow	
5	0014–0017		Print screen	
6	0018–001B		Reserved	
7	001C–001F		Reserved	
8	0020–0023	System-defined hardware	Time of day	
9	0024–0027		Keyboard	
A	0028–002B		Reserved	
B	002C–002F		Communications	
C	0030–0033		Communications	
D	0034–0037		Fixed disk	
E	0038–003B		Floppy disk	
F	003C–003F		Printer	
10	0040–0043	System-defined software	BIOS	BIOS
⋮	⋮			
1F	007C–007F			
20	0080–0083	System-defined software	DOS	DOS
⋮	⋮			
3F	00FC–00FF			
40	0100–0103	System-defined software	Reserved	BIOS
⋮	⋮			
5F	017C–017F			
60	0180–0183	User-defined software	User	User
⋮	⋮			
66	0198–019B			
67	019C–019F	System-defined	Not used	LIM EMS driver
68	01A0–01A3	System-defined software	Not used	BIOS
⋮	⋮			
77	01DC–01DF			
78	01E0–01E3	System-defined	Not used	Not used
⋮	⋮			
7F	01FC–01FF			
80	0200–0203	System-defined software	BASIC	BASIC
⋮	⋮			
F0	03C0–03C3			
F1	03C4–03C7	System-defined	Reserved	Reserved
⋮	⋮			
FF	03FC–03FF			

Predefined Interrupts

Interrupt Types 0–7 are reserved by Intel for **predefined interrupts**, of which five are currently defined and all are nonmaskable.

Type 0 Interrupt—Divide Overflow A Type 0 interrupt is generated whenever a divide operation results in a quotient that is too large to be represented in the number of bits allocated. With unsigned integer division, overflow occurs if the divisor is not greater than the high-order half of the double-length dividend. With signed two's complement integer division, overflow occurs if the n-bit divisor is not greater in magnitude than the high-order $n + 1$ bits of the dividend. DOS provides an interrupt service procedure for the Type 0 interrupt, and it displays the message DIVIDE OVERFLOW and then returns control to DOS rather than to the interrupted procedure.

Type 1 Interrupt—Single Step When the TF bit in the flags register is set, a Type 1 interrupt is generated following most instruction executions. This interrupt allows a program to be executed in the single-step mode, which means that a program can be executed one instruction at a time with program intervention between instruction executions. The program that intervenes is the Type 1 interrupt service procedure. Recall that, when an interrupt occurs, the flags register is saved and the IF and TF bits are cleared in the flags register; this sequence means that the single-step interrupt service procedure will *not* be executing in the single-step mode. However, when the IRET instruction is executed to return control to the interrupted procedure, the flags register is restored, resetting the TF bit in the flags register. Thus, the interrupted procedure executes one instruction before being interrupted again by the Type 1 interrupt. DOS masks the Type 1 interrupt by providing an interrupt service procedure that contains only the IRET instruction. The DEBUG program substitutes its own service procedure for the Type 1 interrupt to implement its trace (T) command. The CodeView program substitutes its own service procedure for the Type 1 interrupt to implement its trace into (F8) command.

Type 2 Interrupt—Nonmaskable Interrupt A Type 2 interrupt is the highest priority interrupt in the Intel 8088/8086. In the IBM PC and IBM PS/2, it is generated whenever a memory or an I/O parity error occurs. BIOS provides an interrupt service procedure for the Type 2 interrupt, and it displays the message PARITY ERROR 1 for memory parity errors and PARITY ERROR 2 for I/O parity errors.

Type 3 Interrupt—Breakpoint A Type 3 interrupt is generated on execution of an INT 3 instruction. The INT instruction is normally a two-byte instruction, one byte for the INT operation code and one byte for the interrupt type. The INT 3 instruction has a special operation code. It is a one-byte instruction that can be used temporarily to replace the first byte of any instruction in the Intel 8088/8086 instruction set for the purpose of setting a breakpoint. DOS masks the Type 3 interrupt by providing an interrupt service procedure that contains only the IRET instruction. The DEBUG program substitutes its own service procedure for the Type 3 interrupt to implement its Go (G) command. When the command G ⟨*offset*⟩ is issued to DEBUG, it replaces the instruction byte at address CS:⟨*offset*⟩ with an INT 3 instruction. Note that CS:⟨*offset*⟩ must be the address of the first byte of an instruction. When the INT 3 instruction is executed and the breakpoint interrupt occurs, the interrupt service procedure (part of DEBUG) restores the instruction byte at address CS:⟨*offset*⟩. DEBUG then produces a current register display and retains control, awaiting another command from the user. The CodeView program substitutes its own service procedure for the Type 3 interrupt to implement its breakpoint (F9) feature. CodeView uses its own Type 3 interrupt service procedure in the implementation of its step over (F10) command.

Type 4 Interrupt—Overflow If the OF bit in the flags register is set, then the execution of an INT 4 instruction generates a Type 4 interrupt. If the OF bit is not set, then this instruction performs no operation. There is an abbreviated form of the INT 4, which has the following general form:

[⟨*label*⟩] `INTO` [⟨*comment*⟩]

DOS masks the Type 4 interrupt by providing an interrupt service procedure that contains only the IRET instruction. The Type 4 interrupt feature can be used in any 8088/8086 assembly language program for detecting and handling arithmetic overflow in signed integer computations. To use this facility, a program must contain the following:

An interrupt service procedure that performs the desired function for the case of arithmetic overflow

The logic to save the Type 4 interrupt vector for DOS

The logic to load the Type 4 interrupt vector with the address of the user's interrupt service procedure

An INTO instruction immediately following each instruction that can cause arithmetic overflow

The logic to restore the Type 4 interrupt vector before returning to DOS

The notion of substituting a user-defined interrupt service procedure for the one provided by DOS or BIOS is demonstrated later in Program Listing 9.1.

Although interrupt Types 5–7 are reserved by Intel for future use, the IBM PC and IBM PS/2 make use of the Type 5 interrupt. BIOS provides a service procedure for the Type 5 interrupt. The procedure performs the same function as does the Print Screen Key (SHIFT–PRTSC key combination on older keyboards) but performs it under program control. That is, execution of an INT 5 instruction causes the cursor position to be saved, the contents of the video screen to be transmitted to the printer, and the cursor position to be restored. On return from the Type 5 interrupt service procedure, memory address 00500 hex contains the status of the print screen operation. A status value of zero indicates that the print operation was successful; a status value of FF hex indicates that an error occurred during the print operation. This status byte contains the value 01 while the print operation is in progress.

System-Defined Interrupts

Interrupt Types 8–F hex are **system-defined hardware interrupts** that arrive at the Intel 8088/8086 via the INTR line under control of the Intel 8259A interrupt controller. Most of these hardware interrupts, the events that cause them, and the procedures that service them are beyond the scope of this book. However, two of them, the timer interrupt and the keyboard interrupt, are discussed briefly. The system-defined hardware interrupts are enabled and disabled by the IF bit of the flags register.

Type 8 Interrupt—System Timer The Intel 8253 programmable timer is a chip in the IBM PC that is programmed to generate an interrupt every 54.9254 milliseconds (approximately 18.2 times per second). BIOS provides an interrupt service procedure for the Type 8 interrupt that keeps a 32-bit count of Type 8 interrupts that DOS uses to keep track of the time of day.

Type 9 Interrupt—Keyboard Interrupt Each time a key is pressed at the keyboard, a Type 9 interrupt is generated. BIOS provides an interrupt service procedure for the Type 9 interrupt that accepts the scan code from the port, converts it to an extended ASCII code, and stores both codes in the next available location in its keyboard input buffer. The service procedure can queue up to 15 scan code:character code pairs.

Interrupt Types 10 hex–1F hex are system-defined software interrupts assigned to BIOS. Many are BIOS entry points. These interrupts are generated by execution of an INT instruction with the appropriate interrupt type. The service procedures for these interrupts provide primitive device-level I/O operations. The BIOS services are discussed in detail in Section 9.3.

Interrupt Types 20 hex–3F hex are system-defined software interrupts assigned to DOS. Many of these are used to provide additional I/O services for user programs. The DOS services are discussed in detail in Section 9.3.

Interrupt Types 40 hex–5F hex are reserved for system use. Interrupt Type 40 hex and interrupt Type 41 hex are used in the IBM PC/XT and the IBM PC/AT versions of BIOS for support of fixed disk operations. Interrupt Types 40 hex–5F hex are all used in the IBM PS/2 versions of BIOS.

Interrupt Types 70 hex–7F hex are also reserved for system use. None of these are currently used in the IBM PC or IBM PC/XT. Interrupt Types 70 hex–77 hex are used by the IBM PC/AT version of BIOS. Interrupt Types 68 hex–77 hex are used by the IBM PS/2 versions of BIOS. Interrupt Type 67 hex is used by the IBM PS/2 in the implementation of expanded memory. In this situation, the Type 67 hex interrupt vector addresses the LIM EMS driver.

Interrupt Types 80 hex–F0 hex are system-defined interrupts assigned to the BASIC interpreter.

IBM PC User-Defined Interrupts

Interrupt Types 60 hex–66 hex are reserved for use in **user-defined software**. Interrupt Types F1 hex–FF hex are classified in the various IBM PC technical reference manuals as "not used." Therefore, these interrupts could be used in user-defined software. However, they could be assigned for other purposes in the future. Interrupt Types 60 hex–66 hex are the only interrupts actually reserved for user-defined software interrupts.

Programming Example—Divide Overflow

Program Listing 9.1 demonstrates the notion of substituting a user-defined interrupt service procedure for one provided by DOS. A Type 0 interrupt is generated whenever execution of a DIV or an IDIV instruction produces a quotient that is too large to fit the AL-register (byte division) or the AX-register (word division). DOS provides an interrupt service procedure for the Type 0 interrupt. The service procedure displays the message DIVIDE OVERFLOW and then returns control to DOS instead of to the interrupted procedure. Suppose a specific application requires that control be returned to the interrupted procedure following the handling of a divide overflow.

The program demonstrates the operation of signed integer division. It prompts the user for a dividend and a divisor, accepts the dividend and divisor from the keyboard, and performs the division. The program repeats this process until the division operation produces no overflow. On execution of a valid division operation, the program displays the dividend, divisor, quotient, and remainder and then returns control to the operating system.

```
            PAGE    80,132
;===========================================================================
;                    PROGRAM LISTING 9.1
;          PROGRAM TO DEMONSTRATE INTEGER DIVISION
;===========================================================================
            .MODEL  SMALL,BASIC
;===========================================================================
                                        ;PROCEDURES TO
            EXTRN   GETDEC:FAR          ;GET 16-BIT DECIMAL INTEGER
            EXTRN   GETDEC32:FAR        ;GET 32-BIT DECIMAL INTEGER
            EXTRN   NEWLINE:FAR         ;DISPLAY NEWLINE CHARACTER
            EXTRN   PUTSTRNG:FAR        ;DISPLAY CHARACTER STRING
            EXTRN   PUTDEC:FAR          ;DISPLAY 16-BIT DECIMAL INT.
            EXTRN   PUTDEC32:FAR        ;DISPLAY 32-BIT DECIMAL INT.
;===========================================================================
; S T A C K   S E G M E N T   D E F I N I T I O N
            .STACK  256
;===========================================================================
; C O N S T A N T   D E F I N I T I O N S
            .CONST
PROMPT1     DB      'ENTER DIVIDEND  '
PROMPT2     DB      'ENTER DIVISOR   '
OUTPUT1     DB      'DIVIDEND   =  '
OUTPUT2     DB      'DIVISOR    =  '
OUTPUT3     DB      'QUOTIENT   =  '
OUTPUT4     DB      'REMAINDER  =  '
DIVO_MSG    DB      'DIVIDE OVERFLOW',0DH,0AH
            DB      'TRY ANOTHER SET OF INPUTS',0DH,0AH
PROMPT_LNG EQU      PROMPT2 - PROMPT1   ;LENGTH OF PROMPT MESSAGES
OUTPUT_LNG EQU      OUTPUT2 - OUTPUT1   ;LENGTH OF OUTPUT MESSAGES
DIVO_LNG    EQU     $ - DIVO_MSG        ;LENGTH OF DIVIDE OVRFLO MSG
;===========================================================================
; V A R I A B L E   D E F I N I T I O N S
            .DATA
DVDEND      DW      ?,?
DVISOR      DW      ?
QUOTIENT    DW      ?
REMAINDR    DW      ?
;===========================================================================
; C O D E   S E G M E N T   D E F I N I T I O N
            .CODE   EX_9_1
;---------------------------------------------------------------------------
;DIVIDE OVERFLOW INTERRUPT SERVICE PROCEDURE
;
DIV_OVFL    PROC    FAR USES CX DI    ;PROCEDURE DIV_OVFL
                                        ;SAVE REGISTERS SPECIFIED
                                        ;      IN USES CLAUSE
            LEA     DI,DIVO_MSG         ;DISPLAY ERROR MESSAGE
            MOV     CX,DIVO_LNG         ;
            CALL    PUTSTRNG            ;
            MOV     BX,1                ;OVRFLO = TRUE
                                        ;RESTORE REGISTERS SPECIFIED
                                        ;      IN USES CLAUSE
            IRET                        ;RETURN FROM INTERRUPT
DIV_OVFL    ENDP                      ;END DIV_OVFL
;---------------------------------------------------------------------------
            .STARTUP                    ;GENERATE STARTUP CODE
;
            MOV     DI,0                ;DI = 0 <OFFSET OF TYPE 0
                                        ;      INTERRUPT VECTOR
                                        ;      WITHIN VECTOR TABLE>
            MOV     ES,DI               ;ES = 0 <ADDRESS OF INTERRUPT
                                        ;      VECTOR TABLE>
            PUSH    ES:[DI]             ;PUSH INT 0 VECTOR ON STACK
            PUSH    ES:[DI+2]           ;    (DIVIDE OVERFLOW)
                                        ;SET INT 0 VECTOR TO ADDRESS
                                        ;PROCEDURE DIV_OVFL
```

```
 68:             MOV    WORD PTR ES:[DI],OFFSET DIV_OVFL
 69:             MOV    WORD PTR ES:[DI+2],SEG DIV_OVFL
 70: ;
 71:             PUSH   DS                      ;SET ES REGISTER TO ADDRESS
 72:             POP    ES                      ;DGROUP
 73: REPEAT1:                                   ;REPEAT
 74:             MOV    BX,0                    ;   OVRFLO = FALSE
 75:             CALL   NEWLINE
 76:             LEA    DI,PROMPT1              ;   PROMPT FOR DIVIDEND
 77:             MOV    CX,PROMPT_LNG
 78:             CALL   PUTSTRNG
 79:             CALL   GETDEC32                ;   GET DIVIDEND
 80:             MOV    DVDEND,AX
 81:             MOV    DVDEND+2,DX
 82:             CALL   NEWLINE
 83:             LEA    DI,PROMPT2              ;   PROMPT FOR DIVISOR
 84:             CALL   PUTSTRNG
 85:             CALL   GETDEC                  ;   GET DIVISOR
 86:             MOV    DVISOR,AX
 87:             CALL   NEWLINE
 88:             MOV    AX,DVDEND
 89:             MOV    DX,DVDEND+2
 90:             IDIV   DVISOR                  ;   DIVIDE DIVIDEND BY DIVISOR
 91:                                            ;   GIVING QUOTIENT & REMAINDER
 92:             CMP    BX,0
 93:             JNE    REPEAT1                 ;UNTIL NOT OVERFLOW
 94:             MOV    QUOTIENT,AX             ;SAVE QUOTIENT
 95:             MOV    REMAINDR,DX             ;SAVE REMAINDER
 96:             LEA    DI,OUTPUT1              ;OUTPUT DIVIDEND
 97:             MOV    CX,OUTPUT_LNG
 98:             CALL   PUTSTRNG
 99:             MOV    AX,DVDEND
100:             MOV    DX,DVDEND+2
101:             CALL   PUTDEC32
102:             CALL   NEWLINE
103:             LEA    DI,OUTPUT2              ;OUTPUT DIVISOR
104:             CALL   PUTSTRNG
105:             MOV    AX,DVISOR
106:             CALL   PUTDEC
107:             CALL   NEWLINE
108:             LEA    DI,OUTPUT3              ;OUTPUT QUOTIENT
109:             CALL   PUTSTRNG
110:             MOV    AX,QUOTIENT
111:             CALL   PUTDEC
112:             CALL   NEWLINE
113:             LEA    DI,OUTPUT4              ;OUTPUT REMAINDER
114:             CALL   PUTSTRNG
115:             MOV    AX,REMAINDR
116:             CALL   PUTDEC
117:             CALL   NEWLINE
118: RETURN:     MOV    DI,0                    ;DI = 0 <OFFSET OF INT 0 VEC.>
119:             MOV    ES,DI                   ;ES = 0 <ADDR OF VECTOR TABLE>
120:             POP    ES:[DI+2]               ;POP INT 0 VECTOR FROM STACK
121:             POP    ES:[DI]                 ;     (DIVIDE OVERFLOW)
122:             .EXIT                          ;RETURN TO DOS
123: ;
124:             END
```

The user-defined interrupt service procedure that handles the divide overflow interrupt appears in lines 42–56 of Program Listing 9.1. This interrupt service procedure is actually defined as a procedure using the PROC and ENDP pseudo-operations (lines 45 and 55). The symbolic name for the service procedure is DIV_OVFL (line 45). The service procedure begins by saving the registers specified in the USES clause (line 45). It then displays a message to the user (lines 48–50). The message displayed is

```
DIVIDE OVERFLOW
TRY ANOTHER SET OF INPUTS
```

and is defined in the program's constant data definitions (lines 27, 28, and 31). The service procedure sets the BX-register to 1 (line 51). The BX-register serves as an overflow flag for the program. The service procedure then restores the registers specified in the USES clause and returns to the interrupted procedure (line 54).

MASM 5.1

With MASM 5.1, the USES clause must not be used in the PROC pseudo-operation that introduces the definition of an interrupt service procedure. MASM 5.1 does not generate the register-restore instructions in response to the IRET instruction as it does in response to the RET instruction.

The program must set the Type 0 interrupt vector to the address of this local interrupt service procedure. The program must also save and restore the Type 0 interrupt vector that exists on entry to the program. In this manner, programs that are executed after this one will have the DOS interrupt service procedure for a divide overflow. The Type 0 interrupt vector appears in memory locations 00000–00003. Locations 00000 and 00001 contain the offset portion of the address of the Type 0 interrupt service procedure, and locations 00002 and 00003 contain the segment portion. The MOV instructions in lines 59 and 62 set the ES:DI register pair to the address of this interrupt vector. Both registers are set to zero, which means that the ES:DI register pair addresses memory location 00000, the location at which the Type 0 interrupt vector begins. The PUSH instructions in lines 64 and 65 save the 4 bytes of the DOS Type 0 interrupt vector on the stack. The MOV instruction in line 68 sets the first word (first 2 bytes) of the Type 0 interrupt vector to the offset portion of the memory address associated with symbolic name DIV_OVFL. The MOV instruction in line 69 sets the second word (last 2 bytes) of the Type 0 interrupt vector to the segment portion of the memory address associated with symbolic name DIV_OVFL. The Type 0 interrupt vector now addresses the interrupt service procedure appearing in lines 42–56.

The REPEAT-UNTIL loop in lines 73–93 accepts the inputs (dividend and divisor) and performs the division. At the beginning of the loop (line 74), the overflow flag (BX-register) is cleared to zero. If the IDIV instruction in line 90 results in a divide overflow, then the Type 0 interrupt is generated and the local interrupt service procedure is executed. The interrupt service procedure displays the diagnostic message and sets the overflow flag (BX-register) to 1. The CMP instruction in line 92 is the loop test that tests the value of the overflow flag (BX-register). If the flag is set, then the jump (line 93) is taken to the top of the loop, which gives the user an opportunity to enter different values for the dividend and divisor. If the flag is not set, then the jump is not taken and the results are displayed (lines 94–117).

Before returning to DOS, the program must restore the DOS Type 0 interrupt vector. The MOV instructions in lines 118 and 119 set the ES:DI register pair to again address the Type 0 interrupt vector. The POP instructions in lines 120 and 121 restore the 4 bytes of the DOS Type 0 interrupt vector.

The following are the results from some sample executions of this program:

```
C>ex_9_1

ENTER DIVIDEND  246810

ENTER DIVISOR   2

DIVIDE OVERFLOW
TRY ANOTHER SET OF INPUTS

ENTER DIVIDEND  246810

ENTER DIVISOR   20

DIVIDEND   =  246810
DIVISOR    =  20
QUOTIENT   =  12340
REMAINDER  =  10

C>ex_9_1

ENTER DIVIDEND  32767

ENTER DIVISOR   0

DIVIDE OVERFLOW
TRY ANOTHER SET OF INPUTS

ENTER DIVIDEND  32767

ENTER DIVISOR   -17

DIVIDEND   =  32767
DIVISOR    =  -17
QUOTIENT   =  -1927
REMAINDER  =  8
```

In general, to set the ES:DI register pair to the address of the Type *t* interrupt vector, set the ES-register to zero (the origin of the interrupt vector table) and the DI-register to 4*t* (the offset within the interrupt vector table of the Type *t* interrupt vector). Note that the DS-register could be used for the segment register, and either the SI-register or the BX-register could be used for the index register.

The program of Program Listing 9.1 executes as shown in the sample executions when it is executed on an 8088- or 8086-based machine. However, when this program is executed on an 80286- or 80386-based machine, the program goes into an endless loop on a divide overflow. This difference in execution is caused by a difference in the way the 80286 and 80386 microprocessors handle the Type 0 interrupt from the way it is handled in the 8088/8086 microprocessor. Execution of an IRET instruction in the Type 0 interrupt service procedure causes the 8088/8086 microprocessor to return control to the instruction that immediately follows the DIV or IDIV instruction that caused the divide overflow. Execution of such an IRET instruction causes the 80286 or 80386 microprocessor to return control to the divide instruction itself. That is, the 80286 and 80386 retry the divide instruction based on the assumption that the interrupt service procedure has done something to modify the operands of the divide operation. Since the interrupt service procedure in lines 45–55 of Program Listing 9.1 does nothing to modify the operands of the divide operation, the retry of the divide instruction causes another divide overflow; consequently, the program goes into an endless loop retrying a divide operation that consistently results in a divide overflow.

Consider the following alternative to the interrupt service procedure for the program of Program Listing 9.1:

```
42: ;
43: ;DIVIDE OVERFLOW INTERRUPT SERVICE PROCEDURE
44: ;
45: DIV_OVFL    PROC    FAR                  ;PROCEDURE DIV_OVFL
46:             POP     BX                      ;SET RETURN ADDRESS TO
47:             LEA     BX,INT_RET              ;    LOCATION INT_RET
48:             PUSH    BX                      ;
49:             PUSH    CX                      ;SAVE REGISTERS
50:             PUSH    DI                      ;
51:             LEA     DI,DIVO_MSG             ;DISPLAY ERROR MESSAGE
52:             MOV     CX,DIVO_LNG             ;
53:             CALL    PUTSTRNG                ;
54:             MOV     BX,1                    ;OVRFLO = TRUE
55:             POP     DI                      ;RESTORE REGISTERS
56:             POP     CX                      ;
57:             IRET                            ;RETURN FROM INTERRUPT
58: DIV_OVFL    ENDP                         ;END DIV_OVFL
59: ;
```

This interrupt service procedure forces the return address to be the address of the instruction with label INT_RET. This label must be added to the instruction that immediately follows the divide instruction. Note that the USES clause is omitted from the PROC pseudo-operation to ensure that the return address is at the top of the stack upon entry to the subprocedure. The POP instruction in line 46 pops the offset portion of the return address from the top of the stack. In the 8088/8086 microprocessor, this would be the offset of the instruction that immediately follows the divide instruction. In the 80286 or 80386 microprocessor, this would be the offset of the divide instruction itself. The LEA instruction in line 47 loads the BX-register with the offset of the instruction labeled INT_RET, the instruction that immediately follows the divide instruction. The BX-register can be used for this operation because it does not need to be saved and restored. The BX-register is used here as a flag from the interrupt service procedure to the main procedure. The PUSH instruction in line 48 pushes the modified return address offset onto the stack. The PUSH instructions in lines 49 and 50 and the POP instructions in lines 55 and 56 save and restore the registers for the interrupted procedure. These instructions are needed because of the elimination of the USES clause from the PROC pseudo-operation. In the previous version, the USES clause caused the assembler to generate these four instructions automatically. The remainder of the interrupt service procedure is the same as in the previous version. The version of Program Listing 9.1 that contains this alternate interrupt service procedure is included on the diskette that accompanies this book under the name EX_9_1A.ASM.

9.2 Single-Step Mode

The Intel 8088/8086 microprocessor is in the single-step mode when the TF bit of the flags register is set to 1. In the single-step mode, the microprocessor generates a Type 1 interrupt following execution of most instructions. A Type 1 interrupt is *not* generated following execution of an instruction that modifies a segment register (e.g., MOV ES,AX), a prefix instruction (e.g., REP), or a WAIT instruction.

There are no instructions in the 8088/8086 assembly language that directly manipulate the TF bit of the flags register. To set the TF bit, the following sequence of instructions can be used:

```
PUSHF
POP    AX
OR     AX,0100H
PUSH   AX
POPF
NOP
```

The first single-step interrupt thus occurs after execution of the instruction that immediately follows the NOP instruction. When the trap flag is set with a POPF instruction, two instructions are executed before the first single-step interrupt is generated.

Recall that, when an interrupt is detected by the microprocessor, the IF and TF bits of the flags register are cleared before transferring control to the interrupt service procedure; thus, the procedure that services the single-step interrupt will *not* be executing in the single-step mode. The interrupt service procedure should return to the interrupted procedure by executing an IRET instruction, which causes the flags register to be restored to its value at the point at which the interrupt occurred. This sequence resets the TF bit in the flags register. When the trap flag is set with an IRET instruction, one instruction is executed before the next single-step interrupt is generated.

To clear the TF bit of the flags register, the following sequence of instructions can be used:

```
PUSHF
POP    AX
AND    AX,0FEFFH
PUSH   AX
POPF
```

The last single-step interrupt occurs immediately after execution of the POPF instruction. When the trap flag is cleared with a POPF instruction, one more single-step interrupt occurs.

The DEBUG utility program uses the single-step mode to implement its trace (T) command. The interrupt service procedure for the single-step interrupt is an entry point within the DEBUG program. The CodeView utility program uses the single-step mode to implement its Trace Into (F8) command. The interrupt service procedure for the single-step interrupt is an entry point within the CodeView program. The single-step interrupt can also be used to perform some function after each instruction of a program. Program Listing 9.2 demonstrates such an application of the single-step mode.

Programming Example—Demonstrates Shift and Rotate Instructions

Program Listing 6.1 was designed to demonstrate shift and rotate instructions in the 8088/8086 assembly language. It loads a value into the AX-register and then performs a series of shifts and rotates. Following each shift and rotate instruction, a call is made to the PUTBIN procedure to display the resulting AX-register in binary form.

The program of Program Listing 9.2 performs the same function as that of Program Listing 6.1; however, Program Listing 9.2 uses a single-step interrupt service

```
            PAGE    80,132
;=====================================================================
;                   PROGRAM LISTING 9.2
;
;PROGRAM TO DEMONSTRATE SHIFT AND ROTATE INSTRUCTIONS
;=====================================================================
            .MODEL  SMALL,BASIC
;=====================================================================
                                        ;PROCEDURES TO
            EXTRN   PUTBIN:FAR          ;DISPLAYT BINARY INTEGER
            EXTRN   PUTDEC:FAR          ;DISPLAY DECIMAL INTEGER
            EXTRN   NEWLINE:FAR         ;DISPLAY NEWLINE CHARACTER
;=====================================================================
; S T A C K   S E G M E N T   D E F I N I T I O N
;
            .STACK  256
;=====================================================================
; C O D E   S E G M E N T   D E F I N I T I O N
;
            .CODE   EX_9_2
            .STARTUP                    ;GENERATE STARTUP CODE
            MOV     DI,4                ;DI = 4 <OFFSET OF TYPE 1
                                        ;        INTERRUPT VECTOR
                                        ;        WITHIN VECTOR TABLE>
            MOV     AX,0                ;ES = 0 <ADDRESS OF INTERRUPT
            MOV     ES,AX               ;        VECTOR TABLE>
            PUSH    ES:[DI]             ;PUSH INT 1 VECTOR ON STACK
            PUSH    ES:[DI+2]           ;     (SINGLE STEP)
                                        ;SET INT 1 VECTOR TO ADDRESS
                                        ;PROCEDURE S_STEP
            MOV     WORD PTR ES:[DI],OFFSET S_STEP
            MOV     WORD PTR ES:[DI+2],SEG S_STEP
            PUSHF                       ;SET TF BIT IN FLAGS REGISTER
            POP     AX
            OR      AX,0100H
            PUSH    AX
            POPF
            NOP
            MOV     AX,0AAABH           ;LOAD AX WITH
                                        ;
                                        ;1010101010101011
                                        ;
            ROL     AX,1                ;LEFT ROTATE AX 1 GIVING
                                        ;
                                        ;0101010101010111
                                        ;
            MOV     CL,3                ;MOVE SHIFT COUNT TO CL
            ROR     AX,CL               ;RIGHT ROTATE AX 3 GIVING
                                        ;
                                        ;1110101010101010
                                        ;
            SAR     AX,1                ;ARITH SHIFT RIGHT 1 GIVING
                                        ;
                                        ;1111010101010101
                                        ;
            SAL     AX,CL               ;ARITH SHIFT LEFT 3 GIVING
                                        ;
                                        ;1010101010101000
                                        ;
;
            MOV     CL,2                ;MOVE SHIFT COUNT TO CL
            SHR     AX,CL               ;LOG. SHIFT RIGHT 2 GIVING
                                        ;
                                        ;0010101010101010
                                        ;
            MOV     CL,3                ;MOVE SHIFT COUNT TO CL
            SHL     AX,CL               ;LOG.SHIFT LEFT 3 GIVING
```

```
 68:                                      ;
 69:                                      ;0101010101010000
 70:                                      ;
 71:                                      ;AND CARRY FLAG = 1
 72:            RCL     AX,1              ;LEFT ROTATE AX 1 THROUGH
 73:                                      ;CARRY GIVING
 74:                                      ;
 75:                                      ;1010101010100001
 76:                                      ;
 77:                                      ;AND CARRY FLAG = 0
 78:            MOV     CL,2
 79:            RCR     AX,CL             ;RIGHT ROTATE AX 2 THROUGH
 80:                                      ;CARRY GIVING
 81:                                      ;
 82:                                      ;1010101010101000
 83:                                      ;
 84:            MOV     CL,4              ;MOVE SHIFT COUNT TO CL
 85:            SAR     AL,CL             ;ARITH RIGHT SHIFT AL 4 GIVING
 86:                                      ;
 87:                                      ;1010101011111010
 88:                                      ;
 89:            ROL     AL,CL             ;LEFT ROTATE AL 4 GIVING
 90:                                      ;
 91:                                      ;1010101010101111
 92:                                      ;
 93:            PUSHF                     ;CLEAR TF BIT IN FLAGS REG.
 94:            POP     AX
 95:            AND     AX,0FEFFH
 96:            PUSH    AX
 97:            POPF
 98:            POP     ES:[DI+2]         ;POP INT 1 VECTOR FROM STACK
 99:            POP     ES:[DI]           ;        (SINGLE STEP)
100:            .EXIT                     ;RETURN TO DOS
101: ;
102: ;------------------------------------------------------------------
103: ; S I N G L E - S T E P   I N T E R R U P T   S E R V I C E
104: ;
105: S_STEP     PROC    FAR USES AX BX  ;PROCEDURE S_STEP
106:                                      ;SAVE REGISTERS SPECIFIED
107:                                      ;     IN USES CLAUSE
108:            STI                       ;ENABLE INTERRUPTS
109:            MOV     BL,1              ;PUTBIN CODE = 1
110:            CALL    PUTBIN            ;DISPLAY AX-REG. IN BINARY
111:            MOV     BH,1              ;PUTDEC CODE = RIGHT JUSTIFY
112:            RCL     AX,1              ;DISPLAY CARRY FLAG
113:            AND     AX,1
114:            CALL    PUTDEC
115:            CALL    NEWLINE           ;DISPLAY NEWLINE CHARACTER
116:                                      ;RESTORE REGISTERS SPECIFIED
117:                                      ;        IN USES CLAUSE
118:            IRET                      ;RETURN TO INTERRUPTED PROC
119: S_STEP     ENDP                    ;END S_STEP
120: ;------------------------------------------------------------------
121:*           END
```

procedure to display the result of each shift operation. In addition to displaying the AX-register value, the single-step interrupt service procedure also displays the value of the carry flag. This discussion concentrates on the changes made to Program Listing 6.1 that produce Program Listing 9.2.

The calls to the PUTBIN procedure and the NEWLINE procedure in Program Listing 6.1 have all been removed from Program Listing 9.2. The function performed by these calls is now achieved with a single-step interrupt service procedure (lines 102–120). This procedure begins by saving the two registers that are specified in the USES clause, which is vital since the interrupted procedure has no method of saving them. The STI instruction in line 108 enables interrupts. Therefore, the remainder of the interrupt service procedure will execute with interrupts enabled—which is a good idea, especially in long interrupt service procedures to avoid the loss of important interrupts, such as the timer interrupt. The PUTBIN procedure is invoked (lines 109 and 110) to display the AX-register value in binary form. The RCL instruction in line 112 moves the CF bit of the flags register to bit 0 of the AX-register. The AND instruction in line 113 clears bits 1–15 of the AX-register. The PUTDEC procedure is invoked (lines 111 and 114) to display the CF bit (now in bit 0 of the AX-register) right-justified in a six-character field. The call to the NEWLINE procedure (line 115) moves the cursor to the beginning of the next line of the display. The service procedure ends by restoring the registers specified in the USES clause and returning control to the interrupted procedure (line 118). The IRET instruction causes the flags register to be restored prior to returning control to the interrupted procedure. Restoring the flags register sets the trap flag again. The interrupted procedure will have its next instruction executed, and then another single-step interrupt will occur.

The Type 1 interrupt vector is stored in locations 00004–00007 of memory. The offset portion of the address of the interrupt service procedure is stored in locations 00004 and 00005, and the segment portion of the address is stored in locations 00006 and 00007. The instructions in lines 22, 25, and 26 set the ES:DI register pair to address memory location 00004, the start of the single-step interrupt vector. The instructions in lines 27 and 28 save the current Type 1 interrupt vector on the stack. The instruction in line 31 sets the first word of the Type 1 interrupt vector (locations 00004 and 00005) to the offset portion of the address of the local interrupt service procedure. The instruction in line 32 sets the second word of the Type 1 interrupt (locations 00006 and 00007) to the segment portion of the address of the local interrupt service procedure. At this point, the Type 1 interrupt vector addresses the interrupt service procedure defined in lines 102–120.

The instructions in lines 33–38 set the trap flag (bit 8) of the flags register. The PUSHF instruction in line 33 pushes a copy of the flags register onto the stack. The POP instruction in line 34 pops this copy of the flags into the AX-register. The OR instruction in line 35 sets bit 8 in this copy of the flags. Bit 8 corresponds to the TF bit in the flags register. The PUSH instruction in line 36 pushes this modified copy of the flags onto the stack, and the POPF instruction in line 37 pops it into the flags register. The TF bit in the flags register is now set. The other bits of the flags register are the same as they were before execution of the instruction in line 33. The NOP instruction in line 38 ensures that the first single-step interrupt will occur following the MOV instruction in line 39.

Since the interrupt service procedure returns to the interrupted procedure via an IRET instruction, a single-step interrupt will occur after each subsequent instruction in the main procedure until the trap flag is cleared by the procedure. The instructions in lines 93–97 clear the TF bit of the flags register. The instructions in lines 93 and 94 copy the flags register value into the AX-register. The AND instruction in line 95 clears the TF bit (bit 8) in this copy of the flags register value. It preserves all of the other bits in this value. The instructions in lines 96 and 97 copy this modified value in the AX-register to the flags register. The TF bit in the flags register is now zero. The other bits of the flags register are the same as they were before execution of the instruction in line 93. The last single-step interrupt occurs after execution of the POPF instruction in line 97.

The two POP instructions in lines 98 and 99 restore the Type 1 interrupt vector to the value that it was prior to program execution. That is, the Type 1 interrupt vector is restored by the value that was placed on the stack by the two PUSH instructions in lines 27 and 28. Note that, when the instruction in line 98 is reached, the ES:DI register pair still contains the address of the Type 1 interrupt vector. This value was set by the MOV instructions in lines 22–26, and there are no instructions in between that modify either the ES- or the DI-register.

The output of this program appears as follows:

```
1010101010101011 0
0101010101010111 1
0101010101010111 1
1110101010101010 1
1111010101010101 0
1010101010101000 1
1010101010101000 1
0010101010101010 0
0010101010101010 0
0101010101010000 1
1010101010100001 0
1010101010100001 0
1010101010101000 0
1010101010101000 0
1010101011111010 1
1010101010101111 1
1010101010101111 1
1111001110000111 1
1111001010000111 0
1111001010000111 0
1111001010000111 1
```

The first line of output shows the value in the AX-register and the value of the CF bit of the flags register just after execution of the MOV instruction in line 39. The AX-register value is AAAB hex, and the CF bit of the flags register is zero. The sixteenth line of output shows the value in the AX-register and the value of the CF bit of the flags register just after execution of the ROL instruction in line 89. The AX-register value is AAAF hex, and the CF bit of the flags register is 1. The seventeenth line of output shows these values just after execution of the PUSHF instruction in line 93. Its output is identical to the preceding output line. A PUSHF instruction modifies neither the AX-register nor the flags register. The eighteenth line of output shows the value in the AX-register and the value of the CF bit of the flags register just after execution of the POP instruction in line 94. The AX-register value, F387 hex, is a copy of the flags register value. Note that bit 8 (corresponding to the TF bit) is set to 1. The CF bit of the flags register is still 1 since the POP instruction has no effect on the flags register. The nineteenth line of output shows the AX-register value, F287 hex, and the value of the carry flag, 0, just after execution of the AND instruction in line 95. Note that bit 8 of the AX-register has been cleared to zero and that the CF bit of the flags register has been cleared to zero by execution of the AND instruction. The twentieth line of output reflects the values of the AX-register and the carry flag just after execution of the PUSH instruction in line 96. Its output is identical to the preceding output line. A PUSH instruction modifies neither the AX-register nor the flags register. The last line of output reflects the values of the AX-register and the carry flag just after execution of the POPF instruction in line 97. The AX-register value was not changed by execution of this instruction, but the CF bit of the flags register was restored to its value at the time of execution of the PUSHF instruction in line 93. The TF bit in the flags register is now zero. Therefore, no further single-step interrupts occur, and no further output is produced by the program.

This program does not produce the exact same results when executed on an 80286- or 80386-based machine—it produces an additional line of output. This extra line of output is caused by the fact that the first single-step interrupt occurs after the NOP instruction in line 38 rather than after the MOV instruction in line 39. For an 8088/8086 microprocessor, when the trap flag is set with a POPF instruction, two instructions are executed before the first single-step interrupt is generated. For an 80286 or 80386 microprocessor, when the trap flag is set with a POPF instruction, only one instruction is executed before the first single-step interrupt is generated.

9.3 Input/Output

Three levels at which I/O operations occur are considered here:

1. The first level is that provided by the BIOS subprocedures. At this level, BIOS controls the actual communications between the microprocessor and the I/O devices. The BIOS routines are accessible from 8088/8086 assembly language programs via software interrupts. Three example procedures are given to demonstrate the use of BIOS procedures in implementing more general I/O operations.
2. The second level is that provided by the DOS subprocedures. The DOS routines are also accessible from 8088/8086 assembly language programs via software interrupts. Some simple examples of DOS I/O services are given in this section. Section 9.4, on file I/O operations, provides several example programs that use DOS I/O procedures.
3. The third level, the most primitive level, is that provided by the machine language. At this level, the assembly language program itself controls the communication between the microprocessor and the I/O devices. Some simple examples of direct device communication are given.

BIOS Service Procedures

BIOS provides a set of subprocedures that removes the burden of direct device communication from the assembly language programmer. These procedures are accessible from assembly language programs via software interrupt Types 10 hex–1C hex. Table 9.2 summarizes these services, and several are described in the following subsections.

TABLE 9.2
BIOS software interrupt services

Interrupt Type (Hex)	Service
10	Video I/O
11	Equipment check
12	Memory size
13	Diskette I/O
14	Communications I/O
15	Cassette I/O
16	Keyboard I/O
17	Printer I/O
18	ROM BASIC
19	Power-on reset
1A	Time of day
1B	Control break
1C	Timer (user supplied)

Video I/O (Interrupt 10H)

Video I/O services are provided through software interrupt Type 10 hex. The BIOS subprocedure that services interrupt Type 10 hex uses the value in the AH-register as a subfunction code. It is via the AH-register that the caller requests the specific video operation to be performed. Depending on the subfunction code in the AH-register, other registers are used for input to and output from the BIOS service procedure. Table 9.3 summarizes the subfunction codes recognized by the BIOS interrupt Type 10 hex service procedure and the other registers used for procedure input and output.

TABLE 9.3 BIOS interrupt Type 10H subfunctions

AH	Function	Procedure Inputs	Procedure Outputs
0	Set video mode	AL = video mode 0—40 × 25 text 1—40 × 25 text 2—80 × 25 text 3—80 × 25 text 4—320 × 200 graphics 4-color 5—320 × 200 graphics 4-color 6—640 × 200 graphics 2-color 7—80 × 25 text PC monochrome mode 8, 9, A—PCjr modes D—320 × 200 graphics 16-color E—640 × 200 graphics 16-color F—640 × 350 graphics monochrome 10—640 × 350 graphics 16-color 11—640 × 480 graphics 2-color 12—640 × 480 graphics 16-color 13—320 × 200 graphics 256-color	None
1	Set cursor type	CH = start line number (0–14) CL = end line number (0–14)	None
2	Set cursor position	BH = page number (0–7) (0–3 for CGA mode 3) DH = row of cursor (0–24) DL = column of cursor (0–79) (0–39 for modes 0 and 1)	None
3	Read cursor type and position	BH = page number (0–7)	CH = start line number CL = end line number DH = row of cursor DL = column of cursor

Table 9.3 Continued

AH	Function	Procedure Inputs	Procedure Outputs
4	Read light pen position	None	AH = status code 0—disabled 1—enabled BX = pixel column CH = raster line DH = row of light pen DL = column of light pen
5	Select active display page	AL = new page number (0–7)	None
6	Scroll up of active page	AL = number of lines BH = display attribute for blank lines CH = upper-left row of scroll window CL = upper-left column of scroll window DH = lower-right row of scroll window DL = lower-right column of scroll window	None
7	Scroll down of active page	AL = number of lines BH = display attribute for blank lines CH = upper-left row of scroll window CL = upper-left column of scroll window DH = lower-right row of scroll window DL = lower-right column of scroll window	None
8	Read attribute/character at current cursor position	BH = page number (0–7)	AL = ASCII character AH = attribute of character in AL
9	Write attribute/character beginning at current cursor position	BH = page number (0–7) BL = attribute of character AL = character to write CX = count of times to write character	None
10	Write character beginning at current cursor position	BH = page number (0–7) BL = color (graphics modes only) AL = character to write CX = count of times to write character	None
11	Set border color for text modes	BH = 0 BL = color code	None
	Set color palette for graphics mode	BH = 1 BL = 0 green/red/yellow = 1 cyan/magenta/white	None

Table 9.3 Continued

AH	Function	Procedure Inputs	Procedure Outputs
12	Plot graphics pixel	AL = color BH = graphics page number DX = row CX = column	None
13	Read graphics pixel	BH = graphics page number DX = row CX = column	AL = color
14	Write character and advance cursor	AL = character to write BH = page number (0–7) BL = color (graphics modes only)	None
15	Read current video state	None	AL = video mode (see AH = 0) AH = screen width BH = active page number

Programming Example—PUTBIN

Program Listing 9.3 illustrates the use of BIOS interrupt Type 10 hex with the PUTBIN procedure from the author's I/O subprocedure library. In Chapters 5 and 6, implementations of algorithms to display 8- or 16-bit integers in binary were presented (see Program Listings 5.1 and 5.3 and Program Listing 6.3). Program Listing 9.3 implements the same algorithm as does the procedure in Program Listing 6.3. The main difference between the two implementations is that Program Listing 6.3 uses the PUTDEC procedure to display the individual bits and Program Listing 9.3 uses BIOS interrupt Type 10 hex to display the individual bits. This discussion concentrates on the I/O procedure differences in Program Listing 9.3.

The STI instruction in line 26 ensures that external interrupts are enabled. This step is simply a precautionary measure performed by all of the author's I/O subprocedures in the library. External interrupts are always enabled when a user program is placed into execution under DOS control. Unless the user program disables external interrupts for some reason, the user program executes with external interrupts enabled. Thus, in case an I/O subprocedure is called when external interrupts are disabled, each I/O procedure performs an STI instruction.

The MOV instruction in line 37 places the subfunction code for BIOS interrupt Type 10 hex in the AH-register. A subfunction code of 15 causes BIOS to return the current status of the video display (Table 9.3). The INT instruction in line 38 calls the BIOS interrupt Type 10 hex service procedure into execution. This call is made to find the current active display page number, which BIOS returns in the BH-register. If the computer on which the program is executing has a monochrome display, then this call is unnecessary as the monochrome display has only one page. However, if the computer on which the program is executing has a color display, then this step is vital as the color display has four or eight pages, numbered 0–3 or 0–7. The active display page is the one that currently appears on the video screen. It is selected by subfunction 5 of BIOS interrupt Type 10 hex (Table 9.3). The active display page number is read into the BH-register by subfunction 15 of BIOS interrupt Type 10 hex. The PUTBIN procedure reads the current active display page number so that it can

```
 1: ;=====================================================================
 2: ;                      PROGRAM LISTING 9.3
 3: ;
 4: ; PROCEDURE TO DISPLAY AN 8 OR 16-BIT VALUE IN BINARY FORM
 5: ;
 6: ; INPUT:   AL-REG  8-BIT  VALUE TO BE DISPLAYED
 7: ;          BL=0     CODE FOR  8-BIT DISPLAY
 8: ;              OR
 9: ;          AX-REG  16-BIT VALUE TO BE DISPLAYED
10: ;          BL<>0   CODE FOR 16-BIT DISPLAY
11: ;
12: ; OUTPUT:  INPUT VALUE DISPLAYED IN BINARY FORM ON THE
13: ;          SCREEN BEGINNING AT CURRENT CURSOR POSITION
14: ;=====================================================================
15:             .MODEL  SMALL,BASIC
16: ;=====================================================================
17: ; C O D E   S E G M E N T   D E F I N I T I O N
18: ;
19:             .CODE   EX_9_3
20: PUTBIN      PROC    FAR PUBLIC USES AX BX CX DX BP
21:                                         ;PROCEDURE PUTBIN (NUMBER,CODE)
22:                                            ;SAVE REGISTERS SPECIFIED
23:                                            ;      IN USES CLAUSE
24:             PUSHF                          ;SAVE FLAGS
25: ;
26:             STI                            ;ENABLE INTERRUPTS
27:             CMP     BL,0                   ;IF    CODE = BYTE (BL=0)
28:             JNZ     ELSE1
29:             MOV     AH,AL                  ;THEN LEFT JUSTIFY 8-BIT NUMBER
30:                                            ;      IN 16-BIT AX-REGISTER
31:             MOV     CX,8                   ;      BIT_COUNT = 8
32:             JMP     ENDIF1
33: ELSE1:                                     ;ELSE
34:             MOV     CX,16                  ;      BIT_COUNT = 16
35: ENDIF1:                                    ;ENDIF
36:             MOV     DX,AX                  ;SAVE NUMBER IN DX
37:             MOV     AH,15                  ;READ ACTIVE DISPLAY PAGE
38:             INT     10H                    ;NUMBER INTO BH-REGISTER
39: PRINT:                                     ;REPEAT
40:             TEST    DX,8000H               ;   IF   BIT 15 OF NUMBER = 0
41:             JNZ     ONE
42:             MOV     AH,14                  ;   THEN DISPLAY 0
43:             MOV     AL,'0'
44:             INT     10H
45:             JMP     ROTATE
46: ONE:        MOV     AH,14                  ;   ELSE
47:             MOV     AL,'1'                 ;        DISPLAY 1
48:             INT     10H                    ;   ENDIF
49: ROTATE:     ROL     DX,1                   ;   ROTATE NUMBER LEFT 1 BIT
50:                                            ;   TO GET NEXT BIT IN POS. 15
51:             LOOP    PRINT                  ;   DECREMENT BIT_COUNT
52:                                            ;UNTIL BIT_COUNT = 0
53:             POPF                           ;RESTORE FLAGS
54:                                            ;RESTORE REGISTERS SPECIFIED
55:                                            ;        IN USES CLAUSE
56:             RET                            ;RETURN
57: PUTBIN      ENDP                        ;END PUTBIN
58:             END
```

display the binary number on the active display page. This process makes **PUTBIN** compatible with both the monochrome display and the color display.

The loop in lines 39–52 displays the 8- or 16-bit binary number based on the loop count determined by the double-alternative decision structure in lines 27–35. The loop body contains a double-alternative decision structure (lines 40–48) that determines whether the next bit of the number is 0 or 1 and displays the appropriate ASCII character. The TEST instruction in line 40 tests bit 15 of the number, and the JNZ instruction in line 41 makes the decision based on this test. If the bit is 0, then the instructions in lines 42–44 are executed; if the bit is 1, then the instructions in lines 46–48 are executed. The rotate instruction in line 49 ensures that the next most significant digit of the number is in bit position 15 for the next iteration of the loop.

The instructions in lines 42–44 display a 0 at the current cursor position on the active display page and advance the cursor to the next character position. The MOV instruction in line 42 places the subfunction code for BIOS interrupt Type 10 hex in the AH-register. A subfunction code of 14 causes BIOS to display the ASCII character in the AL-register on the screen at the current cursor position and then to advance the cursor to the next character position. The MOV instruction in line 43 loads the AL-register with the ASCII representation for the digit 0, the character to be displayed. The BH-register already contains the active display page number. It was set as a result of the BIOS call in line 38, and there are no instructions in the loop body that will change the value in the BH-register. The INT instruction in line 44 calls the BIOS interrupt Type 10 hex service procedure into execution.

The instructions in lines 46–48 display a 1 at the current cursor position on the active display page and advance the cursor to the next character position. The MOV instruction in line 46 places the subfunction code for BIOS interrupt Type 10 hex in the AH-register. The MOV instruction in line 47 loads the AL-register with the ASCII representation for the digit 1, the character to be displayed. The BH-register already contains the active display page number. The INT instruction in line 48 calls the BIOS interrupt Type 10 hex service procedure into execution.

Equipment Check (Interrupt 11H)

By using software interrupt Type 11 hex, BIOS provides a method for an assembly language program to determine the kinds and capacities of resources that are attached to the computer. If programs are being written for a specific personal computer configuration, then this service is of no value. However, if programs are being written to execute on a variety of computer configurations, then this BIOS service allows the program to determine its environment. The BIOS procedure that services the Type 11 hex interrupt returns a value in the AX-register that summarizes the equipment that is available to the computer. Table 9.4 shows the interpretation for each bit in the AX-register value that is returned by the interrupt Type 11 hex service procedure.

Memory Size (Interrupt 12H)

By using software interrupt Type 12 hex, BIOS provides a method for an assembly language program to determine the amount of RAM memory in the computer. This quantity includes both memory on the system board and the add-on memory accessible through I/O ports. The BIOS procedure that services the Type 12 hex interrupt returns in the AX-register a count of the number of 1K RAM memory blocks. For a computer with 256K of RAM, the value returned in the AX-register is 0100 hexadecimal (256 decimal).

Keyboard Input (Interrupt 16H)

Each time a key is pressed at the keyboard, a Type 9 interrupt is generated. The BIOS procedure that services the Type 9 interrupt accepts the scan code from the keyboard

TABLE 9.4 Interpretation of AX-register value returned by Type 11H interrupt service procedure

15	14	13	12	11	10	9	8	7	6	5	4	3	2	1	0

Bit	Meaning
0	0 ⇒ PC has no diskette drives 1 ⇒ PC has at least one diskette drive
1	0 ⇒ no math coprocessor present 1 ⇒ math coprocessor present
3–2	Amount of read/write memory on system board (PC and PC/XT only) 00 ⇒ 16K 01 ⇒ 32K 10 ⇒ 48K 11 ⇒ 64K
2	1 ⇒ pointing device installed (PS/2 only)
5–4	Initial video mode 00 ⇒ not used 01 ⇒ 40 × 25 color 10 ⇒ 80 × 25 color 11 ⇒ monochrome
7–6	Number of diskette drives (if bit 0 = 1) 00 ⇒ 1 01 ⇒ 2 10 ⇒ 3 11 ⇒ 4
8	Not used
11–9	Number of RS-232 communication cards attached
12	0 ⇒ no device attached to game I/O port 1 ⇒ device attached to game I/O port
13	0 ⇒ no serial printer attached 1 ⇒ serial printer attached
15–14	Number of printers attached

input port, converts it to an extended ASCII code, and stores both codes in the next available location in its keyboard input buffer. The Type 9 interrupt service procedure can queue up to 15 scan code:character code pairs in its input buffer. If a Type 9 interrupt occurs and the keyboard input buffer is full, then the interrupt service procedure sends a tone to the speaker on the computer, and the input scan code is discarded. The beep indicates to the user that the keyboard input was not accepted. Because of the BIOS Type 9 interrupt service procedure, assembly language programs do not have to interface directly with the keyboard. BIOS creates a different keyboard interface for assembly language programs.

Keyboard input services are provided through software interrupt Type 16 hex. The BIOS subprocedure that services interrupt Type 16 hex uses the value in the AH-register as a subfunction code. It is via the AH-register that the caller requests the specific keyboard operation to be performed. Depending on the subfunction code in the AH-register, certain registers are used for output from the BIOS service procedure. Table 9.5 summarizes the subfunction codes recognized by the BIOS interrupt Type 16 hex service procedure and the registers used for procedure output.

TABLE 9.5
BIOS interrupt Type 16H subfunctions

AH	Function	Procedure Outputs
0, 10 hex	Read character	AH-register contains scan code of next keyboard character AL-register contains extended ASCII code of next keyboard character Character is deleted from keyboard input buffer
1, 11 hex	Read buffer status	ZF = 0 implies input buffer is not empty AH-register contains scan code of next keyboard character AL-register contains extended ASCII code of next keyboard character Character remains in keyboard input buffer ZF = 1 implies input buffer is empty
2, 12 hex	Read keyboard status	AL-register contains keyboard status byte 7 6 5 4 3 2 1 0

Bit	*Meaning*
7	Status of INSERT $0 \Rightarrow$ INSERT mode off $1 \Rightarrow$ INSERT mode on
6	Status of CAPS LOCK $0 \Rightarrow$ CAPS LOCK off $1 \Rightarrow$ CAPS LOCK on
5	Status of NUM LOCK $0 \Rightarrow$ NUM LOCK off $1 \Rightarrow$ NUM LOCK on
4	Status of SCROLL LOCK $0 \Rightarrow$ SCROLL LOCK off $1 \Rightarrow$ SCROLL LOCK on
3	$0 \Rightarrow$ ALT not depressed $1 \Rightarrow$ ALT depressed
2	$0 \Rightarrow$ CTRL not depressed $1 \Rightarrow$ CTRL depressed
1	$0 \Rightarrow$ LEFT-SHIFT not pressed $1 \Rightarrow$ LEFT-SHIFT depressed
0	$0 \Rightarrow$ RIGHT-SHIFT not pressed $1 \Rightarrow$ RIGHT-SHIFT depressed

Note that there are two sets of subfunction codes for interrupt Type 16 hex. Two sets of services are provided because two types of keyboards are typically used with personal computers. Most of the IBM PC models had an 83-key keyboard. The IBM PS/2 models have a 101-key keyboard. Subfunctions 0, 1, and 2 provide the interface with the old 83-key keyboards. Subfunctions 10 hex, 11 hex, and 12 hex provide the interface with the enhanced 101-key keyboards. The enhanced keyboard subfunctions of interrupt Type 16 hex not only recognize the additional keys, but they also recognize more key combinations. Use of Type 16 hex subfunctions 0, 1, and 2 to interface with an enhanced keyboard simply means that the extra keys and key combinations will be ignored. If your computer has an old 83-key keyboard, then the BIOS on your system probably does not provide subfunctions 10 hex, 11 hex, and 12 hex.

To obtain a character from the keyboard, an assembly language program invokes the interrupt Type 16 hex service procedure with a subfunction code of 0 or 10 hex in the AH-register. That is, to obtain a character from the keyboard, execute the following two assembly language instructions:

```
MOV AH, 0         MOV  AH, 10H
              or
INT 16H           INT  16H
```

The interrupt Type 16 hex service procedure returns the next scan code:character code pair from its keyboard input buffer. The scan code is returned in the AH-register, and the extended ASCII character code is returned in the AL-register. If the keyboard input buffer is empty when the interrupt Type 16 hex service procedure is invoked, then the service procedure goes into an idle loop, waiting until a scan code:character code pair is in its input buffer. The keyboard input buffer is handled as a true **first-in-first-out** (**FIFO**) queue so that assembly language programs receive keyboard characters in the same order as they were depressed at the keyboard.

Programming Example—GETSTRNG and PUTSTRNG

Program Listing 9.4 illustrates the use of BIOS interrupt Type 16 hex with the GETSTRNG procedure from the author's I/O subprocedure library. GETSTRNG also illustrates BIOS interrupt Type 10 hex since each character entered via the keyboard is echoed to the video screen.

The prologue in lines 2–16 explains the function of the GETSTRNG procedure and states its interface requirements. The caller sets the ES:DI register pair to address the first location of the byte array in which the input character string is to be stored, sets the CX-register to the length of this byte array, and then calls GETSTRNG. GETSTRNG accepts characters from the keyboard and stores their extended ASCII codes in the specified byte array until either a RETURN is received or *n* characters have been received, where *n* is the value input to GETSTRNG via the CX-register. That is, the value input in the CX-register instructs GETSTRNG as to the maximum number of characters that the byte array can hold and therefore the maximum size string that GETSTRNG should accept from the keyboard. GETSTRNG returns to the caller with the input character string stored in the specified array, the ES:DI register pair again addressing the first byte of that array, and the CX-register set to the actual length of the input string.

When entering a character string, the user may wish to erase part of the string already entered. The GETSTRNG procedure uses BACKSPACE to provide this capability. Entering a BACKSPACE erases the last character entered into the string; thus, entering *m* consecutive BACKSPACE characters erases the last *m* characters entered into the string. GETSTRNG not only removes the characters from the string, but it also erases them from the echoed copy on the video screen.

Three named constants are defined in this assembly module (lines 20–22). These definitions provide names for the ASCII codes for BACKSPACE, RETURN, and LINE FEED, respectively.

The GETSTRNG procedure begins by saving the registers specified in the USES clause (line 25) and saving the flags register (line 29). The STI instruction in

```
;====================================================================
;                   PROGRAM LISTING 9.4
;
; PROCEDURE TO INPUT A CHARACTER STRING FROM THE KEYBOARD.
; CHARACTERS  WILL  BE ACCEPTED UNTIL THE USER PRESSES THE
; RETURN  KEY  OR N CHARACTERS HAVE BEEN ENTERED,  WHERE N
; IS SUPPLIED BY THE CALLER.
;
; INPUT:  ES:DI POINTS TO THE BUFFER THAT  IS  TO  RECEIVE
;               THE STRING
;         CX    CONTAINS  THE  LENGTH OF THE INPUT  BUFFER
;
; OUTPUT: CX    CONTAINS THE ACTUAL  LENGTH  OF  THE INPUT
;               STRING
;         THE  SPECIFIED  BUFFER  CONTAINS  THE  CHARACTER
;         STRING THAT WAS ENTERED.
;====================================================================
           .MODEL  SMALL,BASIC
;====================================================================
BKSP       EQU     08H                     ;ASCII FOR BACKSPACE
CR         EQU     0DH                     ;ASCII FOR CARRIAGE RETURN
LF         EQU     0AH                     ;ASCII FOR LINE FEED
;====================================================================
           .CODE   EX_9_4
GETSTRNG   PROC    FAR PUBLIC USES AX BX DX DI BP
                                          ;PROCEDURE GETSTRNG (PTR,SIZE)
                                           ;SAVE REGISTERS SPECIFIED
                                           ;     IN USES CLAUSE
           PUSHF                           ;SAVE FLAGS
           STI                             ;ENABLE INTERRUPTS
           CLD                             ;SET DF FOR INCREMENTING
           MOV     AH,15                   ;READ ACTIVE DISPLAY PAGE
           INT     10H                     ;NUMBER INTO BH-REGISTER
           MOV     DX,0                    ;KEY_CNT = 0
LOOP_TOP:                                  ;REPEAT
           MOV     AH,0                    ;   READ CHAR FROM KEYBOARD
           INT     16H
           CMP     AL,CR                   ;   IF   CHAR IS CARRIAGE RTN
           JE      LOOP_END                ;<- THEN EXIT LOOP
                                           ;   ENDIF
           CMP     AL,BKSP                 ;   IF   CHAR IS BACKSPACE
           JNE     ELSE1
           INC     CX                      ;   THEN SIZE = SIZE + 1
           CMP     DX,0                    ;        IF   KEY_CNT > 0
           JE      LOOP_TEST
           DEC     DX                      ;        THEN DECR KEY_CNT
           DEC     DI                      ;             PTR = PTR - 1
           INC     CX                      ;             SIZE = SIZE + 1
           MOV     AH,14                   ;             DISPL BACKSPACE
           MOV     AL,BKSP
           INT     10H
           MOV     AH,14                   ;             DISPLAY BLANK
           MOV     AL,' '
           INT     10H
           MOV     AH,14                   ;             DISPL BACKSPACE
           MOV     AL,BKSP
           INT     10H
           JMP     LOOP_TEST               ;        ENDIF
ELSE1:                                     ;   ELSE
           STOSB                           ;        PTR->BYTE = CHAR
                                           ;        PTR = PTR + 1
           INC     DX                      ;        KEY_CNT = KEY_CNT+1
           MOV     AH,14                   ;        DISPLAY CHAR
           INT     10H                     ;        <ECHO CHAR TO SCREEN>
LOOP_TEST:                                 ;   ENDIF
           LOOP    LOOP_TOP                ;   SIZE = SIZE - 1
LOOP_END:                                  ;UNTIL SIZE = 0
```

```
 68:              MOV     CX,DX                   ;SIZE = KEY_CNT
 69:              MOV     AH,14                   ;DISPLAY CARRIAGE RETURN
 70:              MOV     AL,CR
 71:              INT     10H
 72:              MOV     AH,14                   ;DISPLAY LINE FEED
 73:              MOV     AL,LF
 74:              INT     10H
 75:              POPF                            ;RESTORE FLAGS
 76:                                              ;RESTORE REGISTERS SPECIFIED
 77:                                              ;        IN USES CLAUSE
 78:              RET                             ;RETURN
 79: GETSTRNG     ENDP                         ;END GETSTRNG
 80: ;===================================================================
 81: ; PROCEDURE  TO  DISPLAY  A  CHARACTER STRING ON THE SCREEN
 82: ;
 83: ; INPUT:  ES:DI POINTS TO THE FIRST CHARACTER OF THE STRING
 84: ;         CX    CONTAINS THE LENGTH OF THE CHARACTER STRING
 85: ;
 86: ; OUTPUT: INPUT STRING DISPLAYED ON THE SCREEN BEGINNING AT
 87: ;         THE CURRENT CURSOR POSITION
 88: ;===================================================================
 89: PUTSTRNG     PROC    FAR PUBLIC USES AX BX CX DI BP
 90:                                           ;PROCEDURE PUTSTRNG (PTR,LENGTH)
 91:                                              ;SAVE REGISTERS SPECIFIED
 92:                                              ;     IN USES CLAUSE
 93:              PUSHF                           ;SAVE FLAGS
 94:              STI                             ;ENABLE INTERRUPTS
 95:              MOV     AH,15                   ;READ ACTIVE DISPLAY PAGE
 96:              INT     10H                     ;NUMBER INTO BH-REGISTER
 97:              JCXZ    LOOP_END                ;WHILE LENGTH <> 0
 98: PUT_CHAR:
 99:              MOV     AH,14
100:              MOV     AL,BYTE PTR ES:[DI] ;   DISPLAY PTR -> CHAR
101:              INT     10H
102:              INC     DI                      ;   PTR = PTR + 1
103:              LOOP    PUT_CHAR                ;   LENGTH = LENGTH - 1
104: LOOP_END:                                    ;ENDWHILE
105:              POPF                            ;RESTORE FLAGS
106:                                              ;RESTORE REGISTERS SPECIFIED
107:                                              ;        IN USES CLAUSE
108:              RET                             ;RETURN
109: PUTSTRNG     ENDP                         ;END PUTSTRNG
110: ;===================================================================
111:              END
```

line 30 enables external interrupts, which ensures that the keyboard interrupt will be enabled. The CLD instruction in line 31 sets the DF bit of the flags register for incrementing through the byte array. GETSTRNG uses the STOSB string instruction to store characters in the byte array.

The two instructions in lines 32 and 33 generate a software interrupt Type 10 hex with a subfunction code of 15, which requests the BIOS video I/O service procedure to read the current video state. This step is taken to read the active display page number into the BH-register. GETSTRNG echoes the character string input to the active page of the video screen. Since no other program instructions modify the BH-register value, the active display page number is held in the BH-register until that register is restored (comment lines 76 and 77) just prior to return to the caller.

The GETSTRNG procedure returns to its caller a count of the number of characters in the input string, and the DX-register maintains this count. The MOV instruction in line 34 initializes this key count to zero.

The REPEAT-UNTIL loop in lines 35–67 reads the characters from the keyboard and stores them in the caller's byte array, one character per loop iteration. The loop body executes until a RETURN is received or the length of the input string has reached the maximum allowed, as specified by the value input to GETSTRNG via the CX-register. The CX-register value is used as a loop counter to control the maximum number of characters that can be stored in the caller's byte array.

The two instructions in lines 36 and 37 generate a software interrupt Type 16 hex with a subfunction code of 0, which requests the BIOS keyboard service procedure to obtain a character from the keyboard. The ASCII character code is returned in the AL-register. The CMP instruction in line 38 tests the input character to see if it is a RETURN (0D hex is the ASCII code for a RETURN). The JE instruction in line 39 makes the decision based on this test. If the character is a RETURN, then the jump is taken to line 67, thus exiting the loop body; if the character is not a RETURN, then the jump is not taken and the loop body is continued.

The double-alternative decision structure in lines 41–65 detects the input of a BACKSPACE and performs the necessary adjustments. The CMP instruction in line 41 tests the input character to see if it is a BACKSPACE (08 hex is the ASCII code for a BACKSPACE). The JNE instruction in line 42 makes the decision based on this test. If the character is a BACKSPACE, then the instructions in lines 43–58 are executed; otherwise, the instructions in lines 60–64 are executed.

If the input character is a BACKSPACE, then a character must be logically removed from the caller's byte array unless there is no character in the array to be removed. The single-alternative decision structure in lines 44–58 determines whether there is a character in the array to be removed. The CMP instruction in line 44 tests the key count in the DX-register to see if it is greater than zero. The JE instruction in line 45 makes the decision based on this test. If the key count is greater than zero, then the instructions in lines 46–57 are executed; otherwise, these instructions are skipped. The instructions in lines 46–57 logically remove a character from the caller's byte array and erase the corresponding character from the echoed character string on the video screen. The DEC instruction in line 46 decrements the key count by 1. The DEC instruction in line 47 decrements the DI-register by 1 so that the ES:DI register pair addresses the location in the byte array of the character being erased, which means that the next character entered replaces the one being erased in the byte array. Note that the erased character is not actually removed from the byte array, but, logically, it is no longer a part of the input string. The loop counter in the CX-register (i.e., the maximum number of remaining characters that can be stored in the byte array) is incremented by 1 (line 48). Since a character has been removed from the array, one more iteration of the loop is now possible before the array becomes full. The instructions in lines 49–51 use subfunction 14 of interrupt Type 10 hex to display a BACKSPACE on the screen, which causes the cursor to back up under the character to be erased from the echoed string. To erase this character from the screen, a blank is displayed (lines 52–54), again using subfunction 14 of interrupt Type 10 hex. Displaying the blank character also advances the cursor. The cursor now must be backed up again so that the next character entered will be echoed in the position where the blank was displayed. This step is accomplished by displaying a BACKSPACE (lines 55–57).

If the input character is not a BACKSPACE, then it is stored in the byte array and is echoed to the video screen. The STOSB instruction in line 60 stores the character in the caller's byte array and then increments the DI-register by 1 so that the ES:DI register pair addresses the next byte in the array. The INC instruction in line 62 increments the key count in the DX-register to reflect the character just stored.

The two instructions in lines 63 and 64 generate a software interrupt Type 10 hex with a subfunction code of 14, which requests the BIOS video I/O service procedure to display the character in the AL-register at the current cursor position, on the display page indicated by the value in the BH-register, and then to advance the cursor position. This process echoes the character just stored in the caller's byte array to the video screen.

The LOOP instruction in line 66 decrements the loop counter in the CX-register and returns to the top of the loop (line 35) if the count is nonzero. If the count is zero, then the caller's byte array is full and no more characters can be accepted. Loop exit can occur for one of two reasons: RETURN was entered or the caller's byte array was filled.

On loop exit, the key count, the actual length of the input string, is moved to the CX-register (line 68) for procedure output. Next, a RETURN and a LINE FEED are displayed on the video screen (lines 69–74), which means that the echoed input string terminates a line on the display. The GETSTRNG procedure ends by restoring the flags (line 75), restoring the registers specified in the USES clause, and returning control to the caller (line 78).

The assembly module of Program Listing 9.4 also contains the definition of procedure PUTSTRNG (lines 80–110). The prologue for procedure PUTSTRNG (lines 81–87) explains the function of the PUTSTRNG procedure and states its interface requirements. The caller sets the ES:DI register pair to address the first location of the byte array in which the character string is stored, and sets the CX-register to the length of this string, and then calls PUTSTRNG. PUTSTRNG displays the specified number of characters from the array, beginning with the character addressed by the ES:DI register pair.

The PUTSTRNG procedure begins by saving the registers specified in the USES clause (line 89) and saving the flags register (line 93). The STI instruction in line 94 ensures that external interrupts will be enabled during the execution of procedure PUTSTRNG.

The two instructions in lines 95 and 96 invoke software interrupt Type 10 hex to read the active display page number into the BH-register. PUTSTRNG displays the input character string to the active page of the video screen. Since no other program instructions modify the BH-register value, the active display page number is held in the BH-register until that register is restored (comment lines 106 and 107) just prior to return to the caller.

The WHILE loop in lines 97–104 displays the characters of the string. This loop is controlled by the string length stored in the CX-register. It is a REPEAT-UNTIL loop (see LOOP instruction in line 103) that has been converted into a WHILE loop by the JCXZ instruction in line 97. A WHILE loop is used so that procedure PUTSTRNG can accommodate the null string (a string with length 0). The body of the WHILE loop (lines 99–102) displays one character of the string on each iteration. The instructions in lines 99–101 use subfunction 14 of BIOS interrupt Type 10 hex to display the character addressed by the ES:DI register pair. The INC instruction in line 102 increments the DI-register by 1 so that the ES:DI register pair addresses the next character in the string.

On loop exit, the flags register is restored (line 105), the registers specified in the USES clause are restored, and control is returned to the caller (line 108).

Printer Output (Interrupt 17H)

Printer I/O services are provided through software interrupt Type 17 hex. The BIOS subprocedure that services interrupt Type 17 hex uses the value in the AH-register as a subfunction code. It is via the AH-register that the caller requests the specific printer operation to be performed. Table 9.6 summarizes the subfunction codes recognized by the BIOS interrupt Type 17 hex service procedure and the other registers used for procedure input and output.

TABLE 9.6
BIOS interrupt Type 17H subfunctions

AH	Function	Procedure Inputs	Procedure Outputs
0	Print character	AL = character to print DX = printer number (0, 1, 2)	AH = status byte
1	Initialize printer	DX = printer number (0, 1, 2)	AH = status byte
2	Read printer status	DX = printer number (0, 1, 2)	AH = status byte

Subfunction 0 causes the ASCII character in the AL-register to be output to the printer. Unless the ASCII character is a control character, the character is printed in the next position on the current line. Control characters are discussed in the following paragraphs. Subfunction 1 causes the printer to be initialized, which means a RETURN is output to the printer and the current line is established as the top of page. Subfunction 2 causes no output to the printer; it is simply a request for the current printer status. For all three subfunctions, the DX-register specifies the printer number (0, 1, or 2). BIOS can provide service for up to three printers via interrupt Type 17 hex. For all three subfunctions, the printer status is returned to the caller in the AH-register.

Table 9.7 shows the interpretation for each bit of the printer status byte returned in the AH-register. Some of these bits may have slightly different meanings with some printer interfaces. For example, with some printers, bit 4 = 1 means that

TABLE 9.7
Interpretation of printer status byte

7	6	5	4	3	2	1	0

Bit	Meaning
7	Printer not busy 1 implies printer is not busy
6	Acknowledge 1 implies printer acknowledged receipt of data
5	Out of paper 1 implies printer is out of paper
4	Selected 0 implies printer is offline 1 implies printer is online
3	I/O error 1 implies I/O error occurred on requested print operation
2	Not used
1	Not used
0	Timeout error 1 implies timeout error occurred on requested print operation (printer busy for too long a time)

the printer is switched on; with other printers, bit 4 = 1 means that the printer is switched on and is online. The key bits of interest for most dot matrix printers are bits 7, 5, and 3. Table 9.8 summarizes the settings for these bits for various printer conditions.

TABLE 9.8
Printer status for most dot matrix printers

Status of Printer	Bit 7	Bit 5	Bit 3
Printer power switch is off	1	0	1
Printer power switch is on Printer has paper Printer is offline	0	0	1
Printer power switch is on Printer is out of paper	0	1	1
Printer power switch is on Printer has paper Printer is online	1	0	0
Printer is printing	0	0	0

Most dot matrix printers have several modes. The standard print mode prints 80 characters per line, 6 lines per inch (66 lines per page). The compressed mode prints 132 characters per line, 6 lines per inch. The double-width mode prints 40 characters per line, 6 lines per inch. The number of lines per inch can be changed from 6 to 8, which is convenient when printing in the compressed mode. To change the printer mode, set the number of lines per inch, or perform carriage control operations at the printer. Thus, to print, special control characters are transmitted to the printer.

The extended ASCII character set contains both printable and control characters. When a printable character is transmitted to the printer, it is stored in a buffer in the printer. The characters are not actually printed until a complete print line has been received by the printer. The characters in the buffer are printed when a RETURN, a LINE FEED, or a FORM FEED character is received or when a printable character is received and the printer buffer is full. The printer buffer can hold up to 80 characters in the standard mode, 132 characters in the compressed mode, and 40 characters in the double-width mode. When a line is printed because of a full printer buffer, a RETURN and a LINE FEED are automatically performed. When a control character is transmitted to the printer, the printer performs the requested control operation (e.g., changes mode, advances to top of next page). Table 9.9 summarizes the more useful printer control characters. For a complete set of the printer control characters for your printer, consult your printer manual. The characters in Table 9.9 are standard ASCII characters, so their interpretations apply to most printers. (Illustrations of printer I/O operations are left as programming exercises.)

Time of Day (Interrupt 1AH)

DOS computes the time of day from a count of the number of timer interrupts (Type 8 interrupts) since midnight. This count is initialized to zero (i.e., time of day is initialized to midnight) at time of system start-up. When DOS is loaded, it either prompts the user for the correct date and time or accesses the built-in battery-powered clock for the correct date and time. DOS takes the time entered by the user or the time

TABLE 9.9
Printer control characters

ASCII Code	Interpretation
07 hex	Sounds a beep at the printer
09 hex	Horizontal TAB
0A hex	LINE FEED (advance to next line)
0B hex	Vertical TAB
0C hex	FORM FEED (advance to top of next page)
0D hex	RETURN (return to left margin)
0E hex	Turn on double-width print mode (40 characters per line)
0F hex	Turn on compressed print mode (132 characters per line)
12 hex	Turn off compressed print mode
14 hex	Turn off double-width print mode
18 hex	Clear printer buffer
1B, 30 hex	Set line spacing to 8 lines per inch
1B, 32 hex	Set line spacing to 6 lines per inch
1B, 45 hex	Turn on emphasized printing mode
1B, 46 hex	Turn off emphasized printing mode

retrieved from the battery-powered clock, converts it to a count of timer interrupts since midnight, and reinitializes the count. This count of timer interrupts is maintained by BIOS as a 32-bit value. A program can read or set this count by using software interrupt Type 1A hex.

The BIOS procedure that services interrupt Type 1A hex uses the value in the AH-register as a subfunction code. Table 9.10 summarizes the subfunction codes recognized by the Type 1A hex interrupt service procedure.

TABLE 9.10
BIOS interrupt Type 1AH subfunctions

AH	Function	Procedure Inputs	Procedure Outputs
0	Read count of timer interrupts	None	CX:DX register pair contains timer count
1	Set count of timer interrupts	CX:DX register pair contains timer count	None

The time-of-day interrupt can be used to compute program execution time. Immediately on entry to the program, the program reads and saves the value of the timer count. Just before exit from the program, the program reads the value of the timer count and computes the difference between the value just read and the value saved at the beginning of the program. This difference is the number of timer interrupts (Type 8 interrupts) that occurred during program execution. Since the timer interrupt occurs once every 54.9254 milliseconds, multiplying this difference by 55 gives the approximate number of milliseconds that elapsed during program execution.

The time-of-day interrupt can also be used to provide a delay in a program. The timer interrupt occurs approximately 18.2 times per second. In 5 seconds, the timer interrupt occurs approximately 91 times. To perform a 5-second delay, the following instructions could be used:

```
MOV CX, 0
MOV DX, 0
MOV AH, 1
INT 1AH
```

```
REPEAT:
        MOV AH, 0
        INT 1AH
        CMP DX, 91
        JB  REPEAT
```

The first four instructions set the time count to zero. The last four instructions repeatedly read the timer count until the timer count is found to be 91 or above. The one problem with this delay loop is that it destroys the system's time of day. Some other possibilities for delay loops are considered in the programming exercises at the end of the chapter.

Timer Subfunction (Interrupt 1CH)

BIOS provides the capability for a user program to perform some function on every timer interrupt. The BIOS procedure that services the Type 8 interrupt generates a Type 1C hex software interrupt. BIOS provides an interrupt service procedure for the Type 1C interrupt that contains only an IRET instruction. To perform some function on every timer interrupt, the user program must provide its own Type 1C interrupt service procedure. External interrupts should be disabled while modifying the Type 1C interrupt vector. If a timer interrupt is allowed to occur between setting the segment and offset portions of the interrupt vector, then a bogus Type 1C interrupt service procedure is invoked.

DOS User Services (Interrupt 21H)

DOS provides a set of service procedures that provide a higher level of I/O operations for the assembly language programmer than do the BIOS service procedures. These procedures are accessible from assembly language programs via software interrupt Type 21 hex. The DOS procedure that services interrupt Type 21 hex uses the value in the AH-register as a subfunction code. It is via the AH-register that the caller requests the specific I/O operation to be performed. Depending on the subfunction code in the AH-register, other registers are used for input to and output from the DOS service procedure. Table 9.11 summarizes the subfunction codes recognized by

TABLE 9.11 DOS interrupt Type 21H subfunctions

AH	Function	Procedure Inputs	Procedure Outputs
0	Terminate program (same as INT 20H)	CS = address of PSP	None
1	Wait for one character from keyboard and echo to video screen	None	AL = character
2	Display character and advance cursor	DL = character	None
3	Wait for one character from the asynchronous communications adapter	None	AL = character
4	Output one character to the asynchronous communications adapter	DL = character	None

Continued

TABLE 9.11 Continued

AH	Function	Procedure Inputs	Procedure Outputs
5	Output one character to printer	DL = character	None
6	Input a character from standard input device	DL = FFH	ZF = 1 (no wait) ZF = 0 and AL = character
	Output a character to standard output device	DL < FFH DL = character	None
7	Wait for one character from keyboard (no echo to screen)	None	AL = character
8	Wait for one character from keyboard (no echo to screen); generates interrupt for control break	None	AL = character
9	Display $-terminated character string	DS:DX = address of string	None
A	Input a character string from keyboard	DS:DX = address of BUFFER BUFFER(0) = max length	BUFFER(1) = length BUFFER(*k*) = character *k*–1 of string
B	Check keyboard status	None	AL = FFH if character in buffer AL = 00H if no character in buffer
C	Clear keyboard buffer and invoke keyboard function	AL = keyboard function (1, 6, 7, 8, A)	None
25	Set interrupt vector	AL = interrupt type DS:DX = address of replacement service procedure	None
2A	Get system date	None	CX = year – 1980 DH = month (1–12) DL = day (1–31) AL = day of week (0 = Sunday)
2B	Set system date	CX = year – 1980 DH = month (1–12) DL = day (1–31) AL = day of week (0 = Sunday)	AL = 00H if set date successful AL = FFH if invalid date
2C	Get system time	None	CH = hours (0–23) CL = minutes (0–59) DH = seconds (0–59) DL = hundredths of second (0–99)

Continued

TABLE 9.11 Continued

AH	Function	Procedure Inputs	Procedure Outputs
2D	Set system time	CH = hours (0–23) CL = minutes (0–59) DH = seconds (0–59) DL = hundredths of second (0–99)	AL = 00H if set time successful AL = FFH if invalid time
31	Terminate and stay resident	AL = return code DX = size of program in paragraphs	None
35	Get interrupt vector	AL = interrupt type	ES:BX = interrupt vector
3C	Create file; if file already exists, sets to zero length for overwriting	DS:DX = address of 0-terminated string containing pathname* CX = attribute (see Section 9.4)	CF = 0 and AX = file handle, or CF = 1 and AX = error code
3D	Open file	DS:DX = address of 0-terminated string containing pathname AL = access code 0—open for read 1—open for write 2—open for read/write	CF = 0 and AX = file handle, or CF = 1 and AX = error code
3E	Close file	BX = file handle	CF = 0, or CF = 1 and AX = error code
3F	Read from file	BX = file handle CX = number of bytes to read DS:DX = address of storage area	CF = 0 and AX = number of bytes read, or CF = 1 and AX = error code
40	Write to file	BX = file handle CX = number of bytes to write DS:DX = address of storage area	CF = 0 and AX = number of bytes written, or CF = 1 and AX = error code
41	Delete file	DS:DX = address of 0-terminated string containing pathname	CF = 0, or CF = 1 and AX = error code
4C	Terminate program	AL = return code	None
56	Rename a file	DS:DX = address of 0-terminated string containing pathname ES:DI = address of 0-terminated string containing new path	CF = 0, or CF = 1 and AX = error code
5B	Create file; returns error code 80 if file exists	DS:DX = address of 0-terminated string containing pathname CX = attribute (see Section 9.4)	CF = 0 and AX = file handle, or CF = 1 and AX = error code

*Pathname, in its simplest form, is a complete file specification including disk drive, filename, and filename extension.

the DOS interrupt Type 21 hex and the other registers used for procedure input and output.

EXAMPLES

The following code fragment causes an asterisk (*) to be displayed on the screen, beginning at the current cursor position, and the cursor to be advanced:

```
MOV  AH,2
MOV  DL,'*'
INT  21H
```

Subfunction 2 of the INT 21H service procedure outputs the character to the currently active display page.

The following code fragment causes the current Type 1 interrupt vector to be saved on the stack and the Type 1 interrupt vector to be set to address procedure S_STEP:

```
MOV   AH,35H              ;GET TYPE 1 VECTOR
MOV   AL,1
INT   21H
PUSH  ES                  ;SAVE TYPE 1 VECTOR ON STACK
PUSH  BX

MOV   AX,SEG S_STEP       ;SET TYPE 1 VECTOR TO ADDRESS
MOV   DS,AX               ;PROCEDURE S_STEP
MOV   DX,OFFSET S_STEP
MOV   AH,25H
MOV   AL,1
INT   21H
```

If this code fragment is substituted for the instructions in lines 22–32 of Program Listing 9.2 and the code fragment

```
POP  DX                   ;RESTORE TYPE 1 VECTOR
POP  DS
MOV  AH,25H
MOV  AL,1
INT  21H
```

is substituted for the instructions in lines 98–99, the resulting program will produce the same result as does the program of Program Listing 9.2. ■

Direct Input/Output

Direct input/output involves accessing the I/O ports in the 8088/8086-based machine. The set of I/O ports is like a set of byte registers that holds data that are being transmitted between the microprocessor and an external device (e.g., keyboard, video display). The main difference between a processor register and a port is that a port has an electrical connection to some external device. A port may be used for transmitting data to or from a device, transmitting control information to a device, or receiving status information from a device.

The 8088/8086 can communicate with 65,536 ports, numbered 0–65,535. A specific port is addressed by its unique port number. Addressing a port opens the electrical connection between the port and its external device to allow data to flow from the device to the port or from the port to the device.

There are two 8088/8086 assembly language instructions for accessing the ports: IN and OUT. The **IN instruction** has the following general form:

[⟨*label*⟩] IN ⟨*accumulator*⟩,⟨*port*⟩ [⟨*comment*⟩]

in which ⟨*accumulator*⟩ is either the register designator AL or AX and ⟨*port*⟩ is either an immediate value in the range 0–255 or the register designator DX. If the ⟨*accumulator*⟩ operand is AL, then the IN instruction transfers the byte from the port addressed by the value of the ⟨*port*⟩ operand to the AL-register. If the ⟨*accumulator*⟩ operand is AX, then the IN instruction transfers the byte from the port addressed by the value of the ⟨*port*⟩ operand to the AL-register and transfers the byte from the port addressed by the value of the ⟨*port*⟩ operand plus 1 to the AH-register.

The **OUT instruction** has the following general form:

[⟨*label*⟩] OUT ⟨*port*⟩,⟨*accumulator*⟩ [⟨*comment*⟩]

in which ⟨*port*⟩ is either an immediate value in the range 0–255 or the register designator DX and ⟨*accumulator*⟩ is either the register designator AL or AX. If the ⟨*accumulator*⟩ operand is AL, then the OUT instruction transfers the byte from the AL-register to the port addressed by the value of the ⟨*port*⟩ operand. If the ⟨*accumulator*⟩ operand is AX, then the OUT instruction transfers the byte from the AL-register to the port addressed by the value of the ⟨*port*⟩ operand and transfers the byte from the AH-register to the port addressed by the value of the ⟨*port*⟩ operand plus 1.

EXAMPLES

The instruction

```
IN  AL,2BH
```

transfers the byte from port 2B hex to the AL-register.

The instructions

```
MOV  DX, 3E2H
OUT  DX, AX
```

transfer the byte in the AL-register to port 3E2 hex and the byte in the AH-register to port 3E3 hex. ■

The port assignments in the IBM PC are summarized in the I/O address map in the IBM PC technical reference manual. A few of the ports are discussed here to give examples of IN and OUT instructions. One example that has been used several times in this chapter is that of keyboard input. When a Type 9 interrupt (keyboard interrupt) occurs, the BIOS service procedure reads the scan code for the key by executing the instruction

```
IN  AL, 60H
```

Execution of the IN instruction opens the connection between the keyboard and port 60 hex, allowing the scan code to be transferred to the port, and then copies the scan code from the port to the AL-register. The interrupt service procedure then converts the scan code to an extended ASCII character and stores both codes in the keyboard input buffer.

Programming Example—Demonstrate HLT, IN, and OUT Instructions

Program Listing 9.5 gives a simple illustration of the IN and OUT instructions. It also uses the **HLT instruction**, which halts instruction executions in the microprocessor and has the following general form:

[⟨*label*⟩] HLT [⟨*comment*⟩]

This instruction causes the microprocessor to halt its instruction execution cycle and wait for an interrupt to occur. When an interrupt occurs, instruction execution resumes with the appropriate interrupt service procedure. On return from the interrupt service procedure, execution continues with the instruction immediately following the HLT instruction.

Suppose an HLT instruction has just been executed and that the microprocessor is in the halt state. If all external interrupts are enabled, then the next timer interrupt (Type 8 interrupt) will bring the microprocessor out of the halt state. Suppose there is a need to lock out the timer interrupt so that a keyboard interrupt can be used to awaken the microprocessor from the halt state. If the IF bit of the flags register is used to lock out the timer interrupt, then all other external interrupts, including the keyboard interrupts, are locked out as well. A method is needed for selectively locking out the external interrupts.

```
          PAGE    80,132
;=====================================================================
;                 PROGRAM LISTING 9.5
;
; PROGRAM TO DEMONSTRATE HLT, IN, AND OUT INSTRUCTIONS
;=====================================================================
          .MODEL  SMALL,BASIC
;=====================================================================
                                          ;PROCEDURES TO
          EXTRN   DELAY:FAR               ;DELAY n SECONDS
          EXTRN   NEWLINE:FAR             ;DISPLAY NEWLINE CHARACTER
          EXTRN   PUTBIN:FAR              ;DISPLAY 8- OR 16-BIT BINARY
;=====================================================================
; S T A C K   S E G M E N T   D E F I N I T I O N
;
          .STACK  256
;=====================================================================
; C O D E   S E G M E N T   D E F I N I T I O N
;
          .CODE
EX_9_5:
          MOV     AL,3                    ;DELAY 3 SECONDS TO GET
          CALL    DELAY                   ;DISKETTE MOTOR OFF
;
          IN      AL,21H                  ;READ INTERRUPT MASK REGISTER
          MOV     BL,0                    ;PUTBIN CODE = BYTE
          CALL    PUTBIN                  ;DISPLAY INTERRUPT MASK REG.
          CALL    NEWLINE
          OR      AL,1                    ;MASK TIMER INTERRUPT
          OUT     21H,AL
          HLT                             ;HALT --> WAIT FOR INTERRUPT
          CALL    PUTBIN                  ;DISPLAY INTERRUPT MASK REG.
          AND     AL,0FEH                 ;ENABLE TIMER INTERRUPT
          OUT     21H,AL
          .EXIT                           ;RETURN TO DOS
;
          END     EX_9_5
;=====================================================================
```

The eight external interrupts (Types 8–F hex) are under control of the Intel 8259A interrupt controller. The microprocessor communicates with the interrupt controller via port 20 hex and port 21 hex. The byte at port 21 hex enables or disables each of the eight external interrupts individually, and each bit controls one of the eight external interrupts: Bit 0 controls interrupt Type 8, bit 1 controls interrupt Type 9, bit 2 controls interrupt Type A, and so forth. A 1 in the bit means that the corresponding interrupt type is disabled, and a 0 means that the interrupt is enabled. Therefore, the timer interrupt can be individually disabled by setting bit 0 at port 21 hex.

Program Listing 9.5 demonstrates execution of the HLT instruction with the timer interrupt disabled. The program begins with a 3-second delay. Whenever DOS accesses the disk, it leaves the disk motor on for 2 seconds before turning it off. This policy attempts to avoid excessively turning the disk motor on and off since disk accesses tend to occur in clusters. DOS accesses the disk to load the program. The disk motor is still on when the program begins execution. Without the delay, the disk motor remains on while the processor is in the halt state. The delay ensures that the disk motor will be turned off before the processor is placed into the halt state. (The DELAY subprocedure is left to Programming Exercises 9.9 and 9.10.)

The IN instruction in line 25 reads the current value of port 21 hex into the AL-register. The call to the PUTBIN procedure (lines 26 and 27) displays this byte value in binary. The OR instruction in line 29 sets bit 0 of this byte value in the AL-register, leaving all other bits unchanged. The OUT instruction in line 30 copies this modified byte value to port 21 hex. This instruction disables the timer interrupt, leaving the status of the other seven external interrupts unchanged. The HLT instruction in line 31 places the microprocessor into the halt state. The microprocessor then remains in the halt state until an interrupt occurs. A timer interrupt will not occur because the program has disabled the timer interrupt. Keyboard interrupts are still enabled, so pressing a key at the keyboard will awaken the microprocessor from the halt state.

When the microprocessor does awaken from the halt state, the program displays the value in the AL-register (line 32), which is the value that was transmitted to the interrupt controller via port 21 hex. It is the same value as the value read from port 21 hex (line 25) and displayed earlier (line 27), except that bit 0 is set to 1. The AND instruction in line 33 clears bit 0 of this byte value, leaving all other bits unchanged. The OUT instruction in line 34 transmits this modified byte value to port 21 hex. This instruction enables the timer interrupt once again, leaving the status of the other seven external interrupts unchanged.

When executed on a IBM PC/XT, the program displays the value 10111100 and then halts. When a key is pressed at the keyboard, the program displays the value 10111101 and then returns control to DOS. If the user sets the system time to the correct time before executing this program and waits 2 minutes after the first display before pressing a key, then the system time, after program execution, will be approximately 2 minutes slow.

9.4 Disk File Input/Output

A diskette is physically organized as shown in Figure 9.1. Data are stored on a round, flat surface like that of a phonograph record. Data can be stored on both sides of the disk. Each side is divided into concentric circles, or tracks, and each track is divided into sectors. All tracks have the same number of sectors. Each sector holds a fixed

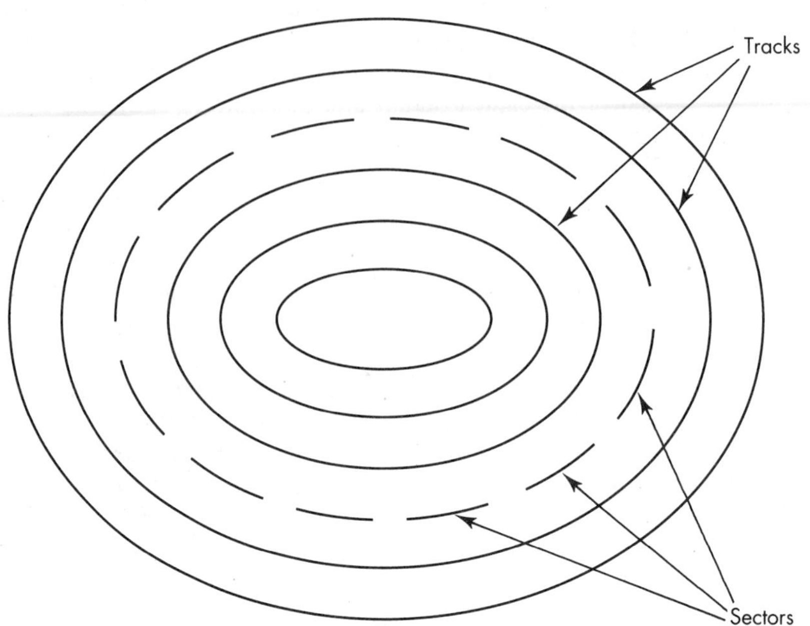

FIGURE 9.1
Diskette organization

number of bytes of data. The sector size is typically 512 bytes for microcomputer systems. The data stored on a disk is addressed by side number, track number, sector number, and position within the sector.

Fortunately, 8088/8086 assembly language programmers do not have to keep track of data by side, track, and sector. DOS takes care of this bookkeeping for us. DOS provides disk file I/O services via interrupt Type 21 hex, which allows assembly language programmers to define a logical structure to data stored in disk files. DOS provides two levels of services for disk I/O operations. At the highest level, a disk file is treated simply as an array of bytes. It is this highest level that is presented here.

Creating Disk Files

DOS interrupt Type 21 hex provides two subfunctions for creating a new file: subfunction 3C hex and subfunction 5B hex. These two subfunctions have the same interface requirements. Two inputs are expected as follows:

1. The DS:DX register pair contains the base address of a null-terminated character string. The string specifies the disk drive, filename, and filename extension for the file.
2. The CX-register contains the attribute for the file. The attribute specifies the type of file to be created. The individual bits of the attribute are defined as follows:

Attribute Bit	File Type
0	Read-only file
1	"Hidden" file
2	DOS system file
3	Volume label
4	Subdirectory
5	Archive file (fixed disk only)

An attribute with all bits of zero specifies a normal file.

The outputs of these functions depend on whether the create operation is successful. For a successful create operation, the outputs are as follows:

1. The CF bit of the flags register is 0, which indicates a successful create.
2. The AX-register contains the file handle, an integer that uniquely identifies the file. The file handle is to be used for all subsequent operations on the file.

For an unsuccessful create operation, the outputs are as follows:

1. The CF bit of the flags register is 1, which indicates an unsuccessful create.
2. The AX-register contains an error code. The error codes returned by subfunctions 3C hex and 5B hex are as follows:

Error Code	Meaning
03	Path not found
04	Too many files open
05	Access denied (directory full or attempt to overwrite a read-only file)
80 (subfunction 5B only)	File exists

The difference between subfunction 3C hex and subfunction 5B hex is in the way they handle the situation in which the file being created already exists. If the file already exists, subfunction 5B returns error code 80 (file exists), but subfunction 3C sets the length of the file to zero so that the file can be overwritten.

EXAMPLE

The following string definition and instructions create and open a file named RAND.DTA on the diskette in drive A (this example assumes that the DS-register has already been set to address the segment or group containing the string):

```
FILENAME DB   'A:RAND.DTA',0
         .
         .
         .
         MOV  AH,5BH            ;CREATE FILE
         LEA  DX,FILENAME       ;       A:RAND.DTA
         MOV  CX,0              ;       AS A NORMAL FILE
         INT  21H
```

If file RAND.DTA already exists on the diskette in drive A, then the INT 21H service procedure returns the error code 80 (file exists). If the create is successful, then the INT 21H service procedure returns the file handle in the AX-register. ■

Opening and Closing Disk Files

A disk file must be opened before it can be read from or written to. The create subfunctions of the INT 21H service procedure (3C hex and 5B hex) also open the file for access. Subfunction 3D hex of interrupt Type 21 hex is used to open an already existing file. Two inputs are expected by subfunction 3D hex as follows:

1. The DS:DX register pair contains the base address of a null-terminated character string. The string specifies the disk drive, filename, and filename extension for the file.
2. The AL-register contains an access code. This code describes how the file is to be accessed by the program. The allowable access codes are as follows:

Access Code	Meaning
0	Open file for read only
1	Open file for write only
2	Open file for read/write

The outputs of subfunction 3D hex depend on whether the open function is successful. For a successful open operation, the outputs are as follows:

1. The CF bit of the flags register is 0, which indicates a successful open.
2. The AX-register contains the file handle, an integer that uniquely identifies the file. The file handle is to be used for all subsequent operations on the file.

For an unsuccessful open operation, the outputs are as follows:

1. The CF bit of the flags register is 1, which indicates an unsuccessful open.
2. The AX-register contains an error code. The error codes returned by subfunction 3D hex are as follows:

Error Code	Meaning
02	File not found
03	Path not found
04	Too many files open
05	Access denied (e.g., attempt to open a read-only file for write access)
12	Invalid access code (access code not 0, 1, or 2)

A disk file should be closed when the program has finished accessing the file. Subfunction 3E hex of interrupt Type 21 hex can be used to close a disk file. One input is expected by subfunction 3E hex, the file handle of the file to be closed in the BX-register. If the close operation is successful, a 0 is returned in the CF bit of the flags register. If the close operation is unsuccessful, a 1 is returned in the CF bit of the flags register and an error code is returned in the AX-register. The only error code returned by subfunction 3E hex is error 6 (invalid handle).

EXAMPLE

The following string definition and instructions open an existing file named RAND.DTA on the diskette in drive A for read/write access and later close the file using its handle (this example assumes that the DS-register has already been set to address the segment or group containing the string and the save location for the handle):

```
FILENAME DB    'A:RAND.DTA',0
HANDLE   DW    ?
         .
         .
         .
         MOV  AH,3DH          ;OPEN FILE
         LEA  DX,FILENAME     ;     A:RAND.DTA
         MOV  AL,2            ;     FOR READ/WRITE ACCESS
         INT  21H
         JC   ERROR           ;IF   NOT ERROR
         MOV  HANDLE,AX       ;THEN SAVE HANDLE
         .
         .
         .
         JMP  ENDIF1
ERROR:                        ;ELSE
           ⟨Code to handle open error⟩
ENDIF1:                       ;ENDIF
         .
         .
         .
         MOV  AH,3EH          ;CLOSE FILE
         MOV  BX,HANDLE       ;      A:RAND.DTA
         INT  21H
```

If the open is successful, then the INT 21H service procedure returns the file handle in the AX-register. The handle is saved as the value of variable HANDLE and is used for all subsequent access to the file including closing the file. ■

Reading From and Writing To Disk Files

Subfunction 3F hex of interrupt Type 21 hex is used to read a sequence of bytes from a disk file. Three inputs are expected by subfunction 3F hex as follows:

1. The BX-register contains the file handle, which was assigned by DOS at the time that the file was created or opened.
2. The CX-register contains the number of bytes to be read from the file.
3. The DS:DX register pair addresses the storage area in the program into which the bytes are to be read.

The outputs of subfunction 3F hex depend on whether the read operation is successful. For a successful read operation, the outputs are as follows:

1. The CF bit of the flags register is 0, which indicates a successful read.
2. The AX-register contains the number of bytes actually read from the file. This value will be less than or equal to the value passed to subfunction 3F hex in the CX-register.

For an unsuccessful read operation, the outputs are as follows:

1. The CF bit of the flags register is 1, which indicates an unsuccessful read.

2. The AX-register contains an error code. The error codes returned by subfunction 3F hex are as follows:

Error Code	Meaning
05	Access defined (e.g., attempt to read from a write-only file)
06	Invalid handle

When a disk file is opened, a pointer is set to point to the first byte in the file. Subfunction 3F hex automatically updates this pointer so that consecutive calls to this subfunction will read contiguous blocks of data from the file. If the number of bytes actually read from the file is equal to the number of bytes that were attempted to be read, then the file may have more data to be read. If the number actually read is less than the number attempted, then the end-of-file was reached during the read. If the number actually read is zero, then the pointer was at the end-of-file when the read was attempted.

EXAMPLE

The following instructions read the next 500 bytes from the disk file whose handle is the value of variable HANDLE into the array named BUFFER (this example assumes that the DS-register has already been set to address the segment or group containing HANDLE and BUFFER):

```
BUFFER DB   500 DUP(?)
HANDLE DW    ?
        .
        .
        .
       MOV  AH,3FH       ;READ
       MOV  CX,500       ;    500 BYTES
       MOV  BX,HANDLE    ;    FROM FILE HANDLE
       LEA  DX,BUFFER    ;    INTO BUFFER
       INT  21H
```

■

Subfunction 40 hex of interrupt Type 21 hex is used to write a sequence of bytes to a disk file. Three inputs are expected by subfunction 40 hex as follows:

1. The BX-register contains the file handle, which was assigned by DOS at the time that the file was created or opened.
2. The CX-register contains the number of bytes to be written to the file.
3. The DS:DX register pair addresses the storage area in the program that contains the bytes that are to be written to the file.

The outputs of subfunction 40 hex depend on whether the write operation is successful. For a successful write operation, the outputs are as follows:

1. The CF bit of the flags register is 0, which indicates a successful write.
2. The AX-register contains the number of bytes actually written to the file.

For an unsuccessful write operation, the outputs are as follows:

1. The CF bit of the flags register is 1, which indicates an unsuccessful write.

2. The AX-register contains an error code. The error codes returned by subfunction 40 hex are as follows:

Error Code	Meaning
05	Access denied (e.g., attempt to write to a read-only file)
06	Invalid handle

EXAMPLE

The following instructions write a 500-byte record to the disk file whose handle is the value of variable HANDLE from the array named BUFFER (this example assumes that the DS-register has already been set to address the segment or group containing HANDLE and BUFFER):

```
BUFFER  DB   500 DUP(?)
HANDLE  DW   ?
        .
        .
        .
        MOV  AH,40H        ;WRITE
        MOV  CX,500        ;     500 BYTES
        MOV  BX,HANDLE     ;     TO FILE HANDLE
        LEA  DX,BUFFER     ;     FROM BUFFER
        INT  21H
```

■

Programming Examples

Disk I/O operations are illustrated in the following subsections by two example programs. The first program builds a file of pseudorandom integers, and the second one reads and displays this file of random integers. (Programming Exercise 9.13 at the end of the chapter specifies a program to read the random-integer file, sort the integers, and create a second file containing the integers in sorted order.)

Building a File of Random Integers

Program Listing 9.6 shows a program that builds a file of random integers. The user is allowed to select the number of integers to be stored in the file. The file must contain at least 1 integer, and it can contain a maximum of 2000 integers. This file-size limit of 2000 is imposed by the program itself. The array used to accumulate the random integers is defined to be 2000 words in length (lines 31 and 32). To increase this limit, the user needs to change only the value of the constant MAX (line 31) and the limit specified in the prompt message (line 23).

The program of Program Listing 9.6 references four external subprocedures (lines 10–13): GETDEC$ and PUTSTRNG, from the I/O subprocedure library; RANDOM, defined in Program Listing 5.4; and DOS_ERROR, which is a procedure to interpret DOS error codes and to display the DOS-defined diagnostic message associated with the code. Procedure DOS_ERROR is not covered here, but its source code (filename EX_9_6E.ASM) is available on the diskette that accompanies this book.

The program begins with a REPEAT-UNTIL loop (lines 40–54), which is used

```
            PAGE    80,132
;====================================================================
;                   PROGRAM LISTING 9.6
;
; PROGRAM TO BUILD A FILE OF RANDOM INTEGERS
;====================================================================
            .MODEL  SMALL,BASIC
;====================================================================
                                        ;PROCEDURES TO
            EXTRN   DOS_ERROR:FAR       ;DISPLAY DOS INT 21H ERROR
            EXTRN   GETDEC$:FAR         ;GET DECIMAL INTEGER
            EXTRN   PUTSTRNG:FAR        ;DISPLAY CHARACTER STRING
            EXTRN   RANDOM:FAR          ;GENERATE RANDOM INTEGERS
;====================================================================
; S T A C K   S E G M E N T   D E F I N I T I O N
            .STACK  256
;====================================================================
; C O N S T A N T   D E F I N I T I O N S
            .CONST
LOWER       DW      0                   ;LOWER END OF RNG RANGE
UPPER       DW      999                 ;UPPER END OF RNG RANGE
PATHNAME    DB      'A:RANDOM.DTA',0
PROMPT_MSG DB       'ENTER FILE SIZE (RANGE IS 1 - 2000) --- '
PROMPT_LNG EQU      $ - PROMPT_MSG
ERROR_MSG   DB      'FILE SIZE OUT OF RANGE',0DH,0AH
ERROR_LNG   EQU     $ - ERROR_MSG
;====================================================================
; V A R I A B L E   D E F I N I T I O N S
            .DATA
HANDLE      DW      ?                   ;HANDLE OF FILE A:RANDOM.DTA
MAX         EQU     2000                ;MAXIMUM FILE SIZE
REC         DW      MAX DUP(?)          ;FILE OUTPUT RECORD
FILE_SIZE   DW      ?                   ;SIZE OF FILE RANDOM.DTA
;====================================================================
; C O D E   S E G M E N T   D E F I N I T I O N
            .CODE
            .STARTUP                    ;GENERATE STARTUP CODE
            PUSH    DS                  ;SET ES REGISTER TO ADDRESS
            POP     ES                  ;DGROUP
            .REPEAT                     ;REPEAT
            LEA     DI,PROMPT_MSG       ;   PROMPT FOR FILE_SIZE
            MOV     CX,PROMPT_LNG
            CALL    PUTSTRNG
            CALL    GETDEC$             ;   GET FILE_SIZE
            .IF     AX == 0 || AX > MAX ;   IF   FILE_SIZE = 0
;
                                        ;     or FILE_SIZE > MAX
;
            LEA     DI,ERROR_MSG        ;   THEN
            MOV     CX,ERROR_LNG        ;        DISPLAY ERROR_MSG
            CALL    PUTSTRNG
            .ENDIF                      ;   ENDIF
            .UNTIL  AX > 0 && AX <= MAX ;UNTIL FILE_SIZE > 0
                                        ;  and FILE_SIZE <= MAX
CREATE:
            MOV     FILE_SIZE,AX
            MOV     AH,5BH              ;CREATE FILE
            LEA     DX,PATHNAME         ;   A:RANDOM.DTA
            MOV     CX,0                ;   AS NORMAL FILE
            INT     21H                 ;AND GET HANDLE
            JC      ERROR               ;IF   NO ERROR
            MOV     HANDLE,AX           ;THEN
            CLD                         ;     SET DF FOR INCR.
            LEA     DI,REC              ;     PTR = ADDR OF REC
            MOV     CX,FILE_SIZE        ;     COUNT = FILE_SIZE
            .REPEAT                     ;     REPEAT
            PUSH    LOWER               ;        X = RANDOM (0,999)
```

```
68:              PUSH     UPPER
69:              CALL     RANDOM
70:              STOSW                      ;         PTR->WORD = X
71:                                         ;         PTR = PTR + 2
72:              .UNTILCXZ                  ;         DECREMENT COUNT
73:                                         ;      UNTIL COUNT = 0
74:              MOV      AH,40H            ;      WRITE REC TO FILE
75:              MOV      BX,HANDLE         ;         A:RANDOM.DTA
76:              MOV      CX,FILE_SIZE
77:              SHL      CX,1
78:              LEA      DX,REC
79:              INT      21H
80:              JNC      ENDIF2            ;      IF   ERROR
81:              CALL     DOS_ERROR         ;      THEN DISPLAY ERROR
82:                                         ;                    MESSAGE
83: ENDIF2:                                 ;      ENDIF
84:              MOV      AH,3EH            ;      CLOSE FILE
85:              MOV      BX,HANDLE         ;            A:RANDOM.DTA
86:              INT      21H
87:              JMP      ENDIF1
88: ERROR:                                  ;ELSE
89:              CALL     DOS_ERROR         ;      DISPLAY ERROR MESSAGE
90: ENDIF1:                                 ;ENDIF
91:              .EXIT                      ;RETURN TO DOS
92: ;
93:              END
94: ;=====================================================================
```

to input a value for the number of random integers to be generated. The loop body prompts the user for the file size (lines 41–43), accepts an input value (line 44), and tests the input value to see if it is in the specified range (lines 45–52). The loop body is repeated until the input value is within the specified range. Upon loop exit, the input file size is stored as the value of variable FILE_SIZE (line 56).

The instructions in lines 57–60 create a file named RANDOM.DTA on the diskette in drive A. The MOV instruction in line 57 loads the AX-register with the subfunction code for the DOS interrupt Type 21 hex service procedure. Subfunction 5B hex is being used so that an error code will be returned on an attempt to create an already existing file. The DX-register is loaded with the offset portion of the address of string constant PATHNAME (line 58). Subfunction 5B hex expects the DS:DX register pair to contain the address of the null-terminated string that specifies the name of the file to be created. The attribute for the file (0 for a normal file) is loaded into the CX-register (line 59). DOS interrupt Type 21 hex is invoked (line 60) to create the file as specified by its inputs. In addition to creating the file, interrupt Type 21 hex opens the file for access.

The double-alternative decision structure in lines 61–90 checks the CF bit of the flags register to determine whether an error occurred on the create operation. If no error occurred, then the instructions in lines 62–87 are executed. These instructions (discussed shortly) save the file handle (line 62) and load the random integers into the file. If an error occurred, then the instruction in line 89 is executed. This instruction invokes procedure DOS_ERROR to display the diagnostic message for the error code returned by DOS interrupt Type 21 hex. Upon completion of this double-alternative decision structure, control is returned to DOS (line 91).

The REPEAT-UNTIL loop in lines 66–73 loads array REC with the specified number of random integers. The instructions in lines 63–65 perform the initialization for this loop. The DF bit of the flags register is set for incrementing through array REC (line 63). The ES:DI register pair is set to the base address of array REC (line

64). The MOV instruction in line 65 sets the loop count in the CX-register to the file size entered by the user (line 44).

The body of the REPEAT-UNTIL loop is the instruction sequence in lines 67–70. Subprocedure RANDOM is invoked to get a random integer in the range 0–999 (lines 67–69). The STOSW instruction in line 70 stores the random integer in array REC and increments the DI-register by 2 so that the ES:DI register pair addresses the next word in array REC.

Upon loop exit, the random integers in array REC are written to the file. The MOV instruction in line 74 loads the AX-register with the subfunction code (40 hex) for the DOS interrupt Type 21 hex service procedure. The MOV instruction in line 75 loads the BX-register with the file handle, which was returned by the create operation (lines 57–60) and saved as the value of variable HANDLE (line 62). The instructions in lines 76 and 77 set the CX-register to the value of variable FILE_SIZE times 2. Variable FILE_SIZE contains the number of random integers (words) to be stored in the file. This value is multiplied by 2 in order to convert it from number of words to number of bytes. Subfunction 40 hex of interrupt Type 21 hex expects the CX-register to contain the number of bytes to be written from the array to the file. The LEA instruction in line 78 loads the DX-register with the offset portion of the address of array REC. Subfunction 40 hex expects the DS:DX register pair to address the array that contains the data to be written to the file. DOS interrupt Type 21 hex (line 79) is invoked to write the specified number of bytes from array REC to the file specified by the file handle.

Following the file write operation, the single-alternative decision in lines 80–83 is executed. If an error occurred during the write operation, then DOS_ERROR is invoked (line 81) to display the diagnostic message for the error code returned by DOS interrupt Type 21 hex.

The instructions in lines 84–86 close the disk file. DOS interrupt Type 21 hex is invoked (line 86) with the subfunction code (3E hex) in the AH-register (line 84) and the file handle in the BX-register (line 85).

Displaying a File of Random Integers

Program Listing 9.7 shows a program that reads integers from the file RANDOM.DTA on the diskette in drive A and displays the integers on the video screen. The integers are displayed one screen at a time with a pause at the end of each screen of output.

The program of Program Listing 9.7 references two external subprocedures (lines 9 and 10): DOS_ERROR, which is a procedure to interpret DOS error codes and to display the DOS-defined diagnostic message associated with the code; and PUTARAY$, which is a procedure to display an array of unsigned integers. PUTARAY$ expects the base address of the array in the DS:SI register pair and the size of array (in words) in the CX-register. The integers of the array are displayed 10 per line, 24 lines per screen. PUTARAY$ pauses after each full screen of output. The detail of procedure PUTARAY$ is not covered here, but its source code (filename PUTARAY$.ASM) is available on the diskette that accompanies this book. A similar procedure, named PUTARRAY, which displays an array of signed integers is also included on the diskette.

The program of Program Listing 9.7 begins by opening the disk file to be read. The DOS interrupt Type 21 hex service procedure is invoked (line 32) with the subfunction code (3D hex) in the AH-register (line 29), the address of the string contain-

```
            PAGE    80,132
;=====================================================================
;                   PROGRAM LISTING 9.7
; PROGRAM TO READ AND DISPLAY A FILE OF RANDOM INTEGERS
;=====================================================================
            .MODEL  SMALL,BASIC
;=====================================================================
                                        ;PROCEDURES TO
            EXTRN   DOS_ERROR:FAR       ;DISPLAY DOS INT 21H ERROR
            EXTRN   PUTARAY$:FAR        ;DISPLAY ARRAY OF UNSIGNED INT
;=====================================================================
; S T A C K   S E G M E N T   D E F I N I T I O N
            .STACK  256
;=====================================================================
; C O N S T A N T   D E F I N I T I O N S
            .CONST
PATHNAME    DB      'A:RANDOM.DTA',0
;=====================================================================
; V A R I A B L E   D E F I N I T I O N S
            .DATA
HANDLE      DW      ?                   ;HANDLE OF FILE A:RANDOM.DTA
REC         DW      240 DUP(?)          ;FILE INPUT RECORD
;=====================================================================
; C O D E   S E G M E N T   D E F I N I T I O N
            .CODE
            .STARTUP                    ;GENERATE STARTUP CODE
            PUSH    DS                  ;SET ES REGISTER TO ADDRESS
            POP     ES                  ;DGROUP
            MOV     AH,3DH              ;OPEN FILE
            LEA     DX,PATHNAME         ;   A:RANDOM.DTA
            MOV     AL,0                ;   FOR INPUT ONLY
            INT     21H                 ;AND GET HANDLE
            JC      ERROR               ;IF  NO ERROR
            MOV     HANDLE,AX           ;THEN
            .REPEAT                     ;     REPEAT
            MOV     AH,3FH              ;        READ 240 WORDS FROM
            MOV     BX,HANDLE           ;           FILE A:RANDOM.DTA
            MOV     CX,480
            LEA     DX,REC              ;           INTO REC
            INT     21H
            JC      READ_ERR            ;        IF  NO ERROR
            .IF     AX > 0              ;        THEN IF  BYTES READ>0
;
            MOV     CX,AX               ;             THEN
            SHR     CX,1                ;                DISPLAY REC
            LEA     SI,REC
            CALL    PUTARAY$
            .ENDIF                      ;             ENDIF
            JMP     ENDIF2
READ_ERR:                               ;        ELSE
            CALL    DOS_ERROR           ;            DISPLAY ERR CODE
            MOV     AX,0                ;            SET END_OF_FILE
ENDIF2:                                 ;        ENDIF
            .UNTIL  AX < 480            ;     UNTIL END_OF_FILE
;
            JMP     ENDIF1
ERROR:                                  ;ELSE
            CALL    DOS_ERROR           ;     DISPLAY ERROR CODE
ENDIF1:                                 ;ENDIF
            MOV     AH,3EH              ;CLOSE FILE A:RANDOM.DTA
            MOV     BX,HANDLE
            INT     21H
            .EXIT                       ;RETURN TO DOS
;
;=====================================================================
            END
```

ing the filename (A:RANDOM.DTA) in the DS:DX register pair (line 30), and the file access code (0 = input only) in the AL-register (line 31).

The double-alternative decision structure in lines 33–59 checks the CF bit of the flags register to determine whether an error occurred on the open operation. If no error occurred, then the instructions in lines 34–56 are executed. These instructions (discussed shortly) save the file handle (line 34) and read and display the random integers from the file. If an error occurred, then the instruction in line 58 is executed. This instruction invokes procedure DOS_ERROR to display the diagnostic message for the error code returned by DOS interrupt Type 21 hex. Upon completion of this double-alternative decision structure, the file is closed (lines 60–62) and control is returned to DOS (line 63).

The REPEAT-UNTIL loop in lines 35–54 reads 240-word (480-byte) records from the file and calls PUTARAY$ to display them. The program does not know the size of the file, so it must read until the end-of-file condition is detected. When the number of bytes actually read from the file is less than the number of bytes requested, the program knows that the end-of-file was reached during the read operation. Therefore, the loop test (line 54) checks to see if the number of bytes actually read, which was returned in the AX-register by subfunction 3F hex of interrupt Type 21 hex, is less than 480. Any convenient number of bytes could have been chosen for each read operation. The number 480 (240 words) was chosen because it corresponds to the number of integers (240) that PUTARAY$ displays on the screen before generating a pause. That is, the program reads a screen's worth of integers from the file and then calls PUTARAY$ to display the integers and execute a pause. Note that PUTARAY$ will not execute the pause if the number of integers being displayed is less than 240. This situation may occur on the last call to PUTARAY$.

The loop body (lines 36–53) begins by reading a 480-byte record from the file. DOS interrupt Type 21 hex is invoked (line 40) with the subfunction code (3F hex) in the AH-register (line 36), the file handle in the BX-register (line 37), the number of bytes to be read in the CX-register (line 38), and the base address of array REC in the DS:DX register pair (line 39). This call to interrupt Type 21 hex is a request to read the next 480 bytes from the file, identified by the handle in the BX-register, into array REC.

The double-alternative decision structure in lines 41–53 checks the CF bit of the flags register to determine whether an error occurred on the read operation. If no error occurred, then the single-alternative decision structure in lines 42–48 is executed. If an error occurred, then the instructions in lines 51 and 52 are executed. The instruction in line 51 invokes procedure DOS_ERROR to display the diagnostic message for the error code returned by DOS interrupt Type 21 hex. The MOV instruction in line 52 sets the AX-register to zero to force loop exit. This operation makes it look as if less than 480 bytes were read from the file.

For a successful read operation, the single-alternative decision structure in lines 42–48 is executed. This decision makes sure that some bytes were actually read from the file before calling procedure PUTARAY$. If the total number of bytes in the file is divisible by 480, then the last read operation will read only the end-of-file marker and return with the actual number of bytes read set to zero. In this case, there is no need to call PUTARAY$. If the number of bytes actually read is greater than zero, then PUTARAY$ is invoked (line 47) with the number of words read in the CX-register (lines 44 and 45) and the base address of array REC in the DS:SI register pair (line 46). Note that the SHR instruction in line 45 converts from number of bytes read to number of words read.

Demonstration of Example Programs

The demonstration of the preceding two programs is left up to you. First, assemble each of the following source code files: EX_9_6.ASM, EX_9_6E.ASM, EX_5_4.ASM, EX_9_7.ASM, and PUTARAY$.ASM. Next, link together EX_9_6.OBJ, EX_9_6E.OBJ, and EX_5_4.OBJ in order to produce the executable file EX_9_6.EXE. Then, link EX_9_7.OBJ, EX_9_6E.OBJ, and PUTARAY$.OBJ in order to produce the executable file EX_9_7.EXE. With a diskette in drive A, perform the following sequence of steps:

1. Execute the program EX_9_7. Because the disk file has not yet been created, the program should display a diagnostic message on the screen.
2. Execute the program EX_9_6 to create the file RANDOM.DTA on the diskette in drive A. When prompted for the file size, first enter 2001, then try 0, and finally enter 1000. You should notice that diskette drive A is activated. When the program completes, request a directory of drive A (DOS DIR A: command) to see that file RANDOM.DTA was, in fact, created.
3. Execute the program EX_9_7 to display the contents of file RANDOM.DTA. There should be five screens of integers, with the last screen containing only four lines.
4. Execute the program EX_9_6 again. Since the disk file has already been created, the program should display a diagnostic message on the screen.

Additional File I/O Capabilities

The file I/O services discussed in this section can also be used to communicate with the keyboard (handle 0), the video monitor (handle 1), and the printer (handle 4). The file write function, subfunction 40 hex of interrupt Type 21 hex, can be used to output a string of characters to the video screen.

EXAMPLE

Consider the following call to procedure PUTSTRNG:

```
LEA   DI,PROMPT       ;DISPLAY PROMPT
MOV   CX,PROMPT_LNG
CALL  PUTSTRNG
```

This instruction sequence assumes that the ES-register contains the origin of the segment or group containing the string PROMPT. This sequence could be replaced with the following reference to subfunction 40 hex of interrupt Type 21 hex:

```
MOV  AH,40H          ;DISPLAY PROMPT
MOV  BX,1
LEA  DX,PROMPT
MOV  CX,PROMPT_LNG
INT  21H
```

This instruction sequence assumes that the DS-register contains the origin of the segment or group containing the string PROMPT. ■

The file read function, subfunction 3F hex of interrupt Type 21 hex, can be used for keyboard input.

EXAMPLE

Consider the following instruction sequence:

```
MOV  AH,3FH       ;INPUT A MAXIMUM OF
MOV  CX,20        ;       20 CHARACTERS
MOV  BX,0         ;       FROM KEYBOARD
LEA  DX,BUFFER    ;       INTO BUFFER
INT  21H
```

This instruction sequence assumes that the DS-register contains the origin of the segment or group containing the string BUFFER. Subfunction 3F hex of interrupt Type 21 hex accepts characters from the keyboard until a RETURN character (ASCII code 0D hex) is received. The RETURN character is included in the string. In addition, the subfunction 3F hex service procedure adds one character to the string following the RETURN character. This additional character is a LINE FEED character (ASCII code 0A hex). The subfunction 3F hex service procedure returns with the actual length of the string, including the RETURN and LINE FEED characters, in the AX-register. If the actual length of the string, including the RETURN and LINE FEED characters, is greater than 20, then the first 20 characters of the string are returned in BUFFER and the value 20 is returned in the AX-register. The remaining characters will be used for the next invocation of subfunction 3F hex of interrupt Type 21 hex. This interface makes it difficult to implement subprocedure GETSTRNG with subfunction 3F hex of DOS interrupt Type 21 hex. ■

9.5 Additional Capabilities in the 80286 Assembly Language

The 80286 assembly language has two kinds of string instructions, input string instructions and output string instructions, that provide the capability for transmitting arrays between memory and the ports.

There are two input string instructions: INSB and INSW. The **INSB instruction** has the following general form:

[⟨*label*⟩] INSB [⟨*comment*⟩]

It causes the byte at the port addressed by the value of the DX-register to replace the byte in memory addressed by the ES:DI register pair and then causes the value of the DI-register to be updated so that the ES:DI register pair addresses the next byte of the string. If the DF bit in the flags register is 0, then the DI-register is incremented by 1; if the DF bit in the flags register is 1, then the DI-register is decremented by 1.

The **INSW instruction** has the following general form:

[⟨*label*⟩] INSW [⟨*comment*⟩]

It causes the word at the port addressed by the value of the DX-register to replace the word in memory addressed by the ES:DI register pair and then causes the value of the DI-register to be updated so that the ES:DI register pair addresses the next word of the array. If the DF bit in the flags register is 0, then the DI-register is incremented by 2; if the DF bit in the flags register is 1, then the DI-register is decremented by 2.

There is a generic form for the input string instructions:

[⟨*label*⟩] INS ⟨*destination*⟩, DX [⟨*comment*⟩]

in which ⟨*destination*⟩ is the symbolic name of an array. When this form is used, the assembler generates the code for either INSB or INSW depending on the type attribute of the ⟨*destination*⟩ operand.

There are two output string instructions: OUTSB and OUTSW. The **OUTSB instruction** has the following general form:

```
[⟨label⟩]  OUTSB                [⟨comment⟩]
```

It causes the byte in memory addressed by the DS:SI register pair to be transmitted to the port addressed by the value of the DX-register and then causes the value of the SI-register to be updated so that the DS:SI register pair addresses the next byte of the string. If the DF bit in the flags register is 0, then the SI-register is incremented by 1; if the DF bit in the flags register is 1, then the SI-register is decremented by 1.

The **OUTSW instruction** has the following general form:

```
[⟨label⟩]  OUTSW                [⟨comment⟩]
```

It causes the word in memory addressed by the DS:SI register pair to be transmitted to the port addressed by the value of the DX-register and then causes the value of the SI-register to be updated so that the DS:SI register pair addresses the next word of the array. If the DF bit in the flags register is 0, then the SI-register is incremented by 2; if the DF bit in the flags register is 1, then the SI-register is decremented by 2.

There is a generic form for the output string instructions:

```
[⟨label⟩]  OUTS  DX, ⟨source⟩   [⟨comment⟩]
```

in which ⟨*source*⟩ is the symbolic name of an array. When this form is used, the assembler generates the code for either OUTSB or OUTSW depending on the type attribute of the ⟨*source*⟩ operand.

None of the flags are affected by input and output string instructions. As well, since these are string instructions, the REP prefix can be used. But, such use causes a high rate of data transfers, and it should be noted that not all I/O devices can handle such a high rate.

9.6 Additional Capabilities in the 80386 Assembly Language

The 80386 assembly language provides for the input and output of double words. The ⟨*accumulator*⟩ operand of the IN and OUT instructions can also be the register designator EAX. If the ⟨*accumulator*⟩ operand is EAX, then the IN instruction transfers the bytes from four consecutive ports, beginning with the port addressed by the value of the ⟨*port*⟩ operand, to the EAX-register. The byte from the first port is transferred to the AL-register, the byte from the second port is transferred to the AH-register, and so on. If the ⟨*accumulator*⟩ operand is EAX, then the OUT instruction transfers the bytes from the EAX-register to four consecutive ports, beginning with the port addressed by the value of the ⟨*port*⟩ operand. The byte from the AL-register is transferred to the first port, the byte from the AH-register is transferred to the second port, and so on.

The 80386 assembly language also includes an additional form for the input string instruction (INSD) and an additional form for the output string instruction (OUTSD). The **INSD instruction** has the following general form:

```
[⟨label⟩]  INSD                 [⟨comment⟩]
```

It causes the double word at the port addressed by the value of the DX-register to replace the double word in memory addressed by the ES:DI register pair and then causes the value of the DI-register to be updated so that the ES:DI register pair addresses the next double word of the array. If the DF bit in the flags register is 0, then the DI-register is incremented by 4; if the DF bit in the flags register is 1, then the DI-register is decremented by 4.

The **OUTSD instruction** has the following general form:

[⟨*label*⟩] `OUTSD` [⟨*comment*⟩]

It causes the double word in memory addressed by the DS:SI register pair to be transmitted to the port addressed by the value of the DX-register and then causes the value of the SI-register to be updated so that the DS:SI register pair addresses the next double word of the array. If the DF bit in the flags register is 0, then the SI-register is incremented by 4; if the DF bit in the flags register is 1, then the SI-register is decremented by 4.

None of the flags are affected by these instructions. As well, since these are string instructions, the REP prefix can be used. But, such use causes a high rate of data transfers, and it should be noted that not all I/O devices can handle such a high rate.

PRACTICAL EXERCISES

9.1 Write the instructions necessary to move the cursor to row 12, column 40 of the currently active display page. (*Hint*: See Table 9.3.)

9.2 Write the instructions necessary to select page 3 as the active display page. (*Hint*: See Table 9.3.)

9.3 Describe the effect of the following program fragment:

```
MOV  AH,15
INT  10H
MOV  AH,3
INT  10H
MOV  CH,0
MOV  AH,1
INT  10H
```

9.4 Write the instructions necessary to set the Type 60 hex interrupt vector to address a procedure called INT60SRV. Assume the procedure is in the currently active code segment.

9.5 Write the data definitions and the instructions necessary to create (or to open for overwrite) a file named TEMP.DTA on the diskette in drive A.

9.6 Describe the effect of the following program fragment:

```
MOV   AH,35H
MOV   AL,1CH
INT   21H
PUSH  ES
PUSH  BX
```

9.7 Describe the effect of the following program fragment:

```
MOV  AH,0CH
MOV  AL,07H
INT  21H
```

PROGRAMMING EXERCISES

Programming Exercises 9.1–9.7 are designed to provide a series of printer I/O subprocedures similar to the video I/O subprocedures in the author's I/O subprocedure library.

9.1 Implement three printer carriage control procedures defined as follows:

a. Implement a FAR subprocedure called FORMFEED that accepts a printer number in the DX-register and sends a FORM FEED to the designated printer.

b. Implement a FAR subprocedure called LINEFEED that accepts a printer number in the DX-register and sends a LINE FEED character to the designated printer.

c. Implement a FAR subprocedure called SAMELINE that accepts a printer number in the DX-register and sends a RETURN to the designated printer.

9.2 Implement a FAR subprocedure called PRTSTAT to test the printer status. Your input should be the printer number in the DX-register. The subprocedure should loop, testing printer status until the printer is ready. If printer power is turned off or the printer is offline, then the subprocedure should display the message

```
PRINTER TURNED OFF OR IS OFFLINE
PRESS ANY KEY WHEN PRINTER IS READY
```

on the video screen and then pause until a keystroke is received. If the printer is out of paper, then the subprocedure should display the message

```
PRINTER OUT OF PAPER
PRESS ANY KEY WHEN PRINTER IS READY
```

on the video screen and then pause until a keystroke is received. The subprocedure should not return to the caller until the printer is ready for output.

9.3 Design and implement a FAR subprocedure called PRTSTRNG to print a character string at the line printer. Your inputs should be as follows:

> ES:DI register pair addresses the first character of the string.
> CX-register contains the length of the string.
> DX-register contains the printer number.

The subprocedure should print the designated string at the specified line printer beginning at the current print position.

9.4 Design and implement a FAR subprocedure called PRTBIN to print an 8- or a 16-bit integer in binary form at the line printer. Your inputs should be as follows:

> AL-register contains the value to be printed for a byte print; AX-register contains the value to be printed for a word print.
> BL-register contains the print code: Zero implies byte print; nonzero implies word print.
> DX-register contains the printer number.

The subprocedure should print the binary value at the specified printer beginning at the current print position.

9.5 Design and implement a FAR subprocedure called PRTHEX to print an 8- or a 16-bit integer in hexadecimal form at the line printer. Your inputs should be as follows:

> AL-register contains the value to be printed for a byte print; AX-register contains the value to be printed for a word print.
> BL-register contains the print code: Zero implies byte print; nonzero implies word print.
> DX-register contains the printer number.

The subprocedure should print the hexadecimal value at the specified printer beginning at the current print position.

9.6 Design and implement a FAR subprocedure called PRTDEC$ to print a 16-bit integer in unsigned decimal form at the line printer. Your inputs should be as follows:

> AX-register contains the value to be printed.
> BH-register contains the print code:
>
> $BH < 0 \rightarrow$ Left-justify in a six-character field
>
> $BH = 0 \rightarrow$ Print with no leading or trailing blanks
>
> $BH > 0 \rightarrow$ Right-justify in a six-character field
>
> DX-register contains the printer number.

The subprocedure should print the unsigned decimal value at the specified printer beginning at the current print position.

9.7 Design and implement a FAR subprocedure called PRTDEC to print a 16-bit integer in signed decimal form on the line printer. Your inputs should be the following:

> AX-register contains the value to be printed.
> BH-register contains the print code:
>
> $BH < 0 \rightarrow$ Left-justify in a six-character field
>
> $BH = 0 \rightarrow$ Print with no leading or trailing blanks
>
> $BH > 0 \rightarrow$ Right-justify in a six-character field
>
> DX-register contains the printer number.

The subprocedure should print the signed decimal value at the specified printer beginning at the current print position.

9.8 Write a subprocedure called a PUTTEXT to display a null-terminated (zero-terminated) character string. The input to your subprocedure should be the address of the string in the ES:DI register pair. Your procedure should use either BIOS or DOS services to perform the I/O operations. It should not call any of the subprocedures in the author's I/O subprocedure library.

Add procedure PUTTEXT to IO.LIB. If you have not done Programming Exercise 8.13, then follow the instructions in that exercise for adding PUTTEXT.OBJ to IO.LIB. If you have done the exercise and already have that version of PUTTEXT.OBJ on IO.LIB, then follow the instructions in that exercise, changing the operation in step 2 to the following operation:

```
-+a:puttext
```

This operation will remove (−) the version of PUTTEXT.OBJ currently on IO.LIB and replace (+) it with the version on the diskette in drive A.

9.9 Implement a subprocedure called DELAY that executes for a specified number of timer interrupts. Your input should be a count in the AX-register that specifies the number of timer interrupts to delay. The subprocedure should repeatedly read the timer counter, decrementing the value in the AX-register each time the count changes. When the AX-register value reaches zero, the subprocedure should return to the caller.

9.10 Implement a subprocedure called DELAY that executes for a specified number of timer interrupts. Your input should be a count in the AX-register that specifies the number of timer interrupts to delay. The procedure should provide a Type 1C interrupt service procedure that decrements the AX-register value on each timer interrupt. When the AX-register value reaches zero, the subprocedure should restore the Type 1C interrupt vector and return control to the caller.

9.11 Modify your solution to Programming Exercise 4.2 to use a Type 4 interrupt service procedure and the INTO instruction to handle the case of arithmetic overflow.

9.12 Modify the program of Program Listing 9.6 to allow the user to choose whether or not to overwrite an already existing file. If the create operation (lines 57–60) returns an error 80, then the program should prompt the user for the choice. If the user chooses to overwrite the file, then the program should create the file using DOS interrupt Type 21 hex, subfunction 3C hex. Otherwise, the program should terminate.

9.13 Write a program to perform the following steps:

a. Read the file A:RANDOM.DTA created by the program of Program Listing 9.6.
b. Display the data read from the file.
c. Sort the random integers in ascending order by using a subprocedure named SORT. (The interface requirements for procedure SORT are described shortly.)
d. Display the sorted array of integers.
e. Create a file on the diskette in drive A named SORTED.DTA. Load the file with the sorted array of integers. If the file already exists, then overwrite the file with the sorted integers.

Write a subprocedure named SORT to sort an array of integers. The inputs to your subprocedure should be the base address of the array in the DS:SI register pair and the count of the number of integers to be sorted in the CX-register. The following are two versions of the *Straight Exchange Sort* (*Bubble Sort*) algorithm (the first version can be implemented directly using indexed addressing; the second one can be implemented directly using base indexed addressing:

```
PROCEDURE SORT(PTR,N)
   PASS_COUNT = N - 1
   REPEAT
      PUSH PTR
      EXCH_FLAG = FALSE
      CMP_COUNT = PASS_COUNT
      REPEAT
            IF   PTR->WORD >
                      (PTR+2)->WORD
            THEN
                 PUSH PTR->WORD
                 PUSH (PTR+2)->WORD
                 POP  PTR->WORD
                 POP  (PTR+2)->WORD
                 EXCH_FLAG = TRUE
            ENDIF
            PTR = PTR + 2
            CMP_COUNT=CMP_COUNT - 1
      UNTIL CMP_COUNT = 0
      POP PTR
      IF   NOT EXCH_FLAG
      THEN PASS_COUNT = 1
           (FORCES LOOP EXIT)
      ENDIF
      PASS_COUNT=PASS_COUNT - 1
   UNTIL PASS_COUNT = 0
   RETURN TO CALLER
END SORT
```

```
PROCEDURE SORT(ARRAY,N)
   PASS_COUNT = N - 1
   REPEAT
      EXCH_FLAG = FALSE
      CMP_COUNT = PASS_COUNT
      I = 0
      REPEAT
         J = I + 2
         IF   ARRAY[I] > ARRAY[J]
         THEN
              PUSH ARRAY[I]
              PUSH ARRAY[J]
              POP  ARRAY[I]
              POP  ARRAY[J]
              EXCH_FLAG = TRUE
         ENDIF
         I = I + 2
         CMP_COUNT=CMP_COUNT-1
      UNTIL CMP_COUNT = 0
      IF   NOT EXCH_FLAG
      THEN PASS_COUNT = 1
           (FORCES LOOP EXIT)
      ENDIF
      PASS_COUNT=PASS_COUNT - 1
   UNTIL PASS_COUNT = 0
   RETURN TO CALLER
END SORT
```

CHAPTER 10

Recursion

Chapter 5 presented subprocedures as a programming tool. The PUT_BIN subprocedure in Program Listing 5.3 contains a call to another subprocedure, PUTDEC, which also makes reference to other subprocedures. This chapter deals with a special kind of procedure, a *recursive procedure*, which is one that can call itself as a subprocedure. The chapter discusses recursion as a programming tool and shows how recursive algorithms are implemented at the machine level.

10.1 Recursive Definitions

A thing is said to be **recursive** if it partially consists of itself or is defined in terms of itself.

EXAMPLES

"A descendant of a person is a son or daughter of the person, or a descendant of a son or daughter." *Elementary Pascal* by Henry Ledgard and Andrew Singer (Science Research Associates, Inc., 1982).

An arithmetic expression can be defined as (a) a variable reference by itself, (b) a constant by itself, (c) a function reference by itself, or (d) if x and y are arithmetic expressions, then so are the following: $x + y$, $x*y$, (x), $-x$, $x - y$, x/y, $x**y$, and $+x$. ■

In the first example, the term *descendant* is used in its definition: A son of a daughter of a daughter of a person is a descendant of that person. In the second example, (d) is the recursive portion of the definition. Part (a) says that the variables x and y are arithmetic expressions, and (b) says that the constant 2 is an arithmetic expression. The recursive portion of the definition, (d), then says that $x + y$ and $x - y$ are arithmetic expressions. It thus follows that $(x + y)$ and $(x - y)$ are arithmetic expressions, that $(x + y)**2$ and $(x - y)**2$ are arithmetic expressions, that $(x + y)**2/(x - y)**2$ is an arithmetic expression, and so on.

With recursion, an infinite set of objects can be defined using a finite statement. An infinite number of arithmetic expressions can be constructed from the definition given.

10.2 Recursive Algorithms

Recursion can often be used in algorithm design. A **recursive algorithm** is one that makes reference to itself. In this section, several recursive algorithms are considered.

Compute 2^n

Consider the trivial problem of calculating 2 to the nth power for some integer value of n:

$$2^n = 2 \times 2^{n-1} = 2^{n-1} + 2^{n-1}$$

The problem of computing 2^{n-1} and adding the result to itself can be substituted for the problem of computing 2^n, which has been restated in a form that is similar to but simpler than the original problem. Continuing in this manner, the problem can be reduced to one that is so simple that it can be solved directly. The original problem is therefore solved:

$$\begin{aligned}
2^n &= 2 \times 2^{n-1} = 2^{n-1} + 2^{n-1} \\
2^{n-1} &= 2 \times 2^{n-2} = 2^{n-2} + 2^{n-2} \\
2^{n-2} &= 2 \times 2^{n-3} = 2^{n-3} + 2^{n-3} \\
&\vdots \\
2^3 &= 2 \times 2^2 = 2^2 + 2^2 \\
2^2 &= 2 \times 2^1 = 2^1 + 2^1 \\
2^1 &= 2 \times 2^0 = 2^0 + 2^0
\end{aligned}$$

The preceding problem leads to the following recursive algorithm for computing 2^n:

```
TWO_TO_N (N):
                IF   N > 0
                THEN
                     RESULT = TWO_TO_N (N-1)
                     RESULT = RESULT + RESULT
                ELSE
                     RESULT = 1
                ENDIF
                RETURN (RESULT)
```

Fibonacci Numbers

The following sequence of numbers

$$1, 1, 2, 3, 5, 8, 13, 21, 34, 55, 89, \ldots$$

is called the **Fibonacci sequence**. The first number in the sequence is 1, the second number in the sequence is 1, and each subsequent number in the sequence is equal to the sum of the two numbers previous to it in the sequence. Consider the problem of finding the *n*th number in the Fibonacci sequence given a positive integer value for *n*. The *n*th Fibonacci number can be defined recursively as follows:

$$F(1) = 1$$

$$F(2) = 1$$

$$F(n) = F(n-1) + F(n-2) \qquad \text{for } n > 2$$

This definition is captured by the following recursive algorithm:

```
FIBONACCI (N):
                IF   N ⩽ 2
                THEN
                     RESULT = 1
                ELSE
                     RESULT = FIBONACCI(N-1) + FIBONACCI(N-2)
                ENDIF
                RETURN (RESULT)
```

Termination of Recursive Algorithms

Like looping constructs, recursive algorithms introduce the possibility of nonterminating computations. The basic technique for demonstrating that a repetition terminates is to define a function F(x), such that F(x) $\leqslant 0$ implies loop termination, and to prove that F(x) decreases during each repetition of the loop. This same technique can be used to ensure termination of a recursive algorithm: Define for the recursive subprocedure a parameter n, such that $n > 0$ implies that the subprocedure is to be called recursively with $n - 1$ as the value of the parameter and $n \leqslant 0$ implies that no recursive call is to be made. This technique is the same as that used in both of the algorithms presented in the two previous sections.

10.3 Implementation of Recursive Algorithms

A subprocedure can be classified as nonreusable, serially reusable, reentrant, or recursive. A **nonreusable** subprocedure can be called only once in an executable program. After its first execution, it leaves itself in such a state that a subsequent execution might produce incorrect results. The MULTIPLY subprocedure in Program Listing 7.3 is an example of a nonreusable subprocedure. The procedure that was used to demonstrate the MULTIPLY subprocedure (procedure EX_7_2 of Program Listing 7.2) referenced MULTIPLY only once. Using EX_7_2, the subprocedure MULTIPLY consistently produces the same product when presented with the same multiplicand and multiplier. However, as pointed out in Programming Exercise 7.3, the MULTIPLY subprocedure does not produce consistent results when called more than once in a program. Using the EX_7_6 procedure from Program Listing 7.6, the MULTIPLY subprocedure might produce two different products if called twice with the same inputs.

A **serially reusable** subprocedure can be used more than once in a program as long as one execution of the subprocedure terminates before another execution of the subprocedure begins. The MULTIPLY subprocedure in Program Listing 7.3 is nonreusable because the flag variable SIGN is initialized as part of the data segment definition (line 22). This initialization is performed only once, just prior to execution of the program. The variable SIGN is conditionally modified during execution of MULTIPLY (lines 47 and 56). On a subsequent call to MULTIPLY, the variable SIGN may or may not be properly initialized. By moving the initialization from the data segment to the code segment, it is performed on each invocation of MULTIPLY. By changing line 22 of Program Listing 7.3 to

```
SIGN  DB  ?  ;SIGN OF PRODUCT
```

and inserting the line

```
MOV  SIGN,1  ;SIGN = +1
```

after line 44, the MULTIPLY procedure is changed from a nonreusable subprocedure to a serially reusable subprocedure.

Consider the RANDOM subprocedure in Program Listing 5.4. This subprocedure is one for which initialization is performed only once. The FIRST_CALL flag (line 24) is initialized prior to execution of the program that contains the subprocedure. The variable SEED is initialized on the first execution of the RANDOM procedure (lines 39–45). Even though the RANDOM subprocedure does not reinitialize itself on each call, it is considered a serially reusable subprocedure. The FIRST_CALL flag is used so that an initial value for variable SEED is selected only on the first execution of RANDOM. The variable SEED is not reinitialized on subsequent executions of RANDOM so that a new value for SEED can be computed from the value that was computed for SEED on the previous execution of RANDOM. In this case, the subprocedure is supposed to compute a potentially different result (i.e., a potentially different random integer) on each execution.

A **reentrant** subprocedure is one that does not modify itself. The important characteristic of reentrant procedures is that multiple instances of one procedure can be executing at the same time without having multiple copies of the subprocedure. This type of subprocedure is important in large, time-shared computer systems. With such systems, multiple users have simultaneous access to the same software resources; they can be using the text editor or the Pascal compiler simultaneously, for example. Having multiple copies of the text editor or the Pascal compiler (one per user) would consume too much storage space—instead, each user shares a common copy. As long as this common copy is reentrant, then one user has no effect on other users of the common copy. However, each instance of the text editor must be able to edit a different text file, and each instance of the compiler must be able to compile a different source code file. This task is accomplished by dividing the shared program into two parts: a fixed part (code and nonchanging data) and a changeable part (changing data). The fixed portion is reentrant, and a single copy of it is shared by all instances of the procedure. The changeable portion is called an **activation record**, and each instance of the procedure must have its own separate activation record. The activation record contains the information that makes one instance of the shared procedure different from other instances of the shared procedure. For a compiler, the activation record might include the following information:

Information needed to return control to the operating system (i.e., the return address)

Name of the file that contains the source code being compiled (i.e., an input argument)

Mass storage address of the file that contains the source code

Compile options selected (i.e., input arguments)

Name of the file to receive the object code (i.e., an input argument)

Mass storage address of the object code file

The operating system tracks each instance of execution of a shared procedure by a set of **state variables** (one state variable for each instance) (Figure 10.1). The state variable for a given instance contains two pointers: a code pointer (CP) and a data pointer (DP). The **code pointer** is the address within the fixed part of the next instruction to be executed for this instance of the shared procedure. The **data pointer** is the base address of the activation record for this instance of execution of the shared procedure. As long as the fixed portion is reentrant (i.e., does not modify itself), the execution of one instance has no effect on other instances.

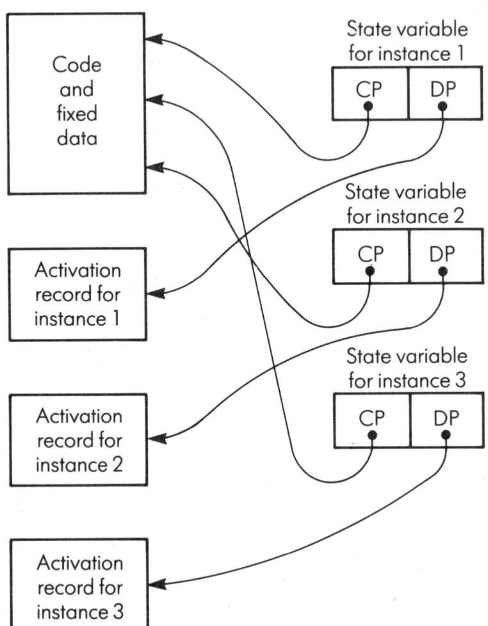

FIGURE 10.1
Reentrant procedure with three instances

The MULTIPLY procedure in Program Listing 7.3, even with the corrections specified in Programming Exercise 7.3, is not a reentrant procedure. It modifies itself by changing the variables in the data segment (e.g., the variable SIGN). Multiple instances of the MULTIPLY procedure could not be allowed because the variables would need to be maintained separately for different instances. (Programming Exercise 10.11 at the end of the chapter deals with a method for changing MULTIPLY into a reentrant procedure.)

A **recursive** subprocedure is one that creates multiple instances of itself by calling itself. Procedure A is said to contain a **direct reference** to procedure B if it contains an explicit call to procedure B. Procedure A is said to contain an **indirect reference** to procedure B if procedure X exists such that procedure A contains a direct reference to procedure X and procedure X contains a direct or indirect reference to procedure B. A subprocedure is said to be **directly recursive** if it contains an explicit call to itself. A subprocedure is said to be **indirectly recursive** if it contains a direct reference to some other procedure that contains a direct or indirect reference to the first procedure. Note that recursion was used in the definitions of indirect reference and indirectly recursive.

Tools for Implementing Recursive Algorithms

Recursive subprocedures are generally implemented as reentrant subprocedures. The items that are different from one invocation of a subprocedure to another include the return address, the arguments passed to the subprocedure, the registers saved for the caller, and local variables used by the subprocedure. These items must be part of the activation record for a reentrant procedure. It is easy to implement a reentrant procedure on a machine that provides a stack: The activation record for a given instance of the procedure can be pushed onto the stack at the beginning of the procedure and popped off at the point of return from the procedure.

In execution of a sequential program, the life span of an instance of execution of one subprocedure cannot overlap the life span of an instance of execution of another subprocedure. That is, the life span of an instance of a subprocedure must be completely contained within the life span of its caller. For example, if the main procedure calls subprocedure A, which in turn calls subprocedure B, then B must return to A before A can return to the main procedure. This sequence must be true for recursive subprocedures as well: If the main procedure calls subprocedure A and subprocedure A calls itself recursively, then the recursive instance of A must return to the original instance of A before the original instance of A can return to the main procedure. This last-called-first-to-return nature of subprocedures coincides with the last-in-first-out (LIFO) nature of the stack (Figure 10.2). The activation record for an instance of the recursive subprocedure is pushed onto the stack as that instance begins execution.

FIGURE 10.2 Relationship of activation records on the stack to instances of a recursive subprocedure

Events	Stack	
Call procedure A Call procedure A recursively	Activation record for instance 3 of procedure A	Top of stack
Call procedure A recursively	Activation record for instance 2 of procedure A	
	Activation record for instance 1 of procedure A	

Events	Stack	
Return from instance 3 to instance 2 of procedure A	Activation record for instance 2 of procedure A	Top of stack
	Activation record for instance 1 of procedure A	

The activation record at the top of the stack always corresponds to the latest instance of the subprocedure, the one that has execution control of the processor. This instance is the **active instance** since it is the one that is actually executing instructions in the recursive procedure. As the active instance of the subprocedure returns to its caller, its activation record is popped from the stack. If the caller is a previous instance of the same subprocedure, then the activation record for that instance (the now active instance) is once again at the top of the stack.

The subprocedure and the stack are the two tools sufficient to implement recursive algorithms. The subprocedure allows a block of instructions to be given a name by which it can be invoked. The stack allows data storage to be allocated and deallocated dynamically, which means that there can be more than one instance of a procedure currently in a state of execution and that each such instance can have its own private set of local objects (i.e., its own activation record). Each instance has its own return address (to a previous instance or to the original caller), its own set of arguments, its own set of saved registers for its caller, and its own set of local variables.

The maximum number of instances of a recursive subprocedure that occurs at one time during execution of an executable program containing that subprocedure is called the **depth of recursion**. Obviously, to ensure termination, the depth of recursion must be finite, and to be practical, it must not only be finite, it must also be small. On each invocation of a recursive procedure, some amount of dynamic storage is required for the activation record. The amount of storage space consumed and the execution time needed to allocate and deallocate dynamic storage space can be significant with a large depth of recursion. It can be even more significant when indirect recursion is involved.

Passing Parameters via the Stack and Local Stack Variables

Parameter passing via the stack, from a user perspective, was introduced in Section 5.4 and illustrated in Section 5.5. The use of base addressing to access stack parameters was discussed and illustrated in Section 8.4. The caller pushes the arguments onto the stack just prior to calling the subprocedure, which uses the **BP**-register as a pointer into the stack and addresses the arguments relative to that pointer. As part of procedure return, the subprocedure pops the arguments from the stack and discards them. Since the return address for the caller is on the stack above the arguments, the popping of the arguments from the stack must be done as part of the return. Recall that the RET instruction has the following general form:

[⟨*label*⟩] RET [⟨*pop-value*⟩] [⟨*comment*⟩]

The ⟨*pop-value*⟩ is an immediate operand that specifies the value that is to be added to the SP-register after the return address is popped from the stack and before the return to the caller is performed. That is, ⟨*pop-value*⟩ is the number of argument bytes to be popped from the stack and discarded.

Local stack variables, from a user perspective, were introduced and illustrated in Section 5.7. The use of base indexed addressing to access a local stack-based array variable was discussed and illustrated in Section 8.4.

EXAMPLE

Consider a subprocedure that has the following header:

```
SUBPROC PROC   FAR PUBLIC, X:WORD, Y:WORD
        LOCAL  K:WORD
```

Subprocedure SUBPROC has two stack parameters, X and Y, and therefore requires a calling sequence of the following form:

```
PUSH  ⟨argument for X⟩
PUSH  ⟨argument for Y⟩
CALL  SUBPROC
```

Figure 10.3(a) shows the state of the stack at time of entry to the SUBPROC procedure.

FIGURE 10.3
State of the stack

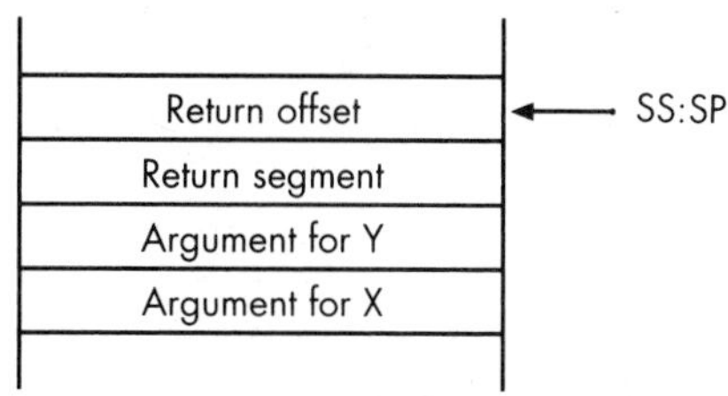

(a) At entry to SUBPROC and just prior to return from SUBPROC

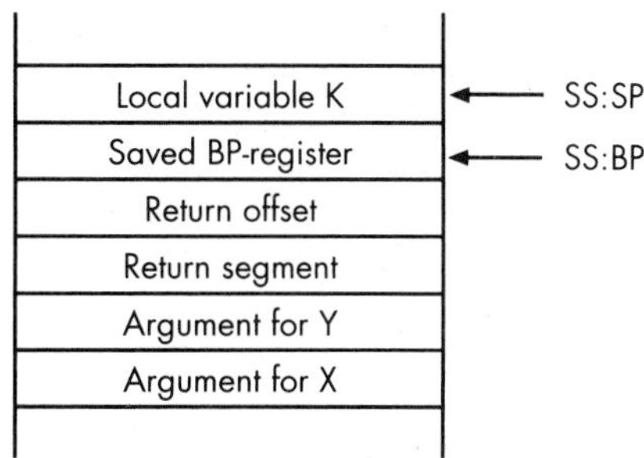

(b) Just after add sp,0FFFEh and just before mov sp,bp

In response to the PROC and LOCAL pseudo-operations, the assembler generates the following instructions at the beginning of SUBPROC:

```
push  bp
mov   bp, sp
add   sp, 0FFFEh
```

The PUSH instruction saves the value of the BP-register for the caller. The MOV instruction sets the BP-register so that the SS:BP register pair addresses a known point in the stack. The ADD instruction adds −2 to (i.e., subtracts 2 from) the SP-register, thus allocating space in the stack for the local variable K. Figure 10.3(b) shows the state of the stack following execution of these three instructions. The six words shown in this stack image make up the activation record for this instance of SUBPROC.

A reference to parameter X causes the assembler to generate the base address 8[BP], a reference to parameter Y causes the assembler to generate the base address 6[BP], and a reference to local variable K causes the assembler to generate the base address −2[BP].

In response to a RET instruction in the subprocedure, the assembler generates the following instructions to replace the RET instruction:

```
mov  sp, bp
pop  bp
ret  00004h
```

Prior to execution of these three instructions, the state of the stack should be as shown in Figure 10.3(b). Otherwise, the PUSH and POP instructions in SUBPROC do not match properly. The MOV instruction deallocates the space in the stack for the local variable K. The POP instruction restores the BP-register for the caller. The state of the stack just prior to execution of the RET 4 instruction is the same as that shown in Figure 10.3(a). Execution of the RET 4 instruction returns control to the caller and pops the arguments from the stack. ■

Programming Example— Compute Fibonacci Numbers

Program Listing 10.1 shows an implementation of the recursive algorithm to compute the *n*th number in the Fibonacci sequence. The program consists of a main procedure and a recursive subprocedure. The main procedure prompts the user for a value for *n* and accepts the input value from the keyboard. It calls the subprocedure (FIBONACCI) to compute the *n*th Fibonacci number and displays the result. The FIBONACCI subprocedure implements the recursive algorithm in Section 10.2.

```
           PAGE    80,132
;===============================================================
;                    PROGRAM LISTING 10.1
;
; PROGRAM TO COMPUTE FIBONACCI NUMBERS
;===============================================================
           .MODEL  SMALL,BASIC
;===============================================================
                                        ;PROCEDURES TO
           EXTRN   GETDEC$:FAR          ;GET UNSIGNED DECIMAL INTEGER
           EXTRN   NEWLINE:FAR          ;DISPLAY NEWLINE CHARACTER
           EXTRN   PUTDEC$:FAR          ;DISPLAY UNSIGNED DEC INTEGER
           EXTRN   PUTSTRNG:FAR         ;DISPLAY CHARACTER STRING
;===============================================================
; S T A C K   S E G M E N T   D E F I N I T I O N
           .STACK  10000
;===============================================================
; C O N S T A N T   D E F I N I T I O N S
           .CONST
;
PROMPT     DB      'COMPUTE N-TH FIBONACCI NUMBER',0DH,0AH
           DB      'ENTER VALUR FOR N',0DH,0AH
ANNOTATE   DB      'FIBONACCI NUMBER = '
;
PROMPT_LNG EQU     ANNOTATE - PROMPT
MSG_LENGTH EQU     $ - ANNOTATE
;
;===============================================================
; C O D E   S E G M E N T   D E F I N I T I O N
;
           .CODE   EX_10_1
;
           .STARTUP                     ;GENERATE STARTUP CODE
;
           PUSH    DS                   ;SET ES-REGISTER TO ADDRESS
           POP     ES                   ;DGROUP
;
```

```
38:             LEA     DI,PROMPT               ;PROMPT FOR N
39:             MOV     CX,PROMPT_LNG
40:             CALL    PUTSTRNG
41:             CALL    GETDEC$                 ;GET N
42:             PUSH    AX
43:             CALL    FIBONACCI               ;COMPUTE FIBONACCI(N)
44:             LEA     DI,ANNOTATE
45:             MOV     CX,MSG_LENGTH
46:             CALL    PUTSTRNG
47:             MOV     BH,0
48:             CALL    PUTDEC$                 ;DISPLAY N-TH FIBONACCI NUMBER
49:             CALL    NEWLINE
50:             .EXIT                           ;RETURN TO DOS
51: ;
52: ;====================================================================
53: ; RECURSIVE SUBROUTINE TO COMPUTE N-TH FIBONACCI NUMBER
54: ; GIVEN A VALUE FOR N. N-TH FIBONACCI NUMBER IS DEFINED
55: ; RECURSIVELY AS FOLLOWS:
56: ;                         F(1)  = 1
57: ;                         F(2)  = 1
58: ;                         F(N)  = F(N-2) + F(N-1)    FOR N > 2
59: ; CALLING SEQUENCE
60: ;           PUSH    <N>
61: ;           CALL    FIBONACCI
62: ; THE RESULT IS RETURNED IN THE AX REGISTER
63: ;====================================================================
64: FIBONACCI   PROC    NEAR, N:WORD        ;FUNCTION FIBONACCI(N)
65:             LOCAL   RESULT:WORD
66:                                             ;GENERATES: push  bp
67:                                             ;           mov   bp,sp
68:                                             ;           add   sp,0FFFEh
69:             CMP     N,2                 ;IF   N <= 2
70:             JG      NGTTWO
71:             MOV     AX,1                ;THEN RESULT = 1
72:             JMP     RETURN
73: NGTTWO:                                 ;ELSE
74:             DEC     N
75:             PUSH    N
76:             CALL    FIBONACCI
77:             MOV     RESULT,AX           ;     RESULT = FIBONACCI(N-1)
78:             DEC     N
79:             PUSH    N
80:             CALL    FIBONACCI
81:             ADD     AX,RESULT           ;     RESULT = RESULT
82:                                         ;            + FIBONACCI(N-2)
83: RETURN:                                 ;ENDIF
84:             RET                         ;POP ARGUMENTS
85:                                         ;RETURN (RESULT)
86:                                             ;GENERATES:  mov    sp,bp
87:                                             ;            pop    bp
88:                                             ;            ret    00002h
89: FIBONACCI   ENDP                        ;END FIBONACCI
90: ;====================================================================
91:             END
```

The program's stack segment is defined in line 16. It has been defined as quite large because recursive algorithms tend to require a large stack (although this size is an overkill because the depth of recursion for this algorithm is not that large). The actual needs of the stack are analyzed later in this section.

The main program (lines 1–51) is rather straightforward and, for the most part, is not discussed here. The portion of the main program that is of interest in this discussion of recursion is the subprocedure interface, lines 41–43. The call to the GETDEC$ procedure in line 41 accepts the positive integer value for n into the AX-register. Lines 42 and 43 contain the calling sequence for the recursive procedure.

The instruction in line 42 pushes the argument, the value of *n*, onto the stack. In line 43, the call is made to the recursive subprocedure FIBONACCI. On return, the *n*th Fibonacci number will be in the AX-register. Figure 10.4 describes the state of the stack segment just prior to execution of the CALL instruction in line 43. It assumes an input value of 4, as do all subsequent figures in this section.

FIGURE 10.4
Stack segment before line 43

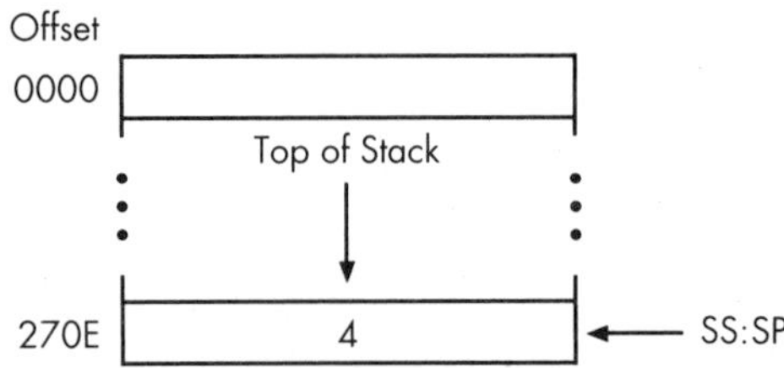

The recursive subprocedure (FIBONACCI) is defined in lines 52–89. Lines 53–62 contain the procedure's prologue, which explains the procedure's function. It also gives the calling sequence for the procedure and specifies how the value of the function is to be returned to the caller. The calling sequence is explicitly shown because the stack is being used to pass the arguments to the procedure. This explanation is especially useful when more than one argument is being passed via the stack because it explicitly shows the order in which the arguments must be pushed onto the stack.

Line 64 defines the recursive subprocedure FIBONACCI as a NEAR subprocedure, which means that only the offset of the return address is pushed onto the stack by execution of the CALL instruction. Line 64 also defines one stack parameter for procedure FIBONACCI, and the LOCAL pseudo-operation in line 65 defines a local stack variable named RESULT. In response to the parameter specification and the LOCAL pseudo-operation, the assembler generates the following instructions at the beginning of the subprocedure:

```
push  bp
mov   bp, sp
add   sp, 0FFFEh
```

These instructions are shown in comment lines 66–68 of Program Listing 10.1. Figure 10.5 shows the state of the stack segment just after invocation of the FIBONACCI subprocedure and just before execution of these three assembler-generated instructions. For ease in hand-tracing the program, the return address offset is shown as a line number and a procedure name; it identifies the position within Program Listing 10.1 of the instruction that follows the CALL instruction.

FIGURE 10.5
Stack segment before assembler-generated instructions

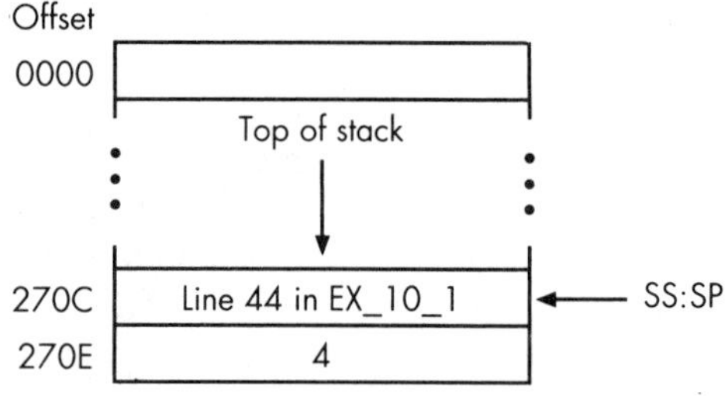

The three assembler-generated instructions save the value in the BP-register for the caller, set it up to point to the stack segment block that contains the local objects for the current instance of the FIBONACCI subprocedure, and allocate stack space for the local variable RESULT. Figure 10.6 shows the state of the stack segment following execution of these three instructions. Note that the figure shows the word in the stack segment that is pointed to by the SS:SP register pair as well as the word that is pointed to by the SS:BP register pair. The SS:SP register pair always points to the current top-of-stack entry. The SS:BP register pair is used to point to the stack segment block that contains the set of local objects (i.e., the activation record) for the active instance of FIBONACCI.

FIGURE 10.6
Stack segment before line 69 (first instance)

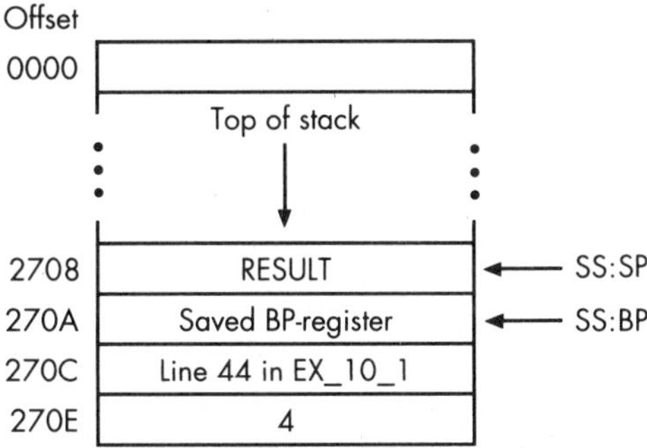

The activation record for the active instance of the FIBONACCI subprocedure contains the following four items:

1. Storage for the local variable RESULT (at offset 2708 within the stack segment)
2. Saved BP-register (at offset 270A)
3. Return address offset (at offset 270C)
4. Input argument (at offset 270E)

Since the BP-register was set to point to this block, the address expression generated by the assembler for references to the input argument is 4[BP], and the address expression generated for references to the local variable RESULT is −2[BP].

The instructions in lines 69 and 70 test the input argument to see if it is less than or equal to 2. In this case, the input argument is greater than 2, so the instruction in line 70 causes a jump to the instruction with label NGTTWO (lines 73 and 74).

The instructions in lines 74–76 carry out the first recursive call to the FIBONACCI subprocedure. The instruction in line 74 decrements the value of the input argument from 4 to 3, and the instruction in line 75 pushes that value onto the stack as the argument for the recursive call to FIBONACCI. Figure 10.7 shows the state of the stack segment just prior to execution of the CALL instruction in line 76.

The recursive call to FIBONACCI in line 76 causes the offset of the return address (the offset of line 77 in FIBONACCI) to be pushed onto the stack and the FIBONACCI subprocedure to be entered for the second time. On entry to the subprocedure, the three assembler-generated instructions (see comment lines 66–68) are executed: The value in the BP-register is saved for the caller, the BP-register is set up to point to the stack segment block that contains the activation record for this second instance of FIBONACCI, and space is allocated in the stack for the local variable RESULT. Figure 10.8 shows the state of the stack segment just prior to execution of the instruction in line 69 in the second instance of the FIBONACCI subprocedure.

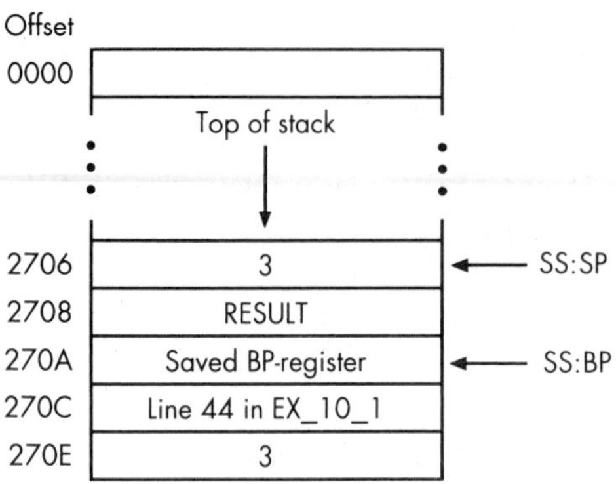

FIGURE 10.7
Stack segment before line 76 (first instance)

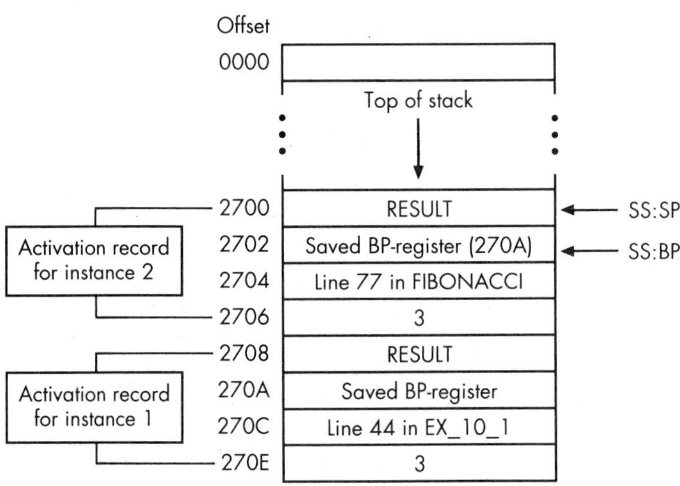

FIGURE 10.8
Stack segment before line 69 (second instance)

Note that there are two activation records on the stack for FIBONACCI: the one pointed to by the SS:BP register pair and the one pointed to by the saved BP-register (SS:270A). The activation record currently in use is *always* the one at the top of the stack.

The value of the input argument for the second instance (3) is greater than 2 (lines 69 and 70), so the jump is made to the instruction in lines 73 and 74. The instruction in line 74 decrements the value of the input argument from 3 to 2, and the instruction in line 75 pushes that value onto the stack as the argument for the next recursive call to FIBONACCI. Figure 10.9 shows the state of the stack segment just prior to execution of the CALL instruction in line 76.

The recursive call to FIBONACCI in line 76 causes the offset of the return address (the offset of line 77 in FIBONACCI) to be pushed onto the stack and the FIBONACCI subprocedure to be entered for the third time. On entry to the subprocedure, the three assembler-generated instructions (see comment lines 66–68) are executed: The value in the BP-register is saved for the caller, the BP-register is set up to point to the stack segment block that contains the activation record for this third instance of FIBONACCI, and space is allocated in the stack for the local variable RESULT. Figure 10.10 shows the state of the stack segment just prior to execution of the instruction in line 69 in the third instance of the FIBONACCI subprocedure. Note that there are now three activation records on the stack for FIBONACCI. The

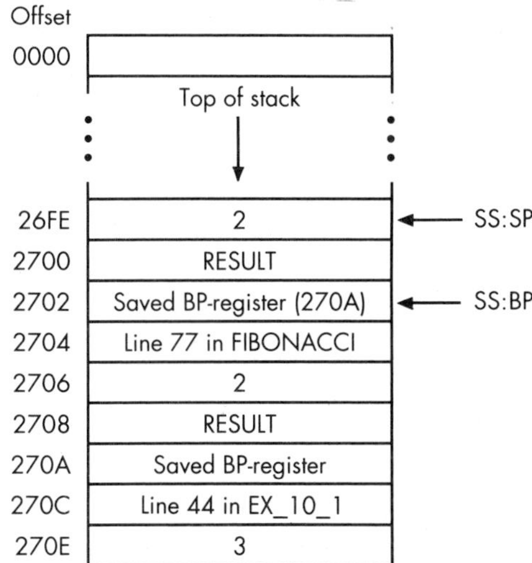

FIGURE 10.9 Stack segment before line 76 (second instance)

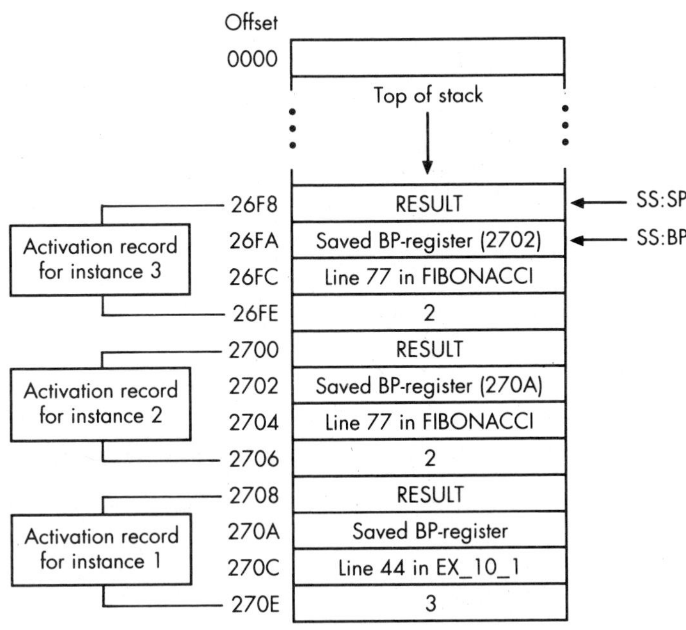

FIGURE 10.10 Stack segment before line 69 (third instance)

one at the top of the stack is the one currently in use. The saved BP-register in each activation record is a partial pointer to the activation record for the previous instance (the caller). It is a partial pointer because it must be combined with the value in the stack segment register to become a complete pointer.

The value of the input argument for the third instance (2) is not greater than 2 (lines 69 and 70), so the jump in line 70 is not taken and the instruction in line 71 is executed. This instruction moves 1, the value of F(2), into the AX-register. The instruction in line 72 causes an unconditional jump to the instruction with label RETURN (lines 83 and 84).

The RET instruction in line 84 causes the assembler to generate the following sequence of instructions to replace the RET instruction:

```
mov  sp, bp
pop  bp
ret  00002h
```

These instructions are shown in comment lines 86–88 of Program Listing 10.1. The MOV instruction deallocates the storage space in the stack for the third instance of the local variable RESULT. The POP instruction restores the BP-register for the caller, the second instance of FIBONACCI. The SS:BP register pair again points to the activation record for the second instance of FIBONACCI. Figure 10.11 shows the state of the stack segment just prior to execution of the RET 2 instruction in the third instance of FIBONACCI. The value in the AX-register at this point is 1, the value of F(2).

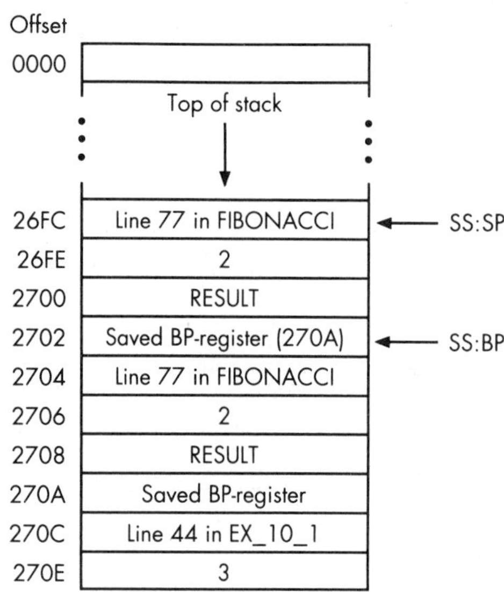

FIGURE 10.11
Stack segment before RET 2 (third instance)

Execution of the RET 2 instruction causes the following sequence of events:

1. The offset of the return address (the offset of line 77 in FIBONACCI) is popped from the stack.
2. The value 2 is added to the SP-register, which, in effect, pops and discards the input argument from the stack.
3. A transfer of control is made to the instruction in line 77 in the previous instance of FIBONACCI with the output value, F(2) = 1, in the AX-register.

Figure 10.12 shows the state of the stack segment just prior to execution of the instruction in line 77 in the second instance of FIBONACCI.

The instruction in line 77 stores the result returned from the third instance of FIBONACCI, F(2) = 1, as the value of the local stack variable RESULT. This value is saved so that it can be added to the result of the next recursive call to FIBONACCI, which produces the result of this, the second, instance of FIBONACCI. The instruction in line 78 decrements the input argument from 2 to 1, and the instruction in line 79 pushes that value onto the stack as the argument for the next recursive call to the FIBONACCI subprocedure. Figure 10.13 shows the state of the stack segment

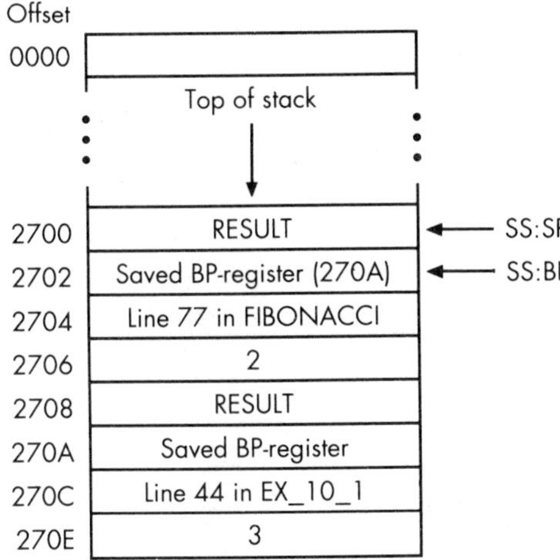

FIGURE 10.12 Stack segment before line 77 (second instance)

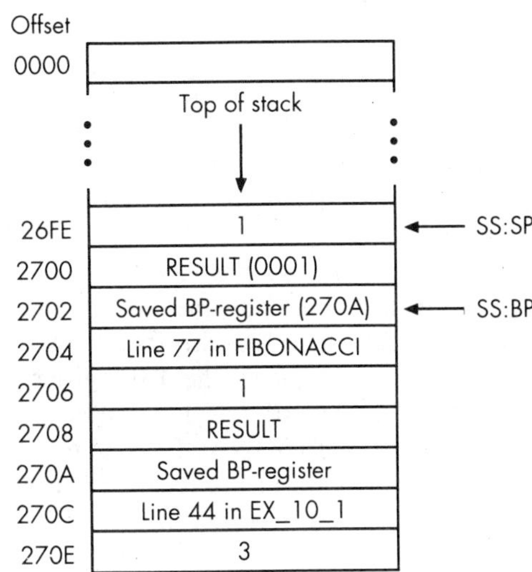

FIGURE 10.13 Stack segment before line 80 (second instance)

just prior to execution of the CALL instruction in line 80. The value at offset 2700 in the stack is the saved value of F(2), and the value at offset 26FE is the argument for the next recursive call to FIBONACCI.

The recursive call to FIBONACCI in line 80 causes the offset of the return address (the offset of line 81 in FIBONACCI) to be pushed onto the stack and the FIBONACCI subprocedure to be entered for the fourth time. On entry to the subprocedure, the three assembler-generated instructions (see comment lines 66–68) are executed: The value in the BP-register is saved for the caller, the BP-register is set up to point to the stack segment block that contains the activation record for this fourth instance of FIBONACCI, and space is allocated in the stack for the local variable RESULT. Figure 10.14 shows the state of the stack segment just prior to execution of the instruction in line 69 in the fourth instance of FIBONACCI. Note again that there are three activation records on the stack for the subprocedure FIBONACCI, one for each existing instance.

The value of the input argument for the fourth instance (1) is not greater than 2 (lines 69 and 70), so the jump in line 70 is not taken and the instruction in line 71 is

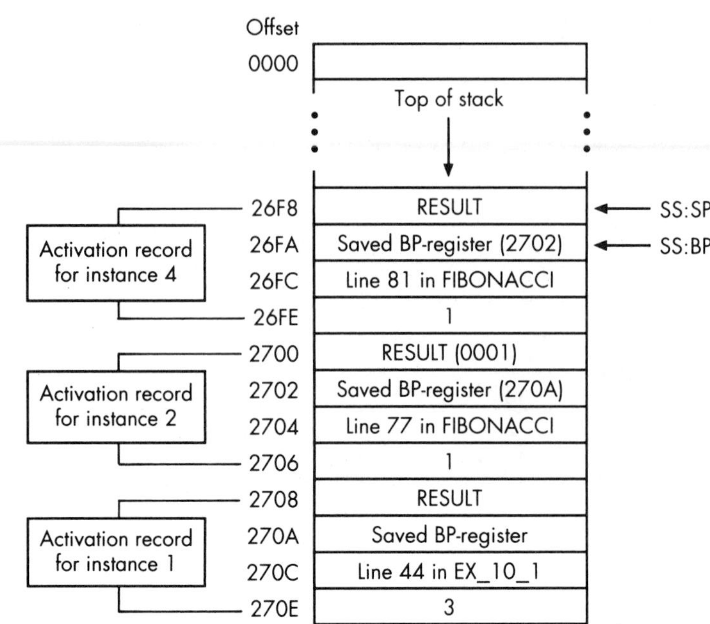

FIGURE 10.14
Stack segment before line 69 (fourth instance)

executed. This instruction moves 1, the value of F(1), into the AX-register. The instruction in line 72 causes an unconditional jump to the instruction with label RETURN (lines 83 and 84).

The RET instruction in line 84 has been replaced by the three assembler-generated instructions shown in comment lines 86–88. The MOV instruction deallocates the storage space in the stack for the fourth instance of the local variable RESULT. The POP instruction restores the BP-register for the caller, the second instance of FIBONACCI. The SS:BP register pair again points to the activation record for the second instance of FIBONACCI. Figure 10.15 shows the state of the stack segment just prior to execution of the RET 2 instruction in the fourth instance of FIBONACCI. The value in the AX-register at this point is 1, the value of F(1).

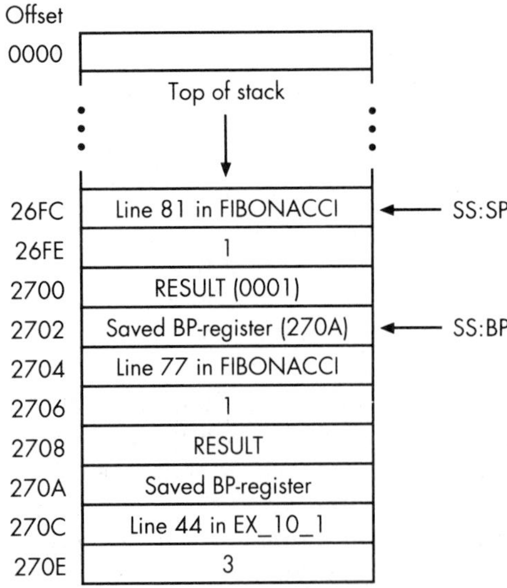

FIGURE 10.15
Stack segment before RET 2 (fourth instance)

Execution of the RET 2 instruction causes the following sequence of events:

1. The offset of the return address (the offset of line 81 in FIBONACCI) is popped from the stack.
2. The value 2 is added to the SP-register, which, in effect, pops and discards the input argument from the stack.
3. A transfer of control is made to the instruction in line 81 in the previous (second) instance of FIBONACCI with the output value, F(1) = 1, in the AX-register.

Figure 10.16 shows the state of the stack segment just prior to execution of the instruction in line 81 in the second instance of FIBONACCI. At this point, the value of F(1) is in the AX-register, and the value of F(2) is the value of the local stack variable RESULT.

FIGURE 10.16
Stack segment before line 81 (second instance)

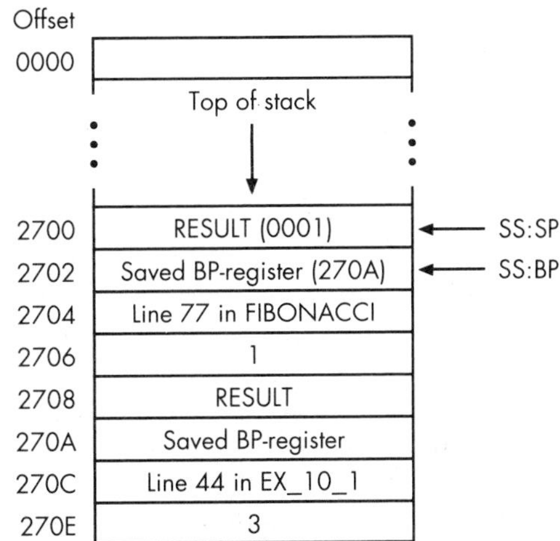

The instruction in line 81 adds the value of F(2) to the value of F(1) in the AX-register, producing the value of F(3). The RET instruction in line 84 has been replaced by the three assembler-generated instructions shown in comment lines 86–88. The MOV instruction deallocates the storage space in the stack for the second instance of the local variable RESULT. The POP instruction restores the BP-register for the caller, the first instance of FIBONACCI. The SS:BP register pair again points to the activation record for the first instance of FIBONACCI. Figure 10.17 shows the

FIGURE 10.17
Stack segment before RET 2 (second instance)

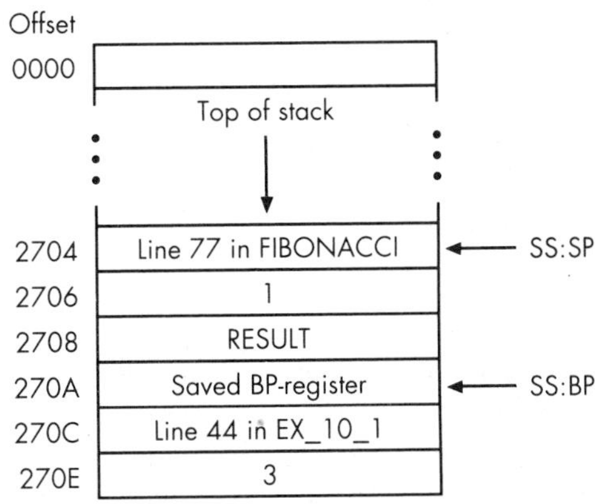

state of the stack segment just prior to execution of the RET 2 instruction in the second instance of FIBONACCI. The value in the AX-register at this point is 2, the value of F(3).

Execution of the RET 2 instruction causes the return address offset (the offset of line 77 in FIBONACCI) to be popped from the stack, the input argument to be popped and discarded from the stack, and a transfer of control to be made to line 77 in the previous (first) instance of FIBONACCI. The value of F(3) is in the AX-register. Figure 10.18 shows the state of the stack segment just prior to execution of the instruction in line 77 in the first instance of FIBONACCI.

FIGURE 10.18
Stack segment before line 77 (first instance)

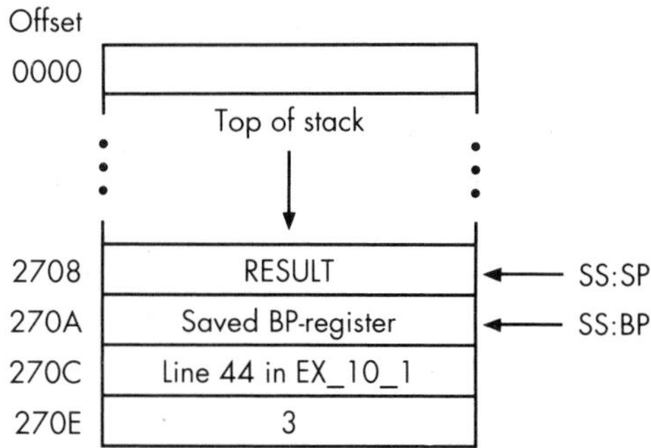

The instruction in line 77 stores the result returned from the second instance of FIBONACCI, F(3) = 2, as the value of the local stack variable RESULT. Again, this value is saved so that it can be added to the result of the next recursive call to FIBONACCI, which produces the result of this, the original, instance of FIBONACCI. The instruction in line 78 decrements the input argument from 3 to 2, and the instruction in line 79 pushes that value onto the stack as the argument for the next recursive call to FIBONACCI. Figure 10.19 shows the state of the stack segment just prior to execution of the CALL instruction in line 80. The value at offset 2708 in the stack is the saved value of F(3), and the value at offset 2706 is the argument for the next recursive call to FIBONACCI.

FIGURE 10.19
Stack segment before line 80 (first instance)

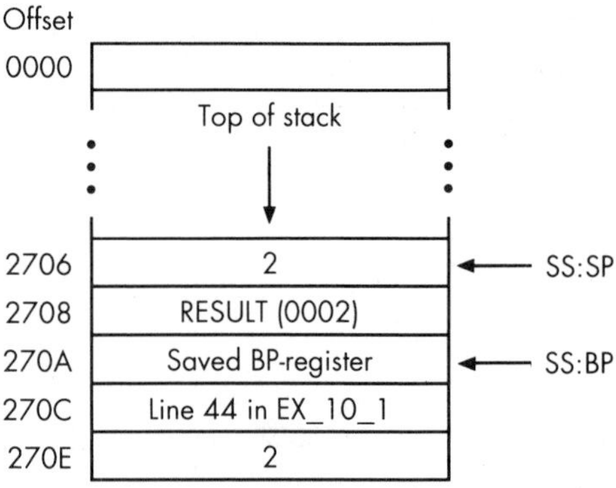

The recursive call to FIBONACCI in line 80 causes the offset of the return address (the offset of line 81 in FIBONACCI) to be pushed onto the stack and the FIBONACCI subprocedure to be entered for the fifth time. On entry to the subprocedure, the three assembler-generated instructions (see comment lines 66–68) are

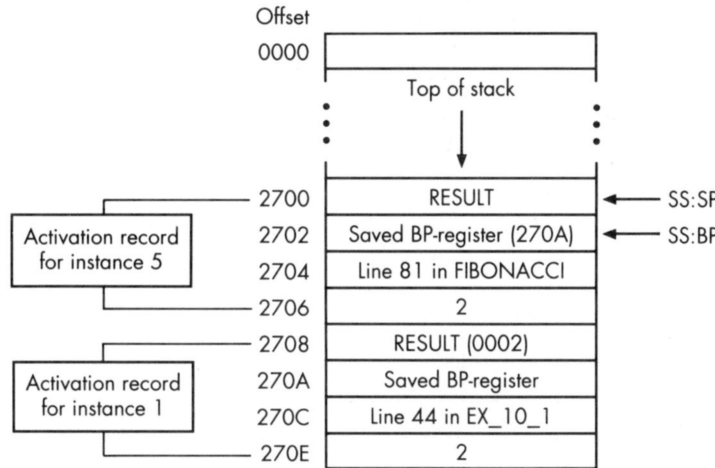

FIGURE 10.20
Stack segment before line 69 (fifth instance)

executed: The value in the BP-register is saved for the caller, the BP-register is set up to point to the stack segment block that contains the activation record for this fifth instance of FIBONACCI, and space is allocated in the stack for the local variable RESULT. Figure 10.20 shows the state of the stack segment just prior to execution of the instruction in line 69 in the fifth instance of FIBONACCI.

The value of the input argument for the fifth instance (2) is not greater than 2 (lines 69 and 70), so the jump in line 70 is not taken and the instruction in line 71 is executed. This instruction moves 1, the value of F(2), into the AX-register. The instruction in line 72 causes an unconditional jump to the instruction with label RETURN (lines 83 and 84).

The RET instruction in line 84 has been replaced by the three assembler-generated instructions shown in comment lines 86–88. The MOV instruction deallocates the storage space in the stack for the fifth instance of the local variable RESULT. The POP instruction restores the BP-register for the caller, the first instance of FIBONACCI. The SS:BP register pair again points to the activation record for the first instance of FIBONACCI. Figure 10.21 shows the state of the stack segment just prior to execution of the RET 2 instruction in the fifth instance of FIBONACCI. The value in the AX-register at this point is 1, the value of F(2).

Execution of the RET 2 instruction causes the return address offset (the offset of line 81 in FIBONACCI) to be popped from the stack, the input argument to be

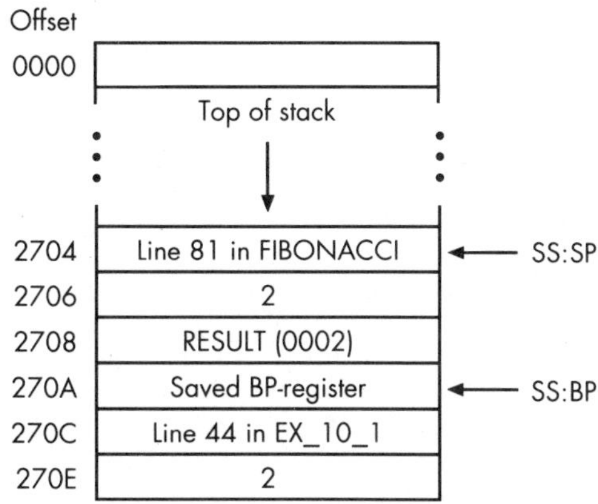

FIGURE 10.21
Stack segment before RET 2 (fifth instance)

popped and discarded from the stack, and a transfer of control to be made to line 81 in the previous (first) instance of FIBONACCI. Figure 10.22 shows the state of the stack segment just prior to execution of the instruction in line 81 in the original instance of FIBONACCI. At this point, the value of F(2) is in the AX-register, and the value of F(3) is the value of the local stack variable RESULT.

FIGURE 10.22
Stack segment before line 81 (first instance)

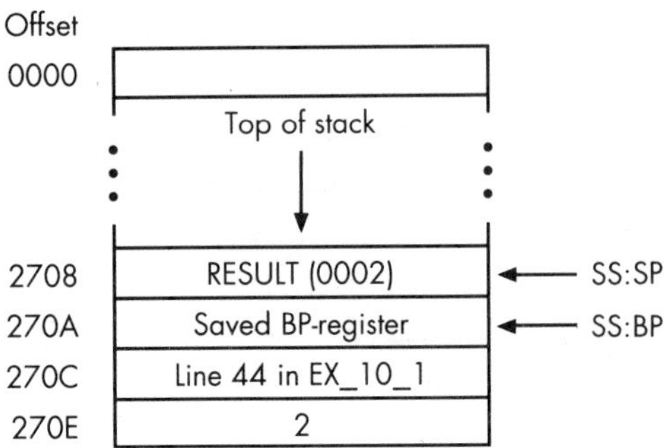

The instruction in line 81 adds the value of F(3) to the value of F(2) in the AX-register, producing the value of F(4). The RET instruction in line 84 has been replaced by the three assembler-generated instructions shown in comment lines 86–88. The MOV instruction deallocates the storage space in the stack for the first instance of the local variable RESULT. The POP instruction restores the BP-register for the caller, the main procedure. At this point, the value of F(4) is in the AX-register. The value of F(4) is the value requested by the original caller, the main procedure. Execution of the RET 2 instruction returns control to the instruction in line 44 of the main procedure with the output value, F(4) = 3, in the AX-register. The argument is popped from the stack as part of the return.

The following are the results from some executions of this program:

```
COMPUTE N-TH FIBONACCI NUMBER
ENTER VALUE FOR N
4
FIBONACCI = 3

COMPUTE N-TH FIBONACCI NUMBER
ENTER VALUE FOR N
12
FIBONACCI = 144

COMPUTE N-TH FIBONACCI NUMBER
ENTER VALUE FOR N
22
FIBONACCI = 17711

COMPUTE N-TH FIBONACCI NUMBER
ENTER VALUE FOR N
23
FIBONACCI = 28657

COMPUTE N-TH FIBONACCI NUMBER
ENTER VALUE FOR N
24
FIBONACCI = 46368
```

Note that $n = 24$ is the largest input value that can be accommodated by this program without overflow. The twenty-fifth FIBONACCI number is

$$F(25) = F(24) + F(23) = 46{,}368 + 28{,}657 = 75{,}025$$

This number is greater than 65,535, the upper limit for 16-bit unsigned integers. Therefore, an input of $n = 25$ would create an arithmetic overflow in the computation. The program as it appears does nothing to detect arithmetic overflow.

The graph in Figure 10.23 is a binary tree that shows the hierarchy of recursive calls to the FIBONACCI procedure in the example execution that was traced in Figures 10.4–10.22. The graph nodes are labeled with the function that is being performed by an invocation of FIBONACCI. The edges are labeled with the value being returned from an invocation back up to its caller. The order of call is that of a **preorder traversal** of the tree, which can be defined recursively by performing the following steps in sequence:

1. Visit the root of the tree.
2. Perform a preorder traversal of the left subtree.
3. Perform a preorder traversal of the right subtree.

For the tree in Figure 10.23, a preorder traversal produces the following sequence of function calls: F(4), F(3), F(2), F(1), and F(2).

FIGURE 10.23
Tree of recursive calls in computing F(4)

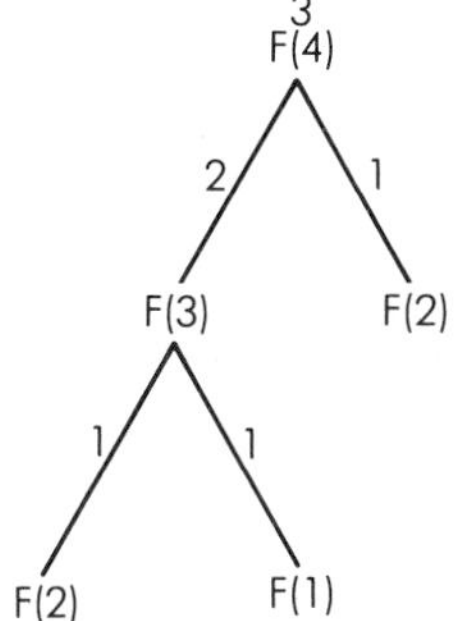

The figure shows that the depth of recursion for this example execution was 3. The depth was reached twice, on the third and fourth invocations (Figures 10.10 and 10.14). Program Listing 10.2 shows the same program with some modifications to compute and display the depth of recursion. A new annotation message appears in line 24, which is used to label the display of the depth of recursion. Two variables have been added in lines 31 and 32. DEPTH is used to track the current level of recursion. It is incremented on each entry to the FIBONACCI procedure (line 77), and it is decremented on each exit from FIBONACCI (line 98). That is, it counts the number of currently existing instances of FIBONACCI. Whenever the value of DEPTH becomes greater than the value of MAX_DEPTH, MAX_DEPTH is set to the current value of DEPTH (lines 93–96). Both DEPTH and MAX_DEPTH are initialized to zero (lines 31 and 32). On return to the main program from FIBONACCI, MAX_DEPTH contains the true depth of recursion. The instructions in lines 53–57 display the value of MAX_DEPTH.

```
            PAGE    80,132
;====================================================================
;                     PROGRAM LISTING 10.2
;
; PROGRAM TO COMPUTE FIBONACCI NUMBERS
;====================================================================
            .MODEL  SMALL,BASIC
;====================================================================
                                        ;PROCEDURES TO
            EXTRN   GETDEC$:FAR         ;GET UNSIGNED DECIMAL INTEGER
            EXTRN   NEWLINE:FAR         ;DISPLAY NEWLINE CHARACTER
            EXTRN   PUTDEC$:FAR         ;DISPLAY UNSIGNED DEC INTEGER
            EXTRN   PUTSTRNG:FAR        ;DISPLAY CHARACTER STRING
;====================================================================
; S T A C K   S E G M E N T   D E F I N I T I O N
            .STACK  10000
;====================================================================
; C O N S T A N T   D E F I N I T I O N S
            .CONST
;
PROMPT      DB      'COMPUTE N-TH FIBONACCI NUMBER',0DH,0AH
            DB      'ENTER VALUR FOR N',0DH,0AH
ANNOTATE    DB      'FIBONACCI NUMBER = '
DEPTH_MSG   DB      'DEPTH OF RECURSION = '
PROMPT_LNG EQU      ANNOTATE - PROMPT
MSG_LENGTH EQU      DEPTH_MSG - ANNOTATE
DEPTH_LNG   EQU     $ - DEPTH_MSG
;====================================================================
; V A R I A B L E   D E F I N I T I O N S
            .DATA
DEPTH       DW      0                   ;CURRENT DEPTH OF RECURSION
MAX_DEPTH   DW      0                   ;DEPTH OF RECURSION
;====================================================================
; C O D E   S E G M E N T   D E F I N I T I O N
;
            .CODE   EX_10_2
            .STARTUP                    ;GENERATE STARTUP CODE
            PUSH    DS                  ;SET ES-REGISTER TO ADDRESS
            POP     ES                  ;DGROUP
;
            LEA     DI,PROMPT           ;PROMPT FOR N
            MOV     CX,PROMPT_LNG
            CALL    PUTSTRNG
            CALL    GETDEC$             ;GET N
            PUSH    AX
            CALL    FIBONACCI           ;COMPUTE FIBONACCI(N)
            LEA     DI,ANNOTATE
            MOV     CX,MSG_LENGTH
            CALL    PUTSTRNG
            MOV     BH,0
            CALL    PUTDEC$             ;DISPLAY N-TH FIBONACCI NUMBER
            CALL    NEWLINE
            LEA     DI,DEPTH_MSG        ;DISPLAY DEPTH OF RECURSION
            MOV     CX,DEPTH_LNG
            CALL    PUTSTRNG
            MOV     AX,MAX_DEPTH
            CALL    PUTDEC$
            .EXIT                       ;RETURN TO DOS
;
;====================================================================
; RECURSIVE SUBROUTINE TO COMPUTE N-TH FIBONACCI NUMBER
; GIVEN A VALUE FOR N. N-TH FIBONACCI NUMBER IS DEFINED
; RECURSIVELY AS FOLLOWS:
;                         F(1) = 1
;                         F(2) = 1
;                         F(N) = F(N-2) + F(N-1)    FOR N > 2
; CALLING SEQUENCE
```

```
;            PUSH     <N>
;            CALL     FIBONACCI
; THE RESULT IS RETURNED IN THE AX REGISTER
;=====================================================================
FIBONACCI    PROC     NEAR, N:WORD       ;FUNCTION FIBONACCI(N)
             LOCAL    RESULT:WORD
                                                ;GENERATES: push  bp
                                                ;           mov   bp,sp
                                                ;           add   sp,OFFFEh
             INC      DEPTH              ;DEPTH = DEPTH + 1
             CMP      N,2                ;IF   N <= 2
             JG       NGTTWO
             MOV      AX,1               ;THEN RESULT = 1
             JMP      CHK_DEPTH
NGTTWO:                                  ;ELSE
             DEC      N
             PUSH     N
             CALL     FIBONACCI
             MOV      RESULT,AX          ;      RESULT = FIBONACCI(N-1)
             DEC      N
             PUSH     N
             CALL     FIBONACCI
             ADD      AX,RESULT          ;      RESULT = RESULT
                                         ;             + FIBONACCI(N-2)
CHK_DEPTH:                               ;ENDIF
             MOV      BX,DEPTH           ;IF   DEPTH > MAX_DEPTH
             CMP      BX,MAX_DEPTH
             JLE      RETURN
             MOV      MAX_DEPTH,BX       ;THEN MAX_DEPTH = DEPTH
RETURN:                                  ;ENDIF
             DEC      DEPTH              ;DEPTH = DEPTH - 1
             RET                         ;POP ARGUMENTS
                                         ;RETURN (RESULT)
                                                ;GENERATES: mov   sp,bp
                                                ;           pop   bp
                                                ;           ret   00002h
FIBONACCI    ENDP                        ;END FIBONACCI
;=====================================================================
             END
```

The following are the results from some executions of this version of the program:

```
COMPUTE N-TH FIBONACCI NUMBER
ENTER VALUE FOR N
4
FIBONACCI NUMBER = 3
DEPTH OF RECURSION = 3

COMPUTE N-TH FIBONACCI NUMBER
ENTER VALUE FOR N
12
FIBONACCI NUMBER = 144
DEPTH OF RECURSION = 11

COMPUTE N-TH FIBONACCI NUMBER
ENTER VALUE FOR N
22
FIBONACCI NUMBER = 17711
DEPTH OF RECURSION = 21

COMPUTE N-TH FIBONACCI NUMBER
ENTER VALUE FOR N
23
FIBONACCI NUMBER = 28657
DEPTH OF RECURSION = 22
```

```
COMPUTE N-TH FIBONACCI NUMBER
ENTER VALUE FOR N
24
FIBONACCI NUMBER = 46368
DEPTH OF RECURSION = 23
```

From these results and from drawing some graphs like the one in Figure 10.23, you can become convinced that the depth of recursion for computing F(n), in which $n > 1$, is $n - 1$. You already have seen that the maximum value for n is 24. On each recursive call, a block of four local objects is pushed onto the stack. Therefore, each call causes four words (8 bytes) to be pushed onto the stack. With a maximum value of $n = 24$, the depth of recursion is 23, and a total of $23 * 8 = 184$ bytes are needed in the stack to support the FIBONACCI procedure. A stack segment of 200 bytes would be more than sufficient, which is far below the estimate of 10,000 bytes that was used. However, with a recursive program, it is much safer to begin with a large stack segment and then reduce it later if analysis shows that a reduction is advisable.

PROGRAMMING EXERCISES

10.1 The factorial function can be defined recursively as follows:

$$0! = 1$$

$$n! = n \times (n - 1)! \qquad \text{for } n > 0$$

Design a recursive algorithm to compute $n!$ given a nonnegative integer value for n. Implement your algorithm with an 8088/8086 assembly language recursive, external FAR subprocedure. Your calling sequence should be

```
PUSH ⟨n⟩
CALL FACT
```

Your subprocedure should return the value of $n!$ in the AX-register. Use a zero result to signify that an overflow occurred in the computation.

10.2 Design an algorithm to compute and display a table of nonnegative integers and their factorial values. Use the recursive subalgorithm in Programming Exercise 10.1 to compute the factorial values. Implement your algorithm with a complete 8088/8086 assembly language program. The table displayed should begin with $n = 0$ and terminate with the first value of n that causes an arithmetic overflow in the factorial computation.

10.3 The binomial coefficients $C(n, k)$, in which $n >= 0$, $k >= 0$, and $n >= k$, are given by the following recursive definition:

$$C(n, n) = 1$$

$$C(n, 0) = 1$$

$$C(n, k) = C(n - 1, k - 1) + C(n - 1, k)$$

$$\text{for } (0 < k < n) \text{ and } n > 1$$

Design a recursive algorithm to compute $C(n, k)$ given nonnegative integer values for n and k. Implement your algorithm with an 8088/8086 assembly language recursive, external FAR subprocedure. Your calling sequence should be

```
PUSH ⟨n⟩
PUSH ⟨k⟩
CALL C
```

Your procedure should return the value of the binomial coefficient, $C(n, k)$, in the AX-register. Use a zero result to signify that an overflow occurred in the computation.

10.4 The first five rows of Pascal's triangle are shown:

```
        1
      1   1
    1   2   1
  1   3   3   1
1   4   6   4   1
```

The nth row of Pascal's triangle produces the coefficients of the expansion of $(a + b)^{n-1}$. For example, row 5 of Pascal's triangle produces the coefficients of

$$(a + b)^4 = a^4 + 4a^3b + 6a^2b^2 + 4ab^3 + b^4$$

The elements in the nth row are the n binomial coefficients $C(n - 1, 0)$, $C(n - 1, 1)$, $C(n - 1, 2)$, . . . , $C(n - 1, n - 1)$. Design an algorithm to compute and display the first 13 rows of Pascal's triangle. Use the recursive subalgorithm in Programming Exercise 10.3 to compute the binomial coefficients. Implement your algorithm with a complete 8088/8086 assembly language program.

10.5 The following recursive function, defined for nonnegative integers m and n, is called *Ackermann's function*:

$$A(m, n) = n + 1 \quad \text{if } m = 0$$

$$A(m, n) = A(m - 1, 1) \quad \text{if } m > 0 \text{ and } n = 0$$

$$A(m, n) = A(m - 1, A(m, n - 1)) \quad \text{if } m > 0 \text{ and } n > 0$$

Design an algorithm to compute and output the value of Ackermann's function given values for m and n. The actual computation of the function should be designed as a recursive subalgorithm.

Implement your algorithm with a complete 8088/8086 assembly language program. Your program should accept values for m and n from the keyboard and output to the display screen the value of Ackermann's function applied to m and n. Implement Ackermann's function with an 8088/8086 assembly language recursive, internal NEAR subprocedure. The calling sequence for the subprocedure is

```
PUSH ⟨m⟩
PUSH ⟨n⟩
CALL ACKERMAN
```

The result of the recursive subprocedure is to be returned in the AX-register. Demonstrate your program with the following computations: A(0, 3), A(3, 0), A(3, 2), A(3, 5), and A(3, 9).

10.6 Ackermann's function has a large depth of recursion. To convince yourself of this, compute A(3, 2) by hand. Now, modify your program from Programming Exercise 10.5 to compute and display the depth of recursion and the total number of calls to the recursive ACKERMAN procedure. Demonstrate your program with the same computations specified in Programming Exercise 10.5.

10.7 The Towers of Hanoi puzzle consists of three pegs and three or more disks of distinct diameters. The disks are all on one peg and are initially arranged in order of decreasing diameter from bottom to top. The object of the puzzle is to transfer all of the disks to another peg by a sequence of moves. Each move involves a *single* disk, the topmost disk from any peg. That disk can be moved to any peg that is either empty or whose topmost disk is larger than the disk being moved. A disk can never be placed on top of a smaller disk. The series of diagrams in Figure 10.24 shows the sequence of moves necessary to transfer three disks from peg 1 to peg 2.

The key of stating an algorithm for solving the Towers of Hanoi puzzle is to realize the following requirement: Before the nth largest disk can be moved from peg X to peg Y, the $n - 1$ smaller disks must first be moved to the third peg, peg Z. Once done, it is trivial to move the nth largest disk from peg X to peg Y. The $n - 1$ smaller disks can then be moved from peg Z to peg Y using a sequence of moves that is similar to the sequence that moved them from peg X to peg Z. The preceding requirement gives rise to the following recursive algorithm for specifying the moves in the Towers of Hanoi puzzle:

FIGURE 10.24
Sequence of moves to transfer three disks from peg 1 to peg 2

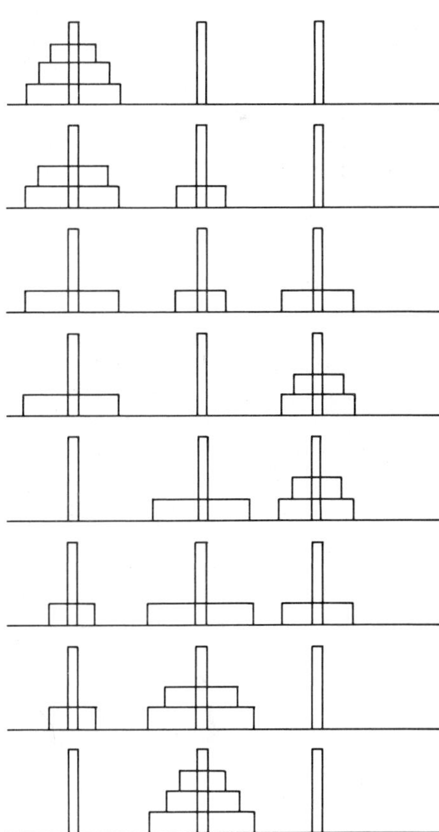

```
MOVDSK (COUNT,FROMPEG,TOPEG):

        IF    COUNT = 1
        THEN
              DISPLAY 'move disk ',COUNT
              DISPLAY ' from peg ',FROMPEG
              DISPLAY ' to peg ',TOPEG
        ELSE
              OTHERPEG = 6 - FROMPEG - TOPEG
              MOVDSK (COUNT-1,FROMPEG,OTHERPEG)
              DISPLAY 'move disk ',COUNT
              DISPLAY ' from peg ',FROMPEG
              DISPLAY ' to peg ',TOPEG
              MOVDSK (COUNT-1,OTHERPEG,TOPEG)
        ENDIF
```

Implement this algorithm with an 8088/8086 assembly language recursive, internal NEAR subprocedure. The calling sequence for the subprocedure is

```
PUSH  〈count〉
PUSH  〈from-peg〉
PUSH  〈to-peg〉
CALL  MOVDSK
```

in which 〈*count*〉 specifies the number of disks to be moved, 〈*from-peg*〉 specifies the number of the peg that contains the disks, and 〈*to-peg*〉 specifies the number of the peg to which the disks are to be moved. Design and implement a main program to test this recursive subprocedure.

10.8 Euclid's algorithm for computing the greatest common divisor (GCD) of two positive integers can be stated recursively as follows:

$$\text{GCD}(x, y) = y \quad \text{if } x \bmod y = 0$$

$$\text{GCD}(x, y) = \text{GCD}(y, x \bmod y) \quad \text{if } x \bmod y \neq 0$$

Design a recursive algorithm that accepts two positive integers as input and returns the GCD of the input integers as output. Implement your algorithm with an 8088/8086 assembly language recursive, external FAR subprocedure called GCD. Your input should be two 16-bit unsigned integers in the AX- and BX-registers. Your subprocedure should return the GCD of these two integers in the AX-register and must protect all registers used. Programming Exercises 10.9 and 10.10 suggest main procedures that can be used to test your subprocedure.

10.9 The least common multiple (LCM) of the two positive integers x and y is defined by

$$\text{LCM}(x, y) = \frac{xy}{\text{GCD}(x, y)}$$

Design an algorithm that accepts the two positive integers x and y as input and outputs the LCM of the two input integers. Assume the existence of a function subalgorithm, GCD(X,Y), that accepts two positive integers as input and returns the greatest common divisor of those two integers. Implement your algorithm with an 8088/8086 assembly language program that accepts two positive integers entered via the keyboard and displays the LCM of the two integers on the screen. Use your solution to Programming Exercise 10.8 as the implementation of the GCD subalgorithm. Demonstrate your program with the following sets of inputs:

x	y
108	60
190	34
12	30
504	540

10.10 Programming Exercises 5.5 and 5.6 involved programs that computed and displayed Pythagorean triples. Both of these programs required a subprocedure (see Programming Exercise 5.4) to compute the GCD of two positive integers. The interface definition for that GCD procedure is the same as that for the GCD procedure in Programming Exercise 10.8. Substitute the recursive GCD subprocedure in Programming Exercise 10.8 for the one in Chapter 5 and then test the modified programs.

10.11 The corrected MULTIPLY procedure (i.e., the solution to Programming Exercise 7.3) can be converted to a reentrant procedure by passing arguments via the stack and maintaining all local variables in the stack rather than in a static data segment. Implement the MULTIPLY procedure as a reentrant subprocedure with the following calling sequence:

```
PUSH  〈least significant word of multiplicand〉
PUSH  〈most significant word of multiplicand〉
PUSH  〈least significant word of multiplier〉
PUSH  〈most significant word of multiplier〉
CALL  MULTIPLY
```

The product is to be returned in the DI:SI:DX:AX register group. The OF and CF bits of the flags register are to reflect whether or not the product overflows 32 bits.

10.12 Implement the algorithm specified in Programming Exercise 10.1 with an 80386 assembly language recursive, external FAR subprocedure. Your calling sequence should be

```
PUSH ⟨n⟩
CALL FACT
```

where $\langle n \rangle$ is a 32-bit unsigned integer. Your procedure should return the value of $n!$ in the EAX-register. Use a zero result to signify that an overflow occurred in the computation.

Implement the algorithm specified in Programming Exercise 10.2 with a complete 80386 assembly language program.

CHAPTER 11

BCD Operations

Chapter 1 introduced the binary number system, the number system of the digital computer. Chapter 2 showed various methods for representing binary integers in the computer. It also discussed how text characters are represented in a computer using ASCII code. This chapter presents the *binary coded decimal* (*BCD*) code for representing the 10 decimal digits. As Chapter 2 presented various methods for using binary bit patterns to represent integers, in a similar manner, various methods can be used to represent decimal numbers with BCD codes. This chapter presents several of these representations.

Since the BCD number system is not the native number system of the digital computer, algorithms are required for performing arithmetic computations in BCD. This chaper presents algorithms for performing BCD arithmetic and provides 8088/8086 assembly language implementations for some of the algorithms. The chapter also introduces a set of 8088/8086 assembly language instructions that aid in implementing BCD arithmetic algorithms. Using the BCD code along with algorithms for performing computations with BCD-coded numbers, the machine is virtually transformed from a binary machine to a decimal machine.

The example programs in previous chapters used I/O procedures like GETDEC and PUTDEC to perform integer I/O operations. The GETDEC procedure converts an input, signed ASCII digit string to a binary integer in two's complement form. The PUTDEC procedure converts a two's complement binary integer to a signed ASCII digit string for output. To perform BCD I/O operations, procedures are needed to convert between BCD and ASCII codes. A procedure for output is provided in this chapter.

11.1 Decimal Encoding

In Chapter 1, an algorithm for converting a fraction from decimal to binary was presented. One example of this algorithm (see Table 1.6) showed that the fraction .1 in decimal is a repeating fraction in binary, which means that the decimal fraction .1 cannot be represented exactly with a finite number of bits. Many such fractions occur in decimal that become infinite fractions when converted to binary.

Consider the problem of representing monetary values (dollars and cents) in the computer. If the binary number system is used, then a value like $45.10 cannot be represented precisely—the value stored in the computer is an approximation of $45.10. Each time this value is used in a computation, the error is compounded. To see the effect of representational error compounded by computation, try the following experiment:

> In a high-level language, such as FORTRAN or Pascal, that provides the data type real, perform the following two computations and print the results to nine decimal places:
>
> 1. Multiply 0.1 by 1000.
> 2. Using a loop, add 0.1 to an initially zero sum 1000 times.
>
> In both cases, the result should be 100. In most high-level language systems, however, neither of the two values will be exactly 100, although the first computation produces a value that is closer to 100 than does the second computation. This situation occurs because the first computation uses an approximation of 0.1 in only one computation but the second uses the approximation in 1000 operations. Following each of the 1000 additions, a rounding off occurs. Each computation and rounding off compounds the error.

To eliminate the representational error caused by conversions between the decimal and binary number systems, a binary code can be used to represent decimal digits in the computer. With such a code, each digit of a decimal number is represented separately and precisely, and a collection of such digit codes represents a complete number.

With n-bit binary numbers, 2^n different objects can be represented. Taking the opposite view, if m objects are to be represented, then a minimum of

$$B = \lceil \log_2 m \rceil$$

bits are needed to represent those objects. The notation, $\lceil x \rceil$, called the **ceiling** of x, is the smallest integer that is greater than or equal to x. The act of selecting m of the 2^B possible bit patterns to represent the m objects (one bit pattern represents one object) is called **encoding** the objects. The set of bit patterns chosen, along with their interpretations, is called a **binary code**.

There are 10 decimal digits (0, 1, 2, 3, 4, 5, 6, 7, 8, and 9), so

$$\lceil \log_2 10 \rceil = \lceil 3.3219281 \rceil = 4$$

bits are required for a binary code. One such code, binary coded decimal (BCD), is presented in this chapter.

11.2 BCD Number System

Binary coded decimal (BCD) is a 4-bit code that is used to represent the 10 digits of the decimal number system. Table 11.1 shows the 4-bit BCD code. Note that the six codes 1010, 1011, 1100, 1101, 1110, and 1111 are not used and in fact are illegal in the BCD number system. To represent a 5-digit decimal number using BCD code, a total of 20 bits (4 bits per decimal digit) are needed. Table 11.2 shows some 4-digit BCD numbers, the corresponding 4-digit decimal number, and the corresponding binary number. From the examples in Table 11.2, you can observe the following:

1. The largest number that can be represented with 4-digit BCD (16 bits) is 9999. In the binary number system, only 14 bits are required to represent the integer 9999.
2. Using the binary number system with 13 bits, the decimal numbers in the range 0–8191 can be represented. However, 16 bits (4 BCD digits) are required to represent this same range in the BCD number system.
3. The decimal number 45.10 can be represented precisely in the BCD number system using a minimum of 16 bits. However, 45.10 cannot be represented precisely in the binary number system with any finite number of bits.

The BCD number system requires more bits to represent a number than does the binary number system. However, the BCD number system provides a more accurate representation for fractions.

With n BCD digits ($4n$ bits), the nonnegative decimal integers in the range 0 to $10^n - 1$ can be represented. That is, the integers in the modulo 10^n number system can be represented.

TABLE 11.1
BCD code

BCD Bit Pattern	Decimal Digit
0000	0
0001	1
0010	2
0011	3
0100	4
0101	5
0110	6
0111	7
1000	8
1001	9

TABLE 11.2
Examples of corresponding numbers in the BCD, decimal, and binary number systems

BCD	Decimal	Binary
0000 0000 0000 0000	0000	0
1001 1001 1001 1001	9999	10011100001111
1000 0001 1001 0001	8191	1111111111111
0010 0111 0011 0101	2735	101010101111
0100 0101.0001 0000	45.10	101101.0001100110011 . . .

Ten's Complement Representation

To represent both negative and nonnegative integers, the ten's complement number system can be used. The **ten's complement number system** for decimal integers is analogous to the two's complement number system for binary integers. With n BCD digits ($4n$ bits), decimal integers in the range $-5(10^{n-1})$ to $+5(10^{n-1}) - 1$ can be represented using the ten's complement number system.

In the n-digit BCD ten's complement number system, negating an integer is a two-step process:

1. Subtract each digit in the number from 1001 (9 in decimal).
2. Add 1 to the result of step 1 using modulo 10^n BCD addition. (BCD addition is discussed shortly.)

An alternate method for negating an integer in the n-digit BCD ten's complement number system is as follows:

1. Start with the rightmost digit of the BCD number and work left.
2. Copy all BCD digits up to but not including the first nonzero digit.
3. Subtract this first nonzero digit from 1010 (10 in decimal).
4. Subtract all of the remaining BCD digits to the left from 1001 (9 in decimal).

The subtractions in these two methods are straight, 4-bit binary subtractions.

EXAMPLE

$n = 5$

0	3	7	0	0	Decimal
0000	0011	0111	0000	0000	BCD
N	N	T	C	C	Operation: C ⇒ Copy BCD digit T ⇒ Subtract from 1010 N ⇒ Subtract from 1001
1001	0110	0011	0000	0000	BCD ten's complement
9	6	3	0	0	Decimal ten's complement

■

Table 11.3 shows the range of decimal integers that can be represented using 4 BCD digits (16 bits) with both the modulo 10,000 and the ten's complement number systems. Note that in the ten's complement number system, the leftmost digit of an integer is an indication of its sign. Nonnegative integers begin with a digit 0–4, (0000–0100 in BCD), and negative integers begin with a digit 5–9 (0101–1001 in BCD).

BCD Arithmetic

Arithmetic in the BCD number system is not as straightforward as it is in the binary number system. This situation occurs because digits in one number system (decimal)

TABLE 11.3
Range of integer values for 4-digit BCD, modulo 10,000, and ten's complement number systems

4-Digit BCD Integer	Modulo 10,000 Interpretation	Ten's Complement Interpretation
0000 0000 0000 0000	0000	0000
0000 0000 0000 0001	0001	0001
0000 0000 0000 0010	0002	0002
0000 0000 0000 0011	0003	0003
0000 0000 0000 0100	0004	0004
0000 0000 0000 0101	0005	0005
0000 0000 0000 0110	0006	0006
0000 0000 0000 0111	0007	0007
0000 0000 0000 1000	0008	0008
0000 0000 0000 1001	0009	0009
0000 0000 0001 0000	0010	0010
0000 0000 0001 0001	0011	0011
.	.	.
.	.	.
.	.	.
0100 1001 1001 0100	4994	4994
0100 1001 1001 0101	4995	4995
0100 1001 1001 0110	4996	4996
0100 1001 1001 0111	4997	4997
0100 1001 1001 1000	4998	4998
0100 1001 1001 1001	4999	4999
0101 0000 0000 0000	5000	−5000
0101 0000 0000 0001	5001	−4999
0101 0000 0000 0010	5002	−4998
0101 0000 0000 0011	5003	−4997
0101 0000 0000 0100	5004	−4996
0101 0000 0000 0101	5005	−4995
.	.	.
.	.	.
.	.	.
1001 1001 1000 1000	9988	−0012
1001 1001 1000 1001	9989	−0011
1001 1001 1001 0000	9990	−0010
1001 1001 1001 0001	9991	−0009
1001 1001 1001 0010	9992	−0008
1001 1001 1001 0011	9993	−0007
1001 1001 1001 0100	9994	−0006
1001 1001 1001 0101	9995	−0005
1001 1001 1001 0110	9996	−0004
1001 1001 1001 0111	9997	−0003
1001 1001 1001 1000	9998	−0002
1001 1001 1001 1001	9999	−0001

are being represented by digits in another number system (binary). Performing arithmetic in BCD requires that you simulate decimal arithmetic using binary arithmetic. In this section, algorithms for BCD addition and subtraction are presented. (An algorithm for BCD multiplication is presented in the programming exercises at the end of the chapter.)

BCD Addition

To add the n-digit BCD number $A_{n-1}A_{n-2} \ldots A_2 A_1 A_0$ to the n-digit BCD number $B_{n-1}B_{n-2} \ldots B_2 B_1 B_0$, the following algorithm can be performed:

```
CARRY = 0
I = 0
WHILE I < n
     CARRY:S_I = A_I + B_I + CARRY
     IF   CARRY = 1 or S_I > 1001
     THEN
          S_I = S_I + 0110
          CARRY = 1
     ENDIF
     I = I + 1
ENDWHILE
```

The output of this algorithm is the n-digit BCD sum $S_{n-1}S_{n-2} \ldots S_2 S_1 S_0$ and the carry out, CARRY, of the most significant digit position. The expression

```
CARRY:S_I = A_I + B_I + CARRY
```

is the straight binary sum of two 4-bit BCD digits plus a 1-bit carry from the previous digit position, producing a 4-bit BCD digit, S_I, and a carry into the next digit position. The result, CARRY:S_I, can be viewed as a 5-bit binary number in the range 00000–10011. If this result is less than or equal to 01001 (9 in decimal), then S_I is a legal BCD digit, the next BCD sum digit, and there is a carry of 0 into the next digit position. If the result is greater than 01001, then S_I has gone beyond 9 (in decimal) and therefore should wrap around to zero and produce a carry of 1 into the next digit position. However, there are six illegal BCD codes (mentioned earlier) that the straight binary sum must count through before the lower 4 bits (the BCD digit) wrap around to zero and produce a carry into the next BCD digit position. To allow the sum to count through the six illegal codes and produce the correct BCD sum digit and carry, 0110 (6 in decimal) is added to S_I.

EXAMPLE

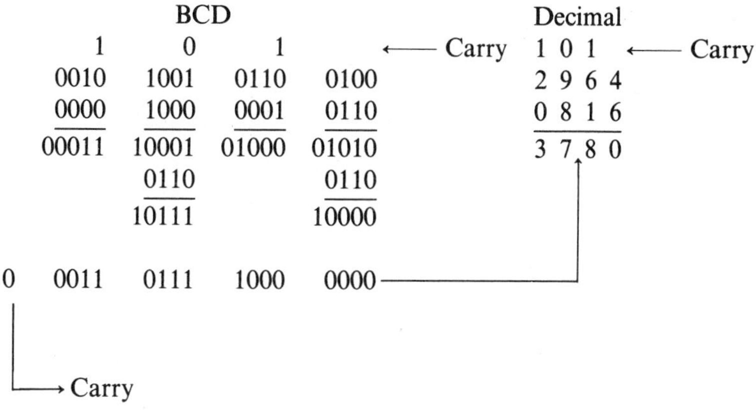

■

BCD Subtraction

To subtract the n-digit BCD number $B_{n-1}B_{n-2} \ldots B_2 B_1 B_0$ from the n-digit BCD number $A_{n-1}A_{n-2} \ldots A_2 A_1 A_0$, the following algorithm can be performed:

```
BORROW = 0
I = 0
WHILE I < n
     CARRY:DI = AI - (BI + BORROW)
     IF   CARRY = 0
     THEN
          DI = DI - 0110
     ENDIF
     BORROW = CARRY inverted
     I = I + 1
ENDWHILE
```

The output of this algorithm is the n-digit BCD difference $D_{n-1}D_{n-2} \ldots D_2 D_1 D_0$ and the borrow into, BORROW, the most significant digit position. The expression

```
CARRY:DI = AI - (BI + BORROW)
```

is the straight binary sum of the 4-bit BCD digit A_I and the two's complement of the sum of the 4-bit BCD digit B_I and the 1-bit BORROW. This binary sum produces a 4-bit BCD digit, D_I, and a carry into the fifth bit position. The borrow into the I-th BCD digit position is this carry inverted.

If the borrow is 0, then the digit D_I is a valid BCD digit and is the correct I-th digit of the difference. However, if the borrow is 1, then the digit D_I is either an invalid BCD digit or the wrong BCD digit for the I-th digit of the difference. The borrow means that the difference has gone below 0 in this digit position and should wrap around to 9. However, six illegal BCD codes (mentioned earlier) must be skipped to wrap around to the legal BCD codes. Therefore, when there is a borrow into the I-th digit position, the value 1010 (−6 in decimal) must be added to D_I to produce the correct I-th digit of the difference.

EXAMPLES

```
                    BCD                                   Decimal
      0110   0101   1000   0001                           6 5 8 1
     -0011   0111   0100   1001                          -3 7 4 9
     ----------------------------                         -------
                                                          2 8 3 2
                                                            ↑
      0011   0111   0100   1001        B_I                  |
     +   1      0      1      0 + Borrow                    |
      ----   ----   ----   ----   ------                    |
      0100   0111   0101   1001        K_I                  |
                                                            |
      0110   0101   1000   0001        A_I                  |
     +1100   1001   1011   0111     (-K_I)                  |
      ----   ----   ----   ----                             |
  ┌--10010  01110  10011  01000        D_I                  |
  |          1010          1010 + (-6)                      |
  |          ----          ----                             |
  |          1000          0010        D_I                  |
  |                                                         |
  0   0010   1000   0011   0010-----------------------------┘
  |
  └→ Borrow
```

BCD					Decimal
0011	0101	1000	0001		3 2 4 9
−0110	0111	0100	1001		−6 2 8 1
					−3 0 3 2
0110	0010	1000	0001	B_I	
+ 1	1	0	0	+ Borrow	
0111	0011	1000	0001	K_I	
0011	0010	0100	1001	A_I	
+1001	1101	1000	1111	$+(-K_I)$	
01100	01111	01100	11000	D_I	
+1010	1010	1010		$+(-6)$	
0110	1001	0110		D_I	
1 0110	1001	0110	1000		

Ten's complement

→ Borrow ■

Note that the algorithm leaves the result in ten's complement form. Note also that the subtraction of each pair of BCD digits and each adjustment of a BCD digit is performed as a binary subtraction; that is, the two's complement of the subtrahend digit is added to the minuend digit.

There is an alternative method for subtracting two BCD numbers: They can be subtracted by adding the ten's complement of the subtrahend to the minuend. Table 11.4 shows some examples of 4-digit BCD subtractions, with interpretations for both the modulo 10,000 and the ten's complement number systems.

TABLE 11.4
BCD subtraction with both modulo 10,000 and ten's complement interpretations

BCD Subtraction				Modulo 10,000 Interpretation	Ten's Complement Interpretation
0010	1001	0110	0100	2 9 6 4	2 9 6 4
−0000	1000	0001	0110	−0 8 1 6	−(+0 8 1 6)
				2 1 4 8	
1	1	0			
0010	1001	0110	0100		2 9 6 4
+ 1001	0001	1000	0100		+(−0 8 1 6)
01100	01011	01110	01000		2 1 4 8
0110	0110	0110			
10010	10001	10100			
1 0010	0001	0100	1000		
→ Borrow = 0					
1000	0100	0110	0011	8 4 6 3	− 1 5 3 7
− 0001	0010	1000	0000	− 1 2 8 0	− (+ 1 2 8 0)
				7 1 8 3	

Continued

Table 11.4 Continued

BCD Subtraction					Modulo 10,000 Interpretation	Ten's Complement Interpretation
	1	0	0			0 1 0
	1000	0100	0110	0011		− 1 5 3 7
+	1000	0111	0010	0000		+ (− 1 2 8 0)
	10001	01011	01000	00011		− 2 8 1 7
	0110	0110				
	10111	10001				
1	0111	0001	1000	0011		
→ Borrow = 0						

11.3 Internal BCD Representations

There are several ways to store BCD numbers in the memory of an IBM PC or IBM PS/2. Each digit of a decimal number is represented by a 4-bit code. The 4-bit codes that make up a BCD number can be stored one per byte (unpacked) or two per byte (packed). The packed or unpacked BCD digits can be stored in sign magnitude form or in ten's complement form. The following sections discuss several internal representations for BCD numbers.

Unpacked BCD Sign Magnitude Representation

A BCD number, entered via the keyboard, appears to a program as a string of ASCII characters stored in a byte array. The GETSTRNG subprocedure can be used to enter an ASCII signed digit string. Figure 11.1 shows the ASCII sign magnitude representation of the decimal number −1,328,745. The ASCII values shown in the figure are given in hexadecimal. The characters are stored in the array in the same order as they would be entered via the keyboard: sign followed by the digits from most significant digit (MSD) to least significant digit (LSD).

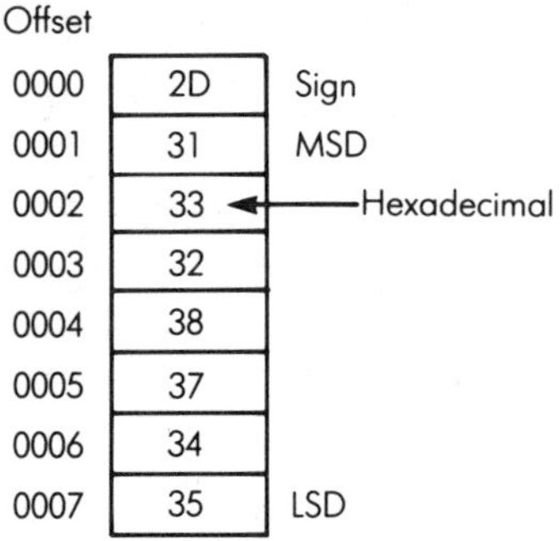

FIGURE 11.1 ASCII sign magnitude representation of −1,328,745

To convert this ASCII number to unpacked BCD sign magnitude form, the following steps can be performed:

1. Convert the sign byte to 00 for positive, 80 for negative.

2. Convert each ASCII digit to its BCD equivalent by subtracting 30 hex from the ASCII code for the digit.

Figure 11.2 shows the unpacked BCD sign magnitude representation of the decimal number −1,328,745.

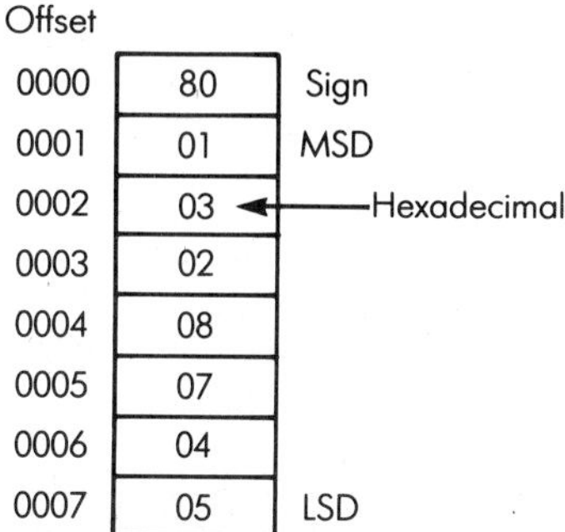

FIGURE 11.2 Unpacked BCD sign magnitude representation of −1,328,745

Packed BCD Sign Magnitude Representation

With the BCD number system, each digit of a decimal number is represented by a 4-bit binary code. When a BCD number is stored in the memory of the microcomputer, two 4-bit BCD codes can be packed into each 8-bit byte of the array that holds the number, which utilizes memory space more efficiently. Figure 11.3(a) shows the packed BCD sign magnitude representation of the decimal number −1,328,745. Note the number is now being stored in reverse order. The least significant pair of digits, 45, is stored in the first byte of the array, the next more significant pair of digits, 87, is stored in the second byte of the array, and so on. Figure 11.3(b) relates digit positions within a decimal number to positions within the array used to store the number. In general, the I-th digit (the LSD is the 0-th digit) is stored in the right nibble of the byte whose index is the floor of I/2 if I is even or is stored in the left nibble of the byte whose index is the floor of I/2 if I is odd. The number is stored in reverse order for compatibility with the Intel 8087 numeric coprocessor. The Intel 8087 represents decimal numbers with a 10-byte array (Figure 11.4).

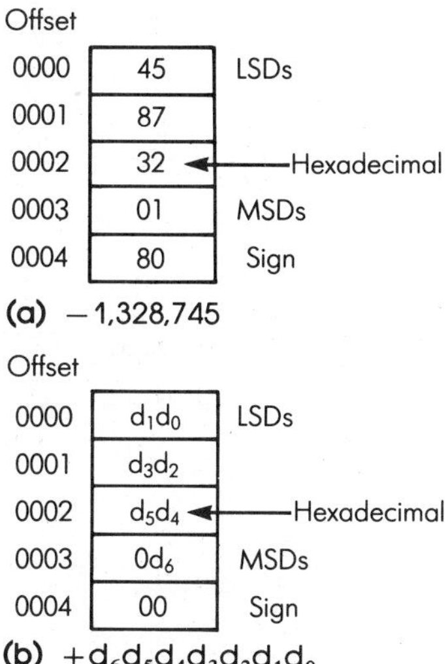

FIGURE 11.3 Packed BCD sign magnitude representations

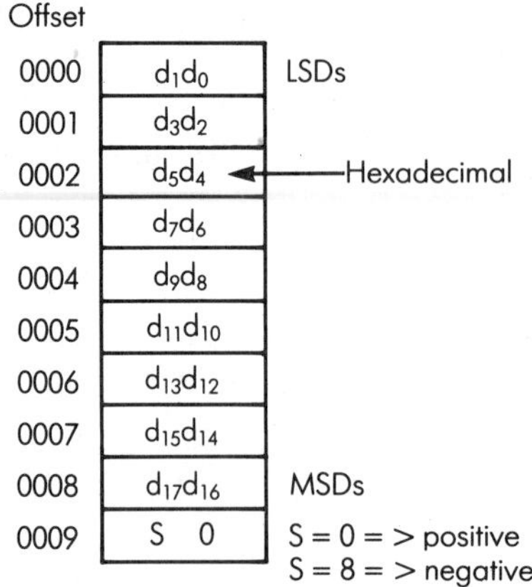

FIGURE 11.4 Packed-decimal representation used by the Intel 8087 numeric processor

Note also that a packed BCD number has an even number of digits. A leading zero is added to convert a BCD number of odd length to one of even length.

Packed BCD Ten's Complement Representation

A packed BCD number also can be stored in ten's complement form rather than in sign magnitude form to facilitate arithmetic computation involving BCD numbers. Figure 11.5 shows the 10-digit, packed BCD ten's complement representation of the decimal number −1,328,745. Again, the number is stored in reverse order.

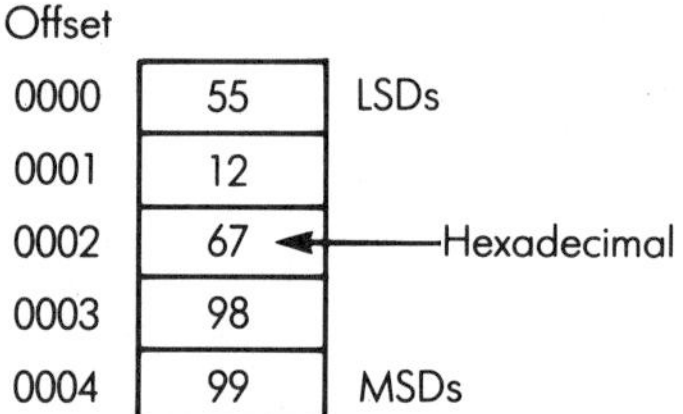

FIGURE 11.5 Packed BCD ten's complement representation of −1,328,745

Defining Packed BCD Data

BCD variables whose initial values are in any of the three forms just mentioned can be defined using the DB pseudo-operation described in Chapter 2. Consider the following data segment definition:

```
DATA     SEGMENT
UNPACKED DB      80H,01H,03H,02H,08H,07H,04H,05H
PACKSMAG DB      45H,87H,32H,01H,80H
PACKTENS DB      55H,12H,67H,98H,99H
DATA     ENDS
```

Figure 11.6 shows the 18-byte memory segment generated by this definition. UNPACKED is defined as a byte array of size 8. Its initial value is the unpacked BCD sign magnitude representation of the decimal number −1,328,745. PACKSMAG is defined as a byte array of size 5. Its initial value is the packed BCD sign magnitude representation of the decimal number −1,328,745. PACKTENS is defined

FIGURE 11.6
BCD data segment—DB pseudo-operation

Offset		Label
0000	80	UNPACKED
0001	01	
0002	03	
0003	02	
0004	08	
0005	07	
0006	04	
0007	05	
0008	45	PACKSMAG
0009	87	
000A	32	
000B	01	
000C	80	
000D	55	PACKTENS
000E	12	
000F	67	
0010	98	
0011	99	

as a byte array of size 5. Its initial value is the packed BCD ten's complement representation of the decimal number $-1{,}328{,}745$.

The 8088/8086 assembly language also provides the DT (define 10 bytes) pseudo-operation to facilitate the definition of packed BCD numbers that are compatible with the Intel 8087 numeric coprocessor. The **DT pseudo-operation** has the following general form:

[⟨*name*⟩] DT ⟨*dec-constant-list*⟩ [⟨*comment*⟩]

in which ⟨*name*⟩ is the symbolic name to be associated with the memory location at which the byte array is to begin and ⟨*dec-constant-list*⟩ is a list of decimal constants separated by commas. A ⟨*dec-constant*⟩ is one of the following:

A signed or unsigned string of up to 18 decimal digits

A question mark (?) to indicate that 10 bytes of storage are to be allocated but that an initial value is not being specified

Each ⟨*dec-constant*⟩ specifies the allocation of 10 consecutive bytes of storage, with the value of the constant being the initial value of the 10-byte array, which is stored in the array using the packed BCD sign magnitude representation.

EXAMPLE

The following data segment definition generates the 20-byte memory segment shown in Figure 11.7:

```
DATA   SEGMENT
ALPHA  DT       1234567890
BETA   DT       -1234567890
DATA   ENDS
```

FIGURE 11.7
BCD data segment—DT pseudo-operation

Offset		Label
0000	90	ALPHA
0001	78	
0002	56	
0003	34	
0004	12	
0005	00	
0006	00	
0007	00	
0008	00	
0009	00	
000A	90	BETA
000B	78	
000C	56	
000D	34	
000E	12	
000F	00	
0010	00	
0011	00	
0012	00	
0013	80	

■

Programming Examples

Each of the internal BCD representations presented previously may be useful in the implementation of algorithms requiring decimal computations. The ASCII sign magnitude representation is useful in input/output operations; the packed sign magnitude representation provides for compatibility with the Intel 8087 numeric processor; and the packed ten's complement representation is useful in performing arithmetic computations. The need often arises for conversion of a BCD number from one of these representations to another. Procedures for two such conversions are presented next. (Two additional conversion procedures are left as programming exercises at the end of the chapter.)

Conversion from Packed Ten's Complement to Packed Sign Magnitude

The FAR procedure defined in Program Listing 11.1 is a PUBLIC procedure called TENSSMAG. It converts a packed BCD number from ten's complement form to sign magnitude form.

The prologue in lines 3–15 describes the function of the procedure and explains its interface requirements. On entry to the procedure, the ES:DI register pair must address the first byte of the array that contains the ten's complement BCD number, and the CX-register must contain the number of digits in the BCD number. The number of digits must be even since the BCD number is stored in packed form. On return to the caller, the array addressed by the ES:DI register pair contains the packed sign magnitude equivalent of the input BCD number. An additional byte is required on the input array to accommodate the sign.

```
 1:              PAGE    80,132
 2: ;===================================================================
 3: ;                      PROGRAM LISTING 11.1
 4: ; PROCEDURE TO CONVERT A PACKED BCD NUMBER
 5: ; FROM TEN'S COMPLEMENT FORM TO SIGN MAGNITUDE FORM
 6: ;
 7: ; INPUTS:    ES:DI   POINTS TO ARRAY CONTAINING TEN'S COMPLEMENT BCD #
 8: ;            CX-REG CONTAINS SIZE OF BCD NUMBER         (MUST BE EVEN)
 9: ; OUTPUTS:   UPON RETURN,  THE ARRAY POINTED TO BY ES:DI WILL CONTAIN
10: ;            A SIGN MAGNITUDE,  PACKED BCD NUMBER  EQUIVALENT  TO THE
11: ;            TEN'S COMPLEMENT,  PACKED BCD NUMBER  THAT  IT CONTAINED
12: ;            UPON ENTRY.
13: ;            CAUTION: ONE BYTE IS ADDED TO THE BCD ARRAY FOR THE SIGN.
14: ;                     HOWEVER, THE SIZE (BCD DIGIT COUNT) REMAINS THE
15: ;                     SAME.
16: ;===================================================================
17:              .MODEL  SMALL,BASIC
18:                                          ;PROCEDURE TO
19:              EXTRN   NEGBCD:FAR          ;NEGATE A PACKED BCD NUMBER
20: ;===================================================================
21: ; C O D E    S E G M E N T    D E F I N I T I O N
22:              .CODE   EX_11_1
23: TENSSMAG     PROC    FAR PUBLIC     ;PROCEDURE TENSSMAG (DPTR,DIGIT_CNT)
24: ;
25:              PUSH    SI                  ;SAVE SI-REGISTER
26:              PUSHF                       ;SAVE FLAGS
27:              MOV     SI,CX               ;PTR = DPTR + DIGIT_CNT/2 - 1
28:              SHR     SI,1
29:              DEC     SI
30:              ADD     SI,DI
31:              CMP     BYTE PTR ES:[SI],50H;IF    PTR -> BYTE >= 50H
32:              JB      ELSE1
33:              CALL    NEGBCD              ;THEN CALL NEGBCD (DPTR,
34:                                          ;                  DIGIT_CNT)
35:              INC     SI                  ;      PTR = PTR + 1
36:              MOV     BYTE PTR ES:[SI],80H;      PTR -> BYTE = 80H
37:              JMP     ENDIF1
38: ELSE1:                                   ;ELSE
39:              INC     SI                  ;      PTR = PTR + 1
40:              MOV     BYTE PTR ES:[SI],0  ;      PTR->BYTE = 0
41: ENDIF1:                                  ;ENDIF
42:              POPF                        ;RESTORE FLAGS
43:              POP     SI                  ;RESTORE SI-REGISTER
44:              RET                         ;RETURN
45: TENSSMAG     ENDP                 ;END TENSSMAG
46: ;===================================================================
47:              END
```

The TENSSMAG procedure references one subprocedure, the procedure NEGBCD (line 19). The NEGBCD procedure performs the ten's complement of a packed BCD number. On entry to NEGBCD, the ES:DI register pair must address the first byte of an array that contains a packed BCD number, and the CX-register must contain the number of digits in the BCD number. Again, the number of digits must be even. When NEGBCD returns to its caller, the array addressed by the ES:DI register pair contains the ten's complement of the input BCD number.

The TENSSMAG procedure begins by saving the registers that it uses (lines 25 and 26). The SI-register and the flags register are the only registers that are modified by the procedure. On entry to the procedure, the ES:DI register pair addresses the first byte of the array that holds the BCD number. The instructions in lines 27–30 set the SI-register to the offset of the last byte of the BCD number, which means that the ES:SI register pair now addresses the byte of the BCD number whose left nibble indicates the sign of the number. Recall that packed BCD numbers are stored with digit pairs in reverse order. The MOV instruction in line 27 moves the digit count to the SI-register. The SHR instruction in line 28 divides the digit count by 2, producing a byte count. The DEC instruction in line 29 decrements the byte count in the SI-register by 1, producing the offset of the last byte in the BCD array relative to the offset of the first byte. The ADD instruction in line 30 adds the offset of the first byte of the BCD array, producing the offset of the last byte of the BCD array relative to the beginning of the segment. The ES:SI register pair now addresses the last byte of the BCD array.

If the left nibble of the most significant digit pair is one of the digits in the range 5–9, then the ten's complement BCD number is negative. If it is one of the digits in the range 0–4, then the BCD number is positive. The double-alternative decision structure in lines 31–41 determines whether the ten's complement BCD number is positive or negative. The CMP instruction in line 31 tests the left nibble of the most significant BCD digit pair; that is, it tests the left nibble of the digit pair addressed by the ES:SI register pair. The JB instruction in line 32 makes the decision based on this test. If the left nibble is a BCD digit in the range 5–9, then the instructions in lines 33–37 are executed; if the left nibble is a BCD digit in the range 0–4, then the instructions in lines 38–40 are executed.

The "then" branch of the double-alternative decision structure (lines 33–37) handles the case of a negative BCD number. The call to NEGBCD in line 33 converts the negative BCD number to the corresponding positive BCD number. The INC instruction in line 35 adjusts the ES:SI register pair so that it addresses the next byte of the BCD array, the byte at which the sign is to be placed. The MOV instruction in line 36 sets the sign bit in this sign byte. The JMP instruction in line 37 causes the "else" portion of the double-alternative decision structure to be skipped.

The "else" branch of the double-alternative decision structure (lines 38–40) handles the case of a positive BCD number. The INC instruction in line 39 adjusts the ES:SI register pair to address the next byte of the BCD array, the byte at which the sign is to be placed. The MOV instruction in line 40 clears the sign bit in this sign byte.

On completion of the double-alternative decision structure, the registers are restored for the caller (lines 42 and 43), and control is returned to the caller (line 44). If the address of the array shown in Figure 11.5 is passed to procedure TENSSMAG with a digit count of 10, then the array is converted to the sign magnitude form shown in Figure 11.8.

FIGURE 11.8 Output of the TENSSMAG procedure for input as shown in Figure 11.5

Offset		
0000	45	LSDs
0001	87	
0002	32	
0003	01	
0004	00	MSDs
0005	80	Sign

The NEGBCD subprocedure provides a significant portion of this conversion, and it is discussed in detail in Section 11.4.

Conversion from Packed BCD Sign Magnitude to ASCII Sign Magnitude

The FAR procedure defined in Program Listing 11.2 is a PUBLIC procedure called BCDASCII. It converts a packed BCD sign magnitude number to ASCII sign magni-

```
            PAGE    80,132
;====================================================================
;                   PROGRAM LISTING 11.2
;
; PROCEDURE TO CONVERT A SIGN MAGNITUDE, PACKED BCD NUMBER TO ASCII
;
; INPUT:  DS:SI POINTS TO ARRAY CONTAINING BCD   NUMBER
;         ES:DI POINTS TO ARRAY TO CONTAIN ASCII NUMBER
;         CX    CONTAINS SIZE OF BCD NUMBER (MUST BE EVEN)
;
; OUTPUT: UPON RETURN, THE ARRAY POINTED TO BY ES:DI WILL
;         CONTAIN AN ASCII NUMBER EQUIVALENT  TO  THE BCD
;         NUMBER IN THE ARRAY POINTED TO BY DS:SI.
;====================================================================
            .MODEL  SMALL,BASIC
;====================================================================
; C O D E   S E G M E N T   D E F I N I T I O N
            .CODE   EX_11_2
BCDASCII    PROC    FAR PUBLIC USES AX CX DX SI DI
                                      ;PROCEDURE BCDASCII (DIGIT_CNT,
                                      ;                     DPTR,SPTR)
                                        ;SAVE REGISTERS SPECIFIED
                                        ;     IN USES CLAUSE
            PUSHF                       ;SAVE FLAGS
            MOV     DX,CX               ;SPTR = SPTR + (DIGIT_CNT/2)
            SHR     DX,1
            ADD     SI,DX
            STD                         ;SET DF FOR DECREMENTING
            LODSB                       ;SIGN = SPTR -> BYTE
                                        ;SPTR = SPTR - 1
            CMP     AL,0                ;IF  LEFT NIBBLE OF SIGN <> 0
            JZ      ELSE1
            MOV     AL,'-'              ;THEN SIGN = '-'
            JMP     ENDIF1
ELSE1:                                  ;ELSE
            MOV     AL,' '              ;     SIGN = ' '
ENDIF1:                                 ;ENDIF
            CLD                         ;SET DF FOR INCREMENTING
            STOSB                       ;DPTR -> BYTE = SIGN
                                        ;DPTR = DPTR + 1
;
;
            MOV     DX,-1               ;LR_FLAG = LEFT
LOOP_TOP:                               ;REPEAT
            CMP     DX,0                ;   IF   LR_FLAG = LEFT
            JG      ELSE2
            STD                         ;   THEN SET DF FOR DECR.
            LODSB                       ;        PAIR = DPTR -> BYTE
                                        ;        SPTR = SPTR - 1
            MOV     AH,AL
            PUSH    CX                  ;        SAVE DIGIT_CNT
            MOV     CL,4                ;        DIGIT = LEFT NIBBLE
            SHR     AL,CL               ;                OF PAIR
            POP     CX                  ;        RESTORE DIGIT_CNT
            JMP     ENDIF2
ELSE2:                                  ;   ELSE
            MOV     AL,AH
            AND     AL,0FH              ;        DIGIT = RIGHT NIBBLE
                                        ;                OF PAIR
ENDIF2:                                 ;   ENDIF
            ADD     AL,'0'              ;   CHAR = DIGIT + ASCII(0)
            CLD                         ;   SET DF FOR INCREMENTING
            STOSB                       ;   SPTR -> BYTE = CHAR
                                        ;   DPTR = DPTR + 1
            NEG     DX                  ;   REVERSE LR_FLAG
            LOOP    LOOP_TOP            ;   DECREMENT DIGIT_CNT
                                        ;UNTIL DIGIT_CNT = 0
```

```
68:              POPF                          ;RESTORE FLAGS
69:                                            ;RESTORE REGISTERS SPECIFIED
70:                                            ;         IN USES CLAUSE
71:              RET                           ;RETURN
72: BCDASCII     ENDP                         ;END BCDASCII
73: ;=================================================================
74:              END
```

tude form. It is similar to the BCDASCII procedure in Program Listing 8.1, although there are two major differences between the procedures:

1. The procedure in Program Listing 11.2 allows for a sign, and the procedure in Program Listing 8.1 does not.
2. The procedure in Program Listing 11.2 reverses the order of the digits as part of the conversion process, and the procedure in Program Listing 8.1 does not. The procedure in Program Listing 11.2 assumes that the packed BCD number is stored in the form described in Figure 11.3, and it converts the BCD number to an ASCII number in the form described in Figure 11.1.

The prologue in lines 3–13 in Program Listing 11.2 describes the function of procedure BCDASCII and explains its interface requirements. On entry to the procedure, the DS:SI register pair must address the first byte of the array that contains the packed BCD number, the ES:DI register pair must address the first byte of the array that is to contain the corresponding ASCII number, and the CX-register must contain the number of digits in the BCD number. The number of digits must be even since the BCD number is stored in packed form. On return to the caller, the array addressed by the ES:DI register pair contains the ASCII sign magnitude equivalent of the input BCD number addressed by the DS:SI register pair.

The BCDASCII procedure begins by saving the registers specified in the USES clause (line 19) and saving the flags register (line 24). The instructions in lines 25–27 set the DS:SI register pair to address the last byte in the input BCD array (the sign byte). The procedure works from the end to the beginning of the BCD array, and it works from the beginning to the end of the ASCII array; thus, it processes both arrays in the following order: sign, then digits from MSD to LSD.

The instructions in lines 28–40 perform the sign conversion. The STD instruction in line 28 sets the direction flag for decrementing through the BCD array. The LODSB instruction in line 29 loads the sign byte of the BCD number into the AL-register and then decrements the SI-register so that the DS:SI register pair addresses the most significant pair of BCD digits. The single-alternative decision structure in lines 31–37 tests the sign byte in the AL-register and then sets it to the ASCII representation of the appropriate sign character: – for negative (line 33) and blank for positive (line 36). The CLD instruction in line 38 clears the direction flag for incrementing through the ASCII array. The STOSB instruction in line 39 stores the ASCII character for the sign in the first byte of the ASCII array and then increments the DI-register so that the ES:DI register pair addresses the second byte of the ASCII array.

The MOV instruction in line 43 initializes a LEFT/RIGHT flag (maintained in the DX-register) to LEFT. The LEFT/RIGHT flag is used to indicate whether the BCD digit currently being processed is from the left or right nibble of a byte. That is, each byte extracted from the BCD array contains two BCD digits, one in the left nibble and one in the right nibble. The flag indicates which of the two is currently being converted to ASCII.

The body (lines 45–65) of the REPEAT-UNTIL loop in lines 44–67 executes once for each digit in the BCD array. The digit count, input to the subprocedure in the CX-register, controls execution of this loop. Each iteration of the loop translates one BCD digit to ASCII and stores the result in the ASCII array. A byte is extracted from the BCD array on every odd iteration of the loop (i.e., every time a left nibble is to be translated).

The double-alternative decision structure in lines 45–60 selects the next BCD digit to be translated. The selection is based on the LEFT/RIGHT flag. The CMP instruction in line 45 tests the flag. If the flag indicates LEFT, then the instructions in lines 47–55 are executed. The STD instruction in line 47 sets the direction flag for decrementing through the BCD array. The LODSB instruction in line 48 extracts the next two BCD digits from the BCD array (the byte addressed by the DS:SI register pair) and decrements the SI-register by 1 so that the DS:SI register pair addresses the previous byte in the BCD array. The byte extracted is placed in the AL-register, and the MOV instruction in line 50 saves a copy of this byte in the AH-register for use in the next iteration of the loop. This iteration of the loop translates the left nibble of the byte just extracted, and the next iteration translates the right nibble of the byte just extracted. The PUSH instruction in line 51 saves the digit count so that the CL-register can be used as a shift count. The instructions in lines 52 and 53 shift the byte in the AL-register right 4 bit positions, which pushes out the right nibble and right-justifies the left nibble; that is, the leftmost BCD digit of the byte is now in the rightmost 4 bits of the AL-register. The POP instruction in line 54 restores the digit count in the CX-register. The JMP instruction in line 55 skips the "else" portion of the double-alternative decision structure. If the flag indicates RIGHT, then the instructions in lines 57 and 58 are executed. The MOV instruction in line 57 moves the copy (saved in line 50) of the byte extracted from the BCD array on the last iteration of the loop from the AH-register back to the AL-register. The AND instruction in line 58 clears the left nibble of the byte, leaving the right nibble in the rightmost 4 bits of the AL-register. When the ENDIF is reached (line 60), the AL-register contains a single BCD digit.

The ADD instruction in line 61 converts the BCD digit in the AL-register to ASCII by adding the ASCII code for zero to the BCD code. The CLD instruction in line 62 clears the direction flag for incrementing through the ASCII array. The STOSB instruction in line 63 stores the ASCII code in the ASCII array at the address specified by the ES:DI register pair, and then it increments the DI-register by 1 so that the ES:DI register pair addresses the next byte in the ASCII array.

The NEG instruction in line 65 reverses the direction of the LEFT/RIGHT flag for the next iteration of the loop. The LOOP instruction in line 66 decrements the digit count in the CX-register by 1 and, if the resulting digit count is nonzero, transfers control to the top of the loop (line 44). Otherwise, the loop is terminated.

At loop exit, the flags are restored for the caller (line 68), the registers specified in the USES clause are restored, and control is returned to the caller (line 71). If the address of the array shown in Figure 11.3(a) is passed to procedure BCDASCII with a digit count of 8, then the output ASCII array will have the values shown in Figure 11.9.

FIGURE 11.9
Output of the BCDASCII procedure for input as shown in Figure 11.3(a)

Offset		
0000	2D	Sign
0001	30	MSD
0002	31	
0003	33	
0004	32	
0005	38	
0006	37	
0007	34	
0008	35	LSD

11.4 BCD Arithmetic Instructions

Arithmetic in the BCD number system was discussed in Section 11.2 and its subsections. The algorithms presented use straight binary addition (or subtraction) to add (or subtract) corresponding digits of two BCD numbers. The result sum (or difference) digit requires an adjustment under certain conditions. This adjustment is an addition (or subtraction) of 0110 (6 in decimal), which is used to skip the six illegal codes. The 8088/8086 assembly language provides six instructions for performing these adjustment operations: Four adjust the result of an arithmetic operation involving unpacked BCD digits, and two adjust the result of an arithmetic operation involving packed BCD digits.

Four of the six BCD adjustment instructions in the 8088/8086 assembly language make use of the AF bit of the flags register, which is a copy of the carry from bit 3 to bit 4 after an addition operation and is a copy of the borrow from bit 4 into bit 3 after a subtraction operation. That is, the AF bit reflects the carry from the low nibble into the high nibble for a byte addition operation, and it reflects the borrow from the high nibble into the low nibble for a byte subtraction.

Unpacked BCD Arithmetic Instructions

The four instructions in the 8088/8086 assembly language that aid in performing arithmetic with unpacked BCD numbers are the ASCII adjust instructions AAA, AAS, AAM, and AAD. The **ASCII adjust for addition (AAA) instruction** has the following general form:

[⟨*label*⟩] AAA [⟨*comment*⟩]

The AAA instruction has no explicit operand. The implicit operand is the contents of the AL-register. The AAA instruction should follow an ADD or ADC instruction that adds two unpacked BCD digits and leaves the result in the AL-register. It adjusts the AL-register to contain a valid, unpacked BCD digit. The carry from this digit is added to the AH-register and is recorded in the CF bit of the flags register. The AAA instruction causes the following steps to be performed:

IF ((*AL-REG and OF hex*) > *9*) *or* (*AF* = *1*)
THEN
AL-REG is incremented by 6
AH-REG is incremented by 1
AF is set to 1

```
ENDIF
```
AF is copied into CF
Upper nibble of AL-REG is cleared

EXAMPLES

Suppose the AL-register contains 1001 (BCD code for 9) and the BL-register contains 0101 (BCD code for 5) before the following two instructions are executed:

```
ADD  AL,BL
AAA
```

The ADD instruction performs the following addition:

```
       1 ←— Carry
00001001
00000101
--------
00001110
```

The carry from bit 3 into bit 4 is 0, so the AF bit of the flags register is cleared to 0 by the ADD instruction.

The AAA instruction performs the following operations:

1. Since the lower nibble of the AL-register is greater than 9, the value 0110 is added to the AL-register:

   ```
        111 ←— Carry
   00001110
   00000110
   --------
   00010100
   ```

   The AH-register is incremented by 1, and the AF bit of the flags register is set to 1.

2. The CF bit of the flags register is set to 1.

3. The upper nibble of the AL-register is cleared, leaving the value 00000100. The result in the AL-register is the BCD code for 4, the correct BCD sum digit, and the CF bit of the flags register is 1, the correct carry into the next BCD digit position.

Suppose the AL-register contains 00111001 (ASCII code for 9) and the BL-register contains 00110111 (ASCII code for 7) before the following two instructions are executed:

```
ADD  AL,BL
AAA
```

The ADD instruction performs the following addition:

```
  111111 ←— Carry
00111001
00110111
--------
01110000
```

The carry from bit 3 into bit 4 is 1, so the AF bit of the flags register is set to 1 by the ADD instruction.

The AAA instruction performs the following operations:

1. Since the AF bit of the flags register is set, the value 0110 is added to the AL-register:

$$\begin{array}{r} 01110000 \\ \underline{00000110} \\ 01110110 \end{array}$$

   The AH-register is incremented by 1, and the AF bit of the flags register is set to 1.

2. The CF bit of the flags register is set to 1.

3. The upper nibble of the AL-register is cleared, leaving the value 00000110. The result in the AL-register is the BCD code for 6, the correct BCD sum digit, and the CF bit of the flags register is 1, the correct carry into the next BCD digit position. ■

Note that the AAA instruction adjusts for the addition of ASCII digits as well as for the addition of unpacked BCD digits. When the sum of two ASCII digits is adjusted, the resulting sum digit is an unpacked BCD digit. To convert this unpacked BCD digit to ASCII, simply add 30 hex to the AL-register. The following loop then adds the ASCII number in the array addressed by the DS:SI register pair to the ASCII number in the array addressed by the ES:DI register pair, leaving the ASCII sum in the array addressed by the ES:DI register pair. The CX-register contains the size of the two ASCII numbers. The addition is ten's complement addition:

```
         MOV    BX,CX
         DEC    BX
         ADD    DI,BX         ;DPTR = DPTR + (SIZE - 1)
         ADD    SI,BX         ;SPTR = SPTR + (SIZE - 1)
         STD                  ;SET DF FOR DECREMENTING
         CLC                  ;CARRY = 0
REPEAT:                       ;REPEAT
         MOV    AL,ES:[DI]    ;    DIGIT = DPTR→ASCII
         ADC    AL,DS:[SI]    ;          + SPTR→ASCII
         AAA                  ;          + CARRY
         PUSHF                ;    PUSH CARRY FROM ADDITION
         ADD    AL,30H        ;    CHAR = DIGIT + 30 HEX
         POPF                 ;    POP CARRY
         STOSB                ;    DPTR→ASCII = CHAR
                              ;    DPTR = DPTR - 1
         DEC    SI            ;    SPTR = SPTR - 1
         LOOP   REPEAT        ;    SIZE = SIZE - 1
                              ;UNTIL SIZE = 0
```

Figure 11.10(a) shows a possible configuration of the two arrays prior to execution of these instructions, and Figure 11.10(b) shows the result after execution.

The **ASCII adjust for subtraction (AAS) instruction** has the following general form:

[⟨*label*⟩] AAS [⟨*comment*⟩]

The AAS instruction has no explicit operand. The implicit operand is the contents of the AL-register. The AAS instruction should follow a SUB or an SBB instruction that subtracts two unpacked BCD digits and leaves the result in the AL-register. It adjusts the AL-register to contain a valid, unpacked BCD digit. The borrow into this digit is

FIGURE 11.10
ASCII addition loop

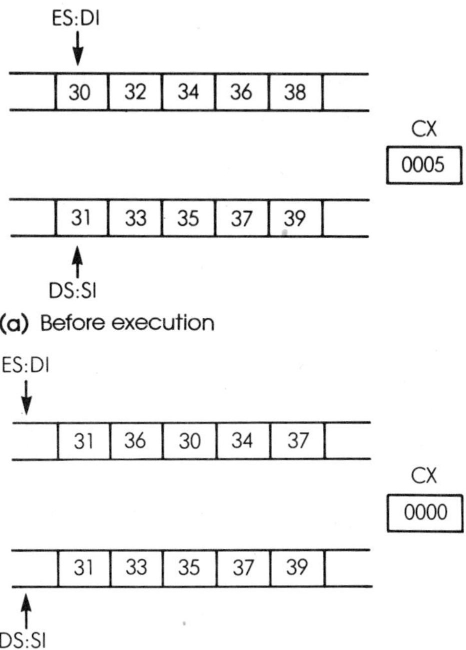

subtracted from the AH-register and is recorded in the CF bit of the flags register. The AAS instruction causes the following steps to be performed.

IF ((*AL-REG and OF hex*) > 9) *or* (*AF* = *1*)
THEN
AL-REG is decremented by 6
AH-REG is decremented by 1
AF is set to 1
ENDIF
AF is copied into CF
Upper nibble of AL-REG is cleared

EXAMPLE

Suppose the AL-register contains 0101 (BCD code for 5) and the BL-register contains 0111 (BCD code for 7) before the following two instructions are executed:

```
SUB  AL,BL
AAS
```

The SUB instruction performs the following subtraction:

$$\begin{array}{r} 00000101 \\ -00000111 \\ \hline \end{array}$$

which is performed by a complement and an add:

$$\begin{array}{r} 1 \longleftarrow \text{Carry} \\ 00000101 \\ +11111001 \\ \hline 11111110 \end{array}$$

The carry from bit 3 into bit 4 is 0, so the borrow from bit 4 into bit 3 is 1. Therefore, the AF bit of the flags register is set to 1 by execution of the SUB instruction.

The AAS instruction performs the following operations:

1. Since the AF bit of the flags register is set, the value 11111010 (−6 in decimal) is added to the AL-register:

$$\begin{array}{r} 111111 \quad \longleftarrow \text{Carry} \\ 11111110 \\ +\,11111010 \\ \hline 11111000 \end{array}$$

   The AH-register is decremented by 1, and the AF bit of the flags register is set to 1.

2. The CF bit of the flags register is set to 1.
3. The upper nibble of the AL-register is cleared, leaving the value 00001000. The result in the AL-register is the BCD code for 8, the correct BCD difference digit, and the CF bit of the flags register is 1, the correct borrow from the next BCD digit position. ■

Note that the AAS instruction adjusts for the subtraction of ASCII digits as well as for the subtraction of unpacked BCD digits. When the difference between two ASCII digits is adjusted, the resulting difference digit is an unpacked BCD digit. To convert this unpacked BCD digit to ASCII, simply add 30 hex to the AL-register. The following loop subtracts the ASCII number in the array addressed by the DS:SI register pair from the ASCII number in the array addressed by the ES:DI register pair, leaving the ASCII difference in the array addressed by the ES:DI register pair. The CX-register contains the size of the two ASCII numbers. The subtraction is ten's complement subtraction:

```
        MOV    BX,CX
        DEC    BX
        ADD    DI,BX         ;DPTR = DPTR + (SIZE - 1)
        ADD    SI,BX         ;SPTR = SPTR + (SIZE - 1)
        STD                  ;SET DF FOR DECREMENTING
        CLC                  ;BORROW = 0
REPEAT:                      ;REPEAT
        MOV    AL,ES:[DI]    ;   DIGIT = DPTR→ASCII
        SBB    AL,DS:[SI]    ;         - SPTR→ASCII
        AAS                  ;         - BORROW
        PUSHF                ;   PUSH BORROW FROM SUBTRACT
        ADD    AL,30H        ;   CHAR = DIGIT + 30 HEX
        POPF                 ;   POP BORROW
        STOSB                ;   DPTR→ASCII = CHAR
                             ;   DPTR = DPTR - 1
        DEC    SI            ;   SPTR = SPTR - 1
        LOOP   REPEAT        ;   SIZE = SIZE - 1
                             ;UNTIL SIZE = 0
```

Figure 11.11(a) shows a possible configuration of the two arrays prior to execution of these instructions, and Figure 11.11(b) shows the result after execution.

The **ASCII adjust for multiplication (AAM) instruction** has the following general form:

[⟨*label*⟩] AAM [⟨*comment*⟩]

The AAM instruction has no explicit operand. The implicit operand is the contents of

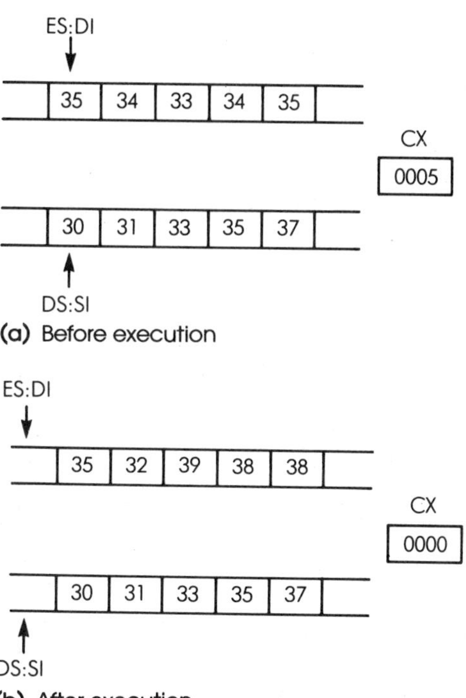

FIGURE 11.11
ASCII subtraction loop

the AX-register. The AAM instruction should follow a MUL instruction that multiplies two unpacked BCD digits and leaves the result in the AX-register. It divides the AX-register value by 10. The quotient (the high-order, unpacked BCD digit of the product) is placed in the AH-register. The remainder (the low-order, unpacked BCD digit of the product) is placed in the AL-register.

EXAMPLE

Suppose the AL-register contains 0110 (BCD code for 6) and the BL-register contains 0111 (BCD code for 7) before the following two instructions are executed:

```
MUL  BL
AAM
```

The MUL instruction produces the product 0000000000101010 in the AX-register, the binary representation of the decimal value 42. The AAM instruction converts this binary product to the unpacked BCD digits 00000100 and 00000010 in the AH- and AL-registers, respectively. ■

An algorithm for the multiplication of two multidigit, unpacked BCD numbers is not considered here. An algorithm for the multiplication of two multidigit, packed BCD numbers is presented in Programming Exercises 11.6, 11.7, and 11.8.

The **ASCII adjust for division (AAD) instruction** has the following general form:

[⟨*label*⟩] AAD [⟨*comment*⟩]

The AAD instruction has no explicit operand. The implicit operand is the two-digit, unpacked BCD number in the AX-register with the high-order digit in the AH-register and the low-order digit in the AL-register. The AAD instruction should precede a DIV instruction to adjust the dividend prior to division of a two-digit, unpacked BCD number by an unpacked BCD digit. The dividend to be adjusted is the two-digit, unpacked BCD number in the AX-register. The most significant BCD digit (AH-register value) is multiplied by 10, and the least significant BCD digit (AL-register value) is added to this product. The resulting binary integer is placed in the AL-register, and the AH-register is cleared.

EXAMPLE

Suppose the AX-register contains 0000010000000010 (unpacked BCD code for 42) and the BL-register contains 00001001 (unpacked BCD code for 9) before the following two instructions are executed:

```
AAD
DIV  BL
```

The AAD instruction converts the two-digit BCD dividend in the AX-register to the binary integer 0000000000101010 in the AX-register. The division is then a binary division producing the quotient 00000100 (BCD code for 4) in the AL-register and the remainder 00000110 (BCD code for 6) in the AH-register. ■

An algorithm for the division of two multidigit, unpacked BCD numbers is not considered here.

Packed BCD Arithmetic Instructions

The two instructions in the 8088/8086 assembly language that aid in performing arithmetic with packed BCD numbers are the decimal adjust instructions DAA and DAS. The **decimal adjust for addition (DAA) instruction** has the following general form:

[⟨*label*⟩] DAA [⟨*comment*⟩]

The DAA instruction has no explicit operand. The implicit operand is the contents of the AL-register. The DAA instruction should follow an ADD or ADC instruction that adds two packed BCD digit pairs and leaves the result in the AL-register. It adjusts the AL-register to contain a valid pair of packed BCD digits. The carry from this digit pair is recorded in the CF bit of the flags register. The DAA instruction causes the following steps to be performed:

```
IF    (lower nibble of AL-REG > 9) or (AF = 1)
THEN
        AL-REG is incremented by 6
        AF is set to 1
ENDIF
IF    (upper nibble of AL-REG > 9) or (CF = 1)
THEN
        AL-REG is incremented by 60 hex
        CF is set to 1
ENDIF
```

EXAMPLE

Suppose the AL-register contains the value 10000101 (packed BCD code for 85) and the BL-register contains 10010110 (packed BCD code for 96) before the following two instructions are executed:

```
ADD  AL,BL
DAA
```

The ADD instruction performs the following addition:

```
  1        ←— Carry
  10000101
  10010110
  --------
1 00011011
```

The carry from bit 3 into bit 4 is 0, so the AF bit of the flags register is cleared to 0 by execution of the ADD instruction. The carry out of the most significant bit is 1, so the CF bit of the flags register is set to 1 by execution of the ADD instruction.

The DAA instruction performs the following operations:

1. Since the lower nibble of the AL-register (1011) is greater than 9 (1001), the value 00000110 is added to the AL-register:

```
    1111   ←— Carry
00011011
00000110
--------
00100001
```

   The AF bit of the flags register is set to 1. Note that this part of the adjustment caused a carry from the lower nibble into the upper nibble.

2. Since the CF bit of the flags register is set, the value 01100000 (60 hex) is added to the AL-register:

```
11         ←— Carry
00100001
01100000
--------
10000001
```

   The CF bit of the flags register is set to 1. The adjusted result is 10000001, which is the packed BCD code for 81 with a carry of 1 into the next higher digit pair. ■

The **decimal adjust for subtraction (DAS) instruction** has the following general form:

[⟨*label*⟩] DAS [⟨*comment*⟩]

The DAS instruction has no explicit operand. The implicit operand is the contents of the AL-register. The DAS instruction should follow a SUB or an SBB instruction that subtracts two packed BCD digit pairs and leaves the result in the AL-register. It adjusts the AL-register to contain a valid pair of packed BCD digits. The borrow into this digit pair is recorded in the CF bit of the flags register. The DAS instruction causes the following steps to be performed:

```
IF    (lower nibble of AL-REG > 9) or (AF = 1)
THEN
      AL-REG is decremented by 6
      AF is set to 1
ENDIF

IF    (upper nibble of AL-REG > 9) or (CF = 1)
THEN
      AL-REG is decremented by 60 hex
      CF is set to 1
ENDIF
```

EXAMPLE

Suppose the AL-register contains the value 01110010 (packed BCD code for 72) and the BL-register contains 00100101 (packed BCD code for 25) before the following two instructions are executed:

```
SUB  AL,BL
DAS
```

The SUB instruction performs the following subtraction:

```
 01110010
-00100101
```

which is performed by a complement and an add:

```
   111  1    <--- Carry
   01110010
  +11011011
1  01001101
```

The carry from bit 3 into bit 4 is 0, so the borrow from bit 4 into bit 3 is 1. Therefore, the AF bit of the flags register is set to 1 by execution of the SUB instruction. The carry out of the most significant bit is 1, so the borrow into the MSB is 0. Therefore, the CF bit of the flags register is cleared to 0 by execution of the SUB instruction.

The DAS instruction performs the following operations:

1. Since the AF bit of the flags register is set, the value 11111010 (-6 in decimal) is added to the AL-register:

   ```
      1111       <--- Carry
      01001101
     +11111010
   1  01000111
   ```

   The AF bit of the flags register is set to 1.

2. Since the upper nibble of the AL-register is not greater than 9 and the CF bit of the flags register is not set, no adjustment is required to the upper nibble of the AL-register. The adjusted result is 01000111, which is the packed BCD code for 47 with no borrow from the next higher digit pair. ■

Arithmetic Overflow in BCD

With the packed BCD ten's complement representation presented in Section 11.3, BCD numbers can be interpreted as either unsigned numbers or signed ten's complement numbers. If the unsigned interpretation is used, then the range of integers that can be represented with n-digit BCD numbers is 0 to $10^n - 1$. If the signed interpretation is used, then the range of integers that can be represented with n-digit BCD numbers is $-5(10^{n-1})$ to $+5(10^{n-1}) - 1$. If an arithmetic operation produces a result that is outside the range of integers for that interpretation, then arithmetic overflow has occurred.

Detection of overflow depends on the interpretation used. With the unsigned integer interpretation, overflow occurs whenever a carry out of the MSD on addition or a borrow into the MSD on subtraction occurs. With the signed integer interpretation, overflow occurs on an addition whenever the signs of the two operands are the same and the sign of the sum is not the same as the signs of the operands. With the signed integer interpretation, overflow occurs on a subtraction operation whenever the signs of the minuend and subtrahend are different and the sign of the difference is not the same as the sign of the minuend. With the signed integer interpretation, overflow occurs on a negation operation whenever the sign of the result is the same as the sign of the operand, which occurs only when the negative number being negated has no corresponding positive number.

Programming Examples

Two BCD arithmetic procedures are presented next. The first performs the sum of two packed BCD numbers, and the second performs the ten's complement of a packed BCD number.

Procedure to Add Two Packed BCD Numbers

The FAR procedure defined in Program Listing 11.3 is a PUBLIC procedure called ADDBCD. It adds two packed BCD numbers. The prologue in lines 3–19 describes the function of the procedure and explains its interface requirements. On entry to the procedure, the DS:SI register pair must address the source BCD number, the ES:DI register pair must address the destination BCD number, and the CX-register must contain the number of digits in the BCD numbers. The two BCD numbers must be the same size. On return to the caller, the array addressed by the ES:DI register pair contains the sum of the two input BCD numbers, and the OF, SF, ZF, and CF bits of the flags register are set to reflect this BCD sum.

```
 1:              PAGE    80,132
 2: ;===================================================================
 3: ;                    PROGRAM LISTING 11.3
 4: ;
 5: ; PROCEDURE TO ADD TWO PACKED BCD NUMBERS
 6: ;
 7: ; INPUTS:   DS:SI POINTS TO THE ARRAY CONTAINING
 8: ;                 THE SOURCE BCD NUMBER
 9: ;           ES:DI POINTS TO THE ARRAY CONTAINING
10: ;                 THE DESTINATION BCD NUMBER
11: ;           CX    CONTAINS THE SIZE OF  THE  TWO
12: ;                 BCD NUMBERS (MUST BE EVEN)
13: ;
14: ; OUTPUTS: THE ARRAY POINTED TO BY ES:DI CONTAINS
15: ;          THE SUM OF THE TWO INPUT  BCD  NUMBERS
16: ;
17: ;          THE FOLLOWING FLAGS ARE SET TO REFLECT
18: ;          THE RESULT
19: ;                     OF  SF  ZF  CF
20: ;===================================================================
21:              .MODEL  SMALL,BASIC
22: ;===================================================================
23: ;
24: ; C O D E   S E G M E N T   D E F I N I T I O N
25: ;
26:              .CODE   EX_11_3
27: ;
28: ADDBCD       PROC    FAR PUBLIC USES AX BX CX DX SI DI
29:                                 ;PROCEDURE ADDBCD(SPTR,DPTR,DIGIT_CNT)
30:                                           ;SAVE REGISTERS SPECIFIED
31:                                           ;      IN USES CLAUSE
32: ;
33:              PUSHF                        ;SAVE FLAGS
```

```
            SHR     CX,1                        ;LOOP_CNT = DIGIT_CNT/2
            CLD                                 ;SET DF FOR INCREMENTING
            MOV     DX,0040H                    ;ZERO_FLAG = 1
            CLC                                 ;CLEAR CF BIT OF FLAGS REG.
            .REPEAT                             ;REPEAT
            MOV     BH,ES:[DI]                  ;   D_SIGN = DPTR -> BYTE
            LODSB                               ;   SUM_PAIR = SPTR -> BYTE
            ADC     AL,ES:[DI]                  ;            + DPTR -> BYTE
                                                ;            + CF
                                                ;   SPTR = SPTR + 1
            DAA                                 ;   BCD_PAIR=ADJUSTED SUM_PAIR
            PUSHF                               ;   SAVE CF AND DF
            CMP     AL,0                        ;   IF   BCD_PAIR <> 0
            JE      END_ZERO
            SUB     DX,DX                       ;   THEN ZERO_FLAG = 0
END_ZERO:                                       ;   ENDIF
            POPF                                ;   RESTORE CF AND DF
            STOSB                               ;   DPTR -> BYTE = BCD_PAIR
                                                ;   DPTR = DPTR + 1
            .UNTILCXZ                           ;   LOOP_CNT = LOOP_CNT - 1
                                                ;UNTIL LOOP_CNT = 0
            PUSHF                               ;SAVE CF
            DEC     DI                          ;DPTR = DPTR - 1
            DEC     SI                          ;SPTR = SPTR - 1
                                                ;<SPTR AND DPTR NOW POINT TO
                                                ; THE HIGHEST PAIR OF DIGITS
                                                ; IN THEIR RESPECTIVE BCD NOS.>
;
;
            CMP     BH,50H                      ;IF   D_SIGN = SIGN OF SOURCE
            JAE     NEG_SIGN                    ;              BCD NUMBER
            CMP     BYTE PTR DS:[SI],50H
            JAE     DIFF
            JMP     SAME
NEG_SIGN:
            CMP     BYTE PTR DS:[SI],50H
            JB      DIFF
SAME:                                           ;THEN
            MOV     BL,1                        ;     CHECK_OVRFLO = TRUE
            JMP     END_SIGN
DIFF:                                           ;ELSE
            MOV     BL,0                        ;     CHECK_OVRFLO = FALSE
END_SIGN:                                       ;ENDIF
;===============================================
;<** S E T   F L A G S   F O R   O U T P U T **>
;===============================================
                                                ;CLEAR OUT_FLAGS
            POP     AX                          ;MOVE SAVED CF TO OUT_FLAGS
            AND     AX,0001
            OR      AX,DX                       ;MOVE ZERO_FLAG TO OUT_FLAGS
            CMP     BYTE PTR ES:[DI],50H        ;IF   BCD SUM IS NEGATIVE
            JB      END_SF
            OR      AX,0080H                    ;THEN SET SF IN OUT_FLAGS
END_SF:                                         ;ENDIF
            CMP     BL,0                        ;IF   CHECK_OVRFLO
            JE      END_OF
            CMP     BH,50H                      ;THEN IF   D_SIGN NOT EQUAL
            JB      POS                         ;          SIGN OF BCD SUM
            CMP     BYTE PTR ES:[DI],50H
            JAE     END_OF
            JMP     SET_OF
POS:
            CMP     BYTE PTR ES:[DI],50H
            JB      END_OF
SET_OF:                                         ;     THEN
            OR      AX,0800H                    ;          SET OF IN OUT_FLAGS
END_OF:                                         ;     ENDIF
                                                ;ENDIF
```

```
102:            POP     CX                        ;TEMP = FLAGS SAVED UPON ENTRY
103:            AND     CX,0F73EH                 ;CLEAR OF SF ZF ZND CF IN TEMP
104:            OR      AX,CX                     ;MERGE TEMP WITH OUT_FLAGS
105:            PUSH    AX                        ;SAVE OUT_FLAGS
106: ;
107:            POPF                              ;RESTORE FLAGS
108:                                              ;RESTORE REGISTERS SPECIFIED
109:                                              ;        IN USES CLAUSE
110: ;
111:            RET                               ;RETURN
112: ADDBCD     ENDP                      ;END ADDBCD
113:            END
```

The ADDBCD procedure begins by saving the registers specified in the USES clause (line 28) and saving the flags register (line 33). It continues by performing initialization for the REPEAT-UNTIL loop that performs the packed BCD addition (lines 34–37). The SHR instruction in line 34 computes the loop count for the REPEAT-UNTIL loop. The loop count is one-half the digit count since each iteration of the loop adds a pair of digits from the source BCD number to the corresponding pair of digits from the destination BCD number and adjusts the sum digit pair. The CLD instruction in line 35 clears the DF bit of the flags register for incrementing through the two BCD arrays from the least significant digit pair to the most significant digit pair. Bit 6 of the DX-register is used as a zero flag and is merged into the flags register value that is returned to the caller. The MOV instruction in line 36 initializes this zero flag to 1. It is cleared in the loop the first time that a nonzero sum digit pair is produced. If all sum digit pairs are zero (i.e., the sum of the two BCD numbers is zero), then the zero flag remains set to 1. The CLC instruction in line 37 clears the CF bit of the flags register so that the carry into the least significant digit position is zero. This operation allows the ADC instruction to be used for the addition of the least significant digit pair as well as for the addition of all subsequent digit pairs.

The REPEAT-UNTIL loop in lines 38–54 performs the addition of the two BCD numbers. The loop body begins with the MOV instruction in line 39, which moves a copy of the digit pair addressed by the ES:DI register pair to the BH-register. At loop exit, the BH-register pair contains the most significant pair of digits from the destination BCD array. The high-order digit of this digit pair indicates the sign of the destination BCD number. This sign would not otherwise be available at loop exit because the sum digit pair replaces the destination BCD digit pair on each iteration of the loop.

The LODSB instruction in line 40 loads the AL-register with a pair of digits from the source BCD number (the pair of digits addressed by the DS:SI register pair) and increments the SI-register by 1 so that the DS:SI register pair addresses the next higher pair of digits in the source BCD number. The ADC instruction in line 41 adds to the digit pair in the AL-register the corresponding pair of digits from the destination BCD number (the pair of digits addressed by the ES:DI register pair) and the carry from the previous digit position. The DAA instruction in line 44 adjusts the sum in the AL-register to the correct pair of packed BCD digits and records the carry from this digit pair in the CF bit of the flags register. The PUSHF instruction in line 45 is used to save the CF bit of the flags register, which is needed in the addition operation in the next iteration of the loop body. Several instructions in the remainder of the loop body affect the CF bit of the flags register.

The single-alternative decision structure implemented in lines 46–49 tests the packed BCD digit pair in the AL-register (the sum digit pair) to see if it is nonzero. If it is nonzero, then the SUB instruction in line 48 is executed, which clears the zero flag in bit 6 of the DX-register.

The POPF instruction in line 50 restores the CF bit of the flags register. None of the remaining instructions in the loop affect the CF bit. The STOSB instruction in line 51 moves a copy of the sum digit pair in the AL-register to the destination BCD array, replacing the pair of digits addressed by the ES:DI register pair, and then increments the DI-register by 1 so that the ES:DI register pair addresses the next higher pair of digits in the destination BCD number. The LOOP instruction generated for the macro directive in line 53 decrements the loop count by 1 and, if the loop count is nonzero, returns control to the top of the loop (line 38).

After the REPEAT-UNTIL loop, the procedure modifies the caller's saved flags to reflect the sum of the two BCD numbers. At loop exit, the destination BCD array contains the BCD sum, the CF bit of the flags register reflects the carry out of the MSD of the sum, and bit 6 of the DX-register reflects whether or not the sum is zero. The PUSHF instruction in line 55 saves the CF bit of the flags register so that it can be merged into the caller's saved flags later in the procedure. The DEC instructions in lines 56 and 57 set the ES:DI register pair and the DS:SI register pair to address the most significant pair of digits in their respective arrays. The single-alternative decision structure implemented in lines 63–76 determines whether or not overflow is possible. The sign of the destination BCD number, recorded in the BH-register on the last iteration of the REPEAT-UNTIL loop, and the sign of the source BCD number are compared to see if they are the same or different (lines 63–70). If the signs of the two input BCD numbers are the same, then the BL-register is set to 1 (line 72), indicating that overflow is possible and that a check for overflow must be made. If the two signs are not the same, then the BL-register is set to 0 (line 75), indicating that overflow is not possible and that a check for overflow is not to be made.

The instructions in lines 80–105 build in the AX-register an image of the OF, SF, ZF, and CF bits of the flags register that reflect the BCD sum. This image is then merged with the flags register value saved for the caller in line 33. The POP instruction in line 81 loads the AX-register with the image of the flags register that existed at exit from the REPEAT-UNTIL loop that was saved in line 55. The AND instruction in line 82 clears all bits except the CF bit in this image of the flags register. The OR instruction in line 83 merges the zero flag in bit 6 of the DX-register with the flag image in the AX-register. The single-alternative decision structure implemented in lines 84–87 sets the SF bit in the flags register image in the AX-register (line 86) if the MSD of the BCD sum is greater than or equal to 5. The single-alternative decision structure implemented in lines 88–101 tests the flag in the BL-register to see if an overflow check needs to be made. If the overflow check is required (BL-register = 1), then the single-alternative decision structure implemented in lines 90–100 is executed. This decision structure compares the sign of the destination BCD number (saved in the BH-register) with the sign of the BCD sum. If the two signs are not the same, then the OF bit in the flags register image in the AX-register is set to 1 (line 99). The POP instruction in line 102 loads the CX-register with the flags register image saved for the caller (line 33). The AND instruction in line 103 clears the OF, SF, ZF, and CF bits in the caller's flags register image in the CX-register. The OR instruction in line 104 merges the flags register image in the CX-register with the one in the AX-register. The PUSH instruction in line 105 pushes the caller's flags register image, modified to reflect the result of the BCD addition, back onto the stack. The instruction in line 107 restores the modified flags for the caller, and the instructions generated for the RET instruction in line 111 cause the registers specified in the USES clause to be restored and control to be returned to the caller.

Procedure to Negate a Packed BCD Number

The FAR procedure defined in Program Listing 11.4 is a PUBLIC procedure called NEGBCD. It performs the ten's complement of a packed BCD number. The prologue in lines 3–12 describes the function of the procedure and explains its interface requirements. On entry to the procedure, the ES:DI register pair must address the first byte of an array that contains a packed BCD number, and the CX-register must contain the number of digits in this BCD number. The digit count in the CX-register must be even. On return to the caller, the array addressed by the ES:DI register pair contains the ten's complement of the input BCD number, and the OF, SF, ZF, and CF bits of the flags register are set to reflect the BCD result. The algorithm used to perform the negation is an application of the alternate method described in Section 11.2.

```
 1:             PAGE    80,132
 2: ;===================================================================
 3: ;                     PROGRAM LISTING 11.4
 4: ;
 5: ; PROCEDURE TO PERFORM TEN'S COMPLEMENT OF A PACKED BCD NUMBER
 6: ;
 7: ; INPUT:    ES:DI POINTS TO ARRAY CONTAINING PACKED BCD NUMBER
 8: ;           CX    CONTAINS SIZE OF BCD NUMBER   (MUST BE EVEN)
 9: ;
10: ; OUTPUT:   THE ARRAY POINTED TO BY ES:DI CONTAINS  THE  TEN'S
11: ;           COMPLEMENT  OF  THE  NUMBER THAT IT CONTAINED UPON
12: ;           ENTRY TO THE PROCEDURE.
13: ;===================================================================
14:             .MODEL  SMALL,BASIC
15: ;===================================================================
16: ; C O D E   S E G M E N T   D E F I N I T I O N
17:             .CODE   EX_11_4
18: NEGBCD      PROC    FAR PUBLIC USES AX BX CX DX DI
19:                                           ;PROCEDURE NEGBCD(PTR,DIGIT_CNT)
20:                                           ;SAVE REGISTERS SPECIFIED
21:                                           ;     IN USES CLAUSE
22:             PUSHF                         ;SAVE FLAGS
23:             SHR     CX,1                  ;LOOP_CNT = DIGIT_CNT / 2
24:             CLD                           ;SET DF FOR INCREMENTING
25:             MOV     BX,0000               ;CLEAR OUT_FLAGS
26: ;
27:             MOV     AL,0                  ;FOUND = FALSE
28:       REPE  SCASB                         ;REPEAT
29:                                           ;   IF   PTR->BYTE <> 0
30:                                           ;   THEN FOUND = TRUE
31:                                           ;   ENDIF
32:                                           ;   PTR = PTR + 1
33:                                           ;   LOOP_CNT = LOOP_CNT - 1
34:                                           ;UNTIL FOUND OR LOOP_CNT = 0
35:             JE      NOTFOUND              ;IF   FOUND
36:             DEC     DI                    ;THEN PTR = PTR - 1
37:             OR      BX,0001               ;     SET CF IN OUT_FLAGS
38:             MOV     DL,ES:[DI]            ;     IN_SIGN = PTR->BYTE
39:             MOV     AL,DL                 ;     IF   RIGHT NIBBLE OF
40:             AND     AL,0FH                ;          PTR->BYTE = 0
41:             JNE     ELSE1
42:             MOV     AL,0A0H               ;     THEN PTR->BYTE =
43:             JMP     SUBTRACT              ;          A0 HEX - PTR->BYTE
44: ELSE1:                                    ;     ELSE PTR->BYTE =
45:             MOV     AL,9AH                ;          9A HEX - PTR->BYTE
46: SUBTRACT:                                 ;     ENDIF
47:             SUB     AL,ES:[DI]
48:             STOSB                         ;     PTR = PTR + 1
49:             JCXZ    LOOP_END              ;     WHILE LOOP_CNT <> 0
```

```
50: LOOP_TOP:
51:             MOV     DL,ES:[DI]              ;         IN_SIGN = PTR->BYTE
52:             MOV     AL,99H                  ;         PTR->BYTE = 99 HEX
53:             SUB     AL,ES:[DI]              ;                - PTR->BYTE
54:             STOSB                           ;         PTR = PTR + 1
55:             LOOP    LOOP_TOP                ;         DECREMENT LOOP_CNT
56: LOOP_END:                                   ;      ENDWHILE
57:             DEC     DI                      ;      PTR = PTR - 1
58:                                             ;      PTR NOW POINTS TO FIRST
59:                                             ;      PAIR OF DIGITS IN BCD NUM
60:             CMP     BYTE PTR ES:[DI],50H;          IF   SIGN OF RESULT = -
61:             JB      OVRFLO_CHK
62:             OR      BX,0080H                ;      THEN SET SF IN OUT_FLAGS
63: OVRFLO_CHK:                                 ;      ENDIF
64:             CMP     DL,ES:[DI]              ;      IF   IN_SIGN =
65:             JNE     MERGE_FLAGS             ;           SIGN OF RESULT
66:             OR      BX,0800H                ;      THEN SET OF IN OUT_FLAGS
67:                                             ;      ENDIF
68:             JMP     MERGE_FLAGS
69: NOTFOUND:                                   ;ELSE
70:             OR      BX,0040H                ;      SET ZF IN OUT_FLAGS
71: MERGE_FLAGS:                                ;ENDIF
72:             POP     AX                      ;TEMP = FLAGS SAVED UPON ENTRY
73:             AND     AX,0F73EH               ;CLEAR OF SF ZF AND CF IN TEMP
74:             OR      AX,BX                   ;MERGE TEMP WITH OUT_FLAGS
75:             PUSH    AX                      ;SAVE OUT_FLAGS
76:             POPF                            ;RESTORE FLAGS
77:                                             ;RESTORE REGISTERS SPECIFIED
78:                                             ;         IN USES CLAUSE
79:             RET                             ;RETURN
80: NEGBCD      ENDP                          ;END NEGBCD
81: ;==================================================================
82:             END
```

The procedure begins by saving the registers specified in the USES clause (line 18), saving the flags register (line 22), and performing loop initialization (lines 23–25). The SHR instruction in line 23 computes the loop count from the digit count input to the procedure in the CX-register. The loop count is one-half the digit count since two digits are processed on each iteration of the loop. The CLD instruction in line 24 clears the DF bit of the flags register for incrementing through the BCD array from the least significant digit pair of the most significant digit pair. The flags register image for the OF, SF, ZF, and CF bits to be returned to the caller is built in the BX-register. The MOV instruction in line 25 initializes this flag image to zero.

The algorithm begins by copying digits from right to left up to but not including the first nonzero digit. The loop in lines 27 and 28 searches the BCD array for the first nonzero digit pair. Each time the string instruction in line 28 is executed, the DI-register is automatically incremented by 1 so that the ES:DI register pair addresses the next higher digit pair of the BCD array, and the loop count in the CX-register is automatically decremented by 1. The repetition of the string instruction in line 28 halts for one of two reasons: Either a nonzero digit pair is found, or the entire BCD array is scanned without finding a nonzero digit pair. The double-alternative decision structure implemented in lines 35–71 determines which of the two conditions cause the repetition of the string instruction to halt. If a nonzero digit pair is found, then the instructions in lines 36–68 (the "then" clause) are executed; otherwise, the instruction in line 70 (the "else" clause) is executed.

The "then" clause of the double-alternative decision structure performs the remaining steps of the alternate method described in Section 11.2. The DEC instruction in line 36 adjusts the ES:DI register pair so that it addresses the first nonzero digit pair in the BCD array. The OR instruction in line 37 sets the CF bit in the flags register image being built in the BX-register. For the purpose of setting flags, a negation is viewed as a subtraction from zero, and the subtraction of a nonzero value from zero always requires a borrow into the MSD. The MOV instruction in line 38 copies the digit pair addressed by the ES:DI register pair into the DL-register. The use of the DL-register is explained in the following paragraphs.

The double-alternative decision structure implemented in lines 39–46 determines whether the first nonzero digit is the left nibble or the right nibble of this digit pair. If the first nonzero digit is the left nibble, then the right nibble must be copied and the left nibble must be subtracted from 1010 (10 in decimal); this step is accomplished by subtracting the digit pair from A0 hex (lines 42 and 47). If the first nonzero digit is the right nibble, then the right nibble must be subtracted from 1010 (10 in decimal) and the left nibble must be subtracted from 1001 (9 in decimal); this step is accomplished by subtracting the digit pair from 9A hex (lines 45 and 47). The STOSB instruction in line 48 replaces the first nonzero digit pair in the BCD array with the result of this subtraction and increments the DI-register so that the ES:DI register pair addresses the next higher digit pair in the BCD array.

The "then" clause continues with the WHILE loop implemented in lines 49–56. The WHILE loop subtracts all remaining BCD digits in the number from 1001 (9 in decimal). The JCXZ instruction (line 49) turns what would normally be a REPEAT-UNTIL loop into a WHILE loop. The loop body begins with the MOV instruction in line 51, which copies the digit pair addressed by the ES:DI register pair into the DL-register. At loop exit, the DL-register pair contains the most significant pair of digits from the input BCD number. That digit indicates the sign of the input BCD number. The instructions in lines 52 and 53 subtract the digit pair addressed by the ES:DI register pair from 99 hex (10011001 binary), and the STOSB instruction in line 54 replaces the digit pair addressed by ES:DI with the result of this subtraction and then increments the DI-register so that the ES:DI register pair addresses the next higher pair of BCD digits. The LOOP instruction in line 55 decrements the loop count by 1 and transfers control to the top of the loop (line 50) if the loop count is not zero. On exit from the WHILE loop, the proper settings for the SF and OF bits of the flags register are determined. The single-alternative decision structure implemented in lines 60–63 determines the sign of the result. If the result is negative, then the OR instruction in line 62 sets the SF bit in the flags register image being built in the BX-register. The single-alternative decision structure implemented in lines 64–67 compares the sign of the input BCD number (indicated by the digit pair in the DL-register) with the sign of the result. If the two signs are the same, then the OR instruction in line 66 sets the OF bit in the flags register image in the BX-register. This last step concludes the "then" clause of the double-alternative decision structure implemented in lines 35–71. The JMP instruction in line 68 skips the "else" clause for this decision structure.

The else clause of the double-alternative decision structure is executed if the scan loop in lines 27 and 28 fails to find a nonzero digit pair in the input BCD array. In this case, the input BCD number is zero and its ten's complement is zero. The OR instruction in line 70 sets the ZF bit in the flags register image in the BX-register.

On completion of the double-alternative decision structure, the flags register image in the BX-register is merged with the flags register value that was saved for the caller. The POP instruction in line 72 loads the AX-register with the flags register value saved for the caller. The AND instruction in line 73 clears the OF, SF, ZF, and CF bits in this flags register image in the AX-register. The OR instruction in line 74 merges the flags register image in the BX-register with the one in the AX-register, which modifies the flags register image saved for the caller to reflect the result of the negation operation. The PUSH instruction in line 75 pushes this modified flags register image back onto the stack, and the POPF instruction in line 76 places this image in the flags register. The instructions generated for the RET instruction in line 79 restore the registers specified in the USES clause and return control to the caller.

11.5 BCD Input/Output

When a BCD number includes both an integer and a fraction, the decimal point that separates the two portions of the number does not have to be part of the internal representation of the number. All BCD numbers can be stored internally as integers. The arithmetic computations performed with these BCD numbers can treat the numbers as integers. The decimal point is only considered in the interpretation of the BCD number. The interpretation is applied when a value is input for the BCD number or when the value represented by the BCD number is output. This section discusses the interpretation of BCD numbers for input/output.

Interpretation of BCD Numbers for Input/Output

The internal representation of a BCD number does not have to have an explicit decimal point. The assumed decimal point can be in any position within the number. For example, consider the packed BCD array shown in Figure 11.12. This array represents the integer 123456 if the decimal point is assumed to follow the digit pair at offset 0000. It represents the real number 1234.56 if the decimal point is assumed to lie between the digit pair at offset 0001 and the digit pair at offset 0000. It represents the real number 1.23456 if the decimal point is assumed to lie between the left nibble and the right nibble of the digit pair at offset 0002.

FIGURE 11.12
Packed BCD array—value depends on interpretation

Offset		
0000	56	LSDs
0001	34	
0002	12	MSDs

The procedures that perform arithmetic computations on packed BCD numbers do not need to know whether their operands represent integers or real numbers. For example, the ADDBCD procedure discussed in Section 11.4 works correctly for real numbers as long as the assumed decimal point is in the same position in the two BCD operands. If so, then the position of the assumed decimal point in the sum is the same as its position in the two operands.

EXAMPLES

Consider the arrays in Figure 11.13(a). Suppose the destination array represents the number 14.5 and the source array represents the number 12.25. Then, for the destination array, the assumed decimal point lies between the left and right nibbles of the digit pair at offset 0001, and, for the source array, the assumed decimal point lies between the digit pair at offset 0001 and the digit pair at offset 0000. The two arrays are *not* compatible for addition since the assumed decimal points are not in the same position. There is no interpretation that can be applied to the sum of these two BCD numbers that can produce the desired result (26.75).

Consider now the arrays in Figure 11.13(b). Suppose the destination array represents the number 14.5 and the source array represents the number 12.25. Then, for both arrays, the assumed decimal point lies between the digit pair at offset 0001 and the digit pair at offset 0000. The two arrays are compatible for addition since the assumed decimal points are in the same position. If the decimal point is assumed to be in the same position in the sum array, then the correct sum (26.75) is produced. ■

FIGURE 11.13
Positions of assumed decimal points must match for correct BCD addition

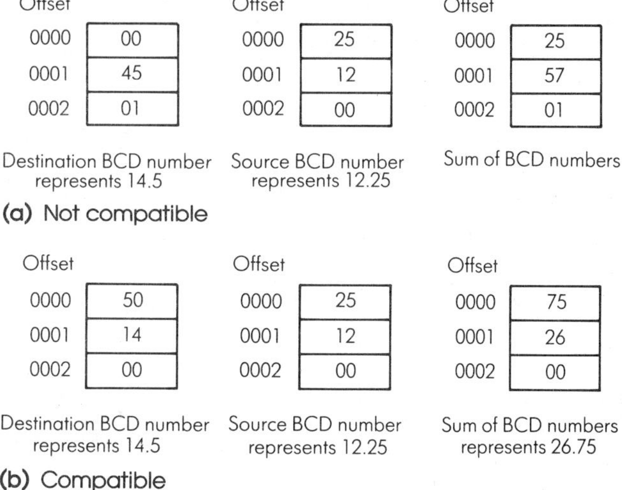

Consistency is required in interpretation of operands supplied to and results received from procedures like ADDBCD. Consistency in interpretation is the responsibility of the caller. ADDBCD simply adds two BCD numbers without regard to interpretation.

Programming Example—BCD Output Procedure

The FAR procedure defined in Program Listing 11.5 is a PUBLIC procedure called PUTBCD. It displays a packed BCD number in signed decimal form. The number is displayed on the screen beginning at the current cursor position. The prologue in lines 3–12 describes the function of the procedure and explains its interface requirements. On entry to the procedure, the DS:SI register pair must address the first byte of an array that contains a packed BCD number, the CH-register must contain the number of digits in this BCD number, and the CL-register must contain the number of digits that follow the assumed decimal point in this BCD number. The output of the procedure is the input BCD number displayed at the screen, in signed decimal form, beginning at the current cursor position. There are no outputs returned to the caller by the PUTBCD procedure.

The field width for the display of the BCD number depends on the count of the number of digits that follow the assumed decimal point. If the number of digits following the assumed decimal point is zero, then the number is displayed in a field of $n + 1$ character positions, in which n is the total number of digits in the BCD number. The extra character position is for the sign. If the number of digits following the assumed decimal point is nonzero, then the number is displayed in a field of $n + 2$ character positions, in which n is the total number of digits in the BCD number. The two extra character positions are for the sign and the decimal point. The sign dis-

```
            PAGE    80,132
;=====================================================================
;                   PROGRAM LISTING 11.5
;
; PROCEDURE TO DISPLAY A PACKED BCD NUMBER IN SIGNED DECIMAL FORM
;
; INPUT:  DS:SI  POINTS TO ARRAY CONTAINING  PACKED BCD NUMBER IN
;                TEN'S COMPLEMENT FORM
;         CH-REG CONTAINS SIZE OF BCD NUMBER        (MUST BE EVEN)
;         CL-REG CONTAINS NUMBER OF FRACTIONAL DIGITS
; OUTPUT: INPUT BCD NUMBER DISPLAYED AT SCREEN IN SIGNED DECIMAL
;         FORM BEGINNING AT THE CURRENT CURSOR POSITION
;=====================================================================
            .MODEL  SMALL,BASIC
;=====================================================================
                                        ;PROCEDURES TO
            EXTRN   BCDASCII:FAR        ;CONVERT BCD NUMBER TO ASCII
            EXTRN   FLT_SIGN:FAR        ;FLOAT SIGN IN ASCII NUMBER
            EXTRN   PUTSTRNG:FAR        ;DISPLAY A CHARACTER STRING
            EXTRN   TENSSMAG:FAR        ;CONVERT TENS COMPLEMENT BCD
                                        ;TO SIGN MAGNITUDE
;=====================================================================
; D A T A   S E G M E N T   D E F I N I T I O N
BCDDATA     SEGMENT COMMON
SIGN        DB      ?                   ;SIGN OF ASCII NUMBER
NUMBER      DB      255 DUP(?)          ;DIGITS OF ASCII NUMBER
DECIMAL_PT  DB      '.'                 ;DECIMAL POINT
BCD_NUM     DB      128 DUP(?)          ;BCD NUMBER
BCDDATA     ENDS
;=====================================================================
; C O D E   S E G M E N T   D E F I N I T I O N
            .CODE   EX_11_5
PUTBCD      PROC    FAR PUBLIC USES AX BX CX DX DI SI DS ES
                                    ;PUTBCD (SPTR,DIGIT_CNT,FRAC_CNT)
                                        ;SAVE REGISTERS SPECIFIED
                                        ;      IN USES CLAUSE
            PUSHF                       ;SAVE FLAGS
;
            MOV     AX,SEG BCDDATA      ;SET ES-REGISTER TO POINT
            MOV     ES,AX               ;TO BCD DATA SEGMENT
            MOV     BX,CX               ;<FRAC_CNT IN BX>
            SUB     BH,BH
            XCHG    CL,CH               ;<DIGIT_CNT IN CX>
            SUB     CH,CH
            MOV     DX,CX               ;INT_CNT = DIGIT_CNT
            SUB     DX,BX               ;            - FRAC_CNT
                                        ;<INT_CNT IN DX>
            PUSH    CX                  ;SAVE DIGIT_CNT
            SHR     CX,1                ;LOOP_CNT = DIGIT_CNT / 2
            CLD                         ;SET DF FOR INCREMENTING
            LEA     DI,BCD_NUM          ;DPTR = ADDRESS OF BCD_NUM
      REP   MOVSB                       ;REPEAT
                                        ;   DPTR->BYTE = SPTR->BYTE
                                        ;   DPTR = DPTR + 1
                                        ;   SPTR = SPTR + 1
                                        ;   LOOP_CNT = LOOP_CNT - 1
                                        ;UNTIL LOOP_CNT = 0
            POP     CX                  ;RESTORE DIGIT_CNT
            PUSH    ES                  ;SET DS-REGISTER TO POINT
            POP     DS                  ;TO BCD DATA SEGMENT
            LEA     DI,BCD_NUM          ;DPTR = ADDRESS OF BCD_NUM
            CALL    TENSSMAG            ;CALL TENSSMAG(DPTR,DIGIT_CNT)
            LEA     SI,BCD_NUM          ;SPTR = ADDRESS OF BCD_NUM
            LEA     DI,SIGN             ;DPTR = ADDRESS OF SIGN:NUMBER
            CALL    BCDASCII            ;CALL BCDASCII (SPTR,DPTR,
                                        ;                DIGIT_CNT)
            MOV     CX,DX               ;CALL FLT_SIGN (DPTR,INT_CNT)
```

```
                CALL     FLT_SIGN
                INC      CX                      ;PRINT_CNT = INT_CNT + 1
                CALL     PUTSTRNG                ;CALL PUTSTRNG(DPTR,PRINT_CNT)
                CMP      BX,0                    ;IF   FRAC_CNT > 0
                JE       NO_FRAC
                PUSH     CX                      ;THEN
                LEA      DI,DECIMAL_PT           ;     DISPLAY DECIMAL POINT
                MOV      CX,1
                CALL     PUTSTRNG
                LEA      DI,SIGN                 ;     DPTR = ADDRESS OF SIGN
                POP      CX                      ;          + PRINT_CNT
                ADD      DI,CX
                MOV      CX,BX                   ;     CALL PUTSTRNG (DPTR,
                CALL     PUTSTRNG                ;                   FRAC_CNT)
      NO_FRAC:                                   ;ENDIF
                POPF                             ;RESTORE FLAGS
                                                 ;RESTORE REGISTERS SPECIFIED
                                                 ;      IN USES CLAUSE
                RET                              ;RETURN
      PUTBCD    ENDP                           ;END PUTBCD
      ;==================================================================
                END
```

played with the BCD number is a blank for positive numbers and a minus sign (−) for negative numbers. Leading zeros in the integer portion of the number are replaced with blanks for display. If the integer portion of the BCD number is zero, then one zero is displayed for the integer with blank fill to the left. If the BCD number has no integer portion (i.e., if the digit count in the CH-register is equal to the fractional digit count in the CL-register), then no characters are displayed for the integer and the decimal point immediately follows the sign. The sign is floated right in the field so that it is displayed adjacent to the first digit displayed in the field. The specified number of fractional digits is displayed, including trailing zeros. Figure 11.14(a) shows a byte array that contains a packed BCD number. The digits of the number are 9999877500, which is the ten's complement of 0000122500. Figure 11.14(b) shows the string that would be displayed by PUTBCD for various interpretations of this BCD

FIGURE 11.14
PUTBCD display formats

Offset		
0000	00	LSDs
0001	75	
0002	87	
0003	99	
0004	99	MSDs

(a) Packed BCD array

Digit count	Fraction digit count	String displayed by PUTBCD
10	4	−12.2500
10	6	−0.122500
6	4	−12.2500
6	6	−.122500
6	0	−122500

(b) Strings displayed by PUTBCD using the packed BCD array shown in (a) for various digit counts

number specified by the digit count in the CH-register and the fractional digit count in the CL-register.

Four external subprocedures are referenced by the PUTBCD procedure and are identified by the EXTRN pseudo-operations in lines 17–20. The BCDASCII and TENSSMAG procedures are the same as those discussed earlier in the chapter. The PUTSTRNG procedure has been used in programming examples throughout the text. The FLT_SIGN procedure has not been used or discussed previously and is not presented here in detail. However, the function of the FLT_SIGN procedure and its interface requirements are discussed briefly. FLT_SIGN accepts a signed ASCII number as input and replaces leading zeros in the integer portion of that number with blanks. The sign of the ASCII number is floated through the field of blanks so that it is adjacent to the first nonblank digit in the ASCII number. On entry to the FLT_SIGN procedure, the ES:DI register pair must address the first byte (i.e., the sign byte) of a byte array that contains an ASCII number, and the CX-register must contain a count of the number of digits in the integer portion of this ASCII number. This integer digit count may be zero. On return to the caller, the array addressed by the ES:DI register pair contains an ASCII number equivalent to the number it contained on entry, except that leading zeros in the integer portion have been replaced by blanks and the sign is adjacent to the first nonblank digit.

The PUTBCD procedure references a local data segment defined in lines 24–29. The data segment is defined as a COMMON data segment (line 24) because the data segment is shared with the BCD input procedure GETBCD. COMMON data segments are discussed in detail in Chapter 12. The variables SIGN and NUMBER (lines 25 and 26) define a byte array of size 256 that is used to build the ASCII number from the input BCD number. Variable SIGN holds the ASCII character that represents the sign of the number, and array NUMBER holds the digits of the ASCII number. The byte variable DECIMAL_PT, defined in line 27, is a single-character string whose initial value is the ASCII code for a period. The variable BCD_NUM, defined in line 28, is a byte array of size 128 that holds a copy of the input packed BCD number. The PUTBCD procedure uses the TENSSMAG procedure to convert the BCD number from ten's complement to sign magnitude, and then it uses the BCDASCII procedure to convert the sign magnitude BCD number to ASCII. The local copy of the BCD number is used for the ten's complement–to–sign magnitude conversion to avoid modifying the BCD number in the caller's environment. (Recall that TENSSMAG returns its output in the same array in which it received its input.)

The PUTBCD procedure begins by saving the registers specified in the USES clause (line 33), saving the flags register (line 37), and initializing the ES-register to address the local data segment (lines 39 and 40). The procedure then isolates the three-digit counts that it needs. The count of the number of digits in the fractional portion of the number is moved from the CL-register to the BX-register (lines 41 and 42); the count of the total number of digits in the number is moved from the CH-register to the CX-register (lines 43 and 44); and the count of the number of digits in the integer portion of the number is computed and placed in the DX-register (lines 45 and 46).

The REPEAT-UNTIL loop implemented by the repeated string instruction in line 52 copies the input BCD number into array BCD_NUM in the local data segment. The PUSH instruction in line 48 saves the digit count so that the CX-register can be used for the count that controls the loop. The SHR instruction in line 49 computes the loop count that is one-half the digit count. The loop count is the count of the number of bytes to be moved, which is one-half the digit count since the digits are packed two per byte. The CLD instruction in line 50 clears the direction flag so that the repeated string instruction increments through the two arrays. The DS:SI register pair already addresses the source array, the BCD array provided by the caller. The LEA instruction in line 51 initializes the DI-register so that the ES:DI register pair addresses the array BCD_NUM in the local data segment. The MOVSB instruction in line 52 with the REP repeat prefix copies the BCD number from the caller's environment into the local environment. The POP instruction in line 58 restores the digit count in the CX-register. Now that the input BCD number has been copied into the local environment, both the ES and DS registers can be used to address the local data segment. The instructions in lines 59 and 60 copy the ES-register value to the DS-register. Recall that only one of the operands of a MOV instruction can be a segment register. To move from one segment register to another, PUSH and POP can be used.

PUTBCD uses a sequence of subprocedure references to convert the BCD number to an ASCII string for output. The instructions in lines 61 and 62 invoke the TENSSMAG procedure to convert the BCD number from ten's complement to sign magnitude form. TENSSMAG is entered with the ES:DI register pair addressing the local BCD array (BCD_NUM) and the CX-register containing the total digit count. The TENSSMAG procedure returns the sign magnitude version of the number in the same array (BCD_NUM). The instructions in lines 63–65 invoke the BCDASCII procedure to convert the sign magnitude BCD number to a sign magnitude ASCII string. BCDASCII is entered with the DS:SI register pair addressing the local BCD array (BCD_NUM), the ES:DI register pair addressing the local ASCII array (SIGN:NUMBER), and the CX-register containing the total digit count. The instructions in lines 67 and 68 invoke the FLT_SIGN procedure to replace leading zeros in the integer portion of the ASCII number with blanks and to float the sign through this field of blanks. FLT_SIGN is entered with the ES:DI register pair addressing the ASCII array (SIGN:NUMBER) and the CX-register containing the integer digit count (line 67). The ASCII string is now ready for output to the video screen.

The PUTBCD procedure displays the ASCII string in two parts. The instructions in lines 69 and 70 invoke the PUTSTRNG procedure to display the sign and the integer portion of the ASCII number. PUTSTRNG is entered with the ES:DI register pair addressing the ASCII array (SIGN:NUMBER) and the CX-register containing the integer digit count plus 1. The addition of 1 to the integer digit count (line 69) is performed to include the sign with the integer digits. The single-alternative decision structure implemented in lines 71–82 displays the decimal point and the fractional portion of the ASCII number if the fraction digit count is nonzero. The CMP instruction in line 71 tests the fraction digit count, and the JE instruction in line 72 makes the decision based on this test. If the fraction digit count is nonzero, then the instructions in lines 73–81 are executed; otherwise, these instructions are skipped. The PUSH instruction in line 73 saves the integer print count so that the CX-register can be used for the display of the decimal point. The instructions in lines 74–76 invoke the PUTSTRNG procedure to display the single character string defined in line 27, the string that contains the decimal point. The instructions in lines 77–81 invoke PUTSTRNG to display the fractional portion of the ASCII number. PUTSTRNG is entered with the ES:DI register pair addressing the fractional portion of the ASCII number in array SIGN:NUMBER (lines 77–79) and the CX-register containing the fraction digit count (line 80).

On completion of the single-alternative decision structure, the flags register is restored (line 83), the registers specified in the USES clause are restored, and control is returned to the caller (line 86).

The object code for the TENSSMAG, BCDASCII, ADDBCD, NEGBCD,

FLT_SIGN, and PUTBCD procedures are in a library named BCD.LIB on the diskette that accompanies this book. This library also contains the object code for a procedure named GETBCD and for several subprocedures that it requires. The interface requirements for the GETBCD procedure are as follows:

1. On entry to GETBCD, the ES:DI register pair must address the first byte of the BCD array that is to contain the BCD number entered via the keyboard, the CH-register is to contain the size (in nibbles) of the BCD array, and the CL-register is to contain the count of the number of digits that are to follow the assumed decimal point in the BCD array.
2. On return to the caller, the specified BCD array contains the BCD number entered via the keyboard, aligned as specified by the inputs to GETBCD in the CX-register.

The programming exercises at the end of this chapter specify several other algorithms whose implementations can be added to this library.

Programming Example— Bank Account Transactions

Program Listing 11.6 displays a report regarding a sequence of transactions on a bank account and demonstrates the use of the subprocedures presented earlier in this chapter. The input data were embedded in the data segment for the program, so this discussion emphasizes computation and output involving BCD numbers. The prologue in line 5 briefly describes the program's function.

```
 1:          PAGE    80,132
 2: ;===================================================================
 3: ;                PROGRAM LISTING 11.6
 4: ;
 5: ; PROGRAM TO PRINT A REPORT OF BANK ACCOUNT TRANSACTIONS
 6: ;===================================================================
 7:          .MODEL  SMALL,BASIC
 8: ;===================================================================
 9:                                     ;PROCEDURES TO
10:          EXTRN   ADDBCD:FAR         ;ADD     PACKED BCD NUMBERS
11:          EXTRN   NEGBCD:FAR         ;NEGATE  PACKED BCD NUMBERS
12:          EXTRN   NEWLINE:FAR        ;DISPLAY NEWLINE CHARACTER
13:          EXTRN   PUTBCD:FAR         ;DISPLAY PACKED BCD NUMBERS
14:          EXTRN   PUTSTRNG:FAR       ;DISPLAY CHARACTER STRING
15: ;===================================================================
16: ; S T A C K   S E G M E N T   D E F I N I T I O N
17:          .STACK  512
18: ;
19: ;===================================================================
20: ; V A R I A B L E   D E F I N I T I O N S
21:          .DATA
22: ;
23: BALANCE    DB    50H,25H,03H,3 DUP(0)
24: TRANSCOUNT DB    12
25: TRANSACTN  DB    'W',00H,50H,00H,3 DUP(0)
26:            DB    'W',25H,25H,02H,3 DUP(0)
27:            DB    'D',00H,25H,00H,3 DUP(0)
28:            DB    'W',25H,75H,00H,3 DUP(0)
29:            DB    'W',50H,07H,00H,3 DUP(0)
30:            DB    'W',00H,20H,00H,3 DUP(0)
31:            DB    'D',00H,00H,01H,3 DUP(0)
```

```
             DB      'D',25H,50H,05H,3 DUP(0)
             DB      'W',50H,82H,00H,3 DUP(0)
             DB      'D',00H,50H,07H,3 DUP(0)
             DB      'W',45H,73H,02H,3 DUP(0)
             DB      'W',50H,27H,00H,3 DUP(0)
SERVICE      DB      6 DUP(0)
CHARGE       DB      65H,5 DUP(99H)
;====================================================================
; C O N S T A N T   D E F I N I T I O N S
             .CONST
HEADER       DB      '       DEPOSIT       WITHDRAWAL       BALANCE'
HEADER_LNG   EQU     $ - HEADER
BLANKS       DB      '                               '
OVERDRAWN    DB      ' OVERDRAWN     '
SERV_CHG     DB      ' SERVICE CHARGE'
MSG_LNG      EQU     $ - SERV_CHG
ONE          DW      1
SIXTEEN      DW      16
SEVENTEEN    DW      17
THIRTY_1     DW      31
;====================================================================
; C O D E   S E G M E N T   D E F I N I T I O N
             .CODE   EX_11_6
             .STARTUP                       ;GENERATE STARTUP CODE
             PUSH    DS                     ;SET ES-REGISTER TO ADDRESS
             POP     ES                     ;DGROUP
             LEA     DI,HEADER              ;DISPLAY HEADER
             MOV     CX,HEADER_LNG
             CALL    PUTSTRNG
             CALL    NEWLINE                ;SKIP TO NEXT LINE
             LEA     DI,BLANKS              ;DISPLAY 31 BLANKS
             MOV     CX,THIRTY_1
             CALL    PUTSTRNG
;
             LEA     SI,BALANCE             ;DISPLAY BEGINNING BALANCE
             MOV     CX,0C02H
             CALL    PUTBCD
             CALL    NEWLINE                ;SKIP TO NEXT LINE
             MOV     CL,TRANSCOUNT          ;LOOP_CNT = TRANSCOUNT
             MOV     CH,0
             LEA     SI,TRANSACTN           ;PTR = ADDRESS OF TRANSACTN
LOOP1:                                      ;REPEAT
             PUSH    CX                     ;   SAVE LOOP_CNT
             MOV     AL,[SI]                ;   CODE = PTR -> BYTE
             INC     SI                     ;   PTR = PTR + 1
             PUSH    SI                     ;   <PTR IS ADDRESS OF AMOUNT>
             CMP     AL,'D'                 ;   IF   CODE = D
             JNE     ELSE1
             LEA     DI,BALANCE             ;   THEN
             MOV     CX,12                  ;        BALANCE = BALANCE
             CALL    ADDBCD                 ;                + AMOUNT
             MOV     CX,0C02H
             CALL    PUTBCD                 ;        DISPLAY AMOUNT
             LEA     DI,BLANKS              ;        DISPLAY 17 BLANKS
             MOV     CX,SEVENTEEN
             CALL    PUTSTRNG
             LEA     SI,BALANCE             ;        DISPLAY BALANCE
             MOV     CX,0C02H
             CALL    PUTBCD
             JMP     ENDIF1
RELAY:       JMP     LOOP1
ELSE1:                                      ;   ELSE
             LEA     DI,BLANKS              ;        DISPLAY 16 BLANKS
             MOV     CX,SIXTEEN
             CALL    PUTSTRNG
             MOV     CX,0C02H               ;        DISPLAY AMOUNT
             CALL    PUTBCD
```

```
 99:            MOV     DI,SI
100:            MOV     CX,12                ;        BALANCE = BALANCE
101:            CALL    NEGBCD               ;                + (-AMOUNT)
102:            LEA     DI,BALANCE
103:            CALL    ADDBCD
104:            PUSHF                        ;        SAVE FLAGS
105:            LEA     DI,BLANKS            ;        DISPLAY A BLANK
106:            MOV     CX,ONE
107:            CALL    PUTSTRNG
108:            LEA     SI,BALANCE           ;        DISPLAY BALANCE
109:            MOV     CX,0C02H
110:            CALL    PUTBCD
111:            POPF                         ;        RESTORE FLAGS
112:            JGE     ENDIF2               ;        IF   BALANCE < 0
113:            LEA     DI,OVERDRAWN         ;        THEN DISP 'OVERDRAWN'
114:            MOV     CX,MSG_LNG
115:            CALL    PUTSTRNG
116: ENDIF2:                                 ;        ENDIF
117:            LEA     DI,SERVICE           ;        SERVICE = SERVICE
118:            LEA     SI,CHARGE            ;                + CHARGE
119:            MOV     CX,12
120:            CALL    ADDBCD
121: ENDIF1:                                 ;   ENDIF
122:            CALL    NEWLINE              ;   SKIP TO NEXT LINE
123:            POP     SI
124:            ADD     SI,6                 ;   PTR = PTR + 6
125:                                         ;   <PTR ADDRESSES NEXT CODE>
126:            POP     CX                   ;   RESTORE LOOP_CNT
127:            LOOP    RELAY                ;   LOOP_CNT = LOOP_CNT - 1
128:                                         ;UNTIL LOOP_CNT = 0
129: ;
130:            LEA     DI,BALANCE           ;BALANCE = BALANCE + SERVICE
131:            LEA     SI,SERVICE
132:            MOV     CX,12
133:            CALL    ADDBCD
134:            LEA     DI,BLANKS            ;DISPLAY 31 BLANKS
135:            MOV     CX,THIRTY_1
136:            CALL    PUTSTRNG
137:            LEA     SI,BALANCE           ;DISPLAY BALANCE
138:            MOV     CX,0C02H
139:            CALL    PUTBCD
140:            MOV     CX,ONE
141:            CALL    PUTSTRNG             ;DISPLAY 1 BLANK
142:            LEA     SI,SERVICE           ;DISPLAY SERVICE
143:            MOV     CX,0C02H
144:            CALL    PUTBCD
145:            LEA     DI,SERV_CHG          ;DISPLAY 'SERVICE CHARGE'
146:            MOV     CX,MSG_LNG
147:            CALL    PUTSTRNG
148:            CALL    NEWLINE              ;SKIP TO NEXT LINE
149:            .EXIT                        ;RETURN TO DOS
150: ;
151: ;=================================================================
152:*           END
```

The subprocedures referenced by the main procedure are identified by the EXTRN pseudo-operations in lines 10–14. You should be familiar with all of these subprocedures.

The stack segment defined in lines 15–18 has been expanded from the 256-byte stack segment used in most of the example programs of this book. This modification accommodates the stack requirements of the BCD subprocedures.

The variable data for the program are defined in lines 19–38. The variable BALANCE (line 23) is a 6-byte (12-nibble) BCD array whose initial value is the beginning balance for the bank account. The initial value for BALANCE is 32550. The program interprets this value as \$325.50 since it interprets all BCD numbers as having two digits following the assumed decimal point. The variable TRANS-COUNT (line 24) is a byte variable whose initial value (12) is a count of the number of transactions that have occurred on the bank account since the beginning balance was recorded. The variable TRANSACTN, defined in lines 25–36, is a data structure that contains the transactions. Each line defines one transaction. A transaction is a one-character string followed by a 12-nibble BCD array. The initial value of the one-character string is either D (for deposit) or W (for withdrawal). The initial value of the BCD array is the amount of the transaction. The value is interpreted as having two digits that follow the assumed decimal point. For example, the transaction defined in line 28 is a withdrawal of \$75.25. The variable SERVICE (line 37) is a 12-nibble BCD array whose initial value is zero. This value represents the total service charge to be deducted from the balance. The variable CHARGE (line 38) is a 12-nibble BCD array whose initial value is −0.35, which is the amount of the service charge to be applied to each withdrawal from the account. Each time the program processes a withdrawal, it adds the value of CHARGE to SERVICE. At the end of the program, the value of SERVICE is added to BALANCE. Since CHARGE and SERVICE are negative, this addition to BALANCE represents a reduction of the BALANCE.

The constant data for the program are defined in lines 39–51. These items are character strings that are used to annotate the report. The string HEADER (line 42) is the column headers for the report. The report is displayed in three columns: one column for deposits, one column for withdrawals, and one column for the resulting balance. Each transaction fills one line of the report. If the transaction is a deposit, then the amount of the transaction is displayed under the DEPOSIT column, and the resulting balance is displayed under the BALANCE column. If the transaction is a withdrawal, then the amount of the transaction is displayed under the WITH-DRAWAL column, and the resulting balance is displayed under the BALANCE column. To align values in specific columns, the program must output different size strings of blanks. The string BLANKS (line 44) is a string of 31 spaces. The string OVERDRAWN (line 45) is displayed next to any negative BALANCE. The string SERV_CHG (line 46) is displayed to annotate the service charge deduction on the last line of the report.

The code segment defined in lines 52–149 contains the definition of the main procedure for the program. The program begins by setting the DS- and ES-registers to address DGROUP (lines 55–57). The program then displays the header for the report (lines 58–61) and the beginning balance (lines 62–69). The reference to the PUTSTRNG procedure (lines 62–64) displays 31 blanks. This step is taken so that the value of the beginning balance is displayed in the BALANCE column. The PUTBCD procedure is called (line 68) with the DS:SI register pair addressing the BCD array BALANCE (line 66), the CH-register containing the total digit count (12), and the CL-register containing the fraction digit count (2). The two digit counts are set up by the MOV instruction in line 67.

The REPEAT-UNTIL loop implemented in lines 73–128 processes the transactions. Each iteration of the loop processes one transaction and displays one line of the report. The initialization for the loop is performed by the instructions in lines 70–72. The count of the number of transactions is moved to the CX-register (lines 70 and 71), and the DS:SI register pair is set to address the beginning of the data structure that contains the transactions (line 72). At this point, the DS:SI register pair addresses the code for the first transaction. The loop body begins with the PUSH instruction in line 74. The loop count in the CX-register is saved so that the register can be used for input to the PUTSTRNG and PUTBCD procedures referenced in the loop body. The MOV instruction in line 75 moves the code for the transaction to the AL-register. The INC instruction in line 76 increments the SI-register so that the DS:SI register pair addresses the first byte of the transaction amount. The PUSH instruction in line 77 saves the SI-register so that the current position within the transaction data structure is not lost when the SI-register is used for another purpose later in the loop.

The double-alternative decision structure implemented in lines 78–121 determines whether the transaction is a deposit or a withdrawal. The CMP instruction in line 78 tests the transaction code that was loaded into the AL-register by the MOV instruction in line 75, and the JNE instruction in line 79 makes the decision based on this test. If the transaction code is D, then the instructions in lines 80–91 (the "then" clause) are executed; if the transaction code is not D, then it is assumed to be W and the instructions in lines 93–120 (the "else" clause) are executed.

The "then" clause of the double-alternative decision structure processes a deposit transaction. The ADDBCD procedure is invoked (lines 80–82) to add the transaction amount (addressed by the DS:SI register pair) to the balance (addressed by the ES:DI register pair). The PUTBCD procedure is invoked (lines 83 and 84) to display the transaction amount (addressed by the DS:SI register pair) in the DEPOSIT column. The PUTSTRNG procedure is invoked (lines 85–87) to display 17 spaces, which skips the WITHDRAWAL column. The PUTBCD procedure is invoked (lines 88–90) to display the new balance (addressed by the DS:SI register pair) in the BALANCE column. The JMP instruction in line 91 causes the "else" clause to be skipped.

The "else" clause of the double-alternative decision structure processes a withdrawal transaction. The PUTSTRNG procedure is invoked (lines 94–96) to display 16 spaces, which skips the DEPOSIT column. The PUTBCD procedure is invoked (lines 97 and 98) to display the transaction amount (addressed by the DS:SI register pair) in the WITHDRAWAL column. The NEGBCD procedure is invoked (lines 99–101) to negate the transaction amount (addressed by the ES:DI register pair). The ADDBCD procedure is invoked (lines 102 and 103) to add the negated transaction amount (addressed by the DS:SI register pair) to the balance (addressed by the ES:DI register pair). Negating the transaction amount and adding the result to the balance is equivalent to subtracting the transaction amount from the balance. (The implementation of a BCD subtraction procedure and its integration into this program are left as an exercise at the end of the chapter.) The PUSHF instruction in line 104 saves the flags produced by this addition operation. The flags are used to determine whether the account is overdrawn as a result of this withdrawal. The PUTSTRNG procedure is invoked (lines 105–107) to display a space. The PUTBCD procedure is invoked (lines 108–110) to display the new balance (addressed by the DS:SI register pair) in the BALANCE column. The POPF instruction in line 111 restores the flags (saved in line 104) to reflect the new balance. The single-alternative decision structure implemented in lines 112–116 displays the string 'OVERDRAWN' if the new balance is less than zero. Following this decision structure, the ADDBCD procedure is invoked (lines 117–120) to add the value of BCD array CHARGE (−0.35) to array SERVICE (the negative of the total service charge).

Following the double-alternative decision structure, preparations are made for the next iteration of the loop. The call to the NEWLINE procedure in line 122 terminates a line of the report. The POP instruction in line 123 restores the SI-register so that the DS:SI register pair again addresses the transaction amount for the transaction just processed. The ADD instruction in line 124 increments the SI-register so that the DS:SI register pair addresses the code for the next transaction to be processed. The POP instruction in line 126 restores the loop count in the CX-register. The LOOP instruction in line 127 decrements the loop count by 1 and transfers control to the top of the loop (line 73) if the resulting loop count is nonzero. The label LOOP1 in line 73 is outside the short label range (−128 to +127) from the instruction following the LOOP instruction in line 127. Therefore, the branch to the top of the loop requires a relay jump, and the LOOP instruction causes a branch to the line labeled RELAY (line 92). The instruction at that location is an unconditional jump to the top of the loop. Relay jumps are easily embedded in programs by placing them after any unconditional jump that is within range. The instruction immediately following an unconditional jump must be labeled; otherwise, there would be no way of reaching that instruction. The relay jump instruction can then be placed between that unconditional jump instruction (JMP in line 91 in this case) and the label of the next instruction (label ELSE1 in line 93 in this case) with no adverse effect on the program.

On exit from the REPEAT-UNTIL loop, the service charge line of the report is displayed. The ADDBCD procedure is invoked (lines 130–133) to add the value of BCD array SERVICE, the negative of the service charge, to the value of BCD array BALANCE, producing the ending balance for the account. The PUTSTRNG procedure is invoked (lines 134–136) to display 31 spaces, which skips the DEPOSIT and WITHDRAWAL columns. The PUTBCD procedure is invoked (lines 137–139) to display the ending balance in the BALANCE column. The PUTSTRNG procedure is again invoked (lines 140 and 141) to display a space. The PUTBCD procedure is invoked (lines 142–144) to display the value of BCD array SERVICE, the total service charge. The PUTSTRNG procedure is invoked (lines 145–147) to display the string 'SERVICE CHARGE'. The call to NEWLINE in line 148 terminates the last line of the report.

The main procedure of this program consists largely of calling sequences for subprocedures. Most of the operations required for this program already exist in previously developed subprocedures. Assembly language programming becomes much more efficient once a good library of subprocedures has been developed. The following report was generated by this program:

```
C>EX_11_6
       DEPOSIT  WITHDRAWAL  BALANCE
                              325.50
                     50.00    275.50
                    225.25     50.25
        25.00                  75.25
                     75.25      0.00
                      7.50     -7.50  OVERDRAWN
                     20.00    -27.50  OVERDRAWN
       100.00                  72.50
       550.25                 622.75
                     82.50    540.25
       750.00                1290.25
                    273.45   1016.80
                     27.50    989.30
                              986.50          -2.80 SERVICE CHARGE
```

NUMERIC EXERCISES

11.1 Fill in the blanks in the following table:

4-Digit (16-Bit) BCD Bit Pattern	Modulo 10,000 Interpretation	Ten's Complement Interpretation
1000 0101 0111 0010		
0001 0100 0011 0110		
	6347	
		−4095
	7200	

11.2 Perform the following additions involving 4-digit BCD integers in the ten's complement number system:

a.
```
  0001 1001 0010 0000
+ 0010 0011 1000 0101
```

b.
```
  1000 1001 0101 0100
+ 0000 0001 1000 0100
```

11.3 Perform the following subtractions involving 4-digit BCD integers in the ten's complement number system; add the ten's complement of the subtrahend to the minuend:

a.
```
  0001 1001 0010 0000
− 0010 0011 1000 0101
```

b.
```
  1000 1001 0101 0100
− 0000 0001 1000 0100
```

PROGRAMMING EXERCISES

11.1 Design an algorithm to accept as input a nibble array that contains a packed BCD number in sign magnitude form and to produce as output a nibble array that contains the same packed BCD number in ten's complement form. The number of digits in the BCD number is also an input to the algorithm. Implement your algorithm with an 8088/8086 assembly language FAR subprocedure. The name of your subprocedure should be SMAGTENS. Your inputs should be as follows:

> ES:DI register pair addresses the first byte of the packed BCD array.
> CX-register contains a count of the number of digits in the BCD number (must be even).

On return from your subprocedure, the array addressed by the ES:DI register pair should contain the packed BCD number in ten's complement form that is equivalent to the sign magnitude number that the array contained on entry to the subprocedure. Your subprocedure should save and restore all registers used.

11.2 Design an algorithm to accept as input a byte array that contains an ASCII number in sign magnitude form and to produce as output a nibble array that contains the corresponding BCD number in sign magnitude form. The number of digits in the ASCII number is also an input to the algorithm. Implement your algorithm with an 8088/8086 assembly language external FAR subprocedure. The name of your subprocedure should be ASCIIBCD. Your inputs should be as follows:

> DS:SI register pair addresses the first byte of the array that contains the ASCII number.
> ES:DI register pair addresses the first byte of the array that is to contain the corresponding BCD number.
> CX-register contains a count of the number of digits in the ASCII number.

On return from your subprocedure, the array addressed by the ES:DI register pair should contain the packed BCD number in sign magnitude form that is equivalent to the ASCII number in the array addressed by the DS:SI register pair, and the CX-register should contain $n + (n \bmod 2)$, in which n is the input digit count. Your subprocedure should save and restore all registers used, except for the CX-register that is used for subprocedure output.

11.3 Design an algorithm to subtract two packed BCD numbers in ten's complement form. Do *not* use the complement-and-add method that was used in Program Listing 11.6. Instead, use the SBB and DAS instructions in a method analogous to that used in the procedure in Program Listing 11.3. Implement your algorithm with an 8088/8086 assembly language external FAR subprocedure. The name of your subprocedure should be SUBBCD. Your inputs should be as follows:

> DS:SI register pair addresses the first byte of the array that contains the source BCD number.

ES:DI register pair addresses the first byte of the array that contains the destination BCD number.
CX-register contains a count of the number of digits in one of the BCD numbers (must be even).

The size of the two BCD numbers must be the same.

On return from your subprocedure, the array addressed by the ES:DI register pair should contain the packed BCD difference of the two input BCD numbers (i.e., the difference replaces the destination BCD number), and the OF, SF, ZF, and CF bits of the flags register should reflect this difference. Your subprocedure should save and restore all registers used. Only the OF, SF, ZF, and CF bits of the flags register should be modified. Make your subprocedure a PUBLIC procedure and add it to the BCD subprocedure library BCD.LIB.

11.4 Modify Program Listing 11.6 to use your subprocedure SUBBCD (i.e., your solution to Programming Exercise 11.3) instead of using the negate-and-add method to process a withdrawal. Also, maintain the service charge as a positive number rather than as a negative number and use SUBBCD to deduct the service charge from the balance.

11.5 Design an algorithm to compare two packed BCD numbers in ten's complement form. Recall that a compare is like a subtraction in which the result is not saved. Implement your algorithm with an 8088/8086 assembly language external FAR subprocedure. The name of your subprocedure should be CMPBCD. Your inputs should be as follows:

DS:SI register pair addresses the first byte of the array that contains the source BCD number.
ES:DI register pair addresses the first byte of the array that contains the destination BCD number.
CX-register contains the count of the number of digits in one of the BCD numbers (must be even).

The size of the two BCD numbers must be the same.

On return from your subprocedure, the OF, SF, ZF, and CF bits of the flags register should reflect the result of the subtraction (i.e., destination BCD number minus source BCD number). However, neither of the BCD numbers should be modified. Your procedure should save and restore all registers used. Only the OF, SF, ZF, and CF bits of the flags register should be modified. Make your subprocedure a PUBLIC procedure and add it to the BCD subprocedure library BCD.LIB.

11.6 Design an algorithm to multiply a packed BCD number in ten's complement form by 10. (*Hint*: This exercise can be accomplished by shifting the number left one digit position.) Implement your algorithm with an 8088/8086 assembly language external FAR subprocedure. The name of your subprocedure should be MULBCD10. Your inputs should be as follows:

ES:DI register pair addresses the first byte of the array that contains the BCD number.
CX-register contains a count of the number of digits in the BCD number (must be even).

On return from your subprocedure, the array addressed by the ES:DI register pair should contain the product of the input BCD number and 10 (i.e., the product replaces the input BCD number), and the OF and CF bits of the flags register should reflect whether or not an overflow occurred. Your subprocedure should save and restore all registers used. Only the OF and CF bits of the flags register should be modified. Make your subprocedure a PUBLIC procedure and add it to the BCD subprocedure library BCD.LIB.

11.7 Design an algorithm to divide a packed BCD number in ten's complement form by 10. (*Hint*: This exercise can be accomplished by shifting the number right one digit position. The digit shifted out is the remainder of the division.) Implement your algorithm with an 8088/8086 assembly language external FAR subprocedure. The name of your subprocedure should be DIVBCD10. Your inputs should be as follows:

ES:DI register pair addresses the first byte of the array that contains the BCD number.
CX-register contains a count of the number of digits in the BCD number (must be even).

On return from your subprocedure, the array addressed by the ES:DI register pair should contain the quotient of the input BCD number and 10 (i.e., the quotient replaces the input BCD number), and the AL-register should contain the one-digit remainder. Your subprocedure should save and restore all registers used, except for the AL-register that is used for subprocedure output. Make your subprocedure a PUBLIC procedure and add it to the BCD subprocedure library BCD.LIB.

11.8 Using the MULBCD10 and DIVBCD10 procedures from Programming Exercises 11.6 and 11.7 and a modified version of the Russian Peasant's Method, a procedure can be developed to multiply two packed BCD numbers in ten's complement form. The algorithm is as follows:

```
PROCEDURE MULBCD (MPCAND,MPLIER)
          IF   MPLIER < 0
          THEN
               MPLIER = -MPLIER
               MPCAND = -MPCAND
          ENDIF
          PRODUCT = 0
          WHILE MPLIER > 0
               COUNT = MPLIER mod 10
               WHILE COUNT > 0
                    PRODUCT = PRODUCT + MPCAND
                    COUNT = COUNT - 1
               ENDWHILE
               MPCAND = MPCAND * 10
               MPLIER = MPLIER / 10
          ENDWHILE
          MPCAND = PRODUCT
END MULBCD
```

Implement this algorithm with an 8088/8086 assembly language external FAR subprocedure. The name of your subprocedure should be MULBCD. Your inputs should be as follows:

> ES:DI register pair addresses the first byte of the BCD array that contains the multiplicand.
> DS:SI register pair addresses the first byte of the BCD array that contains the multiplier.
> CH-register contains a count of the number of digits in the multiplicand (must be even).
> CL-register contains a count of the number of digits in the multiplier (must be even).

On return from your subprocedure, the array addressed by the ES:DI register pair should contain the product of the two BCD numbers (i.e., the product replaces the multiplicand), and the OF and CF bits of the flags register should reflect whether or not overflow occurred. Your subprocedure should save and restore all registers used. Only the OF and CF bits of the flags register should be modified. Make your subprocedure a PUBLIC subprocedure and add it to the BCD subprocedure library BCD.LIB.

Note that, when BCD numbers are interpreted for output, the number of digits that follow the assumed decimal point in the product is the sum of the number of digits that follow the assumed decimal point in the multiplicand and the number of digits that follow the assumed decimal point in the multiplier. Note also that the number of digits that follow the assumed decimal point in the multiplier does not have to equal the number of digits that follow the assumed decimal point in the multiplicand.

11.9 Rewrite Program Listing 8.7 (the program to compute arbitrarily large factorial values) to use packed BCD numbers for the factorial values. The MULBCD subprocedure from Programming Exercise 11.8 is needed in the solution.

CHAPTER 12

Segment Linking

Chapter 1 discussed the two general forms of an 8088/8086 assembly module and identified their three kinds of segment definitions. The first program form presented in Chapter 1 used full segment definitions (see Program Listing 1.1), and the second form used simplified segment directives (see Program Listing 1.2). With simplified segment directives, the assembler (MASM) and the Linkage Editor (LINK) have most of the control over the alignment and the interrelationships of segments in the executable program. With full segment definitions, the way in which segments are organized in the executable program module depends on information provided by the segment pseudo-operations in the assembly modules that make up the corresponding assembly language program.

In the example programs in previous chapters, segments were defined with simplified segment directives, which cause the LINK program to use default rules in organizing the machine language segments into an executable program. In the example programs of this chapter, segments are defined with full segment definitions; that is, the segment definition begins with the SEGMENT pseudo-operation and ends with the ENDS pseudo-operation. The SEGMENT pseudo-operation can have up to five operands that provide information to the LINK program. This information guides LINK in organizing the machine language segments into an executable program. This chapter discusses the SEGMENT pseudo-operation and its operands in detail, demonstrating the advantages of some of the program segmentation features provided by the assembler and LINK. This chapter also discusses the interface between assembly language procedures and those written in a high-level language.

12.1 SEGMENT Pseudo-Operation

The SEGMENT pseudo-operation marks the physical beginning of a segment definition, indicates how that segment is to be aligned in memory, and specifies the relationship of the segment to other segments of the executable program. The **SEGMENT pseudo-operation** has the following general form:

⟨*seg-name*⟩ `SEGMENT [`⟨*align*⟩`] [READONLY] [`⟨*combine*⟩`][`⟨*use*⟩`][`⟨*class*⟩`]`

in which ⟨*seg-name*⟩ is the symbolic name associated with the memory location at which the segment is to begin, ⟨*align*⟩ identifies the type of boundary for the beginning of the segment, READONLY tells the assembler to generate an error for any instruction whose execution would modify an item in the segment, ⟨*combine*⟩ indicates the way in which this segment is to be combined with other segments by the Linkage Editor (LINK), ⟨*use*⟩ indicates whether the segment is to be executed in real mode or in protected mode for 80386/80486 assembly language programs, and ⟨*class*⟩ is a symbolic name used to group segments at link time. All of the operands for the SEGMENT pseudo-operation are optional.

The ⟨*align*⟩ operand specifies how the segment is to be aligned in memory. The align type, if specified, must be one of the following: PAGE, PARA, DWORD, WORD, or BYTE.

PAGE An align type of PAGE specifies that the segment must begin on a page boundary, which is an address divisible by 256. That is, the start address for the segment must be an address of the hexadecimal form XXX00, in which X represents any hexadecimal digit. For example, the addresses 00000, 00100, and F3C00 all mark the beginning of a new page in memory.

PARA An align type of PARA specifies that the segment must begin on a paragraph boundary, which is an address divisible by 16. That is, the start address for the segment must be an address of the hexadecimal form XXXX0, in which X represents any hexadecimal digit. For example, the addresses 00000, 00010, F3C00, and FF3E0 all mark the beginning of a new paragraph in memory. Note that any page boundary is also a paragraph boundary; however, a paragraph boundary is not necessarily a page boundary.

DWORD An align type of DWORD specifies that the segment must begin on a double-word boundary, which is an address divisible by 4. For example, 00000, 00004, 00008, 0000C, and 00010 are double-word boundary addresses.

WORD An align type of WORD specifies that the segment must begin on a word boundary, which is an even address. For example, 00000, 00002, and 00004 are word boundary addresses.

BYTE An align type of BYTE specifies that the segment is to begin at the next available byte in memory. That is, the start address for the segment can be any address in memory.

The default value for the align type is PARA. That is, unless otherwise specified, all segments begin on a paragraph boundary. Recall that all segments must begin on a paragraph boundary so that the start address of the segment can be stored in a 16-bit segment register. The only reason for using DWORD, WORD, or BYTE as the align type is to allow a segment to be combined with another segment without memory space being skipped.

The ⟨*combine*⟩ operand specifies the relationship between the segment being defined and other segments of the executable program. The combine type, if specified, must be one of the following: PRIVATE, PUBLIC, STACK, COMMON, MEMORY, or AT ⟨*expr*⟩.

PRIVATE A combine type of PRIVATE specifies that the segment is to be logically separate from other segments.

PUBLIC A combine type of PUBLIC specifies that the segment is to be concatenated with other segments having the same ⟨*seg-name*⟩ and ⟨*class*⟩, producing a single physical segment.

STACK A combine type of STACK specifies that the segment is to be concatenated with other segments having the same ⟨*seg-name*⟩ and ⟨*class*⟩, producing a single physical segment. This single segment is to be the run-time stack segment for the program. When program execution begins, the SS-register specifies the origin of this segment, and the SP-register contains the offset from this origin to the location immediately following the segment. This setup denotes that the run-time stack segment is empty.

After combining segments, if more than one segment is of combine type STACK, then the last segment encountered by the LINK program is the run-time stack segment for the program. This situation occurs when the segments with a combine type of STACK do not all have the same ⟨*seg-name*⟩ and ⟨*class*⟩.

COMMON A combine type of COMMON specifies that the segment is to be overlaid with other segments having the same ⟨*seg-name*⟩ and ⟨*class*⟩, producing a single segment whose length is the length of the largest such common segment. Common segments allow procedures in separate assembly modules to reference the same physical data segment using a private set of symbolic names.

MEMORY A combine type of MEMORY specifies that the segment is to be located at a higher memory address than any other segment of the executable program. If more than one segment being linked has a combine type of MEMORY, then only the first such segment encountered is to be treated in this way. Any subsequent segment with a combine type of MEMORY is to be treated as a COMMON segment. The Microsoft Linkage Editor (MS-LINK Version 5.13) does not support the MEMORY combine type; it treats the combine type MEMORY as if it were combine type PUBLIC.

AT ⟨*expr*⟩ A combine type of AT ⟨*expr*⟩ specifies that the segment is to begin at the paragraph identified by the 16-bit value of the address expression, ⟨*expr*⟩. The AT combine type cannot be used to load values into fixed locations in memory. It is used to assign symbolic names to fixed offsets within fixed areas of memory (e.g., the video display buffer).

The default value for the combine type is PRIVATE. That is, if the combine type is omitted, then the segment is to be logically separate from other segments, regardless of its placement relative to other segments. The combine type should not be mixed for segments with the same ⟨*seg-name*⟩ and ⟨*class*⟩.

The ⟨*use*⟩ operand specifies the type of segment to be generated for 80386/80486 assembly language programs. The ⟨*use*⟩ operand, if specified, must be one of the following: USE16, USE32, or FLAT.

USE16 The operand USE16 specifies that the segment is to be generated for real-mode execution. Thus, data and instructions in the segment are addressed with 16-bit offsets, and the default operand size for the segment is 16 bits.

USE32 The operand USE32 specifies that the segment is to be generated for protected-mode execution. Thus, data and instructions in the segment are addressed with 32-bit offsets, and the default operand size for the segment is 32 bits.

FLAT The operand FLAT specifies a nonsegmented configuration, which is used primarily in the development of operating systems.

The ⟨*class*⟩ operand is a symbolic name that is used to group segments at link time. (The class name must be enclosed in apostrophes.) All segments with the same class name are contiguous in memory.

12.2 Combining Segments

Combining several logical segments into one physical segment is done primarily to conserve memory space. Since each physical segment must begin on a paragraph boundary, segments consume memory in 16-byte (1-paragraph) units. For example, if a data segment definition specifies 18 bytes of storage, the corresponding physical segment consumes 32 bytes (2 paragraphs) because the next contiguous segment cannot begin until the next paragraph boundary. The last paragraph of any physical segment is likely to include some unused storage cells. On the average, you can expect 8 unused storage cells in the last paragraph of a physical segment. By combining n logical segments into one physical segment, the number of "last paragraphs" is reduced from n to 1, which reduces the expected number of unused storage cells from $8n$ to 8. In small programs, like the example programs in this book, the savings is insignificant. However, in large programs, like a high-level language compiler, the savings can be quite significant.

Several segments can be combined into one physical segment by using the PUBLIC combine type. The segments being combined must all have the same segment name and class name. The first such segment encountered by the LINK program must have the PARA (default) align type so that the physical segment begins on a paragraph boundary. All subsequent segments to be included in the same physical segment should have the BYTE align type to avoid embedded blocks of unused storage cells.

Programming Example—Simulate Flipping a Coin

Program Listings 12.1 and 12.2 show two parts of a single program that simulates the flipping of a coin. The program prompts the user for an integer that specifies the number of times to flip the coin, simulates flipping the coin the specified number of times, and displays a count of the number of heads and tails in the simulation. The assembly module in Program Listing 12.2 contains the definition of one subprocedure and the definition of a local data segment for that subprocedure. The subprocedure is the random number generator used in the simulation, which is the same random number generator presented in Program Listing 5.4. The assembly module in Program Listing 12.1 contains the definition of the main procedure and the definition of its data segment. The assembly module of Program Listing 12.1 references the external subprocedure PUTTEXT (lines 9, 35, 55, and 59), which is the subprocedure described in Programming Exercises 8.13 and 9.8. Its object code is not contained in IO.LIB. (The implementation of PUTTEXT is left to you as an exercise.)

The main procedure uses the random number generator to obtain an integer in the range 0–1. One such integer simulates a single flip of the coin: The value 0 represents tails; the value 1 represents heads. The detail of the main procedure is not discussed here because you should have no difficulty in following the logic of this program at this point in the text.

Program Listings 12.1 and 12.2 have two data segments. The data segment defined in Program Listing 12.1 (lines 18–26) requires 65 bytes of storage. The physical data segment corresponding to this definition consumes 5 paragraphs (80 bytes).

```
 1:             PAGE    80,132
 2: ;===================================================================
 3: ;                   PROGRAM LISTING 12.1
 4: ;           PROGRAM TO SIMULATE THE FLIPPING OF A COIN
 5: ;===================================================================
 6:                                             ;PROCEDURES TO
 7:             EXTRN   GETDEC$:FAR             ;GET UNSIGNED DECIMAL INTEGER
 8:             EXTRN   PUTDEC$:FAR             ;DISPL. UNSIGNED DEC. INTEGER
 9:             EXTRN   PUTTEXT:FAR             ;DISPLAY A TEXT STRING
10:             EXTRN   RANDOM:FAR              ;GENERATE PSEUDO-RANDOM NUMBER
11: ;===================================================================
12: ; S T A C K   S E G M E N T   D E F I N I T I O N
13: STACK       SEGMENT STACK
14:             DB      256 DUP(?)
15: STACK       ENDS
16: ;===================================================================
17: ; D A T A   S E G M E N T   D E F I N I T I O N
18: DATA        SEGMENT
19: HEADS       DW      0                       ;COUNT OF NUMBER OF HEADS
20: TAILS       DW      0                       ;COUNT OF NUMBER OF TAILS
21: PROMPT      DB      'ENTER NUMBER OF TIMES TO FLIP THE COIN  ',0
22: HEADSMSG    DB      ' HEADS  ',0
23: TAILSMSG    DB      ' TAILS',0
24: ZERO        DW      0
25: ONE         DW      1
26: DATA        ENDS
27: ;===================================================================
28: ; C O D E   S E G M E N T   D E F I N I T I O N
29: CODE        SEGMENT
30:             ASSUME  CS:CODE,SS:STACK,DS:DATA,ES:DATA
31: COINFLIP:   MOV     AX,SEG DATA             ;SET DS AND ES REGISTERS
32:             MOV     DS,AX                   ;TO ADDRESS DATA SEGMENT
33:             MOV     ES,AX
34:             LEA     DI,PROMPT               ;PROMPT FOR NUMBER_OF_FLIPS
35:             CALL    PUTTEXT
36:             CALL    GETDEC$                 ;GET NUMBER_OF_FLIPS
37:             MOV     CX,AX                   ;LOOP_CNT = NUMBER_OF_FLIPS
38:             .REPEAT                         ;REPEAT
39:             PUSH    ZERO                    ;   NUMBER = RANDOM(0,1)
40:             PUSH    ONE
41:             CALL    RANDOM
42:             .IF     AX > 0                  ;   IF   NUMBER > 0
43:                                             ;   THEN
44:             INC     HEADS                   ;        HEADS = HEADS + 1
45: ;
46:             .ELSE                           ;   ELSE
47:             INC     TAILS                   ;        TAILS = TAILS + 1
48:             .ENDIF                          ;   ENDIF
49:             .UNTILCXZ                       ;   LOOP_CNT = LOOP_CNT - 1
50:                                             ;UNTIL LOOP_CNT = 0
```

```
            MOV     BH,1
            MOV     AX,HEADS              ;DISPLAY HEADS
            CALL    PUTDEC$
            LEA     DI,HEADSMSG
            CALL    PUTTEXT
            MOV     AX,TAILS              ;DISPLAY TAILS
            CALL    PUTDEC$
            LEA     DI,TAILSMSG
            CALL    PUTTEXT
            MOV     AH,4CH                ;RETURN TO DOS
            INT     21H
CODE        ENDS
            END     COINFLIP
;====================================================================
```

```
            PAGE    80,132
;====================================================================
;                     PROGRAM LISTING 12.2
;        r a n d o m   n u m b e r   g e n e r a t o r
;
; GENERATES PSEUDO-RANDOM INTEGERS IN THE RANGE LOWER TO UPPER
; INPUT:  TWO STACK PARAMETERS - LOWER AND UPPER ENDS OF RANGE
; OUTPUT: AX-REG CONTAINS RANDOM INTEGER
; CALLING SEQUENCE:     PUSH    <LOWER END OF RANGE>
;                       PUSH    <UPPER END OF RANGE>
;                       CALL    RANDOM
;====================================================================
FALSE       EQU     0                     ;CONSTANT FALSE
TRUE        EQU     1                     ;CONSTANT TRUE
;====================================================================
; D A T A   S E G M E N T   D E F I N I T I O N
RAND_DATA   SEGMENT
SEED        DW      ?                     ;SEED FOR RANDOM NUMBER GEN.
MULTIPLIER  DW      25173                 ;MULTIPLIER AND
ADDEND      DW      13849                 ;ADDEND FOR MIXED
                                          ;LINEAR CONGRUENTIAL METHOD
FIRST_CALL  DB      TRUE                  ;FIRST CALL FLAG
RAND_DATA   ENDS
;====================================================================
; C O D E   S E G M E N T   D E F I N I T I O N
;
CODE        SEGMENT
            ASSUME  DS:RAND_DATA
RANDOM      PROC    FAR BASIC PUBLIC USES CX DX DS, LOWER:WORD,
                    UPPER:WORD       ;FUNCTION RANDOM(LOWER,UPPER)
                                          ;push    bp      INSTRUCTIONS
                                          ;mov     bp, sp  GENERATED IN
                                          ;push    cx      RESPONSE TO
                                          ;push    dx      PROC
                                          ;push    ds      PSEUDO OP
            PUSHF                         ;SAVE FLAGS
            MOV     AX,SEG RAND_DATA      ;SET DS-REGISTER TO POINT
            MOV     DS,AX                 ;TO LOCAL DATA SEGMENT
            .IF     FIRST_CALL == TRUE    ;IF   FIRST_CALL
                                          ;THEN
            MOV     FIRST_CALL,FALSE      ;     FIRST_CALL = FALSE
            MOV     AH,0                  ;     SEED = LOWER HALF OF
            INT     1AH                   ;            TIME OF DAY CLOCK
            MOV     SEED,DX
            .ENDIF                        ;ENDIF
            MOV     AX,SEED               ;X = SEED * MULTIPLIER mod
            MUL     MULTIPLIER            ;                        65536
            ADD     AX,ADDEND             ;SEED = (X + ADDEND) mod 65536
            MOV     SEED,AX
            MOV     CX,UPPER              ;RANGE = UPPER - LOWER + 1
            SUB     CX,LOWER
```

```
52:             INC     CX
53:             MUL     CX                      ;RANDOM = SEED/65536 * RANGE
54:             ADD     DX,LOWER                ;                    + LOWER
55:             MOV     AX,DX
56:             POPF                            ;RESTORE FLAGS
57:                                             ;RESTORE REGISTERS SPECIFIED
58:                                             ;        IN USES CLAUSE,
59:                                             ;   RESTORE BP-REGISTER, AND
60:                                             ;   POP ARGUMENTS WITH RETURN
61:             RET                             ;RETURN (RANDOM)
62: RANDOM      ENDP                        ;END RANDOM
63: CODE        ENDS
64:             END
```

The last 15 bytes in this 5-paragraph memory segment are unused. The data segment defined in Program Listing 12.2 (lines 17–23) requires 7 bytes of storage. The physical data segment corresponding to this definition consumes 1 paragraph (16 bytes). The last 9 bytes in this 1-paragraph memory segment are unused. A total of 24 bytes of unused space is encompassed in these two memory segments, as Load Map Listing 12.3 illustrates (the load map was generated when the object modules for this program were linked):

1. The segment named DATA (defined in Program Listing 12.1) begins at zero-relative location 00100 hex and is 41 hex (65 decimal) bytes in length (line 6 in Load Map Listing 12.3). However, the next contiguous segment (the code segment for the main procedure) begins at zero-relative location 00150 hex, so the data segment actually consumes 50 hex (80 decimal) bytes of storage space.
2. The segment named RAND_DATA (defined in Program Listing 12.2) begins at location 001B0 hex and is 7 bytes in length (line 8 in Load Map Listing 12.3). However, the next contiguous segment (the code segment for the random number generator) begins at location 001C0, so the data segment actually consumes 10 hex (16 decimal) bytes of storage space.

```
 1:                 LOAD MAP LISTING 12.3
 2:
 3:
 4:  Start   Stop    Length Name                   Class
 5:  00000H 000FFH 00100H STACK
 6:  00100H 00140H 00041H DATA
 7:  00150H 001A9H 0005AH CODE
 8:  001B0H 001B6H 00007H RAND_DATA
 9:  001C0H 00203H 00044H CODE
10:  00210H 00266H 00057H IO_DATA
11:  00270H 0028AH 0001BH CODE                   IO_CODE
12:  00290H 002ADH 0001EH CODE                   IO_CODE
13:  002B0H 00304H 00055H CODE                   IO_CODE
14:  00310H 0032FH 00020H CODE                   IO_CODE
15:  00330H 00387H 00058H CODE                   IO_CODE
16:  00390H 00430H 000A1H CODE                   IO_CODE
17:  00440H 0045DH 0001EH CODE                   IO_CODE
18:
19:*Program entry point at 0015:0000
```

*

The following are the results from some sample executions of the coin-flip simulation program:

```
C>ex_12_1
ENTER NUMBER OF TIMES TO FLIP THE COIN: 10000
  4935 HEADS    5065 TAILS
```

```
C>ex_12_1
ENTER NUMBER OF TIMES TO FLIP THE COIN: 10000
  5066 HEADS    4934 TAILS

C>ex_12_1
ENTER NUMBER OF TIMES TO FLIP THE COIN: 10000
  5017 HEADS    4983 TAILS

C>ex_12_1
ENTER NUMBER OF TIMES TO FLIP THE COIN: 10000
  5002 HEADS    4998 TAILS
```

Consider the modified version of this program defined in Program Listings 12.4 and 12.5. The assembly module in Program Listing 12.4 differs from the assembly module in Program Listing 12.1 in only one place. The DATA segment is defined with combine type PUBLIC (line 18 in Program Listing 12.4). The assembly module in Program Listing 12.5 differs from the assembly module in Program Listing 12.2 in several places. The name of the local data segment for the random number generator has been changed from RAND_DATA to DATA (line 17 in Program Listing 12.5). The names of the two data segments being combined must be the same. The local data segment for the random number generator is defined with combine type PUBLIC and align type BYTE (line 17 in Program Listing 12.5). This definition causes the LINK program to concatenate this segment with other PUBLIC segments that have the name DATA and have no class name. Since this piece of the segment has align type BYTE, it is concatenated with any existing portion of the segment, leaving no unused storage locations in between.

```
 1:             PAGE    80,132
 2: ;===================================================================
 3: ;                   PROGRAM LISTING 12.4
 4: ;       PROGRAM TO SIMULATE THE FLIPPING OF A COIN
 5: ;===================================================================
 6:                                             ;PROCEDURES TO
 7:             EXTRN   GETDEC$:FAR             ;GET UNSIGNED DECIMAL INTEGER
 8:             EXTRN   PUTDEC$:FAR             ;DISPL. UNSIGNED DEC. INTEGER
 9:             EXTRN   PUTTEXT:FAR             ;DISPLAY A TEXT STRING
10:             EXTRN   RANDOM:FAR              ;GENERATE PSEUDO-RANDOM NUMBER
11: ;===================================================================
12: ; S T A C K   S E G M E N T   D E F I N I T I O N
13: STACK       SEGMENT STACK
14:             DB      256 DUP(?)
15: STACK       ENDS
16: ;===================================================================
17: ; D A T A   S E G M E N T   D E F I N I T I O N
18: DATA        SEGMENT PUBLIC
19: HEADS       DW      0                       ;COUNT OF NUMBER OF HEADS
20: TAILS       DW      0                       ;COUNT OF NUMBER OF TAILS
21: PROMPT      DB      'ENTER NUMBER OF TIMES TO FLIP THE COIN  ',0
22: HEADSMSG    DB      ' HEADS   ',0
23: TAILSMSG    DB      ' TAILS',0
24: ZERO        DW      0
25: ONE         DW      1
26: DATA        ENDS
27: ;===================================================================
28: ; C O D E   S E G M E N T   D E F I N I T I O N
29: CODE        SEGMENT
30:             ASSUME  CS:CODE,SS:STACK,DS:DATA,ES:DATA
31: COINFLIP:   MOV     AX,SEG DATA             ;SET DS AND ES REGISTERS
32:             MOV     DS,AX                   ;TO ADDRESS DATA SEGMENT
33:             MOV     ES,AX
34:             LEA     DI,PROMPT               ;PROMPT FOR NUMBER_OF_FLIPS
```

```
            CALL    PUTTEXT
            CALL    GETDEC$                 ;GET NUMBER_OF_FLIPS
            MOV     CX,AX                   ;LOOP_CNT = NUMBER_OF_FLIPS
            .REPEAT                         ;REPEAT
            PUSH    ZERO                    ;   NUMBER = RANDOM(0,1)
            PUSH    ONE
            CALL    RANDOM
            .IF     AX > 0                  ;   IF   NUMBER > 0
                                            ;   THEN
            INC     HEADS                   ;        HEADS = HEADS + 1
;
            .ELSE                           ;   ELSE
            INC     TAILS                   ;        TAILS = TAILS + 1
            .ENDIF                          ;   ENDIF
            .UNTILCXZ                       ;   LOOP_CNT = LOOP_CNT - 1
                                            ;UNTIL LOOP_CNT = 0
            MOV     BH,1
            MOV     AX,HEADS                ;DISPLAY HEADS
            CALL    PUTDEC$
            LEA     DI,HEADSMSG
            CALL    PUTTEXT
            MOV     AX,TAILS                ;DISPLAY TAILS
            CALL    PUTDEC$
            LEA     DI,TAILSMSG
            CALL    PUTTEXT
            MOV     AH,4CH                  ;RETURN TO DOS
            INT     21H
CODE        ENDS
            END     COINFLIP
;====================================================================
```

```
            PAGE    80,132
;====================================================================
;                    PROGRAM LISTING 12.5
;       r a n d o m   n u m b e r   g e n e r a t o r
;
; GENERATES PSEUDO-RANDOM INTEGERS IN THE RANGE LOWER TO UPPER
; INPUT:  TWO STACK PARAMETERS - LOWER AND UPPER ENDS OF RANGE
; OUTPUT: AX-REG CONTAINS RANDOM INTEGER
; CALLING SEQUENCE:     PUSH    <LOWER END OF RANGE>
;                       PUSH    <UPPER END OF RANGE>
;                       CALL    RANDOM
;====================================================================
FALSE       EQU     0                       ;CONSTANT FALSE
TRUE        EQU     1                       ;CONSTANT TRUE
;====================================================================
; D A T A   S E G M E N T   D E F I N I T I O N
DATA        SEGMENT PUBLIC BYTE
SEED        DW      ?                       ;SEED FOR RANDOM NUMBER GEN.
MULTIPLIER  DW      25173                   ;MULTIPLIER AND
ADDEND      DW      13849                   ;ADDEND FOR MIXED
                                            ;LINEAR CONGRUENTIAL METHOD
FIRST_CALL  DB      TRUE                    ;FIRST CALL FLAG
DATA        ENDS
;====================================================================
; C O D E   S E G M E N T   D E F I N I T I O N
;
CODE        SEGMENT
            ASSUME  DS:DATA
RANDOM      PROC    FAR BASIC PUBLIC USES CX DX, LOWER:WORD,
                    UPPER:WORD        ;FUNCTION RANDOM(LOWER,UPPER)
                                            ;push    bp       INSTRUCTIONS
                                            ;mov     bp, sp   GENERATED IN
                                            ;push    cx       RESPONSE TO
```

```
34:                                              ;push    dx        PROC
35:            PUSHF                             ;SAVE FLAGS
36:            .IF     FIRST_CALL == TRUE        ;IF    FIRST_CALL
37:                                              ;THEN
38:            MOV     FIRST_CALL,FALSE          ;      FIRST_CALL = FALSE
39:            MOV     AH,0                      ;      SEED = LOWER HALF OF
40:            INT     1AH                       ;             TIME OF DAY CLOCK
41:            MOV     SEED,DX
42:            .ENDIF                            ;ENDIF
43:            MOV     AX,SEED                   ;X = SEED * MULTIPLIER mod
44:            MUL     MULTIPLIER                ;                       65536
45:            ADD     AX,ADDEND                 ;SEED = (X + ADDEND) mod 65536
46:            MOV     SEED,AX
47:            MOV     CX,UPPER                  ;RANGE = UPPER - LOWER + 1
48:            SUB     CX,LOWER
49:            INC     CX
50:            MUL     CX                        ;RANDOM = SEED/65536 * RANGE
51:            ADD     DX,LOWER                  ;                    + LOWER
52:            MOV     AX,DX
53:            POPF                              ;RESTORE FLAGS
54:                                              ;RESTORE REGISTERS SPECIFIED
55:                                              ;         IN USES CLAUSE,
56:                                              ;    RESTORE BP-REGISTER, AND
57:                                              ;    POP ARGUMENTS WITH RETURN
58:            RET                               ;RETURN (RANDOM)
59: RANDOM     ENDP                            ;END RANDOM
60: CODE       ENDS
61:            END
```

The assembly modules in Program Listings 12.2 and 12.5 also differ in the code segment. Since the local data segment for the random number generator in Program Listing 12.2 is physically separate from the caller's data segment, the random number generator must save the DS-register for the caller (line 29), set the DS-register to address its local data segment (lines 37 and 38), and restore the DS-register before returning to the caller. These items have been removed from the random number generator in Program Listing 12.5. Since the local data for the random number generator is part of the caller's data segment, the DS-register has already been initialized by the caller (lines 31 and 32 in Program Listing 12.4) to address this shared data segment. Note the ASSUME pseudo-operation in line 28 in Program Listing 12.5. The assembler must know that the DS-register will address the DATA segment during execution of the RANDOM procedure, regardless of where the DS-register is actually initialized.

The load map for the second version of this program appears in Load Map Listing 12.6 and was produced in response to the following LINK command:

```
C>LINK A:EX_12_4 A:EX_12_5 PUTTEXT,A:,A:,IO;
```

The load map was placed on the diskette in drive A under the name EX_12_4.MAP. Note that the first two object modules must be presented to the LINK program in the order shown. The first part of the combined segment must be defined with align type PARA (the default) so that the physical segment begins on a paragraph boundary. All subsequent parts can be defined with align type BYTE.

The segment named DATA, the shared data segment, begins at zero-relative location 00100 hex and is 48 hex (72 decimal) bytes in length (line 6 in Load Map Listing 12.6). Note that the length is the sum of the lengths of the two segments that were combined. The next contiguous segment (the code segment for the main procedure) begins at zero-relative location 00150 hex, so the data segment actually consumes 50 hex (80 decimal) bytes of storage space, which is the same amount of storage space consumed for segment DATA in Program Listing 12.1 (line 6 in Load

```
 1:                   LOAD MAP LISTING 12.6
 2:
 3:
 4:  Start   Stop    Length Name                    Class
 5:  00000H 000FFH 00100H STACK
 6:  00100H 00147H 00048H DATA
 7:  00150H 001A9H 0005AH CODE
 8:  001B0H 001ECH 0003DH CODE
 9:  001F0H 00246H 00057H IO_DATA
10:  00250H 0026AH 0001BH CODE                      IO_CODE
11:  00270H 0028DH 0001EH CODE                      IO_CODE
12:  00290H 002E4H 00055H CODE                      IO_CODE
13:  002F0H 0030FH 00020H CODE                      IO_CODE
14:  00310H 00367H 00058H CODE                      IO_CODE
15:  00370H 00410H 000A1H CODE                      IO_CODE
16:  00420H 0043DH 0001EH CODE                      IO_CODE
17:
18:*Program entry point at 0015:0000
```

Map Listing 12.3). The storage space consumed by the data segment for the main procedure did not increase when the data required by the subprocedure was included. The paragraph consumed by the local data segment for the random number generator in the first version has been eliminated in the second version. Note that the second code segment (the code segment for the random number generator) begins a paragraph lower in Load Map Listing 12.6 than in Load Map Listing 12.3. The combining of data segments saved 1 paragraph (16 bytes) of storage.

Another observation can be made by comparing Load Map Listings 12.3 and 12.6. The length of the second code segment (the code segment for the random number generator) was reduced from 44 hex (68 decimal) bytes to 3D hex (61 decimal) bytes (line 9 in Load Map Listing 12.3 and line 8 in Load Map Listing 12.6). This reduction is due to the segment register initialization instructions that were removed from the random number generator when the two data segments were combined. This code segment now consumes 4 paragraphs of storage space, as opposed to the 5 paragraphs it consumed in the previous version of the program. Note that all subsequent segments begin 2 paragraphs lower in Load Map Listing 12.6 than in Load Map Listing 12.3. The combining of data segments saved 2 paragraphs (32 bytes) of storage (1 data paragraph and 1 code paragraph).

By combining segments, a program's storage requirements can be reduced. In the coin-flip illustration, combining the data segment for the random number generator with the data segment for the caller reduced the storage requirements of the program by 2 paragraphs (32 bytes). The user of the random number generator must be familiar with the name of the random number generator's data segment and must use the same name for its data segment. The caller's data segment must also be defined with combine type PUBLIC. If the caller uses a different name for its data segment or defines its data segment as nonPUBLIC, then the data segment for the random number generator is physically separate and independent from the caller's data segment. In this case, the random number generator would execute with the DS-register addressing the caller's data segment rather than its local data segment, and the results would not be the desired results. Also, the data segment for the random number generator might not begin on a paragraph boundary as required for a physically separate segment. The reduction in storage requirements, achieved by combining segments, comes at the expense of a loss in flexibility for the random number generator.

Code segments can also be combined into a single physical segment, which is illustrated in Program Listings 12.9 and 12.10 later in this chapter.

12.3 Stack Segments

An 8088/8086 machine language program has exactly one run-time stack segment whose top-of-stack element is addressed by the SS:SP register pair. The various assembly modules from which the machine language program was generated can each contribute to the size of the run-time stack segment. All segments that have the combine type STACK and have the same segment name and class name are combined into a single physical segment by the LINK program. The length of this segment is the sum of the lengths of the segments being combined. At execution time, the SS-register is automatically initialized to specify the origin of this combined stack segment, and the SP-register is initialized to contain the offset, relative to the SS-register value, of the location immediately following the segment.

If the LINK program encounters segments with combine type STACK that have different segment and/or class names, then the run-time stack segment (i.e., the one addressed by the SS:SP register pair) is the last such segment encountered.

EXAMPLES

Table 12.1 specifies the order in which four segments with combine type STACK are encountered by the LINK program. LINK combines these four segments into two physical segments. The first segment, named STACK, is 192 bytes in length (offsets 0000–00BF hexadecimal). The second segment, named STAK, is 256 bytes in length (offsets 0000–00FF hexadecimal). Since the last segment encountered is a part of segment STAK, it is the run-time stack segment for the program. The SS-register is initialized to specify the origin of segment STAK, and the SP-register is initialized to the hexadecimal value 0100 (256 decimal).

TABLE 12.1
Stack segments being linked

Segment Name	Class Name	Combine Type	Size in Bytes
STACK	None	STACK	64
STAK	None	STACK	192
STACK	None	STACK	128
STAK	None	STACK	64

Suppose the LINK program encountered the same segments in the order shown in Table 12.2. Since the last segment encountered is a part of segment STACK, it is the run-time stack segment for the program. The SS-register is initialized to specify the origin of segment STACK, and the SP-register is initialized to the hexadecimal value 00C0 (192 decimal). ■

TABLE 12.2
Stack segments being linked

Segment Name	Class Name	Combine Type	Size in Bytes
STACK	None	STACK	64
STAK	None	STACK	192
STAK	None	STACK	64
STACK	None	STACK	128

Note that during program execution, the SS:SP register pair can be switched from one physical segment to another, but this technique is beyond the scope of this book.

The example programs used in this book contain one stack segment definition, and this stack segment definition appears in the assembly module that contains the definition of the main procedure. This one stack segment must be large enough to accommodate the stack needs for the entire program. An alternative would be to define a portion of the stack segment in each assembly module. The size of the portion defined in a given assembly module would depend on the needs of the procedures defined in that assembly module. With either approach, knowledge of the dynamic structure is requred to define the size of the stack segment properly.

EXAMPLES

Suppose a program consists of a main procedure and four subprocedures named A, B, C, and D, and suppose the main procedure requires 4 words of the stack segment, procedure A requires 10 words of the stack segment, procedure B requires 12 words of the stack segment, procedure C requires 8 words of the stack segment, and procedure D requires 6 words of the stack segment.

Now, suppose the dynamic structure of the program is described by the chart in Figure 12.1. The main procedure references each of the subprocedures in sequence, and the subprocedures themselves do not call any subprocedures. In this case, the stack must be large enough to accommodate the main procedure and the subprocedure with the largest stack need. Therefore, the stack must be 16 words (4 for the main procedure and 12 for procedure B) in length.

FIGURE 12.1 Dynamic structure of a program

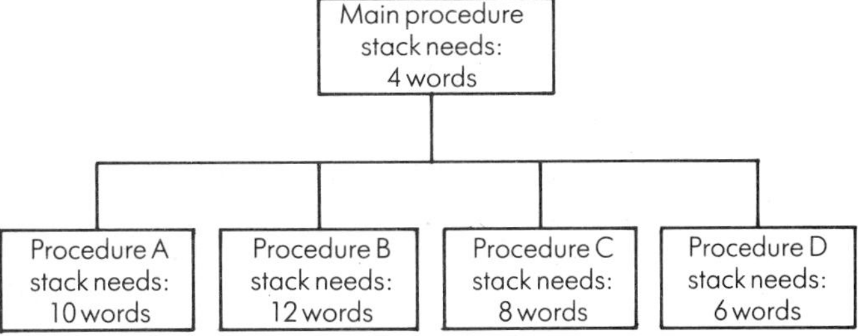

Then, suppose the dynamic structure of the program is described by the chart in Figure 12.2. The main procedure references subprocedures A and C in sequence. Sub-

FIGURE 12.2 Dynamic structure of a program

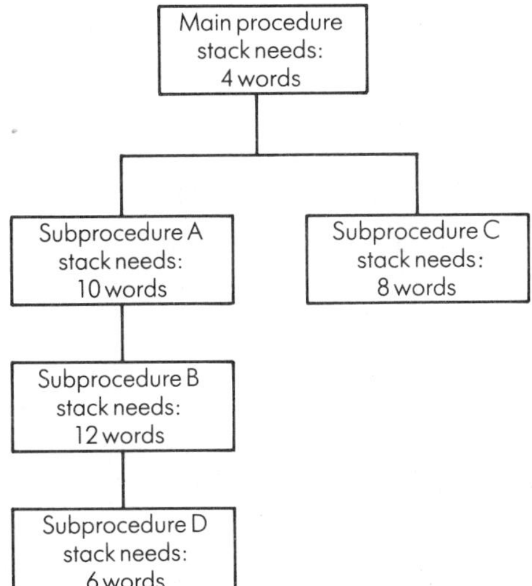

procedure A calls subprocedure B, which in turn calls subprocedure D. In this case, the stack segment must be large enough to accommodate the main procedure and subprocedures A, B, and D at the same time. Therefore, the stack must be 32 words (4 for the main procedure, 10 for subprocedure A, 12 for subprocedure B, and 6 for subprocedure D) in length. Consequently, twice as much stack space is required for the program structure of Figure 12.2 than is required for the structure of Figure 12.1. ■

Since you cannot know the dynamic structure or the stack needs for the I/O subprocedures provided by the I/O subprocedure library that accompanies this text, it is suggested that a stack of at least 256 bytes be defined when using these subprocedures. Except for the example programs in Chapters 10 and 11, a 256-byte stack is sufficient for the example programs in this book; however, for a number of the programs, reducing the stack size to 128 bytes would produce an incorrect program due to an insufficient stack.

12.4 Overlay Segments

In the 8088/8086 assembly language, it is possible to define a data segment that is accessible to procedures in separate assembly modules. This accessibility is accomplished by having each assembly module define its own version of the common data segment. The various versions overlay one another to produce one physical segment. The definition of the common data segment in a specific assembly module is simply a symbolic name template to be used by assembly module procedures in referencing the common data.

The combine type COMMON specifies that the segment being defined is to be overlaid with other COMMON segments that have the same segment name and class name. The segments being overlaid do not have to be the same size. The size of the physical segment produced is the same as the size of the largest of the segments being overlaid. Initial values for the storage cells in the common data segment can be specified in any of the segment definitions for the common segment. If more than one initial value is supplied for a specific storage cell, then the last value encountered by the LINK program is the one that prevails.

EXAMPLE

Suppose the following three segment definitions appear in separate assembly modules of an 8088/8086 assembly language program:

Assembly module A:

```
DATA    SEGMENT  COMMON
STRING  DB       4 DUP(?)
V       DW       300
W       DW       500
DATA    ENDS
```

Assembly module B:

```
DATA    SEGMENT  COMMON
STRING  DB       4 DUP(' ')
X       DW       ?
Y       DW       ?
Z       DW       0
DATA    ENDS
```

Assembly module C:

```
DATA  SEGMENT  COMMON
      DB       4 DUP(?)
Z     DW       6
Y     DW       12
DATA  ENDS
```

Table 12.3 shows the name template for use by procedures in each of the three assembly modules to reference the locations of the common data segment. The 4-byte string that begins at offset 0000 can be referenced by the name STRING in assembly module A and B procedures. This string cannot be referenced by name in assembly module C procedures. The word variable that begins at offset 0006 can be referenced by the name Y in assembly module B and C procedures and by the name W in assembly module A procedures.

TABLE 12.3

Label templates for a common data segment

Offset	Label for Use in Assembly Module A	Label for Use in Assembly Module B	Label for Use in Assembly Module C
0000	STRING	STRING	
0001			
0002			
0003			
0004	V	X	Z
0005			
0006	W	Y	Y
0007			
0008		Z	
0009			

TABLE 12.4

Common data segment: (a) after assembly module A, (b) after assembly module B, and (c) after assembly module C

(a) Offset	(a) Value	(b) Offset	(b) Value	(c) Offset	(c) Value
0000	?	0000	20	0000	20
0001	?	0001	20	0001	20
0002	?	0002	20	0002	20
0003	?	0003	20	0003	20
0004	2C	0004	2C	0004	06
0005	01	0005	01	0005	00
0006	F4	0006	F4	0006	0C
0007	01	0007	01	0007	00
		0008	00	0008	00
		0009	00	0009	00

Suppose the assembly modules are presented to the LINK program in the order shown previously (A followed by B followed by C). Table 12.4 shows the steps in building the common data segment from the three definitions:

1. On encountering the data segment definition in assembly module A, the LINK program allocates 8 bytes for the data segment. No initial values are specified for the first 4 bytes. The fifth and sixth bytes are initialized to 2C hex and 01 hex,

respectively, which is the word value 300 (012C hex). The seventh and eighth bytes are initialized to F4 hex and 01 hex, respectively, which is the word value 500 (01F4 hex). The status of the data segment at this point in the linking process is shown in Table 12.4(a).

2. On encountering the data segment definition in assembly module B, the LINK program appends 2 bytes to the common data segment. The data segment is now 10 bytes in length. Each of the first 4 bytes is initialized to the ASCII representation for a space (20 hex). No initial values are specified for the next 2 words (4 bytes), thus leaving the initial values specified by the data segment definition in assembly module A. The last 2 bytes (the 2 bytes just appended) are each initialized to 00. The status of the data segment at this point in the linking process is shown in Table 12.4(b).

3. On encountering the data segment definition in assembly module C, the LINK program makes no modification in the size of the common data segment because the size specified by this definition (8 bytes) is smaller than the current size of the segment (10 bytes). No initial values are specified for the first 4 bytes, thus leaving the initial values specified by the data segment definition in assembly module B. The next 2 words are assigned the initial values 0006 and 000C hex, thus replacing the initial values specified by the data segment definition in assembly module A. The physical data segment produced by the complete linking process has the initial values shown in Table 12.4(c). ■

Programming Example—Sieve of Eratosthenes Revisited

The Sieve of Eratosthenes, introduced in Section 8.5, is a technique for computing prime numbers. Program Listing 8.5 shows part of an implementation of an algorithm for computing prime numbers using this technique. The assembly module contains a data segment definition (lines 28–32) that defines the sieve as a word array. It also contains the definition of a code segment that contains the definitions of a main procedure and two NEAR subprocedures. The program shows the definition of the main procedure (lines 37–89) and one of the subprocedures (lines 99–116). (The definition of the other subprocedure was left to Programming Exercise 8.10.)

Program Listings 12.7 and 12.8 illustrate an alternative approach for implementing the same algorithm—implementing the main procedure and the two NEAR subprocedures in separate assembly modules. The sieve is defined in a data segment that is common to the three assembly modules. Such a definition allows the subprocedure interface for the two NEAR subprocedures to remain the same. If the two subprocedures are to be NEAR subprocedures, then they must be defined in the same code segment as the main procedure. The code segments in the three assembly modules are given the same name and are defined with combine type PUBLIC, which causes the LINK program to combine the three code segments into one physical code segment containing all three procedures. Program Listings 12.7 and 12.8 show two of these three assembly modules. (The third module is left to Programming Exercise 12.1.)

The assembly module in Program Listing 12.7 contains the definition of the stack segment for the program (lines 19–21), a definition of the common data segment (lines 30–35), and the definition of the main procedure (lines 41–94). The main procedure references the two subprocedures FINDPRIM and SIFTSIEVE. Since the two subprocedures are external (i.e., defined in separate assembly modules), they must be

```
            PAGE    80,132
;=====================================================================
;                   PROGRAM LISTING 12.7
;
; PROGRAM TO DISPLAY THE PRIME NUMBERS THAT ARE LESS THAN 16000.
; THE PROGRAM USES THE SIEVE OF ERATOSTHENES.
;
;=====================================================================
                                         ;PROCEDURES TO
            EXTRN   FINDPRIM:NEAR        ;FIND NEXT PRIME IN SIEVE
            EXTRN   NEWLINE:FAR          ;DISPLAY NEWLINE CHARACTER
            EXTRN   PAUSE:FAR            ;PAUSE UNTIL KEYSTROKE
            EXTRN   PUTDEC$:FAR          ;DISPLAY UNSIGNED DECIMAL INT.
            EXTRN   SIFTSIEVE:NEAR       ;SIFT MULTIPLES OF PRIME
                                         ;FROM SIEVE
;=====================================================================
; S T A C K   S E G M E N T   D E F I N I T I O N
;
STACK       SEGMENT STACK
            DB      256 DUP(?)
STACK       ENDS
;=====================================================================
; C O N S T A N T   D E F I N I T I O N S
;
SIZE$       EQU     15999
MAX_INDEX   EQU     2*SIZE$
;=====================================================================
; D A T A   S E G M E N T   D E F I N I T I O N
;
DATA        SEGMENT COMMON
;
SIEVE       DW      SIZE$ DUP(?)
PAUSE_MSG   DB      'PRESS ANY KEY TO CONTINUE'
;
DATA        ENDS
;=====================================================================
; C O D E   S E G M E N T   D E F I N I T I O N
;
CODE        SEGMENT PUBLIC
            ASSUME  CS:CODE,SS:STACK,DS:DATA,ES:DATA
EX_12_7:
            MOV     AX,SEG DATA          ;SET ES AND DS REGISTERS TO
            MOV     DS,AX                ;POINT TO DATA SEGMENT
            MOV     ES,AX
                                         ;<INITIALIZE SIEVE>
            CLD                          ;SET DF FOR INCREMENTING
            MOV     CX,SIZE$             ;LOOP_COUNT = SIZE OF SIEVE
            LEA     DI,SIEVE             ;SET ES:DI TO BASE ADDRESS
                                         ;              OF SIEVE
            MOV     AX,2                 ;VALUE = 2
LOADLOOP:                                ;REPEAT
            STOSW                        ;   ES:DI -> WORD = VALUE
                                         ;   DI = DI + 2
            INC     AX                   ;   VALUE = VALUE + 1
            LOOP    LOADLOOP             ;   LOOP_COUNT = LOOP_COUNT - 1
                                         ;UNTIL LOOP_COUNT = 0
;
            MOV     BX,0                 ;INDEX = 0
            MOV     CX,0                 ;PRIME_COUNT = 0
            CALL    FINDPRIM             ;CALL FINDPRIME(INDEX,PRIME)
;
PRIMELOOP:                               ;REPEAT
            CALL    SIFTSIEVE            ;   CALL SIFTSIEVE(PRIME,INDEX)
                                         ;   <SIFT OUT MULTIPLES OF PRIME>
            PUSH    BX                   ;   SAVE SIEVE INDEX
            MOV     BH,1                 ;   DISPLAY PRIME
            CALL    PUTDEC$
            INC     CX                   ;   PRIME_COUNT = PRIME_COUNT + 1
            MOV     AX,CX                ;   IF   PRIME_COUNT mod 10 = 0
            MOV     DX,0
            MOV     BX,10
            DIV     BX
```

```
               CMP     DX,0
               JNE     NEXTPRIME
               CALL    NEWLINE                 ;   THEN DISPLAY NEWLINE CHAR
               MOV     DX,0                    ;        IF   PRIME_COUNT mod 240
               MOV     BX,24                   ;             = 0
               DIV     BX
               CMP     DX,0
               JNE     NEXTPRIME
               PUSH    CX                      ;        THEN
               LEA     DI,PAUSE_MSG            ;             PAUSE FOR PRINT
               MOV     CX,25                   ;             OF DISPLAY SCREEN
               CALL    PAUSE
               POP     CX
                                               ;        ENDIF
NEXTPRIME:                                     ;   ENDIF
               POP     BX                      ;   RESTORE SIEVE INDEX
               CALL    FINDPRIM                ;   CALL FINDPRIME(INDEX,PRIME)
               CMP     AX,0
               JNE     PRIMELOOP               ;UNTIL SIEVE IS EMPTY
               CALL    NEWLINE
               MOV     AH,4CH                  ;RETURN TO DOS
               INT     21H
CODE           ENDS
               END     EX_12_7
```

```
               PAGE    80,132
;===================================================================
;                      PROGRAM LISTING 12.8
;
; SIFT MULTIPLES OF PRIME OUT OF SIEVE
;
; INPUT:  AX-REG CONTAINS PRIME NUMBER
;         BX-REG CONTAINS SIEVE INDEX OF PRIME NUMBER
;
; OUTPUT: SIEVE WITH MULTIPLES OF PRIME REMOVED
;
;===================================================================
; C O N S T A N T   D E F I N I T I O N S
;
SIZE$          EQU     15999
MAX_INDEX      EQU     2*SIZE$
;===================================================================
; D A T A   S E G M E N T   D E F I N I T I O N
;
DATA           SEGMENT COMMON
;
SIEVE          DW      SIZE$ DUP(?)
;
DATA           ENDS
;===================================================================
; C O D E   S E G M E N T   D E F I N I T I O N
;
CODE           SEGMENT PUBLIC BYTE
               ASSUME  CS:CODE,DS:DATA
;
SIFTSIEVE      PROC    NEAR PUBLIC        ;PROCEDURE SIFTSIEVE(PRIME,INDEX)
               PUSH    AX                       ;SAVE REGISTERS
               PUSH    BX
               MOV     SIEVE[BX],0              ;SIEVE(INDEX) = 0
               SAL     AX,1                     ;OFFSET = PRIME * 2
                                                ;<OFFSET BETWEEN MULTIPLES
                                                ;           OF PRIME>
SIFTLOOP:                                       ;WHILE (INDEX+OFFSET) < MAX_INDEX
               ADD     BX,AX                    ;   INDEX = INDEX + OFFSET
               CMP     BX,MAX_INDEX
               JAE     RETURN1
```

```
42:               MOV      SIEVE[BX],0             ;    SIEVE(INDEX) = 0
43:               JMP      SIFTLOOP
44: RETURN1:                                         ;ENDWHILE
45:               POP      BX                        ;RESTORE REGISTERS
46:               POP      AX
47:               RET                                ;RETURN
48: SIFTSIEVE     ENDP                             ;END SIFTSIEVE
49: CODE          ENDS
50: ;=====================================================================
51:               END
```

identified to the assembler with the EXTRN pseudo-operation (lines 10 and 14). These pseudo-operations notify the assembler that the symbolic names FINDPRIM and SIFTSIEVE, defined in other assembly modules, are used in this assembly module as NEAR procedure names. Since these are NEAR procedures, the code segments containing these procedures must be combined with the code segment for the main procedure, producing a single code segment for the three procedures.

Two named constants are defined in lines 25 and 26. The named constant SIZE$ defines the word size of the sieve. To modify the program to process a different size sieve, you only need to modify the value of this named constant. Since this named constant appears in all three assembly modules, it must be consistent in all three. The named constant MAX_INDEX is the index of the last word in the sieve.

A definition of the common data segment appears in lines 30–35. The data segment is defined with combine type COMMON so that it is overlaid with the definitions appearing in the other assembly modules, producing a single data segment. The segment contains the definition of the sieve (line 32) and the definition of a message to be displayed whenever the display screen is full (line 33).

The code segment (lines 39–95) is defined with combine type PUBLIC, which causes this code segment to be combined with other PUBLIC code segments having the same segment name and class name, producing a single code segment. The code segments containing the NEAR subprocedures must be defined in exactly the same way. The procedure defined in this code segment, the main procedure (lines 41–94), is virtually the same as the main procedure in Program Listing 8.5.

The assembly module in Program Listing 12.8 contains a definition of the common data segment (lines 20–24) and the definition of the subprocedure SIFTSIEVE (lines 31–48). The named constants that were defined in the assembly module in Program Listing 12.7 are also defined in this assembly module (lines 15 and 16). Both constants are needed in the SIFTSIEVE procedure.

The data segment (lines 20–24) is defined with combine type COMMON so that it is overlaid with the data segment defined in the assembly module in Program Listing 12.7. Note that the same segment name is used in these two data segment definitions. The LINK program will not overlay COMMON segments that have different segment names. The version of the common data segment definition in Program Listing 12.8 only defines the sieve; it does not include the string that was defined in Program Listing 12.7. The SIFTSIEVE subprocedure does not use the character string, so it has no need for access to it. If the data segment definition in Program Listing 12.7 had been

```
DATA        SEGMENT  COMMON
PAUSE_MSG   DB       'PRESS ANY KEY TO CONTINUE'
SIEVE       DW       SIZE$ DUP(?)
DATA        ENDS
```

then the data segment definition in Program Listing 12.8 would have to be

```
DATA   SEGMENT  COMMON
       DB       25 DUP(?)
SIEVE  DW       SIZE$ DUP(?)
DATA   ENDS
```

Space needs to be allocated for the string so that the sieve overlays properly. The name can be omitted since the SIFTSIEVE procedure does not need to access the string. Its initial value has already been defined, so this definition must protect that initial value. The use of the question mark (?) protects any initial value that might have already been established.

The code segment is defined with combine type PUBLIC so that it is combined with the code segment defined in the assembly module in Program Listing 12.7. It is defined with align type BYTE so that no unused storage space appears between the SIFTSIEVE procedure and the procedure that precedes it in the physical code segment. The code segment contains an ASSUME pseudo-operation (line 29) that notifies the assembler that the CS-register will address the code segment and the DS-register will address the data segment during execution of SIFTSIEVE. SIFTSIEVE does not have to be concerned with initialization of either of these registers. Since one code segment contains all three procedures, the CS-register is initialized on invocation of the main procedure and does not change when the SIFTSIEVE procedure is invoked. The main procedure initializes the DS-register to address the common data segment that is shared by the three procedures (lines 42 and 43 in Program Listing 12.7). The name SIFTSIEVE is declared as PUBLIC (line 31 in Program Listing 12.8) so that it is available for reference in other assembly modules. The definition of the SIFTSIEVE procedure (lines 31–48 in Program Listing 12.8) is exactly the same as the definition of the SIFTSIEVE procedure in Program Listing 8.5.

When the object modules for these assembly modules are presented to the LINK program, the object module for the assembly module in Program Listing 12.7 must be presented first because the PUBLIC code segment in that assembly module has align type PARA (the default) and the PUBLIC code segment must begin on a paragraph boundary. The other two object modules can be presented in any order.

12.5 Combining Code Segments with Data Segments

A code segment and a data segment can be combined into the same physical segment. This feature might be accomplished so that an external subprocedure can access its local data segment via the CS-register rather than the DS- or ES-register, which avoids having to save, initialize, and restore the DS- or ES-register.

As an example, consider again the coin-flip simulation program. Program Listings 12.9 and 12.10 show a version of this program that specifies the combining of the main procedure, its data segment, the random number generator, and its data segment into one physical segment. Note that all four segments have the same name, PROG (lines 19 and 30 in Program Listing 12.9 and lines 17 and 27 in Program Listing 12.10). All four of these segments are defined with combine type PUBLIC. The first of these four segments, the data segment in Program Listing 12.9, is defined with align type PARA (the default); the other three are defined with align type BYTE.

```
             PAGE    80,132
;=====================================================================
;                     PROGRAM LISTING 12.9
;
;        PROGRAM TO SIMULATE THE FLIPPING OF A COIN
;=====================================================================
                                              ;PROCEDURES TO
             EXTRN   GETDEC$:FAR              ;GET UNSIGNED DECIMAL INTEGER
             EXTRN   PUTDEC$:FAR              ;DISPL. UNSIGNED DEC. INTEGER
             EXTRN   PUTTEXT:FAR              ;DISPLAY A TEXT STRING
             EXTRN   RANDOM:NEAR              ;GENERATE PSEUDO-RANDOM NUMBER
;=====================================================================
; S T A C K   S E G M E N T   D E F I N I T I O N
STACK        SEGMENT STACK
             DB      256 DUP(?)
STACK        ENDS
;=====================================================================
; D A T A   S E G M E N T   D E F I N I T I O N
PROG         SEGMENT PUBLIC
HEADS        DW      0                        ;COUNT OF NUMBER OF HEADS
TAILS        DW      0                        ;COUNT OF NUMBER OF TAILS
PROMPT       DB      'ENTER NUMBER OF TIMES TO FLIP THE COIN  ',0
HEADSMSG     DB      ' HEADS  ',0
TAILSMSG     DB      ' TAILS',0
ZERO         DW      0
ONE          DW      1
PROG         ENDS
;=====================================================================
; C O D E   S E G M E N T   D E F I N I T I O N
PROG         SEGMENT PUBLIC BYTE
             ASSUME  CS:PROG,SS:STACK,ES:PROG
COINFLIP:    MOV     AX,SEG PROG              ;SET ES-REGISTER TO ADDRESS
             MOV     ES,AX                    ;PROGRAM SEGMENT
             LEA     DI,PROMPT                ;PROMPT FOR NUMBER_OF_FLIPS
             CALL    PUTTEXT
             CALL    GETDEC$                  ;GET NUMBER_OF_FLIPS
             MOV     CX,AX                    ;LOOP_CNT = NUMBER_OF_FLIPS
             .REPEAT                          ;REPEAT
             PUSH    ZERO                     ;   NUMBER = RANDOM(0,1)
             PUSH    ONE
             CALL    RANDOM
             .IF     AX > 0                   ;   IF   NUMBER > 0
                                              ;   THEN
             INC     HEADS                    ;        HEADS = HEADS + 1
;
             .ELSE                            ;   ELSE
             INC     TAILS                    ;        TAILS = TAILS + 1
             .ENDIF                           ;   ENDIF
             .UNTILCXZ                        ;   LOOP_CNT = LOOP_CNT - 1
                                              ;UNTIL LOOP_CNT = 0
             MOV     BH,1
             MOV     AX,HEADS                 ;DISPLAY HEADS
             CALL    PUTDEC$
             LEA     DI,HEADSMSG
             CALL    PUTTEXT
             MOV     AX,TAILS                 ;DISPLAY TAILS
             CALL    PUTDEC$
             LEA     DI,TAILSMSG
             CALL    PUTTEXT
             MOV     AH,4CH                   ;RETURN TO DOS
             INT     21H
PROG         ENDS
             END     COINFLIP
;=====================================================================
```

```
            PAGE    80,132
;=====================================================================
;                        PROGRAM LISTING 12.10
;      r a n d o m   n u m b e r   g e n e r a t o r
;
; GENERATES PSEUDO-RANDOM INTEGERS IN THE RANGE LOWER TO UPPER
; INPUT:  TWO STACK PARAMETERS - LOWER AND UPPER ENDS OF RANGE
; OUTPUT: AX-REG CONTAINS RANDOM INTEGER
; CALLING SEQUENCE:      PUSH    <LOWER END OF RANGE>
;                        PUSH    <UPPER END OF RANGE>
;                        CALL    RANDOM
;=====================================================================
FALSE       EQU     0                       ;CONSTANT FALSE
TRUE        EQU     1                       ;CONSTANT TRUE
;=====================================================================
; D A T A   S E G M E N T   D E F I N I T I O N
PROG        SEGMENT PUBLIC BYTE
SEED        DW      ?                       ;SEED FOR RANDOM NUMBER GEN.
MULTIPLIER  DW      25173                   ;MULTIPLIER AND
ADDEND      DW      13849                   ;ADDEND FOR MIXED
                                            ;LINEAR CONGRUENTIAL METHOD
FIRST_CALL  DB      TRUE                    ;FIRST CALL FLAG
PROG        ENDS
;=====================================================================
; C O D E   S E G M E N T   D E F I N I T I O N
;
PROG        SEGMENT PUBLIC BYTE
            ASSUME  CS:PROG
RANDOM      PROC    NEAR BASIC PUBLIC USES CX DX, LOWER:WORD,
                    UPPER:WORD        ;FUNCTION RANDOM(LOWER,UPPER)
                                            ;push   bp      INSTRUCTIONS
                                            ;mov    bp, sp  GENERATED IN
                                            ;push   cx      RESPONSE TO
                                            ;push   dx      PROC
            PUSHF                           ;SAVE FLAGS
            .IF     FIRST_CALL == TRUE      ;IF  FIRST_CALL
                                            ;THEN
            MOV     FIRST_CALL,FALSE        ;     FIRST_CALL = FALSE
            MOV     AH,0                    ;     SEED = LOWER HALF OF
            INT     1AH                     ;            TIME OF DAY CLOCK
            MOV     SEED,DX
            .ENDIF                          ;ENDIF
            MOV     AX,SEED                 ;X = SEED * MULTIPLIER mod
            MUL     MULTIPLIER              ;                      65536
            ADD     AX,ADDEND               ;SEED = (X + ADDEND) mod 65536
            MOV     SEED,AX
            MOV     CX,UPPER                ;RANGE = UPPER - LOWER + 1
            SUB     CX,LOWER
            INC     CX
            MUL     CX                      ;RANDOM = SEED/65536 * RANGE
            ADD     DX,LOWER                ;                    + LOWER
            MOV     AX,DX
            POPF                            ;RESTORE FLAGS
                                            ;RESTORE REGISTERS SPECIFIED
                                            ;        IN USES CLAUSE,
                                            ;  RESTORE BP-REGISTER, AND
                                            ;  POP ARGUMENTS WITH RETURN
            RET                             ;RETURN (RANDOM)
RANDOM      ENDP                      ;END RANDOM
PROG        ENDS
            END
```

Use of the DS-register has been eliminated from the program. The CS-register must be used to address the segment in order to access the procedures' instructions. It can also be used as the segment register for accessing the data items in the segment, which eliminates the need for the DS-register. The ASSUME pseudo-operation in line 31 in Program Listing 12.9 indicates that the main procedure uses both the CS- and ES-registers to address the segment PROG. The ES-register is needed because the PUTTEXT procedure is being used. PUTTEXT expects the address of the string to be displayed to be in the ES:DI register pair. Note that only the ES-register is initialized (lines 32 and 33). Initialization of the DS-register has been eliminated. The ASSUME pseudo-operation in line 28 in Program Listing 12.10 indicates that the random number generator uses only the CS-register to address the segment PROG, which means that the CS-register is used by the random number generator to reference its data.

The random number generator has been changed from a FAR procedure to a NEAR procedure in this version of the program (line 11 in Program Listing 12.9 and line 29 in Program Listing 12.10). There is no need for the random number generator to be a FAR procedure since it is in the same code segment as its caller. By making it a NEAR procedure, the CALL instruction that invokes the NEAR procedure is 2 bytes shorter.

The following LINK command was used to create the executable module for this program:

```
C>LINK A:EX_12_9 A:EX_12_10 PUTTEXT,A:,A:,IO;
```

The load map produced and stored on the diskette in drive A under the name EX_12_9.MAP is shown in Load Map Listing 12.11. The load map shows a segment named STACK (the stack segment for the program) and a segment named PROG (the combined data and code segment for the program). The remainder of the segments listed in the load map came from the I/O subprocedure library. The segment PROG is E8 hex (232 decimal) bytes in length.

```
                    LOAD MAP LISTING 12.11


 Start   Stop    Length Name                     Class
 00000H 000FFH 00100H STACK
 00100H 001E7H 000E8H PROG
 001F0H 00246H 00057H IO_DATA
 00250H 0026AH 0001BH CODE                       IO_CODE
 00270H 0028DH 0001EH CODE                       IO_CODE
 00290H 002E4H 00055H CODE                       IO_CODE
 002F0H 0030FH 00020H CODE                       IO_CODE
 00310H 00367H 00058H CODE                       IO_CODE
 00370H 00410H 000A1H CODE                       IO_CODE
 00420H 0043DH 0001EH CODE                       IO_CODE

*Program entry point at 0010:0041
```

DEBUG Listing 12.12 shows the four parts that make up the PUBLIC segment named PROG. The first command issued to DEBUG, the R command, requests a register display. The value of the CS-register (1FCB) indicates that segment PROG is loaded in memory beginning at location 1FCB0 hex. The value of the IP-register (0041) indicates that the main procedure begins at offset 0041 hex within the segment.

The next command issued to DEBUG

```
D CS:0,40
```

DEBUG LISTING 12.12

```
C>DEBUG A:EX_12_9.EXE
-R
AX=0000  BX=0000  CX=043E  DX=0000  SP=0100  BP=0000  SI=0000  DI=0000
DS=1FAB  ES=1FAB  SS=1FBB  CS=1FCB  IP=0041   NV UP EI PL NZ NA PO NC
1FCB:0041 B8CB1F        MOV     AX,1FCB
-D CS:0,40
1FCB:0000  00 00 00 00 45 4E 54 45-52 20 4E 55 4D 42 45 52   ....ENTER NUMBER
1FCB:0010  20 4F 46 20 54 49 4D 45-53 20 54 4F 20 46 4C 49    OF TIMES TO FLI
1FCB:0020  50 20 54 48 45 20 43 4F-49 4E 20 20 00 20 48 45   P THE COIN  . HE
1FCB:0030  41 44 53 20 20 00 20 54-41 49 4C 53 00 00 00 01   ADS  . TAILS....
1FCB:0040  00
-U CS:41,9C
1FCB:0041 B8CB1F        MOV     AX,1FCB
1FCB:0044 8EC0          MOV     ES,AX
1FCB:0046 BF0400        MOV     DI,0004
1FCB:0049 9A0000EA1F    CALL    1FEA:0000
1FCB:004E 9A0000F21F    CALL    1FF2:0000
1FCB:0053 8BC8          MOV     CX,AX
1FCB:0055 26            ES:
1FCB:0056 FF363D00      PUSH    [003D]
1FCB:005A 26            ES:
1FCB:005B FF363F00      PUSH    [003F]
1FCB:005F E84200        CALL    00A4
1FCB:0062 83F800        CMP     AX,+00
1FCB:0065 7607          JBE     006E
1FCB:0067 26            ES:
1FCB:0068 FF060000      INC     WORD PTR [0000]
1FCB:006C EB05          JMP     0073
1FCB:006E 26            ES:
1FCB:006F FF060200      INC     WORD PTR [0002]
1FCB:0073 E2E0          LOOP    0055
1FCB:0075 B701          MOV     BH,01
1FCB:0077 26            ES:
1FCB:0078 A10000        MOV     AX,[0000]
1FCB:007B 9A0000EC1F    CALL    1FEC:0000
1FCB:0080 BF2D00        MOV     DI,002D
1FCB:0083 9A0000EA1F    CALL    1FEA:0000
1FCB:0088 26            ES:
1FCB:0089 A10200        MOV     AX,[0002]
1FCB:008C 9A0000EC1F    CALL    1FEC:0000
1FCB:0091 BF3600        MOV     DI,0036
1FCB:0094 9A0000EA1F    CALL    1FEA:0000
1FCB:0099 B44C          MOV     AH,4C
1FCB:009B CD21          INT     21
-D CS:9D,A3
1FCB:0090                                          00 00 55              ..U
1FCB:00A0  62 19 36 01                                       b.6.

-U CS:A4,E7
1FCB:00A4 55            PUSH    BP
1FCB:00A5 8BEC          MOV     BP,SP
1FCB:00A7 51            PUSH    CX
1FCB:00A8 52            PUSH    DX
1FCB:00A9 9C            PUSHF
1FCB:00AA 2E            CS:
1FCB:00AB 803EA30001    CMP     BYTE PTR [00A3],01
1FCB:00B0 750F          JNZ     00C1
1FCB:00B2 2E            CS:
1FCB:00B3 C606A30000    MOV     BYTE PTR [00A3],00
1FCB:00B8 B400          MOV     AH,00
1FCB:00BA CD1A          INT     1A
1FCB:00BC 2E            CS:
1FCB:00BD 89169D00      MOV     [009D],DX
1FCB:00C1 2E            CS:
1FCB:00C2 A19D00        MOV     AX,[009D]
1FCB:00C5 2E            CS:
```

```
1FCB:00C6 F7269F00      MUL     WORD PTR [009F]
1FCB:00CA 2E            CS:
1FCB:00CB 0306A100      ADD     AX,[00A1]
1FCB:00CF 2E            CS:
1FCB:00D0 A39D00        MOV     [009D],AX
1FCB:00D3 8B4E04        MOV     CX,[BP+04]
1FCB:00D6 2B4E06        SUB     CX,[BP+06]
1FCB:00D9 41            INC     CX
1FCB:00DA F7E1          MUL     CX
1FCB:00DC 035606        ADD     DX,[BP+06]
1FCB:00DF 8BC2          MOV     AX,DX
1FCB:00E1 9D            POPF
1FCB:00E2 5A            POP     DX
1FCB:00E3 59            POP     CX
1FCB:00E4 5D            POP     BP
1FCB:00E5 C20400        RET     0004
-Q
```

requests a dump of the first 65 bytes of the segment addressed by the CS-register, which is the part of the segment produced from the data segment definition in Program Listing 12.9. The first 2 bytes (offsets 0000 and 0001) make up the memory word that contains the value of the variable HEADS, whose initial value is 0000. The next 2 bytes (offsets 0002 and 0003) make up the memory word that contains the value of the variable TAILS, whose initial value is 0000. The next 41 bytes (offsets 0004–002C hex) are the bytes of the character string PROMPT. The ASCII interpretation at the right-hand side of the dump shows the actual characters of the string. The next 9 bytes (offsets 002D–0035) are the bytes of the character string HEADSMSG. The next 7 bytes (offsets 0036–003C) are the bytes of the character string TAILSMSG. The next 2 bytes (offsets 003D and 003E) make up the memory word that contains the value of the variable ZERO, whose initial value is 0000. The last 2 bytes (offsets 003F and 0040) make up the memory word that contains the value of the variable ONE, whose initial value is 0001.

The next command issued to DEBUG

```
U CS:41,9C
```

requests a dump of the next 92 bytes of the segment addressed by the CS-register. The command U (unassemble) instructs the DEBUG program to interpret the bytes being dumped as machine language instruction bytes. DEBUG dumps each instruction in hexadecimal form and then unassembles that instruction to give an assembly language interpretation of the instruction. The instruction bytes being dumped are the portion of the segment produced from the main procedure definition in Program Listing 12.9.

The next command issued to DEBUG

```
D CS:9D,A3
```

requests a dump of the next 7 bytes of the segment addressed by the CS-register, which is the part of the segment produced from the data segment definition in Program Listing 12.10. The first 2 bytes (offsets 009D and 009E) make up the memory word that contains the value of the variable SEED. The next 2 bytes (offsets 009F and 00A0) make up the memory word that contains the value of the variable MULTIPLIER, whose initial value is 6255 hexadecimal (25,173 decimal). The next 2 bytes (offsets 00A1 and 00A2) make up the memory word that contains the value of the variable ADDEND, whose initial value is 3619 hexadecimal (13,849 decimal). The last byte (offset 00A3) contains the value of the variable FIRST_CALL, whose initial value is the constant TRUE (01).

The next command issued to DEBUG

```
U CS:A4,E7
```

requests an instruction dump of the last 68 bytes of the segment addressed by the CS-register, which is the part of the segment produced from the subprocedure definition in Program Listing 12.10. The eleventh instruction of this dump

```
1FCB:00BC 2E        CS:
1FCB:00BD 89169D00  MOV  [009D],DX
```

corresponds to the instruction

```
MOV  SEED,DX
```

in line 41 in Program Listing 12.10. The variable SEED is located at offset 009D hex within the segment addressed by the CS-register. The first byte of the instruction

```
1FCB:00BC 2E  CS:
```

is called a **segment override prefix**. The machine language representation of a memory-referencing instruction such as the instruction

```
MOV  SEED,DX
```

indicates an offset relative to the paragraph address specified by the contents of the DS-register unless this default segment register is overriden by a 1-byte segment prefix. That is, using the CS-register rather than the DS-register to address the data portions of segment PROG causes each memory-referencing instruction to be expanded by 1 byte, the segment override prefix. (Whether or not this override has an impact on the number of paragraphs consumed by segment PROG is left as an exercise.)

This chapter has presented a number of the segmentation features provided by the assembler (MASM) in conjunction with the Linkage Editor (LINK). The discussion is by no means exhaustive, but it gives you a good basis from which to experiment further.

12.6 High-Level Language Interface

Procedures and functions written in assembly language can be linked with high-level language programs. Assembly language subprocedures are frequently used in high-level language programming for time-critical operations, bit manipulation operations, and interrupt control operations. The interface between an assembly language subprocedure and a high-level language program is specific to the particular high-level language. An exhaustive coverage of high-level language interface is beyond the scope of this book. However, some of the basic principles of high-level language interface can be illustrated through an example program involving one high-level language.

The high-level language used here is Turbo Pascal. Turbo Pascal was chosen for two reasons: First, Pascal is the standard language in the curriculum of many undergraduate computer science programs. Second, many undergraduate students have or have access to a Turbo Pascal compiler.

An assembly module must adhere to certain rules if the corresponding object module is to be successfully linked to a Turbo Pascal program. These rules are as follows:

1. All functions and procedures must be defined in a segment named CODE (or in a segment named Cseg).
2. All variables must be defined in a segment named DATA (or in a segment named Dseg).
3. Turbo Pascal only recognizes segments named CODE (or Cseg) and DATA (or Dseg). All other segments and all groups are ignored by Turbo Pascal.
4. The segment definitions can specify an align type of either BYTE or WORD. However, all assembly language segments are word-aligned when they are linked to a Turbo Pascal program.
5. All variables defined in the DATA (or Dseg) segment should be specified without initial value; that is, the question mark initializer should be used. Turbo Pascal ignores any initial values specified in the data definitions.
6. The Turbo Pascal program and the assembly language subprocedure may share common data. As well, the Turbo Pascal program may pass arguments to the parameters of the assembly language subprocedure, and the assembly language subprocedure may return a function value to the Pascal program. These shared and passed data items must be defined with compatible data types. Table 12.5 shows some of the Turbo Pascal data types and the corresponding MASM type attributes.

TABLE 12.5
Compatibility of data types between 8088/8086 assembly language and Turbo Pascal

Turbo Pascal Data Type	MASM Type Attribute
Char	BYTE
Boolean	BYTE
Byte	BYTE
Shortint	SBYTE
Word	WORD
Integer	SWORD
Longint	SDWORD
Enumerated type (256 or fewer values)	BYTE
Enumerated type (more than 256 values)	WORD

The coin-flip simulation is again used for illustration. The main program is implemented in Turbo Pascal, and the random number generator is implemented in assembly language. Program Listing 12.13 shows the assembly language implementation of the random number generator. This random number generator implementation differs from that of Program Listing 12.2 in several key places. These differences are the focus of the discussion here.

The name of the data segment has been changed from RAND_DATA to DATA (compare lines 17, 23, and 28 of Program Listing 12.13 to lines 17, 23, and 28 of Program Listing 12.2). The variables SEED, MULTIPLIER, and ADDEND have been defined without initial values (compare lines 18–20 of Program Listing 12.13 to lines 18–20 of Program Listing 12.2), but MULTIPLIER and ADDEND require initial values. Because the random number generator must detect its first call in order

```
            PAGE    80,132
;==================================================================
;                   PROGRAM LISTING 12.13
;      r a n d o m   n u m b e r   g e n e r a t o r
;
; GENERATES PSEUDO-RAND   INTEGERS IN THE RANGE LOWER TO UPPER
; INPUT:  TWO STACK PARAMETERS - LOWER AND UPPER ENDS OF RANGE
; OUTPUT: AX-REG CONTAINS RAND   INTEGER
; CALLING SEQUENCE:     PUSH    <LOWER END OF RANGE>
;                       PUSH    <UPPER END OF RANGE>
;                       CALL    RAND
;==================================================================
FALSE       EQU     0                       ;CONSTANT FALSE
TRUE        EQU     1                       ;CONSTANT TRUE
;==================================================================
; D A T A   S E G M E N T   D E F I N I T I O N
DATA        SEGMENT BYTE
SEED        DW      ?                       ;SEED FOR RAND   NUMBER GEN.
MULTIPLIER  DW      ?                       ;MULTIPLIER AND
ADDEND      DW      ?                       ;ADDEND FOR MIXED
                                            ;LINEAR CONGRUENTIAL METHOD
            EXTRN   FIRST_CALL:BYTE         ;FIRST CALL FLAG
DATA        ENDS
;==================================================================
; C O D E   S E G M E N T   D E F I N I T I O N
;
CODE        SEGMENT WORD
            ASSUME  DS:DATA
RAND        PROC    FAR PASCAL PUBLIC USES CX DX, LOWER:WORD,
                    UPPER:WORD        ;FUNCTION RAND(LOWER,UPPER)
                                            ;push    bp      INSTRUCTIONS
                                            ;mov     bp, sp  GENERATED IN
                                            ;push    cx      RESPONSE TO
                                            ;push    dx      PROC
            PUSHF                           ;SAVE FLAGS
            .IF     FIRST_CALL == TRUE      ;IF   FIRST_CALL
                                            ;THEN
            MOV     FIRST_CALL,FALSE        ;     FIRST_CALL = FALSE
            MOV     AH,0                    ;     SEED = LOWER HALF OF
            INT     1AH                     ;            TIME OF DAY CLOCK
            MOV     SEED,DX
            MOV     MULTIPLIER,25173        ;     MULTIPLIER = 25173
            MOV     ADDEND,13849            ;     ADDEND = 13849
            .ENDIF                          ;ENDIF
            MOV     AX,SEED                 ;X = SEED * MULTIPLIER mod
            MUL     MULTIPLIER              ;                      65536
            ADD     AX,ADDEND               ;SEED = (X + ADDEND) mod 65536
            MOV     SEED,AX
            MOV     CX,UPPER                ;RANGE = UPPER - LOWER + 1
            SUB     CX,LOWER
            INC     CX
            MUL     CX                      ;RAND   = SEED/65536 * RANGE
            ADD     DX,LOWER                ;                    + LOWER
            MOV     AX,DX
            POPF                            ;RESTORE FLAGS
                                            ;RESTORE REGISTERS SPECIFIED
                                            ;         IN USES CLAUSE,
                                            ;   RESTORE BP-REGISTER, AND
                                            ;   POP ARGUMENTS WITH RETURN
            RET                             ;RETURN (RAND)
RAND        ENDP                        ;END RAND
CODE        ENDS
            END
```

to initialize the value of SEED, the values of MULTIPLIER and ADDEND can also be initialized on the first call to the subprocedure (see lines 42 and 43 of Program Listing 12.13). However, the value of the variable FIRST_CALL must be initialized prior to the first call of the random number generator, so the variable FIRST_CALL is defined in the interface unit between the Turbo Pascal program and the assembly language subprocedure and initialized in the interface unit. (Turbo Pascal interface units are discussed in a subsequent paragraph.) The assembly module can reference a variable in the Turbo Pascal interface unit via an external definition. The EXTRN pseudo-operation in line 22 of Program Listing 12.13 identifies FIRST_CALL as an externally defined variable of type BYTE. BYTE is the appropriate assembly language type attribute for a Turbo Pascal variable of type Boolean (see Table 12.5).

It should be noted that the variables defined in the DATA (or Dseg) segment are stored with the global variables of the Turbo Pascal program. Therefore, their values persist from one invocation of the subprocedure to the next, which is precisely what is needed for the random number generator. On each call to the subprocedure, the previous SEED value is used to compute a new value for SEED, and the new SEED value is used to compute the pseudorandom integer to be returned to the caller. The SEED value must persist from one invocation of the subprocedure to the next.

The DATA segment is defined with align type BYTE (line 17), and the CODE segment is defined with align type WORD (line 27). Both segments are aligned on a word boundary when linked to the Turbo Pascal program.

The name of the subprocedure has been changed from RANDOM to RAND (compare lines 29 and 61 of Program Listing 12.13 to lines 29 and 62 of Program Listing 12.2). Turbo Pascal has its own random number generator, the standard function Random. To avoid confusion for readers who are familiar with Turbo Pascal, the name of the subprocedure was changed from RANDOM to RAND.

The procedure RAND is defined with language type PASCAL (see line 29) so that the assembler (MASM) is consistent with Turbo Pascal in regard to the following subprocedure interface conventions:

1. Identifiers are case-insensitive (e.g., FIRST_CALL and First_Call are identical identifiers).
2. Arguments to a subprocedure are passed via the stack and are pushed onto the stack in left-to-right order.
3. Arguments are popped from the stack as part of procedure return.
4. Function values are returned in CPU registers as follows:
   a. A double-word function value is returned in the DX:AX register pair.
   b. A word function value is returned in the AX-register.
   c. A byte function value is returned in the AL-register.

The saving and restoring of the DS-register (see the USES clause in line 29 of Program Listing 12.2) and the initialization of the DS-register to address the local data segment (see lines 37 and 38 of Program Listing 12.2) have been removed from the assembly module of Program Listing 12.13. The variable defined in the DATA (or Dseg) segment are placed in the same physical segment as the Turbo Pascal global variables. Since the Turbo Pascal global variables are accessed through the DS-register, the variables in the DATA (or Dseg) segment can be accessed through the DS-register as well. The assembly language subprocedure does not need to initialize the DS-register. Turbo Pascal takes care of the DS-register initialization.

Program Listing 12.14 shows the Turbo Pascal interface unit for the random number generator. Pascal was designed with the idea that each program would be produced through a single compilation. The notion of modular programming (i.e., producing programs by linking together separately compiled pieces of the program) is foreign to Pascal. Many implementations of Pascal include nonstandard features that facilitate modular programming. The **interface unit** is the Turbo Pascal feature that facilitates modular programming. A Turbo Pascal interface unit has the following general form:

```
UNIT ⟨unit-name⟩
     INTERFACE
          [USES ⟨unit-list⟩]
          ⟨public declarations⟩
     IMPLEMENTATION
          ⟨private declarations⟩
     BEGIN
          ⟨initialization code⟩
     END.
```

in which the optional USES clause identifies other interface units that are used by this interface unit; ⟨*public declarations*⟩ declares the constants, data types, variables, procedures, and functions of this interface unit that are to be made available to any program or interface unit that uses this interface unit; ⟨*private declarations*⟩ declares the constants, data types, variables, procedures, and functions that are private to this interface unit (i.e., are not to be made available to programs and interface units that use this interface unit); and ⟨*initialization code*⟩ contains the Turbo Pascal statements necessary to perform the initialization of variables declared in the ⟨*public declarations*⟩ and in the ⟨*private declarations*⟩.

```
 1: {==================================================================
 2:                      PROGRAM LISTING 12.14
 3:
 4:     INTERFACE UNIT FOR RANDOM NUMBER GENERATOR --- EX_12_13.OBJ
 5:  ==================================================================}
 6:    UNIT EX_12_14;
 7:       INTERFACE
 8:          FUNCTION Rand(Lower,Upper:Word): Word;
 9:       IMPLEMENTATION
10:          VAR
11:             First_Call : Boolean;
12:          {$L EX_12_13}
13:          FUNCTION Rand; External;
14:    BEGIN
15:       First_Call := TRUE
16:    END.
```

Lines 1–5 of Program Listing 12.14 are comment lines. They explain that the listing contains the definition of an interface unit for the random number generator whose object code is found in file EX_12_13.OBJ. The name of the interface unit being defined in Program Listing 12.14 is EX_12_14 (line 6).

The interface unit of Program Listing 12.14 contains one public declaration (line 8). This declaration defines the interface requirements for the random number generator using Turbo Pascal syntax. It states that the subprocedure is a function named Rand, which has two parameters of type Word (i.e., 16-bit unsigned integer) and which returns a value of type Word.

The interface unit of Program Listing 12.14 contains two private declarations (lines 11 and 13). The declaration in line 11 declares the variable First_Call to be of type Boolean, which is compatible with the variable FIRST_CALL, declared in line 22 of Program Listing 12.13, as an external variable with type attribute BYTE. This variable is referenced twice in the random number generator (see lines 36 and 38 of Program Listing 12.13). The declaration in line 13 of Program Listing 12.14 states that the function Rand is implemented externally to the interface unit. The comment in line 12 is actually a directive to the Turbo Pascal compiler to link the file EX_12_13.OBJ to this interface unit. The file EX_12_13.OBJ contains the implementation of the external function RAND.

Line 15 of Program Listing 12.14 is the initialization code for the interface unit. The variable First_Call is initialized to the constant value TRUE. The random number generator uses variable First_Call to detect its first invocation. The initialization code in the interface unit is executed only once, prior to the invocation of any procedure or function defined in the interface unit. Therefore, the variable First_Call has the value TRUE on the first invocation of subprocedure RAND. On entry to subprocedure RAND, the FIRST_CALL flag is tested; if RAND finds that the FIRST_CALL flag is TRUE, it sets FIRST_CALL to FALSE (see lines 36–38 of Program Listing 12.13). Therefore, the variable First_Call will have the value FALSE on all subsequent invocations of subprocedure RAND.

Program Listing 12.15 shows the Turbo Pascal program that simulates the flipping of a coin. This program is a Turbo Pascal implementation of the same algorithm

```
 1: {=================================================================
 2:                              PROGRAM LISTING 12.15
 3:
 4:         TURBO PASCAL PROGRAM TO SIMULATE THE FLIPPING OF A COIN
 5:  =================================================================}
 6: PROGRAM CoinFlip;
 7:    USES EX_12_14;
 8:    VAR
 9:       Heads   : Word;
10:       Tails   : Word;
11:       Number  : Word;
12:       Flips   : Word;
13:    BEGIN
14:       Heads := 0;
15:       Tails := 0;
16:       Write ('Enter number of times to flip the coin: ');
17:       Readln (Flips);
18:       REPEAT
19:          Number := Rand(0,1);
20:          IF   Number > 0
21:          THEN Heads := Heads + 1
22:          ELSE Tails := Tails + 1;
23:          Flips := Flips - 1
24:       UNTIL Flips = 0;
25:       Writeln (Heads:4,' Heads   ',Tails:4, ' Tails')
26:    END.
```

that is implemented by the assembly language code of Program Listing 12.1. In fact, the Turbo Pascal statements in lines 17–24 of Program Listing 12.15 look very similar to the pseudocode statements in lines 36–50 of Program Listing 12.1. The Turbo Pascal code is not explained here. The only statements to be considered are the one that specifies the use of the interface unit (line 7) and the one that invokes subprocedure RAND (line 19). The USES statement (line 7) indicates that this program uses an interface unit that is stored in a file named EX_12_14.TPU. (The creation of the .TPU file is discussed in a subsequent paragraph.) Subprocedure RAND is invoked as a function, with argument 0 for the parameter LOWER and argument 1 for the parameter UPPER (line 19). The value returned by subprocedure RAND is assigned as the value of variable Number. RAND returns its value in the AX-register.

Consider the assembly module of Program Listing 12.13, the interface unit of Program Listing 12.14, and the program of Program Listing 12.15. Suppose these three source files are on a diskette with filenames EX_12_13.ASM, EX_12_14.PAS, and EX_12_15.PAS, respectively. Suppose further that we have a fixed disk system, the assembler (MASM) and the Turbo Pascal compiler are on the fixed disk, the three source files are on the diskette in drive A, and the fixed disk drive is the default drive.

The command

```
ml /c /Foa: a:ex_12_13.asm
```

instructs MASM 6.0 to translate the assembly module in file EX_12_13.ASM to machine language. MASM 6.0 places the object code file on the diskette in drive A with EX_12_13.OBJ as the filename.

MASM 5.1

The command

```
masm a:ex_12_13,a:;
```

instructs MASM 5.1 to translate the assembly module in file EX_12_13.ASM to machine language. MASM 5.1 places the object code file on the diskette in drive A with EX_12_13.OBJ as the filename.

The command

```
tpc /oa: a:ex_12_14
```

instructs the Turbo Pascal compiler to translate the source code in file EX_12_14.PAS. The /oa: option tells the compiler to search the diskette in drive A for any object code files specified in the source code. In this case, the object code file specified in line 12 of Program Listing 12.14 (EX_12_13.OBJ) will be found on the diskette in drive A. Turbo Pascal places the translated unit on the diskette in drive A with EX_12_14.TPU as the filename.

The command

```
tpc /ua: a:ex_12_15
```

instructs the Turbo Pascal compiler to translate the source code in file EX_12_15.PAS. The /ua: option tells the compiler to search the diskette in drive A for any unit files specified in the source code. In this case, the interface unit file specified in line 7 of Program Listing 12.15 (EX_12_14.TPU) will be found on the diskette in drive A. Turbo Pascal places the executable code file on the diskette in drive A with EX_12_15.EXE as the filename.

The following are the results from some sample executions of this program:

```
C>a:ex_12_15
Enter number of times to flip the coin: 10000
5013 Heads  4987 Tails
```

```
C>a:ex_12_15
Enter number of times to flip the coin: 10000
5018 Heads  4982 Tails

C>a:ex_12_15
Enter number of times to flip the coin: 10000
5001 Heads  4999 Tails

C>a:ex_12_15
Enter number of times to flip the coin: 10000
4994 Heads  5006 Tails

C>a:ex_12_15
Enter number of times to flip the coin: 10000
5000 Heads  5000 Tails

C>a:ex_12_15
Enter number of times to flip the coin: 10000
4972 Heads  5028 Tails
```

PROGRAMMING EXERCISES

12.1 Complete Program Listings 12.7 and 12.8 by implementing the NEAR subprocedure FINDPRIM with interface specifications as described in Section 8.5. This subprocedure should be defined in a separate assembly module, which should also have a definition of the common data segment that contains the sieve. If your implementation requires the size of the sieve or the maximum index within the sieve, then use named constants similar to those defined in lines 25 and 26 in Program Listing 12.7. Assemble, link, and execute the completed program.

12.2 In Program Listings 12.7 and 12.8 and Programming Exercise 12.1, the named constants SIZE$ and MAX_INDEX appear in more than one assembly module. To change the size of the sieve, the value of SIZE$ must be changed in each assembly module. Modify this program so that the named constant SIZE$ appears in only one of the three assembly modules and so that only that one named constant needs to be modified to change the size of the sieve. Demonstrate the modified version of the program with sieve sizes 1199, 3099, and 15999. (This is a nontrivial problem.)

12.3 Modify Program Listings 12.9 and 12.10 to use the DS-register to address the data portions of segment PROG. Does this impact the number of paragraphs consumed by segment PROG?

12.4 Programming Exercises 8.2–8.6 make up the problem statement for a set of modules that are to solve for the detection of palindromes. Character strings are communicated from one procedure to another in this system by passing the addresses of character strings in the ES:DI register pair and/or DS:SI register pair and by passing the lengths of strings in the CX-register. Redesign the procedures of this system so that all communication is handled through a common data segment. Make all of the procedures NEAR procedures, but define them in separate assembly modules.

12.5 Program Listing 9.3 shows a version of the PUTBIN subprocedure. Modify this subprocedure to receive its arguments via the stack. The calling sequence for this new version of PUTBIN will be as follows:

```
PUSH  ⟨value⟩
PUSH  ⟨code⟩
CALL  PUTBIN
```

If ⟨*code*⟩ has a zero value, then PUTBIN should display the low-order 8 bits of ⟨*value*⟩ in binary form beginning at the current cursor position. If ⟨*code*⟩ has a nonzero value, then PUTBIN should display the 16-bit ⟨*value*⟩ in binary form beginning at the current cursor position.

Write a Turbo Pascal program to implement the Ulam's conjecture algorithm of Programming Exercise 4.1. Use the Turbo Pascal data type Word for the elements of the Ulam sequence, and use the data type BYTE for the length of the Ulam sequence. Display all numeric output in binary form. Use your modified PUTBIN subprocedure for the binary output.

CHAPTER 13

Two-Dimensional Arrays and Text Graphics

Chapter 8 introduced the notion of an array. It discussed methods for defining arrays in the data segment of an assembly language program and presented various techniques for accessing an array's elements. This chapter explores a special kind of array, an array whose elements are themselves arrays—the *multidimensional array*. Restricted to a discussion of *two-dimensional* arrays, the chapter presents the two classic methods of representing two-dimensional arrays in the linear memory of a computer, along with the address calculations needed in each case to compute the memory address of a two-dimensional array element given its row and column position.

Chapter 9 discussed video input/output at the BIOS level (Section 9.3). All models of the IBM PC and the IBM PS/2 have a *video subsystem* that provides the hardware interface between the microprocessor and the video monitor. All models of the IBM PS/2 have a built-in video subsystem that resides on the main system circuit board. The video subsystem for the IBM PC is on a separate circuit board, the video adapter. In both cases, the video subsystem includes some memory space for the video buffer, which holds the text characters (or graphics pixels) currently being displayed on the video screen. For text modes, the video buffer can be viewed as a two-dimensional array with one element for each character position on the video screen. This chapter discusses direct access to the video buffer as an application involving a two-dimensional array.

13.1 One-Dimensional Array Revisited

Array applications often involve a translation process. When transferring text data from an IBM PC to an IBM mainframe, the data must be translated from ASCII code to EBCDIC code. Chapter 11 presented algorithms for translating numbers between ASCII and BCD code. The secret message program presented in Program Listing 8.4 performed a translation from one alphabet to another. The two alphabets were related by position. Translating a character of the secret message was a two-step process:

1. Find the position of the character in the ENCODED alphabet.
2. Extract the character in the same position of the DECODED alphabet.

The 8088/8086 assembly language provides an instruction to aid in translations that are based on position, the **translate (XLAT) instruction**, which has the following general form:

[⟨*label*⟩] XLAT [⟨*source*⟩] [⟨*comment*⟩]

in which ⟨*source*⟩ is the symbolic name of the byte array that is assumed to be addressed by the DS:BX register pair. Prior to execution of an XLAT instruction, the DS:BX register pair must be set up to address the first byte of the translation table, and the AL-register must be set up to contain the offset from this address to the translation table element of interest. Execution of the XLAT instruction replaces the AL-register value with the byte in the data segment whose offset is specified by the contents of the BX-register plus the contents of the AL-register. Because the index into the translation table (i.e., the AL-register value) is an 8-bit index, the translation table can be a maximum of 256 bytes in length.

The optional ⟨*source*⟩ operand is provided for documentation and type-checking purposes. The assembler checks to see if it is a symbolic name defined in the segment to be addressed by the DS-register and defined with type attribute BYTE. The assembler does not attempt to determine whether or not, at execution time, the DS:BX register pair will correctly address the memory location associated with the symbolic name specified in the operand field of the XLAT instruction.

EXAMPLE

Consider the following hexadecimal-to-ASCII translation table:

```
HEX_ASCII DB '0123456789ABCDEF'
```

The 16-byte array HEX_ASCII is a character string whose characters are the ASCII representations of the 16 hexadecimal digits in numerical order (Figure 13.1). A 4-bit binary number serves as an index into this string. The contents of the byte indexed by a 4-bit binary number are the ASCII code for the hexadecimal digit that corresponds to that 4-bit binary number. The following instruction sequence translates the integer in the AL-register to a two-character ASCII string in the AH:AL register pair (AX-register). This code sequence assumes that the DS-register specifies the start address of the segment that contains the array HEX_ASCII:

```
LEA   BX,HEX_ASCII
MOV   AH,AL
MOV   CL,4
SHR   AL,CL
XLAT
XCHG  AH,AL
AND   AL,0FH
XLAT  HEX_ASCII
```

The LEA instruction loads the BX-register with the offset within the data segment of

FIGURE 13.1
Array HEX_ASCII

Index	Contents	
0	30	HEX_ASCII
1	31	
2	32	
3	33	
4	34	
5	35	
6	36	
7	37	
8	38	
9	39	
A	41	
B	42	
C	43	
D	44	
E	45	
F	46	

the first byte of array HEX_ASCII. The DS:BX register pair now addresses the first byte of array HEX_ASCII.

Suppose the AL-register contains the integer 01011100 (5C hex). The first MOV instruction saves a copy of this value in the AH-register. The AX-register now contains the value 5C5C hex. The second MOV instruction loads the CL-register with a shift count of 4. The SHR instruction shifts the AL-register value 4 bit positions to the right, which isolates the left nibble (first hex digit) of the integer being translated. The AL-register now contains 00000101 (05 hex). The first XLAT instruction uses this AL-register value as an index into the translation table addressed by the DS:BX register pair (array HEX_ASCII). It loads the AL-register with the byte value at index 05 within array HEX_ASCII. The AL-register now contains 35 hex (the ASCII code for the digit 5). The XCHG instruction moves the 35-hex value to the AH-register and moves the saved copy of the integer being translated to the AL-register. The AND instruction isolates the right nibble (second hex digit) of the integer being translated. The AL-register now contains 00001100 (0C hex). The second XLAT instruction uses this AL-register value as an index into the translation table (HEX_ASCII). It loads the AL-register with the byte value at index 12 (0C hex) within array HEX_ASCII. The AL-register now contains 43 hex (the ASCII code for the letter C). The value in the AX-register is 3543 hex, which is the ASCII representation of the two-digit number 5C, which is the hexadecimal number that was in the AL-register at the beginning of the instruction sequence.

Note that the first XLAT instruction specifies no operand and that the second one specifies the operand HEX_ASCII. The two XLAT instructions translate to the same machine language instruction. In the case of the instruction

```
XLAT HEX_ASCII
```

the assembler provides some additional error checking—checking to see if HEX_ASCII is defined with type attribute BYTE and is defined in the segment that is to be addressed by the DS-register. Recall that the ASSUME pseudo-operation tells the assembler which segment register is to address a specific segment. ■

Programming Example—Secret Message Revisited

Consider again Program Listing 8.4, which translates a secret message. Program Listing 13.1 is an alternate implementation of this algorithm that uses the XLAT

```
            PAGE    80,132
;===================================================================
;                   PROGRAM LISTING 13.1
;
;PROGRAM TO TRANSLATE A SECRET MESSAGE
;===================================================================
            .MODEL  SMALL,BASIC
;===================================================================
                                        ;PROCEDURES TO
            EXTRN   GETSTRNG:FAR        ;INPUT A CHARACTER STRING
            EXTRN   PUTSTRNG:FAR        ;DISPLAY CHARACTER STRING
            EXTRN   NEWLINE:FAR         ;DISPLAY NEWLINE CHARACTER
;===================================================================
; S T A C K   S E G M E N T   D E F I N I T I O N
;
            .STACK  256
;===================================================================
; C O N S T A N T   D E F I N I T I O N S
;
            .CONST
DECODED     DB      'ABCDEFG.HIJKLMNO PQRSTUVWXYZ'
ENCODED     DB      'JEKPQBWALR.MSCUTDVNFZGYHIOX$'
PROMPT      DB      'ENTER SECRET MESSAGE',0DH,0AH
TMSG        DB      'TRANSLATED MESSAGE',0DH,0AH
CODE_LNGTH  EQU     ENCODED-DECODED     ;LENGTH OF CODE STRINGS
PROMPT_LNG  EQU     TMSG - PROMPT       ;LENGTH OF PROMPT MESSAGE
TMSG_LNG    EQU     $ - TMSG            ;LENGTH OF TMSG
;
;===================================================================
; V A R I A B L E   D E F I N I T I O N S
;
            .DATA
SECRTMSG    DB      40 DUP(?)           ;SECRET MESSAGE
TRANSMSG    DB      40 DUP(?)           ;TRANSLATED MESSAGE
COUNT       DW      ?                   ;CHARACTER COUNT OF MESSAGE
MSG_LNG     EQU     TRANSMSG - SECRTMSG ;LENGTH OF SECRET MESSAGE
;
;===================================================================
; C O D E   S E G M E N T   D E F I N I T I O N
            .CODE   EX_13_1
            .STARTUP                    ;GENERATE STARTUP CODE
            PUSH    DS                  ;SET ES-REGISTER TO ADDRESS
            POP     ES                  ;DGROUP
            CALL    NEWLINE
            LEA     DI,PROMPT           ;PROMPT FOR SECRET_MSG
            MOV     CX,PROMPT_LNG
            CALL    PUTSTRNG
            LEA     DI,SECRTMSG         ;GET SECRET_MSG AND MSG_LENGTH
            MOV     CX,MSG_LNG
            CALL    GETSTRNG
            CALL    NEWLINE
            CLD                         ;SET DF FOR INCREMENTING
            LEA     BX,DECODED
            MOV     COUNT,CX            ;COUNT = MSG_LENGTH
```

```
55:            MOV     SI,0                ;INDEX = 0
56: NEXT_CHAR:                             ;REPEAT
57:            MOV     AL,SECRTMSG[SI]     ;   CHAR = SECRET_MSG (INDEX)
58:            PUSH    CX
59:            MOV     CX,CODE_LNGTH       ;   SRCH_CNT = CODE_LNGTH
60:            LEA     DI,ENCODED          ;   SET EPTR TO BASE ADDRESS
61:                                        ;       OF ENCODED STRING
62:      REPNE SCASB                       ;   FOUND = FALSE
63:                                        ;   REPEAT
64:                                        ;      IF   EPTR->BYTE = CHAR
65:                                        ;      THEN FOUND = TRUE
66:                                        ;      ENDIF
67:                                        ;      EPTR = EPTR + 1
68:                                        ;      DECREMENT SRCH_CNT
69:                                        ;   UNTIL FOUND OR SRCH_CNT=0
70:            JE      FOUND               ;   IF   NOT FOUND
71:            MOV     TRANSMSG[SI],'*'    ;   THEN TRANS_MSG(INDEX) = *
72:            JMP     LOOPEND
73: FOUND:                                 ;   ELSE
74:            DEC     DI                  ;      EPTR = EPTR - 1
75:            MOV     AX,DI               ;      J = EPTR
76:            SUB     AX,OFFSET ENCODED   ;        - BASE ADDR OF ENCODED
77:            XLAT                        ;     CHAR = DECODED(J)
78:            MOV     TRANSMSG[SI],AL     ;      TRANS_MSG(INDEX) = CHAR
79: LOOPEND:                               ;   ENDIF
80:            INC     SI                  ;   INDEX = INDEX + 1
81:            POP     CX
82:            LOOP    NEXT_CHAR           ;   DECREMENT MSG_LENGTH
83:                                        ;UNTIL MSG_LENGTH = 0
84:            LEA     DI,TMSG             ;DISPLAY TRANS_MSG
85:            MOV     CX,TMSG_LNG
86:            CALL    PUTSTRNG
87:            LEA     DI,TRANSMSG
88:            MOV     CX,COUNT
89:            CALL    PUTSTRNG
90:            CALL    NEWLINE
91:            .EXIT                       ;RETURN TO DOS
92: ;
93:            END
94:*;=====================================================================
```

instruction to translate a character from the ENCODED alphabet to the DECODED alphabet. The stack segment and data segment definitions are the same for the two versions of the program, and both programs have the same basic structure. There is a REPEAT-UNTIL loop (lines 56–83 in Program Listing 13.1) that executes once for each character in the secret message; that is, each iteration of the loop body translates one character of the secret message. Nested within the REPEAT-UNTIL loop is a second REPEAT-UNTIL loop (lines 62–69). The inner REPEAT-UNTIL loop searches the ENCODED alphabet to find the occurrence of the character being translated, and it is followed by a double-alternative decision structure (lines 70–79) that determines whether or not the character being translated is found in the ENCODED alphabet. If it is not found, then an asterisk (*) is inserted into the translated message (line 71); if it is found, then the character in the same position of the DECODED alphabet is inserted into the translated message. The difference between Program Listing 13.1 and Program Listing 8.4 is in the "else" clause of this double-alternative decision structure.

The "else" clause (lines 74–78) translates a character from the ENCODED alphabet to the DECODED alphabet. On entry into the "else" clause, the ES:DI register pair addresses the character of the ENCODED alphabet that immediately follows the occurrence of the character being translated. The DEC instruction in line 74 adjusts the DI-register so that the ES:DI register pair addresses the character in the ENCODED alphabet that matches the character being translated. The DI-register is the offset of this ENCODED element relative to the beginning of the data segment. The MOV instruction in line 75 copies this offset to the AX-register. The SUB instruction in line 76 converts this offset to an index relative to the beginning of array ENCODED. This index is an integer in the range 0 through (CODE_LNGTH – 1) in the AL-register. The character at the same index within array DECODED is the character to be inserted in the translated message. The XLAT instruction in line 77 loads the AL-register with a copy of this character from the DECODED alphabet. The MOV instruction in line 78 inserts this character into the appropriate position of the translated message.

The XLAT instruction in line 77 assumes that the DS:BX register pair addresses the first byte of a translation table, and it uses the AL-register value as an index into this table. At the time that the XLAT instruction is executed, the BX-register has already been set to the offset within the data segment of array DECODED. This initialization was accomplished by the LEA instruction in line 53. It is done outside the outer REPEAT-UNTIL loop to ensure that the LEA instruction is executed only once. Since the BX-register is used for no other purpose, the DS:BX register pair addresses array DECODED throughout the remainder of the program execution.

Note that the XLAT instruction in line 77 has no operand specified. The instruction

```
XLAT DECODED
```

could have been used. The machine language translation would have been exactly the same. However, the assembler would have verified that DECODED was defined in the data segment with type attribute BYTE. The instruction

```
XLAT ENCODED
```

could also have been used. Again, the machine language translation would have been exactly the same. The array ENCODED is defined in the data segment with type attribute BYTE. The program still executes correctly since the DS:BX register pair correctly addresses array DECODED during execution. The incorrect operand on the XLAT instruction simply means that the program documentation is incorrect. Recall that a similar occurrence can happen with the generic form of the string instructions.

13.2 Two-Dimensional Arrays

A **two-dimensional array** is an ordered list of homogeneous data items that is logically arranged into rows and columns as shown in Table 13.1. The array in the table has *m* rows and *n* columns, and it is referred to as an *m* by *n* (written $m \times n$) array. Applications often involve data that are more conveniently viewed and processed from a two-dimensional standpoint. The grades of *m* students on each of *n* tests can be arranged in an $m \times n$ array. The element in row *i*, column *j* is the test score for student *i* on test *j*. To find the average test score for student *i*, simply sum all *n* elements of row *i* and divide this sum by *n* (the number of tests). To find the class average for test *j*, simply sum all *m* elements of column *j* and divide this sum by *m* (the number of students).

TABLE 13.1
Two-dimensional array

	Column 1	Column 2	Column 3	Column 4	...	Column n
Row 1	Row 1 Column 1	Row 1 Column 2	Row 1 Column 3	Row 1 Column 4	...	Row 1 Column n
Row 2	Row 2 Column 1	Row 2 Column 2	Row 2 Column 3	Row 2 Column 4	...	Row 2 Column n
Row 3	Row 3 Column 1	Row 3 Column 2	Row 3 Column 3	Row 3 Column 4	...	Row 3 Column n
Row 4	Row 4 Column 1	Row 4 Column 2	Row 4 Column 3	Row 4 Column 4	...	Row 4 Column n
⋮	⋮	⋮	⋮	⋮		⋮
Row m	Row m Column 1	Row m Column 2	Row m Column 3	Row m Column 4	...	Row m Column n

Linear Representations for Two-Dimensional Arrays

A computer's memory can be viewed as a one-dimensional array. In fact, the segment–offset approach to memory addressing is based on this viewpoint. A segment is like a byte array. The segment origin address, specified by the contents of a segment register, is the base address of the array. The offset is the index from this base address to the element (memory location) of interest.

Defining a two-dimensional array in terms of one-dimensional arrays leads to two natural ways of representing that array in the linear memory of a computer. A two-dimensional array can be defined as a one-dimensional array whose elements are each a row of the $m \times n$ array (an n-element, one-dimensional array). This view fits the definition of a one-dimensional array given in Chapter 8: It is an ordered list of data items; that is, there is a first element (the first row), a second element (the second row), and so on. It is a list of homogeneous data items; that is, each element of the array is an n-element, one-dimensional array. This array of arrays can be stored in memory in the same way that a byte or word array is stored in memory. That is, the array elements are stored in contiguous memory locations beginning with the first element, followed immediately by the second element, followed immediately by the third element, and so on. In the case of the $m \times n$ array viewed as a one-dimensional array of rows, the elements can be stored by row as shown in Figure 13.2, which is known as **row-major order**.

The $m \times n$ array in Table 13.1 can also be viewed as an n-element, one-dimensional array whose elements are each a column of the $m \times n$ array (an m-element, one-dimensional array). With this view, the elements can be stored by column as shown in Figure 13.3, which is known as **column-major order**.

Address Calculations

To select and use a specific element of a two-dimensional array, the subscripting operation is used. To identify an element of a two-dimensional array, two subscripts are needed: A row subscript identifies the row in which the element appears, and a column subscript identifies the column in which the element appears. An address calculation is needed to translate the row and column position to a physical memory

FIGURE 13.2 Two-dimensional array in row-major order (S is the size of an element: 1 for byte, 2 for word, 4 for double word)

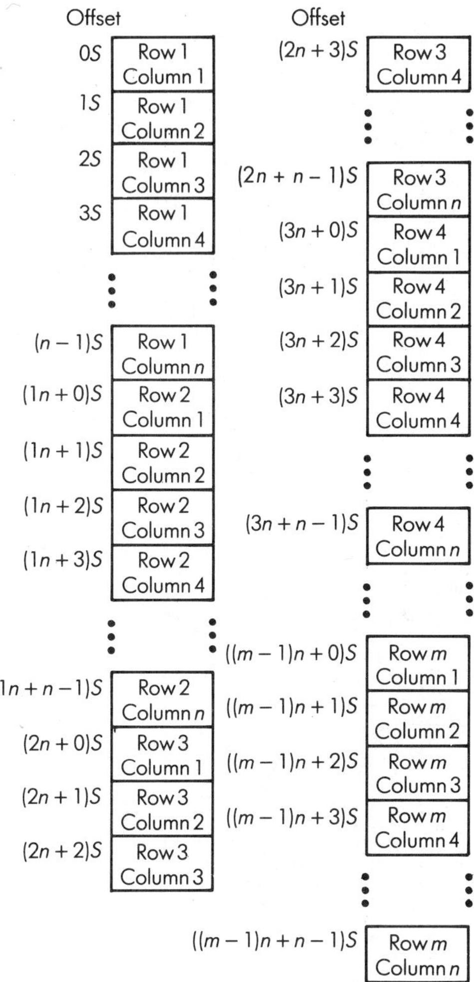

address. The formula used for the address calculation depends on whether the array is stored in row-major order or column-major order.

Consider the problem of computing the address of the element in row r, column c of an $m \times n$ array stored in row-major order. Assume that the array begins at address BASE and that each element is of size S bytes. To get to row r of the array, the first $(r - 1)$ rows must be skipped. There are $(r - 1)n$ elements in the first $(r - 1)$ rows, and each element is of size S bytes. Therefore, $(r - 1)nS$ bytes must be skipped to get to the rth row. That is, $(r - 1)nS$ is the offset from the beginning of the array to the first element of the rth row. To get to column c within a given row, $(c - 1)$ elements must be skipped. Each element is of size S bytes. Therefore, $(c - 1)S$ bytes must be skipped to get to the cth column. That is, $(c - 1)S$ is the offset from the beginning of the rth row to the element in the cth column of the rth row. The sum of these two offsets produces the offset from the beginning of the array to the element in the rth row, cth column. Therefore, for an $m \times n$ array stored in row-major order, the

FIGURE 13.3 Two-dimensional array in column-major order (S is the size of an element: 1 for byte, 2 for word, 4 for double word)

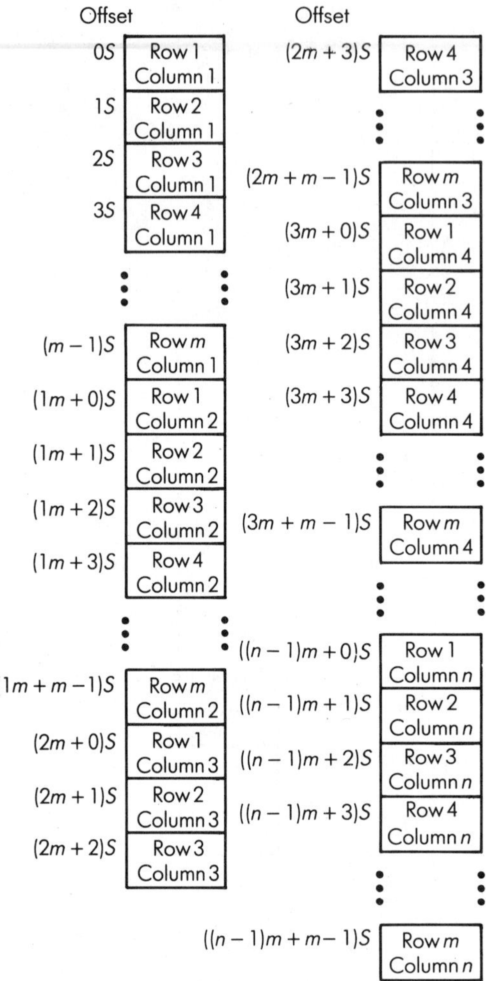

address of the element at row r, column c is computed by either

$$\text{BASE} + (r - 1)nS + (c - 1)S$$

or

$$\text{BASE} + [(r - 1)n + (c - 1)]S$$

in which BASE is the base address of the array.

EXAMPLE

Consider the two-dimensional array in Table 13.1 stored in row-major order (Figure 13.2). The offset of the element in row 3, column 4, relative to the beginning of the array, is computed as follows:

$$[(r - 1)n + (c - 1)]S$$

$$[(3 - 1)n + (4 - 1)]S$$

$$(2n + 3)S$$

Compare this result to the offset shown for that element in Figure 13.2. ■

Consider now the problem of computing the address of the element in row r, column c of an $m \times n$ array stored in column-major order. Again, assume that the array begins at address BASE and that each element is of size S bytes. To get to column c of the array, the first $(c - 1)$ columns must be skipped. There are $(c - 1)m$ elements in the first $(c - 1)$ columns, and each element is of size S bytes. Therefore, $(c - 1)mS$ is the offset from the beginning of the array to the first element of the cth column. To get to the rth element of a column, $(r - 1)$ elements must be skipped. Therefore, $(r - 1)S$ is the offset from the beginning of the cth column to the element in the rth row of the cth column. For an $m \times n$ array stored in column-major order, the address of the element at row r, column c is computed by

$$\text{BASE} + [(c - 1)m + (r - 1)]S$$

in which BASE is the base address of the array.

EXAMPLE

Consider the two-dimensional array of Table 13.1 stored in column-major order (Figure 13.3). The offset of the element in row 3, column 4, relative to the beginning of the array, is computed as follows:

$$[(c - 1)m + (r - 1)]S$$

$$[(4 - 1)m + (3 - 1)]S$$

$$(3m + 2)S$$

Compare this result to the offset shown for that element in Figure 13.3. ■

Programming Example—Procedure to Compute the Address of a Two-Dimensional Array Element Given the Row and Column

The procedure presented in this section implements one of the formulas derived in the previous section: the address calculation formula for two-dimensional arrays stored in row-major order. This example introduces the notion of an **array descriptor**, which is a data structure that contains the information necessary to describe an array's characteristics. In this chapter, an array descriptor describes a two-dimensional array. It is a seven-byte data structure that has the general form shown in Table 13.2. The type of the array (byte 4 of the descriptor) describes the size in bytes of each element of the array. Integer values greater than 4 can be used for the type. For example, a type of 8 would be used for a two-dimensional array whose elements are 64-bit

TABLE 13.2
Array descriptor

Byte(s)	Meaning
0–1	Segment portion of base address of array
2–3	Offset portion of base address of array
4	Type of array: 1 ⇒ byte array 2 ⇒ word array 4 ⇒ double-word array
5	Number of rows in array
6	Number of columns in array

integer values. The number of rows and columns in the array (bytes 5 and 6 of the descriptor) describes the overall size of the array and can be used to check out-of-range subscripts.

EXAMPLE The following data segment definition allocates storage for a 4 × 5 word array named SALES and defines a descriptor for this array:

```
DATA    SEGMENT
SALES   DW      20 DUP(?)
S_DSCR  DW      SEG SALES
        DW      OFFSET SALES
        DB      2
        DB      4
        DB      5
DATA    ENDS
```

■

The procedure in Program Listing 13.2 computes the address of a two-dimensional array element given the row and column position of the element and the

```
           PAGE    80,132
;=====================================================================
;                        PROGRAM LISTING 13.2
; PROCEDURE TO COMPUTE THE ADDRESS OF A TWO-DIMENSIONAL ARRAY
; ELEMENT  GIVEN  THE  ROW  AND COLUMN OF THE ELEMENT AND THE
; ARRAY DESCRIPTOR.  THE  ARRAY  DESCRIPTOR IS A 7-BYTE  DATA
; STRUCTURE THAT HAS THE FOLLOWING GENERAL FORM:
;
;     BYTE(S) | CONTENTS                                  | NAME
;    ---------+-------------------------------------------+-------
;       0-1   | SEGMENT PORTION OF BASE ADDRESS OF ARRAY  | SEG
;       2-3   | OFFSET  PORTION OF BASE ADDRESS OF ARRAY  | OFFSET
;        4    | TYPE OF ARRAY : 1 => BYTE; 2 => WORD      | TYPE
;             |                 4 => DOUBLEWORD           |
;        5    | NUMBER OF ROWS    IN ARRAY                | ROWS
;        6    | NUMBER OF COLUMNS IN ARRAY                | COLS
;    ---------+-------------------------------------------+-------
; INPUTS:  DS:SI  REGISTER PAIR  CONTAINS BASE ADDRESS OF ARRAY DSCR
;          DH-REG CONTAINS   ROW  NUMBER
;          DL-REG CONTAINS COLUMN NUMBER
; OUTPUTS: ES:DI  REG. PAIR  ADDRESSES 1ST ELEMENT  IN SPECIFIED ROW
;          BP-REG CONTAINS  OFFSET  WITHIN  ROW  OF SPECIFIED COLUMN
;          DX-REG CONTAINS DI-REGISTER OFFSET NEEDED TO MOVE  1  ROW
;          OF-BIT OF FLAGS REGISTER  (1  =>  OUT OF RANGE SUBSCRIPT)
;=====================================================================
           .MODEL  SMALL,BASIC
           .CODE   EX_13_2
ADDR_RM    PROC    FAR PUBLIC USES AX BX
                      ;PROCEDURE ADDR_RM(DSCR,ROW,COL,RPTR,COFF,RINC)
                                       ;SAVE REGISTERS - USES CLAUSE
           PUSHF                       ;SAVE FLAGS
           POP     BX                  ;TMP_FLGS = SAVED FLAGS
           .IF     DH==0 || DH > 5[SI] || DL==0 || DL > 6[SI]
                                       ;IF   ROW=0 OR ROW>DSCR.ROWS
                                       ;  OR COL=0 OR COL>DSCR.COLS
                                       ;THEN
           OR      BX,0800H            ;     SET OF BIT IN TMP_FLGS
           PUSH    BX                  ;     SAVED FLAGS = TMP_FLGS
           .ELSE                       ;ELSE
           AND     BX,0F7FFH           ;     CLEAR OF BIT IN TMP_FLGS
           PUSH    BX                  ;     SAVED FLAGS = TMP_FLGS
           MOV     ES,[SI]             ;     ES-REG = DSCR.SEG
           MOV     AL,4[SI]            ;     COFF = DSCR.TYPE
           DEC     DL                  ;          * (COL - 1)
           MUL     DL
           MOV     BP,AX
```

```
47:              MOV     DI,2[SI]              ;      RPTR = DSCR.OFFSET
48:              MOV     AL,4[SI]              ;           + [DSCR.TYPE
49:              DEC     DH                    ;             * (ROW - 1)
50:              MUL     DH
51:              MOV     DL,6[SI]              ;             * DSCR.COLS]
52:              MOV     DH,0
53:              MUL     DX
54:              ADD     DI,AX
55:              MOV     AL,6[SI]              ;      RINC = DSCR.COLS
56:              MUL     BYTE PTR 4[SI]        ;           * DSCR.TYPE
57:              MOV     DX,AX
58:              .ENDIF                        ;ENDIF
59:              POPF                          ;RESTORE FLAGS
60:                                            ;RESTORE REGISTERS-USES CLAUSE
61:              RET                           ;RETURN TO CALLER
62: ADDR_RM      ENDP         ;END ADDR_RM
63:*            END
```

address of the array descriptor. The prologue in lines 3–24 describes the function of the procedure, shows the general form of the array descriptor, and describes the procedure's interface requirements. On entry to the procedure, the DS:SI register pair must address the first byte of the array descriptor, the DH-register must contain the row number of the desired element, and the DL-register must contain the column number of the desired element. On return to the caller, the ES:DI register pair addresses the first element of the row that contains the desired element, the BP-register contains the offset within that row of the desired element, the DX-register contains the amount to be added to (or subtracted from) the DI-register to move one row in the array, and the OF bit of the flags register indicates whether the address generated is out of the bounds of the array. The range of legal row subscripts is from 1 to the number of rows, inclusive; the range of legal column subscripts is from 1 to the number of columns, inclusive.

The procedure begins by saving the registers specified in the USES clause (line 28) and saving the flags register (line 31). The POP instruction in line 32 pops the flags register image, saved for the caller, into the BX-register. The double-alternative decision structure in lines 33–58 checks the subscripts for an out-of-range condition. The condition for the decision structure (line 33) is a compound condition. If the row number is zero or is greater than the number of rows in the array or if the column number is zero or is greater than the number of columns in the array, then at least one of the subscripts is out of range and the instructions in lines 37 and 38 are executed. Otherwise, the subscripts are in range and the instructions in lines 40–57 are executed.

In the case of an out-of-range subscript, the OF bit of the caller's saved flags must be set. The OR instruction in line 37 sets the OF bit of the flags register image in the BX-register. The PUSH instruction in line 38 pushes the modified flags register image back onto the stack.

In the case of in-range subscripts, the OF bit of the caller's saved flags must be cleared and the address of the specified array element must be calculated. The AND instruction in line 40 clears the OF bit of the flags register image in the BX-register. The PUSH instruction in line 41 pushes the modified flags register image back onto the stack.

The instructions in lines 42–54 perform the address calculation. The MOV instruction in line 42 sets the ES-register to address the segment that contains the array. This segment address is obtained from bytes 0 and 1 of the descriptor. The operand [SI] is an example of register indirect addressing (Section 8.4).

The instructions in lines 43–46 implement the $(c - 1)S$ portion of the address calculation formula. The MOV instruction in line 43 loads the AL-register with the element size (the array type from byte 4 of the descriptor), which is the S in the formula. The DEC instruction in line 44 decrements the column subscript by 1, which is the $(c - 1)$ in the formula. The MUL instruction in line 45 computes the product of these two values, and the MOV instruction in line 46 copies this product into the BP-register. The BP-register now contains the offset from the beginning of a row to the element in the cth column of that row, in which c is the column subscript entered via the DL-register. The operand 4[SI] is an example of indexed addressing (Section 8.4).

The instructions in lines 47–54 implement the BASE + $(r - 1)nS$ portion of the address calculation formula. The MOV instruction in line 47 loads the DI-register with the offset portion of the base address of the array (bytes 2 and 3 of the descriptor), which is the BASE in the formula. The MOV instruction in line 48 loads the AL-register with the element size (the array type from byte 4 of the descriptor), which is the S in the formula. The DEC instruction in line 49 decrements the row subscript by 1, which is the $(r - 1)$ in the formula. The MUL instruction in line 50 computes the product of these two values, which produces the $(r - 1)S$ in the formula and leaves it in the AX-register. The MOV instructions in lines 51 and 52 load the DX-register with the number of columns in the array (byte 6 of the descriptor), which is the n in the formula. The MUL instruction in line 53 computes the product of this value and the value in the AX-register, which produces the $(r - 1)nS$ portion of the formula. The ADD instruction in line 54 adds this value to the base address offset in the DI-register. The ES:DI register pair now addresses the first element of the rth row of the array, in which r is the row subscript entered via the DH-register.

The instructions in lines 55–57 compute the offset increment needed to move one complete row in the array (i.e., the number of bytes in one row of the array). The MOV instruction in line 55 loads the AL-register with the number of columns in the array (byte 6 of the descriptor). The MUL instruction in line 56 multiplies this value by the element size (the array type from byte 4 of the descriptor). The MOV instruction in line 57 copies this product (the number of bytes per row in the array) to the DX-register.

The procedure terminates by restoring the flags register (line 59), with the OF bit modified, restoring the registers specified in the USES clause, and returning control to the caller (line 61). The caller can access the specified array element by the operand ES:[DI][BP], which is an example of base indexed addressing with a segment override prefix (Section 8.4). The operand ES:[DI][BP] addresses the element in row r, column c of the array, in which r is the row subscript and c is the column subscript passed to the ADDR_RM procedure. To increment this address to the next element in the array, the instruction

```
ADD BP,4[SI]
```

can be used, which adds the element size to the column offset in the BP-register. Similarly, to decrement this address to the previous element in the array, the instruction

```
SUB BP,4[SI]
```

can be used. To increment this address to the corresponding element in the next row of the array, the instruction

```
ADD DI,DX
```

can be used, which adds the number of bytes per row to the row offset in the DI-register. Similarly, to decrement this address to the corresponding element in the previous row of the array, the instruction

```
SUB DI,DX
```

can be used. A procedure that uses ADDR_RM is presented in Section 13.5.

13.3 Video Subsystems and Video Monitors

The two standard video monitors for the IBM PC and PC/XT, the IBM Monochrome Display and the IBM Color Display, each require an adapter card. The display adapter is a circuit board that contains a video controller and some random-access memory (RAM). The standard adapter for the monochrome display is the IBM Monochrome Display and Printer Adapter (MDA), and the standard adapter for the color display is the IBM Color/Graphics Adapter (CGA).

The video monitor determines the maximum number of colors that can be displayed, and the video adapter determines the subset of colors that can be displayed simultaneously. The monochrome monitor of the IBM PC can display one color, green characters on a black background. Other common monochrome monitors display amber characters on a black background. The color monitor of the IBM PC/XT is commonly referred to as an "RGB" monitor because it is driven by four digital signals, one for each of the primary additive colors (red, green, blue) and one for intensity. With four digital signals, an RGB monitor can display up to $2^4 = 16$ possible colors. MDA provides high-quality text display, but it supports only one color and provides no graphics capability. CGA provides both text and graphics display capabilities, and it supports up to 16 colors. All 16 colors can be displayed simultaneously in text mode, and 4 of the 16 colors can be displayed simultaneously in graphics mode. The quality of the text display with CGA is not as good as it is with MDA. MDA was designed to drive a monochrome monitor, and it was designed exclusively for text applications. CGA was designed to drive an RGB monitor, and it was designed primarily for graphics applications and secondarily for text applications.

IBM later introduced the IBM Enhanced Color Display along with its standard adapter, the IBM Enhanced Graphics Adapter (EGA). EGA combines the capabilities of MDA and CGA with some enhancements. IBM's Enhanced Color Display can be referred to as an "enhanced RGB" monitor because it is driven by six digital signals, two red, two green, and two blue. Two signals per color provides $2^2 = 4$ intensities (or shades) for each of the primary additive colors. With six digital signals, an enhanced RGB monitor can display up to $2^6 = 64$ possible colors. EGA can be used with a monochrome monitor, an RGB monitor, or an enhanced RGB monitor. When used with a monochrome monitor, EGA not only provides the same high-quality text display of MDA but also provides one-color graphics display capability. When used with an RGB monitor, EGA not only provides 16-color text and 4-color graphics but also provides one-color, high-quality text. When used with an enhanced RGB monitor, EGA provides high-quality, 16-color text and graphics and supports up to 64 colors. Any 16 of the 64 possible colors can be displayed simultaneously in both text and graphics modes. EGA was designed to drive monochrome, RGB, and enhanced RGB monitors, and it was designed for both text and graphics applications.

The video monitors used in the various models of the IBM PS/2 are driven by continuous analog signals rather than discrete digital signals. An analog monitor provides a much finer gradation of possible colors. Consider the analogy of an electric lamp: Most lamps have a simple on–off switch (a digital device); the lamp is either on (full intensity) or off (no intensity). However, some lamps have a continuous dimmer dial (an analog device); as the dial is rotated, the lamp goes through a fine gradation of intensities from no intensity to full intensity.

An RGB monitor is analogous to a lamp with an on–off switch. Each of the three color signals (red, green, blue) is either on or off. These three signals provide a total of $2^3 = 8$ distinct colors. The intensity signal is also either on or off. With the intensity signal, each of the 8 color combinations can be displayed with either normal intensity or high intensity. Therefore, an RGB monitor can display 16 distinct colors.

An analog monitor is analogous to a lamp with a dimmer dial. Each of the primary colors (red, green, blue) can be displayed with a fine gradation of intensities from no intensity to high intensity. Combining the primary colors provides an almost limitless number of possible colors. The number of possible colors is not limited by the video monitor but is determined by the video subsystem.

All models of the IBM PS/2 have a built-in video subsystem that resides on the main system circuit board, so a separate video adapter board is not required. Originally, the standard video subsystem for the low-end models (Models 25 and 30) was the IBM Multi-Color Graphics Array (MCGA), and the standard video subsystem for the other models (Models 50, 60, and 80) was the IBM Video Graphics Array (VGA). The standard video subsystem for some of the newer models of the IBM PS/2 (e.g., Models 85 and 90) is the IBM Extended Graphics Array (XGA). MCGA, VGA, and XGA take an 18-bit digital color signal and convert it to an analog signal using a digital-to-analog converter (DAC). The 18-bit digital signal consists of 6 bits for red, 6 bits for green, and 6 bits for blue. That is, the color signal is a combination of 1 of 64 (2^6) shades of red, 1 of 64 shades of green, and 1 of 64 shades of blue. This combination provides a total of $2^{18} = 262{,}144$ possible colors. Any 16 of the 262,144 possible colors can be displayed simultaneously in text mode, and up to 256 of the 262,144 possible colors can be displayed in graphics mode. MCGA, VGA, and XGA were designed to drive analog monitors, and they were designed for both text and graphics applications.

All of these video subsystems are capable of displaying text data on the screen. The text data being displayed at any point in time is maintained in a display buffer in the video subsystem's RAM. This display buffer is organized as a two-dimensional word array with 25 rows and 80 columns. The 25 rows correspond to the 25 lines on the video screen, and the 80 columns correspond to the 80 character positions in each line on the video screen. (It should be noted that video modes exist for which the display buffer is organized with 25 rows and 40 columns, but these modes are not covered in detail here.) Each word of this array contains the 8-bit ASCII code for a character to be displayed and an 8-bit attribute that indicates how the character is to be displayed (e.g., normal, blinking, with underscore). To display a character in the jth character position of the ith line on the screen, simply place the ASCII code and the desired attribute for the character in the word at row i, column j of this two-dimensional array.

The video controller in the video subsystem contains the circuitry to convert a character:attribute pair to an array of dots and to display that array of dots at the appropriate position on the screen. This hardware includes a character generator and an attribute decoder. The **character generator** generates an array of dots from the ASCII code, and the **attribute decoder** determines exactly how that array of dots is to appear on the screen. The video controller displays the first character in the buffer in character position 1 of line 1, the second character in the buffer in character position 2 of line 1, and so on. This method of display means that the character:

attribute pairs are stored in the video buffer in row-major order. The video controller cycles through the video buffer at least 50 times per second; that is, the complete display screen is refreshed at least 50 times per second. This cycling virtually eliminates flicker on the screen. It also means that new data placed in the buffer are displayed almost immediately.

Graphics Symbols (Extended ASCII Character Set)

The ASCII code is the 7-bit code adopted by the American National Standards Institute (ANSI). With a 7-bit code, a total of 128 characters can be represented. The first 32 binary codes in the ASCII character set, 0000000–0011111 (00 hex–1F hex), represent control characters (e.g., form feed and line feed for the printer). The remaining binary codes, 0100000–1111111 (20 hex–7F hex), represent the printable characters, including the uppercase and lowercase letters, the decimal digits, and special characters such as $, ?, SPACE,], and /.

For the PC and PS/2 families of computers, IBM has extended the standard ASCII code to an 8-bit code called **Extended ASCII**. The first 128 codes in the Extended ASCII character set, 00000000–01111111 (00 hex–7F hex), represent the standard ASCII character set. The remaining 128 binary codes, 10000000–11111111 (80 hex–FF hex), represent a variety of symbols that include graphics symbols. In addition, the binary codes 00000000–00011111 (00 hex–1F hex), are interpreted as special graphics symbols when the codes are output to the video monitor. For example, the binary code 00000011 displays a heart-shaped symbol. (See Appendix E for the complete set of symbols in the Extended ASCII character set.) All of the video subsystems are capable of generating the symbols of the Extended ASCII character set.

Video Buffer Organization

The video buffer in the video subsystem's RAM is organized as a 25 × 80 two-dimensional word array stored in row-major order. The number of elements in the array is 2000 (25 × 80), and the size of each element is 2 bytes. Therefore, 4000 bytes of memory are required for the video buffer. The address of the element at row r, column c is computed by

$$\text{BASE} + [(r - 1)80 + (c - 1)]2$$

Each element of the array contains a character:attribute pair. The first byte is the character, and the second byte is the attribute. The size and location of the video memory and the interpretation of the attribute byte depend on whether a monochrome or a color/graphics adapter is being emulated.

MDA Video Buffer

MDA has 4K RAM (4096 bytes). This memory has physical addresses B0000 hex–B0FFF hex. The video buffer is normally the first 4000 bytes of this memory space, the bytes of addresses B0000 hex–B0F9F hex. The position of the 4000-byte video buffer within this 4096-byte memory space can be altered; however, the position of the video buffer is normally kept static. The address of the element at row r, column c of the video buffer is computed by

$$\text{B0000 hex} + [(r - 1)80 + (c - 1)]2$$

The attribute byte of the character:attribute pair indicates how the character is to be displayed. Table 13.3 shows the different ways that a character can be displayed on a monochrome display and, in each case, the attribute that can be used to display a character in that way. The attributes given in Table 13.3 are the ones typically used; however, any 8-bit pattern is legal as an attribute. Figure 13.4 shows the interpretations for all possible attribute bytes.

TABLE 13.3
Attributes for MDA

Attribute (Hex)	Interpretation
00	No display
01	Normal video (green on black) with underscore beneath character
07	Normal video (green on black)
09	Intense normal video (green on black) with underscore beneath character
0F	Intense normal video (green on black)
70	Reverse video (black on green)
81	Normal video (green on black) with underscore beneath character and character and underscore blinking
87	Normal video (green on black) with character blinking
89	Intense normal video (green on black) with underscore beneath character and character and underscore blinking
8F	Intense normal video (green on black) with character blinking
F0	Reverse video (black on green) with character blinking

CGA Video Buffer

CGA has 16K RAM (16,384 bytes). This memory has physical addresses B8000 hex–BBFFF hex and houses four text video buffers, one for each of four display pages (numbered 0–3). Only one of the four pages, the **active display page**, is displayed at any point in time. The active display page is selectable via BIOS interrupt 10H. The four video buffers are normally the first 4000 bytes of each 4K block of this memory space. The physical addresses for these four video buffers are as follows: page 0, B8000–B8F9F; page 1, B9000–B9F9F; page 2, BA000–BAF9F; and page 3, BB000–BBF9F. The position of the 4000-byte active display page within this 16K memory space can be altered; however, the positions of the four pages are normally kept static. The address of the element at row r, column c of the active display page is

$$\text{B8000 hex} + 4096\,(\text{page\#}) + [(r - 1)80 + (c - 1)]2$$

in which page# is the number of the active display page.

The attribute byte of the character:attribute pair indicates how the character is to be displayed, including the colors to be used in displaying the character. The bits of the attribute byte are interpreted as shown in Figure 13.5. The blink bit (bit 7) controls whether the character is displayed blinking (bit 7 = 1) or solid (bit 7 = 0).

The background color for the character is controlled by bits 6, 5, and 4 of the attribute byte: Bit 6 selects the color red (R), bit 5 selects the color green (G), and bit 4 selects the color blue (B). Combinations of these bits are used to select a color other than the three basic colors; for example, the color magenta (purple) is achieved by

FIGURE 13.4 Complete MDA attribute interpretation

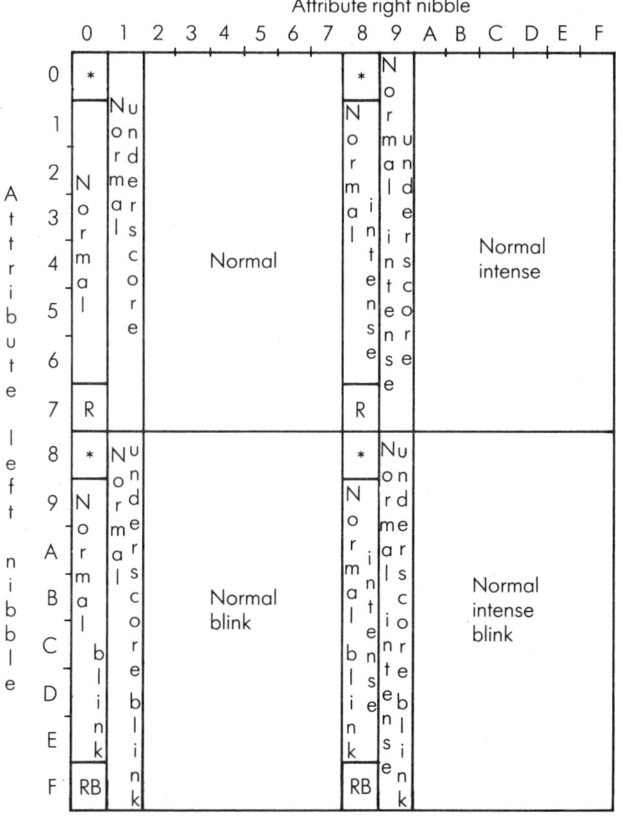

* No display
R Reverse video (black on green)
RB Reverse video blinking

FIGURE 13.5 Attribute byte for CGA

7	6	5	4	3	2	1	0
BL	Background color R	G	B	I	Foreground color R	G	B

BL Blink bit
I Intensity bit (extends foreground colors)
R Red bit
G Green bit
B Blue bit

selecting both red and blue (bits 6 and 4). Figure 13.6 describes the background color produced for each possible combination of the RGB bits (bits 6–4) of the attribute byte.

The foreground color for the character (i.e., the color of the character itself) is controlled by bits 2, 1, and 0 of the attribute byte: Bit 2 selects the color red, bit 1 selects the color green, and bit 0 selects the color blue. Again, combinations of these bits are used to select a color other than the basic colors. In addition, the intensity bit (bit 3) is used to produce a light shade of the foreground color. Figure 13.6 also describes the foreground color produced for each possible combination of the intense (I) RGB bits (bits 3–0) of the attribute byte.

Note that there is some amount of compatibility between the attribute byte for

FIGURE 13.6
Color combinations available with CGA

R	G	B	Background color
0	0	0	Black
0	0	1	Blue
0	1	0	Green
0	1	1	Cyan
1	0	0	Red
1	0	1	Magenta
1	1	0	Brown
1	1	1	Light gray

I	R	G	B	Foreground color
0	0	0	0	Black
0	0	0	1	Blue
0	0	1	0	Green
0	0	1	1	Cyan
0	1	0	0	Red
0	1	0	1	Magenta
0	1	1	0	Brown
0	1	1	1	Light gray
1	0	0	0	Dark gray
1	0	0	1	Light blue
1	0	1	0	Light green
1	0	1	1	Light cyan
1	1	0	0	Light red
1	1	0	1	Light magenta
1	1	1	0	Yellow
1	1	1	1	White

CGA and that for MDA: Bit 7 is the blink bit, and bit 3 is the intensity bit in both cases. The CGA attribute for white on black is the same as the MDA attribute for normal video (green on black). The CGA attribute for black on white is the same as the MDA attribute for reverse video (black on green). These compatibilities make it easier to produce programs that are compatible with both monitors.

EGA and VGA Video Buffer

EGA and VGA have 128K RAM (131,072 bytes). This memory has physical addresses A0000 hex–BFFFF hex and houses eight text video buffers, one for each of eight display pages (numbered 0–7). Only one of the eight pages, the active display page, is displayed at any point in time. The active display page is selectable via BIOS interrupt 10H. EGA and VGA can emulate either CGA text display (video modes 2 and 3) or MDA text display (video mode 7). The video mode is selectable via BIOS interrupt 10H. For MDA emulation, the default text mode is video mode 7, and the physical addresses for the eight video buffers are as follows: page 0, B0000–B0F9F; page 1, B1000–B1F9F; page 2, B2000–B2F9F; and so on, to page 7, B7000–B7F9F. For CGA emulation, the default text mode is video mode 3, and the physical addresses for the eight video buffers are as follows: page 0, B8000–B8F9F; page 1, B9000–B9F9F; page 2, BA000–BAF9F; and so on, to page 7, BF000–BFF9F. The address of the element at row r, column c of the active display page is

MDA emulation

$$\text{B0000 hex} + 4096\,(\text{page\#}) + [(r - 1)80 + (c - 1)]2$$

CGA emulation

$$\text{B8000 hex} + 4096\,(\text{page\#}) + [(r - 1)80 + (c - 1)]2$$

in which page # is the number of the active display page.

The attribute byte of the character:attribute pair indicates how the character is to be displayed. In MDA emulation, the attribute byte is interpreted as shown in Table 13.3. It should be noted that the additional interpretations shown in Figure 13.4 are not all valid for EGA (or VGA) emulation of MDA. In CGA emulation, the attribute byte is interpreted in exactly the same way as it is with CGA. The colors shown in Figure 13.6 are the default colors for the EGA emulation of CGA. However, these colors can be replaced with any 16 of the 64 possible colors when EGA is used with an enhanced RGB monitor. The colors shown in Figure 13.6 are also the default colors for the VGA emulation of CGA. However, these colors can be replaced with any 16 of the 262,144 possible VGA colors. Changing color palettes with EGA and VGA is beyond the scope of this discussion.

MCGA Video Buffer

MCGA has 64K RAM (65,536 bytes). This memory has physical addresses A0000 hex–AFFFF hex. For compatibility with CGA, the second half of this memory space (addresses A8000–AFFFF) can also be referenced with addresses B8000–BFFFF. This second half houses eight text video buffers, one for each of eight display pages (numbered 0–7). Only one of the eight pages, the active display page, is displayed at any point in time. The active display page is selectable via BIOS interrupt 10H. MCGA emulates CGA for text display. The physical addresses for the eight video buffers are as follows: page 0, A8000–A8F9F (or B8000–B8F9F); page 1, A9000–A9F9F (or B9000–B9F9F); page 2, AA000–AAF9F (or BA000–BAF9F); and so on, to page 7, AF000–AFF9F (or BF000–BFF9F). The address of the element at row r, column c of the active display page is either

$$\text{A8000 hex} + 4096\,(\text{page}\#) + [(r-1)80 + (c-1)]2$$

or

$$\text{B8000 hex} + 4096\,(\text{page}\#) + [(r-1)80 + (c-1)]2$$

in which page# is the number of the active display page.

The attribute byte is interpreted in exactly the same way as it is with CGA. The colors shown in Figure 13.6 are the default colors for the MCGA emulation of CGA. However, these colors can be replaced with any 16 of the 262,144 possible MCGA colors. Changing color palettes with MCGA is beyond the scope of this discussion.

13.4 Text Graphics (A Two-Dimensional Array Application)

The text video buffer can be viewed as a two-dimensional array of character:attribute pairs. Direct access of the video buffer facilitates the display of textual shapes on the video screen. BIOS service procedures available through software interrupt Types 10 hex and 11 hex are useful in accessing the video buffers. Procedure ADDR_RM, presented in Section 13.2, is also useful in accessing the video buffers.

BIOS Interrupts Revisited

Section 9.3 discussed the BIOS service procedures available through software interrupts Types 10 hex–1F hex. Interrupt 10 hex provides video I/O services, of which several options are useful in accessing the video buffers. Interrupt 11 hex provides the capability for determining the equipment that is attached to the microcomputer system, and it can be used to determine the microcomputer's initial video mode.

The BIOS procedure that services interrupt Type 10 hex uses the value in the AH-register as a subfunction code (Table 9.3). A subfunction code of 0 selects the video mode. The video mode number is passed to the interrupt 10 hex service procedure via the AL-register. The legal mode numbers are summarized in Table 9.3. For example, to select video mode 3, the following instruction sequence can be used:

```
MOV  AH,0
MOV  AL,3
INT  10H
```

BIOS sets the initial video mode at the time of system start-up. The initial video mode is always a text mode. For MDA, the initial video mode is mode 7, the standard monochrome text mode. Mode 7 is the only video mode available with MDA. For CGA, MCGA, and VGA, the initial video mode is mode 3, the standard 25-line by 80-column text mode. For EGA, the initial video mode is mode 7 or mode 3, depending on whether the EGA is driving a monochrome or a color monitor. Mode 1, the standard 25-line by 40-column text mode, was used as the initial video mode when a TV set was used as the video monitor. There are two additional text modes, mode 0 and mode 2. When CGA is used with a monochrome video monitor, mode 0 is used instead of mode 1 for 25-line by 40-column text mode, and mode 2 is used instead of mode 3 for 25-line by 80-column text mode. With EGA, MCGA, and VGA, mode 0 is equivalent to mode 1, and mode 2 is equivalent to mode 3.

An interrupt 10 hex subfunction code of 5 selects the active display page for CGA, EGA, MCGA, and VGA. The page number of the page being selected is passed to the interrupt 10 hex service procedure via the AL-register. The legal page numbers are 0, 1, 2, and 3 for CGA and 0, 1, 2, 3, 4, 5, 6, and 7 for EGA, MCGA, and VGA. For example, to select page 2 (the third page) as the active page, the following instruction sequence can be used:

```
MOV  AH,5
MOV  AL,2
INT  10H
```

A subfunction code of 15 reads the current video mode, the current screen width (40 or 80 characters), and the active display page number. For instance, the instruction sequence

```
MOV  AH,15
INT  10H
```

causes the screen width to be loaded into the AH-register, the current video mode to be loaded into the AL-register, and the active display page number to be loaded into the BH-register. Several interrupt 10 hex subfunctions require the page number as an input (Table 9.3). To communicate with the active page, it is necessary first to determine which is the active page.

The BIOS procedure that services interrupt Type 11 hex returns a value in the AX-register that summarizes the equipment attached to the microcomputer system (Table 9.4). Bits 5 and 4 indicate the initial video mode and therefore can be used to set the video mode to an appropriate text mode if the video subsystem is not currently in a text mode. If both bits are set, then the initial video mode is mode 7; if only bit 5 is set, then the initial video mode is mode 3; if only bit 4 is set, then the initial video mode is mode 1.

Program Listing 13.3 shows a function, named IN_TMODE, that checks to see if the video subsystem is currently in a text mode. The function expects no inputs. If the video subsystem is in a text mode, then the function simply returns the screen width in the AH-register and the mode number in the AL-register. However, if the video subsystem is not in a text mode, then the function sets it to the text mode specified by the initial video mode and returns control to the caller with that mode number in the AL-register and the screen width in the AH-register. The function

```
            PAGE    80,132
;=====================================================================
;                   PROGRAM LISTING 13.3
;
; FUNCTION TO VERIFY THAT THE VIDEO SUBSYSTEM IS CURRENTLY IN A TEXT
; MODE. IF NOT IN A TEXT MODE, THE FUNCTION SETS THE VIDEO SUBSYSTEM
; TO THE MODE SPECIFIED BY THE INITIAL VIDEO MODE, WHICH IS RETURNED
; BY SOFTWARE INTERRUPT TYPE 11 HEX.
; THE FUNCTION VALUE,  <SCREEN WIDTH:MODE>,  IS RETURNED  IN THE AX.
;
; INPUT:    NONE
; OUTPUTS:  AH-REGISTER CONTAINS SCREEN WIDTH
;           AL-REGISTER CONTAINS  VIDEO  MODE
;=====================================================================
            .MODEL  SMALL,BASIC
;=====================================================================
            .CODE   EX_13_3
IN_TMODE    PROC    FAR PUBLIC          ;FUNCTION IN_TMODE
;
            PUSH    BX                      ;SAVE BX-REGISTER
            PUSHF                           ;SAVE FLAGS
            MOV     AH,15                   ;GET <WIDTH:MODE>
            INT     10H
            .IF   AL > 3 && AL != 7
                                            ;IF   MODE IS NOT A TEXT MODE
;
;
            INT     11H                     ;THEN
            AND     AX,30H                  ;      GET INIT_MODE
            .IF     AX == 10H               ;      IF   INIT_MODE = 1
                                            ;      THEN
            MOV     AX,2801H                ;           WIDTH = 40
                                            ;           MODE  = 1
;
            .ELSE                           ;      ELSE
            .IF     AX == 20H               ;           IF   INIT_MODE = 2
                                            ;           THEN
            MOV     AX,5003H                ;                WIDTH = 80
                                            ;                MODE  = 3
;
            .ELSE                           ;           ELSE
            MOV     AX,5007H                ;                WIDTH = 80
                                            ;                MODE  = 7
            .ENDIF                          ;           ENDIF
            .ENDIF                          ;      ENDIF
            PUSH    AX                      ;      PUSH <WIDTH:MODE>
            MOV     AH,0                    ;      SET VIDEO MODE = MODE
            INT     10H
            POP     AX                      ;      POP  <WIDTH:MODE>
            .ENDIF                          ;ENDIF
            POPF                            ;RESTORE FLAGS
            POP     BX                      ;RESTORE BX-REGISTER
            RET                             ;RETURN (<WIDTH:MODE>)
IN_TMODE    ENDP                        ;END IN_TMODE
;=====================================================================
            END
```

begins by saving the BX-register (line 20) and the flags register (line 21). Subfunction 15 of interrupt Type 10 hex is invoked to read the screen width into the AH-register and the video mode number into the AL-register (lines 22 and 23).

The single-alternative decision structure in lines 24–50 tests the mode number to determine whether the video subsystem is currently in a text mode. If the current video mode is a text mode, then control goes to the ENDIF in line 50 with the screen width in the AH-register and the mode number in the AL-register. If the current video mode is not a text mode, then the instructions in lines 28–49 are executed. The INT instruction in line 28 invokes the interrupt Type 11 hex service procedure to determine the initial video mode. The code in bits 5 and 4 of the value returned in the AX-register indicates the initial video mode. The AND instruction in line 29 isolates this two-bit code, and the nested double-alternative decision structure in lines 30–45 sets the AL-register to the mode number specified by this code and sets the AH-register to the appropriate screen width. The instructions in lines 47 and 48 set the video subsystem to this initial mode. Since the AH-register is needed as an input to the interrupt 10 hex service procedure (line 47), the screen width stored in the AH-register must be saved and restored. The PUSH instruction in line 46 and the POP instruction in line 49 perform this function.

When the ENDIF in line 50 is reached, the AH-register contains the screen width and the AL-register contains the video mode number, which is a text video mode. The function terminates by restoring the flags register (line 51), restoring the BX-register (line 52), and returning control to the caller (line 53). The screen width is in the AH-register and the video mode number is in the AL-register when control is returned to the caller.

Video Buffer Descriptor

Section 13.2 presented the procedure ADDR_RM, which computes the physical address of a two-dimensional array element given that element's row and column position and the array descriptor's address. If array descriptors are defined for the text video buffers, then the ADDR_RM procedure can be used to access the video buffers.

Program Listing 13.4 shows a subprocedure, named BLD_DSCR, that builds a video descriptor for the specified page of the video buffer. The inputs to the subprocedure are the video page number in the BH-register and the address of an array in the DS:SI register pair. The subprocedure builds the video descriptor in the array addressed by the DS:SI register pair. The subprocedure begins by saving the registers specified in the USES clause (line 25) and saving the flags register (line 29). The CALL instruction in line 30 invokes the function IN_TMODE to verify that the video subsystem is in a text mode and to obtain the screen width and the mode number. On return from this function, the screen width is in the AH-register and the mode number is in the AL-register.

The remainder of the subprocedure builds the video buffer descriptor in the caller's array. The MOV instruction in line 31 sets the fifth byte of the descriptor to 2, the size of the elements in the video buffer (2 bytes or 1 word). The MOV instruction in line 32 sets the sixth byte of the descriptor to 25, the number of rows in the video buffer. The MOV instruction in line 33 sets the seventh byte of the descriptor to the screen width returned by IN_TMODE. The screen width is either 40 or 80, the number of columns in the video buffer.

The double-alternative decision structure in lines 34–40 sets the first word (bytes 0 and 1) of the descriptor to the segment origin of the video buffer. If the video

```
 1:             PAGE     80,132
 2: ;======================================================================
 3: ;                        PROGRAM LISTING 13.4
 4: ;
 5: ; PROCEDURE TO BUILD  A VIDEO BUFFER DESCRIPTOR IN THE ARRAY POINTED
 6: ; TO BY THE DS:SI REGISTER PAIR. THE PROCEDURE BUILDS THE DESCRIPTOR
 7: ; FOR ANY MDA, CGA, EGA, MCGA, OR VGA TEXT MODE.  PROCEDURE IN_TMODE
 8: ; IS USED TO VERIFY  THAT THE VIDEO SUBSYSTEM IS CURRENTLY IN A TEXT
 9: ; MODE.  IF NOT  IN A TEXT MODE,  PROCEDURE IN_TMODE  SETS THE VIDEO
10: ; SUBSYSTEM TO THE MODE SPECIFIED BY THE INITIAL VIDEO MODE RETURNED
11: ; BY SOFTWARE INTERRUPT TYPE 11 HEX.
12: ;
13: ; INPUTS: BH-REGISTER CONTAINS PAGE NUMBER  (CGA, EGA, MCGA AND VGA)
14: ;         DS:SI REGISTER PAIR  CONTAINS ADDRESS  OF ARRAY,  IN WHICH
15: ;               DESCRIPTOR IS TO BE BUILT.
16: ; OUTPUT: VIDEO DESCRIPTOR IN ARRAY ADDRESSED BY DS:SI REGISTER PAIR
17: ;======================================================================
18:             .MODEL   SMALL,BASIC
19: ;======================================================================
20:                                            ;FUNCTION TO
21:             EXTRN    IN_TMODE:FAR          ;VERIFY THAT VIDEO SUBSYSTEM
22:                                            ;IS IN A TEXT MODE
23: ;======================================================================
24:             .CODE    EX_13_4
25: BLD_DSCR    PROC     FAR PUBLIC USES AX BX DX
26:                                          ;PROCEDURE BLD_DSCR (PAGE_#,PTR)
27:                                            ;SAVE REGISTERS SPECIFIED
28:                                            ;     IN USES CLAUSE
29:             PUSHF                          ;SAVE FLAGS
30:             CALL     IN_TMODE              ;<WIDTH:MODE> = IN_TMODE()
31:             MOV      BYTE PTR 4[SI],2      ;[PTR+4]->BYTE = 2
32:             MOV      BYTE PTR 5[SI],25     ;[PTR+5]->BYTE = 25
33:             MOV      BYTE PTR 6[SI],AH     ;[PTR+6]->BYTE = WIDTH
34:             .IF      AL == 7               ;IF   MODE = 7
35: ;                                          ;THEN
36:             MOV      WORD PTR [SI],0B000H;      PTR->WORD = B000 HEX
37: ;
38:             .ELSE                          ;ELSE
39:             MOV      WORD PTR [SI],0B800H;      PTR->WORD = B800 HEX
40:             .ENDIF                         ;ENDIF
41:             AND      AX,1800H              ;CONVERT WIDTH TO PAGE_SIZE
42:             MOV      BL,BH                 ;[PTR+2]->BYTE = PAGE_SIZE
43:             MOV      BH,0                  ;                * PAGE_#
44:             MUL      BX
45:             MOV      WORD PTR 2[SI],AX
46:             POPF                           ;RESTORE FLAGS
47:                                            ;RESTORE REGISTERS SPECIFIED
48:                                            ;      IN USES CLAUSE
49:             RET                            ;RETURN TO CALLER
50: BLD_DSCR    ENDP                         ;END BLD_DSCR
51: ;======================================================================
52:*            END
```

mode is mode 7, then the segment origin in the descriptor is set to B000 hex, the origin of the MDA text video buffer (line 36). For all other video modes, the segment origin is set to B800 hex, the origin of the CGA, EGA, MCGA, and VGA text video buffers (line 39).

The AND instruction in line 41 converts the screen width in the AH-register to page size in the AX-register. The value in the AX-register, before execution of the AND instruction, is either 28*xx* hex or 50*xx* hex, where *xx* is the mode number in the AL-register. The value in the AH-register is either 28 hex (40 decimal) or 50 hex (80 decimal). Execution of the AND instruction leaves the AX-register with either 0800 hex (2048 decimal) or 1000 hex (4096 decimal), which is the correct page size for the corresponding screen width.

The instructions in lines 42–44 compute the offset from the origin of the video buffer to the beginning of the specified page within that buffer. The MOV instructions in lines 42 and 43 expand the page number from an 8-bit value in the BH-register to a 16-bit value in the BX-register. The MUL instruction in line 44 multiplies the page number in the BX-register by the page size in the AX-register, producing the offset from the beginning of the video buffer to the beginning of the specified page. The MOV instruction in line 45 sets the second word (bytes 2 and 3) of the descriptor to this offset.

The subprocedure terminates by restoring the flags (line 46), restoring the registers specified in the USES clause, and returning control to the caller (line 49). The array addressed by the DS:SI register pair contains the descriptor for the specified page of the appropriate video buffer.

13.5 Programming Examples

Program Listing 13.5 uses the two-dimensional array components developed in Program Listings 13.2, 13.3, and 13.4 and one additional component to display and move a face around on a video screen. The additional component, shown in Program Listing 13.5, is a procedure to display a predefined figure (shape) on the screen.

Procedure to Display a Predefined Shape

The procedure in Program Listing 13.5 moves a predefined shape into a specified

```
            PAGE    80,132
;===================================================================
;                   PROGRAM LISTING 13.5
; DISPLAY  A TEXTUAL SHAPE  AT A SPECIFIED POSITION  ON VIDEO SCREEN
; INPUTS:  DS:SI  REGISTER PAIR  ADDRESSES ARRAY  CONTAINING  SHAPE.
;                 FIRST 2 BYTES OF ARRAY CONTAIN SHAPE SIZE  (NUMBER
;                 OF ROWS & COLUMNS).  EACH SUBSEQUENT PAIR OF BYTES
;                 IS A <CHAR:ATTR> PAIR TO BE STORED IN VIDEO BUFFER
;          BH-REG CONTAINS VIDEO PAGE NUMBER
;          DH:DL  CONTAINS  (ROW,COL)  OF STARTING  DISPLAY POSITION
; OUTPUT:  SHAPE DISPLAYED AT SPECIFIED POSITION ON THE VIDEO SCREEN
;===================================================================
            .MODEL  SMALL,BASIC
                                          ;PROCEDURE TO
            EXTRN   ADDR_RM:FAR           ;COMPUTE ADDR OF 2D ARRAY REF
            EXTRN   BLD_DSCR:FAR          ;BUILD VIDEO BUFFER DESCRIPTOR
;======D A T A  S E G M E N T  D E F I N I T I O N===============
            .FARDATA DSCR_DATA
DSCR        DB      7 DUP(?)              ;VIDEO BUFFER DESCRIPTOR
;======C O D E  S E G M E N T  D E F I N I T I O N===============
            .CODE   EX_13_5
PUTSHAPE    PROC    FAR PUBLIC USES AX BX CX DX DI SI BP ES
                           ;PROCEDURE PUTSHAPE(SPTR,PAGE_#,ROW,COL)
                                          ;SAVE REGISTERS - USES CLAUSE
            PUSHF                         ;SAVE FLAGS
            PUSH    DS                    ;SAVE SPTR
            PUSH    SI
            MOV     AX,SEG DSCR_DATA      ;SET DS-REGISTER TO ADDRESS
            MOV     DS,AX                 ;SEGMENT DSCR_DATA
            LEA     SI,DSCR               ;DPTR = ADDRESS OF DSCR
            CALL    BLD_DSCR              ;CALL BLD_DSCR (PAGE_#,DPTR)
            CALL    ADDR_RM               ;CALL ADDR(DPTR,ROW,COL,
                                          ;          RPTR,COFF,RINC)
```

```
34:             POP     SI                      ;RESTORE SPTR
35:             POP     DS
36:             CLD                             ;SET DF FOR INCREMENTING
37:             LODSB                           ;#_ROWS = SPTR->BYTE
38:             MOV     AH,0                    ;SPTR = SPTR + 1
39:             MOV     CX,AX
40:             LODSB                           ;#_COLS = SPTR->BYTE
41:             MOV     BX,AX                   ;SPTR = SPTR + 1
42:             .REPEAT                         ;REPEAT
43:             PUSH    BX                      ;   SAVE #_COLS
44:             PUSH    BP                      ;   SAVE COFF
45: _REPEAT:                                    ;   REPEAT
46:             LODSW                           ;      (RPTR+COFF)->WORD =
47:             MOV     ES:[DI][BP],AX          ;                 SPTR->WORD
48:                                             ;      SPTR = SPTR + 2
49:             ADD     BP,2                    ;      COFF = COFF + 2
50:             DEC     BX                      ;      #_COLS = #_COLS - 1
51:             JNE     _REPEAT                 ;   UNTIL #_COLS = 0
52:             POP     BP                      ;   RESTORE COFF
53:             POP     BX                      ;   RESTORE #_COLS
54:             ADD     DI,DX                   ;   RPTR = RPTR + RINC
55:             .UNTILCXZ                       ;   #_ROWS = #_ROWS - 1
56:                                             ;UNTIL #_ROWS = 0
57:             POPF                            ;RESTORE FLAGS
58:                                             ;RESTORE REGISTERS SPECIFIED
59:                                             ;        IN USES CLAUSE
60:             RET                             ;RETURN TO CALLER
61: PUTSHAPE    ENDP                ;END PUTSHAPE
62: ;==================================================================
63:             END
```

position of the video buffer. The shape must be stored in a data structure of the form shown in Figure 13.7. The first word of the structure specifies the size of the shape. The first byte of this word contains the number of rows (*m*), and the second byte contains the number of columns (*n*) required to display the shape. The remainder of the structure is an $m \times n$ two-dimensional word array stored in row-major order that contains the character:attribute pairs that define the shape.

EXAMPLE

The face in Figure 13.8 is a textual shape that requires 7 rows and 11 columns. Figure 13.9 shows the data structure used to represent this shape in memory. The row offsets and the contents of this data structure are shown in hexadecimal. The first word of the structure (the word at offset 0000) contains the size of the shape (7×11). The remainder of the structure is a 7×11 two-dimensional array that contains the character:attribute pairs that describe the shape.

Consider row 3 of the shape (the row that contains the eyes). This row begins at offset 002E relative to the beginning of the data structure. The first and last columns of this row contain the value 2A07 hex. The byte value 2A hex is the ASCII code for an asterisk (*). The byte value 07 is the attribute for normal video with a monochrome adapter or for white on black with a color/graphics adapter. The fourth and eighth columns of this row contain the value 2B07 hex. The byte value 2B hex is the ASCII code for a plus sign (+). Again, the attribute is normal video (white on black). The remaining columns of this row contain the value 2007 hex. The byte value 20 hex is the ASCII code for a space (blank). Again, the attribute is normal video (white on black). ■

The procedure in Program Listing 13.5 displays a textual shape at a specified position on the video screen. The prologue in lines 3–11 explains the function of the procedure and describes its interface requirements. On entry to the procedure, the

FIGURE 13.7
Word array to store a shape

Offset		
0000	Number of rows (m)	Number of columns (n)
0002	Character for row 1 column 1	Attribute for row 1 column 1
0004	Character for row 1 column 2	Attribute for row 1 column 2
0006	Character for row 1 column 3	Attribute for row 1 column 3
⋮	⋮	⋮
$(2n)$	Character for row 1 column n	Attribute for row 1 column n
$(2n + 2)$	Character for row 2 column 1	Attribute for row 2 column 1
$(2n + 4)$	Character for row 2 column 2	Attribute for row 2 column 2
$(2n + 6)$	Character for row 2 column 3	Attribute for row 2 column 3
⋮	⋮	⋮
$(4n)$	Character for row 2 column n	Attribute for row 2 column n
⋮	⋮	⋮
$2(m - 1)n + 2$	Character for row m column 1	Attribute for row m column 1
$2(m - 1)n + 4$	Character for row m column 2	Attribute for row m column 2
$2(m - 1)n + 6$	Character for row m column 3	Attribute for row m column 3
⋮	⋮	⋮
$(2mn)$	Character for row m column n	Attribute for row m column n

FIGURE 13.8
Face described by Figure 13.9

FIGURE 13.9
Two-dimensional array describing face in Figure 13.8

Offset											
0000	070B										
0002	2007	2007	2A07	2A07	2A07	2A07	2A07	2A07	2A07	2007	2007
0018	2007	2A07	2007	2007	2007	2007	2007	2007	2007	2A07	2007
002E	2A07	2007	2007	2B07	2007	2007	2007	2B07	2007	2007	2A07
0044	2A07	2007	2007	2007	2007	5E07	2007	2007	2007	2007	2A07
005A	2A07	2007	2007	5C07	5F07	5F07	5F07	2F07	2007	2007	2A07
0070	2007	2A07	2007	2007	2007	2007	2007	2007	2007	2A07	2007
0086	2007	2007	2A07	2A07	2A07	2A07	2A07	2A07	2A07	2007	2007

DS:SI register pair must address the data structure that contains the shape, the BH-register must contain the video page number, and the DH and DL registers must contain the row and column, respectively, at which the shape is to begin on the screen. The PUTSHAPE procedure simply copies the shape into the appropriate position of the video buffer.

The PUTSHAPE procedure references two external procedures as indicated by the EXTRN pseudo-operations in lines 15 and 16. The external procedure ADDR_RM, from Program Listing 13.2, is used to compute the address of the element in a specified row and column of the video buffer. The external procedure BLD_DSCR, from Program Listing 13.4, is used to build the two-dimensional array descriptor for the specified page of the video buffer. Recall that procedure BLD_DSCR references procedure IN_TMODE from Program Listing 13.3.

The local data segment defined in lines 18 and 19 contains a seven-byte array named DSCR. This array will hold the descriptor for the specified page of the video buffer. The address of this array is an input to procedures BLD_DSCR and ADDR_RM.

PUTSHAPE begins by saving the registers specified in the USES clause (line 22) and saving the flags register (line 25). The instructions in lines 26–35 set the ES:DI:BP register group to address the element in the video buffer specified by the row and column values input to PUTSHAPE via the DH- and DL-registers. The PUSH instructions in lines 26 and 27 save the pointer to the data structure containing the shape so that the DS:SI register pair can be used to address the descriptor for the video buffer. The instructions in lines 28–30 set the DS:SI register pair to address the array DSCR in the local data segment. The CALL instruction in line 31 invokes the BLD_DSCR procedure with the DS:SI register pair addressing the array into which the video buffer descriptor is to be loaded and the BH-register containing the video page number. The video page number was input to PUTSHAPE also via the BH-register. BLD_DSCR loads the specified array with the descriptor for the specified page of the video buffer. The CALL instruction in line 32 invokes the ADDR_RM procedure with the DS:SI register pair addressing the descriptor for the video buffer, the DH-register containing the row number, and the DL-register containing the column number. ADDR_RM returns with the ES:DI register pair addressing the beginning of the desired row in the video buffer, the BP-register containing the offset within that row of the desired column, and the DX-register containing the offset increment needed to move one row within the video buffer. The POP instructions in lines 34 and 35 restore the DS:SI register pair to readdress the data structure that contains the shape to be displayed. The descriptor for the video buffer is no longer needed.

To display the shape beginning at row r, column c on the video screen, a copy of the $m \times n$ two-dimensional array that describes the shape must be stored in the video buffer as follows:

1. Row 1 of the shape array must be copied into row r of the video buffer in column positions c through $(c + n - 1)$.
2. Row 2 of the shape array must be copied into row $(r + 1)$ of the video buffer in column positions c through $(c + n - 1)$.
3. Row 3 of the shape array must be copied into row $(r + 2)$ of the video buffer in column positions c through $(c + n - 1)$.

.
.
.

m. Row m of the shape array must be copied into row $(r + m - 1)$ of the video buffer in column positions c through $(c + n - 1)$.

The nested REPEAT-UNTIL loops in lines 42–56 perform this copy operation. The body of the outer loop is executed once for each row in the shape array, and the body of the inner loop is executed once for each column in the shape array. The instructions in lines 36–41 perform the initialization for this nested loop structure. The CLD instruction in line 36 sets the DF bit of the flags register for incrementing through the shape array. The LODSB instruction in line 37 loads the AL-register with the number of rows in the shape array, and the MOV instructions in lines 38 and 39 expand this value to 16 bits and move it to the CX-register. The CX-register is used as the loop counter for the outer REPEAT-UNTIL loop. The LODSB instruction in line 40 loads the AL-register with the number of columns in the shape array, and the MOV instructions in lines 38 and 41 expand this value to 16 bits and move it to the BX-register. The BX-register is used as the loop counter for the inner REPEAT-UNTIL loop.

The outer REPEAT-UNTIL loop is implemented by the instructions in lines 42–56. The body of the outer loop begins by saving the data needed for performing reinitialization for the inner loop. The PUSH instruction in line 43 saves the number of columns in the shape array, the loop counter for the inner loop. The PUSH instruction in line 44 saves the offset from the beginning of a row to the column at which the display of the shape is to begin. Next, the inner REPEAT-UNTIL loop copies one row of the shape array to the video buffer.

The inner REPEAT-UNTIL loop is implemented by the instructions in lines 45–51. The body of the inner loop executes once for each column in the shape array. The LODSW instruction in line 46 loads the AX-register with a word (character:attribute pair) from the shape array (the array addressed by the DS:SI register pair) and then increments the SI-register by 2 so that the DS:SI register pair addresses the next word of the shape array. The MOV instruction in line 47 copies this character:attribute pair from the AX-register to the element of the video buffer that is addressed by the ES:DI:BP register group. The ADD instruction in line 49 increments the BP-register by 2 so that the ES:DI:BP register group addresses the next element of the video buffer. The operand ES:[DI][BP] is an example of base indexed addressing (Section 8.4). The segment portion of the address is specified by the contents of the ES-register. The offset portion of the address is the sum of the contents of the DI-register and the contents of the BP-register. The ES:DI register pair addresses the element at the beginning of a row, and the BP-register contains the offset from the beginning of the row to the element of interest. The DEC instruction in line 50 decrements the inner loop counter by 1, and the JNE instruction in line 51 transfers control back to the top of the inner loop (line 45) if this loop counter is nonzero.

Suppose that the shape is described by an $m \times n$ two-dimensional array and that the shape is to be displayed beginning at row r, column c on the video screen. On the kth iteration of the outer loop ($k \leqslant m$), the inner loop copies the kth row of the shape into row $(r + k - 1)$ of the video buffer in column positions c through $(c + n - 1)$. On entering the inner loop, the DS:SI register pair addresses the first element of the kth row of the shape, the ES:DI register pair addresses the first element of row $(r + k - 1)$ of the video buffer, and the BP-register contains the offset from the beginning of the row to the element in the cth column. The inner loop moves the kth row of the shape array to the video buffer as follows:

1. The first iteration of the inner loop copies the first element of the kth row of the shape array to row $(r + k - 1)$, column c of the video buffer.

2. The second iteration of the inner loop copies the second element of the kth row of the shape array to row $(r + k - 1)$, column $(c + 1)$ of the video buffer.
3. The third iteration of the inner loop copies the third element of the kth row of the shape array to row $(r + k - 1)$, column $(c + 2)$ of the video buffer.

.
.
.

n. The nth iteration of the inner loop copies the nth element of the kth row of the shape array to row $(r + k - 1)$, column $(c + n - 1)$ of the video buffer.

The LODSW instruction in line 46 increments the SI-register so that the DS:SI register pair increments through the kth row of the shape array. The ADD instruction in line 49 increments the BP-register so that the ES:DI:BP register group increments through row $(r + k - 1)$ of the video buffer from column c through column $(c + n - 1)$. On exit from the kth execution of the inner loop, the DS:SI register pair addresses the first element of row $(k + 1)$ of the shape array.

Following execution of the inner loop, the outer loop body continues by performing inner loop initialization in preparation for the next iteration of the outer loop body. The POP instruction in line 52 restores the column offset to the offset from the beginning of a row to the column at which the shape's display is to begin (saved in line 44). The POP instruction in line 53 restores the inner loop counter to the number of columns in the shape array. The ADD instruction in line 54 increments the DI-register by the number of bytes in one row of the video buffer (returned by the ADDR_RM procedure in line 32). The ES:DI register pair now addresses the first element in the next row of the video buffer, and the ES:DI:BP register group now addresses the element in the cth column of the next row (in which c is the value input to PUTSHAPE in the DL-register). The expansion for the macro instruction in line 55 decrements the outer loop counter by 1 and transfers control back to the top of the outer loop (line 42) if this loop counter is nonzero.

Suppose again that the shape is described by an $m \times n$ two-dimensional array and that the shape is to be displayed beginning at row r, column c on the video screen. On entering the outer loop, the DS:SI register pair addresses the first element of the first row of the shape, the ES:DI register pair addresses the first element of the rth row of the video buffer, and the BP-register contains the offset from the beginning of the row to the element in the cth column. The outer loop copies the shape array to the video buffer as follows:

1. The first iteration of the outer loop copies row 1 of the shape array to row r of the video buffer in column positions c through $(c + n - 1)$.
2. The second iteration of the outer loop copies row 2 of the shape array to row $(r + 1)$ of the video buffer in column positions c through $(c + n - 1)$.
3. The third iteration of the outer loop copies row 3 of the shape array to row $(r + 2)$ of the video buffer in column positions c through $(c + n - 1)$.

.
.
.

m. The mth iteration of the outer loop copies row m of the shape array to row $(r + m - 1)$ of the video buffer in column positions c through $(c + n - 1)$.

The inner loop body increments the SI-register through a complete row of the shape array (one element per iteration). Therefore, the DS:SI register pair addresses the first element of a different row of the shape array at the beginning of each iteration of the outer loop. At the beginning of the kth iteration of the outer loop, the ES:DI register pair addresses the first element of row $(r + k - 1)$ of the video buffer, and the BP-register contains the offset from the beginning of that row to the element in the cth column of the row. The inner loop body increments the BP-register through n elements of that row of the video buffer (one element per iteration). The POP instruction in line 52 sets the BP-register to the offset from the beginning of the row to the element in the cth column. The ADD instruction in line 54 increments the DI-register so that the ES:DI register pair addresses the first element of row $(r + k)$ of the video buffer on the next iteration (iteration $k + 1$) of the outer loop.

On exit from the outer loop, the flags register is restored (line 57), the registers specified in the USES clause are restored, and control is returned to the caller (line 60).

Program to Move a Face Around the Video Screen by Moving the Face in the Video Buffer

The main procedure presented in Program Listing 13.6 uses the PUTSHAPE procedure, developed in the previous section, to display a face on the video screen. By

```
            PAGE    80,132
;====================================================================
;                   PROGRAM LISTING 13.6
;
;
; PROGRAM TO MOVE A FACE AROUND THE SCREEN
;====================================================================
                                        ;PROCEDURES TO
            EXTRN   CLEAR:FAR           ;CLEAR VIDEO SCREEN
            EXTRN   DELAY:FAR           ;DELAY n SECONDS
            EXTRN   PUTSHAPE:FAR        ;DISPLAY A TEXTUAL SHAPE
;====================================================================
            .MODEL  SMALL,BASIC
;====================================================================
; S T A C K   S E G M E N T   D E F I N I T I O N
;
            .STACK  256
;====================================================================
; D A T A   S E G M E N T   D E F I N I T I O N
            .DATA
FACE        DB      07,11               ;7 x 11 SHAPE
            DB      20H,07H,20H,07H,2AH,07H,2AH,07H,2AH,07H,2AH,07H
            DB              2AH,07H,2AH,07H,2AH,07H,20H,07H,20H,07H
            DB      20H,07H,2AH,07H,20H,07H,20H,07H,20H,07H,20H,07H
            DB              20H,07H,20H,07H,20H,07H,2AH,07H,20H,07H
            DB      2AH,07H,20H,07H,20H,07H,2BH,07H,20H,07H,20H,07H
            DB              20H,07H,2BH,07H,20H,07H,20H,07H,2AH,07H
            DB      2AH,07H,20H,07H,20H,07H,20H,07H,20H,07H,5EH,07H
            DB              20H,07H,20H,07H,20H,07H,20H,07H,2AH,07H
            DB      2AH,07H,20H,07H,20H,07H,5CH,07H,5FH,07H,5FH,07H
            DB              5FH,07H,2FH,07H,20H,07H,20H,07H,2AH,07H
            DB      20H,07H,2AH,07H,20H,07H,20H,07H,20H,07H,20H,07H
            DB              20H,07H,20H,07H,20H,07H,2AH,07H,20H,07H
            DB      20H,07H,20H,07H,2AH,07H,2AH,07H,2AH,07H,2AH,07H
            DB              2AH,07H,2AH,07H,2AH,07H,20H,07H,20H,07H
SAD_MOUTH   DB      02,11               ;2 x 11 SHAPE
            DB      2AH,07H,20H,07H,20H,07H,20H,07H,5FH,07H,5FH,07H
```

```
37:               DB               5FH,07H,20H,07H,20H,07H,20H,07H,2AH,07H
38:               DB       20H,07H,2AH,07H,20H,07H,2FH,07H,20H,07H,20H,07H
39:               DB               20H,07H,5CH,07H,20H,07H,2AH,07H,20H,07H
40: WINK          DB       1,1,2BH,87H            ;1 X 1 SHAPE
41: ;=======================================================================
42: ; C O D E   S E G M E N T   D E F I N I T I O N
43: ;
44:               .CODE    EX_13_6
45:               .STARTUP                        ;GENERATE STARTUP CODE
46: ;
47:               MOV      AH,15                  ;GET PG <ACTIVE PAGE NO.>
48:               INT      10H
49:               LEA      SI,FACE                ;SPTR = ADDRESS OF FACE
50:               MOV      DH,3                   ;I = 3
51:               MOV      DL,18                  ;J = 18
52:               MOV      AL,1
53:               MOV      CX,12                  ;LOOP_CNT = 12
54:               .REPEAT                         ;REPEAT
55:               CALL     CLEAR                  ;   CLEAR SCREEN
56:               INC      DH                     ;   I = I + 1
57:               INC      DL                     ;   J = J + 1
58:               CALL     PUTSHAPE               ;   CALL PUTSHAPE(SPTR,PG,I,J)
59:               CALL     DELAY                  ;   DELAY 1 SECOND
60:               .UNTILCXZ                       ;   LOOP_CNT = LOOP_CNT - 1
61:                                               ;UNTIL LOOP_CNT = 0
62:               ADD      DH,4                   ;I = I + 4
63:               LEA      SI,SAD_MOUTH           ;SPTR = ADDRESS OF SAD_MOUTH
64:               CALL     PUTSHAPE               ;CALL PUTSHAPE(SPTR,PG,I,J)
65:               MOV      AL,5                   ;DELAY 5 SECONDS
66:               CALL     DELAY
67:               LEA      SI,WINK                ;SPTR = ADDRESS OF WINK
68:               SUB      DH,2                   ;I = I - 2
69:               ADD      DL,7                   ;J = J + 7
70:               CALL     PUTSHAPE               ;CALL PUTSHAPE(SPTR,PG,I,J)
71:               CALL     DELAY                  ;DELAY 5 SECONDS
72:               .EXIT                           ;RETURN TO DOS
73: ;
74: ;=======================================================================
75:               END
```

repeatedly clearing the video screen and displaying the face in a slightly different position, the procedure causes the face to move across the screen. The assembly module in Program Listing 13.6 contains the definition of this main procedure along with the definition of a data segment that contains the data structure for the face.

The assembly module references three external subprocedures identified by the EXTRN pseudo-operations in lines 8–10. The CLEAR procedure sets every character in the appropriate video buffer to blank, which, in effect, clears the video screen. CLEAR also homes the cursor (i.e., moves it to the upper left-hand corner of the video screen). The CLEAR procedure has no inputs, and it is available in the I/O subprocedure library, I/O.LIB. The DELAY procedure cycles (doing nothing) for approximately *n* seconds, in which *n* is the unsigned integer value in the AL-register. DELAY is similar to a solution to Programming Exercise 9.10. This version of DELAY must perform a conversion from seconds to a count of timer interrupts, and it is *not* available in the I/O subprocedure library. The PUTSHAPE procedure is, of course, the procedure from Program Listing 13.5.

The data segment definition in lines 19–40 contains the definitions of the data structures for three shapes. The data structure FACE, defined in lines 20–34, is the data structure from Figure 13.9 that describes the face from Figure 13.8. The data structure SAD_MOUTH, defined in lines 35–39, describes a 2×11 shape that transforms the smiling face in Figure 13.8 into the frowning face in Figure 13.10. By replac-

FIGURE 13.10 Shape described by data structure FACE with changes described by data structure SAD_MOUTH

ing rows 5 and 6 of the shape described by data structure FACE with the two rows of the shape described by data structure SAD_MOUTH, the transformation is accomplished. The data structure WINK, defined in line 40, describes a 1 × 1 shape that is a plus sign (+) with an attribute of normal video with the blink bit set. By replacing one of the eyes of the face with this shape, the face is made to wink.

The code segment defined in lines 44–73 contains the definition of the main procedure. The program begins by setting the DS-register to address DGROUP (line 45). Subfunction 15 of software interrupt Type 10 hex is invoked to read the active video page number into the BH-register (lines 47 and 48).

The instructions in lines 49–53 perform the initialization for the REPEAT-UNTIL loop implemented in lines 54–61. The LEA instruction in line 49 loads the SI-register with the offset of data structure FACE. That is, after execution of the LEA instruction, the DS:SI register pair addresses the first byte of data structure FACE. The MOV instruction in line 50 sets the row number in the DH-register to 3, and the MOV instruction in line 51 sets the column number in the DL-register to 18. The DH- and DL-registers specify a row and column within the video buffer and are inputs for the PUTSHAPE procedure. The MOV instruction in line 52 loads the AL-register with the input for the DELAY procedure. The MOV instruction in line 53 sets the loop counter for the REPEAT-UNTIL loop to 12.

The REPEAT-UNTIL loop is implemented by the instructions in lines 54–61. The loop body is executed 12 times. On each iteration of the loop body, the video screen is cleared (line 55), the row and column positions in the DH- and DL-registers are both incremented by 1 (lines 56 and 57), the face is displayed at the specified row and column (line 58), and a 1-second delay is performed (line 59). The LOOP instruction generated in response to the macro instruction in line 60 decrements the loop counter and transfers control back to the top of the loop (line 54) if this loop counter is nonzero. On the first iteration of the loop body, the face is displayed beginning at row 4, column 19 on the video screen. On the second iteration, it is displayed beginning at row 5, column 20. On the *n*th iteration ($1 \leqslant n \leqslant 12$), it is displayed beginning at row $(3 + n)$, column $(18 + n)$. The face is left in each display position for approximately 1 second. Since the screen is cleared between display positions, the face moves down the screen diagonally.

On loop exit, the face is displayed beginning at row 15, column 30 on the video screen. Rows 5 and 6 of the face are on rows 19 and 20 of the video screen, beginning at column 30. The ADD instruction in line 62 increments the DH-register value from 15 to 19 so that the DH- and DL-registers specify row 19, column 30. The LEA instruction in line 63 sets the DS:SI register pair to address the data structure for the shape SAD_MOUTH. The call to the PUTSHAPE procedure in line 64 transforms the happy mouth into a sad mouth (i.e., transforms the face in Figure 13.8 into the face in Figure 13.10). The instructions in lines 65 and 66 perform a delay of approximately 5 seconds.

With the face displayed beginning at row 15, column 30 on the video screen, the face's left eye is at row 17, column 37. The DH- and DL-register values currently specify row 19, column 30. The LEA instruction in line 67 sets the DS:SI register pair to address the data structure for the shape WINK, and the instructions in lines 68 and 69 adjust the DH- and DL-registers to specify row 17, column 37. The call to the PUTSHAPE procedure in line 70 transforms the frowning face to a frowning face with its left eye winking. The call to the DELAY procedure in line 71 produces a delay of approximately 5 seconds before control is returned to DOS (line 72).

13.6 Using Multiple Video Pages

MDA has just enough video memory to display one screen's worth of data. CGA, EGA, MCGA, and VGA have larger video memories. The video memory is divided into equal-size regions, or **video pages**, each of which is large enough to hold one screen's worth of data. At any point in time, only one of the pages, the **active page**, is displayed on the screen. Subfunction 5 of software interrupt Type 10 hex can be used to select which of the display pages is to be the active page. Table 13.4 lists the number of video pages that are available in the video memory for the various modes of each video subsystem.

TABLE 13.4
Video pages available for video modes of each video subsystem

Video Subsystem	Text Mode	Description of Mode	Number of Pages
MDA	7	25 × 80 monochrome	1
CGA	0	25 × 40 black and white	8
	1	25 × 40 color	8
	2	25 × 80 black and white	4
	3	25 × 80 color	4
EGA	0, 1	25 × 40 color	8
	2, 3	25 × 80 color	8
	7	25 × 80 monochrome	8
MCGA	0, 1	25 × 40 color	8
	2, 3	25 × 80 color	8
VGA	0, 1	25 × 40 color	8
	2, 3	25 × 80 color	8
	7	25 × 80 monochrome	8

Two advantages of having multiple pages in the video buffer are as follows:

1. It facilitates the illusion of the instantaneous display of an entire screen's worth of data. The screen is built on one of the inactive pages, and then the active page number is set to that page.
2. It facilitates the creation of an animation effect. Slightly different versions of a textual shape can be stored in the available video pages. By rapidly cycling through the pages (i.e., by rapidly changing the active video page), the shape appears to be animated.

The example program of this section illustrates the second of these two advantages. This program requires an EGA, MCGA, VGA, or XGA video subsystem (the availability of eight video pages is assumed), and it requires a color video monitor.

Program Listing 13.7 shows a program that moves a stack of cards diagonally

```
            PAGE    80,132
;====================================================================
;                   PROGRAM LISTING 13.7
;
; PROGRAM TO MOVE A STACK OF CARDS DIAGONALLY UP THE VIDEO SCREEN
; (THIS PROGRAM  DEMONSTRATES  THE USE  OF MULTIPLE VIDEO PAGES.)
;====================================================================
            .MODEL  SMALL,BASIC
;====================================================================
                                            ;PROCEDURES TO
            EXTRN   DELAY:FAR               ;DELAY n SECONDS
            EXTRN   PUTSHAPE:FAR            ;DISPLAY A TEXTUAL SHAPE
;====================================================================
; S T A C K   S E G M E N T   D E F I N I T I O N
            .STACK  256
;====================================================================
; C O N S T A N T   D E F I N I T I O N S
            .CONST
CARD0       DB      07,12                   ;7 x 12 SHAPE
            DB      7*12 DUP('█',78H)
CARD1       DB      07,12                   ;7 x 12 SHAPE
            DB      7*12 DUP('█',79H)
CARD2       DB      07,12                   ;7 x 12 SHAPE
            DB      7*12 DUP('█',7AH)
CARD3       DB      07,12                   ;7 x 12 SHAPE
            DB      7*12 DUP('█',7BH)
CARD4       DB      07,12                   ;7 x 12 SHAPE
            DB      7*12 DUP('█',7CH)
CARD5       DB      07,12                   ;7 x 12 SHAPE
            DB      7*12 DUP('█',7DH)
CARD6       DB      07,12                   ;7 x 12 SHAPE
            DB      7*12 DUP('█',7EH)
CARD7       DB      07,12                   ;7 x 12 SHAPE
            DB      7*12 DUP('█',7FH)
;====================================================================
; C O D E   S E G M E N T   D E F I N I T I O N
            .CODE   EX_13_7
            .STARTUP                        ;GENERATE STARTUP CODE
;
            MOV     AH,0                    ;SET VIDEO MODE TO 3
            MOV     AL,3
            INT     10H
            MOV     BH,0                    ;PG = 0
            LEA     SI,CARD0                ;SPTR = ADDRESS OF CARD0
            MOV     CX,8                    ;PAGE_COUNT = 8
            .REPEAT                         ;REPEAT
            PUSH    CX
            MOV     AH,9                    ;   SET ATTRIBUTE OF ENTIRE
            MOV     AL,' '                  ;   PAGE TO BROWN ON LT. GRAY
            MOV     BL,76H
            MOV     CX,2000
            INT     10H
            MOV     DH,2                    ;   r = 2
            MOV     DL,18                   ;   c = 18
            MOV     CX,17                   ;   CARD_CNT = 17
            .REPEAT                         ;   REPEAT
            CALL    PUTSHAPE                ;      CALL PUTSHAPE(SPTR,PG,
                                            ;                        r,c)
            INC     DH                      ;      r = r + 1
            ADD     DL,2                    ;      c = c + 2
            ADD     SI,2+7*12*2             ;      SPTR = SPTR+CARD_SIZE
            .IF     SI > OFFSET CARD7       ;      IF   SPTR > CARD7
                                            ;      THEN
            LEA     SI,CARD0                ;          SPTR=ADDR OF CARD0
            .ENDIF                          ;      ENDIF
            .UNTILCXZ                       ;      CARD_CNT = CARD_CNT-1
                                            ;   UNTIL CARD_CNT = 0
```

```
68:          POP    CX
69:          INC    BH                    ;    PG = PG + 1
70:          .UNTILCXZ                    ;    PAGE_COUNT=PAGE_COUNT-1
71:                                       ;UNTIL PAGE_COUNT = 0
72:          MOV    BH,0                  ;PAGE_# = 0
73:          MOV    CX,50                 ;LOOP_CNT = 50
74:          .REPEAT                      ;REPEAT
75:          MOV    AH,5                  ;    ACTIVE PAGE_# = PAGE_#
76:          MOV    AL,BH
77:          INT    10H
78:          MOV    AL,1                  ;    DELAY 1 SECOND
79:          CALL   DELAY
80:          INC    BH                    ;    PAGE_# = PAGE_# + 1
81:          AND    BH,07H                ;                          mod 8
82:          .UNTILCXZ                    ;    LOOP_CNT = LOOP_CNT - 1
83:                                       ;UNTIL LOOP_CNT = 0
84:          MOV    AH,15                 ;GET PAGE_#
85:          INT    10H
86:          MOV    AH,10                 ;SET PAGE_# TO ALL BLANKS
87:          MOV    AL,' '
88:          MOV    CX,2000
89:          INT    10H
90:          MOV    AH,11                 ;SET BORDER COLOR TO LT. GRAY
91:          MOV    BX,0007H
92:          INT    10H
93:          .EXIT                        ;RETURN TO DOS
94: ;
95: ;=====================================================================
96:          END
```

up the video screen. It uses the multiple pages of the video buffer to achieve the effect of animation. The constant data segment for the program contains the definitions of eight shapes named CARD0, CARD1, CARD2, ..., CARD7 (lines 19–34). Each card structure defines the shape shown in Figure 13.11. The only difference between these

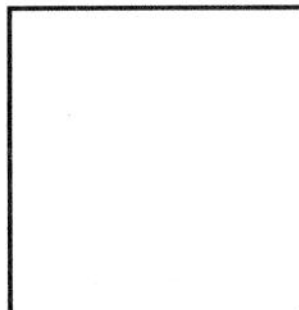

FIGURE 13.11
Shape described by each data structure of Program Listing 13.7

eight shape structures is the display attribute used. Each of the card shapes has a different color. Table 13.5 shows the color used for each of the eight cards. Seventeen cards are displayed, one on top of the other, separated by one row and two columns, as shown in Figure 13.12. This stack of cards is displayed on each of the eight pages of the video buffer. The cards are displayed in a different order on each of the eight pages, as shown in Table 13.6. Note that as you move from one page to the next-highest page in Table 13.6, each card moves up one position and the next-highest card replaces the bottom card. Moving from page 7 back to page 0 has the same effect. By periodically changing the active video page, from page 0 up to page 7 and back to page 0 again, the cards appear to move diagonally up the screen. Note also that each column of Table 13.6 is a continuation of the previous column. This sequence means that the cards go in sequence from the first card on page 0 through the last card on page 7 and back to the first card on page 0 again.

Two external subprocedures are referenced by this program, DELAY and PUTSHAPE (lines 11 and 12). These subprocedures were discussed earlier in the chapter.

TABLE 13.5
Colors for the eight cards defined in Program Listing 13.7

Data Structure	Color
CARD0	Dark gray
CARD1	Light blue
CARD2	Light green
CARD3	Light cyan
CARD4	Light red
CARD5	Light magenta
CARD6	Yellow
CARD7	White

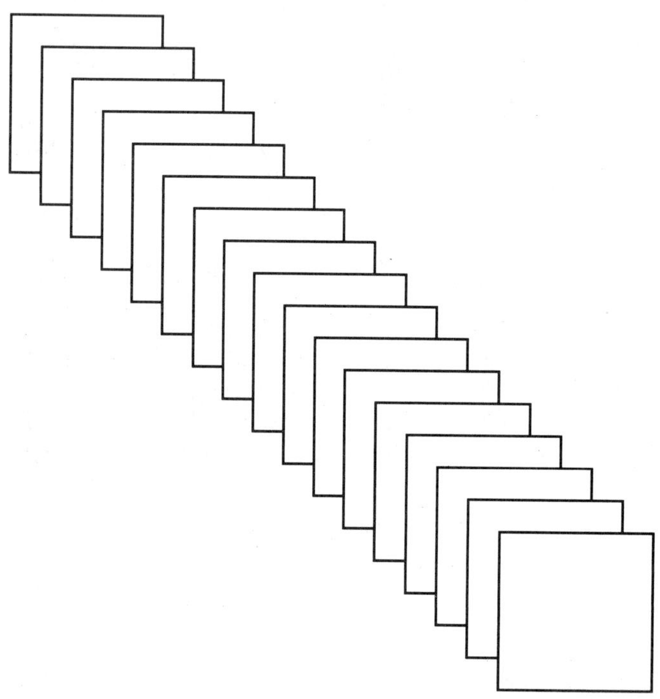

FIGURE 13.12
Shape displayed by the program of Program Listing 13.7

The program begins by setting the DS-register to address DGROUP (line 38). The program then sets the video mode to mode 3 (lines 40–42), the 25-line by 80-column color text mode. Explicitly setting the video mode automatically clears each page of the video buffer and homes the cursor on each page.

The instructions in lines 43–45 perform the initialization for the REPEAT-UNTIL loop in lines 46–71. This loop loads the eight pages of the video buffer with the card shapes. The MOV instruction in line 43 sets the BH-register to zero. The BH-register is used to hold the video page number. The subfunctions of software interrupt Type 10 hex that require the video page number as an input expect that input to be in the BH-register. The LEA instruction in line 44 sets the DS:SI register pair to address the CARD0 shape structure. The MOV instruction in line 45 loads the CX-register with the page count. The page count is the loop count for the REPEAT-UNTIL loop in lines 46–71. This loop executes once for each video page. Each iteration of this loop loads one page of the video buffer.

The body of the REPEAT-UNTIL loop begins by saving the loop counter (line

TABLE 13.6 Order of the cards on the eight pages of the video buffer

Page 0	Page 1	Page 2	Page 3	Page 4	Page 5	Page 6	Page 7
CARD0	CARD1	CARD2	CARD3	CARD4	CARD5	CARD6	CARD7
CARD1	CARD2	CARD3	CARD4	CARD5	CARD6	CARD7	CARD0
CARD2	CARD3	CARD4	CARD5	CARD6	CARD7	CARD0	CARD1
CARD3	CARD4	CARD5	CARD6	CARD7	CARD0	CARD1	CARD2
CARD4	CARD5	CARD6	CARD7	CARD0	CARD1	CARD2	CARD3
CARD5	CARD6	CARD7	CARD0	CARD1	CARD2	CARD3	CARD4
CARD6	CARD7	CARD0	CARD1	CARD2	CARD3	CARD4	CARD5
CARD7	CARD0	CARD1	CARD2	CARD3	CARD4	CARD5	CARD6
CARD0	CARD1	CARD2	CARD3	CARD4	CARD5	CARD6	CARD7
CARD1	CARD2	CARD3	CARD4	CARD5	CARD6	CARD7	CARD0
CARD2	CARD3	CARD4	CARD5	CARD6	CARD7	CARD0	CARD1
CARD3	CARD4	CARD5	CARD6	CARD7	CARD0	CARD1	CARD2
CARD4	CARD5	CARD6	CARD7	CARD0	CARD1	CARD2	CARD3
CARD5	CARD6	CARD7	CARD0	CARD1	CARD2	CARD3	CARD4
CARD6	CARD7	CARD0	CARD1	CARD2	CARD3	CARD4	CARD5
CARD7	CARD0	CARD1	CARD2	CARD3	CARD4	CARD5	CARD6
CARD0	CARD1	CARD2	CARD3	CARD4	CARD5	CARD6	CARD7

47) because the CX-register is used for two other purposes in the loop body. The attribute of each character of the page is set to brown on light gray (lines 48–52). Subfunction 9 of software interrupt Type 10 hex is invoked to display 2000 blanks, each with attribute 76 hex. This attribute is used to set the background color to light gray. The foreground color (brown) is insignificant to this program. The instructions in lines 53–55 perform the initialization for the nested REPEAT-UNTIL loop in lines 56–67. The MOV instructions in lines 53 and 54 set the row number to 2 and the column number to 18. These are inputs to the PUTSHAPE procedure. The MOV instruction in line 55 sets the loop counter for the nested loop to 17. Each iteration of the nested loop stores one card shape in the specified page of the video buffer, and there are 17 card shapes to be stored in each video page.

The body of the nested REPEAT-UNTIL loop begins by calling the PUTSHAPE subprocedure (line 57). PUTSHAPE moves the shape addressed by the DS:SI register pair to the page of the video buffer specified by the BH-register value. The shape will be stored in the specified page of the video buffer beginning at the row and column specified by the DH- and DL-register values, respectively. The instructions in lines 59–65 prepare for the next iteration of this nested loop. The row number is incremented by 1 (line 59), and the column number is incremented by 2 (line 60). Thus, the card shape moved on the next iteration of the loop will be separated from the card shape moved on this iteration by one row and two columns. The ADD instruction in line 61 increments the SI-register so that the DS:SI register pair addresses the beginning of the next card shape structure. The size of a card structure is $2 + (7 \times 12 \times 2)$. Each card structure contains 2 bytes, which specify the shape size, plus 7 times 12 elements, each of which is 2 bytes in size. The single-alternative decision structure in lines 62–65 checks this updated pointer to see if it was incremented beyond the CARD7 shape. If it was, then the instruction in line 64 is executed to set the pointer to address the CARD0 shape once again. That is, this decision structure ensures that CARD0 will always follow CARD7. The LOOP instruction generated in response to the macro instruction in line 66 decrements the nested loop counter and returns control to the top of the loop (line 56) if the updated loop counter value is nonzero.

On completion of the nested loop, the instructions in lines 68 and 69 are executed. These instructions prepare for the next iteration of the outer REPEAT-UNTIL loop. The INC instruction in line 69 increments the video page number in the BH-register so that the next iteration of the outer loop will load the next page of the video buffer. The POP instruction in line 68 restores the outer loop counter in preparation for the loop test. The LOOP instruction generated in response to the macro instruction in line 70 decrements the outer loop counter and returns control to the top of the loop (line 46) if the updated loop counter value is nonzero.

On completion of the outer loop, the instructions in lines 72–83 are executed. When control reaches the instruction in line 72, the eight video pages have been loaded with the card images specified in Table 13.6. Page 0 is the only video page that has been active (i.e., the only page that has been displayed) up to this point in the program. The next section of the program cycles through the display of the eight video pages, creating the effect of animation. The active display page is changed approximately once per second over a 50-second period.

The instructions in lines 72 and 73 perform the initialization for the REPEAT-UNTIL loop in lines 74–83. The MOV instruction in line 72 sets the BH-register to zero. The BH-register is again used to hold the video page number. The MOV instruction in line 73 sets the loop counter to 50, the approximate number of seconds for the animation. The body of the loop sets the active video page to the page specified by the BH-register (lines 75–77) and then performs a 1-second delay (lines 78 and 79). The instructions in lines 80 and 81 increment the video page number in the BH-register in a mod 8 fashion so that each successive iteration of the loop selects the next page of the video buffer as the active page, with page 0 following page 7. The LOOP instruction generated in response to the macro instruction in line 82 decrements the loop counter and returns control to the top of the loop (line 74) if the updated loop counter value is nonzero.

On completion of the outer loop, the instructions in lines 84–92 are executed. The instructions in lines 84 and 85 invoke subfunction 15 of interrupt Type 10 hex to load the BH-register with the active page number. The instructions in lines 86–89 invoke subfunction 10 of interrupt Type 10 hex to fill the active page of the video buffer with blanks. These operations are performed so that the cards will be cleared from the active page of the video screen before control is returned to DOS. (What is the active video page number at this point? What effect do you expect that to have when control is returned to DOS?) The instructions in lines 90–92 invoke subfunction 11 of interrupt Type 10 hex to set the border color of the video monitor to light gray (the same as the current background color). The macro instruction in line 93 causes control to be returned to DOS.

When control returns to DOS, you will notice that brown characters are displayed on a light gray background, which is a rather soothing color combination. Try it for a while—you may like it. On some video monitors, the brown may be closer to a yellow, and yellow on light gray may not be as pleasant. You now know how to write a program to set the color combination to whatever you desire, so go ahead and experiment with various color combinations.

On return to DOS, display the text of this program using the DOS TYPE command. As the program text is being displayed, you will notice that some of the character positions have a foreground color other than brown. Why do you think that this situation occurs? As these lines scroll off the screen, you will also notice that the screen eventually displays brown on light gray in all character positions. Why do you think that this situation occurs? (The reader is encouraged to experiment with this program to answer these and other questions regarding text display and color attributes.)

NUMERIC EXERCISES

13.1 Compute the hexadecimal address of the element in row 6 and column 4 of an 8 × 12 two-dimensional byte array, with base address 2C000 hex, whose elements are stored in (a) row-major order and (b) column-major order.

13.2 Compute the hexadecimal address of the element in row 7 and column 5 of a 9 × 6 two-dimensional word array, with base address 3B000 hex, whose elements are stored in (a) row-major order and (b) column-major order.

13.3 Compute the hexadecimal address of the element in row 2 and column 4 of an 8 × 6 two-dimensional double-word array, with base address 12000 hex, whose elements are stored in (a) row-major order and (b) column-major order.

13.4 Compute the hexadecimal address of the character: attribute pair for line 12, column 40 in the MDA video buffer.

13.5 Compute the hexadecimal address of the character: attribute pair for line 12, column 40 in page 0 of the CGA mode 1 video buffer.

13.6 Compute the hexadecimal address of the character: attribute pair for line 25, column 10 in page 2 of the CGA mode 3 video buffer.

13.7 Compute the hexadecimal address of the character: attribute pair for line 16, column 80 in page 5 of the EGA mode 3 video buffer.

13.8 Fill in the blanks in the following table:

Foreground Color	Background Color	Character Blink	CGA Attribute (Hex)
Cyan	Blue	Off	
Black	Light gray	On	
			1E
			AF
Blue	Cyan	Off	
Light blue	Brown	On	

PROGRAMMING EXERCISES

13.1 Write an external FAR subprocedure named PUTHEX to display an 8- or a 16-bit integer in hexadecimal form beginning at the current cursor position on the video screen. Your inputs should be one of the following:

> AL-register contains an 8-bit value to be displayed, and the BL-register contains 0, the code for the 8-bit display.

or

> AX-register contains a 16-bit value to be displayed, and the BL-register contains a nonzero value, the code for the 16-bit display.

Your subprocedure should use the array HEX_ASCII from Figure 13.1 and the XLAT instruction to perform the translation.

13.2 Write an external FAR subprocedure named PUTATTR to display a character:attribute pair in hexadecimal form with a colon between the two-digit character value and the two-digit attribute value. Your inputs should be as follows:

> BH-register contains the video page number.
> DH-register contains the row number (1–25).
> DL-register contains the column number (1–80).

Your procedure should display the specified character:attribute pair on the screen beginning at the current cursor position. Your procedure should be sensitive to all text modes.

13.3 The ADDR_RM subprocedure in Program Listing 13.2 applies to two-dimensional arrays stored in row-major order. Write a similar subprocedure called ADDR_CM that applies to two-dimensional arrays stored in column-major order. Your inputs should be the same as those for the ADDR_RM procedure. Your outputs should be as follows:

> ES:DI register pair addresses the first element in the specified column of the array.
> BP-register contains the offset within the column of the specified row.
> DX-register contains the DI-register offset needed to move one column in the array (i.e., the number of bytes per column).
> OF bit of the flags register is set to 1 for an out-of-range subscript.

13.4 Design an algorithm to display a two-dimensional array of signed integers that is stored in row-major order. The array is to be displayed in two-dimensional form with the number of rows and columns specified by a descriptor of the form described in Table 13.2. Implement your algorithm with an 8088/8086 assembly language external FAR subprocedure called PUT2DRM. Your input should be the address of the array descriptor in the DS:SI register pair. Your output should be the elements of the two-dimensional array displayed in rows and columns beginning on the next line of the video screen. Your procedure should be able to handle both byte and word arrays.

13.5 Design an algorithm to display a two-dimensional array of signed integers that is stored in column-major order. The array is to be displayed in two-dimensional form with the number of rows and columns specified by a descriptor of the form described in Table 13.2. Implement your algorithm with an 8088/8086 assembly language external FAR subprocedure called PUT2DCM. Your input should be the address of the array descriptor in the DS:SI register pair. Your output should be the elements of the two-dimensional array displayed in rows and columns beginning on the next line of the video screen. Your procedure should be able to handle both byte and word arrays.

13.6 Rework Programming Exercises 13.4 and 13.5 for unsigned integer arrays. Name the new procedures PUT2DRM$ and PUT2DCM$, respectively.

13.7 Define a two-dimensional array as follows:

```
ARRAY DW  -501, -502, -503, -504
      DW  -505, -506, -507, -508
      DW  -509, -510, -511, -512
```

Write a program that uses the ADDR_RM procedure and the procedures developed in Programming Exercises 13.3, 13.4, and 13.5 to perform the following sequence of operations:

a. Interpret the array as a 3 × 4 array stored in row-major order and display it on the screen.
b. Interpret the array as a 3 × 4 array stored in column-major order and display it on the screen.
c. Interpret the array as a 4 × 3 array stored in row-major order and display it on the screen.
d. Interpret the array as a 4 × 3 array stored in column-major order and display it on the screen.
e. Interpret the array as a 2 × 6 array stored in column-major order and display it on the screen.

13.8 Design an algorithm to clear a specified window on the video screen given the row and column of the upper left-hand and lower right-hand corners of the window. Implement your algorithm with an 8088/8086 assembly language external FAR subprocedure named CLEAR_W. Your inputs should be as follows:

> DH-register contains the row at the upper left-hand corner of the window.
> DL-register contains the column at the upper left-hand corner of the window.
> BH-register contains the row at the lower right-hand corner of the window.
> BL-register contains the column at the lower right-hand corner of the window.

Your subprocedure should clear the specified window of the video screen and should work for both MDA and CGA. For CGA, your procedure should be page-sensitive.

13.9 Design an algorithm to fill the video screen with a specified character:attribute pair. Implement your algorithm with an 8088/8086 assembly language external FAR subprocedure named FILL_SCR. Your inputs should be as follows:

> AH-register contains the attribute to be displayed in every position on the video screen.
> AL-register contains the character to be used in each position.

Your procedure should fill the appropriate video buffer with the specified character:attribute pair and should work for both MDA and CGA. For CGA, your procedure should be page-sensitive.

13.10 Write a main procedure that uses the procedures in Programming Exercises 13.8 and 13.9 to perform the following sequence of operations:

a. Fill the screen with the character DB hex using the attribute 07 hex.
b. Clear a window from row 1, column 1 to row 5, column 16.
c. Clear a window from row 6, column 17 to row 10, column 32.
d. Clear a window from row 11, column 33 to row 15, column 48.
e. Clear a window from row 16, column 49 to row 20, column 64.
f. Clear a window from row 21, column 65 to row 25, column 80.

(*Note*: Your presentation of this program will be better with a delay between each step.)

13.11 Modify the program of Program Listing 13.7 so that the cards move diagonally down the screen.

13.12 Modify the program of Program Listing 13.7 so that the cards move diagonally from the middle outward.

13.13 Write a program to load the (first) four pages of the mode 3 video buffer (CGA, EGA, MCGA, VGA, or XGA) with the following shapes:

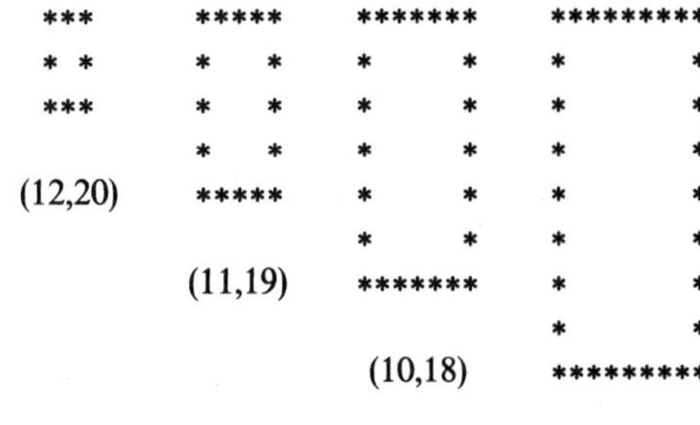

(9,17)

The coordinates below each shape identify the row and column where that shape is to begin on the page. Your program should systematically cycle through the pages so that the shape appears to expand and contract on the screen. (*Note*: You may wish to write your own delay subprocedure so that you can use delays of less than 1 second. The smaller delay times will enhance the animation.)

APPENDIX A

Instruction Summary

The following diagram shows the general format used in this appendix to describe the individual instructions that make up the instruction set of the Intel 8088/8086 family of microprocessors. The instructions described are available on all microprocessors in the family, unless otherwise noted below the Operation Code Mnemonic. For those instructions that are available on all microprocessors, the 8088/8086 operands are shown. It should be noted that the operands are expanded to include double word operands on the 80386 and 80486 microprocessors.

Operation Code Mnemonic

Description of operation performed										
General form of instruction Notation: Items in capital letters must be coded exactly as shown. <> encloses items supplied by the programmer [] encloses optional items The optional label field, denoted by [<label>] in the general form of each instruction, is the symbolic name to be associated with the memory location at which the instruction is to begin.										
Explanation of operands										
	OF	DF	IF	TF	SF	ZF	AF	PF	CF	

U -> unchanged
UD -> undefined
R -> reflects result of operation
S -> set to 1
C -> cleared to 0
T -> toggled (i.e., set to the opposite state)
LB -> last bit shifted out
SC -> reflects sign bit change on last bit shifted
SV -> saved value popped from top of stack

AAA
ASCII Adjust for Addition

Adjusts the result of a previous addition of two unpacked BCD digits. Adjusts the AL-register to contain a valid, unpacked BCD digit. The upper nibble of the AL-register is cleared. The carry from this digit is added to the AH-register. AAA causes the following steps to be performed:

```
IF    ((AL-REG and 0F hex) > 9) or (AF = 1)
THEN
      AL-REG is incremented by 6
      AH-REG is incremented by 1
      AF is set to 1
ENDIF
AF is copied into CF
Upper nibble of AL-REG is cleared
```

[<label>] AAA [<comment>]

The operand is implied by the instruction. It is always the contents of the AL-register.

OF	DF	IF	TF	SF	ZF	AF	PF	CF
UD	U	U	U	UD	UD	R	UD	R

AAD
ASCII Adjust for Division

Adjusts the dividend prior to division of a two-digit, unpacked BCD number by an unpacked BCD digit. The dividend to be adjusted is the two-digit, unpacked BCD number in the AX-register. The most significant BCD digit (AH-register) is multiplied by 10, and the least significant BCD digit (AL-register) is added to this product. The resulting binary integer is placed in the AL-register, and the AH-register is cleared.

[<label>] AAD [<comment>]

The operand is implied by the instruction. It is always the contents of the AX-register.

OF	DF	IF	TF	SF	ZF	AF	PF	CF
UD	U	U	U	R	R	UD	R	UD

AAM
ASCII Adjust for Multiply

Adjusts the result of a previous multiplication of two unpacked BCD digits, producing two unpacked BCD digits. The result of the multiplication (AX-register value) is divided by 10. The quotient (the high-order, unpacked BCD digit) is placed in the AH-register. The remainder (the low-order, unpacked BCD digit) is placed in the AL-register.

[<label>] AAM [<comment>]

The operand is implied by the instruction. It is always the contents of the AX-register.

OF	DF	IF	TF	SF	ZF	AF	PF	CF
UD	U	U	U	R	R	UD	R	UD

AAS
ASCII Adjust for Subtraction

Adjusts the result of a previous subtraction of two unpacked BCD digits. Adjusts the AL-register to contain a valid, unpacked BCD digit. The upper nibble of the AL-register is cleared. The borrow into this digit is subtracted from the AH-register. AAS causes the following steps to be performed:

```
   IF   ((AL-REG and OF hex) > 9) or (AF = 1)
   THEN
        AL-REG is decremented by 6
        AH-REG is decremented by 1
        AF is set to 1
   ENDIF
   AF is copied into CF
   Upper nibble of AL-REG is cleared
```

[<label>] AAS [<comment>]

The operand is implied by the instruction. It is always the contents of the AL-register.

OF	DF	IF	TF	SF	ZF	AF	PF	CF
UD	U	U	U	UD	UD	R	UD	R

ADC
Add with Carry

ADD
Addition

The ADC instruction adds the source operand, the destination operand, and the carry flag, replacing the destination operand with the sum.
The ADD instruction adds the source operand to the destination operand, replacing the destination operand with the sum.

```
[<label>]     ADC     <destination>,<source>     [<comment>]

[<label>]     ADD     <destination>,<source>     [<comment>]
```

<source> identifies the location of the addend, and
<destination> identifies the location of the augend that will be replaced by the sum.

The types of the two operands must match (i.e., both must be byte or both must be word). Both operands may be double word for the 80386 and 80486 microprocessors.

<destination>	<source>
General register	General register Memory location Immediate
Memory location	General register Immediate

OF	DF	IF	TF	SF	ZF	AF	PF	CF
R	U	U	U	R	R	R	R	R

AND
Logical AND

ANDs each bit of the destination operand with the corresponding bit of the source operand, replacing the bit in the destination operand with the result.

```
[<label>]      AND      <destination>,<source>      [<comment>]
```

<destination> identifies the location of the operand that is to be replaced with the result, and
<source> identifies the location of the operand that is not to be modified.

The types of the two operands must match (i.e., both must be byte or both must be word). Both operands may be double word for the 80386 and 80486 microprocessors.

<destination>	<source>
General register	General register Memory location Immediate
Memory location	General register Immediate

OF	DF	IF	TF	SF	ZF	AF	PF	CF
C	U	U	U	R	R	UD	R	C

BSF Bit Scan Forward / BSR Bit Scan Reverse (80386/80486)

The BSF instruction scans the source operand from bit 0 toward the MSB to find the first set bit.
The BSR instruction scans the source operand from the MSB toward bit 0 to find the first set bit.
If a set bit is found, then the value of the destination operand is replaced by the bit index of the first set bit found, and the ZF bit of the flags register is cleared.
If no set bit is found, then the ZF bit of the flags register is set, and the destination operand is not modified.

```
[<label>]     BSF     <destination>,<source>     [<comment>]

[<label>]     BSR     <destination>,<source>     [<comment>]
```

<destination> identifies the general register, whose value is to be replaced by the bit index of the first set bit found, and

<source> identifies the location of the binary value that is to be scanned.

The types of the two operands must match (i.e., both must be word or both must be double word).

<destination>	<source>
General register	General register Memory location

OF	DF	IF	TF	SF	ZF	AF	PF	CF
U	U	U	U	U	R	U	U	U

BT	BTC	BTR	BTS
Bit Test	Bit Test and Complement	Bit Test and Reset	Bit Test and Set

(80386/80486)

The BT instruction copies the bit of the destination operand, whose bit position is specified by the source operand, into the CF bit of the flags register.
The BTC instruction copies the bit of the destination operand, whose bit position is specified by the source operand, into the CF bit of the flags register, and then complements the specified bit in the destination operand.
The BTR instruction copies the bit of the destination operand, whose bit position is specified by the source operand, into the CF bit of the flags register, and then clears the specified bit in the destination operand.
The BTS instruction copies the bit of the destination operand, whose bit position is specified by the source operand, into the CF bit of the flags register, and then sets the specified bit in the destination operand.

```
[<label>]     BT      <destination>,<source>      [<comment>]

[<label>]     BTC     <destination>,<source>      [<comment>]

[<label>]     BTR     <destination>,<source>      [<comment>]

[<label>]     BTS     <destination>,<source>      [<comment>]
```

<destination> identifies the location of the operand that is to have a bit copied and toggled (BTC), reset (BSR), or set (BTS), and

<source> specifies the bit position of the bit in the destination operand that is to be copied and toggled (BTC), reset (BSR), or set (BTS).

Except for the case of an immediate source operand, the types of the two operands must match (i.e., both must be word or both must be double word). An immediate source operand is always a byte value.

<destination>	<source>
General register	General register Immediate
Memory location	General register Immediate

OF	DF	IF	TF	SF	ZF	AF	PF	CF
U	U	U	U	U	U	U	U	R

CALL

The procedure that begins at the memory location specified by the operand is invoked. The return address is pushed onto the stack.

[<label>] CALL <target> [<comment>]

<target> is the name of the procedure that is being invoked (direct call), or an address expression that specifies the memory location that contains the address of the procedure being invoked (indirect call).

<target>	Description
Procedure name with attribute NEAR	The machine language operand is the difference between the offset of the memory location specified by the target and the offset of the memory location immediately following the CALL instruction. At execution, this difference is added to the IP-reg.
Procedure name with attribute FAR	The machine language operand is the segment and offset of the specified target. At execution, this segment and offset replace the value in the CS:IP register pair.
Address expression of variable with attribute WORD	The machine language operand is the segment register number and offset of the variable. At execution, the contents of the memory location specified by this segment and offset replaces the IP-register value.
Address expression of variable with attribute DBL WORD	The machine language operand is the segment register number and offset of the variable. At execution, the contents of the memory location specified by this segment and offset replaces the value of the CS:IP register pair.
General register (16-bit register)	The contents of the general register replaces the value in the IP-reg.

OF	DF	IF	TF	SF	ZF	AF	PF	CF
U	U	U	U	U	U	U	U	U

CBW
Convert Byte to Word

Expands the signed, 8-bit integer in the AL-register to a signed, 16-bit integer in the AX-register. Extends the sign bit (bit 7 of the AL-register) into bits 0 through 7 of the AH-register.

[<label>] CBW [<comment>]

OF	DF	IF	TF	SF	ZF	AF	PF	CF
U	U	U	U	U	U	U	U	U

CDQ
Convert Double Word to Quadword
(80386/80486)

Expands the signed, 32-bit integer in the EAX-register to a signed, 64-bit integer in the EDX:EAX-register pair. Extends the sign bit (bit 31 of the EAX-register) into bits 0 through 31 of the EDX-register.

[<label>] CDQ [<comment>]

OF	DF	IF	TF	SF	ZF	AF	PF	CF
U	U	U	U	U	U	U	U	U

CLC
Clear Carry Flag

Resets the carry flag to zero.

[<label>] CLC [<comment>]

OF	DF	IF	TF	SF	ZF	AF	PF	CF
U	U	U	U	U	U	U	U	C

CLD
Clear Direction Flag

Resets the direction flag to zero, which causes the automatic update of the DI- and/or SI-register following execution of a string instruction to be an increment.

[<label>] CLD [<comment>]

OF	DF	IF	TF	SF	ZF	AF	PF	CF
U	C	U	U	U	U	U	U	U

CLI
Clear Interrupt Flag

Resets the interrupt flag to zero, which disables external interrupts. That is, it causes the processor to ignore external interrupts.

[<label>] CLI [<comment>]

OF	DF	IF	TF	SF	ZF	AF	PF	CF
U	U	C	U	U	U	U	U	U

CMC
Complement Carry Flag

Changes the state of (i.e., toggles) the CF bit of the flags register.

[<label>] CMC [<comment>]

OF	DF	IF	TF	SF	ZF	AF	PF	CF
U	U	U	U	U	U	U	U	T

CMP
Compare

Compares the first operand to the second operand, and sets the flags accordingly. The source operand is subtracted from the destination operand, and the flags are set to reflect the difference. Neither the source nor the destination operand is modified.

```
[<label>]      CMP      <destination>,<source>      [<comment>]
```

<destination> identifies the location of the left-hand operand of the comparison, and

<source> identifies the location of the right-hand operand of the comparison.

The types of the two operands must match (i.e., both must be byte or both must be word). Both operands may be double word for the 80386 and 80486 microprocessors.

<destination>	<source>
General register	General register Memory location Immediate
Memory location	General register Immediate

OF	DF	IF	TF	SF	ZF	AF	PF	CF
R	U	U	U	R	R	R	R	R

CMPS

CMPSB	CMPSW	CMPSD
Compare String Byte	Compare String Word	Compare String Double Word (80386/80486)

Compares the byte, word, or double word identified by the DS:SI register pair to the byte, word, or double word identified by the ES:DI register pair, and sets the flags accordingly. The operand identified by the ES:DI register pair is subtracted from the operand identified by the DS:SI register pair, and the flags are set to reflect the difference. Neither operand is modified. If the direction flag (DF) is 0, both the SI and DI registers are incremented by 1 (CMPSB), 2 (CMPSW), or 4 (CMPSD); if DF is 1, both the SI and DI registers are decremented by 1 (CMPSB), 2 (CMPSW), or 4 (CMPSD).

```
[<label>]     CMPS    <source>,<destination>     [<comment>]

[<label>]     CMPSB                              [<comment>]

[<label>]     CMPSW                              [<comment>]

[<label>]     CMPSD                              [<comment>]
```

<source> identifies the array addressed by the DS:SI register pair, and
<destination> identifies the array addressed by the ES:DI register pair.

The types of the two operands must match (i.e., both must be byte or both must be word). Both operands may be double word for the 80386 and 80486 microprocessors. For byte operands, a CMPSB instruction is generated; for word operands, a CMPSW instruction is generated; for double word operands, a CMPSD instruction is generated.

OF	DF	IF	TF	SF	ZF	AF	PF	CF
R	U	U	U	R	R	R	R	R

CMPXCHG
Compare and Exchange
(80486)

Compares the destination operand to the accumulator (AL, AX, or EAX), and sets the flags accordingly. If equal, replaces the value of the destination operand with a copy of the value of the source operand. If not equal, replaces the value of the accumulator with a copy of the value of the destination operand.

```
[<label>]     CMPXCHG <destination>,<source>     [<comment>]
```

<destination> identifies the location of the left-hand operand of the comparison, and
<source> identifies the location of the right-hand operand of the comparison.

The types of the two operands must match (i.e., both must be byte, both must be word, or both must be double word).

<destination>	<source>
General register or Memory location	General register

OF	DF	IF	TF	SF	ZF	AF	PF	CF
R	U	U	U	R	R	R	R	R

CWD
Convert Word to Double Word

Expands the signed, 16-bit integer in the AX-register to a signed, 32-bit integer in the DX:AX register pair. Extends the sign bit (bit 15 of the AX-register) into bits 0-15 of the DX-register.

```
[<label>]     CWD                                [<comment>]
```

OF	DF	IF	TF	SF	ZF	AF	PF	CF
U	U	U	U	U	U	U	U	U

CWDE
Convert Word to Double Word Extended
(80386/80486)

Expands the signed, 16-bit integer in the AX-register to a signed, 32-bit integer in the EAX register. Extends the sign bit (bit 15 of the AX-register) into bits 16-31 of the the EAX-register.

[<label>] CWDE [<comment>]

OF	DF	IF	TF	SF	ZF	AF	PF	CF
U	U	U	U	U	U	U	U	U

DAA
Decimal Adjust for Addition

Adjusts the result of a previous addition of two packed BCD digit pairs. Adjusts the AL-register to contain a valid pair of packed BCD digits. The carry from this digit pair is recorded in the CF bit of the flags register. DAA causes the following steps to be performed:

```
IF    (lower nibble of AL-REG > 9) or (AF = 1)
THEN
      AL-REG is incremented by 6
      AF is set to 1
ENDIF
IF    (upper nibble of AL-REG > 9) or (CF = 1)
THEN
      AL-REG is incremented by 60 hex
      CF is set to 1
ENDIF
```

[<label>] DAA [<comment>]

The operand is implied by the instruction. It is always the contents of the AL-register.

OF	DF	IF	TF	SF	ZF	AF	PF	CF
UD	U	U	U	R	R	R	R	R

DAS
Decimal Adjust for Subtraction

Adjusts the result of a previous subtraction of two packed BCD digit pairs. Adjusts the AL-register to contain a valid pair of packed BCD digits. The borrow into this digit pair is recorded in the CF bit of the flags register. DAS causes the following steps to be performed:

```
IF    (lower nibble of AL-REG > 9) or (AF = 1)
THEN
      AL-REG is decremented by 6
      AF is set to 1
ENDIF
IF    (upper nibble of AL-REG > 9) or (CF = 1)
THEN
      AL-REG is decremented by 60 hex
      CF is set to 1
ENDIF
```

[<label>] DAS [<comment>]

The operand is implied by the instruction. It is always the contents of the AL-register.

OF	DF	IF	TF	SF	ZF	AF	PF	CF
UD	U	U	U	R	R	R	R	R

DEC
Decrement

Decrements the value in the specified register or memory location by 1.

[<label>] DEC <destination> [<comment>]

<destination> identifies the location of the value to be decremented.

<destination>
General register
Memory location

OF	DF	IF	TF	SF	ZF	AF	PF	CF
R	U	U	U	R	R	R	R	U

DIV
Divide

For a byte operand, divides the 16-bit, unsigned integer value in the AX-register by the 8-bit, unsigned integer value of the operand, and leaves the quotient in the AL-register and the remainder in the AH-register.
For a word operand, divides the 32-bit, unsigned integer value in the DX:AX register pair by the 16-bit, unsigned integer value of the operand, and leaves the quotient in the AX-register and the remainder in the DX-register.
For a double word operand (80386/80486 only), divides the 64-bit, unsigned integer value in the EDX:EAX register pair by the 32-bit, unsigned integer value of the operand, and leaves the quotient in the EAX-register and the remainder in the EDX-register.

[<label>] DIV <source> [<comment>]

<source> identifies the location of the divisor.

<source>
General register
Memory location

OF	DF	IF	TF	SF	ZF	AF	PF	CF
UD	U	U	U	UD	UD	UD	UD	UD

HLT
Halt

Stops the instruction execution cycle of the microprocessor. The microprocessor waits for an interrupt before continuing.

[<label>] HLT [<comment>]

OF	DF	IF	TF	SF	ZF	AF	PF	CF
U	U	U	U	U	U	U	U	U

IDIV
Integer Divide

For a byte operand, divides the 16-bit, signed integer value in the AX-register by the 8-bit, signed integer value of the operand, and leaves the quotient in the AL-register and the remainder in the AH-register.
For a word operand, divides the 32-bit, signed integer value in the DX:AX register pair by the 16-bit, signed integer value of the operand, and leaves the quotient in the AX-register and the remainder in the DX-register.
For a double word operand (80386/80486 only), divides the 64-bit, signed integer value in the EDX:EAX register pair by the 32-bit, signed integer value of the operand, and leaves the quotient in the EAX-register and the remainder in the EDX-register.

[<label>] IDIV <source> [<comment>]

<source> identifies the location of the divisor.

<source>
General register
Memory location

OF	DF	IF	TF	SF	ZF	AF	PF	CF
UD	U	U	U	UD	UD	UD	UD	UD

IMUL
Integer Multiply

For a byte operand, multiplies the signed integer value in the AL-register by the 8-bit, signed integer value specified by the operand, and leaves the 16-bit product in the AX-register.
For a word operand, multiplies the signed integer value in the AX-register by the 16-bit, signed integer value specified by the operand, and leaves the 32-bit product in the DX:AX register pair.
For a double word operand (80386/80486 only), multiplies the signed integer value in the EAX-register by the 32-bit, signed integer value specified by the operand, and leaves the 64-bit product in the EDX:EAX register pair.

```
[<label>]      IMUL     <source>                        [<comment>]

   <source>      identifies the location of the  multiplier.
```

<source>

General register
Memory location

OF	DF	IF	TF	SF	ZF	AF	PF	CF
R	U	U	U	UD	UD	UD	UD	R

IMUL
Integer Multiply
(Additional Form 80286/80386/80486)

Multiplies the signed integer value specified by the destination operand by the immediate value and replaces the destination operand with the single-length product.

```
[<label>]      IMUL     <destination>,<immediate>  [<comment>]

   <destination> identifies the general register  containing
                 the multiplicand, and
   <immediate>   identifies the constant multiplier.
```

OF	DF	IF	TF	SF	ZF	AF	PF	CF
R	U	U	U	UD	UD	UD	UD	R

IMUL
Integer Multiply
(Additional Form 80286/80386/80486)

Multiplies the signed integer value specified by the source operand by the immediate value and replaces the destination operand with the single-length product.

[<label>] IMUL <destination>,<source>,<immediate> [<comment>]

<destination> identifies the general register whose value is replaced by the single-length product,
<source> identifies the location of the multiplicand, and
<immediate> identifies the constant multiplier.

The types of the <destination> and <source> operands must match (i.e., both must be byte or both must be word). Both operands may be double word for the 80386 and 80486 microprocessors.

<source>
General register
Memory location

OF	DF	IF	TF	SF	ZF	AF	PF	CF
R	U	U	U	UD	UD	UD	UD	R

IMUL
Integer Multiply
(Additional Form 80386/80486)

Multiplies the signed integer value specified by the destination operand by the signed integer value specified by the source operand and replaces the destination operand with the single-length product.

```
[<label>]      IMUL     <destination>,<source>      [<comment>]

   <destination> identifies  the general register containing
                 the multiplicand,  whose value  is replaced
                 by the single-length product, and
   <source>      identifies  the location of the multiplier.

   The types of the two operands must match (i.e., both must
   be byte, both must be word, or both must be double word).
```

<source>
General register
Memory location

OF	DF	IF	TF	SF	ZF	AF	PF	CF
R	U	U	U	UD	UD	UD	UD	R

IN
Input Byte or Word from Port
Input Byte, Word, or Double Word from Port (80386/80486)

Transfers a byte from the specified port to the AL-register, or transfers a word from the specified port pair to the AX-register. May also transfer a double word from four consecutive ports to the EAX-register on the 80386 and 80486 microprocessors.

```
[<label>]     IN      AL,<port>                  [<comment>]

[<label>]     IN      AX,<port>                  [<comment>]

[<label>]     IN      EAX,<port>                 [<comment>]
```

<port> specifies the port number for a byte transfer, the first of two consecutive ports for a word transfer, or the first of four consecutive ports for a double word transfer.

The <port> operand can be an immediate value in the range 0-255 or the register designator DX.

OF	DF	IF	TF	SF	ZF	AF	PF	CF
U	U	U	U	U	U	U	U	U

INC
Increment

Increments the value in the specified register or memory location by 1.

```
[<label>]     INC     <destination>              [<comment>]
```

<destination> identifies the location of the value to be incremented.

<destination>
General register
Memory location

OF	DF	IF	TF	SF	ZF	AF	PF	CF
R	U	U	U	R	R	R	R	U

INS

INSB	INSW	INSD
Input String Byte	Input String Word	Input String Double Word
(80286/80386/80486)		(80386/80486)

Transfers the byte, word, or double word value beginning at the port addressed by the value of the DX-register to the memory byte, word, or double word addressed by the ES:DI register pair. If the direction flag (DF) is 0, the DI-register is incremented by 1 (INSB), 2 (INSW), or 4 (INSD); if the DF is 1, the DI-register is decremented by 1 (INSB), 2 (INSW), or 4 (INSD).

```
[<label>]     INS     <destination>,DX           [<comment>]

[<label>]     INSB                               [<comment>]

[<label>]     INSW                               [<comment>]

[<label>]     INSD                               [<comment>]
```

<destination> is the symbolic name that identifies the array addressed by the ES:DI register pair.

OF	DF	IF	TF	SF	ZF	AF	PF	CF
U	U	U	U	U	U	U	U	U

INT
Interrupt

Pushes the flags register value onto the stack, clears the trap flag and the interrupt flag, pushes the CS-register value onto the stack, multiplies the interrupt type by 4 to compute the address of the interrupt vector, loads the second word of the interrupt vector into the CS-register, pushes the IP-register value onto the stack, and loads the first word of the interrupt vector into the IP-register.

[<label>] INT <int-type> [<comment>]

<int-type> is an integer in the range 0-255 that identifies the interrupt.

The interrupt type identifies an interrupt vector that contains the segment and offset of the service procedure for the specified type of interrupt.

OF	DF	IF	TF	SF	ZF	AF	PF	CF
U	U	C	C	U	U	U	U	U

INTO
Interrupt on Overflow

If the overflow flag (OF) is set, then the INTO instruction causes the processor to perform the following steps: Pushes the flags register value onto the stack, clears the trap flag and the interrupt flag, pushes the CS-register value onto the stack, loads the second word of the Type 4 interrupt vector into the CS-register, pushes the IP-register value onto the stack, and loads the first word of the Type 4 interrupt vector into the IP-register. If OF is not set, then no operation is performed for INTO.

[<label>] INTO [<comment>]

OF	DF	IF	TF	SF	ZF	AF	PF	CF
U	U	C/U	C/U	U	U	U	U	U

IRET
Interrupt Return

Pops the top-of-stack item into the IP-register, pops the new top-of-stack item into the CS-register, and pops the new top-of-stack item into the flags register.

[<label>] IRET [<comment>]

OF	DF	IF	TF	SF	ZF	AF	PF	CF
SV	SV	SV	SV	SV	SV	SV	SV	SV

Jxxx
Conditional JUMP
(Unsigned Integer)

This group of conditional JUMP instructions provides the capability to make decisions based on the results of computations involving unsigned numbers.

[<label>] Jxxx <short label> [<comment>]

<short label> is the label of an instruction whose memory location is within -128 to 127 bytes from the memory location immediately following the conditional JUMP instruction.

OF	DF	IF	TF	SF	ZF	AF	PF	CF
U	U	U	U	U	U	U	U	U

Operation Code Mnemonic	Description	Will Jump If
JA/JNBE	Jump if Above Jump if Not Below nor Equal	CF = 0 and ZF = 0
JAE/JNB	Jump if Above or Equal Jump if Not Below	CF = 0
JB/JNAE	Jump if Below Jump if Not Above nor Equal	CF = 1
JBE/JNA	Jump if Below or Equal Jump if Not Above	CF = 1 or ZF = 1
JE/JZ	Jump if Equal to Zero	ZF = 1
JNE/JNZ	Jump if Not Equal to Zero	ZF = 0

Jxxx
Conditional JUMP
(Signed Integer)

This group of conditional JUMP instructions provides the capability to make decisions based on the results of computations involving signed numbers.

[<label>] Jxxx <short label> [<comment>]

<short label> is the label of an instruction whose memory location is within -128 to 127 bytes from the memory location immediately following the conditional JUMP instruction.

OF	DF	IF	TF	SF	ZF	AF	PF	CF
U	U	U	U	U	U	U	U	U

Operation Code Mnemonic	Description	Will Jump If
JG/JNLE	Jump if Greater than Jump if Not Less nor Equal	ZF = 0 and SF = OF
JGE/JNL	Jump if Greater than or Equal Jump if Not Less than	(SF xor OF) = 0 (i.e., SF = OF)
JL/JNGE	Jump if Less than Jump if Not Greater nor Equal	(SF xor OF) = 1 (i.e., SF <> OF)
JLE/JNG	Jump if Less than or Equal Jump if Not Greater than	ZF = 1 or SF <> OF
JE/JZ	Jump if Equal to Zero	ZF = 1
JNE/JNZ	Jump if Not Equal to Zero	ZF = 0

Jxx
Conditional JUMP
(Specific Flag)

This group of conditional JUMP instructions provides the capability to make decisions based on the current state of a specific flag in the flags register.

[<label>] Jxx <short label> [<comment>]

<short label> is the label of an instruction whose memory location is within -128 to 127 bytes from the memory location immediately following the conditional JUMP instruction.

OF	DF	IF	TF	SF	ZF	AF	PF	CF
U	U	U	U	U	U	U	U	U

Operation Code Mnemonic	Description	Will Jump If
JC	Jump if Carry	CF = 1
JNC	Jump if No Carry	CF = 0
JO	Jump if Overflow	OF = 1
JNO	Jump if No Overflow	OF = 0
JS	Jump if negative Sign	SF = 1
JNS	Jump if Nonnegative Sign	SF = 0
JZ	Jump if Zero	ZF = 1
JNZ	Jump if Not Zero	ZF = 0
JP/JPE	Jump if Parity Even	PF = 1
JNP/JPO	Jump if Parity Odd	PF = 0

The 80386 and 80486 microprocessors have a second set of conditional jump instructions with the exact same operation code mnemonics but with <extended short label> as the operand. An extended short label is the label of a memory location, in the machine language translation, that is in the range -32,768 to +32,767 bytes from the memory location following the jump instruction.

JCXZ
Jump if CX-Register Zero

If the value in the CX-register is zero, then control is transferred to the instruction that begins at the memory location specified by the operand.

[<label>] JCXZ <short label> [<comment>]

<short label> is the label of an instruction whose memory location is within -128 to 127 bytes from the memory location immediately following the JCXZ instruction.

OF	DF	IF	TF	SF	ZF	AF	PF	CF
U	U	U	U	U	U	U	U	U

JECXZ
Jump if ECX-Register Zero
(80386/80486)

If the value in the ECX-register is zero, then control is transferred to the instruction that begins at the memory location specified by the operand.

[<label>] JECXZ <short label> [<comment>]

<short label> is the label of an instruction whose memory location is within -128 to 127 bytes from the memory location immediately following the JECXZ instruction.

OF	DF	IF	TF	SF	ZF	AF	PF	CF
U	U	U	U	U	U	U	U	U

JMP

Control is unconditionally transferred to the instruction that begins at the memory location specified by the operand.

[<label>] JMP <target> [<comment>]

<target> is the label of the instruction to which control is being transferred (direct jump) or an address expression that specifies the memory location that contains the address of the instruction to which control is being transferred (indirect jump).

<target>	Description
Label with type attribute NEAR	The machine language operand is the difference between the offset of the memory location specified by the target and the offset of the memory location immediately following the JMP instruction. At execution, this difference is added to the IP-reg.
Label with type attribute FAR	The machine language operand is the segment and offset of the specified target. At execution, this segment and offset replace the value in the CS:IP register pair.
Address expression of variable with attribute WORD	The machine language operand is the segment register number and offset of the variable. At execution, the contents of the memory location specified by this segment and offset replaces the IP-register value.
Address expression of variable with attribute DBL WORD	The machine language operand is the segment register number and offset of the variable. At execution, the contents of the memory location specified by this segment and offset replaces the value of the CS:IP register pair.
General register (16-bit register)	The contents of the general register replaces value in the IP-register.

OF	DF	IF	TF	SF	ZF	AF	PF	CF
U	U	U	U	U	U	U	U	U

LAHF
Load AH-Register from Flags

Loads the AH-register with a copy of the value in the low-order half of the flags register.

[<label>] LAHF [<comment>]

OF	DF	IF	TF	SF	ZF	AF	PF	CF
U	U	U	U	U	U	U	U	U

LDS LES LFS LGS LSS

Load Pointer Using
DS-Register ES-Register FS-Register (80386/80486) GS-Register (80386/80486) SS-Register

Loads the 16-bit general register designated by the destination operand with a copy of the lower 16 bits of the double word in memory addressed by the source operand. Loads the segment register specified by the operation code mnemonic (DS, ES, FS, GS, or SS) with a copy of the upper 16 bits of the double word in memory addressed by the source operand.

[<label>] LDS <destination>,<source> [<comment>]

[<label>] LES <destination>,<source> [<comment>]

[<label>] LFS <destination>,<source> [<comment>]

[<label>] LGS <destination>,<source> [<comment>]

[<label>] LSS <destination>,<source> [<comment>]

<destination> is the designator of the 16-bit general register that is to receive the offset portion of the value of the pointer, and

<source> is an address expression that identifies a double word memory operand that contains the pointer (segment and offset of a physical memory location).

OF	DF	IF	TF	SF	ZF	AF	PF	CF
U	U	U	U	U	U	U	U	U

LEA
Load Effective Address

Computes the offset of the memory location specified by the source operand. Loads this offset into the 16-bit register specified as the destination operand.

```
[<label>]      LEA      <destination>,<source>      [<comment>]

   <destination> is the designator of the 16-bit register
                 whose value is to be replaced by the offset,
                 and
   <source>      is the address expression from which the
                 offset is to be computed.
```

OF	DF	IF	TF	SF	ZF	AF	PF	CF
U	U	U	U	U	U	U	U	U

LODS

LODSB	LODSW	LODSD
Load String Byte	Load String Word	Load String Double Word (80386/80486)

Loads the accumulator register (AL, AX, or EAX) with the byte, word, or double word addressed by the DS:SI register pair. If the direction flag (DF) is 0, the SI-register is incremented by 1 (LODSB), 2 (LODSW), or 4 (LODSD); if DF is 1, the SI-register is decremented by 1 (LODSB), 2 (LODSW), or 4 (LODSD).

```
[<label>]      LODS     <source>                    [<comment>]

[<label>]      LODSB                                [<comment>]

[<label>]      LODSW                                [<comment>]

[<label>]      LODSD                                [<comment>]

   <source>      identifies the array addressed by the DS:SI
                 register pair.
```

OF	DF	IF	TF	SF	ZF	AF	PF	CF
U	U	U	U	U	U	U	U	U

LOOP	LOOP (real mode) (80386/80486)	LOOPW (real or protected mode) (80386/80486)

The value in the CX-register is decremented by 1. If the resulting value in the CX-register is nonzero, then control is transferred to the instruction that begins at the memory location specified by the operand.

```
[<label>]     LOOP    <short label>              [<comment>]

[<label>]     LOOPW   <short label>              [<comment>]
```

<short label> is the label of an instruction whose memory location is within -128 to 127 bytes from the memory location immediately following the LOOP/LOOPW instruction.

OF	DF	IF	TF	SF	ZF	AF	PF	CF
U	U	U	U	U	U	U	U	U

LOOP (protected mode) (80386/80486)	LOOPD (real or protected mode) (80386/80486)

The value in the ECX-register is decremented by 1. If the resulting value in the ECX-register is nonzero, then control is transferred to the instruction that begins at the memory location specified by the operand.

```
[<label>]     LOOP    <short label>              [<comment>]

[<label>]     LOOPD   <short label>              [<comment>]
```

<short label> is the label of an instruction whose memory location is within -128 to 127 bytes from the memory location immediately following the LOOP/LOOPD instruction.

OF	DF	IF	TF	SF	ZF	AF	PF	CF
U	U	U	U	U	U	U	U	U

LOOPE/LOOPZ | **LOOPE/LOOPZ (real mode) (80386/80486)** | **LOOPEW/LOOPZW (real or protected mode) (80386/80486)**

Loop on Equal/Loop on Zero

The value in the CX-register is decremented by 1. If the resulting value in the CX-register is nonzero and ZF = 1, then control is transferred to the instruction that begins at the memory location specified by the operand.

```
[<label>]    LOOPE    <short label>             [<comment>]

[<label>]    LOOPZ    <short label>             [<comment>]

[<label>]    LOOPEW   <short label>             [<comment>]

[<label>]    LOOPZW   <short label>             [<comment>]
```

<short label> is the label of an instruction whose memory location is within -128 to 127 bytes from the memory location immediately following the LOOPE/LOOPZ (LOOPEW/LOOPZW) instruction.

OF	DF	IF	TF	SF	ZF	AF	PF	CF
U	U	U	U	U	U	U	U	U

LOOPE/LOOPZ (protected mode) (80386/80486) | **LOOPED/LOOPZD (real or protected mode) (80386/80486)**

Loop on Equal/Loop on Zero

The value in the ECX-register is decremented by 1. If the resulting value in the ECX-register is nonzero and ZF = 1, then control is transferred to the instruction that begins at the memory location specified by the operand.

```
[<label>]    LOOPE    <short label>             [<comment>]

[<label>]    LOOPZ    <short label>             [<comment>]

[<label>]    LOOPED   <short label>             [<comment>]

[<label>]    LOOPZD   <short label>             [<comment>]
```

<short label> is the label of an instruction whose memory location is within -128 to 127 bytes from the memory location immediately following the LOOPE/LOOPZ (LOOPED/LOOPZD) instruction.

OF	DF	IF	TF	SF	ZF	AF	PF	CF
U	U	U	U	U	U	U	U	U

LOOPNE/LOOPNZ	LOOPNE/LOOPNZ (real mode) (80386/80486)	LOOPNEW/LOOPNZW (real or protected mode) (80386/80486)

Loop on Not Equal/Loop on Not Zero

The value in the CX-register is decremented by 1. If the resulting value in the CX-register is nonzero and ZF = 0, then control is transferred to the instruction that begins at the memory location specified by the operand.

```
[<label>]     LOOPNE   <short label>          [<comment>]

[<label>]     LOOPNZ   <short label>          [<comment>]

[<label>]     LOOPNEW  <short label>          [<comment>]

[<label>]     LOOPNZW  <short label>          [<comment>]
```

<short label> is the label of an instruction whose memory location is within -128 to 127 bytes from the memory location immediately following the LOOPNE/LOOPNZ (LOOPNEW/LOOPNZW) instruction.

OF	DF	IF	TF	SF	ZF	AF	PF	CF
U	U	U	U	U	U	U	U	U

LOOPNE/LOOPNZ (protected mode) (80386/80486)

LOOPNED/LOOPNZD (real or protected mode) (80386/80486)

Loop on Not Equal/Loop on Not Zero

The value in the ECX-register is decremented by 1. If the resulting value in the ECX-register is nonzero and ZF = 0, then control is transferred to the instruction that begins at the memory location specified by the operand.

```
[<label>]     LOOPNE  <short label>          [<comment>]

[<label>]     LOOPNZ  <short label>          [<comment>]

[<label>]     LOOPNED <short label>          [<comment>]

[<label>]     LOOPNZD <short label>          [<comment>]
```

<short label> is the label of an instruction whose memory location is within -128 to 127 bytes from the memory location immediately following the LOOPNE/LOOPNZ (LOOPNED/LOOPNZD) instruction.

OF	DF	IF	TF	SF	ZF	AF	PF	CF
U	U	U	U	U	U	U	U	U

LSS
Load Pointer Using SS Register

See entry for LDS instruction.

MOV
Move Byte or Word
Move Double Word (80386/80486)

Replaces the value of the destination operand with a copy of the value of the source operand.

[<label>] MOV <destination>,<source> [<comment>]

<source> identifies the location of the value that is to be copied, and
<destination> identifies where the value is to be moved.

The types of the two operands must match (i.e., both must be byte or both must be word). Both operands may be double word for the 80386 and 80486 microprocessors.

<destination>	<source>
General register	General register Segment register Memory location Immediate
Segment register	General register Memory location
Memory location	General register Segment register Immediate

OF	DF	IF	TF	SF	ZF	AF	PF	CF
U	U	U	U	U	U	U	U	U

MOVS

MOVSB	MOVSW	MOVSD
Move String Byte	Move String Word	Move String Double Word (80386/80486)

Replaces the byte, word, or double word addressed by the ES:DI register pair with a copy of the byte, word, or double word addressed by the DS:SI register pair. If the direction flag (DF) is 0, both the SI and DI registers are incremented by 1 (MOVSB), 2 (MOVSW), or 4 (MOVSD); if DF is 1, both the SI and DI registers are decremented by 1 (MOVSB), 2 (MOVSW), or 4 (MOVSD).

```
[<label>]     MOVS     <destination>,<source>     [<comment>]

[<label>]     MOVSB                               [<comment>]

[<label>]     MOVSW                               [<comment>]

[<label>]     MOVSD                               [<comment>]
```

<destination> identifies the array addressed by the ES:DI register pair, and
<source> identifies the array addressed by the DS:SI register pair.

OF	DF	IF	TF	SF	ZF	AF	PF	CF
U	U	U	U	U	U	U	U	U

MOVSX
Move with Sign-Extension
(80386/80486)

MOVZX
Move with Zero-Extension
(80386/80486)

The MOVSX instruction replaces the value of the destination operand with a sign-extended copy of the source operand.
The MOVZX instruction replaces the value of the destination operand with a zero-extended copy of the source operand.

```
[<label>]      MOVSX   <destination>,<source>      [<comment>]

[<label>]      MOVZX   <destination>,<source>      [<comment>]
```

<source> identifies the location of the value that is to be copied, and
<destination> identifies where the extended value is to be moved.

The type of the destination operand must be larger than the type of the source operand (i.e., if the source operand type is byte, then the destination operand type must be word or double word; if the source operand type is word, then the destination operand type must be double word).

<destination>	<source>
General register	General register Memory location

OF	DF	IF	TF	SF	ZF	AF	PF	CF
U	U	U	U	U	U	U	U	U

MUL
Multiply

For a byte operand, multiplies the unsigned integer value in the AL-register by the 8-bit, unsigned integer value specified by the operand, and leaves the 16-bit product in the AX-register.
For a word operand, multiplies the unsigned integer value in the AX-register by the 16-bit, unsigned integer value specified by the operand, and leaves the 32-bit product in the DX:AX register pair.
For a double word operand (80386/80486 only), multiplies the unsigned integer value in the EAX-register by the 32-bit, unsigned integer value specified by the operand, and leaves the 64-bit product in the EDX:EAX register pair.

[<label>] MUL <source> [<comment>]

<source> identifies the location of the multiplier.

<source>
General register
Memory location

OF	DF	IF	TF	SF	ZF	AF	PF	CF
R	U	U	U	UD	UD	UD	UD	R

NEG
Negate

Performs the two's complement of the value in the specified register or memory location, leaving the result in the specified register or memory location.

[<label>] NEG <destination> [<comment>]

<destination> identifies the location of the value to be negated.

<destination>
General register
Memory location

OF	DF	IF	TF	SF	ZF	AF	PF	CF
R	U	U	U	R	R	R	R	R

NOP
No Operation

Causes the microprocessor to do nothing (i.e., to perform no operation). In effect, the instruction causes a delay of 3 clock cycles. Produces the same machine code as XCHG AX,AX.

[<label>] NOP [<comment>]

OF	DF	IF	TF	SF	ZF	AF	PF	CF
U	U	U	U	U	U	U	U	U

NOT
Logical NOT

Performs the one's complement of the value in the specified register or memory location, leaving the result in the specified register or memory location.

[<label>] NOT <destination> [<comment>]

<destination> identifies the location of the value to be logically inverted.

<destination>
General register
Memory location

OF	DF	IF	TF	SF	ZF	AF	PF	CF
U	U	U	U	U	U	U	U	U

OR
Logical OR

Inclusive ORs each bit of the destination operand with the corresponding bit of the source operand, replacing the bit in the destination operand with the result.

[<label>] OR <destination>,<source> [<comment>]

<destination> identifies the location of the operand that is to be replaced with the result, and
<source> identifies the location of the operand that is not to be modified.

The types of the two operands must match (i.e., both must be byte or both must be word). Both operands may be double word for the 80386 and 80486 microprocessors.

<destination>	<source>
General register	General register Memory location Immediate
Memory location	General register Immediate

OF	DF	IF	TF	SF	ZF	AF	PF	CF
C	U	U	U	R	R	UD	R	C

OUT
Output Byte or Word to Port
Output Byte, Word, or Double Word to Port (80386/80486)

Transfers a byte from the AL-register to the specified port, or transfers a word from the AX-register to the specified port pair. May also transfer a double word from the EAX-register to four consecutive ports on the 80386 and 80486 microprocessors.

```
[<label>]     OUT     <port>,AL                 [<comment>]

[<label>]     OUT     <port>,AX                 [<comment>]

[<label>]     OUT     <port>,EAX                [<comment>]
```

<port> specifies the port number for a byte transfer, the first of two consecutive ports for a word transfer, or the first of four consecutive ports for a double word transfer.

The <port> operand can be an immediate value in the range 0-255, or the register designator DX.

OF	DF	IF	TF	SF	ZF	AF	PF	CF
U	U	U	U	U	U	U	U	U

OUTS

OUTSB	OUTSW	OUTSD
Output String Byte	Output String Word	Output String Double Word
(80286/80386/80486)		(80386/80486)

Transfers the byte, word, or double word addressed by the DS:SI register pair to the port(s) addressed by the value of the DX-register. If the direction flag (DF) is 0, the SI-register is incremented by 1 (OUTSB), 2 (OUTSW), or 4 (OUTSD); if the DF is 1, the SI-register is decremented by 1 (OUTSB), 2 (OUTSW), or 4 (OUTSD).

```
[<label>]     OUTS    DX,<source>               [<comment>]

[<label>]     OUTSB                             [<comment>]

[<label>]     OUTSW                             [<comment>]

[<label>]     OUTSD                             [<comment>]
```

<source> is the symbolic name that identifies the array addressed by the DS:SI register pair.

OF	DF	IF	TF	SF	ZF	AF	PF	CF
U	U	U	U	U	U	U	U	U

POP

Replaces the value of the destination operand with a copy of the 16-bit value at the top of the stack, and increments the SP-register by 2.
On the 80386 and 80486 microprocessors, the destination operand may be a word or a double word operand. For a word operand, a 16-bit value is popped from the stack, and the SP-register (ESP in protected mode) is incremented by 2. For a double word operand, a 32-bit value is popped from the stack, and the SP-register (ESP in protected mode) is incremented by 4.

```
[<label>]     POP     <destination>                 [<comment>]
```

<destination> identifies where the value popped from the top of the stack is to be placed.

<destination>

General register
Segment register
Memory location

OF	DF	IF	TF	SF	ZF	AF	PF	CF
U	U	U	U	U	U	U	U	U

POPA
Pop All General Registers
(80286/80386/80486)

Copies the top-of-stack value into the DI-register, and increments the SP-register by 2.
Copies the new top-of-stack value into the SI-register, and increments the SP-register by 2.
Copies the new top-of-stack value into the BP-register, and increments the SP-register by 4 (discards SP-register value).
Copies the new top-of-stack value into the BX-register, and increments the SP-register by 2.
Copies the new top-of-stack value into the DX-register, and increments the SP-register by 2.
Copies the new top-of-stack value into the CX-register, and increments the SP-register by 2.
Copies the new top-of-stack value into the AX-register, and increments the SP-register by 2.

```
[<label>]     POPA                                  [<comment>]
```

OF	DF	IF	TF	SF	ZF	AF	PF	CF
U	U	U	U	U	U	U	U	U

POPAD
Pop All 32-Bit General Registers
(80386/80486)

Copies the top-of-stack double word into the EDI-register, and increments the SP-register (ESP in protected mode) by 4.
Copies the new top-of-stack double word into the ESI-register, and increments the SP-register (ESP in protected mode) by 4.
Copies the new top-of-stack double word into the EBP-register, and increments the SP-register (ESP in protected mode) by 8 (discards ESP-register value).
Copies the new top-of-stack double word into the EBX-register, and increments the SP-register (ESP in protected mode) by 4.
Copies the new top-of-stack double word into the EDX-register, and increments the SP-register (ESP in protected mode) by 4.
Copies the new top-of-stack double word into the ECX-register, and increments the SP-register (ESP in protected mode) by 4.
Copies the new top-of-stack double word into the EAX-register, and increments the SP-register (ESP in protected mode) by 4.

```
[<label>]      POPAD                          [<comment>]
```

OF	DF	IF	TF	SF	ZF	AF	PF	CF
U	U	U	U	U	U	U	U	U

POPF — Pop Flags / POPFD — Pop Eflags (80386/80486)

The POPF instruction copies the top-of-stack value into the flags register, and increments the SP-register by 2.
The POPFD instruction copies the top-of-stack double word into the Eflags register, and increments the SP-register (ESP in protected mode) by 4.

```
[<label>]      POPF                           [<comment>]

[<label>]      POPFD                          [<comment>]
```

OF	DF	IF	TF	SF	ZF	AF	PF	CF
SV	SV	SV	SV	SV	SV	SV	SV	SV

PUSH **PUSHW** **PUSHD**
(80386/80486)

The PUSH and PUSHW instructions decrement the SP-register by 2, and store a copy of the value of the 16-bit operand as the new top-of-stack value.
The PUSHD instruction decrements the SP-register (ESP in protected mode) by 4, and stores a copy of the value of the 32-bit operand as the new top-of-stack value.

```
[<label>]     PUSH     <source>                    [<comment>]

[<label>]     PUSHW    <source>                    [<comment>]

[<label>]     PUSHD    <source>                    [<comment>]
```

<source> identifies the location of the data to be pushed onto the stack.

The type of the operand must be word for PUSH and PUSHW; double word for PUSHD.

<source>
General register
Segment register
Memory location
Immediate value (80286/80386/80486)

OF	DF	IF	TF	SF	ZF	AF	PF	CF
U	U	U	U	U	U	U	U	U

PUSHA
Push All General Registers
(80286/80386/80486)

Pushes the eight general registers onto the stack as follows: Decrements the SP-register by 2, and stores a copy of the AX-register value as the new top-of-stack value. Decrements the SP-register by 2, and stores a copy of the CX-register value as the new top-of-stack value. Decrements the SP-register by 2, and stores a copy of the DX-register value as the new top-of-stack value. Decrements the SP-register by 2, and stores a copy of the BX-register value as the new top-of-stack value. Decrements the SP-register by 2, and stores a copy of the SP-register value as the new top-of-stack value. Decrements the SP-register by 2, and stores a copy of the BP-register value as the new top-of-stack value. Decrements the SP-register by 2, and stores a copy of the SI-register value as the new top-of-stack value. Decrements the SP-register by 2, and stores a copy of the DI-register value as the new top-of-stack value. The value that is pushed for the SP-register is the value of the SP-register prior to the push of the AX-register value.
[<label>] PUSHA [<comment>]

OF	DF	IF	TF	SF	ZF	AF	PF	CF
U	U	U	U	U	U	U	U	U

PUSHAD
Push All 32-Bit General Registers
(80386/80486)

Pushes the eight 32-bit general registers onto the stack as follows:
Decrements the SP-register (ESP in protected mode) by 4, and stores a copy of the EAX-register value as the new top-of-stack double word.
Decrements the SP-register (ESP in protected mode) by 4, and stores a copy of the ECX-register value as the new top-of-stack double word.
Decrements the SP-register (ESP in protected mode) by 4, and stores a copy of the EDX-register value as the new top-of-stack double word.
Decrements the SP-register (ESP in protected mode) by 4, and stores a copy of the EBX-register value as the new top-of-stack double word.
Decrements the SP-register (ESP in protected mode) by 4, and stores a copy of the ESP-register value as the new top-of-stack double word.
Decrements the SP-register (ESP in protected mode) by 4, and stores a copy of the EBP-register value as the new top-of-stack double word.
Decrements the SP-register (ESP in protected mode) by 4, and stores a copy of the ESI-register value as the new top-of-stack double word.
Decrements the SP-register (ESP in protected mode) by 4, and stores a copy of the EDI-register value as the new top-of-stack double word.
The value that is pushed for the ESP-register is the value of the ESP-register prior to the push of the EAX-register value.

[<label>] PUSHAD [<comment>]

OF	DF	IF	TF	SF	ZF	AF	PF	CF
U	U	U	U	U	U	U	U	U

PUSHF
Push Flags

PUSHFD
Push Eflags
(80386/80486)

The PUSHF instruction decrements the SP-register by 2, and stores a copy of the flags register value as the new top-of-stack value.
The PUSHFD instruction decrements the SP-register (ESP in protected mode) by 4, and stores a copy of the Eflags register value as the new top-of-stack double word.

```
[<label>]      PUSHF                                   [<comment>]

[<label>]      PUSHFD                                  [<comment>]
```

OF	DF	IF	TF	SF	ZF	AF	PF	CF
U	U	U	U	U	U	U	U	U

RCL
Rotate Through Carry Left

Rotates the contents of the specified register or memory location left the number of bit positions specified by the shift count (1 or the value in the CL-register). The last bit shifted out on the left is recorded in the carry flag. Bits shifted from the carry flag are shifted in on the right.

```
[<label>]     RCL     <destination>,1                [<comment>]

[<label>]     RCL     <destination>,CL               [<comment>]

----------------------(80286/80386/80486)----------------------
[<label>]     RCL     <destination>,<immediate>      [<comment>]
```

<destination> specifies the general register or memory location that contains the value to be shifted.

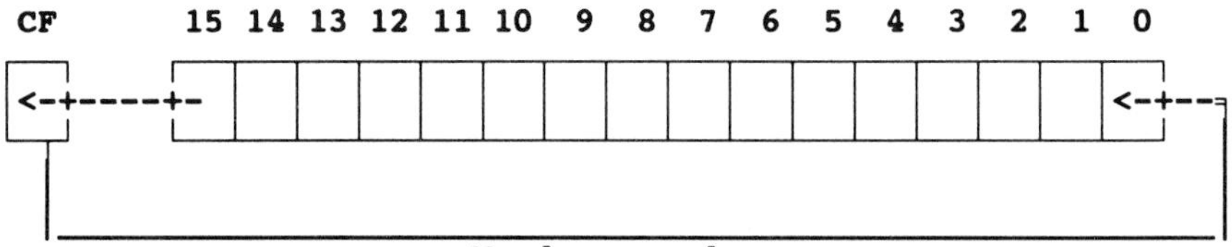

```
 CF       15 14 13 12 11 10  9  8  7  6  5  4  3  2  1  0
+--+     +--+--+--+--+--+--+--+--+--+--+--+--+--+--+--+--+
|<-+-----+- |  |  |  |  |  |  |  |  |  |  |  |  |  |  |<-+--+
+--+     +--+--+--+--+--+--+--+--+--+--+--+--+--+--+--+--+  |
 |                                                          |
 +----------------------------------------------------------+
                      Word operand

                    CF        7  6  5  4  3  2  1  0
                   +--+     +--+--+--+--+--+--+--+--+
                   |<-+-----+- |  |  |  |  |  |  |<-+--+
                   +--+     +--+--+--+--+--+--+--+--+  |
                    |                                  |
                    +----------------------------------+
                                Byte operand
```

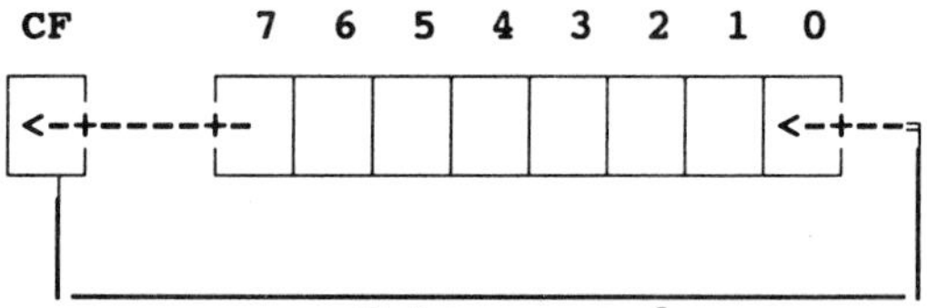

OF	DF	IF	TF	SF	ZF	AF	PF	CF
SC	U	U	U	U	U	U	U	LB

RCR
Rotate Through Carry Right

Rotates the contents of the specified register or memory location right the number of bit positions specified by the shift count (1 or the value in the CL-register). The last bit shifted out on the right is recorded in the carry flag. Bits shifted from the carry flag are shifted in on the left.

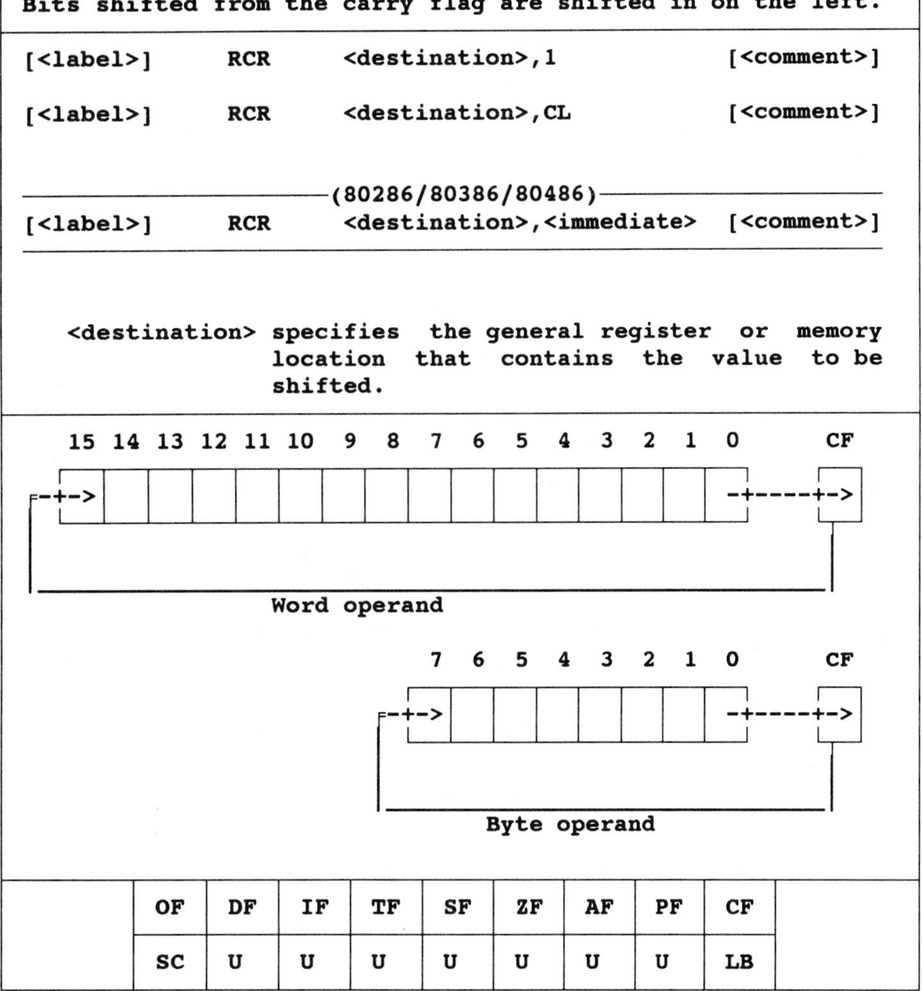

```
[<label>]     RCR     <destination>,1               [<comment>]

[<label>]     RCR     <destination>,CL              [<comment>]

--------------------(80286/80386/80486)--------------------
[<label>]     RCR     <destination>,<immediate>     [<comment>]
```

<destination> specifies the general register or memory location that contains the value to be shifted.

OF	DF	IF	TF	SF	ZF	AF	PF	CF
SC	U	U	U	U	U	U	U	LB

REP
Repeat

```
This repeat prefix can be placed before the  operation  code
of a string instruction, and it produces the following loop:
REPEAT
   Execute following string instruction
   Decrement CX-register by 1
UNTIL CX-register is 0
```

```
[<label>]     REP <string-op>    <operands>         [<comment>]

   <string-op>    is  the operation code mnemonic  of  one of
                  the string instructions, and
   <operands>     is the operand list (if any) for the string
                  instruction.
```

The prefix REP should be used only with the MOVE, LOAD, and STORE string instructions. If REP is used with the COMPARE or SCAN string instructions, it behaves exactly like the REPE/REPZ prefix.

OF	DF	IF	TF	SF	ZF	AF	PF	CF
U	U	U	U	U	U	U	U	U

REPE/REPZ
Repeat on Equal/Repeat on Zero

```
This repeat prefix can be placed before the  operation  code
of a string instruction, and it produces the following loop:
REPEAT
   Execute following string instruction
   Decrement CX-register by 1
UNTIL CX-register is 0  or  ZF is 0
```

```
[<label>]     REPE <string-op>    <operands>        [<comment>]

[<label>]     REPZ <string-op>    <operands>        [<comment>]

   <string-op>    is  the operation code mnemonic  of  one of
                  the string instructions, and
   <operands>     is the operand list (if any) for the string
                  instruction.
```

The prefix REPE/REPZ should be used only with the COMPARE and SCAN string instructions. If REPE/REPZ is used with the MOVE, LOAD, or STORE string instructions, it behaves exactly like the REP prefix.

OF	DF	IF	TF	SF	ZF	AF	PF	CF
U	U	U	U	U	U	U	U	U

REPNE/REPNZ
Repeat on Not Equal/Repeat on Not Zero

```
This repeat prefix can be placed before the operation code
of a string instruction, and it produces the following loop:
REPEAT
   Execute following string instruction
   Decrement CX-register by 1
UNTIL CX-register is 0 or ZF is 1
```

```
[<label>]    REPNE <string-op>   <operands>      [<comment>]

[<label>]    REPNZ <string-op>   <operands>      [<comment>]

   <string-op>   is the operation code mnemonic of one of
                 the string instructions, and
   <operands>    is the operand list (if any) for the string
                 instruction.
```

The prefix REPNE/REPNZ should be used only with the COMPARE and SCAN string instructions. If REPNE/REPNZ is used with the MOVE, LOAD, or STORE string instructions, it behaves exactly like the REP prefix.

OF	DF	IF	TF	SF	ZF	AF	PF	CF
U	U	U	U	U	U	U	U	U

RET
Return

Pops the return address from the top of the stack and transfers control to the instruction at that address. Adds the value of the immediate operand to the SP-register (i.e., pops the arguments from the stack).

[<label>] RET [<pop-value>] [<comment>]

<pop-value> is an immediate value that specifies the number of argument bytes to be popped from the stack and discarded.

Procedure Type	Operation of RET Instruction
NEAR	Pops the top-of-stack value into the IP-register, and then adds the optional operand value to the SP-register.
FAR	Pops the top-of-stack value into the IP-register, pops the new top-of-stack value into the CS-register, and then adds the optional operand value to the SP-register.

OF	DF	IF	TF	SF	ZF	AF	PF	CF
U	U	U	U	U	U	U	U	U

ROL
Rotate Left

Rotates the contents of the specified register or memory location left the number of bit positions specified by the shift count (1 or the value in the CL-register). The last bit shifted out on the left is recorded in the carry flag. Bits shifted out on the left are shifted in on the right.

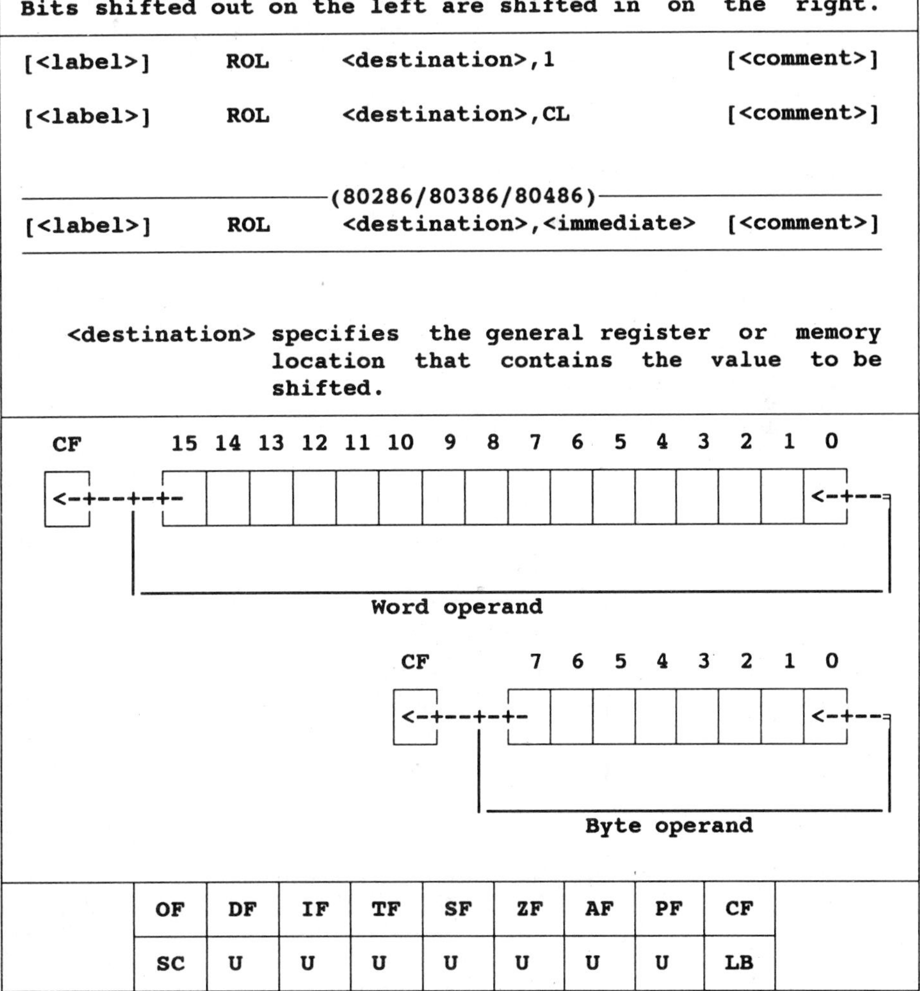

```
[<label>]     ROL     <destination>,1                 [<comment>]

[<label>]     ROL     <destination>,CL                [<comment>]

              (80286/80386/80486)
[<label>]     ROL     <destination>,<immediate>       [<comment>]
```

<destination> specifies the general register or memory location that contains the value to be shifted.

	OF	DF	IF	TF	SF	ZF	AF	PF	CF	
	SC	U	U	U	U	U	U	U	LB	

ROR
Rotate Right

Rotates the contents of the specified register or memory location right the number of bit positions specified by the shift count (1 or the value in the CL-register). The last bit shifted out on the right is recorded in the carry flag. Bits shifted out on the right are shifted in on the left.

```
[<label>]     ROR     <destination>,1                [<comment>]

[<label>]     ROR     <destination>,CL               [<comment>]

------------------(80286/80386/80486)-------------------
[<label>]     ROR     <destination>,<immediate>      [<comment>]
```

<destination> specifies the general register or memory location that contains the value to be shifted.

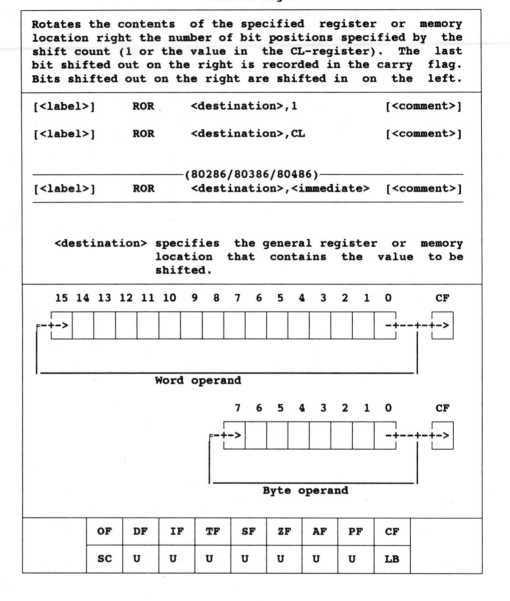

```
 15 14 13 12 11 10  9  8  7  6  5  4  3  2  1  0      CF
┌-+-> |  |  |  |  |  |  |  |  |  |  |  |  |  |  -+--+-+->  
|                                               |
|_______________________________________________|
               Word operand

                          7  6  5  4  3  2  1  0      CF
                        ┌-+-> |  |  |  |  |  |  -+--+-+->
                        |                       |
                        |_______________________|
                              Byte operand
```

	OF	DF	IF	TF	SF	ZF	AF	PF	CF	
	SC	U	U	U	U	U	U	U	LB	

SAHF
Store AH-Register into Flags

Stores a copy of the AH-register value in the low-order half of the flags register.

```
[<label>]     SAHF                                   [<comment>]
```

	OF	DF	IF	TF	SF	ZF	AF	PF	CF	
	U	U	U	U	R	R	R	R	R	

SAL
Shift Arithmetic Left

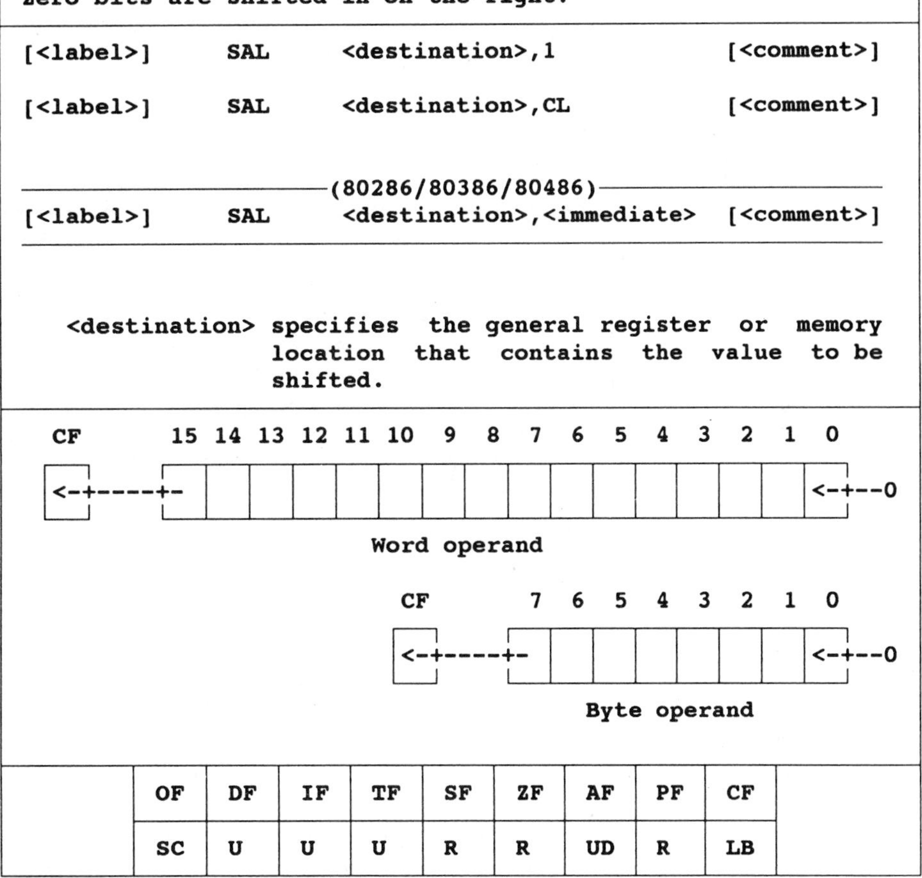

Shifts the contents of the specified register or memory location left the number of bit positions specified by the shift count (1 or the value in the CL-register). The last bit shifted out on the left is recorded in the carry flag. Zero bits are shifted in on the right.

```
[<label>]     SAL     <destination>,1              [<comment>]

[<label>]     SAL     <destination>,CL             [<comment>]

              (80286/80386/80486)
[<label>]     SAL     <destination>,<immediate>    [<comment>]
```

<destination> specifies the general register or memory location that contains the value to be shifted.

OF	DF	IF	TF	SF	ZF	AF	PF	CF
SC	U	U	U	R	R	UD	R	LB

SAR
Shift Arithmetic Right

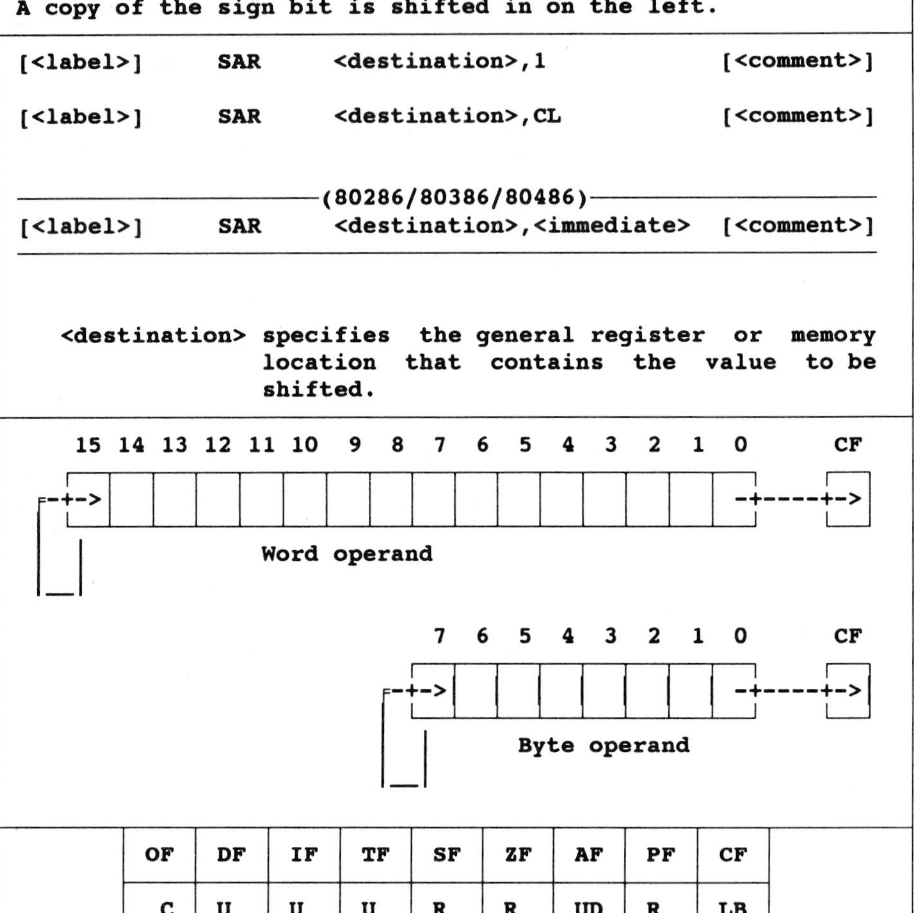

Shifts the contents of the specified register or memory location right the number of bit positions specified by the shift count (1 or the value in the CL-register). The last bit shifted out on the right is recorded in the carry flag. A copy of the sign bit is shifted in on the left.

[<label>] SAR <destination>,1 [<comment>]

[<label>] SAR <destination>,CL [<comment>]

(80286/80386/80486)

[<label>] SAR <destination>,<immediate> [<comment>]

<destination> specifies the general register or memory location that contains the value to be shifted.

OF	DF	IF	TF	SF	ZF	AF	PF	CF
C	U	U	U	R	R	UD	R	LB

SBB
Subtract with Borrow

Subtracts the source operand and the borrow flag from the destination operand, replacing the destination operand with the difference.

[<label>] SBB <destination>,<source> [<comment>]

<source> identifies the location of the subtrahend, and

<destination> identifies the location of the minuend that will be replaced by the difference.

The types of the two operands must match (i.e., both must be byte or both must be word). Both operands may be double word for the 80386 and 80486 microprocessors.

<destination>	<source>
General register	General register Memory location Immediate
Memory location	General register Immediate

OF	DF	IF	TF	SF	ZF	AF	PF	CF
R	U	U	U	R	R	R	R	R

SCAS

SCASB	SCASW	SCASD
Scan String Byte	Scan String Word	Scan String Double Word (80386/80486)

Compares the byte, word, or double word in the accumulator register (AL, AX, or EAX) to the byte, word, or double word addressed by the ES:DI register pair, and sets the flags accordingly. The byte, word, or double word addressed by the ES:DI register pair is subtracted from the byte, word, or double word in the accumulator register, and the flags are set to reflect the difference. Neither operand is modified. If the direction flag (DF) is 0, the DI-register is incremented by 1 (SCASB), 2 (SCASW), or 4 (SCASD); if DF is 1, the DI-register is decremented by 1 (SCASB), 2 (SCASW), or 4 (SCASD).

```
[<label>]     SCAS     <destination>          [<comment>]

[<label>]     SCASB                           [<comment>]

[<label>]     SCASW                           [<comment>]

[<label>]     SCASD                           [<comment>]
```

<destination> identifies the array addressed by the ES:DI register pair.

OF	DF	IF	TF	SF	ZF	AF	PF	CF
R	U	U	U	R	R	R	R	R

SETxxx
Conditional SET
(Unsigned Integer)
(80386/80486)

This group of conditional SET instructions provides the capability to set or clear a byte based on the results of computations involving unsigned numbers.

[<label>] SETxxx <destination> [<comment>]

<destination> identifies the 8-bit general register or memory location that is to be set or cleared.

OF	DF	IF	TF	SF	ZF	AF	PF	CF
U	U	U	U	U	U	U	U	U

Operation Code Mnemonic	Description	Will Set If
SETA/SETNBE	SET if Above SET if Not Below nor Equal	CF = 0 and ZF = 0
SETAE/SETNB	SET if Above or Equal SET if Not Below	CF = 0
SETB/SETNAE	SET if Below SET if Not Above nor Equal	CF = 1
SETBE/SETNA	SET if Below or Equal SET if Not Above	CF = 1 or ZF = 1
SETE/SETZ	SET if Equal to Zero	ZF = 1
SETNE/SETNZ	SET if Not Equal to Zero	ZF = 0

SETxxx
Conditional SET
(Signed Integer)
(80386/80486)

This group of conditional SET instructions provides the capability to set or clear a byte based on the results of computations involving signed numbers.

[<label>] SETxxx <destination> [<comment>]

<destination> identifies the 8-bit general register or memory location that is to be set or cleared.

OF	DF	IF	TF	SF	ZF	AF	PF	CF
U	U	U	U	U	U	U	U	U

Operation Code Mnemonic	Description	Will Set If
SETG/SETNLE	SET if Greater than SET if Not Less nor Equal	ZF = 0 and SF = OF
SETGE/SETNL	SET if Greater or Equal SET if Not Less than	(SF xor OF) = 0 (i.e., SF = OF)
SETL/SETNGE	SET if Less than SET if Not Greater nor Equal	(SF xor OF) = 1 (i.e., SF <> OF)
SETLE/SETNG	SET if Less than or Equal SET if Not Greater than	ZF = 1 or SF <> OF
SETE/SETZ	SET if Equal to Zero	ZF = 1
SETNE/SETNZ	SET if Not Equal to Zero	ZF = 0

SETxx
Conditional SET
(Specific Flag)
(80386/80486)

This group of conditional SET instructions provides the capability to set or clear a byte based on the current state of a specific flag in the flags register.

[<label>] SETxx <destination> [<comment>]

<destination> identifies the 8-bit general register or memory location that is to be set or cleared.

OF	DF	IF	TF	SF	ZF	AF	PF	CF
U	U	U	U	U	U	U	U	U

Operation Code Mnemonic	Description	Will Set If
SETC	SET if Carry	CF = 1
SETNC	SET if No Carry	CF = 0
SETO	SET if Overflow	OF = 1
SETNO	SET if No Overflow	OF = 0
SETS	SET if negative Sign	SF = 1
SETNS	SET if Nonnegative Sign	SF = 0
SETZ	SET if Zero	ZF = 1
SETNZ	SET if Not Zero	ZF = 0
SETP/SETPE	SET if Parity Even	PF = 1
SETNP/SETPO	SET if Parity Odd	PF = 0

SHL
Shift Logical Left

Shifts the contents of the specified register or memory location left the number of bit positions specified by the shift count (1 or the value in the CL-register). The last bit shifted out on the left is recorded in the carry flag. Zero bits are shifted in on the right.

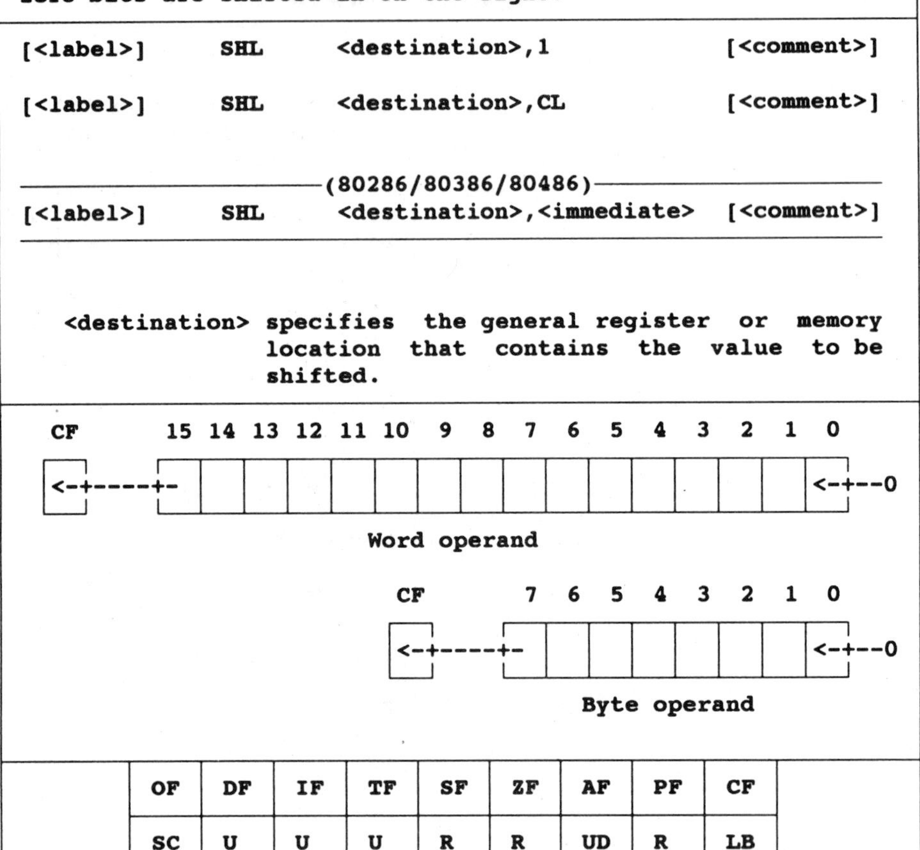

```
[<label>]     SHL     <destination>,1                [<comment>]

[<label>]     SHL     <destination>,CL               [<comment>]

------------------(80286/80386/80486)------------------
[<label>]     SHL     <destination>,<immediate>      [<comment>]
```

<destination> specifies the general register or memory location that contains the value to be shifted.

OF	DF	IF	TF	SF	ZF	AF	PF	CF
SC	U	U	U	R	R	UD	R	LB

SHR
Shift Logical Right

Shifts the contents of the specified register or memory location right the number of bit positions specified by the shift count (1 or the value in the CL-register). The last bit shifted out on the right is recorded in the carry flag. Zero bits are shifted in on the left.

```
[<label>]    SHR    <destination>,1                [<comment>]

[<label>]    SHR    <destination>,CL               [<comment>]

-------------------(80286/80386/80486)-------------------
[<label>]    SHR    <destination>,<immediate>      [<comment>]
```

<destination> specifies the general register or memory location that contains the value to be shifted.

```
   15 14 13 12 11 10  9  8  7  6  5  4  3  2  1  0       CF
0--+->[  ][  ][  ][  ][  ][  ][  ][  ][  ][  ][  ][  ][  ][  ][  ]-+----+->[  ]
                  Word operand

                              7  6  5  4  3  2  1  0       CF
                        0--+->[  ][  ][  ][  ][  ][  ][  ]-+----+->[  ]
                                   Byte operand
```

OF	DF	IF	TF	SF	ZF	AF	PF	CF
SC	U	U	U	R	R	UD	R	LB

SHLD
Double Precision
Left Shift

SHRD
Double Precision
Right Shift

(80386/80486)

Shifts the contents of the specified register or memory location left (SHLD) or right (SHRD) the number of bit positions specified by the shift count operand. The last bit shifted out on the left (SHLD) or right (SHRD) is recorded in the carry flag. The n most significant bits (SHLD) or the n least significant bits (SHRD) of the source operand are shifted in on the right (SHLD) or on the left (SHRD), where n is the value of the shift count operand.

```
[<label>] SHLD <destination>,<source>,<shift-count> [<comment>]

[<label>] SHRD <destination>,<source>,<shift-count> [<comment>]
```

<destination> specifies the general register or memory location that contains the value to be shifted,

<source> specifies the general register containing the bits that are to replace the bits vacated by the shift, and

<shift-count> specifies the number of bit positions to shift the destination operand.

The types of the two operands must match (i.e., both must be word or both must be double word).

OF	DF	IF	TF	SF	ZF	AF	PF	CF
SC	U	U	U	R	R	UD	R	LB

STC
Set Carry/Borrow Flag

Sets the carry flag to 1.

```
[<label>]     STC                              [<comment>]
```

OF	DF	IF	TF	SF	ZF	AF	PF	CF
U	U	U	U	U	U	U	U	S

STD
Set Direction Flag

Sets the direction flag to 1, which causes the automatic update of the DI- and/or SI-register following execution of a string instruction to be a decrement.

[<label>] STD [<comment>]

OF	DF	IF	TF	SF	ZF	AF	PF	CF
U	S	U	U	U	U	U	U	U

STI
Set Interrupt Flag

Sets the interrupt flag to 1, which enables external interrupts. That is, it causes the processor to accept external interrupts.

[<label>] STI [<comment>]

OF	DF	IF	TF	SF	ZF	AF	PF	CF
U	U	S	U	U	U	U	U	U

STOS

STOSB	STOSW	STOSD
Store String Byte	Store String Word	Store String Double Word (80386/80486)

Stores a copy of the byte, word, or double word from the accumulator register (AL, AX, or EAX) into the byte, word, or double word addressed by the ES:DI register pair. If the direction flag (DF) is 0, the DI-register is incremented by 1 (STOSB), 2 (STOSW), or 4 (STOSD); if DF is 1, the DI-register is decremented by 1 (STOSB), 2 (STOSW), or 4 (STOSW).

```
[<label>]      STOS    <destination>              [<comment>]

[<label>]      STOSB                              [<comment>]

[<label>]      STOSW                              [<comment>]

[<label>]      STOSD                              [<comment>]
```

<destination> identifies the array addressed by the ES:DI register pair.

OF	DF	IF	TF	SF	ZF	AF	PF	CF
U	U	U	U	U	U	U	U	U

SUB
Subtract

Subtracts the source operand from the destination operand, replacing the destination operand with the difference.

[<label>] SUB <destination>,<source> [<comment>]

<source> identifies the location of the subtrahend, and
<destination> identifies the location of the minuend that will be replaced by the difference.

The types of the two operands must match (i.e., both must be byte or both must be word). Both operands may be double word for the 80386 and 80486 microprocessors.

<destination>	<source>
General register	General register Memory location Immediate
Memory location	General register Immediate

OF	DF	IF	TF	SF	ZF	AF	PF	CF
R	U	U	U	R	R	R	R	R

TEST

ANDs each bit of the destination operand with the corresponding bit of the source operand, and sets the flags according to the result. Neither the source operand nor the destination operand is modified.

[<label>] TEST <destination>,<source> [<comment>]

<destination> identifies the location of one operand, and
<source> identifies the location of the other operand.

The types of the two operands must match (i.e., both must be byte or both must be word). Both operands may be double word for the 80386 and 80486 microprocessors.

<destination>	<source>
General register	General register Memory location Immediate
Memory location	General register Immediate

OF	DF	IF	TF	SF	ZF	AF	PF	CF
C	U	U	U	R	R	UD	R	C

XADD
Exchange and Add
(80486)

Adds the source operand to the destination operand, replacing the destination operand with the sum, and replacing the source operand with the original value of the destination operand.

```
[<label>]     XADD     <destination>,<source>     [<comment>]
```

<source> identifies the location of the addend that will be replaced by the original value of the destination operand, and
<destination> identifies the location of the augend that will be replaced by the sum.

The types of the two operands must match (i.e., both must be byte, both must be word, or both must be double word).

<destination>	<source>
General register Memory location	General register

OF	DF	IF	TF	SF	ZF	AF	PF	CF
R	U	U	U	R	R	R	R	R

XCHG
Exchange

Exchanges the values of the two operands.

```
[<label>]     XCHG     <destination>,<source>     [<comment>]
```

<source> identifies the location of one of the two values to be exchanged, and
<destination> identifies the location of the other value to be exchanged.

The types of the two operands must match (i.e., both must be byte or both must be word). Both operands may be double word for the 80386 and 80486 microprocessors.

<destination>	<source>
General register	General register Memory location
Memory location	General register

OF	DF	IF	TF	SF	ZF	AF	PF	CF
U	U	U	U	U	U	U	U	U

XLAT
Translate

Replaces the AL-register value with a copy of the byte addressed by the DS:BX+AL register group.

```
[<label>]      XLAT     [<source>]                    [<comment>]

   <source>        is the symbolic name of the byte array
                   addressed by the DS:BX register pair.
```

OF	DF	IF	TF	SF	ZF	AF	PF	CF
U	U	U	U	U	U	U	U	U

XOR
Exclusive OR

Exclusive ORs each bit of the destination operand with the corresponding bit of the source operand, replacing the bit in the destination operand with the result.

```
[<label>]      XOR      <destination>,<source>      [<comment>]

   <destination> identifies the location of the operand that
                 is to be replaced with the result, and
   <source>      identifies the location of the operand that
                 is not to be modified.
```

The types of the two operands must match (i.e., both must be byte or both must be word). Both operands may be double word for the 80386 and 80486 microprocessors.

<destination>	<source>
General register	General register Memory location Immediate
Memory location	General register Immediate

OF	DF	IF	TF	SF	ZF	AF	PF	CF
C	U	U	U	R	R	UD	R	C

APPENDIX B

Pseudo-Operations

The following diagram shows the general format used in this appendix to describe the individual pseudo-operations recognized by the Macro Assembler (MASM).

Pseudo-Operation Code

Description of operation to be performed by the assembler
General form of pseudo-operation Notation: <> encloses items supplied by the programmer. [] encloses optional items.
Additional information

.286

Instructs the assembler to accept and assemble nonprivileged instructions for the 80286 microprocessor.

.286	[<comment>]

.286P

Instructs the assembler to accept and assemble all privileged and nonprivileged instructions for the 80286 microprocessor.

.286P	[<comment>]

.287

Instructs the assembler to accept and assemble instructions for the 80287 coprocessor.

.287	[<comment>]

.386

Instructs the assembler to accept and assemble nonprivileged instructions for the 80386 microprocessor.

.386	[<comment>]

.386P

Instructs the assembler to accept and assemble all privileged and nonprivileged instructions for the 80386 microprocessor.

.386P	[<comment>]

.387

Instructs the assembler to accept and assemble instructions for the 80387 coprocessor.

.387	[<comment>]

.486

Instructs the assembler to accept and assemble nonprivileged instructions for the 80486 microprocessor.	
.486	[<comment>]

.486P

Instructs the assembler to accept and assemble all privileged and nonprivileged instructions for the 80486 microprocessor.	
.486P	[<comment>]

ASSUME
Segment Register Assumptions

Instructs the assembler as to how the segment registers will be associated with the assembly module segments at execution time.

```
ASSUME <seg-reg-assign-list>      [<comment>]
```

<seg-reg-assign-list>	is a list of segment register assignments of the form <seg-reg>:<seg-name> or <seg-reg>:NOTHING or <seg-reg>:ERROR
<seg-reg>	is one of the segment register designators CS, SS, DS, or ES (CS, SS, DS, ES, FS, or GS on 80386 and 80486), and
<seg-name>	is the symbolic name of a segment defined by a SEGMENT pseudo-operation, or by a simplified segment directive.

NOTHING states that the specified segment register is not being used, but requests no error-checking.
ERROR states that an assembly error is to be generated if the register is used in the assembly module.

ASSUME
General Register Assumptions

Instructs the assembler as to the data types allowed for the general registers at execution time.

ASSUME <gen-reg-assign-list> [<comment>]

<gen-reg-assign-list> is a list of general register assignments of the form

<gen-reg>:<type>
or
<gen-reg>:PTR <type>
or
<gen-reg>:NOTHING
or
<gen-reg>:ERROR

<gen-reg> is one of the general register designators, and

<type> is one of the data types: BYTE, SBYTE, WORD, SWORD, DWORD, or SDWORD.

NOTHING states that the specified general register is not being used, but requests no error-checking.
ERROR states that an assembly error is to be generated if the register is used in the assembly module.

BYTE
Define Unsigned Byte

See DB pseudo-operation.

.CODE

Indicates the beginning (or the continuation) of a code segment definition. Must be preceded by a .MODEL directive.

```
.CODE    [<seg-name>]              [<comment>]

<seg-name>   is the symbolic name to be associated with
             the memory location at which the segment is
             to begin.
```

The default segment name is _TEXT for TINY, SMALL, COMPACT, and FLAT memory models; <source-name>_TEXT for MEDIUM, LARGE, and HUGE memory models, in which <source-name> is the name of the source code file that contains the segment definition.

The align type is WORD for TINY, SMALL, MEDIUM, COMPACT, LARGE, and HUGE memory models; DWORD for FLAT memory model.
The combine type is PUBLIC.
The class name is 'CODE'.

COMMENT

Provides a method for entering a sequence of comment lines without the requirement of a semicolon (;) at the beginning of each line.

```
COMMENT <delimiter> <text>
        <text>
        <text>
          .
          .
          .
        <text> <delimiter>
```

The first nonblank character following the COMMENT keyword is taken as the <delimiter>. All subsequent characters are taken as part of the comment, <text>, until another occurrence of the <delimiter> is detected.

.CONST
Constant Data Segment Definition

Indicates the beginning (or the continuation) of a data segment definition in which only constants are to be defined (i.e., the definition of a data segment that has the read-only attribute). Must be preceded by a .MODEL directive.
.CONST [<comment>]
The segment name is CONST. The align type is WORD for all memory models, except FLAT; DWORD for memory model FLAT. The combine type is PUBLIC. The class name is 'CONST'. The data segment is part of DGROUP for all memory models, except FLAT.

.DATA **.DATA?**
NEAR Data Segment Definition
(Initialized Variables) **(Uninitialized Variables)**

Indicates the beginning (or the continuation) of a NEAR data segment definition in which variables are to be defined. With .DATA, the variables may be given initial values. Must be preceded by a .MODEL directive.
.DATA [<comment>] .DATA? [<comment>]
The segment name is _DATA for .DATA and _BSS for .DATA?. The align type is WORD for all memory models, except FLAT; DWORD for memory model FLAT. The combine type is PUBLIC. The class name is 'DATA' for .DATA and 'BSS' for .DATA?. The data segment is part of DGROUP for all memory models, except FLAT.

.DOSSEG/DOSSEG
DOS Segment Conventions

Causes the segments of the executable program to be organized in memory according to segment type.
.DOSSEG [<comment>] or DOSSEG [<comment>]
All code segments appear first in memory, followed by all data segments, followed by the stack segment. Within a given type, the segments are grouped according to class name. When defined using simplified segment directives, segments are given a default class name.

DB Define Byte | **BYTE** Define Byte (Unsigned) | **SBYTE** Define Byte (Signed)

Allocates one or more consecutive data bytes of storage, and initializes their values.

```
[<var-name>]  DB      <constant-list>          [<comment>]

[<var-name>]  BYTE    <constant-list>          [<comment>]

[<var-name>]  SBYTE   <constant-list>          [<comment>]
```

<var-name> is the symbolic name to be associated with the memory location at which the sequence of data bytes is to begin, and

<constant-list> is a list of constant expressions separated by commas.

<constant>	<form>
Binary	A string of binary digits followed by the letter B.
Octal	A string of octal digits followed by the letter O or the letter Q.
Decimal	A string of decimal digits optionally followed by the letter D.
Hexadecimal	A string of hex digits followed by the letter H. The first character must be a digit 0-9.
String	A string of characters enclosed in apostrophes (') or quotation marks (").
Null	? - means that no initial value is specified for the allocated byte.
Duplicate clause	<repeat-count> DUP(<constant-list>)

A minus sign (-) in front of a binary, octal, decimal, or hexadecimal constant instructs the assembler to perform the two's complement of the binary representation of the constant.

DD	DWORD	SDWORD
Define Double Word	Define Double Word (Unsigned)	Define Double Word (Signed)

Allocates one or more consecutive double words of storage, and initializes their values.

```
[<var-name>]  DD      <constant-list>        [<comment>]

[<var-name>]  DWORD   <constant-list>        [<comment>]

[<var-name>]  SDWORD  <constant-list>        [<comment>]
```

<var-name> is the symbolic name to be associated with the memory location at which the sequence of double words is to begin, and

<constant-list> is a list of constant expressions separated by commas.

<constant>	<form>
Binary	A string of binary digits followed by the letter B.
Octal	A string of octal digits followed by the letter O or the letter Q.
Decimal	A string of decimal digits optionally followed by the letter D.
Hexadecimal	A string of hex digits followed by the letter H. The first character must be a digit 0-9.
Address	A label that represents a segment and an offset within the segment.
Null	? - means that no initial value is specified for the allocated double word.
Duplicate clause	<repeat-count> DUP(<constant-list>)

A minus sign (-) in front of a binary, octal, decimal, or hexadecimal constant instructs the assembler to perform the two's complement of the binary representation of the constant.

DT TBYTE
Define Ten Bytes

Allocates one or more ten-byte data blocks of storage, and initializes their values. It is used to define BCD variables.

```
[<var-name>]  DT      <constant-list>          [<comment>]

[<var-name>]  TBYTE   <constant-list>          [<comment>]
```

<var-name> is the symbolic name to be associated with the memory location at which the sequence of data bytes is to begin, and

<constant-list> is a list of constant expressions separated by commas.

<constant>	<form>
BCD	A signed or unsigned string of up to 18 significant decimal digits
Binary	A string of binary digits followed by the letter B.
Octal	A string of octal digits followed by the letter O or the letter Q.
Hexadecimal	A string of hex digits followed by the letter H. The first character must be a digit 0-9.
Null	? - means that 10 bytes of storage are to be allocated but that initial values are not specified.
Duplicate clause	<repeat-count> DUP(<constant-list>)

A minus sign (-) in front of a binary, octal, decimal, or hexadecimal constant instructs the assembler to perform the two's complement of the binary representation of the constant.

DW	WORD	SWORD
Define Word	Define Word (Unsigned)	Define Word (Signed)

Allocates one or more consecutive data words of storage, and initializes their values.

```
[<var-name>]  DW      <constant-list>          [<comment>]

[<var-name>]  WORD    <constant-list>          [<comment>]

[<var-name>]  SWORD   <constant-list>          [<comment>]
```

<var-name> is the symbolic name to be associated with the memory location at which the sequence of data words is to begin, and

<constant-list> is a list of constant expressions separated by commas.

<constant>	<form>
Binary	A string of binary digits followed by the letter B.
Octal	A string of octal digits followed by the letter O or the letter Q.
Decimal	A string of decimal digits optionally followed by the letter D.
Hexadecimal	A string of hex digits followed by the letter H. The first character must be a digit 0-9.
Address	A label that represents an offset within a segment.
Null	? - means that no initial value is specified for the allocated word.
Duplicate clause	<repeat-count> DUP(<constant-list>)

A minus sign (-) in front of a binary, octal, decimal, or hexadecimal constant instructs the assembler to perform the two's complement of the binary representation of the constant.

DWORD
Define Unsigned Double Word

See DD pseudo-operation.

END
End of Assembly Module

Defines the physical end of an assembly module. It must be the last line of every assembly language source module.

```
              END      [<label>]                  [<comment>]

   <label>        is the symbolic name that specifies the
                  entry point for the executable program.
```

ENDM
End of Macro Definition

Defines the physical end of a macro definition.

```
              ENDM                                [<comment>]
```

ENDP
End of Procedure Definition

Defines the physical end of a procedure definition.

```
<proc-name>   ENDP                                [<comment>]

   <proc-name>    is the symbolic name of the procedure and
                  must match the <proc-name> on the PROC
                  pseudo-operation at the beginning of the
                  procedure.
```

ENDS
End of Segment Definition

Defines the physical end of a segment definition.

```
<seg-name>    ENDS                                [<comment>]

   <seg-name>     is the symbolic name to be associated with
                  the segment and must match the <seg-name>
                  used on the SEGMENT pseudo-operation at the
                  beginning of the segment.
```

EQU
Equate

Assigns a symbolic name to the value of a constant expression.
<name> EQU <constant-expr> [<comment>]
<name> is the symbolic name to be associated with the value of the <constant-expr>, and <constant-expr> is an expression that consists of constants and operators.
The symbolic name will have the value of the constant expression throughout the entire assembly module.

=
Equate

Assigns a symbolic name to the value of a constant expression.
<name> = <constant-expr> [<comment>]
<name> is the symbolic name to be associated with the value of the <constant-expr>, and <constant-expr> is an expression that consists of constants and operators.
From this point until it is reassigned by another = pseudo-operation, the symbolic name will have the value of the constant expression.

EVEN

Instructs the assembler to advance the location counter to the next even address so that the next item assembled begins on a word boundary.
EVEN [<comment>]
The assembler inserts a NOP instruction, if necessary, to to reach a word boundary.

.EXIT

Directs the assembler to generate the instructions that, when executed, will return control to DOS.

```
.EXIT    [<constant-expr>]          [<comment>]
```

<constant-expr> is an expression that consists of byte constants and operators.

When the optional operand is omitted, the assembler generates the instructions:

```
mov     ah, 04Ch
int     21h
```

When the optional operand is present, the assembler generates the instructions:

```
mov     al, <constant>
mov     ah, 04Ch
int     21h
```

in which <constant> is the value of the <constant-expr> in the .EXIT macro directive.

EXITM
Exit Macro

Is used in conjunction with a conditional assembly pseudo-operation to terminate a macro expansion under a specified condition.

```
EXITM                               [<comment>]
```

EXTRN/EXTERN
External Declaration

Identifies symbolic names used in this assembly module whose attributes are defined in a separate assembly module.

```
EXTRN    <ext-name-list>            [<comment>]
           or
EXTERN   <ext-name-list>            [<comment>]
```

<ext-name-list> is a list of external name specifications of the form <name>:<type>, and
<type> is one of the following type attributes: BYTE, SBYTE, WORD, SWORD, DWORD, SDWORD, FWORD, QWORD, TBYTE, REAL4, REAL8, REAL10, NEAR, FAR, or ABS.

May be placed anywhere in an assembly module as long as it appears before the first reference to the names that it defines.

.FARDATA **.FARDATA?**

FAR Data Segment Definition

(Initialized Variables) **(Uninitialized Variables)**

Indicates the beginning (or the continuation) of a FAR data segment definition in which variables are to be defined. With .FARDATA, the variables may be given initial values.
Must be preceded by a .MODEL directive.

```
.FARDATA   [<seg-name>]              [<comment>]

.FARDATA?  [<seg-name>]              [<comment>]
```

<seg-name> is the symbolic name to be associated with the memory location where the segment is to begin.

The default segment name is FAR_DATA for .FARDATA and FAR_BSS for .FARDATA? with all memory models, except FLAT; _DATA for .FARDATA and _BSS for .FARDATA? with memory model FLAT.
The align type is PARA for all memory models, except FLAT; DWORD for memory model FLAT.
The combine type is PRIVATE for all memory models, except FLAT; PUBLIC for memory model FLAT.
The class name is 'FAR_DATA' for .FARDATA and 'FAR_BSS' for .FARDATA? with all memory models, except FLAT; 'DATA' for .FARDATA and 'BSS' for .FARDATA? with memory model FLAT.

GROUP

Indicates that the specified segments are to be added to the named group.

```
<group-name>  GROUP  <seg-name-list>            [<comment>]
```

<group-name> is the name of the group to which the specified segments are to be added, and
<seg-name-list> is a list of segment names separated by commas.

IFxxxx
Conditional Assembly

Identifies a sequence of instructions and pseudo-operations that are to be included in or omitted from the assembly depending on a condition that can be evaluated at assembly time.

```
                IFxxxx  <argument>               [<comment>]
                        <block>
                [ELSE                            [<comment>]
                        <block>]
                ENDIF                            [<comment>]
```

IFxxxx is one of the conditional pseudo-operations from the following list,

<argument> is a constant expression, symbolic name, or macro argument used for the condition, and

<block> is a sequence of instructions and pseudo-operations to be included in or omitted from the assembly.

Pseudo-Operation	Explanation
IF <expr>	True if the constant expression, <expr>, evaluates to a nonzero value.
IFE <expr>	True if the constant expression, <expr>, evaluates to zero.
IFDEF <symbol>	True if the symbolic name, <symbol>, is defined or has been declared with EXTRN.
IFNDEF <symbol>	True if the symbolic name, <symbol>, is not defined and has not been declared with EXTRN.
IFB <<arg>>	The pointed brackets around <arg> are required. IFB can be used in a macro definition. True in a specific macro expansion if the operand corresponding to the dummy argument, <arg>, is blank or <>.
IFNB <<arg>>	The pointed brackets around <arg> are required. IFNB can be used in a macro definition. True in a particular macro expansion if the operand corresponding to the dummy argument, <arg>, is not blank and not <>.

.IF ··· .ENDIF
Single-Alternative Decision

Facilitates the implementation of a single-alternative decision structure.

```
.IF      <conditional-expr>         [<comment>]
<instruction-list>
.ENDIF                              [<comment>]
```

<conditional-expr> is a conditional expression, and
<instruction-list> is the list of assembly language instructions to be executed if the <conditional-expr> evaluates to True.

<conditional-expr>, in its simplest form, is a relational expression of the form:

<destination> <rel-op> <source>

in which <destination> is the destination operand for the CMP instruction to be generated by the assembler, <source> is the source operand for the CMP instruction, and <rel-op> is one of the following relational operators:

< <= == != >= >

<conditional-expr> may be a compound expression formed by combining relational expressions using the following logical operators:

&& (AND), || (OR), ! (NOT)

.IF ··· .ELSE ··· .ENDIF
Double-Alternative Decision

Facilitates the implementation of a double-alternative decision structure.

```
.IF     <conditional-expr>          [<comment>]
<first-instruction-list>
.ELSE
<second-instruction-list>
.ENDIF                              [<comment>]
```

<conditional-expr>	is a conditional expression,
<first-instruction-list>	is the list of assembly language instructions to be executed if the <conditional-expr> evaluates to True, and
<second-instruction-list>	is the list of assembly language instructions to be executed if the <conditional-expr> evaluates to False.

<conditional-expr>, in its simplest form, is a relational expression of the form:

<destination> <rel-op> <source>

in which <destination> is the destination operand for the CMP instruction to be generated by the assembler, <source> is the source operand for the CMP instruction, and <rel-op> is one of the following relational operators:

< <= == != >= >

<conditional-expr> may be a compound expression formed by combining relational expressions using the following logical operators:

&& (AND), || (OR), ! (NOT)

INCLUDE

Provides the capability to embed text from one source code file into the text from another source code file during the assembly process.

```
INCLUDE <file-spec>                 [<comment>]
```

<file-spec> is an explicit file specification that identifies the disk drive and the filename.

The assembler replaces the INCLUDE pseudo-operation with the text from the file specified by the <file-spec> operand.

INCLUDELIB

Indicates that the object module, produced from this assembly module, must be linked to object modules from the named library.

```
            INCLUDELIB  <library-name>        [<comment>]

   <library-name> is an explicit file specification that
                  identifies the disk drive and the library
                  name.
```

The <library-name> must be enclosed in angle brackets if it includes any of the following characters: < > \ ; ' "

EXAMPLES:

```
            INCLUDELIB  <A:\MASM\BCD.LIB>
            INCLUDELIB  IO.LIB
```

LABEL

Assigns a symbolic name to a memory location.

```
<name>         LABEL   <type>                   [<comment>]

   <type>  is one of the following type attributes:
           BYTE, SBYTE, WORD, SWORD, DWORD, SDWORD, FWORD,
           QWORD, TBYTE, REAL4, REAL8, REAL10, NEAR, or FAR.
```

EXAMPLES:

```
         ELSE       LABEL   NEAR
                    MOV     AX,1

         is equivalent to

         ELSE:
                    MOV     AX,1
```

```
         BTABLE     LABEL   BYTE
         WTABLE     DW      100 DUP(?)

         allows the array to be accessed by byte or by word.
```

LOCAL
Local Macro Labels

Identifies dummy labels used in a macro body. The assembler generates a unique label for each occurrence of a dummy label as part of macro expansion.

```
LOCAL    <dummy-label-list>         [<comment>]
```

<dummy-label-list> is a list of dummy labels separated by commas.

The LOCAL pseudo-operation must appear between the MACRO pseudo-operation that marks the beginning of the macro definition and the first instruction of the macro body. The labels generated by the assembler are the labels in the range ??0000–??FFFF.

LOCAL
Local Stack Variables

Identifies stack-based variables that exist for a single invocation of a subprocedure.

```
LOCAL    <local-stack-variable-list>
```

<local-stack-variable-list> is a list of variable definitions separated by commas.

The variable definitions in the list have the following form:

```
<name> [[<count>]][:<type>]
```

<name> is the symbolic name to be associated with the stack location in which storage for the variable is to begin,
<count> is the number of elements for an array variable, and
<type> is the type attribute for the variable.

Note that the optional <count>, if present, must be enclosed in square brackets. If [<count>] is omitted, then the variable being defined is a scalar variable.

The LOCAL pseudo-operation must appear between the PROC pseudo-operation and the first instruction of the procedure body.

MACRO

Defines the beginning of a macro definition, and identifies the macro arguments.

```
<mac-name>    MACRO   <arg-list>                 [<comment>]

   <mac-name> is the  symbolic  name of  the macro (the user-
              defined operation code), and
   <arg-list> is a  list  of  dummy  arguments  separated  by
              commas.
```

The dummy arguments in the <arg-list> are symbolic names that are used as operation codes or operands in the instructions of the macro body. These dummy arguments are replaced by actual arguments whenever macro expansion occurs.

.MODEL
Memory Model

Enables use of simplified segment directives.

```
    .MODEL  <mem-model>[,<lang-type>][,<os>][,<stack-type>]

   <mem-model>  specifies the memory model (TINY, SMALL,
                MEDIUM, COMPACT, LARGE, HUGE, or FLAT),
   <lang-type>  specifies compatibility with a high-level
                language (BASIC, C, FORTRAN, PASCAL, STDCALL,
                or SYSCALL) in terms of naming conventions,
                and procedure calling conventions,
   <os>         identifies the operating system being used
                (OS_DOS or OS_OS2), and
   <stack-type> specifies whether the stack is to be placed
                in DGROUP (NEARSTACK) or is to be a segment
                by itself (FARSTACK).
```

The .MODEL directive must appear in the assembly module prior to any simplified segment directive.

The default operating system is OS_DOS.
The default stack type is NEARSTACK.

PAGE
Listing Page Size

```
Defines the page size for the assembler-generated listing.

               PAGE     <lines/page>,<char/line>    [<comment>]

   <lines/page> is  an integer constant  in the range  10-255
                that  specifies  the maximum number  of lines
                per page for the listing, and
   <char/line>  is  an integer constant  in the range  60-255
                (60-132  in previous versions  of MASM)  that
                specifies  the maximum number  of  characters
                per line for the listing.
```

PAGE
Page Break

```
Generates a page break in the assembler-generated listing.

               PAGE
```

PROC
Procedure Definition

Defines the beginning of a procedure definition.

```
<proc-name>   PROC    [<attributes>] [USES <reg-list>]
                          [,<parameter-list>]   [<comment>]
```

<proc-name>	is the symbolic name by which the procedure is invoked,
<attributes>	is a list of attributes for the procedure separated by spaces,
<reg-list>	is the list of register designators for the registers used by the subprocedure that must be saved and restored, and
<parameter-list>	is the list of parameters, separated by commas, whose arguments are to be passed via the stack.

The <attributes> include the type attribute (NEAR or FAR), the language attribute (BASIC, C, FORTRAN, PASCAL, STDCALL, or SYSCALL), and the visibility attribute (PUBLIC, PRIVATE, or EXPORT).

Type Attribute	Meaning
NEAR (Default)	The procedure is local to this code segment and can only be invoked by the procedures in this code segment.
FAR	The procedure can be made available to be invoked by procedures in any code segment in the program.

The <parameter-list> is a list of parameter specifications of the form:

<parameter-name>:<type>

<parameter-name>	is the symbolic name of the parameter, and
<type>	is one of the following type attributes: BYTE, SBYTE, WORD, SWORD, DWORD, SDWORD, FWORD, QWORD, TBYTE, REAL4, REAL8, REAL10, NEAR, or FAR.

PUBLIC

Identifies symbolic names defined in the assembly module that are to be made available for use in other assembly modules.

```
                PUBLIC  <public-def-list>            [<comment>]

   <public-def-list> is a list of public definitions
                     separated by commas. A public definition
                     has the following form:

                                        [<lang-type>] <name>

                    <lang-type> specifies compatibility with
                                a high-level language (BASIC,
                                C, FORTRAN, PASCAL, STDCALL,
                                or SYSCALL), and
                    <name>      is a symbolic name defined in
                                the assembly module.
```

May be placed anywhere in an assembly module.

A symbolic name in the list can be either the label of an instruction, the name of a data item, a procedure name, or the name of a numeric equate.

PURGE

Deletes the named macro definitions from the assembler's macro table.

```
                PURGE   <macro-name-list>            [<comment>]

   <macro-name-list> is a list of macro names separated by
                     commas.
```

Any name in the <macro-name-list> that corresponds to an IBM PC instruction mnemonic or assembler pseudo-operation that was redefined by a macro definition reverts to its original function.

.RADIX

Allows the programmer to change the default radix from decimal to any base within the range 2-16.

```
.RADIX  <constant-expr>            [<comment>]
```

<constant-expr> is a constant expression that evaluates to an integer in the range 2-16.

The <constant-expr> always uses a radix of 10 (decimal), regardless of the current default radix. The .RADIX pseudo-operation does not affect floating-point constants appearing in DD, DQ, DT, REAL4, REAL8, or REAL10 pseudo-operations.

.REPEAT ··· .UNTIL
Repeat-Until Loop

Facilitates the implementation of a Repeat-Until loop structure.

```
.REPEAT                                  [<comment>]
<instruction-list>
.UNTIL <conditional-expr>                [<comment>]
```

<conditional-expr> is a conditional expression, and
<instruction-list> is the list of assembly language instructions to be executed until the <conditional-expr> evaluates to True.

<conditional-expr>, in its simplest form, is a relational expression of the form:

<destination> <rel-op> <source>

in which <destination> is the destination operand for the CMP instruction to be generated by the assembler, <source> is the source operand for the CMP instruction, and <rel-op> is one of the following relational operators:

<   <=   ==   !=   >=   >

<conditional-expr> may be a compound expression formed by combining relational expressions using the following logical operators:

&& (AND), || (OR),   ! (NOT)

SBYTE
Define Signed Byte

See DB pseudo-operation.

SDWORD
Define Signed Double Word

See DD pseudo-operation.

SEGMENT
Segment Definition

Defines the beginning of a segment definition and defines the relationships of this segment to other segments in the executable program.

```
<seg-name>    SEGMENT [READONLY] [<align>] [<combine>]
                                    [<use>] [<class>]
```

<seg-name>	is the symbolic name to be associated with the memory location at which the segment is to begin,
READONLY	tells the assembler to generate an error for any instruction whose execution would modify an item in the segment,
<align>	identifies the type of boundary for the beginning of the segment,
<combine>	indicates the way in which this segment is to be combined with other segments by the Linkage Editor (LINK),
<use>	indicates whether the segment is to be executed in real mode or in protected mode for 80386/80486 assembly language programs, and
<class>	is a symbolic name used to group segments at link time. All segments with the same class name are placed contiguous in memory.

<align>	Beginning Address
PAGE	XXX00
PARA	XXXX0 (Default)
DWORD	XXXX#
WORD	XXXXE
BYTE	XXXXX

in which X is any hexadecimal digit,
is the hexadecimal digit 0, 4, 8, or C
E is any even hexadecimal digit, and
0 is the hexadecimal digit 0.

SEGMENT (Continued)

<combine>	Meaning
Blank	Indicates the segment is to be logically separate from other segments, regardless of its placement relative to other segments.
PRIVATE	Indicates that the segment is to be logically separate from other segments.
PUBLIC	Indicates that this segment is to be combined with other segments having the same <seg-name> and <class>, producing a single, physical segment.
COMMON	Indicates that this segment is to be overlaid with other segments having the same <seg-name> and <class>. Each of the overlaid segments begins at the same address.
STACK	Indicates that the segment is to be part of the run-time stack segment for the program.
AT <expr>	Indicates that the segment is to begin at the paragraph specified by the value of <expr>.

.STACK
Stack Segment Definition

Defines a stack segment of the specified size.
Must be preceded by a .MODEL directive.

```
.STACK  [<stack-size>]            [<comment>]
```

<stack-size> specifies the size of the stack segment in bytes.

The default stack size is 1024 bytes.

The name of the stack segment is STACK.
The align type is PARA for all memory models, except TINY and FLAT; DWORD for FLAT.
The combine type is STACK for all memory models, except TINY and FLAT; PUBLIC for FLAT.
The class name is 'STACK'.
If the .MODEL directive specifies NEARSTACK (the default), the stack segment is part of DGROUP for all memory models, except TINY and FLAT. If the .MODEL directive specifies FARSTACK, the stack segment is a physically separate segment for all memory models, except TINY and FLAT.

The .STACK directive cannot be used with the TINY memory model.

.STARTUP

Directs the assembler to generate the instructions that, when executed, set the DS-register to address DGROUP and, if the .MODEL directive specifies NEARSTACK, adjust the SS:SP register pair so that it is relative to DGROUP.

```
.STARTUP                          [<comment>]
```

SWORD
Define Signed Word

See DW pseudo-operation.

TBYTE
Define Ten Bytes

See DT pseudo-operation.

TITLE

Specifies a title for the assembler-generated listing.

```
                TITLE    <text>

   <text> is the title to be placed on the second line of
          every page of the assembler-generated listing.
```

.WHILE ··· .ENDW
While Loop

Facilitates the implementation of a While loop structure.

```
                .WHILE <conditional-expr>          [<comment>]
                <instruction-list>
                .ENDW                              [<comment>]

   <conditional-expr> is a conditional expression, and
   <instruction-list> is the list of assembly language
                      instructions to be executed until the
                      <conditional-expr> evaluates to True.
```

<conditional-expr>, in its simplest form, is a relational expression of the form:

<destination> <rel-op> <source>

in which <destination> is the destination operand for the CMP instruction to be generated by the assembler, <source> is the source operand for the CMP instruction, and <rel-op> is one of the following relational operators:

<   <=   ==   !=   >=   >

<conditional-expr> may be a compound expression formed by combining relational expressions using the following logical operators:

&& (AND), || (OR),   ! (NOT)

WORD
Define Unsigned Word

See DW pseudo-operation.

APPENDIX C

Pseudocode

The comments used in the assembly language procedures presented in this book provide a pseudocode description of the algorithm that is implemented by the procedure. The control structures used in the pseudocode are described in this appendix.

A program is a sequence of control structures. A subprogram is either a function or a procedure. The pseudocode for a function subprogram is as follows:

```
FUNCTION <f-name> (<arg-list>)
     <sequence of control structures>
     RETURN (<value>)
END <f-name>
```

in which

```
<f-name>    is the symbolic name of the function,
<arg-list>  is the list of symbolic names that is used
            for the arguments of the function,
<sequence of control structures>
            describes the algorithm implemented by the
            function, and
<value>     is an expression that specifies the value
            being returned by the function.
```

The pseudocode for a procedure subprogram is as follows:

```
PROCEDURE <p-name> (<arg-list>)
     <sequence of control structures>
     RETURN
END <p-name>
```

in which

```
<p-name>    is the symbolic name of the procedure,
<arg-list>  is the list of symbolic names that is used
            for the arguments of the procedure, and
<sequence of control structures>
            describes the algorithm implemented by the
            procedure.
```

A <control structure> is either a simple sequence, a decision structure, or a loop structure. The pseudocode statements to be used for each of these control structures are described in this appendix.

Simple Sequence

A simple sequence is a set of instructions that contains no transfer of control instructions. The instructions are executed strictly in the sequence that they appear. The comment on an instruction or group of instructions in a simple sequence describes the logical steps of the algorithm that are performed by that instruction or group of instructions. The pseudocode statements for sequential instructions include the following:

Statement	Meaning
PROMPT FOR <var-name>	Outputs a prompt message to the user to request a value for the pseudocode variable specified by <var-name>.
GET <var-name>	Inputs a value into the pseudocode variable specified by <var-name>.
DISPLAY <disp-item-list>	Displays, on the screen, the values of the items specified in the <disp-item-list>. The items in the list are separated by commas and may include both pseudocode variables and character strings.
PRINT <print-item-list>	Prints, at the printer, the values of the items specified in the <print-item-list>. The items in the list are separated by commas and may include both pseudocode variables and character strings.
RETURN TO DOS	Returns control to the Disk Operating System (DOS).
<var-name> = <expression>	The <expression> is evaluated and the resulting value is assigned as the value of the pseudocode variable specified by <var-name>.
INCREMENT <var-name>	Adds 1 to the value of the pseudocode variable specified by <var-name>.
DECREMENT <var-name>	Subtracts 1 from the value of the pseudocode variable specified by <var-name>.
PUSH <var-name>	Pushes the value of the pseudocode variable specified by <var-name> onto the stack.
POP <var-name>	Pops the top-of-stack data item and replaces the value of the pseudocode variable specified by <var-name> with that value.
CALL <p-name> (<arg-list>)	Invokes the <p-name> procedure, and passes to it the data items specified in <arg-list>.

CREATE FILE <file-spec> AS <attribute> AND GET <file-handle>
Creates a disk file with the disk drive and filename as specified by <file-spec> and the file attribute specified by <attribute>, and accepts the DOS file handle for the file as the value of the pseudocode variable specified by <file-handle>.

OPEN FILE <file-spec> FOR <access-type> AND GET <file-handle>
Opens the disk file with the disk drive and filename as specified by <file-spec> for the type of access specified by <access-type>, and accepts the DOS file handle for the file as the value of the pseudocode variable specified by <file-handle>.

READ <amount> FROM <file-handle> INTO <buffer>
Reads the amount of data specified by <amount> from the disk file whose DOS file handle is specified by the value of pseudocode variable <file-handle>, and loads that data into the array specified by the pseudocode variable <buffer>.

WRITE <amount> TO <file-handle> FROM <buffer>
Writes the amount of data specified by <amount> from the array specified by the pseudocode variable <buffer> to the disk file whose DOS file handle is specified by the value of pseudocode variable <file-handle>.

CLOSE FILE <file-handle>
Closes the disk file with the DOS file handle specified by <file-handle>.

In an <expression>, an operand can be a constant, a variable, (i.e., <var-name>), or a function reference of the form <f-name> (<arg-list>). The value of a function reference is the value returned by the function when invoked with the arguments of <arg-list>.

In an <expression>, +, -, *, and ** are used for addition, subtraction, multiplication, and exponentiation, respectively. Integer division is shown with the operator /, real division is shown with the operator //, the remainder of an unsigned integer division is shown with the operator mod, and the remainder of a signed integer division is shown with the operator rem.

EXAMPLES:

```
COUNT = NUMBER / 2
```

means that variable COUNT is assigned the quotient of the division of variable NUMBER divided by 2.

```
COUNT = NUMBER mod 2
```

means that variable COUNT is assigned the remainder of the unsigned division of variable NUMBER divided by 2.

Decision Structures

There are two simple decision structures that are used in the pseudocode.

Single-Alternative Decision

A single-alternative decision structure either performs a sequence of control structures or skips that sequence of control structures depending on the value of a condition. If the condition evaluates to True, then the sequence of control structures is performed. If the condition evaluates to False, then the sequence of control structures is not performed. The pseudocode for a single-alternative decision structure is as follows:

```
IF   <condition>
THEN
     <sequence of control structures>
ENDIF
```

in which

<condition> is a logical expression that evaluates to either True or False, and

<sequence of control structures> describes the set of steps to be performed if the <condition> evaluates to True.

Double-Alternative Decision

A double-alternative decision structure selects one of two sequences of control structures depending on the value of a condition. If the condition evaluates to True, then the first sequence of control structures is selected. If the condition evaluates to False, then the second sequence of control structures is selected. The pseudocode for a double-alternative decision structure is as follows:

```
IF   <condition>
THEN
     <first sequence of control structures>
ELSE
     <second sequence of control structures>
ENDIF
```

in which

<condition> is a logical expression,

<first sequence of control structures> describes the set of steps to perform if the <condition> evaluates to True, and

<second sequence of control structures> describes the set of steps to perform if the <condition> evaluates to False.

Loop Structures

Loop structures provide a mechanism for repeating a sequence of control structures based on the value of a condition. A loop consists of two parts: the loop test and the loop body. The loop body is the sequence of control structures to be repeated. The loop test is the evaluation of the condition on which the decision to execute the loop body is based. There are two loop structures used in the pseudocode appearing in this book.

WHILE Loop

With a WHILE loop, the loop test is at the top of the loop. While the condition evaluates to True, the loop body is executed. When the condition evaluates to False, the loop is terminated. Since the test is at the top of the loop, it is possible that the loop body will not be executed at all. The pseudocode for a WHILE loop is as follows:

```
WHILE <condition>
     <sequence of control structures>
ENDWHILE
```

in which

<condition> is a logical expression, and

<sequence of control structures> describes the set of steps to be repeated while the <condition> evaluates to True.

REPEAT-UNTIL Loop
With a REPEAT-UNTIL loop, the loop test is at the bottom of the loop. The loop body is executed, and as long as the condition evaluates to False, the loop body is repeated. When the condition evaluates to True, the loop is terminated. Since the test is at the bottom of the loop, the loop body is always executed at least once. The pseudocode for the REPEAT-UNTIL loop is as follows:

```
REPEAT
     <sequence of control structures>
UNTIL <condition>
```

in which

<condition> is a logical expression, and

<sequence of control structures> describes the set of steps to be repeated until the <condition> becomes True.

Nesting of control structures is allowed as long as one control structure is completely contained within another. That is, a nested control structure must be completely contained within the loop body of a loop structure or within one of the alternatives of a decision structure. No overlapping of control structures is allowed. Loop bodies and decision alternatives are always indented at least three spaces.

EXAMPLE:

The following is the pseudocode description of an algorithm to classify each of the positive integers in the range 2-100 as deficient, abundant, or perfect.

```
LOOP_COUNT = 99
NUMBER = 2
REPEAT
   DIVISOR_SUM = 1
   DIVISOR = 2
   UPPER_LIMIT = NUMBER / 2
   WHILE DIVISOR <= UPPER_LIMIT
      QUOTIENT = NUMBER / DIVISOR
      REMAINDER = NUMBER mod DIVISOR
      IF   REMAINDER = 0
      THEN
           DIVISOR_SUM = DIVISOR_SUM + DIVISOR
           IF   DIVISOR <> QUOTIENT
           THEN
                DIVISOR_SUM = DIVISOR_SUM + QUOTIENT
           ENDIF
           UPPER_LIMIT = QUOTIENT - 1
      ENDIF
      DIVISOR = DIVISOR + 1
   ENDWHILE
   IF   DIVISOR_SUM = NUMBER
   THEN
        DISPLAY 'PERFECT'
   ELSE
        IF   DIVISOR_SUM < NUMBER
        THEN
             DISPLAY 'DEFICIENT'
        ELSE
             DISPLAY 'ABUNDANT'
        ENDIF
   ENDIF
   DISPLAY NUMBER
   NUMBER = NUMBER + 1
   LOOP_COUNT = LOOP_COUNT - 1
UNTIL LOOP_COUNT = 0
```

APPENDIX D

Input/Output Procedures

This appendix describes the input/output subprocedures referenced in the example programs used in the book, for both the original version and the 80386 version. Many of the subprocedures have the same interface requirements in both versions. For those subprocedures that have different interface requirements in the two versions, both descriptions are presented. In addition, there are descriptions for subprocedures that exist only in the 80386 version. The object code for both versions of these subprocedures is available on diskette.

BLANKS

This procedure displays a specified number of blanks on the screen beginning at the current cursor position.

Inputs:
- BH-register contains the active display page number.
- DX-register contains the number of blanks to be displayed.

Outputs:
- The specified number of blanks is displayed on the screen beginning at the current cursor position.

CLEAR

This procedure clears the display screen.

Inputs:
- None.

Outputs:
- The display screen is cleared.

DIV32 —— Original Version Only ——

This procedure performs a 32-bit, unsigned integer divide using the Restoring Method.

Inputs:
- DX:AX register pair contains the dividend.
- CX:BX register pair contains the divisor.

Outputs:
- DX:AX register pair contains the quotient.
- CX:BX register pair contains the remainder.

DIV64 —— 80386 Version Only ——

This procedure performs a 64-bit, unsigned integer divide using the Restoring Method.

Inputs:
- EDX:EAX register pair contains the dividend.
- ECX:EBX register pair contains the divisor.

Outputs:
- EDX:EAX register pair contains the quotient.
- ECX:EBX register pair contains the remainder.

GETDEC

This procedure accepts a 16-bit integer in signed decimal form from the keyboard and returns it to the caller. The range of integers allowed is -32,768 to +32,767. This procedure does not prompt for the input; that responsibility belongs to the caller. Error messages are output in response to input errors, and then another input is accepted.

Inputs:
An integer in signed decimal form from the keyboard.
No input from the caller.

Outputs:
AX-register contains the 16-bit, signed integer value received from the keyboard.

GETDEC$

This procedure accepts a 16-bit integer in unsigned decimal form from the keyboard and returns it to the caller. The range of integers allowed is 0 to 65,535. This procedure does not prompt for the input; that responsibility belongs to the caller. Error messages are output in response to input errors, and then another input is accepted.

Inputs:
An integer in unsigned decimal form from the keyboard.
No input from the caller.

Outputs:
AX-register contains the 16-bit, unsigned integer value received from the keyboard.

GETDEC32 — Original Version

This procedure accepts a 32-bit integer in signed decimal form from the keyboard and returns it to the caller. The range of integers allowed is -2,147,483,648 to +2,147,483,647. This procedure does not prompt for the input; that responsibility belongs to the caller. Error messages are output in response to input errors, and then another input is accepted.

Inputs:
An integer in signed decimal form from the keyboard.
No input from the caller.

Outputs:
DX:AX register pair contains the 32-bit, signed integer value received from the keyboard.

GETDC32$ —| Original Version |—

This procedure accepts a 32-bit integer in unsigned decimal form from the keyboard and returns it to the caller. The range of integers allowed is 0 to 4,294,967,295. This procedure does not prompt for the input; that responsibility belongs to the caller. Error messages are output in response to input errors, and then another input is accepted.

Inputs:
  An integer in unsigned decimal form from the keyboard.
  No input from the caller.
Outputs:
  DX:AX register pair contains the 32-bit, unsigned integer value received from the keyboard.

GETDEC32 —| 80386 Version |—

This procedure accepts a 32-bit integer in signed decimal form from the keyboard and returns it to the caller. The range of integers allowed is -2,147,483,648 to +2,147,483,647. This procedure does not prompt for the input; that responsibility belongs to the caller. Error messages are output in response to input errors, and then another input is accepted.

Inputs:
  An integer in signed decimal form from the keyboard.
  No input from the caller.
Outputs:
  EAX-register pair contains the 32-bit, signed integer value received from the keyboard.

GETDC32$ —| 80386 Version |—

This procedure accepts a 32-bit integer in unsigned decimal form from the keyboard and returns it to the caller. The range of integers allowed is 0 to 4,294,967,295. This procedure does not prompt for the input; that responsibility belongs to the caller. Error messages are output in response to input errors, and then another input is accepted.

Inputs:
  An integer in unsigned decimal form from the keyboard.
  No input from the caller.
Outputs:
  EAX-register pair contains the 32-bit, unsigned integer value received from the keyboard.

GETDEC64 —| 80386 Version Only |—

This procedure accepts a 64-bit integer in signed decimal form from the keyboard and returns it to the caller. The range of integers allowed is -9,223,372,036,854,775,808 to +9,223,372,036,854,775,807. This procedure does not prompt for the input; that responsibility belongs to the caller. Error messages are output in response to input errors, and then another input is accepted.

Inputs:
- An integer in signed decimal form from the keyboard.
- No input from the caller.

Outputs:
- EDX:EAX register pair contains the 64-bit, signed integer value received from the keyboard.

GETDC64$ —| 80386 Version Only |—

This procedure accepts a 64-bit integer in unsigned decimal form from the keyboard and returns it to the caller. The range of integers allowed is 0 to 18,446,744,073,709,551,615. This procedure does not prompt for the input; that responsibility belongs to the caller. Error messages are output in response to input errors, and then another input is accepted.

Inputs:
- An integer in unsigned decimal form from the keyboard.
- No input from the caller.

Outputs:
- EDX:EAX register pair contains the 64-bit, unsigned integer value received from the keyboard.

GETSTRNG

This procedure accepts a character string from the keyboard and returns it to the caller. Characters are accepted until either the user presses RETURN or a total of n characters has been entered, in which n is supplied by the caller.

Inputs:
- ES:DI register pair addresses the buffer that is to receive the input string.
- CX-register contains the length of the input buffer.

Outputs:
- CX-register contains the actual length of the input string.
- The specified buffer contains the character string that was entered.

IDIV32 ——| **Original Version Only** |——

This procedure performs a 32-bit, signed integer divide using the Restoring Method.

Inputs:
- DX:AX register pair contains the dividend.
- CX:BX register pair contains the divisor.

Outputs:
- DX:AX register pair contains the quotient.
- CX:BX register pair contains the remainder.

IDIV64 ——| **80386 Version Only** |——

This procedure performs a 64-bit, signed integer divide using the Restoring Method.

Inputs:
- EDX:EAX register pair contains the dividend.
- ECX:EBX register pair contains the divisor.

Outputs:
- EDX:EAX register pair contains the quotient.
- ECX:EBX register pair contains the remainder.

NEWLINE

This procedure displays a RETURN and LINE FEED to the display.

Inputs:
- None.

Outputs:
- A RETURN and LINE FEED are displayed on the screen at the current cursor position.

PAUSE

This procedure displays a character string on the screen beginning at the current cursor position, clears the BIOS keyboard input buffer, and then waits for a keystroke before returning to its caller.

Inputs:
- ES:DI register pair addresses the first character of the string.
- CX-register contains the length of the character string.

Outputs:
- The input string is displayed on the screen beginning at the current cursor position.

PUTBIN

This procedure displays an 8- or a 16-bit integer in binary form beginning at the current cursor position.

Inputs:

AL-register contains the 8-bit value to be displayed.
BL-register contains 0, the code for the 8-bit display.

or

AX-register contains the 16-bit value to be displayed.
BL-register contains a nonzero value, the code for the 16-bit display.

Outputs:

The input value is displayed in binary form on the screen beginning at the current cursor position.

PUTBIN32 — 80386 Version Only

This procedure displays a 32-bit integer in binary form beginning at the current cursor position.

Inputs:

EAX-register contains the 32-bit value to be displayed.

Outputs:

The input value is displayed in binary form on the screen beginning at the current cursor position.

PUTDEC

This procedure displays a 16-bit integer in signed decimal form beginning at the current cursor position.

Inputs:

AX-register contains the signed integer value to be displayed.
BH-register contains the display code:

BH < 0 => left-justify in a 6-character field.
BH = 0 => display with no blanks.
BH > 0 => right-justify in a 6-character field.

Outputs:

The input value is displayed in signed decimal form on the screen beginning at the current cursor position.

PUTDEC$

This procedure displays a 16-bit integer in unsigned decimal form beginning at the current cursor position.

Inputs:

AX-register contains the unsigned integer value to be displayed.
BH-register contains the display code:

BH < 0 => left-justify in a 6-character field.
BH = 0 => display with no blanks.
BH > 0 => right-justify in a 6-character field.

Outputs:

The input value is displayed in unsigned decimal form on the screen beginning at the current cursor position.

PUTDEC32 —| Original Version |—

```
This procedure displays a 32-bit  integer in  signed decimal
form beginning at the current cursor position.

Inputs:
     DX:AX register  pair contains the signed  integer value
            to be displayed.
     BH-register contains the display code:
            BH < 0 => left-justify in an 11-character field.
            BH = 0 => display with no blanks.
            BH > 0 => right-justify in an 11-character field.
Outputs:
     The input value is displayed in signed decimal  form on
     the screen beginning at the current cursor position.
```

PUTDC32$ —| Original Version |—

```
This procedure displays a 32-bit integer in unsigned decimal
form beginning at the current cursor position.

Inputs:
     DX:AX register pair contains the unsigned integer value
            to be displayed.
     BH-register contains the display code:
            BH < 0 => left-justify in an 11-character field.
            BH = 0 => display with no blanks.
            BH > 0 => right-justify in an 11-character field.
Outputs:
     The input value is  displayed in  unsigned decimal form
     on the screen beginning at the current cursor position.
```

PUTDEC32 —| 80386 Version |—

```
This procedure displays  a 32-bit integer  in signed decimal
form beginning at the current cursor position.

Inputs:
     EAX-register pair contains the signed integer  value to
                  be displayed.
     BH-register contains the display code:
            BH < 0 => left-justify in an 11-character field.
            BH = 0 => display with no blanks.
            BH > 0 => right-justify in an 11-character field.
Outputs:
     The input value is displayed in signed decimal  form on
     the screen beginning at the current cursor position.
```

PUTDC32$ —| 80386 Version |—

```
This procedure displays a 32-bit integer in unsigned decimal
form beginning at the current cursor position.

Inputs:
     EAX-register pair  contains the  unsigned integer value
                    to be displayed.
     BH-register contains the display code:
            BH < 0 => left-justify in an 11-character field.
            BH = 0 => display with no blanks.
            BH > 0 => right-justify in an 11-character field.
Outputs:
     The input value  is displayed in unsigned  decimal form
     on the screen beginning at the current cursor position.
```

PUTDEC64 —| 80386 Version Only |—

```
This procedure displays a 64-bit  integer in  signed decimal
form beginning at the current cursor position.

Inputs:
     EDX:EAX register pair contains the signed integer value
             to be displayed.
     BH-register contains the display code:
            BH < 0 => left-justify in a 21-character field.
            BH = 0 => display with no blanks.
            BH > 0 => right-justify in a 21-character field.
Outputs:
     The input value is displayed in signed decimal  form on
     the screen beginning at the current cursor position.
```

PUTDC64$ —| 80386 Version Only |—

```
This procedure displays a 64-bit integer in unsigned decimal
form beginning at the current cursor position.

Inputs:
     EDX:EAX register  pair  contains  the  unsigned integer
             value to be displayed.
     BH-register contains the display code:
            BH < 0 => left-justify in a 21-character field.
            BH = 0 => display with no blanks.
            BH > 0 => right-justify in a 21-character field.
Outputs:
     The input value is  displayed in  unsigned decimal form
     on the screen beginning at the current cursor position.
```

PUTHEX

This procedure displays an 8- or a 16-bit integer in hexadecimal form beginning at the current cursor position.

Inputs:
- AL-register contains the 8-bit value to be displayed.
- BL-register contains 0, the code for the 8-bit display.

or
- AX-register contains the 16-bit value to be displayed.
- BL-register contains a nonzero value, the code for the 16-bit display.

Outputs:
- The input value is displayed in hexadecimal form on the screen beginning at the current cursor position.

PUTHEX32 —| 80386 Version Only |—

This procedure displays a 32-bit integer in hexadecimal form beginning at the current cursor position.

Inputs:
- EAX-register contains the 32-bit value to be displayed.

Outputs:
- The input value is displayed in hexadecimal form on the screen beginning at the current cursor position.

PUTOCT

This procedure displays an 8- or a 16-bit integer in octal form beginning at the current cursor position.

Inputs:
- AL-register contains the 8-bit value to be displayed.
- BL-register contains 0, the code for the 8-bit display.

or
- AX-register contains the 16-bit value to be displayed.
- BL-register contains a nonzero value, the code for the 16-bit display.

Outputs:
- The input value is displayed in octal form on the screen beginning at the current cursor position.

PUTOCT32 —| 80386 Version Only |—

This procedure displays a 32-bit integer in octal form beginning at the current cursor position.

Inputs:
- EAX-register contains the 32-bit value to be displayed.

Outputs:
- The input value is displayed in octal form on the screen beginning at the current cursor position.

PUTSTRNG

This procedure displays a character string on the screen beginning at the current cursor position.

Inputs:

ES:DI register pair addresses the first character of the string.

CX-register contains the length of the character string.

Outputs:

The input string is displayed on the screen beginning at the current cursor position.

APPENDIX E

ASCII Character Set

Video Display Character Set

The following table, reprinted by permission from IBM PC Technical Reference (1502234) (c) 1981, 1982, 1983 by International Business Machines Corporation, lists the characters of the IBM Extended ASCII character set. These characters can be generated by all of the video subsystems presented in Chapter 13 (MDA, CGA, MCGA, EGA, VGA, and XGA).

DECIMAL VALUE	➡	0	16	32	48	64	80	96	112
⬇	HEXA DECIMAL VALUE	0	1	2	3	4	5	6	7
0	0	BLANK (NULL)	►	BLANK (SPACE)	0	@	P	‘	p
1	1	☺	◄	!	1	A	Q	a	q
2	2	☻	↕	"	2	B	R	b	r
3	3	♥	‼	#	3	C	S	c	s
4	4	♦	¶	$	4	D	T	d	t
5	5	♣	§	%	5	E	U	e	u
6	6	♠	▬	&	6	F	V	f	v
7	7	•	↨	'	7	G	W	g	w
8	8	◘	↑	(	8	H	X	h	x
9	9	○	↓	)	9	I	Y	i	y
10	A	◙	→	*	:	J	Z	j	z
11	B	♂	←	+	;	K	[	k	{
12	C	♀	∟	,	<	L	\	l	¦
13	D	♪	↔	—	=	M	]	m	}
14	E	♫	▲	.	>	N	∧	n	~
15	F	☼	▼	/	?	O	_	o	△

DECIMAL VALUE	➡	128	144	160	176	192	208	224	240
⬇	HEXA DECIMAL VALUE	8	9	A	B	C	D	E	F
0	0	Ç	É	á	░	└	╨	α	≡
1	1	ü	æ	í	▒	┴	╤	β	±
2	2	é	Æ	ó	▓	┬	╥	Γ	≥
3	3	â	ô	ú	│	├	╙	π	≤
4	4	ä	ö	ñ	┤	─	╘	Σ	⌠
5	5	à	ò	Ñ	╡	┼	╒	σ	⌡
6	6	å	û	ª	╢	╞	╓	µ	÷
7	7	ç	ù	º	╖	╟	╫	τ	≈
8	8	ê	ÿ	¿	╕	╚	╪	Φ	°
9	9	ë	Ö	⌐	╣	╔	┘	Θ	•
10	A	è	Ü	¬	║	╩	┌	Ω	·
11	B	ï	¢	½	╗	╦	█	δ	√
12	C	î	£	¼	╝	╠	▄	∞	^{n}
13	D	ì	¥	¡	╜	═	▌	φ	^{2}
14	E	Ä	₧	«	╛	╬	▐	∈	■
15	F	Å	ƒ	»	┐	╧	▀	∩	BLANK 'FF'

Printer Character Set

The following table summarizes the more useful control characters recognized by dot matrix printers.

ASCII Code	Interpretation
07 hex	Sound a beep at the printer
09 hex	Horizontal TAB
0A hex	LINE FEED (advance to the next line)
0B hex	Vertical TAB
0C hex	FORM FEED (advance to the top of the next page)
0D hex	RETURN (return to the left margin)
0E hex	Turn on the double-width print mode (40 characters per line)
0F hex	Turn on the compressed print mode (132 characters per line)
12 hex	Turn off the compressed print mode
14 hex	Turn off the double-width print mode
18 hex	Clear printer buffer
1B, 30 hex	Set line spacing to 8 lines per inch
1B, 32 hex	Set line spacing to 6 lines per inch
1B, 45 hex	Turn on emphasized printing mode
1B, 46 hex	Turn off emphasized printing mode

The following table lists the printable characters for most dot matrix printers. The ASCII codes for these characters are given in decimal, binary, and hexadecimal.

Decimal	Binary	Hex	ASCII	Decimal	Binary	Hex	ASCII
32	00100000	20		160	10100000	A0	á
33	00100001	21	!	161	10100001	A1	í
34	00100010	22	"	162	10100010	A2	ó
35	00100011	23	#	163	10100011	A3	ú
36	00100100	24	$	164	10100100	A4	ñ
37	00100101	25	%	165	10100101	A5	Ñ
38	00100110	26	&	166	10100110	A6	ª
39	00100111	27	'	167	10100111	A7	º
40	00101000	28	(	168	10101000	A8	¿
41	00101001	29	)	169	10101001	A9	⌐
42	00101010	2A	*	170	10101010	AA	¬
43	00101011	2B	+	171	10101011	AB	½
44	00101100	2C	,	172	10101100	AC	¼
45	00101101	2D	-	173	10101101	AD	¡
46	00101110	2E	.	174	10101110	AE	«
47	00101111	2F	/	175	10101111	AF	»
48	00110000	30	0	176	10110000	B0	░
49	00110001	31	1	177	10110001	B1	▒
50	00110010	32	2	178	10110010	B2	▓
51	00110011	33	3	179	10110011	B3	│
52	00110100	34	4	180	10110100	B4	┤
53	00110101	35	5	181	10110101	B5	╡
54	00110110	36	6	182	10110110	B6	╢
55	00110111	37	7	183	10110111	B7	╖
56	00111000	38	8	184	10111000	B8	╕
57	00111001	39	9	185	10111001	B9	╣
58	00111010	3A	:	186	10111010	BA	║
59	00111011	3B	;	187	10111011	BB	╗
60	00111100	3C	<	188	10111100	BC	╝
61	00111101	3D	=	189	10111101	BD	╜
62	00111110	3E	>	190	10111110	BE	╛
63	00111111	3F	?	191	10111111	BF	┐

Decimal	Binary	Hex	ASCII	Decimal	Binary	Hex	ASCII
64	01000000	40	@	192	11000000	C0	└
65	01000001	41	A	193	11000001	C1	┴
66	01000010	42	B	194	11000010	C2	┬
67	01000011	43	C	195	11000011	C3	├
68	01000100	44	D	196	11000100	C4	─
69	01000101	45	E	197	11000101	C5	┼
70	01000110	46	F	198	11000110	C6	╞
71	01000111	47	G	199	11000111	C7	╟
72	01001000	48	H	200	11001000	C8	╚
73	01001001	49	I	201	11001001	C9	╔
74	01001010	4A	J	202	11001010	CA	╩
75	01001011	4B	K	203	11001011	CB	╦
76	01001100	4C	L	204	11001100	CC	╠
77	01001101	4D	M	205	11001101	CD	═
78	01001110	4E	N	206	11001110	CE	╬
79	01001111	4F	O	207	11001111	CF	╧
80	01010000	50	P	208	11010000	D0	╨
81	01010001	51	Q	209	11010001	D1	╤
82	01010010	52	R	210	11010010	D2	╥
83	01010011	53	S	211	11010011	D3	╙
84	01010100	54	T	212	11010100	D4	╘
85	01010101	55	U	213	11010101	D5	╒
86	01010110	56	V	214	11010110	D6	╓
87	01010111	57	W	215	11010111	D7	╫
88	01011000	58	X	216	11011000	D8	╪
89	01011001	59	Y	217	11011001	D9	┘
90	01011010	5A	Z	218	11011010	DA	┌
91	01011011	5B	[	219	11011011	DB	█
92	01011100	5C	\	220	11011100	DC	▄
93	01011101	5D	]	221	11011101	DD	▌
94	01011110	5E	^	222	11011110	DE	▐
95	01011111	5F	_	223	11011111	DF	▀

Decimal	Binary	Hex	ASCII	Decimal	Binary	Hex	ASCII
96	01100000	60	`	224	11100000	E0	α
97	01100001	61	a	225	11100001	E1	β
98	01100010	62	b	226	11100010	E2	Γ
99	01100011	63	c	227	11100011	E3	π
100	01100100	64	d	228	11100100	E4	Σ
101	01100101	65	e	229	11100101	E5	σ
102	01100110	66	f	230	11100110	E6	μ
103	01100111	67	g	231	11100111	E7	τ
104	01101000	68	h	232	11101000	E8	Φ
105	01101001	69	i	233	11101001	E9	Θ
106	01101010	6A	j	234	11101010	EA	Ω
107	01101011	6B	k	235	11101011	EB	δ
108	01101100	6C	l	236	11101100	EC	∞
109	01101101	6D	m	237	11101101	ED	ø
110	01101110	6E	n	238	11101110	EE	∈
111	01101111	6F	o	239	11101111	EF	∩
112	01110000	70	p	240	11110000	F0	≡
113	01110001	71	q	241	11110001	F1	±
114	01110010	72	r	242	11110010	F2	≥
115	01110011	73	s	243	11110011	F3	≤
116	01110100	74	t	244	11110100	F4	⌠
117	01110101	75	u	245	11110101	F5	⌡
118	01110110	76	v	246	11110110	F6	÷
119	01110111	77	w	247	11110111	F7	≈
120	01111000	78	x	248	11111000	F8	°
121	01111001	79	y	249	11111001	F9	•
122	01111010	7A	z	250	11111010	FA	·
123	01111011	7B	{	251	11111011	FB	√
124	01111100	7C	¦	252	11111100	FC	^{n}
125	01111101	7D	}	253	11111101	FD	^{2}
126	01111110	7E	~	254	11111110	FE	■
127	01111111	7F		255	11111111	FF	

APPENDIX F

Support Software

Notation:

<> encloses items to be supplied by the user.
[] encloses optional items.

Definitions:

1. Filename <filename> - from 1 to 8 characters optionally followed by a filename extension.

2. Filename extension - a period (.) followed by from 1 to 3 characters.

3. Disk drive identifier <drive-id> - the letter designator for the disk drive (e.g., A, B, or C) followed by a colon (:).

4. Explicit file specification - a disk drive identifier followed by a filename. If the disk drive identifier is omitted, then the default disk drive identifier, specified in the DOS prompt, is assumed.

The following characters are allowed in filenames (including the filename extension):

A-Z, 0-9, and $, &, #, @, !, %, `, ', (,), -, {, }, and _.

Disk Operating System (DOS)

DOS Commands

Command	Description
CHKDSK	Function: Checks the disk on the specified drive, and produces a status report on the disk and on the size of the memory, used and available. Command line: CHKDSK [<drive-id>]
CLS	Function: Clears the video screen. Command line: CLS
COMP	Function: Compares two disk files. The asterisk (*) may be used as a universal qualifier in a filename. If the optional filename is omitted, then it is assumed to be the same as the required filename, and the disk drives must be different. Command line: COMP [<drive-id>]<filename> [<drive-id>][<filename>] Examples: COMP SORT1.ASM B: Compares the file named SORT1.ASM on the disk in the default drive to the file named SORT1.ASM on the disk in drive B. COMP A:*.ASM B: Compares each file on the disk in drive A that has a filename extension of .ASM to the file on the disk in drive B that has the same filename.

COPY

```
Function: Copies file(s) from the source disk (identified by
          the first operand) to the destination disk
          (identified by the second operand). The asterisk
          (*) may be used in a <filename> as a universal
          qualifier. If the destination filename is omitted,
          then the source filename is used and the disk
          drives must be different.
Command line:
    COPY [<drive-id>]<filename> [<drive-id>][<filename>][/V]
Options:
     /V  Specifies that each sector transferred to the
         destination disk is to be verified by reading that
         sector back into memory and comparing the data read
         with the data written.
Examples:
         COPY B:PROG.ASM PROG1.ASM
            Copies the file named PROG.ASM from the disk in
            drive B to the disk in the default drive using
            the filename PROG1.ASM.

         COPY B:PROG.EXE
            Copies the file named PROG.EXE from the disk in
            drive B to the disk in the default drive using
            the same filename (PROG.EXE).

         COPY *.ASM B:
            Copies any file with a filename extension of
            .ASM from the disk in the default drive to the
            disk in drive B using the same filename in each
            case.
```

DATE

```
Function: Sets and/or displays the date stored in the
          computer's memory.
Command line:
              DATE [mm-dd-yy]
Examples:
         DATE 1-17-83
              Sets the date to January 17, 1983.

         DATE
              Displays the date stored in the computer's
              memory, and waits for a user response. To keep
              the date as displayed, the user presses
              RETURN. To change the date, the user enters
              the date in the numeric form mm-dd-yy, and
              presses RETURN.
```

DEL

```
Function: Deletes one or more filenames from the directory
          on a disk. This command behaves exactly like the
          ERASE command. The asterisk (*) may be used as a
          universal qualifier in a filename.
Command line:
             DEL [<drive-id>]<filename>
Examples:
         DEL EX1.ASM
             Deletes the file named EX1.ASM on the disk in
             the default drive.

         DEL B:*.OBJ
             Deletes all files on the disk in drive B that
             have a filename extension of .OBJ.
```

DIR

```
Function: Displays a list with an entry for each file stored
          on the specified disk. A file's entry in the list
          includes the complete filename, the size (in
          bytes) of the file, and the date and time that the
          file was last updated. If the optional filename
          is specified, then only the files with the
          specified name are listed.
Command line:
           DIR [<drive-id>][<filename>][/W][/P]
Options:
     /W  Specifies that only the filenames are to be listed,
         5 per line.
     /P  Specifies that a pause is to occur after each page
         of the listing. The listing is continued by
         pressing any key.
Examples:
         DIR
             Lists all files on the disk in the default
             drive.

         DIR B:/P
             Lists all files on the disk in drive B, pausing
             after each page of the listing.

         DIR B:*.ASM
             Lists all files on the disk in drive B that
             have a filename extension of .ASM.
```

DISKCOMP

Function: Compares two diskettes, sector by sector, to determine if they are identical. This operation is used to verify a DISKCOPY operation. The DISKCOMP command is not part of the memory-resident portion of DOS. Therefore, DOS must be available on the disk in the default drive when the command is issued. DOS then prompts the user to place the two diskettes in the appropriate disk drives.

If the first diskette is formatted with 8 sectors per track (see the FORMAT command) and the second diskette is formatted with 9 sectors per track, then each track of the first diskette is compared to the first 8 sectors of the same track on the second diskette. If the first diskette is formatted with 9 sectors per track and the second diskette is formatted with 8 sectors per track, then the /8 option must be used so that only the first 8 sectors of each track on the first diskette are compared to the same track on the second diskette.

DISKCOMP should only be used to compare diskettes of the same size and storage capacity.

Command line:

```
DISKCOMP [<drive-id>] [<drive-id>][/1]

DISKCOMP [<drive-id>] [<drive-id>][/8]
```

Options:

- **/1** Specifies that only the first sides of the two diskettes are to be compared. This option is normally used when single-sided diskettes are involved.
- **/8** Specifies that only the first 8 sectors of each track are to be compared. This option is used when one or both of the diskettes are formatted with 8 sectors per track.

DISKCOPY

Function: Copies the contents of a source diskette onto a destination diskette of the same size and capacity (see FORMAT command), producing a backup copy of the source diskette. The DISKCOPY command is not part of the memory-resident portion of DOS. Therefore, DOS must be available on the disk in the default drive when the command is issued. DOS then prompts the user to place the source and target diskettes in the appropriate disk drives.

If the source diskette is formatted with 8 sectors per track (see the FORMAT command) and the destination diskette is formatted with 9 sectors per track, then each track of the source diskette is copied into the first 8 sectors of the same track on the destination diskette. A diskette that is formatted with 9 sectors per track cannot be copied to a diskette that is formatted with 8 sectors per track.

The DISKCOPY operation formats the destination diskette, if it has not already been formatted.

DISKCOPY cannot be used to copy between a 5¼" diskette and a 6½" diskette.

Command line:

DISKCOPY [<drive-id>] [<drive-id>][/1]

Options:

/1 Specifies that only the first side of the source diskette is to be copied, and is copied to the first side of the destination diskette. This option is normally used when single-sided diskettes are involved.

Examples:

DISKCOPY A: B:

Copies both sides of the diskette in drive A to the diskette in drive B.

DISKCOPY B: /1

Copies only the first side of the diskette in drive B to the diskette in the default drive.

ERASE

Function: Erases one or more filenames from the directory on a disk. This command behaves exactly like the DEL command. The asterisk (*) may be used as a universal qualifier in a filename.

Command line:

ERASE [<drive-id>]<filename>

Examples:

See the DEL command.

F
O
R
M
A
T

Function: Initializes a diskette. The format operation divides each surface of a diskette into concentric circles called tracks. Each track is divided into sectors. Each sector holds 512 bytes of data.

The FORMAT operation also places a directory on the diskette for DOS to use in keeping track of the files that are stored on the diskette. The following table summarizes the types of diskettes supported by DOS and their storage capacities.

The FORMAT command is not part of the memory-resident portion of DOS. Therefore, DOS must be available on the disk in the default drive when the command is issued. DOS then prompts the user to place the disk to be formatted in the specified drive.

Diskette Type & DOS Version	Tracks /Side	Sectors /Track	Bytes/ Sector	Total Bytes
5¼" Single-sided (DOS 1.0 and up)	40	8	512	163,840
5¼" Double-sided (DOS 1.1 and up)	40	8	512	327,680
5¼" Single-sided (DOS 2.0 and up)	40	9	512	184,320
5¼" Double-sided (DOS 2.0 and up)	40	9	512	368,640
5¼" High-Density (DOS 3.0 and up)	80	15	512	1,228,800
3½" Low-Density (DOS 3.2 and up)	80	9	512	737,280
3½" High-Density (DOS 3.2 and up)	80	18	512	1,474,560

FORMAT

Command line:

```
        FORMAT [<drive-id>][/S][/V][/1][/8][/4][/F:720]
```

Options:

- /S Specifies that the hidden files IBMBIO.COM and IBMDOS.COM are to be copied from the DOS diskette to the diskette being formatted.
- /V Specifies that the user desires to place a volume label on the diskette. DOS prompts the user for the label after the FORMAT operation is complete.
- /1 Specifies that the 5¼" diskette is to be formatted for use as a single-sided diskette, whether or not it actually is a single-sided diskette.
- /8 Specifies that the 5¼" diskette is to be formatted with 8 sectors per track. The default is 9 sectors per track for double-density, 5¼" disk drives and 15 sectors per track for high-density, 5¼" disk drives.
- /4 Specifies that a double-density, 5¼" diskette is being formatted in a high-density, 5¼" disk drive.
- /F:720 Specifies that a double-density, 3½" diskette is being formatted in a high-density, 3½" disk drive.

MODE

Function: Sets the mode of the video display or the printer.

Command line:

```
        MODE <char/line>
```

<char/line> is the number of characters per line for the video display (40 or 80).

```
        MODE LPT<#>:[<char/line>][,[<lines/inch>][,P]]
```

<#> is the printer number (1, 2, or 3),
<char/line> is the number of characters per line for the printer (80 or 132),
<lines/inch> is the number of lines per inch for the printer (6 or 8), and
P specifies continuous retry on time-out errors on prints.

Examples:

MODE 40
Sets the video monitor to display 40 characters per line.

MODE LPT1:132,8
Sets printer number 1 to print 132 characters per line and 8 lines per inch (88 lines per page).

P R I N T	Function: Outputs the contents of a file to the printer. DOS prompts the user for the print device to be used. Device PRN (LPT1) is the default. DOS outputs a form feed character (ASCII 0C hex) following the output of the file. To ensure a readable output, this command should only be used for ASCII text files. Command line: PRINT [<drive-id>]<filename> Example: PRINT SORT.ASM Outputs to the printer the contents of the file SORT.ASM from the disk in the default drive.
R E N A M E	Function: Change the name of a file or group of files. The asterisk (*) may be used in a <filename> as a universal qualifier. Command line: RENAME [<drive-id>]<filename> <filename> Examples: RENAME B:PROG.BAK PROG.OLD Changes the name of file PROG.BAK on the disk in drive B to PROG.OLD. RENAME SEARCH.* BIN_SRCH.* For all files on the disk in the default drive that have a filename of SEARCH (regardless of the filename extension), the filename is changed to BIN_SRCH, and the filename extension remains the same.
T I M E	Function: Sets and/or displays the time stored in the computer's memory. Command line: TIME [hh:mm[:ss[.hs]]] Examples: TIME 18:43 Sets the time to 6:43 PM. TIME Displays the time stored in the computer's memory, and waits for a user response. To keep the time as displayed, the user presses RETURN. To change the time, the user enters the time in the numeric form hh:mm[:ss[.hs]], and presses RETURN.

TYPE

Function: Displays the contents of a file on the video screen. To ensure a readable output, this command should only be used for ASCII text files.

Command line:

```
TYPE [<drive-id>]<filename>
```

Example:

```
TYPE SORT.ASM
```

Displays the contents of the file named SORT.ASM from the disk in the default drive.

VERIFY

Function: Determines the status of the VERIFY option, or sets the VERIFY option. When the VERIFY option is "on," each sector transferred to a disk is verified by reading that sector into memory and comparing the data read with the data written.

Command line:

```
VERIFY

VERIFY ON

VERIFY OFF
```

Examples:

```
VERIFY
```

Displays the status of the VERIFY option.

```
VERIFY ON
```

Sets the VERIFY option to "on."

DEBUG Program

```
To invoke DEBUG:
   a. DOS must be available on the default disk drive.

   b. Enter the following command line:

      DEBUG [[<drive-id>]<filename>]

      DOS loads DEBUG from the disk in the default drive  and
      then transfers control to the DEBUG program. If a file-
      name  is specified,  then  the DEBUG program  loads the
      requested file into memory. DEBUG prompts the user with
      a hyphen (-). The user can enter commands to display or
      modify  the contents of registers  or memory locations,
      and to execute instructions contained in memory.  DEBUG
      expects all numeric values to be in hexadecimal.

Abbreviations and notation:
          <> encloses items to be supplied by the user.
          [] encloses optional items.

   <address> denotes  the  segment  and  offset  of a  memory
             location. A colon (:) separates the two parts of
             the memory address.  The segment portion  of the
             address can be specified as follows:

                A segment register designator (CS, SS, DS, or
                ES), or
                A 1-4 digit hexadecimal number that specifies
                the  upper  16 bits  of  the  address  of the
                origin of the segment  (e.g.,  0914 specifies
                the origin address 09140), or
                Omitted,  specifying  that a default  segment
                register is to be used.

             The offset portion of the address must be  a 1-4
             digit  hexadecimal  number  that  specifies  the
             offset relative  to the segment origin.  If  the
             segment portion of the address is omitted,  then
             the separating colon must also be omitted.

     <range> denotes  a  block   of   memory   locations   by
             specifying where the block begins  and  ends  in
             memory.  A  range  of memory  locations  can  be
             specified in either of the following two ways:

                <address> [<offset>]

                in which <address> specifies the segment  and
                                offset of the memory location at
                                which the block begins  and
                         <offset> specifies the offset within
                                the   segment   of   the   memory
                                location at which the block ends.
```

```
            <address> [L <length>]

            in which <address> specifies the segment  and
                          offset of the memory location at
                          which the block begins  and
                      <length>  specifies  the  number  of
                          bytes in the block.

         In either case,  if  the optional  parameter  is
         omitted, then a default end of range is used.
```

DEBUG Commands

```
  Function: Translates 8088/8086 assembly language instructions
A           into  machine  language   and  loads  the  machine
S           language  instructions  into  consecutive   memory
S           locations  beginning  at  the  specified  address.
E           DEBUG   prompts   for   each   assembly   language
M           instruction  by displaying  the memory address  at
B           which the machine language representation  of  the
L           instruction will begin. Pressing RETURN terminates
E           the  entry  of  an  assembly language instruction.
            Pressing RETURN by itself  terminates the assemble
            command.
               All   immediate  operands  must  be  entered  in
            hexadecimal,  and  all  memory  operands  must  be
            hexadecimal  offsets  enclosed  in square brackets
            (e.g.,   [4A]).  A segment override mnemonic  (CS:,
            SS:, DS:, or ES:)  is  entered  just prior  to the
            operation code.
               RETF is used for return  from a FAR  procedure.
            RET is used for return from a NEAR procedure.
               The generic forms  for the string  instructions
            cannot be used,  and a repeat  prefix  is  entered
            just prior to the string operation code.

 Command lines:
                 A [<address>]
                 <assembly language instruction>
                 <assembly language instruction>
                           .
                           .
                           .
                 <assembly language instruction>
                 <assembly language instruction>
```

DUMP

Function: Displays the contents of a block of memory locations in hexadecimal and as ASCII characters.

Command line:

```
D [<range>]
```

If only the start address for the range is specified, then a total of 128 bytes (8 rows of 16 bytes each) is displayed. If the range is omitted, then the dump begins at the memory location immediately following the end location for the previous dump. The DS-register contents are used as the default segment origin address for the start address of the range.

Examples:

```
D SS:0 1F
```

Displays the contents of stack segment locations beginning at offset 0000 and terminating at offset 001F.

```
D DS:08 L 30
```

Displays 48 (30 hex) locations of the data segment beginning at offset 0008.

ENTER

Function: Changes the contents of a block of memory locations.

Command line:

```
E <address> [<byte-constant-list>]
```

<byte-constant-list> is a list of hexadecimal byte constants separated by spaces or commas.

The DS-register contents are used as the default segment origin address for the address in an E command.

If the <byte-constant-list> is omitted, then DEBUG displays the contents of the specified memory location and prompts the user to change the value. To leave the value as is, the user presses RETURN. To change the value, the user types the the new byte value in hexadecimal and then presses RETURN.

If the <byte-constant-list> is present, then the constants from the list are entered into consecutive memory locations beginning with the specified memory location. The constants are entered into memory in the order that they appear in the list.

Example:

```
E 9A4:0 1A 2B 3C
```

Enters the hex value 1A into memory location 09A40, the hex value 2B into memory location 09A41, and the hex value 3C into memory location 09A42.

G
O

Function: Sets one or more breakpoints in a program so that a selected block of instructions can be executed. Execution begins with the next instruction to be executed in the program being debugged (identified by the saved CS:IP register pair) or with the instruction at a specified address. Execution continues until one of the breakpoints is reached.

Command line:

```
G [=<address>] [<address-list>]
```

<address-list> is a list of addresses separated by spaces or commas.

The optional parameter, =<address>, specifies the memory location at which execution is to begin. If omitted, then execution begins with the next instruction in the program being debugged.

The addresses in the <address-list> specify breakpoints for the program. Execution is interrupted when the instruction at one of the breakpoint addresses is reached. The instruction at the breakpoint is not executed.

Each address specified with the G command must be the address of the first byte of an instruction in the program being debugged. DEBUG replaces the instruction byte at each breakpoint address with the 1-byte INT 3 instruction (CC hex). On detection of a Type 3 interrupt (i.e., on reaching a breakpoint), DEBUG receives control. DEBUG saves the state of the processor for the program being debugged, displays the processor state to the user, restores the instruction byte at each breakpoint address, and waits for another command from the user. Another G, P, or T command causes DEBUG to restore the state of the processor for and return control to the program being debugged.

The CS-register contents are used as the default segment origin address for any address used in the G command.

The G command uses 6 bytes in the user's stack segment.

If no breakpoints are specified, execution continues until the program being debugged terminates normally.

Examples:

G 10A

Begins execution with the instruction that begins in the memory location specified by the saved CS:IP register pair, and stops execution just prior to the instruction at offset 010A in the segment addressed by the CS-register.

GO	G =91A:0 91A:A8 91A:B2 Begins execution with the instruction that begins in memory location 091A0, and stops execution just prior to the instruction that begins in location 09248 (091A:00A8) or just prior to the instruction that begins in location 09252 (091A:00B2).
HEX ARITH	Function: Displays the hexadecimal sum and difference of two hexadecimal numbers. Command line: H <hex-integer> <hex-integer> <hex-integer> is a hexadecimal integer in the range 0-FFFF. Example: H 1AC F8 Displays the sum of 1AC hex and F8 hex followed by the difference between 1AC and F8. In this case, the display would be 02A4 00B4.

PROCESS

Function: Executes one or more instructions, beginning with the next instruction in the program being debugged (identified by the saved CS:IP register pair) or beginning with the instruction at a specified address. Execution continues until the next n interruptions occur. The default value for n is 1. The P command uses 6 bytes in the user's stack segment. See also the TRACE (T) command. The P and T commands differ in the way in which they handle the CALL, loop, repeated string, and INT instructions. For the CALL instruction, the P command causes DEBUG to execute the entire subprocedure as if it were a single step; that is, DEBUG allows instructions to be executed continuously stopping just prior to the execution of the instruction that immediately follows the CALL instruction. The P command handles loop instructions, string instructions with repeat prefixes, and INT instructions in a simpler manner.

Command line:

P [=<address>] [<n>]

<n> is a count of the number of interruptions to service before execution is suspended to wait for another command.

The optional parameter, =<address>, specifies the memory location at which execution is to begin. If omitted, then execution begins with the next instruction in the program being debugged.

On each interruption, DEBUG saves the state of the processor for the program being debugged and displays this processor state to the user. On each interruption except for the last, DEBUG restores the state of the processor and returns control to the program being debugged. On the last interruption, DEBUG waits for another command from the user. Another G, P, or T command causes DEBUG to restore the state of the processor for and return control to the program being debugged.

Examples:

P

Processes the next instruction in the program being debugged.

P 10

Processes the execution of the next 16 (10 hex) instructions in the program being debugged. Note that a subprocedure, an interrupt service routine, a string instruction with a repeat prefix, and the iterations of a loop are treated as single instructions.

QUIT

Function: Terminates execution of the DEBUG program, and returns control to DOS.

Command line:

```
Q
```

REGISTER

Function: Displays the contents of the processor registers for the program being debugged.

Displays the contents of a selected processor register, and prompts the user for a new value for the selected register. To keep the register value as is, the user presses RETURN. To change the register value, the user types the new value, in hexadecimal, and then presses RETURN.

Command line:

```
R[<reg-name>]
```

<reg-name> is one of the following register designators: AX, BX, CX, DX, SP, BP, DI, SI, CS, SS, DS, ES, IP, PC (same as IP), or F (for the flags register).

The following abbreviations are used for the display and modification of the individual bit of the flags register:

FLAG	0	1
OF	NV	OV
DF	UP	DN
IF	DI	EI
SF	PL	NG
ZF	NZ	ZR
AF	NA	AC
PF	PO	PE
CF	NC	CY

Examples:

R

Displays the contents of the processor registers.

R CX

Displays the contents of the CX-register, and waits for the user to enter a new value.

T
R
A
C
E

Function: Executes one or more instructions, beginning with the next instruction in the program being debugged (identified by the saved CS:IP register pair) or beginning with the instruction at a specified address. Execution continues until the next n single-step interrupts occur. The default value for n is 1. The T command uses 6 bytes in the user's stack segment. See also the PROCESS (P) command. The T and P commands differ in the way in which they handle the CALL, loop, repeated string, and INT instructions. The P command causes DEBUG to execute the CALL instruction, in single-step mode, thus allowing the user to trace into a subprocedure. The user can then trace the instructions of the subprocedure in single-step mode. The T command handles loop instructions, string instructions with repeat prefixes, and INT instructions in a simpler manner.

Command line:

```
T [=<address>] [<n>]
```

<n> is a count of the number of single-step interrupts to service before execution is suspended to wait for another command.

The optional parameter, =<address>, specifies the memory location at which execution is to begin. If omitted, then execution begins with the next instruction in the program being debugged.

On each single-step interrupt, DEBUG saves the state of the processor for the program being debugged and displays this processor state to the user. On each single-step interrupt except for the last, DEBUG restores the state of the processor and returns control to the program being debugged. On the last single-step interrupt, DEBUG waits for another command from the user. Another G P, or T command causes DEBUG to restore the state of the processor for and return control to the program being debugged.

Examples:

T

Traces the execution of the next instruction in the program being debugged.

T 10

Traces the execution of the next 16 (10 hex) instructions in the program being debugged.

U N A S S E M B L E

Function: Interprets the contents of memory locations as machine language instructions, and translates these instructions to assembly language.

All immediate operands are displayed in base 16. All memory operands are displayed as hexadecimal offsets enclosed in square brackets.

A prefix operator is displayed on a separate line immediately preceding the instruction to which it applies.

Command line:

```
U [<range>]
```

If only the start address for the range is specified, then a maximum of 37 bytes (minimum 32) is unassembled. The number of instructions displayed can vary since instructions are from 1 to 6 bytes in length.

If the range is omitted, then the display begins with the instruction immediately following the last instruction displayed for the previous U command.

The CS-register contents are used as the default segment origin address for the start address of the range.

Example:

U 100 11F

Interprets the bytes from offset 0100 through 011F in the segment whose origin is specified by the contents of the CS-register as a sequence of machine language instructions. The first instruction is the one that begins at offset 0100, and the last instruction is the last one that begins at or before offset 011F. Displays the assembly language interpretations for this sequence of instructions.

Macro Assembler (MASM 6.0)

Function:
Translates an assembly module from assembly language to machine language.

Command line:
ML [<options>] <source>

Explanation of arguments:
<options> is a list of commands that control the way the assembler performs its task.
<source> identifies the input source code file.

Legal entries for arguments:

<source>	Explicit file specification that identifies the disk drive, the filename, and the filename extension. The filename extension cannot be omitted.
<options>	/Zi specifies the generation of CodeView information in the object file.
(option codes are case-sensitive)	/Fo <filename> identifies the output object code file. The default for this entry is to use the same filename as the <source> filename with the .OBJ filename extension.
	/Fl [<filename>] identifies the output file for the assembler-generated listing. The default filename is the same as the <source> filename with the .LST filename extension.
	/Sa specifies that all available information is to be included in the assembler-generated listing.
	/Sg specifies that assembler-generated code is to be included in the assembler-generated listing.
	/Sn specifies that the symbol table is not to be included in the assembler-generated listing.

Macro Assembler (MASM 5.1)

Function:

Translates an assembly module from assembly language to machine language.

Command line:

MASM [<opt>] <source>,[<object>],[<listing>],[<cross-ref>]

A semicolon (;) may terminate the command line after any file specification, and in that case, the remaining output files (except for <object>) are simply not generated (the <object> file specification is treated as if it had been left blank).

Explanation of arguments:

<opt>	is a list of assembly options.
<source>	identifies the input source code file.
<object>	identifies the output object code file.
<listing>	identifies the output file for the assembler-generated listing.
<cross-ref>	identifies the output file for cross-reference data.

Legal entries for arguments:

<opt>	/ZI specifies the generation of CodeView information in the object file.
<source>	Explicit file specification Default filename extension: .ASM
<object> <listing> <cross-ref>	Explicit file specification Default filename extensions: .OBJ for <object> .LST for <listing> .CRF for <cross-ref> NUL indicates that the specific output file is not to be generated. Blank indicates that the specific output file is to be placed on the diskette in the default drive using the <source> filename with the filename extension replaced by the appropriate suffix (.OBJ, .LST, or .CRF). Disk drive identifier indicates that the specific output file is to be placed on the diskette in the specified drive using the <source> filename with the filename extension replaced by the appropriate suffix (.OBJ, .LST, or .CRF).
<listing>	CON indicates that the assembler-generated listing is to be displayed on the video screen.

Linkage Editor (LINK)

Function:

Combines separately assembled object code modules into a single executable module.

Command line:

LINK [/CO] <obj-list>,[<runfile>],[<mapfile>],[<lib-list>]

A semicolon (;) may terminate the command line after any file specification, and in that case, the remaining output files (except for <runfile>) are simply not generated (the <runfile> file specification is treated as if it had been left blank).

Explanation of arguments:

/CO	specifies that the executable file is to be produced in the CodeView format.
<obj-list>	is a list of object code file specifications separated by spaces or plus signs (+).
<runfile>	identifies the output file for the executable machine code.
<mapfile>	identifies the output file for the load map.
<lib-list>	is a list of library specifications separated by spaces or plus signs (+).

Legal entries for arguments:

<obj-list> <lib-list>	List of explicit file specifications Default filename extensions: .OBJ for <obj-list> items .LIB for <lib-list> items
<runfile> <mapfile>	Explicit file specification Default filename extensions: .EXE for <runfile> .MAP for <mapfile> NUL indicates that the specific output file is not to be generated. Blank indicates that the particular output file is to be placed on the diskette in the default drive using the first object filename with the filename extension replaced by the appropriate suffix (.EXE or .MAP). Disk drive identifier indicates that the specific output file is to be placed on the diskette in the specified drive using the first object filename with the filename extension replaced by the appropriate suffix (.EXE or .MAP).
<mapfile>	CON indicates that the load map listing is to be displayed on the video screen.

Library Utility (LIB)

Function:

Creates and maintains libraries of object code files.

Command line:

```
LIB <old-lib> [<commands>][,<listfile>][,<new-lib>][;]
```

Explanation of arguments:

```
<old-lib>  identifies the library to be created or updated.
<commands> is a list of library commands separated by
           spaces.
<listfile> identifies the output file for the library
           listing.
<new-lib>  identifies the output library file. This entry
           is ignored if <old-lib> is being created.
;          marks the end of the command line.
```

Legal entries for arguments:

<old-lib>	Explicit file specification Default filename extension: .LIB
<commands>	+<filename> indicates that the specified object code file is to be added to the library. +<libname> indicates that all object code files from the specified library are to be added to the library. -<module> indicates that the specified library module is to be deleted from the library. -+<module> indicates that the specified library module is to be replaced by the object code file whose filename is <module>.OBJ. *<module> indicates that the specified library module is to be copied to the object code file whose filename is <module>.OBJ. -*<module> indicates that the specified library module is to be copied to the object code file whose filename is <module>.OBJ and then deleted.
<listfile>	Explicit file specification
<new-lib>	Explicit file specification Default filename extension: .LIB Default entry: <old-lib>

Cross Reference (CREF)

Function:

Produces an alphabetical listing of the symbolic names used in an assembly module. The listing contains a list of line numbers for each symbolic name, indicating where in the assembly module the name is defined (denoted by #) and referenced.

Command line:

CREF <cross-ref>,<cref-listing>

Explanation of arguments:

<cross-ref> identifies the input file that contains the cross-reference data.

<cref-listing> identifies the output file for the cross-reference listing.

Legal entries for arguments:

<cross-ref>	Explicit file specification Default filename extension: .CRF
<cref-listing>	Explicit file specification Default filename extension: .REF Blank indicates that the output <cref-listing> file is to be placed on the diskette in the default drive using the <cross-ref> filename with the filename extension replaced by the suffix .REF. Disk drive identifier indicates that the output <cref-listing> file is to be placed on the diskette in the specified drive using the <cross-ref> filename with the filename extension replaced by the suffix .REF. CON indicates that the output listing file is to be displayed on the video screen. PRN indicates that the output listing file is to be output to the printer.

Index